The Complete Works Of Stephen Charnock, B. D.

Volume 1

Sovereign Grace Publishers, Inc.
P.O. Box 4998
Lafayette, IN 47903

Printed In the United States of America
By Lightning Source, Inc.

THE COMPLETE WORKS

OF

STEPHEN CHARNOCK, B.D.

With Introduction

BY THE REV. JAMES M'COSH, LL.D.,

PROFESSOR OF LOGIC AND METAPHYSICS, QUEEN'S COLLEGE, BELFAST.

VOL. I.

CONTAINING

DISCOURSES ON DIVINE PROVIDENCE,

AND

THE EXISTENCE AND ATTRIBUTES OF GOD.

EDINBURGH : JAMES NICHOL.

LONDON: JAMES NISBET AND CO.   DUBLIN: W. ROBERTSON.

———

M.DCCC.LXIV.

CONTENTS.

INTRODUCTION TO CHARNOCK'S WORKS.

I. HIS LIFE.

THE memorials of the life of Charnock are much scantier than those who have profited by his writings, or who are interested in the history of the time, could wish. We have some notices of him in the sermon preached at his funeral by his 'bosom friend' Mr Johnson ; a vague general account of him in an epistle 'To the Reader,' prefixed by Mr Adams and Mr Veal, the editors, to his 'Discourse of Divine Providence,' published shortly after his death; a brief life of him by Calamy in his 'Account of the Ejected and Silenced ;' his collegiate positions detailed by Wood in his *Athenæ Oxonienses* and *Fasti* ; and this is all the original matter that we have been able to discover regarding the author of the great work 'On the Attributes.' Mr Johnson says, 'he heard a narrative of his life would be drawn up by an able hand ;' and Calamy mentions that *Memoirs of Mr Steph. Charnock* were written by Mr John Gunter, his 'chamber-fellow' at Oxford ; but of these we have not been able to find any trace. We have made researches in London, in Cambridge, and in Dublin, without being rewarded by the discovery of many new facts, not given by the original authorities. All that we have aimed at in the following Memoir is to combine the scattered accounts of him, to allot the incidents the proper place in his life and in the general history of the times, and thus to furnish, if not a full, yet a faithful, picture of the man and his work.*

Stephen Charnock was born in the parish of Saint Catherine Cree (or Creechurch), London, in the year 1628. He was the son of Mr Richard Charnock, a solicitor, who was descended from an ancient Lancashire family, the Charnocks of Charnock. We have no account of his childish or boyish years, or of his training in the family. But we know what was the spirit that reigned around him among the great body of the middle classes

---

* The writer is under deep obligations to the Rev. Alexander B. Grosart, Kinross; the Rev. Dr Halley, New College, London; Joshua Wilson, Esq., Tunbridge Wells; and Charles Henry Cooper, Esq., author of the *Annals of Cambridge*, for directing him in his researches.

in the best parts of the metropolis. An awe sat upon their minds in consequence of the great national collisions which were impending or had commenced; public sports were discouraged, as agreeing not with 'public calamities,' and the Lord's day was observed with great strictness. The churches were crowded with earnest hearers, and 'religious exercises were set up in private families, as reading the Scriptures, family prayer, repeating sermons, and singing psalms, which were so universal in the city of London, that you might walk the streets on the evening of the Lord's day without seeing an idle person, or hearing anything but the voice of prayer or praise from churches or private houses.'*

In those times students entered college at a much earlier age than they now do, and had their university career over in sufficient time to enable them to enter when yet young on their several professional employments. Stephen was matriculated as a sizar at Cambridge July 8. 1642. Whether by the design of his father, or by the leadings of providential circumstances, we have no means of knowing, but young Charnock was sent to Emmanuel, the 'Puritan College,' so called, it is said, from a conversation between Queen Elizabeth and its founder, Sir Walter Mildmay. 'Sir Walter,' said the Queen, 'I hear you have erected a puritan foundation at Cambridge.' 'Madam,' said Sir Walter, 'far be it from me to countenance anything contrary to your Majesty's established laws; but I have set an acorn which, when it becomes an oak, God alone knows what will be the fruit thereof.' In 1641, it had 204 students attending, standing next to St John's and Trinity in respect of numbers;† and occupying a still higher place in respect of the eminence of its pupils. 'Sure I am,' says Fuller, 'it has overwhelmed all the university, more than a moiety of the present masters of colleges having been bred therein.'

Charnock entering in 1642, is proceeding B.A. in 1645–6, and commencing M.A. in 1649. We have no difficulty in apprehending the spirit which reigned in Cambridge when he began his college life. The Reformation struggle was over, and earnest men saw that the Reformed Church, with its worldly, often immoral and ill-educated, clergy, and its ignorant people, was yet very far from coming up to the pattern which Christ was supposed to have shewn to his apostles. Two manner of spirits had sprung up and were contending with each other. Each had an ideal, and was labouring to bring the church into accordance with it. The one looked to the written word, and was seeking to draw forth, systematize, and exhibit its truths; the other looked more to the church, and was striving to display its visible unity before the world, that men's looks and hearts might be attracted towards it. The one was internal, personal, puritan, anxious to keep up the connection between the church and its Head, and between the members of the church in and

* Neal's *History of the Puritans*, 1642. † Cooper's *Annals of Cambridge*, 1641.

through Christ; the other was external, ecclesiastical, priestly, seeking to retain the connection of the Church of England with the church of the past and the church universal, and to organize it into a powerful body, which might put down all error and all schism, and mould the whole institutions and sentiments of the country.

Every public event of interest, and every collegiate influence, must have tended to press religious questions upon the attention of the student at the time when his character was being formed. The Thirty Years' War, which had begun in 1618, was dragging its weary length along, and was essentially a religious conflict which the continental nations were seeking to settle by arms and by policy. The colonies of Plymouth and Massachussets, Connecticut and Newhaven, had been founded in the far west, and Herbert had sung, in a sense of his own,

> " Religion stands a tiptoe in our land,
> Ready to pass to the American strand."

In 1641, the three kingdoms had been moved by the reports of the popish massacres in Ireland, in which it was said two hundred thousand protestants were put to death. In 1642, Charles had made his attempt to seize the 'five members,' and soon after the civil war began, and the king had rather the worst of it at the battle of Edge Hill. By the autumn it was ordained that the prelatic form of government should be abolished from and after November 5. 1643; and it was farther resolved that an assembly of divines should be called to settle the intended reformation, which assembly actually met at Westminster in July 1643, and continued its sittings for five years and a half.

In Cambridge, the feeling has risen to a white heat, and is ready to burst into a consuming flame. For years past there had been a contest between those who were for modelling the colleges after the ecclesiastical, and those who wished to fashion them after the puritan type. In a paper drawn up in the university in 1636, and endorsed by Laud as 'Certain disorders in Cambridge to be considered in my visitation,' there is a complaint that the order as to vestments is not attended to; that the undergraduates wear new-fashioned gowns of any colour whatsoever, and that their other garments are light and gay; that upon Fridays and all fasting days, the victualling houses prepare flesh for all scholars and others that will come and send to them, and that many prefer their own invented and unapproved prayers before all the liturgy of the church. When the report comes to Emmanuel, it says, 'Their Chappel is not consecrate. At surplice prayers they sing nothing but certain riming psalms of their own appointment, instead of Hymnes between the Lessons. And Lessons they read not after the order appointed in the Callendar, but after another continued course of their own,' &c. But by 1643 the complaint takes an entirely different turn; and an ordinance of both houses of parliament is made, directing that in all churches and chapels, all altars and tables of stone shall be taken away and demolished ; that all communion tables shall be removed from the east end of the churches; that all crucifixes, crosses, images, and pictures of any one or more persons of the Trinity, or of the Virgin Mary, and all other images and pictures of saints or superstitious inscriptions in churches or chapels shall be taken away or defaced.' One William Downing puts this order in execution, and at Queen's he beats down one hundred superstitious pictures; but when he comes to Emmanuel, 'there is nothing to be done.' These scenes must have fallen under the notice of the boy Charnock during the first year of his collegiate life. More startling sounds still must have reached the ears of the young student. Oliver Cromwell, who had been elected one of the burgesses of the town in 1640, has a close and intimate connection with the inhabitants ; and in 1642 he is sending down arms to the county; the Parliament has committed the care of the town to him, the mayor, and three aldermen, who raise and exercise trained bands and volunteers ; and he seizes a portion of the plate which the colleges are sending to the king. By the beginning of the following year, Cromwell has taken the magazine in the castle, the town is fortified, and a large body of armed men are in the place; the colleges are being beset and broken open, and guards thrust into them, sometimes at midnight, whilst the scholars are asleep in their beds, and multitudes of soldiers are quartered in them. By this time Holdsworth, the Master of Emmanuel, is in custody, and Dr Beale, Master of St John's, Dr Martin, President of Queen's College, and Dr Sterne, Master of Jesus, are sent up to parliament as prisoners.* In 1644, the royalists are ejected, and their places supplied by friends of the parliament.

At the time young Charnock entered, the sentiment of the members of the university was very much divided. Even in Emmanuel the opinion was not altogether puritan. The tutor from whom Charnock received his chief instruction was Mr W. Sancroft (afterwards Archbishop of Canterbury), who was attached to the royalist cause, and had joined in the congratulatory addresses to the king on his return from Scotland in 1641. Dr Holdsworth, who was Master of Emmanuel when Charnock entered, was appointed by the Lords, and approved by the Commons, as one of the divines to sit at Westminster; but he never attended, and in 1643 he was imprisoned, and in the following year ejected. The spirit of Emmanuel had been all along reforming and parliamentary, and after the ejectments all the colleges became so. Dr Anthony Tuckney, who succeeded Holdsworth in the Mastership of Emmanuel, was an active member of the Westminster Assembly, and 'had a considerable hand,' says Calamy, 'in the preparation of the Confession and Catechisms.' Dr Arrowsmith, made Master of St

* These facts are gathered out of Cooper's *Annals of Cambridge*, vol. iii. 1642-4.

John's, and Dr Hill, appointed Master of Trinity, were of the same puritan spirit. Cudworth, Culverwel, and Whichcote, who had all been connected with Emmanuel, and held places in the university after the ejection, could scarcely be described as of the puritan type, but they were opposed to the policy which the king had been pursuing, and the ecclesiastical system which Laud intended to set up. In the university and the town, the popular preaching was decidedly evangelical and Calvinistic. In particular, Dr Samuel Hammond preached in St Giles 'with such pious zeal, liveliness, and Christian experience, that his ministry was attended by persons from all parts of the town and the most distant colleges; and it was crowned with the conversion of some scores (Mr Stancliff says some hundreds) of scholars. It was generally allowed that there was not a more successful minister in Cambridge since the time of Perkins.'*

This state of things, the conflicts of the time, the talk of the tutors and students, the earnest preaching in the churches, the spiritual struggles in many a bosom, and the necessity for understanding the questions at issue, and coming to a decision with its life consequences, all these must have tended to press religion on the personal attention of so earnest a youth as Charnock was. Without any living faith when he came to Cambridge, he was there led to search and pray; he was for a time in darkness, and beset with fears and temptations, but he got light and direction from above, and he devoted himself to God for life. He subsequently wrote out a paper explaining the way by which he was led, and declaring his dedication, but it perished in the great fire of London. Mr Johnson met him in 1644; and in the sermon which he delivered at his funeral, represents him 'as venerable and grave, like an aged person from his youth,' and gives the following account of his conversion and his Cambridge life:—
'The deed of gift, or rather copy of it, which shewed his title to heaven, I believe perished with his books in London's flames, and I have forgot the particular places of Scripture by which he was most wrought upon, and which were there inserted.' 'He would deeply search into and prove all things, and allow only what he found pure and excellent.' 'In this I had him in my heart at my first acquaintanceship with him in Cambridge thirty-six years since. I found him one that, Jonah-like, had turned to the Lord with all his heart, all his soul, and all his might, and none like him; which did more endear him to me. How had he hid the word of God in a fertile soil, "in a good and honest heart," which made him "flee youthful lusts," and antidoted him against the infection of youthful vanities. His study was his recreation; the law of God was his delight. Had he it not, think ye, engraven in his heart? He was as choice, circumspect, and prudent in his election of society, as of books, to converse with; all his delight being in such as excelled in the divine art of directing, furthering, and quickening him in the

* Calamy's 'Account of Ejected,' Art. Samuel Hammond.

way to heaven, the love of Christ and souls. Most choice he was of the ministers that he would hear; what he learned from books, converse, or sermons, that which affected and wrought most upon him he prayed over till he was delivered into the form of it, and had Christ, grace, and the Spirit formed in him. True, he had been in darkness, and then he said full of doubtings, fears, and grievously pestered with temptations. How oft have we found him (as if he had lately been with Paul caught up into the third heavens, and heard unspeakable words) magnifying and adoring the mercy, love, and goodness of God.'

We know from general sources what was the course of secular instruction imparted in the colleges at this time. Aristotle still ruled, though no longer with an undisputed sway, in the lessons of the tutors. There is an account left by a pupil, Sir Simonds D'Ewes, of the books prescribed by Dr Holdsworth in 1618-19, when he was a tutor in St John's, and probably there was not much difference in Emmanuel when he became master: 'We went over all Seton's Logic exactly, and part of Keckerman and Molinæus. Of ethics or moral philosophy, he read to me Gelius and part of Pickolomineus; of physics, part of Magirus; and of history, part of Florus.' 'I spent the next month (April 1619) very laboriously in the perusal of Aristotle's physics, ethics, and politics; and I read logic out of several authors.' [*] But for an age or two there had been a strong reaction against Aristotle on the part of the more promising pupils. Bacon had left Trinity College in the previous century with a profound dissatisfaction with the scholastic studies, and already cogitating those grand views which he gave to the world in his *Novum Organum* (1620), as to the importance of looking to things instead of notions and words. Milton, in his College Exercises (1625 to 1632), had in his own grandiose style, and by help of mythological fable, given expression to his discontent with the narrow technical method followed, and to his breathings after some undefined improvement.[†] The predominant philosophic spirit in Cambridge prior to the Great Rebellion was Platonic rather than Aristotelian. This was exhibited by a number of learned and profound writers who rose about this time, and who continue to be known by the name of the 'Cambridge Moralists.' In Emmanuel College, before the ejectment, there were Whichcote, author of *Moral and Religious Aphorisms*, and of *Letters to Tuckney* (1651); Nathanael Culverwel, author of the masterly work *Of the Light of Nature*[‡] (1651); and Ralph Cudworth, who produced the great work on *The True Intellectual System of the Universe*,—all promoted to important offices in Cambridge under the Commonwealth. There were also in Cambridge Henry More, author of the *Enchiridion Metaphysicum*, and John

[*] Masson's *Life of Milton*, p. 229.
[†] *Familiar Letters* in Masson's Milton, p. 249.
[‡] See the valuable edition by John Brown, D.D., with a critical essay by John Cairns, D.D.

Smith, author of the *Select Discourses*. All of those great men had caught, and were cherishing, a lofty Platonic spirit. While they implicitly received and devoutly revered the Bible as the inspired book of God, they entertained at the same time a high idea of the office of reason, and delighted in the contemplation of the eternal verities which they believed it to sanction, and sought to unite them with the living and practical truths of Christianity. Nor is it to be forgotten that John Howe, who entered Christ College in 1647, imbibed from Cudworth, More, and Smith his 'Platonic tincture,' which however was more thoroughly subordinated in him to the letter of Scripture. But in those times there was probably a still greater number of students whose college predilections would be those of Heywood: 'My time and thoughts were more employed in practical divinity, and experimental truths were more vital and vivifical to my soul. I preferred Perkins, Bolton, Preston, Sibbes, far above Aristotle, Plato, Magirus, and Wendeton, though I despise no laborious authors in these subservient studies.' *

Charnock was all his life a laborious student. We can infer what must have been his favourite reading, begun at college and continued to his death. While not ignorant of the physical science of his time, there is no reason to believe that he entered deeply into it. However, we are expressly told by Adams and Veal that he had arrived at a considerable knowledge of medicine, and that he was prevented from giving himself farther to it only by his dedication to a higher work. There are no traces of his having fallen under the bewitching spirit of Platonism, which so prevailed among the profounder students of Cambridge; but he characterises Plato as 'the divine philosopher,' he quotes More and Culverwel, and his own philosophy is of a wide and catholic character. It is quite clear from his systematic method, that he had received lessons from the Aristotelian logic, as modified by the schoolmen; but he never allowed it to bind and shackle him. He shews a considerable acquaintance with the ancient Greek philosophy, including the mystics of the Neoplatonist school. He is familiar with the writings of many of the fathers, and quotes from them in a way which shews that he understood them. He does not disdain to take instruction from Aquinas and the schoolmen when it serves his purpose. Among contemporary philosophic writers, he quotes from Gassendi and Voetius. His favourite uninspired writers were evidently the reformers, and those who defended and systematised their theology. Amyraut, and Suarez, and Daille were evidently favourites; and he was familiar with Turretine, Ames, Zanchius, Cocceius, Crellius, Cameron, Grotius, and many others; nay, he is not so bigoted as to overlook the high church Anglican divines of his own age. But we venture to say that, deeply read as he was in the works of uninspired men, he devoted more time to the study of the word

* Hunter's *Life of Oliver Heywood*, p. 46.

of God than to all other writings whatsoever. As to his linguistic accomplishments Mr Johnson, himself a scholar, says, 'I never knew any man who had attained near unto that skill which he had in both their originals [that is, of the Scriptures], except Mr Thomas Cawton;' and Mr Cawton, it seems, knew Latin, Greek, Hebrew, Arabic, French, Dutch, Italian, and Spanish.

Thus furnished by divine gift and acquired scholarship, he set out on the work to which he had devoted himself. 'Not long after he had received light himself,' says Johnson, 'when the Lord by his blessing on his endeavours had qualified him for it, such was his love, he gave forth light unto others, inviting them, and saying, "Come and see Jesus." In Southwark, where seven or eight, in that little time Providence continued him there, owed their conversion under God to his ministry; then in the university of Oxford and adjacent parts; after in Dublin, where it might be said of his as it was of the Lord's preaching in the land of Zebulon, "the people which sat in darkness saw a great light." '

On leaving college, he is represented by Adams and Veal as spending some time in a private family, but whether as a tutor or a chaplain does not appear. He seems to have commenced his ministry in Southwark, where he knew of seven or eight persons who owned him as the instrument of their conversion; and we may hope there were others profited, at a time when the mercantile and middle classes generally so crowded to the house of God, and the preaching of the word was so honoured. In 1649 or thereabouts, says Wood, he retired to Oxford, purposely to obtain a fellowship from the visitors appointed by the parliament when ' they ejected scholars by whole shoals ;' and in 1650, he obtained a fellowship in New College. November 19. 1652, he is incorporated Master of Arts in Oxford, as he had stood in Cambridge. April 5. 1654 (not 1652, as Calamy says), he and Thomas Cracroft of Magdalene College are appointed Proctors of the university. Charnock, greatly respected for his gifts, his learning, and his piety, was frequently put upon ' public works.' In particular, he seems to have been often employed in preaching in Oxford and the adjacent parts. Here he had as his chamber-fellow,. Mr John Gunter, who purposed to write, or did write, a life of him ; and here he gained or renewed a friendship with Richard Adams, formerly, like himself, of Cambridge, and now of Brazennose, and Edward Veal of Christ's Church, and afterwards with him in Dublin, the two who joined, many years after, in publishing his posthumous works. Here he connected himself with ' a church gathered among the scholars by Dr Goodwin,' a society which had the honour to have enrolled among its members Thankful Owen, Francis Howel, Theophilus Gale, and John Howe,* who must no doubt have enjoyed much sweet fellowship together, and helped to edify one another. Oliver Cromwell,

* See Life of Goodwin, in folio edition of Works, Vol. V. ; and Calamy's *Account of Ejected*, John Howe.

Lord Protector, was chancellor of the university, and Dr Owen, vice-chancellor; and an energetic attempt was made to produce and foster a high, though perhaps a somewhat narrow, scholarship, and to exercise a discipline of a moral and religious character, such as Christian fathers set up in their families. Notwithstanding all that has been said against it, it was by no means of an uncheerful character, and young men of virtue and piety delighted in it; but others, we fear, felt it irksome, because of the constant supervision, and the restraints meeting them on every hand, and the number of religious services imposed on them, and which could have been enjoyed only by converted persons. Lord Clarendon thinks that such a state of things might have been expected to extirpate all 'learning, religion, and loyalty,' and to be 'fruitful only in ignorance, profaneness, atheism, and rebellion;' but is obliged to admit that, 'by God's wonderful providence, that fruitful soil could not be made barren,' and that it yielded an harvest of extraordinary good knowledge in all parts of learning.' It could easily be shewn that the fruit was what might have been expected to spring from the labour bestowed and the seed sown. It is a matter of fact, as Neal remarks, that all the great philosophers and divines of the Church of England, who flourished in the reigns of Charles II. and William III., such as Tillotson, Stillingfleet, Patrick, South, Cave, Sprat, Kidder, Whitby, Bull, Boyle, Newton, Locke, and others, were trained under teachers appointed by parliament and Cromwell.*

The scene of Charnock's labours and usefulness was now shifted. Cromwell had subdued Ireland to the Commonwealth, and he and others longed to have the protestants in that country supplied with a pure and fervent gospel ministry. Dr John Owen had been in Ireland a year and a half, overseeing the affairs of Dublin College and preaching the gospel. He dates a work from 'Dublin Castle, December 20. 1649,' and speaks of himself as 'burdened with manifold employments, with constant preaching to a numerous multitude of as thirsty people after the gospel as ever I conversed withal.' In the January following he returns to England, and has to preach before the Commons. Referring to Cromwell's victories, he says:—'How is it that Jesus Christ is, in Ireland, only as a lion staining all his garments with the blood of his enemies, and none to hold him forth as a lamb sprinkled with his own blood for his friends? Is it the sovereignty and interest of England that is alone to be thus transacted? For my part, I see no farther into the mystery of these things, but that I would heartily rejoice that innocent blood being expiated, the Irish might enjoy Ireland so long as the moon endureth, so that Jesus might possess the Irish.' 'I would there were, for the present, one gospel preacher for every walled town in the English possession in Ireland.' 'They are sensible of their wants, and cry out for supply. The tears and cries of the inha-

* The History of the Puritans, 1647.

bitants of Dublin are ever in my view.' In the course of the year, grants of land are made for the better support of Dublin University, and the Commissioners brought with them several Christian ministers. Among them was Samuel Winter, who afterwards became Provost of Trinity College, and who preached every Lord's day in Christ Church Cathedral before Deputy Fleetwood and the Commissioners, his services being reserved specially for the afternoons, when was the 'greatest auditory.' By 1654, Mr Veal, who had been in Oxford with Charnock, is a fellow of Dublin College, and some years after, is often exercising his ministry in and about the city of Dublin. Nor should we omit Mr John Murcot, who came from Lancashire in 1653, and preached with great fervour and acceptance to large numbers in Dublin and the south-west of Ireland, till the close of the following year, when he was cut off suddenly at the early age of twenty-nine, to the great grief of the Protestant inhabitants,—the Lord Deputy, and the Mayor, with a large body of citizens, following the body to the grave.*

Cromwell finding it necessary to restrain the republican Commissioners in Ireland, sent over his ablest son Henry to watch their proceedings, and to succeed them in the government. When he came to Ireland in August 1655, he brought with him some eminent ministers of religion, among whom was Samuel Mather, who, 'with Dr Harrison, Dr Winter, and Mr Charnock,' attended on Lord Harry Cromwell.† Mather was one of a famous nonconformist family, well known on both sides of the Atlantic. A native of England, he received his education in Harvard College, but returned to his native country, and having spent some time at Oxford and Cambridge, and in Scotland, he now came to Dublin, where he was appointed a fellow of the University, and chosen colleague to Dr Winter, and had to preach every Lord's day at the church of St Nicholas, besides taking his turn every five or six weeks before the Lord Deputy and Council. Dr Thomas Harrison was born at Kingston-upon-Hull, but, like Mather, was brought up in America, and had returned to England, where he was chosen to succeed Dr Goodwin in London ; and now in Dublin he is chaplain to Henry Cromwell, with a salary of £300 a year, and preaches in St Werburgh's.

It was in such company that Stephen Charnock acted as one of the chaplains of the chief governor of Ireland, living with much respect in his family, we may suppose whether he resided at the Castle or in Phœnix Park, and enjoying a stipend of £200 a year, worth ten times the same nominal sum in the present day.‡ When in Dublin, he was also officially minister of St

---

* See *Several Works of Mr John Murcot.* It may be mentioned here that there is a valuable sketch of the state of religion in Dublin at that time, in a lecture, *Independency in Dublin in the Olden Time,* by William Urwick, D.D.

† Calamy's *Noncon. Mem.,* by Palmer, Art. Samuel Mather.

‡ See Extracts from 'The Civil Establishment of the Commonwealth for Ireland, for the year 1665,' in Appendix to vol. ii. of Reid's 'History of the Presbyterian Church in Ireland.'

Werburgh's, and lecturer at Christ Church. St Werburgh's Church, in its foundation going back to near the time of the Norman settlement, was in the time of Cromwell, and is still, close by the very walls of Dublin Castle; and the Lord-Depute must have attended there or at Christ Church, at one or both. In 1607, the famous Usher had been appointed to this church, and was succeeded by William Chappel, who had been John Milton's tutor at Cambridge, and who, according to Symmonds, was the reputed author of 'The Whole Duty of Man.' 'The church is described in 1630 as "in good repair and decency," worth sixty pounds per annum, there being two hundred and thirty-nine householders in the parish, all Protestants, with the exception of twenty-eight Roman Catholics. "St Warburr's," says a writer in 1635, "is a kind of cathedral, wherein preacheth the judicious Mr Hoile about ten in the morning and three in the afternoon,—a most zealous preacher, and general scholar in all manner of learning, a mere cynic." Mr Hoyle, the friend of Usher, and "the tutor and chamber-fellow" of Sir James Ware, was elected professor of divinity in, and fellow of, Trinity College, Dublin; he sat in the Assembly of Divines, witnessed against Laud, and in 1648 was appointed Master of University College, Oxford.'* In this famous church, where the gospel had been proclaimed with such purity and power by Usher and by Hoyle, Charnock officiated, down, we may suppose, to the Restoration.

But his most conspicuous field of usefulness seems to have been on the afternoons of the Lord's day, when the great audiences of the citizens of Dublin assembled, and to them he *lectured*—that is, delivered an elaborate discourse, discussing fully the subject treated of—we may suppose either at St Werburgh's or Christ Church. Calamy says, 'he exercised his ministry on the Lord's day afternoons to the admiration of the most judicious Christians, having persons of the greatest distinction in the city of Dublin for his auditors, and being applauded by such as were of very different sentiments from himself. Many commended his learning and abilities who had no regard for his piety.' God was now giving his servant, who had been so thoroughly prepared for his work by a long course of training, a wide sphere to labour in. In future years, when he was partially silenced, he must have looked to his Dublin opportunities with feelings of lively interest. Though a counsellor, and a wise counsellor, to Henry Cromwell, and at times employed on public duty, in which his good sense, his moderation, and his truly catholic spirit gained him universal confidence, yet preaching was his peculiar gift, and to this he devoted all his talents. His preaching powers had now reached their full maturity. At a later period his memory somewhat failed him, and he had to read in a disadvantageous way with a glass. But at this time he used no notes, and he poured forth the riches of his original endowments and of his acquired treasures to the great delight of

* *The History of the City of Dublin* by J. T. Gilbert, vol. i. p 29.

his audience. His solid judgment, his weighty thoughts, his extensive learning, and his cultivated imagination, were all engaged in the work of recommending the gospel of Jesus Christ to the principal inhabitants of the capital of Ireland. Most careful in husbanding time, on which he ever set great value, spending most of it in his study, in reading and writing, meditation and prayer, accustomed to muse on profound topics in his restless hours in the night, and when walking in the streets during the day, constantly jotting down (as many of the puritans did) the thoughts that occurred to him on these occasions, and employing them as materials for his projected discourses,* he made it appear on the Lord's day how well he had been employed. We know what the discourses which he preached were from those given to the world after his death, and which were printed from his manuscripts as he left them. Characterised as those of most of the preachers of the time were by method, Charnock's were specially eminent for solidity of thought, for clear enunciation of important truth, for orderly evolution of all the parts of a complicated subject, for strength and conclusiveness of argument, coming forth with a great flow of expression, recommended by noble sentiment and enlivened by brilliant fancy,—with the weight he ever had the lustre of the metal.† Except in the discourses of Usher, there never had been before, and it is doubtful whether there ever has been since, such able and weighty evangelical preaching in the metropolis of Ireland; and we do not wonder that the thinking and the 'judicious' should have waited eagerly on his ministry, specially on his 'lectures,' seeking not so much excitement as instruction, presented in a clear and pleasant manner. Doing much good during the brief period allowed him, we are convinced that he helped to raise up a body of intelligent Christian men and women among the English settlers, who within the Established Church, or beyond it as Presbyterians or Independents, handed down the truth to the generations following, and that the lively protestant religion of Dublin in the present day owes not a little to the seed which was then scattered, and which in due time, spite of many blights, grew into a forest.

But his days of usefulness in Ireland speedily came to a close.‡ When Oliver Cromwell died, he left no one who could wield his sceptre. Henry was certainly fittest of his kindred for the work of government; but he had one disqualification (for such it is in our crooked world), he was too upright and

---

* Adams and Veal mention these habits.

† Cotton Mather, in his *History of New England*, speaking of Nathanael Mather, who succeeded his brother Samuel as pastor in Dublin, says:—' It was commonly remarked that Mr Charnock's invention, Dr Harrison's expression, and Mr Mather's logic, would have made the perfectest preacher in the world.'

‡ His editors make Charnock B.D. Wood conceives that he was made so by Dublin University. Mr Armstrong and Dr Seaton Reid make him a fellow of Trinity College. There is no register of this in the college books; but the records both of Trinity College and of Dublin Castle are very defective as to the Commonwealth period.

honourable to descend to the base means necessary to keep the various conflicting parties in subjection. His soul was expressed in one of his letters: 'I will rather submit to any sufferings with a good name, than be the greatest man on earth without it.'* He had to complain during his whole rule in Ireland of the selfishness of the English settlers, of the extravagancies of the sectaries, and of the jealousy of the army of the Commonwealth. He seems, however, to have been efficiently supported in his wise and impartial rule by such men as Winter† and Charnock. Nearly all parties in Ireland, Church of England, Presbyterians, and Roman Catholics, were opposed to the Commonwealth and his father's rule; but all respected and loved Henry Cromwell. He got his brother Richard proclaimed in Ireland; but the incapable parliament, out of jealousy, summoned him to England, and the royalists, at the Restoration, expelled him, without his offering any resistance.

Charnock had now to sink for a time into obscurity, with rare and limited opportunities compared with those which he had enjoyed for four or five years in the court of the lord deputy, and in St Werburgh's and Christ Church Cathedral. It was necessary to shew that he could not only act, but suffer, for Christ's name. Adams and Veal say, that 'about the year 1660, being discharged from the public exercise of his ministry, he returned back into England, and in and about London spent the greatest part of fifteen years, without any call to his old work in a settled way.' Wood and Calamy make statements to the same effect, and we must believe the account to be correct. But there is some reason to think, that though for the most part in London, he had not altogether abandoned Dublin for some time after 1660. At the close of the year 1661 (Dec. 31), he signs a certificate in favour of his friend Mr Veal, dated at Dublin.‡ It is stated that he and Mr Veal ministered in Dublin after the Restoration; and it is certain that at that time the meetings of nonconformists were winked at in Ireland, and that the Presbyterian and Independent ministers there took and were allowed an amount of liberty denied to their brethren in England and Scotland. It is stated that both Charnock and Veal preached in a Presbyterian church in Wood Street (afterwards Strand Street), which continued for many years to have a flourishing congregation, with such pastors as the Rev. Samuel Marsden, one of the ejected fellows of Dublin College, the Rev.

---

* Letter in *Thurloe Papers*.

† There is a work, *Life and Death of Winter*, 1677; also *Sermons* by him against the Anabaptists, preached before the lord deputy.

‡ The certificate is given by Calamy in *Continuation*, p. 88. It is 'Dated at Dublin, Dec. 31. 1661,' and is signed 'Steph. Charnock, formerly Minister at Warbouroughs, and late Lecturer at Christ Church, Dublin; Edward Baines, late Minister of St John's Parish, Dublin; Nath. Hoyle, late Minister at Donobrock, and late Fellow of Trinity College, Dublin; Robert Chambres, late Minister of St Patrick's Church, Dublin; Samuel Coxe, late Minister at Katherine's, Dublin; William Leclew, late Minister of Dunborn; Josiah Marsden, late Fellow of the above said Trin. College, Dublin.'

Dr Daniel Williams, who founded the Dissenters' Library in Red Cross Street, London; Dr Gilbert Rule, afterwards principal of the university of Edinburgh; and the Rev. Joseph Boyse, an able defender of the doctrine of the Trinity, and of Protestant nonconformists. On the supposition that this is correct, we find Charnock's ministry in Ireland after the Restoration followed by a train of important consequences, reaching forward into coming ages.*

This is the proper place for referring to and examining a scandalous story about Charnock given by Bishop Parker in the '*History of his own Times.*' He tells us that, Jan. 6. 1662–3, one Philip Alden voluntarily discovered to Vernon, one of the king's officers, a conspiracy to subvert the government in all the three kingdoms. This Alden had been an old rebel, and one who dealt in proscriptions and forfeited estates; but Vernon had so much obliged him by begging his life of the lord lieutenant, that he promised to discover the designs of the rebels. The principal leaders being chosen in March, determined on May 11. to open the war with the siege of Dublin : but many forces were in readiness, and they were dispersed. Lackey, a Presbyterian teacher, was hanged; but it is said he had seven accomplices, among whom was Charnock. 'This Charnock had been chaplain of Henry Cromwell, advanced to that dignity by John Owen. He was sent by the conspirators as their ambassador to London, and promised them great assistance, as Gibbs, Carr, and others had done in Scotland and Holland. But the conspiracy being now discovered, he fled again into England, and changed his name from Charnock to Clarke. He was a man of great authority among the fanatics, and for a long time was at the head of a great assembly, and did not die till twenty years after, *anno* 1683, and his corpse was carried through the city with the pomp of almost a royal funeral.'† This statement lays itself open to obvious criticism. First, Bishop Parker, so inconsistent in his life and so hasty in his charges, is by no means a safe authority in any question of fact. Next, the original informer is described as an old rebel, and a dealer in proscriptions and forfeited estates, and by no means to be trusted in the charges which he brings. Then our author makes Charnock live till 1683, whereas we have documentary evidence that he died in 1680. These considerations might seem sufficient to justify us in dismissing the statement as a fabrication, or an entire mistake.

But we know from better authorities that there was a general discontent, in the spring of 1663, among the protestants of Ireland, indeed among the nonconformists all over the three kingdoms, and that there was a conspiracy formed to seize Dublin

* See *Sermon*, &c., at the ordination of Rev. James Martineau, with an appendix containing a Summary History of the Presbyterian Churches in the City, by the Rev. James Armstrong, 1829.

† The statement of the Latin edition is 'neque enim ante vicennium obiit anno, 1683 cujus exequias pene regali funeris pompâ per urbem extulerant.'

Castle. In Ireland, the dissatisfaction was very keen among the English settlers, because they thought their interests neglected; among the soldiers of the Commonwealth, who were now stripped of their importance; but especially among zealous protestants, who were bitterly disappointed, because they saw the work of reformation thrown back. The leader seems to have been the notorious Blood, who involved in it his brother-in-law, the Rev. W. Lecky, formerly a fellow of Trinity College, who seems to have become maddened in the course of the trial. Leland says that ' some lawyers, several Presbyterian ministers, Blood, who was afterwards so distinguished in London, some members of the Irish Commons, and several republican officers, embarked in this design.' ' On the eve of the day appointed for seizing the Castle of Dublin and publishing their declaration, about five-and-twenty conspirators were seized, and a reward published for the apprehension of those who escaped.'* It appears, farther, that some intimation had been sent to London which raised the suspicion of the Government there against Charnock, for there is issued, ' 1663, June 19., warrant to Joel Hardy to apprehend Stephen Charnock,' and, ' June 20., an examination of Rob. Littlebury. Knows Mr Charnock, who visits at his house, and told him he had an overture to go beyond seas. Has had no letter from Ireland for him these six weeks;' and under the same year, ' Note of address of Robt. Littlebury at the Unicorn, Little Britain, London, with note not to miss him.' The country is evidently in a very moved state, in consequence of the ejection of the two thousand ministers, and the refusal to allow the non-conformists to meet for the worship of God. Thus William Kingsley to Secretary Bennet, June 20. 1663 :—' There are daily great conventicles in these parts ; on Whitsunday, 300 persons met at Hobday's house, Waltham parish, &c.' The news from Carlisle give indications of an understanding among the discontented. Thus Sir Phil. Musgrave reports to Williamson, June 22., Carlisle :—' There is much talk of the more than ordinary meeting of the sectaries, and the passing of soldiers between Ireland and Scotland before the public discovery of the horrid plot.'† The conclusion which we draw from these trustworthy statements is, that there was deep discontent over all the three kingdoms, among those who had been labouring to purify the church, and who were now claiming liberty of worship ; that there was a correspondence carried on among the aggrieved ; that there was a disposition among some to resist the Government, the anticipation and precursor of the covenanting struggle in Scotland, and the revolution of 1688 ; and that there was an ill-contrived conspiracy in Dublin, which was detected and put down. But there is no evidence whatever to shew that Charnock was identified in any way with the projected rising in Dublin. His name does not appear in the proclamation from Dublin Castle, 23d May

* *History of Ireland*, vol. iii. p. 434
† *Calendar State Papers*, edited by Mrs Green, vol. iii.

1663. That the government should have proceeded against him, is no presumption of his guilt, though it may have been quite sufficient to lead Bishop Parker to propagate the story. We know that 'the generality of the ministers of the north (Ulster) were at this time either banished, imprisoned, or driven into corners, upon occasion of a plot of which they knew nothing,'* these Presbyterians having in fact stood throughout by the family of Stuart, and given evidence of loyalty in very trying times. We can readily believe that Charnock should deeply sympathise with the grievances of his old friends in Dublin ; but his sober judgment, his peaceable disposition, his retiring and studious habits, all make it very unlikely that he should have taken any active part in so ill-conceived and foolish a conspiracy.†

From whatever cause, Charnock disappears very much from public view for twelve or fifteen years. We must be satisfied with such a general statement as that of Wood, who says that, returning to England about 1660, 'in and about London he did spend the greater part of fifteen years without any call to his own work, whereby he took advantage to go now and then either into France or Holland.' In France he would see a lordly church, enjoying full privileges under Louis XIV., and meet with many protestants deprived of political and military power, but having a precarious liberty under the Edict of Nantes not yet revoked. In Holland were already gathering those refugees who in due time were to bring over with them William of Orange to rescue England from oppression. Calamy represents him as 'following his studies without any stated preaching.' Yes, it was now a necessity of his nature to study. Adams and Veal say, 'Even when providence denied him opportunities, he was still laying in more stock, and preparing for work against he might be called to it.' During these years when he was in some measure out of sight, he was probably revolving those thoughts which were afterwards embodied in his great work on

* Adair MSS., quoted in Reid's *History of the Presbyterian Church in Ireland*, vol. ii. p. 284.

† In reference to Parker's charge, Bliss, the editor, in Notes to Wood's *Athenæ*, says :—' Quære—if Stephen Charnock? Grey. Probably it was the same, the bishop having mistaken the time of his death.' Mr T. Y. Gilbert, the famous antiquarian, writes us :—' Among the names of those committed on account of the alleged conspiracy, is that of "Eduard Baines, a fanatic preacher, formerly Harry Cromwell's chaplain." Could Bishop Parker have confounded the two men ? Baines was rector of St John's Church, close to Werburgh's, during the Commonwealth, and subsequently founded the Cooke Street congregation in Dublin.' It is proper to explain, as to this alleged 'fanatic preacher and the congregation in Cooke Street (first Wine Tavern Street), that Mr Baines was 'a clergyman of learning and good sense, of rational piety and zeal for the truth, and of great integrity and simplicity of spirit ;' and that in the congregation there were many persons of rank and fortune, particularly Sir John Clotworthy, afterwards Lord Massareene, Lady Chichester, afterwards Countess of Donegal, and Lady Cole of the Enniskillen family. Dr Harrison became co-pastor with Mr Baines in this congregation, and John Howe often officiated there when Lord Massareene, to whom Howe was chaplain, happened to reside in the capital. In all this we have another example of the continuance of the puritan influence in Dublin. See Armstrong's 'History of the Presbyterian Churches,' in Appendix to *Sermon*.

the 'Attributes.' Now, as at all times, he lived much in his
library, which, say Adams and Veal, was his 'workshop,'
furnished, 'though not with a numerous, yet a curious, collection
of books;' and we can conceive that one so dependent on his
reading, and who had it in view to prepare deep theological
works, must have felt it to be a great trial when his books were
burnt in the great fire of London.

About 1675, he seems to be in a position to receive a call to
minister to a fixed congregation. It appears that a portion of
the congregation were anxious to secure him as joint pastor with
Dr Thomas Jacomb, and successor to Dr Lazarus Seaman, who
died Sept. 9. 1675. John Howe, however, was settled in this
office;* and Charnock was appointed joint pastor to the Rev.
Thomas Watson in Crosby Hall. The congregation worshipping
there had been collected soon after the Restoration by Mr Watson,
formerly rector of the parish of St Stephen's, Walbrook, whose
little work, *Heaven taken by Storm*, was the means, under God,
of Colonel Gardiner's conversion. Upon the indulgence in 1674
he licensed the hall in Crosby House, on the east side of Bishops-
gate Street, which had been built in the fifteenth century by Sir
John Crosby, had at a later date been the residence of Richard
Duke of Gloucester, afterwards Richard III., and was now
the property of Sir John Langham, who patronised the nonconformists, and devoted its very beautiful Gothic hall to the
preaching of the word. Charnock was settled there in 1675, and
officiated there to the time of his death, and there a numerous
and wealthy congregation, presbyterian or independent, continued to worship for some ages.† Charnock could not be
described at this part of his life as specially a popular preacher.
On account of his memory failing, he had to read his sermons;
and on account of his weak eyesight he had to read them with
a glass, and his delivery was without the flow and impressiveness
which it had in his younger years. Besides, his compositions
were too full of matter, and were far too elaborate to be relished
by the unthinking multitude, who complained of his discourses
as being "but morality or metaphysics," their only fault being
that they were too thoughtful. Adams and Veal say, 'Yet it
may withal be said that if he were sometimes deep, he was
never abstruse; he handled the great mysteries of the gospel
with much clearness and perspicuity, so that in his preaching, if
he were above most, it was only because most were below it.'
Those who were educated up to him, as many of the middle
classes were in that age, when the word of God and theological
treatises were so studied, and when the public events of the
times compelled men to think on profound topics, waited upon
his ministry with great eagerness, and drank in greedily the

---

* Roger's *Life of Howe*, p. 144.

† Wilson's *History and Antiquities of Dissenting Churches*, vol. i. pp. 331, *et seq.*,
where is a history of Crosby Hall and an account of its ministers. Crosby Hall is
now a merchant's wareroom, but retains traces of its beauty in its timber roof and
splendid bow window.

instruction which he communicated from sabbath to sabbath. Mr Johnson tells us that 'many able ministers loved to sit at his feet, for they received by one sermon of his those instructions which they could not get by many books or sermons of others.'

We can readily picture him at this time from the scattered notices left of him. We have two portraits of him; one a painting in Williams' Library, the other a plate in the folio edition of his works. Both exhibit him with marked and bony features, and a deep expressive eye. The painting makes him appear more heavy looking and sunken, as if he often retreated into himself to commune with his own thoughts. The plate is more lively, as if he could be drawn out by those who understood and reciprocated him. Adams and Veal say he 'was somewhat reserved when he was not very well acquainted, otherwise very affable and communicative where he understood and liked his company.' We now extract from his funeral sermon. Those who did not know him cast upon him 'foul and false aspersions' ' as if he was melancholy, reserved, unsociable to all, while his acquaintances will give a character of him diametrically opposite. How cheerful, free, loving, sweet-dispositioned was he in all companies where he could take delight; he was their love, their delight.' By this time ' our Timothy was somewhat obscured by manifold infirmities, a crazy body, weak eyes, one dark, the other dim, a hand that would shake, sometimes an infirm stomach, an aching head, a fugitive memory, which, after it had failed him sometimes, he would never trust again, but *verbatim* penned and read all his notes, whereas till of late years he never looked within them.' From such a temperament we might expect a little 'passion or choler,' which is acknowledged by his friend, but which, he assures us, 'through grace he turned into the right channel.' 'He was careful to watch over his heart and against spiritual pride.' Five days each week, and twelve hours each day, he spent in his study, 'I will not say, as some, to make one sermon; I know he had other work there.' When some one told him if he studied too much it would cost him his life, he replied, 'Why, it cost Christ his life to redeem and save me.' When he went out from his books and meditations, it was to visit and relieve his patients, he having had all along a taste for medicine, and having given much time to the study of it. His bodily infirmities, his trials and spiritual conflicts, gave him a peculiar fitness for guiding the anxious and comforting the afflicted. 'He had bowels of compassion for sinners to snatch them out of the flames, and for saints to direct them unto the love of Christ.' 'I need not speak unto you of his preaching; how oft went he to children of light walking in darkness, to cheer and revive them with cordials wherewith the Lord had usually refreshed him.' 'Your teacher was,' said the preacher in the face of the congregation, 'though not a perfect man, a perfect minister, thoroughly accomplished by the Spirit and the word of truth.'

The ambition of able and thinking ministers in those times

was to draw out a system of theology. Watson, his colleague, has left us a '*Body of Divinity*,' which long continued to train the common people in the puritan theology, and may still be found, as we can testify, in the cottages of the Scottish peasantry. Charnock ' intended to have given forth a complete body of divinity' to the congregation which met in Crosby Hall, the result, we doubt not, of long reading and much thought. He began with treating of the being, and went on to the attributes of God ; but 'his sun set before he had gone over half of his transcendent excellencies and perfections. The last subject he treated on and finished was the patience of God. He was looking what to say next of the mercy, grace, and goodness of God, which he is gone to see and admire, for he found that which he most looked and longed for, the mercy of our Lord Jesus Christ unto eternal life, in heaven whence he shines now. Indeed, all the while he was upon the attributes of God, he moved with that extraordinary strength and celerity, 'twas an argument of his near approach unto his centre and everlasting rest; and if it be true, as some say, that the soul doth *prominere in morte*, his words were too true predictions, and from his soul when he said, that concerning divine patience would be his last sermon.' ' It was his longing desire, and his hopes were, that he should shortly be in that sinless state where there is the acme, the perfection of grace and holiness.'

He died July 27. 1680, at the comparatively early age of fifty-two, in the house of Richard Tymms, a glazier in the parish of Whitechapel. On July 30th, his body was conveyed to Crosby Hall, and thence accompanied by great numbers of his brethren to St Michael's Church, in Cornhill, where * his bosom friend Mr Johnson, gained at Emmanuel, adhering to him at New College, preached his funeral sermon from Mat. xiii. 43, ' Then shall the righteous shine forth as the sun in the kingdom of their Father.'† His remains were buried ' over Mr Sykes, under the steeple' of St Michael's, where the worshippers have ever since passed over them in going in to the church.

He published himself nothing but a sermon ' On the Sinfulness and cure of Evil Thoughts,' Gen. vi. 5, which appeared in the supplement to the Morning Exercises at Cripplegate; and it is an indication of his disposition to keep his name from public

* We might have doubted whether a nonconformist minister could have been permitted to preach the funeral sermon of a nonconformist minister in a parish church, but the statement is made by Wood. The entry in the register of St Michael's is, ' July 30. was buryed Stephen Charnock, minister, under the steeple.'

† 'ΕΚΛΑΜΨΙΣ ΤΩΝ ΔΙΚΑΙΩΝ. On the shining of the righteous, a sermon preached partly on the Death of that Reverend and Excellent Divine, Mr Stephen Charnock, and in part at the funeral of a godly friend, by John Johnson, M.A.' 1680. In explanation, he states that the body of the discourse had been prepared on the occasion of the death of another friend ; but, as being called suddenly to preach at Mr Charnock's funeral, he had used the same sermon, but accommodated to the different person. The discourse is somewhat rambling. We have embodied most of what relates to Charnock in this memoir. We have used the copy in the Williams' Library.

view, that in the title there is nothing more than the initials S. C., whereas in every other sermon in the collection there appears the name of the preacher. His posthumous works were given to the world by Mr Richard Adams and Mr Edward Veal, both Oxford friends, the latter also a Dublin friend, the one then a nonconformist minister in Southwark, and the other in Wapping. They first published 'A Discourse on Divine Providence,' 1680, and announce that 'this comes out first as a prodromus to several works designed to be made public as soon as they can be with conveniency transcribed,' declaring that 'the piece now published is a specimen of the strain and spirit of this holy man, this being his familiar and ordinary way of preaching.' The same year there appeared 'A Sermon on Reconciliation to God in Christ.' His discourses 'On the Existence and Attributes of God,' appeared in a large folio in 1681–82, and were followed by another folio in 1683, containing discourses on regeneration, reconciliation, the Lord's supper, and other important subjects. A second edition of his works, in two volumes folio, appeared in 1684, and a third in 1702. In 1699, were published with 'An Advertisement to the Reader,' by Edward Veal, two discourses, one on *Man's Enmity to God*, the other on *Mercy for the Chief of Sinners*.

His great work is that on the 'Attributes.' Prior to his time the subject had been treated of near the opening of systems of theology, but never in the particular and minute way in which it is done in Charnock's discourses. There had been two works on the special topic published in the English tongue in the early part of the century. The one was *A Treatise containing the Original of Unbelief, Misbelief, or Mispersuasion concerning the Veritie, Unitie, and Attributes of the Deity, by Thomas Jackson, Doctor in Divinity, Vicar of St Nicholas Church, Newcastle-upon-Tyne, and late Fellow of Corpus Christi College, Oxford, 1625.* The work is a philosophico-religious one, treating profoundly, if not clearly, of the origin of ideas as discussed by Plato and Aristotle, and of belief in God; but not unfolding, as Charnock does, the nature of the several attributes. A work more nearly resembling that of our author, and very probably suggesting it, was written by Dr Preston, one of the ablest of the Cambridge divines, and who had been master of Emmanuel some years before Charnock's time, and left a great name behind him. It is *Life Eternal, or a Treatise of the Knowledge of the Divine Essence and Attributes*, by the late John Preston. It reached a fourth edition in 1634. In the eighteen sermons of which the work is composed, the author first proves the existence and unity of God, and then dwells on eight of his perfections.* The whole is

---

* These are (1.) that God is perfect; (2.) that he is without all causes, having his being and beginning from himself; (3.) that he is eternal; (4.) that he is simple and spiritual; (5.) immutable; (6.) infinite (beyond all we can conceive), including goodness; (7.) omnipresent; (8.) omnipotent. The arrangement is very imperfect.

under 400 pages, of by no means close printing. The analysis and distribution of the attributes are by no means the same with those followed by Charnock, whose method is much more logical and judicious, while his illustration is much more full and ample. Charnock's work is at this day the most elaborate that has appeared on the subject.

Some in our day object to the separation of the divine attributes, such as we have in Charnock's work, and in systems of theology, that it is a division of the divine unity; that it is fitted to leave the impression that the perfections are so many different entities ; and that it exhibits the divine being in dry and abstract forms, which do not engage and win the affections of the heart. Now, it should be admitted at once, that a theological treatise on the attributes, or on any other subject, cannot serve every good purpose. No treatise of divinity can accomplish the high ends secured by the Word of God, with its vivid narratives, its typical events and ordinances, its instructive parables, and its attractive exhibition of God as living, acting, and loving—all suited to the heart and imagination of man as well as his understanding. A theological system when compared with the word of God, is at best like a *hortus siccus*, when compared with the growing plants in nature, or a skeleton in reference to the living frame, clothed with flesh and skin. The most useful and effective preaching must follow the Word of God as a model rather than bodies of divinity, and present God and his love in the concrete and not in the abstract form. Still, systematic theology has important purposes to secure, not only in testing and guarding purity of doctrine in a church, but in combining the scattered truths of God's Word, so that we may clearly apprehend them : in exhibiting the unity of the faith ; and in facing the misapprehensions, mistakes, and errors which may arise. In particular, great good may be effected by a full display, and a reflective contemplation of the divine character; and in order to this, there must be some order, plan, and division, and the more logical these are the better for every purpose, speculative or practical. Care must be taken always, in drawing such a portraiture, to shew that the attributes are not distinct parts of the divine essence, but simply different aspects of the one God, viewed separately because of the infirmity of our minds, and the narrowness of our vision, which prevent us from taking in the whole object at once, and constrain us to survey it part after part. As it is not the abstract quality, but the concrete being that calls forth feeling and affection, we must ever contemplate his perfections, as combined in the unity of his living person. It is to be said, in behalf of Charnock, that he never leaves the impression that the attributes are separate existences; they are simply different manifestations presented to us, and views taken by us of the one God, who is at once Great and Good, Holy and Gracious.

II. THE PURITAN PREACHING AND THE PURITAN LECTURE.

'Say not thou, What is the cause that the former days were better than these? for thou dost not inquire wisely concerning this,' Eccles. vii. 10. There are some ever telling us that the theology of former times is much superior to that of our day. Some prefer the theology of the so-called fathers of the church, some that of the middle ages, some that of the Reformation, some that of the puritans. Now we believe that it may be good for us to look to the way in which great and good men have conceived, expressed, and enforced the truth in divers ages, were it only to widen the narrowness of our views, and recall attention to catholic verities which particular ages or sects have allowed to sink out of sight. Let us by all means rise from time to time above the contracted valleys in which we dwell, and ascend a height whence we may observe the whole broad and diversified territory which God has given us as an inheritance, and the relation of the varied parts which branch out from Christ as the centre, as do the hills and valleys of our country from some great mountain, the axis of its range. There is, we should acknowledge, an attractive simplicity in the expositions of divine truth by the early fathers; and we are under deep obligations to the divines of the fourth century for establishing on Scripture evidence the doctrine of the Trinity. Those who look into it with a desire to discover what is good, will find not a few excellencies even in the mediæval divinity, notwithstanding the restraints laid on it by crutches and bandages. It is not to be forgotten that Thomas à Kempis lived in what are called the dark ages; and that we owe to a philosophic divine of that time, not certainly the doctrine of the atonement, which had been in the revealed religion of God since Adam and Abel offered lambs in sacrifice, but a very masterly and comprehensive exposition of that cardinal truth. Free grace, which had been so limited and hindered in the priestly and ecclesiastical ages, breathes from every page of the Reformers as fragrance does from the flower. The puritan preaching is unsurpassed for clear enunciation of divine truth, accompanied with close, searching, and fervent appeal, which now shakes the whole soul, as the earthquake did the prison at Philippi, and anon relieves it by the command and promise, 'Believe in the Lord Jesus Christ, and thou shalt be saved.'

But we should put implicit trust in no human, or hereditary, or traditional theology, in no theology except what comes direct from the Bible, interpreted according to the letter, but received after the spirit. How often does it happen that you will know what sect a man belongs to by the favourite passages which he quotes in his sermons, and in his very prayers, shewing how apt we are to take our very Scriptures from the traditions of our churches. We act as if the well were shut up from us, and as if we were obliged to go to the streams, which may have caught earthliness in their course, and which at the best cannot be so fresh as the fountain. That is the theology best suited to the age which is put forth by living men of the age, drinking of the living word for themselves by the power of the living Spirit.

The peculiarities of the puritan preaching arose from the circumstances in which they were placed, combined always with their deep piety. Most of them were highly educated men, trained in classics, logics, and ethics at the old universities. In their colleges, and in the Established Church, they had acquired habits of careful study and preparation for the pulpit, which they retained all their lives, whether they remained in or removed from the communion of the Church of England. Meanwhile, in the prosecution of their high aims, they were thrown into the midst of most exciting scenes, which moved society from its base to its summit. They had to make up their minds on most momentous questions, and to come to a public decision, and take their side,—it may be at an immense sacrifice of worldly wealth and status. With a great love for the national Church, and a desire to keep the unity of the faith, they declined, in obedience to what they believed to be the commands of God in his word, to conform to practices which the government, political and ecclesiastical, was imposing on them. In taking their part in the movements of these times, they had to mingle with men of all classes, to write papers of defence and explanation, and at times of controversy, and to transact a multifarious business, with bearings on statesmen on the one hand, and the mass of the people on the other. Out of this state of things arose a style of exposition different from that of the retired scholar on the one hand, and from that of the man of bustle on the other; equally removed from the manner of the independent churchman and of the ever stirring dissenter. The discourses are by men of thought and erudition, who must draw their support from the great body of the people, and address in one and the same sermon both men and women belonging to all ranks and classes. We see those characteristics in every treatise of Owen and Baxter, and they come out in the discourses of Charnock.

The works of Charnock, and of the puritans generally, labour under two alleged imperfections. With the exception of Howe's 'Living Temple,' and one or two other treatises, they are without that subdued and quiet reflection which gives such a charm to books which have come out of retired parsonages or the cloisters of colleges. In most of the writings of the puritans, there is a movement, and in many of them a restlessness, which shew that they were composed for hearers or readers who were no doubt to be instructed, but whose attention required also to be kept alive. Their profound discussions and their erudite disquisitions, having reference commonly to expected, indeed immediate action, are ever mixed with practical lessons and applications which interrupt the argument, and at times give a strain and bias to the interpretation of a passage. In this respect their discourses, written with the picture of a mixed auditory before them, are very different from the essays or dissertations, philosophic or critical, of certain of the Anglican or German divines, who, themselves mere scholars or thinkers, write only for the learned; but possess an interest to them such as cannot attach to spoken addresses in which the popular and the scientific are mixed in every page.

Because of this attempted combination, the puritans labour under another alleged disadvantage. Most of their writings contain too much thought, too much erudition, and above all too many logical distinctions, to admit of their being appreciated by vulgar readers. With the living voice and the earnest manner to set them off, the sermons may have been listened to with profound interest by large mixed audiences; but in the yellow pages of the old volume they scare those who do not wish to be troubled with active or earnest thought. In this respect they are inferior—some would rather say immeasurably superior—to the popular works produced in our day by evangelical writers both within and beyond the established churches of England and Scotland. They are not characterised by that entire absence, in some cases studious abnegation, of reflective thought and convincing argument, which is a characteristic of some of our modern preachers, who cast away their manhood and pule like infants; nor do they indulge in those stories and anecdotes by which some of our most successful ministers of the word attract and profit large audiences in our times. The puritans had learning, and they gave the results of it to their congregations. They thought profoundly themselves, and they wished to stimulate and gratify thought in their hearers and readers.

The consequence of all this is, that there is a class who reckon themselves above, and there is a class certainly below, the puritan. There are contemplatists who are disturbed by their feverishness, and scholars who complain of the intrusion of unasked practical lessons. But if these persons would only exercise a little of that patience on which they set so high a value, they would find imbedded in the rich conglomerate of the puritans profound reflections and wise maxims, which could have come only from deep thinkers and scholars, who spent long hours in their studies reading, meditating, and, we may add, praying over the deepest questions which the mind of man can ponder. It is also true that there are men and women of all ranks and conditions who are below the puritans, such as the devourers of novels in our circulating libraries, our men of pleasure and of mere business and agriculture, who have never been led to entertain a thought above their amusements, or their shops and their warehouses, their crops and their cattle; and such are the masses in our great cities, and in our scattered rural districts too, who have been allowed to spring up in utter ignorance, but who would not have been left in such utter degradation if the puritans had been allowed to carry out their system of inspection, catechising, and careful Bible instruction. We allow that persons so untrained to thinking would speedily fall asleep if made to read a puritan treatise, with its deep thoughts and its logical distinctions. The puritan preachers no doubt required a prepared audience; but they had succeeded so far in training intelligent audiences in their own day, and they had a discipline which, if they had been allowed to carry it out, might have prepared the great body of the people for listening to the systematic exposition of the divine word. Nor is it to be forgotten that there are passages in the writings of the best puritans more fitted than any composed by uninspired men to awaken the unthinking and arouse the careless, and compel them to think of the things which belong to their everlasting peace. These passages continue to be regularly quoted to this day, and often constitute the very best parts of the articles in our popular religious literature. Charnock's discourses, in particular, have been a mine in which many have dug, and found there gold wherewithal to enrich themselves, without exhausting the numberless veins. The preachers who have caught the spirit of the puritans, but have avoided their technicality and mannerism, have commonly been the most successful in rousing the sunken and the dead from their apathy, and in stirring them to anxiety and prayer.

Some of the critical commentaries furnished by the puritans, such as those of Owen, are among the ablest, and altogether the best, that have ever been published. It is all true that modern German industry has dug up and collected materials unknown in the sixteenth and seventeenth centuries, and the more recent contests with the rationalists and infidels, while producing it may be much immediate mischief, have in the end led to a larger and more minute acquaintance with ancient thought and history, and with eastern languages and customs. But the puritans have been left behind merely by the onward march of knowledge; and the time may come when even the most advanced German critics may in this sense become antiquated. It is true that the puritans, keeping before them a living audience, ever mingled practical reflections and applications with their most erudite criticism, in a way which is now avoided by learned commentators. But over against this we have to place the counterbalancing circumstance, that the Scriptures were written for practical purposes, and will ever be better interpreted by practical men, who have felt the truth themselves, and who have had enlarged and familiar intercourse with men, women, and children in the actual world, than by the mere book scholar, who is ever tempted to attribute motives to historical actors such as real human beings were never swayed by, and to discard passages because they contain improbabilities such as one who mingles with mankind is meeting with every day. We have sometimes thought, in comparing the puritan with the modern German criticism, that the one of these circumstances is quite fitted to outweigh the other; of course, the one should be used to counteract the other, and a perfect commentary should seek to embrace both advantages.

The multiplied divisions, and ramified subdivisions, employed in their discourses, furnish matter of very common complaint against them. The habit arose from the training in a narrow scholastic logic in the universities, and is to be found in the ethical, the juridical, the legal, and the parliamentary quite as much as in the theological writings of the age, and in the high Anglican as well as in the puritan theology. We are not prepared to vindicate the peculiar manner of the times. The excess in one direction led in the immediately succeeding age to an excess in the other direction. The new method, or want of method, was introduced from France, and came in with a very light and superficial literature. It was espoused by such writers as Lord Shaftesbury in his ' *Characteristics of Men, and Manners, and Times;*' and appeared in a very graceful dress in the *Tatler, Spectator*, and *Guardian*. Shaftesbury tells us that the miscellaneous manner was in the highest esteem in his day, that the old plan of dividing into firsts and seconds had grown out of fashion, and that 'the elegant court divine exhorts in miscellany, and is ashamed to bring his twos and threes before a fashionable assembly.' 'Ragouts and fricassees are the reigning dishes; so authors, in order to become fashionable, have run into the more savoury way of learned ragout and medley.' In adopting the style of the times, the preachers no doubt supposed that they could thereby recommend religion to the world, especially to the gay and fashionable classes, who had been repelled by the old manner, and might be won, it was alleged, by the new. The comment of the clerical satirist Witherspoon, in his ' *Characteristics*,' is very pertinent. After stating the allegation that the old system had driven most of the fashionable gentry from the churches, he says: 'Now the only way to regain them to the church, is to accommodate the worship as much as may be to their taste;' and then remarks slily, 'I confess there has sometimes been an ugly objection thrown up against this part of my argument, viz., that this desertion of public worship by those in high life seems in fact to be contemporary with, and to increase in a pretty exact proportion to, the attempts that have been made, and are made, to suit it to their taste.' Not that we have any right to condemn the preachers of the eighteenth century because they did not choose to follow the formalism of the seventeenth. A much graver charge can be brought against them; that of sinking out of sight, or diluting, some of the convincing and saving truths of Christianity. The minister of God's Word, if he is not to make himself ridiculous, must wear the dress and accommodate himself to the innocent manners of his age; but he is never to forget that he is a minister of the word, prepared to declare the whole counsel of God, and he is not to imagine that he can deliver himself from the offence of the cross. The polite, the gay, and the refined admired the preaching of the eighteenth century, but never thought of allowing themselves to fall under the power of the religion recommended. The puritan preachers are still read and have power, 'being dead they yet speak unto us;' but who remembers the names of the admired pulpit orators of last century? Who, except the lovers of *belles lettres*, ever think of looking into the polished sermons of Hugh Blair and his school?

It may be allowed that the puritan preachers, like all the didactic writers of their time, carried their subdivisions too far. They sought by abstraction to bring out into distinct view all the attributes of the concrete object; and by mental analysis to distribute a complex subject into its parts. As correct thinkers, their judgment would have been offended if a single one of the parts which go to make up the whole had been left out. But comprehensive minds now see that it is beyond the capacity of man to find out all the elements of any one existing object 'in the heavens above, or in the earth beneath, or the waters under the earth.' In the subject, for example, discussed by Charnock, the nature of God, no one should profess, (certainly Charnock does not) to be able to discover or to unfold all the perfections of Jehovah; and it would be simple pretension to make the propositions we utter assume the appearance of completeness of knowledge and explanation. The mind feels burdened when a speaker or writer would lay the whole weight of a comprehensive subject upon it. Charles II. was offering a just criticism on the whole preaching of the age when he charged Isaac Barrow with being an unjust preacher, inasmuch as he left nothing for any other man to say. All people weary of an enumeration which would count all gifts bestowed in minute coins; independent thinkers feel offended when any one would dogmatically settle everything for them; and enlarged minds would rather have a wide margin left for them to write on, and prefer suggestive to exhaustive writers.

But on the other hand, definition and division are important logical instruments; and when they are kept in their proper place as means, they serve important purposes. The puritan preachers all aimed at vastly more than mere tickling, rousing, and interesting their hearers; they aimed at instructing them. For this purpose it was needful first of all to give their hearers clear notions; and how could that be done except by the speakers themselves acquiring distinct and adequate ideas, and then uttering a clear expression of them? They were quite aware that speculative notions and linked ratiocinations were not fitted to raise feeling, and that there could be no religion without affection; and hence they ever mingled appeals to the conscience, and addresses to the feelings, and even pictures for the fancy, with their methodical arrangements and reasoning processes.

c

But they knew at the same time that mere feeling, unsustained by the understanding, would die out like an unfed flame, and hence they ever sought to convey clear apprehensions, and to convince the judgment. Then they wished their audience to retain what they heard in their memories for future rumination. But the memory, at least of the intelligent, proceeds in its reminiscences by correlation; it cannot bring up the unconnected, the dismembered; it needs hooks on which to hang the thoughts, compartments in which to arrange them, that we may know where to find them, and to be able to bring them out for use when we need them. All skilful teachers of youth know that if their pupils would make progress they must employ method, and have division and enumeration in the lessons on which they examine. And it is certain that the puritans aimed at nothing less than thoroughly *teaching* their flocks; and many of their hearers, male and female, took notes of the sermons and afterwards expanded them. Such a process would be quite impossible in regard to much of the preaching of our times, satisfying itself with a loose general view of a subject, which may produce a transient impression for good, but which does not give a distinct apprehension at the time, and which could not possibly be recalled afterwards, much less expressed, by any but the original speaker. Depend upon it, two centuries hence these writers will be far less read than the puritans are at this present time.

An objection has frequently been taken to the too graphic illustrations and quaintnesses of the puritans. An excuse can easily be pled for it by those who may not be prepared to recommend it for general adoption. It was the habit of the time, and was adopted in all departments of literature, poetical and prose, and by the adherents of the Anglican establishment as well as the nonconformists. The puritan preachers felt as if they were necessitated to employ some such means of keeping alive the attention of hearers to the weighty instruction they were in the habit of imparting to their large mixed audiences. It is a curious circumstance that the present age has come back to the same practice under a somewhat different form, and with less excuse for it in the solidity of its thinking; and it cannot with any consistency object to the fashion of the good old puritans as long as it calls for and favours so many *sensation* means of summoning the attention, not only in novels, but in every species of writing, including our religious literature, which is advertised by catch titles and read for the sake of excitement. It is to be said in behalf of the puritans, that though there may be at times an overstrained ingenuity in their illustrations, yet these always bear directly and pointedly upon the doctrinal truth which they are expounding, and the practical lessons which they enforce. The puritans ever sought to enlighten the intellect; but their aim was also to gain the heart, and in order to both one and the other, to awaken the conscience—in the addresses to which they have not been surpassed, perhaps not equalled, by any class of teachers in ancient or in modern times.

The best puritan preaching ever tended to take the form of what they called the 'lecture.' We often meet with this phrase in reading the history of the times. There were lectures delivered weekly in certain churches in London, and in some of the principal towns throughout the three kingdoms; Laud, we know, endeavoured to put down the puritan lecture. Charnock describes himself as officially lecturer at Christ Church, where the lecture was delivered at three o'clock on the afternoons of the Lord's day. We are not to suppose that the puritans always preached in this elaborate style, but the ablest of them did so when they could get fit audience; and the sermons which they thought worthy of publication were commonly of this elaborately-expository type. In particular, Charnock always discourses to us as if he were lecturing in a college chapel at Oxford, or in Christ Church, Dublin.

While it is not desirable that all preaching, or even ordinary preaching, should be of this stamp, it would surely be for the benefit of the church of Christ to have a few lecturers or doctors, fitted for such work, in all our great cities; or to secure the same end by systematic lectures delivered by a judicious combination of competent men, not merely on attractive and popular, but on profound theological, subjects. To accomplish the purpose in our day, it is not needful that this elaborate exposition should proceed in the manner of the puritans; in particular, it should avoid the minute dissection of texts in which they so delighted, but in which the living truth was apt to be killed in the process. In order to be profitable, the lectures must be addressed to the age, by men who sympathise with the age; and it is only thus that they can accomplish in this century, what the puritan lecture effected two hundred years ago. Ever founded on the word of God, they should endeavour to bring out its broad and simple meaning, rather than exercise their ingenuity in drawing out significations which were never seen by the writers of the Scriptures. Thus may the church of God expect to raise up a body of intelligent people, to maintain and defend the truth in our day, by better weapons than were employed even by the soldiers of Cromwell in the seventeenth century.

III. PHILOSOPHICAL PRINCIPLES INVOLVED IN THE PURITAN THEOLOGY.

The author of this Introduction feels that, on being asked to write about the divine who discussed the profound subject of the 'Attributes of God,' it will be expected of him, from the character of his favourite studies, that he should say something of the philosophy of the puritans, or rather of the philosophic principles involved in the puritan theology. For in truth the puritans were not, really nor professedly, philosophers, but theologians and preachers. Not that their religious views discouraged the study of philosophy. It could be shewn that some of the greatest thinkers that England has produced, owed not a little to puritan influence. Francis Bacon had certainly none of the self-sacrificing spirit of the puritans, but he owed much to a puritan mother. The puritans generally were too much engrossed with practical questions, to write calm philosophic treatises. But it is not to be forgotten that Culverwel and Cudworth, about the most learned and profound thinkers of their age, took the reforming side in Cambridge; and Howe, who wrote his 'Living Temple' (at least the first part of it) in his calm retirement in the family of Lord Massarene at Antrim, was altogether a puritan. Locke (like Milton) did not keep by the deep religious faith of those among whom he was brought up, but he cherished their reverence for the Bible and liberty of thought.

The phrase 'puritan divines' is understood to apply to those who sought to construct a biblical theology. But Christian theology, which is a co-ordination of the scattered truths of God's word, cannot be constructed without philosophic principles, more or fewer, being involved explicitly, or more frequently implicitly. If we try to connect truths which in the Bible are left unconnected; if we generalise what in the Scriptures is particular; if we infer from what is revealed; if we argue from the analogy of the faith, or from any other principle; above all, if we would arrange the truth into a system, we must, whether we avow it or not, whether we know it or not, proceed on some principle of reason. We often find that those who affect to be the most determined to avoid all scholastic forms, are all the while, in their statements and reasonings, proceeding on principles which are really metaphysical, the metaphysics being very confused and ill-founded. It would be very curious and very instructive withal, to have a full and clear enunciation of the philosophic principles involved in the theologies of all different ages and creeds. It is only by having such a statement spread out articulately, that we can find what is human and what is divine in systems of divinity. In this article we are to endeavour to bring out to view the philosophy implied in the construction of the puritan theology.

Bible theologians, as such, should always avoid identifying their systems with, or founding them upon, any peculiar metaphysical system. But let us not be misunderstood. We do not mean to affirm that no attempt should be made to wed religion and philosophy. We hold that all philosophy should be thought out in a religious spirit, and that much good may be effected by philosophic works on religious topics, such as those of Pascal, and Culverwel, and Cudworth in the seventeenth century. But in all such cases the philosophy and the Scriptural theology should be kept separate, not, it may be, in separate chapters, but first in the mind of the writer, and second in the composition of his work ; so separate, that the reader may discern the difference, and that the certainties of God may not be confounded by the dullest apprehension with the speculations of men.

The puritans professed to be students of the Bible, and not philosophers, and to avoid all mere speculative questions. And we are prepared to affirm that neither before nor since, has there been a body of profound divines assuming fewer doubtful metaphysical principles. But the very puritans did proceed, in the construction of their systems, on certain logical or metaphysical maxims. We allow that, like all dogmatic theologians, they carried their method of technical formulæ too far ; that they did at times squeeze a text, written in an eastern language, to suit it to a western article ; and that they professed to reach a completeness of system such as is altogether beyond the limited capacities of man, in dealing with the boundless truths of God's Word. But we maintain that in their theology they ground on no peculiar philosophy ; that the maxims involved in their construction and inferences are found in the very nature of the human mind, and of the reason with which man is endowed, are such as man must ever take with him, if he is not to abnegate his rational nature, are such as have had a place allotted them in all profound philosophies, whether in ancient, in mediæval, or in modern times ; in short, the puritans proceed on the principles of a catholic philosophy, which is the expression of the laws of man's intellectual constitution.

It may be allowed indeed that they employed at times the forms and expressions of authors, and of systems that were favourites with them. In particular, they used the distinctions and the phrases of Aristotle, of Augustine, and of the scholastic logicians. But then it is to be remembered that Aristotle and Augustine were about the most comprehensive thinkers that ever lived ; and it is a fact that the schoolmen, all narrow and technical as they were in their spirit, were the main instruments of giving definiteness to the expressions used in the western world in our modern literature,—in fact, in our very speeches, sermons, and common conversation. The puritans in their learned treatises had to ·employ the phraseology of the learning of their times, just as they had to use the language of their country. The inspired writers themselves had their nationalities and their individualities—the speech of the disciples still ' bewrayeth ' them. They had to speak of the sun rising, and the earth standing, according to the ideas of their time ; and in regard to man's nature they had to use the phrases, ' reins,' ' bowels,' ' heart,' and employ the distinction of ' body,' ' soul,' and ' spirit,' because they were accepted in their times. The puritans must use the language they found ready for them, and the distinctions understood by their readers ; but just as the writers of Scripture did not mean authoritatively to sanction any theories of the world or of the mind, so the puritans did not intend to adopt any peculiar philosophic system, Platonic or Aristotelian, Greek or Latin, ancient or modern, but to proceed on the universal principles of reason.

In establishing the divine existence, Charnock had to make references to the material universe, as furnishing evidence of order, design, and beneficence. In doing so, he has to make his statements according to the views of the time. The Copernican theory of the universe had been adopted for some ages by men of science, but had not yet been brought down to the common belief of the people. Bacon had rejected it, and Milton in his great poem forms his pictures on the idea of the earth being reckoned the stable centre, with the stars moving round it in cycles and epicycles. When Charnock was in Dublin, the Royal Society was formed in Oxford; and while Charnock was meditating his discourses on the Attributes, Newton was cogitating the law of universal gravitation. But the preacher feels that it was not for him to go in advance of the popular apprehension. He usually supposes, as all men in fact still do, that the sun moves round the earth, but he states in a note, 'whether it be the sun or the earth that moves, it is all one,' that is for his purpose, which is to shew that 'the things in the world declare the existence of a God in their production, harmony, preservation, and answering their several ends.' 'Every plant, every atom, as well as every star, at the first meeting, whispers this in our ears, "I have a Creator, I am witness to a Deity." Who ever saw statues or pictures, but presently thinks of a statuary and limner?' 'The spider, as if it understood the art of weaving, fits its web both for its own habitation, and a net to catch its prey. The bee builds its cell, which serves for chambers to reside in, and a repository for its provision.' 'The whole model of the body is grounded upon reason. Every member hath its exact proportion, distinct office, regular motion.' 'The mouth takes in the meat, the teeth grind it for the stomach, the stomach prepares it.' 'Every member hath a signature and mark of God, and of his wisdom.'* It is the office of natural theology to unfold the order and the adaptation which everywhere fall under our notice in the works of God, but in doing so it should never profess to expound the ultimate constitution of things: 'No man can find out the work that God maketh from the beginning to the end.' In order to the conclusiveness of the argument for the divine existence, it is not necessary that we should know the final composition and laws of the substances in which the order and design are exhibited. We may see at once that there are plan and purpose in the dispositions of an army in march, though we know not meanwhile whence it has come or whither it is going. In like manner we are sure that there are skill and contrivance in the movements of the hosts of nature, though we cannot tell their ultimate properties. Charnock lived in an age of transition in physical science, and some of his representations are antiquated; but his arguments are still conclusive, and his illustrations need only to be expressed in a new form to become apposite. We should not forget that we, too, live in an age of transition, and

* *Attributes*, Dis. I.

when the grand discoveries of our day in regard to the conservation of energy and the correlation of all the physical forces, and in regard to the unity of all organic forms, are wrought out to their full consequences, we suspect that the most advanced works in our century, that the Natural Theology of Paley, and the Bridgewater and Burnet Treatises, will be found as antiquated in the twentieth century as the works of the seventeenth century are to us.

But the divines of the seventeenth century had to deal much more with mental philosophy than with physical science. It may serve some good ends to exhibit the exact historical position in respect of philosophy of the puritans, and more especially of Charnock. The puritan divines generally were well acquainted with the philosophy of Aristotle, with his logic, his psyche, his ethics, and metaphysics. They were also conversant with the theology of Augustine, of the middle ages, and of the reformers. The exclusive reverence for the scholastic system had passed away among advanced thinkers, but the scholastic training still lingered in the colleges, and the new and experiential method had not yet been expounded. Charnock was born four years before Locke, and the ‘ Discourses on the Attributes’ appeared ten years before the ‘ Essay on the Human Understanding,’ the work which founded modern English philosophy. Charnock died fifty-nine years before David Hume published the sceptical work on *Human Nature*, which compelled thinkers to review all old philosophic principles, even those involved in theology ; eighty years before Thomas Reid began the work of reconstruction on observational principles ; and a century before Emmanuel Kant made his attack on rational theology, and appealed to man’s moral nature as furnishing the only argument for the divine existence. This was no doubt one reason why the puritan theology was not appreciated except by earnest Christians in the eighteenth century ; it did not speak to those who had been trained in the new philosophy. But we have now arrived at a time in which neither the philosophy of Locke, nor that of Kant, can be allowed to reign supremely. We are at a sufficient distance to regard them, not as suns in our sky, but as stars, with Plato and Aristotle and Augustine, and many others, their equals in light and splendour. In particular, those who most admire Locke and his fresh observational spirit, now see his great defects in deriving all our ideas from sensation and reflection, and setting aside the constitutional principles of the mind. The superficial theology which grounded itself on the philosophy of Locke has died an unlamented death, and no one wishes to see it raised from the grave to which it has been consigned. We shall certainly never return to the phraseology employed by the puritans, nor bind ourselves to follow them in their favourite distinctions. Let us copy them only in this, that in our arguments we proceed on the principles which, in some modification or other, have appeared in all deep philosophies, and have done so because they are in the very structure of our minds, and in the nature of human reason, as reflecting the divine reason.

I. Let us glance at the PURITAN PSYCHOLOGY.

The Faculties of the Mind.—These come out only incidentally. The following is Charnock's summary, 'The essential faculties of the rational soul—the mind, the repository of principles, the faculty whereby we should judge of things honest or dishonest; the understanding, the discursive faculty, and the reducer of those principles into practical dictates; that part whereby we reason and collect one thing from another, framing conclusions from the principles in the mind; the heart, *i. e.*, the will, conscience, affections, which were to apply those principles, draw out those reasonings upon the stage of the life.'* Though not a perfect, this is not a bad, distribution of the mental powers. The account of our intellectual capacities is certainly superior to that given by Locke, who denied innate ideas, and allowed an inadequate place to intuition. Charnock mentions first 'the mind, the repository of principles.' What is this but Plato's λόγος and Aristotle's νοῦς described by both, each, however, with a different explanation, as τόπος εἰδῶν (see Aris. *Psyche*, iii. c. 4 s. 4)? What but Locke's *intuition*—not properly unfolded by him? What but Reid's *principles of common sense*, Kant's *forms*, and Sir William Hamilton's *regulative faculty?* Then in regard to the other, or motive, department of the mind, we may mark how English thinkers had not yet come to the miserably defective psychology of the last century and beginning of this, in which man's powers are represented as consisting simply in the understanding and feelings. Man's heart is spoken of as having three essential elements, the will, the conscience, and the affections, each with a province, each serving a purpose, and all to be dedicated to God. There was no such narrow and confused controversy such as that which has been started in our day as to whether religion be an affair of the head or of the heart. In their 'repository of principles,' as distinguished from the discursive faculty and reasoning, they had all that is good and true in the modern Germano-Coleridgean distinction between the reason and the understanding; and they had it in a better form; and they never proposed, as some in our day have done, to make reason the sole discerner and judge of religion. With the puritan, religion was an affair of the whole man, including head and heart, and the heart having not only emotive sensibility and attachment, but a conscience to discern good and evil, and a will to choose.

Knowledge.—As opposing themselves to scepticism, both in natural and revealed religion, they held that man could reach knowledge, positive and correct. They represented some knowledge as being intuitive, and other knowledge as obtained by a process, both the one and the other being real. They held that man could rise to a true knowledge of God, to some knowledge by means of his works within and without us, but to a still closer and more satisfactory knowledge by the revelation he has given in his Word, very specially by the manifestation he has made of himself

* Sermon on *The Knowledge of God*, p. vi.

in the face of his Son. The divines of that century did not countenance the doctrine advocated by Archbishop King and Bishop
Peter Brown in the beginning of the next, and revived in our day,
as to man being incapacitated by his very nature from knowing
God as he is, a doctrine supposed to be favourable to religion, but
which may quite as readily serve the purposes of a philosophy
which affirms that man can know nothing, and terminate in scepticism. Charnock declares, as to this knowledge, first, that it is not
immediate or intuitive, such as we have of a man when we see him
face to face, but through 'his excellent works of creation, providence, redemption, and the revelation of invisible mysteries in the
Word.' He says, secondly, it is not *comprehensive.* 'To know
comprehensively is to contain, and the thing contained must be
less than that which contains, and therefore, if a creature could
comprehend the essence of God, he would be greater than God.'
He says that we cannot comprehend the nature of the creatures
that are near us, and that not even in heaven shall God be comprehensively known. But still we are represented as knowing
God. We know God as we know the sea ; we behold the vastness
of its waters, but we cannot measure the depths and abysses of it.
Yet we may be said truly to see it, as we may touch a mountain
with our hands, but not grasp it in our arms.'

Knowledge and faith.—The puritans do not enter into any
minute inquiries as to the natural exercises of knowledge and faith.
The precise nature and relation of knowledge and faith as psychological acts cannot be said to be yet settled by the professors of
mental science. We here come to a *desideratum,* which we venture to think might be supplied by inductive investigation. There
is a constant reference in the present day to knowledge and faith
as different, and each with a province, but we are furnished with
no definition of terms, or explanation of the precise difference of
the exercises. The puritans confined themselves, as the schoolmen
of the age of Anselm and Abelard did, to their own province, the
relation of the two as religious acts. Their views, especially those
of Charnock, are clear and distinctly announced, and they seem to
us to be sound and judicious. Charnock declares unequivocally
that knowledge is necessary in order to faith : 'It is impossible an
act can be without an object ; nothing is grace but as it is conversant about God, or hath a respect to God. There can be no act
about an unknown object.' 'Faith cannot be without the knowledge of God and Christ.' 'Knowledge is antecedent to faith in the
order of nature. *I know whom I have believed,* 2 Tim. i. 12.
That ye may know and believe that I am he, Is. xliii. 10.' The
divines of that century have not started the question whether faith
belongs to the understanding or the feelings. Their view seems to
us to be sounder both psychologically and theologically. 'This
grace (faith), therefore, is set in a double seat by divines, in the
understanding and will: *it is properly a consent of the will, which
cannot be without an assent in the mind.*' 'Faith is in the understanding in regard of disposition, but in the will in regard of the

fiducial apprehension; for faith is not one simple virtue, but compounded of two, knowledge and trust.'*

The conscience.—In respect of the place they give to the conscience, the puritans have passed far beyond Aristotle, whom they so far follow in their psychology. Aristotle, in his Ethics, does allot to 'right reason' (ὡρισμενη λόγῳ καὶ ὡς ἄν ὁ φρόνιμος ὁρίσειεν, see *Ethics* ii. c. 6, § 15), a function in the determination of virtue; but he does not mention the conscience. The puritans, founding on the passage in Paul (Rom. ii. 15), make constant references to the conscience; no preachers before their time, and few since, have made such direct and powerful appeals to this mental faculty. 'Conscience,' says Charnock, 'is natural to man, and an active faculty.' They attempt no psychological analysis of the power; they do not inquire whether it is an exercise of the reason on the one hand, or a sense, sentiment, or feeling on the other. This was a question started in the next age by Samuel Clarke on the one side, and Shaftesbury and Francis Hutcheson on the other. Charnock, we have seen, makes the heart embrace 'the conscience, will, affections.' In the 'mind, the repository of principles,' he places the faculty 'whereby we should judge of things honest or dishonest;' and the office of conscience seems to be that of following this up by 'accusing, or else excusing.' He argues resolutely that the conscience testifieth in behalf of the existence of God. 'Man witnesseth to God in the operations and reflections of conscience.' 'There is a law in the minds of men which is a rule of good and evil. There is a notion of good and evil in the consciences of men, which is evident by those laws which are common to all countries.' 'Man, in the first instant of the use of reason, finds natural principles within himself; directing and choosing them, he finds a distinction between good and evil; how could this be if there were not some rule to him to try and distinguish good and evil.' 'Common reason supposeth that there is some hand which hath fixed this distinction in man; how could it else be universally impressed? No law can be without a lawgiver.' 'As there is a rule in us, there must be a judge.' 'From this a man may rationally be instructed that there is a God; for he may thus argue: I find myself naturally obliged to do this thing and avoid that, I have therefore a superior that doth oblige me.'† Has Emmanuel Kant, with his 'practical reason' and 'categorical imperative,' said anything more direct and convincing than this?

The affections and the will. These two were never resolved into each other by the puritans. They asserted that all knowledge should lead on to affection, and that all genuine faith does produce

* The above extracts from the sermon on *The Knowledge of God.*

† *Attributes,* Disc. I. The puritans generally appealed to first principles, intellectual and moral. Thus Baxter says, *Reasons of the Christian Religion,* P. 1, 'And if I could not answer a sceptic, who denied the certainty of my judgment by sensation and reflexive intuition (how near to Locke), yet nature would not suffer me to doubt.' 'By my actions I know that I am; and that I am a sentient, intelligent, thinking, willing, and operative being.' 'It is true that there is in the nature of man's soul a certain aptitude to understand certain truths as soon as they are revealed; that is, as soon as the very *natura rerum* is observed. And it is true that

affection.   But they ever insisted that above the affections there is
a more important power, the power of will.   It is thus that Charnock puts the relation of these attributes :—'The choice of the will
in all true knowledge treads upon the heel of the act of understanding, and men naturally desire the knowledge of that which is true,
in order to the enjoyment of that which is good in it.   The end
of all the acts of the understanding is to cause a motion in the will
and affections suitable to the apprehension.'   'Knowledge is but
as a cloud that intercepts the beams of the sun, and doth not advantage the earth, unless melted into drops, and falling down into the
bosom of it.   Let the knowledge of the word of the truth drop down
in a kindly shower upon your hearts, let it be a knowledge of the
word heated with love.'*

II. PHILOSOPHIC PRINCIPLES.—We have seen that among the
mental attributes he places 'the repository of principles.' The puritan
divines do not attempt to expound the nature of these principles, and
the accounts given by metaphysicians since that time, as well as prior

this disposition is brought to actual knowledge as soon as the mind comes to actual
consideration of the things.   But it is not true that there is any actual knowledge
of any principles born in man.' It is wrong to 'make it consist in certain axioms
(as some say) born in us, or written in our hearts from our birth (as others say),
dispositively there.' These distinctions do not exhaust the subject, but they contain
important truth; and if Locke had attended to them, he would have been saved
from extravagant statements. Owen, in his *Dissertation on Divine Justice*, appeals,
in proving the existence of justice, (1.) to the 'common opinion' and innate conceptions of all; (2.) to the consciences of all mankind; (3.) to the public consent
of all nations.

* Sermons on *Knowledge of God* and *Regeneration*. David Clarkson, in his
account of the 'New Creature,' speaks of the following mental acts as involved
in the religious exercises of the soul:—I. THE MIND OR UNDERSTANDING. And
under this (1.) apprehensions, view, or notion; (2.) judgment and assent arising from apprehensions; (3.) valuations proceeding from the estimative power
of the mind; (4.) designs or contrivances of ends; (5.) inventions, whereby
finds means towards ends; (6.) reasonings, or discursive power; (7.) thoughts,
or cogitations; (8.) consultations, the advising power which philosophers call
Βουλευτική, which shews by what means the good end may be secured. II. THE
WILL, under which we have (1.) new inclinations,—Aristotle calls the act Βούλησις,
and the schoolmen, *simplex volitio*, in it the mind has a new object; (2.) new intentions, aiming at something new, intending God and aiming at him; (3.) fruitions,
in which the mind rests and is contented; (4.) new elections in choice of means for
promoting ends, Aristotle's προαίρεσις τῶν πρὸς τὸ τέλος; (5.) new consents, in
particular the soul consenting to enter into covenant with God; (6.) new applications, whereby the will applies the faculties to prosecute what it has pitched on;
(7.) new purposes, determinations, resolves, these being fixed and permanent. This
analysis, taken with modifications from Aristotle and the scholastic divines, is too
minute, but it shews how expanded a view the puritans took of the higher attributes
of the mind as engaged in spiritual acts. In his sermon 'Of Faith,' he says—Faith
implies (1.) knowledge; (2.) assent; (3) dependence or procumbence. 'To rely upon
Christ alone for salvation is saving faith.' See *Sermons and Discourses on Several
Divine Subjects, by the late Reverend and learned David Clarkson, B.D., and sometime
Fellow of Clare Hall, Cambridge*, 1696. In these sermons, the scholastic phrases,
objective, subjective, effective, formaliter, interpretive, habitualiter, cast up in all profound
discussion. The account of the mental faculties is the most extended we have seen
in the puritan writings. That of Charnock is more succinct and judicious. But all
the puritans proceed substantially on the same views. The view of faith is the
same with that of Charnock, and it could easily be shewn that it is that held by the
puritan divines generally.

to it, have been sufficiently confused. So far as Charnock incidentally sketches their nature, his views are both just and profound. He speaks of them as *connatural*,* a phrase the praise of which has been ascribed to Shaftesbury; but Culverwel, with whose writings Shaftesbury was well acquainted, uses *connate*, and Whichcote (see *Aphorisms*) uses *connatural;* and *connate* and *connatural* were probably familiar phrases among the Platonic thinkers in Emmanuel College. Charnock is fond of characterising these principles as 'common reason,' 'nature within man;' he speaks of 'the common principles in the conscience,' and in this form they are 'a law of nature writ upon the hearts of men, which will direct them to commendable actions if they will attend to the writings in the conscience.'

In establishing the existence of God in the opening of his most elaborate work, Charnock ever appeals to these principles of reason. 'What is the general dictate of nature is a certain truth,' and with Cicero he appeals to common consent; 'a general consent of all nations is to be esteemed as a law of nature.' He shews in regard to the conviction of the divine existence; (1) that it hath been universal, no nation being without it; (2) that it hath been consistent and uninterrupted in all kinds and conditions of men; and (3) natural and innate. 'Every man is born with a restless instinct to be of some kind of religion or other, which implies some object of religion. The impression of a Deity is as common as reason, and of the same age with reason. It is a relic of knowledge after the fall of man, like fire under ashes, which sparkles as soon as ever the heap of ashes is opened. A notion is sealed up in the soul of every man: how could these people, who were unknown to one another, separate by seas and mountains, differing in various customs and manner of living, had no mutual intelligence one with another, light upon this as a common sentiment, if they had not been guided by one uniform reason in all their minds, by one nature common to them all?" While he represents the belief in God as thus a dictate of nature, he does not allege that it is formed independent of the observation of objects, or without the exercise of discursive thought. 'The notion of a God seems to be twisted with the nature of man, and is the first natural branch of common reason, or upon either the first inspection of a man into himself and his own state and constitution, or upon the first sight of any external visible object.'†

He has occasion to make use of important metaphysical principles, but he does not discuss them as a metaphysician. He incidentally refers to our ideas of Time and Eternity. He accords with those divines who hold that God may stand in a different relation to time from that in which man does; but he does not give any countenance to the statements of those schoolmen, who, founding upon certain mystic expressions of Augustine, spoke of time as having no existence, no reality in the view of God. His view is characterised by his usual judgment. 'Since God knows time, he knows all things as they were in time; he doth not know all things

* Sermon on *Regeneration*, p. 111.   † *Attributes*, Discourse I.

to be at once, though he knows at once what is, has been, and will be. All things are past, present, and to come, in regard to their existence ; but there is not past, present, and to come, in regard to God's knowledge of them, because he sees and knows not by any other but by himself ; he is his own light by which he sees, his own glass wherein he sees ; beholding himself, he beholds all things.'*

David Hume had not yet risen to compel philosophers to discuss the precise nature of causation. Charnock proceeds as Bacon had done, and as all thinkers of his time still did, upon the Aristotelian distinction of causes into material, efficient, formal, and final, a distinction, we may remark, founded on the nature of things, and having a deep but somewhat confused meaning. In regard to efficient cause he assumes that every occurrence has a cause, and with Aristotle, that there cannot be an infinite series of causes, and reckons this a principle of reason, though not formed independent of the observation of things.

But the metaphysical topic which fell more especially under the notice of the puritan theologians was that of the freedom of the will, which they had to consider and discuss as against the rising Arminianism. Really and professedly they followed Augustine and Calvin, whose doctrines however have often been misunderstood. These profound thinkers were most sensitively anxious to have their doctrine of predestination distinguished from the fatalism of the Stoics.† They held that man had an essential freedom given him by his Maker, a freedom which made him a responsible being, and of which he could never be deprived. At the same time, they maintained that this freedom had been much impaired by sin, which has injured man first morally and then physically, so that the will is now enslaved. This is the doctrine resolutely defended by Augustine (see *De Libero Arbitrio*), and by Calvin (see his *De Servitute et Liberatione Humani Arbitrii* in reply to Pighius). They were followed by the puritans generally. Thus Owen in his ' Display of Arminianism' :—' We grant man in the substance of all his actions as much power, liberty, and freedom, as a mere created nature is capable of. We grant him to be free in his choice from all outward exaction or inward natural necessity to work according to election and deliberation, spontaneously embracing what seemeth good unto him.'‡ The puritans clung to the Scrip-

* *Attributes*, Discourse on Eternity.

† It is a circumstance worthy of being noted, that in modern times, we have reversed the meaning of the phrases used by the ancient philosophers, and thus produced some confusion. The Stoics resolutely denied *Necessitas*, but held by *Fatum* (see Cicero *De Fato*), by which they meant what was spoken or decreed by God, whom they represented as an intellectual fire, developing all things in cycles, according to a fixed and eternal order. The arguments advanced by them in favour of fatalism are substantially the same with those urged in modern times in behalf of Philosophical Necessity.

‡ In the same treatise, Owen speaks of that ' effectual working of his, according to his eternal purpose, whereby though some agents as the wills of men are causes free and indefinite or unlimited, lords of their own actions, in respect of their internal principle of operations (that is, their own nature), they are yet all, in respect of his decree, and by his powerful working, determined to this and that

ture doctrine of predestination, but they did not identify it with the philosophic doctrine of Necessity as Jonathan Edwards did in the next century. They drew their doctrine from the Word of God, and founded it upon the perfection of God's Knowledge looking into the future as well as the past and present, and upon his Sovereignty doing all things, but all things wisely, justly, and beneficently. Some Calvinistic divines we acknowledge have drawn distinctions to save the freedom of the will which have rather wrecked it, and have used expressions which make our moral nature shudder. Charnock is wonderfully clear of all such extremes :— 'God's foreknowledge of man's voluntary actions doth not necessitate the will of man.' 'It is certain all necessity doth not take away liberty ; indeed, a compulsive necessity takes away liberty, but a necessity of immutability removes not liberty from God. Why should then a necessity of infallibility in God remove liberty from the creature ?' 'God did not only know that we should do such actions, but that we should do them freely ; he foresaw that the will would freely determine itself to this or that.' 'God did not foreknow the actions of men as necessary but as free ; so that liberty is rather established by this foreknowledge than removed.' 'That God doth foreknow every thing, and yet that there is liberty in the rational creature, are both certain ; but how fully to reconcile them, may surmount the understanding of man.' As to his sovereignty and election, he declares. what the experience of every Christian responds to, 'It could not be any merit in the creature that might determine God to choose him. If the decree of election falls not under the merit of Christ's passion, as the procuring cause, it cannot fall under the merit of any part of the corrupted mass.' But he ever falls back upon the goodness and justice of God as regulating his sovereignty, 'As it is impossible for him not to be sovereign, it is impossible for him to deny his deity and his purity. It is lawful to God to do what he will, but his will being ordered by the righteousness of his nature,

effect in particular; not that they are compelled to do this, or hindered from doing that, but are inclined and disposed to do this or that according to their proper manner of working, that is most freely.' 'We grant as large a freedom and dominion to our wills over their own acts as a creature subject to the supreme rule of God's providence is capable of. Endued we are with such a liberty of will as is free from all outward compulsion and inward necessity, having an elective faculty of applying itself unto that which seems good unto it, in which it has a free choice, notwithstanding it is subservient to the decree of God.' 'The acts of will being positive entities,' 'cannot have their essence and existence solely from the will itself, and cannot be thus, αὐτὸ ὄν, a first and supreme cause endued with an underived being.' He distinguishes between will 'as it was at first by God created,' and 'will as it is now by sin corrupted;' yet being considered in that estate also, they ascribe more unto it than it was ever capable of.' 'There is both an impotency and an enmity in corrupted nature to anything spiritually good.' 'Even in spiritual things we deny that our wills are at all debarred or deprived of their proper liberty, but here we say indeed, that we are not properly free until the Son makes us free.' In his *Saint's Perseverance*, he says, 'The impotency that is in us to do good is not amiss termed *ethico-physica*, both natural and moral.' These extracts give the views entertained by the puritans generally, who meant simply to express the doctrines written on the very face of Scripture, but sometimes did so by doubtful metaphysical distinctions.

as infinite as his will, he cannot do any thing but what is good.'*

The inspired writers as little profess to give a system of the faculties of the mind as of the material world. In mentioning the sun, moon, and stars, and the earth with its rocks, plants, and animals, they proceed upon the ideas of their time; and in the same manner they refer to the attributes of the soul in language understood by those whom they addressed—very often, we may add, imparting to the phrases and the notions embodied in them, a comprehensiveness and an elevation which they never could have had but for their association with spiritual verities. In the Old Testament, constant allusions are made to the special senses of seeing, hearing, touching, tasting, and smelling; to remembrances, imaginations, and knowledge; to thoughts, understanding, and comprehending; to belief, trust, and confidence; to devices, counsels, purposes, and intents; to fear and hope, grief and joy, pity and compassion, anger and mercy, hatred and love. Among the Hebrews, as indeed in most nations, particular faculties were connected with particular parts of the body; and we read of 'bowels,' the seat of sympathy; of the 'reins,' the seat of deep and anxious thought; and of the 'heart,' the seat of all inward reflection. And here we think it of some importance to call attention to the circumstance that the Scriptures do not distinguish, as we do, the heart from the head; and do not make the heart signify mere emotion, but use it to include all that passes through the mind prior to action; and we read of the 'imaginations' and of the 'thoughts' of man's heart,—hence the absurdity of arguing that faith consists in feeling, from the fact that we are said to believe with the heart. In the New Testament, we have a more advanced view; and we read of the 'mind' and 'conscience,' the 'soul' and 'spirit,' and 'will' has a higher place allotted to it. The preacher and divine must, like the inspired writers, proceed so far upon the distribution of the mental powers understood by their hearers and readers; but it will be found that when they take a limited view of the human mind and its capacities, both their preaching and their theology will be very much narrowed. It could easily be shewn that the inspired writers have something suited to every essential quality of man's complex nature, providing symbols for the senses, images for the fancy, types for the imagination, aiding the memory by interesting correlations of time and number, presenting arguments to the understanding, rousing appeals to the conscience, a lovely object to draw forth the affections, and motives to persuade the will. The broad and comprehensive views of the faculties taken by the puritan preachers led them to address all the parts of man's complex nature.

As the Bible is not a book of science, mental or material, so it is not a book of philosophy. Nor should preaching, nor should theology, affect to be metaphysics. If any thinker is discontented with

* *Attributes*, Discourses on God's Knowledge and Dominion.

past speculative philosophy, he is at liberty to attempt to amend it. But let him do so in a professedly philosophic work, written always in a religious spirit, but without identifying religion with his theories. Still it will be difficult for the theologian, difficult even for the preacher, to avoid proceeding on an implied philosophy. If we do nothing more than exhort persons to beware of satisfying themselves, with a *speculative* without a *practical* knowledge, we are proceeding, whether we know it or not, on an Aristotelian distinction. A profound philosophy has in all ages sought to ally itself with theology. Religion may be inconsistent with a superficial or a one-sided, but not with a deep or a catholic philosophy. A shallow philosophy will always tend to produce a shallow theology. Suppose, for instance, we adopt the principle of Hobbes and the sensational school of France, and hold that all our ideas are got from the senses, it will be difficult to establish any of the higher truths of religion; or suppose we assert that virtue is mere utility, it will be difficult to vindicate the justice of God in the awful punishment of the sinner. Philosophic principles should certainly not obtrude themselves in the disquisitions of the divine; but philosophic conceptions may underlie his whole mode of thought and discussion, and impart a coherency and consistency to the system constructed by him. The profound views of human reason, in its strength and in its weakness, taken by the puritan divines, enabled them to construct a theology in some measure corresponding to the profundity of Scripture, and defective only in this, that at times it proposed to settle what should have been left free, and to embrace all revealed truths, which, in their entireness, will always refuse to be compressed within human systems.

A TREATISE OF DIVINE PROVIDENCE.

TO THE READER.

READER,—Thou art here presented with a little piece of a great man; great, indeed, if great piety, great parts, great learning, and great wisdom, may be admitted to claim that title; and we verily believe that none well acquainted with him will deny him his right, however malevolent persons may grudge him the honour. It hath been expected and desired by many that some account of his life might be given to the world; but we are not willing to offer violence to his ashes by making him so public now he is dead, who so much affected privacy while he lived. Thou art therefore desired to rest satisfied with this brief account of him: That being very young he went to Cambridge, where, in Immanuel College, he was brought up under the tuition of the present Archbishop of Canterbury. What gracious workings and evidences of the new birth appeared in him while there, hath already been spoken of by* one who was at that time his fellow-collegiate and intimate. Some time he afterward spent in a private family, and a little more in the exercise of his ministry in Southwark, then removed to New College in Oxon, where he was fellow, and spent several years; being then taken notice of for his singular gifts, and had in reputation by the most learned and godly in that university, and upon that account the more frequently put upon public work. Being thence (the year after he had been proctor) called over into Ireland to a constant public employment, he exercised his ministry for about four or five years, not with the approbation only, but to the admiration of the most wise and judicious Christians, and with the concurrent applause of such as were of very different sentiments from him in the things of religion. Nay, even those that never loved his piety, yet would commend his learning and gifts, as being beyond exception, if not above compare. About the year 1660, being discharged from the public exercise of his ministry, he returned back into England, and in and about London spent the greatest part of fifteen years, without any call to his old work in a settled way, but for about these five years last past hath been more known by his constant preaching, of which we need not speak, but let them that heard him speak for him; or, if they should be silent, his works will do it.

He was a person of excellent parts, strong reason, great judgment, and (which do not often go together) curious fancy, of high improvements, and general learning, as having been all his days a most diligent and methodical student, and a great redeemer of time, rescuing not only his restless hours in the night, but his very walking time in the streets, from those impertinencies and fruitless vanities which do so customarily fill up men's minds, and steal away their hearts from those better and more noble objects, which do so justly challenge their greatest regards. This he did by not only carefully watching (as every good Christian should do), but constantly writing down his thoughts, whereby he both governed them better, and furnished

* Mr Johnson, in his Sermon on occasion of Mr Charnock's death.

himself with many materials for his most elaborate discourses. His chief talent was his preaching-gift, in which, to speak modestly, he had few equals. To this, therefore, as that for which his Lord and Master had best fitted him (neglecting the practice of physic, in which he had arrived at a considerable measure of knowledge), he did especially addict himself, and direct his studies; and even when providence denied him opportunities, yet he was still laying in more stock, and preparing for work against he might be called to it. When he was in employment, none that heard him could justly blame his retiredness, he being, even when most private, continually at work for the public; and had he been less in his study, he would have been less liked in the pulpit. His library, furnished, though not with a numerous, yet a curious collection of books, was his workhouse, in which he laboured hard all the week, and on the Lord's day made it appear he had not been idle; and that though he consulted his privacy, yet he did not indulge his sloth. He was somewhat reserved where he was not well acquainted, otherwise very free, affable, and communicative, where he understood and liked his company. He affected not much acquaintance, because he would escape visitants, well knowing how much the ordinary sort of friends were apt to take up of his time, which he could ill spare from his beloved studies, meeting with few that could give him better entertainment with their company than he could give himself alone. They had need be very good, and very learned, by whose converse he could gain more than by his own thoughts and books. He was a true son of the Church of England, in that sound doctrine laid down in the articles of religion, and taught by our most famous ancient divines and reformers; and a real follower of their piety, as well as a strenuous maintainer of the truth they professed. His preaching was mostly practical, yet rational and argumentative, to his hearers' understandings as well as affections; and where controversies came in his way, he shewed great acuteness and judgment in discussing and determining them, and no less skill in applying them to practice: so that he was indeed ' a workman that needed not to be ashamed,' being able ' by sound doctrine both to exhort and convince gainsayers.' Some have thought his preaching too high for vulgar hearers; and it cannot be denied but his gifts were suited to the more intelligent sort of Christians; yet it must withal be said, that if he were sometimes deep, he was never abstruse; he handled the great mysteries of the gospel with much clearness and perspicuity; so that if in his preaching he were above most, it was only because most were below him. Several considerable treatises on some of the most important points of religion he finished in his ordinary course, which he hath left behind him, in the same form he usually wrote them for the pulpit. This comes out first, as a *prodromus* to several others designed to be made public, as soon as they can be with conveniency transcribed, which (if the Lord will, and spare life) shall be attested with our hands; and whatever any else shall publish, can be but imperfect notes (his own copies being under our revisal at the request of his friends) taken from him in the pulpit; in which, what mistakes do often happen, every one knows, and we have found by experience in the case of this very author more than once. This was thought fit to be said to secure the reputation of the dead, and prevent the abuse of the living. These sermons might have come out with the solemn ceremony of large recommendations, the author's worth being so well known to, and his preaching so highly esteemed by, the most eminent ministers about this city; but it was judged needless, his own works being sufficient to praise him.

One thing more is to be added: that such as he is here, such he is in his other pieces. So that thou hast here, reader, a specimen of the strain and spirit of this holy man, this being his familiar and ordinary way of preaching, and these sermons coming out first, not as if they were the nonsuch of what he left behind him, but because they could soonest be despatched, and to obviate the injuries might else be done by spurious treatises both to him and thee; and likewise by this little taste to gratify the appetites of such who, having been his auditors, did long even with greediness to feast themselves again upon those excellent truths which in the delivery were so sweet to them. Perhaps too it may quicken their appetites who never heard him, it may be never yet heard of him. If thou like this cluster, fear not but the vintage will be answerable; if this little earnest be good metal, the whole sum will be no less current. That a blessing from heaven may be upon this work, and upon thee in reading and studying the nature, and beauty, and ends of divine providence, and that the Lord of the harvest (especially when so many are daily called home) would send forth more and more *such* labourers into the harvest, is the hearty prayer of

Thine in the Lord,

RICHARD ADAMS.
EDWARD VEAL.

A DISCOURSE OF DIVINE PROVIDENCE.

For the eyes of the Lord run to and fro throughout the whole earth, to shew himself strong in the behalf of them whose heart is perfect towards him.— 2 CHRON. XVI. 9.

In the beginning of the chapter you find Baasha king of Israel raising walls about, and fortifying Ramah, a place about twelve miles from Jerusalem, the metropolis of Judah, intending by that means to block Asa up, because Ramah lay just upon the road between Jerusalem and Samaria, the seats of the two kings, ver. 1.

Baasha was probably afraid of the revolt of Israel to Judah, upon that reformation of religion wrought by Asa, and therefore would fortify that place, to be a hindrance, and to intercept any that should pass upon that account; and to this purpose makes great preparation, as appears ver. 6, for with the provision Baasha had made for the fortification of Ramah, Asa, after the seizing of the materials, builds two towns, Geba and Mispah.

Asa seeing Baasha so busy about this design, and fearing the consequence of it, hath recourse to carnal policy rather than to God; and therefore enters into league with Benhadad, a neighbour, though an idolatrous prince, and purchaseth his assistance with the sacrilegious price of the treasure of the temple, ver. 2, 3; and hereby engageth him to invade the king of Israel's territories, that he might thereby find work for Baasha in another part, and so divert him from that design upon which he was so bent: ver. 3, ' Go, break thy league with Baasha, that he may depart from me.'

Benhadad is easily persuaded by the quantity of gold, &c., to break his league, and make an inroad, and proves victorious, and takes many cities where the magazines and stores were laid up, ver. 4.

Baasha now, to save his country, and make head against his enemies, is forced to leave Ramah; whereupon Asa, who watched his opportunity, seizeth the materials he had left for the fortifying of Ramah, and puts them to another use, ver. 5, 6.

Hanani the seer is presently sent by God with a threatening of war, because he applies himself to a heathen prince rather than to the Lord of hosts, ver. 7; his sin is aggravated by God's former kindness to him, and experience he had given him of his miraculous providence in his success against that vast army of the Ethiopians and Lubims, or Lybians, and that upon his recourse to or reliance on God; and that he should afterwards have recourse to the arm of flesh was a disparagement to God's providential kindness, ver. 8. He further aggravates his sin by the consideration of God's general providential care of his creatures, and the particular end of it, and of all his providences, viz., the good of his church and people, ver. 9, ' For the eyes of the Lord,' &c.

Eyes of the Lord, in Scripture, signify,

1. His knowledge : Job. xxxiv. 21, ' For his eyes are upon all the ways of man, and he sees all his goings.' Heb. iv. 13, ' All things are naked and opened unto the eyes of him with whom we have to do.'*

2. His providence.

(1.) For good, so it notes his grace and good will; so his eyes and his heart are joined together : I Kings vi. 3, ' Mine eyes and my heart shall be there perpetually,' viz., in his temple, the place which he had hallowed to put his name there for ever. Ps. xxxii. 8, ' I will guide him with mine eye ;' that is, I will counsel him, and direct him in a gracious and a favourable way. Therefore, to be cut off from the eye of the Lord, is to be deprived of his favour, Ps. xxxi. 22, for none can be cut off from a simple knowledge of God ; so Zech. iii. 9, ' seven eyes upon one stone,' that is, the providence of God was in an especial manner with Christ in the midst of his passion.

(2.) For evil, so it notes his anger and vindictive justice. Isa. iii. 8, ' Their doings are against the Lord, to provoke the eyes of his glory.' Kindness and anger appear first in the eye, one by its pleasantness, the other by its redness.

' Run,' that notes diligence and care, an industrious inspection into all things. Ps. cxix. 32, ' I will run the ways of thy commandments,' noting speed and diligence.

In the verse we have,

I. A description of God's providence.

II. The end of it.

I. The description of God's providence.

1. The immediateness of it ; ' his eyes,' his own eyes, not another's. Not like princes, who see by their servants' eyes more than by their own, what is done in their kingdoms ; his care is immediate. Though angels are ministers of his providence, the guardians and watchers of the world, yet God is their captain, and is always himself upon the watch.

2. Quickness and speed of providence ; ' run.' His eyes do not only walk, but run the round ; they are not slumbering eyes, nor drowsy eyelids ; their motion is quick and nimble.

3. Extent of providence ; ' the whole earth ;' all things in the earth, all the hairs on the heads of these men : the meanest worm as well as the mightiest prince; the lowest shrub as well as the tallest cedar ; every cranny, corner, or chink of the earth.

4. Diligence of providence ; ' to and fro.' His care is repeated, he looks this way and that way, again and again ; his eyes are not confined to one place, fixed on one object, but are always rolling about from one place to another.

5. The efficacy of his providence ; his care doth engage his strength ; he doth not only discover dangers, but prevent them ; he hath eyes to see, and power to order all things according to his pleasure ; wise to see, and strong to save.

II. The end of providence ; ' to shew himself strong,' &c.

* τραχηλὸς significat spinam dorsi, et in mactatis animalibus per spinam omnia apparent interiora, ita ut nihil latere potest.—Glassius, vol. iii. 1, 106.

1. *Finis cujus*, ' to shew himself strong.' *Heb.* to ' make himself strong,' but best translated, to ' shew himself strong.' It is not an addition of strength, but an exercise of strength that is here meant.

2. *Finis cui*, or the persons for whom, ' those that are perfect in heart.' *Doctrines.*

1. There is a providence exercised by God in the world.

2. All God's providences in the world are in order to the good of his people.

3. Sincerity in God's way gives a man an interest in all God's providences, and the good of them.

1. For the first, there is a providential inspection and government of all things in the world by God. It is not a bare sight of things that is here meant by God's eye, but a sight and knowledge in order to the governing and disposing of them. View this doctrine at your leisure, preached by God himself, with an inconceivable elegancy, and three whole chapters spent in the sermon, Job xxxviii., xxxix., xl., and by the psalmist, Ps. cxlvii. cxlviii.

Some observe that the society of angels and heavenly creatures is represented, Ezek. i., by a quaternarian number, because the world is divided into four dimensions, east, west, north, and south, as intimating the extension of God's providence over all parts.*

Things are not ordered in the world *cæco impetu*, not by blind fortune, but an all-seeing Deity, who hath the management of all sublunary affairs. Τίς μεγάλη δύναμις τῆς προνοίας ; † πάντα ὑπ' ἀρίστου νοῦ γίνεται, was the theological maxim of the Stoics.

Before I come particularly to explain the providence of God, I shall lay down some propositions as the foundations of this doctrine.

1. God hath an indisputable and peculiar right to the government of the world. None ever questioned God's right, no, nor his act, but those that were swelled with an unreasonable ambition, such as Nebuchadnezzar, who for this cause underwent the punishment of a seven years' banishment from the society of men, Dan. iv. 17.

None indeed that acknowledge a God, did or can question God's right, though they may question his will and actual exercise of his right. He is the creator, and therefore is the sovereign Lord and Ruler. The world is his family, and, as a master, he hath an undoubted right to govern his own family : he gave all creatures their beings, and therefore hath a right to enact their laws, appoint their stations, and fix their ends. It is as much his property and prerogative to rule, as it is to create. Creation is so peculiarly proper to God, that it is not communicable to any creature, no, not to angels, though of a vast capacity in other things, and that because they are creatures themselves. It is as impossible for one creature, or all, to govern the world, and manage all the boisterous passions of men to just and glorious ends, as to create them. It is true, God useth instruments in the executive part of his providence ; but he doth not design the government of the world only by instruments. He useth them not for necessity, but ornament. He created the world without them, and therefore can govern the world without them.

Virtus creativa est fundamentum providentiæ, et argumentum ad providentiam. This right is founded upon that of creation, as he is the efficient cause of it. This right is also founded upon the excellency of his being ; that which is excellent having a right to rule, in the way of that excellency, that which is inferior. Every man hath a natural right to rule another in

---

* Hudson's Divine Right of Government, chap. vi. p. 8.
† Clemens ad Corinth, p. 84.

his own art and skill wherein he excels him.   If it be the right of a chief magistrate to manage the concerns of his kingdom, with what reason can we deny that right to God ?

2. God only is qualified for the universal government of the world.   All creatures, as they were unable to create themselves, so are unable to manage themselves without the direction of a superior power, much more unable to manage the vast body of the world.   God is only fit in regard of,

(1.) Power.   Conservation is *continuata creatio ;* that power which is fit to create, is only fit to preserve.   A continued creation belongs as much to omnipotency as the first creation.

The government of it requires no less power, both in regard of the numerousness of the objects, and the strange contrariety of passions in rational creatures, and qualities in irrational ; conservation is but one continued act with creation, following on from an instant to duration, as a line from its mathematical point.*

(2.) Holiness and righteousness.   If he that hates right is not fit to govern, Job xxxiv. 17, then he that is infinitely righteous, and hath an infinite love to righteousness, is the fittest to undertake that task ; without righteousness there would be nothing but confusion in the whole creation. Disorder is the effect of unrighteousness, as order is the effect of justice. The justest man is fittest for subordinate government among men, and the infinite just God is fittest for the universal government of the world.

(3.) Knowledge.   An infinite knowledge to decry all the contrivances and various labyrinths of the hearts of men, their secret intentions and aims, is necessary.   The government of the world consists more in ordering the inward faculties of men, touching the hearts, and tuning them to play what note he pleases, than in external things.   No creature hath the skill or power to work immediately upon the will of man ; neither angels nor devils can do it immediately, but by proposing objects, and working upon the fancy, which is not always successful.   He that created the heart, knows all the wards of it, and hath only the skill to turn it and incline it as he pleases ; he must needs know all the inclinations of the creatures and their proper activities, since he alone conferred all those several principles and qualities upon them.   'Known unto God are all his works from the beginning of the world,' Acts xv. 8, viz., the particular natures, inclinations, inward motions, which no creature fully understands ; he needs no deputy to inform him of what is done, he is everywhere, and sees all things.   Worldly governors cannot be everywhere essentially present.

God is so perfect in his knowledge of all things, that he cannot be imposed upon by the evil suggestions and flatteries of men or angels.

In nature it is so : the eye guides the body, because that is the chief organ of sensitive knowledge ; the mind, which is the seat of wisdom, guides the whole.

(4.) Patience.   Infinite patience is requisite to the preservation and government of the world, in the circumstances wherein it hath stood ever since the fall.   What angel, though the meekest, or can all the angels in heaven, be masters of so much patience as is needful for this work of governing the world, though for the space of one day ?   Could they bear with all those evils which are committed in the world in the space of twenty-four hours ?   Might we not reasonably conceive, that they would be so tired with the obliquities, disorders, deformities which they would see in the acts of men (besides all the evil which is in the hearts of men, which lie without the verge of their

---

* Taylor's Exemplar, preface.

knowledge), that they would rather call for fire from heaven to burn the world to ashes.

Averröes* thought that because of God's slowness to anger, he meddled not with sublunary concerns. This rather fits him for it, because he can bear with the injuries of wicked men, otherwise the world would not continue a moment.

Angels, though powerful, holy, wise and patient creatures, yet being creatures, they want the infiniteness of all these qualifications which are necessary to this government. Though they are knowing, yet they know not men's hearts ; though they are wise, yet they may be charged with a folly uncapable of this ; though holy, yet not able in this respect to manage it to the ends and designs of an infinite holiness ; though nimble, yet cannot be in all parts of the world at every turn : but the providence of God is infallible, because of his infinite wisdom ; indefatigable, because of his omnipotency ; and righteous, because of his goodness.

3. There can be no reason rendered why God should not actually govern the world, since he only hath a right and fitness. If God doth not actually govern it, it is either because he cannot, or because he will not.

(1.) Not because he cannot. This inability must be either for want of knowledge, or want of power. The one, if asserted, would deny his omnipotence, the other his omniscience ; the one would make him a weak God, the other an ignorant God, and consequently no God.

(2.) Not because he will not ; if he can and will not, it is, say some, a testimony of envy, that he maligns the good of his creatures ; but not to insist upon this ; this must be either because of the,

[1.] Difficulty. This cannot be. What difficulty can there be in a single word, or one act of his will, which can be done by God without any molestation, were there millions of worlds as well as this ? For still they would be finite, and so governable by an infinite superior. May we not more reasonably think the forming such a mass would require more pains than the government of it ? The right stringing an instrument is more trouble to a skilful musician, than the tripping over the strings afterwards to make an harmony. What difficulty can it be to Omnipotence ? Is it a greater labour to preserve and govern, than it was to create ? Doth not the soul order every part of the body, and all its functions, without any pain to it ? and shall not the God that made that soul so indefatigable, much more manage the concernments of the world without labour to himself ? Is it not as easy with God to guide all these things by one single act of his will, as for me, by an act of my soul, to do many things without a distinct act of cogitation or consideration before ? Can it be more laborious to him to govern the world, than it is to know all things in the world ? He sees all things in an instant by one act of his understanding, and he orders all creatures in a moment by one act of his will. Can one act of his will be more painful than one act of his understanding ? Can he with a word make this great ball ? and can he not with as much ease order all to conform to the law of his own righteous will ? Can a continual eruption of goodness be a difficulty to an infinite being, which we find natural to the sun, to the fountains, to the sea, to many works of that omnipotent goodness ? Or,

[2.] Disparagement. Denial of God's providence over the lesser things of the world did arise from the consideration of the state of monarchs, who thought it an abridgment of their felicity and dignity, to stoop to such low considerations as the *minutula* of their estates might exact from them, but left them to their vice-gerents. But they consider not that the felicity of

* Trap on Exod. xxxiv.

God as it respects the creature, is to communicate his goodness to as many subjects as he had made capable of his care. If it were his glory to create the world, can it be his dishonour to govern it? The glorifying his wisdom is as honourable to him as the magnifying his power; though both are eminent in creation and providence, yet his wisdom is more signal in the governing, as his power was in framing of the world.

Why was it not as much a disparagement to God to create things contemptible in our eyes, as since he hath created them to take care of them, and marshal them for his glorious ends? The sun in the heavens is a shadow of God, which doth not disdain to communicate its natural goodness, and emit its beams to the meanest creatures, and let the little flies sport themselves in them, as well as the greatest princes, and transmits an influence upon things obscure and at a distance from it, whereby it manifests an universal regard to all. And would it not be a disparagement to an infinite goodness to be outstripped by a creature, which he hath set up for a natural communication of goodness to the rest of the world? The very consideration of the sun, and the nature of it, gives us as much an account of God as any inanimate being whatsoever. It is as much the sun's honour to produce a small insect, as the growth of the greatest plant.

Have not all creatures, a natural affection in them to preserve and provide for their own?* hath not God much more, who endued all creatures with that disposition? Whatsoever is a natural perfection in creatures, is eminently an infinite perfection in God. If it be therefore a praise to you to preserve your own, can it be a disgrace to God? You may as well say it is as much a dishonour to him to be good, as to have a tender regard to his creatures. Censure him as well you may for creating them for your delight, as preserving and governing them for the same end. They are all good, for he pronounced them so; and being so, a God of goodness will not account them unworthy of his care. Are they now the products of his omnipotent wisdom? and shall not they be the objects of his directing wisdom? If they are not unworthy of God to create, how can they be unworthy of God to govern them? It would be as much below him to make them, as to rule them when they were made.

4. Therefore, God doth actually preserve and govern the world; though angels are in ministry in some particular works of his providence, yet God is the steersman who gives out his particular orders to them.

Jacob's ladder had the top in heaven, where God stood to keep it firm, its foot on earth, and the angels going up and down upon several errands at their master's beck.

As God made all things for himself, so he orders the ends of all things made by him for his own glory. For being the most excellent and intelligent agent, he doth reduce all the motions of his creatures to that end for which he made them.

This actual government of the world by God brancheth itself out in three things.

1. Nothing is acted in the world without God's knowledge. The vision of the wheels in Ezekiel presents us with an excellent portraiture of providence, there are eyes round about the wheels: Ezek. i. 18, 'Their wings were full of eyes,' &c.

The eye of God is upon the whole circle of the creatures' motion. In all the revolutions in the world, there is the eye of God's omniscience to see them, and the arm of his omnipotence to guide them. Not the most retired corner, or the darkest cell, not the deepest cavern, or most inward projecc- nor the most secret wickedness, not the closest goodness, but the eye of

* Mornæ. de Verit. Relig. Christian, chap. xi.

the Lord beholds it: Prov. xv. 8, 'The eyes of the Lord are in every place, beholding the evil and the good.' He hears the words, sees the actions, knows the thoughts, registers the gracious discourses, bottles up the penitent tears, and considers all the ways of men; not a whispered oath, not an atheistical thought, though but only peeping upon the heart, and sinking down again in that mass of corruption, not a disorderly word, but he knows and marks it. The soul hath a particular knowledge of every act, because it is the spring of every act in any member, and nothing is done in this little world, but the soul knows it. Surely, then, there is not an act done in the world, nor the motion of any creature, but as God doth concur to it, he must needs know what he doth concur to. The knowledge and ordaining every thing is far less to the infinite being of God, than the knowledge and ordaining every motion of the body is to a finite soul.

Or, suppose a soul clothed with a body of as big a proportion as the matter of the whole creation, it would actuate this body, though of a greater bulk, and know every motion of it; how much more God, who hath infinity and excellency and strength of all angels and souls, must need actuate this world, and know every motion of it! There is nothing done in the world but some creature or other knows it; he that acts it doth at least know it. If God did not know it, the creatures then in that particular knowledge would be superior to God, and know something more than God knows; can this be possible?

2. Nothing is acted in the world without the will of God. His will either commands it, or permits it: Eph. i. 11, 'He works all things after the counsel of his own will,' Ps. cxxxv. 6, 'Whatsoever the Lord pleased, that did he in heaven and in earth.'

Even the sins of the world his will permits them, his power assists in the act, and his wisdom orders the sinfulness of the act for holy ends. The four chariots in Zech. vi. 2–5, by which some understand angels, are sent upon commission into the several parts of the world, and compared to chariots, both for their strength, their swiftness, their employment in a military way to secure the church. These are said to come out of the two mountains of brass, ver. 1, which signify the irreversible decrees of God, which the angels are to execute.* He alarms up the winds, when he would have Jonah arrested in his flight. He sounds a retreat to them, and locks them up in their chambers, Ps. cvii. 25–29. Bread hath a natural virtue in it to nourish, but it must be accompanied with his secret blessing, Mat. iv. 4.

Virtute primi actus, agunt agentia omnia quicquid agunt.

3. Nothing doth subsist without God's care and power. His eyes running to and fro, implies not only knowledge, but care. He doth not carelessly behold what is done in the world, but, like a skilful pilot, he sits at the helm, and steers the world in what course it should sail. Our being we owe to his power, our well-being to his care, our motion and exerting of every faculty to his merciful providence and concurrence; 'in him we live, and move, and have our being,' Acts xvii. 28. He frames our being, preserves our life, concurs with our motion. This is an idea that bears date in the minds of men with the very notion of a God. Why else did the heathen in all their straits fly to their altars, and fill their temples with cries and sacrifices? To what purpose was this, if they had not acknowledged God's superintendency, his taking notice of their cause, hearing their prayers, considering their cries? Why should they do this, if they thought that God did not regard human affairs, but stood untouched with a sense of their miseries?

* Reynolds.

If all things were done by chance, there could be no predictions of future things, which we frequently find in Scripture, and by what ways accomplished. Impossible it is that anything can be continued without his care. If God should in the least moment withhold the influence of his providence, we should melt into nothing, as the impression of a seal upon the water vanishes as soon as the seal is removed; or as the reflection of the face in the glass disappears upon the first instant of our removal from it. The light in the air is by participation of the light of the sun; the light in the air withdraws upon the departure of the sun. The physical and moral goodness [of] the creature would vanish upon the removal of God from it, who is the fountain of both.

What an artificer doth work, may continue, though the workman dies, because what he doth is materially, as to the matter of it, ready to his hands; he creates not the matter, but only sets materials together, and disposeth them into such a form and figure. But God gives a being to the matter and form of all things, and therefore the continuance of that being depends upon his preserving influence.* God upholds the world, and causes all those laws which he hath impressed upon every creature, to be put in execution: not as a man that makes a watch, and winds it up, and then suffers it to go of itself; or that turns a river into another channel, and lets it alone to run in the graff he hath made for it; but there is a continual concurrence of God to this goodly frame. For they do not only live, but move in him, or by him; his living and omnipotent power runs through every vein of the creation, giving it life and motion, and ordering the acts of every part of this great body. All the motions of second causes are ultimately resolved into the providence of God, who holds the first link of them in his hands, Hosea ii. 21, 22. More particularly, the nature of providence may be explained by two propositions.

Prop. 1. The universality of it. His eyes run to and fro throughout the whole earth.

1. It is over all creatures, (1.) the highest, (2.) the lowest.

(1.) The highest and most magnificent pieces of the creation.

[1.] Over Jesus Christ, the first-born of every creature. God's providence was in an especial manner conversant about him, and fixed upon him. It was by the determinate counsel of God, that he was delivered up, Acts ii. 23. His providence was diligently exercised about him in his whole course. Christ answers his mother's solicitousness with the care his Father took of him: Luke ii. 49, 'Wist you not that I must be about my Father's business?' Do you not know that I am about those things my Father takes care of? This exposition best agrees with his reproof, who blames them for creating so much trouble to themselves upon their missing him in the town. It is not, Why do you interrupt me in my dispute with the Jewish doctors? But 'How is it that you sought me? Do you think I am not under the care of my Father?'† It was particularly exercised on him in the midst of his passion, Zech. iii. 9. Seven eyes were upon the stone; seven, a number of perfection, a perfect and peculiar care of God attended him.

[2.] Over angels and men. The soul of the least animal, and the smallest plant, is formed and preserved by God, but the breath of mankind is more particularly in his hand: Job xii. 10, 'In whose hand is the soul of every living thing, and the breath of all mankind.'

First, Over good angels and men. He charges his angels with folly and weakness. They cannot direct themselves without his wisdom, nor preserve

---

* Stillingfleet, Orig. sacræ. lib. iii. cap. 3, sect. 3.

† ἐν τοῖς τοῦ πατρός.   *Hammond in loc.*

themselves without his power. God hath a book of providence, wherein he writes down who shall be preserved, and this book Moses understands : Exod. xxxii. 83, ' Whosoever hath sinned against me, him will I blot out of my book;' not the book of election,—no names written there are blotted out,—but out of the book of providence. As it is understood, Isa. iv. 3, ' Every one that is written among the living in Jerusalem,' *i. e.* every one whom God designs to preservation and deliverance.* That God, surely, that hath a care of the mean animals, will not be careless of his affectionate worshippers. He that feeds the ravens will not starve his doves. He that satisfies the ravening wolf, will not famish his gentle lambs and harmless sheep. He shelters Jacob from Laban's fury, Gen. xxxi., and tutors him how he should carry himself towards the good man. He brought Haman out of favour, and set Mordecai in his place for the deliverance of the Jews which were designed for slaughter.

Secondly, Over evil angels and men. God's power preserves them, his patience suffers them, his wisdom orders them, and their evil purposes and performances, to his own glory. The devil cannot arrest Job, nor touch a lamb of his flock, nor a hair of his head, without a commission from God. He cannot enter into one filthy swine in the Gaderenes' herd, without asking our Saviour leave. Whatever he doth, he hath a grant or permission from heaven for it. God's special providence is over his people, but his general providence over all kingdoms and countries.

He takes care of Syria, as well as of Judea ; and sends Elisha to anoint Hazael king of Syria, as well as Jehu king of Israel, 1 Kings xix. 15. Though Ishmael had mocks for Isaac, yet the God of Isaac provided for the wants of Ishmael ; Gen. xxv. 16–18, ' He causeth his sun to shine upon the unjust,' as well as ' the just,' to produce fruits and plants for their preservation.

(2.) Over the meanest creatures. As the sun's light, so God's providence disdains not the meanest worms. It is observed, that in the enumeration of the works of creation, Gen. i. 21, only the great whales and small creeping things are mentioned, and not the intermediate creatures, to shew that the least as well as the greatest are under his care. It is one of his titles to be the preserver of beasts as well as men, Neh. ix. 6. He is the great caterer for all creatures ; Ps. civ. 21, ' The young lions seek their meat from God.' They attend him for their daily portion, and what they gather and meet with in their pursuit, is God's gift to them, ver. 27, 28. He listens to the cries of the young ravens, though they are birds of prey. ' He gives to the beast his food, and to the young ravens which cry,' Ps. cxlvii. 9. In Ps. civ. David throughout the whole reads a particular lecture of this doctrine, wherein you may take a prospect of God's providence all over the world. He acts them by a commandment and imprinted law upon their natures, and makes them observe exactly those statutes he enacts for the guidance of them in their proper operations. Ps. cxlvii. 15, ' He sendeth forth his commandment upon earth, and his word runs very swiftly,' viz., his word of providence. God keeps them in the observation of their first ordinance. Ps. cxix. 91, ' They continue this day according to thine ordinances, for all are thy servants,' *i. e.* the earth and what is upon it. They observe their stations, the law God hath set them, as if they had a rational knowledge of their duty in their particular motions ; Ps. civ. 19, ' the sun knoweth his going down.' Sometimes he makes them instruments of his ministry to us, sometimes executioners of his judgments. Lice and frogs arm themselves at his command to punish Egypt. He makes a whale to attend Jonas dropping into the sea, to be an instrument both to punish and preserve him.

* Horton's Serm. Ps. lxxxvii. p. 56.

Yea, and which is more wonderful, the multitude of the very cattle is brought among others as a reason of a people's preservation from destruction, Jonah iv. 11 ; the multitude of the cattle are joined with the multitude of the infants, as an argument to spare Nineveh.   He remembers Noah's cattle as well as his sons ; Gen viii. 1, ' God remembered Noah, and every living thing, and all the cattle that were with him in the ark.'   He numbers the very hairs of our heads, that not one falls without his will.   Not only the immortal soul, but the decaying body ; not only the vital parts of that body, but the inconsiderable hairs of the head, are under his care.

Obs. 1. This is no dishonour to God, to take care of the meanest creatures. It is as honourable for his power to preserve them, and his wisdom to govern them, as for both to create them.   It is one part of a man's righteousness to be merciful to his beasts, which he never made ; and is it not a part of God's righteousness, as the rector of the world, to take care of those creatures, which he did not disdain to give a being to ?

Obs. 2. It rather conduceth to his honour.

(1.) The honour of his goodness.   It shews the comprehensiveness of his goodness, which embraceth in the arms of his providence the lowest worm, as well as the highest angel.   Shall infinite goodness frame a thing, and make no provision for its subsistence ?   At the first creation he acknowledged whatever he had created good in his kind, good in themselves, good in order to the end for which he created them ; it is therefore an honourable thing for his goodness to conduct them to that end which in their creation he designed them for ; and not leave them wild disorders, unsuitable to the end of that goodness which first called them into being.   If he grow out of love with the operations of his hands, he would seem to grow out of love with his own goodness that formed them.

(2.) The honour of his power and wisdom.   The power of God is as much seen in making an insect full of life and spirit in all the parts of it, to perform all the actions suitable to its life and nature, as in making creatures of a greater bulk ; and is it not for the honour of his power to preserve them, and the honour of his wisdom to direct these little animals to the end he intended in their creation ?   For as little as they seem to be, an end they have, and glorious too, for *natura nihil facit frustra*.   It seems not to consist with his wisdom to neglect that which he hath vouchsafed to create.   And though the apostle seems to deny God's care of brutes,—1 Cor. ix. 9, ' Doth God take care for oxen ?'—it is true God did not in that law only take care of oxen, *i. e.* with a legislative care, as making a law only for them, though with a providential care he doth ; but the apostle there doth not deny God's care for oxen, but makes an argument *a minore ad majus*.

2. Providence extends to all the actions and motions of the creature. Every second cause implies a dependence upon a first cause in its operation. If God did not extend his providence over the actions of creatures, he would not every where, and in all things and beings, be the first cause.

(1.) To natural actions.   What an orderly motion is there in the natural actions of creatures, which evidenceth a guidance by an higher reason, since they have none of their own!   How do fish serve several coasts at several seasons, as if sent upon a particular message by God ?   This cannot be by any other faculty than the instinct their Maker hath put into them.   Plants that grow between a barren and fruitful soil, shoot all their roots towards the moist and fruitful ground, by what other cause than a secret direction of providential wisdom ?*   There is a law impressed upon them and their motions, that are so orderly, as if they were acted according to a covenant

* Andrew's Catechistical Doctrine, p. 60.

and agreement between them and their Creator, and therefore called ' the covenant of the day and night,' Jer. xxxiii. 20.   What avails the toil and labour of man in ploughing, trading, watching, unless God influence, unless he bless, unless he keep the city !   The proceed of all things depends upon his goodness in blessing, and his power in preserving.   God signified this, when he gave the law from mount Sinai, promising the people, that if they kept his commandments, he would give them rain in due season, and that the earth should bring forth her fruit : Lev. xxvi. 3, 4, ' Then will I give you rain, and the land shall yield her increase, and the trees of the field shall yield their fruit ;' evidencing thereby, that those natural causes can produce nothing without his blessing ; that though they have natural principles to produce such fruits according to their natures, yet he can put a stop to their operations, and make all their fruits abortive.   He weighs the waters, how much shall be poured out in showers of rain upon the parched earth. He makes a decree for the rain, and gives the clouds commission to dissolve themselves so much and no more, Job xxviii. 23-26.   Yea, he doth order the conduct of them by counsel, as employing his wisdom about these things which are of concern to the world.   Job xxxvii. 11, 12, ' He scattereth his bright cloud, and it is turned round about by his counsels, that they may do whatsoever he commands them upon the face of the world in the earth.'

(2.) To civil actions.   Counsels of men are ordered by him to other ends than what they aim at, and which their wisdom cannot discover.   God stirred up Sennacherib to be the executioner of his justice upon the Jews, and afterwards upon the Egyptians, when that great king designed only the satisfaction of his ambition in the enlarging his kingdom, and supporting his greatness.   Isa. x. 6, 7, ' I will send him against an hypocritical nation, and against the people of my wrath.   Howbeit he means not so, neither doth his heart think so,'—he designs not to be an instrument of my justice,— ' but it is in his heart to destroy and cut off nations not a few.'   His thoughts and aims were far different from God's thoughts.   The hearts of kings are in his hands, as wax in the hands of a man, which he can work into what form and shape he pleases.   He hath the sovereignty over, and the ordering the hearts of magistrates ; Ps. xlvii. 9, ' The shields of the earth belong unto God.'   Counsels of men for the good of his people are his act.   The princes advised Jeremiah and Baruch, Jer. xxxvi. 19, to hide themselves, which they did, yet, verse 26, it is said the Lord hid them.   Though they followed the advice of their court-friends, yet they could not have been secured, had not God stepped in by his providential care, and covered them with his hand.   It was the courtiers' counsel, but God challenges the honour of the success.

Military actions are ordered by him.   Martial employments are ordered by his providence.   He is the great general of armies.   It is observed that in the two prophets, Isaiah and Jeremiah, God is called *the Lord of Hosts* no less than a hundred and thirty times.[*]

(3.) To preternatural actions.   God doth command creatures to do those things which are no way suitable to their inclinations, and gives them sometimes for his own service a writ of ease from the performance of the natural law he hath impressed upon them.   A devouring raven is made by the providence of God the prophets' caterer in time of famine, 1 Kings xvii. 4.   God instructs a ravenous bird in a lesson of abstinence for Elijah's safety, and makes it both a cook and a serving-man to the prophet.   The whale, that delights to play about the deepest part of the ocean, approaches to the shore, and attends upon Jonah to transport him to the dry land, Jonah ii. 10,

* Arrowsmith, ' Chain of Principles,' Exercit. i. sect 1.

The fire was slacked by God, that it should not singe the least hair of the three children's heads, but was let loose to consume the officers of the court, Dan. iii. The mouths of the ravenous lions, which had been kept with an empty stomach, were muzzled by God, that they should not prey upon Daniel in a whole night's space. God taught them an heroical temperance with so dainty a dish at their mouths, and yet they tore the accusers in a trice.

(4.) To all supernatural and miraculous actions of the creatures, which are as so many new creations. As when the sun went backward in Hezekiah's time, when it stood still in the valley of Ajalon, that Joshua might complete his victory on the Canaanites. The boisterous waves stood on a heap like walls to secure the Israelites' passage ; but, returning to their natural motion, were the Egyptians' sepulchre. When creatures have stepped out of their natural course, it could not be the act of the creature, it being so much against and above their natures, but it must be by the order of some superior power.

(5.) To all fortuitous actions. What is casual to us is ordained by God ; as effects stand related to the second cause, they are many times contingent, but as they stand related to the first cause, they are acts of his counsel, and directed by his wisdom. God never left second causes to straggle and operate in a vagabond way ; though the effect seem to us to be a loose act of the creature, yet it is directed by a superior cause to a higher end than we can presently imagine. The whole disposing of the lot which is cast into the lap, is from the Lord, Prov. xvi. 33. A soldier shoots an arrow at random, and God guides it to be the executioner of Ahab for his sin, 1 Kings xxii. 34, which death was foretold by Micaiah, ver. 17, 28. God gives us a certain rule to judge of such contingencies, Exod. xxi. 13, ' And if a man lie not in wait, but God deliver him into his hand.' A man accidentally kills another, but it is done by a secret commission from God. God delivered him into his hands. Providence is the great clock, keeping time and order, not only hourly, but instantly, to its own honour.*

(6.) To all voluntary actions.

[1.] To good actions. Not by compelling, but sweetly inclining, determining the will, so that it doth that willingly, which, by an unknown and unseen necessity, cannot be omitted. It constrains not a man to good against his will, but powerfully moves the will to do that by consent, which God hath determined shall be done : ' The way of man is not in himself,' the motion is man's, the action is man's, but the direction of his steps is from God. Jer. x. 23, ' It is not in man that walketh to direct his steps.'

[2.] To evil actions.

First, In permitting them to be done. Idolatries and follies of the heathen were permitted by God. He checked them not in their course, but laid the reins upon their necks, and suffered them to run what race they pleased : Acts xiv. 16, ' Who in times past suffered all nations to walk in their own ways.' Not the most execrable villany that ever was committed in the world could have been done without his permission. Sin is not *amabile propter se*, and therefore the permission of it is not desirable in itself, but the permission of it is only desirable, and *honestatur ex fine*. God is good, and wise, and righteous in all his acts, so likewise in this act of permitting sin ; and therefore he wills it out of some good and righteous end, which belongs to the manifestation of his glory, which is that he intends in all the acts of his will, of which this is one. Wicked men are said to be a staff in God's hand ; as a man manages a staff which is in his own power, so

* Fuller, Eccles. Hist. Cent. 6, book ii. p. 51.

doth God manage wicked men for his own holy purposes, and they can go
no further than God gives them license.

Secondly, In ordering them. God governs them by his own unsearchable
wisdom and goodness, and directs them to the best and holiest ends, contrary to the natures of the sins, and the intentions of the sinner. Joseph's
brothers sold him to gratify their revenge, and God ordered it for their preservation in a time of famine. Pharaoh's hardness is ordered by God for his
own glory and that king's destruction. God decrees the delivering up Christ
to death; and Herod, Pilate, the Pharisees, and common rout of people, in
satisfying their own passion, do but execute what God had before ordained :
Acts iv. 28, ' For to do whatsoever thy hand and thy counsel determined
before to be done.' Judas his covetousness, and the devil's malice, are
ordered by God to execute his decree for the redemption of the world. Titus
the emperor, his ambition led him to Jerusalem, but God's end is the fulfilling of his threatenings, and the taking revenge upon the Jews for their murdering of Christ. The aim of the physician is the patient's health, when the
intent of the leeches is only to suck the blood. God hath holy ends in permitting sin, while man hath unworthy ends in committing it. The rain,
which makes the earth fruitful, is exhaled out of the salt waters, which would
of themselves spoil the ground and make it unfruitful. ' The deceiver and
the deceived are his,' Job xii. 16. Both the action of the devil the
seducer, and of wicked men the seduced, are restrained by God within due
bounds, in subserviency to his righteous will. For ' with him is strength
and wisdom.'

Prop. 2. As providence is universal, so it is mysterious. Who can trace
the motions of God's eyes in their race ? ' He makes the clouds his chariot,'
Ps. civ. 3, in his motions about the earth, and his throne is in the dark. He
walks upon the wings of the wind, his providential speed makes it too quick
for our understanding. His ways are mysterious, and put the reason and
wisdom of men to a stand. The clearest-sighted servants of God do not see
the bottom of his works, the motion of God's eyes is too quick for ours.

John Baptist is so astonished at the strange condescension of his Saviour
to be baptized of him, that he forbids it, Mat. iii. 14 ; man is a weak creature, and cannot trace or set out the wisdom of God.

But this mysteriousness and darkness of providence adds a lustre to it,
as stones set in ebony, though the grounds be dark, make the beauty and
sparkling the clearer.

1. His ways are above human methods. Dark providences are often
the groundwork of some excellent piece he is about to discover to the world.
His methods are like a plaited picture, which on the one side represents a
negro, on the other a beauty. He lets Sarah's womb be dead, and then
brings out the root of a numerous progeny. He makes Jacob a cripple, and
then a prince to prevail with God ; he gives him a wound and then a blessing. He sends not the gospel till reason was nonplussed, and that the world,
in that highest wisdom it had at that time attained unto, was not able to
arrive to the knowledge of God. 1 Cor. i. 21, ' After that the world by
wisdom knew not God, it pleased God, by the foolishness of preaching, to
save them that believe.'

2. His ends are of a higher strain than the aims of men. Who would
have thought that the forces Cyrus raised against Babylon, to satisfy his own
ambition, should be a means to deliver the Israelites, and restore the worship
of God in the temple ? God had this end, which Isaiah prophesied of, and
Cyrus never dreamt of : Isa. xliv. 28, ' That saith of Cyrus, Thou art my
shepherd, and shalt perform all my pleasure, even saying that Jerusalem

shall be built,' &c.; and this a long time before Cyrus was born, Isa, xlv. 1. Pharaoh sent Israel away in the very night, at the end of the four hundred and thirty years, the time prefixed by God. He could not keep them longer because of God's promise, he would not because of God's plagues. God aims at the glorifying his truth, in keeping touch with his word. Pharaoh designs not the accomplishing God's will, but his deliverance from God's judgments.

There is an observable consideration to this purpose, how God's ends are far different from man's, Luke ii. 1, 4, in the taxing the whole world by Augustus. Augustus, out of pride, to see what a numerous people he was prince of, would tax the whole world. Some tell us he had appointed the enrolling the whole empire twenty-seven years before the birth of our Saviour, and had proclaimed it at Tarracon, in Spain. But soon after this proclamation, Augustus found a breaking out of some stirs, and thereupon deferred his resolution to some other fit time, which was the very time of the birth of Christ. See now God's wise disposal of things, in changing Augustus's resolution, and deferring it till the forty-fourth year of his reign, when Christ was ready to come into the world! And this by giving occasion, yea, necessitating Mary to come from Nazareth, where Joseph and Mary dwelt, who perhaps being big with child, without this necessity laid upon her by the emperor's edict, would not have ventured upon the journey to Bethlehem. There she falls in travail, that so Christ, the seed of David, being conceived in Nazareth, should be born at Bethlehem, where Jesse lived, and David was born. How wisely doth God order the ambition and pride of men to fulfil his own predictions, and to publish the truth of Christ's birth of the seed of David, for the names of Joseph and Mary were found in the records of Rome in Tertullian's time.

3. God hath several ends in the same action. Jacob is oppressed with famine, Pharaoh enriched with plenty, but Joseph's imprisonment is in order to his father's relief, and Pharaoh's wealth; his mistress's anger flings him into a prison. Joseph is wronged, and hath captivity for a reward of his chastity. God makes it a step to his advancement, and by this way brings him from a captive to be a favourite. What is God's end? Not only to preserve the Egyptian nation, but old Jacob and his family. Was this all that God aimed at? No; he had a further design, and lays the foundation of something to be acted in the future age. By this means Jacob is brought into Egypt, leaves his posterity there, makes way for that glory in the working of the future miracles for their deliverance, such an action that the world should continually ring of, and which should be a type of the spiritual deliverance by Christ.

4. God has more remote ends than short-sighted souls are able to espy. God doth not eye the present advantage of himself and his creature, but hath an eye to his own glory in all, yea, in the very last ages of the world. In small things are often great designs laid by God, and mysteries in the least of his acts. Isaac was delivered from his father's sword, when he was intentionally dead, to set forth to the world a type of Christ's resurrection, and a ram is conducted thither by God, and entangled in the thickets, and appointed to sacrifice, whereby God sets forth a type of Christ's death.* He useth the captivities of the people, to enlarge the bounds of the gospel.

The wise men were guided by a star to Christ as King of the Jews, and come to pay homage to him in his infancy. When was the foundation of this remarkable event laid? Probably in Balaam's prophecy, Num. xxiv. 17. ' I shall see him, but not now; I shall behold him, but not nigh. There

* Hall's Contemp. p. 796.

shall come a star out of Jacob, and a sceptre shall rise out of Israel,' &c. transmitted by tradition to those wise men, and perhaps renewed by *Sibilla Chaldœa*, and confirmed in their minds by the Jews, whilst in the Babylonish captivity they conversed with them. Thus God many ages before in this prophecy had an end in promoting the readier entertainment of Christ among this people, when he should be born; what the wise men's end was, the Scripture doth not acquaint us; but, however, their gifts were a means to preserve our Saviour, Joseph, and Mary, from the rage of a tyrant, and affording them wherewithal to support them in Egypt, whither they were ordered by God to fly for security. So God, 2 Kings vii. 1, 2, 17, threatens by the prophet the nobleman for his scoffing unbelief, that though he should see the plenty, that he should not taste of it. See how God doth order second causes, naturally to bring about his own decree! The king gives this person charge of the gate; whilst the people crowd for provision to satisfy their hunger, they accomplish the threatening, which they had no intentions to do, and trod him to death. Now I come to shew that there is a providence.

Obs. 1. The wisdom of God would not be so perspicuous, were there not a providence in the world. It is eminent in the creation, but more illustrious in the government of the creatures. A musician discovers more skill in the touching an instrument, and ordering the strings, to sound what notes he pleaseth, than he doth in the first framing and making of it. Isa. xxviii. 29, 'This also comes from the Lord of hosts, which is wonderful in counsel, and excellent in working.' All God's providences are but his touch of the strings of this great instrument of the world. And all his works are excellent, because they are the fruit of his wonderful counsel, and unsearchable wisdom, which is most seen in his providence, as in reading the verses before. His power is glorified in creating and upholding this fabric. How shall his wisdom be glorified but in his government of it? Surely God will be no less intent upon the honour of his wisdom than upon that of his power. For if any attribute may be said to excel another, it is his wisdom and holiness, because those are perfections which God hath stamped upon the nobler part of his creation. Inferior creatures have more power and strength than man, but wisdom is the perfection of a rational creature. Now it is God's wisdom to direct all things to their proper end, as well as to appoint them their ends, which direction must be by a particular providence, especially in those things which know not their end, and have no reason to guide them. We know in the world it is not a part of wisdom to leave things to chance, but to state our ends, and lay a platform of those means which direct to an attaining of them. And wisdom is most seen in drawing all things together, and making them subservient to the end he hath fixed to himself; and, therefore, one of the great things that shall be admired at last, next to the great work of redemption, will be the harmony and consent of those things which seemed contrary, how they did all conspire for the bringing about that end which God aimed at.

Obs. 2. The means whereby God acts discover a providence. He acts,

1. By small means. The considerable actions in the world have usually very small beginnings. As of a few letters how many thousand words are made! of ten figures, how many thousand numbers! And a point is the beginning of all geometry. A little stone flung into a pond makes a little circle, then a greater, till it enlargeth itself to both the sides. So from small beginnings, God doth cause an efflux through the whole world.

(1.) He useth small means in his ordinary works. The common works of nature spring from small beginnings. Great plants are formed from small seeds. The clouds which water the great garden of the world are but a collection of vapours. The noblest operations of the soul are wrought in an organ, viz. the brain, composed of coagulated phlegm. Who would imagine that Saul, in seeking his father's asses, should find a kingdom?

(2.) In his extraordinary works he useth small means. Elisha, that waited upon Elijah, and poured water upon his hands, shall do greater miracles than his master. And the apostles shall do greater works than Christ, John xiv. 12, that the world may know that God is not tied to any means that men count excellent; that all creatures are his, and act not of themselves, but by his spirit and power.

In his extraordinary works of justice. He makes a rod in the hands of Moses to confound the skill of the Egyptian magicians. He commissioned frogs and flies to countercheck a powerful and mighty people. When Benhadad was so proud as to say, the dust of Samaria should not suffice for handfuls for his army, God scattered his army by the lacqueys of the princes,—1 Kings xx. 14, 'The young men of the princes of the provinces,'—about two hundred thirty-two, ver. 15. The little sling in the hand of David a youth, guided by God's eye and hand, is a match fit enough for a blasphemous giant, and defeats the strength of a weaver's beam.

In his extraordinary works of mercy.

[1.] In the deliverance of a people or person. A dream was the occasion of Joseph's greatness and Joseph's preservation. He used the cacklings of geese to save the Roman Capitol from a surprise by the Gauls. He picks out Gideon to be a general, who was least in his father's esteem, Judges vi. 15; and what did his army consist of, but few, and those fearful, Judges vii. 6, 7; those that took water with their hands (which, as Josephus saith, is a natural sign of fear) did God choose out to overthrow the Midianites, who had overspread the land as grasshoppers, to shew that he can make the most fearful men to be sufficient instruments against the greatest powers, when the concernments of his church and people lie at stake.

God so delights in thus baffling the pride of men, that Asa uses it as an argument to move God to deliver him in the strait he was in, when Zerah the Ethiopian came against him with a great multitude, when he was but a small point and centre in the midst of a wide circumference: 2 Chron. xiv. 11, 'Lord, it is nothing with thee to help with many or with few.' Hereby God sets off his own power, and evidenceth his superintendent care of his people. It was more signally the arm of God for Moses to confound Pharaoh with his lice and frogs, than if he had beaten him in a plain field with his six hundred thousand Israelites.

[2.] In the salvation of the soul. Our Saviour himself, though God, the great redeemer of the world, was so mean in the eyes of the world, that he calls himself 'a worm, and no man,' Ps. xxii. 6. He picks out many times the most unlikely persons to accomplish the greatest purposes for men's souls. He lodgeth the treasures of wisdom in vessels of earth; he chose not the cedars of Lebanon, but the shrubs of the valley; not the learned Pharisees of Jerusalem, but the poor men of Galilee: 'Out of the mouths of babes and sucklings, he ordains praise to himself.'

The apostles' breeding was not capable of ennobling their minds, and fitting them for such great actions as Christ employed them in. But after he had new moulded and inflamed their spirits, he made them of fishermen, greater conquerors of the world, than the most magnified grandees could pretend to.

Thus salvation is wrought by a crucified Christ: and that God who made the world by wisdom, would save it by the foolishness of preaching. And make Paul, the least of the apostles as he terms himself, more successful than those who had been instructed at the feet of Christ, 1 Cor. xv. 9, 10.

2. By contrary means. God by his providence makes contrary things contribute to his glory, as contrary colours in a picture do to the beauty of the piece. Nature is God's instrument to do whatsoever he pleases; and therefore nothing so contrary but he may bring to his own ends; as in some engines you shall see wheels have contrary motions, and yet all in order to one and the same end. God cured those by a brazen serpent, which were stung by the fiery ones; whereas brass is naturally hurtful to those that are bit by serpents.*

(1.) Afflictions. Joseph is sold for a slave, and God sends him as a harbinger; his brothers sold him to destroy him, and God sends him to save them. Paul's bonds, in the opinion of some, might have stifled the gospel; but he tells us that they had fallen out to the furtherance of the gospel, Phil. i. 12.

(2.) Sins.† God doth often effect his just will by our weakness; neither thereby justifying our infirmities, nor blemishing his own action. Jacob gets the blessing by unlawful means, telling no less than two lies to attain it,—I am Esau, and this is venison,—but hereby God brings about the performance of his promise, which Isaac's natural affection to Esau would have hindered Jacob of.

The breach of the first covenant was an occasion of introducing a better. Man's sinning away his first stock, was an occasion to God to enrich him with a surer. The loss of his original righteousness made way for a clearer and more durable. The folly of man made way for the evidence of God's wisdom, and the sin of man for the manifestation of his grace; and by the wise disposal of God, opens a way for the honour of those attributes which would not else have been experimentally known by the sons of men.

3. Casual means. The viper which leapt upon Paul's hand out of the bundle of sticks was a casual act, but designed by the providence of God for the propagation of the gospel. Pharaoh's daughter comes casually to wash herself in the river, but, indeed, conducted by the secret influence of God upon her, to rescue Moses, exposed to a forlorn condition, and breed him up in the Egyptian learning, that he might be the fitter to be his kindred's deliverer. Saul had been hunting David, and at last had lodged him in a place whence he could not well escape, and being ready to seize upon him in that very instant of time, a post comes to Saul, and brings the news that the Philistines had invaded the land, which cut out other work for him, and David for that time escapes, 1 Sam. xxiii. 26, 27, 28.

Prop. 3. Reason. Such actions and events of things are in the world, which cannot rationally be ascribed to any other cause than a supreme providence. It is so in common things. Men have the same parts, the same outward advantages, the same industry, and yet prosper not alike. One labours much, and gets little; another uses not altogether such endeavours, and hath riches flowing in upon him. Men lay their projects deep, and question not the accomplishment of them, and are disappointed by some strange and unforeseen accident. And sometimes men attain what they desire in a different way, and many times contrary to the method they had projected. This is evidenced,

1. By the restraints upon the passions of men. The waves of the sea, and the tumults of the people are much of the same impetuous natures, and are quelled by the same power: Ps. lxv. 7, ' Which stilleth the noise of

---

* Grotius, Num. xxi. 9. *Æs naturaliter nocet* τοῖς ὀφιοδήκτοις.
† Hall, Contemp. book iii. p. 806, 807.

the sea, and tumult of the people.' Tumults of the people could no more be stilled by the force of a man, than the waves of the sea by a puff of breath. How strangely did God qualify the hearts of the Egyptians willingly to submit to the sale of their land, when they might have risen in a tumult, broke open the granaries, and supplied their wants, Gen. xlvii. 19, 21. Indeed, if the world were left to the conduct of chance and fortune, what work would the savage lusts and passions of men make among us ! How is it possible that any but an almighty power can temper so many jarring principles, and rank so many quarrelsome and turbulent spirits in a due order ! If those brutish passions which boil in the hearts of men were let loose by that infinite power that bridles them, how soon would the world be run headlong into inconceivable confusions, and be rent in pieces by its own disorders ?

2. By the sudden changes which are made upon the spirits of men for the preservation of others. God takes off the spirit of some as he did the wheels from the Egyptian chariots, in the very act of their rage. Paul was struck down and changed while he was yet breathing out threatenings, &c. God sees all the workings of men's hearts, all those cruel intentions in Esau against his brother Jacob, but God on a sudden turns away that torrent of hatred, and disposeth Esau for a friendly meeting, Gen. xxxiii. 4. And he who had before an exasperated malice by reason of the loss of his birthright and blessing, was in a moment a changed man. Thus was Saul's heart changed towards David, and from a persecutor turns a justifier of him, confesseth David's innocence and his own guilt : 1 Sam. xxiv. 17, 18, ' Thou art more righteous than I, for thou hast rewarded me good, whereas I have rewarded thee evil,' &c. What reason can be rendered for so sudden a change in Saul's revengeful spirit, which had all the force of interest to support it, and considered by him at that very time ? For, ver. 24, he takes special notice that his family should be disinherited, and David be his successor in the throne. How suddenly did God turn the edge of the sword and the heart of an enemy from Jehoshaphat, 2 Chron. xviii. 31. Jehoshaphat cried out, and the Lord helped him, and God moved them to depart from him. The Holy Ghost emphatically ascribes it to God's motion of their wills, by twice expressing it. But stranger is the preservation of the Jews from Haman's bloody designs, after the decree was gone out against them. Mordecai the Jew is made Ahasuerus's favourite by a strange wheeling of providence. First, the king's eyes are held waking, Esther vi. 1, 2, and he is inclined to pass away the solitariness of the night with a book, rather than a game, or some other court pastime ; no book did he fix on but the records of that empire, no place in that voluminous book but the chronicle of Mordecai's service in the discovery of a treason against the king's life ; he doth not carelessly pass it over, but inquires what recompence had been bestowed on Mordecai for so considerable a service, and this just before Mordecai should have been destroyed. Had Ahasuerus slept, Mordecai and all his countrymen had been sacrificed, notwithstanding all his loyalty. Could this be a cast of blind chance, which had such a concatenation of evidences in it for a superior power ?

3. In causing enemies to do things for others which are contrary to all rule of policy. It is wonderful that the Jews, a people known to be of a stubborn nature, and tenacious of their laws, wherein they differed from all the nations, should in the worst of their captivities be so often befriended by their conquerors, not only to rebuild their city, and re-edify their temple, but at the charge of their conquerors too. The very enemies that had captived the Jews, though they knew them to be a people apt to rebel : that the people

whose temple they had helped to build would keep up a distinct worship and difference in religion, which is usually attended with the greatest animosities; and when they knew it to be so strong in situation as to be a fort as well as a place of worship; that for this their enemies should furnish them with materials, when they were not in a condition to procure any for themselves, and give them money out of the public exchequer, and timber out of the king's forest, as we read, Ezra i. 1, 2, 4, 7; iv. 12, 15, 19; vi. 4, 5, 8, 9, 11; Neh. ii. 8. And all this they looked upon as the hand of God: Ezra, vi. 22, 'The Lord hath turned the heart of the king of Assyria unto them, to strengthen their hands in the work of the house of God.' And the heathen Artaxerxes takes notice of it. Cicero tells us, that in his time gold was carried out of Italy for the ornament of the temple. They had their rites in religion preserved entire under the Roman government, though more different from the Roman customs than any nation subdued by them. Dion and Seneca, and others, observe, that wherever they were transplanted they prospered and gave laws to the victors. And this was so generally acknowledged, that Haman's cabinet counsel (who were surely none of the meanest statesmen) gave him no hopes of success, when he appeared against Mordecai, because he was of the race of the Jews, Esth. vi. 13, so much did God own them by his gracious providence. They were also so entire in all their captivities before their crucifying of our Lord and Saviour, that they count their genealogies.

4. In infatuating the counsels of men. God sets a stamp of folly upon the wisdom of men, Isa. xliv. 25, 'that turns the wise men backward, and makes their knowledge foolishness, and makes their counsels as chaff and stubble.' Isa. xxxiii. 11, 'Ye shall conceive chaff, and bring forth stubble.' Herod was a crafty person, insomuch that Christ calls him fox.* How foolish was he in managing his project of destroying Christ, his supposed competitor in the kingdom! When the wise men came to Jerusalem, and brought the news of the birth of a king of the Jews, he calls a synod of the ablest men among the Jews! The result of it is to manifest the truth of God's prediction in the place of our Saviour's birth, and to direct the wise men in their way to him. Herod had no resolutions but bloody concerning Christ, Mat. ii. 3–8. God blinds his mind in the midst of all his craft, that he sees not those rational ways which he might make use of for the destruction of that which he feared: he sends those wise men, mere strangers to him, and entrusts them with so great a concern; he goes not himself, nor sends any of his guard with them to cut him off immediately upon the discovery, but leaves the whole conduct of the business to those he had no acquaintance with, and of whose faithfulness he could have no assurance. God crosses the intentions of men. Joab slew Amasa because he thought him his rival in David's favour, and then imagined he had rid his hands of all that could stand in his way; yet God raised up Benaiah, who drew Joab from the horns of the altar, and cut him in pieces at Solomon's command. God doth so order it, many times, that when the most rational counsel is given to men, they have not hearts to follow it. Ahithophel gave as suitable counsel for Absalom's design as the best statesman in the world could give, 2 Sam. xvii. 1, 2, to surprise David while he was amused† at his son's rebellion, and dejected with grief at so unnatural an action, and whilst his forces had not yet made their rendezvous, and those that were with him were

---

* This is a singular inadvertence on the part of the author. It was not the Herod who slew the babes at Bethlehem whom our Lord so designated.—Ed.

† That is, his attention was occupied, or perhaps it may be a misprint for 'amazed.' —Ed.

tired in their march. Speed was best in attempts of this nature. David in all probability had been cut off, and the hearts of the people would have melted at the fall of their sovereign. But Absalom inclines rather to Hushai's counsel, which was not so proper for the business he had engaged in, ver. 7–14. Now this was from God. 'For the Lord had appointed to defeat the good counsel of Ahithophel, to the intent that the Lord might bring evil upon Absalom.' So foolish were the Egyptians against reason, in entering into the Red Sea after the Israelites ; for could they possibly think that that God, who had by a strong hand and an army of prodigies brought Israel out of their captivity, and conducted them thus far, and now by a miracle opened the Red Sea and gave them passage through the bowels of it, should give their enemies the same security in pursuing them, and unravel all that web he had been so long a working ?

5. In making the counsels of men subservient to the very ends they design against. God brings a cloud upon men's understandings, and makes them the contrivers of their own ruin, wherein they intend their own safety, and gains honour to himself by outwitting the creature. The Babel projectors, fearing to be scattered abroad, would erect a power to prevent; and this proved the occasion of dispersing them over the world in such a confusion that they could not understand one another, Gen. xi. 4, 8. God ordered Pharaoh's policies to accomplish the end against which they were directed. He is afraid Israel should grow too mighty, and so wrest the kingdom out of his hands, and therefore he would oppress them to hinder their increase, which made them both stronger and more numerous. Exercise strengthens men, and luxury softens the spirit. The Jews fear if they suffered Christ to make a farther progress in his doctrine and miracles, they should lose Cæsar's favour, and expose their country as a prey to a Roman army : this caused their destruction by those enemies they thought by this means to prevent; God ordering it so, that a Roman army was poured in upon them which swept them into all corners of the earth. Priests and Pharisees sit close together in counsel how to hinder men's believing in Christ, and the result of their consultation was to put him to death, and no man then would believe in a dead person, not capable of working any miracles, John xi. 47–50, for the amusing of the people ; and by this means there were a greater number of believers on him than in the time of his life, according to his own prediction, John xii. 32, 'And I, if I be lifted up from the earth, will draw all men unto me.'

6. In making the fancies of men subservient to their own ruin. God brings about strange events by the mere imaginations and conceits of men, which are contrary to common and natural observation, and the ordinary course of rational consequences, 2 Kings iii. 22, 23. The army of the Moabites which had invaded Israel thought the two kings of Judah and Israel had turned their swords against one another, because the rising sun had coloured those unexpected waters and made them look red, which they took for the blood of their enemies, and so disorderly run without examination of the truth of their conceit ; but instead of dividing the spoil, they left their lives upon the points of the Israelites' swords. So the Syrian army are scared with a panic fear, and scatter themselves upon an empty sound, 2 Kings vii. 6. Thus a dream struck a terror into the Midianites, and the noise of the broken potsherds made them fear some treason in their camp, and caused them to turn their swords into one another's bowels: Judges vii. 19–22, ' The Lord set every man's sword against his fellow.'

Quest. First, If God's providence orders all things in world, and concurs to every thing, how will you free God from being the author of sin ?

Answer, in several propositions.

1. It is certain God hath a hand about all the sinful actions in the world. The selling Joseph to the Ishmaelites was the act of his brethren ; the sending him into Egypt was the act of God : Ps. cv. 17, 'He sent a man before them, even Joseph, who was sold for a servant ;' Gen. xlv. 8, 'It was not you that sent me hither, but God,' where Joseph ascribes it more to God than to them. Their wicked intention was to be rid of him, that he might tell no more tales of them to his father. God's gracious intention was to advance him for his honour and their good; and to bring about this gracious purpose, he makes use of their sinful practice. God's end was righteous, when theirs was wicked. It is said God moved David to number the people : 2 Sam. xxiv. 1, 'The anger of the Lord was kindled against Israel, and he moved David against them to say, Go number Israel and Judah.' Yet Satan is said to provoke David to number the people : 1 Chron. xxi. 1, 'And Satan stood up against Israel, and provoked David to number Israel.' Here are two agents; but the text mentions God's hand in it out of justice to punish Israel ; Satan's end, no question, was out of malice to destroy. Satan wills it as a sin, God as a punishment: God, say some, *permissivè*, Satan *efficaciter*. In the most villanous and unrighteous action that ever was done, God is said to have an influence on it. God is said to deliver up Christ: Acts ii. 23, 'Him, being delivered by the determinate counsel and foreknowledge of God, ye have taken, and by wicked hands have crucified and slain :' Acts iv. 28, 'For to do whatsoever thy hand and thy counsel determined before to be done.' Not barely as an act of his presence, but his counsel, and that determinate, *i. e.* stable and irreversible. He makes a distinction between these two acts. In God it was an act of counsel, in them an act of wickedness, 'by wicked hands ;' there was God's counsel about it, an actual tradition : Rom. viii. 32, 'He that spared not his own Son, but delivered him up for us all.' All the agents had several ends. God in that act aimed at the redemption of the world, Satan at the preventing it, Judas to satisfy his covetousness, the Jews to preserve themselves from the Roman invasion, and out of malice to him for so sharply reproving them. God had a gracious principle of love to mankind, and acted for the salvation of the world in it ; the instruments had base principles and ends, and moved freely in obedience to them. So in the affliction of Job, both God and Satan had an hand in it : Job. i. 12, 'The Lord said unto Satan, Behold, all that he hath is in thy power ;' ver. 11, 'Touch all that he hath, and he will curse thee to thy face ;' their ends were different: the one righteous, for trial; the other malicious, against God, that he might be cursed; against Job that he might be damned. God's end was the brightening of his grace, and the devil's end was the ruin of his integrity, and despoiling him of God's favour.

2. In all God's acts about sin there is no stain to God's holiness.* In second causes, one and the same action, proceeding from divers causes, in respect of one cause, may be sinful ; in respect of the other, righteous. As when two judges condemn a guilty person, one condemns him out of love to justice, because he is guilty ; the other condemns him out of a private hatred and spleen : one respects him as a malefactor only, the other as a private enemy chiefly. Here is the same action with two concurring causes, one being wicked in it, the other righteous. Much more may we conceive it in the concurrence of the Creator with the action of the creature.

(1.) God moves every thing in his ordinary providence according to their particular natures. God moves every thing ordinarily according to the nature he finds it in. Had we stood in innocency, we had been moved

* Senguer. Metaph. lib. ii. cap. 15. sect. 5.

according to that originally righteous nature; but since our fall we are moved according to that nature introduced by us with the expulsion of the other. Our first corruption was our own act, not God's work; we owe our creation to God, our corruption to ourselves. Now, since God will govern his creature, I do not see how it can be otherwise, than according to the present nature of the creature, unless God be pleased to alter that nature. God forces no man against his nature; he doth not force the will in conversion, but graciously and powerfully inclines it. He doth never force nor incline the will to sin, but leaves it to the corrupt habits it hath settled in itself: Ps. lxxxi. 12, 'So I gave them up to their own hearts' lusts, and they walked in their own counsels;' counsels of their own framing, not of God's. He moves the will, which is *sponte mala*, according to its own nature and counsels. As a man flings several things out of his hand, which are of several figures, some spherical, tetragons, cylinders, conics, some round and some square, though the motion be from the agent, yet the variety of their motions is from their own figure and frame; and if any will hold his hand upon a ball in its motion, regularly it will move according to his nature and figure; and a man by casting a bowl out of his hand, is the cause of the motion, but the bad bias is the cause of its irregular motion. The power of action is from God, but the viciousness of that action from our own nature. As when a clock or watch hath some fault in any of the wheels, the man that winds it up, or putting his hand upon the wheels moves them, he is the cause of the motion, but it is the flaw in it, or deficiency of something, is the cause of its erroneous motion; that error was not from the person that made it, or the person that winds it up, and sets it on going, but from some other cause; yet till it be mended it will not go otherwise, so long as it is set upon motion. Our motion is from God,—Acts xvii. 28, 'In him we move',—but not the disorder of that motion. It is the foulness of a man's stomach at sea is the cause of his sickness, and not the pilot's government of the ship.

(2). God doth not infuse the lust, or excite it, though he doth present the object about which the lust is exercised. God delivered up Christ to the Jews, he presented him to them, but never commanded them to crucify him, nor infused that malice into them, nor quickened it; but he, seeing such a frame, withdrew his restraining grace, and left them to the conduct of their own vitiated wills. All the corruption in the world ariseth from lust in us, not from the object which God in his providence presents to us: 2 Peter i. 4, 'The corruption that is in the world through lust.' The creature is from God, but the abuse of it from corruption. God created the grape, and filled the vine with a sprightliness, but he doth never infuse a drunken frame into a man, or excite it. Providence presents us with the wine, but the precept is to use it soberly. Can God be blamed if that which is good in itself be turned into poison by others? No more than the flower can be called a criminal, because the spider's nature turns that into venom which is sweet in itself. Man hath such a nature, not from creation, wherein God is positive, but from corruption, wherein God is permissive. Providence brings a man into such a condition of poverty, but it doth not encourage his stubbornness and impatience. There is no necessity upon thee from God to exercise thy sin under affliction, when others under the same exercise their graces. The rod makes the child smart, but it is its own stubbornness makes it curse. In short, though it be by God's permission that we *can* do evil, yet it is not by his inspiration that we *will* to do evil; that is wholly from ourselves.

(3.) God supports the faculties wherewith a man sinneth, and supports a man in that act wherein he sinneth, but concurs not to the sinfulness of that act. No sin doth properly consist in the act itself, as an act, but in the deficiency of that act from the rule. No action wherein there is sin but may be done as an action, though not as an irregular action. Killing a man is not in itself unlawful, for then no magistrate should execute a malefactor for murdering another, and justice would cease in the world ; man also must divest himself of all thoughts of preserving his life against an invader ; but to kill a man without just cause, without authority, without rule, contrary to rule, out of revenge, is unlawful. So that it is not the act, as an act, is the sin, but the swerving of that act from the rule, makes it a sinful act. So speaking, as speaking, is not a sin, for it is a power and act God hath endued us with, but speaking irreverently and dishonourably of God, or falsely and slanderously of man, or any otherwise irregularly, therein the sin lies ; so that it is easy to conceive that an act and the viciousness of it are separable. That act which is the same in kind with another, may be laudable, and the other base and vile in respect of its circumstances. The mind wherewith a man doth this or that act, and the irregularity of it, makes a man a criminal. There is a concurrence of God to the act wherein we sin, but the sinfulness of that act is purely from the inherent corruption of the creature ; as the power and act of seeing is communicated to the eye by the soul, but the seeing doubly or dimly is from the viciousness of the organ, the eye. God hath no manner of immediate efficiency in producing sin ; as the sun is not the efficient cause of darkness, though the darkness immediately succeeds the setting of the sun, but it is the deficient cause. So God withdraws his grace, and leaves us to that lust which is in our wills : Acts xiv. 16, ' Who in times past suffered all nations to walk in their own ways.' He bestowed no grace upon them, but left them to themselves. As a man who lets a glass fall out of his hand is not the efficient cause that the glass breaks, but its own brittle nature ; yet he is the deficient cause, because he withdraws his support from it. God is not obliged to give us grace, because we have a total forfeiture of it. He is not a debtor to any man, by way of merit, of anything but punishment. He is indeed in some sense a debtor to those that are in Christ, upon the account of Christ's purchase and his own promise, but not by any merits of theirs.

(4.) God's providence is conversant about sin as a punishment, yet in a very righteous manner. God did not will the first sin of Adam as a punishment, because there was no punishment due to him before he sinned, but he willed the continuance of it as a punishment to the nature *sub ratione boni*. This being a judicial act of God, is therefore righteously willed by him. Punishment is a moral good. It is also a righteous thing to suit the punishment to the nature of the offence ; and what can be more righteous than to punish a man by that wherein he offends ? Hence God is said to give up men to sin,—Rom. i. 26, 27, ' For this cause God gave them up unto vile affections,'—and to send ' strong delusions that they may believe a lie.' And the reason is rendered, 2 Thess. ii. 12, ' that they all might be damned who believed not the truth, but had pleasure in unrighteousness.' What more righteous than to make those vile affections and that unrighteousness their punishment which they make their pleasure, and to leave them to pursue their own sinful inclinations, and make them (as the psalmist speaks) Ps. v. 10, ' fall by their own counsels' ? A drunkard's beastliness is his punishment as well as his sin. Thus God delivers up some to their own lusts, as a punishment both to themselves and others, as he hardened Pharaoh's heart for the destruction both of himself and his people.

(5.) God by his providence draws glory to himself and good out of sin. It is the highest excellency to draw good out of evil, and it is God's right to manifest his excellency when he pleases, and to direct that to his honour which is acted against his law. The holiness of God could never intend sin as sin. But the wisdom of God foreseeing it, and decreeing to permit it, intended the making it subservient to his own honour. He would not permit it but for some good, because he is infinitely good, and could not by reason of that goodness suffer that which is purely evil, if by his wisdom he could not raise good out of it. It is purely evil, as it is contrary to law; it is good *ratione finis*, as God orders it by his providence; yet that goodness flows not from the nature of sin, but from the wise disposal of God.

As God at the creation framed a beautiful world out of a chaos, out of matter without form, and void, so by his infinite wisdom he extracts honour to himself out of the sins of men. As sin had dishonoured him at its entrance, in defacing his works and depraving his creature, so he would make use of the sins of men in repairing his honour and restoring the creature.

It is not conceivable by us what way there could be more congruous to the wisdom and holiness of God, as the state of the world then stood, to bring about the death of Christ, which in his decree was necessary to the satisfaction of his justice, without ordering the evil of some men's hearts to serve his gracious purpose. If we could suppose that Christ could commit some capital crime, for which he should deserve death, which was impossible by reason of the hypostatical union, the whole design of God for redemption had sunk to the ground. Therefore God doth restrain or let out the fury of men's passions and the corrupt habits of their wills to such a degree as should answer directly to the full point of his most gracious will, and no further. He lets out their malice so far as was conducing to the grand design of his death, and restrains it from everything that might impair the truth of any prediction, as in the parting his garments, or breaking his bones. If God had put him to death by some thunder or otherwise, and after raised him, how could the voluntariness of Christ appear, which was necessary to make him a perfect oblation? How would his innocency have appeared? The strangeness of the judgment would have made all men believe him some great and notorious sinner. How then could the gospel have been propagated? Who would have entertained the doctrine of one whose innocency could not be cleared? If it be said, God might raise him again, what evidences would have been had that he had been really dead? But as the case was, his enemies confess him dead really, and many witnesses there were of his resurrection.

[1.] God orders the sins of men to the glory of his grace. As a foil serves to make the lustre of a diamond more conspicuous, so doth God make use of the deformities of men to make his own grace more illustrious, and convey it with a more pleasing relish to them. Never doth grace appear more amiable, never is God entertained with so high admirations, as by those who, of the worst of sinners, are made the choicest of saints. Paul often takes occasion, from the greatness of his sin, to admire the unsearchable riches of that grace which pardoned him.

[2.] God orders them to bring forth temporal mercies. In providence there are two things considerable. *First*, Man's will. *Secondly*, God's purpose. What man's will intends as a harm in sin, God in his secret purpose orders to some eminent advantage. In the selling of Joseph, his brothers intend the execution of their revenge; and God orders it for the advancement of himself, and the preservation of his unrighteous enemies, who might otherwise have starved. His brothers sent him to frustrate his dream, and God to fulfil it. Our reformation and return from under the yoke of antichrist was, by the wise disposal of God, occasioned by the three great idols of the world, the lust of the eye, the lust of the flesh, and the pride of life; lust, covetousness, and ambition, three vices notoriously eminent in Henry the Eighth, the first instrument in that work. What he did for the satisfaction of his lust is ordered by God for the glory of his mercy to us. And though the papists upon that account reflect upon our Reformation, they may as well reflect upon the glorious work of redemption, because it was in the wisdom of God brought about by Judas his covetousness, and the Jews' malice.

[3.] God orders them for the glory of his justice upon others. Nathan had threatened David that one in his house should lie with his wives in the sight of the sun, 2 Sam. xii. 11. Ahithophel adviseth Absalom to do so, not with any design to fulfil God's threatening, but secure his own stake, by making the quarrel between the father and the son irreconcilable, because he might well fear that upon a peace between David and Absalom he might be offered up as a sacrifice to David's justice. God orders Ahithophel's counsel and Absalom's sin to the glory of his justice in David's punishment.

The ambition of Vespasian and Titus was only to reduce Judea to the Roman province after the revolt of it. But God orders hereby the execution of his righteous will in the punishment of the Jews for their rejecting Christ, and the accomplishment of Christ's prediction. Luke xix. 43, ' For the days shall come, that thy enemy shall cast a trench about thee,' &c. To conclude; if we deny God the government of sin in the course of his providence, we must necessarily deny him the government of the world, because there is not an action of any man's in the world, which is under the government of God, but is either a sinful action or an action mixed with sin.

God therefore in his government doth advance his power in the weakness, his wisdom in the follies, his holiness in the sins, his mercy in the unkindness, and his justice in the unrighteousness of men;* yet God is not defiled with the impurities of men, but rather draws forth a glory to himself, as a rose doth a greater beauty and sweetness from the strong smell of the garlic set near it.†

Quest. 2. If there be a providence, how comes those unequal distributions to happen in the world? How is it so bad with good men, as if they were the greatest enemies to God, and so well with the wicked, as if they were the most affectionate friends? Doth not virtue languish away in obscurity, whiles wickedness struts about the world? What is the reason that splendid virtue is oppressed by injustice, and notorious vices triumph in prosperity? It would make men believe that the world was governed rather by a blind and unrighteous, than by a wise, good, and just governor, when they see things in such disorder, as if the devil had, as he pretends, the whole power of the world delivered to him, Luke iv. 6, and God had left all care of it to his will.

Ans. This consideration has heightened the minds of many against a providence. It was the notion of many heathens,‡ when they saw many who had acted with much gallantry for their countries afflicted, they questioned whether there were a superintendent power over the world. This hath also been the stumbling-block of many taught in a higher school than

---

* Vid. Ovid Amor. lib. iii. Eleg. iii. v. 1, and v. 27.
† Boetius de Conso. lib. i.
‡ See instances in Jackson. Vol. i. 8, chap. iv. sect. 5.

that of nature, the Jews: Mal. ii. 17, 'Ye say, every one that doth evil is good in the sight of the Lord, and he delighteth in them; and where is the God of judgment?' Yea, and the observation of the outward felicities of vice, and the oppression of goodness, have caused fretting commotions in the hearts of God's people; the Psalm lxxiii. is wholly designed to answer this case. Jeremiah, though fixed in the acknowledgment of God's righteousness, would debate the reason of it with God: Jer. xii. 1, 'Righteous art thou, O Lord, yet let me talk with thee of thy judgments: Wherefore doth the way of the wicked prosper? wherefore are all they happy that deal very treacherously? Thou hast planted them; yea, they have taken root: they grow; yea, they bring forth fruit.' He perceiving it a universal case,—'Wherefore are all they happy,' &c.—did not know how to reconcile it with the righteousness of God, nor Habakkuk with the holiness of God: Hab. i. 13, 'Thou art of purer eyes than to behold iniquity: wherefore holdest thou thy tongue when the wicked devoureth the man that is more righteous than he?' In point of God's goodness, too, Job expostulates the case with God: Job x. 3, 'Is it good unto thee that thou shouldst oppress? that thou shouldst despise the work of thy hands? and shine upon the counsel of the wicked?' You see upon the account of holiness, righteousness, goodness, the three great attributes of God, it hath been questioned by good men, and upon the account of his wisdom by the wicked Jews.

Ans. 1. Answer in general, Is it not a high presumption for ignorance to judge God's proceedings? In the course of providence such things are done that men could not imagine could be done without injustice; yet when the whole connection of their end is unravelled, they appear highly beautiful, and discover a glorious wisdom and righteousness. If it had entered into the heart of man to think that God should send his Son in a very low estate to die for sinners, would it not have been judged an unjust and unreasonable act, to deliver up his Son for rebels, the innocent for the criminals, to spare the offender and punish the observer of his law? Yet when the design is revealed and acted, what an admirable connection is there of justice, wisdom, mercy, and holiness, which men could not conceive of! It will be known to be so at last in God's dealing with all his members. We are incompetent judges of the righteousness and wisdom of God, unless we were infinitely righteous and wise ourselves; we must be gods, or in another state, before we can understand the reason of all God's actions. We judge according to the law of sense and self, which are inferior to the rules whereby God works. 'Judge nothing then before the time,' 1 Cor. iv. 5. It is not a time for us to pass a judgment upon things. A false judgment is easily made, when neither the counsels of men's hearts, nor the particular laws of God's actions, are known to us. In general it is certain, God doth righteously order his providences; he may see some inward corruptions in good men to be demolished by afflictions, and some good moral affections, some useful designs, or some services he employs wicked men in, to be rewarded in this life.

Ans. 2. God is sovereign of the world. He is *sui juris*: 'The earth is his, and the fulness thereof,' may he not 'do what he will with his own'? Mat. xx. 15. Who shall take upon them to control God, and prescribe laws to him how to deal with his creatures? Why should a finite understanding prescribe measures and methods to an infinite majesty?

Ans. 3. God is wise and just, and knows how to distribute. If we question his providence, we question his wisdom. Is it fit for us, who are but of yesterday, and know nothing, to say to an infinite wisdom, What dost thou? and to direct the only wise God to a method of his actions? His own wisdom will best direct him to the time when to punish the insolence of the wicked, and relieve the miseries of his people. We see the present dispensations, but are we able to understand the internal motives? May there not be some sins of righteous men's parents that he will visit upon their children? some virtues of their ancestors, that he will reward even in their wicked posterity? He may use wicked men as instruments in some service. It is part of his distributive justice to reward them. They aim at these things in their service, and he gratifies them according to their desires. Let not, then, his righteousness be an argument against his providence; it is righteous with God not to be in arrears with them. Sometimes God gives them not to them as rewards of any moral virtue, but puts power into their hands, that they may be instruments of his justice upon some offenders against him: Isa. x. 5, the staff in the Assyrian's hand was God's indignation.

Ans. 4. There is a necessity for some seeming inequality, at least, in order to the good government of the world. Can all in any community of men be of an equal height? A house hath not beams and rafters of an equal bigness, some are greater and some less. The world is God's family. It is here as in a family; all cannot have the same office, but they are divided according to the capacities of some persons, and the necessity of others. Providence would not be so apparent in the beauty of the world, if all men were alike in their stations. Where would the beauty of the body be, if all the members had one office, and one immediate end? Man would cease to be man, if every member had not some distinct work, and a universal agreement in the common profit of the body. All mankind is but one great body, constituted of several members, which have distinct offices, but all ordered to the good of the whole; the apostle argues this excellently in a parallel case of the diversities of gifts in the church: 1 Cor. xii. 19, 'If all were one member, where were the body?' ver. 23, 'Those members of the body which we think to be less honourable, upon those we bestow more abundant honour;' ver. 24, 'God hath tempered the body together, having given more abundant honour to that part which lacked.' What harmony could there be, if all the voices and sounds were exactly the same in a concert? Who can be delighted with a picture that hath no shadows? The afflictions of good men are a foil to set off the beauty of God's providence in the world.

Ans. 5. Unequal dispensations do not argue carelessness. A father may give one child a gayer coat than he gives another, yet he extends his fatherly care and tenderness over all. According to the several employments he puts his children upon, he is at greater expense, and yet loves one as well as another, and makes provision for all. As the soul takes care of the lowest member, and communicates spirits to every part for their motions; so though God place some in a higher, some in a lower condition, yet he takes care of all: God 'divides to every man as he will,' 1 Cor. xii. 11. Every man hath a several share, according to God's pleasure, of a goodness in the world, as well as of gifts in the church.

Ans. 6. Yet upon due consideration the inequality will not appear so great as the complaint of it. If the wants of one, and the enjoyment of another, were weighed in the balance, the scales might not appear so uneven; we see such a man's wealth, but do you understand his cares? A running sore may lie under a purple robe. Health, the salt of blessing, as one calls it, is bestowed upon a labourer, when many that wallow in abundance have those torturing diseases which embitter their pleasures. If some want those worldly ornaments which others have, may they not have more wisdom than those that enjoy them (the noblest perfection of a rational creature)? Prov. iii. 13, 14, ' The merchandise of it is better than the merchandise of silver, and the gain thereof than fine gold:' Prov. xv. 16, ' Better is a little with the fear of the Lord, than great treasure, and trouble therewith.' As some are stripped of wealth and power, so they are stripped of their incumbrances they bring with them. One hath that serenity and tranquillity of mind, which the cares and fears of others will not suffer them to enjoy, and a grain of contentment is better than many pounds of wealth. It is not a desirable thing to be a great prince, attended with as many cares and fears as he hath subjects in his empire. He made a true estimate of his greatness, that said he would not stoop to take up a crown if it lay at his feet. But more particularly to the parts of the case.

1. It is not well with bad men here.

(1.) Is it well with them who are tortured by their own lusts? What peace can worldly things bestow upon a soul filled with impurity? In 2 Cor. vii. 1, sin is called filthiness: Can it be well with them that have nasty souls? Is it well with them who are racked by pride, stung with cares, gnawn with envy, distracted by insatiable desires, and torn in pieces by their own fears? Can it be well with such who have a multitude of vipers in their breasts, sticking all their stings into them, though the sun shine, and the shadows drop upon them? You are spectators of their felicity, but do you understand their inward gripes? Prov. xiv. 13, ' Even in laughter the heart is sorrowful.' Can silken curtains or purple clothes confer a happiness upon those who have a mortal plague-sore poisoning their bodies, and are ready to expire? Sin is their plague, whatever is their happiness. 1 Kings viii. 38, sin is called the plague of the heart. Their insolent lusts are a far greater misery than the possession of all the kingdoms in the world can be a happiness.

(2.) Is it well with them who have so great an account to make, and know not how to make it? Those that enjoy much are more in God's debt, and therefore more accountable. The account of wicked men is the greater, because of their abundance; and their unfitness to make that account is the greater, because of their abuse. Would any reckon themselves happy to be called upon to give an account of their stewardship for talents, and know not how to give a good account of one farthing? Luke xvi. 2, ' Give an account of thy stewardship.'

(3.) Is it well with them who are the worse for what they have? Is it a happiness to command others, and be more slaves to the worst of creatures than any can be to them? The wicked man's well-spread table sometimes proves his snare, Ps. lxix. 22, and his destruction is bound up in his very prosperity: Prov. i. 32, ' And the prosperity of fools shall destroy them.' Prosperity falling upon an unregenerate heart, like the sun and rain upon bad ground, draws forth nothing but weeds and vermin. Would you think it your happiness to be masters of their concerns, and slaves to their pride? Is a stubbornness against God so desirable a thing, which is strengthened by those things in the hands of the wicked?

(4.) Is it well with them who in the midst of their prosperity are reserved for justice? Can that traitor be accounted happy, that is fed in prison by the prince with better dishes than many a loyal subject hath at his table, but only to keep him alive for his trial, and a public example of justice? God raises some for greater falls. Miserable was the felicity of Pharaoh, to be raised up by God for a subject to shew in him the power of his wrath, Exod. ix. 16. It is but a little time before they shall be ' cut down as grass, and wither as the green herb,' Ps. xxxvii. 2. None would value the condition of that soldier, who, leaping into a river to save a king's crown, and putting it upon his own head, that he might be enabled to swim out with it, was rewarded for saving it, and executed for wearing it. God rewards wicked men for their service, and punishes them for their insolence.

2. Neither is it bad here with good men, if all be well considered. Other men's judgment of a good man is frivolous, they cannot rightly judge of his state and concerns, but he can make a judgment of theirs: 1 Cor. ii. 15, 'A spiritual man judgeth all things, but he himself is judged of no man.' No man can make a sound judgment and estimate of a righteous man's state in any condition, unless he hath had experience of the like in all the circumstances, the inward comforts as well as the outward crosses. For,

(1.) Adversity cannot be called absolutely an evil, as prosperity cannot be called absolutely a good. They are rather indifferent things, because they may be used either for the honour or dishonour of God. As they are used for his honour, they are good, and as used for his dishonour, they are evil. The only absolutely bad thing in the world is sin, which cannot be, in its own nature, but a dishonour to God. The only absolutely good thing in the world is holiness, and a likeness to God, which cannot be, in its own nature, but for his glory. As for all other things, I know no true satisfaction can be in them, but as they are subservient to God's honour, and give us an advantage for imitating some one or other of his perfections. Crosses in the Scripture are not excluded from those things we have a right to by Christ, when they may conduce to our good: 1 Cor. iii. 22, 'Life and death, things present, and things to come, are yours, and you are Christ's.' Since the revelation of the gospel, I do not remember that any such complaint against the providence of God fell from any holy man in the New Testament; for our Saviour had given them another prospect of those things. The holy men in the Old Testament comforted themselves against this objection by the end of the wicked which should happen, and the rod cease, Ps. lxxiii. In the New Testament we are more comforted by the certain operation of crosses to our good and spiritual advantage, Rom. viii. Our Saviour did not promise wealth and honour to his followers, nor did he think it worth his pains of coming and dying, to bestow such gifts upon his children. He made heaven their happiness, and the earth their hell; the cross was their badge here, and the crown their reward hereafter; they seemed not to be a purchase congruous to so great a price of blood. Was God's providence to Christ the more to be questioned because he was poor? Had he the less love to him because he was 'a man of sorrows,' even while he was a God of glory? Such groundless conceits should never enter into Christians, who can never seriously take up Christ's yoke without a proviso of afflictions, who can never be God's sons without expecting his corrections.

(2.) God never leaves good men so bare, but he provides for their necessity: Ps. lxxxiv. 11, 'The Lord will give grace and glory, and no good thing will he withhold from them that walk uprightly.' If any thing be good, an upright man may expect it from God's providence; if it be not good, he should not desire it: Howsoever grace, which is necessary for preparing thee for happiness and glory, which is necessary for fixing thee in it, he will be sure to give; we have David's experience for it in the whole course of his life, Ps. xxxvii. 5.

(3.) The little good men have is better than the highest enjoyments of wicked men: Ps. xxxvii. 16, 'A little that a righteous man hath is better than the riches of many wicked;' not better than many riches of the wicked, but better than the riches of many wicked, better than all the treasures of the whole mass of the wicked world. Others have them in a providential way, good men in a gracious way: Prov. xvi. 8, 'Better is a little with righteousness, than great revenues without right,' without a covenant right. Wicked prosperity is like a shadow that glides away in a moment, whereas a righteous man's little is a part of Christ's purchase, and part of that inheritance which shall endure for ever: Ps. xxxvii. 18, 'Their inheritance shall be for ever,' *i. e.*, God regards the state of the righteous, whether good or evil, all that befalls them. God doth all with a respect to his everlasting inheritance. No man hath worldly things without their wings. And though the righteous have worldly things with their wings, yet that love whereby they have them hath no wings ever to fly away from them. How can those things be good to a man that can never taste them, nor God in them?

(4.) No righteous man would in his sober wits be willing to make an exchange of his smartest afflictions for a wicked man's prosperity, with all the circumstances attending it. It cannot therefore be bad with the righteous in the worst condition. Would any man be ambitious of snares that knows the deceit of them? Can any but a madman exchange medicines for poison? Is it not more desirable to be upon a dunghill with an intimate converse with God, than upon a throne without it? They gain a world in prosperity, a righteous man gains his soul by afflictions, and possesses it in patience. Is the exchange of a valuable consideration? God strips good men of the enjoyment of the world, that he may wean them from the love of it; keeps them from idolatry, by removing the fuel of it; sends afflictions that he may not lose them, nor they their souls. Would any man exchange a great goodness 'laid up for him that fears God,' Ps. xxxi. 19, for a lesser goodness laid out upon them that are enemies to him?

Who would exchange a few outward comforts with God's promise, inward comforts with assurance of heaven, godliness with contentment, a sweet and spiritual life, sovereignty over himself and lusts, though attended with sufferings, for the government of the whole world?

(5.) It is not ill with the righteous in afflictions, because they have high advantages by them. That cannot be absolutely evil which conduceth to a greater good; as,

First, Sensible experiments of the tender providence of God over them. If the righteous had not afflictions in this life, God would lose the glory of his providence, and they the sweetness in a gracious deliverance from them, in ways which makes the affliction the sweeter as well as the mercy; they would lose the comfort of them, in not having such sensible evidences of God's gracious care.

The sweetness of the promises made for times of trouble would never be tasted: Ps. xxxvii. 19, 'They shall not be ashamed in the evil time;' that is, they shall be mightily encouraged and supported. God's people do best understand God's strength when they feel the smart of men's malice: 2 Tim. iv. 17, 'The Lord stood with me, and strengthened me.' He had never felt so much of God's strength if he had not tasted much of man's wickedness in forsaking him. Ps. xxxvii. 39, 'He is their strength,' when in times of trouble they experiment more of his care in preserving them, and his strength in supporting them, than at other times. Abundance of consolations are manifested in abundance of sufferings, 2 Cor. i. 5, 1 Peter iv. 13, 14. A greater sense of joy and glory lights upon them in a storm of persecutions. Men see the sufferings of the godly, but they do not behold that inward peace which composeth and delights their souls, worth the whole mass of the world's goodness, and pleasures of the unrighteous.

Secondly, Inward improvements, opportunities to manifest more love to God, more dependence on him, the perfection of the soul: 1 Tim. v. 5, 'Now she that is a widow indeed, and desolate, trusts in God, and continues in supplications and prayers night and day.' There is a ground of more exercise of trust in God and supplication to him. The poor and desolate have an advantage for the actual exercise of those graces, which a prosperous condition wants. God changeth the metal by it; what was lead and iron he makes come forth as gold: Job xxiii. 10, 'When he hath tried me, I shall come forth as gold.' Crosses and sufferings, which fit good men for special service here, and eternal happiness hereafter, can no more be said to be evil, than the fire which refines the gold, and prepares it for a prince's use. If there were not such evils, what ground could you have to exercise patience? what heroic acts of faith could you put forth without difficulties? how could you believe against hope, if you had not sometimes something to contradict your hopes? And if a good man should have a confluence of that which the ignorant and pedantical world calls happiness, he might undervalue the pleasures of a better life, deface the beauty of his own soul, and withdraw his love from the most gratifying as well as the most glorious object, unto that which is not worth the least grain of his affection.

Thirdly, Future glory. The great inquiry at the day of Christ's appearing will be, how good men bare their sufferings, what improvements they had; and the greater their purity by them, the greater will be their praise and honour: 1 Peter i. 7, 'That the trial of your faith,' viz., by manifold temptations, 'may be found to praise, and honour, and glory, at the appearing of Jesus Christ.' For a good improvement by them, they will have a public praise from God's mouth, and a crown of honour set upon their heads. Providence sends even light afflictions as so many artificers, to make the crown more massy and more bright: 2 Cor. iv. 17, 'Works for us a far more exceeding and eternal weight of glory.' They are at work about a good man's crown while they make him smart. They prepare him for heaven, and make it more grateful to him when he comes to possess it. A Christian carriage in them prepares for greater degrees of glory. Every stroke doth but more beautify the crown.

Fourthly, Sufferings of good men for the truth highly glorifies the providence of God. This is a matter of glory and honour: 1 Peter iv. 16, 'If any man suffer as a Christian, let him not be ashamed; but let him glorify God on this behalf.' They thereby bear a testimony to the highest act of providence that God ever exercised, even the redemption of the world by the blood of his Son. And the church, which is the highest object of his providence in the world, takes the deeper root, and springs up the higher; the foundation of it was laid in the blood of Christ, and the growth of it is furthered by the blood of martyrs. The carriage of the righteous in them makes the truth they profess more valued. It enhanceth the excellency of religion, and manifests it to be more amiable for its beauty than for its dowry, since they see it desirable by the sufferers, not only without worldly enjoyments, but with the sharpest miseries. This consideration hath wrought upon many to embrace the religion of the sufferers. If it reaches as far as death, they are but despatched to their Father's house, and the day of their death is the day of their coronation; and what evil is there in all this?

Fifthly, To conclude; this argument is stronger (upon the infallible righteousness of God's nature) for a day of reckoning after this life, than against providence. It is a more rational conclusion that God will have a time to justify the righteousness and wisdom of his providential government, and repair the honour of the righteous, oppressed by the injustice of the wicked. And indeed, unless there be a retribution in another world, the question is unanswerable, and all the reason in the world knows not how to salve the holiness and righteousness of God in his providential dispensations in this life, since we see here goodness unrewarded and debased to the dunghill, vice glorying in impunity, and ranting to the firmament. We cannot see how it can consist with the nature of God's wisdom, righteousness, and holiness, if there were not another life, wherein God will manifest his righteousness in the punishing sin and rewarding goodness; for it is impossible that a God of infinite justice should leave sin unpunished, and grace unrewarded, here or hereafter. The Scripture gives us so full an account of a future state, that may satisfy all Christians in this business.

The wicked rich man is in his purple, and Lazarus in his rags; yet Abraham's bosom is prepared for the one, and an endless hell for the other. Jeremiah resolves the case in his dispute with God about it: Jer. xii. 3, 'Pull them out like sheep to the slaughter, and prepare them for the day of slaughter.' They are but fattening for the knife of justice; and the day will come when they shall be consumed like the fat of lambs in the sacrifice, which shall wholly evaporate into smoke; so the psalmist resolves it in Ps. xxxvii. 20, a psalm written for the present case. God laughs at their security in a way of mockery: Ps. xxxvii. 13, 'The Lord shall laugh at him, for he sees that his day is coming,'—God's day for the justification of his proceedings in the world, and the wicked man's day for his own destruction, wherein they shall all be destroyed together, Ps. xxxvii. 38; the whole mass of them in one bundle. Who then will charge God with unequal distributions at that day, which is appointed for the clearing up of his righteousness, which is here masked in the world? Who can be fond of the state of the wicked? Who would be fond of a dead man's condition, because he lies in state, whose soul may be condemned, whilst his body, with a pompous solemnity, is carried to the grave, and both body and soul, joined together at the resurrection, adjudged to eternal misery?

Quest. 2. What hath been said in this will also answer another question, Why God doth not immediately punish notorious offenders, since the best governments in the world are such as call the violators of the law to a speedy account, to keep up the honour of justice? Thus the Epicures charge God with neglects of providence, because if he doth punish wicked men, it is later than is fit and just: 'Because sentence against an evil work is not executed speedily, therefore the heart of the sons of men is fully set in them to do evil,' Eccles. viii. 11. Delay of justice is an encouragement to sin.

Ans. 1. This is an argument for God's patience, none against his providence. Should he make such quick work, what would become of the world? Could it have held out to this day? If God had instantly taken revenge upon those that thus disparage his providence, the frame of such an objection had not been alive. No man is so perfectly good but he might fall under the revenging stroke of his sword, if he pleased to draw it. Suffer God to evidence his patience here, since after the winding up of the world he will have no time to manifest it. God doth indeed sometimes send the sharp arrow of some judgment upon a notorious offender, to let him understand that he hath not forgotten how to govern; but he doth not always do so, that his patience may be glorified in bearing with his rebellious creature.

Ans. 2. God is just in that wherein the question supposeth him unjust;

he suffers wicked men to continue to be the plagues of the places where they live, and the executioners of his justice upon offenders against him, Ps. xvii. 18. The wicked are God's sword, Jer. xlvii. 6. Those that God would stir up against the Philistines are called the sword of the Lord, Isa. x. 5. Asshur is said to be the rod of his anger; would it consist with his wisdom to drop the instruments out of his hand as soon as he begins to use them? to cast his rods out of his hand as soon as he takes them up? The rules of justice are as much unknown to us as the communications of his goodness to his people are unknown to the world.

Ans. 3. Let me ask such a one whether he never injured another man, and whether he would not think it very severe, if not unjust, that the offended person should presently take revenge of him? If every man should do the like, how soon would mankind be despatched, and the world become a shambles, men running furiously to one another's destructions for the injuries they have mutually received! Do we praise the lenity of parents to their children, and dispraise the mercy of God, because he doth not presently use his right? Is, then, forbearance of revenge accounted a virtue in a man, and shall it be an imperfection in God? With what reason can we thus blame the eminent patience of God, which we have reason to adore, and which every one of us are monuments of? The use is,—

Use 1. Of information.

How unworthy and absurd a thing is it to deny providence! Some of the heathens fancied that God walked his circuit in heaven, or sat with folded arms there, taking no cognizance of what was done in the world. Some indeed, upon some great emergencies, have acknowledged the mercies and justice of God, which are the two arms of his providence. The barbarians his justice, when they saw a viper leap upon Paul's hand, Acts xxviii. 4, they say among themselves, 'No doubt this man is a murderer, whom, though he hath escaped the sea, yet vengeance suffers not to live.' The mariners in Jonah implored his mercy in their distress at sea; yet they generally attributed affairs to blind chance, and worshipped fortune as a deity. For this vain conceit the psalmist calls the atheist fool: Ps. xiv. 1, 'The fool hath said in his heart, There is no God.' Potiphar acknowledged it, he saw that the Lord was with Joseph, and favoured his designs: Gen. xxxix. 3, 'And his master saw that the Lord was with him, and that the Lord made all things that he did to prosper in his hand.'

It will not be amiss to consider this, for the root of denial of providence is in the hearts of the best men, especially under affliction. Asaph was a holy man, Ps. lxxiii. 13, saith he, 'Verily I have cleansed my heart in vain, and washed my hands in innocency.' He had taken much pains with his heart, and had been under much affliction: ver. 14, 'All the day long have I been plagued, and chastened every morning.' And the consideration of this, that he should have so much affliction with so much holiness, so strangely puzzled him, that he utters that dreadful speech, as if he had a mind to cast off all cares about the worship of God, and sanctifying his heart, and repent of all that he had done in that business, as much as to say, Had I been as very a villain as such or such a man, I might have prospered as well as they, but I was a fool to have any fear of God.

Therefore we will consider,

1. The evil of denying providence.

2. The grounds of the denial of it by the heathen, which we shall find in our own hearts.

3. The various ways wherein men practically deny providence.

1. The evil of denying it.

(1.) It gives a liberty to all sin. It give an occasion for an unbounded licentiousness, for what may not be done where there is no government? The Jews tell us* that the dispute between Cain and Abel was this: Cain said, because his sacrifice was not accepted, that there was no judge, no reward of good works, or punishment of bad, which when Abel opposed, Cain slew him. They ground it upon the discourse of God with Cain, Gen. iv. 7, 8, which had been about his providence and acceptation of men, if they did well, and punishment of men if they did ill; whence they gather the discourse, ver. 8, Cain had with his brother was about the same subject, for Cain talked with Abel, and upon that discourse rose up against him, and slew him. And his discourse afterwards with God, ver. 9, seems to favour it, 'Am I my brother's keeper?' Thou dost say thou art the Governor of the world, it is not my concern to look after him. Their conjecture is not improbable. If it were so, we see how early this opinion began in the world, and what was the horrid effect of it, the first sin, the first murder that we read of after the sin of Adam. And what confusion would grow upon the entertainment of such a notion.

Indeed, the Scripture everywhere places sin upon this root: Ps. x. 11, 'God hath forgotten: he hides his face; he will never see it.' He hath turned his back upon the world. This was the ground of the oppression of the poor by the wicked which he mentions, ver. 9, 10. So Isa. xxvi. 10, 'The wicked will not learn righteousness, he will deal unjustly.' The reason is, 'he will not behold the majesty of the Lord; he will not regard God's government of the world, 'though his hand be lifted up to strike.' There is no sin but receives both its birth and nourishment from this bitter root. Let the notion of providence be once thrown out, or the belief of it faint, how will ambition, covetousness, neglect of God, distrust, impatience, and all other bitter gourds, grow up in a night! It is from this topic all iniquity will draw arguments to encourage itself; for nothing doth so much discountenance those rising corruptions, and put them out of heart, as an actuated belief that God takes care of human affairs. Upon the want of this actuated knowledge God charges all the sin of Ephraim: Hosea vii. 2, 'They consider† not in their hearts that I remember all their wickedness;' as if God were blind and did not see, or stupid and did not concern himself, or of a very frail memory soon to forget.

(2.) It destroys all religion. The first foundation of all religion is, first, the being, secondly, the goodness, of God in the government of the world: Heb. xi. 6, 'He that comes to God must believe that he is, and that he is a rewarder of them that diligently seek him.' He is the object of religion as he is the governor of the world. This denial would shut up Bibles and temples, and bring irreligious disorder into all societies.

[1.] All worship. He that hath not design to govern, is supposed to expect no homage; if he regards not his creatures, he cares for no worship from them. How is it possible to persuade men to regard him for God, who takes no care of them? Who will adore him who regards no adoration?

[2.] Prayer. To what purpose should they beg his directions, implore his assistance in their calamities, if he had no regard at all to his creatures? What favour can we expect from him who is regardless of dispensing any?

[3.] Praise. Who would make acknowledgments to one from whom they never received any favour, and hath no mind to receive any acknowledgments

---

* Targum Hierosolymit, Mercer in Gen. iv. 7.
† Heb., 'They speak not to their hearts.'

from them, because he takes no care of them? If the Deity have no relation to us, how can we have relation to him? To what purpose will it be either to call upon him, or praise him, which are the prime pieces of religion, if he concern not himself with us?

[4.] Dependence, trust, and hope. What reason have we to commit our concerns to him, and to depend upon him for relief? Hence the apostle saith, Eph. ii. 12, the Gentiles were 'without hope, and without God in the world.' The reason they were without hope was because they were without God. They denied a settled providence, and acknowledged a blind chance, and therefore could have no sound hope; so some understand it of denial of God's government. It might well give occasion to people to utter Pharaoh's speech: Exod. v. 2, 'Who is the Lord, that I should obey his voice, to let Israel go? I know not the Lord, neither will I let Israel go.' What is God that I should serve him? I have no such notion of a God that governs the world. The regardlessness of his creature disobligeth the creature from any service to him.

(3.) It is a high disparagement of God. To believe an impotent, ignorant, negligent God, without care of his works, is as bad or worse than to believe no God at all. The denial of his providence is made equal with the denial of God: Ps. xiv. 1, 'The fool hath said in his heart, There is no God.' He denied God, *Elohim*, which word denotes God's providence; not, there is no *Jehovah*, which notes his essence, he denied not God *quoad essentiam*, but *quoad providentiam*, whereupon the psalmist dubs the atheist fool. It strips God of his judicial power. How shall he judge his creatures, if he know not what they think, and regards not what they do? How easy will it be for him to be imposed upon by the fair pretences and lying excuses of men! It is diabolical. The devil denies not God s right to govern, but he denies God's actual government; for he saith, Luke iv. 6, 'The power and glory of the world is delivered' unto him, 'and to whomsoever,' saith he, 'I will, I give it.' God had cast off all care of all things, and made the devil his deputy. He that denies providence denies most of God's attributes, he denies at least the exercise of them. He denies his omniscience, which is the eye of providence; mercy and justice, which are the arms of it; power, which is the life and motion of providence; wisdom, which is the rudder of providence, whereby it is steered; and holiness, which is the compass and rule of the motion of providence.

(4.) It is clearly against natural light. Socrates an heathen could say, Whosoever denied providence did Δαιμονιᾶν, was possessed with a devil.* Should God create a man anew with a sound judgment, and bring him into the world, when he should see the harmony, multitudes, virtues, and operations of all creatures, the stated times and seasons, must he not needs confess that some invisible, inconceivable wisdom did both frame, and doth govern all the motions of it? And it is a greater crime in any of us to deny providence, either in opinion or practice, than it was or could have been in heathens; because we have not only that natural reason which they had, sufficient to convince us, but supernatural revelation in the Scripture, wherein God hath declared those methods of his providence which reason could not arrive to; as to deny his creation of the world is a greater crime in a man that knows the Scripture than in a heathen, because that hath put it out of doubt. And the asserting of this being the end of all God's judgments in the world—Job xix. 29, 'Wrath brings the punishment of the sword, that you may know there is a judgment,' *i. e.*, providence—the denial of it is a sin against all past or present judgments, which God hath or doth

* Montague against Selden, p. 525.

exercise, the Scripture frequently declaring the meaning of such and such judgments to be, that men may know that the Lord is God.

2. The second thing is, the grounds of the denial of providence. This atheism has been founded,

(1.) Upon an overweening conceit of men's own worths. When men saw themselves frustrated of the rewards they expected, and saw others that were instruments of tyranny and lust graced with the favours they thought due to their own virtue, they ran into a conceit that God did not mind the actions of men below. So that it was pride, interest, self-conceit, and opinion of merit, rather than any well-grounded reason, introduced this part of atheism into the world; for upon any cross this opinion of merit swelled up into blasphemous speeches against God. When we have any thoughts (as we are apt to have) by our religious acts to merit at God's hand, we act against the absoluteness of his providence, as though God could be obliged to us by any other than his own promise. Methinks Job hath some spice of this in speaking so often of his own integrity, as though God dealt injuriously with him in afflicting him. God seems to charge him with it: Job xl. 8, 'Wilt thou also disannul my judgment? wilt thou condemn me, that thou mayest be righteous?' As though in speaking so much of his own integrity, and in complaining expressions, he would accuse God of injustice, and condemn him as an unrighteous governor; and in Job's answer you find no syllable or word of his integrity to God, but a self-abhorrency: Job xlii. 16, 'Wherefore I abhor myself in dust and ashes.' I doubt that from this secret root arise those speeches which we ordinarily have among men, What have I done that God should so afflict me? though in a serious way it is a useful question, tending to an inquiry into the sin that is the cause of it; but I doubt ordinarily there is too much of a reflection upon God, as though they had deserved other dealing at his hands. Take heed therefore of pride and conceits of our own worth, we shall else be led by it to disparaging conceits of God, which indeed are the roots of all actions contradictory to God's will.

(2.) It is founded upon pedantical and sensual notions of God. As though it might detract from his pleasures and delight to look down upon this world, or as though it were a molestation of an infinite power to busy himself about the cares of sublunary things. They thought it unsuitable to the felicity of God, that it should interrupt his pleasure, and make a breach upon his blessedness. As though it were the felicity of a prince not to take care of the government of his kingdom, nor so much as provide for the well-being of his children. I doubt that from such or as bad conceptions of God may spring ordinarily our distrust of God upon any distress. Take heed therefore of entertaining any conceptions of God but what the Scripture doth furnish you with.

(3.) Or else, this sort of atheism was ushered in by a flattering conceit of the majesty of God. They thought it unbecoming the excellency of the divine majesty to descend to a regard of the petty things of the world. This seems to be the fancy of them, Ps. lxxiii. 11, 'How doth God know? is there knowledge in the Most High?' They think him too high to know, too high to consider. How unreasonable is it to think God most high in place, and not in perfection; and if in perfection, not in knowledge and discerning? They imagined of him as of a great prince, taking his pleasure upon the battlements of his palace, not beholding the worms upon the ground; muffled with clouds, as Job xxii. 13, 14, 'How doth God know? Can he judge through the dark clouds? thick clouds are a covering to him, that he sees not, and he walks in the circuit of heaven. We cannot indeed have too high apprehensions of God's majesty and excellency ; but must take heed of entertaining superstitious conceits of God, and such as are dishonourable to him, or make the grandeur and ambition of men the measure of the greatness and majesty of God. Upon this root sprung superstition and idolatry, and the worship of demons, who, according to the heathens' fancy, were mediators between God and men. And I doubt such a conceit might be the first step to the introducing the popish saint-worship into the Christian world ; and this lies at the root of all our omissions of duty, or neglects of seeking God. Let us therefore have raised thoughts of God's majesty, and admiring thoughts of his condescension, who, notwithstanding his greatness, humbles himself to behold what is done upon the earth. The psalmist sets a pattern for both, Ps cxiii. 5, 6.

(4.) From their wishes upon any gripes of conscience. They found guilt staring them in the face, and were willing to comfort themselves with the embraces of this doctrine, wherein they might find a security and ease to their prostituted consciences, and unbounded liberty in the ways of sin. Those in Zephaniah were first settled upon their lees, and then, to drive away all fears of punishment, deny God's government : Zeph. i. 12, ' The Lord will not do good, neither will he do evil.' A brave liberty, for a city to be without a magistrate, a house without a governor, a ship without a pilot, exposed to the mercy of winds and waves ; a man to be without reason, that passion and lust should act their pleasure ; a liberty that beasts themselves would not have, to be without a shepherd, and one to take care of them ! Such wishes certainly there are in men upon a sense of guilt ; they wish, for their own security, there were no providential eye to inspect them. Take heed therefore of guilt, which will draw you to wish God deprived of the government of the world, and all those attributes which qualify him for it. The readiness to entertain the motions of Satan, rather than the motions of the Spirit, implies a willingness in them that Satan might be the god of the world, who favours them in sin, rather than the Creator who forbids it. But indeed the fears of conscience evidence a secret belief in men of a just providence, whatever means they use to stifle it ; else why is man, upon the commission of some notorious sinful act, afraid of some evil hap to betide him ? Why is he restless in himself ? There is no sinner, unless extremely hardened, but hath some secret touch of conscience upon notorious enormities ; while the work of the law is written in their heart, their conscience will bear witness and accuse them, Rom. ii. 15. In the most flagitious courses which the apostle reckons up, Rom. i. 29–32, they cannot put off the knowledge of ' the judgment of God, that they which commit such things are worthy of death,' that is, worthy of death by the . judgment of God, which judgment is discovered in the law of nature.

3. The third thing is, the various ways wherein men practically deny providence, or abuse it, or contemn it.

(1.) When we will walk on in a way contrary to checks of providence, when we will run against the will of God manifested in his providence, we do deny his government, and refuse subjection to him ; when we will be peremptory in our resolves against the declaration of God's will by his checks of providence, we contend with him about the government of us and our actions. Such a dispute had Pharaoh with God, notwithstanding all the checks by the plagues poured out upon him, he would march against Israel to take them out of God's hand into his own service again, Exod. xv. 9, ' The enemy said, I will overtake, I will divide the spoil ; my lust shall be satisfied upon them ; I will draw my sword, my hand shall destroy them.' Here is the will of man vaunting against the governor of the world, resolved to dispute God's royalty with him in spite of all the blastings of his designs, and the smart blows he had had from that powerful arm, which cost him and his subjects their lives; they would not understand the taking off their wheels, but would run headlong into the Red Sea. A remarkable example of this is in a good man not so peremptory in words, but against the revelations of God's mind both by the prophet and his providence; Jehoshaphat had made a league with Ahab, 2 Chron. xviii. 1–3, and God had ordered Micaiah to acquaint him with the ill success of the affair they went about, ver. 16, 19, which Jehoshaphat found true, for his own life was in danger, he was hardly beset by the enemy upon a mistake, ver. 31, 32, he had an eminent answer of prayer, for upon his cry he had a quick return; God engaged his providence over his enemies' hearts for him: ver. 31, ' The Lord helped him, and God moved them to depart from him.' And for this conjunction and continuance in it against Micaiah's prophecy, God sends a prophet to reprove him, 2 Chron xix. 2, ' Should thou help the ungodly, and love them that hate the Lord ? therefore is wrath upon thee from the Lord;' he reproves him sharply for this confederacy, yet Jehoshaphat after had a signal providence in delivering him from another army, chap. xx. 24. Yet after this he goes on in this way, chap. xx. 35, ' after this,' *i. e.*, after a reproof by a prophet, after ill success in his league, after eminent care of God in his deliverance, after a signal freeing him from a dangerous invasion in a miraculous way, he enters into a league with Ahab's son, as wicked as his father, ver. 36 ; he joined himself with him to make ships to go to Tarshish, and after that a third prophet is sent to reprove him, and the ships were broken, ver. 37. Here is a remarkable opposition to checks of providence, and manifest declarations of God's will, as if he would be the commander of the world instead of God. Abner's action is much of the same kind, who would make the house of Saul strong against David, though he knew and was satisfied that God had promised the kingdom to David.

(2.) In omissions of prayer. One reason to prove the fools' denying God's government of the world is, that they call not upon the Lord, Ps. xiv. 2, ' The Lord looked down from heaven, to see if there were any that did understand and seek God.' 'Tis certainly either a denying of God's sufficiency to help us, when we rather beg of every creature, than ask of God ; or a charging him with a want of providence, as though he had thrown off all care of worldly matters: 2 Kings i. 3, ' Is it not because there is not a God in Israel, that you go to inquire of Baal-zebub the god of Ekron ?' Seeking of anything else with a neglect of God, is denying the care of God over his creature. Do we not in this case make ourselves our own governors and lords, as though we could subsist without him, or manage our own affairs without his assistance ? If we did really believe there was a watchful providence, and an infinite powerful goodness to help us, he would hear from us oftener than he doth. Certainly those who never call upon him disown his government of the world, and do not care whether he regards the earth or no. They think they can do what they please, without any care of God over them. The restraining prayer is a casting off the fear of God: Job xv. 4, ' Thou castest off fear,' why ? ' and restrainest prayer before God.' The neglect of prayer ariseth from a conceit of the unprofitableness of it. Job xxi. 15, ' What profit should we have if we prayed unto him ?' Which conceit must be grounded upon a secret notion of God's carelessness of the world ; such fruit could not arise but from that bitter root. But the prophet Malachi plainly expresses it: Malachi iii. 14, ' Ye have said it is in vain to serve God, and what profit is it that we have kept his ordinance ?' Whence did this arise, but from a denial of providence upon the observation of the outward happiness of the wicked? ver. 15, 'And now we call the proud happy; yea, they that work wickedness are set up; yea, they that tempt God are even delivered.' Sometimes it ariseth from an apprehension that God in the way of his providence dealeth unjustly with us. A good prophet utters such a sinful speech in his passion, 2 Kings vi. 33, 'Behold, this evil is of the Lord, what should I wait for the Lord any longer?'

(3.) When men will turn every stone to gain the favourable assistance of men in their designs, and never address to God for his direction or blessing. When they never desire God to move the hearts of those whose favour they court, as though providence were an unuseful and unnecessary thing in the world. It was the case of those Elihu speaks of: Job xxxv. 9, 10, 'They cry out by reason of the arm of the mighty. But none saith, Where is God my maker, who gives songs in the night?' &c. None in the midst of their oppressions and cries under them, did consider either the power of God in the creation, as he was their maker, nor his providence in the government of the world, as he raised up men from low estates, and gave matter of cheerfulness even in a time of darkness. This was the charge God by his prophet brought against Asa: 2 Chron. xvi. 7 (before the text, ver. 9), 'Thou hast relied on the king of Syria, and not relied on the Lord thy God;' herein thou hast done foolishly,' where he sets a reliance on the creature, and a reliance on God, in direct opposition. In several cases men do thus deny and put a contempt on God as the governor of the world, when we will cast about to find out some creature-refuge, rather than have recourse to God for any supply of our necessities. Doth not he slight his father's care, that will not seek to him in his distress? This was Asa's sin: 2 Chron. xvi. 12, 'In his disease he sought not to the Lord, but to the physicians.' The Jews think, that one reason why Joseph continued two years in prison, was his confiding too much upon the butler's remembrance of him, and interest for his deliverance, which they ground upon the request he makes to him: Gen. xl. 14, 'But think on me when it shall be well with thee, and shew kindness to me, and make mention of me unto Pharaoh, and bring me out of this house.' I must confess the expressions are very urgent, being so often repeated, and seems to carry a greater confidence at present in the arm of flesh than in God. We do not read that Joseph prayed so earnestly to God, though no doubt but being a good man he did. Methinks the setting down his request with that repetition in the Scripture, seems to intimate a probability of the Jews' conceit; or also when we do seek to him, but it is out of a general belief of his providence and sufficiency, not out of an actuated consideration; or when we seek to him with colder affections than we seek to creatures, as if we did half despair of his ability or will to help us; as when a man thinks to get learning by the sagacity of his own wit, his indefatigable industry, and never desires with any ardent affection the blessing of God upon his endeavours. When we lean to our own wisdom, we distrust the providence of God: Prov. iii. 5, 'Trust in the Lord with all thine heart, and lean not to thine own understanding.' Trust in God, and leaning to our own wisdom, are opposed to one another as inconsistent; or when a man hath some great concern, suppose a suit at law, to think to carry his cause by the favour of friends, the help of his money, the eloquence of his advocate, and never interest God in his business: this is not to acknowledge God in thy ways, which is the command: ver. 6, 'In all thy ways acknowledge him;' as though our works were not 'in the hand of God,' Eccles. ix. 1. This is to take them out of God's hand, and put them into the hands of men. To trust in our wealth, it is to make God a dead and a stupid God, and disown his providence in the bestowing it upon us. The apostle seems to intimate this in the opposition which he makes between ' uncertain riches,' and ' the living God,' 1 Tim. vi. 17. These, and many more actions suitable to them, are virtual denials of God's superintendency, as though God had left off the government of the world to the wits, or rather follies of men. These are to magnify the things we seek to, above God, as the chief authors of all our good. It is to imagine him less careful than man, more insufficient than man. It is a departure from a full fountain to a shallow stream; not to desire God's assistance, is either from some check of conscience that our business is sinful, that we dare not interest him in it, or a disowning God's care, as if we could hide our counsels from him (Isa. xxix. 15, ' Woe unto them that seek deep to hide their counsel from the Lord, and they say, Who seeth us, and who knoweth us?'), and bring our business to pass before he shall know of it; at least it is a slighting God's government, since we will not engage God by prayer in the exercise of it on our behalf, and disdain to acquaint him with our concerns. It is a reflection upon God's wisdom to do so, which the prophet mentions with a woe: Isa. xxxi. 1, 2, ' Woe unto them that go down to Egypt for help: but they look not to the Holy One of Israel! Yet he also is wise.' It is a disparagement to God's providential wisdom, not to look to him in our concerns, yea, and of his righteousness too; ' they look not to the Holy One of Israel.' In this they neither regard his holiness nor his wisdom. When we consult not with him upon emergent occasions, we trust more to our own wisdom, counsel, and sufficiency, than to God's; and set up ourselves as our own lords, and independent upon him, as though we could manage things according to our pleasure.

(4.) When upon the receiving any good, they make more grateful acknowledgment to the instruments, than to God the principal author of it; as if God had no hand in bestowing those blessings upon them, as if the instruments had dispossessed God of his governing providence, and engrossed it in their own hands. This men are guilty of when they ascribe their wealth to their own wit and fortune, their health to their own care, or the physician's skill; their learning to their own industry, their prosperity to their friends or merits. When men thus return their thank-offering to second causes, and ascribe to them what is due to God, they give the glory of his providence to a miserable creature. Thus was the foolish boasting of the Assyrian: Isa. x. 13, 14, ' By the strength of my hand I have done this, and by my wisdom: for I am prudent: for I have removed the bounds of the people,' &c. Belshazzar's offence also, Dan. v. 23, ' Thou hast lifted up thyself against the Lord of heaven: and praised the gods of silver,' as though they were the authors of all thy greatness; so Hab. i. 16, ' They sacrifice to their net, and burn incense to their drag, because by them their portion is fat,' alluding to those that then worshipped their warlike weapons, and the tools whereby they had got their wealth, in the place of God, as the heathen used to do.* How base a usage is this of God, to rifle him of all his glory, and bestow it upon the unworthiest instruments, inanimate creatures! It is as high idolatry as that of the heathens, inasmuch as it is a stripping God of the glory of his providential care, though the object to which we direct our acknowledgments is not so mean as theirs, which was a stock or stone. But is it not the same injury to a person to rifle him of his goods, to bestow it upon a beggar, as to give it to a prince? It is a depriving a man of his right.† Yet, is not this ordinary! Do not men ascribe more to the physician, that saves an eye in danger of being lost by a defluxion, than to God, who hath given them both, with the enjoyment of the light of the sun; yea, more to the medicine than to that God who hath a witness of his deity in

---

* Dought Analect. Sacr. Excurs. 182.   † Amirant sur les religions.

every drug? It is as if the kindness a prince shews to his subjects should be attributed to a scullion in his kitchen rather than to himself. This is to ' belie God, and say it is not he,' Jer. v. 12. It is applicable to the case of mercies as well as afflictions and judgments, of which it is properly meant. And this contempt is the greater, by how much the greater mercy we have received in a way of providence : Hos. ii. 8, ' She did not know that I gave her corn, and wine, and oil, and multiplied her silver and gold, which they prepared for Baal ;' she that had most reason to know, because she had enjoyed so much ; she that had experience how by a strong and mighty hand I brought her out of Egypt into the land now possessed by her : she would not know that I gave her those good things she prepared for Baal. It would be a natural consequence from this Scripture, that those that employ the good things they enjoy upon their lusts, do deny the providential goodness of God in their possession and enjoyment of them, because they prepare God's goodness for their sinful pleasures, as though their own lusts had been the authors of them ; and also their instruments, that receive too high and flattering thanks of this nature, are much like Herod, that tickled himself with the people's applause, that his voice was the voice of God, and not of man.

(5.) When we use indirect courses, and dishonest ways to gain wealth or honour. This is to leave God, to seek relief at hell's gates, and adore the devil's providence above God's : when God doth not answer us, like Saul, we will go to the witch of Endor, and have our ends by hell when heaven refuseth us. It is a covenanting with the devil, and striking up a bargain and agreement with hell, and acknowledging Satan to be the god of the world. No man will doubt but in express covenants with the devil, as witches and conjurors are reported to make, that the devil shall give them such knowledge, such wealth, or bring them to such honour ; it is no doubt, I say, but such do acknowledge the devil the god of the world, because they agree by articles to have those things conferred upon them by Satan, which are only in the power of God absolutely to promise or bestow. So when a man will commit sin to gain the ends of his ambition or covetousness, does he not implicitly covenant with the devil, who is the head of sinners, and set up his sin in the place of God, because he hopes to attain those things by sinful means, which are only in the hand of God, and on whom he only can have a dependence ? This is the devil's design out of an enmity to providence. He tempted Christ to be his own carver, thereby to put him upon a distrust of his Father's care of him': Mat. iv. 3, ' Command that these stones be made bread,' as though God would not provide for him ; which design of the devil is manifest by our Saviour's answer. This is to prostitute providence to our own lusts, and to pull it down from the government of the world, to be a lacquey to our sinful pleasure ; to use means which God doth prohibit, is to set up hell to govern us, since God will not govern our affairs in answer to our greedy desires. It is to endeavour that by God's curse which we should only expect by God's blessing ; for when God hath forbid sinful ways, severely threatened them, perhaps cursed them in examples before our eyes, what is it but to say, that we will rather believe God's curse will further us than his blessing ? It is to disparage his blessing, and prefer his curse, to slight his wisdom and adore our folly. When we go out of God's way, we go out of God's protection, we have no charter for the blessing of providence without that condition : Ps. xxxvii. 3, ' Trust in the Lord, and do good : so shalt thou dwell in the land, and verily thou shalt be fed.' To do evil, then, is not to trust in God, or have any regard to his providential care.

(6.) When we distrust God when there is no visible means. A distrust of God renders* him impotent, or false and mutable, or cruel and regardless, and what not. We detract from his power, as if it depended upon creatures, or that he were like an artificer, that could not act without his tools; as if God were tied to means, and were beholding to creatures for his operating power; as if that God who created the world without instruments could not providentially apply himself to our particular exigencies without the help of some of his creatures. If he cannot work without this or that means you did expect your mercy by, it supposeth that God hath made the creature greater than himself, and more necessary to thy well-being than himself is; or else we conceit him false or foolish, as if he had undertaken a task of government too hard for him; as if he were grown weary of his labour, and must have some time to recruit his strength; or as if he were unfaithful, not walking by rules of unerring goodness; or if we acknowledge him wise, and able, and faithful, yet it must then be a denial of his gracious tenderness, which is as great as his power and wisdom, and a perfection equal with any of the rest. If his caring for us be a principal argument to move us to cast our care upon him,—as it is 1 Peter v. 7, 'Casting all your care upon him, for he careth for you;' then if we cast not our care upon him, it is a denial of his gracious care of us,—this is to imagine him a tenderer governor of beasts than men, as though our Saviour had spoke a palpable untruth, when he told us, not an hair of our heads doth fall without his leave; as if he regarded sparrows only, and not his children; or else it implies that God cannot mind us in a crowd of business, in such multitudes in the world, which he hath to take care of. But certainly as the multitude of things doth not hinder his knowledge of them, so neither do they hinder his care. The arms of his goodness are as large to embrace all creatures, as the eyes of his omniscience are to behold them. From this root do all our fears of the power of men grow: Isa. li. 12, 13, 'Who art' thou, that art afraid of a man that shall die, &c., and forgettest the Lord thy Maker, that hath stretched forth the heavens?' &c. Our forgetfulness at least, if not a secret denial of God's power in the works of creation and providence, ushers in distrust of him, and that introduceth a fear of man. If they that know his name, will put their trust in him: Ps. ix. 10, 'For thou, Lord, hast not forsaken them that seek thee;' then a distrust of him discovers an ignorance and inconsideration of his name and his ways of working, and implies his forsaking of his creatures. He that trusts in anything else besides God, denies all the powerful operations of God, and conceives him not a strength sufficient for him, Ps. lii. 7; that man doth not 'make God his strength, who trusts in the abundance of his riches.' How gross is it not to trust God under the very sense of his powerful goodness, but question whether he can or will do this or that for us. When we will have jealousies of him, when he doth compass us round about with mercy, and encircle us with his beams, it is to question whether the summer sun will warm me, though it shine directly upon me, and I feel the vigour of its beams upon my body; much more base is this, then to distrust him when we have no means. What doth this imply, but that he cares not what becomes of his children, that no advantage can be expected from him, that his intentions towards us are not gracious even whiles we feel him!

(7.) Stoutness under God's afflicting or merciful hand, is a denial or contempt of providence. This was the aggravation of Belshazzar's sin: Dan. v. 23, 'And the God in whose hand thy breath is, and whose are all thy ways, hast thou not glorified.' He glorified not God in the way of his providence, but was playing the epicure, and was sacrilegiously quaffing in the

* That is, interprets, or represents.—Ed.

vessels of the temple when the city was besieged; he seemed to dare the providence of God upon a presumption that the city was impregnable, by reason of Euphrates, and the provision they had within their walls, which Xenophon saith was enough for twenty years, yet was taken that night when the hand-writing was. And by how much God's judgments have been more visible to us, and upon some well known by us, or related to us, so much the greater is the contempt of his providential government, as ver. 22, 'And thou his son, Belshazzar, hast not humbled thy heart, though thou knewest all this,' &c. He had known God's judgments upon his grandfather Nebuchadnezzar, a domestic example of God's vindicating his government of the world, and yet went in the same steps; so Jer. v. 3, 4. 'Thou hast consumed them, but they have refused to receive correction: they have made their faces harder than a rock. What is the reason? The prophet renders it, ver. 4, 'They are foolish: for they know not the way of the Lord, nor the judgment of their God.' Correction calls for submission; but those, like a rock under God's hand, were correction-proof, they would not consider the ways of God's providence, and the manner of them; it is as if by our peevishness we would make God weary of afflicting us, which is the worst case can happen. This is God's complaint of the ten tribes, Hos. vii. 9, 'gray hairs are upon them, and they know it not; strangers have devoured his strength,' &c. There was a consumption of their strength; the Assyrians and Egyptians, to whom they gave gifts, had drained their treasure; but they would not consider God as the author, or acknowledge whence their misery came; they would not 'seek God for all this, ver. 10. It is like a man's picking a pocket, or cutting a throat under the gallows in contempt of justice;* whereas good men are both afflicted with, and remember God's judgments. Eber called his son Peleg, *division*, because in his days the earth was divided, that in the daily sight of the sun† he might remember that sharp providence in scattering of the Babel builders. Judgments affect us when they are before our eyes, as the thunder and plagues did Pharaoh; but when they are removed, men return to their beloved ways, as though God had shot away all his arrows, and was departed to mind them no more. Take heed of this, it is a sin highly provoking; God is so tender that his providence should be minded and improved, that a sin of this nature he follows with his displeasure, in this life at least: Isa. xxii. 12, 13, 'And in that day did the Lord God of hosts call to weeping, and to mourning; and behold joy and gladness, eating flesh and drinking wine: let us eat and drink, for to-morrow we shall die.' When God in any judgment shews himself to be the Lord God of hosts, and calls us to weeping, and we behave ourselves jollily in spite of his government, it is a sin he will remember, and bind the guilt upon us, ver 14, 'And it was revealed in mine ears by the Lord of hosts, Surely this iniquity shall not be purged from you till ye die.'

(8.) Envy also is a denial of providence. To be sad at the temporal good, or the gifts of another, as counting him unworthy of them, it is a reflection upon the author of those gifts; an accusing providence of an unjust or unwise distribution.‡ Since God may do what he will with his own, if our eye be evil, because God is good, we intrench upon his liberty, and deny him the disposal of his own goods, as if God were but our steward, and we his lords. It is a temper we are all subject to: Ps. xxxvii. 1, 'Fret not thyself because of evil-doers, neither be thou envious against the workers of iniquity.' It is peculiarly the product of self-love, which affects the principality in the world, and particularly affects the conduct of God in

---

* Jenkin.   † Qu. 'his son'?—ED.   ‡ Cajetan *Summa*, p. 4, 28.

distributing his goods, that he must not give but to whom they please. It ariseth indeed from a sense of our wants; but the language of it is, God is unjust in his providence to me, because he bestows not upon me that good which he gives to another. It is such a sin that it seems to be a companion of our first parents' pride, which was the cause of their fall. They envied God a felicity by himself, for they would be like him, they would be as gods. Hence, perhaps, the Jews say Cain denied the providence of God, as envying his brother, because God accepted Abel's sacrifice and not his. Jonah's passion arose from this pride, for fear he should be accounted a false prophet; whereupon he envies God the glory of his mercy, and the poor Ninevites the advantage of it; he would have God conform the way of his providence to his pleasure and reputation. Indeed, it is to envy God the honour of his providence in those gifts or good things another possesses, whereby he is instrumental to glorify God and advantage others. Thus, we would direct God what instruments he should employ; when no artificer in his own art would endure to be directed by any ignorant person what tools he should use in his work.

(9.) Impatience under cross providence is a denial and contempt of God's government. Men quarrel with God's revealed will, and therefore no wonder that they quarrel with his providential will; whereby we deny him his right of governing, and slight his actual exercise of his right. As if God were accountable to us for his dispensations, and must have only a respect to us or our humour in his government: Job xviii. 4, 'He tears himself in his anger; shall the earth be forsaken for thee? and shall the rock be removed out of his place?' Must God alter the scene of his affairs according to our model and platform? And because he doth not observe our rules and methods, must we tear ourselves in anger? This is a secret cursing of God and flying in his face, when we see providence so cross, that there seems to be no help at any time either in heaven or earth: Isa. viii. 21, 22, 'They shall fret themselves, and curse their king and their God, and look upwards. And they shall look unto the earth; and behold trouble and darkness.' Take heed of fretting at God's management of things in the world, or thy own particular concerns; this may lead to a cursing of God, and is indeed an initial secret swelling against him, and cursing of him. Man is ambitious to become a god. Adam's posterity have in one sort or other imitated him. This,

[1.] Is a wrong to the sovereignty of providence. It was a good admonition of Luther's to Melancthon, when he was troubled much about the affairs of the church, *Monendus est Philippus ut desinat esse rector mundi.* By this temper we usurp God's place, and set ourselves in his throne; we invade his supremacy, by desiring everything to be at our beck, and are displeased with him, because he doth not put the reins of the world's government into our hands; as if we would command his will and become his sovereigns. It is a striving with our Maker for the superintendency, when we will sit judge upon him, or censure his acts, and presume to direct him: Isa. xlv. 9, 'Woe to him that strives with his Maker. Shall the clay say to him that fashions it, What makest thou? or thy work, He hath no hands.' How do men summon God to the bar of their interest, and expostulate with him about his works, why he did not order them thus and thus; and if he doth so, to tell him he hath no hand, no hand of providence in the world! The design of that place is to stop such peevishness and invasions of God's right; I will not have my sovereign will disputed, as if I were but the creature's servant. I am content you should 'ask of me things to come,' ver. 11, and pray to me, but notwithstanding yet to submit to my pleasure, without a peevish endeavouring to wrest the sovereignty out of my hand, and pull the crown from my head.

[2.] It is a wrong to the goodness and righteousness of providence. It is a charging God with ill management, and an implicit language, that if we were the commanders of providence, things should be managed more justly and righteously; as it was Absalom's pretence in wishing to be the king of Israel in David's stead, 2 Sam. xv. 4. If patience be a giving God the honour of his righteousness in his judgments—Ps. cxix. 75, ' I know, O Lord, that thy judgments are right, and that thou in faithfulness hast afflicted me;'—impatience must be a charge against God for unrighteousness in his judicial proceedings, and a saying, ' the way of the Lord is not equal,' Ezek. xviii. 25. It is implied in that complaint, Isa. lviii. 2, 3, ' They ask of me the ordinances of justice, &c. Wherefore have we fasted, and thou seest not ? wherefore have we afflicted our souls, and thou takest no knowledge ? ' We demand justice of thee, since thou dost not seem to do that which is fit and righteous, in not regarding us in our suits, and not bestowing that which we have fasted for. God governs the world according to his will, our murmuring implies that God's will is not the rule of righteousness. We affront the care of God towards his creatures, as if the products of our shallow reasons were more beautiful and just than God's contrivances for us, who hath higher and more glorious ends in everything, both for ourselves and the world, of which we are members, and for his own glory, to which we ought to subject ourselves, when perhaps our projects tend immediately to gratify some sensual or spiritual lust in us. It is the commendation the Holy Ghost gives of Job, chap. i. 22, ' In all this Job sinned not, neither charged God foolishly,' as a character peculiar to him, implying that most men in the world do, upon any emergency, charge God with their crosses, as dealing unjustly with them, in inflicting punishment when they think they have deserved rewards. Jeremiah is not innocent in this case: Jer. xx. 7, ' O Lord, thou hast deceived me, and I was deceived,' in the ill success of his prophecy, as though an immense goodness would, and a sovereign power needed to deal in a fraudulent way with his creatures to bring his ends about.

[3.] It is a wrong to the wisdom of providence. We would degrade his omniscience and wisdom, and sway him by our foolish and purblind dictates; it is as if we would instruct him better in the management of the world, and direct him to a reformation of his methods : Job xl. 2, ' Shall he that contends with the Almighty instruct him ? He that reproves God let him answer it.' It is a reproving God, and reproofs imply a greater authority, or righteousness, or wisdom, in the person reproving. We reprove God, as if God should have consulted with us, and asked our advice; it is to take upon us to be God's counsellors, and to conclude the only wise God by our imperfect reason : Rom. xi. 34, ' Who hath been his counsellor ? ' It is a secret boasting of some excellency in ourselves, as if God did not govern well, or we could govern better. Shall a silly passenger, that understands not the use of the compass, be angry that the skilful pilot will not steer the vessel according to his pleasure ? Must we give out our orders to God, as though the counsels of infinite wisdom must roll about according to the conceits of our fancy ? Is not the language of our hearts in our fits of impatience as prodigiously proud against God's providence as the speech of that monster was against the creation, who said if he had been by God at the creation of the world, he could have directed him to a better platform ? All this, and much more, is virtually in this sin of impatience.

(10.) In charging our sins and miscarriages by them upon providence, in this we contemn it. Some think Cain doth so: Gen iv. 9, 'Am I my brother's keeper?' Thou art the keeper and governor of the world, why didst thou not hinder me from killing my brother? It is certain the first man did so: Gen. iii. 12, 'The woman thou gavest to be with me, she gave me of the tree;' thy gift is the cause of my sin and ruin. It is as certain David laid the sin of Uriah's murder at the door of providence: 2 Sam. xi. 25, when he heard that Uriah was dead, 'The sword,' saith he, 'devours one as well as another.' Man conjures up trouble to himself when by his folly he brings himself into sin, and from thence to misery, and then his heart frets against the Lord, and lays the blame both of his sin and following mischiefs upon him: Prov. xix. 3, 'The foolishness of man perverts his way, and his heart frets against the Lord.' There are many other ways wherein we deny or slight providence.

[1.] When we do things with a respect to the pleasure of men more than of God, as though God were careless both of himself and his own honour, and regarded not the principles and ends of our actions.

[2.] In vain boasting and vaunting of ourselves. As Benhadad would have such a multitude of men in his army as that there should not be dust enough in Samaria to afford every man a handful, 1 Kings xx. 10, wherein he swaggers with God, and vaunts as if he were the governor of the world; yet this man, with his numerous host, was routed by a troop of lacqueys, ver. 15, 20; they are called 'the young men of the princes.' Such is the folly of men against the orders of God, when they boast in their hearts that their house shall continue for ever, Ps. xlix. 11.

[3.] Oppression. 'They slay the fatherless, and say, The God of Jacob shall not regard it,' Ps. xciv. 6, 7. Their denial of providence was the cause of their oppression of the poor, and where this is found in any, it is an argument it ariseth principally from a like cause. This is also made the cause why they eat up God's people as they eat bread, Ps. xiv. 1, 4.

[4.] Misinterpretations of providence.

Such cursed jealousies had the Jews of God: Num. xiv. 3, 'And wherefore hath the Lord brought us into this land to fall by the sword? were it not better for us to return into Egypt?' As though God in that mighty deliverance had cheated them with a design to destroy them in the wilderness, when one of those plagues poured out upon Pharaoh being turned upon their heads, had destroyed them in Egypt. So foolish are they to think that God would ruin them upon dry land who might have drowned them as well as their enemies in the Red Sea; so unreasonable is man in his disputes against God.

[5.] In limiting providence. In bounding it to time, manner, and other circumstances, as they did: Ps. lxxviii. 41, 'They limited the holy one of Israel, for they remembered not his hand.' As though God must manage everything according to the will of a simple creature. It was a forgetfulness of providence, at least, that was the cause of it.

Use 2. The second use is of comfort. As the justice and righteousness of God is the highest comfort to a good man since the evangelical dispensation, in that he hath to deal with a righteous God, who can as soon deny himself as his righteousness, so it is none of the meanest comforts that we acknowledge and worship that God, who exerciseth himself in a constant government of the world, and leaves not anything to the capriciousness of that which we call fortune and chance. What satisfaction can any man in his sober wits have, to live in a world cast off from all care of the Creator of it? Wisdom without providence would make any man mad, and the greatest advantage would be to be a stupid and senseless fool. Can there be any worse news told to men than this, that let them be as religious as they will, there is no eye above takes notice of it ? What can be bitterer to a rational man than that God should be careless of the world ? * What a door would be opened by it for all sin in the wicked, and despair in the godly ! It is as great a matter of joy to the godly that God reigns as it is of terror to the wicked : Ps. xcvii. 1, 'The Lord reigns, let the earth rejoice ; Ps. xcix. 1, 'The Lord reigns, let the people tremble.'

It is a comfort that,

1. Man is a special object of providence. God provides for all creatures, even those that are the works of his hands, much more for man, who is more peculiarly the work of his head, in whose creation he took counsel : Gen. i. 26, 'Let us make man in our image, after our likeness.' The work of his heart, in being made according to his image, and intended as a sub-ordinate end of his whole creation, next to the principal, that of God's glory. He is the preserver of man and beast ; of man principally, of beasts in subserviency to man's good and preservation.

2. Holy men a more special object of it. God preserves and provides for all things, and all persons. But his eye is more peculiarly fixed upon those that fear him : Ps. xxxiii. 18, 'Behold, the eye of the Lord is upon them that fear him, upon them that hope in his mercy,' so fixed as if he had no regard to anything else. If God hath a care of man created after his own image, though his image be depraved, much more of those wherein his image is restored. If God loves himself, he loves his image and his works. A man loves the works which he hath made of some external matter ; much more doth a father love his son, much more doth God love his own, and therefore will work their good, and dispose of them well. God exerciseth a special providence over the actions of a good man, as well as his person, Ps. xxxvii. 23, 'The steps of a good man are ordered by the Lord, and he delighteth in his ways ;' it is a special, because a delight-ful providence, he delights in his way. How highly may it cheer a man to be in covenant with that God which rules the world, and hath all things at his beck, to be under not only the care of his wisdom, but of his goodness. The governor of the world, being such an only friend, will do him no hurt, being such an only father, will order all things to his good out of a fatherly affection ; he is the world's sovereign, but a good man's father ; he rules the heavens and the earth, but he loves his holy ones. Other things are the objects of his providence, and a good man is the end of it. For ' His eyes run to and fro throughout the whole earth, to shew himself strong for him whose heart is perfect towards him,' 2 Chron. xvi. 8.

3. Hence it will follow that the spirits of good men have sufficient grounds to bear up in their innocent sufferings and storms in the world. Innocent sufferings. There is a righteous governor who orders all, and will reward them for their pains as well as their service : Heb. vi. 10, 'For God is not unrighteous to forget your work and labour of love ;' there is one that pre-sides in the world, who sees all their calamities, and cannot be mistaken in their cause, who hath as much power and wisdom as will to help them. It would be an affliction indeed if there were no sovereign power to whom they might make their moan in their distress, to whom they might ease their con-sciences, if there were no governor to whom they might offer up their petitions in the storms they meet with in the world. How doth the presence of a skilful pilot in a weather-beaten ship cheer the hearts of the fearful passen-

---

* It was an excellent speech of a Stoic, οὐκ ᾿εστὶ ζῆν ἐν τῷ κόσμῳ κενῷ θεῶν καὶ προνοίας.

gers ! What a dread would it be to them to have the vessel wherein their lives and all are concerned left to the fury of winds and waves, without an able hand to manage it ? God hath a bridle to check the passions of men, to marshal them according to his pleasure ; they are all but his instruments in the government, not the lords of it. God can lay a plot with more wisdom for a good man's safety than the enemy can for his destruction ; he can countermine their plots with more power than they can execute them ; he can out-wit their craft, overpower their strength, and turn their designed cruelty against them, as a knife into their own breasts.

4. Hence follows a certain security against a good man's want. If God take care of the hairs, the ornamental superfluities, why should we doubt his care of our necessary supply ? If he be the guardian of our hairs, which fall off without our sense of their departure, shall he be careless of us when we are at a pinch for our all ? Will God reach out his care to beasts, and deny it to his children ? What would you judge of that father who should feed his servants and starve his sons ? He supplies his enemies, and hath he no bowels for his friends ? The very unjust as well as the just are enlightened by his sun, and refreshed by his rain ; and shall he not have a providence for those that have a special interest in that Mediator, whose interposition kept up those standing mercies after our forfeiture of them by sin ? If he bless with those blessings those who are the objects of his curse, will he not bless those that are in his special favour with them, so far as they may prove blessings to them ? Ps. xxxiv. 10, ' The young lions do lack and suffer hunger, but they that seek the Lord shall not want any good thing,' ver. 9, ' for there is no want to them that fear him.' A good man shall have what he needs, not always what he thinks he needs. Providence intends the supply of our necessities, not of our desires; he will satisfy our wants, but not our wantonness. When a thing is not needful, a man cannot properly be said to want it ; when it is needful, a good man shall not be without it. What is not bestowed upon us may not be so beautiful at that time wherein we desire it, for everything is beautiful in its season, Eccles. iii. 11. He that did not want God's kindness to renew him, shall never want God's kindness to supply him ; his hand shall not be wanting to give, where his heart has been so large in working. Others live that have an interest only in common providence, but good men have providence cabineted in a promise, and assured to them by a deed of covenant conveyance ; he was a provider before, he hath made himself now your debtor. You might pray for his providential care before with a common faith, now with a more special expostulation, for in his promise he hath given a good man the key of the chest of his providence, because it is ' the promise of this life, and that which is to come,' 1 Tim. iv. ; of this life, not to our desires, but necessities ; of the life to come to both, wherein they shall have whatsoever they can want and whatsoever they can desire.

Again consider, God doth exercise a more special providence over men, as clothed with miserable circumstances, and therefore among his other titles this is one, to be ' a helper of the fatherless,' Ps. x. 14. It is the argument the church used to express her return to God : Hosea xiv. 3, ' For in thee the fatherless find mercy.' Now what greater comfort is there than this, that there is one presides in the world who is so wise he cannot be mistaken, so faithful he cannot deceive, so pitiful he cannot neglect his people, and so powerful that he can make stones even to be turned into bread if he please !

Further, take this for a comfortable consideration ;

God doth not govern the world only by his will as an absolute monarch, but by his wisdom and goodness as a tender father. ⁕ It is not his greatest pleasure to shew his sovereign power, or his unconceivable wisdom, but his immense goodness, to which he makes the other attributes subservient. What was God's end in creating is his end in governing, which was the communication and diffusion of his goodness ; we may be sure from hence that God will do nothing but for the best, his wisdom appointing it with the highest reason, and his goodness ordering it to the most gracious end ; and because he is the highest good, he doth not only will good, but the best good in everything he acts.

What greater comfort can there be than that we are under the care of an infallible, unwearied, and righteous governor! infallible because of his infinite wisdom, unwearied because of his incomprehensible omnipotency, and righteous because of his unbounded goodness and holiness.

Use 3. Of exhortation.

The duties arising from hence will run as a thread through the web of our whole lives, and all the motions of them. This doctrine hath an influence upon our whole course ; there is nothing we meet with but is an act of providence, and there is no act of providence but calls for some particular duty. Is there any good we want? We must seek it at his hands, we must depend upon him for it ; we must prescribe no methods to him, but leave the conduct of it to his own wisdom. Is it a cross providence, and contrary to our desires and expectations? Murmur not at it. Is it afflictive and troublesome? Submit to it. Is it either good or bad, and present? We must study to understand it. Is it a good and present? Give God the glory of it.

1. Seek everything you need at the hands of God. It is not only the skilfulness of the pilot, but a favourable gale from heaven, which must conduct the ship to the intended port. As his providence is the foundation, so it is the encouragement of all prayer. The end of the Lord's prayer is, ' For thine is the kingdom, the power, and the glory.' The providential kingdom belongs to God. Power he hath to manage it, and his glory is the end of all. Seek to him therefore for the exercise of his power in thy concerns, and for his directing them to his glory in his providential administrations. Every one of our days, and both the mercy and the misery of them, depend upon him : Prov. xxvii. 1, ' Thou knowest not what a day may bring forth,' but God foresees all events; have recourse therefore to his care for every day's success. What are our contrivances without the leave and blessing of providence ? Like the bubbles blown up from a nut-shell, easily broken by the next puff. Our labour will be as fruitless as Peter's, with all his toil, and catch nothing till. God speaks the word, and sends the fish into our net, Luke v. 5. The way of man is not in himself : Jer. x. 23, ' O Lord, I know that the way of man is not in himself; it is not in man that walks to direct his steps.' Dangers are not within the reach of our eye to foresee, nor within the compass of our power to prevent. Human prudence may lay the platform, and God's power blast the execution when it seems to be grown up nearest to maturity. Hezekiah was happy in his affairs, because he was assisted by God ; Ahaz unhappy, because he is deserted by God. If we would have a clock go well, we must look chiefly to the motion of the chief wheel ; a failure in that makes an error in all the rest. Nothing can terminate its motion to our benefit without providence. Coloured glass can reflect no beams without the sun's light, nor fruits be ripened without its influence. Our dependence on God is greater than theirs on the sun. God lets men play with their own wit and strength, and come to the brink of execution of their designs, and then blows upon them, that they

may know there is a God in the earth. Pythagoras could say it was
γελοῖον, a ridiculous thing to seek that which is brave and virtuous anywhere
else than of God.*   Cyrus is a brave pattern, who is mentioned in Scripture, and represented by Xenophon calling upon God when he was first
chosen general; † and in his speech to his captains to encourage them to
hope for a good success of the expedition, tells them they might expect it,
because I have begun with God, which you know, saith he, is my custom,
not only when I attempt great matters, but also τὰ μικρὰ, the things of lesser
concernment.   The seeking of God should be the prologue to all our affairs.
We are enjoined first to pray, and then to determine : Job xxii. 27, ' Thou
shalt make thy prayer unto him, thou shalt also decree a thing, and it shall .
be established unto thee.'   The interesting providence in our concerns is
the highway to success. The reason we miscarry, is because we consult not
God, but determine without him; and then we have no reason to complain
of him for not prospering our way, when we never commended our affairs to
his conduct.   It hath been the practice of holy men.   Nehemiah first
petitioned God before he would use his interest in the king's favour : Neh.
ii. 4, ' Then the king said unto me, For what dost thou make request ? So
I prayed to the God of heaven, and I said unto the king,' &c.   So Abraham's
steward put up his request to God, before he would put the business he came
upon in execution, Gen. xxiv. 12. David frequently in particular cases, 1 Sam.
xxiii. 9, 2 Sam. ii. 1, 2 Sam. xvi. 12. God only doth what he pleases in heaven
and in earth. He only can bless us, he only can blast us. Shall we be careless in any undertaking, whether we have his favour or no ? It is a ridiculous madness to resolve to do anything without God, without whose assisting
and preserving of us we had not been able to make that resolution.

   2. Trust providence. To trust God when our warehouses and bags are
full, and our tables spread, is no hard thing; but to trust him when our
purses are empty, but a handful of meal and a cruse of oil left, and all ways
of relief stopped, herein lies the wisdom of a Christian's grace. Yet none
are exempted from this duty, all are bound to acknowledge their trust in
him by the daily prayer for daily bread, even those that have it in their cup-
boards as well as those that want it, the greatest prince as well as the meanest
beggar. Whatever your wants are, want not faith, and you cannot want
supplies. It is the want of this binds up his hand from doing great works
for his creatures ; the more we trust him the more he concerns himself in
our affairs. The more we trust ourselves, the more he delights to cross us ;
for he hath denounced such an one cursed that maketh flesh his arm, Jer.
xvii. 5, though it be the best flesh in the world, because it is a departing
from the Lord. No wonder then that God departs from us, and carries away
his blessing with him ; while we trust ourselves, we do but trouble ourselves,
and know not how to reconcile our various reasons for hopes and fears, but
the committing our way to the Lord renders our minds calm and composed :
Prov. xvi. 3, ' Commit thy works unto the Lord, and thy thoughts shall be
established.'   Thou shalt have no more of those quarrelling disturbing
thoughts what the success shall be.

   (1.) Trust providence in the greatest extremities. He brings us into
straits, that he may see the exercise of our faith : Zeph. iii. 12, ' I will leave
in the midst of thee an afflicted and poor people, and they shall trust in the
name of the Lord.'   When we are most desolate, we have most need of this
exercise, and have the fittest season to practise it ; he is always our refuge
and our strength, but in time of trouble a present help, Ps. xlvi. 1. Daniel's
new advancement by Belshazzar but a day before the city was taken by the

* Jamblich. Vita. Pythag , lib. i. cap. 18.   † Xenophon περὶ Κύρου Παιδ. lib. i.

enemy, Dan. v. 29, the king slain, and (no doubt) many of his nobility, and those that were nearest in authority with him, it being the interest of the enemy to despatch them, was a danger, yet God by ways not expressed preserved Daniel, and gave him favour with the conqueror.   God sometimes leads his people into great dangers, that they may see and acknowledge his hand in their preservation.   Daniel had not had so signal an experience of God's care of him, had he been in the lower condition he was in before his new preferment.   God's eye is always upon them that fear him, not to keep distress from them, but to quicken them in it, and give them as it were a new life from the dead: Ps. xxxiii. 18, 19, 'To deliver their soul from death, and to keep them alive in famine.'   God brings us into straits, that we may have more lively experiments of his tenderness in his seasonable relief. If he be angry, he will repent himself for his servants, when he sees their power is gone, because then the glory of his providence is appropriated to himself: Deut. xxxii. 36, 39, 'See now that I, even I, am he, and there is no god with me: I kill, and I make alive.'   No creature can have any pretence to share in it; he delights thereby to blow up both our affections to him and admirations of him, and store up in us a treasure of experiments to encourage our trusting in him in the like straits.   We should therefore repose ourselves in God in a desert as well as in the cities; with as much faith among savage beasts as in the best company of the most sociable men;* and answer the greatest strait with Abraham's speech to Isaac, 'GOD WILL PROVIDE.' For we have to do with a God who is bound up to no means, is at no expense in miraculous succours, who delights to perfect his strength in the creature's weakness.   We have to do with a God who only knows what may further our good, and accordingly orders it; what may hinder it, and therefore prevents it.   He can set all causes in such a posture as shall conspire together as one link to bring about success, and make even contrary motions meet in one gracious end; as the rivers which run from north and south, the contrary quarters of the world, agree in the surges of one sea.   Though providences may seem to cross one another, they shall never cross his word and promise, which he hath magnified above all his names.   And his providence is but a servant to his truth.

(2.) Trust it in the way of means.   Though we are sure God hath decreed the certain event of such a thing, yet we must not encourage our idleness, but our diligence.   Though Moses was assured of the victory when Amalek came armed against him, yet he commands Joshua to draw up the valiant men into a body, himself goes to the mount to pray, and is as diligent in the use of all means as if he had been ignorant of God's purpose, and had rather suspected the rout of his own than his enemies' forces.   Neither doth Joshua afterwards, though secured by promise in his conquest of Canaan, omit any part of the duty of a wise and watchful general; he sends spies, disciplines his forces, besiegeth cities, and contrives stratagems.   Providence directs us by means, not to use them is to tempt our guardian; where it intends any great thing for our good, it opens a door, and puts such circumstances into our hands as we may use without the breach of any command, or the neglect of our own duty.   God could have secured Christ from Herod's fury by a miraculous stroke from heaven upon his enemy, but he orders Joseph and Mary's flight into Egypt as a means of his preservation.   God rebukes Moses for praying, and not using the means in continuing the people's march: Exod. xiv. 15, 'Wherefore criest thou unto me?   Speak unto the children of Israel, that they go forwards.'   To use means without respect to God, is proudly to contemn him; to depend upon God without the use of

* Durant de Tentat. p. 168.

means, is irreligiously to tempt him; in both we abuse his providence. In the one we disobey him in not using the means he hath appointed; in the other presumptuously impose upon him for the encouragement of our laziness.   Diligence on our part, and the blessing on God's, Solomon joins together, Prov. x. 4, 'The hand of the diligent makes rich,' but, ver. 22, 'The blessing of the Lord maketh rich.'   So Eccles. ix. 1, 'Our works are in the hand of God;' our works, but God's blessing; God's blessing, but not without our works.   It was the practice of good men.   Jacob wrestles with God to divert his brother's fury, yet sends a present to his brother to appease him, Gen. xxxii. 9, 13.   David trusts in the name of the Lord his God in his duel with Goliah, but not without his sling; our labour should rather be more vigorous than more faint, when we are assured of the blessing of providence by the infallibility of the promise.

(3.) Trust providence in the way of precept.   Let not any reliance upon an ordinary providence induce you into any way contrary to the command. Daniel had many inducements from an appearance of providence to eat the king's meat: his necessity of compliance in his captivity, probability of preferment by learning the wisdom of the country, whereby he might both have advanced himself and assisted his countrymen, the greatness of the consideration for a captive to be fed from the king's table, the ingratitude he might be accused of for despising so kind a treatment; but none of these things moved him against a command; because the law of God forbade it, he would not eat of the king's meat, Dan. i. 8–10, &c.   'But Daniel purposed in his heart that he would not defile himself with the portion of the king's meat.'   Daniel might have argued, I may wind myself into the king's favour, do the church of God a great service by my interest in him, which may be dashed in pieces by my refusal of this kindness; but none of these things wrought upon him.   No providences wherein we have seeming circumstances of glorifying God, must lead us out of the way of duty; this is to rob God one way to pay him another.   God brought Daniel's ends about: he finds favour with the governor, his request is granted, the success is answerable, and all those ends attained which he might in a sinful way, by an ill construction of providence, have proposed to himself, all which he might have missed of had he run on in a carnal manner.   This, this is the way to success: Ps. xxxvii. 5, 'Commit thy way unto the Lord, trust also in him, and he shall bring it to pass.'   Commit thy way to the guidance of his providence, with an obedience to his precept and reliance on his promise, and refer all success in it to God.   If we set up our golden calves made of our own ear-rings, our wit, and strength, and carnal prudence, because God seems to neglect us, our fate may be the same with theirs, and the very dust of our demolished calf may be a bitter spice in our drink, as it was in theirs.

(4.) Trust him solely, without prescribing any methods to him; leave him to his wise choice, wait upon him because he is a God of judgment, Isa. xxx. 18, who goes judiciously to work, and can best time the executions of his will.   The wise God observes particular periods of time for doing his great works,—John ii. 4, 'My hour is not yet come; woman, what have I to do with thee?'—which man is no competent judge of: I will do this miracle, but the season is not yet come wherein it will be most beautiful. God hath as much wisdom to pitch the time of performance of his promise, as he hath mercy at first to make it.   How presumptuous would it be for the shallow world, a thing worse than nothing, and vanity, to prescribe rules to the Creator! much more for a single person, a little atom of dust, infinitely worse than nothing, and vanity, to do it.   Since we had no hand in creating the world or ourselves, let us not presume to direct God in the government of it: Job xxxviii. 4, 'Where wast thou when I laid the foundation of the earth? declare, if thou hast understanding.' Would it not be a disparagement to God to stoop to thy foolish desires? yea, would you not yourselves have a lower conceit of him, if he should degrade his wisdom to the wrong bias of your blind reason?

3. Submit to providence. It is God's right to govern the world, and dispose of his creature; it is his glory in heaven to do what he will: Ps. cxv. 3, 'But our God is in the heaven: he hath done whatsoever he pleased.' Let us not, by our unsubmissive carriage, deprive him of the same glory on earth; he brings to pass his will by ways the creature cannot understand. It is the wisest speech in the medley of fooleries, the Turkish Alcoran.* We must walk by the rule of reason which God hath placed in us for our guide; yet if providence brings to pass any other event contrary to our rational expectations, because it is a clear evidence of his will, we must acquiesce. As when a traveller hath two ways to come to his journey's end, the one safe and the other dangerous, reason persuades him to choose the safest way, wherein he falls among thieves; now having used his reason, which in that case was to be his director, he must acquiesce; God's providence bringeth forth an event, which he could not without violence to his reason avoid. And therefore it is a great vanity, when a man hath resolved the most probable way in a business, and fails in it, to torment himself; because though our consultations depend upon ourselves, yet the issues of them are solely in the hand of God. It concerns us therefore to submit to God's disposal of us and our affairs, since nothing can come to pass but by the will of God effecting it, or permitting it. If the fall of a sparrow is not without his will, Mat. x. 29, much less can the greater events which befall men, the nobler creatures, be without the same concurrence of God's pleasure; therefore submit: for,

(1.) Whatsoever God doth, he doth wisely. His acts are not sudden and rash, but acts of counsel; not taken up upon the present posture of things, but the resolves of eternity. As his is the highest wisdom, so all his acts relish of it, and he guides his will by counsel: Eph. i. 11, 'Who worketh all things after the counsel of his own will.' If God took counsel in creating the world, much more in laying a platform of government, much more in the act of government; for men can frame models of government that can never reduce them into practice. Now God being infinitely wise, and his will infinitely good, it must needs be that goodness and wisdom are the rules whereby he directs himself in his actions in the world. And what greater motive can there be to persuade our submission, than wisdom and goodness transacting all things? God's counsel being the firmest, as well as the wisest, it is a folly both ways to resist it.

(2.) God discovers his mind to us by providences. Every work of God being the result of his counsel, when we see it actually brought forth into the world, what else doth it discover to us but that counsel and will of his? Every single providence hath a language wherein God's mind is signified, much more a train and contexture of them: Luke vii. 22, 'Tell John what things you have seen and heard: how that the blind see, the lame walk, the lepers are cleansed, the deaf hear, the dead are raised to life, to the poor the gospel is preached.' Our Saviour informs John's disciples from acts of providence, he gives them no other answer, but turns him over to interpret and construe his works in the case. Providence therefore must not be resisted, when God's mind in it is discovered. It is disingenuous to act against his pleasure and manifest mind; it is the devil's sin. Aaron,

* *Deus triumphat in sua causa, &c.*

when he lost his two sons in so judicial manner by fire from heaven, yet
held his peace, Lev. x. 1–3 ; because God had declared his mind positively,
' I will be glorified.'   It is dangerous to resist the mind of God, for the
word of his providence shall prosper in spite of men and devils : Isa. lv. 11,
' My word that goes forth of my mouth, shall not return unto me void ; it
shall prosper in the thing whereto I sent it ;' and therefore a resisting of it
is termed θεομαχεῖν, a fighting against God, by Gamaliel, no great friend to
the church, Acts v. 38, 39.

4. Murmur not at providence.   Though we do not clearly resist it, if
there be a repining submission, it is a partial opposition to the will of God.
We might as well murmur at God's creation as at his providence, for that
is as arbitrary as this ; he is under no law but his own righteous will : we
should therefore leave the government of the world to God's wisdom, as we
acknowledge the frame of it to be an act of his power.   If God should
manage his ways according to our prescriptions, what satisfaction would
God have ? what satisfaction would the world have ? He might be unjust
to himself, and unjust to others.   Your own complaints would not be stilled,
when you should feel the smart of your own counsels ; yet if they were,
what satisfaction could there be to the complaints of others, whose interests
and therefore judgments and desires lie cross to yours ?   Man is a cross
creature.   The Israelites exclaimed to God against Pharaoh, and when the
scene was changed, they did no less murmur against Moses in the wilderness.   They were as troublesome when they were delivered, as when they
were afflicted.   In Egypt they would have their liberty, and in the wilderness their stomachs turn, and they long for the onions and garlic, though
attended with their former slavery.   Let God govern the world according to
his own wisdom and will, till all mankind can agree in one method to offer
to him, and that I think will never be, though the world should last for ever.
Murmur not, therefore ; whatsoever is done in the world is the work of a
wise agent, who acts for the perfection of the whole universe ; and why
should I murmur at that which promotes the common happiness and perfection, that being better and more desirable than the perfection of any one
particular person ?   Must a lutenist break all his strings because one is out
of tune ?   And must God change his course because things are out of order
with one man, though in regard of divine providence things are not out of
order in themselves, or without any care, for God is a God of order ?   This
temper will hinder our prayers ; with what face can we pray to that God
whose wisdom we thus repine at ?   If God doth exercise a providence in
the world, why do we murmur ?   If he doth not take care of those things,
why do we pray to him ?   It is a contradiction.   It also hinders us from
giving God the glory, and ourselves the comfortable sight of his providence.
God may have taken something from us, which is the matter of our sorrow,
and give another thing to us, which might be the matter of our joy.   Jacob
lost a joint, and got a blessing, Gen. xxxii. 29, 31.   What advantage can it
be to murmur ?   Can all your cries stop the motions of the heavens, when
a storm reaches you ?   Can your clamours make the clouds move the
faster, or persuade the showers from drenching us ?   Murmuring at any
afflictive providence, is the way to make the rod smarter in itself, and
sharper to us.

5. Study providence.   It is a part of atheism not to think the acts of God
in the world worth our serious thoughts.   And if you would know the meaning of his administrations, grow up in the fear of God : Ps. xxv. 14, ' The
secret of the Lord is with them that fear him.'   God is highly angry with
those that mind him not : Ps. xxviii. 5, ' Because they regard not the ope-

ration of his hands, he shall destroy them, and not build them up.' He shall utterly root them out.

(1.) Study providence universally. The darkest: God brings order out of the world's confusion, even as he framed a beautiful heaven and earth out of a rude mass. The terriblest: these offer something worth our observation; the dreadful providence of God makes Sodom an example to after ages: Jude 7, they are 'set forth for an example, suffering the vengeance of eternal fire,' &c. The smallest: God is a wise agent, and so the least of his actions are significant. There is nothing superfluous in those acts we account the meanest; for to act vainly and lightly argues imperfection, which cannot be attributed to God. The wisdom of God may be much seen in those providences the blind world counts small; as a little picture is oft-times of more value, and hath more of the workman's skill than a larger, which an ignorant person might prize at a higher rate; the lilies, flowers, sparrows, our Saviour raises excellent observations from.

(2.) Regularly. By the word: compare providence and the promise together; God's manner of administrations, and the meaning of them, is understood by the word: Ps. lxxvii. 13, 'Thy way, O God, is in the sanctuary.' By faith: we many times correct our sense by reason; when we look through a blue or green glass, and see all things blue or green, though our sense represents them so, yet our reason discovers the mistake. Why should we not correct reason by faith? Indeed, our purblind reason stands in as much need of a regulation by faith, as our deceitful sense doth of a regulation by reason. We may often observe in the gospel, that the Holy Ghost taking notice of the particular circumstances in the bringing Christ into the world, and in the course of his life, often hath those expressions, ' as it is written; that the Scriptures might be fulfilled.' There is not a providence happens in the world, but there are some general rules in the word whereby we may apprehend the meaning of it. From God's former work discovered in his word, we may trace his present footsteps. Observe the timings of providence wherein the beauty of it appears, since ' God hath made every thing beautiful in its time.'

(3.) Entirely. View them in their connection. A harsh touch single would not be pleasing, but may rarely affect the concert. The providences of God bear a just proportion to one another, and are beautiful in their entire scheme; but when regarded apart, we shall come far short of a delightful understanding of them. As in a piece of arras folded up, and afterwards particularly opened, we see the hand or foot of a man, the branch of a tree; or if we look on the outside, we see nothing but knots and threads, and uncouth shapes that we know not what to make of; but when it is fully opened, and we have the whole web before us, we see what histories and pleasing characters are interwoven in it. View them in their end; there is no true judgment to be made of a thing in motion, unless we have a right prospect of the end to which it tends. Many things which may seem terrible in their motion, may be excellent in their end. Providence is crowned by the end of it. Asaph was much troubled about the prosperity of the wicked, and affliction of the godly, but he was well satisfied when he understood their end, which was the end of providence too: Ps. lxxiii. 16, 17, ' When I thought to know this, it was too painful for me, until I went into the sanctuary, then understood I their end.' Moses his rod was a serpent in its motion upon the ground; but when taken up, it was a rod again to work miracles. God set us a pattern for this in the creation. He views the creatures as they came into being, and pronounced them GOOD; he takes a review of them afterward in their whole frame, and the subordination of them to one another, and the ends he had destined them to, and then pronounceth them *very good*. The merciful providences of God, if singly looked upon, will appear *good*, but if reviewed in the whole web, and the end of them, will commence *very good* in our apprehensions.

(4.) Calmly. Take heed of passion in this study, that is a mist before the eye of the mind; several pleasures also disturb and stifle the nobler operation of the intellective part, and all improving thoughts of God's providence: Isa. v. 12, 'And the harp, and the viol, and wine, are in their feasts, but they regard not the work of the Lord, nor consider the operations of his hands.' All thoughts of them are choked by the pleasures of sense. Passions and sensual pleasures are like flying clouds in the night, interposing themselves between the stars and our eyes, that we cannot observe the motions of them. Turbulent passions, or swinish pleasures prevailing, obscure the providence of God. Our own humour and interest we often make the measures of our judgment of providence. Shimei, when Absalom rebels against his father, looks no further than his own interest, and therefore interprets it as a judgment of God in revenging the house of Saul: 2 Sam. xvi. 7, 8, 'The Lord hath returned upon thee all the blood of the house of Saul, in whose stead thou hast reigned.' Therefore the Spirit of God takes particular notice that he was of the house of Saul, ver. 5, when indeed this judgment was quite another thing, for David's sin in the matter of Uriah was written in the forehead of it.

(5.) Seriously. It is not an easy work; for the causes of things are hid, as the seminal virtues in plants, not visible till they manifest themselves. Providence is God's lantern in many affairs; if we do not follow it close, we may be left in the dark, and lose our way. With much prayer, for we cannot of ourselves find out the reason of them; being shallow creatures, we cannot find out those infinite wise methods God observes in the managing of them; but if we seriously set to work, and seek God in it, God may inform us, and make them intelligible to us. Though a man may not be able of himself to find out the frame and motions of an engine, yet when the artificer hath explained the work, discovered the intent of the fabric, it may be easily understood: if it be dark, whilst you seriously muse on it, God may send forth a light into you, and give you an understanding of it: Mat. i. 20, Joseph thought of those things, and whilst he thought on them, the angel of the Lord appeared to him in a dream; God made them known to him. The Israelites saw God's acts in the bulk of them, but Moses saw his way, and the manner how he wrought them; Ps. ciii. 7, 'He made known his ways unto Moses, his acts unto the children of Israel.' Moses had more converse with God than they, and therefore was admitted into his secrets.

(6.) Holily; with a design to conform to that duty providence calls for. Our motions should be according to the providence of God, when we understand the intent of them. There is a call of providence: Isa. xxii. 12, 'In that day the Lord called to weeping and mourning,' sometimes to sorrow, sometimes to joy. If it be a providence to discover our sin, let us comply with it by humiliation; if it be to further our grace, suit it by lively and fresh actings. As the sap in plants descends with the sun's declination, and ascends at the return of the sun from the tropic, there are several graces to be exercised upon several acts of providence, either public to the church and nation, or particular to our own persons—sometimes faith, sometimes joy, sometimes patience, sometimes sorrow for sin. There are spiritual lessons in every providence, for it doth not only offer something to be understood, but some things to be practised. Mark x. 15, a child is brought to

Christ, and Christ from thence teaches them a lesson of humility. Luke xiii. 1–3. When Christ discourses of that sad providence of the blood of the Galileans, and the tower of Siloam, he puts them upon the exercise of repentance. The ruler inquired the time when his son began to recover, that his faith in Christ might be confirmed, for upon that circumstance it did much hang ; and in doubtful cases, after a serious study of it, and thou knowest not which way to determine, consider what makes most for God's glory and thy spiritual good, for that is the end of all. Let us therefore study providence, not as children do histories, to know what men were in the world, or to please their fancy only, but as wise men, to understand the motions of states, and the intrigues of councils, to enrich them with a knowledge whereby they might be serviceable to their country. So let us inquire into the providence of God, to understand the mind of God, the interest of the church, the wisdom and kindness of God, and our own duty in conformity thereunto.

6. Ascribe the glory of every providence to God. Abraham's steward petitioned God at the beginning of his business, Gen. xxiv. 12 ; and he blesses God at the success of it, ver. 26, 27. We must not thank the tools which are used in the making an engine, and ascribe unto them what we owe to the workman's skill. Man is but the instrument, God's wisdom is the artist. Let us therefore return the glory of all where it is most rightly placed. We may see the difference between Rachel and Leah in this respect; when Rachel had a son by her maid Bilhah, she ascribes it to God's care, and calls his name Dan, which signifies *judging*—Gen. xxx. 6, ' God hath judged me, and heard my voice'—that the very name might put her in remembrance of the kindness of God in answering her prayer; and the next, Naphthali, she esteems as the fruit of prayer, ver. 8; whereas Leah takes no notice of God, but vaunts of the multitude of her children: ver. 11, ' Behold, a troop comes.' She imposeth the name of Gad upon them, which also signifies *fortune* or good luck; and the next, Asher, ver. 13, which is *fortunate* or *blessed*. And we find Leah of the same mind afterward, ver. 17. It is said God hearkened unto her, so that her son Issachar was an answer of prayer; but she ascribes it to a lower cause which had moved God, because she had given her maid to her husband, ver. 18. ' Not unto us, not unto us, O Lord, but to thy name be the glory.'

Doct. 2. All the motions of providence in the world are ultimately for the good of the church, of those whose heart is perfect towards him. Providence follows the rule of Scripture. Whatsoever was written, was written for the church's comfort, Rom. xv. 4; whatsoever is acted in order to anything written, is acted for the church's good. All the providences of God in the world are conformable to his declarations in his word. All former providences were ultimately in order to the bringing a mediator into the world, and for the glory of him; then surely all the providences of God shall be in order to the perfecting the glory of Christ in that mystical body whereof Christ is head, and wherein his affection and his glory are so much concerned. See the proof of this by a scripture or two: Ps. xxv. 10, ' All the paths of the Lord are mercy and truth unto such as keep his covenant and his testimonies.' Not one path, but *all* the works and motions; not one particular act or passage of providence, but the whole tract of his proceedings; not only those which are more smooth and pleasant, but those which are more rugged and bitter. All *mercy and truth* suitable to that affection he bears in his heart to them, and suitable to the declaration of that affection he hath made in his promise. There is a contexture and a friendly connection of kindness and faithfulness in every one of them. They both kiss and embrace each other in every motion of God towards them. As mercy made the covenant, so truth shall perform it. And there shall be as much mercy as truth in all God's actings towards those that keep it: Rom. viii. 28, 'We know that all things work together for good to them that love God, to them who are the called according to his purpose.' *We know*, we do not conjecture or guess so, but we have an infallible assurance of it; *all things*, even the most frightful, and so those that have, in respect of sense, nothing but gall and wormwood in them; *work together*, they all conspire with an admirable harmony and unanimous consent for a Christian's good. One particular act may seem to work to the harm of the church, as one particular act may work to the good of wicked men; but the whole series and frame of things combine together for the good of those that are affectionate to him. Both the lance that makes us bleed, and the plaster which refresheth the wounds, both the griping purges and the warming cordials, combine together for the patient's cure. To them who are *called according to his purpose*. Here the apostle renders a reason of this position, because they are called not only in the general amongst the rest of the world, to whom the gospel comes, but they are such that were in God's purpose and counsel from eternity to save, and therefore resolved to incline their will to faith in Christ; therefore all his other counsels about the affairs of the world shall be for their good. Another reason of this the apostle intimates, verse 27, 'The Spirit makes intercession for the saints, according to the will of God.' The intercessions of the Spirit, which are also according to God's will and purpose, will not be fruitless in the main end, which both the intercessions of the Spirit and purpose of God, and the will and desire of the saints, do aim at, which is their good. Indeed, where any is the object of this grand purpose of God, he is the object of God's infinite and innumerable thoughts: Ps. xl. 5, 'Many, O Lord my God, are thy wonderful works which thou hast done, and thy thoughts which are to us-ward; they cannot be reckoned up in order unto thee: if I would declare and speak of them, they are more than can be numbered.' The psalmist seems to intimate that, in all the wonderful works which God hath done, his thoughts are towards his people. He thinks of them in all his actions; and those thoughts are infinite, and cannot be numbered and reckoned up by any creature. He seems to restrain the thoughts of God towards his people in all those works of wonder which he doth in the world, and which others are the subjects of; but his thoughts or purposes and intentions in all (for the word signifies purposes too) are chiefly, next to his own glory, directed towards his people, those that trust in him, which, verse 4, he has pronounced blessed. They run in his mind, as if his heart was set upon them, and none but them.

Here I shall premise two things as the groundwork of what follows:

1. God certainly in all his actions has some end; that is without question, because he is a wise agent; to act vainly and lightly is an evidence of imperfection, which cannot be ascribed to the only wise God. The wheels of providence are full of eyes, Ezek. i. 18; there is motion, and a knowledge of the end of that motion. And Jesus Christ, who is God's deputy in the providential government, hath seven eyes as well as seven horns, Rev. v. 6; a perfect strength, and a perfect knowledge how to use that strength, and to what end to use it, seven being the number of perfection in Scripture.

2. That certainly is God's end which his heart is most set upon, and that

which is last in execution. What doth God do at the folding up of the world but perfect his people, and welcome them into glory? Therefore God principally next to himself loves his church. The whole earth is his, but the church is his treasure: Exod. xix. 5, 'If you will keep my covenant, then shall you be a peculiar treasure unto me above all people; for all the earth is mine,' *segullah;* such a treasure, that a man, a king, will entrust in no hands but his own. 'All the earth is mine' is not a reason why the church was his treasure, but an incentive of thankfulness; that when the whole earth was his, and lay before him, and there were many people that he might have chosen and loved before them, yet he pitched upon them to make them his choicest treasure. And when the blessed God hath pitched upon a people, and made them his treasure, what he doth for them is with his whole heart and with his whole soul. Jer. xxxii. 41, 42, speaking of making an everlasting covenant, he adds, 'Yea, I will rejoice over them to do them good,' &c., 'assuredly with my whole heart, and with my whole soul.' As though God minded nothing else but those people he had made an everlasting covenant with, which is the highest security, and most pregnant expression of his affection that can be given to any; not to give them a parcel or moiety of his heart, but the whole, infinite, entire piece, and to engage it all with the greatest delight in doing good to them. That infinite heart of God, and all the contrivances and workings of it, centre in the church's welfare. The world is a wilderness, but the church is a garden. If he water the wilderness, will he not much more dress his garden? If the flights of birds be observed by him, shall not also the particular concernments of the church? He hath a repository for them and all that belong to them; he hath a book of life for their names, Luke x. 20, a book of record for their members, Ps. cxxxix. 16; a note-book for their speeches, Mal. iii. 16, 'A book of remembrance was written before him for them that feared the Lord;' and a book of providence for their preservation, Exod. xxxii. 32. In the prosecution of this I shall shew,

1. That it is so *de facto*, and hath been so.

2. That according to the state of things, and God's economy, it must be so.

3. The improvement of it, by way of use.

1. That all providence is for the good of the church *de facto*, and has been so.

It will appear by an enumeration of things.

(1.) First, All good things.

(2.) Secondly, All bad things are for their good.

(1.) First, All good things.

[1.] The world.

[2.] Gifts and common graces of men in the world.

[3.] Angels.

[1.] The world. The whole world was made and ordained for the good of the church, next to the glory of God. This will appear in three things:

First, The continuance of the world is for their sakes. God would have destroyed the world because of the ignorance and wickedness of it, before this time, but he overlooked it all, and had respect to the times of Christ, and the publishing faith in him, and repentance: Acts xvii. 30, 'And the times of this ignorance God winked at,' God overlooked,* he looked not so upon them, as to be provoked to destroy the world, but his eyes were fixed on the times of Christianity, therefore would not take notice, in the extremity of his justice, of the wickedness of those foregoing ages. Believers are the

* ὑπεριδών.

salt of the earth, Mat. v. 13, which makes the world savoury to God, and keeps it from corrupting. It is meant not only of the apostles, but of Christ's disciples, of all Christians, for to them was that sermon made, ver. 1. ' If the salt have lost his savour,' if the salt be corrupted, and Christianity overthrown in the world, wherewith shall the world be salted ? How can it be kept from corruption ? If they that persecuted the prophets before you in Judea (which is sometimes called the earth in Scripture), cannot relish you, and find nothing grateful to their palates in your doctrine and conversation, wherewith shall they be salted ? How shall they be preserved from corruption ? The land will be good for nothing but to be given as a prey to the Romans, to be trodden under their feet, as being cast out of God's protection. They are the foundation of the world : Prov. x. 25, ' The righteous are an everlasting foundation.' Maimonides understands it thus, that the world stands for the righteous' sakes. When God had Noah and his family lodged in the ark, he cares not what deluge and destruction he brings upon the rest of the world. When he had conducted Lot out of Sodom, he brings down that dreadful storm of fire.* He cares for no place, no, nor for the whole world, any longer than whilst his people are there, or he hath some to bring in, in time. For the meanest believer is of more worth than a world ; therefore when God hath gathered all together, he will set fire upon this frame of the creation ; for what was the end of Christ's coming and dying, but to gather all things together in one ? Eph. i. 10, ' That in the dispensation of the fulness of time he might gather together in one all things in Christ.' When Christ hath summed up all together, he hath attained his end. And to what purpose, then, can we imagine God should continue the world any longer ? for his delight is not simply in the world, but in the saints there : Ps. xvi. 3, ' But to the saints that are in the earth, in whom is all my delight ;' not in the earth, but in the saints there, which are the only excellent things in it, which Christ speaks (of whom that psalm is meant) who knew well what was the object of his Father's pleasure. The sweet savour God smelt in Noah's sacrifice, was the occasion of God's declaration for the world's standing : Gen. viii. 21, ' And the Lord said in his heart, I will not curse the ground any more for man's sake,' that he would no more smite it with a totally destroying judgment. It was his respect to Christ represented in that sacrifice, and to the faith and grace of Noah the sacrificer. What savour could an infinitely pure spirit smell in the blood and flames of beasts ?

Secondly, The course of natural things is for the good of the church, or particular members of it. God makes articles of agreement with the beasts and fowls, whose nature is raging and ravenous, and binds them in sure bonds for the performance of those articles : Hosea ii. 18, ' And in that day will I make a covenant for them with the beasts of the field, and with the fowls of heaven, and with the creeping things of the ground, and will make them to lie down safely.' As upon our sin God can arm them against us, so upon our obedience he can make them serviceable even against their natures, as if he had made a covenant with them, and they had both the reason and virtue to observe it. I do not remember any instance in Scripture, that God went out of the usual tract of his providence, and acted in an extraordinary manner, but where his people were one way or other concerned. It was for Joshua's and the Israelites' sake that the sun was arrested to stand still in the valley of Ajalon, that they might have light enough to defeat their enemies, and pursue their victory, Josh. x. 12, 13. The sea shall, against its natural course, stand in heaps like walls of brass

* Grotius on the place.

to assist the Israelites' escape, Exod. xiv. 22. The fire is restrained in the operation of its nature, even whilst it retains its burning quality, when the lives of the three valiant believing children are in danger, Dan. iii. 25. The mouths of lions are muzzled when the safety of his beloved Daniel is concerned, Dan. vi. 22. And the shadow goes back upon the dial for Hezekiah's sake, 2 Kings xx. 11. When God would at any time deliver his people, he can muster up lightnings and thunders for their assistance; 1 Sam. vii. 10; he can draw all the regiments of heaven into battle array, and arm the stars to fight against Sisera, when Israel's condition needs it; and make even the lowest creatures to list themselves as auxiliaries in the service. God hath not a displeasure with senseless creatures, neither is transported with strains of fury against such objects, when he alters their natural course. Hab. iii. 8, 'Was the Lord displeased against the rivers? was thy wrath against the sea, that thou didst ride upon thy horses and chariots of salvation?' No; but he made those creatures the horses and chariots, to speed assistance and salvation to his people, which the psalmist elegantly describes, Ps. cxiv. All creatures are his host; and that God that created them hath still the sovereign command over them, and can embody them in an army to serve his purpose for the deliverance of his people, as he did against Pharaoh.

Thirdly, The interest of nations is ordered as is most for the church's good. He orders both the course of natural things, and of civil affairs for their interest. He alters the state of things, and changeth governors and governments for the sake of his people. For these causes God sent Elisha to crown Jehu king: 2 Kings ix. 6, 7, 'I have anointed thee king over the people of the Lord, &c., that I may avenge the blood of my servants the prophets, and the blood of all the servants of the Lord at the hand of Jezebel.' For the sakes of the godly in that nation, and the revenging the blood of the prophets which had been shed, was he raised up by the Lord. He sent such judgments upon Egypt, that it was as much the interest of that nation to let Israel go, as it was before to keep them their vassals. God orders the interest and affairs of nations for those ends; and according to this disposition of affairs, Christ times his intercession for his church. The angels had been sent out to view the state of the world, and found it in peace: Zech. i. 11, 'Behold, all the earth sits still, and is at rest;' there had been wars in Artaxerxes and Xerxes his time, but in the time of Darius that part of the world had an universal peace, which was the fittest time for the restoration of the Jews, and building the temple, because it could not be built but by the king's cost, whose treasure in the time of war was expended another way; nor would it consist with their policy to restore the Jews to their government at such a time when they had wars with the neighbour-parts of Egypt. See how God orders the state of the world in subserviency to his gracious intentions towards his church. The time of the Jewish captivity was now out, according to the promise of God, and God gives that part of the world a general peace, that the restoration of the Jews, and the rebuilding of the temple, might be facilitated, and the truth of his promise in their deliverance accomplished. Upon the news of this general peace in that part of the world, Christ expostulates with God for the restoration of Jerusalem; ver. 12, 'How long, O Lord, wilt thou not have mercy on Jerusalem, and on the cities of Judah, against which thou hast had indignation these threescore and ten years?' The time of the captivity determined by God was now expired. The first Reformation in Germany was backed by reasons of state as it was then altered, it being the interest of many princes of that country to countenance Luther's doctrine, for the putting a stop to the growing greatness of Charles the Fifth, who had evident designs to enslave them. I might mention many more; only by the way let me advise those that have an inclination to read histories of former transactions, to which men naturally are addicted, to make this your end, to observe the strange providences of God in the world, and how admirably he hath made them subservient to the interest of the church, which will be the most profitable way of reading them, whereby they will not only satisfy your curiosity, but establish your Christianity. Calvin understands that place: Deut. xxxii. 8, 'He sets the bounds of the people according to the number of the children of Israel,' that in the whole ordering of the state of the world, God proposeth this as his end, to consult for the good of his people, and his care extends to the rest only in order to them; and though they are but a small number, yet he orders his whole government of the world's affairs as may best tend to their salvation. Therefore God sets the people bounds, or enlargeth them according as they may be serviceable one way or other to this end. And the reason is rendered, ver. 9, 'For the Lord's portion is his people, and Jacob is the lot of his inheritance.' Therefore God orders all the rest of the world in subserviency to the maintaining and improving his portion and inheritance.

[2.] As the world, so the gifts and common graces of men in the world, are for the good of the church, which is a great argument for providence in general; since there is nothing so considerable in government as the disposing of places to men according to their particular endowments and abilities for them. And the bestowing such gifts upon men is none of the meanest arguments for God's providential government of the world. As,

First, The gifts of good men. The gifts conferred upon Paul were deposited in him, not only to be possessed by him, but used and laid out for the good of the church: Col. i. 25, 'Whereof I am made a minister, according to the dispensation of God which is given to me for you;' 'The manifestation of the Spirit to any man is given to profit withal,' 1 Cor. xii. 7. And this is the great end for which men should seek to excel, viz., for the edifying of the church: 1 Cor. xiv. 12, 'Forasmuch as you are zealous of spiritual gifts, seek that you may excel to the edifying of the church.'

Secondly, The gifts and common graces of bad men. There is something that is amiable in men, though they have not grace. As in stones, plants, and flowers, though they have not sense, there is something grateful in them, as colour and smell, &c. And all those things that are lovely in men are for the church's good; the best life, and the worst death, things present, let who will be the possessor, all things between life and death, are for the good of believers, because they are Christ's: 1 Cor. iii. 22, 'Whether Paul, or Apollos, or Cephas, or the world,'—*i. e.*, whether the gifts of the prime lights in the church, or the common gifts of the world,—'are all yours, and ye are Christ's, and Christ is God's.' God is the dispenser of them, Christ is the governor of them, and all for your sakes. As the medicinal qualities of waters are not for the good of themselves, but the accommodation of the indigencies of men. By the common works of the Spirit God doth keep men from the evil of the world. For it cannot be supposed that the Spirit, whose mission is principally for the church, should give such gifts out of love to men which hate him, and are not the objects of his eternal purpose; but he hath some other ends in doing it, which is the advantage of his church and people; and this God causes by the preaching of the gospel, which when it works gracious works in some, produceth common works in others for the good of those gracious ones. As a seed of corn hath straw, husks, and chaff come up with it, which are shelters to that little seed which lies in the midst, so in the preaching of the gospel there are some husks come up among natural men, which God makes to be shelters to the church, as those common works, and restraining men through the knowledge of Christ. God gives gifts to them, not out of love to them, but love to his church. As nurses of great men's children are fed with better meat than the other servants, not out of any particular personal respect to them, but to their office, that the milk whereby the child is nourished may be the sweeter and wholesomer; were it not for that relation, she must be content with the diet allowed to the rest of the servants. Some stinking plants may have medicinal virtues, which the physician extracts for the cure of a disease, and flings the rest upon the dunghill. God bestows such qualities upon men otherwise unsavoury to him, which he draws forth upon several occasions for the good of those that are more peculiarly under his care, and then casts them away. These gifts are indeed the ruin of bad men, because of their pride, but the church's advantage in regard of their excellency, and are often as profitable to others as dangerous to themselves. As all that good which is in plants and animals is for the good of man, so all the gifts of natural men are for the church's good; for they are for that end as the principal, next the glory of God, because every inferior thing is ordained to something superior as its end. Plants are ordained for the nourishment of beasts, and both plants and beasts for men; the inferior men for the service of higher; and all for the community: yet still there is a higher end beyond those, viz., the glory of God, to which they are ultimately ordained, which is so connected with the church's good, that what serves one serves the other.

[3.] Angels, the top creatures in the creation, are ordered for the good of the church. If the stars are not cyphers in the world only to be gazed upon, but have their influences both upon plants and animals; as the sun in impregnating the earth, and enlivening the plants, and assisting the growth of fruits for the good of mankind; if the stars have those natural influences upon the sensible world, the angels, which are the morning stars, have no less interest as instruments in the government of it. The heathens had such a notion of demons working those things which were done in the world, but according to the will and order of the supreme God. The angels are called watchers: Dan. iv. 13, 'A watcher, and an holy one;' ver. 17, 'This is by the decree of the watchers, and the demand by the word of the holy ones;' they watch for God's orders, and watch for God's honour, and the church's good. There are orders of state among them, for we read of their decree; it is called their decree ministerially, as they execute it; approbativè, as they subscribe to the equity and goodness of it. As the saints are said to judge the world, not authoritativè, as in commission with Christ, but as they approve of Christ's sentence. They seem to request those things of God which may make for his glory, and they decree among themselves what is fit to be presented to God in order to his glory. They cannot endure that men should trample upon God's authority, despoil him of his right, and tread down his inheritance, and therefore they send such requests to God to act so as men may acknowledge him and his government, 'to the intent that the living may know that the most high rules in the kingdoms of men.' Their care therefore must be for the church, since God rules all things in order to that, and since that is God's portion and inheritance, so that as they have a care of God's glory, they must also have a care of God's portion, and his peculiar treasure. The inward part of the temple was to be adorned with cherubims, to note the special attendance of the holy angels in the assemblies of the saints.*   As evil angels plot against the church, so good angels project for it.   Though in the Scripture we find angels sometimes employed in affairs of common providence, and doing good to them that are not of the church; as one is sent to comfort Hagar, and relieve Ishmael upon his cry, though he had scoffed at Isaac the heir of the covenant when he was in Abraham's family, Gen. xxi. 17; yet for the most part they were employed in the concerns of some of his special servants.   Angels thrust Lot out of Sodom, Gen. xix. 25, 26.   An angel stopped the lions' mouths when Daniel was in the den: Dan. vi. 22, 'My God hath sent his angel, and hath shut the lions' mouths.'   God employs angels in the preserving and ruining of empires, which is clear in the prophecy of Daniel, and some understand Isa. x. 34, 'And Lebanon shall fall by a mighty one,' of an angel.   As the soul sends forth a multitude of spirits swiftly into the nerves for the supply of the lowest member, which runs thither upon the least motion, so do the angels, which are God's ministers, run at the appointment of God, and are employed in all the wheels of providence. The spirit of the living creatures was in the wheels of providence, Ezek. i. 20.

First, The highest orders among them are not exempted from being officers for the church.   Though they are called God's angels in respect of their immediate attendance on God, yet they are called man's angels in respect of the service they do for them, Mat. xviii. 10, '*Their* angels do always behold the face of my Father which is in heaven.'   They are not the ordinary sort of angels which attend upon those little ones, upon young converts, humble souls, those little ones in the kingdom of heaven; but they are the highest courtiers there, such as see the face of God, and stand before him.   A king hath many servants, but not every servant, only the chief of the nobility stand before him; so they are not angels of the meanest order and rank in heaven, that are ordered to attend the lowest Christian. The apostles make no doubt of this: Heb. i. 14, 'Are they not all ministering spirits'—there is no question but they are—'sent forth to minister for them who shall be heirs of salvation?'   He asserts confidently that not one of them is blotted out of the list for this employment.   'Are they not all?'   None are exempted from the service of God, so none are exempted from the end of that service, which is the good of believers.   They are God's servants, but for the church's good, for them which shall be heirs. Are they not all?   It is irrational to deny it.   And they are sent forth, every one of them hath his commission signed by God for this purpose, and not only for the church in general, but for every member in particular; 'for the heirs of salvation.'   And not only for them which are already called and enrolled, but for them who shall be called, whose names are written in the book of God's election; 'who shall be heirs.'   And they are not only faintly sent, as if they might go if they will, but they have a strict charge to look after them well, not in one or two of their works, or ways, but in all: Ps. xci. 11, 'He shall give his angels charge over thee, to keep thee in all thy ways; to bear thee up in their hands, lest thou dash thy foot against a stone.'   They are to use all their strength to this purpose, to bear them up in their hands; as the elder children are appointed by parents to have a care of the younger in their works and motions, and to use both their widsom and strength for them.   The angels are a guard to secure them here, and at last to convey them to their Father's house, Luke xvi. 22. When a man is in favour with a prince, all the courtiers will be observant of him.

* Trap on Numb. p. 58.

Secondly, Armies of them are employed upon this occasion. There are great multitudes of them, as Bildad speaks, Job xxv. 3, 'Is there any number of his armies?' that is, of his angels. When Joel speaks of the heathens gathering together, 'Thither,' saith he, 'Lord, cause thy mighty ones to come down,' chap. iii. 11. A whole squadron of them shall attend upon a gracious man, according to the circumstances he is involved in. Gen. xxxiii. 1, 2, 'And Jacob went on his way, and the angels of God met him. And when Jacob saw them, he said, This is God's host.' Regiments of angels, enough to make up an army (for so Jacob terms them) met him upon the way, to secure his brother Esau, and to encourage him in his journey. So some interpret 2 Sam. v. 24, 'The sound of a going in the tops of the mulberry trees,' the sign of the marching of the brigade of angels, with the Lord at the head of them, for the discomfiture of David's enemies; 'then shall the Lord go out before thee, to smite the host of the Philistines.' And this they do not of their own heads, but by the pleasure of God; not only by a bare will, but a delight: Ps. ciii. 21, 'Bless the Lord, all ye his hosts; ye ministers of his, that do his pleasure.' רצונו his choicest pleasure, he delights to see this his militia upon action.

Thirdly, Christ hath the government of them to this end for his church. Angels are all put in subjection to him: Heb. ii. 7, 8, 'In that he put all in subjection under him, he left nothing that is not put under him.' He is 'exalted above all principality and power.' 'God hath put all things under his feet, and gave him to be the head over all things to the church,' Eph. i. 21, 22; all things, even principalities and powers, are put under his feet, to be commissioned and influenced by him for the good of his church: Ezek. i. 12, 'Whither the Spirit was to go, they went.' They are ordered by the Spirit of Christ to this purpose: Zech. i. 10, 'Those are they whom the Lord hath sent to walk to and fro through the earth.' They are his faithful messengers, despatched into the world by him, as scouts and spies, to take notice of the state of the world, and to give him intelligence, and an exact account of affairs, and, ver. 11, they gave an account to Christ. Christ is the head and general of them, Col. ii. 10. They are his host, always in a warlike posture, with Christ in the head of them, Zech. i. 8, upon their horses, which notes readiness to move and speed in motion: and as an host they are said to pitch their tents round about them that fear him, and are in a continual conflict with the evil angels to prevent their designs, in the behalf of Christ, whom they acknowledge as their head by their worship of him, Heb. i. 6. Christ orders them to take care to seal his servants in the foreheads, that they may be preserved in the storms which shall happen in the world at the time of the ruin of the Romish papacy, Rev. vii. 2, 3. An angel comes that had the seal of the living God (commission of God), saying, 'Hurt not the earth, nor the sea, nor the trees, till we have sealed the servants of our God in the foreheads.'

Fourthly, The great actions which have been done in the world, or shall be done for the church, are performed by them. Angels were sent as expresses by God with his great decrees concerning the revolutions of times, Dan. vii. 16; viii. 16, 'And I heard a man's voice, which called, and said, Gabriel, make this man to understand the vision.' An angel was sent to Daniel with the message of a Redeemer, and the clearest prophecy of Christ, which the Jews are not able to answer to this day, which they most startle at, Dan. ix. 21. Part of the discovery of the revelation to John, which is a standing almanac to the church, was made us by an angel, Rev. x. 8, 9; xxii. 8, 9. And when by the course of time those turnings are to happen in the world, the angels must have their share of service in them. The trumpets are sounded by angels, and the vials which are filled with the causes of such alterations, are poured out by the hands of angels. Some indeed, by the angels there mentioned, understand the visible instruments of reformation, not excluding the angels, who are the invisible ministers in the affairs of the world.*

Fifthly, They engage in this work for the church with delight; they act as God's ministers in his providence with a unanimous consent: Ezek, i. 9, ' Their wings were joined one to another;' so that they perform their office with the same swiftness, and with the same affection, without emulation to go one before another, which makes many actions succeed ill among men; but they go hand in hand. They do it with affection, both in respect of the kind disposition of their natures, and as they are fellow-members of the same body, for they are parts of the church and of the heavenly Jerusalem: Heb. xii. 22, ' Ye are come to the heavenly Jerusalem, and to an innumerable company of angels, and to the general assembly and church of the firstborn;' and therefore act out of affection to that which is a part of their body, as well as out of obedience to their head. They do it in respect of their own improvement too, and increase of their knowledge (which is the desire of all intellectual creatures); for they complete their understandings by the sight of the methods of infinite wisdom in the perfecting his gracious designs. And it is God's intent that they should grow in the knowledge of his great mystery by their employment: Eph. iii. 10, ' To the intent that now, unto the principalities and powers in heavenly places, might be known by the church the manifold wisdom of God,' *i. e.*, By the gracious works of God towards the church, and in the behalf of it, for the security and growth of the church, and in the executions of those decrees which as instruments they are employed in; for I do not understand how it can be meant of the knowledge of Christ, for that they know more than the church below can acquaint them with: for without question they have a clear insight into the offices of Christ, who is the head, and whom they are ordered to worship. They understand the aim of his death and resurrection, and can better explain the dark predictions of Scripture, than purblind man can. But by observing the methods which God uses in the accomplishment of them, they become more intelligent, and commence masters of knowledge in a higher degree, which it is probable is one reason of their joy, when they see God's infinite wisdom and grace in the conversion of a sinner; without affection to them, and their employment about them, they could not rejoice so much. And their rejoicing in their first bringing in to God, argues their joy in all their employments which concerns their welfare.

(2.) As all good things, so all bad things are ordered by providence for the good of the church. That which in its own nature is an injury, by God's ordering puts on the nature of a mercy; and what is poison in itself, by the almighty art becomes a sovereign medicine. Are God's dispensations in their own nature destructive? That wise physician knows how to make poisons work the effect of purges. Are they sharp? It is to humble and purge the church. As shadows serve to set out the pictures, so the darkest passages of providence are made by God to commend the beauty of those glorious things he works for his church. We may see this in,

[1.] Bad persons. As,

First, The devil. God manageth him for his own glory, and the strengthening of believers. Mat. viii. 31, 32, the devils desired to enter into the herd of swine, with an intent, probably, not only to destroy the swine, but to incense the Gadarenes against him, out of whom they had been cast, to do

* Lightfoot, Temple. chap. 38, p. 253, 256.

him some considerable mischief. But what is the issue? As they discover their malice, so they enhance the value of Christ's kindness to the distressed man, whom he had freed from this tyranny. Hereby also was the law of God justified in commanding the Jews to abstain from swine's flesh, which the Gadarenes, being apostate Jews, had broken; he magnified his own power in the routing such a number of unclean spirits, which had not been so conspicuous in the turning them out of one man, had not this regiment discovered themselves among the swine, and brought such a loss upon the Gadarenes, whereby as they shewed their own strength and malice, so they discovered occasionally the greatness of Christ's charity, and his power over them; so that in granting the malicious petition of this exasperated legion, the law of God is justified, our Saviour's love glorified, his power manifested, and a foundation laid for the gaining proselytes in that country, to which purpose he left the man he had cured, Luke viii. 39, and to strengthen the faith of those poor believers which then followed him. God makes use of the devils by the sovereignty of providence, to bring about ends unknown to themselves, for all their wisdom. The malice of the devil against Job hath rendered him a standing miracle of patience for ever. They are the 'rulers of the darkness of this world,' Eph. vi. 12, not of the light of the world; they are the rulers of the wicked, and the scullions of the saints, to scour and cleanse them. They are the rulers of the world, but subordinate to serve the providence of God, wherein God declares his wisdom by serving himself of the worst of his enemies. The devil thought he had brought a total destruction upon mankind when he persuaded our first parents to eat of the forbidden fruit, but the only wise God ordered it to bring about a greater glory to himself, and a more firm stability to his people, in introducing an everlasting covenant which could not be broken, and establishing their happiness upon surer terms than it was settled in paradise; and afterwards in filling the heart of Judas to betray Christ, and the hearts of the Jews to crucify him. Even by that way whereby he thought to hinder the good of mankind, he occasionally promotes their perpetual redemption; and I do not much question but those very principles which the devil had distilled into the Gentile world, of shedding human blood in sacrifices for expiation of guilt, and the gods conversing with men in human ways, and the imagination of the intercessions of demons for them,—the first out of rage against mankind, and both that and the other to induce them to idolatry,—might facilitate the entertainment of Christ as the great expiatory sacrifice, and the receiving of him as the Son of God, though in an human shape, and the belief of his intercession. God overreaches the devil, and makes him instrumental for good where he designs hurt and mischief.

Secondly, Wicked men. All the wicked in the midst of the church are for the good of it, either for the exercise of their grace, or security of their persons, or interest: Prov. xvi. 7, 'When a man's ways please the Lord, he will make his enemies to be at peace with him.' Sometimes he will incline their hearts intentionally to favour, or order even their actions against them to procure their peace, contrary to their intentions. Sometimes God makes them his sword to cut his people, sometimes physic to purge them, sometimes fire to melt and refine them, sometimes hedges to preserve them, sometimes a ransom to redeem them, Prov. xxi. 18. A traveller makes use of the mettle of a headstrong horse to carry him to his journey's end. That wind which would overturn a little boat, the skilful pilot makes use of to drive his ship into the harbour, and the husbandman to cleanse his corn from the chaff. Though the ends of the workers, viz., God and wicked men, are different, yet the end of the work is but one, which is ordered by

God's sovereign pleasure. It was promised in the promise of the gospel to the Gentiles: Gen. ix. 27, ' God shall enlarge Japhet, and he shall dwell in the tents of Shem, and Canaan shall be his servant.' God shall allure Japhet, the Gentiles of Europe, to dwell in the tents of Shem, and Canaan the head of the cursed posterity, shall be servants to the church beside their will, and sometimes against it, by an overruling hand. And Christ hath bought them to be his servants: 2 Peter ii. 1, ' Denying the Lord that bought them,' and therefore hath the disposing of them, whether they voluntarily give up themselves to him or no. He is a Lord by purchase over them, who own him not as a Saviour. The hatred of the church's enemies sometimes conduceth more to her good than the affections of all her worldly friends. Now this appears,

First, In furthering the gospel. The Jews, who speak not of Christ among themselves, but with opprobrious terms,* have been the exact pre-servers of the Old Testament, even to the very number of the letters, wherein Christians have sufficient to confirm them in the belief of Christ's being the Messiah, and unanswerable arguments against their adversaries ; whereupon St Austin terms them *capsarios ecclesiæ*, such that carry the books of the children of great men after them to school. When the authority of the Revelation was anciently questioned, the Church of Rome was instru-mental to keep it in the number of the canonical books, not thinking they should find their own church so plainly deciphered in it to be the mother of abominations. To this we may refer the action of Ptolemy Philadelphus, king of Egypt, in causing the Scripture to be translated about three hundred years before the coming of Christ, through which the nations† might better discern (as it were through a prospective glass) the new star of Jacob which was shortly to arise. No doubt but many of the Gentiles, by com-paring the old Scripture prophecies, which they could read in the Greek language, might be more easily induced to an embracing the gospel, and acknowledging Christ to be the Messiah, when it came to be divulged among them. Herod is the cause of the consultation about the place of Christ's birth, not for any goodwill he had to him whom he intended to murder, but God makes use of this to clear up the truth of the prophecy concerning Bethlehem, the place of his birth: Mat. ii. 6, ' Out of thee shall come a Governor that shall rule my people Israel.' And they certainly were not very good who preached Christ out of envy, and propagated the gospel, wherein Paul rejoiced ; not in their sin, but in the providential fruit of it : Philip. i. 15, 18, ' Some indeed preach Christ even of envy and strife. What then ? notwithstanding, every way, whether in pretence or truth, Christ is preached ; and I therein do rejoice, yea, and will rejoice.'

Secondly, In furthering the temporal good of the church.

(1.) In its preservation. Wicked men are often serviceable to the church, as the filthy raven was to holy Elijah, or as the lion which would have devoured Samson is a storehouse to provide him food ; for in his hunger he finds a table spread in the belly of his enemy. Pharaoh's design was to destroy Israel, and the daughter of that irreconcilable enemy is directed to preserve Moses, who was to be the ruin of her family, the destruction of the Egyptian glory, and the deliverer of the church. She saves him out of charity, and God out of a wise design ; she, by his education in the Egyptian learning, fits him for the court, and God for the deliverance of his church. Egypt had corn to relieve, first Abraham, Gen. xii. 10, after-ward Jacob in a time of famine, the family wherein the church of God was only then bound up. Herod lies in wait for Christ's destruction, and Egypt,

* Helvicus contra Judæos.   † Jackson, vol. i. fol. f, p. 62.

the most idolatrous country in the world, and an ancient enemy to God's church, affords him shelter, God makes 'Moab to hide his outcasts and be their covert from the face of the spoiler,' Isa. xvi. 3, 4. Some think God's design in sending Jonah to Nineveh to work so remarkable a change by repentance, was to soften some of their hearts, and the hearts of their posterity, to deal more tenderly with those gracious Israelites, who, in the captivity of the ten tribes some years after, should be their guests, God making thereby provision for his own people in that common judgment which should come upon the nation. This God doth sometimes by reviving the law of nature and the common sentiments of religion in the hearts of natural men, whereby their own consciences, bearing witness to the innocency and excellency of the church of God, put them upon thoughts for its security. Sometimes it is above their own sphere and besides their own intentions. The whale which swallowed Jonah intended him as a morsel to quell his hunger, but proves his security, and disgorgeth him upon the shore; they understand their own aim, but not the design of God. The leech that sucks the patient's blood knows not the chirurgeon's design, who useth it for the cure of a disease. Sometimes their rage proves their own ruin, and the church's safety; as the leech bursts itself sometimes, and saves the patient. The very earth, whereby is meant the carnal world, is said to help the woman, the church, by swallowing up the flood which the dragon casts out of his mouth against her, Rev. xii. 16, just as the old rags were the instruments whereby Jeremiah was drawn out of the dungeon.

(2.) In the advancement of the church or persons eminent. Abner had a plot for bringing Israel to David's sceptre, which concurred both with God's purpose and promises, but sprung from an ill cause, a disdain to be checked by Ishbosheth, though his king, for an unjustifiable act, for having too much familiarity with one of Saul's concubines, 2 Sam. iii. 6–10. And from this animosity he contrives the deposing of Ishbosheth, and the exaltation of David; yet dissembles the ground, and pretends the promise of God to David, ver. 18, 'For the Lord hath spoken of David, By the hand of my servant David I will save my people Israel out of the hand of the Philistines.' He is the first engine that moves in this business, and by him and his correspondents after his death, ver. 17, the business is brought about by God's overruling hand, wherein God's promise is accomplished, and David a type of Christ, and the great champion for the church against its enemies round about is advanced. Very remarkable is the advancement of Mordecai, in order to the advancing of the Jews as well as preserving them, when the necks of all the visible church God had in the world were upon the block. Haman ignorantly is the cause of this preferment of Mordecai, and at that time too when he came to petition for his death: Esther vi. 4, 'He was come to speak to the king to hang Mordecai upon the gallows which he had prepared for him.' The king asks him what should be done to the man whom the king delights to honour, ver. 16. He imagineth that the king's question did respect himself, lays out a scheme of what honour he was ambitious of, ver. 8, 9, which was by the king designed for Mordecai, and Haman made the herald to proclaim him. Here Haman, not only a wicked man in himself, but the greatest enemy Mordecai and the whole church of God had, is made unwittingly an instrument to exalt Mordecai, and in him the whole church of God.

(3.) In enriching the church, or some persons in it, whereby it may become more serviceable to God. How wonderful was it, that when the Israelites were abominated by the Egyptians, God should so order their hearts that the Egyptians should lend them gold and jewels, Exod. xii. 35, 36, and dismiss them with wealth as well as safety, and not so much as one person molest them till they arrived at the Red Sea! The very gain and honour of the enemies is sometimes consecrated to the Lord of the whole earth: Micah iv. 13, 'Arise and thresh, O daughter of Zion; I will make thy horn iron, and thou shalt beat in pieces many people: and I will consecrate their gain unto the Lord, and their substance to the Lord of the whole earth.' This was when many nations were gathered against Sion, ver. 11; 'the wealth of the sinner is laid up for the just,' Prov. xiii. 22. And God sometimes makes the wicked, unwittingly to themselves, in their carking, be the factors for good men, into whose lap providence pours the fruit of their labour. God gave Cyrus the spoils of Babylon and the treasures of Crœsus, to enable him to furnish the Jews with materials for building the temple: Isa. xlv. 3, 4, 'And I will give thee the treasures of darkness, and hidden treasures of secret places (speaking of Cyrus), that thou mayest know that I the Lord which call thee by thy name, am the God of Israel, for Jacob my servant's sake,' &c. That he might acknowledge him the God of Israel, and lay his wealth out in the service of God, and the service of Jacob his servant.

Thirdly, As bad persons, so bad things are ordered to the good of the church, whether they be sinful evils or afflictive.

1. Sin.

(1.) A man's own sin. Onesimus runs from his master, and finds a spiritual father; his being a runagate is the occasion of his being a convert. By flying from his master he becomes a brother in the Lord, Philem. 10, 12, 16. What Joseph's brethren sinfully intended for revenge against their brother, and security from their father's checks (who acquainted Jacob with their miscarriages), God ordered for the preservation of them who were the only visible church in the world. Their sin against their brother, contrary both to their intentions and expectations, became the means of their safety. God makes the remainder of sin in a good man an occasion to exercise his grace, discover his strength, and shew his loyalty to God.

(2.) Other men's sins. That might be in Sarah but a heady passion, for hearing her son mocked by Ishmael, that made her so desirous to have the bond-woman and her first son thrust out, Gen. xxi. 10; but God makes use of it to make a separation between Isaac, the heir of the covenant, and Ishmael, that he might not be corrupted by an evil example from him; God orders Abraham to hearken to her voice, because in Isaac his seed should be called, ver. 12. And the revengeful threatening of Esau was the occasion of Jacob's flight, whereby he was hindered from marrying with any of the people of the land, by whom he might have been induced to idolatry, Gen. xxvii. 43, 46. Why should we mistrust that God that can make use of the lusts of men to bring about his own gracious purposes?

2. Commotions in the world. There is the eye of God, that eye which runs to and fro throughout the whole earth in the wheels of worldly motions, even in the most dreadful providences in the world that stare upon men with a grim countenance: Ezek. i. 18, 'Their wings were dreadful, and their wings were full of eyes.' All the overturnings in the world are subservient to the church's interest, though they are not visibly so, unless diligently attended.* God orders the confusions of the world, and is in the midst of the tumults of the people: Ps. xxix. 10, 11, 'The Lord sits upon the. flood; yea, the Lord sits King for ever. The Lord will give strength to his people; the Lord will bless his people with peace.' He sits upon the flood as a charioteer in his chariot, guiding it with holy and merciful intentions to his people, to give them both strength and peace in the midst of them, and

* Broughton on Rev. xiii. sect. 177.

as the issue of them. By water and floods is frequently meant tumults and confusions in the world. If it were not so, why should our Saviour encourage his disciples, and all their successors in the same profession, to lift up their heads when they hear of wars, if their redemption were not designed by God in them? Luke xxi. 25-28; they are all testimonies of the nearer approaches of Christ in power and glory to judge the earth, and glorify his people. God's great end in the shaking of nations is the performing those gracious promises to his church which yet remained unaccomplished. These earthquakes in the world will bring heaven to the church. The great revolutions in the eastern part of the world, the ruin of the Babylonian empire, the erecting the Persian, and all the means whereby it was brought about, God ordered, God foretold, God directed, for Jacob's service. Cyrus, led by ambition, levies an army against Babylon; yet though he was a ravenous bird he was to execute the counsel of God: Isa. xlvi. 11, 'Calling a ravenous bird from the east, the man that executeth my counsel,' to be an instrument for the delivery of the captived Jews, and the restorer of the ruined temple. He had called him out by name to make a great revolution of the world. He foretold by his prophet Isaiah many years before, the means he should use in the siege of Babylon to attain the victory, the very dividing Euphrates, which was the great confidence of the Babylonian: Isa. xliv. 27, 'That say to the deep, Be dry; and I will dry up the rivers;' whereby it was as it were dried up for them to pass over the very opening of the gates: Isa. xlv. 1, 'And the gates shall not be shut;' the Babylonians in a presumptuous security had left them open, thinking it impossible the city could be taken, because of the river Euphrates: 'I will go before thee, and make the crooked places straight;' and what was the end of that great revolution and motion in that part of the world? See Isa. xlv. 4, 'For Jacob my servant's sake, and Israel, mine elect, I have even called thee by thy name.' This prophecy was when Jerusalem and the temple were standing. God casts about long before his people needs, for their welfare in the great revolutions and changes of the world. In Isa. xliv. 28, 'That saith of Cyrus, He is my shepherd, and shall perform all my pleasure; even saying to Jerusalem, Thou shalt be built; and to the temple, Thy foundation shall be laid.' Cyrus had no knowledge of this end of God, 'though thou hast not known me,' Isa. xlv. 4, 5, twice repeated. Cyrus did not know God, neither did he know God's end; he acts his own purposes, and is acted by God to higher purposes than he understood. In all the siftings of nations, and sifting the church among the nations, as corn is sifted in a sieve, God designs not the destruction of his people, but the cleansing them, the separating the flour from the bran.

3. Destroying judgments, yea, and the very curses sometimes are turned into blessings.

Destroying judgments. The desolation of the Jews was not only in order to the fulfilling God's truth in his threatenings, but useful for the great gospel design; the fall of the Jews was the calling of the Gentiles: Rom. xi. 11, 12, 'Through their fall salvation is come unto the Gentiles.' And also their fall and dispersion among the Gentiles was prophesied of as the occasion of their return to God: Ezek. xx. 36, 37, 'Like as I pleaded with your fathers in the wilderness, so will I plead with you; and cause you to pass under the rod, and bring you into the bond of the covenant;' when they are in the wilderness of captivity, then God shall plead with them, and make them to pass under the rod of propriety, and bring them into covenant. The like also is prophesied of that captivity of the ten tribes to this day, not known where they are: Hosea ii. 14, the time of God's speaking kindly to her should be in the wilderness, and then ' I will give her the valley of Achor for a door of hope.' No question but God hath performed his promise, and brought many of the posterity of the ten tribes into the church among the mass of the Gentiles, among whom they were dispersed.

Curses sometimes, as God orders them, prove blessings. The curse of inspired Jacob upon Levi,—Gen. xlix. 7, ' Cursed be their anger, for it was fierce ; and their wrath, for it was cruel : I will divide them in Jacob, and scatter them in Israel,'—was the advantage both of Levi and the Israelites ; that they were dispersed among the several tribes without any universal cohabitation as the rest, was a curse ; but that they should be the instructors of the people in the matters of the law, was an honour God put upon the head of that tribe, and a public blessing to the people.

4. Divisions in the church. One would think this of all other things should shake the foundation of it ; yet God orders even these to the good of the church. Paul and Barnabas, two great apostles, fell out, Acts xv. 36–39, &c. ; the contention comes to be very sharp, a thing naturally of very ill consequence in two of the prime guides of Christianity, and at the laying the first foundation of it ; but the gospel gains ground, one sails to Cyprus, and the other travels into Syria. Perhaps had not this quarrel been between them, and they thus disjointed from one another, some of those poor souls had never, or at least not so soon, have heard of the gospel mercy.

5. Persecutions. These naturally tend to the dissolution and utter extirpation of it, but God orders them otherwise. God doth often lay the scene of his amazing providences in very dismal afflictions ; as the limner first puts on the dusky colours on which he intends to draw the portraiture of some illustrious beauty. The oppression of Israel immediately before their deliverance was the dusky colour whereupon God drew those gracious lines of their salvation from Egypt, the pattern of all the after deliverances of the church in all ages, and a type of our spiritual redemption by Christ. The humiliation, persecution, and death of the Son of God, was the dusky colour upon which God drew that amazing piece of divine love and wisdom in man's salvation, which the eyes of saints and angels will be fixed on with ravishing admirations to all eternity. All afflictions in the world, which God doth exercise the church with, are parts of his providence, and like mournful notes in music, which make the melody of the tune more pleasant, and set off those sweeter airs which follow upon them. Afflictions here cause the joys of heaven to appear more glorious in the eyes of glorified saints. The persecutions of the martyrs did but heighten their graces, send them to the place of rest, and enlarge their robes of glory. God many times saves his people by sufferings, and brings them to the shore upon the planks of a broken ship, and makes that which was the occasion of their loss to be a means of their safety ; they sometimes evidence that which they would destroy. Herod's murdering the children, to destroy him that was born king of the Jews, made his birth more conspicuous in the world ; snuffing the candle makes it burn the clearer.

They sometimes make,

1. To the improvement of the church. One of the sorest judgments God brought upon the Jewish church is expressly asserted by God to be for their good : Jer. xxiv. 5, speaking of the captived Jews, ' Whom I have sent out of this place into the land of the Chaldeans for their good.' The Chaldeans had overrun their land, carried them captives, made them slaves, destroyed the temple ; yet God tells them this was for their good, when there was no present appearance of any good in it. It should be good in respect of God's favour towards them, which retired to return with the greater force : ver. 6,

' I will set mine eyes upon them for good ; I will build them, and not pull them down.' God will give them a more durable settlement. In respect also of that frame of heart they should have toward God, their knowledge of him and cleaving to him, ver. 7, ' I will give them a heart to know me ; and they shall return to me with their whole heart.' God had but a moiety of their hearts before, but then he should have the whole. And indeed it was remarkably for their good ; for they who before were addicted to idolatry were never guilty of the same sin after ; and God kept them from being drawn away to it by the example and solicitation of those among whom they were. The church grows by tears and withers by smiles. God's vine thrives the better for pruning. God makes our persecutions fit us for that for which we are persecuted ; as Saul by his persecution of David for the title God had given him to the kingdom, made him fitter to succeed him in the throne, and manage the government. God uses persecutors as lances, which, whiles they wound us, let out the purulent and oppressive matter ; and makes them instruments of his providence to work out his people's happiness, and thus makes the very wrath of man to be an occasion of his people's praise : Ps. lxxvi. 10, ' The wrath of man shall praise thee.' God doth in this as a father deals with his son, sends him to a sharp school, that he may be trained up in learning.

2. In the increase of the church. The Jews crucified our Saviour to diminish the multitude of his followers, and by this means the number is increased. The whole world runs after him by that means they used to stop their course, which Christ foretold, that when he was lifted up he should draw all men after him ; and that a grain of corn brings not forth more seed unless it be cast into the ground and die.

1. In the increase of it within its own bounds. When the Israelites were most oppressed in Egypt, the more they multiplied, Exod. i. 20. When the dragon's fury did most swell against the woman, she brought forth a man child, Rev. xii. 1, 3, 4. When the Roman empire was at the highest, and was most inflamed with anger against the Christians ; when the learning of the philosophers, the witchcrafts of heretics, the power of the emperors, and the strength of the whole world was set against them, the Christians grew more flourishing and numerous by those very means which were used to destroy them. Not only a new succession of saints sprung up from the martyrs' ashes, but their flames were the occasion of warming some so much with a heavenly fire, that some persecutors have become preachers. Their very bonds for the truth have sometimes a seminal virtue in them to beget men to faith in Christ : Philip. i. 12, ' The things which have happened unto me, have fallen out rather to the furtherance of the gospel.'

2. In the increase of it in other parts. Paul's prison made his preaching famous in Rome, and was an occasion of bringing Christianity into Nero's court, that monster of mankind, Philip. i. 13, iv. 22 ; one might have looked for saints in hell as soon ; his bonds were as great a confirmation of the truth of his doctrine as his eloquence. When Saul made havoc of the church, and by that storm dispersed the Christians, they, like so many grains of corn scattered in several parts of a greater field, produced the greater harvest : Acts viii. 3, 4, ' Therefore they that were scattered abroad went everywhere preaching the word.' As clouds scattered by the winds, they rained down the gospel in several quarters. The Jews when scattered in their several flights did scatter among the heathen the notions of the true religion. When they shall go down to Egypt to secure themselves from Sennacherib's invasion, they shall be a means to make many converts among that idolatrous nation : Isa. xix. 18, ' In that day ' (the day of the Jews'

trouble) ' shall five cities in the land of Egypt speak the language of Canaan, and swear to the Lord of hosts ;' so one expounds it, but I rather think it meant of the times of the gospel. The flight of the Israelites shall be the occasion of some Egyptians' conversion. A poor slave in Naaman's family was an occasion both of the cure of his body and of that of his soul, 2 Kings v. 2, 3, 17. So much for the first reason, drawn from an enumeration of things.

Reason 2. To prove that all providence is for the good of the church, is, because God hath sometimes preferred mercy to the church, and care of it, above his own concernments of justice. He values his mercy to them above his justice upon his enemies. He consults their safety before he brings ruin upon the wicked whose sins are full. He first prepared the ark for Noah, and sees him lodged in it before he begins to shower down destruction upon the world. He hath sometimes punished a nation more for their offences against his people, than their sins against himself. Amalek was guilty of many idolatries and other sins against God, but God chargeth none of them upon them but their malicious hindering the Israelites in their march to Canaan : 1 Sam. xv. 2, ' Thus saith the Lord of hosts, I remember that which Amalek did to Israel, how he laid wait for him in the way, when he came up from Egypt.' He shews his love to them, and how much he values them, that when he is acting justice and pouring out his wrath, when he is (as it were) cutting and slashing on all sides, and is in fury with wicked men, he hath nothing but sweetness and tenderness towards his own. Amos ix. 9, 10, in the sifting of Israel and the nations ' Not the least grain shall fall upon the earth. All the sinners of my people shall die by the sword.' While he thunders out his fury upon wicked men, he hath his eyes upon the least grain of the true Israel. What would it be for God, when he is raising the glory of his justice upon the people that have provoked him, not to regard the concernments of this or that, or many sincere souls, but put no stop to his fury ? Yet he doth, not a grain shall perish. He is more desirous to hear of the preservation and welfare of a few righteous, than of the just punishment of the wicked wherein his justice is gloriously interested. The man clothed with linen, that was to mark the mourners, returned to God and gave an account that he had done according to his command, Ezek. ix. 11 ; the other five, which were to kill, returned not to give any account of their severe and sharp proceedings. The angels that held the four winds of the earth, Rev. vii. 1, which some understand of wars and commotions in the world for the overthrow of the Romish power, were ordered not to let the winds go till the servants of God were sealed in their foreheads.

Reason 3. God takes particular notice of the meanest of his people, and mightily condescends to them, much more of the church. It is strange to consider that the Scripture mentions none of those great potentates among the heathen, but either as they were instruments of his people's good, or executioners of his justice upon them, or subjects of his people's triumph. Cyrus and Darius are mentioned as their friends ; Nebuchadnezzar, and Sennacherib, and others, as God's instruments in scourging them ; Chedorlaomer and the other kings with him, as they were the subjects of Abraham's valour and triumph, Gen. xiv. 9, 10. He takes no notice of the names of any in his word but upon such accounts ; Cyrus and Nebuchadnezzar had done no doubt many actions before, but none taken notice of but those; but he takes notice of the meanest wherein was grace, and the meanest of their concerns and actions.* He mentions in his word Jacob's flocks, &c., things of no great moment, the actions, speeches, gestures of his people, to shew

* Rivet in Gen. exercit, 129.

how his providence wrought for them, and how much he is concerned in the least of their affairs; but the great empires of the world, their original and progress, and the magnified founders of them, he speaks not of but as they have some relation or other to his people. As we love to use the names of our friends, so doth God love the relish of the names of his servants. The name of Noah is repeated several times, as the Jews observe, Gen. vii., viii. The Spirit of God loves the very mention of their names, he delights to dwell upon the catalogue of their names. The Scripture uses to reckon the genealogies of wicked men in short characters. Cain's generation is numbered in haste, as if God had no care at all of them, Gen. iv. 17, 18; he puts them off with a kind of &c. But he insists much upon the generation of the godly. Seth's posterity are written in a large scroll and more legible hand, Gen. v., with the number of the years which they lived, which in Cain's posterity there is no notice taken of. His whole respect, his heart, his eye, his all is fixed upon them. And Christ himself stands more astonished and wondering at the faith of the centurion, the importunity of the Canaanitish woman, condescends to them to grant them what they would have. You never find him taking notice of the learning of the rabbis, the magnificence of Herod, or the glorious building of the temple. See how condescending God is, to work a miracle for the support and strengthening of a weak faith, and the peevish distrust of his people. Gideon's faith was weak, yet how compassionate is God towards him (Judges vi. 36, &c., he would have one time the fleece dry, another time wet; God condescends to them in all), in ordering his providence as Gideon would have it, without upbraiding him, just as a tender mother cherishes a weak child! And this miracle was in order to the church's deliverance from a present oppressive enemy. Certainly when we find God taking care and ordering even the very pins, snuffers, and basins of the temple, the place of his worship, as well as the more stately ornaments of it, we may say, Doth his care extend to the meanest utensils in his temple, and not much more to the worshippers in it? Doth he give order for the candlesticks, and will he not have much more care of the lights in them? His care to the least implies his care of the greatest too. In a building, the little stones must be well laid as well as the greatest. Every believer is a stone in the spiritual building.

Reason 4. God reveals often to his people what he will do in the world, as if he seemed to ask their advice; and therefore surely all his providences shall work for their good. God would not surely acquaint them, and advise with them what he should do, did he intend to do anything to their hurt. There is not anything in the heart of Christ wherein the church is concerned but he doth reveal it to them: John xv. 15, 'I have called you friends; for all things I have heard of my Father I have made known to you.' He discovered all to them, the ends of his coming, his Father's love, his death, and resurrection, what he would do after his ascension, the progress of his affairs, and the glory of heaven, and the end of all. John must be the penman of the Revelation which concerned the future state of the church in all ages. Joseph must know the interpretation of dreams in order to the church's preservation. Moses must be acquainted with God's methods in the Israelites' deliverance, with the Egyptians' ruin. Daniel must know the future state of the eastern parts of the world; he must know the turnings of the times, and the end of the world, Dan. x. 11, 19, 20. It is to Noah, and none else, that he immediately discovers his intended destruction of the world. And all those revelations ended in his people's advantage; nay, he doth not only reveal, but as it were consult with him in his affairs. God doth as it were unbosom himself to Abraham, as one friend to another; as it were adviseth with him concerning his intention on Sodom: Gen. xviii. 17, 'And the Lord said, Shall I hide from Abraham the thing which I do?' *i. e.* I will by no means do it, it will not consist with my love and friendship to him to hide anything from him. And see the reason of it: ver. 18, 'Seeing that Abraham shall surely become a great and mighty nation, and all the nations of the earth shall be blessed in him.' It was, first, his great affection to him, because he had advanced him, and promised that a mighty nation should spring out of his loins. And he had not withheld from him the secret of giving the Messias, which was a universal blessing, and so many ages were to run out before it was to be accomplished; he had discovered to him his acts of mercy, and therefore would not hide from him his acts of justice, he would know his mind in it and what he thought of it. And you know the story, how God regulated himself by Abraham's prayer, and denied him nothing, till Abraham left off suing any more. It would make one conjecture, that if Abraham had proceeded farther, he had quite diverted the judgment from Sodom. And when the Israelites had provoked God by a golden calf, he would not do anything against them till he had consulted Moses, and therefore lays the whole case before him, and seeks to take him off from pleading with the Lord, and promising to make of him a great nation (Exod. xxxii. 9, 10, 'And the Lord said to Moses, I have seen this people, and, behold, it is a stiff-necked people: now therefore let me alone, that my wrath may wax hot against them'), and in such terms that one would wonder at: 'Now therefore let me alone;' as if God did fear Moses's interposition would prevent him and dissuade him from it. Do not you stand in the way; my wrath will cool if you interpose yourself; as much as to say, God could not do it unless Moses gave his consent; Moses would not be quiet, but pleads the providences of God, which had been all for him, the promise of God made to Abraham concerning them. And he would not leave till God repented of the evil which he thought to do unto his people, ver. 14. If angels, as Calvin saith, are God's counsellor in heaven, believers are (as it were) his counsellors on earth.

5. God has given the choicest things he hath to his people; he hath given his law. The church is the sphere wherein the light of the gospel is fixed, and wherein it shines, from whence its beams do dart out to others: Isa. ii. 3, 'Out of Sion shall go forth the law.' The oracles of God, the great things of the law, as it is phrased, Hosea viii. 12, his covenant, and the counsel of his will, are entrusted with the church. Now, this being a mercy which exceeds all other things in the world, is therefore comprehensive of all other, as the greater comprehends the lesser. And the psalmist considers it as the top-stone of all blessings; for after summing up the providences of God, he shews how God had distinguished Jacob by more eminent marks of his favour: Ps. cxlvii. 19, 20, 'He shews his word to Jacob, his statutes and his judgments unto Israel. He hath not dealt so with any nation;' he hath not left so rich a legacy to any, or given any so much of his heart. Others are ordered by the word of his power (for that is meant by *word* in the foregoing verse), but Jacob hath the word of his grace too. And this being the choicest piece of affection which God hath shewed to the church, implies the making all lesser providences subservient to it. The church, wherein God hath laid up his gospel, and those souls which are as the ark wherein God hath deposited his law, shall be shadowed with the wings of his merciful providence, in a perpetual succession of all true blessings. All the providences of God are to preserve his law in the

world; his severest judgments are to quicken up the law of nature in men
that know no other, and the law of his gospel in men that sit under it.
And he hath given Christ to his church, and thereby hath given an earnest
that still their good shall be promoted. It is not to be thought that God
will spare anything else, when he hath given them his Son.

The second thing. It must needs be that all providences is for the good
of the church.

1. All the providence of God is for the glorifying his grace in Christ.
The whole economy or dispensation of the fulness of time, to the latter ages
of the world, is for the gathering of all things together in him: Eph. i. 10,
'That in the dispensation of the fulness of time he might gather together in
one all things in Christ, both which are in heaven, and which are in earth,
even in him;' in him as their head. This was the design in all his dispensations, both before his coming and since, ever since the promise made to
Adam, though it be more manifest in the latter age. This the apostle
represents as the main purpose of God, ver. 9. This was the mystery of
his will, which accordingly to his good pleasure he had purposed in himself,
that is, purposed in himself as a thing he was mightily pleased with; and,
ver. 11, saith he, he works all things after, or κατὰ, 'according to the
counsel of his own will,' or of that purpose which he had purposed in himself, to gather all things in one in Christ. All the things that God acts are
referred to this as their end, and ordered by this counsel as their rule. As
it was the design of God's providence to make way for Christ's entrance
into the world, and all the prophecies in the Old Testament tended to the
discovery of it, so since the coming of Christ the end of all is to advance
him in respect of his headship: Eph. i. 22, 23, 'And hath put all things
under his feet, and gave him to be the head over all things to the church,
which is his body, the fulness of him that fills all in all.' God would
advance Christ to the highest pitch, ver. 21, far above all principality and
power, both in this world and in the world to come; and there is still a
fulness wanting to Christ to complete him,—not any personal fulness, but a
fulness belonging to him as head, which is the advancement God designs
him. He is already advanced above all principality and power; he is
already given as a head to the church, but the completeness of it is not till
all his members be perfected, to which all his providences in the world doth
ultimately tend. Therefore if the design of God be to honour Christ, and
if the spiritual happiness of the church be part of that glory and fulness of
Christ, it must needs be carried on by God, else he will want part of his
completeness as a head. But this shall not be wanting, since, as all things
are squared according to that counsel of glorifying Christ as head, so all
things are acted for believers by that power whereby he raised Christ from
the grave to be their head, which power is the copy according to which all
acts which respect the church are framed: ver. 19, 'And what is the
exceeding greatness of his power to us-ward who believe, according to the
working of his mighty power, which he wrought in Christ when he raised
him up from the dead.' God intended the good of the church in this very act
of glorifying Christ, for he is made the 'head over all things to the church;'
as if God then had prescribed him that order, that the glory he gave him
should be also managed for the church's interest. Christ is Lord of the
rest of the world, but head of the church. All things are under his feet,
but are not his members; he is head over all things to the church, and
therefore to every member of the church, the least as well as the greatest;
and to the whole church, even that part of it which is on earth, as well as
that part which is in heaven, who are completed. This church is the ful-

ness of Christ, he would be bodiless without it; therefore since Christ will be a head without a body if the church be not preserved, in order to the preservation of it, all things must necessarily concur by the wise disposal of affairs. Therefore since they are travelling to be where their head is, he having the government of the world, will make all things contribute assistance to them in their journey. That Christ may have that completeness of glory which God intends him, he expressly tells his Father that he is glorified in his people: John xvii. 10, 'And I am glorified in them.' And at the sound of the seventh trumpet, 'the kingdoms of this world are to become the kingdoms of the Lord and of his Christ, and he shall reign for ever and ever,' Rev. xi. 15. Now, since all the motions in the world are that the kingdoms of the world may become the kingdoms of his Christ, peculiarly his, as being anointed King by him, it must needs be that all things must be subservient one time or other to this end, wherein the good of his people doth consist; otherwise they would not bless God so highly for it as they do: ver. 17, 'We give thee thanks, O Lord God Almighty; because thou hast taken to thee thy great power, and hast reigned.' And where there is a resistance of this glory of Christ, it is a natural effect of that decree whereby Christ is constituted King, that the resisters should be broken in pieces, and dashed like a potter's vessel, Ps. ii. 6, 9; and the issue of all is the blessedness of those that put their trust in him, ver. 12. The care that God hath of Christ and the church in the types of them, seems to be equal. The ark, which was a type of Christ, and the table of shew-bread, a figure of the church, had three coverings, whereas all the rest of the vessels, &c., belonging to the ceremonial part, had but two, Num. iv. 5–8. On the ark there was the veil, and covering of badgers' skins, and a covering of blue; on the table of shew-bread there was a cloth of blue, a cloth of sclarlet, and a covering of badgers' skins. God orders as much for the security of the church as for the security of Christ, therefore the same things that tend to the glorifying of Christ shall tend to the advantage of the church.

2. God hath given the power of the providential administration of things to Christ, to this very end, for the good of the church. If God had constituted him head over all things to the church, can there be any doubt but that he will manage the government for that which is the principal end of his government, which he hath shed his blood for, and which is chiefly intended by God who appointed him?

(1.) All power of government is given to Christ : Mat. xi. 27, ' All things are delivered to me of my Father.' And, John v. 22, ' The Father judges no man, but hath committed all judgment to the Son,' that is, the whole government and administration of affairs. It is not to be understood of the last judgment, for then it would be a limitation of that word all; not that the Father lays aside all care of things, but as the Father discovers himself only in him, so he governs things only by him. All this power was committed to him upon his interposition after the fall of man. He was made Lord and Christ, that is, anointed by God to the government of the world; for, upon the fall, God as a rector, had overturned all. Man could not with any comfort have treated with the Father, had not Christ stepped in and pleaded for the creation, whereupon God commits all judgment to the Son, that he might temper it. It was by Christ as a covenanting mediator, that the earth was established, Isa. xlix. 8. He had this government anciently, and it was confirmed to him upon his death: Heb. i. 3, ' Who being the brightness of his glory, and the express image of his person, and upholding all things by the word of his power.' Calvin understands the first word not only of the deity of Christ, but of the discovery the Father made of himself in and through him as a mediator. The latter words some understand both of his providential and mediatory kingdom : ' by the word of his power :' this, say some, is referred to the Father, whose image Christ is, as acting by a delegated authority and commission from his Father; others, to Christ, as, that Christ upholds or bears up all things by his own powerful word. Calvin thinks both may be taken, but embraceth the second as being more generally received.

I may offer, whether it may not be meant also of the powerful interposition of Christ as mediator, whose interest in God was so great, that he kept up the world by his powerful intercession, when all was forfeited ; and God put it, upon that interposition, into his hands, as ' heir of all things' (who having a hand with him in creation, understood both the rights of God and the duty of the creature), upon the condition of ' purging sin' by his death, which he did, and thereupon went to heaven to take possession of the government, at the right hand of God ; ' sat down,' took his seat at the right hand of the Majesty on high, as due to him by covenant and articles agreed on between them. I know nothing at present against such an interpretation of the words ; but I will not contend about it. All this honour was confirmed unto him upon his death. For having performed the condition requisite on his part, God deputes him, and entrusts him with the government of things, that he might order all things so as to see the full travail of his soul.

(2.) All this power was intended by God for this end, the good of the church. As God appointed Christ a priest for his church to sacrifice for them, a prophet to teach them, so the other office of king is conferred upon him for the same end, the advantage of the church. God acquaints us of this end, aimed at him, in the promise of the government to him : Jer. xxxiii. 15, 16, ' In those days, and at that time, will I cause the branch of righteousness to grow up to David ; and he shall execute judgment and righteousness in the land.' What is the end ? ' In those days shall Judah be saved, and Jerusalem shall dwell safely.' He should execute judgment, that is, administer the government for the salvation of Judah, and security of Jerusalem. It was his office both to build the temple, and to bear the glory, and to rule upon his throne ; to be a priest upon his throne, to rule as king and priest : Zech. vi. 12, 13, ' He shall build the temple of the Lord, even he shall build the temple of the Lord.' The erecting a church is the sole work of Christ by God's appointment; and he was to bear up the glory of it. He should rule to this end, ' for the counsel of peace shall be between them both.' If by *both* be meant, the Lord, and the man whose name is the Branch, it then chiefly aims at our reconciliation, as wrought by covenant between them. If by *both* be meant the two offices of king and priest, and that the counsel of peace be between them, it will extend to all the blessings of the church, to the good and glory of the church, which is the fruit of his kingly, as well as the first reconciliation was the fruit of his priestly, office. By *peace*, in Scripture, is meant the confluence of all blessings ; so that the intent of God in bestowing those offices upon Christ, and so great a rule, was for the good and advantage of that church or temple, which he appointed him only to build. And in Isa. xi. 9, where the prophecy of the government of Christ is, the end is expressed to be, that ' none should hurt or destroy in all his holy mountain.' And certainly, since God set him at his right hand, and confirmed this power unto him, after he had purged our sins, it was certainly out of the high value God had for him, and therefore must be the intent of God, that he should govern all things in reference to the design of that death, and for the good of those whose sins he had by himself purged. For the possessing this government was the very end why Christ died and rose again: Rom. xiv. 9, ' For to this end Christ both died, and rose, and revived, that he might be Lord both of dead and living.' If this were Christ's end in dying and rising, it was his Father's end too, who appointed him to death, and raised him by his mighty power. And since he was ' delivered for our offences, and rose again for our justification,' Rom. iv. 25, the government he is invested with, being Lord of the dead and of the living, must be for the sakes of those for whom he was delivered, and for whom he rose. His regal power, which was one end of his death, cannot cross the other main end, the constituting a church, and carrying on the good of them that believe. The government, being in the hands not of God as creator, but in and through the hands of a mediator, and that mediator which both died and rose again peculiarly for them, therefore it cannot in the least be for their hurt, but advantage. The whole management of Christ's kingly office in relation to the church, is prescribed unto Christ by God. God reveals to him what shall be done in the world, what acts he shall perform for the church, and gives him a history of all that was to be done upon the stage, together with an order to communicate it unto his servants: Rev. i. 1, ' The Revelation of Jesus Christ, which God gave unto him, to shew unto his servants' (to be communicated to the whole church), ' things that must shortly come to pass.' Whether this revelation was made to the human nature of Christ at his incarnation, as Tirinus thinks, or rather upon his ascension, is not material. The whole scheme of what was to be done in the world is revealed here by God to Christ; and you find all the motions in the world relating to the church, and the end of all is the good of the heavenly Jerusalem.

(3.) All power thus given, and intended for this end, is actually administered by Christ for this end. Christ, as the head of the church, doth like a natural head. It never sees, nor hears, nor exerciseth any act of sense only for itself, but for the good of the whole body. The eye watches for the body, the tongue speaks for it, the understanding contrives for it ; every part of the head is active for the whole body. Now Christ as head is more bound to act for the church militant than for the church triumphant, because the greatest part of his work for the church triumphant, viz., the bringing them to heaven, is already performed. And they are above the reach of all things in the world, and all the actions and motions in the world cannot touch or disorder them. But the command of God concerning the other part behind is not yet performed, and even they are the members of Christ as well as those in heaven. The apostle, Col. i. 16–18, seems to refer both Christ's creation, and the preservation of things, to this title of headship: ' All things were created by him, and for him, and by him all things consist, and he is the head of the body the church;' and therefore the conservation and government of all things shall be subservient to the church, which is the body of this governing head. The chief seat of Christ's sovereignty is the church: Ps. ii. 6, ' Yet have I set my king upon my holy hill of Sion;' and he stands upon mount Sion, Rev. xiv. 1. The church is the proper seat and metropolis of his empire, the royal chamber of this great king. All the conquests of princes redound to the advantage of that place where they fix their residence. He is king of the world, but for the sake of Sion. Christ did manage this charge anciently for his people ; when Joshua had passed over Jordan, and first entered upon the conquest of Canaan, he sees a man over against him with a sword drawn in his hand: Josh. v. 13, 14, ' And Joshua said unto him, Art thou for us, or for our adversaries? And he said, Nay; but as captain of the hosts of the Lord am I now come.' This was Christ, that came armed for his people, according to his charge, as their captain and general. It was not an angel, because Joshua worshipped him, ver. 14. An angel did not use to receive any worship from men; and he accepts the worship, and commands him to loose his shoe from his foot, for the place whereon he stood was holy, ver. 15. And the same person, Josh. vi. 2, is called Jehovah; and there he gives him orders how he should manage his war. Christ came here to direct his people in their concerns; he employs his wisdom for his church, as well as his other excellencies. He is called a Counsellor, Isa. ix. 5: it is one of the great letters in his name; and this, as the rest there mentioned, hath a relation to the church. 'For unto us a Child is born, unto us a Son is given.' And the first use he makes of his power, after the confirmation of it to us, upon his resurrection, is for the church: Mat. xxviii. 18, 'All power is given unto me in heaven and in earth; all authoritative power over angels, and the affairs of the world; 'Go you therefore and teach all nations, baptizing them,' &c.; 'and lo, I am with you always, even unto the end of the world.' He commands the apostles to gather a church among all nations; and doth, by virtue of this authority committed to him, promise his presence with them, in all such services they should do to this end, even to the end of the world. He promises his Spirit, and his providential presence; as his power should endure to the end of the world, so the exercise of it for this end should run parallel with the continuance of it. There should be no alteration or change in this great end of his, as long as the world lasts. How can Christ be with them, and that to the end of the world, if all the parts of his providential government were not ordered to serve this end, the good of the church? For the church is 'the fulness of him that fills all in all,' Eph. i. 23, that fills all in all places, all in all actions and motions, for the good of his church, which is his body.

8. Thirdly, God in the church discovers the glory of all his attributes. It is in a man's house where his riches and state is seen: it is in the church God makes himself known in his excellency, more than in all the world besides: Ps. lxxvi. 1, 'In Judah is God known; his name is great in Israel. In Salem also is his tabernacle, and his dwelling-place in Sion.' It is in his church he doth manifest his power. It is called, therefore, 'a glorious high throne: Jer. xvii. 12, 'A glorious high throne from the beginning is the place of our sanctuary.' Kings use to display all their glory and majesty upon their thrones; in this sense heaven is called God's throne, Isa. lx. 1, because the prospect of the heavens affords us discoveries of the wisdom and power of God, more than in any other visible thing, both in their essence, magnitude, and motion: so is there a greater discovery of God's attributes in the church (which is also styled heaven in Scripture) than in the whole world besides; there it is that the angels look to learn more of the wisdom of God than they understood before, Eph. iii. 10. It is there the day of his power dawns, Ps. cx. 3. It is there his saints see his power and his glory, Ps. lxiii. 2; the sanctuary is called the firmament of his power, Ps. cl. 1. The glory of God's attributes is centred in Christ in a higher manner than in the creation; and in that work did excel themselves in what they had done in the framing of the world; and the church being the glory of Christ, all those attributes which are glorified in Christ, do in and through him shine forth more clearly upon the church, than upon any other part of the world. He styles himself their Creator, as much as the Creator of the whole frame of heaven and earth: Isa. xliii. 15, 'I am the Lord, your Holy One, the Creator of Israel, your King.' As though all

the attributes of God, his power in creation, his holiness in redemption, were designed for none else but them : and indeed by virtue of the covenant they were to be so ; for if God be their God, then all of God is theirs. What wisdom, power, sufficiency, grace, and kindness he hath, is principally for them. If God be their God, it is in their concerns he will glorify himself as a God in the manifestation of his perfections. This cannot be without the ordering all providences for their advantage.

4. Fourthly, There is a peculiar relation of God and Christ to the church ; upon which account this doctrine must needs be true. God is set out in all relations to manifest his great care of his people. He is a Father to provide for them, Isa. lxiv. 8 ; a mother to suckle them, Isa. xlix. 15. Christ is a husband to love and protect them, Eph. v. 29 ; a brother to counsel them, John xx. 17. And when all these relations meet in one and the same person, the result of it must be very strong. Any one relation where there is affection is a great security ; but here all the relations are twisted together with the highest affections of them in God to the church. A father will order all for the good of his child, a mother for her infant, a husband for his wife, and one kind brother for another ; so doth God for his people ; and whatsoever those relations bind men to on earth, in respect of care, love, and faithfulness, that is God to his church. The church hath the relation to God which none in the world have besides. They are his jewels, therefore he will keep them ; they are his children, therefore he will spare them, Mal. iii. 17. They shall have protection from him as they are his jewels, and compassion from him as they are his sons. The church is Christ's flesh, as dear to him as our flesh is to us ; as much his, as our flesh is ours : Eph. v. 29, ' No man hates his own flesh, but nourisheth it, as Christ doth his church.' No man can have a higher value for his own flesh than Christ hath for his church. The church, as Tertullian speaks, is nothing else but *Christus explicatus ;** and as considered in union with Christ, is called Christ, 1 Cor. xii. 12. It is ' the apple of his eye,' Zech. ii. 8, a tender and beloved part. The church is Christ's spouse ; the contract is made, the espousals shall be at the last day. The members are picked out one by one to be presented to the Lamb at last as a glorious bride for him, Rev. xxi. 2.

And all God's dealings with them in the world are but preparations of them for that state. Upon the making of the match God promises a communion of goods : Hosea ii. 20, ' I will even betroth thee unto me in faithfulness,' which is a fruit of marriage, the wife being invested in her husband's estate. When God hath given the blood of his Son for the church, he will not deny her the service of the creatures, but jointure her in that as one part of her dowry. ' In that day will I hear the heavens,' &c., ver. 21. In what day ? In the day of betrothing, in the day of the evangelical administration, when the contract shall be made between me and my church. Heavens, earth, corn, wine, and oil, the voice and motions of all creatures, are for Jezreel, which signifies *the seed of God*. This great prince he hath a care of all his subjects, so more peculiarly of his spouse and princess, which is his seed too, and all creatures shall be her servants. This fatherly relation and affection is strong and pure, not as the love which acts au ambitious man to ambition, or a covetous man to wealth ; which respects nothing but the grasping and possessing the objects they doat upon, and have nothing of love for the objects themselves, therefore deserves not the name of love. But it is the love of a father, whose love is pure towards his children ; he seeks their good as his own.

* Christ unfolded.

Consider these two things.

1. God hath a peculiar love to this very relation, and often mentions it with delight, as if he loved to hear the sound of it in his own lips : Cant. viii. 12, ' My vineyard which is mine, is before me.' *Me, my, mine.* The church is always under his eye, seated in his affection, and God is pleased with his propriety in them. God never calls the world *my* world, though he 'created it ; sometimes he saith, the earth is mine, but it is either to check the presumptions of men, who ascribe that to themselves which is due to the first cause ; or to encourage his people in the expectation of deliverance, because all things in the earth are at his beck ; or to shew his own sufficiency, without the services of his people; as when he saith, the earth is mine, and the fulness thereof ; but it is never mentioned in such a way, as to discover any pleasure he hath in the relation between him and it, simply considered ; but *my* vineyard, *my* people, *my* children, *my* jewels, *my* sanctuary, very often. So much doth God esteem his propriety in them.

2. This relation is prevalent with God in the highest emergencies and distresses of his people. The very consideration that they are his people, kindles his affection, and enlivens his strength for them : Isa. lxiii. 8, ' And he said, Surely they are my people, children that will not lie : so he was their Saviour.' God is brought in, as one that had heard the cries of his church, and had not been moved ; but when he recollects himself, and considers that they were his people, and that he was in a special manner related to them, he became their Saviour ; he could no longer bear it, but stirs up himself to relieve them. Nay, it hath so strong an influence upon him, that if this note be often sounded in his ears, it doth as it were change his voice, and when he seems to have a mind to cast them off he cannot. When Israel had offended by erecting and worshipping a golden calf, he calls them no more his people, but Moses's people: Exod. xxxii. 7, ' And the Lord said unto Moses, Go, get thee down; for *thy* people, which thou broughtest out of the land of Egypt, have corrupted themselves.' As though God had not been concerned in this miraculous conduct out of Egypt ; and ver. 9, ' *this* people,' as if he had had no interest in them, but particularises them with disdain. God had here discarded them, and turned them over upon Moses's hands, as if he would have no longer anything to do with them ; but Moses in prayer turns them upon God again, and would not own them as his, but pleads that they were God's proper goods : ver. 11, ' Lord, why doth thy wrath wax hot against *thy* people, which thou hast brought forth out of the land of Egypt ?' And ver. 12, again, ' *thy* people;' and God at last resumes his former notes, ver. 14, ' And the Lord repented him of the evil he thought to do unto *his* people.' Now they are God's people again ; the repetition of this relation is a powerful rhetoric to persuade him to own them again, which he had cashiered and turned off.

5. Fifthly, The whole interest of God in the world lies in his church and people. He sees little of himself in any part of the corrupted world, but only in them. It is in the church he hath put his name ; it is there he sees his image, and therefore places his love there; and shall all this signify nothing? Shall the Governor of the world let things go contrary to his own interest ? They are like to him in that which is one of his greatest perfections, viz., his holiness, which gives him a greater interest in them. It is his interest that is opposed by an opposition to the church. All the hatred any bear it grows from the inward root of enmity against God himself : Ps. xliv. 22, ' Yea, for thy sake are we killed all the day long.' God surely will concern himself in the church's interest, since it is his own. His interest lies, •

(1.) In the persons of his people. It is his inheritance, Isa. xix. 25. It is his portion: Deut. xxxii. 9, 'The Lord's portion is his people, Jacob is the lot of his inheritance.' Every part of an inheritance and a portion doth as particularly belong to the owner as the whole. Every part of the ground which belongs to the inheritance is the heir's, as well as the whole field. He will not suffer the world, which is but the work of his hands, to lay waste his church, which is his proper inheritance. It is his treasure, and where a man's treasure is, there is his heart; and where God's treasure is, there is God's heart.

(2.) In the services and actions of the church. If the church should be destroyed, whom hath God to love and imitate him, and to shew forth his glory? If the candlestick is broken, what is fit to hold out the light to the world? He hath none in the world besides, that do intentionally mind his honour, that take pleasure in glorifying his name, and writing after his copy, and observing his works. And will it stand with his interest to govern things contrary to theirs, which is really his own?

When God had made the world, and pronounced it good, what would it have signified if he had not brought in man as his rent-gatherer, and the collector of his tribute, to return it to him! And what would man signify, since the corrupted world embezzles that which is God's right, and turns it to its own use, if God had not some honest stewards, who faithfully act for him, and give him the glory of his works! And God will spare them, as a man spares his own son that serves him. God hath no voluntary service in the world but from them, therefore he is more interested in their good than in the good of the world besides. The services of the church are all the delight God hath in the world: Hosea ix. 10, 'I found Israel like grapes in the wilderness; I saw your fathers as the first ripe in the fig-tree at her first time.' They are as the refreshing wine and grapes, as the delicious fruit of the first ripe figs, wherewith a weary traveller recruits his spirits after a long and trying journey. And God hath a greater delight in the fruit he receives from the church, than in it simply as it is his inheritance; for no inheritance is valued but for the fruit and revenue it yields; and therefore God orders all his blackest providences in the world, like dark clouds, to be the watering-pots of this his garden, that the fruit and flowers of it may be brought to maturity, which yield him so much pleasure and honour. God only is acknowledged by them and in them, as the Jews were bound to acknowledge God the author of their mercies, by presenting the first fruits of their increase to God. And believers are called so: Rev. xiv. 4, 'These were redeemed from among men, being the first fruits to God and the Lamb.' It is by and in them that God hath the acknowledgment of all his mercies and blessings to the world.

6. It cannot be but all the providences of God shall work to the good of his church, if we consider the affections of God.

(1.) His love. What hath God in the world as an object to bestow his affections upon, and communicate the rays of his love unto, since he created it, but his church? The men of the world hate him; he can see nothing amiable in them; for what was first lovely they have defaced and blotted out, but the church hath God's comeliness put upon her: Ezek. xvi. 14, 'It was perfect through my comeliness which I had put upon thee, saith the Lord God;' and he did not lay those glorious colours upon her, to manage his government, or any part of it against her, to deface her. Besides their loveliness, which is conferred upon them by God, they have a love to God, and no man will act against those whom he thinks to be his friend. God being *purus actus*, there being nothing but purity and activity in God, his love must be the purest and highest love, the most vigorous and glowing; as fire, which sets all other bodies, so this all other powers in the world in motion for them. God cannot love them, but he must wish all good to them, and do all good for them; for his love is not a lazy love, but hath its raptures and tenderness, and his affection is twisted with his almighty power to work that good for them, which in their present condition in the world they are capable of. Now it is certain God loves his church; for,

[1.] He carries them in his hand, Deut xxxiii. 3; and that not in a loose manner to be cast out, but they are engraven upon the palms of his hands, Isa. xlix. 16, that he cannot open his hand to bestow a blessing upon any person but the picture of his church doth dart in his eye. God alludes to the rings wherein men engrave the image of those that are dear to them. And the Jews did in their captivity engrave the effigies of their city Jerusalem upon their rings, that they might not forget it.* If his eye be alway upon the church, his thoughts can never be off it in all his works.

[2.] He loves the very gates and outworks: Ps. lxxxvii. 2, 'The Lord loveth the gates of Sion;' he loves a cottage where a church is more than the stately palaces of princes. The gates were the places where they consulted together, and gave judgment upon affairs. God loved the assemblies of his saints because of the truths revealed, the ordinances administered, the worship presented to him.

[3.] Nay, one saint is more valued by him than the whole world of the wicked. God is the God of all creatures, but peculiarly the God of Abraham and of his seed. One Abraham is more deeply rooted in his heart than all the world, and he doth more entitle himself the God of Abraham than the God of the whole world; for in that style he speaks to Isaac: Gen. xxvi. 24, 'I am the God of Abraham thy father,' much more the God of Israel, the God of the whole church, of which Abraham was but a member, though the father of the faithful, and a feoffee of the covenant. God hath a greater value for one sincere soul than for a whole city. He saves a Lot, and burns a Sodom; yea, than for a whole world, he drowns a world and reserves a Noah; he secures his jewels, whilst he flings away the pebbles.

[4.] He loves them so, that he overlooks their crabbed and perverse misconstructions of his providence. When the Israelites had jealous thoughts of him, and of Moses his instrument, when they saw that mighty Egyptian army just at their heels, and themselves cooped up between mountains, forts, and waters, God doth not upon this provoking murmuring draw up his cloudy pillar to heaven, but puts it in the rear of them, when before it had marched in the van, Exod. xiv. 19, and wedgeth himself in between them and Pharaoh's enraged host, to shew that they should as soon sheath their swords in his heart as in their bowels; and if they could strike them, it should be through his own deity, which was the highest expression of his affection. And though they often murmured against his providence after they were landed on the shore, yet he left them not to shift for themselves, but bore them all the way in his arms, as a father doth his child, Deut. i. 31, and bare them like an eagle upon his wings, Deut. xxxii. 11. And God loves them magnificently and royally: Hosea xiv. 4, 'I will love them freely,'† without any doubting, without any reluctancy. I will love thee without any repugnancy in my heart to draw me back from thee; 'for mine anger is turned away,' as the streams of a river, quite another way. Now, all this considered, can the Governor of the world, the King of saints,

* Sanctius in Isa. xlix. 16.

† Hosea xiv. 4, נְדָבָה; Sept., ὁμολόγως.

act anything against his own affections? Yea, will he not make all things subservient to them whom he loves?

(2.) His delight. See what an inundation of sweetening joy there was in him, for which he had not terms of expression to suit the narrow apprehensions of men: Zeph. iii. 17, 'The Lord thy God in the midst of thee is mighty; he will save, he will rejoice over thee with joy; he will rest in his love; he will joy over thee with singing.' He seems in his expression to know no measure of his delight in the church, and no end of it: 'I will rejoice over thee with joy.' Joy sparkles up fresh after joy; it is his rest, where the soul and all that is within him centres itself with infinite contentment. 'Joy over thee with singing:' a joy that blossoms into triumph. Never had any such charming transports in the company of any he most affected as God hath in his church; he doth so delight in the graces of his people, that he delights to mention them. He twice mentions Enoch's walking with him, Gen. v. 22, 24. And certainly God cannot but delight in it more than in the world, because it is a fruit of greater pains than the creation of the world. The world was created in the space of six days by a word, the erecting a church hath cost God more pains and time. Before the church of the Jews could be settled, he hath both a contest with the peevishness of his people and the malice of their enemies. And his own Son must bleed and die before the church of the Gentiles could be fixed. Men delight in that which hath cost them much pains and a great price. God hath been at too much pains, and Christ at too great price, to have small delight in the church; will he then let wild beasts break the hedges, and tread down the fruit of it? Shall not all things be ordered to the good of that which is the object of his greatest delight in the world?

7. Seventhly, The presence of God in his church will make all providences tend to the good of it.

It would be an idle, useless presence if it were not operative for their good. 'The Lord is there' is the very name of the gospel church, Ezek. xlviii. 35; what would it signify if it were a useless presence? Christ stands upon mount Sion, his throne is in the church, when the great things in the world shall be acted for the ruin of antichrist, Rev. xiv. 1. God's presence in his church is the glory and defence of it, as the presence of the king is the glory of the court: Zech. ii. 5, 'For I, saith the Lord, will be unto her a wall of fire round about, and will be the glory in the midst of her.' His presence is a covenant presence: Isa. xli. 10, 'Fear not, I am with thee; be not dismayed, for I am thy God;' whence follows strength, help, and support: 'I will strengthen thee; yea, I will help thee; yea, I will uphold thee with the right hand of my righteousness;' that is, with my righteous power, with my power engaged to thee in a righteous covenant. His presence and providence in the world is in a way of absolute dominion, but in his church in a way of federal relation. He is the God *of* Israel, and God *to* Israel, or *for* Israel, 1 Chron. xvii. 24, yea, and a God *in the midst of* Israel,—every one of them sufficient engagements to protect Israel, and provide for Israel, and govern everything for Israel's good. God is under an oath to do good to Israel; will he violate his oath, tear his seal, break his covenant, who never broke his league with any of his people yet?

8. Eighthly, The prayers of the church have a mighty force with God to this end. God is entitled a God hearing prayer; and what prayers should God hear, if not the prayers of his church, which aim at God's glory in their own good? Though the prayers of the church may in some particulars fail, yet in general they do not; because they submit their desires to the will of God, which always works what is best for them.

When God would do any mighty work in the world, he stirs up his people to pray for it; and their prayers by his own appointment have a mighty influence upon the government of the world, for when they come before him in behalf of the church in general, he doth indulge them a greater liberty and boldness, and as it were a kind of authority over him, than upon other occasions of their own: Isa. xlv. 11, 'Thus saith the Lord, the Holy One of Israel, and his Maker, Ask of me things to come concerning my sons; and concerning the work of mine hands command you me.' God would be more positively, confidently, and familiarly dealt with about the concerns of his sons, though they were things to come to pass in after ages. And indeed the prayers of the church have a powerful and invisible efficacy on the great actions and overturnings which are in the world. The being of the world is maintained by them from sinking; according to the Jews' saying, *sine stationibus non subsisteret mundus* (standing in prayer was their usual prayer gesture). And that they have actually such a force is evident: Rev. viii. 3, 4, an angel hath a golden censer with incense, to offer it with the prayers of the saints upon the altar which was before the throne. And, verse 5, the censer wherein their prayers were offered was filled with the fire of the altar, and cast into the earth; and there were voices, thunderings, lightnings, and earthquakes. When the prayer of the saints were offered to God, and ascended up before him, that is, were very pleasing to him, the issue is, the angel fills the censer with fire of the altar, and thereby causes great commotions and alterations in the world, signifying that the great changes of the world are an answer unto those prayers which are offered unto God; for fire is taken from that altar upon which they were offered, and flung into the world. And it must needs be that the prayers of the church should have an influence on the government of the world. ·

(1.) Because God hath a mighty delight in the prayers of his people. 'The prayer of the upright is his delight;' and he loves to hear the church's voice: Cant. ii. 14, 'O my dove, let me hear thy voice, for sweet is thy voice' (*Chaldee*, 'Thy voice is sweet in prayer'). In the times of the gospel, God promises that the offerings of Judah and Jerusalem should be pleasant to him, Mal. iii. 4. When Christ shall sit as a refiner, ver. 3, what is the issue of those prayers? ver. 5, '1 will come near to you to judgment, and I will be a swift witness against the sorcerers,' &c. Prayer awakes providence to judge the enemies of the church. A parent delights not in the bare crying, or the voice of his child simply considered in itself, but in the significations and effects of it. He delights in the matter of their prayers, it being so agreeable to his own heart and will, and in the sense they have of the sufferings of the whole body.

(2.) Because prayer is nothing else but a pleading of God's promises. Unto this they are directed by that Spirit which knows the mind of God, and marshals their petitions according to his will. Now as God turns his own decrees and purposes concerning his church into promises to them, so the church turns those promises into prayers for them; so that promises being for the good of the church, and there being an exact harmony between those promises and the church's prayers, all those providences which are the issue of those promises, and the answer of the church's prayers, must needs be for the church's good.

(3.) Because there are united supplications and pleadings both in heaven and earth. All the hands of the whole family in heaven and earth are concerned in their petitions.

[1.] Christ intercedes for the church, who always desires mercy and deliverance for them in the appointed time: Zech. i. 12; 'How long wilt thou not have mercy on Jerusalem?' and the issue is always gracious; for, ver. 13, God answers him with 'good and comfortable words;' and thereupon carpenters are raised to 'cut off the horns which had scattered Judah,' ver. 20.

[2.] Angels in all probability plead for the church, as we have already heard; it is likely they offer and present that to God which makes for his glory, and that is the good of the church. Angels surely desire that which their head doth, which is described as one of their own order, and called an angel, Zech. i. 12. Do they rejoice at the repentance of a sinner, and do they not likewise triumph at the happiness of the church, which is part of that family they are of? And we know that the greatness of our joy is suited to the mercies of our desires; where our joy is most triumphant, it implies that our desires before were most vehement.

[3.] Glorified saints are not surely behind. The rich man in the parable desired his friends on earth might not come into that place of torment, Luke xvi. 28. If there be so much charity in hell, can there be less in heaven? If he desired it, that by the presence of his companions in sin, his own torments might not be increased, do not the saints in heaven desire the presence of the whole church, that their happiness in that of the whole body may be completed? If the head Christ be not complete without the body, the members of the body cannot be complete without one another. The souls of them that were slain for the word of God cry under the altar for vengeance on them that dwell on the earth; as Rev. vi. 9, 10, 'How long, O Lord holy and true, dost thou not judge and avenge our blood on them that dwell on the earth?' Will not their kindness to their fellow-members be as strong as their justice, and their love for the good of their friends draw out their prayers as well as their desire of vengeance on their enemies? Why may they not as well pray for us as we praise God for them? Had they not some likeness to their great Master whilst they were on earth, and shall they not be more like to him now they are in heaven, and behold his face, and feel all the stirrings of his heart? And if they have no sense at all of the church's sufferings, how shall they be like to him who hath? As their bodies shall be like the glorious body of Christ at the resurrection, are not their souls now like his glorious soul, merciful, and compassionate, and sympathising in all the afflictions of the church? And can this be without some breathings for a full completing of the church's freedom? Are such desires and pleas any hindrance to their present happiness? It is so far from that, that it doth rather further their glory, which cannot be complete, as the glory of Christ, as head, is not mounted to the highest pitch of glory, till his mystical body be all gathered in and lodged with him. If it be thus, will God do anything prejudicial to the church, and contrary to the combined desires of all those that are so near him? If God doth sometimes stir up himself upon the supplication of one man, and grant an order upon his petition according to his mind; and if the prayers of one faithful Moses, or Elias, or Samuel have such a kind of almighty power in them, much more is the joint force of so many prayers twisted together.

Use 1. For information. Is it so that all providence is for the good of the church? Then,

1. God will always have a church in the world, he will have some to serve him. The whole course of his providence being designed for it, as long as the world, which is the object of his providence, doth endure, he will have a church. God would otherwise lose the end of the motion of his eyes,* the

---

* As in the text, 2 Chron. xvi. 9.

operation of his providence, since it is to shew himself strong for the church and every member of it. As long as the candle and light of the gospel burns and shines, God will have a candlestick to set the candle in.* His great design in making a world was not to have sun, moon, and stars, but a church, a company of men that might bear his mark, and honour him, to whom he might speak, and extend his grace abroad, which he was so full of within. As a limner who would draw an excellent draught, draws his design in the midst of the cloth, and fills the void places with clouds, and landscapes, and other fancies at his pleasure, which communicate some beauty and lustre to the work, but that was not the principal design of the workman. That Redeemer which bears the church upon his heart, will create a stability for it ; it is a part of his priestly office to have a care of the lamps ; it is one of his titles to be he that walks in the midst of the seven golden candlesticks, Rev. ii. 1. Priests under the law were to look to the great candlestick in the temple, supply the lamps with oil, and make them clean, Lev. xxiv. 3, 4. The church indeed may be eclipsed, but not extinguished ; if it be not conspicuous on the mountain, yet it shall be hid in the wilderness. There shall be sprinklings of professors among all people. God will leaven the places where they are into Christianity, and cause them to fructify and grow up in purity and glory : Micah v. 7, ‘And the remnant of Jacob shall be in the midst of many people, as a dew from the Lord, as the showers upon the grass, that tarrieth not for man, nor waiteth for the sons of men.’ It tarries not for man. It attends not the power of man, the precepts of man, or inventions of man ; but whose descent is from heaven, and is carried on not by human power, but by the divine Spirit and providence ; it shall be firmer than all worldly power, and the strongest kings : Isa. ii. 2, ‘And the mountain of the Lord’s house shall be established upon the top of the mountains, and shall be exalted above the hills.’ Above mountains and hills, to which sometimes the powers of the world are compared, Zech. iv. 7. That providence which gave the church at first a footing in the world upon a weak foundation to outward appearance, in spite of men and devils will preserve it, and not suffer it to be blown up ; he will shadow the church with his wings in a perpetual succession of the choicest mercies.

2. God will in the greatest exigencies find out means for the protection of his church. This will be till his providence be at an end. When God hath removed one instrument of his church’s protection, he hath his choice of others, whom he can raise and spirit for his work. When those upon whom the church’s hopes hang are taken off, he can raise things that are unlikely to supply the place. As the lutenist accidentally had a grasshopper leapt upon his instrument, to supply by its noise the place of a string which had newly cracked, whereby his music was continued without interruption. God can spirit men against their own natural fears. It is very improbable, that Nicodemus, one of a fearful disposition, who came to our Saviour by night for fear of the Jews, should have the courage to assert his cause in the face of a whole council of pharisees, contriving his death, and at present blunt the edge of their malice, though we read of none at that time in the council to second him, John vii. 50, 51. The Holy Ghost takes particular notice that it was he that came to Jesus by night.

Joseph of Arimathea, whose name we meet not with' in the catalogue of any of our disciples,† till the time of his death, and then he appears boldly to beg the body of Jesus of Pilate. God will never want instruments for the preserving that church, which he owns as his. It is observed by some,

* Cham. Les trais verit. liv. 3 chap i. p. 16.
† Qu. ‘in any of the catalogues of our Lord’s disciples’?—Ed.

that God so ordered it, that the same day that Pelagius, the great poisoner of the Christian doctrine, was born in Britain, Austin, the most famous defender of the truth, was born in Africa; that the horn which pushed the truth should no sooner appear, but the carpenter to cut it off should be provided too. As it is observed where poisons grow, antidotes grow near them by the indulgent provision of the God of nature.

As there is the wisdom of the serpent against the church, so there is the wisdom of God for it. God's goodness upon his church in former ages is not all laid out, he hath his stores still, neither is his wisdom nonplussed, nor his power weakened; neither is he, nor can he be weary of his care.

3. The church shall in the end prove victorious against all its adversaries, or providence must miss of its aim. The church is compared to an olive tree, Hosea xiv. 6, in respect of beauty, 'his beauty shall be as the olive tree.' It is so also in respect of victory. Olive branches were used in triumph. God is on the church's side, and he is stronger than the strongest, and wiser than the wisest, and higher than the highest. Jesus Christ is the church's head and general; Christ the head watcheth for the good of the church, the body. He must be destroyed before the church can. There is a mighty arm, which, though it may for a time seem withered, will in the end be stretched out, and get itself the victory. Whilst Christ is in the ship, it may be tossed, but it shall not be sunk. It may be beaten down, but like a ball to rebound the higher. The young tree that is shaken by the wind may lose some leaves, and some fruit too, but the root gets greater strength and strikes itself deeper into the earth, and makes the branches more capable of a rich return of fruit the following year. The church's stature is compared to a palm tree, Cant. vii. 7, which cannot be depressed by the weights which hang upon it, but riseth the higher. God uses the same method in the church's, as in Christ's advancement. Our Saviour's death was necessary to his glory, Luke xxiv. 26, and the church's affliction sometimes to its exaltation. A nation may lose some battles, and yet be victorious; the church may have many a cross, but in the end will surmount all difficulties. Though judgments and apostasies may be great in a nation, yet God will have a care of his own plants, Isa. vi. 12, 13; 'There shall be a tenth; it shall return, the holy seed shall be the substance thereof.' As a tree in winter, which seems dead, but its juice shall revive into rich and generous blossoms. The ark shall float above the waters. Babylon shall fall, the Lamb shall stand upon mount Zion. Men may as well stop the rising of the sun in its mounting to the meridian, bridle in the tide of the ocean, as hinder the current of an almighty providence.

4. The interest of nations is to bear a respect to the church, and countenance the worship of God in it. This is to concur with God's main end, and imitate him in his providential administrations. God's people, whatever their enemies suggest to the contrary, are a blessing in the midst of a land, Isa. xix. 24; their interest is greater than the interest of all the world besides; though they be but a handful, their fruit shall shake like Lebanon, Ps. lxxii. 16. The neglect of religion is the ruin of nations. It is observed that Cyrus was slain in the war in Scythia, a little after he neglected the building of the temple of Jerusalem which he had begun.* Those Persian kings reigned the longest that favoured the Jews in that and their other just requests. God honoured or disgraced them as they were kind or cruel to his people. And when they act for the good of his people, they shall not be without their reward. When Cyrus should let the Jewish captives go free without ransom, he should be no loser by it. God would

* Broughton on Dan. x. 10.

give him the labour of Egypt, the merchandise of Ethiopia, and the strength of the Sabeans into his hand for the price of his people's delivery, Isa. xlv. 13, 14. Those nations which should favour them in the times of their persecutions and flights, and give them shelter in their countries, should thrive and prosper by the blessing of God upon them. If Moab give entertainment to the flying Israelites in the time of the invasion of Shalmanezer, God will preserve their land that the spoiler shall not enter into the confines of it, and they shall have kings and judges under the protection of the house of David, *i. e.* under the kings of Israel, as some understand it, Isa. xvi. 4, 5. Saints are the guardians of the places where they live, their prayers have a greater influence than the wisest counsels, or the mightiest force, 2 Kings ii. 12 : 'And Elisha cried, My father, my father ! the chariot of Israel, and the horsemen thereof.' The *Chaldee* paraphraseth thus : 'Thou art better to Israel by thy prayers than chariots and horsemen.' This is the elogy of one single prophet ; what influence then hath the whole church of God in a place ? The whole world is the better for the church of God. The Chaldee paraphrase hath a notion upon that, Ps. xxii. 3 : 'But thou art holy, O thou that inhabitest the praises of Israel ;' thou that establishest the world for the praises of Israel. God hath nothing to do in the world but the saving of his people. When that is once done, he will put an end to this frame of things. When he hath gathered his wheat into his garner, he will burn up the chaff. His people are the spirit and quintessence of the world. When this is extracted, the rest are flung upon the dunghill, as a *caput mortuum*.

5. We may see hence the ground of most of the judgments in the world. Men by their rage against the church, will not acknowledge God's government of the world for the church's good ; therefore the psalmist, Ps. lix. 13, 'Consume them in wrath, consume them that they may not be, and let them know that God rules in Jacob unto the ends of the earth.' The church is the seat of his government, and from thence he extends it to the uttermost parts of the earth. In Jacob he rules, and for the sake of Jacob he orders his government to the ends of the earth ; the not acknowledging this brings wrathful consumptions upon men ; and it is also the end of his judgments to make men know it. It is likely enough the four kings, Gen. xiv. 9, might have gone clear away with all their booty, had not they laid their fingers upon Lot ; but when they would pack him up among the rest, they did but solicit their own ruin, and arm the almighty God against them. God did not think any of the people worth the mention, verse 11 ; only Lot a righteous person, verse 12, he is named, as having God's eye only upon him. And when Abraham returns from the victory, ver. 16, the rest of the delivered captives are mentioned in the bulk, Lot only in particular, as though all that had been done had been done by God only for Lot's sake. They might have preserved the whole prey to themselves, had it not been for this jewel, too precious in God's account for their custody. And the fearful curse that God pronounced against the Ammonite and Moabite, that they should not come into the congregation for ten generations, though any of them turned proselytes, was because they came not out with so much as bread and water to meet the Israelites, and because they hired Balaam to curse them, Deut. xxiii. 3, 4. The utter wasting of nations and kingdoms, is because they will not serve the interest of God in his people : Isa. lx. 12, 'For the nation and kingdom that will not serve thee shall perish ; yea, those nations shall be utterly wasted.' God will bring an utter consumption upon those people that refuse to love them, much more upon those that hate them.

6. What esteem, then, should there be of the godly in the world ? The providence of God, being chiefly for the good of his people, cannot well fall upon them, but some drops will fall upon those involved with them in a common interest. When the corn, and wine, and oil hear Jezreel (the seed of God), and the earth hears the corn, and the heavens hear the earth, and God hears the heavens, Hosea ii. 21, 22 ; when their supplications come up to the great superintendent of the world, many of the wicked will fare the better for that providence which is given only in answer to Jezreel's prayer ; God causes his sun to shine upon the unjust, upon them, not for their sakes. When Nebuchadnezzar issued out that unjust order for the slaying the Chaldeans for not performing an impossible command in telling him the dream he had forgotten, Dan. ii. 12, Daniel was sought out to undergo the same fate ; yet by his wisdom God bends the heart of Arioch, the executioner of this decree, to stay his hand. Daniel goes to the king, God stays Nebuchadnezzar's fury, and moves his heart to give them time. The providence is chiefly intended for the preservation of Daniel and his godly companions, but the rest of the wise men have the benefit of it. As the water with which a man waters his choicest plants and flowers in his garden is intended only for them, yet some falling off from those flowers refresheth the weeds that grow under them. If God had not had such flowers as Daniel and his companions, the weeds in Chaldea had been plucked up. Yet the ungrateful world takes no notice of the benefits they receive from this salt of the earth, which preserves them, and to whom they are all so much beholding. Lot had been the occasion of restoring Zoar from captivity, as I mentioned before, for the inhabitants of that city were engaged with those of Sodom in the fight against the four kings (' And the king of Bela, the same is Zoar,' Gen. xiv. 8) ; and perhaps were carried captives with the rest of their neighbours ; and it had been saved from the flames which fell upon Sodom merely by Lot's prayer : Gen. xix. 21, ' See, I have accepted thee concerning this thing, that I will not overthrow this city for the which thou hast spoken ; ' yet he found them a surly people, and was requited with a rude reception, notwithstanding his kindness : ver. 18, ' He went up out of Zoar, for he feared to dwell in Zoar.' It was not likely he was so distrustful of God, that he should overthrow it, when he had absolutely promised him the contrary ; therefore most likely for some churlish threatenings from them. Nay, Sodom itself was beholden to him for a small respite of the judgment intended against them. For God tells him he could do nothing till he were come thither, Gen. xix. 22. And it was so, for Lot was entered into Zoar before a drop of brimstone and fire was rained down upon Sodom : ver. 23, 24, ' Then the Lord rained upon Sodom ; ' when ? When Lot was entered into Zoar. This good the wicked world get by God's people is so evident, that sometimes wicked men cannot but take notice of it : Laban, a selfish idolater, was sensible of it : Gen. xxx. 27, ' I have found by experience that the Lord hath blessed me for thy sake.' It was a lesson so legible that he might have learned it sooner than in fourteen years. The church is the chief object of preservation, wicked men are preserved for their sakes ; as dung is preserved, not for its own sake, but for the manuring a fruitful field, and thorns in the hedge are preserved for the garden's sake.

7. It is then a very foolish thing for any to contend against the welfare of God's people. It is to strive against an almighty and unwearied providence. Men may indeed sometimes be suffered by God for holy ends to have their wills, in some measure, upon the church, but not altogether ; they must first depose him from his throne, blind his eyes, or hold his arm.

It is as foolish as if a worm should design to dig down a mountain, or chaff to martial itself in battle array against the wind, or for a poor fly to stop the motion of a millstone.

(1.) It is foolish, because it is exceeding sinful. What is done against the church is rather done against God than against it ; since all her constitution, worship, observances, are directed to God as their ultimate end ; so that to endeavour to destroy the church is to deny God a worship, deprive him of his sanctuary, break open his house, ravish his spouse, cut off Christ's body, rob him of his jewels, and will be so interpreted by God at the last, upon the scanning of things. If the church be God's house, the enemies shall answer for every invasion, every forcible entry, for the breaking down the gates and bars of it, God will sue them at last for dilapidations.

(2.) Very unsuccessful. Shall God be afraid of the multitudes and power of men ? No more than ' a lion, or a young lion roaring after his prey, when a multitude of shepherds are called forth against them, shall he be afraid of their voice, or abase himself for their noise,' Isa. xxxi. 4. Noise and clamour is all they can do, and that not long; the fierceness of the lion quickly scatters them. The associations, and men's girding themselves against the church, is but a preparation to their own ruin : Isa. viii. 9, ' Associate yourselves together, O ye people, and ye shall be broken in pieces,' three times repeated. Your counsels, saith he, shall not stand against that presence of God that is with us, ' for God is with us.'

(3.) It is very destructive too. God will not alway be still and refrain himself ; he seems to do so for a while, but when he doth arise he will destroy and devour at once, Isa. xlii. 14, he will make but ʻone morsel of them. When God is angry with his people, and gives them into the hands of men to execute his justice upon them, and punish them, he will even punish those enemies for their cruelty, and going beyond their commission, in satisfying their own immoderate passions upon them. Upon this account God threatens Babylon : Isa. xlvii. 6, ' I was wroth with my people ; I have polluted mine inheritance, and given them into thy hand : thou didst shew them no mercy ;' whereupon God threatens them afterwards, &c. ; so Zech. i. 15, God was sore displeased with the heathen, for when he was ' but a little displeased' with his people, ' they helped forward the affliction.'

Use 2. Is for comfort.

If all the providence of God be for the good of the church, if his eyes run to and fro to shew himself strong for them, it affords matter of great comfort. His providence is continual for them, Zech. iv. 2. He hath seven pipes to convey kindness to them, as well as seven lamps whereby to discern their straits. His providence is as vast as his omniscience. The number of pipes belonging to the candlestick of the church is exact according to the number of lamps. The church's misery cannot be hid from God's eye, let it be in what part of the earth soever, for his eyes run to and fro throughout the whole earth, and his sight excites his strength. Upon the sight of their distressed condition he watches only for the fittest opportunity to shew himself strong for them. And when that opportunity comes he is speedy in the deliverance of them : Ps. xviii. 10, ' He rode upon a cherub, and did fly ; yea, he did fly upon the wings of the wind.' He doth not only ride upon a cherub, but fly. His wings are nothing but wind, which hath the quickest and strongest motion, which moves the greatest bodies, and turns down all before it. What is for the good of the whole hath an influence upon every member of the body.

1. It is comfort in duties and special services. Nothing shall be wanting for encouragement to duty, and success in it when God calls any to it, since all his providence is for the good of the church. Let there be but sincerity on our parts, in our attempts of service upon God's call, and we need not fear a want of providence on God's part. God never calls any to serve his church in any station, but he doth both spirit and encourage them. God hath in his common providence suited the nature of every creature to that place in which he hath set it in the world; and will he not much more in his special providence suit every one to that place he calls them to, for the service of his church? He did not forsake Christ in redeeming his church, neither will he forsake any in assisting his church. When Joseph of Arimathea would boldly demand the body of our Saviour, providence made the way plain before him; he meets with no check, neither from Pilate nor the priests, Mat. xxvii. 58, Mark xv. 43.

2. In meanness and lowness. It is one and the same God that rules the affairs of the whole world, of the church and of every particular member of it. As it is the same soul that informs the whole body, the meanest member as well as that which is most excellent. Not the meanest sincere Christian but is under God's eye for good. The Spirit acts and animates every member in the church, the weakest as well as the most towering Christian. Baruch was but the prophet Jeremiah's amanuensis or scribe, and servant to Jeremiah (who was no great man in the world himself), yet God takes notice so of his service, that he would particularly provide for him, and commands Jeremiah in a way of prophecy to tell him as much: Jer. xlv. 5, 'I will bring evil upon all flesh, but thy life will I give unto thee for a prey, whithersoever thou goest.'

3. In the greatest judgments upon others. In an epidemical judgment upon the whole nation of the Jews, God would have a special care of Baruch. If he should cast his people far off among the heathen, and scatter them among the countries, yet even there he would be a little sanctuary unto them. His own presence should supply the want of a temple, so he is pleased to express himself, Ezek. xi. 16. But how is it possible the great God can be but a little sanctuary? His eye is upon them to see their danger, and his hand upon them to secure them from it. His promise shall shield them, and his wings shall cover them, Ps. xci. 4. While he hath indignation, he hath a secret chamber for their security, Isa. xxvi. 20, an almighty shadow under which they abide, Ps. xci. 1. In times of the most devouring danger he hath a seal to set upon their foreheads as a mark of his special protection. We never have so much experience of God's care and strength as in times of trouble: Ps. xxxvii. 39, 'He is their strength in time of trouble.' He is a friend who is as able as willing, and as willing as able to help them, whose watchfulness over them is as much above their apprehension as it is above their merits.

4. In the greatest extremities wherein his people may be, there are promises of comfort, Isa. xliii. 2. Both in overflowing waters and scorching fires he will be with them; his providence shall attend his promise, and his truth shall be their shield and buckler, Ps. xci. 4. That surely is a sufficient support; Christ thought it so, when he only said to his disciples, 'It is I, be not afraid,' John vi. 17, 18. What though there be a storm, a darkness, and trouble, 'It is I am he.' The darkness of the night troubles not the pilot whilst he hath his compass to steer by. If all his providences be for the good of them that fear him, he can never want means to bring them out of trouble, because he is always actually exercised in governing that which is for their good, and till he sees it fit to deliver them, he will be

with them. Great mercies succeed the sharpest afflictions, Jer. xxx. 5, 6, 7, &c. When there should be a voice of trembling, and men with their hands upon their loins, as women in travail, and paleness in their faces from the excess of their fears, in that day God would break the yoke from them, and they should serve the Lord their God, and David their king. Though the night be never so dark, yet it is certain the sun will rise and disperse its light next morning, and one time or other shew itself in its brightness. We have no reason to despond in great extremities, since he can think us into safety,—Ps. xl. 17, ' Lord, think on me,'—much more look us into it ; his thoughts and his eyes move together.

5. In fear of wants. The power of the government of the world cannot be doubted. His love, as little as it seems, since it hath moved him to prepare heaven to entertain his people at the end of their journey, it will not be wanting to provide accommodation for them upon the way, since all things, both good and bad, are at his beck, and under the government of his gracious wisdom. His eyes run to and fro through the whole earth, not only to defend them in dangers, but supply them in wants, for his strength is shewed both ways. Doth he providentially regard them that have no respect for him, and will he not employ his power for, and extend his care to them that adore and love him, and keep up his honour in the world? He will not surely be regardless of the afflictions of his creatures. His people are not only his creatures, but his new creatures ; their bodies are not only created by him, but redeemed by his Son. The purchase of the Redeemer is joined to the providence of the Creator. If he take care of you when he might have damned you for your sins, will he not much more since you are believers in Christ? And he cannot damn you believing, unless he renounce his Son's mediation and his own promise. A natural man provides for his own, much more a righteous man : Pro. xiii. 22, ' A good man leaves an inheritance to his children,' much more the God of righteousness, a God who hath his eye always upon them. His eye will affect his heart, and his heart spirit the hand of his power to relieve them. He hath ' prepared of his goodness for the poor,' Ps. lxviii. 10.

6. It is comfort in the low estate of the church at any time. God's eye is upon his church even whilst he seems to have forsaken them. If he seem to be departed, it is but in some other part of the earth, to shew himself strong for them ; wherever his eye is fixed in any part of the world, his church hath his heart, and his church's relief is his end. Though the church may sometimes lie among the pots in a dirty condition, yet there is a time of resurrection, when God will restore it to its true glory, and make it as white as a dove with its silver wings, Ps. lxviii. 13. The sun is not alway obscured by a thick cloud, but will be freed from the darkness of it. ' God will judge his people, and repent himself concerning his servants,' Ps. cxxxv. 14.* It is a comfort to God to deliver his people, and he will do it in such a season when it shall be most comfortable to his glory and their hearts. The very name Jerusalem some derive from *Jireh Salem*, ' God will provide in Salem.' The new Jerusalem is the title given to God's church, Rev. xxi., and is still the object of his providence, and he will provide for it at a pinch : Gen. xxii. 14, ' Jehovah Jireh,' God will raise up the honour and beauty of his church ; great men shall be servants to it, and employ their strength for it when God shall have mercy on it, Isa. lx. 10, 12 ; yea, the learning and knowledge of the world shall contribute to the building of it ; ver. 13, ' The glory of Lebanon shall come unto thee, the fir-tree, the pine-tree, and the box together, to beautify the place of my sanctuary.

* יתנחם, *comfort himself.*

It shall be called the city of the Lord, the Zion of the Holy One of Israel, that she may know that the Lord is her Saviour, and her Redeemer, the mighty one of Jacob.' As Christ rose in his natural, so he will in his spiritual body. If Christ when dead could not be kept from rising, Christ now living shall not be hindered from rising and helping his church. His own glory is linked with his people's security, and though he may not be moved for anything in them because of their sinfulness, he will for his own name, because of its excellency: Ezek. xxxvi. 22, 'I do not this for your sakes, O house of Israel, but for my holy name's sake.' As sorrows increased upon the Israelites, the nearer their deliverance approached.

Because this method of God is the greatest startling even to good men, let us consider this a little, that God doth, and why God doth, leave his church to extremities before he doth deliver it.

Take the resolution of this in some propositions.

1. It is indeed God's usual method to leave the church to extremity before he doth command help. You never heard of any eminent deliverance of the church but was ushered in by some amazing distress. The Israelites were not saved till they were put in between sea, hills, and forts, that their destruction was inevitable, unless heaven relieved them. Pharaoh resolves to have his will, and God resolves to have his; but he lets him come with his whole force and open mouth at the Israelites' backs, and then makes the waters his sepulchre. Constantine, the man-child in the Revelation, was preceded by Diocletian, the sharpest persecutor. When his people are at a loss, it is his usual time to do his greatest works for them; God had promised Christ many ages, and yet no appearance of him; still promise after promise, and no performance, Ps. xl. 8. It was then, 'Lo, I come,' yet many hundred years rolled away, and no sight of him yet. Captivity and affliction, and no Redeemer; but when the world was overrun with idolatry, the Jews oppressed by the Romans, the sceptre departed from Judah, Herod an Edomite and stranger-king, and scarce any faith left, then, then he comes. The world will be in much the like case at his next coming: Luke xviii. 8, 'When the Son of man comes, shall he find faith in the earth?' There shall be faintings, despondency, unbelief of his promise, as though he had cast off all care of his church's concerns. It is not meant of a justifying faith, but a faith in that particular promise of his coming. The faith of the Israelites must needs begin to flag when they saw their males murdered by the Egyptians; could they believe the propagation of the seed of Abraham, when murder took off the infants, and labour and age would in time the old ones? Whilst their children were preserved, the promise might easily be believed. But consider, this was but just before their deliverance; like a violent crisis before recovery. He doth then 'judge his people, and repent himself for his servants, when he sees their power is gone, and there is none shut up or left,' Deut. xxxii. 36. He doth so for the wicked many times. When the affliction of idolatrous Israel was bitter, when there was not any shut up, nor any left, nor any helper for Israel, then he saved them by the hand of Jeroboam, the son of Joash, 2 Kings xiv. 26, 27. He doth so with private persons; Peter might have been delivered by God's power out of prison when he was first sent thither, but God thought it fittest for him to lie in chains, and free him but the night before his intended execution, Acts xii. 6, 7. Lot had his goods rifled and carried away captive before God stirred up Abraham to rescue him. When the hand of the wicked lies heaviest upon the heads of the righteous, and wrings the most mournful sighs from them; when they are needy, and the wicked securely puffing at them, as though they had brought them to so low a condition as to blow them away with a blast; 'Now,' saith

God, 'will I arise:' Ps. xii. 5, 'For the oppression of the poor, for the sighing of the needy, now will I arise, saith the Lord; I will set him at safety from him that puffeth at him.' *Now*, this is the time I watched for as fittest for my own glory and their safety. Then God disappoints them, when they seem to have got to the goal, with the ball at their foot.

Secondly, God hereby doth glorify himself. He then discovers that there is nothing too high for his power to check, nothing too subtle for his wisdom to disappoint, nothing too low for his love to embrace. That is the season wherein his mercy will be most prized, his power most admired, his wisdom most adored, and his justice most cleared. God lets the concerns of his church go backward, that he may bring them on with more glory to himself and satisfaction to his creature. God will divide the benefit and the honour between himself and the creature; he will have the whole glory, and his creature shall have the sensible advantage. They shall enjoy salvation, there is their benefit, but 'not by sword or bow, but by the Lord their God,' Hosea i. 7. Saved they should be, but in such a way wherein the honour of God might most appear, without any mixture of the creature.

1. God glorifies his power. His eyes run to and fro to shew himself strong. He will then pitch upon such a season when his strength may appear most illustrious, and none else have any pretence to claim an equal strength with him. A time of extremity is the fittest opportunity for this, when his power cannot be clouded by any interpositions of the creature for challenging a share in it. The greater the malice against the church, the weaker the church's ability to help itself, the more glorious is the power of God magnified in deliverance; little dangers are not so suitable for the triumph of an infinite strength. As God let Christ lie three days in the grave, that his resurrection might be known to be the fruit of a divine power, for the same end he lets his mystical body lie in the same condition. Had God brought Israel out of Egypt in the time of the kings that were friends to them from a kindly remembrance of Joseph, there had been no character of a divine power, though there had been of a divine truth apparent in the case; but he set apart that time for their deliverance, when he was to contest with the mightiest opposition from the whole body of the Egyptian nation, who had forgot Joseph their great benefactor. Had not the disciples been in a great storm, ready to be cast away, and Christ asleep till they were in extremity, they had not seen such visible marks of the extensiveness of their Master's power, Isa. xxxiii. 7, 8, &c. When the hearts of the strong men fainted, when the Assyrians would not hear the ambassadors of peace, when they had broke their former covenant, resolved to invade the land, when their calamity and despair had arrested all their hopes, 'Now,' when all things are in such a deplorable state, 'will I rise, saith the Lord, now will I be exalted; now will I lift up myself.' God was not asleep or unconcerned, but he sat still watching for such a season; *now* is three times repeated. The Psalmist gives us a record of this in his particular case. When the waters of his affliction were many, the enemy strong, and too strong for him, their strength edged with an intense hatred, then God appears to be his stay, and prevents them in the day of his calamity, Ps. xviii. 16–18. God lets his enemies be too strong for him, that he might appear his only stay, without any mixture of David's strength in the case. When the Jews thrust Christ out of Nazareth, led him to the brow of the hill, and were ready to cast him down, then, and not till then, he frees himself out of their hands, and disappoints the effects of their rage, Luke iv. 29. As Christ dealt thus for himself, so he deals for his church in all ages.

2. God glorifies his wisdom. 'His eyes run to and fro throughout the

whole earth, to shew himself strong.' It is not a bare strength that God would shew, or such a power which we call in man a brutish valour, without wit or skill, but to shew his strength with his wisdom, when all his other attributes may be glorified with that of his power. When all worldly helps are departed, we can as little ascribe our security to our own wisdom and industry as to our own strength and power. The physician's skill is best evidenced in mastering a desperate disease. He will bring the counsels of the heathen to nought, Ps. xxxiii. 10. He will let them counsel, he will let them devise and carry on their counsels near to execution, that he may shew that, as the strength of hell is no match for his power, so the craft of Satan is no mate for his wisdom. But he raises the trophies of his wisdom upon the subtle devices of his enemies.

3. God glorifies his care and compassion. When his people are nearest crushing, God is nearest preserving. God's mercy is greatest when his saints' misery is deepest ; when Zion is as an outcast, it shall be taken into God's protection : Jer. xxx. 16, 17, ' I will heal thee of thy wounds, because they called thee an outcast, saying, This is Zion whom no man seeks after.' When none stood up to plead for her, when her lovers she depended on, had forgotten and forsaken her, when they thought her cast out of the care of any creature, the Creator would take her up. When the ruin was inevitable as to man, their preservation was most regarded by God. Had God stopped Pharaoh at his first march, by raising some mutiny in his army, his mercy to his people, as well as his power against his enemies, had not been so conspicuous. The more desperate things are, the fitter subject for the advancement of God's kindness. Had God conducted the Israelites through a rich and fruitful country, it would have obscured the glory of his care of them, which was more signal in directing them through a barren desert, crowded with fiery serpents, without bread to nourish them, or water to cool them, wherein he manifested himself to be both their caterer and physician. Moses was never more peculiarly under God's protection, no, not when he had the whole guard of Israel about him in the wilderness, than when his mother had exposed him to the river forlorn, in a pitched ark, and forsaken by his sister, who stood aloof off to see how providence would conduct him. When Laban was possessed with fury against Jacob, God countermands it, and issues out his own order to him, how he should behave himself towards his son, Gen. xxxi. 24, 29. God times his kindness, so that it may appear to be nothing else but grace, grace with a witness, that his people may be able to understand the very particularities of it : Isa. xxx. 18, ' Therefore will the Lord wait that he may be gracious unto you.' He leaves them therefore for a while to the will of their enemies : verse 17, ' At the rebuke of five shall you flee, till you be left as a beacon upon the top of a mountain, and as an ensign upon a hill.' Never is salvation sweeter, and mercy better relished, than when it snatcheth us out of the teeth of danger. God would have his mercy valued, and it is fit it should. And when is a calm more grateful than after the bitterest storm, attended with the highest despair ? God's mercy in sparing Isaac after the knife was at his throat, was more welcome and more delicious both to father and son, than if God had revealed his intent to Abraham in the three days' journey to the mount Moriah. But God suspending his soul in bitterness all that time, prepared his heart for the valuation of that mercy. When human help forsaketh us, God most embraceth us : Ps. xxvii. 10, ' When my father and mother forsake me, then the Lord will take me up.'

4. God glorifies his righteousness and justice. There is a measure of wickedness God stays for, which will be an object of his justice without

exception. When the measure of a people's covetousness is come, ' then their end is come, and God will fill them with men as with caterpillars, and they shall lift up a shout against them,' Jer. li. 13, 14. Hereby God clears the justice of his proceedings, that he exercised patience so long, that things were come to that pass, that either his people or his enemies must be destroyed. As the case was with the Israelites, had not God marvellously appeared, every man of them had been cut off or reduced to slavery. The die was cast, either the Egyptians or Israelites must be defeated ; either God must appear for his church, or none would be left in the world to profess him. In such a case the justice of God is more unexceptionable. No man has any semblance for complaining of him ; for he struck not till the safety of his adversaries was inconsistent with his own honour and interest of the world. When men come to such a height, as to slight and resolve to break the laws of God, then is the time for the honour of his righteousness in his own institutions, to vex them in his sore displeasure : Ps. ii. 3, 5, ' Then shall he speak to them in his wrath, and vex them,' &c. When ? When they resolve to ' cast away his bands and cords from them,' ver. 2. He is forced to rise then, when men make void his law, and tread down the honour of it ; when they would not have God to have a standing law in the world, or a people to profess him : Ps. cxix. 126, ' It is time for the Lord to work, for they have made void thy law.' When the grapes of wickedness are thus fully ripe, then is God's time for the honour of his justice to cast them into the wine-press of his wrath, Rev. xiv. 19, 20. This is God's set time, when he may glorify, without any exception, his justice in punishing his enemies' sins, his wisdom in defeating his enemies' plots, his power in destroying his enemies' strength, and his mercy in relieving his people's wants.

Thirdly, Such extremities and deliverance in them, are most advantageous for his people.

1. It being a season to improve and know their interest. Men do not usually seek to God, or at least so earnestly, as when they are in distress ; the time of the tempest was the time of the disciples' praying to Christ. The Israelites, you scarce find them calling upon God but in times of danger and distress ; hereby God doth encourage and give an argument for prayer. The Psalmist useth the extremity of the church often as an argument to move God to pity : Ps. cxxiii. 3, ' Have mercy upon us, O Lord, have mercy upon us, for we are exceedingly filled with contempt.' We are glutted with contempt, as low as low can be : so Ps. xliv. 23, 24, ' Awake, why sleepest thou, O Lord ? arise, cast us not off for ever ; our soul is bowed to the dust.' That is the most successful time for prayer, which is the time of the stirring of God's bowels. He hath been a ' strength to the poor, a strength to the needy in his distress, a refuge from the storm, a shadow from the heat, when the blast of the terrible ones is as a storm against the wall,' Isa. xxv. 4. They in such a time find how considerable their interest is with God, when upon their prayer they shall find relief suitable to every kind of danger they are in. The spirit of prayer upon the church is but the presage of their adversaries' ruin. When God seeks to destroy the nations that come against Jerusalem, he will pour upon the inhabitants of it a spirit of grace and of supplication : Zech. xii. 9, ' And in that day I will seek to destroy all the nations that come against Jerusalem, and I will pour upon the house of David, and the inhabitants of Jerusalem, the spirit of grace and of supplication.' This time of extremity, when all their hands fail, should edge the church's prayers. Our great intercessor seems in this case to set us a pattern : Zech. i. 12, ' O Lord of hosts, how long wilt thou not have mercy

upon Jerusalem!' (אֲתָה single by itself, not in an affix.) When all the earth sits still and is at rest, unconcerned in the affairs of thy church, if *thou* wilt not have mercy on them in this strait, who shall relieve them? none else have any mind to it; then issue out comfortable words to the angel from the mouth of God. This is an advantage of extremity; it sets Christ a pleading, and the church on praying.

2. As a season for acting faith at present, and an encouragement of reliance upon him in future straits. As a season for acting faith at present. Our Saviour lets Lazarus die and stink in the grave, before he raised him, that he might both confirm faith in his disciples' hearts, and settle it in the hearts of some of the Jews. John xi. 15, 45, 'I am glad for your sakes that I was not there, to the intent that ye may believe.' What, let Lazarus die, one that he loved, one so strongly pleaded for by two sisters that he loved too, and solicited upon his friendship to relieve him! ver. 3, 'Behold, he whom thou lovest is sick,' and our Saviour glad he was not there to prevent it! yes, not glad of Lazarus his extremity, nor of the church's, but of the opportunity to give them greater ground of faith and encouragement to trust him. The church's faith is God's glory. He that hath many things to trust to, is in suspense which he should take hold of; but when there is but one left, with what greediness will he clasp about that! God cuts down worldly props, that we might make him our stay. How will the church in extremity recollect all the deliverances of it in former ages, and put them up in pleas to God, for a renewal of his wonted kindness and new successions of deliverance, whereby God gets the glory of his former work, and his church the present comfort in renewing fiducial acts upon him! How doth Jehoshaphat put God in mind of his gracious assistance acted some ages before, when he was in a strait, by the invasion of a powerful army: 2 Chron. xx. 7, 'Art not thou our God that didst drive out the inhabitants of this land before thy people Israel?' ver. 12, 'We know not what to do, but our eyes are upon thee.' Never are the church's eyes so fixed upon God, never God's eyes so fixed upon the church, as in times of their distress. Then there is a sweet communion with, and recounting of all their former friendships. The church then throws itself wholly upon God; its prosperity is but like a troubled sea, its distress is the time of its rest. So Asa, when assaulted by a million of men under Zerah the Ethiopian, how doth he throw himself and the whole weight of his concerns upon the hands of God, and makes his cause God's! 2 Chron. xiv. 11, 'Help us, O Lord our God, for we rest on thee; O Lord, thou art our God, let not man prevail against thee.'

And there is an encouragement also in the deliverance for future faith. It gives a ground for future faith from the riches of the present experience; in such distresses there is the highest experience of God, and hope is the fruit of experience. How apt are we to believe God in other straits, when we have had assistance (like they that dreamed) come unexpectedly upon us. God overthrew Pharaoh's host in the Red Sea, when they were upon the heels of the affrighted Israelites and ready to crush them, but God gave them ' to be meat to the people inhabiting the wilderness,' Ps. lxxiv. 14, as a standing excellent dish to feed their hopes for all future deliverances upon their trust in God. And indeed that deliverance was an earnest of their perpetual security, by special providence in any succeeding trouble. And God often gives them a particular charge to remember that deliverance, with a practical remembrance to still their fear and support their faith: Deut. vii. 18, ' Thou shalt not be afraid of them, but shalt well remember what the Lord thy God did unto Pharaoh, and to all the Egyptians.' He would have them remember it as a covenant-mercy, ' what the Lord *thy God* did,' thy God in covenant, not what *the Lord* did barely by an arm of power, but what he did by a vastness of affection, and as a God of truth and firmness in his covenant.

3. In fitting them by the extremity for a holy reception of the mercy intended.

God keeps up the distress of his church to expel self-confidence. Trust in earthly things are the great checks of God's kindness. We hardly forsake this temper till we are forsaken by all those things we confide in. Times of extremity make us more humble; and humility, like the plough, fits us for the seed of mercy. The gardener's digging up the clods is but to prepare the earth for the receiving and nourishing some excellent plants he intends to put into its womb. There is a certain set time for God's great actions. He lets the powers of darkness have their hour, and God will take his hour: Ps. cii. 13, 'Thou shalt arise and have mercy upon Sion: for the time to favour her, yea, the set time, is come.' He hath a set time for the discovery of his mercy, and he will not stay a jot beyond it. What is this time? ver. 9, &c. When they 'eat ashes like bread, and mingle their drink with weeping;' when they are most humble, and when the servants of God have more affection to the church; when their humble and ardent affections are strong, even to the ruin and rubbish of it; when they have a mighty desire and longing for the reparation of it, as the Jews in captivity had for the very dust of the temple: ver. 14, 'For thy servants take pleasure in her stones, and favour the dust thereof.' *For* there notes it to be a reason why the set time was judged by them to be come. That is God's set time when the church is most believing, most humble, most affectionate to God's interest in it, and most sincere. Without faith we are not fit to desire mercy, without humility we are not fit to receive it, without affection we are not fit to value it, without sincerity we are not fit to improve it. Times of extremity contribute to the growth and exercise of those qualifications.

4. In securing them against future straits. For God's disappointing enemies when they think themselves sure of all, is the highest discouragement to them, and those of the like temper, to renew the like attempt; but if they do, it is an evidence they shall meet with the like success; it is the highest vexation to see their projects diverted, when they have lighted their match, and are ready to give fire. Men may better take notice how God loves his people, when he apprehends their adversaries in the very pinnacle of their pride, and flings them down from the mount of their hopes. It doth not only dash the present designs, but dishearten future attempts. The Egyptians, after their overthrow at the Red Sea, never attempted to disturb them in their journey in the wilderness. It was a bridle to all their enemies except Amalek, upon whose country they travelled in the wilderness, when it was the interest of state in all those nations to rout that swarm of people that must have some seat to dwell in; and every nation might justly fear to be dispossessed by them; yet we read of no league among those nations bordering upon the wilderness, such a terror did God strike into them by that relief he gave his people in their extremity at the Red Sea, whereby he provided for their future security in their whole journey. It was this melted the hearts of the Gibeonites, one of the nations of Canaan, and brought them to a submission to Joshua, as the sentiment of all their neighbours: Josh. ix. 9, 'We are come, because of the name of the Lord thy God; for we have heard the fame of him, and all that he did in Egypt.' And for this and other reasons it may be, that the times before the church's last deliverance shall be sharper than any before, which our Saviour intimates, Mat. xxiv. 21, 'For then there shall be great tribulation, such as

was not since the beginning of the world, no, nor ever shall be.' In discoursing his disciples of the troubles at the destruction of Jerusalem, which was a type of the trouble preceding the end of the world, he adds a discourse of what shall be at the end of the world, in the last attempt of the enemies of the church ; for, ver. 29, he saith, 'immediately after the tribulation of those days,' he speaks of his coming in the clouds of heaven with great power and glory. And also in the Revelation : Rev. xvi. 18, 'And there was a great earthquake, such as was not since men were upon the earth, so mighty an earthquake, and so great.' This, perhaps, at the pouring out of the seventh vial, may concern the Christian church as well as the antichristian party. But the reason why it may be sharper just before that last deliverance, than it was in former ages, may be because it is the last effort the enemy shall make ; the last demonstration of God's power and wisdom for, and care of his church, and justice upon his enemies in such cases ; the last season for their multiplying their cries, and acting their faith for such a concern.

Use 3. Of exhortation.

If it be so, that the providence of God is chiefly designed for the good of the church,—

First, Fear not the enemies of the church. It is a wrong to God. Fear of man is always attended with a forgetfulness of God : Isa. li. 12, 13, 'I, even I, am he that comforteth you : who art thou, that art afraid of a man that shalt die, and of the son of man that shalt be made as grass : and forgettest the Lord thy Maker, who hath stretched forth the heavens,' &c. It is to value the power of grass above the power of the Creator, as though that had more ability to hurt than God to help. As if men were as strong as mountains, and God as weak as a bulrush. It is a wrong to his truth ; hath he not comforted you in his promise ? What creature should then deject you ? It is a wrong to his mercy. Is he not the Lord thy Maker ? Calvin refers this to regeneration, and not creation. Hath he not renewed you by his Spirit ? and will he not protect you by his strength ? and that you may not question his power, look up to the heavens which he hath stretched out, and the foundations of the earth which he hath laid. And is that arm which hath done such mighty works, too weak to defend that work, which is choicer in his eye than either the extended heaven or the established earth ? We vilify God, and defile his glory, when our fear of man's power stifles our faith in God : Isa. viii. 12, 13, 'Neither fear you their fear, nor be afraid : sanctify the Lord of Hosts himself, and let him be your fear.' Let the wicked fear the Assyrians, and engage in confederacies against them ; but let your eyes be lifted up to me and my providence. God will either turn away the mouth of the cannon from the church, or arm it against the shot ; either preserve it from a danger, protect it in it, or sanctify it to the church ; and who need fear a sword in a father's hand ?

1. Will you fear man, who have a God to secure you ? The church belongs to God, not to man as a just propriety : Isa. xliii. 1, 'Fear not : for I have redeemed thee, I have called thee by my name : thou art mine. When thou passest through the waters, I will be with thee,' &c. 'Thou art *mine*,' not man's. Thou art mine, I am thine. I will be with thee as thine, I will secure thee as mine. Is my creating, is my forming, is my redeeming thee to no purpose ? I will not secure you from trouble ; but surely my redemption of you, the propriety I have in you, should secure you from fears in those troubles. None shall hurt you whilst I have power to defend you. God with us, if well considered and believed, is sufficient to still those fears which have the greatest outward objects for their encouragement :

Ps. xxvii. 1, ' The Lord is the strength of my life, of whom shall I be afraid ?'
If God be our strength to support us, why should the weakness of dust and
ashes scare us ?   Alliance to great men, and protection of princes, prop up
men's hearts against the fear of others ; and shall alliance to God be of a
weaker efficacy ? A heathen* could so argue, that knew nothing of redemption. Let the counsels of enemies be crafty, Ps. lxxxiii. 3 ; yet they consult against God's hidden ones, hidden by God, whilst plotted against by
men : who would fear the stratagems of men, whilst protected in an impregnable tower ? God hides, when men are ready to seize the prey. How did
the angel protect a sincere trembling Lot against the invasion of a whole
city, and secured his person whilst he blinded his enemies' eyes that they
could not find the door. Instruments cannot design more maliciously, than
Christ watches over them affectionately. Christ hath his eye to see your
works and danger where Satan hath his throne, Rev. ii. 13.

2. Will you fear men, who have a God to watch over their motions ?
What counsels can prevail where God intends to overrule their resolves ?
There is no place so close as to keep private resolutions from his knowledge.
This was the thought of those statesmen against whom the prophet Isaiah
thunders, Isa. xxix. 15, 16 : ' Woe unto them that seek deep to hide their
counsel from the Lord, and their works are in the dark ; surely your turning of things upside down shall be esteemed as the potter's clay.' Their
counsels were as well known to him as the potter's clay is to the potter,
which he can either frame into a vessel, or fling away into the mass from
whence he took it.   God hath not despoiled himself of his government ; nor
will devolve his right upon any men to dispose of his concerns.   When men
think to act so secretly, as though they framed themselves, as though God's
eye were not upon them, he will watch and trace all their motions, and
make them insignificant to their purposes. Satan himself, the slyest and
subtilest agent, is too open to God to hide his counsels from him.   Never
fear man till the whole combined policies of hell can control the resolves of
heaven, till God wants omniscience to dive into their secrets, skill to defeat their counsels, and an arm to abate their power.

3. Will you fear men or devils, who have a God to restrain them ?
The great dragon and general of the serpent's seed is under a binding
power, who can bind him not only a thousand years, Rev. xx. 2, but a thousand ages.   Have his seed more force to resist almightiness than their
captain ?   The prophet, speaking of the Assyrians threatening Jerusalem,
and the confusion in some cities for fear of them, yet, saith he, ' he shall
remain at Nob,' a city of the Levites, not far from Jerusalem, where he
might have a full prospect of the city.   He shall but ' shake his hand,' he
shall not gripe it in his talons : he shall shew his teeth, but not bite, snarl
but not worry, Isa. x. 32.   God will let out so much of the enemies' wrath
as may answer his gracious ends to the church in purging of them, but ' the
remainder of wrath,' which remains in their hearts for the church's destruction, ' he will restrain,' Ps. lxxvi. 9, 10 ; as the physician weighs out as
much as may curb the disease, not kill the patient.   The chain of providence
controls the power of Satan, when it doth not change his desires.   The
Egyptian's will against the Israelites was strong, but his power was weak.
Might and power is only in the hand of God, who reigns over all, 1 Chron.
xxix. 12.   And God will exert so much of power to bridle the inclinations
of nature in the wicked for the good of his people.   He will give them so
much line as may serve his holy purposes, but not so much as shall prejudice
the church's standing.   A staff is not capable of giving a smart blow with-

* Arram. in Epist. lib. i. c. 9.

out the force of the hand that holds it.   Wicked men are no more than a staff in God's hand: Isa. x. 5, 'The rod of my anger, the staff in their hand is my indignation;' he can either strike with it, or break it in pieces.   The staff is still in the hand of God, and can do no more than what his merciful arm moves it to ; as he can restrain it, so he can divert it.   What should we fear those whose hearts are in God's hands, whose enmity is under God's restraint, who can change their fury into favour, or at least bridle it as he doth the waves of the sea ?   No enemy's shot can exceed God's commission.   God often laughs when men plot, and disappoints when they begin to act.   Some- times he makes them act contrary to their intentions.   Balaam comes to curse the people, and God turns his tongue to bless them, which, if guided by his own heart, would have poured out execrations upon them, Num. xxiii. 7, 8.   God puts the words into his mouth, but not in his heart, ver. 5, and makes him bless that which his heart hates.

4. Will you fear them who have a God to ruin them ?   Though the beast in the Revelations hath seven heads, a reaching wisdom, and ten horns, a mighty power, Rev. xvii. 3 (both the numbers of seven and ten being num- bers of perfection in Scripture), yet, with all his wisdom and strength, he shall tumble down to destruction ; they can no more resist God's power than blustering winds or raging waves can cross his will.   When the enemies of the church are in combination, like thorns full of prickles 'folded together,' then shall they ' be consumed like stubble that is dry,' Nahum i. 10.   God loves to defeat pride : Exod. xviii. 11, 'In the thing wherein they dealt proudly, he was above them.'   God waits but the time of their swelling to make them burst.   Absalom kills his brother, withdraws the people from their obedience to the king, stirs them up to revolt, enters Jerusalem in his father's absence, pollutes his concubines, engages his designs against his life, raiseth an army against him ; who would not say David was in extremity, and Absalom alone prospering in his designs ?   But when Absalom comes to open force, God arises, an oak catches him, his mule forsakes him, and Joab despatches him.   Sennacherib had prospered in his conquest of Judea, taken many strong towns, laid siege to Jerusalem, solicits the people to revolt, blasphemes the God of heaven, and then an angel comes and makes a dreadful slaughter in a night, and he, returning to his own country, is killed by his own sons, 2 Kings xix. 7, 35, 36, 37.   God's arrows shall never miss their mark, and he hath more than one to strike into the hearts of his enemies : Ps. xviii. 14, 'He sent out his arrows and scattered them.' What reason then to fear even multitudes, who can never be too strong for that God who gave them that little strength they have !

Secondly, The second duty to which we are exhorted.   If all God's pro- vidences tend to the good of his church and people,

2. Then censure not God in his dark providences.   As we are often too hasty in our desires for mercy, and are not content to stay God's time, so we are too hasty in making constructions of providence, and will not stay God's leisure of informing us.   When God seems at the beginning of every providence to speak the same language as Christ did to Peter in washing his feet, John xiii. 7, 'What I do thou knowest not now, but thou shalt know hereafter,' the instruments are visible, the action sensible, but the inward meaning still lies obscured from our view.   We are too short-sighted to apprehend and judge of God's works ; man cannot understand his own way, Prov. xx. 24, much less the ways of an infinite God.   God's judgments are a great deep, Ps. xxxvi. 6 ; we may sooner fathom the deepest part in the sea, understand all the turnings of those subterranean passages, lave out the ocean with a spoon, or suck in, into our bellies, that great mass of

waters, than understand the ways of God with our shallow brains. He makes darkness his pavilion; he is sometimes very obscure in his ways. Neither the greatness of his means, nor the wisdom of his workings, can be fully apprehended by men. We have sense to feel the effects, but not heads to understand the reasons and methods of the divine government. Eccles. iii. 11, 'No man can find out the work that God makes from the beginning to the end.' Though a man may see the beginning of God's works, yet is he able to walk understandingly along with divine wisdom in every step it takes? will he not lose the track often before it comes to an end? It is not the face, but the back parts of providence which we behold; why then should we usurp an authority beyond our ability, and make ourselves God's judges, as if infinite wisdom and power were bounded within the narrow compass of our purblind reasons? His ways are beyond our tracing, and his counsels too high for our short measures. Since therefore God satisfies the righteousness of his own will, let us submit our curiosity to his wisdom, and forbear our censures of that exact righteousness and superlative wisdom which we cannot comprehend.

1. Therefore, first fix this in your minds, that God is righteous, wise, and good in everything. Good, therefore nothing can be hurtful to his people; righteous, therefore nothing unjust; wise, therefore nothing in vain; our injurious thoughts of him make us so uncharitable towards him, and greater censurers of his righteous ways than we are of men's wicked actions. Clouds and darkness are about him; our eye cannot pierce through his darkness, or see the frame of his counsels; yet let these principles be kept as the centre, that 'righteousness and judgment are the habitation of his throne,' Ps. lxxxix. 14. He is righteous in his darkness, wise in his cloudiness; though his judgments are unsearchable to us, and his ways past finding out by our most industrious inquisitions, and a depth of knowledge and wisdom there is in them too deep for us to measure, Rom. xi. 33. God was always righteous, wise, and good; he is the same still. Though the motions of the planets be contrary, yet the sphere where they are fixed, the natures wherewith they are created, are the same still. Though the providences of God have various motions, yet the spring of his counsel, the rule of his goodness, the eye of his wisdom, the arm of his power, are not altered. He acts by the same rule, disposeth by the same wisdom, orders according to the same righteousness; he is unchangeable in the midst of the changeable effects of providence. The sun is the same body, which admits of no inward alteration, keeps exactly its own motion, though its appearances are sometimes ruddy, sometimes clear; its heat sometimes more faint, at another time more scorching; its distance sometimes nearer, sometimes farther off. He must be very ignorant that thinks the objects upon which we look through a prism or trigonal glass change their colours as often as they are represented so in the various turnings of the glass. You see the undulations and wavings of a chain which hangs perpendicularly, one part moves this way and another that way, but the hand that holds it, or the beam to which it is fastened, is firm and steady.

2. Distinguish between preparations to the main work and the perfection of the work, between the motions of God's eyes and the discovery of his strength; his eyes move before his power. The neglect of this was the cause of the Israelites' uncharitable censures of the kindness of God; they interpret God's reducing them into the straits near the Red Sea a design for their destruction, which was but the preparation for their complete deliverance, in a way most glorious to God, and most comfortable and advantageous to themselves.

He that knows not the use of the grape, would foolishly censure a man who should fling them into a wine-press, and squeeze them into mash, which is but a preparation of them to afford that generous liquor which was the end of their growth.* God treads his grapes in a wine-press to draw from thence a delicate wine, and preserve the juice for his own use, which would else wither upon the stalk, and dry up to nothing. We judge not the husbandman angry with his ground for tearing it with his plough, nor censure an artificer for hewing his stones or beating his iron, but expect patiently the issue of the design. Why should we not pay the same respect to God which we do to men in their arts, since we are less capable of being judges of his incomprehensible wisdom than of the skill of our fellow-creatures? God in his cross providence prepares the church for fruitfulness whilst he ploughs it. He may seem to be digging up the bowels of the church, while he is only preparing to lay the foundation in Sion for the raising a noble structure; and in what shape soever he appears in his preparations, he will in his perfection of it appear in glory: Ps. cii. 16, 'When the Lord shall build up Sion, he shall appear in glory;' and evidence that he was restoring whilst we thought him destroying, and healing whilst we thought him wounding. As God hath settled a gradual progress in his works of creation, so by degrees he brings his everlasting counsels to perfection. The seasons of the year are not jumbled together, but orderly succeed one another; and the coldness of the winter is but a preparation for a seasonable spring and a summer harvest. We do not unrighteously accuse God of disorder in his common works, why should we do it in his special works of providence? Do we disparage the musician's skill for the jarring and intelligible touches in the tuning the instrument, but rather wait for the lesson he intends to play? If we stay for God's fuller touches of this great instrument of the world in the way of his providence, it will, like David's harp, chase away that evil spirit from us which is now too apt to censure him.

3. Fix not your eye only upon the sensible operations of providence, but the ultimate end. As in a watch the various wheels have different motions, yet all subservient to one end, to tell the true hour of the day and the motion of the sun, so are all the providences of God. Should any have been preserved in the deluge upon some high mountain who had not known the design of the ark, and had seen it floating upon such a mass of waters, he would have judged the people in it in a deplorable condition, and have concluded that it would have broke against the mountain, or been overturned by the waves; yet that was Noah's preservative. Had any of us been with Christ, and acknowledged him the Saviour of the world, and yet seen him crucified in such a manner by men, and judged only by that, what wise and just constructions should we have made of that providence? Much the same as some of his disciples did: Luke xxiv. 21, 'We trusted that it had been he which should have redeemed Israel;' but the whole design is spoiled, we are fools, and he an impostor. Yet this, which seemed to be the ruin of redemption, was the necessary highway to it by God's constitution. No other way was it to be procured: ver. 26, 'Ought not Christ to have suffered these things, and to have entered into his glory?' His entrance into glory to perfect our salvation was the end of the sensible suffering wherein he laid the foundation. As they charge Christ with imposture, not considering the end, so do we God with unrighteousness when we consider not his aim. The end both beautifies and crowns the work; the remarks of God's glory in the creation are better drawn from the ends of

* Morn. de verit. Rel. Christian, cap. xii. p. 210, 211.

the creatures, and their joint subserviency to them, than from any one single piece of the creation. We must not only consider the present end, but the remote end, because God in his providence towards his church hath his end for after times. God acts for ends at a great distance from us, which may not be completed till we are dead and rotten. How can we judge of that which respects a thing so remote from us, unless we view it in that relation? God's aims in former providences were things to come, his aims in present providences are things to come. As the matter of the church's prayers, so the objects of God's providences are things to come: Isa. xlv. 11, 'Ask me of things to come, concerning my sons.' The matter of their prayers then were, that God would order all things for the coming of the Messiah. The matter of the church's prayer now is, that God would order all things for the perfecting the Messiah in his mystical body. The whole frame of providence is for one entire design; it is one entire book with seven seals, Rev. v. 1. The beginning of a book, as well as the middle, hath relation to the end. The design of God's book of providence is but one in all the seven seals and periods of time.

4. Consider not only one single act of providence, but the whole scheme, to make a conclusion. The motions of his eyes are various, but all ends in discoveries of his strength. Men do not argue from one single proposition, but draw the conclusion from several propositions knit together. It is by such a spiritual logic we are to make our conclusions from the way of providence; as in the reading Scripture, if we take not the whole period, we may make not only nonsense, but blasphemy;[*] as in that of the psalmist, 'Thou art not a God that hath pleasure in unrighteousness.' If a man should read only, *Thou art not a God*, and make a full stop there, it would be blasphemy; but reading the whole verse, it is an excellent sense, and an honourable declaration of God's holiness. Such errors will be committed in reading the books of providence, if we fix our eyes only in one place, and make a full stop where God hath not made any. We judge not of a picture by the first draught, but the last lines; not by one shadow or colour, but by the whole composure. The wisdom of God is best judged of by the view of the harmony of providence. The single threads of providence may seem very weak or knotty and uneven, and seem to administer just occasion of censure; but will it not as much raise the admiration to see them all woven into a curious piece of branched work? Consider therefore God's ways of working, but fully judge nothing till the conclusion, for that is to judge before the time. Judge not then of providence at the first appearance; God may so lose the glory of his work, and you the comfort.

Thirdly. The third duty. Inquire into providence, and interpret all public providences by this rule. We must search into it, though we are not able to find out all the reasons of it. What can be a braver study than that which is the object of God's eternal counsel? We are conformed to God in our wills, when we have the same ends in our motions; and we are conformed to God in our understandings, when we have the same object of our thoughts. Some providences have their interpretation written in their foreheads, we may run and read: such as his signal judgments in the world, which express the very sin for which they are inflicted; others are wrapped up in a harder shell and more covers, and therefore more labour to reach the kernel; some are too high for our knowledge, none for our inquiry. It is our duty to seek after God, though we can never arrive to a perfect knowledge of him: Job xi. 7, 'Canst thou by searching find out God? canst thou find out the Almighty unto perfection?' He prohibits not the searching, though he

[*] Burgess of Justification, part ii. serm. 2, p. 12.

asserts the impossibility of finding him out to perfection. What hath God given us faculties for, but to search after him? And we must not do it to satisfy our curiosity, but to increase our knowledge, and consequently our admiration of his wise and powerful care. Diligence must be used too. Our first thoughts about things of concernment are usually confused; so are our first sights of providence. Providence is a great deep; deep things are not seen without stooping down. We must παρακυψαι, as the angels do when they search into the things of the gospel, 1 Pet. i. 12. But let this aim of God at the good of his church be the rule of your interpretation. Without this compass to steer our judgments by, we may both lose and rack ourselves in the wilderness of providence, and fortify our natural atheism and ignorance instead of our faith. I must confess the study of providence is in some respect more difficult than in the former ages of the world, because God seems to manage things in the church more by his wisdom than power, which is not so intelligible by man as the sensible effects of his strength. That attribute he manifested most in miraculous ways and the visible minis- try of angels, as we read in Scripture stories; now he employs his wisdom more in ordering second causes, in ordinary ways, to his own high, merciful, and just ends. Yet since the discovering of Christ, God hath given us a rule whereby we may discern much of his wisdom in the knowledge of his end, as the knowledge of Christ removes the veil from the Scripture in our reading of it: 2 Cor. iii. 14–16, 'The same veil remains in the reading of the Old Testament, which veil is done away in Christ' (which veil is still upon the Jews), and makes us understand those parts of the Old Testament which otherwise would be utterly obscure; so in the reading the books of provi- dence, the knowledge of this end of God in them, will help us to understand the meaning of that which otherwise would non-plus the reason of man. He that knows the end of one that is making a watch, will not wonder at his framing small wheels and filing little pins; but he that understands nothing of the design, would count it ridiculous for a man so to trifle away his time. Without the knowledge of this end, we shall expose ourselves to miserable mistakes; as Plutarch mistook the cause of the ceasing of oracles, ascribing it to the change of the nature of the soil, not affording those exhalations as formerly, or the death of the demons which gave those oracles. He had judged otherwise, had he known or believed the rising of a higher power, the Sun of righteousness in the world, who imposed silence upon those angels of darkness, the most famous oracles in the world ceasing about the time of Christ. To imagine to interpret the motions of providence, without a know- ledge of Christ and the design of God for his church, is as vain as to imagine we can paint a sound, or understand a colour by our smell. Correct sense by reason in this work, and reason by faith. To what end hath God pre- scribed faith to succour us in the weakness of reason, if it had been capable to understand his ways without it, and if we make no use of it upon such occasions?

Fourthly. A fourth duty. Consider the former providences God hath wrought for the church in the past ages. Let him not lose the present glory of his past works: Ps. cii. 18, 'This shall be written for the generation to come, and the people which shall be created shall praise the Lord,' even for that work of his which is written to be done in former ages. God loves to have his former works read and pleaded. It is a keeping a standing praise of him in the world. We have had the benefit of them; it is fit God should have the glory of them from us, as well as from those who immediately en- joyed them. Our good was bound up in every former preservation of the church. If the candlestick had been broken, where had the candle been?

H

Had the church been destroyed, how could the gospel have been transmitted to us ?   Let the duty we owe to God's glory engage us to a consideration of them, and the benefit we have had by them also incite us.   We usually forget not things that are strange, nor things that are profitable ; his works of old have been works of wonder in themselves, and profitable to us.   To what end are the praises of God discovered to the generations to come, but that they should reflect those praises to heaven again, and convey them down to the generations following ? Ps. lxxviii. 4, 'Shewing to the generation to come the praises of the Lord.'

1. This will help us in our inquiries in present providences.

There is a beautiful connection between former and latter providences ; they are but several links of one chain.   The principle and end is the same ; that God from whence they come, that Christ to which they tend, is the same yesterday, to-day, and for ever.   What God doth now, is but a copy of what he portrayed in his word as done in former ages ; there are the same goodness, the same design in both.   The births of providence are all of a like temper and disposition.   We cannot miss of the understanding of them, if we compare them with the ancient copies ; for God is in the generation of the righteous, the same God still.   God is the same, his ends are the same, the events will be the same.

2. It will support our faith.   The reason of our diffidence of God in the cause of the church, is the forgetfulness of his former appearances for her.   Oh if we did remember his former goodness, we should not be so ready to doubt of his future care.   This was the psalmist's care in his despondencies, and in his overwhelming troubles of spirit : Ps. lxxvii. 9, 'Hath God forgotten to be gracious ? hath he in anger shut up his tender mercies ?' but, ver. 10, he concludes it his infirmity, and resolves upon a review of the records of God's ancient works for his people, ' and the years of the right hand of the Most High,' these times wherein he declared his power and his glory, and so proceeds to the top of all their deliverances, viz., that out of Egypt.   Doth God's wisdom decay, or his power grow feeble ? Is not his interest the same ? Is he not a God still like himself ? Is not his glory as dear to him as before ? Hath he cast off his affection to his own name ? Why should not he then do the same works, since he hath the same concern ? God himself, to encourage us, calls them to our remembrance : Isa. l. 2, 'Is my hand shortened, that I cannot redeem ? or have I no power to deliver ? Behold, at my rebuke I do dry up the sea, I make the rivers a wilderness,' &c.   Am not I the same God that dried up the sea, that wrought those ancient wonders which amazed the world ?   What doth your distrust signify but the impair of my power ? Rouse up yourselves to a consideration of them, and thence gather fresh supplies to strengthen you in your present dependence upon me !   He puts us in mind of them, because we are apt to forget them.   Gen. xv. 6, when it is said Abraham ' believed in the Lord, and it was accounted to him for righteousness,' God answered him, ver. 7, ' I am the Lord that brought thee out of Ur of the Chaldees.'   Keep up thy faith ; and to that end, remember what I did for thee before in calling thee.   Cast thy eye upon that place whence I delivered thee, either from the idolatries of the place, or the persecution he was in for the true worship of God.   And as God puts him in mind of his mercy he had shewn to him before, for the encouragement of his faith, so the people of God have made use of them to this end.   Goliah's sword was counted by David the fittest for his defence in his flight, because it had been a monument of God's former deliverance of him, 1 Sam. xxi. 9.   When he asks for a sword or spear, Abimelech said, ' The sword of Goliah, whom thou slewest, is here ;' and David said, ' There

is none like that: give it me.' How hasty he catches at it! There is none like that sword, that hath so signal a mercy writ upon it. That very sword will not only defend me against my enemies, but guard my faith against those temptations that would invade it. This encouragement of faith and hope is the end of God in his transmission of the records of his former providences to us: Ps. lxxviii. 6, 7, 'That the generation to come might know them, and declare them to their children' from one posterity to another, 'that they might set their hope in God.'

3. It will enliven our prayer.

It is a mighty plea in prayer. How often doth David urge it! Thou hast been my help, thou hast delivered my soul from death, wilt thou not deliver my feet from falling? But in the church's concerns too: 1 Chron. xvi. 11, 12, 'Seek the Lord and his strength, seek his face continually. Remember the marvellous works that he hath done.' A reflection upon what God hath done should be enjoined* with our desires of what we would have God to do for us. When Moses was praying upon the top, while Israel was fighting with Amalek at the foot of the hill, he had the rod of God in his hand, Exod. xvii. 9; that miraculous rod which had amazed Pharaoh, whose motion summoned all the plagues upon them; that rod which had split the sea for their passage, broached the rock for their thirst, and had been instrumental in many miracles: certainly Moses shewed this rod to God, and pleaded all those wonderful deliverances God had wrought instrumentally by it. No doubt but he carried it with him to shew to God for a plea, as well as to the Israelites, to spirit their resolutions against their enemies.

4. It will prevent much sin.

A forgetfulness of his former works is one cause of our present provocations. It was so in the case of the Israelites' sin: Ps. cvi. 7, 'They remembered not the multitude of his mercies; but provoked thee at the sea, even at the Red Sea;' they had lost the memory of so many miracles in Egypt, and which aggravated their sin, ' they provoked him at the sea, at the Red Sea;' they provoked him under a present indigency, as well as against former mercy; they provoked him in that place of straits where all the powers on earth could not have relieved them had heaven neglected them. The provocation you may see, Exod. xiv. 11, 12, which sprang from a forgetfulness of his kindness so lately shewed to them. How apt are we to forget old mercies, when we are so naturally apt to blot out of our memories mercies newly received! If this were well considered by men, it would prevent their enterprises against the church, and consequently their shame and ruin. Are there records of any who have hardened themselves against God and prospered? Job ix. 4. How might in that reflection be seen the frustrations of counsels, disgracing of attempts, showers of fury and vengeance from heaven upon the heads of such! The reason why the wonderful works of God were to be made known to posterity, was ' that they might not be as their fathers, a stubborn and rebellious generation of men,' Ps. lxxviii. 6, 8. If they did consider those transactions of God in and for his church, they could no more think to stop the breath of perpetual powerful providence, than to bridle in a storm, or stop the motion of the sun. To conclude this : God's providential judgments are to be remembered; though they are for the punishment of the age that feel them, they are also for the instruction of the age which succeeds them; tell, מרדן, number, be as exact as in your accounts, wherein you take notice of every number, minute, and cypher. The works of providence as well as the

* That is, 'joined in,' or incorporated.—ED.

doctrine of God are parts of a child's catechism, they are to keep up the consideration of them in themselves, and hand them in instruction to their children.

F.fthly, The fifth duty. Act faith on God's providence.

Times of trouble should be times of confidence; fixedness of heart on God would prevent fears of heart : Ps. cxii. 7, 'He shall not be afraid of evil tidings : his heart is fixed.' How? 'Trusting in the Lord. His heart is established, they shall not be moved.' Otherwise without it we shall be as light as a cock* moved with every blast of evil tidings, our hopes will swim or sink according to the news we hear. Providence would seem to sleep, unless faith and prayer awakened it. The disciples had but little faith in their Master's account, yet that little faith awakened him in a storm, and he relieved them. Unbelief doth only discourage God from shewing his power in taking our parts. 'Every one will walk in the name of his god, and we will walk in the name of the Lord our God for ever and ever,' Micah iv. 5. Heathens will trust in their idols, and shall not we in that God that lives for ever? Have we any reason to have a less esteem of our confidence in God than heathens had of and in their idols ? We should do our duty, which is faith and hope, and leave God to do his work, which is mercy and kindness. By unbelief we deny his providence, disparage his wisdom, and strip him of his power ; we have none else to trust ; no creature can order anything for the church's good without God's commission and direction. What should we trust him for ? For that wherein his glory is concerned, which is more worth to him than all the world besides. Trust him most when instruments fail. God takes them off some time, to shew that he needs not any, and to have our confidence rightly placed on him, which staggered before between him and the creature.

1. All the godly formerly did act faith on a less foundation. The godly patriarchs who lived eight or nine hundred years, depended upon providence that long time, and shall not we for seventy years, the usual term of man's life ! They had promises to support them, we have not only the same promises, but the performances of them too. They had providences, we have the same and more, all upon record in Scripture, all since the canon of Scripture was closed, whatsoever God hath remarkably done for his people in all ages. Adam had but one promise, and but little experience of God's providence, yet no doubt trusted in him. We have a multitude of promises, not only pronounced, but sealed, confirmed by many repetitions, which are fresh obligations laid by God upon himself, the experience of all the providences of God towards his church for above five thousand years, and shall our faith stagger when upon us are come the ends of the world ? Doth it become us to have our obligations to faith so strong, and our exercise of it so weak ? The promise of Christ, Isa. vii. 14, that a virgin should bring forth a Son, was thought by God a sufficient security to support their confidence in him against the fury of their enemies ; it being a greater wonder that a virgin without loss of her virginity should bring forth a son, than the routing of an host of enemies. Is not then the performance of this, God's actual sending his Son to us through the womb of a virgin, a higher ground of confidence for the church's success in every thing else, than barely the promise could be ? All creatures in danger have a natural confidence in God : 'He is the confidence of all the ends of the earth ;' but the church's confidence may be more firmly placed in him, because he is particularly the God of their salvation : Ps. lxv. 5, 'By terrible things in

---

* That is, a weather-cock or vane.—ED.

righteousness wilt thou answer us, O God of our salvation; who art the confidence of all the ends of the earth.'

2. It is your only way to have mercy for the church, and for ourselves.

If he 'take pleasure in them that hope in his mercy,' as it is in Ps. cxlvii. 11, he will take pleasure to relieve them, he will 'strengthen the bars of their gates,' ver. 13. If he take pleasure in them that hope in his mercy, then the stronger and more lively their hope is, the more intense is God's pleasure in them. If they do not hope in his mercy, he hath no pleasure in them, and no delight to them. He hath a goodness laid up for them that fear him, and he will lay it out too for them that trust in him: Ps. xxxi. 19, 'Oh how great is thy goodness which thou hast laid up for them that fear thee, which thou hast wrought for them that trust in thee before the sons of men!' It is laid up for all that fear him, but it is wrought for them that trust in him. It is manifested upon special acts of trust and reliance, and wrought before the sons of men. Those that own God publicly in a way of reliance, God will own them publicly in a way of kindness. Faith is the key that unlocks the cabinet of special providence. Those eyes which move about all the world are fixed upon those that trust in him: Ps. xxxiii. 18, 'The eye of the Lord is upon them that hope in his mercy.'

The sixth duty. Wait upon God in the way of his providence. Wait upon him as he is 'a faithful Creator,' 1 Pet. iv. 19; much more since the title of being our Redeemer is added to that of our Creator, which strengthens his relation to us. Not to wait disparageth his care, bounds his power, or reflects upon his wisdom, as if he had stripped himself of his immense goodness, and forgot both his promise and his people; as if he had cancelled the covenant, and given up his whole interest to the lusts of men. Wait in the saddest appearances. The hour of Christ's death was dismal in the world, and darkness upon the earth; a miraculous eclipse of the sun taken notice of by the very heathens; yet were we never nearer to happiness, than in that dreadful time when our Saviour was most dyed in his own blood. The sanguine complexion of the evening sky is a presage of a fair succeeding morning; so many times is the red vesture of the church.

1. Wait upon him obedientially.

Commit your souls to God, but in 'well-doing,' 1 Pet. iv. 19. Use no indirect means; a contempt of the precept cannot consist with faith in either promise or providence. The obeying part is ours, the governing part is God's: Prov. xxiii. 17, 18, 'Let not thine heart envy sinners, but be thou in the fear of the Lord all the day long; for surely there is an end, and thine expectation shall not be cut off.' God will govern all the day, but we must fear him all the day. When fear on our part attends government on God's part, there will be an end of our carnal fears, and a good issue of our hopes. The greatest deliverances of his church have been when his people has stood still, Exod. xiv. 13. As that deliverance was a type of all future and a ground of faith, so the carriage God enjoined was a rule to his people in all future straits. It is against the laws of God's government for those listed in his service to stir without order. The law is our standing rule of duty. Providence cannot be a standing visible rule, because of the variety and seeming crossness of it sometimes to our apprehensions. Do not presume to lead God, but be led by him. It is our safety to follow him; it is our sin and danger to presume to be his directors. We may lose ourselves when we are our own blind guides, and fall into a ditch; but when we follow God, he hath wisdom to foresee the precipices we may stumble into, and goodness to divert us from them. By interposing carnal devices, men may perhaps have their ends, but with little comfort, perhaps much bitterness to themselves. Jacob by his hasty using his own and his mother's sinful project for the blessing, got it indeed, but a cross too, for he was a man of sorrows all his days. By waiting in God's way, we shall have our ends with more sweetness, because purely a fruit of God's care and goodness.

2. Wait patiently. How often are our spirits troubled about future events, and are afraid of the evil which threatens us, as if we were in pain for God, and in doubt of his wise conduct! Think not God's time too long. He waits as much for a fit opportunity to shew his mercy, as you can wait for the enjoyment of it: Isa. xxx. 18, ' Therefore will the Lord wait, that he may be gracious unto you ; blessed are all they that wait for him.' It is a part of our blessedness to wait for God, since it is a part of God's kindness to wait for a fit season to be gracious to us. It is not for us to prescribe rules to God, but follow the rules he prescribes to us. He hath freely made his promise ; let him be master of his own time to make it good. He will shew as much wisdom in accomplishing, as he did mercy in declaring it. God can do things in a moment, but it is his wisdom to take time, that his people may have time to exercise their trust, their hope, and their patience. He will take time in the ways of his providence, as well as he did in the works of creation. He allotted six days to that which he could have framed in a minute. He is judge of what is needful for us, and when it is needful for us. If God should give us that which is a mercy in its own nature, many times when we desire it, it might not be a mercy. If we will trust the skill of his wisdom for the best season, it cannot but be a mercy, for he will give it us with his own glory and grace wrapped up in it, which will make it sweeter to himself when his wisdom is honoured, and sweeter to us when our good is promoted. God's methods appear in the end both wiser and better than our frames. Infinite goodness aims more at our welfare than our shallow self-love ; and infinite wisdom can conduct things to our welfare, better than our short-sighted skill. He that knows all the moments of time, knows best how to time his actions. As God stayed for a fulness of time to bring the great redemption by Christ into the world, so he stays for a fulness of time to bring all the great consequences and appendices of it unto his church. ' Everything is beautiful in his time,' Eccles. iii. 11 ; in its own time ; in God's time, not in ours, &c.

3. Wait constantly. Though the wheels of providence seem sometimes to stand still, Ezek. i. 21, and God seems to put a period to the care of his church, yet let not us neglect our duty. Wait a while, and the wheels will be put upon their former rolling. Some particular passages of providence may trouble us for a while ; but in the issue, God may answer our desires above our expectations, and thereby confute our fears. His providences are sometimes like rivers that run under ground, out of sight, but will rise again with a delightful stream, with some new medicinal quality, contracted from the earth by the way. Joseph a prisoner waits upon God for his liberty, and God gives him freedom with preferment. God can bring about his people's safety by unexpected ways. Who would have imagined before, that his own dream should make him a captive, and Pharaoh's dream make him a favourite ? The chief butler remembers him not till he was in an exigency, and the divining skill of the wise men of Egypt confounded. Joseph lost nothing by waiting upon God, who made so many circumstances concur to promote his honour. Wait therefore upon him in the sorest afflictions. The church is only afflicted in mercy, but the enemies of it are pulled up by the roots : Jer. xxx. 11, ' I am with thee to save thee ; though I make a full end of the nations whither I have scattered thee, yet I will not make a full end of thee, but I will correct thee in measure.' God deals with his people

as a father, who corrects to reform, not to destroy; but with his enemies he deals as a judge. God's providence, like Moses his rod, may seem sometimes a devouring serpent, but it is to convince the Egyptians, and deliver the Israelites.

4. Wait in the use of lawful means for preservation. Not to use means, is to slight his providence, not to trust it. It seems not to consist with the wisdom of God to order things always so, as to be necessitated to put forth an extraordinary power in things which his creatures, by a common providence, can naturally accomplish. God saves by natural means; when they will not serve the turn, he will save by supernatural. God chose an ark to preserve Noah in. He did not want supernatural means for his preservation. He might have catched him up in a cloud, and continued him there till the drying of the waters. Noah doth not dispute the business with God, but prepares an ark according to his order; and he was righteous in his obedience, as well as in his trust. God would not preserve our Saviour by a miracle, when ordinary means would serve the turn. He commands Joseph, by his angel, to flee into Egypt with the child, Mat. ii. 13. Joseph desires not God to preserve him by an extraordinary power, to save his pains of travelling; he submits to God's order, and God quickly clears the way for his return. Indeed, sometimes the wheels of providence are lifted up from the earth, and do not go in the ordinary tracts, Ezek. i. 19; but miracles must be left to God's pleasure. For us to desire them, is to tempt our great governor.

The seventh duty. Pray for the church.

It is an encouragement that our suit in this case will not be denied. The desire of welfare is conformable to his counsel, which shall stand, Prov. xix. 21, notwithstanding the devices of men. His counsel in particular concerns of men shall stand; much more is the stability of his counsel for the church. He is a God hearing prayer in a way of common providence, and a God hearing prayer in a way of special attention: Ps. lxi. 1, 'Hear my cry, O God, attend unto my prayer.' David desires that God would hear him, as more particularly concerned in his case. He is so in the concerns of his church. Will he hear an Ishmael crying for himself, and young lions roaring for their prey, and stop his ears to the voice of his own Spirit in his people, pleading for the church, dearer to him than the whole mass of nature? We have greater arguments to use than in any other case. The relation the church hath to God; the affection God hath to the church. 'Lazarus whom thou lovest is sick,' was Martha's argument to Christ. What greater encouragement to our petitions than God's affection, than God's relation? God loves to have our affection comply with his; God loves others the better for soliciting its welfare. Moses had the greatest manifestation of God's love after he had prayed for the Israelites, Exod. xxxii. 32, though in a case of sin; and presently after, in Exod. xxxiii. 11, God 'speaks with him face to face, as a man speaks to his friend;' and in the same chapter, and the beginning of Exod. xxxiv., God shews him his glory as much as he was capable to bear. Daniel was a great petitioner for the church, Dan. ix. 3, 21. He was God's great favourite upon that account, x. 2, 5, and had the clearest and highest revelations made to him of the course of providence in the world.

The eighth duty. When you receive any mercy for the church in answer of prayer, give God the glory of it.

The variety of his providences gives us matter for new songs and compositions, Ps. cxlix. 1. What volleys of joyful shouts, what hallelujahs to God do we find upon the ruin of antichrist; Rev. xix. 1–3, God calls for praise out of the throne, ver. 5, and the church returns it, ver. 6, 7. It is God rides upon the cherub, it is God that sits upon the wings of the wind, it is God who is in all instruments to quicken their motions and direct them to their scope, Ps. xviii. 10.

The ninth duty.   Imitate God in his affection to the church.

Christ did what he did for the good of his church, God doth what he doth for the advantage of the church.   Let the same mind be in us that was in Christ, let the same end be ours which is the end of God.   Thus we shall be like our Creator, thus we shall be like our Governor, thus we shall be like our Redeemer.   Men take it kindly from others that love those they have a respect for.   God loves all that love his people, and blesses them that bless them : Gen. xii. 3, ' I will bless them that bless thee, and curse them that curse thee.'

The tenth duty.   Look after sincerity before God.

It is for the security of such that God shews himself strong.   No man that fully believes and understands this doctrine but should be glad to be of that happy society, that assembly of the first-born, who are under the care of a watchful eye, and the mighty power of the God of the whole earth. When God chose Israel, the very strangers should for their own interest join with them, Isa. xiv. 1.   And to such as ' take hold of his covenant' he promises to ' give a name in his house that shall not be cut off,' Isa. lvi. 4, 5 ; yea, even ' to the sons of the strangers that shall join themselves to the Lord,' ver. 6.   Let this encourage us to Christianity.   God never encouraged men to be Christians by promises of worldly greatness, but by promises of a constant care of them for their happiness, by promises of making all things work together for their good.   If God will shew himself strong for those that are perfect in heart towards him, then he hath no strength for those that are unsound and false in heart towards him.   No man hath an interest in his special providence without faith.   The power, knowledge, wisdom of God, are all set against him.   Though the whole world be in commotions, the earth be removed, and the mountains cast into the depths of the sea, there is no ground of fear to faith ; but what buckler against them hath unbelief and hypocrisy ?   What security against wrath can riches give you ?   What defence against his power can your potsherd strength afford you ?   It was not for Job s wealth that God made his boasts of him, but for his sincerity : Job i. 8, ' Hast thou considered my servant Job, that there is none like him in the earth, a perfect and an upright man ?' And for the want of this he loathes a world.   Labour therefore for sincerity towards God, beg it of God ; get the evidence of it and preserve it.

DISCOURSE ON THE EXISTENCE AND ATTRIBUTES OF GOD.

TO THE READER.

THIS long since promised and greatly expected volume of the reverend author upon the divine attributes, being transcribed out of his own manuscripts by the unwearied diligence of those worthy persons that undertook it,* is now at last come to thy hands. Doubt not but thy reading will pay for thy waiting, and thy satisfaction make full compensation for thy patience. In the epistle before his *Treatise of Providence*, it was intimated that his following discourses would not be inferior to that, and we are persuaded that ere thou hast perused one half of this, thou wilt acknowledge that it was modestly spoken. Enough, assure thyself, thou wilt find here for thy entertainment and delight, as well as profit. The sublimeness, variety, and rareness of the truths here handled, together with the elegancy of the composure, neatness of the style, and whatever is wont to make any book desirable, will all concur in the recommendation of this. What so high and noble a subject, what so fit for his meditations or thine, as the highest and noblest being, and those transcendently glorious perfections wherewith he is clothed! A mere contemplation of the divine excellencies may afford much pleasure to any man that loves to exercise his reason, and is addicted to speculation; but what incomparable sweetness will holy souls find in viewing and considering those perfections now, which they are more fully to behold hereafter, and seeing what manner of God, how wise and powerful, how great, and good, and holy is he in whom the covenant interests them, and in the enjoyment of whom their happiness consists! If rich men delight to sum up their vast revenues, to read over their rentals, look upon their hoards; if they bless themselves in their great wealth, or, to use the prophet's words, Jer. ix. 23, 'glory in their riches,' well may believers rejoice and glory in their 'knowing the Lord,' ver. 24, and please themselves in seeing how rich they are in having an immensely full and all-sufficient God for their inheritance. Alas, how little do most men know of that Deity they profess to serve, and own, not as their sovereign only, but their portion! To such this author might say, as Paul to the Athenians, Acts xvii. 23, 'Whom you ignorantly worship, him declare I unto you.' These treatises, reader, will inform thee who he is whom thou callest thine, present thee with a view of thy chief good, and make thee value thyself a thousand times more upon thy interest in God, than upon all external accomplishments and worldly possessions. Who but delights to hear well of one whom he loves? God is thy love, if thou be a believer, and then it cannot but fill thee with delight and ravishment to hear so much spoken in his praise. David desired to 'dwell in the house of the Lord,' that he might there 'behold his beauty;' how much of that beauty (if thou art but capable of seeing it) mayest thou behold in this volume, which was our author's main business for about three years before he died, to display before his hearers! True, indeed, the Lord's glory, as shining forth before his heavenly courtiers above, is unapproachable by mortal men; but what of it is visible in his works, creation, providence, redemption, falls under the cognisance of his inferior subjects here; and this is in a great measure presented to view in these discourses, and so much, we may well say, as may, by the help of grace, be effectual to raise thy admiration,

* Mr J. Wichens and Mr Ashton.

attract thy love, provoke thy desires, and enable thee to make some guess at what is yet unseen; and why not likewise to clear thy eyes and prepare them for future sight, as well as turn them away from the contemptible vanities of this present life? Whatever is glorious in this world, yet (as the apostle in another case, 2 Cor. iii. 10) 'hath no glory by reason of the glory that excels.' This excellent glory is the subject of this book, to which all created beauty is but mere shadow and duskiness. If thy eyes be well fixed on this, they will not be easily drawn to wander after other objects; if thy heart be taken with God, it will be mortified to everything that is not God.

But thou hast in this book, not only an excellent subject in the general, but great variety of matter, for the employment of thy understanding, as well as enlivening thy affections, and that too such as thou wilt not readily find elsewhere; many excellent things which are out of the road of ordinary preachers and writers, and which may be grateful to the curious, no less than satisfactory to the wise and judicious. It is not therefore a book to be played with, or slept over, but read with the most intent and serious mind; for though it afford much pleasure for the fancy, yet much more work for the heart, and hath indeed enough in it to busy all the faculties. The dress is complete and decent, yet not garish or theatrical; the rhetoric masculine and vigorous, such as became a pulpit, and was never borrowed from the stage; the expressions full, clear, apt, and such as are best suited to the weightiness and spirituality of the truths here delivered. It is plain he was no empty preacher, but was more for sense than sound, filled up his words with matter, and chose rather to inform his hearers' mind than to claw any itching ears. Yet we will not say but some little things, a word or a phrase now and then he may have, which no doubt had he lived to transcribe his own sermons, he would have altered. If in some lesser matters he differ from thee, it is but in such as godly and learned men do frequently, and may without breach of charity differ in among themselves; in some things he may differ from us too, and it may be we from each other, and where are there any two persons who have in all, especially the more disputable points of religion, exactly the same sentiments, at least express themselves altogether in the same terms? But this we must say, that though he treat of many of the most abstruse and mysterious doctrines of Christianity, which are the subjects of great debates and controversies in the world, yet we find no one material thing in which he may justly be called heterodox (unless old heresies be of late grown orthodox, and his differing from them must make him faulty), but generally delivers (as in his former pieces*) what is most consonant to the faith of this, and other the best reformed churches. He was not indeed for that modern divinity which is so much in vogue with some, who would be counted the only sound divines; having 'tasted the old,' he did not 'desire the new,' but said 'the old] is better.' Some errors, especially the Socinian, he sets himself industriously against, and cuts the very sinews of them, yet sometimes almost without naming them.

In the doctrinal part of several of his discourses thou wilt find the depth of polemical divinity, and in his inferences from thence the sweetness of practical; some things which may exercise the profoundest scholar, and others which may instruct and edify the weakest Christian; nothing is more nervous than his reasonings, and nothing more affecting than his applications. Though he make great use of schoolmen, yet they are

* Treatise of Providence and of Thoughts. [The former of which precedes this, and the latter will be given in a subsequent volume.—ED.]

certainly more beholden to him than he to them ; he adopts their notions, but he refines them too, and improves them, and reforms them from the barbarousness in which they were expressed, and dresseth them up in his own language (so far as the nature of the matter will permit, and more clear terms are to be found), and so makes them intelligible to vulgar capacities, which in their original rudeness were obscure and strange, even to learned heads.

In a word, he handles the great truths of the gospel with that perspicuity, gravity, and majesty which best becomes the oracles of God ; and we have reason to believe, that no judicious and unbiassed reader but will acknowledge this to be incomparably the best practical treatise the world ever saw in English upon this subject. What Dr Jackson did (to whom our author gave all due respect) was more brief, and in another way. Dr Preston did worthily upon the attributes in his day, but his discourses likewise are more succinct, when this author's are more full and large. But whatever were the mind of God in it, it was not his will that either of these two should live to finish what he had begun, both being taken away when preaching upon this subject. Happy souls, whose last breath was spent in so noble a work, ' praising God while they had any being,' Ps. cxlvi. 2.

His method is much the same in most of these discourses, both in the doctrinal and practical part, which will make the whole more plain and facile to ordinary readers. He rarely makes objections, and yet frequently answers them, by implying them in those propositions he lays down for the clearing up the truths he asserts. His dexterity is admirable in the applicatory work, where he not only brings down the highest doctrines to the lowest capacities, but collects great variety of proper, pertinent, useful, and yet (many times) unthought of inferences, and that from those truths, which however they afford much matter for inquisition and speculation, yet might seem (unless to the most intelligent and judicious Christians) to have a more remote influence upon practices. He is not like some school writers, who attenuate and rarefy the matter they discourse of to a degree bordering upon annihilation ; at least beat it so thin, that a puff of breath may blow it away ; spin their thread so fine, that the cloth, when made up, proves useless ; solidity dwindles into niceties, and what we thought we had got by their assertions we lose by their distinctions. But if our author have some subtilties and superfine notions in his argumentations, yet he condenseth them again, and consolidates them into substantial and profitable corollaries in his applications. And in them his main business is, as to discipline a profane world for its neglect of God and contempt of him in his most adorable and shining perfections, so likewise to shew how the divine attributes are not only infinitely excellent in themselves, but a grand foundation for all true divine worship, and should be the great motives to provoke men to the exercise of faith, and love, and fear, and humility, and all that holy obedience they are called to by the gospel ; and this without peradventure is the great end of all those rich discoveries God hath in his word made of himself to us, Ps. cix. 1. And, reader, if these elaborate discourses of this holy man, through the Lord's blessing, become a means of promoting holiness in thee, and stir thee up to love, and live to the God of his praise, we are well assured that his end in preaching them is answered, and so is ours in publishing them. :

Thine in the Lord,

EDW. VEEL.
RI. ADAMS.

THE EXISTENCE OF GOD.

The fool hath said in his heart, There is no God. They are corrupt; they have done abominable works; there is none that doth good.—Ps. XIV. 1.

THIS psalm is a description of the deplorable corruption by nature of every son of Adam, since the withering of that common root. Some restrain it to the gentiles, as a wilderness full of briars and thorns, as not concerning the Jews, the garden of God, planted by his grace and watered by the dew of heaven. But the apostle, the best interpreter, rectifies this in extending it by name to Jews as well as Gentiles: Rom. iii. 9, 'We have before proved both Jews and Gentiles, that they are all under sin;' and ver. 10, 11, 12, cites part of this psalm and other passages of Scripture for the further evidence of it; concluding both Jews and Gentiles, every person in the world, naturally in this state of corruption.

The psalmist first declares the corruption of the faculties of the soul: 'The fool hath said in his heart.' Secondly, The streams issuing from thence, 'they are corrupt,' &c.; the first in atheistical principles, the other in unworthy practices; and lays all the evil, tyranny, lust, and persecutions by men, as if the world were only for their sake, upon the neglects of God, and the atheism cherished in their hearts.

'The fool,' a term in Scripture signifying a wicked man, used also by the heathen philosophers to signify a vicious person, נָבָל as coming from נָבֵל signifies the extinction of life in men, animals, and plants; so the word נָבֵל is taken,—Isa. xl. 7, נָבֵל צִיץ 'the flower fadeth,' Isa. xxviii. 1,—a plant that hath lost all that juice that made it lovely and useful. So a fool is one that hath lost his wisdom and right notion of God and divine things, which were communicated to man by creation; one dead in sin, yet one not so much void of rational faculties, as of grace in those faculties; not one that wants reason, but abuses his reason. In Scripture the word signifies foolish.*

'Said in his heart;' that is, he thinks, or he doubts, or he wishes. The thoughts of the heart are in the nature of words to God, though not to men. It is used in the like case of the atheistical person: Ps. x. 11, 13, 'He hath said in his heart, God hath forgotten,' 'he hath said in his heart thou wilt not require it.' He doth not form a syllogism, as Calvin speaks, that there is no God; he dares not openly publish it, though he dares secretly think

* Muis. נבל and לא חכם put together, Deut. xxxii. 6, 'O foolish people and nwise.'

it; he cannot rase out the thoughts of a deity, though he endeavours to blot those characters of God in his soul; he hath some doubts whether there be a God or no: he wishes there were not any, and sometimes hopes there is none at all; he could not so ascertain himself by convincing arguments to produce to the world, but he tampered with his own heart to bring it to that persuasion, and smothered in himself those notices of a deity, which is so plain against the light of nature that such a man may well be called a fool for it.

'There is no God.'* לִית שׁוּלְטָנָא *non potestas Domini* (*Chaldee*). It is not *Jehovah*, which name signifies the essence of God as the prime and supreme being, but *Eloahim*, which name signifies the providence of God, God as a rector and judge. Not that he denies the existence of a supreme being that created the world, but his regarding the creatures, his government of the world, and consequently his reward of the righteous or punishments of the wicked.

There is a threefold denial of God.† 1. *Quoad existentiam*, this is absolute atheism. 2. *Quoad providentiam*, or his inspection into, or care of the things of the world, bounding him in the heavens. 3. *Quoad naturam*, in regard of one or other of the perfections due to his nature.

Of the denial of the providence of God most understand this,‡ not excluding the absolute atheist, as Diagoras is reported to be, nor the sceptical atheist, as Protagoras, who doubted whether there were a God. Those that deny the providence of God, do in effect deny the being of a God; for they strip him of that wisdom, goodness, tenderness, mercy, justice, righteousness, which are the glory of the Deity. And that principle of a greedy desire to be uncontrolled in their lusts, which induceth men to a denial of providence, that thereby they might stifle those seeds of fear which infect and embitter their sinful pleasures, may as well lead them to deny that there is any such being as a God. That at one blow their fears may be dashed all in pieces, and dissolved by the removal of the foundation; as men who desire liberty to commit works of darkness would not have the lights in the house dimmed but extinguished. What men say against providence, because they would have no check in their lusts, they may say in their hearts against the existence of God upon the same account; little difference between the dissenting from the one, and disowning the other.

'They are corrupt, they have done abominable works, there is none that doth good.'

He speaks of the atheist in the singular, *the fool*; of the corruption issuing in the life, in the plural; intimating that some few may choke in their hearts the sentiments of God and his providence, and positively deny them, yet there is something of a secret atheism in all, which is the fountain of the evil practices in their lives, not an utter disowning of the being of a God, but a denial or doubting of some of the rights of his nature.§ When men deny the God of purity, they must needs be polluted in soul and body, and grow brutish in their actions; when the sense of religion is shaken off, all kinds of wickedness is eagerly rushed into, whereby they become as loathsome to God as putrefied carcases are to men.‖ Not one or

---

‖ אֵין אֱלֹהִים   No God.—*Muis.*   † Cocceius.

‡ Not owning him as the Egyptians called, θεὸν ἐγκόσμιον.—*Eugubin. in loc.*
§ Atheism absolute is not in all men's judgments, but practical is in all men's actions.
‖ The apostle in the Romans, applying the later part of it to all mankind, but not the former, as the word translated *corrupt* signifies.

two evil actions is the product of such a principle, but the whole scene of a man's life is corrupted, and becomes execrable.

No man is exempted from some spice of atheism by the deprivation of his nature, which the Psalmist intimates, ' there is none that doth good.' Though there are indelible convictions of the being of a God, that they cannot absolutely deny it, yet there are some atheistical bubblings in the hearts of men which evidence themselves in their actions; as the apostle, Titus i. 16, ' They profess that they know God, but in works they deny him.' Evil works are a dust stirred up by an atheistical breath. He that habituates himself in some sordid lust can scarcely be said seriously and firmly to believe that there is a God in being; and the apostle doth not say that they know God, but they ' profess to know him.' True knowledge and profession of knowledge are distinct. It intimates also to us the unreasonableness of atheism in the consequences; when men shut their eyes against the beams of so clear a sun, God revengeth himself upon them for their impiety by leaving them to their own wills, lets them fall into the deepest sink and dregs of iniquity; and since they doubt of him in their hearts, suffers them above others to deny him in their works; this the apostle discourseth at large, Rom. i. 24.

The text, then, is a description of man's corruption.

1. Of his mind. ' The fool hath said in his heart.' No better title than that of a fool is afforded to the atheist.

2. Of the other faculties. 1. In sins of commission, expressed by the loathsomeness, ' corrupt,' ' abominable.' 2. In sins of omission, ' there is none that doth good;' he lays down the corruption of the mind as the cause, the corruption of the other faculties as the effect.

I. It is a great folly to deny or doubt of the existence or being of God; or, an atheist is a great fool.

II. Practical atheism is natural to man in his corrupt state. It is against nature as constituted by God, but natural as nature is depraved by man. The absolute disowning of the being of a God is not natural to men, but the contrary is natural; but an inconsideration of God, or misrepresentation of his nature, is natural to man as corrupt.

III. A secret atheism, or a partial atheism, is the spring of all the wicked practices in the world; the disorders of the life spring from the ill dispositions of the heart.

I. For the first, every atheist is a grand fool. If he were not a fool, he would not imagine a thing so contrary to the stream of the universal reason in the world, contrary to the rational dictates of his own soul, and contrary to the testimony of every creature and link in the chain of creation. If he were not a fool, he would not strip himself of humanity, and degrade himself lower than the most despicable brute.

It is a folly; for though God be so inaccessible that we cannot know him perfectly, yet he is so much in the light, that we cannot be totally ignorant of him; as he cannot be comprehended in his essence, he cannot be unknown in his existence; it is as easy by reason to understand that he is, as it is difficult to know what he is.

The demonstrations reason furnisheth us with for the existence of God will be evidences of the atheist's folly. One would think there were little need of spending time in evidencing this truth, since in the principle of it, it seems to be so universally owned, and at the first proposal and demand gains the assent of most men.

But, 1, doth the growth of atheism among us render this necessary? May it not justly be suspected that the swarms of atheists are more numerous in our times than history records to have been in any age, when men will not only say it in their hearts, but publish it with their lips, and boast that they have shaken off those shackles which bind other men's consciences? Doth not the barefaced debauchery of men evidence such a settled sentiment, or at least a careless belief of the truth, which lies at the root, and sprouts up in such venomous branches in the world? Can men's hearts be free from that principle wherewith their practices are so openly depraved? It is true the light of nature shines too vigorously for the power of man totally to put it out, yet loathsome actions impair and weaken the actual thoughts and considerations of a deity, and are like mists, that darken the light of the sun though they cannot extinguish it; their consciences, as a candlestick, must hold it, though their unrighteousness obscure it: Rom. i. 18, 'Who hold the truth in unrighteousness.' The engraved characters of the law of nature remain, though they daub them with their muddy lusts to make them illegible, so that since the inconsideration of a deity is the cause of all the wickedness and extravagancies of men; and, as Austin saith, the proposition is always true, 'The fool hath said in his heart,' &c., and more evidently true in this age than any; it will not be unnecessary to discourse of the demonstrations of this first principle.

The apostles spent little time in urging this truth, it was taken for granted all over the world, and they were generally devout in the worship of those idols they thought to be gods; that age ran from one God to many, and our age is running from one God to none at all.

2. The existence of God is the foundation of all religion. The whole building totters if the foundation be out of course; if we have not deliberate and right notions of it, we shall perform no worship, no service, yield no affection to him. If there be not a God, it is impossible there can be one; for eternity is essential to the notion of a God; so all religion would be vain and unreasonable, to pay homage to that which is not in being, nor can ever be. We must first believe that he is, and that he is what he declares himself to be, before we can seek him, adore him, and devote our affections to him, Heb. xi. 6. We cannot pay God a due and regular homage unless we understand him in his perfections, *what* he is; and we can pay him no homage at all, unless we believe *that* he is.

3. It is fit we should know why we believe, that our belief of a God may appear to be upon undeniable evidence, and that we may give a better reason for his existence than that we have heard our parents and teachers tell us so, and our acquaintance think so. It is as much as to say there is no God, when we know not why we believe there is, and would not consider the arguments for his existence.

4. It is necessary to depress that secret atheism which is in the heart of every man by nature. Though every visible object which offers itself to our sense presents a deity to our minds, and exhorts us to subscribe to the truth of it, yet there is a root of atheism springing up sometimes in wavering thoughts and foolish imaginations, inordinate actions and secret wishes. Certain it is that every man that doth not love God denies God; now can he that disaffects him, and hath a slavish fear of him, wish his existence, and say to his own heart with any cheerfulness, there is a God, and make it his chief care to persuade himself of it? He would persuade himself there is no God, and stifle the seeds of it in his reason and conscience, that he might have the greatest liberty to entertain the allurements of the flesh.

It is necessary to excite men to daily and actual considerations of God and his nature, which would be a bar to much of that wickedness which overflows in the lives of men.

5. Nor is it unuseful to those that effectually believe and love him ;* for those who have had a converse with God, and felt his powerful influences in the secrets of their hearts, to take a prospect of those satisfactory accounts which reason gives of that God they adore and love, to see every creature justify them in their owning of him, and affections to him ; indeed, the evidences of a God striking upon the conscience of those who resolve to cleave to sin as their chiefest darling, will dash their pleasures with unwelcome mixtures.

I shall further premise this,

That the folly of atheism is evidenced by the light of reason. Men that will not listen to Scripture, as having no counterpart of it in their souls, cannot easily deny natural reason, which riseth up on all sides for the justification of this truth. There is a natural as well as a revealed knowledge, and the book of the creatures is legible in declaring the being of a God, as well as the Scriptures are in declaring the nature of a God ; there are outward objects in the world, and common principles in the conscience; whence it may be inferred.

For (1.) God, in regard of his existence, is not only the discovery of faith, but of reason. God hath revealed not only his being, but some sparks of his eternal power and Godhead in his works as well as in his word. Rom. i. 19, 20, 'God hath shewed it unto them.' How?† In his works, by the things that are made ; it is a discovery to our reason as shining in the creatures, and an object of our faith as breaking out upon us in the Scriptures ; it is an article of our faith, and an article of our reason. Faith supposeth natural knowledge, as grace supposeth nature. Faith indeed is properly of things above reason, purely depending upon revelation. What can be demonstrated by natural light is not so properly the object of faith, though in regard of the addition of a certainty by revelation it is so.

The belief that God is, which the apostle speaks of, Heb. xi. 6, is not so much of the bare existence of God, as what God is in relation to them that seek to him, viz., 'a rewarder.' The apostle speaks of the faith of Abel, the faith of Enoch, such a faith that pleases God ; but the faith of Abel testified in his sacrifice, and the faith of Enoch testified in his walking with God, was not simply a faith of the existence of God. Cain, in the time of Abel, other men in the world in the time of Enoch, believed this as well as they ; but it was a faith joined with the worship of God, and desirous to please him in the way of his own appointment ; so that they believed that God was such as he had declared himself to be in his promise to Adam, such an one as would be as good as his word, and bruise the serpent's head ; he that seeks to God according to the mind of God, must believe that he is such a God that will pardon sin and justify a seeker of him ; that he is a God of that ability and will to justify a sinner in that way he hath appointed for the clearing the holiness of his nature, and vindicating the honour of his law violated by man.

No man can seek God, or love God, unless he believe him to be thus, and he cannot seek God without a discovery of his own mind how he would be sought ; for it is not a seeking God in any way of man's invention that renders him capable of this desired fruit of a reward : he that believes God as a rewarder, must believe the promise of God concerning the Messiah. Men, under the conscience of sin, cannot tell, without a divine discovery, whether God will reward, or how he will reward, the seekers of him, and therefore cannot act towards him as an object of faith. Would any man seek God merely because he is, or love him because he is, if he did not

* Coccei Sum. Theol. c. 8, § 1.   † Aquin.

know that he should be acceptable to him ? The bare existence of a thing is not the ground of affection to it, but those qualities of it, and our interest in it which render it amiable and delightful. How can men whose consciences fly in their faces seek God or love him, without this knowledge that he is a rewarder ? Nature doth not shew any way to a sinner how to reconcile God's provoked justice with his tenderness. The faith the apostle speaks of here is a faith that eyes the reward as an encouragement, and the will of God as the rule of its acting, he doth not speak simply of the existence of God.

I have spoken the more of this place, because the Socinians* use this to decry any natural knowledge of God, and that the existence of God is only to be known by revelation, so that by that reason any one that lived without the Scripture hath no ground to believe the being of a God.

The Scripture ascribes a knowledge of God to all nations in the world, Rom. i. 19; not only a faculty of knowing, if they had arguments and demonstrations, as an ignorant man in any art hath a faculty to know, but it ascribes an actual knowledge: ver. 19, 'manifest in them;' ver. 21, ' they knew God,'—not they might know him, they knew him when they did not care for knowing him. The notices of God are as intelligible to us by reason as any object in the world is visible; he is written in every letter.

(2.) We are often in the Scripture sent to take a prospect of the creatures for a discovery of God. The apostles drew arguments from the topics of nature when they discoursed with those that owned the Scripture, Rom. i. 19, as well as when they treated with those that were ignorant of it, as Acts xiv. 15, 16; and among the philosophers of Athens, Acts xvii. 27, 29. Such arguments the Holy Ghost in the apostles thought sufficient to convince men of the existence, unity, spirituality, and patience of God.† Such arguments had not been used by them and the prophets from the visible things in the world to silence the Gentiles with whom they dealt, had not this truth, and much more about God, been demonstrated by natural reason; they knew well enough that probable arguments would not satisfy piercing and inquisitive minds.

In Paul's account the testimony of the creatures was without contradiction. God himself justifies this way of proceeding by his own example, and remits Job to the consideration of the creatures, to spell out something of his divine perfections, Job xxxviii. xxxix. xl. &c. It is but one truth in philosophy and divinity, that what is false in one cannot be true in another. Truth, in what appearance soever, doth never contradict itself. And this is so convincing an argument of the existence of God, that God never vouchsafed any miracle, or put forth any act of omnipotency, besides what was evident in the creatures, for satisfaction of the curiosity of any atheist, or the evincing of his being,‡ as he hath done for the evidencing those truths which were not written in the book of nature, or for the restoring a decayed worship, or the protection or deliverance of his people. Those miracles in publishing the gospel indeed did demonstrate the existence of some supreme power; but they were not seals designedly affixed for that, but for the confirmation of that truth which was above the ken of purblind reason, and purely the birth of divine revelation. Yet what proves the truth of any spiritual doctrine, proves also in that act the existence of the divine Author of it. The revelation always implies a revealer; and that which manifests it to be a revelation, manifests also the supreme revealer of it. By the

* Voet. Theol. natural. cap. iii. § 1, p. 22.   † Ibid.
‡ Lord Bacon has almost the same words in his sixteenth essay.—Ed.

same light the sun manifests other things to us it also manifests itself. But what miracles could rationally be supposed to work upon an atheist, who is not drawn to a sense of the truth proclaimed aloud by so many wonders of the creation?

Let us now proceed to the demonstration of the atheist's folly.

It is folly to deny or doubt of a sovereign being, incomprehensible in his nature, infinite in his essence and perfections, independent in his operations, who hath given being to the whole frame of sensible and intelligible creatures, and governs them according to their several natures, by an unconceivable wisdom, who fills the heavens with the glory of his majesty, and the earth with the influences of his goodness.

It is a folly inexcusable to renounce in this case all appeal to universal consent, and the joint assurances of the creatures.

Reason 1. It is a folly to deny or doubt of that which has been the acknowledged sentiment of all nations, in all places and ages. There is no nation but hath owned some kind of religion, and therefore no nation but hath consented in the notion of a supreme Creator and Governor.

1. This hath been universal.

2. It hath been constant and uninterrupted.

3. Natural and innate.

1. It hath been universally assented to by the judgments and practices of all nations in the world.

(1.) No nation hath been exempt from it. All histories of former and later ages have not produced any one nation but fell under the force of this truth. Though they have differed in their religions, they have agreed in this truth; here both heathen, Turk, Jew, and Christian centre without any contention. No quarrel was ever commenced on this score, though about other opinions wars have been sharp and enmities irreconcilable. The notion of the existence of a deity was the same in all, Indians as well as Britons, Americans as well as Jews.

It hath not been an opinion peculiar to this or that people, to this or that sect of philosophers, but hath been as universal as the reason whereby men are differenced from other creatures; so that some have rather defined man by *animal religiosum* than *animal rationale*. It is so twisted with reason, that a man cannot be accounted rational unless he own an object of religion; therefore he that understands not this renounces his humanity when he renounceth a divinity.

No instance can be given of any one people in the world that disclaimed it. It hath been owned by the wise and ignorant, by the learned and stupid, by those who had no other guide but the dimmest light of nature, as well as by those whose candles were snuffed by a more polite education; and that without any solemn debate and contention. Though some philosophers have been known to change their opinions in the concerns of nature, yet none can be proved to have absolutely changed their opinion concerning the being of a God. One died for asserting one God, none in the former ages upon record hath died for asserting no God. Go to the utmost bounds of America: you may find people without some broken pieces of the law of nature, but not without this signature and stamp upon them, though they wanted commerce with other nations, except as savage as themselves, in whom the light of nature was as it were sunk into the socket, who were but one remove from brutes, who clothe not their bodies, cover not their shame, yet were they as soon known to own a God as they were known to be a people. They were possessed with the notion of a supreme being, the author of the world, had an object of religious adoration, put up prayers to the deity they owned for the good things they wanted and the diverting the evils they feared.   No people so untamed, where absolute, perfect atheism had gained a footing.

Not one nation of the world known in the time of the Romans that were without their ceremonies, whereby they signified their devotion to a deity. They had their places of worship, where they made their vows, presented their prayers, offered their sacrifices, and implored the assistance of what they thought to be a god, and in their distresses ran immediately, without any deliberation, to their gods; so that the notion of a deity was as inward and settled in them as their own souls, and indeed runs in the blood of mankind.   The distempers of the understanding cannot utterly deface it; you shall scarce find the most distracted bedlam in his raving fits to deny a God, though he may blaspheme and fancy himself one.

(2.) Nor doth the idolatry and multiplicity of gods in the world weaken, but confirm this universal consent.   Whatsoever unworthy conceits men have had of God in all nations, or whatsoever degrading representations they have made of him, yet they all concur in this, that there is a supreme power to be adored.   Though one people worshipped the sun, others the fire ; and the Egyptians, gods out of their rivers, gardens, and fields ; yet the notion of a deity existent, who created and governed the world, and conferred daily benefits upon them, was maintained by all, though applied to the stars, and in part to those sordid creatures.   All the Dagons of the world establish this truth, and fall down before it.   Had not the nations owned the being of a God, they had never offered incense to an idol ; had there not been a deep impression of the existence of a deity, they had never exalted creatures below themselves to the honour of altars : men could not so easily have been deceived by forged deities, if they had not had a notion of a real one.   Their fondness to set up others in the place of God, evidenced a natural knowledge that there was one who had a right to be worshipped.   If there were not this sentiment of a deity, no man would ever have made an image of a piece of wood, worshipped it, prayed to it, and said, ' Deliver me, for thou art my god,' Isa. xliv. 17.   They applied a general notion to a particular image.   The difference is in the manner and immediate object of worship, not in the formal ground of worship.   The worship sprung from a true principle, though it was not applied to a right object : while they were rational creatures they could not deface the notion; yet while they were corrupt creatures it was not difficult to apply themselves to a wrong object from a true principle.   A blind man knows he hath a way to go as well as one of the clearest sight, but because of his blindness he may miss the way and stumble into a ditch.   No man would be imposed upon to take a Bristol stone instead of a diamond, if he did not know that there were such things as diamonds in the world ; nor any man spread forth his hands to an idol, if he were altogether without the sense of a deity. Whether it be a false or a true God men apply to, yet in both, the natural sentiment of a God is evidenced ; all their mistakes were grafts inserted in this stock, since they would multiply gods rather than deny a deity.

How should such a general submission be entered into by the world, so as to adore things of base alloy, if the force of religion were not such, that in any fashion a man would seek the satisfaction of his natural instinct to some object of worship.*   This great diversity confirms this consent to be a good argument, for it evidenceth it not to be a cheat, combination, or conspiracy to deceive, or a mutual intelligence, but every one finds it in his climate, yea, in himself.   People would never have given the title of a god to men

* Charron de la Sagesse, livr. i. chap. 7.

or brutes, had there not been a pre-existing and unquestioned persuasion, that there was such a being.* How else should the notion of a God come into their minds? The notion that there is a God must be more ancient.

(3.) Whatsoever disputes there have been in the world, this of the existence of God was never the subject of contention. All other things have been questioned. What jarrings were there among philosophers about natural things, into how many parties were they split, with what animosities did they maintain their several judgments? But we hear of no solemn controversies about the existence of a Supreme Being. This never met with any considerable contradiction. No nation, that had put other things to question, would ever suffer this to be disparaged, so much as by a public doubt.† We find among the heathen contentions about the nature of God, and the number of gods. Some asserted an innumerable multitude of gods; some affirmed him to be subject to birth and death; some affirmed the entire world was God; others fancied him to be a circle of a bright fire; others, that he was a spirit diffused through the whole world: yet they unanimously concurred in this, as the judgment of universal reason, that there was such a sovereign being. And those that were sceptical in every thing else, and asserted that the greatest certainty was that there was nothing certain, professed a certainty in this. The question was not whether there was a first cause, but what it was.‡ It is much the same thing as the disputes about the nature and matter of the heavens, the sun and planets; though there be a great diversity of judgments, yet all agree that there are heavens, sun, planets. So all the contentions among men about the nature of God, weaken not, but rather confirm, that there is a God, since there was never a public formal debate about his existence. Those that have been ready to pull out one another's eyes for their dissent from their judgments, sharply censured one another's sentiments, envied the births of one another's wits, always shook hands with an unanimous consent in this: never censured one another for being of this persuasion, never called it into question. As what was never controverted among men professing Christianity, but acknowledged by all, though contending about other things, has reason to be judged a certain truth belonging to the Christian religion; so what was never subjected to any controversy, but acknowledged by the whole world, hath reason to be embraced as a truth without any doubt.

(4.) This universal consent is not prejudiced by some few dissenters. History doth not reckon twenty professed atheists in all ages in the compass of the whole world; § and we have not the name of any one absolute atheist upon record in Scripture: yet it is questioned, whether any of them, noted in history with that infamous name, were downright deniers of the existence of God, but rather because they disparaged the deities commonly worshipped by the nations where they lived, as being of a clearer reason to discern that those qualities, vulgarly attributed to their gods, as lust and luxury, wantonness and quarrels, were unworthy of the nature of a God. But suppose they were really what they are termed to be, what are they to the multitude of men that have sprung out of the loins of Adam? Not so much as one grain of ashes is to all that were ever turned into that form by any fires in your chimneys. And many more were not sufficient to weigh down the contrary consent of the whole world, and bear down an universal impression. Should the laws of a country, agreed universally to by the whole body of the people, be accounted vain, because a hundred men of those millions disapprove of them, when not their reason, but their folly and base interest,

---

* Gassend. Phys. ¿ 1. lib. 4. cap. 2.   ‡ Gassend. Phys. ¿ 1. lib. 4. cap. 2.
† Amyrant de Religion, page 50.   ¿ Gassend. Phys. ¿ 1. lib. 4. cap. 7.

persuades them to dislike them, and dispute against them?* What if some men be blind, shall any conclude from thence that eyes are not natural to men? Shall we say that the notion of the existence of God is not natural to men, because a very small number have been of a contrary opinion? Shall a man in a dungeon, that never saw the sun, deny that there is a sun, because one or two blind men tell him there is none, when thousands assure him there is? Why should then the exceptions of a few, not one to millions, discredit that which is voted certainly true by the joint consent of the world? Add this too, that if those that are reported to be atheists had had any considerable reason to step aside from the common persuasion of the whole world, it is a wonder it met not with entertainment by great numbers of those, who, by reason of their notorious wickedness and inward disquiets, might reasonably be thought to wish in their hearts that there were no God. It is strange, if there were any reason on their side, that in so long a space of time as hath run out from the creation of the world, there could not be engaged a considerable number to frame a society for the profession of it. It hath died with the person that started it, and vanished as soon as it appeared.

To conclude this, is it not folly for any man to deny or doubt of the being of a God, to dissent from all mankind, and stand in contradiction to human nature? What is the general dictate of nature is a certain truth. It is impossible that nature can naturally and universally lie; and therefore those that ascribe all to nature, and set it in the place of God, contradict themselves, if they give not credit to it in that which it universally affirms. A general consent of all nations is to be esteemed as a law of nature.† Nature cannot plant in the minds of all men an assent to a falsity, for then the laws of nature would be destructive to the reason and the minds of men. How is it possible that a falsity should be a persuasion spread through all nations, engraven upon the minds of all men, men of the most towering and men of the most creeping understanding; that they should consent to it in all places, and in those places where the nations have not had any known commerce with the rest of the known world? A consent not settled by any law of man to constrain people to a belief of it; and indeed it is impossible that any law of man can constrain the belief of the mind. Would not he deservedly be accounted a fool, that should deny that to be gold which had been tried and examined by a great number of knowing goldsmiths, and hath passed the test of all their touchstones? What excess of folly would it be for him to deny it to be true gold, if it had been tried by all that had skill in that metal in all nations in the world!

2. It hath been a constant and uninterrupted consent. It hath been as ancient as the first age of the world; no man is able to mention any time from the beginning of the world, wherein this notion hath not been universally owned; it is as old as mankind, and hath run along with the course of the sun, nor can the date be fixed lower than that.

(1.) In all the changes of the world this hath been maintained. In the overturnings of the government of states, the alteration of modes of worship, this hath stood unshaken. The reasons upon which it was founded were in all revolutions of time accounted satisfactory and convincing, nor could absolute atheism, in the changes of any laws, ever gain the favour of any one body of people to be established by a law. When the honour of the heathen idols was laid in the dust, this suffered no impair. The being of one God was more vigorously owned when the unreasonableness of multiplicity of gods was manifest, and grew taller by the detection of counterfeits.

* Gassend. Phys. § 1. lib. 4. cap. 2.   † Cicero.

When other parts of the law of nature have been violated by some nations, this hath maintained its standing. The long series of ages hath been so far from blotting it out, that it hath more strongly confirmed it, and maketh further progress in the confirmation of it. Time, which hath eaten out the strength of other things, and blasted mere inventions, hath not been able to consume this. The discovery of all other impostures never made this by any society of men to be suspected as one. It will not be easy to name any imposture that hath walked perpetually in the world without being discovered and whipped out by some nation or other. Falsities have never been so universally and constantly owned without public control and question. And since the world hath detected many errors of the former age, and learning been increased, this hath been so far from being dimmed, that it hath shone out clearer with the increase of natural knowledge, and received fresh and more vigorous confirmations.

(2.) The fears and anxieties in the consciencies of men have given men sufficient occasion to root it out, had it been possible for them to do it. If the notion of the existence of God had been possible to have been dashed out of the minds of men, they would have done it rather than have suffered so many troubles in their souls upon the commission of sin; since they did [not] want wickedness and wit in so many corrupt ages to have attempted it and prospered in it, had it been possible. How comes it therefore to pass that such a multitude of profligate persons, that have been in the world since the fall of man, should not have rooted out this principle, and dispossessed the minds of men of that which gave birth to their tormenting fears? How is it possible that all should agree together in a thing which created fear, and an obligation against the interest of the flesh, if it had been free for men to discharge themselves of it? No man, as far as corrupt nature bears sway in him, is willing to live controlled.

The first man would rather be a god himself than under one, Gen. iii. 5. Why should men continue this notion in them, which shackled them in their vile inclinations, if it had been in their power utterly to deface it? If it were an imposture, how comes it to pass that all the wicked ages of the world could never discover that to be a cheat, which kept them in continual alarms? Men wanted not will to shake off such apprehensions; as Adam, so all his posterity are desirous to hide themselves from God upon the commission of sin, ver. 9, and by the same reason they would hide God from their souls. What is the reason they could never attain their will and their wish by all their endeavours? Could they possibly have satisfied themselves that there were no God, they had discarded their fears, the disturbers of the repose of their lives, and been unbridled in their pleasures. The wickedness of the world would never have preserved that which was a perpetual molestation to it, had it been possible to be razed out.

But since men, under the turmoils and lashes of their own consciences, could never bring their hearts to a settled dissent from this truth, it evidenceth, that as it took its birth at the beginning of the world, it cannot expire, no, not in the ashes of it, nor in anything, but the reduction of the soul to that nothing from whence it sprung. This conception is so perpetual, that the nature of the soul must be dissolved before it be rooted out, nor can it be extinct whilst the soul endures.

(3.) Let it be considered also by us that own the Scripture, that the devil deems it impossible to root out this sentiment. It seems to be so perpetually fixed, that the devil did not think fit to tempt man to the denial of the existence of a deity, but persuaded him to believe, he might ascend to that dignity, and become a god himself: Gen. iii. 1, 'Hath God said?' and he there owns him, ver. 5, ' Ye shall become as gods.' He owns God in the question he asks the woman, and persuades our first parents to be gods themselves. And in all stories, both ancient and modern, the devil was never able to tincture men's minds with a professed denial of the deity, which would have opened a door to a world of more wickedness than hath been acted, and took away the bar to the breaking out of that evil, which is naturally in the hearts of men, to the greater prejudice of human societies. He wanted not malice to raze out all the notions of God, but power ; he knew it was impossible to effect it, and therefore in vain to attempt it. He set up himself in several places of the ignorant world as a god, but never was able to overthrow the opinion of the being of a God. The impressions of a deity were so strong as not to be struck out by the malice and power of hell.

What a folly is it then in any to contradict or doubt of this truth, which all the periods of time have not been able to wear out ; which all the wars and quarrels of men with their own consciences have not been able to destroy ; which ignorance,and debauchery, its two greatest enemies, cannot weaken ; which all the falsehoods and errors which have reigned in one or other part of the world, have not been able to banish ; which lives in the consents of men in spite of all their wishes to the contrary, and hath grown stronger and shone clearer by the improvements of natural reason !

3. Natural and innate, which pleads strongly for the perpetuity of it. It is natural, though some think it not a principal writ in the heart of man ; * it is so natural that every man is born with a restless instinct to be of some kind of religion or other, which implies some object of religion. The impression of a deity is as common as reason, and of the same age with reason.† It is a relic of knowledge after the fall of Adam, like fire under ashes, which sparkles as soon as ever the heap of ashes is open ; a notion sealed up in the soul of every man ;‡ else how could those people, who were unknown to one another, separate by seas and mounts, differing in various customs and manner of living, had no mutual intelligence one with another, light upon this as a common sentiment, if they had not been guided by one uniform reason in all their minds, by one nature common to them all ; though their climates be different, their tempers and constitutions various, their imaginations in some things as distant from one another as heaven is from earth, the ceremonies of their religion not all of the same kind, yet wherever you find human nature, you find this settled persuasion. So that the notion of a God seems to be twisted with the nature of man, and is the first natural branch of common reason, or upon either the first inspection of a man into himself and his own state and constitution, or upon the first sight of any external visible object. Nature within man, and nature without man, agree upon the first meeting together to form this sentiment, that there is a God. It is as natural as anything we call a common principle. One thing which is called a common principle and natural is, that the whole is greater than the parts. If this be not born with us, yet the exercise of reason, essential to man, settles it as a certain maxim; upon the dividing anything into several parts, he finds every part less than when they were all together. By the same exercise of reason, we cannot cast our eyes upon anything in the world, or exercise our understandings upon ourselves, but we must presently imagine there was some cause of those things, some cause of myself and my own being, so that this truth is as natural to man as anything he can call most natural or a common principle.

* Pink. Eph. vi. p. 10, 11.　　　　‡ Amyrant des Religions, p. 6–9.
† King on Jonah, p. 16.

It must be confessed by all, that there is a law of nature writ upon the hearts of men, which will direct them to commendable actions, if they will attend to the writing in their own consciences. This law cannot be considered without the notice of a lawgiver. For it is but a natural and obvious conclusion, that some superior hand engrafted those principles in man, since he finds something in him twitching him upon the pursuit of uncomely actions, though his heart be mightily inclined to them; man knows he never planted this principle of reluctancy in his own soul; he can never be the cause of that which he cannot be friends with. If he were the cause of it, why doth he not rid himself of it? No man would endure a thing that doth frequently molest and disquiet him, if he could cashier it. It is therefore sown in man by some hand more powerful than man, which riseth so high and is rooted so strong, that all the force that man can use cannot pull it up. If therefore this principle be natural in man, and the law of nature be natural, the notion of a lawgiver must be as natural as the notion of a printer, or that there is a printer is obvious upon the sight of a stamp impressed; after this the multitude of effects in the world step in to strengthen this beam of natural light, and the direct conclusion from thence is, that that power which made those outward objects, implanted this inward principle; this is sown in us, born with us, and sprouts up with our growth; or as one saith,* it is like letters carved upon the bark of a young plant, which grows up together with us, and the longer it grows the letters are more legible.

This is the ground of this universal consent, and why it may well be termed natural.

This will more evidently appear to be natural, because,

[1.] This consent could not be by mere tradition.

[2.] Nor by any mutual intelligence of governors to keep people in awe, which are two things the atheist pleads. The first hath no strong foundation, and that other is as absurd and foolish as it is wicked and abominable.

[3.] Nor was it fear first introduced it.

[1.] It could not be by mere tradition. Many things indeed are entertained by posterity, which their ancestors delivered to them, and that out of a common reverence to their forefathers, and an opinion that they had a better prospect of things than the increase of the corruption of succeeding ages would permit them to have.

But if this be a tradition handed from our ancestors, they also must receive it from theirs; we must then ascend to the first man, we cannot else escape a confounding ourselves with running into infinite. Was it then the only tradition he left to them? Is it not probable he acquainted them with other things in conjunction with this, the nature of God, the way to worship him, the manner of the world's existence, his own state? We may reasonably suppose him to have a good stock of knowledge; what is become of it? It cannot be supposed, that the first man should acquaint his posterity with an object of worship, and leave them ignorant of a mode of worship, and of the end of worship. We find in Scripture his immediate posterity did the first in sacrifices, and without doubt they were not ignorant of the other. How come men to be so uncertain in all other things, and so confident of this, if it were only a tradition? How did debates and irreconcilable questions start up concerning other things, and this remain untouched, but by a small number? Whatsoever tradition the first man left besides this, is lost, and no way recoverable, but by the revelation God hath made in his word.

* Charleton.

How comes it to pass, this of a God is longer lived than all the rest, which we may suppose man left to his immediate descendants? How come men to retain the one and forget the other? What was the reason this survived the ruin of the rest, and surmounted the uncertainties into which the other sunk? Was it likely it should be handed down alone without other attendants on it at first? Why did it not expire among the Americans, who have lost the account of their own descent, and the stock from whence they sprung, and cannot reckon above eight hundred or a thousand years at most? Why was not the manner of the worship of a God transmitted, as well as that of his existence? How came men to dissent in their opinions concerning his nature, whether he was corporeal or incorporeal, finite or infinite, omnipresent or limited? Why were not men as negligent to transmit this of his existence as that of his nature? No reason can be rendered for the security of this above the other, but that there is so clear a tincture of a Deity upon the minds of men, such traces and shadows of him in the creatures, such indelible instincts within, and invincible arguments without to keep up this universal consent. The characters are so deep that they cannot possibly be razed out, which would have been one time or other, in one nation or other, had it depended only upon tradition, since one age shakes off frequently the sentiments of the former.

I cannot think of above one which may be called a tradition, which indeed was kept up among all nations, viz., sacrifices, which could not be natural but instituted. What ground could they have in nature, to imagine that the blood of beasts could expiate and wash off the guilt and stains of a rational creature? Yet they had in all places (but among the Jews, and some of them only) lost the knowledge of the reason and end of the institution, which the Scripture acquaints us was to typify and signify the redemption by the promised seed. This tradition hath been superannuated and laid aside in most parts of the world, while this notion of the existence of a God hath stood firm.

But suppose it were a tradition, was it likely to be a mere intention* and figment of the first man? Had there been no reason for it, his posterity would soon have found out the weakness of its foundation. What advantage had it been to him to transmit so great a falsehood, to kindle the fears or raise the hopes of his posterity, if there were no God? It cannot be supposed he should be so void of that natural affection men in all ages bear to their descendants, as so grossly to deceive them, and be so contrary to the simplicity and plainness which appears in all things nearest their original.

[2.] Neither was it by any mutual intelligence of governors among themselves, to keep people in subjection to them. If it were a political design at first, it seems it met with the general nature of mankind very ready to give it entertainment.

First, It is unaccountable how this should come to pass. It must be either by a joint assembly of them, or a mutual correspondence. If by any assembly, who were the persons? Let the name of any one be mentioned. When was the time? Where was the place of this appearance? By what authority did they meet together? Who made the first motion, and first started this great principle of policy? By what means could they assemble from such distant parts of the world? Human histories are utterly silent in it, and the Scripture, the ancientest history, gives an account of the attempt of Babel, but not a word of any design of this nature.

What mutual correspondence could such have, whose interests are for the most part different, and their designs contrary to one another? How could

* Qu. 'invention'?—Ed.

they, who were divided by such vast seas, have this mutual converse? How could those, who were different in their customs and manners, agree so unanimously together in one thing to gull the people? If there had been such a correspondence between the governors of all nations, what is the reason some nations should be unknown to the world till of late times? How could the business be so secretly managed, as not to take vent, and issue in a discovery to the world? Can reason suppose so many in a joint conspiracy, and no man's conscience in this life under sharp afflictions, or on his deathbed, when conscience is most awakened, constrain him to reveal openly the cheat that beguiled the world? How came they to be so unanimous in this notion, and to differ in their rites almost in every country? Why could they not agree in one mode of worship throughout all the world, as well as in this universal notion? If there were not a mutual intelligence, it cannot be conceived how in every nation such a state engineer should rise up with the same trick to keep people in awe. What is the reason we cannot find any law in any one nation, to constrain men to the belief of the existence of a God, since politic stratagems have been often fortified by laws? Besides, such men make use of principles received to effect their contrivances, and are not so impolitic as to build designs upon principles that have no foundation in nature. Some heathen law-givers have pretended a converse with their gods to make their laws be received by the people with a greater veneration, and fix with stronger obligation the observance and perpetuity of them; but this was not the introducing of a new principle, but the supposition of an old received notion, that there was a God, and an application of that principle to their present design. The pretence had been vain had not the notion of a God been ingrafted. Politicians are so little possessed with a reverence of God, that the first mighty one in the Scripture (which may reasonably gain with the atheist the credit of the ancientest history in the word), is represented without any fear of God. Gen. x. 9, 'Nimrod was a mighty hunter before the Lord.' An invader and oppressor of his neighbours, and reputed the introducer of a new worship, and being the first that built cities after the flood (as Cain was the first builder of them before the flood), built also idolatry with them, and erected a new worship, and was so far from strengthening that notion the people had of God, that he endeavoured to corrupt it; the first idolatry in common histories being noted to proceed from that part of the world, the ancientest idol being at Babylon, and supposed to be first invented by this person. Whence by the way perhaps Rome is in the Revelations called Babylon, with respect to that similitude of their saint-worship, to the idolatry first set up in that place.* It is evident politicians have often changed the worship of a nation, but it is not upon record, that the first thoughts of an object of worship ever entered into the minds of people by any trick of theirs.

But to return to the present argument; the being of a God is owned by some nations that have scarce any form of policy among them. It is as wonderful how any wit should hit upon such an invention, as it is absurd to ascribe it to any human device, if there were not prevailing arguments to constrain the consent. Besides, how is it possible they should deceive themselves? What is the reason the greatest politicians have their fears of a deity upon their unjust practices, as well as other men, they intended to befool? How many of them have had forlorn consciences upon a deathbed, upon the consideration of a God to answer an account to in another world?

* Or if we understand it, as some think, that he defended his invasions under a pretext of the preserving religion, it assures us that there was a notion of an object of religion before, since no religion can be without an object of worship.

Is it credible they should be frighted by that wherewith they knew they beguiled others ? No man satisfying his pleasures would impose such a deceit upon himself, or render and make himself more miserable than the creatures he hath dominion over.

Secondly, It is unaccountable how it should endure so long a time ; that this policy should be so fortunate as to gain ground in the consciences of men, and exercise an empire over them, and meet with such an universal success. If the notion of a God were a state-engine, and introduced by some politic grandees for the ease of government, and preserving people with more felicity in order, how comes it to pass the first broachers of it were never upon record ? There is scarce a false opinion vented in the world, but may as a stream be traced to the first head and fountain. The inventors of particular forms of worship are known, and the reasons why they prescribed them known ; but what grandee was the author of this ? who can pitch a time and person that sprung up this notion ? If any be so insolent as to impose a cheat, he can hardly be supposed to be so successful as to deceive the whole world for many ages. Impostures pass not free through the whole world without examination and discovery. Falsities have not been universally and constantly owned without control and question. If a cheat imposeth upon some towns and countries, he will be found out by the more piercing inquiries of other places ; and it is not easy to name any imposture that hath walked so long in its disguise in the world, without being unmasked and whipped out by some nation or other. If this had been a mere trick, there would have been as much craft in some to discern it as there was in others to contrive it. No man can be imagined so wise in a kingdom, but others may be found as wise as himself ; and it is not conceivable that so many clear-sighted men in all ages should be ignorant of it, and not endeavour to free the world from so great a falsity.* It cannot be found that a trick of state should always beguile men of the most piercing insights, as well as the most credulous. That a few crafty men should befool all the wise men in the world, and the world lie in a belief of it, and never like to be freed from it. What is the reason the succeeding politicians never knew this stratagem, since their maxims are usually handed to their successors ?†

This persuasion of the existence of God, owes not itself to any imposture or subtlety of men. If it had not been agreeable to common nature and reason, it could not so long have borne sway. The imposed yoke would have been cast off by multitudes. Men would not have charged themselves with that which was attended with consequences displeasing to the flesh, and hindered them from a full swing of their rebellious passions ; such a shackle would have mouldered of itself, or been broke by the extravagances human nature is inclined unto. The wickedness of men, without question, hath prompted them to endeavour to unmask it, if it were a cozenage, but could never yet be so successful as to free the world from a persuasion, or their own consciences from the tincture, of the existence of a deity. It must be, therefore, of an ancienter date than the craft of statesmen, and descend into the world with the first appearance of human nature. Time, which hath rectified many errors, improves this notion, makes it shock down its roots deeper, and spread its branches larger.

It must be a natural truth that shines clear by the detection of those errors that have befooled the world, and the wit of man is never able to name any human author that first insinuated it into the beliefs of men.

[3.] Nor was it fear first introduced it. Fear is the consequent of wicked-

---

* Fotherby, A theomastrix, p. 64.

† 'And there is not a Richelieu, but leaves his axioms to a Mazarin.'

ness. As man was not created with any inherent sin, so he was not created with any terrifying fears ; the one had been against the holiness of the Creator, the other against his goodness. Fear did not make this opinion, but the opinion of the being of a deity was the cause of this fear, after his sense of angering the deity by his wickedness. The object of fear is before the act of fear ; there could not be an act of fear exercised about the deity, till it was believed to be existent, and not only so, but offended. For God, as existent only, is not the object of fear or love : it is not the existence of a thing that excites any of those affections, but the relation a thing bears to us in particular. God is good, and so the object of love, as well as just, and thereby the object of fear. He was as much called love (Εϱως) and *mens*, or mind, in regard of his goodness and understanding, by the heathens, as much as by any other name. Neither of those names were proper to insinuate fear, neither was fear the first principle that made the heathens worship a god. They offered sacrifices out of gratitude to some, as well as to others out of fear ; the fear of evils in the world, and the hopes of belief and assistance from their gods, and not a terrifying fear of God, was the principal spring of their worship. When calamities from the hands of men, or judgments by the influences of heaven, were upon them, they implored that which they thought a deity. It was not their fear of him, but a hope in his goodness, and persuasion of remedy from him, for the averting those evils, that rendered them adorers of a god. If they had not had pre-existent notions of his being and goodness, they would never have made addresses to him, or so frequently sought to that they only apprehended as a terrifying object.* When you hear men calling upon God in a time of affrighting thunder, you cannot imagine that the fear of thunder did first introduce the notion of a God, but implies that it was before apprehended by them, or stamped upon them, though their fear doth at present actuate that belief, and engage them in a present exercise of piety ; and whereas the Scripture saith, 'the fear of God is the beginning of wisdom,' Prov. ix. 10, Ps. cxi. 10, or of all religion, it is not understood of a distracted and terrifying fear, but a reverential fear of him, because of his holiness, or a worship of him, a submission to him, and sincere seeking of him.

Well then, is it not a folly for an atheist to deny that which is the reason and common sentiment of the whole world, to strip himself of humanity, run counter to his own consience, prefer a private before a universal judgment, give the lie to his own nature and reason, assert things impossible to be proved, nay, impossible to be acted, forge irrationalities for the support of his fancy against the common persuasion of the world, and against himself, and so much of God as is manifest in him and every man ? Rom. i. 19.

Reason 2. It is a folly to deny that which all creatures, or all things in the world manifest.† Let us view this in Scripture since we acknowledge it, and after consider the arguments from natural reason.

The apostle resolves it : Rom. i. 19, 20, 'The invisible things of him from the creation of the world are clearly seen, being understood by the things that are made, even his eternal power and Godhead, so that they are without excuse.' They know, or might know, by the things that were made, the eternity and power of God ; their sense might take circuit about every object, and their minds collect the being, and something of the perfections of the deity. The first discourse of the mind upon the sight of a delicate piece of workmanship, is the conclusion of the being of an artificer, and the admiration of his skill and industry. The apostle doth not say, the invisible things

---

* Gassend. Phys., sect. 1, l. 4, c. 2, p. 291, 292.
† Jupiter est quodcunque vides, &c.

of God are *believed*, or they have an opinion of them, but they are *seen*, and *clearly seen*. They are like crystal glasses, which give a clear representation of the existence of a deity, like that mirror reported to be in a temple in Arcadia, which represented to the spectator, not his own face, but the image of that deity which he worshipped.

The whole world is like a looking-glass, which whole and entire represents the image of God, and every broken piece of it, every little shred of a creature, doth the like; not only the great ones, elephants and the leviathan, but ants, flies, worms, whose bodies rather than names we know; the great cattle and the creeping things, Gen. i. 24. Not naming there any intermediate creature, to direct us to view him in the smaller letters, as well as the greater characters of the world. His name is glorious, and his attributes are excellent ' in all the earth,' Ps. viii. 1, in every creature, as the glory of the sun is in every beam and smaller flash; he is seen in every insect, in every spire of grass. The voice of the Creator is in the most contemptible creature.* The apostle adds that they are so clearly seen, that men are inexcusable if they have not some knowledge of God by them; if they might not certainly know them, they might have some excuse. So that his existence is not only probably, but demonstratively, proved from the things of the world.

Especially the heavens declare him, which God ' stretches out like a curtain,' Ps. civ. 2, or as some render the word, ' a skin,' whereby is signified, that heaven is as an open book, which was anciently made of the skins of beasts, that by the knowledge of them we may be taught the knowledge of God. Where the Scripture was not revealed, the world served for a witness of a God; whatever arguments the Scripture uses to prove it are drawn from nature (though indeed it doth not so much prove as suppose the existence of a God), but what arguments it uses are from the creatures, and particularly the heavens, which are the public preachers of this doctrine. The breath of God sounds to all the world through those organ pipes. His being is visible in their existence, his wisdom in their frame, his power in their motion, his goodness in their usefulness; for ' their voice goeth to the end of the earth,' Ps. xix. 1, 2. They have a voice, and their voice is as intelligible as any common language. And those are so plain heralds of a deity, that the heathen mistook them for deities, and gave them a particular adoration which was due to that god they declared. The first idolatry seems to be of those heavenly bodies, which began probably in the time of Nimrod. In Job's time it is certain they admired the glory of the sun and the brightness of the moon, not without kissing their hand, a sign of adoration, Job xxxi. 25, 27. It is evident a man may as well doubt whether there be a sun, when he sees his beams gilding the earth, as doubt whether there be a God, when he sees his works spread in the world.

The things in the world declare the existence of a God.

1, In their production; 2, harmony; 3, preservation; 4, answering their several ends.

1. In their production. The declaration of the existence of God was the chief end for which they were created, that the notion of a supreme and independent eternal being might easier incur into the active understanding of man from the objects of sense dispersed in every corner of the world, that he might pay a homage and devotion to the Lord of all: Isa. xl. 12, 13, 18, 19, &c., ' Have you not understood from the foundation of the earth, it is he that sits upon the circle of the heaven,' &c. How could this great heap be brought into being unless a God had framed it? Every

* Banes in Aquin., Par. 2, Qu. 2, Artic. 2, p. 78, col. 2.

plant, every atom, as well as every star, at the first meeting whispers this in our ears, I have a Creator, I am witness to a deity. Who ever saw statues or pictures, but presently thinks of a statuary and limner? Who beholds garments, ships, or houses, but understands there was a weaver, a carpenter, an architect?* Who can cast his eyes about the world, but must think of that power that formed it, and that the goodness which appears in the formation of it hath a perfect residence in some being? 'Those things that are good must flow from something perfectly good; that which is chief in any kind is the cause of all of that kind. Fire, which is most hot, is the cause of all things which are hot. There is some being therefore which is the cause of all that perfection which is in the creature, and this is God' (Aquin. i. qu. 2, art. 3). All things that are demonstrate something from whence they are. All things have a contracted perfection, and what they have is communicated to them. Perfections are parcelled out among several creatures. Anything that is imperfect cannot exist of itself. We are led therefore by them to consider a fountain which bubbles up in all perfection, a hand which distributes those several degrees of being and perfection to what we see. We see that which is imperfect, our minds conclude something perfect to exist before it; our eye sees the streams, but our understanding riseth to the head; as the eye sees the shadow, but the understanding informs us whether it be the shadow of a man or of a beast.

God hath given us sense to behold the objects in the world, and understanding to reason his existence from them; the understanding cannot conceive a thing to have made itself, that is against all reason, Rom. i. 20. As they are made, they speak out a maker, and cannot be a trick of chance, since they are made with such an immense wisdom, that is too big for the grasp of all human understanding. Those that doubt whether the existence of God be an implanted principle, yet agree that the effects in the world lead to a supreme and universal cause; and that if we have not the knowledge of it rooted in our natures, yet we have it by discourse, since by all masters of reason a *processus in infinitum* must be accounted impossible in subordinate causes.

This will appear in several things.

(1.) The world and every creature had a beginning. The Scripture ascertains this to us, Gen. i. David, who was not the first man, gives the praise to God of his being 'curiously wrought,' &c., Ps. cxxxix. 14, 15. God gave being to men, and plants, and beasts, before they being to one another. He gives being to them now as the fountain of all being, though the several modes of being are from the several natures of second causes.

It is true indeed we are ascertained that they were made by the true God, that they were made by his word ('By faith we understand that the worlds were framed by the word of God,' &c., Heb. xi. 3), that they were made of nothing, and not only this lower world wherein we live, but according to the Jewish division, the world of men, the world of stars, and the world of spirits and souls. We do not waver in it, or doubt of it, as the heathen did in their disputes; we know they are the workmanship of the true God, of that God we adore, not of false gods. 'By his word:' without any instrument or engine as in earthly structures; 'of things which do not appear:' without any pre-existent matter, as all artificial works of men are framed.

Yet the proof of the beginning of the world is affirmed with good reason; and if it had a beginning, it had also some higher cause than itself; every effect hath a cause.

* Philo, ex Petav. Theol. Dog. tom. i. lib. 1, cap. 1, p. 4, somewhat changed.

The world was not eternal or from eternity.* The matter of the world cannot be eternal; matter cannot subsist without form, nor put on any form without the action of some cause; this cause must be in being before it acted; that which is not cannot act. The cause of the world must necessarily exist before any matter was endued with any form; that therefore cannot be eternal before which another did subsist. If it were from eternity, it would not be subject to mutation; if the whole was from eternity, why not also the parts? What makes the changes so visible, then, if eternity would exempt it from mutability?

¶ [1.] Time cannot be infinite, and therefore the world not eternal; † all motion hath its beginning; if it were otherwise, we must say the number of heavenly revolutions of days and nights, which are past to this instant, is actually infinite, which cannot be in nature. If it were so, it must needs be granted that a part is equal to the whole; because infinite being equal to infinite, the number of days past in all ages to the beginning of one year being infinite (as they would be, supposing the world had no beginning), would by consequence be equal to the number of days which shall pass to the end of the next; whereas the number of days past is indeed but a part, and so a part would be equal to the whole.

[2.] Generations of men, animals, and plants could not be from eternity.‡ If any man say the world was from eternity, then there must be propagation of living creatures in the same manner as are at this day, for without this the world could not consist. What we see now done must have been perpetually done, if it be done by a necessity of nature; but we see nothing now that doth arise but by a mutual propagation from another. If the world were eternal, therefore, it must be so in all eternity. Take any particular species, suppose a man, if men were from eternity, then there were perpetual generations, some were born into the world and some died. Now the natural condition of generation is, that a man doth not generate a man, nor a sheep a lamb, as soon as ever itself is brought into the world, but gets strength and vigour by degrees, and must arrive to a certain stated age before they can produce the like; for whilst anything is little and below the due age, it cannot increase its kind. Men therefore and other creatures did propagate their kind by the same law, not as soon as ever they were born, but in the interval of some time, and children grew up by degrees in the mother's womb till they were fit to be brought forth. If this be so, then there could not be an eternal succession of propagating; for there is no eternal continuation of time. Time is always to be conceived as having one part before another; but that perpetuity of nativities is always after some time, wherein it could not be for the weakness of age. If no man, then, can conceive a propagation from eternity, there must be then a beginning of generation in time, and consequently the creatures were made in time.

To express it in the words of one of our own : ' If the world were eternal, it must have been in the same posture as it is now, in a state of generation and corruption; and so corruption must have been as eternal as generation, and then things that do generate and corrupt must have eternally been, and eternally not have been : there must be some first way to set generation on work.' § We must lose ourselves in our conceptions; we cannot conceive a father before a child, as well as we cannot conceive a child before a father; and reason is quite bewildered, and cannot return into a right way of con-

* Daille, 20 Serm. Psa. cii. p. 13, 14.
† Daille *ut supra*.   ‡ Petav. Theo. Dogmat. tom. i. lib. 1, cap. 2, p. 15.
§ Wolseley of Atheism, page 47.

ception till it conceive one first of every kind : one first man, one first animal, one first plant, from whence others do proceed. The argument is unanswerable, and the wisest atheist (if any atheist can be called wise) cannot unloose the knot. We must come to something that is first in every kind, and this first must have a cause, not of the same kind, but infinite and independent ; otherwise men run into inconceivable labyrinths and contradictions.

Man, the noblest creature upon earth, hath a beginning. No man in the world but was some years ago no man. If every man we see had a beginning, then the first man had also a beginning, then the world had a beginning; for the earth, which was made for the use of man, had wanted that end for which it was made. ' We must pitch upon some one man that was unborn ;'* that first man must either be eternal,—that cannot be, for he that hath no beginning hath no end,—or must spring out of the earth, as plants and trees do,—that cannot be. Why should not the earth produce men to this day, as it doth plants and trees ? He was therefore made ; and whatsoever is made hath some cause that made it, which is God. If the world were uncreated, † it were then immutable, but every creature upon the earth is in a continual flux, always changing. If things be mutable, they were created ; if created, they were made by some author ; whatsoever hath a beginning must have a maker ; if the world hath a beginning, there was then a time when it was not : it must have some cause to produce it. That which makes is before that which is made, and this is God ; which will appear further in this

Prop. No creature can make itself : the world could not make itself.

If every man had a beginning, every man then was once nothing ; he could not then make himself, because nothing cannot be the cause of something : Ps. c. 3, ' The Lord he is God : he hath made us, and not we ourselves.' Whatsoever begun in time, was not ; and when it was nothing, it had nothing, and could do nothing : and therefore could never give to itself nor to any other to be, or to be able to do ; for then it gave what it had not, and did what it could not. ‡ Since reason must acknowledge a *first* of every kind, a first man, &c., it must acknowledge him created and made, not by himself. Why have not other men since risen up by themselves ? Not by chance ; why hath not chance produced the like in that long time the world hath stood ? If we never knew any thing give being to itself, how can we imagine any thing ever could ? If the chiefest part of this lower world cannot, nor any part of it hath been known to give being to itself, then the whole cannot be supposed to give any being to itself. Man did not form himself : his body is not from himself ; it would then have the power of moving itself, but that is not able to live or act without the presence of the soul. Whilst the soul is present, the body moves ; when that is absent, the body lies as a senseless log, not having the least action or motion. His soul could not form itself ; can that which cannot form the least mote, the least grain of dust, form itself a nobler substance than any upon the earth ?

This will be evident to every man's reason, if we consider,

1. Nothing can act before it be. The first man was not, and therefore could not make himself to be : for any thing to produce itself is to act; if it acted before it was, it was then something and nothing at the same time ; it had then a being before it had a being ; it acted when it brought itself into being. How could it act without a being, without it was ? So that if it were the cause of itself, it must be before itself as well as after itself : it

---

* Petav. *ut supra*, page 10.   † Damason.
‡ Petav. Theol. Dog. tom. i. lib. i. cap. 2, page 14.

was before it was; it was as a cause before it was as an effect. Action always supposes a principle from whence it flows; as *nothing* hath no existence, so it hath no operation; there must be therefore something of real existence to give a being to those things that are, and every cause must be an effect of some other before it be a cause. To be and not be at the same time, is a manifest contradiction, which would be if any thing made itself. That which makes is always before that which is made. Who will say the house is before the carpenter, or the picture before the limner? The world as a creator must be before itself as a creature.

2. That which doth not understand itself, and order itself, could not make itself. If the first man fully understood his own nature, the excellency of his own soul, the manner of its operations, why was not that understanding conveyed to his posterity? Are not many of them found, who understand their own nature almost as little as a beast understands itself, or a rose understands its own sweetness, or a tulip its own colours? The Scripture indeed gives us an account how this came about, viz., by the deplorable rebellion of man, whereby death was brought upon them, a spiritual death, which includes ignorance as well as an inability to spiritual action, Gen. ii. 17, Ps. xlix. 8. Thus he fell from his honour, and became like the beasts that perish, and not retaining God in his knowledge, retained not himself in his own knowledge.

But what reply can an atheist make to it, who acknowledges no higher cause than nature? If the soul made itself, how comes it to be so muddy, so wanting in its knowledge of itself and of other things? If the soul made its own understanding, whence did the defect arise? If some first principle was settled by the first man in himself, where was the stop, that he did not implant all in his own mind, and consequently in the minds of all his descendants? Our souls know little of themselves, little of the world, are every day upon new inquiries, have little satisfaction in themselves, meet with many an invincible rub in their way; and when they seem to come 'to some resolution in some cases, stagger again, and like a stone rolled up to the top of the hill, quickly find themselves again at the foot. How come they to be so purblind in truth? so short of that which they judge true goodness? How comes it to pass they cannot order their own rebellious affections, and suffer the reins they have to hold over their affections to be taken out of their hands by the unruly fancy and flesh?

Thus no man that denies the being of a God, and the revelation in Scripture, can give an account of. Blessed be God that we have the Scripture, which gives us an account of those things, that all the wit of men could never inform us of; and that when they are discovered and known by revelation, they appear not contrary to reason.

3. If the first man made himself, how came he to limit himself? If he gave himself being, why did he not give himself all the perfections and ornaments of being? Nothing that made itself could sit down contented with a little, but would have had as much power to give itself that which is less, as to give itself being when it was nothing. The excellencies it wanted had not been more difficult to gain than the other which it possessed, as belonging to its nature. If the first man had been independent upon another, and had his perfection from himself, he might have acquired that perfection he wanted, as well as have bestowed upon himself that perfection he had; and then there would have been no bounds set to him. He would have been omniscient and immutable. He might have given himself what he would; if he had had the setting his own bounds, he would have set none at all; for what should restrain him? No man now wants ambition to be what he is

not; and if the first man had not been determined by another, but had given himself being, he would not have remained in that determinate being, no more than a toad would remain a toad, if it had power to make itself a man, and that power it would have had, if it had given itself a being. Whatsoever gives itself being, would give itself all degrees of being, and so would have no imperfection, because every imperfection is a want of some degree of being.* He that could give himself matter and life, might give himself every thing. The giving of life is an act of omnipotence, and what is omnipotent in one thing, may be in all. Besides, if the first man had made himself, he would have conveyed himself to all his posterity in the same manner; every man would have had all the perfections of the first man, as every creature hath the perfections of the same kind; from whence it naturally issues, all are desirous to communicate what they can to their posterity. Communicative goodness belongs to every nature. Every plant propagates its kind in the same perfection it hath itself; and the nearer anything comes to a rational nature, the greater affection it hath to that which descends from it; therefore this affection belongs to a rational nature much more. The first man, therefore, if he had had power to give himself being, and consequently all perfection, he would have had as much power to convey it down to his posterity; no impediment could have stopped his way: then all souls proceeding from that first man would have been equally intellectual. What should hinder them from inheriting the same perfections? whence should they have diverse qualifications and differences in their understandings? No man then would have been subject to those weaknesses, doubtings, and unsatisfied desires of knowledge and perfection. But being all souls are not alike, it is certain they depend upon some other cause for the communication of that excellency they have. If the perfections of men be so contracted and kept within certain bounds, it is certain that they were not in his own power, and so were not from himself. Whatsoever hath a determinate being must be limited by some superior cause. There is therefore some superior power, that hath thus determined the creature by set bounds and distinct measures, and hath assigned to every one its proper nature, that it should not be greater or less than it is; who hath said of every one, as of the waves of the sea, Job xxxviii. 11, 'Hitherto shalt thou come, but no further;' and this is God. Man could not have reserved any perfection from his posterity; for since he doth propagate not · by choice but nature, he could no more have kept back any perfection from them than he could, as he pleased, have given any perfection belonging to his nature to them.

4. That which hath power to give itself being, cannot want power to preserve that being. Preservation is not more difficult than creation. If the first man made himself, why did he not preserve himself? He is not now among the living in the world. How came he to be so feeble as to sink into the grave? Why did he not inspire himself with new heat and moisture, and fill his languishing limbs and declining body with new strength? Why did he not chase away diseases and death at the first approach? What creature can find the dust of the first man? All his posterity traverse the stage and retire again; in a short space again their 'age departs, and is removed from them as a shepherd's tent, and is cut off with pining sickness,' Isa. xxxviii. 12. The life of man is as a wind, and like a cloud that is consumed and vanishes away. 'The eye that sees him shall see him no more. He returns not to his house, neither doth his place know him any more,'

---

* Therefore the heathens called God τὸ ὄν, the only being. Other things were not beings, because they had not all degrees of being.

Job vii. 8, 10. The Scripture gives us the reason of this, and lays it upon the score of sin against his Creator, which no man without revelation can give any satisfactory account of.

Had the first man made himself, he had been sufficient for himself, able to support himself without the assistance of any creature. He would not have needed animals and plants, and other helps to nourish and refresh him, nor medicines to cure him. He could not be beholding to other things for his support, which he is certain he never made for himself. His own nature would have continued that vigour which once he had conferred upon himself. He would not have needed the heat and light of the sun; he would have wanted nothing sufficient for himself in himself; he needed not have sought without himself for his own preservation and comfort. What depends upon another is not of itself, and what depends upon things inferior to itself is less of itself. Since nothing can subsist of itself, since we see those things upon which man depends for his nourishment and subsistence growing and decaying, starting into the world and retiring from it, as well as man himself, some preserving cause must be concluded upon which all depends.

5. If the first man did produce himself, why did he not produce himself before?

It hath been already proved that he had a beginning, and could not be from eternity. Why then did he not make himself before? Not because he would not. For having no being, he could have no will; he could neither be willing nor not willing. If he could not then, how could he afterwards? If it were in his own power he could have done it, he would have done it; if it were not in his own power, then it was in the power of some other cause, and that is God. How came he by that power to produce himself? If the power of producing himself were communicated by another, then man could not be the cause of himself. That is the cause of it which communicated that power to it. But if the power of being was in and from himself, and in no other, nor communicated to him, man would always have been in act, and always have existed, no hindrance can be conceived. For that which had the power of being in itself was invincible by anything that should stand in the way of its own being.

We may conclude from hence the excellency of the Scripture, that it is a word not to be refused credit. It gives us the most rational account of things in the 1st and 2d of Genesis, which nothing in the world else is able to do.

Prop. 2. No creature could make the world. No creature can create another. If it creates of nothing, it is then omnipotent, and so not a creature. If it makes something of matter unfit for that which is produced out of it, then the inquiry will be, Who was the cause of the matter? and so we must arrive to some uncreated being, the cause of all. Whatsoever gives being to any other must be the highest being, and must possess all the perfections of that which it gives being to. What visible creature is there which possesses the perfections of the whole world? If, therefore, an invisible creature made the world, the same inquiries will return, whence that creature had its being? For he could not make himself. If any creature did create the world, he must do it by the strength and virtue of another, which first gave him being; and this is God. For whatsoever hath its existence and virtue of acting from another is not God. If it hath its virtue from another, it is then a second cause, and so supposeth a first cause. It must have some cause of itself, or be eternally existent. If eternally existent, it is not a second cause, but God; if not eternally existent, we must come to something at length which was the cause of it, or else be bewildered without being able to give an account of anything. We must come at last to an infinite, eternal, independent being that was the first cause of this structure and fabric wherein we and all creatures dwell. The Scripture proclaims this aloud: Isa. xlv. 6, 7, Deut. iv. 35, 'I am the Lord, and there is none else. I form the light, and I create darkness.' Man, the noblest creature, cannot of himself make a man, the chiefest part of the world. If our parents only, without a superior power, made our bodies or souls, they would know the frame of them; as he that makes a lock knows the wards of it; he that makes any curious piece of arras knows how he sets the various colours together, and how many threads went to each division in the web; he that makes a watch, having the idea of the whole work in his mind, knows the motions of it, and the reason of those motions. But both parents and children are equally ignorant of the nature of their souls and bodies, and of the reason of their motions. God only, that had the supreme hand in informing us, 'in whose book all our members are written, which in continuance were fashioned,' Ps. cxxxix, 16, knows what we all are ignorant of. If man hath, in an ordinary course of generation, his being chiefly from an higher cause than his parents, the world then certainly had its being from some infinitely wise intelligent being, which is God. If it were, as some fancy, made by an assembly of atoms, there must be some infinite intelligent cause that made them, some cause that separated them, some cause that mingled them together for the piling up so comely a structure as the world. It is the most absurd thing to think they should meet together by hazard, and rank·themselves in that order we see without a higher and a wise agent. So that no creature could make the world. For supposing any creature was formed before this visible world, and might have a hand in disposing things, yet he must have a cause of himself, and must act by the virtue and strength of another, and this is God.

Prop. 3. From hence it follows, that there is a first cause of things, which we call God. There must be something supreme in the order of nature, something which is greater than all, which hath nothing beyond it or above it, otherwise we must run *in infinitum.* We see not a river but we conclude a fountain; a watch, but we conclude an artificer. As all number begins from unity, so all the multitude of things in the world begins from some unity, oneness, as the principle of it. It is natural to arise from a view of those things to the conception of a nature more perfect than any. As from heat mixed with cold, and light mixed with darkness, men conceive and arise in their understanding to an intense heat and a pure light, and from a corporeal or bodily substance joined with an incorporeal (as man is an earthly body and a spiritual soul), we ascend to a conception of a substance purely incorporeal and spiritual, so from a multitude of things in the world, reason leads us to one choice being above all. And since, in all natures in the world, we still find a superior nature, the nature of one beast above the nature of another, the nature of man above the nature of beasts, and some invisible nature, the worker of strange effects in the air and earth, which cannot be ascribed to any visible cause, we must suppose some nature above all those, of inconceivable perfection.

Every sceptic, one that doubts whether there be anything real or no in the world, that counts everything an appearance, must necessarily own a first cause.* They cannot reasonably doubt but that there is some first cause, which makes the things appear so to them. They cannot be the cause of their own appearance. For as nothing can have a being from

* Coccei. Sum. Theol. cap. 8, sec. 33.

itself, so nothing can appear by itself and its own force. Nothing can be and not be at the same time. But that which is not, and yet seems to be, if it be the cause why it seems to be what it is not, it may be said to be and not to be. But certainly such persons must think themselves to exist. If they do not, they cannot think; and if they do exist, they must have some cause of that existence. So that, which way soever we turn ourselves, we must in reason own a first cause in the world.

Well, then, might the psalmist term an atheist a fool, that disowns a God against his own reason. Without owning a God as the first cause of the world, no man can give any tolerable or satisfactory account of the world to his own reason.

And this first cause,

1. Must necessarily exist. It is necessary that he by whom all things are should be before all things, and nothing before him.* And if nothing be before him, he comes not from any other; and then he always was, and without beginning. He is from himself; not that he once was not, but because he hath not his existence from another, and therefore of necessity he did exist from all eternity. Nothing can make itself or bring itself into being; therefore there must be some being which hath no cause, that depends upon no other, never was produced by any other, but was what he is from eternity, and cannot be otherwise, and is not what he is by will, but nature, necessarily existing, and always existing without any capacity or possibility ever not to be.

2. Must be infinitely perfect. Since man knows he is an imperfect being, he must suppose the perfections he wants are seated in some other being, which hath limited him, and upon which he depends. Whatsover we conceive of excellency or perfection must be in God; for we can conceive no perfection but what God hath given us a power to conceive. And he that gave us power to conceive a transcendent perfection above whatsoever we saw or heard of, hath much more in himself, or else he could not give us such a conception.

II. As the production of the world, so the harmony of all the parts of it declare the being and wisdom of a God. Without the acknowledging God, the atheist can give no account of those things. The multitude, elegancy, variety, and beauty of all things are steps whereby to ascend to one fountain and original of them.

Is it not a folly to deny the being of a wise agent, who sparkles in the beauty and motions of the heavens, rides upon the wings of the wind, and is writ upon the flowers and fruits of plants? As the cause is known by the effects, so the wisdom of the cause is known by the elegancy of the work, the proportion of the parts to one another. Who can imagine the world could be rashly made, and without consultation, which in every part of it is so artificially framed?† No work of art springs up of its own accord. The world is framed by an excellent art, and therefore made by some skilful artist. As we hear not a melodious instrument but we conclude there is a musician that touches it, as well as some skilful hand that framed and disposed it for those lessons,—and no man that hears the pleasant sound of a lute but will fix his thoughts, not upon the instrument itself, but upon the skill of the artist that made it, and the art of the musician that strikes it, though he should not see the first when he saw the lute, nor see the other when he hears the harmony,—so a rational creature confines not his thoughts to his sense when he sees the sun in its glory and the moon walking in its

* Petav. Theol. Dog. tom. i. lib. i. cap. 2, page 10, 11.
† Philo. Judæ. Petav. Theol. Dogmat. tom. i. lib. i. cap. 1, page 9.

brightness, but riseth up in a contemplation and admiration of that infinite spirit that composed and filled them with such sweetness.

This appears,

1. In the linking contrary qualities together. All things are compounded of the elements. Those are endued with contrary qualities, dryness and moisture, heat and cold ; these would always be contending with and infesting one another's rights, till the contest ended in the destruction of one or both. Where fire is predominant, it would suck up the water ; where water is prevalent, it would quench the fire : the heat would wholly expel the cold, or the cold overpower the heat. Yet we see them chained and linked one within another in every body upon the earth, and rendering mutual offices for the benefit of that body wherein they are seated, and all conspiring together in their particular quarrels for the public interest of the body. How could those contraries, that of themselves observed no order, that are always preying upon one another, jointly accord together of themselves for one common end, if they were not linked in a common band, and reduced to that order by some incomprehensible wisdom and power, which keeps a hand upon them, orders their motions, and directs their events, and makes them friendly pass into one another's natures ? Confusion had been the result of the discord and diversity of their natures ; no composition could have been of those conflicting qualities for the frame of any body, nor any harmony arose from so many jarring strings, if they had not been reduced into concord by one that is supreme Lord over them, and knows how to dispose their varieties and enmities for the public good.* If a man should see a large city or country, consisting of great multitudes of men of different tempers, full of frauds, and factions, and animosities in their natures against one another, yet living together in good order and peace, without oppressing and invading one another, and joining together for the public good, he would presently conclude there were some excellent governor, who tempered them by his wisdom and preserved the public peace, though he had never yet beheld him with his eye. It is as necessary to conclude a God, who moderates the contraries in the world, as to conclude a wise prince, who overrules the contrary dispositions in a state, making every one to keep his own bounds and confines. Things that are contrary to one another subsist in an admirable order.

2. In the subserviency of one thing to another. All the members of living creatures are curiously fitted for the service of one another, destined to a particular end, and endued with a virtue to attain that end, and so distinctly placed, that one is no hindrance to the other in its operations.† Is not this more admirable than to be the work of chance, which is incapable to settle such an order, and fix particular and general ends, causing an exact correspondency of all parts with one another, and every part to conspire together for one common end ? One thing is fitted for another. The eye is fitted for the sun, and the sun fitted for the eye. Several sorts of food are fitted for several creatures, and those creatures fitted with organs for the partaking of that food.

(1.) Subserviency of heavenly bodies. The sun, the heart of the world, is not for itself but for the good of the world,‡ as the heart of man is for the good of the body. How conveniently is the sun placed, at a distance from the earth and the upper heavens, to enlighten the stars above and enliven the earth below ! If it were either higher or lower, one part would want its influences. It is not in the higher parts of the heavens ; the earth then,

* Athanasius, Petav. Theol., Dog. tom. i. lib. i. cap. 1, p. 4, 5.
† Gassend. Physic, sect. i. lib. iv. cap. 2, page 315.　　　　‡ Lessius.

which lives and fructifies by its influence, would have been exposed to a perpetual winter and chillness, unable to have produced anything for the sustenance of man or beast; if seated lower, the earth had been parched up, the
world made uninhabitable, and long since had been consumed to ashes by
the strength of its heat.   Consider the motion, as well as the situation, of
the sun.   Had it stood still, one part of the world had been cherished by
its beams, and the other left in a desolate widowhood, in a disconsolate
darkness.   Besides, the earth would have had no shelter from its perpendi-
cular beams striking perpetually and without any remission upon it.   The
same incommodities would have followed upon its fixedness as upon its too
great nearness.   By a constant day the beauty of the stars had been obscured, the knowledge of their motions been prevented, and a considerable
part of the glorious wisdom of the Creator in those choice ' works of his
fingers,' Ps. viii. 8, had been veiled from our eyes.   It moves in a fixed
line, visits all parts of the earth, scatters in the day its refreshing blessings
in every creek of the earth, and removes the mask from the other beauties
of heaven in the night, which sparkle out to the glory of the Creator.   It
spreads its light, warms the earth, cherisheth the seeds, excites the spirit
in the earth, and brings fruit to maturity.   View also the air, the vast
extent between heaven and earth, which serves for a watercourse, a cistern
for water to bedew the face of the sunburnt earth, to satisfy the desolate
ground, and to cause the ' bud of the tender herb to spring forth,' Job
xxxviii. 25, 27. Could chance appoint the clouds of the air to interpose as fans
before the scorching heat of the sun and the faint bodies of the creatures ?
Can that be the ' father of the rain,' or ' beget the drops of dew ' ? ver. 28.
Could anything so blind settle those ordinances of heaven for the preservation of creatures on the earth ?   Can this either bring or stay the bottles of
heaven, when ' the dust grows into hardness and the clods cleave fast
together ' ? ver. 37, 38.

(2.) Subserviency of the lower world, the earth and sea, which was
created to be inhabited, Isa. xlv. 18.   The sea affords water to the rivers ;
the rivers, like so many veins, are spread through the whole body of the
earth to refresh and enable it to bring forth fruit for the sustenance of man
and beast: Ps. civ. 10, 11, ' He sends the springs into the valleys, which
run among the hills.   They give drink to every beast of the field : the wild
asses quench their thirst.   He causes the grass to grow for the cattle, and
the herb for the service of man, that he may bring forth food out of the
earth,' ver. 14.   The trees are provided for shades against the extremity of
heat, a refuge for the panting beasts, ' an habitation for birds' wherein to
make their nests, ver. 17, and a basket for their provision.   How are the
valleys and mountains of the earth disposed for the pleasure and profit of
man !   Every year are the fields covered with harvests, for the nourishing
the creatures; no part is barren, but beneficial to man.   The mountains that
are not clothed with grass for his food are set with stones to make him an
habitation ; they have their peculiar services of metals and minerals, for
the conveniency, and comfort, and benefit of man.   Things which are not
fit for his food are medicines for his cure under some painful sickness.
Where the earth brings not forth corn, it brings forth roots for the service
of other creatures.   Wood abounds more in those countries where the cold
is stronger than in others.   Can this be the result of chance, or not rather
of an infinite wisdom ?

Consider the usefulness of the sea for the supply of rivers to refresh the
earth, ' which go up by the mountains and down by the valleys into the
place God hath founded for them,' Ps. civ. 8: a storehouse for fish for the

nourishment of other creatures, a shop of medicines for cure, and pearls for ornament; the band that ties remote nations together, by giving opportunity of passage to, and commerce with one another. How should that natural inclination of the sea to cover the earth submit to this subserviency to the creatures? Who hath pounded in this fluid mass of water in certain limits, and confined it to its own channel for the accommodation of such creatures, who by its common law can only be upon the earth? Naturally the earth was covered with the deep as with a garment, the waters stood above the mountains: 'Who set a bound that they might not pass over, that they return not again to cover the earth?' Ps. civ. 6, 9. Was it blind chance, or an infinite power, that 'shut up the sea with doors, and made thick darkness a swaddling band for it, and said, Hitherto shall thou come, and no further; and here shall thy proud waves be stayed'? Job xxxviii. 8, 9, 11.

All things are so ordered that they are not *propter se*, but *propter aliud*. What advantage accrues to the sun by its unwearied rolling about the world? Doth it increase the perfection of its nature by all its circuits? No, but it serves the inferior world, it impregnates things by its heat. Not the most abject thing, but hath its end and use. There is a straight connection: the earth could not bring forth fruit without the heavens, the heavens could not water the earth without vapours from it.

(3.) All this subserviency of creatures centres in man. Other creatures are served by those things as well as ourselves, and they are provided for their nourishment and refreshment as well as ours;* yet both they and all creatures meet in man, as lines in their centres. Things that have no life or sense are made for those that have both life and sense, and those that have life and sense are made for those that are endued with reason. When the psalmist admiringly considers the heavens, moon, and stars, he intimates man to be the end for which they were created: Ps. viii. 3, 4, 'What is man that thou art mindful of him?' He expresseth more particularly the dominion that man hath over 'the beasts of the fields, the fowl of the air, and whatsoever passes through the paths of the sea,' ver. 6–8, and concludes from thence the 'excellency of God's name in all the earth.' All things in the world, one way or other, centre in an usefulness for man: some to feed him, some to clothe him, some to delight him, others to instruct him, some to exercise his wit, and others his strength. Since man did not make them, he did not also order them for his own use. If they conspire to serve him who never made them, they direct man to acknowledge another, who is the joint Creator both of the lord and the servants under his dominion. And therefore, as the inferior natures are ordered by an invisible hand for the good of man, so the nature of man is by the same hand ordered to acknowledge the existence and the glory of the Creator of him. This visible order man knows he did not constitute, he did not settle those creatures in subserviency to himself; they were placed in that order before he had any acquaintance with them, or existence of himself, which is a question God puts to Job, to consider of: Job xxxviii. 4, 'Where wast thou when I laid the foundation of the earth? Declare if thou hast understanding.' All is ordered for man's use, the heavens answer to the earth as a roof to a floor, both composing a delightful habitation for man; 'vapours ascend from the earth,' and the heavens concocts them, and returns them back in welcome showers for the supplying of the earth, Jer. x. 13. The light of the sun descends to beautify the earth, and employs its heat to midwife its fruits, and this for the good of the community, whereof man is the head; and though all creatures have distinct natures, and must act for particular ends,

* Amyrald. de Trinitate, p. 13 and p. 18.

according to the law of their creation, yet there is a joint combination for the good of the whole as the common end ; just as all the rivers in the world, from what part soever they come, whether north or south, fall into the sea, for the supply of that mass of waters ; which loudly proclaims some infinitely wise nature who made those things in so exact an harmony. ' As in a clock, the hammer which strikes the bell leads us to the next wheel, that to another, the little wheel to a greater, whence it derives its motion, this at last to the spring, which acquaints us that there was some artist that framed them in this subordination to one another for this orderly motion.'*

(4.) This order or subserviency is regular and uniform. Everything is determined to its peculiar nature.† The sun and moon make day and night, months and years, determine the seasons, never are defective in coming back to their station and place, they wander not from their roads, shock not against one another, nor hinder one another in the functions assigned them. From a small grain or seed a tree springs, with body, root, bark, leaves, fruit of the same shape, figure, smell, taste ; that there should be as many parts in one as in all of the same kind, and no more, and that in the womb of a sensitive creature should be formed one of the same kind, with all the due members and no more, and the creature that produceth it knows not how it is formed or how it is perfected. If we say this is nature, this nature is an intelligent being ; if not, how can it direct all causes to such uniform ends ? If it be intelligent, this nature must be the same we call God, who ordered every herb to yield seed, and every fruit-tree to yield fruit after its kind, and also every beast and every creeping thing after its kind, Gen. i. 11, 12, 24.

And everything is determined to its particular season. The sap riseth from the root at its appointed time, enlivening and clothing the branches with a new garment at such a time of the sun's returning, not wholly hindered by any accidental coldness of the weather, it being often colder at its return than it was at the sun's departure. All things have their seasons of flourishing, budding, blossoming, bringing forth fruit; they ripen in their seasons, cast their leaves at the same time, throw off their old clothes, and in the spring appear with new garments, but still in the same fashion.

The winds and the rain have their seasons,‡ and seem to be administered by laws for the profit of man. No satisfactory cause of those things can be ascribed to the earth, the sea, to the air or stars. ' Can any understand the spreading of his clouds, or the noise of his tabernacle ?' Job xxxvi. 29. The natural reason of those things cannot be demonstrated without recourse to an infinite and intelligent being. Nothing can be rendered capable of the direction of those things but a God.

This regularity in plants and animals is in all nations. The heavens have the same motion in all parts of the world ; all men have the same law of nature in their mind ; all creatures are stamped with the same law of creation. In all parts the same creatures serve for the same use; and though there be different creatures in India and Europe, yet they have the same subordination, the same subserviency to one another, and ultimately to man, which shews that there is a God, and but one God, who tunes all those different strings to the same notes in all places. It is nature merely conducts these natural causes in due measures to their proper effects, without interfering with one another! Can mere nature be the cause of those musical proportions of time ? You may as well conceive a lute to sound its

* Morn. de Verit. cap. i. p. 7.   † Amyrant.
‡ Coccei. Sum. Theol. cap. viii. sec. 77.

own strings without the hand of an artist, a city well governed without a governor, an army keep its stations without a general, as imagine so exact an order without an orderer. Would any man, when he hears a clock strike, by fit intervals, the hour of the day, imagine this regularity in it, without the direction of one that had understanding to manage it? He would not only regard the motion of the clock, but commend the diligence of the clock-keeper.

(5.) This order and subserviency is constant. Children change the customs and manners of their fathers, magistrates change the laws they have received from their ancestors, and enact new ones in their room; but in the world all things consist as they were created at the beginning; the law of nature in the creatures hath met with no change.* Who can behold the sun rising in the morning, the moon shining in the night, increasing and decreasing in its due spaces, the stars in their regular motions night after night, for all ages, and yet deny a president over them? And this motion of the heavenly bodies, being contrary to the nature of other creatures, who move in order to rest, must be from some higher cause. But those, ever since the settling in their places, have been perpetually rounding the world.—Whether it be the sun or the earth that moves, it is all one ; whence have either of them this constant and uniform motion?—What nature, but one powerful and intelligent, could give that perpetual motion to the sun, which being bigger than the earth a hundred sixty-six times, runs many thousand miles with a mighty swiftness in the space of an hour, with an unwearied diligence performing its daily task, and as a strong man, rejoicing to run its race for above five thousand years together, without intermission but in the time of Joshua? Josh. x. 13. It is not nature's sun, but God's sun, which he 'makes to rise upon the just and unjust,' Mat. v. 45.

So a plant receives its nourishment from the earth, sends forth its juice to every branch, forms a bud which spreads it into a blossom and flower; the leaves of this drop off, and leave a fruit of the same colour and taste, every year, which being ripened by the sun, leaves seed behind it for the propagation of its like, which contains in the nature of it the same kind of buds, blossoms, fruit, which were before; and, being nourished in the womb of the earth, and quickened by the power of the sun, discovers itself at length in all the progresses and motions which its predecessor did. Thus, in all ages, in all places, every year it performs the same task, spins out fruit of the same colour, taste, virtue, to refresh the several creatures for which they are provided.

This settled state of things comes from that God who laid the foundations of the earth, that it should not be removed for ever, Ps. civ. 5, and set ordinances for them to act by a stated law, Job xxxviii. 33, according to which they move as if they understood themselves to have made a covenant with their Creator, Jer. xxxiii. 20.

3. Add to this union of contrary qualities, and the subserviency of one thing to another, the admirable variety and diversity of things in the world. What variety of metals, living creatures, plants! What variety and distinction in the shape of their leaves, flowers, smell resulting from them! Who can number up the several sorts of beasts on the earth, birds in the air, fish in the sea? How various are their motions! Some creep, some go, some fly, some swim ; and in all this variety each creature hath organs or members fitted for their peculiar motion. If you consider the multitude of stars, which shine like jewels in the heavens, their different magnitudes, or the variety of colours in the flowers and tapestry of the earth, you could

* Petav. ex Athanas. Theol., Dog. tom. i. lib. i. sec. 4.

no more conclude they made themselves, or were made by chance, than you can imagine a piece of arras, with a diversity of figures and colours, either wove itself or were knit together by hazard.

How delicious is the sap of the vine, when turned into wine, above that of a crab? Both have the same womb of earth to conceive them, both agree in the nature of wood and twigs as channels to convey it into fruit. What is that which makes the one so sweet, the other so sour, or makes that sweet which was a few weeks before unpleasantly sharp? Is it the earth? No; they both have the same soil; the branches may touch each other, the strings of their roots may under ground entwine about one another. Is it the sun? Both have the same beams; why is not the taste and colour of the one as gratifying as the other? Is it the root? The taste of that is far different from that of the fruit it bears. Why do they not, when they have the same soil, the same sun, and stand near one another, borrow something from one another's natures? No reason can be rendered, but that there is a God of infinite wisdom hath determined this variety, and bound up the nature of each creature within itself. 'Everything follows the law of its creation, and it is worthy observation that the Creator of them hath not given that power to animals, which arise from different species, to propagate the like to themselves; as mules, that arise from different species. No reason can be rendered of this but the fixed determination of the Creator that those species which were created by him should not be lost in those mixtures, which are contrary to the law of the creation.'* This cannot possibly be ascribed to that which is commonly called nature, but unto the God of nature, who will not have his creatures exceed their bounds or come short of them.

Now, since among those varieties there are some things better than other, yet all are good in their kind, Gen. i. 31, and partake of goodness, there must be something better and more excellent than all those, from whom they derive that goodness, which inheres in their nature and is communicated by them to others. And this excellent being must inherit in an eminent way in his own nature, the goodness of all those varieties, since they made not themselves, but were made by another. All that goodness which is scattered in those varieties must be infinitely concentrated in that nature, which distributed those various perfections to them: Ps. xciv. 9, 'He that planted the ear, shall not he hear? he that formed the eye, shall not he see? he that teacheth man knowledge, shall not he know?' The Creator is greater than the creature, and whatsoever is in his effects is but an impression of some excellency in himself; there is therefore some chief fountain of goodness, whence all those various goodnesses in the world do flow.

From all this it follows, if there be an order and harmony, there must be an orderer, one that 'made the earth by his power, established the world by his wisdom, and stretched out the heavens by his discretion,' Jer. x. 12. Order being the effect, cannot be the cause of itself. Order is the disposition of things to an end, and is not intelligent, but implies an intelligent orderer; and therefore it is as certain that there is a God as it is certain there is order in the world. Order is an effect of reason and counsel; this reason and counsel must have its residence in some being before this order was fixed. The things ordered are always distinct from that reason and counsel whereby they are ordered; and also after it, as the effect is after the cause. No man begins a piece of work but he hath the model of it in his own mind; no man builds a house or makes a watch but he hath the

* Amyrald. de Trinitate, page 21.

idea or copy of it in his own head. This beautiful world bespeaks an idea of it or a model, since there is such a magnificent wisdom in the make of each creature, and the proportion of one creature to another; this model must be before the world, as the pattern is always before the thing that is wrought by it. This therefore must be in some intelligent and wise agent, and this is God. Since the reason of those things exceed the reason and all the art of man, who can ascribe them to any inferior cause? Chance it could not be; the motions of chance are not constant, and at seasons, as the motions of creatures are. That which is by chance is contingent, this is necessary; uniformity can never be the birth of chance. Who can imagine that all the parts of a watch can meet together, and put themselves in order and motion, by chance? ' Nor can it be nature only, which indeed is a disposition of second causes. If nature hath not an understanding, it cannot work such effects. If nature therefore uses counsel to begin a thing, reason to dispose it, art to effect it, virtue to complete it, and power to govern it, why should it be called nature rather than God?' * Nothing so sure as that that which hath an end to which it tends hath a cause by which it is ordered to that end. Since therefore all things are ordered in subserviency to the good of man, they are so ordered by him that made both man and them. And man must acknowledge the wisdom and goodness of his Creator, and act in subserviency to his glory, as other creatures act in subserviency to his good. Sensible objects were not made only to gratify the sense of man, but to hand something to his mind as he is a rational creature, to discover God to him as an object of love and desire to be enjoyed.† If this be not the effect of it, the order of the creature, as to such an one, is in vain, and falls short of its true end.

To conclude this ; as when a man comes into a palace, built according to the exactest rule of art, and with an unexceptionable conveniency for the inhabitants, he would acknowledge both the being and skill of the builder, so whosoever shall observe the disposition of all the parts of the world,—their connection, comeliness, the variety of seasons, the swarms of different creatures, and the mutual offices they render to one another,—cannot conclude less than that it was contrived by an infinite skill, effected by infinite power, and governed by infinite wisdom. None can imagine a ship to be orderly conducted without a pilot, nor the parts of the world to perform their several functions without a wise guide, considering the members of the body cannot perform theirs without the active presence of the soul. The atheist then is a fool, to deny that which every creature in his constitution asserts, and thereby renders himself unable to give a satisfactory account of that constant uniformity in the motions of the creatures.

Prop. 4. As the production and harmony, so particular creatures, pursuing and attaining their ends, manifest that there is a God. All particular creatures have natural instincts, which move them for some end. The intending of an end is a property of a rational creature; since the lower creatures cannot challenge that title, they must act by the understanding and direction of another. And since man cannot challenge the honour of inspiring the creatures with such instincts, it must be ascribed to some nature infinitely above any creature in understanding. No creature doth determine itself. Why doth the fruits and grain of the earth nourish us, when the earth, which instrumentally gives them that fitness, cannot nourish us, but because their several ends are determined by one higher than the world?

1. Several creatures have several natures. How soon will all creatures,

* Lactant.   † Coccei. Sum. Theol. cap. 8, sec. 63, 64.

even as soon as they see the light, move to that whereby they must live, and make use of the natural arms God hath given their kind for their defence, before they are grown to any maturity to afford them that defence. The Scripture makes the appetite of infants to their milk a foundation of the divine glory: Ps. viii. 8, 'Out of the mouths of babes and sucklings hast thou ordained strength;' that is, matter of praise and acknowledgment of God, in the natural appetite they have to their milk, and their relish of it. All creatures have a natural affection to their young ones, all young ones by a natural instinct move to and receive the nourishment that is proper for them. Some are their own physicians as well as their own caterers, and naturally discern what preserves them in life, and what restores them when sick. The swallow flies to its celandine, and the toad hastens to its plantain.

Can we behold the spider's nets or silkworm's web, the bee's closets or the ant's granaries, without acknowledging a higher being than a creature, who hath planted that genius in them? The consideration of the nature of several creatures God commended to Job (chap. xxxix., where he discourseth to Job of the natural instincts of the goat, the ostrich, horse, and eagle, &c.), to persuade him to the acknowledgment and admiration of God, and humiliation of himself.

The spider, as if it understood the art of weaving, fits its web both for its own habitation and a net to catch its prey. The bee builds a cell which serves for chambers to reside in and a repository for its provision. Birds are observed to build their nests with a clammy matter without, for the firmer duration of it, and with a soft moss and down within, for the conveniency and warmth of their young: 'The stork knows his appointed time,' Jer. viii. 7; 'and the swallows observe the time of their coming;' they go and return according to the seasons of the year. This they gain not by consideration, it descends to them with their nature; they neither gain nor increase it by rational deductions. It is not in vain to speak of these. How little do we improve by meditation those objects, which daily offer themselves to our view, full of instruction for us? And our Saviour sends his disciples to spell God in the lilies, Mat. vi. 28. It is observed also that the creatures offensive to man go single; if they went by troops, they would bring destruction upon man and beast. This is the nature of them for the preservation of others.

2. They know not their end. They have a law in their natures, but have no rational understanding, either of the end to which they are appointed, or the means fit to attain it. They naturally do what they do, and move by no counsel of their own, but by a law impressed by some higher hand upon their natures.

What plant knows why it strikes its root into the earth? Doth it understand what storms it is to contest with, or why it shoots up its branches towards heaven? Doth it know it needs the droppings of the clouds to preserve itself, and make it fruitful? These are acts of understanding: the root is downward to preserve its own standing, the branches upward to preserve other creatures. This understanding is not in the creature itself, but originally in another. Thunders and tempests know not why they are sent, yet by the direction of a mighty hand they are instruments of justice upon a wicked world.

Rational creatures that act for some end, and know the end they aim at, yet know not the manner of the natural motion of the members to it.* When we intend to look upon a thing, we take no counsel about the natural motion

* Coccei. Sum. Theolog. cap. 8. sec. 67, &c.

of our eyes, we know not all the principles of their operations ; or how that dull matter whereof our bodies are composed, is subject to the order of our minds. We are not of counsel with our stomachs about the concoction of our meat, or the distribution of the nourishing juice to the several parts of the body.* Neither the mother nor the fœtus sit in council how the formation should be made in the womb. We know no more than a plant knows what stature it is of, and what medicinal virtue its fruit hath for the good of man ; yet all those natural operations are perfectly directed 'to their proper end, by an higher wisdom than any human understanding is able to conceive, since they exceed the ability of an inanimate or fleshly nature, yea, and the wisdom of a man. Do we not often see reasonable creatures acting for one end, and perfecting a higher than what they aimed at, or could suspect ? When Joseph's brethren sold him for a slave, their end was to be rid of an informer, Gen. xxxvii. 12 ; but the action issued in preparing him to be the preserver of them and their families. Cyrus his end was to be a conqueror, but the action ended in being the Jews' deliverer : Prov. xvi. 9, ' A man's heart deviseth his way, but the Lord directs his steps.'

3. Therefore there is some superior understanding and nature which so acts them. That which acts for an end unknown to itself, depends upon some overruling wisdom that knows that end. Who should direct them in all those ends, but he that bestowed a being upon them for those ends,† who knows what is convenient for their life, security, and propagation of their natures ? An exact knowledge is necessary, both of what is agreeable to them, and the means whereby they must attain it ; which, since it is not inherent in them, is in that wise God, who puts those instincts into them, and governs them in the exercise of them to such ends. Any man that sees a dart flung, knows it cannot hit the mark without the skill and strength of an archer ; or he that sees the hand of a dial pointing to the hours successively, knows that the dial is ignorant of its own end, and is disposed and directed in that motion by another. All creatures ignorant of their own natures could not universally in the whole kind, and in every climate and country, without any difference in the whole world, tend to a certain end, if some over-ruling wisdom did not preside over the world and guide them ; and if the creatures have a conductor, they have a creator. All things are ' turned round about by his counsel, that they may do whatsoever he commands them upon the face of the world in the earth,' Job xxxvii. 12.

So that in this respect the folly of atheism appears. Without the owning a God no account can be given of those actions of creatures, that are an imitation of reason. To say the bees, &c., are rational, is to equal them to man ; nay, make them his superiors, since they do more by nature than the wisest man can do by art. It is their own counsel whereby they act, or another's : if it be their own, they are reasonable creatures ; if by another's, it is not mere nature that is necessary ; then other creatures would not be without the same skill : there would be no difference among them. If nature be restrained by another, it hath a superior ; if not, it is a free agent : it is an understanding being that directs them. And then it is something superior to all creatures in the world ; and by this, therefore, we may ascend to the acknowledgment of the necessity of a God.

Prop. 5. Add to the production and order of the world, and the creatures acting for their end, the preservation of them. Nothing can depend upon itself in its preservation, no more than it could in its being. If the order of the world was not fixed by itself, the preservation of that order cannot be continued by itself.

---

* Pearson on the Creed, page 85.   † Lessius. de providen. lib. i. page 652.

Though the matter of the world after creation cannot return to that nothing whence it was fetched, without the power of God that made it (because the same power is as requisite to reduce a thing to nothing as to raise a thing from nothing), yet without the actual exerting of a power that made the creatures they would fall into confusion. Those contesting qualities which are in every part of it could not have preserved, but would have consumed and extinguished one another, and reduced the world to that confused chaos wherein it was before the Spirit moved upon the waters. As contrary parts could not have met together in one form, unless there had been one that had conjoined them, so they could not have kept together after their conjunction unless the same hand had preserved them. Natural contrarieties cannot be reconciled. It is as great power to keep discords knit, as at first to link them. Who would doubt, but that an army made up of several nations and humours, would fall into a civil war, and sheathe their swords in one another's bowels, if they were not under the management of some wise general, or a ship dash against the rocks without the skill of a pilot ?* As the body hath neither life nor motion, without the active presence of the soul, which distributes to every part the virtue of acting, sets every one in the exercise of its proper function, and resides in every part, so there is some powerful cause which doth the like in the world, that rules and tempers it. There is need of the same power and action to preserve a thing, as there was at first to make it. When we consider that we are preserved, and know that we could not preserve ourselves, we must necessarily run to some first cause which doth preserve us. All works of art depend upon nature, and are preserved while they are kept by the force of nature. As a statue depends upon the matter whereof it is made, whether stone or brass, this nature therefore must have some superior by whose influx it is preserved. Since therefore we see a stable order in the things of the world, that they conspire together for the good and beauty of the universe, that they depend upon one another, there must be some principle upon which they depend, something to which the first link of the chain is fastened, which himself depends upon no superior, but wholly rests in his own essence and being. It is the title of God to be the ' preserver of man and beast,' Ps. xxxvi. 6. The psalmist elegantly describeth it: Ps. civ. 24, &c., ' The earth is full of his riches ; all wait upon him, that he may give them their meat in due season; when he opens his hand, he fills them with good; when he hides his face, they are troubled: if he take away their breath, they die and return to dust ; he sends forth his Spirit, and they are created, and renews the face of the earth. The glory of the Lord shall endure for ever, and the Lord shall rejoice in his works.' Upon the consideration of all which the psalmist, ver. 34, takes a pleasure in the meditation of God, as the cause and manager of all those things, which issues into a joy in God and a praising of him. And why should not the consideration of the power and wisdom of God in the creatures produce the same effect in the hearts of us, if he be our God ? Or as some render it, ' my meditation shall be sweet,' or acceptable ' to him,' whereby I find matter of praise in the things of the world, and offer it to the Creator of it.

Reason 3. It is a folly to deny that which a man's own nature witnesseth to him. The whole frame of bodies and souls bears the impress of the infinite power and wisdom of the Creator. A body framed with an admirable architecture, a soul endowed with understanding, will, judgment, memory, imagination. Man is the epitome of the world, contains in himself the substance of all natures, and the fulness of the whole universe, not only

* Gassend. Phys., sect. 6, lib. 4, cap. 2, p. 101.

in regard of the universalness of his knowledge, whereby he comprehends the reasons of many things, but as all the perfections of the several natures of the world are gathered and united in man for the perfection of his own, in a smaller volume. In his soul he partakes of heaven, in his body of the earth. There is the life of plants, the sense of beasts, and the intellectual nature of angels. Gen. ii. 7, 'The Lord breathed into his nostril the breath of life, and man,' &c., חיים, *of lives.* Not one sort of life, but several, not only an animal, but a rational life, a soul of a nobler extract and nature than what was given to other creatures.

So that we need not step out of doors, or cast our eyes any further than ourselves to behold a God. He shines in the capacity of our souls and the vigour of our members. We must flee from ourselves and be stripped of our own humanity before we can put off the notion of a deity. He that is ignorant of the existence of God must be possessed with so much folly as to be ignorant of his own make and frame.

1. In the parts whereof he doth consist, body and soul.

First, Take a prospect of the body. The psalmist counts it a matter of praise and admiration : Ps. cxxxix. 14, 15, 'I will praise thee ; for I am fearfully and wonderfully made. When I was made in secret, and curiously wrought in the lowest parts of the earth, in thy book all my members were written.' The scheme of man and every member was drawn in his book ; all the sinews, veins, arteries, bones, like a piece of embroidery or tapestry, were wrought by God, as it were, with deliberation, like an artificer that draws out the model of what he is to do in writing, and sets it before him when he begins his work.

And indeed the fabric of man's body, as well as his soul, is an argument for a divinity. The artificial structure of it, the elegancy of every part, the proper situation of them, their proportion one to another, the fitness for their several functions, drew from Galen* (a heathen, and one that had no raised sentiments of a deity) a confession of the admirable wisdom and power of the Creator, and that none but God could frame it.

(1.) In the order, fitness, and usefulness of every part. The whole model of the body is grounded upon reason. Every member hath its exact proportion, distinct office, regular motion. Every part hath a particular comeliness and convenient temperament bestowed upon it according to its place in the body. The heart is hot to enliven the whole ; the eye clear to take in objects to present them to the soul. Every member is fitted for its peculiar service and action. Some are for sense, some for motion, some for preparing, and others for dispensing nourishment to the several parts ; they mutually depend upon and serve one another. What small strings fasten the particular members together, as 'the earth that hangs upon nothing,' Job xxvi. 7. Take but one part away, and you either destroy the whole, or stamp upon it some mark of deformity. All are knit together by an admirable symmetry ; all orderly perform their functions, as acting by a settled law, none swerving from their rule but in case of some predominant humour ; and none of those in so great a multitude of parts stifled in so little a room, or jostling against one another to hinder their mutual actions, none can be better disposed. And the greatest wisdom of a man could not imagine it, till his eyes present them with the sight and connection of one part and member with another.

[1.] The heart.† How strongly it is guarded with ribs like a wall, that it might not be easily hurt ! It draws blood from the liver through a

---

* Lib. 3, de usu partium. Petav. Theol. Dog., tom. 1, lib. 1, cap. 1, p. 6.
† Theod. de providentiâ, Orat. 3.

channel made for that purpose, rarefies it, and makes it fit to pass through the arteries and veins, and to carry heat and life to every part of the body, and by a perpetual motion, it sucks in the blood and spouts it out again, which motion depends not upon the command of the soul, but is pure natural.

[2.] The mouth takes in the meat, the teeth grind it for the stomach, the stomach prepares it, nature strains it through the milky veins, the liver refines it and mints it into blood, separates the purer from the drossy parts, which go to the heart, circuits through the whole body, running through the veins like rivers through so many channels of the world, for the watering of the several parts, which are framed of a thin skin for the straining the blood through for the supplying of the members of the body, and framed with several valves or doors for the thrusting the blood forwards to perform its circular motion.

[3.] The brain, fortified by a strong skull to hinder outward accidents, a tough membrane or skin to hinder any oppression by the skull, the seat of sense, that which coins the animal spirits, by purifying and refining those which are sent to it, and seems like a curious piece of needlework.

[4.] The ear, framed with windings and turnings, to keep anything from entering to offend the brain; so disposed as to admit sounds with the greatest safety and delight, Eccles. xii. 4; filled with an air within, by the motion whereof the sound is transmitted to the brain, as sounds are made in the air by diffusing themselves, as you see circles made in the water by the flinging in a stone. This is the gate of knowledge, whereby we hear the oracles of God, and the instruction of men for arts. It is by this they are exposed to the mind, and the mind of another man framed in our understandings.

[5.] What a curious workmanship is that of the eye, which is in the body as the sun in the world; set in the head as in a watch-tower, having the softest nerves for the receiving the greater multitude of spirits necessary for the act of vision! How is it provided with defence, by the variety of coats, to secure and accommodate the little humour and part whereby the vision is made! Made of a round figure, and convex, as most commodious to receive the species of objects; shaded by the eyebrows and eyelids, secured by the eyelids, which are its ornament and safety, which refresh it when it is too much dried by heat, hinder too much light from insinuating itself into it to offend it, cleanse it from impurities, by their quick motion preserve it from invasion, and by contraction confer to the more evident discerning of things; both the eyes seated in the hollow of the bone for security, yet standing out that things may be perceived more easily on both sides. And this little member can behold the earth, and in a moment view things as high as heaven.

[6.] The tongue* for speech framed like a musical instrument; the teeth serving for variety of sounds; the lungs serving for bellows to blow the organs, as it were, to cool the heart: by a continual motion transmitting a pure air to the heart, expelling that which was smoky and superfluous. It is by the tongue that communication of truth hath a passage among men; it opens the sense of the mind; there would be no converse and commerce without it. Speech among all nations hath an elegancy and attractive force, mastering the affections of men.

Not to speak of other parts, or of the multitude of spirits that act every part, the quick flight of them where there is a necessity of their presence. Solomon, Eccles. xii., makes an elegant description of them in his speech of

* Coccei. Sum. Theolog., cap. 8, sec. 49.

old age ; and Job speaks of this formation of the body, Job x. 9–11, &c. Not the least part of the body is made in vain. The hairs of the head have their use, as well as are an ornament. The whole symmetry of the body is a ravishing object. Every member hath a signature and mark of God and his wisdom ; he is visible in the formation of the members, the beauty of the parts, and the vigour of the body. This structure could not be from the body : that only hath a passive power, and cannot act in the absence of the soul ; nor can it be from the soul. How comes it then to be so ignorant of the manner of its formation ? The soul knows not the internal parts of its own body, but by information from others, or inspection into other bodies. It knows less of the inward frame of the body than it doth of itself. But he that makes the clock can tell the number and motions of the wheels within, as well as what figures are without.

This short discourse is useful to raise our admirations of the wisdom of God, as well as to demonstrate that there is an infinite, wise Creator. And the consideration of ourselves every day, and the wisdom of God in our frame, would maintain religion much in the world, since all are so framed that no man can tell any error in the constitution of him. If thus the body of man is fitted for the service of his soul by an infinite God, the body ought to be ordered for the service of this God, and in obedience to him.

(2.) In the admirable difference of the features of men, which is a great argument that the world was made by a wise Being. This could not be wrought by chance, or be the work of mere nature, since we find never, or very rarely, two persons exactly alike. This distinction is a part of infinite wisdom ; otherwise, what confusion would be introduced into the world ! Without this, parents could not know their children, nor children their parents, nor a brother his sister, nor a subject his magistrate. Without it there had been no comfort of relations, no government, no commerce. Debtors would not have been known from strangers, nor good men from bad ; propriety could not have been preserved, nor justice executed ; the innocent might have been apprehended for the nocent ; wickedness could not have been stopped by any law.

The faces of men are the same for parts, not for features. A dissimiltude in a likeness ; man, like to all the rest in the world, yet unlike to any, and differenced by some mark from all, which is not to be observed in any other species of creatures. This speaks some wise agent which framed man ; since for the preservation of human society and order in the world, this distinction was necessary.

Secondly, As man's own nature witnesseth a God to him in the structure of his body, so also in the nature of his soul.* We know that we have an understanding in us : a substance we cannot see, but we know it by its operations, as thinking, reasoning, willing, remembering, and as operating about things that are invisible and remote from sense. This must needs be distinct from the body, for that, being but dust and earth in its original, hath not the power of reasoning and thinking, for then it would have that power when the soul were absent, as well as when it is present. Besides, if it had that power of thinking, it could think only of those things which are sensible and made up of matter, as itself is. This soul hath a greater excellency. It can know itself, rejoice in itself, which other creatures in this world are not capable of. The soul is the greatest glory of this lower world ; and as one saith,† there seems to be no more difference between the soul and an angel, than between a sword in the scabbard and when it is out of the scabbard.

* Coccei. Sum. Theolog., cap. 8, sec. 50, 51.   † More.

1. Consider the vastness of its capacity. The understanding can conceive the whole world, and paint in itself the invisible pictures of all things. It is capable of apprehending and discoursing of things superior to its own nature. 'It is suited to all objects, as the eye to all colours, or the ear to all sounds.'* How great is the memory to retain such varieties, such diversities! The will also can accommodate other things to itself. It invents arts for the use of man, prescribes rules for the government of states, ransacks the bowels of nature, makes endless conclusions, and steps in reasoning from one thing to another, for the knowledge of truth; it can contemplate and form notions of things higher than the world.

2. The quickness of its motions. 'Nothing is more quick in the whole course of nature. The sun runs through the world in a day: this can do it in a moment. It can, with one flight of fancy, ascend to the battlements of heaven.'† The mists of the air, that hinder the sight of the eye, cannot hinder the flights of the soul; it can pass in a moment from one end of the world to the other, and think of things a thousand miles distant. It can think of some mean thing in the world, and presently, by one cast, in the twinkling of an eye, mount up as high as heaven. As its desires are not bounded by sensual objects, so neither are the motions of it restrained by them. It will break forth with the greatest vigour, and conceive things infinitely above it; though it be in the body, it acts as if it were ashamed to be cloistered in it. This could not be the result of any material cause. Who ever knew mere matter understand, think, will? And what it hath not, it cannot give. That which is destitute of reason and will, could never confer reason and will. It is not the effect of the body, for the body is fitted with members to be subject to it.‡ It is in part ruled by the activity of the soul, and in part by the counsel of the soul. It is used by the soul, and knows not how it is used. Nor could it be from the parents, since the souls of the children often transcend those of the parents in vivacity, acuteness, and comprehensiveness. One man is stupid, and begets a son with a capacious understanding; one is debauched and beastly in morals, and begets a son who from his infancy testifies some virtuous inclinations, which sprout forth in delightful fruit with the ripeness of his age.§ Whence should this difference arise, a fool begat the wise man, and a debauched the virtuous man? The wisdom of the one could not descend from the foolish soul of the other, nor the virtues of the son from the deformed and polluted soul of the parent. It lies not in the organs of the body; for if the folly of the parent proceeded not from their souls, but the ill disposition of the organs of their bodies, how comes it to pass that the bodies of the children are better organised beyond the goodness of their immediate cause? We must recur to some invisible hand, that makes the difference, who bestows upon one at his pleasure richer qualities than upon another. You can see nothing in the world endowed with some excellent quality, but you must imagine some bountiful hand did enrich it with that dowry. None can be so foolish as to think that a vessel ever enriched itself with that sprightly liquor wherewith it is filled; or that anything worse than the soul should endow it with that knowledge and activity which sparkles in it. Nature could not produce it. That nature is intelligent, or not; if it be not, then it produceth an effect more excellent than itself, inasmuch as an understanding being surmounts a being that hath no understanding. If the supreme cause of the soul be intelligent, why do we

---

* Culverwell.   † Theodoret.   ‡ Coccei. Sum. Theolog., cap. 8, sec. 51, 52.
§ I do not dispute whether the soul were generated or no. Suppose the substance of it was generated by the parents, yet those more excellent qualities were not the result of them.

not call it God as well as nature ? We must arise from hence to the notion of a God. A spiritual nature cannot proceed but from a spirit higher than itself, and of a transcendent perfection above itself. If we believe we have souls, and understand the state of our own faculties, we must be assured that there was some invisible hand which bestowed those faculties and the riches of them upon us. A man must be ignorant of himself before he can be ignorant of the existence of God. By considering the nature of our souls, we may as well be assured that there is a God, as that there is a sun by the shining of the beams in at our windows. And indeed the soul is a statue and representation of God, as the landscape of a country or map represents all the parts of it, but in a far less proportion than the country itself is. The soul fills the body, and God the world ; the soul sustains the body, and God the world ; the soul sees, but is not seen ; God sees all things, but is himself invisible. How base are they then that prostitute their souls, an image of God, to base things unexpressibly below their own nature !

β. I might add the union of soul and body. Man is a kind of compound of angel and beast, of soul and body ; if he were only a soul, he were a kind of angel ; if only a body, he were another kind of brute. Now, that a body as vile and dull as earth, and a soul that can mount up to heaven and rove about the world with so quick a motion, should be linked in so strait an acquaintance ; that so noble a being as the soul should be an inhabitant in such a tabernacle of clay, must be owned to some infinite power that hath so chained it.

4. Man witnesseth to a God in the operations and reflections of conscience : Rom. ii. 15, ' Their thoughts are accusing or excusing.' An inward comfort attends good actions, and an inward torment follows bad ones ; for there is in every man's conscience fear of punishment and hope of reward. There is therefore a sense of some superior judge, which hath the power both of rewarding and punishing. If man were his supreme rule, what need he fear punishment, since no man would inflict any evil or torment on himself; nor can any man be said to reward himself, for all rewards refer to another, to whom the action is pleasing, and is a conferring some good a man had not before. If an action be done by a subject or servant, with hopes of reward, it cannot be imagined that he expects a reward from himself, but from the prince or person whom he eyes in that action, and for whose sake he doth it.

1. There is a law in the minds of men which is a rule of good and evil. There is a notion of good and evil in the consciences of men, which is evident by those laws which are common in all countries, for the preserving human societies, the encouragement of virtue and discouragement of vice ; what standard should they have for those laws but a common reason ? The design of those laws was to keep men within the bounds of goodness, for mutual commerce ; whence the apostle calls the heathen magistrate ' a minister of God for good,' Rom. xiii. 4 ; and the Gentiles ' do by nature the things contained in the law,' Rom. ii. 14.

Man in the first instant of the use of reason finds natural principles within himself, directing and choosing them ; he finds a distinction between good and evil ; how could this be if there were not some rule in him to try and distinguish good and evil ? If there were not such a law and rule in man, he could not sin ; for where there is no law, there is no transgression. If man were a law to himself, and his own will his law, there could be no such thing as evil ; whatsoever he willed would be good and agreeable to the law, and no action could be accounted sinful ; the worst act would be as commendable as the best. Every thing at man's appointment would be good or evil. If there were no such law, how should men that are naturally inclined to evil disapprove of that which is unlovely, and approve of that good which they practise not? No man but inwardly thinks well of that which is good while he neglects it, and thinks ill of that which is evil while he commits it. Those that are vicious do praise those that practise the contrary virtues. Those that are evil would seem to be good, and those that are blameworthy, yet will rebuke evil in others. This is really to distinguish between good and evil; whence doth this arise, by what rule do we measure this, but by some innate principle?

And this is universal, the same in one man as in another, the same in one nation as in another; they are born with every man, and inseparable from his nature: Prov. xxvii. 19, 'As in water face answers to face, so the heart of man to man.' Common reason supposeth that there is some hand which hath fixed this distinction in man. How could it else be universally impressed? No law can be without a law-giver; no sparks but must be kindled by some other. Whence should this law then derive its original? Not from man; he would fain blot it out, and cannot alter it when he pleases. Natural generation never intended it; it is settled therefore by some higher hand, which, as it imprinted it, so it maintains it against the violences of men, who, were it not for·this law, would make the world, more than it is, an Aceldama and field of blood; for, had there not been some supreme good, the measure of all other goodness in the world, we could not have had such a thing as good. The Scripture gives us an account that this good was distinguished from evil before man fell, they were *objecta scibilia;* good was commanded and evil prohibited, and did not depend upon man. From this a man may rationally be instructed that there is a God; for he may thus argue: I find myself naturally obliged to do this thing and avoid that, I have therefore a superior that doth oblige me; I find something within me that directs me to such actions, contrary to my sensitive appetite, there must be something above me therefore that put this principle into man's nature. If there were no superior, I should be the supreme judge of good and evil. Were I the lord of that law which doth oblige me, I should find no contradiction within myself between reason and appetite.

2. From the transgression of this law of nature fears do arise in the consciences of men. Have we not known or heard of men struck by so deep a dart that could not be drawn out by the strength of men, or appeased by the pleasure of the world, and men crying out with horror upon a death-bed of their past life, when 'their fear hath come as a desolation, and destruction as a whirlwind'? Prov. i. 27. And often in some sharp affliction the dust hath been blown off from men's consciences, which for a while hath obscured the writing of the law. If men stand in awe of punishment, there is then some superior to whom they are accountable. If there were no God, there were no punishment to fear. What reason of any fear, upon the dissolution of the knot between the soul and body, if there were not a God to punish, and the soul remained not in being to be punished?

How suddenly will conscience work upon the appearance of an affliction, rouse itself from sleep like an armed man, and fly in a man's face before he is aware of it? It will 'surprise the hypocrites,' Isa. xxxiii. 14. It will bring to mind actions committed long ago, and set them in order before the face, as God's deputy acting by his authority and omniscience. As God hath not left himself without a witness among the creatures, Acts xiv. 17, so he hath not left himself without a witness in a man's own breast.

1. This operation of conscience hath been universal. No nation hath been any more exempt from it than from reason; not a man but hath one

time or other more or less smarted under the sting of it. All over the world conscience hath shot its darts. It hath torn the hearts of princes in the midst of their pleasures; it hath not flattered them whom most men flatter, nor feared to disturb their rest whom no man dares to provoke. Judges have trembled on a tribunal, when innocents have rejoiced in their condemnation; the iron bars upon Pharaoh's conscience were at last broke up, and he acknowledged the justice of God in all that he did: Exod. ix. 27, 'I have sinned, the Lord is righteous, and I and my people are wicked.' Had they been like childish frights at the apprehension of bug-bears, why hath not reason shaken them off? But, on the contrary, the stronger reason grows, the smarter those lashes are; groundless fears had been short-lived, age and judgment would have worn them off, but they grow sharper with the growth of persons. The Scripture informs us they have been of as ancient a date as the revolt of the first man: Gen. iii. 10, 'I was afraid,' saith Adam, 'because I was naked,' which was an expectation of the judgment of God. All his posterity inherit his fears, when God expresseth himself in any tokens of his majesty and providence in the world. Every man's conscience testifies that he is unlike what he ought to be according to that law engraven upon his heart. In some, indeed, conscience may be seared or dimmer; or, suppose some men may be devoid of conscience, shall it be denied to be a thing belonging to the nature of man? Some men have not their eyes, yet the power of seeing the light is natural to man, and belongs to the integrity of the body; who would argue, that because some men are mad, and have lost their reason by a distemper of the brain, that therefore reason hath no reality, but is an imaginary thing? But I think it is a standing truth, that every man hath been under the scourge of it, one time or other, in a less or greater degree; for, since every man is an offender, it cannot be imagined conscience, which is natural to man and an active faculty, should always lie idle, without doing this part of its office? The apostle tells us of the thoughts, accusing or excusing one another, or by turns, according as the actions were. Nor is this truth weakened by the corruptions in the world, whereby many have thought themselves bound in conscience to adhere to a false and superstitious worship and idolatry, as much as any have thought themselves bound to adhere to a worship commanded by God. This very thing infers that all men have a reflecting principle in them; it is no argument against the being of conscience, but only infers that it may err in the application of what it naturally owns. We can no more say, that because some men walk by a false rule, there is no such thing as conscience, than we can say that because men have errors in their minds, therefore they have no such faculty as an understanding; or, because men will that which is evil, they have no such faculty as a will in them.

2. These operations of conscience are when the wickedness is most secret. These tormenting fears of vengeance have been frequent in men who have had no reason to fear man, since, their wickedness being unknown to any but themselves, they could have no accuser but themselves. They have been in many acts which their companions have justified them in; persons above the stroke of human laws, yea, such as the people have honoured as gods, have been haunted by them. Conscience hath not been frighted by the power of princes, or bribed by the pleasures of courts. David was pursued by his horrors, when he was by reason of his dignity above the punishment of the law, or at least was not reached by the law; since, though the murder of Uriah was intended by him, it was not acted by him. Such examples are frequent in human records. When the crime hath been above any punishment by man, they have had an accuser, judge, and executioner in

their own breasts.   Can this be originally from a man's self ?   He who loves
and cherishes himself would fly from anything that disturbs him.   It is a
greater power and majesty from whom man cannot hide himself, that holds
him in those fetters.   What should affect their minds for that which can
never bring them shame or punishment in this world, if there were not some
supreme judge to whom they were to give an account, whose instrument
conscience is ?   Doth it do this of itself ; hath it received an authority from
the man himself to sting him ?   It is some supreme power that doth direct
and commission it against our wills.

3. These operations of conscience cannot be totally shaken off by man.
If there be no God, why do not men silence the clamours of their consciences, and scatter those fears that disturb their rest and pleasures ?   How
inquisitive are men after some remedy against those convulsions ?   Sometimes they would render the charge insignificant, and sing a rest to themselves, though they ' walk in the wickedness of their own hearts,' Deut.
xxix. 19.   How often do men attempt to drown it by sensual pleasures, and
perhaps overpower it for a time ; but it revives, reinforceth itself, and acts
a revenge for its former stop.   It holds sin to a man's view, and fixes his
eyes upon it, whether he will or no: ' The wicked are like a troubled sea,
and cannot rest,' Isa. lvii. 20.   They would wallow in sin without control,
but this inward principle will not suffer it ; nothing can shelter men from
those blows.   What is the reason it could never be cried down ?   Man is
an enemy to his own disquiet ; what man would continue upon the rack, if
it were in his power to deliver himself ?   Why have all human remedies been
without success, and not able to extinguish all those operations, though all
the wickedness of the heart hath been ready to assist and second the attempt ?
It hath pursued men notwithstanding all the violence used against it, and
renewed its scourges with more severity, as men deal with their resisting
slaves.   Man can as little silence those thunders in his soul, as he can the
thunders in the heavens.   He must strip himself of his humanity before he
can be stripped of an accusing and affrighting conscience : it sticks as close
to him as his nature.   Since man cannot throw out the process it makes
against him, it is an evidence that some higher power secures its throne and
standing.   Who should put this scourge into the hand of conscience, which
no man in the world is able to wrest out ?

4. We may add, the comfortable reflections of conscience.   There are
excusing as well as accusing reflections of conscience, when things are done
as works of the law of nature, Rom. ii. 15.   As it doth not forbear to accuse
and torture, when a wickedness, though unknown to others, is committed,
so when a man hath done well, though he be attacked with all the calumnies
the wit of man can forge, yet his conscience justifies the action, and fills
him with a singular contentment.   As there is torture in sinning, so there
is peace and joy in well-doing.   Neither of those it could do, if it did not
understand a sovereign judge, who punishes the rebels and rewards the well-
doer.   Conscience is the foundation of all religion ; and the two pillars upon
which it is built, are the being of God, and the bounty of God to those that
diligently seek him, Heb. xi. 6.

This proves the existence of God.   If there were no God, conscience were
useless ; the operations of it would have no foundation, if there were not an
eye to take notice, and a hand to punish or reward the action.   The accusations of conscience evidence the omniscience and the holiness of God ;
the terrors of conscience, the justice of God ; the approbations of conscience, the goodness of God.   All the order in the world owes itself, next
to the providence of God, to conscience : without it the world would be a

Golgotha. As the creatures witness there was a first cause that produced them, so this principle in man evidenceth itself to be set by the same hand for the good of that which it had so framed. There could be no conscience if there were no God, and man could not be a rational creature if there were no conscience. As there is a *rule* in us, there must be a *judge*, whether our actions be according to the rule; and since conscience in our corrupted state is in some particular misled, there must be a power superior to conscience to judge how it hath behaved itself in its deputed office: we must come to some supreme judge, who can judge conscience itself. As a man can have no surer evidence that he is a being, than because he thinks, he is a thinking being, so there is no surer evidence in nature that there is a God, than that every man hath a natural principle in him, which continually cites him before God, and puts him in mind of him, and makes him one way or other fear him, and reflects upon him whether he will or no. A man hath less power over his conscience than over any other faculty. He may choose whether he will exercise his understanding about, or move his will to, such an object, but he hath no such authority over his conscience; he cannot limit it, or cause it to cease from acting and reflecting; and therefore both that, and the law about which it acts, are settled by some supreme authority in the mind of man, and this is God.

Prop. 4. The evidence of a God results from the vastness of the desires in man, and the real dissatisfaction he hath in every thing below himself. Man hath a boundless appetite after some sovereign good. As his understanding is more capacious than any thing below, so is his appetite larger. This affection of desire exceeds all other affections. Love is determined to something known: fear to something apprehended; but desires approach nearer to infiniteness, and pursue, not only what we know, or what we have a glimpse of, but what we find wanting in what we already enjoy. That which the desire of man is most naturally carried after, is *bonum;* some fully satisfying good. We desire knowledge by the sole impulse of reason; but we desire good before the excitement of reason, and the desire is always after good, but not always after knowledge.

Now the soul of man finds an imperfection in every thing here, and cannot scrape up a perfect satisfaction and felicity. In the highest fruitions of worldly things, it is still pursuing something else, which speaks a defect in what it already hath. The world may afford a felicity for our dust, the body, but not for the inhabitant in it; it is too mean for that. Is there any one soul among the sons of men, that can upon due inquiry say, it was at rest and wanted no more, that hath not sometimes had desires after an immaterial good? The soul 'follows hard' after such a thing, and hath frequent looks after it, Ps. lxiii. 8. Man desires a stable good, but no sublunary thing is so; and he that doth not desire such a good, wants the rational nature of a man. This is as natural as understanding, will, and conscience. Whence should the soul of man have those desires? How came it to understand that something is still wanting to make its nature more perfect, if there were not in it some notion of a more perfect being, which can give it rest?

Can such a capacity be supposed to be in it without something in being able to satisfy it? If so, the noblest creature in the world is miserablest, and in a worse condition than any other: other creatures obtain their ultimate desires, 'they are filled with good,' Ps. civ. 28; and shall man only have a vast desire without any possibility of enjoyment? Nothing in man is in vain: he hath objects for his affections, as well as affections for objects. Every member of his body hath its end, and doth attain it. Every affection of his soul hath an object, and that in this world; and shall there be none for his desire, which comes nearest to infinite of any affection planted in him? This boundless desire had not its original from man himself. Nothing would render itself restless; something above the bounds of this world implanted those desires after a higher good, and made him restless in everything else. And since the soul can only rest in that which is infinite, there is something infinite for it to rest in. Since nothing in the world, though a man had the whole, can give it a satisfaction, there is something above the world only capable to do it, otherwise the soul would be always without it, · and be more in vain than any other creature.

There is therefore some infinite being that can only give a contentment to the soul, and this is God. And that goodness which implanted such desires in the soul would not do it to no purpose, and mock it in giving it an infinite desire of satisfaction, without intending it the pleasure of enjoyment, if it doth not by its own folly deprive itself of it. The felicity of human nature must needs exceed that which is allotted to other creatures.

Reason 4, and last. As it is a folly to deny that which all nations in the world have consented to, which the frame of the world evidenceth, which man in his body, soul, operations of conscience, witnesseth to, so it is a folly to deny the being of God, which is witnessed unto by extraordinary occurrences in the world.

1. In extraordinary judgments. When a just revenge follows abominable crimes, especially when the judgment is suited to the sin, by a strange concatenation and succession of providences, methodised to bring such a particular punishment; when the sin of a nation or person is made legible in the inflicted judgment, which testifies that it cannot be a casual thing. The Scripture gives us an account of the necessity of such judgments, to keep up the reverential thoughts of God in the world: Ps. ix. 16, ' The Lord is known by the judgment which he executes, the wicked is snared in the work of his own hand.' And jealousy is the name of God: Exod. xxxiv. 14, ' Whose name is Jealous.' He is distinguished from false gods by the judgments which he sends, as men are by their names.

Extraordinary prodigies in many nations have been the heralds of extraordinary judgments, and presages of the particular judgments which afterwards they have felt, of which the Roman histories and others are full. That there are such things is undeniable, and that the events have been answerable to the threatening, unless we will throw away all human testimonies, and count all the histories of the world forgeries. Such things are evidences of some invisible power which orders those affairs. And if there be invisible powers, there is also an efficacious cause which moves them; a government certainly there is among them as well as in the world, and then we must come to some supreme governor which presides over them.

Judgments upon notorious offenders have been evident in all ages, the Scripture gives many instances. I shall only mention that of Herod Agrippa, which Josephus * mentions. He receives the flattering applause of the people, and thought himself a god; but by the sudden stroke upon him was forced by his torture to confess another, Acts xii. 21–23. I am God, saith he, in your account, but a higher calls me away; the will of the heavenly Deity is to be endured. The angel of the Lord smote him. The judgment here was suited to the sin; he that would be a god is eaten up of worms, the vilest creatures. Tully Hostilius, a Roman king, who counted it the most unroyal thing to be religious, or own any other God but his sword, was consumed himself and his whole house by lightning from heaven.

Many things are unaccountable unless we have recourse to God. The

* Lib. 19, Antiq.

strange revelations of murderers, that have most secretly committed their crimes ; the making good some dreadful imprecations, which some wretches have used to confirm a lie, and immediately have been struck with that judgment they wished ; the raising often unexpected persons to be instruments of vengeance on a sinful and perfidious nation ; the overturning the deepest and surest counsels of men, when they have had a successful progress, and came to the very point of execution ; the whole design of men's preservation hath been beaten in pieces by some unforeseen circumstances, so that judgments have broken in upon them without control, and all their subtilties been outwitted ; the strange crossing of some in their estates, though the most wise, industrious, and frugal persons, and that by strange and unexpected ways ; and it is observable how often everything contributes to carry on a judgment intended, as if they rationally designed it. All those loudly proclaim a God in the world ; if there were no God, there would be no sin ; if no sin, there would be no punishment.

2. In miracles. The course of nature is uniform, and when it is put out of its course it must be by some superior power invisible to the world, and by whatsoever invisible instruments they are wrought, the efficacy of them must depend upon some first cause above nature. Ps. lxxii. 18, ' Blessed be the Lord God of Israel, who only doth wondrous things,' by himself and his sole power.

That which cannot be the result of a natural cause, must be the result of something supernatural ; what is beyond the reach of nature is the effect of a power superior to nature. For it is quite against the order of nature, and is the elevation of something to such a pitch, which all nature could not advance it to. Nature cannot go beyond its own limits ; if it be determined by another, as hath been formerly proved, it cannot lift itself above itself without that power that so determined it. Natural agents act necessarily. The sun doth necessarily shine, fire doth necessarily burn. That cannot be the result of nature which is above the ability of nature. That cannot be the work of nature which is against the order of nature. Nature cannot do anything against itself, or invert its own course.

We must own that such things have been, or we must accuse all the records of former ages to be a pack of lies, which whosoever doth destroys the greatest and best part of human knowledge. The miracles mentioned in the Scripture, wrought by our Saviour, are acknowledged by the heathen, by the Jews at this day, though his greatest enemies. There is no dispute whether such things were wrought, the dead raised, the blind restored to sight. The heathens have acknowledged the miraculous eclipse of the sun at the passion of Christ, quite against the rule of nature, the moon being then in opposition to the sun ; the propagation of Christianity contrary to the methods whereby other religions have been propagated, that in a few years the nations of the world should be sprinkled with this doctrine, and give in a greater catalogue of martyrs courting the devouring flames than all the religions of the world.

To this might be added the strange hand that was over the Jews, the only people in the world professing the true God, that should so often be befriended by their conquerors, so as to rebuild their temple, though they were looked upon as a people apt to rebel. Dion and Seneca observe, that wherever they were transplanted they prospered and gave laws to the victors ; so that this proves also the authority of the Scripture, the truth of Christian religion, as well as the being of a God, and a superior power over the world.

To this might be added the bridling the tumultuous passions of men for the preservation of human societies, which else would run the world into unconceivable confusions : Ps. lxv. 7, ' Which stilleth the noise of the sea, and the tumults of the people ; ' as also the miraculous deliverance of a person or nation, when upon the very brink of ruin ; the sudden answer of prayer when God hath been sought to, and the turning away a judgment, which in reason could not be expected to be averted, and the raising a sunk people from a ruin which seemed inevitable, by unexpected ways.

3. Accomplishments of prophecies. Those things which are purely contingent, and cannot be known by natural signs and in their causes, as eclipses and changes in nations, which may be discerned by an observation of the signs of the times, such things that fall not within this compass, if they be foretold and come to pass, are solely from some higher hand, and above the cause of nature. This in Scripture is asserted to be a notice of the true God : Isa. xli. 23, ' Shew the things that are to come hereafter, that we may know that you are God ; ' and Isa. xlvi. 10, ' I am God, declaring the end from the beginning, and from ancient times, the things that are not yet done, saying, My counsel shall stand, and I will do all my pleasure.' And prophecy was consented to by all the philosophers to be from divine illumination. That power which discovers things future, which all the foresight of men cannot ken and conjecture, is above nature. And to foretell them so certainly as if they did already exist, or had existed long ago, must be the result of a mind infinitely intelligent ; because it is the highest way of knowing, and a higher cannot be imagined; and he that knows things future in such a manner must needs know things present and past. Cyrus was prophesied of by Isaiah, chap. xliv. 28 and xlv., long before he was born ; his victories, spoils, all that should happen in Babylon, his bounty to the Jews, came to pass, according to that prophecy; and the sight of that prophecy which the Jews shewed him, as other historians report, was that which moved him to be favourable to the Jews.

Alexander's sight of Daniel's prophecy concerning his victories moved him to spare Jerusalem. And are not the four monarchies plainly deciphered in that book, before the fourth rose up in the world ? That power which foretells things beyond the reach of the wit of man, and orders all causes to bring about those predictions, must be an infinite power, the same that made the world, sustains it and governs all things in it according to his pleasure, and to bring about his own ends ; and this being is God.

Use 1. If atheism be a folly, it is then pernicious to the world, and to the atheist himself. Wisdom is the band of human societies, the glory of man. Folly is the disturber of families, cities, nations, the disgrace of human nature.

1. It is pernicious to the world.

(1.) It would root out the foundations of government. It demolisheth all order in nations. The being of a God is the guard of the world. The sense of a God is the foundation of civil order ; without this there is no tie upon the consciences of men. What force would there be in oaths for the decisions of controversies, what right could there be in appeals made to one that had no being ? A city of atheists would be a heap of confusion; there could be no ground of any commerce when all the sacred bands of it in the consciences of men were snapped asunder, which are torn to pieces and utterly destroyed by denying the existence of God. What magistrate could be secure in his standing, what private person could be secure in his right ?* Can that then be a truth that is destructive of all public good ? If the atheist's sentiment, that there were no God, were a truth, and the contrary, that there were a God, were a falsity, it would then follow that falsity made men

* Lessius de Provid., p. 665.

good and serviceable to one another; that error were the foundation of all
the beauty, and order, and outward felicity of the world, the fountain of all
good to man. If there were no God, to believe there is one would be an error,
and to believe there is none would be the greatest wisdom, because it would be
the greatest truth. And then as it is the greatest wisdom to fear God upon
the apprehension of his existence, Ps. cxi. 10, so it would be the greatest
error to fear him, if there were none. It would unquestionably follow, that
error is the support of the world, the spring of all human advantages, and
that every part of the world were obliged to a falsity for being a quiet
habitation, which is the most absurd thing to imagine. It is a thing impossible to be tolerated by any prince, without laying an axe to the root of the
government.

(2.) It would introduce all evil into the world. If you take away God,
you take away conscience, and thereby all measures and rules of good and
evil. And how could any laws be made when the measure and standard of
them were removed? All good laws are founded upon the dictates of conscience and reason, upon common sentiments in human nature, which
spring from a sense of God; so that if the foundation be demolished, the
whole superstructure must tumble down. A man might be a thief, a murderer, an adulterer, and could not in a strict sense be an offender. The
worst of actions could not be evil if a man were a god to himself, a law to
himself. Nothing but evil deserves a censure, and nothing would be evil if
there were no God, the rector of the world, against whom evil is properly
committed. No man can make that morally evil that is not so in itself.
As where there is a faint sense of God, the heart is more strongly inclined
to wickedness, so where there is no sense of God, the bars are removed,
the flood-gates set open for all wickedness to rush in upon mankind.
Religion pinions men from abominable practices, and restrains them from
being slaves to their own passions; an atheist's arms would be loose to do
anything.* Nothing so villanous and unjust but would be acted, if the
natural fear of a deity were extinguished. The first consequence issuing
from the apprehension of the existence of God, is his government of the
world. If there be no God, then the natural consequence is that there is
no supreme government of the world. Such a notion would cashier all
sentiments of good, and be like a Trojan horse, whence all impurity,
tyranny, and all sorts of mischiefs would break out upon mankind. Corruption and abominable works in the text are the fruit of the fool's persuasion that there is no God. The perverting of the ways of men, oppression,
and extortion, owe their rise to a forgetfulness of God: Jer. iii. 21, 'They
have perverted their way, and they have forgotten the Lord their God;'
Ezek. xxii. 12, 'Thou hast greedily gained by extortion, and hast forgotten
me, saith the Lord.' The whole earth would be filled with violence, all
flesh would corrupt their way as it was before the deluge, when probably
atheism did abound more than idolatry; and if not a disowning the being,
yet denying the providence of God by the posterity of Cain, those of the
family of Seth only calling upon the name of the Lord, Gen. vi. 11, 12
compared with Gen. iv. 26.

The greatest sense of a deity in any hath been attended with the greatest
innocence of life and usefulness to others, and a weaker sense hath been
attended with a baser impurity.† If there were no God, blasphemy would
be praiseworthy; as the reproach of idols is praiseworthy, because we testify that there is no divinity in them. What can be more contemptible
than that which hath no being? Sin would be only a false opinion of a

* Lessius de Provid., p. 664.   † Lessius de Provid., p. 665.

violated law and an offended deity. If such apprehensions prevail, what a wide door is opened to the worst of villanies? If there be no God, no respect is due to him; all the religion in the world is a trifle and error, and thus the pillars of all human society, and that which hath made commonwealths to flourish, are blown away.

Secondly, 2, It is pernicious to the atheist himself. If he fear no future punishment, he can never expect any future reward; all his hopes must be confined to a swinish and despicable manner of life, without any imaginations of so much as a dram of reserved happiness. He is in a worse condition than the silliest animal, which hath something to please it in its life; whereas an atheist can have nothing here to give him a full content, no more than any other man in the world, and can have less satisfaction hereafter. He deposeth the noble end of his own being, which was to serve a God and have a satisfaction in him, to seek a God and be rewarded by him; and he that departs from this end, recedes from his own nature. All the content any creature finds is in performing its end, moving according to its natural instinct; as it is a joy to the sun to run its race, Ps. xix. 5, in the same manner it is a satisfaction to every other creature, and its delight, to observe the law of its creation. What content can any man have that runs from his end, opposeth his own nature, denies a God by whom and for whom he was created, whose image he bears, which is the glory of his nature, and sinks into the very dregs of brutishness? How elegantly is it described by Bildad: Job xviii. 7, 8, &c., to the end, 'His own counsel shall cast him down, terrors shall make him afraid on every side; destruction shall be ready at his side, the first-born of death shall devour his strength. His confidence shall be rooted out, and it shall bring him to the king of terrors: brimstone shall be scattered upon his habitation. He shall be driven from light into darkness, and chased out of the world. They that come after him shall be astonished at his day, as they that went before were affrighted. And this is the place of him that knows not God.' If there be a future reckoning (as his own conscience cannot but sometimes inform him of), his condition is desperate, and his misery dreadful and unavoidable. It is not righteous a hell should entertain any else if it refuse him.

Use 2. How lamentable is it that in our times this folly of atheism should be so rife! that there should be found such monsters in human nature, in the midst of the improvements of reason and shinings of the gospel, who not only make the Scripture the matter of their jeers, but scoff at the judgments and providences of God in the world, and envy their Creator a being, without whose goodness they had had none themselves; who contradict in their carriage what they assert to be their sentiment, when they dreadfully imprecate damnation to themselves! Whence should [come] that damnation they so rashly wish be poured forth upon them, if there were not a revenging God? Formerly atheism was as rare as prodigious, scarce two or three known in an age. And those that are reported to be so in former ages, are rather thought to be counted so for mocking at the senseless deities the common people adored, and laying open their impurities. A mere natural strength would easily discover that those they adored for gods could not deserve that title, since their original was known, their uncleanness manifest and acknowledged by their worshippers. And probably it was so, since the Christians were termed ἄθεοι, as Justin informs us, because they acknowledged not their vain idols.

I question whether there ever was or can be in the world an uninterrupted and internal denial of the being of God, or that men (unless we can suppose conscience utterly dead) can arrive to such a degree of impiety. For before they can stifle such sentiments in them (whatsoever they may assert), they must be utter strangers to the common conceptions of reason, and despoil themselves of their own humanity. He that dares to deny a God with his lips, yet sets up something or other as a god in his heart. Is it not lamentable that this sacred truth, consented to by all nations, which is the band of civil societies, the source of all order in the world, should be denied with a bare face and disputed against in companies, and the glory of a wise Creator ascribed to an unintelligent nature, to blind chance? Are not such worse than heathens? They worshipped many gods, these none; they preserved a notion of God in the world under a disguise of images, these would banish him both from earth and heaven, and demolish the statues of him in their own consciences; they degraded him, these would destroy him; they coupled creatures with him—Rom. i. 25, 'Who worshipped the creature with the Creator,' as it may most properly be rendered. And these would make him worse than a creature, a mere nothing. Earth is hereby become worse than hell. Atheism is a persuasion, which finds no footing anywhere else. Hell, that receives such persons, in this point reforms them; they can never deny or doubt of his being while they feel his strokes. The devil, that rejoices at their wickedness, knows them to be in an error; for he 'believes, and trembles' at the belief, James ii. 19. This is a forerunner of judgment; boldness in sin is a presage of vengeance, especially when the honour of God is more particularly concerned therein. It tends to the overturning human society, taking off the bridle from the wicked inclinations of men. And God appears not in such visible judgments against sin immediately committed against himself, as in the case of those sins that are destructive to human society. Besides, God as governor of the world will uphold that, without which all his ordinances in the world would be useless. Atheism is point blank against all the glory of God in creation, and against all the glory of God in redemption, and pronounceth at one breath both the Creator and all acts of religion and divine institutions useless and insignificant.

Since most have had, one time or other, some risings of doubt, whether there be a God, though few do in expressions deny his being, it may not be unnecessary to propose some things for the further impressing this truth, and guarding themselves against such temptations.

1. It is utterly impossible to demonstrate there is no God. He can choose no medium, but will fall in as a proof for his existence, and a manifestation of his excellency rather than against it. The pretences of the atheist are so ridiculous, that they are not worth the mentioning.

They never saw God, and therefore know not how to believe such a being; they cannot comprehend him. He would not be God if he could fall within the narrow model of an human understanding; he would not be infinite if he were comprehensible, or to be terminated by our sight. How small a thing must that be which is seen by a bodily eye, or grasped by a weak mind! If God were visible or comprehensible, he would be limited. Shall it be a sufficient demonstration from a blind man that there is no fire in the room, because he sees it not, though he feel the warmth of it? The knowledge of the effect is sufficient to conclude the existence of the cause. Who ever saw his own life? Is it sufficient to deny a man lives, because he beholds not his life, and only knows it by his motion? He never saw his own soul, but knows he hath one by his thinking power. The air renders itself sensible to men in its operations, yet was never seen by the eye.

If God should render himself visible, they might question as well as now whether that which was so visible were God or some delusion. If he should appear glorious, we can as little behold him in his majestic glory as an owl can behold the sun in its brightness; we should still but see him in his effects, as we do the sun by his beams. If he should shew a new miracle, we should still see him but by his works; so we see him in his creatures, every one of which would be as great a miracle as any can be wrought to one that had the first prospect of them. To require to see God, is to require that which is impossible: 1 Tim. vi. 16, 'He dwells in the light which no man can approach unto; whom no man hath seen, nor can see.' It is visible *that* he is, for 'he covers himself with light as with a garment,' Ps. civ. 2; it is invisible *what* he is, for 'he makes darkness his secret place,' Ps. xviii. 11. Nothing more clear to the eye than light, and nothing more difficult to the understanding than the nature of it; as light is the first object obvious to the eye, so is God the first object obvious to the understanding. The arguments from nature do with greater strength evince his existence, than any pretences can manifest there is no God. No man can assure himself by any good reason there is none; for as for the 'likeness of events to him that is righteous and him that is wicked, to him that sacrificeth and to him that sacrificeth not,' Eccles. ix 2, it is an argument for a reserve of judgment in another state, which every man's conscience dictates to him, when the justice of God shall be glorified in another world as much as his patience is in this.

2. Whosoever doubts of it makes himself a mark, against which all the creatures fight.

All the stars fought against Sisera for Israel; all the stars in heaven, and the dust on earth, fight for God against the atheist. He hath as many arguments against him as there are creatures in the whole compass of heaven and earth. He is most unreasonable that denies or doubts of that whose image and shadow he sees round about him; he may sooner deny the sun that warms him, the moon that in the night walks in her brightness, deny the fruits he enjoys from earth, yea, and deny that he doth exist. He must tear his own conscience, fly from his own thoughts, be changed into the nature of a stone, which hath neither reason nor sense, before he can disengage himself from those arguments which evince the being of a God. He that would make the natural religion professed in the world a mere romance, must give the lie to the common sense of mankind; he must be at an irreconcilable enmity with his own reason, resolve to hear nothing that it speaks, if he will not hear what it speaks in this case with a greater evidence than it can ascertain anything else. God hath so settled himself in the reason of man, that he must vilify the noblest faculty God hath given him, and put off nature itself, before he can blot out the notion of a God.

3. No question but those that have been so bold as to deny that there was a God have sometimes been much afraid they have been in an error, and have at least suspected there was a God, when some sudden prodigy hath presented itself to them and roused their fears. And whatsoever sentiments they might have in their blinding prosperity, they have had other kind of motions in them in their stormy afflictions, and, like Jonah's mariners, have been ready to cry to him for help, whom they disdained to own so much as in being while they swam in their pleasures. The thoughts of a deity cannot be so extinguished but they will revive and rush upon a man, at least under some sharp affliction. Amazing judgments will make them question their own apprehensions. God sends some messengers to keep alive the apprehension of him as a judge, while men resolve not to own or reverence him as a governor. A man cannot but keep a scent of what was born with

him; as a vessel that hath been seasoned first with a strong juice will preserve the scent of it, whatsoever liquors are afterwards put into it.

4. What is it for which such men rack their wits, to form notions that there is no God? Is it not that they would indulge some vicious habit, which hath gained the possession of their soul, which they know cannot be favoured by that holy God, whose notion they would raze out? Ps. xciv. 6, 7. Is it not for some brutish affection, as degenerative of human nature, as derogatory to the glory of God; a lust as unmanly as sinful?

The terrors of God are the effects of guilt; and therefore men would wear out the apprehensions of a deity, that they might be brutish without control. They would fain believe there were no God, that they might not be men, but beasts. How great a folly is it to take so much pains in vain for a slavery and torment! to cast off that which they call a yoke for that which really is one! There is more pains and toughness of soul requisite to shake off the apprehensions of God than to believe that he is, and cleave constantly to him. What a madness is it in any to take so much pains to be less than a man, by razing out the apprehensions of God, when with less pains he may be more than an earthly man, by cherishing the notions of God, and walking answerably thereunto.

5. How unreasonable is it for any man to hazard himself at this rate in the denial of a God! The atheist saith he knows not that there is a God; but may he not reasonably think there may be one for aught he knows? And if there be, what a desperate confusion will he be in, when all his bravadoes shall prove false! What can they gain by such an opinion? A freedom, say they, from the burdensome yoke of conscience, a liberty to do what they list, that doth not subject them to divine laws. It is a hard matter to persuade any that they can gain this. They can gain but a sordid pleasure, unworthy the nature of man. But it were well that such would argue thus:—If there be a God, and I fear and obey him, I gain a happy eternity; but if there be no God, I lose nothing but my sordid lusts by firmly believing there is one. If I be deceived at last, and find a God, can I think to be rewarded by him for disowning him? Do not I run a desperate hazard to lose his favour, his kingdom, and endless felicity, for an endless torment? By confessing a God, I venture no loss; but by denying him, I run the most desperate hazard if there be one.

He is not a reasonable creature that will not put himself upon such a reasonable arguing.

What a doleful meeting will there be between the God who is denied and the atheist that denies him, who shall meet with reproaches on God's part, and terrors of his own! All that he gains is a liberty to defile himself here, and a certainty to be despised hereafter, if he be in an error, as undoubtedly he is.

6. Can any such person say he hath done all that he can to inform himself of the being of God, or of other things which he denies? Or rather, they would fain imagine there is none, that they may sleep securely in their lusts, and be free (if they could) from the thunder-claps of conscience? Can such say they have used their utmost endeavours to instruct themselves in this, and can meet with no satisfaction? Were it an abstruse truth, it might not be wondered at; but not to meet with satisfaction in this which everything minds us of and helpeth, is the fruit of an extreme negligence, stupidity, and a willingness to be unsatisfied, and a judicial process of God against them. It is strange any man should be so dark in that upon which depends the conduct of his life, and the expectation of happiness hereafter.

I do not know what some of you may think, but I believe these things are not useless to be proposed for ourselves to answer temptations. We know not what wicked temptation in a debauched and sceptic age, meeting with a corrupt heart, may prompt men to, and though there may not be any atheist here present, yet I know there is more than one who have accidentally met with such who openly denied a deity. And if the like occasion happen, these considerations may not be unuseful to apply to their consciences. But I must confess, that since those that live in this sentiment do not judge themselves worthy of their own care, they are not worthy of the care of others; and a man must have all the charity of the Christian religion, which they despise, not to contemn them, and leave them to their own folly. As we are to pity madmen, who sink under an unavoidable distemper, we are as much to abominate them who will fully hug this prodigious frenzy.

Use 3. If it be the atheist's folly to deny or doubt of the being of God, it is our wisdom to be firmly settled in this truth, that God is. We should never be without our arms in an age wherein atheism appears barefaced without a disguise.

You may meet with suggestions to it; though the devil formerly never attempted to demolish this notion in the world, but was willing to keep it up, so the worship due to God might run in his own channel; and was necessitated to preserve it, without which he could not have erected that idolatry which was his great design in opposition to God; yet since the foundations of that are torn up, and never like to be rebuilt, he may endeavour, as his last refuge, to banish the notion of God out of the world, that he may reign as absolutely without it, as he did before by the mistakes about the divine nature. But we must not lay all upon Satan; the corruption of our own hearts ministers matter to such sparks. It is not said, Satan hath suggested to the fool, but ' The fool hath said *in his heart*, There is no God.' But let them come from what principle soever, silence them quickly, give them their dismiss, oppose the whole scheme of nature to fight against them, as the stars did against Sisera. Stir up sentiments of conscience to oppose sentiments of corruption. Resolve sooner to believe that yourselves are not than that God is not. And if you suppose they at any time come from Satan, object to him that you know he believes the contrary to what he suggests. Settle this principle firmly in you, let us behold him that is invisible, as Moses did, Heb. xi. 27. Let us have the sentiments following upon the notion of a God, to be restrained by a fear of him, excited by a love to him, not to violate his laws and offend his goodness. He is not a God careless of our actions, negligent to inflict punishment and bestow rewards: ' He forgets not the labour of our love,' Heb. vi. 10, nor the integrity of our ways. He were not a God if he were not a governor; and punishments and rewards are as essential to government as a foundation to a building. His being and his government in rewarding, Heb. xi. 6, which implies punishment (for the neglects of him are linked together), are not* to be separated in our thoughts of him.

1. Without this truth fixed in us, we can never give him the worship due to his name. When the knowledge of any thing is fluctuating and uncertain, our actions about it are careless. We regard not that which we think doth not much concern us. If we do not firmly believe there is a God, we shall pay him no steady worship ; and if we believe not the excellency of his nature, we shall offer him but a slight service; Mal. i. 13, 14. The Jews† call the knowledge of the being of God, the foundation and pillar of wisdom. The

---

* Qu. ' His being and government in rewarding, which implies punishment for the neglect of him, are linked together, and are not,' &c. ?—Ed.

† Maimon. Funda. Legis, cap. i.

whole frame of religion is dissolved without this apprehension, and totters if this apprehension be wavering. Religion in the heart is as water in a weather glass, which rises or falls according to the strength or weakness of this belief. How can any man worship that which he believes not to be, or doubts of? Could any man omit the paying an homage to one whom he did believe to be an omnipotent, wise being, possessing (infinitely above our conceptions) the perfections of all creatures? He must either think there is no such being, or that he is an easy, drowsy, inobservant God, and not such a one as our natural notions of him, if listened to, as well as the Scripture, represent him to be.

2. Without being rooted in this, we cannot order our lives. All our baseness, stupidity, dulness, wanderings, vanity, spring from a wavering and unsettledness in this principle. This gives ground to brutish pleasures, not only to solicit but conquer us. Abraham expected violence in any place where God was not owned: Gen. xx. 11, 'Surely the fear of God is not in this place, and they will slay me for my wife's sake.' The natural knowledge of God firmly impressed, would choke that which would stifle our reason and deface our souls. The belief that God is, and what he is, would have a mighty influence to persuade us to a real religion, and serious consideration, and casting about how to be like to him and united with him.

3. Without it we cannot have any comfort of our lives. Who would willingly live in a stormy world, void of a God? If we waver in this principle, to whom should we make our complaints in our afflictions? Where should we meet with supports? How could we satisfy ourselves with the hopes of a future happiness? There is a sweetness in the meditation of his existence, and that he is a creator, Ps. civ. 24. Thoughts of other things have a bitterness mixed with them: houses, lands, children now are, shortly they will not be; but God is, that made the world; his faithfulness as he is a creator, is a ground to deposit our souls and concerns in our innocent sufferings, 1 Peter iv. 19. So far as we are weak in the acknowledgment of God, we deprive ourselves of our content in the view of his infinite perfections.

4. Without the rooting of this principle, we cannot have a firm belief of Scripture. The Scripture will be a slight thing to one that hath weak sentiments of God. The belief of a God must necessarily precede the belief of any revelation; the latter cannot take place without the former as the foundation. We must firmly believe the being of a God, wherein our happiness doth consist, before we can believe any means which conduct us to him. Moses begins with the author of creation, before he treats of the promise of redemption. Paul preached God as a creator to a university, before he preached Christ as mediator, Acts xvii. 24. What influence can the testimony of God have in his revelation upon one that doth not firmly assent to the truth of his being? All would be in vain that is so often repeated, *Thus saith the Lord*, if we do not believe there is a Lord that speaks it. There could be no awe from his sovereignty in his commands, nor any comfortable taste of his goodness in his promises. The more we are strengthened in this principle, the more credit we shall be able to give to divine revelation, to rest in his promise, and to reverence his precept; the authority of all depends upon the being of the revealer.

To this purpose, since we have handled this discourse by natural arguments,

1. Study God in the creatures as well as in the Scriptures. The primary use of the creatures, is to acknowledge God in them; they were made to be witnesses of himself and his goodness, and heralds of his glory, which

glory of God as creator 'shall endure for ever,' Ps. civ. 31. That whole psalm is a lecture of creation and providence. The world is a sacred temple, man is introduced to contemplate it, and behold with praise the glory of God in the pieces of his art. As grace doth not destroy nature, so the book of redemption blots not out that of creation. Had he not shewn himself in his creatures, he could never have shewn himself in his Christ. The order of things required it. God must be read wherever he is legible ; the creatures are one book, wherein he hath writ a part of the ' excellency of his name,' Ps. viii. 9, as many artists do in their works and watches. God's glory, like the filings of gold, is too precious to be lost wherever it drops ; nothing so vile and base in the world, but carries in it an instruction for man, and drives in further the notion of a God. As he said of his cottage, enter here, *sunt hic etiam Dii*, God disdains not this place, so the least creature speaks to man, every shrub in the field, every fly in the air, every limb in a body : Consider me, God disdains not to appear in me ; he hath discovered in me his being and a part of his skill, as well as in the highest. The creatures manifest the being of God and part of his perfections. We have indeed a more excellent way, a revelation setting him forth in a more excellent manner, a firmer object of dependence, a brighter object of love, raising our hearts from self-confidence to a confidence in him. Though the appearance of God in the one be clearer than in the other, yet neither is to be neglected. The Scripture directs us to nature to view God ; it had been in vain else for the apostle to make use of natural arguments. Nature is not contrary to Scripture, nor Scripture to nature, unless we should think God contrary to himself, who is the author of both.

2. View God in your own experiences of him. There is a taste and sight of his goodness, though no sight of his essence, Ps. xxxiv. 38. By the taste of his goodness you may know the reality of the fountain, whence it springs and from whence it flows. This surpasseth the greatest capacity of a mere natural understanding. Experience of the sweetness of the ways of Christianity is a mighty preservative against atheism. Many a man knows not how to prove honey to be sweet by his reason, but by his sense ; and if all the reason in the world be brought against it, he will not be reasoned out of what he tastes.

Have not many found the delightful illapses of God into their souls, often sprinkled with his inward blessings upon their seeking of him ; had secret warnings in their approaches to him ; and gentle rebukes in their consciences upon their swervings from him ? Have not many found sometimes an invisible hand raising them up when they were dejected, some unexpected providence stepping in for their relief, and easily perceived that it could not be a work of chance, nor many times the intention of the instruments he hath used in it ? You have often found that he is, by finding that he is a rewarder, and can set to your seals that he is what he hath declared himself to be in his word: Isa. xliii. 12, ' I have declared, and have saved, therefore you are my witnesses, saith the Lord, that I am God.' The secret touches of God upon the heart, and inward converses with him, are a greater evidence of the existence of a supreme and infinitely good being, than all nature.

Use 4. Is it a folly to deny or doubt of the being of God ? It is a folly also not to worship God, when we acknowledge his existence. It is our wisdom then to worship him. As it is not indifferent whether we believe there is a God or no, so it is not indifferent whether we will give honour to that God or no. A worship is his right as he is the author of our being, and fountain of our happiness. By this only we acknowledge his deity. Though we profess his being, yet we deny that profession in neglects of worship. To deny him a worship is as great a folly as to deny his being. He that renounceth all homage to his Creator, envies him the being which he cannot deprive him of. The natural inclination to worship is as universal as the notion of a God; idolatry else had never gained footing in the world. The existence of God was never owned in any nation, but a worship of him was appointed; and many people who have turned their backs upon some other parts of the law of nature, have paid a continual homage to some superior and invisible being. The Jews gave a reason why man was created in the evening of the Sabbath, because he should begin his being with the worship of his Maker. As soon as ever he found himself to be a creature, his first solemn act should be a particular respect to his Creator. 'To fear God and keep his commandment, is the whole of man,' Eccles. xii. 13, or is 'whole man' (*Hebrew*); he is not a man but a beast, without observance of God. Religion is as requisite as reason to complete a man. He were not reasonable if he were not religious; because by neglecting religion, he neglects the chiefest dictate of reason. Either God framed the world with so much order, elegancy, and variety, to no purpose, or this was his end at least, that reasonable creatures should admire him in it, and honour him for it. The notion of God was not stamped upon men, the shadows of God did not appear in the creatures to be the subject of an idle contemplation, but the motive of a due homage to God. He created the world for his glory, a people for himself, that he might have the honour of his works; that since we live and move in him and by him, we should live and move to him and for him. It was the condemnation of the heathen world, that when they knew there was a God, they did not give him the glory due to him, Rom. i. 21. He that denies his being is an atheist to his essence: he that denies his worship is an atheist to his honour.

5. If it be a folly to deny the being of God, it will be our wisdom then, since we acknowledge his being, often to think of him. Thoughts are the first issue of a creature as reasonable, Prov. iv. 23. He that hath given us the faculty whereby we are able to think, should be the principal object about which the power of it should be exercised. It is a justice to God the author of our understandings, a justice to the nature of our understandings, that the noblest faculty should be employed about the most excellent object. Our minds are a beam from God; and therefore, as the beams of the sun, when they touch the earth, should reflect back upon God. As we seem to deny the being of God, not to think of him, we seem also to unsoul our souls, in misemploying the activity of them any other way: like flies, to be oftener on dunghills than flowers.

It is made the black mark of an ungodly man or an atheist, that 'God is not in all his thoughts,' Ps. x. 4. What comfort can be had in the being of God without thinking of him with reverence and delight! A God forgotten is as good as no God to us.

PRACTICAL ATHEISM.

The fool hath said in his heart, There is no God.—Ps. XIV. 1.

Doct. 2. Practical atheism is natural to man in his depraved state, and very frequent in the hearts and lives of men.

'The fool hath said in his heart, There is no God.' He regards him as little as if he had no being. He said in his heart, not with his tongue, nor in his head; he never firmly thought it, nor openly asserted it; shame put a bar to the first, and natural reason to the second. Yet perhaps he had sometimes some doubts whether there were a God or no; he wished there were not any, and sometimes hoped there were none at all. He could not raze out the notion of a deity in his mind, but he neglected the fixing the sense of God in his heart, and made it too much his business to deface and blot out those characters of God in his soul which had been left under the ruins of original nature.

Men may have atheistical hearts without atheistical heads. Their reasons may defend the notion of a deity, while their hearts are empty of affection to the Deity; Job's children may 'curse God in their hearts,' Job i. 5, though not with their lips.

'There is no God.' Most understand it of a denial of the providence of God, as I have said in opening the former doctrine.

He denies some essential attribute of God, or the exercise of that attribute in the world.*

He that denies any essential attribute may be said to deny the being of God. Whosoever denies angels or men to have reason and will, denies the human and angelical nature, because understanding and will are essential to both those natures; there could neither be angel nor man without them. No nature can subsist without the perfections essential to that nature, nor God be conceived of without his. The apostle tells us, Eph. ii. 12, that the Gentiles were 'without God in the world.' So in some sense all unbelievers may be termed atheists; for rejecting the mediator appointed by God, they reject that God who appointed him.

But this is beyond the intended scope, natural atheism being the only subject; yet this is deducible from it, that the title of ἄθεοι doth not only belong to those who denied the existence of God, or to those who contemn all sense of a deity, and would root the conscience and reverence of God out of their souls, but it belongs also to these who give not that worship to God which is due to him; who worship many gods, or who worship one

* So the Chaldee reads, לית שולטנא, *non potestas*, denying the authority of God in the world.

God in a false and superstitious manner; when they have not right conceptions of God, nor intend an adoration of him according to the excellency of
his nature. All those that are unconcerned for any particular religion fall
under this character; though they own a God in general, yet are willing
to acknowledge any god that shall be coined by the powers under whom they
live. The Gentiles were without God in the world; without the true notion
of God, not without a god of their own framing.

This general or practical atheism is natural to men.

1. Not natural by created, but by corrupted, nature. It is against nature,
as nature came out of the hand of God; but universally natural, as nature
hath been sophisticated and infected by the serpent's breath. Inconsideration of God, or misrepresentations of his nature, are as agreeable to corrupt
nature as the disowning the being of a God is contrary to common reason.
God is not denied *naturâ sed vitiis.**

2. It is universally natural: 'The wicked are estranged from the womb,'
Ps. lviii. 2, 'They go astray as soon as they be born, their poison is like
the poison of a serpent.' The wicked; and who by his birth hath a better
title? They go astray from the dictates of God and the rule of their creation as soon as ever they be born; their poison is like the poison of a
serpent, which is radically the same in all of the same species. It is seminally and fundamentally in all men, though there may be a stronger restraint
by a divine hand upon some men than upon others. This principle runs
through the whole stream of nature. The natural bent of every man's heart
is distant from God; when we attempt anything pleasing to God, it is like
the climbing up a hill against nature; when anything is displeasing to him,
it is like a current running down the channel in its natural course; when
we attempt anything that is an acknowledgment of the holiness of God, we
are fain to rush with arms in our hands through a multitude of natural
passions, and fight the way through the oppositions of our own sensitive
appetite. How softly do we naturally sink down into that which sets us at
a greater distance from God! There is no active, potent, efficacious sense
of a God by nature. 'The heart of the sons of men is fully set in them to
do evil,' Eccl. viii. 11; *the heart* in the singular number, as if there were
but one common heart beat in all mankind, and bent, as with one pulse,
with a joint consent and force to wickedness, without a sense of the authority of God in the earth; as if one heart acted every man in the world.

The great apostle cites the text to verify the charge he brought against
all mankind, Rom. iii. 9–12. In his interpretation, the Jews, who owned
one God, and were dignified with special privileges, as well as the Gentiles,
that maintained many gods, are within the compass of this character. The
apostle leaves out the first part of the text, 'The fool hath said in his heart,'
but takes in the latter part, and the verses following. He charges all,
because all, every man of them, was under sin: 'There is none that seeks
God;' and, ver. 19, he adds, 'What the law saith, it speaks to those that
are under the law,' that none should imagine he included only the Gentiles,
and exempted the Jews from this description. The leprosy of atheism had
infected the whole mass of human nature. No man among Jews or Gentiles
did naturally seek God, and therefore all were void of any spark of the
practical sense of the deity. The effects of this atheism are not in all ex-
ternally of an equal size; yet, in the fundamentals and radicals of it, there
is not a hair's difference between the best and the worst men that ever tra-
versed the world. The distinction is laid either in the common grace,
bounding and suppressing it; or in special grace, killing and crucifying it.

* Augustin. de Civit. Dei.

It is in every one either triumphant or militant, reigning or deposed. No man is any more born with sensible acknowledgments of God than he is born with a clear knowledge of the nature of all the stars in the heavens or plants upon the earth. 'None seeks after God.' None seeks God as his rule, as his end, as his happiness, which is a debt the creature naturally owes to God; he desires no communion with God; he places his happiness in anything inferior to God; he prefers everything before him, glorifies everything above him; he hath no delight to know him; he regards not those paths which lead to him; he loves his own filth better than God's holiness; his actions are tinctured and dyed with self, and are void of that respect which is due from him to God.

The noblest faculty of man, his understanding, wherein the remaining lineaments of the image of God are visible, the highest operation of that faculty, which is wisdom, is in the judgment of the Spirit of God 'devilish,' whiles it is 'earthly and sensual,' James iii. 15. And the wisdom of the best man is no better by nature; a legion of impure spirits possess it; devilish as the devil, who though he believe there is a God, yet acts as if there were none, and wishes he had no superior to prescribe him a law, and inflict that punishment upon him which his crimes have merited. Hence the poison of man by nature is said to be like 'the poison of a serpent,' alluding to that serpentine temptation which first infected mankind, and changed the nature of man into the likeness of that of the devil, Ps. lviii. 4. So that notwithstanding the harmony of the world, that presents men not only with the notice of the being of a God, but darts into their minds some remarks of his power and eternity, yet the thoughts and reasonings of man are so corrupt, as may well be called diabolical, and as contrary to the perfection of God and the original law of their nature, as the actings of the devil are; for since every natural man is a child of the devil, and is acted by the diabolical spirit, he must needs have that nature which his father hath, and the infusion of that venom which the spirit that acts him is possessed with, though the full discovery of it may be restrained by various circumstances, Eph. ii. 2. To conclude: though no man, or at least very few, arrive to a round and positive conclusion in their hearts that there is no God, yet there is no man that naturally hath in his heart any reverence of God.

In general, before I come to a particular proof, take some propositions.

Prop. 1. Actions are a greater discovery of a principle than words. The testimony of works is louder and clearer than that of words, and the frame of men's hearts must be measured rather by what they do than by what they say. There may be a mighty distance between the tongue and the heart, but a course of actions is as little guilty of lying as interest is, according to our common saying. All outward impieties are the branches of an atheism at the root of our nature, as all pestilential sores are expressions of the contagion in the blood. Sin is therefore frequently called ungodliness in our English dialect. Men's practices are the best indexes of their principles. The current of a man's life is the counterpart of the frame of his heart: who can deny an error in the spring or wheels, when he perceives an error in the hand of the dial? Who can deny atheism in the heart, when so much is visible in the life? The taste of the water discovers what mineral it is strained through. A practical denial of God is worse than a verbal, because deeds have usually more of deliberation than words; words may be the fruit of a passion, but a set of evil actions are the fruit and evidence of a predominant evil principle in the heart. All slighting words of a prince do not argue an habitual treason, but a succession of overt treasonable attempts signify a settled treasonable disposition in the mind. Those, therefore, are more deservedly termed atheists, who acknowledge a God and walk as if there were none, than those (if there can be any such) that deny a God, and walk as if there were one.

A sense of God in the heart would burst out in the life. Where there is no reverence of God in the life, it is easily concluded there is less in the heart. What doth not influence a man when it hath the addition of the eyes and censures of outward spectators, and the care of a reputation (so much the god of the world), to strengthen it and restrain the action, must certainly have less power over the heart when it is single, without any other concurrence. The flames breaking out of a house discover the fire to be much stronger and fiercer within. The apostle judgeth those of the circumcision, who gave heed to Jewish fables, to be deniers of God, though he doth not tax them with any notorious profaneness: Tit. i. 16, 'They profess that they know God, but in works they deny him;' he gives them epithets contrary to what they arrogated to themselves.* They boasted themselves to be holy, the apostle calls them abominable. They bragged that they fulfilled the law, and observed the traditions of their fathers; the apostle calls them disobedient, or unpersuadable. They boasted that they only had the rule of righteousness, and a sound judgment concerning it; the apostle said they had a reprobate sense, and unfit for any good work; and judges against all their vain-glorious brags, that they had not a reverence of God in their hearts; there was more of the denial of God in their works, than there was acknowledgment of God in their words. Those that have neither God in their thoughts, nor in their tongues, nor in their works, cannot properly be said to acknowledge him. Where the honour of God is not practically owned in the lives of men, the being of God is not sensibly acknowledged in the hearts of men. The principle must be of the same kind with the actions; if the actions be atheistical, the principle of them can be no better.

Prop. 2. All sin is founded in a secret atheism. Atheism is the spirit of every sin; all the flood of impieties in the world break in at the gate of a secret atheism; and though several sins may disagree with one another, yet like Herod and Pilate against Christ, they join hand in hand against the interest of God. Though lusts and pleasures be divers, yet they are united in disobedience to him, Tit. iii. 3. All the wicked inclinations in the heart, and struggling motions, secret repinings, self-applauding confidences in our own wisdom, strength, &c., envy, ambition, revenge, are sparks from this latent fire; the language of every one of these is, I would be a lord to myself, and would not have a God superior to me.

The variety of sins against the first and second table, the neglects of God, and violences against man, are derived from this in the text, first, 'The fool hath said in his heart,' and then follows a legion of devils. As all virtuous actions spring from an acknowledgment of God, so all vicious actions rise from a lurking denial of him. All licentiousness goes glib down where there is no sense of God. Abraham judged himself not secure from murder, nor his wife from defilement in Gerar, if there were no fear of God there, Gen. xx. 11. He that makes no conscience of sin has no regard to the honour, and consequently none to the being, of God. 'By the fear of God men depart from evil,' Prov. xvi. 6. By the non-regarding of God men rush into evil. Pharaoh oppressed Israel because he knew not the Lord. If he did not deny the being of a deity, yet he had such an unworthy notion of God as was inconsistent with the nature of a deity; he, a poor creature, thought himself a mate for the Creator.

* Illyric.

In sins of omission we own not God, in neglecting to perform what he enjoins. In sins of commission we set up some lust in the place of God, and pay to that the homage which is due to our Maker. In both we disown him; in the one by not doing what he commands, in the other by doing what he forbids.

We deny his sovereignty when we violate his laws; we disgrace his holiness when we cast our filth before his face; we disparage his wisdom when we set up another rule as the guide of our actions than that law he hath fixed; we slight his sufficiency when we prefer a satisfaction in sin before a happiness in him alone, and his goodness, when we judge it not strong enough to attract us to him. Every sin invades the rights of God, and strips him of one or other of his perfections. It is such a vilifying of God .as if he were not God; as if he were not the supreme creator and benefactor of the world; as if we had not our being from him; as if the air we breathed in, the food we lived by, were our own by right of supremacy, not of donation: for a subject to slight his sovereign is to slight his royalty; or a servant a master, is to deny his superiority.

Prop. 3. Sin implies that God is unworthy of a being. Every sin is a kind of cursing God in the heart, Job i. 5; an aim at the destruction of the being of God, not actually, but virtually; not in the intention of every sinner, but in the nature of every sin. That affection which excites a man to break his law, would excite him to annihilate his being if it were in his power. A man in every sin aims to set up his own will as his rule, and his own glory as the end of his actions, against the will and glory of God; and could a sinner attain his end, God would be destroyed: God cannot out-live his will and his glory; God cannot have another rule but his own will, nor another end but his own honour. Sin is called a 'turning the back' upon God, Jer. xxxii. 33; a 'kicking against him,' Deut. xxxii. 15; as if he were a slighter person than the meanest beggar. What greater contempt can be shewed to the meanest, vilest person, than to turn the back, lift up the heel, and thrust away with indignation? All which actions, though they signify that such a one hath a being, yet they testify also that he is unworthy of a being, that he is an unuseful being in the world, and that it were well the world were rid of him.

All sin against knowledge is called a reproach of God, Num. xv. 10, Ezek. xx. 27. Reproach is a vilifying a man as unworthy to be admitted into company. We naturally judge God unfit to be conversed with. God is the term turned from by a sinner; sin is the term turned to; which implies a greater excellency in the nature of sin than in the nature of God. And as we naturally judge it more worthy to have a being in our affections, so consequently more worthy to have a being in the world, than that infinite nature from whom we derive our beings, and our all, and upon whom with a kind of disdain we turn our backs. Whosoever thinks the notion of a deity unfit to be cherished in his mind by warm meditation, implies that he cares not whether he hath a being in the world or no. Now though the light of a deity shines so clearly in man, and the stings of conscience are so smart, that he cannot absolutely deny the being of a God, yet most men endeavour to smother this knowledge, and make the notion of a God a sapless and useless thing: Rom. i. 28, 'They like not to retain God in their knowledge.'

It is said Cain 'went out from the presence of the Lord,' Gen. iv. 16; that is, from the worship of God. Our refusing or abhorring the presence of a man implies a carelessness whether he continue in the world or no, it is a using him as if he had no being, or as if he were not concerned in it. Hence all men in Adam, under the emblem of the prodigal, are said to go into a far country. Not in respect of place, because of God's omnipresence, but in respect of acknowledgment and affection; they mind and love anything but God. And the descriptions of the nations of the world, lying in the ruins of Adam's fall, and the dregs of that revolt, is that they know not God; they forget God, as if there were no such being above them; and indeed, he that doth the works of the devil, owns the devil to be more worthy of observance, and consequently of a being, than God, whose nature he forgets, and whose presence he abhors.

Prop. 4. Every sin in its own nature would render God a foolish and impure being. Many transgressors esteem their acts, which are contrary to the law of God, both wise and good; if so, the law against which they are committed must be both foolish and impure. What a reflection is there then upon the law-giver! The moral law is not properly a mere act of God's will considered in itself, or a tyrannical edict, like those of whom it may well be said, *stat pro ratione voluntas*, but it commands those things which are good in their own nature, and prohibits those things which are in their own nature evil, and therefore is an act of his wisdom and righteousness, the result of his wise counsel, and an extract of his pure nature; as all the laws of just lawgivers are not only the acts of their will, but of a will governed by reason and justice, and for the good of the public, whereof they are conservators. If the moral commands of God were only acts of his will, and had not an intrinsic necessity, reason, and goodness, God might have commanded the quite contrary, and made a contrary law, whereby that which we now call vice might have been canonised for virtue; he might then have forbid any worship of him, love to him, fear of his name; he might then have commanded murders, thefts, adulteries. In the first, he would have united the link of duty from the creature, and dissolved the obligations of creatures to him, which is impossible to be conceived; for from the relation of a creature to God, obligations to God, and duties upon those obligations, do necessarily result. It had been against the rule of goodness and justice to have commanded the creature not to love him, and fear and obey him; this had been a command against righteousness, goodness, and intrinsic obligations to gratitude. And should murder, adulteries, rapines have been commanded instead of the contrary, God would have destroyed his own creation; he would have acted against the rule of goodness and order; he had been an unjust tyrannical governor of the world; public society would have been cracked in pieces, and the world become a shambles, a brothel house, a place below the common sentiments of a mere man. All sin therefore being against the law of God, the wisdom and holy rectitude of God's nature is denied in every act of disobedience. And what is the consequence of this, but that God is both foolish and unrighteous in commanding that which was neither an act of wisdom as a governor, nor an act of goodness as a benefactor to his creature?

As was said before, presumptuous sins are called reproaches of God: Num. xv. 30, 'The soul that doth aught presumptuously reproacheth the Lord.' Reproaches of men are either for natural, moral, or intellectual defects. All reproaches of God must imply a charge either of unrighteousness or ignorance; if of unrighteousness, it is a denial of his holiness; if of ignorance, it is a blemishing his wisdom. If God's laws were not wise and holy, God would not enjoin them; and if they are so, we deny infinite wisdom and holiness in God by not complying with them. As when a man believes not God when he promises, he 'makes him a liar,' 1 John v. 10, so he that obeys not a wise and holy God commanding, makes him guilty either of folly or unrighteousness.

Now, suppose you knew an absolute atheist, who denied the being of a God, yet had a life free from any notorious spot or defilement, would you in reason count him so bad as the other that owns a God in being, yet lays, by his course of action, such a black imputation of folly and impurity upon the God he professeth to own, an imputation which renders any man a most despicable creature ?

Prop. 5. Sin in its own nature endeavours to render God the most miserable being. It is nothing but an opposition to the will of God. The will of no creature is so much contradicted as the will of God is by devils and men ; and there is nothing under the heavens that the affections of human nature stand more point blank against, than against God. There is a slight of him in all the faculties of man ; our souls are as unwilling to know him as our wills are averse to follow him : Rom. viii. 7, ' The carnal mind is enmity against God ; it is not subject to the law of God, nor can be subject.' It is true God's will cannot be hindered of its effect, for then God would not be supremely blessed, but unhappy and miserable ; all misery ariseth from a want of that which a nature would have and ought to have ; besides, if anything could frustrate God's will, it would be superior to him ; God would not be omnipotent, and so would lose the perfection of the deity, and consequently the deity itself ; for that which did wholly defeat God's will would be more powerful than he. But sin is a contradiction to the will of God's revelation ; to the will of his precept, and therein doth naturally tend to a superiority over God, and would usurp his omnipotence, and deprive him of his blessedness. For if God had not an infinite power to turn the designs of it to his own glory, but the will of sin could prevail, God would be totally deprived of his blessedness. Doth not sin endeavour to subject God to the extravagant and contrary wills of men, and make him more a slave than any creature can be ? For the will of no creature, not the meanest and most despicable creature, is so much crossed as the will of God is by sin : Isa. xliii. 24, ' Thou hast made me to serve with thy sins ; ' thou hast endeavoured to make a mere slave of me by sin. Sin endeavours to subject the blessed God to the humour and lust of every person in the world.

Prop. 6. Men sometimes in some circumstances do wish the not being of God. This some think to be the meaning of the text, ' The fool hath said in his heart, there is no God ; ' that is, he wishes there were no God. Many tamper with their own hearts to bring them to a persuasion that there is no God, and when they cannot do that, they conjure up wishes that there were none. Men naturally have some conscience of sin, and some notices of justice : Rom. i. 32, ' They know the judgment of God,' and they know the demerit of sin ; they know the judgment of God, and ' that they which do such things are worthy of death.' What is the consequent of this but fear of punishment ? and what is the issue of that fear but a wishing the judge either unwilling or unable to vindicate the honour of his violated law? When God is the object of such a wish, it is a virtual undeifying of him. Not to be able to punish, is to be impotent ; not to be willing to punish, is to be unjust : imperfections inconsistent with the deity. God cannot be supposed without an infinite power to act, and an infinite righteousness as the rule of acting. Fear of God is natural to all men ; not a fear of offending him, but a fear of being punished by him. The wishing the extinction of God has its degree in men, according to the degree of their fears of his just vengeance ; and though such a wish be not in its meridian but in the damned in hell, yet it hath its starts and motions in affrighted and awakened consciences on the earth, under this rank of wishers, that there were no God, or that God were destroyed, do fall,—

1. Terrified consciences, that are *magor missabib*,* see nothing but matter of fear round about. As they have lived without the bounds of the law, they are afraid to fall under the stroke of his justice ; fear wishes the destruction of that which it apprehends hurtful. It considers him as a God to whom 'vengeance belongs,' as the 'judge of all the earth,' Ps. xciv. 1, 2. The less hopes such a one hath of his pardon, the more joy he would have to hear that his judge should be stripped of his life; he would entertain with delight any reasons that might support him in the conceit that there were no God ; in his present state, such a doctrine would be his security from an account ; he would as much rejoice if there were no God to inflame a hell for him, as any guilty malefactor would if there were no judge to order a gibbet for him. Shame may bridle men's words, but the heart will be casting about for some arguments this way to secure itself. Such as are at any time in Spira's case, would be willing to cease to be creatures, that God might cease to be judge. 'The fool hath said in his heart, there is no Elohim,' no judge, fancying God without any exercise of his judicial authority. And there is not any wicked man under anguish of spirit, but, were it within the reach of his power, would take away the life of God, and rid himself of his fears by destroying his avenger.

2. Debauched persons are not without such wishes sometimes. An obstinate servant wishes his master's death, from whom he expects correction for his debaucheries. As man stands in his corrupt nature, it is impossible but one time or other most debauched persons, at least have some kind of velleities, or imperfect wishes. It is as natural to men to abhor those things which are unsuitable and troublesome, as it is to please themselves in things agreeable to their minds and humours. And since man is so deeply in love with sin, as to count it the most estimable good, he cannot but wish the abolition of that law which checks it, and consequently the change of the lawgiver which enacted it ; and in wishing a change in the holy nature of God, he wishes a destruction of God, who could not be God, if he ceased to be immutably holy. They do as certainly wish, that God had not a holy will to command them, as despairing souls wish, that God had not a righteous will to punish them ; and to wish conscience extinct for the molestations they receive from it, is to wish the power conscience represents out of the world also.

Since the state of sinners is a state of distance from God, and the language of sinners to God is, 'Depart from us,' Job xxi. 14, they desire as little the continuance of his being as they desire the knowledge of his ways. The same reason which moves them to desire God's distance from them, would move them to desire God's not being. Since the greatest distance would be most agreeable to them, the destruction of God must be so too ; because there is no greater distance from us, than in not being. Men would rather have God not to be, than themselves under control, that sensuality might range at pleasure. He is like a ' heifer sliding from the yoke,' Hosea iv. 16. The cursing of God in the heart, feared by Job of his children, intimates a wishing God despoiled of his authority, that their pleasure might not be damped by his law ; besides, is there any natural man that sins against actuated knowledge, but either thinks or wishes that God might not see him, that God might not know his actions ? And is not this to wish the destruction of God, who could not be God unless he were immense and omniscient ?

3. Under this rank fall those who perform external duties only out of a principle of slavish fear. Many men perform those duties that the law enjoins, with the same sentiments that slaves perform their drudgery, and are

* That is, מגור מסביב, Jer. xx. 3.—Ed.

constrained in their duties by no other considerations but those of the whip and the cudgel. Since, therefore, they do it with reluctancy, and secretly murmur while they seem to obey, they would be willing that both the commands were recalled, and the master that commands them were in another world. The Spirit of adoption makes men act towards God as a father, a Spirit of bondage only eyes him as a judge. Those that look upon their superiors as tyrannical, will not be much concerned in their welfare, and would be more glad to have their nails pared, than be under perpetual fear of them.

Many men regard not the infinite goodness in their service of him, but consider him as cruel, tyrannical, injurious to their liberty. Adam's posterity are not free from the sentiments of their common father, till they are regenerate. You know what conceit was the hammer whereby the hellish Jael struck the nail into our first parents, which conveyed death, together with the same imagination to all their posterity: Gen. iii. 5, 'God knows that in the day you eat thereof, your eyes shall be opened, and you shall be as gods, knowing good and evil.' Alas, poor souls! God knew what he did when he forbade you that fruit; he was jealous you should be too happy; it was a cruelty in him to deprive you a food so pleasant and delicious. The apprehension of the severity of God's commands riseth up no less in desires that there were no God over us, than Adam's apprehension of envy in God, for the restraint of one tree moved him to attempt to be equal with God; fear is as powerful to produce the one in his posterity, as pride was to produce the other in the common root. When we apprehend a thing hurtful to us, we desire so much evil to it, as may render it uncapable of doing us the hurt we fear. As we wish the preservation of what we love or hope for, so we are naturally apt to wish the not being of that whence we fear some hurt or trouble. We must not understand this as if any man did formally wish the destruction of God, as God. God in himself is an infinite mirror of goodness and ravishing loveliness. He is infinitely good, and so universally good, and nothing but good, and is therefore so agreeable to a creature, as a creature, that it is impossible that the creature, while it bears itself to God as a creature, should be guilty of this, but thirst after him and cherish every motion to him. As no man wishes the destruction of any creature, as a creature, but as it may conduce to something which he counts may be beneficial to himself, so no man doth, nor perhaps can wish the cessation of the being of God, as God; for then he must wish his own being to cease also; but as he considers him clothed with some perfections, which he apprehends as injurious to him; as his holiness in forbidding sin, his justice in punishing sin. And God being judged in those perfections contrary to what the revolted creature thinks convenient and good for himself, he may wish God stripped of those perfections, that thereby he may be free from all fear of trouble and grief from him in his fallen state. In wishing God deprived of those, he wishes God deprived of his being, because God cannot retain his deity without a love of righteousness and hatred of iniquity; and he could not testify his love to the one, or his loathing of the other, without encouraging goodness, and witnessing his anger against iniquity.

Let us now appeal to ourselves, and examine our own consciences. Did we never please ourselves sometimes in the thoughts, how happy we should be, how free in our vain pleasures, if there were no God? Have we not desired to be our own lords without control, subject to no law but our own, and be guided by no will but that of the flesh? Did we never rage against God under his afflicting hand? Did we never wish God stripped of his holy will to command, and his righteous will to punish, &c.

Thus much for the general.

For the proof of this, many considerations will bring in evidence ; most may be reduced to these two generals.

Man would set himself up, first, as his own rule ; secondly, as his own end and happiness.

I. Man would set himself up as his own rule instead of God. This will be evidenced in this method.

1. Man naturally disowns the rule God sets him.

2. He owns any other rule rather than that of God's prescribing.

3. These he doth in order to the setting himself up as his own rule.

4. He makes himself not only his own rule, but would make himself the rule of God, and give laws to his creator.

1. Man naturally disowns the rule God sets him. It is all one to deny his royalty and to deny his being. When we disown his authority, we disown his Godhead. It is the right of God to be the sovereign of his creatures ; and it must be a very loose and trivial assent that such men have to God's superiority over them (and consequently to the excellency of his being, upon which that authority is founded), who are scarce at ease in themselves, but when they are invading his rights, breaking his bands, casting away his cords, and contradicting his will.

Every man naturally is a son of Belial, would be without a yoke, and leap over God's enclosures ; and in breaking out against his sovereignty, we disown his being as God. For to be God and sovereign are inseparable ; he could not be God, if he were not supreme ; nor could he be a creator without being a lawgiver. To be God, and yet inferior to another, is a contradiction. To make rational creatures without prescribing them a law, is to make them without holiness, wisdom, and goodness.

(1.) There is in man naturally an unwillingness to have any acquaintance with the rule God sets him : Ps. xiv. 2, ' None that did understand and seek God.' The ' refusing instruction,' and ' casting his word behind the back,' is a part of atheism, Ps. l. 17. We are heavy in hearing the instructions either of law or gospel, Heb. v. 11, 12, and slow in the apprehension of what we hear. The people that God had hedged in from the wilderness of the world for his own garden were foolish, and did not know God ; were sottish, and had no understanding of him, Jer. iv. 22. The law of God is accounted a strange thing, Hos. viii. 12, a thing of a different climate and a far country from the heart of man, wherewith the mind of man had no natural acquaintance, and had no desire to have any, or they regarded it as a sordid thing. What God accounts great and valuable, they account mean and despicable. Men may shew a civility to a stranger, but scarce contract an intimacy ; there can be no amicable agreement between the holy will of God and the heart of a depraved creature : one is holy, the other unholy ; one is universally good, the other stark naught. The purity of the divine rule renders it nauseous to the impurity of a carnal heart. Water and fire may as well friendly kiss each other and live together without quarrelling and hissing, as the holy will of God and the unregenerate heart of a fallen creature.

The nauseating a holy rule is an evidence of atheism in the heart, as the nauseating wholesome food is of putrified phlegm in the stomach. It is found more or less in every Christian, in the remainders, though not in a full empire. As there is a law in his mind whereby he delights in the law of God, so there is a law in his members whereby he wars against the law of God, Rom. vii. 22, 23, 25. How predominant is this loathing of the law of God, when corrupt nature is in its full strength, without any principle to control it! There is in the mind of such a one a darkness whereby it is ignorant of it, and in the will a depravedness whereby it is repugnant to it. If man were naturally willing and able to have an intimate acquaintance with, and delight in the law of God, it had not been such a signal favour for God to promise to write the law in the heart. A man may sooner engrave the chronicle of a whole nation, or all the records of God in the Scripture, upon the hardest marble with his bare finger, than write one syllable of the law of God in a spiritual manner upon his heart. For,

[1.] Men are negligent in using the means for the knowledge of God's will. All natural men are fools, who know not how to use the 'price God puts into their hands,' Prov. xvii. 16; they put not a due estimate upon opportunities and means of grace, and account that law folly which is the birth of an infinite and holy wisdom. The knowledge of God which they may glean from creatures, and is more pleasant to the natural gust of men, is not improved to the glory of God, if we will believe the indictment the apostle brings against the Gentiles, Rom. i. 21. And most of those that have dived into the depths of nature, have been more studious of the qualities of the creatures than of the excellency of the nature, or the discovery of the mind of God in them; who regard only the rising and motions of the star, but follow not with the wise men, its conduct to the king of the Jews. How often do we see men filled with an eager thirst for all other kind of knowledge, that cannot acquiesce in a twilight discovery, but are inquisitive into the causes and reasons of effects, yet are contented with a weak and languishing knowledge of God and his law, and are easily tired with the proposals of them.

He now that nauseates the means whereby he may come to know and obey God, has no intention to make the law of God his rule. There is no man that intends seriously an end, but he intends means in order to that end; as when a man intends the preservation or recovery of his health, he will intend means in order to those ends, otherwise he cannot be said to intend his health. So he that is not diligent in using means to know the mind of God, has no sound intention to make the will and law of God his rule. Is not the inquiry after the will of God made a work by the by, and fain to lacquey after other concerns of an inferior nature, if it hath any place at all in the soul? which is a despising the being of God. The notion of the sovereignty of God bears the same date with the notion of his Godhead; and by the same way that he reveals himself, he reveals his authority over us, whether it be by creatures without, or conscience within. All authority over rational creatures consists in commanding and directing; the duty of rational creatures, in compliance with that authority, consists in obeying. Where there is therefore a careless neglect of those means which convey the knowledge of God's will and our duty, there is an utter disowning of God as our sovereign and our rule.

[2.] When any part of the mind and will of God breaks in upon men, they endeavour to shake it off; as a man would a sergeant that comes to arrest him: 'They like not to retain God in their knowledge,' Rom. i. 28. 'A natural man receives not the things of the Spirit of God;' that is, into his affection; he pusheth them back as men do troublesome and importunate beggars. They have no kindness to bestow upon it. They thrust with both shoulders against the truth of God, when it presseth in upon them; and dash as much contempt upon it as the Pharisees did upon the doctrine our Saviour directed against their covetousness. As men naturally delight to be without God in the world, so they delight to be without any offspring of God in their thoughts. Since the spiritual palate of man is depraved, divine truth is unsavoury and ungrateful to us, till our taste and relish is restored by grace. Hence men damp and quench the motions of the Spirit to obedience and compliance with the dictates of God; strip them of their life and vigour, and kill them in the womb. How unable are our memories to retain the substance of spiritual truth, but like sand in a glass, put in at one part and runs out at the other! Have not many a secret wish that the Scripture had never mentioned some truths, or that they were blotted out of the Bible, because they face their consciences, and discourage those boiling lusts they would with eagerness and delight pursue? Methinks that interruption John gives our Saviour, when he was upon the reproof of their pride, looks little better than a design to divert him from a discourse so much against the grain, by telling him a story of their prohibiting one to cast out devils, because he followed not them, Mark ix. 33, 38. How glad are men when they can raise a battery against a command of God, and raise some smart objection, whereby they may shelter themselves from the strictness of it!

[3.] When men cannot shake off the notices of the will and mind of God, they have no pleasure in the consideration of them; which could not possibly be, if there were a real and fixed design to own the mind and law of God as our rule. Subjects or servants that love to obey their prince and master, will delight to read and execute their orders. The devils understand the law of God in their minds, but they loathe the impressions of it upon their wills. Those miserable spirits are bound in chains of darkness, evil habits in their wills, that they have not a thought of obeying that law they know. It was an unclean beast under the law that did not chew the cud; it is a corrupt heart that doth not chew truth by meditation. A natural man is said not to know God, or the things of God; he may know them notionally, but he knows them not affectionately. A sensual soul can have no delight in a spiritual law. To be sensual and not to have the Spirit are inseparable, Jude 19.

Natural men may indeed meditate upon the law and truth of God, but without delight in it; if they take any pleasure in it, it is only as it is knowledge, not as it is a rule; for we delight in nothing that we desire, but upon the same account that we desire it. Natural men desire to know God and some part of his will and law, not out of a sense of their practical excellency, but a natural thirst after knowledge; and if they have a delight, it is in the act of knowing, not in the object known, not in the duties that stream from that knowledge; they design the furnishing their understandings, not the quickening their affections; like idle boys that strike fire, not to warm themselves by the heat, but sport themselves with the sparks; whereas a gracious soul accounts not only his meditation, or the operations of his soul about God and his will to be sweet, but he hath a joy in the object of that meditation, Ps. civ. 34. Many have the knowledge of God, who have no delight in him or his will. Owls have eyes to perceive that there is a sun, but by reason of the weakness of their sight have no pleasure to look upon a beam of it; so neither can a man by nature love or delight in the will of God, because of his natural corruption. That law that riseth up in men for conviction and instruction, they keep down under the power of corruption, making their souls not the sanctuary, but prison of truth, Rom. i. 18. They will keep it down in their hearts, if they cannot keep it out of their heads, and will not endeavour to know and taste the spirit of it.

[4.] There is further a rising and swelling of the heart against the will of God. (1.) Internal. God's law cast against a hard heart is like a ball thrown against a stone wall, by reason of the resistance rebounding the further from it. The meeting of a divine truth and the heart of man, is like the meeting of two tides, the weaker swells and foams. We have a natural antipathy against a divine rule, and therefore when it is clapped close to our consciences, there is a snuffing at it, high reasonings against it, corruption breaks out more strongly; as water poured on lime sets it on fire by an *antiperistasis*, and the more water is cast upon it, the more furiously it burns; or as the sunbeams shining upon a dunghill makes the steams the thicker and the stench the noisomer, neither being the positive cause of the smoke in the lime, or the stench in the dunghill, but by accident the causes of the eruption : Rom. vii. 8, ' But sin taking occasion by the commandment, wrought in me all manner of concupiscence, for without the law sin was dead.' Sin was in a languishing posture, as if it were dead, like a lazy garrison in a city, till upon an alarm from the adversary it takes arms and revives its courage; all the sin in the heart gathers together its force to maintain its standing, like the vapours of the night, which unite themselves more closely to resist the beams of the rising sun. Deep conviction often provokes fierce opposition; sometimes disputes against a divine rule end in blasphemies : Acts xiii. 45, ' Contradicting and blaspheming' are coupled together. Men naturally desire things that are forbidden, and reject things commanded, from the corruption of nature, which affects an unbounded liberty, and is impatient of returning under that yoke it hath shaken off, and therefore rageth against the bars of the law, as the waves roar against the restraint of a bank. When the understanding is dark and the mind ignorant, sin lies as dead : ' A man scarce knows he hath such motions of concupiscence in him, he finds not the least breath of wind, but a full calm in his soul; but when he is awakened by the law, then the viciousness of nature being sensible of an invasion of its empire, arms itself against the divine law, and the more the command is urged, the more vigorously it bends its strength, and more insolently lifts up itself against it.'[*] He perceives more and more atheistical lusts than before; ' all manner of concupiscence,' more leprous and contagious than before. When there are any motions to turn to God, a reluctancy is presently perceived; atheistical thoughts bluster in the mind like the wind, they know not whence they come nor whither they go, so unapt is the heart to any acknowledgment of God as his ruler, and any reunion with him. Hence men are said to ' resist the Holy Ghost,' Acts vii. 51, to fall against it, as the word signifies, as a stone or any ponderous body falls against that which lies in its way; they would dash to pieces or grind to powder that very motion which is made for their instruction, and the Spirit too which makes it, and that not from a fit of passion, but an habitual repugnance. ' Ye always resist,' &c.

(2.) External, it is a fruit of atheism, in the fourth verse of this Psalm : ' Who eat up my people as they eat bread.' How do the revelations of the mind of God meet with opposition! And the carnal world like dogs bark against the shining of the moon! So much men hate the light, that they spurn at the lanterns that bear it; and because they cannot endure the treasure, often fling the earthen vessels against the ground wherein it is held. If the entrance of truth render the market worse for Diana's shrines, the whole city will be in an uproar, Acts xix. 24, 28, 29. When Socrates upon natural principles confuted the heathen idolatry, and asserted the unity of God, the whole cry of Athens, a learned university, is against him, and because he opposed the public received religion, though with an undoubted truth, he must end his life by violence. How hath every corner of the world steamed with the blood of those that would maintain the authority of

[*] Thes. Salmur. De Spiritu Servitutis, Thes. 19.

God in the world! The devil's children will follow the steps of their father, and endeavour to bruise the heel of divine truth, that would endeavour to break the head of corrupt lust.

[5.] Men often seem desirous to be acquainted with the will of God, not out of any respect to his will and to make it their rule, but upon some other consideration. Truth is scarce received as truth. There is more of hypocrisy than sincerity in the pale of the church, and attendance on the mind of God. The outward dowry of a religious profession makes it often more desirable than the beauty. Judas was a follower of Christ for the bag, not out of any affection to the divine revelation. Men sometimes pretend a desire to be acquainted with the will of God, to satisfy their own passions, rather than to conform to God's will. The religion of such is not the judgment of the man, but the passion of the brute. Many entertain a doctrine for the person's sake, rather than a person for the doctrine's sake. and believe a thing because it comes from a man they esteem, as if his lips were more canonical than Scripture.

The apostle implies in the commendation he gives the Thessalonians, 1 Thes. ii. 13, that some receive the word for human interest, not ' as it is in truth the word and will of God,' to command and govern their consciences by its sovereign authority; or else they ' have the truth of God' (as St James speaks of the faith of Christ) ' with respect of persons,' James ii. 1, and receive it not for the sake of the fountain, but of the channel; so that many times the same truth delivered by another is disregarded, which when dropping from the fancy and mouth of a man's own idol, is cried up as an oracle. This is to make not God, but man, the rule; for though we entertain that which materially is the truth of God, yet not formally as his truth, but as conveyed by one we affect; and that we receive a truth and not an error, we owe the obligation to the honesty of the instrument, and not to the strength and clearness of our own judgment. Wrong considerations may give admittance to an unclean as well as a clean beast into the ark of the soul; that which is contrary to the mind of God may be entertained as well as that which is agreeable. It is all one to such, that have no respect to God, what they have; as it is all one to a spunge to suck up the foulest water or the sweetest wine, when either is applied to it.

[6.] Many that entertain the notions of the will and mind of God admit them with unsettled and wavering affections. There is a great levity in the heart of man. The Jews that one day applaud our Saviour with *Hosannahs* as their king, vote his crucifixion the next, and use him as a murderer. We begin in the Spirit and end in the flesh. Our hearts, like lute-strings, are changed with every change of weather, with every appearance of a temptation; scarce one motion of God in a thousand prevails with us for a settled abode. It is a hard task to make a signature of those truths upon our affections, which will with ease pass current with our understandings; our affections will as soon loose them as our understandings embrace them. The heart of man is unstable as water, Gen. xlix. 4, James i. 8. Some were willing to rejoice in John's light, which reflected a lustre on their minds, but not in his heat, which would have conveyed a warmth to their hearts; and the light was pleasing to them but for a season, John v. 35, while their corruptions lay as if they were dead, not when they were awakened. Truth may be admitted one day, and the next day rejected. As Austin saith of a wicked man, he loves the truth shining, but he hates the truth reproving. This is not to make God, but our own humour, our rule and measure.

[7.] Many desire an acquaintance with the law and truth of God, with a design to improve some lust by it, to turn the word of God to be a pander to the breach of his law. This is so far from making God's will our rule, that we make our own vile affections the rule of his law. How many forced interpretations of Scripture have been coined to give consent to the lusts of men, and the divine rule forced to bend and be squared to men's loose and carnal apprehensions! It is a part of the instability or falseness of the heart to 'wrest the Scriptures to their own destruction,' 2 Peter iii. 16, which they could not do, if they did not first wring them to countenance some detestable error or filthy crime. In paradise, the first interpretation made of the first law of God was point blank against the mind of the law-giver, and venomous to the whole race of mankind. Paul himself feared that some might put his doctrine of grace to so ill a use, as to be an altar and sanctuary to shelter their presumption: Rom. vi. 1, 15, 'Shall we then continue in sin, that grace may abound?' Poisonous consequences are often drawn from the sweetest truths; as when God's patience is made a topic whence to argue against his providence, Ps. xciv. 1, or an encourage-ment to commit evil more greedily, as though because he had not presently a revenging hand, he had not an all-seeing eye; or when the doctrine of justification by faith is made use of to depress a holy life; or God's readi-ness to receive returning sinners an encouragement to defer repentance till a death-bed. A liar will hunt for shelter in the reward God gave the midwives that lied to Pharaoh for the preservation of the males of Israel, and Rahab's saving the spies by false intelligence. God knows how to distinguish between grace and corruption, that they may lie close together, or between something of moral goodness and moral evil which may be mixed. We find their fidelity rewarded, which was a moral good; but not their lie approved, which was a moral evil. Nor will Christ's conversing with sinners be a plea for any to thrust themselves into evil company. Christ conversed with sinners as a physician with diseased persons, to cure them, not approve them; others with profligate persons to receive infec-tion from them, not to communicate holiness to them. Satan's children have studied their father's art, who wanted not perverted Scripture to second his temptations against our Saviour, Mat. iv. 4, 6. How often do carnal hearts turn divine revelation to carnal ends, as the sea fresh water into salt! As men subject the precepts of God to carnal interests, so they subject the truths of God to carnal fancies. When men will allegorise the word, and make a humorous and crazy fancy the interpreter of divine oracles, and not the Spirit speaking in the word, this is to enthrone our own imaginations as the rule of God's law, and depose his law from being the rule of our reason; this is to rifle truth of its true mind and intent. It is more to rob a man of his reason, the essential constitutive part of man, than of his estate. This is to refuse an intimate acquaintance with his will. We shall never tell what is the matter of a precept, or the matter of a promise, if we impose a sense upon it contrary to the plain meaning of it; thereby we shall make the law of God to have a distinct sense according to the variety of men's imaginations, and so make every man's fancy a law to himself.

Now, that this unwillingness to have a spiritual acquaintance with divine truth is a disowning God as our rule, and a setting up self in his stead, is evident, because this unwillingness respects truth,

First, As it is most spiritual and holy. A fleshly mind is most contrary to a spiritual law, and particularly as it is a searching and discovering law, that would dethrone all other rules in the soul. As men love to be without a holy God in the world, so they love to be without a holy law, the transcript and image of God's holiness, in their hearts, and without holy men, the lights kindled by the Father of lights. As the holiness of God, so the holiness of the law most offends a carnal heart: Isa. xxx. 11, ' Cause the Holy One of Israel to cease from before us ; prophesy [not] to us right things.' They could not endure God as a holy one. Herein God places their rebellion, rejecting him as their rule : ver. 9, ' Rebellious children, that will not hear the law of the Lord.' The more pure and precious any discovery of God is, the more it is disrelished by the world. As spiritual sins are sweetest to a carnal heart, so spiritual truths are most distasteful. The more of the brightness of the sun any beam conveys, the more offensive it is to a distempered eye.

Secondly, As it doth most relate to, or lead to God. The devil directs his fiercest batteries against those doctrines in the word, and those graces in the heart, which most exalt God, debase man, and bring men to the lowest subjection to their Creator. Such is the doctrine and grace of justifying faith. That men hate not knowledge as knowledge, but as it directs them to choose the fear of the Lord, was the determination of the Holy Ghost long ago : Prov. i. 29, ' For that they hated knowledge, and did not choose the fear of the Lord.' Whatsoever respects God, clears up guilt, witnesses man's revolt to him, rouseth up conscience, and moves to a return to God, a man naturally runs from, as Adam did from God, and seeks a shelter in some weak bushes of error, rather than appear before it. Not that men are unwilling to inquire into and contemplate some divine truths which lie furthest from the heart, and concern not themselves immediately with the rectifying the soul. They may view them with such a pleasure as some might take in beholding the miracles of our Saviour, who could not endure his searching doctrine. The light of speculation may be pleasant, but the light of conviction is grievous, that which galls their conciences, and would affect them with a sense of their duty to God.

Is it not easy to perceive that when a man begins to be serious in the concerns of the honour of God and the duty of his soul, he feels a reluctancy within him, even against the pleas of conscience, which evidenceth that some unworthy principle has got footing in the hearts of men, which fights against the declarations of God without and the impressions of the law of God within, at the same time when a man's own conscience takes part with it, which is the substance of the apostle's discourse, Rom. vii. 15, 16, &c.

Close discourses of the honour of God and our duty to him are irksome, when men are upon a merry pin. They are like a damp in a mine, that takes away their breath ; they shuffle them out as soon as they can, and are as unwilling to retain the speech of them in their mouths, as the knowledge of them in their hearts. Gracious speeches, instead of bettering many men, distemper them, as sometimes sweet perfumes affect a weak head with aches.

Thirdly, As it is most contrary to self. Men are unwilling to acquaint themselves with any truth that leads to God, because it leads from self. Every part of the will of God is more or less displeasing, as it sounds harsh against some carnal interest men would set above God, or as a mate with him. Man cannot desire any intimacy with that law which he regards as a bird of prey, to pick out his right eye or gnaw off his right hand, his lust dearer than himself. The reason we have such hard thoughts of God's will, is because we have such high thoughts of ourselves. It is a hard matter to believe or will that which hath no affinity with some principle in the understanding, and no interest in our will and passions. Our unwillingness to be acquainted with the will of God, ariseth from the disproportion between that and our corrupt hearts ; we are ' alienated from the life of God in our minds,' Eph. iv. 18, 19. As we live not like God, so we neither think or will as God.

There is an antipathy in the heart of man against that doctrine which teaches us to deny ourselves, and be under the rule of another ; but whatsoever favours the ambition, lusts, and profits of men is easily entertainable. Many are fond of those sciences which may enrich their understandings, and grate not upon their sensual delights. Many have an admirable dexterity in finding out philosophical reasons, mathematical demonstrations, or raising observations upon the records of history, and spend much time and many serious and affectionate thoughts in the study of them. In those they have not immediately to do with God ; their beloved pleasures are not impaired. It is a satisfaction to self, without the exercise of any hostility against it. But had those sciences been against self, as much as the law and will of God, they had long since been rooted out of the world. Why did the young man turn his back upon the law of Christ ? Because of his worldly self. Why did the Pharisees mock at the doctrine of our Saviour, and not at their own traditions ? Because of covetous self. Why did the Jews slight the person of our Saviour, and put him to death, after the reading so many credentials of his being sent from heaven ? Because of ambitious self, that the Romans might not come and take away their kingdom. If the law of God were fitted to the humours of self, it would be readily and cordially observed by all men. Self is the measure of a world of seeming religious actions ; while God seems to be the object and his law the motive, self is the rule and end : Zech. vii. 5, ' Did you fast unto me ? ' &c.

(2.) As men discover their disowning the will of God as a rule by unwillingness to be acquainted with it, so they discover it by the contempt of it, after they cannot avoid the notions and some impressions of it. The rule of God is burdensome to a sinner ; he flies from it as from a frightful bugbear and unpleasant yoke. Sin against the knowledge of the law is therefore called a ' going back from the commandment of God's lips,' Job xxiii. 12 ; a ' casting God's word behind them,' Ps. l. 17, as a contemptible thing, fitter to be trodden in the dirt than lodged in the heart. Nay, it is a casting it off as an abominable thing, for so the word רגז signifies : Hos. viii. 3, ' Israel hath cast off the thing that is good ; ' an utter refusal of God : Jer. xliv. 16, ' As for the word which thou hast spoken to us in the name of the Lord, we will not hearken.' In the slight of his precepts, his essential perfections are slighted. In disowning his will as a rule, we disown all those attributes which flow from his will, as goodness, righteousness, and truth. As an act of the divine understanding is supposed to precede the act of the divine will, so we slight the infinite reason of God. Every law, though it proceeds from the will of the lawgiver, and doth formally consist in an act of the will, yet it doth presuppose an act of the understanding. If ' the commandment be holy, just, and good,' as it is (Rom. vii. 12), if it be the image of God's holiness, a transcript of his righteousness and the efflux of his goodness, then in every breach of it, dirt is cast upon those attributes which shine in it, and a slight of all the regards he hath to his own honour, and all the provisions he makes for his creature. This atheism or contempt of God, is more taken notice of by God than the matter of the sin itself ; as a respect to God, in a weak and imperfect obedience, is more than the matter of the obedience itself, because it is an acknowledgment of God, so a contempt of God, in an act of disobedience, is more than the matter of disobedience. The creature stands, in such an act, not only in a posture of distance from God, but defiance of him. It was not the bare act of murder and adultery which Nathan charged upon David, but the atheistical principle which spirited those evil acts. The ' despising the commandment of the Lord' was the venom of them, 2 Sam. xii. 9, 10. It is possible to break a law without contempt ; but when men pretend to believe there is a God, and that this is the law of God, it shews a contempt of his majesty. Men naturally account God's laws too strict, his yoke too heavy, and his limits too strait ; and he that liveth in a contempt of this law, curseth God in his life. How can they believe there is a God, who despise him as a ruler ? How can they believe him to be a guide, that disdain to follow him ? To think we firmly believe a God, without living conformably to his law, is an idle and vain imagination. The true and sensible motion* of a God cannot subsist with disorder and an affected unrighteousness.

This contempt is seen,

[1.] In any presumptuous breach of any part of his law. Such sins are frequently called in Scripture rebellions, which are a denial of the allegiance we owe to him. By a wilful refusal of his right in one part, we root up the foundation of that rule he doth justly challenge over us. His right is as extensive to command us in one thing as in another. And if it be disowned in one thing, it is virtually disowned in all, and the whole statute-book of God is contemned: James ii. 10, 11, 'Whosoever shall keep the whole law, and yet offend in one point, is guilty of all.' A willing breaking one part, though there be a willing observance of all the other points of it, is a breach of the whole, because the authority of God, which gives sanction to the whole, is slighted. The obedience to the rest is dissembled; for the love which is the root of all obedience is wanting, for 'love is the fulfilling the whole law,' Rom. xiii. 10. The rest are obeyed because they cross not carnal desire so much as the other, and so it is an observance of himself, not of God. Besides, the authority of God, which is not prevalent to restrain us from the breach of one point, would be of as little force with us to restrain us from the breach of all the rest, did the allurements of the flesh give us as strong a diversion from the one as from the other. And though the command that is transgressed be the least in the whole law, yet the authority which enjoins it is the same with that which enacts the greatest. And it is not so much the matter of the command, as the authority commanding, which lays the obligation.

[2.] In the natural averseness to the declarations of God's will and mind, which way soever they tend. Since man affected to be as God, he desires to be boundless; he would not have fetters, though they be golden ones, and conduce to his happiness; though the law of God be a strength to them, yet they will not: Isa. xxx. 15, 'In returning shall be your strength; and you would not.' They would not have a bridle to restrain them from running into the pit, nor be hedged in by the law, though for their security, as if they thought it too slavish and low-spirited a thing to be guided by the will of another. Hence man is compared to a wild ass, that loves to 'snuff up the wind in the wilderness at her pleasure,' rather than come under the guidance of God, Jer. ii. 24. From whatsoever quarter of the heavens you pursue her, she will run to the other.

The Israelites could not endure what was commanded, Heb. xii. 20, though in regard of the moral part, agreeable to what they found written in their own nature, and to the observance whereof they had the highest obligations of any people under heaven, since God had by many prodigies delivered them from a cruel slavery, the memory of which prefaced the Decalogue: Exod. xx. 2, 'I am the Lord thy God, which have brought thee out of the land of Egypt, out of the house of bondage.' They could not think of the rule of their duty but they must reflect upon the grand incentive of it in their redemption from Egyptian thraldom ; yet this people were

* Qu. 'notion'?—ED.

cross to God, which way soever he moved. When they were in the brick-kilns, they cried for deliverance; when they had heavenly manna, they longed for their onions and garlic. In Num. xiv. 3, they repent of their deliverance from Egypt, and talk of returning again to seek the remedy of their evils in the hands of their cruellest enemies; and would rather put themselves into the irons whence God had delivered them, than believe one word of the promise of God for giving them a fruitful land. But when · Moses tells them God's order, that they should turn back by the way of the Red Sea, ver. 25, and that God had confirmed it by an oath that they should not see the land of Canaan, ver. 28, they then run cross to this com-mand of God, and instead of marching towards the Red Sea, which they had wished for before, they will go up to Canaan, as in spite of God and his threatening, 'We will go to the place which the Lord hath promised,' ver. 40, which Moses calls a 'transgressing the commandments of the Lord,' ver. 41. They would presume to go up, notwithstanding Moses his pro-hibition, and are smitten by the Amalekites. When God gives them a precept, with a promise to go up to Canaan, they long for Egypt; when God commands them to return to the Red Sea, which was nearer to the place they longed for, they will shift sides and go up to Canaan, Num. xxi. 4, 5, &c.;* and when they found they were to traverse the solitudes of the desert, they took pet against God, and instead of thanking him for the late victory against the Canaanites, they reproach him for his conduct from Egypt, and the manna wherewith he nourished them in the wilderness. They would not go to Canaan the way God had chosen, nor preserve them-selves by the means God had ordained. They would not be at God's dis-posal, but complain of the badness of the way and the lightness of manna, empty of any necessary juice to sustain their nature. They murmuringly solicit the will and power of God to change all that order which he had resolved in his counsel, and take another, conformable to their vain, foolish desires. And they signified thereby that they would invade his conduct, and that he should act according to their fancy, which the psalmist calls a 'tempting of God, and limiting the Holy One of Israel,' Ps. lxxviii. 41.

To what point soever the declarations of God stand, the will of man turns the quite contrary way. Is not the carriage of this nation, the best then in the world, a discovery of the depth of our natural corruption, how cross man is to God? And that charge God brings against them may be brought against all men by nature, that they 'despise his judgment,' and have a rooted abhorrency of his statutes in their soul, Lev. xxvi. 43. No sooner had they recovered from one rebellion, but they revolted to another; so difficult a thing it is for man's nature to be rendered capable of conforming to the will of God. The carriage of his people is but a copy of the nature of mankind, and is 'written for our admonition,' 1 Cor. x. 11. From this temper men are said to 'make void the law of God,' Ps. cxix. 126; to make it of no obligation, an antiquated and moth-eaten record. And the Pharisees, by setting up their traditions against the will of God, are said to make his law 'of none effect,' to strip it of all its authority, as the word signifies, Mat. xv. 6, ἠκυρώσατε.

[3.] We have the greatest slight of that will of God which is most for his honour and his greatest pleasure. It is the nature of man, ever since Adam, to do so: Hosea vi. 6, 7, 'God desired mercy, and not sacrifice; the know-ledge of himself more than burnt-offering. But they, like men,' as Adam, 'have transgressed the covenant,' invade God's rights, and not let him be Lord of one tree.

* Daille, Serm. 1 Cor. x. Serm. 9.

We are more curious observers of the fringes of the law than of the greater concerns of it. The Jews were diligent in sacrifices and offerings, which God did not urge upon them as principals, but as types of other things, but negligent of the faith which was to be established by him; holiness, mercy, pity, which concerned the honour of God as governor of the world, and were imitations of the holiness and goodness of God, they were strangers to. This is God's complaint, Isa. i. 11, 12, and 16, 17.

We shall find our hearts most averse to the observation of those laws which are eternal and essential to righteousness; such that he could not but command, as he is a righteous governor; in the observation of which we come nearest to him, and express his image more clearly, as those laws for an inward and spiritual worship, a supreme affection to him. God, in regard of his righteousness and holiness of his nature, and the excellency of his being, could not command the contrary to these; but this part of his will our hearts most swell against, our corruption doth most snarl at, whereas those laws which are only positive, and have no intrinsic righteousness in them, but depend purely upon the will of the lawgiver, and may be changed at his pleasure (which the other, that have an intrinsic righteousness in them, cannot), we better comply with than that part of his will that doth express more of the righteousness of his nature, Ps. l. 6, 17, 19, such as the ceremonial part of worship, and the ceremonial law among the Jews. We are more willing to observe order in some outward attendances and glavering devotions, than discard secret affections to evil, crucify inward lusts and delightful thoughts. A 'hanging down the head like a bulrush' is not difficult, but the breaking the heart like a potter's vessel to shreds and dust (a sacrifice God delights in, whereby the excellency of God and the vileness of the creature is owned), goes against the grain. To cut off an outward branch is not so hard as to hack at the root. What God most loathes, as most contrary to his will, we most love. No sin did God so severely hate, and no sin were the Jews more inclined unto, than that of idolatry. The heathen had not 'changed their God' as the Jews had 'changed their glory,' Jer. ii. 11; and all men are naturally tainted with this sin, which is so contrary to the holy and excellent nature of God. By how much the more defect there is of purity in our respects to God, by so much the more respect there is to some idol within or without us, to humour, custom, and interest, &c.

Never did any law of God meet with so much opposition as Christianity, which was the design of God from the first promise to the exhibiting the Redeemer, and from thence to the end of the world. All people drew swords at first against it. The Romans prepared yokes for their neighbours, but provided temples for the idols those people worshipped. But Christianity, the choicest design and most delightful part of the will of God, never met with a kind entertainment at first in any place. Rome, that entertained all others, persecuted this with fire and sword, though sealed by greater testimonies from heaven than their own records could report in favour of their idols.

[4.] In running the greatest hazards, and exposing ourselves to more trouble to cross the will of God, than is necessary to the observance of it. It is a vain charge men bring against the divine precepts, that they are rigorous, severe, difficult, when, besides the contradiction to our Saviour, who tells us his yoke is easy and his burden light, they thwart their own calm reason and judgment. Is there not more difficulty to be vicious, covetous, violent, cruel, than to be virtuous, charitable, kind? Doth the will of God enjoin that that is not conformable to right reason and secretly delightful in the exercise and issue? And, on the contrary, what doth Satan and the world engage us in that is not full of molestation and hazard? Is it a sweet and comely thing to combat continually against our own consciences, and resist our own light, and commence a perpetual quarrel against ourselves, as we ordinarily do when we sin? They, in the prophet, Micah vi. 6, 7, 8, would be at the expense of ' thousands of rams and ten thousand rivers of oil,' if they could compass them; yea, would strip themselves of their natural affection to their first-born to expiate the ' sin of their soul,' rather than to ' do justice, love mercy, and walk humbly with God;' things more conducible to the honour of God, the welfare of the world, the security of their souls, and of a more easy practice than the offerings they wished for.

Do not men then disown God, when they will walk in ways hedged with thorns, wherein they meet with the arrows of conscience at every turn in their sides, and slide down to an everlasting punishment, sink under an intolerable slavery, to contradict the will of God? When they will prefer a sensual satisfaction, with a combustion in their consciences, violation of their reasons, gnawing cares and weary travels, before the honour of God, the dignity of their natures, the happiness of peace and health, which might be preserved at a cheaper rate than they are at to destroy them?

[5.] In the unwillingness and awkwardness of the heart, when it is to pay God a service. Men ' do evil with both hands earnestly,' Micah vii. 3, but do good with one hand faintly; no life in the heart nor any diligence in the hand. What slight and loose thoughts of God doth this unwillingness imply! It is a wrong to his providence, as though we were not under his government, and had no need of his assistance; a wrong to his excellency, as though there were no amiableness in him to make his service desirable; an injury to his goodness and power, as if he were not able or willing to reward the creature's obedience, or careless, not to take notice of it. It is a sign we receive little satisfaction in him, and that there is a great unsuitableness between him and us.

First, There is a kind of constraint in the first engagement. We are rather pressed to it than enter ourselves volunteers. What we call service to God, is done, naturally, much against our wills; it is not a delightful food, but a bitter potion; we are rather haled than run to it. There is a contradiction of sin within us against our service, as there was a contradiction of sinners without our Saviour against his doing the will of God. Our hearts are unwieldy to any spiritual service of God; we are fain to use a violence with them sometimes. Hezekiah, it is said, ' walked before the Lord with a perfect heart,' 2 Kings xx. 3; he walked, he made himself to walk. Man naturally cares not for a walk with God; if he hath any communion with him, it is with such a dulness and heaviness of spirit, as if he wished himself out of his company. Man's nature, being contrary to holiness, hath an aversion to any act of homage to God, because holiness must at least be pretended; in every duty wherein we have a communion with God, holiness is requisite; now, as men are against the truth of holiness because it is unsuitable to them, so they are not friends to those duties which require it, and for some space divert them from the thoughts of their beloved lusts. The word of the Lord is a yoke, prayer a drudgery, obedience a strange element. We are like fish, that ' drink up iniquity like water,' Job xv. 16, and come not to the bank without the force of an angle; no more willing to do service for God than a fish is of itself to do service for man. It is a constrained act to satisfy conscience, and such are servile, not son-like performances, and spring from bondage more than affection; if conscience, like a task-master, did not scourge them to duty, they would never perform it.

Let us appeal to ourselves whether we are not more unwilling to secret, closet, hearty duty to God, than to join with others in some external service; as if those inward services were a going to the rack, and rather our penance than privilege. How much service hath God in the world from the same principle that vagrants perform their task in Bridewell! How glad are many of evasions to back them in the neglect of the commands of God, of corrupt reasonings from the flesh to waylay an act of obedience, and a multitude of excuses to blunt the edge of the precept! The very service of God shall be a pretence to deprive him of the obedience due to him. Saul will not be ruled by God's will in the destroying the cattle of the Amalekites, but by his own; and will impose upon the will and wisdom of God, judging God mistaken in his command, and that the cattle God thought fittest to be meat to the fowls were fitter to be sacrifices on the altar, 1 Sam. xv. 3, 9, 15, 21.

If we do perform any part of his will, is it not for our own ends, to have some deliverance from trouble? Isa. xxvi. 16, 'In trouble have they visited thee, they poured out a prayer, when thy chastening was upon them.' In affliction, he shall find them kneeling in homage and devotion; in prosperity, he shall feel them kicking with contempt; they can pour out a prayer in distress, and scarce drop one when they are delivered.

Secondly, There is a slightness in our service of God. We are loath to come into his presence, and when we do come, we are loath to continue with him. We pay not an homage to him heartily, as to our lord and governor; we regard him not as our master, whose work we ought to do, and whose honour we ought to aim at.

First, In regard of the matter of service. When the torn, the lame, and the sick is offered to God, Mal. i. 13, 14, so thin and lean a sacrifice that you might have thrown it to the ground with a puff, so some understand the meaning of 'you have snuffed at it.' Men have naturally such slight thoughts of the majesty and law of God that they think any service is good enough for him, and conformable to his law. The dullest and deadest times we think fittest to pay God a service in; when sleep is ready to close our eyes, and we are unfit to serve ourselves, we think it a fit time to open our hearts to God. How few *morning sacrifices* hath God from many persons and families! Men leap out of their beds to their carnal pleasures or worldly employments, without any thought of their Creator and Preserver, or any reflection upon his will as the rule of our daily obedience; and as many reserve the dregs of their lives, their old age, to offer up their souls to God, so they reserve the dregs of the day, their sleeping time, for the offering up their service to him. How many grudge to spend their best time in the serving the will of God, and reserve for him the sickly and rheumatic part of their lives; the remainder of that which the devil and their own lusts have fed upon!

Would not any prince or governor judge a present half eaten up by wild beasts, or that which died in a ditch, a contempt of his royalty? A corrupt thing is too base and vile for so great a king as God is, whose name is dreadful, Mal. i. 14. When by age men are weary of their own bodies, they would present them to God, yet grudgingly, as if a tired body were too good for him, snuffing at the command for service. God calls for our best, and we give him the worst.

Secondly, In respect of frame. We think any frame will serve God's turn; which speaks our slight of God as a ruler. Man naturally performs duty with an unholy heart, whereby it becomes an abomination to God:

Prov. xxviii. 9, 'He that turns away his ear from hearing the law, even his prayers shall be an abomination to God.' The services which he commands he hates for their evil frames or corrupt ends: Amos v. 21, 'I hate, I despise your feast-days, I will not smell in your solemn assemblies.' God requires gracious services, and we give him corrupt ones. We do not rouse up our hearts, as David called upon his lute and harp to awake, Ps. lvii. 8. Our hearts are not given to him, we put him off with bodily exercise; the heart is but ice to what it doth not affect. There is not that natural vigour in the observance of God which we have in worldly business. When we see a liveliness in men in other things, change the scene into a notion towards God, how suddenly doth their vigour shrink, and their hearts freeze into sluggishness! Many times we serve God as languishingly as if we were afraid he should accept us, and pray as coldly as if we were unwilling he should hear us, and take away that lust by which we are governed, and which conscience forces us to pray against; as if we were afraid God should set up his own throne and government in our hearts. How fleeting are we in divine meditation, how sleepy in spiritual exercises, but in other exercises active! The soul doth not awaken itself, and excite those animal and vital spirits which it will in bodily recreations and sports, much less the powers of the soul; whereby it is evident we prefer the latter before any service to God. Since there is a fulness of animal spirits, why might they not be excited in holy duties as well as in other operations, but that there is a reluctancy in the soul to exercise its supremacy in this case, and perform anything becoming a creature in subjection to God as a ruler?

It is evident also in the distractions we have in his service. How loath are we to serve God fixedly one hour, nay, a part of an hour, notwithstanding all the thoughts of his majesty, and the eternity of glory set before our eye! What man is there since the fall of Adam that served God one hour without many wanderings and unsuitable thoughts unfit for that service! How ready are our hearts to start out and unite themselves with any worldly objects that please us!

Weariness in it evidenceth it. To be weary of our dulness signifies a desire; to be weary of service signifies a discontent to be ruled by God. How tired are we in the performance of spiritual duties, when in the vain triflings of time we have a perpetual motion. How will many willingly revel whole nights, when their hearts will flag at the threshold of a religious service; like Dagon, 1 Sam. v. 4, lose both our heads to think, and hands to act, when the ark of God is present. Some in the prophet wished the new moon and the Sabbath over, that they might sell their corn, and be busied again in their worldly affairs, Amos viii. 5. A slight and weariness of the Sabbath was a slight of the Lord of the Sabbath, and of that freedom from the yoke and rule of sin which was signified by it. The design of the sacrifices in the new moon was to signify a rest from the tyranny of sin, and a consecration to the spiritual service of God. Servants that are quickly weary of their work are weary of the authority of their master that enjoins it. If our hearts had a value for God, it would be with us as with the needle to the loadstone, there would be upon his beck a speedy motion to him, and a fixed union with him. When the judgments and affections of the saints shall be fully refined in glory, they shall be willing to behold the face of God, and be under his government to eternity, without any weariness; as the holy angels have owned God as their sovereign near these six thousand years without being weary of running on his errands. But, alas! while the flesh clogs us, there will be some relics of unwillingness to hear his injunctions, and weariness in performing them; though men may excuse those things by extrinsic causes, yet God's unerring judgment calls it a weariness of himself: Isa. xliii. 22, 'Thou hast not called upon me, O Jacob, but thou hast been weary of me, O Israel.' Of this he taxeth his own people, when he tells them he would have 'the beasts of the field, the dragons, and the owls;' the Gentiles, that the Jews counted no better than such, to honour him, and acknowlege him their rule in a way of duty, ver. 20, 21.

[6.] This contempt is seen in a deserting the rule of God, when our expectations are not answered upon our service. When services are performed from carnal principles, they are soon cast off when carnal ends meet not with desired satisfaction. But when we own ourselves God's servants, and God our master, 'our eyes will wait upon him till he have mercy on us,' Ps. cxxiii. 2. It is one part of the duty we owe to God as our master in heaven to 'continue in prayer,' Col. iv. 1, 2. And by the same reason in all other service, and to 'watch in the same with thanksgiving;' to watch for occasions of praise, to watch with cheerfulness for further manifestations of his will, strength to perform it, success in the performance, that we may from all draw matter of praise. As we are in a posture of obedience to his precepts, so we should be in a posture of waiting for the blessing of it.

But naturally we reject the duty we owe to God if he do not speed the blessing we expect from him. How many do secretly mutter the same as they in Job xxi. 15, 'What is the Almighty that we should serve him, and what profit shall we have if we pray to him?' They serve not God out of conscience to his commands, but for some carnal profit; and if God make them to wait for it, they will not stay his leisure, but cease soliciting him any longer. Two things are expressed; that God was not worthy of any homage from them,—'What is the Almighty that we should serve him?'— and that the service of him would not bring in a good revenue or an advantage of that kind they expected. Interest drives many men on to some kind of service, and when they do not find an advance of that, they will acknowledge God no more; but like some beggars, if you give them not upon their asking and calling you good master, from blessing they will turn to cursing.

How often do men do that secretly, practically if not plainly, which Job's wife advised him to, curse God, and cast off that disguise of integrity they had assumed! Job ii. 9, 'Dost thou still retain thy integrity? Curse God.' What a stir, and pulling, and crying is here! Cast off all thoughts of religious service, and be at daggers drawing with that God, who for all thy service of him has made thee so wretched a spectacle to men, and a banquet for worms. The like temper is deciphered in the Jews: Mal. iii. 14, 'It is in vain to serve God; and what profit is it that we have kept his ordinances, that we have walked mournfully before the Lord?' What profit is it that we have regarded his statutes, and carried ourselves in a way of subjection to God as our sovereign, when we inherit nothing but sorrow, and the idolatrous neighbours swim in all kind of pleasures? As if it were the most miserable thing to acknowledge God. If men have not the benefits they expect, they think God unrighteous in himself, and injurious to them, in not conferring the favour they imagine they have merited; and if they have not that recompence, they will deny God that subjection they owe to him as creatures. Grace moves to God upon a sense of duty, corrupt nature upon a sense of interest; sincerity is encouraged by gracious returns, but is not melted away by God's delay or refusal. Corrupt nature would have God at its beck, and steers a course of duty by hope of some carnal profits, not by a sense of the sovereignty of God.

[7.] This contempt is seen in breaking promises with God. One while the conscience of a man makes vows of new obedience, and perhaps binds himself with many an oath ; but they prove like Jonah's gourd, withering the next day after their birth. This was Pharaoh's temper ; under a storm he would submit to God, and let Israel go, but when the storm is ended, he will not be under God's control, and Israel's slavery shall be increased. The fear of divine wrath makes many a sinner turn his back upon his sin, and the love of his ruling lust makes him turn his back upon his true Lord. This is from the prevalency of sin, that disputes with God for the sovereignty.*

When God hath sent a sharp disease, as a messenger to bind men to their beds, and make an interruption of their sinful pleasures, their mouths are full of promises of a new life, in hope to escape the just vengeance of God. The sense of hell, which strikes strongly upon them, makes them full of such pretended resolutions when they howl upon their beds. But if God be pleased in his patience to give them a respite, to take off the chains wherewith he seemed to be binding them for destruction, and recruit their strength, they are more earnest in their sins than they were in their promises of a reformation, as if they had got the mastery of God, and had outwitted him. How often doth God charge them of not returning to him after a succession of judgments ! Amos iv. 6–11. So hard it is, not only to allure, but to scourge men to an acknowledgment of God as their ruler.

Consider, then,

Are we not naturally inclined to disobey the known will of God ? Can we say, Lord, for thy sake we refrain the thing to which our hearts incline ? Do we not allow ourselves to be licentious, earthly, vain, proud, revengeful, though we know it will offend him ? Have we not been peevishly cross to his declared will ? Run counter to him and those laws which express most of the glory of his holiness ? Is not this to disown him as our rule ? Did we never wish there were no law to bind us, no precept to check our idols ? What is this, but to wish that God would depose himself from being our governor, and leave us to our own conduct ? or else to wish that he were as unholy as ourselves, as careless of his own laws as we are ; that is, that he were no more a God than we, a God as sinful and unrighteous as ourselves ? He whose heart riseth against the law of God to unlaw it, riseth against the author of that law to undeify him. He that casts contempt upon the dearest thing God hath in the world, that which is the image of his holiness, the delight of his soul ; that which he hath given a special charge to maintain, and that because it is holy, just, and good ; would not stick to rejoice at the destruction of God himself. If God's holiness and righteousness in the beam† be despised, much more will an immense goodness and holiness in the fountain be rejected ? He that wisheth a beam far from his eyes, because it offends and scorcheth him, can be no friend to the sun from whence that beam doth issue. How unworthy a creature is man, since he only, a rational creature, is the sole being that withdraws itself from the rule of God in this earth ? And how miserable a creature is he also, since, departing from the order of God's goodness, he falls into the order of his justice ; and while he refuseth God to be the rule of his life, he cannot avoid him being the judge of his punishment. It is this is the original of all sin, and the fountain of all our misery.

This is the first thing man disowns, the rule which God sets him.

2. Man naturally owns any other rule rather than that of God's prescribing. The law of God orders one thing, the heart of man desires another.

---

* Reyn.   † Qu. 'stream'?—Ed.

There is not the basest thing in the world, but man would sooner submit to be guided by it, rather than by the holiness of God; and when anything that God commands crosses our own wills, we value it no more, than we would the advice of a poor despicable beggar.

How many are 'lovers of pleasure, more than lovers of God!' 2 Tim. iii. 4. To make something which contributes to the perfection of nature, as learning, wisdom, moral virtues, our rule, would be more tolerable. But to pay that homage to a swinish pleasure, which is the right of God, is an inexcusable contempt of him. The greatest excellency in the world is infinitely below God; much more a bestial delight, which is both disgraceful and below the nature of man. If we made the vilest creature on earth our idol, it is more excusable than to be the slave of a brutish pleasure. The viler the thing is that doth possess the throne in our heart, the greater contempt it is of him who can only claim a right to it and is worthy of it. Sin is the first object of man's election, as soon as the faculty whereby he chooses comes to exercise its power; and it is so dear to man, that it is, in the estimate of our Saviour, counted as the right hand and the right eye, dear, precious, and useful members.

(1.) The rule of Satan is owned before the rule of God. The natural man would rather be under the guidance of Satan than the yoke of his Creator. Adam chose him to be his governor in paradise. No sooner had Satan spoke of God in a way of derision—Gen. iii. 1, 5, 'Yea, hath God said?'—but man follows his counsel and approves of the scoff; and the greatest part of his posterity have not been wiser by his fall, but would rather ramble in the devil's wilderness than to stay in God's fold. It is by the sin of man that the devil is become the god of the world, as if men were the electors of him to the government. Sin is an election of him for a lord, and a putting the soul under his government. Those that live according to the course of the world, and are loath to displease it, are under the government of the prince of it. The greatest part of the works done in the world is to enlarge the kingdom of Satan. For how many ages were the laws whereby the greatest part of the world was governed in the affairs of religion, the fruits of his usurpation and policy! When temples were erected to him, priests consecrated to his service, the rites used in most of the worship of the world were either of his own coining, or the misapplying the rites God had ordained to himself under the notion of a god; whence the apostle calls all idolatrous feasts 'the table of devils,' 'the cup of devils,' 'sacrifice to devils,' 'fellowship with devils,' 1 Cor. x. 20, 21. Devils being the real object of the pagan worship, though not formally intended by the worshipper, though in some parts of the Indies the direct and peculiar worship is to the devil, that he might not hurt them; and though the intention of others was to offer to God and not the devil, yet since the action was contrary to the will of God, he regards it as a sacrifice to devils. It was not the intention of Jeroboam to establish priests to the devil when he consecrated them to the service of his calves, for Jehu afterwards calls them 'the servants of the Lord:' 2 Kings x. 23, 'See if there be here none of the servants of the Lord,' to distinguish them from the servants of Baal, signifying that the true God was worshipped under those images, and not Baal, nor any of the gods of the heathens; yet Scripture couples the calves and devils together, and ascribes the worship given to one to be given to the other. 2 Chron. xi. 15, 'He ordained him priests for the high places, and for the devils, and for the calves which he had made;' so that they were sacrifices to devils, notwithstanding the intention of Jeroboam and his subjects that had set them up and worshipped them, because they were contrary to the mind of God, and agreeable to the doctrine and mind of Satan, though the object of their worship in their own intention were not the devil, but some deified man or some canonised saint. The intention makes not a good action ; if so, when men kill the best servants of God with a design to do God service, as our Saviour foretells, John xvi. 2, the action would not be murder, yet who can call it otherwise, since God is wronged in the persons of his servants ? Since most of the worship of the world, which men's corrupt natures incline them to, is false and different from the revealed will of God, it is a practical acknowledgment of the devil as the governor, by acknowledging and practising those doctrines which have not the stamp of divine revelation upon them, but were minted by Satan to depress the honour of God in the world. It doth concern men then to take good heed, that in their acts of worship they have a divine rule, otherwise it is an owning the devil as the rule, for there is no medium. Whatsoever is not from God is from Satan.

But to bring this closer to us, and consider that which is more common among us. Men that are in a natural condition, and wedded to their lusts, are under the paternal government of Satan: John viii. 44, ' Ye are of your father the devil, and the lusts of your father you will do.' If we divide sin into spiritual and carnal, which division comprehends all, the devil's authority is owned in both : in spiritual, we conform to his *example*, because those he commits ; in carnal, we obey his *will*, because those he directs ; he acts the one, and sets us a *copy ;* he tempts to the other, and gives us a kind of a *precept.* Thus man by nature being a willing servant of sin, is more desirous to be bound in the devil's iron chains than in God's silken cords.

What greater atheism can there be than to use God as if he were inferior to the devil ! to take the part of his greatest enemy, who drew all others into the faction against him ! to pleasure Satan by offending God, and gratify our adversary with the injury of our Creator ! For a subject to take arms against his prince with the deadliest enemy both himself and prince hath in the whole word, adds a greater blackness to the rebellion.

(2.) The more visible rule preferred before God in the world is man. The opinion of the world is more our rule than the precept of God, and many men's abstinence from sin is not from a sense of the divine will, no, nor from a principle of reason, but from an affection to some man on whom they depend, or fear of punishment from a superior ; the same principle with that in a ravenous beast, who abstains from what he desires for fear only of a stick or club. Men will walk with the herds, go in fashion with the most, speak and act as the most do. While we ' conform to the world,' we cannot perform a ' reasonable service' to God, nor prove, nor approve practically, ' what the good and acceptable will of God is.' The apostle puts them in opposition to one another, Rom. xii. 1, 2.

This appears,

[1.] In complying more with the dictates of men than the will of God. Men draw encouragement from God's forbearance, to sin more freely against him, but the fear of punishment for breaking the will of man lays a restraint upon them ; the fear of man is a more powerful curb to restrain men in their duty than the fear of God. So we may please a friend, a master, a governor, we are regardless whether we please God or no ; men-pleasers are more than God-pleasers. Man is more advanced as a rule than God, when we submit to human orders, and stagger and dispute against divine. Would not a prince think himself slighted in his authority, if any of his servants should decline his commands, by the order of one of his subjects ? And will not God make the same account of us when we deny or delay our obedience for fear of one of his creatures? In the fear of man we as little acknowledge God for our sovereign as we do for our comforter: Isa. li. 12, 13, 'I, even I, am he that comforteth you: who art thou, that thou shouldest be afraid of a man that shall die, &c., and forgettest the Lord thy maker,' &c. We put a slight upon God, as if he were not able to bear us out in our duty to him, and uncapable to balance the strength of an arm of flesh.

[2.] In observing that which is materially the will of God, not because it is his will, but the injunctions of men. As the word of God may be received, yet not as his word, so the will of God may be performed, yet not as his will. It is materially done, but not formally obeyed. An action, and obedience in that action, are two things; as when man commands the ceasing from all works of the ordinary calling on the Sabbath, it is the same that God enjoins; the cessation or attendance of his servants on the hearing the word are conformable in the matter of it to the will of God, but it is only conformable in the obediential part of the acts to the will of man, when it is done only with respect to a human precept. As God hath a right to enact his laws without consulting his creature in the way of his government, so man is bound to obey those laws without consulting whether they be agreeable to men's laws or no. If we act the will of God, because the will of our superiors concurs with it, we obey not God in that, but man; a human will being the rule of our obedience, and not the divine, this is to vilify God, and make him inferior to man in our esteem, and a valuing the rule of man above that of our Creator.

Since God is the highest perfection, and infinitely good, whatsoever rule he gives the creature must be good, else it cannot proceed from God. A base thing cannot be the product of an infinite excellency, and an unreasonable thing cannot be the product of an infinite wisdom and goodness; therefore as the respecting God's will before the will of man is excellent and worthy of a creature, and is an acknowledging the excellency, goodness, and wisdom of God, so the eyeing the will of man before and above the will of God, is, on the contrary, a denial of all those in a lump, and a preferring the wisdom, goodness, and power of man in his law above all those perfections of God in his. Whatsoever men do that looks like moral virtue or abstinence from vices, not out of obedience to the rule God hath set, but because of custom, necessity, example,'or imitation, they may in the doing of it be rather said to be apes than Christians.

[3.] In obeying the will of man when it is contrary to the will of God. As the Israelites willingly 'walked after the commandment,' Hosea v. 11, not of God, but of Jeroboam in the case of the calves, and 'made the king's heart glad with their lies,' Hosea vii. 3. They cheered him with their ready obedience to his command for idolatry (which was a lie in itself, and a lie in them) against the commandment of God and the warnings of the prophets, rather than cheer the heart of God with their obedience to his worship instituted by him; nay, and when God offered them to cure them their wound, their iniquity breaks out afresh; they would neither have him as a Lord to rule them, nor a physician to cure them: Hosea vii. 1, 'When I would have healed Israel, then the iniquity of Ephraim was discovered.' The whole Persian nation shrunk at once from a duty due by the light of nature to the Deity, upon a decree that neither God or man should be petitioned to for thirty days, but only their king, Dan. vi. One only, Daniel, excepted against it, who preferred his homage to God above obedience to his prince. An adulterous generation is many times made the rule of men's professions, as is implied in those words of our Saviour, Mark

viii. 38, ' Whosoever shall be ashamed of me and my words in this adulterous and sinful generation.' Own him among his disciples, and be ashamed of him among his enemies. Thus men are said to deny God, Titus i. 16, when they attend to Jewish fables and the precepts of men rather than the word of God ; when the decrees or canons of fallible men are valued at a higher rate, and preferred before the writings of the Holy Ghost by his apostles.

As man naturally disowns the rule God sets him, and owns any other rule than that of God's prescribing, so

(3.) He doth this in order to the setting himself up as his own rule, as though our own wills, and not God's, were the true square and measure of goodness. We make an idol of our own wills ; and as much as self is exalted, God is deposed ; the more we esteem our own wills, the more we endeavour to annihilate the will of God ; account nothing of him, the more we account of ourselves ; and endeavour to render ourselves his superiors by exalting our own wills. No prince but would look upon his authority as invaded, his royalty derided, if a subject should resolve to be a law to himself in opposition to his known will. True piety is to hate ourselves, deny ourselves, and cleave solely to the service of God. To make ourselves our own rule, and the object of our chiefest love, is atheism. If self-denial be the greatest part of godliness, the great letter in the alphabet of religion, self-love is the great letter in the alphabet of practical atheism. Self is the great antichrist and antigod in the world, that ' sets up itself above all that is called God ; ' self-love is the captain of that black band, 2 Tim. iii. 2. It sits in the temple of God, and would be adored as God ; self-love begins, but denying the power of godliness, which is the same with denying the ruling power of God, ends the list ; it is so far from bending to the righteous will of the Creator, that it would have the eternal will of God stoop to the humour and unrighteous will of a creature ; and this is the ground of the contention between the flesh and the Spirit in the heart of a renewed man ; flesh wars for the godhead of self, and Spirit fights for the Godhead of God ; the one would settle the throne of the Creator, and the other maintain a law of covetousness, ambition, envy, lust, in the stead of God.

The evidence of this will appear in these propositions.

Prop. 1. This is natural to man as he is corrupted. What was the venom of the sin of Adam, is naturally derived with his nature to all posterity. It was not the eating a forbidding apple, or the pleasing his palate, that Adam aimed at, or was the chief object of his desire ; but to live independently on his Creator, and be a god to himself : Gen. iii. 5, ' You shall be as gods.' That which was the matter of the devil's temptation, was the incentive of man's rebellion. A likeness to God he aspired to in the judgment of God himself, an infallible interpreter of man's thoughts : ' Behold, man is become as one of us, to know good and evil,' in regard of self-sufficiency and being a rule to himself. The Jews understand the ambition of man to reach no further than an equality with the angelical nature ; but Jehovah here understands it in another sense. God had ordered man by this prohibition not to eat the fruit of the tree of knowledge of good and evil ; not to attempt the knowledge of good and evil of himself, but to wait upon the dictates of God ; not to trust to his own counsels, but to depend wholly upon him for direction and guidance. Certainly he that would not hold off his hand from so small a thing as an apple, when he had his choice of the fruit of the garden, would not have denied himself any thing his appetite had desired, when that principle had prevailed upon him. He would not have stuck at a greater matter to pleasure himself with the displeasing of God, when for so small a thing he would incur the anger of his Creator.

Thus would he deify his own understanding against the wisdom of God, and his own appetite against the will of God. This desire of equality with God, a learned man* thinks the apostle intimates: Phil. ii. 6, 'Who being in the form of God, thought it not robbery to be equal with God.' The Son's being in the form of God, and thinking it not robbery to be equal with God, implies that the robbery of sacrilege committed by our first parents, for which the Son of God humbled himself to the death of the cross, was an attempt to be equal with God, and depend no more upon God's directions, but his own conduct, which could be no less than an invasion of the throne of God, and endeavour to put himself into a posture to be his mate. Other sins, adultery and theft, &c., could not be committed by him at that time, but he immediately puts forth his hand to usurp the power of his Maker. This treason is the old Adam in every man. The first Adam contradicted the will of God to set up himself: the second Adam humbled himself, and did nothing but by the command and will of his Father. This principle, wherein the venom of the old Adam lies, must be crucified to make way for the throne of the humble and obedient principle of the new Adam, or quickening Spirit. Indeed, sin in its own nature is nothing else but a willing according to self, and contrary to the will of God. Lusts are therefore called the wills of the flesh and of the mind, Eph. ii. 3. As the precepts of God are God's will, so the violations of these precepts is man's will; and thus man usurps a godhead to himself, by giving that honour to his own will which belongs to God; appropriating the right of rule to himself, and denying it to his Creator. That servant that acts according to his own will with a neglect of his master's, refuseth the duty of a servant, and invades the right of his master. This self-love, and desire of independency on God, has been the root of all sin in the world. The great controversy between God and man hath been, whether he or they shall be God; whether his reason or theirs, his will or theirs, shall be the guiding principle. As grace is the union of the will of God and the will of the creature, so sin is the opposition of the will of self to the will of God. 'Leaning to our own understanding' is opposed as a natural evil to 'trusting in the Lord,' a supernatural grace, Prov. iii. 5. Men commonly love what is their own, their own inventions, their own fancies; therefore the ways of a wicked man are called 'the ways of his own heart,' Eccles. xi. 9; and the ways of a superstitious man his own devices: Jer. xviii. 12, 'We will walk after our own devices;' we will be a law to ourselves. And what the psalmist says of the tongue,—'our tongues are our own, who shall control us?'— is as truly the language of men's hearts, our wills are our own, who shall check us?

Prop. 2. This is evident in the dissatisfaction of men with their own consciences, when they contradict the desires of self. Conscience is nothing but an actuated or reflex knowledge of a superior power and an equitable law; a law impressed, and a power above it impressing it. Conscience is not the law-giver, but the remembrancer to mind us of that law of nature imprinted upon our souls, and actuate the considerations of the duty and penalty, to apply the rule to our acts, and pass judgment upon matter of fact. It is to give the charge, urge the rule, enjoin the practice of those notions of right, as part of our duty and obedience.

But man is much displeased with the directions of conscience, as he is out of love with the accusations and condemning sentence of this officer of

* Dr Jackson.

God. We cannot naturally endure any quick and lively practical thoughts of God and his will, and distaste our own consciences for putting us in mind of it; they therefore 'like not to retain God in their knowledge,' Rom. i. 28; that is, God in their own consciences; they would blow it out as it is the candle of the Lord in them to direct them, and their acknowledgments of God, to secure themselves against the practice of its principles. They would stop all the avenues to any beam of light, and would not suffer a sparkle of divine knowledge to flutter in their minds, in order to set up another directing rule suited to the fleshly appetite; and when they cannot stop the light of it from glaring in their faces, they rebel against it, and cannot endure to abide in its paths, Job xxiv. 13. He speaks not of those which had the written word or special revelations, but only a natural light or traditional handed from Adam. Hence are all the endeavours to still it when it begins to speak, by some carnal pleasures, as Saul's evil spirit with a fit of music; or bribe it with some fits of a glavering devotion when it holds the law of God in its commanding authority before the mind; they would wipe out all the impressions of it when it presses the advances of God above self, and entertain it with no better compliment than Ahab did Elijah, ' Hast thou found me, O my enemy ?'

If we are like to God in anything of our natural fabric, it is in the superior and more spiritual part of our souls. The resistance of that which is most like to God, and instead of God in us, is a disowning of the sovereign represented by that officer. He that would be without conscience, would be without God, whose vicegerent it is, and make the sensitive part, which conscience opposes, his lawgiver. Thus a man out of respect to sinful self, quarrels with his natural self, and cannot comport himself in a friendly behaviour to his internal implanted principles. He hates to come under the rebukes of them, as much as Adam hated to come into the presence of God, after he turned traitor against him. The bad entertainment God's deputy hath in us, reflects upon that God whose cause it pleads. It is upon no other account that men loathe the upright language of their own reasons in those matters, and wish the eternal silence of their own consciences, but as they maintain the rights of God, and would hinder the idol of self from usurping his Godhead and prerogative. Though this power be part of a man's self, rooted in his nature, as essential to him, and inseparable from him, as the best part of his being; yet he quarrels with it as it is God's deputy, and stickling for the honour of God in his soul, and quarrelling with that sinful self he would cherish above God. We are not displeased with this faculty barely as it exerciseth a self-reflection, but as it is God's vicegerent, and bears the mark of his authority in it. In some cases this self-reflecting act meets with good entertainment, when it acts not in contradiction to self, but suitable to natural affections: as suppose a man hath in his passion struck his child, and caused thereby some great mischief to him, the reflection of conscience will not be unwelcome to him, will work some tenderness in him, because it takes the part of self and of natural affection; but in the more spiritual concerns of God it will be rated as a busy body.

Prop. 3. Many, if not most actions, materially good in the world, are done more because they are agreeable to self, than as they are honourable to God. As the word of God may be heard not *as* his word, 1 Thes. ii. 13, but as there may be pleasing notions in it, or discourses against an opinion or party we disaffect, so the will of God may be performed, not as his will, but as it may gratify some selfish consideration, when we will please God so far as it may not displease ourselves, and serve him as our master, so far as his command may be a servant to our humour; when we consider not who it is that commands, but how short it comes of displeasing that sin which rules in our heart, pick and choose what is least burdensome to the flesh and distasteful to our lusts.

He that doth the will of God, not out of conscience of that will, but because it is agreeable to himself, casts down the will of God, and sets his own will in the place of it, takes the crown from the head of God, and places it upon the head of self. If things are done, not because they are commanded by God, but desirable to us, it is a disobedient obedience; a conformity to God's will in regard of the matter, a conformity to our own will in regard of the motive; either as the things done are agreeable to natural and moral self, or sinful self.

1. As they are agreeable to natural or moral self. When men will practise some points of religion, and walk in the track of some divine precepts, not because they are divine, but because they are agreeable to their humour or constitution of nature; from the sway of a natural bravery, the bias of a secular interest, not from an ingenuous sense of God's authority, or a voluntary submission to his will; as when a man will avoid excess in drinking, not because it is dishonourable to God, but as it is a blemish to his own reputation, or an impair of the health of his body, doth this deserve the name of an observance of the divine injunction, or rather an obedience to ourselves? Or when a man will be liberal in the distribution of his charity, not with an eye to God's precept, but in compliance with his own natural compassion, or to pleasure the generosity of his nature. The one is obedience to a man's own preservation, the other an obedience to the interest or impulse of a moral virtue. It is not respect to the rule of God, but the authority of self, and, at the best, is but the performance of the material part of the divine rule, without any concurrence of a spiritual motive or a spiritual manner. That only is a maintaining the rights of God, when we pay an observance to his rule, without examining the agreeableness of it to our secular interest, or consulting with the humour of flesh and blood; when we will not decline his service, though we find it cross, and hath no affinity with the pleasure of our own nature; such an obedience as Abraham manifested in his readiness to sacrifice his son; such an obedience as our Saviour demands in cutting off the right hand. When we observe anything of divine order upon the account of its suitableness to our natural sentiments, we shall readily divide from him, when the interest of nature turns its point against the interest of God's honour; we shall fall off from him according to the change we find in our own humours: and can that be valued as a setting up the rule of God, which must be deposed upon the mutable interest of an inconstant mind? Esau had no regard to God in delaying the execution of his resolution to shorten his brother's days, though he was awed by the reverence of his father to delay it; he considered, perhaps, how justly he might lie under the imputation of hastening crazy Isaac's death, by depriving him of a beloved son. But had the old man's head been laid, neither the contrary command of God, nor the nearness of a fraternal relation, could have bound his hands from the act, no more than they did his heart from the resolution: Gen. xxvii. 41, 'Esau hated Jacob, because of the blessing wherewith his father blessed him: and Esau said in his heart, The days of mourning for my father are at hand; then will I slay my brother.'

So many children, that expect at the death of their parents great inheritances or portions, may be observant of them, not in regard of the rule fixed by God, but to their own hopes, which they would not frustrate by a disobligement. Whence is it that many men abstain from gross sins, but in love to their reputation? Wickedness may be acted privately, which a man's own credit puts a bar to the open commission of. The preserving his own esteem may divert him from entering into a brothel-house, to which he hath set his mind before, against a known precept of his Creator. As Pharaoh parted with the Israelites, so do some men with their blemishing sins; not out of a sense of God's rule, but the smart of present judgments, or fear of a future wrath. Our security, then, and reputation, is set up in the place of God.

This also may be, and is, in renewed men, who have the law written in their hearts, that is, an habitual disposition to an agreement with the law of God; when what is done is with a respect to this habitual inclination, without eyeing the divine precept, which is appointed to be their rule. This also is to set up a creature, as renewed self is, instead of the Creator, and that law of his in his word, which ought to be the rule of our actions. Thus it is when men choose a moral life, not so much out of respect to the law of nature, as it is the law of God, but as it is a law become one with their souls and constitutions. There is more of self in this, than consideration of God; for if it were the latter, the revealed law of God would upon the same reason be received as well as his natural law. From this principle of self, morality comes by some to be advanced above evangelical dictates.

2. As they are agreeable to sinful self. Not that the commands of God are suited to bolster up the corruptions of men, no more than the law can be said to excite or revive sin, Rom. vii. 8, 9. But it is like a scandal taken, not given; an occasion taken by the tumultuousness of our depraved nature. The Pharisees were devout in long prayers, not from a sense of duty or a care of God's honour, but to satisfy their ambition, and rake together fuel for their covetousness (Mat. xxiii. 14, 'You devour widows' houses, and for a pretence make long prayers'), that they might have the greater esteem and richer offerings, to free by their prayers the souls of deceased persons from purgatory; an opinion that some think the Jewish synagogue had then entertained,* since some of their doctors have defended such a notion. Men may observe some precepts of God to have a better conveniency to break others. Jehu was ordered to cut off the house of Ahab; the service he undertook was in itself acceptable, but corrupt nature misacted that which holiness and righteousness commanded. God appointed it to magnify his justice, and check the idolatry that had been supported by that family. Jehu acted it to satisfy his revenge and ambition; he did it to fulfil his lust, not the will of God who enjoined him. Jehu applauds it as zeal, and God abhors it as murder, and therefore would 'avenge the blood of Jezreel on the house of Jehu,' Hosea i. 4. Such kind of services are not paid to God for his own sake, but to ourselves for our lust's sake.

4. This is evident in neglecting to take God's direction upon emergent occasions. This follows the text, 'None did seek God.' When we consult not with him, but trust more to our own will and counsel, we make ourselves our own governors and lords, independent upon him; as though we could be our own counsellors, and manage our concerns without his leave and assistance; as though our works were in our own hands, and not in the hands of God, Eccles. ix. 1, that we can by our own strength and sagacity direct them to a successful end without him. If we must 'acquaint ourselves with God' before we decree a thing, Job xxii. 28, then to decree a thing without acquainting God with it, is to prefer our purblind wisdom before the infinite wisdom of God; to resolve without consulting God, is to depose God and deify self, our own wit and strength. We would rather, like Lot, follow our own humour and stay in Sodom, than observe the angel's order to go out of it.

* Gerrard in loc.

5. As we account the actions of others to be good or evil, as they suit with or spurn against our fancies and humours. Virtue is a crime, and vice a virtue, as it is contrary or concurrent with our humours. Little reason have many men to blame the actions of others, but because they are not agreeable to what they affect and desire. We would have all men take directions from us, and move according to our beck; hence that common speech in the world, Such an one is an honest friend. Why? Because he is of their humour, and lacqueys according to their wills. Thus we make self the measure and square of good and evil in the rest of mankind, and judge of it by our own fancies, and not by the will of God, the proper rule of judgment.

Well, then, let us consider,

Is not this very common, are we not naturally more willing to displease God than displease ourselves, when it comes to a point that we must do one or other? Is not our own counsel of more value with us than conformity to the will of the Creator? Do not our judgments often run counter to the judgment of God? Have his laws a greater respect from us than our own humours? Do we scruple the staining his honour when it comes in competition with our own? Are not the lives of most men a pleasing themselves, without a repentance that ever they displeased God? Is not this to undeify God, to deify ourselves, and disown the propriety he hath in us by the right of creation and beneficence? We order our own ways by our own humours, as though we were the authors of our own being, and had given ourselves life and understanding. This is to destroy the order that God hath placed between our wills and his own, and a lifting up of the foot above the head; it is the deformity of the creature. The honour of every rational creature consists in the service of the First Cause of his being; as the welfare of every creature consists in the orders and proportionable motion of its members, according to the law of its creation.

He that moves and acts according to a law of his own, offers a manifest wrong to God, the highest wisdom and chiefest good, disturbs the order of the world, nulls the design of the righteousness and holiness of God. The law of God is the rule of that order he would have observed in the world. He that makes another law his rule, thrusts out the order of the Creator, and establishes the disorder of the creature.

But this will yet be more evident in the fourth thing.

(4.) Man would make himself the rule of God, and give laws to his Creator. We are willing God should be our benefactor, but not our ruler; we are content to admire his excellency and pay him a worship, provided he will walk by our rule. 'This commits a riot upon his nature; to think him to be what we ourselves would have him and wish him to be, Ps. l. 21. We would amplify his mercy and contract his justice, we would have his power enlarged to supply our wants, and straitened when it goes about to revenge our crimes; we would have him wise to defeat our enemies, but not to disappoint our unworthy projects; we would have him all eye to regard our indigence, and blind, not to discern our guilt; we would have him true to his promises, regardless of his precepts, and false to his threatenings; we would new mint the nature of God according to our models, and shape a God according to our fancies, as he made us at first according to his own image.'* Instead of obeying him, we would have him obey us; instead of owning and admiring his perfections, we would have him strip himself of his infinite excellency, and clothe himself with a nature agreeable to our own.

---

* Decay of Christian piety, p. 169, somewhat changed.

This is not only to set up self as the law of God, but to make our own imaginations the model of the nature of God.

Corrupted man takes a pleasure to accuse or suspect the actions of God. We would not have him act conveniently to his nature, but act what doth gratify us, and abstain from what distastes us. Man is never well but when he is impeaching one or other perfection of God's nature, and undermining his glory; as if all his attributes must stand indicted at the bar of our pur-blind reason. This weed shoots up in the exercise of grace. Peter intended the refusal of our Saviour's washing his feet as an act of humility, but Christ understands it to be a prescribing a law to himself, a correcting his love, John xiii. 8, 9.

This is evidenced,

(1.) In the strivings against his law. How many men imply by their lives that they would have God deposed from his government, and some unrighteous being step into his throne; as if God had or should change his laws of holiness into laws of licentiousness, as if he should abrogate his old eternal precepts and enact contrary ones in their stead. What is the language of such practices, but that they would be God's lawgivers and not his subjects; that he should deal with them according to their own wills, and not according to his righteousness; that they could make a more holy, wise, and righteous law than the law of God; that their imaginations, and not God's righteousness, should be the rule of his doing good to them? Jer. ix. 13, 'They have forsaken my law, and walked after the imaginations of their own heart.'

When an act is known to be a sin, and the law that forbids it acknowledged to be the law of God, and after this we persist in that which is contrary to it, we tax his wisdom as if he did not understand what was convenient for us; we would 'teach God knowledge,' Job xxi. 22; it is an implicit wish that God had laid aside the holiness of his nature, and framed a law to pleasure our lusts. When God calls for weeping, and mourning, and gird-ing with sackcloth upon approaching judgments, then the corrupt heart is for joy and gladness, eating of flesh and drinking of wine, because to-morrow they should die, Isa. xxii. 12, 13; as if God had mistaken himself when he ordered them so much sorrow when their lives were so near an end, and had lost his understanding when he ordered such a precept. Disobedience is therefore called contention—Rom. ii. 8, 'Contentious, and obey not the truth'—contention against God, whose truth it is that they disobey; a dis-pute with him, which hath more of wisdom in itself and conveniency for them, his truth or their imaginations. The more the love, goodness, and holiness of God appears in any command, the more are we naturally averse from it, and cast an imputation on him, as if he were foolish, unjust, cruel, and that we could have advised and directed him better. The goodness of God is eminent to us in appointing a day for his own worship, wherein we might converse with him and he with us, and our souls be refreshed with spiritual communications from him; and we rather use it for the ease of our bodies than the advancement of our souls, as if God were mistaken and injured his creature when he urged the spiritual part of duty. Every dis-obedience to the law is an implicit giving law to him, and a charge against him that he might have provided better for his creature.

(2.) In disapproving the methods of God's government of the world. If the counsels of heaven roll not about according to their schemes, instead of adoring the unsearchable depths of his judgments, they call him to the bar, and accuse him, because they are not fitted to their narrow vessels, as if a nut-shell could contain an ocean. As corrupt reason esteems the highest truths foolishness, so it counts the most righteous ways unequal. Thus we commence a suit against God, as though he had not acted righteously and wisely, but must give an account of his proceedings at our tribunal. This is to make ourselves God's superiors, and presume to instruct him better in the government of the world; as though God hindered himself and the world in not making us of his privy council, and not ordering his affairs according to the contrivances of our dim understandings.

Is not this manifest in our immoderate complaints of God's dealings with his church, as though there were a coldness in God's affections to his church, and a glowing heat towards it only in us? Hence are those importunate desires for things which are not established by any promise, as though we would overrule and over-persuade God to comply with our humour. We have an ambition to be God's tutors, and direct him in his counsels; 'Who hath been his counsellor,' saith the apostle? Rom. xi. 34. Who ought not to be his counsellor, saith corrupt nature? Men will find fault with God in what he suffers to be done according to their own minds, when they feel the bitter fruit of it. When Cain had killed his brother, and his conscience racked him, how saucily and discontentedly doth he answer God: Gen. iv. 9, 'Am I my brother's keeper?' Since thou dost own thyself the rector of the world, thou shouldst have preserved his person from my fury; since thou dost accept his sacrifice before my offering, preservation was due as well as acceptance. If this temper be found on earth, no wonder it is lodged in hell. That deplorable person, under the sensible stroke of God's sovereign justice, would oppose his *nay* to God's will: Luke xvi. 30, 'And he said, Nay, father Abraham: but if one went to them from the dead, they will repent.' He would presume to prescribe more effectual means than Moses and the prophets to inform men of the danger they incurred by their sensuality. 'David was displeased,' it is said, 2 Sam. vi. 8, 'when the Lord had made a breach upon Uzzah;' not with Uzzah, who was the object of his pity, but with God, who was the inflicter of that punishment.

When any of our friends have been struck with a rod against our sentiments and wishes, have not our hearts been apt to swell in complaints against God, as though he disregarded the goodness of such a person, did not see with our eyes, and measure him by our esteem of him? As if he should have asked our counsel before he had resolved, and managed himself according to our will rather than his own. If he be patient to the wicked, we are apt to tax his holiness, and accuse him as an enemy to his own law. If he inflict severity upon the righteous, we are ready to suspect his goodness, and charge him to be an enemy to his affectionate creature. If he spare the Nimrods of the world, we are ready to ask, 'Where is the God of judgment?' Mal. ii. 17. If he afflict the pillars of the earth, we are ready to question, Where is the God of mercy? It is impossible, since the depraved nature of man, and the various interests and passions in the world, that infinite power and wisdom can act righteously for the good of the universe, but he will shake some corrupt interest or other upon the earth; so various are the inclinations of men, and such a weather-cock judgment hath every man in himself, that the divine method he applauds this day, upon a change of his interest, he will cavil at the next. It is impossible for the just orders of God to please the same person many weeks, scarce many minutes together. God must cease to be God, or to be holy, if he should manage the concerns of the world according to the fancies of men.

How unreasonable is it thus to impose laws upon God? Must God revoke his own orders? govern according to the dictates of his creature? Must God, who hath only power and wisdom to sway the sceptre, become the obedient subject of every man's humour, and manage everything to serve the design of a simple creature ?   This is not to be God, but to set the creature in his throne.   Though this be not formally done, yet that it is interpretatively and practically done is every hour's experience.

(3.) In impatience in our particular concerns.   It is ordinary with man to charge God in his complaints in the time of affliction.   Therefore it is the commendation the Holy Ghost gives to Job: Job i. 22, that 'in all this,' that is, in those many waves that rolled over him, 'he did not charge God foolishly;' he never spake nor thought anything unworthy of the majesty and righteousness of God.   Yet afterwards, we find him warping; he nicknames the affliction to be God's oppression of him, and no act of his goodness: Job x. 3, 'Is it good for thee that thou shouldst oppress ?'   He seems to charge God with injustice for punishing him when he was not wicked, for which he appeals to God, 'Thou knowest that I am not wicked,' ver. 7, and that God acted not like a Creator, ver. 8.

If our projects are disappointed, what fretfulness against God's management are our hearts racked with !   How do uncomely passions bubble up in us, interpretatively at least, wishing that the arms of his power had been bound, and the eye of his omniscience been hoodwinked, that we might have been left to our own liberty and design ; and this oftentimes when we have more reason to bless him than repine at him.   The Israelites murmured more against God in the wilderness, with manna in their mouths, than they did at Pharaoh in the brick kilns, with their garlic and onions between their teeth.   Though we repine at instruments in our afflictions, yet God counts it a reflection upon himself.   The Israelites speaking against Moses, was in God's interpretation a rebellion against himself, Num. xvi. 41 compared with xvii. 10.   A rebellion is always a desire of imposing laws and conditions upon those against whom the rebellion is raised.   The sottish dealings of the vine-dressers in Franconia with the statue of St Urban, the protector of the vines, upon his own day, is an emblem of our dealing with God.   If it be a clear day, and portend a prosperous vintage, they honour the statue, and drink healths to it; if it be a rainy day, and presage a scantiness, they daub it with dirt in indignation.   We cast out our mire and dirt against God when he acts cross to our wishes, and flatter him when the wind of his providence joins itself to the tide of our interest.

Men set a high price upon themselves, and are angry God values them not at the same rate, as if their judgment concerning themselves were more piercing than his.   This is to 'disannul God's judgment,' and 'condemn him,' and 'count ourselves righteous,' as it is Job xl. 8.   This is the epidemical disease of human nature ; they think they deserve caresses instead of rods, and upon crosses are more ready to tear out the heart of God than reflect humbly upon their own hearts.   When we accuse God, we applaud ourselves, and make ourselves his superiors, intimating that we have acted more righteously to him than he to us, which is the highest manner of imposing laws upon him, as that emperor accused the justice of God for snatching him out of the world too soon.*   What an high piece of practical atheism is this, to desire that that infinite wisdom should be guided by our folly, and asperse the righteousness of God rather than blemish our own.   Instead of silently submitting to his will and adoring his wisdom, we declaim against him as an unwise and unjust governor.   We would invert his order, make him the steward, and ourselves the proprietors of what we are and have.   We deny ourselves to be sinners, and our mercies to be forfeited.

(4.) It is evidenced in envying the gifts and prosperities of others.   Envy

* Cœlum suspiciens vitam, &c.   Vita Titi, ca. 10.

hath a deep tincture of practical atheism, and is a cause of atheism.* We are unwilling to leave God to be the proprietor, and do what he will with his own, and as a Creator to do what he pleases with his creatures; we assume a liberty to direct God what portions, when and how he should bestow upon his creatures; we would not let him choose his own favourites, and pitch upon his own instruments for his glory. As if God should have asked counsel of us how he should dispose of his benefits. We are unwilling to leave to his wisdom the management of his own judgments to the wicked, and the dispensation of his own love to ourselves. This temper is natural; it is as ancient as the first age of the world. Adam envied God a felicity by himself, and would not spare a tree that he had reserved as a mark of his sovereignty. The passion that God had given Cain to employ against his sin he turns against his Creator; he was wroth with God, Gen. iv. 5, and with Abel; but envy was at the root, because his brother's sacrifice was accepted and his refused. How could he envy his accepted person without reflecting upon the acceptor of his offering! Good men have not been free from it. Job questions the goodness of God, that he should 'shine upon the counsel of the wicked,' Job x. 3. Jonah had too much of self in fearing to be counted a false prophet, when he came with absolute denunciations of wrath, Jonah iv. 2. And when he could not bring a volley of destroying judgments upon the Ninevites, he would shoot his fury against his master, envying those poor people the benefit, and God the honour of his mercy; and this after he had been sent into the whale's belly to learn humiliation, which, though he exercised there, yet those two great branches of self-pride and envy were not lopped off from him in the belly of hell. And God was fain to take pains with him, and by a gourd scarce makes him ashamed of his peevishness. Envy is not like to cease, till all atheism be cashiered, and that is in heaven.

This sin is an imitation of the devil, whose first sin upon earth was envy, as his first sin in heaven was pride. It is a wishing that to ourselves which the devil asserted as his right, to give the kingdoms of the world to whom he pleased, Luke iv. 6. It is an anger with God because he hath not given us a patent for government. It utters the same language in disparagement of God as Absalom did in reflection on his father: If I were king in Israel, justice should be better managed; if I were Lord of the world, there should be more wisdom to discern the merits of men, and more righteousness in distributing to them their several portions. Thus we impose laws upon God, and would have the righteousness of his will submit to the corruptions of ours, and have him lower himself to gratify our minds rather than fulfil his own. We charge the author of those gifts with injustice, that he hath not dealt equally, or with ignorance, that he hath mistook his mark. In the same breath that we censure him by our peevishness, we would guide him by our wills.

This is an unreasonable part of atheism. If all were in the same state and condition, the order of the world would be impaired. Is God bound to have a care of thee, and neglect all the world besides? 'Shall the earth be forsaken for thee? Job xviii. 4. Joseph had reason to be displeased with his brothers, if they had muttered, because he gave Benjamin a double portion, and the rest a single. It was unfit that they, who had deserved no gift at all, should prescribe him rules how to dispense his own doles. Much more unworthy is it to deal so with God; yet this is too rife.

(5.) It is evidenced in corrupt matters or ends of prayer and praise. When we are importunate for those things that we know not whether the

* Because wicked men flourish in the world; *Sollicitor nullos esse putare Deos.*

righteousness, holiness, and wisdom of God can grant, because he hath not discovered his will in any promise to bestow them, we would then impose such conditions on God which he never obliged himself to grant, when we pray for things not so much to glorify God, which ought to be the end of prayer, as to gratify ourselves. We acknowledge, indeed, by the act of petitioning, that there is a God, but we would have him un-God himself to be at our beck, and debase himself to serve our turns. When we desire those things which are repugnant to those attributes whereby he doth manage the government of the world; when by some superficial services we think we have gained indulgence to sins, which seems to be the thought of the strumpet in her paying her vows to wallow more freely in the mire of her sensual pleasures: Pro. vii. 14, 'I have peace-offerings with me; this day I have paid my vows:' I have made my peace with God, and have entertainment for thee. Or when men desire God to bless them in the commission of some sin. As when Balak and Balaam offered sacrifices that they might prosper in the cursing of the Israelites, Num. xxv. 1, &c.

So for a man to pray to God to save him, while he neglects the means of salvation appointed by God, or to renew him when he slights the word, the only instrument to that purpose, this is to impose laws upon God contrary to the declared will and wisdom of God, and to desire him to slight his own institutions. When we come into the presence of God with lusts reeking in our hearts, and leap from sin to duty, we would impose the law of our corruption on the holiness of God. While we pray the will of God may be done, self-love wishes its own will may be performed, as though God should serve our humours when we will not obey his precepts. And when we make vows under any affliction, what is it often but a secret contrivance to bend and flatter him to our conditions! We will serve him if he will restore us; we think thereby to compound the business with him, and bring him down to our terms.

(6.) It is evidenced in positive and bold interpretations of the judgments of God in the world. To interpet the judgments of God to the disadvantage of the sufferer, unless it be an unusual judgment, and have a remarkable hand of God in it, and the sin be rendered plainly legible in the affliction, is a presumption of this nature. When men will judge the Galileans, whose blood Pilate mingled with the sacrifices, greater sinners than others, and themselves righteous, because no drops of it were dashed upon them; or when Shimei, being of the house of Saul, shall judge according to his own interest, and desires David's flight upon Absalom's rebellion to be a punishment for invading the rights of Saul's family, and depriving him of the succession in the kingdom, 2 Sam. xvi. 5, as if he had been of God's privy council when he decreed such acts of justice in the world.

Thus we would fasten our own wills as a law or motive upon God, and interpret his acts according to the motions of self. Is it not too ordinary, when God sends an affliction upon those that bear ill will to us, to judge it to be a righting of our cause, to be a fruit of God's concern for us in revenging our wrongs, as if we had heard the secrets of God, or as Eliphaz saith, had turned over the records of heaven, Job xv. 8. This is a judgment according to self-love, not a divine rule, and imposeth laws upon heaven, implying a secret wish that God would take care only of them, make our concerns his own, not in ways of kindness and justice, but according to our fancies. And this is common in the profane world, in those curses they so readily spit out upon any affront; as if God were bound to draw his arrows and shoot them into the heart of all their offenders at their beck and pleasure.

(7.) It is evidenced, in mixing rules for the worship of God, with those which have been ordered by him. Since men are most prone to live by sense, it is no wonder that a sensible worship, which affects their outward sense with some kind of amazement, is dear to them, and spiritual worship most loathsome.

Pompous rites have been the great engine wherewith the devil hath deceived the souls of men, and wrought them to a nauseating the simplicity of divine worship, as unworthy the majesty and excellency of God, 2 Cor. xi. 3. Thus the Jews would not understand the glory of the second temple in the presence of the Messiah, because it had not the pompous grandeur of that of Solomon's erecting.

Hence in all ages men have been forward to disfigure God's models, and dress up a brat of their own; as though God had been defective in providing for his own honour in his institutions without the assistance of his creature. This hath always been in the world: the old world had their imaginations, and the new world hath continued them. The Israelites, in the midst of miracles, and under the memory of a famous deliverance, would erect a calf. The Pharisees, that sat in Moses's chair, would coin new traditions, and enjoin them to be as current as the law of God, Mat. xxiii. 6. Papists will be blending the Christian appointments with pagan ceremonies, to please the carnal fancies of the common people. Altars have been multiplied, under the knowledge of the law of God, Hos. viii. 12. Interest is made the balance of the conveniency of God's injunctions. Jeroboam fitted a worship to politic ends, and posted up calves to prevent his subjects revolting from his sceptre, which might be occasioned by their resort to Jerusalem, and converse with the body of the people from whom they were separated, 1 Kings xii. 27. Men will be putting their own dictates with God's laws, and are unwilling he should be the sole governor of the world without their counsel: they will not suffer him to be the Lord of that which is purely and solely his concern. How often hath the practice of the primitive church, the custom wherein we are bred, the sentiments of our ancestors, been owned as a more authentic rule in matters of worship, than the mind of God delivered in his word! It is natural by creation to worship God; and it is as natural by corruption for man to worship him in a human way, and not in a divine. Is not this to impose laws upon God? to esteem ourselves wiser than he? to think him negligent of his own service, and that our feeble brains can find out ways to accommodate his honour better than himself hath done? Thus do men for the most part equal their own imaginations to God's oracles: as Solomon built a high place to Moloch and Chemosh, upon the mount of Olives, to face on the east part Jerusalem and the temple, 1 Kings xi. 7. This is not only to impose laws on God, but also to make self the standard of them.

(8.) It is evidenced, in fitting interpretations of Scripture to their own minds and humours. Like the Lacedæmonians, that dressed the images of their gods according to the fashion of their own country, we would wring Scripture to serve our own designs, and judge the law of God by the law of sin, and make the serpentine seed in us to be the interpreter of divine oracles. This is like Belshazzar; to drink healths out of the sacred vessels. As God is the author of his law and word, so he is the best interpreter of it; the Scripture having an impress of divine wisdom, holiness, and goodness, must be regarded according to that impress, with a submission and meekness of spirit and reverence of God in it. But when in our inquiries into the word, we inquire not of God, but consult flesh and blood, the temper of the times wherein we live, or the satisfaction of a party we side withal, and impose glosses upon it according to our own fancies, it is to put laws upon God, and make self the rule of him. He that interprets the law to bolster up some eager appetite against the will of the lawgiver, ascribes to himself as great an authority as he that enacted it.

(9.) In falling off from God after some fair compliances, when his will grateth upon us and crosseth ours. They will walk with him as far as he pleaseth them, and leave him upon the first distaste, as though God must observe their humours more than they his will. Amos must be suspended from prophesying, because ' the land could not bear his words,' Amos vii. 10, &c., and his discourses condemned their unworthy practices against God. The young man came not to receive directions from our Saviour, but expected a confirmation of his own rules, rather than an imposition of new, Mark x. 17, 22. He rather cares for commendations than instructions, and upon the disappointment turns his back: ' he was sad,' that Christ would not suffer him to be rich and a Christian together, and leaves him because his command was not suitable to the law of his covetousness. Some truths that are at a further distance from us we can hear gladly; but when the conscience begins to smart under others, if God will not observe our wills, we will with Herod be a law to ourselves, Mark vi. 20, 27.

More instances might be observed.

Ingratitude is a setting up self, and an imposing laws on God. It is as much as to say God did no more than he was obliged to do; as if the mercies we have were an act of duty in God, and not of bounty. Insatiable desires after wealth: hence are those speeches, James iv. 13, ' We will go into such a city, and buy and sell,' &c., ' to get gain;' as though they had the command of God, and God must lacquey after their wills. When our hearts are not contented with any supply of our wants, but are craving an overplus for our lust; when we are unsatisfied in the midst of plenty, and still, like the grave, cry, Give, give.

Incorrigibleness under affliction, &c.

II. The second main thing. As man would be a law to himself, so he would be his own end and happiness in opposition to God.

Here four things shall be discoursed on:

1. Man would make himself his own end and happiness.
2. He would make any thing his end and happiness rather than God.
3. He would make himself the end of all creatures.
4. He would make himself the end of God.

1. Man would make himself his own end and happiness. As God ought to be esteemed the first cause, in point of our dependence on him, so he ought to be our last end, in point of our enjoyment of him. When we therefore trust in ourselves, we refuse him as the first cause; and when we act for ourselves, and expect a blessedness from ourselves, we refuse him as the chiefest good, and last end, which is an undeniable piece of atheism; for man is a creature of a higher rank than others in the world, and was not made, as animals, plants, and other works of the divine power, materially to glorify God; but a rational creature, intentionally to honour God by obedience to his rule, dependence on his goodness, and zeal for his glory. It is therefore as much a slighting of God, for man, a creature, to set himself up as his own end, as to regard himself as his own law.

For the discovery of this, observe that there is a threefold self-love.

(1.) Natural, which is common to us by the law of nature with other creatures, inanimate as well as animate, and so closely twisted with the nature of every creature, that it cannot be dissolved but with the dissolution of nature itself. It consisted not with the wisdom and goodness of God to create an unnatural nature, or to command any thing unnatural:

nor doth he; for when he commands us to sacrifice ourselves, and dearest lives for himself, it is not without a promise of a more noble state and being in exchange. for what we lose.   This self-love is not only commendable, but necessary, as a rule to measure that duty we owe to our neighbour, whom we cannot love as ourselves, if we do not first love ourselves: God having planted this self-love in our nature, makes this natural principle the measure of our affection to all mankind of the same blood with ourselves.

(2.) Carnal self-love; when a man loves himself above God, in opposition to God, with a contempt of God; when our thoughts, affections, designs, centre only in our own fleshly interest, and rifle God of his honour, to make a present of it to ourselves.   Thus the natural self-love, in itself good, becomes criminal by the excess, when it would be superior and not subordinate to God.

(3.) A gracious self-love.   When we love ourselves for higher ends than the nature of a creature, as a creature dictates, viz., in subserviency to the glory of God, this is a reduction of the revolted creature to his true and happy order.   A Christian is therefore said to be ' created in Christ to good works,' Eph. ii. 10.   As all creatures were created, not only for themselves, but for the honour of God, so the grace of the new creation carries a man to answer this end, and to order all his operations to the honour of God and his well-pleasing.

The first is from nature, the second from sin, the third from grace.   The first is implanted by creation, the second the fruit of corruption, the third is by the powerful operation of grace.

This carnal self-love is set up in the stead of God as our last end; like the sea, which all the little and great streams of our actions run to, and rest in.   And this is,

1. Natural.   It sticks as close to us as our souls; it is as natural as sin, the foundation of all the evil in the world.   As self-abhorrency is the first stone that is laid in conversion, so an inordinate self-love was the first inlet to all iniquity.   As grace is a rising from self to centre in God, so is sin a shrinking from God into the mire of a carnal selfishness.   Since every creature is nearest to itself, and, next, to God, it cannot fall from God, but must immediately sink into self;* and therefore all sins are well said to be branches or modifications of this fundamental passion.   What is wrath but a defence and strengthening self against the attempts of some real or imaginary evil?   Whence springs envy, but from a self-love, grieved at its own wants in the midst of another's enjoyment, able to supply it?   What is impatience, but a regret that self is not provided for at the rate of our wish, and that it hath met with a shock against supposed merit?   What is pride, but a sense of self-worth, a desire to have self of a higher elevation than others?   What is drunkenness, but a seeking a satisfaction for sensual self in the spoils of reason?   No sin is committed as sin, but as it pretends a self-satisfaction.   Sin indeed may well be termed a man's self, because it is, since the loss of original righteousness, the form that overspreads every part of our souls.   The understanding assents to nothing false, but under the notion of true, and the will embraceth nothing evil, but under the notion of good; but the rule whereby we measure the truth and goodness of proposed objects is not the unerring word, but the inclinations of self, the gratifying of which is the aim of our whole lives.

Sin and self are all one.   What is called a ' living to sin' in one place, Rom. vi., is called a living to self in another: 2 Cor. v. 15, ' That they that live should not live unto themselves.'   And upon this account it is

* More, Dial. ii. sect. 17, page 274.

that both the Hebrew word חָטָא, and the Greek word ἁμαρτάνειν, used in Scripture to express sin, properly signify to miss the mark, and swerve from that *white* to which all our actions should be directed, viz., the glory of God. When we fell to loving ourselves, we fell from loving God ; and therefore, when the psalmist saith, Ps. xiv. 2, there were none that sought God, viz., as the last end, he presently adds, 'they are all gone aside,' viz., from their true mark, and therefore become filthy.

2. Since it is natural, it is also universal. The not seeking God is as universal as our ignorance of him. No man in a state of nature but hath it predominant ; no renewed man on this side heaven but hath it partially : the one hath it flourishing, the other hath it struggling. If to aim at the glory of God as the chief end, and not to live to ourselves, be the greatest mark of the restoration of the divine image, 2 Cor. v. 15, and a conformity to Christ, who glorified not himself, Heb. v. 5, but the Father, John xvii. 4, then every man wallowing in the mire of corrupt nature pays a homage to self, as a renewed man is biassed by the honour of God.

The Holy Ghost excepts none from this crime : Philip. ii. 21, ' All seek their own.' It is rare for them to look above or beyond themselves ; whatsoever may be the immediate subject of their thoughts and inquiries, yet the utmost end and stage is their profit, honour, or pleasure. Whatever it be, that immediately possesses the mind and will, self sits like a queen, and sways the sceptre, and orders things at that rate, that God is excluded, and can find no room in all his thoughts : Ps. x. 4, ' The wicked through the pride of his countenance will not seek after God ; God is not in all his thoughts.' The whole little world of man is so overflowed with a deluge of self, that the dove, the glory of the Creator, can find no place where to set its foot ; and if ever it gain the favour of admittance, it is to disguise and be a vassal to some carnal project ; as the glory of God was a mask for the murdering his servants.

It is from the power of this principle that the difficulty of conversion ariseth. As there is no greater pleasure to a believing soul than the giving itself up to God, and no stronger desire in him than to have a fixed and unchangeable will to serve the designs of his honour, so there is no greater torment to a wicked man than to part with his carnal ends, and lay down the Dagon of self at the feet of the ark. Self-love and self-opinion in the Pharisees, waylaid all the entertainment of truth : John v. 44, ' They sought honour one of another, and not the honour which comes from God.' It is of so large an extent, and so insinuating nature, that it winds itself into the exercise of moral virtues, mixeth with our charity, Mat. vi. 2, and finds nourishment in the ashes of martyrdom, 1 Cor. xiii. 3.

This making ourselves our end will appear in a few things.

(1.) In frequent self-applauses, and inward overweening reflections. Nothing more ordinary in the natures of men, than a dotage on their own perfections, acquisitions, or actions in the world. Most ' think of themselves above what they ought to think,' Rom. xii. 3, 4. Few think of themselves so meanly as they ought to think : this sticks as close to us as our skin ; and as humility is the beauty of grace, this is the filthiest soil of nature. Our thoughts run more delightfully upon the track of our own perfections than the excellency of God ; and when we find any thing of a seeming worth, that may make us glitter in the eyes of the world, how cheerfully do we grasp and embrace ourselves ! When the grosser profanenesses of men have been discarded, and the floods of them dammed up, the head of corruption, whence they sprang, will swell the higher within, in self-applauding speculations of their own reformation, without acknowledgments of their own weaknesses, and desires of divine assistance to make a further progress. 'I thank God I am not like this publican,' Luke xviii. 11. A self-reflection, with a contempt rather than compassion to his neighbour, is frequent in every Pharisee. The vapours of self-affections in our clouded understandings, like those in the air in misty mornings, alter the appearance of things, and make them look bigger than they are. This is thought by some to be the sin of the fallen angels, who, reflecting upon their own natural excellency, superior to other creatures, would find a blessedness in their own nature, as God did in his, and make themselves the last end of their actions. It is from this principle we are naturally so ready to compare ourselves, rather with those that are below us, than with those that are above us; and often think those that are above us inferior to us, and secretly glory that we are become none of the meanest and lowest in natural or moral excellencies.

How far were the gracious penmen of the Scripture from this, who when possessed and directed by the Spirit of God, and filled with a sense of him, instead of applauding themselves, publish upon record their own faults to all the eyes of the world! And if Peter, as some think, dictated the Gospel, which Mark wrote as his amanuensis, it is observable that his crime in denying his Master, is aggravated in that gospel in some circumstances, and less spoken of his repentance than in the other evangelists: 'When he thought thereon, he wept,' Mark xiv. 72; but in the other, 'he went out, and wept bitterly,' Luke xxii. 62.

This is one part of atheism and self-idolatry, to magnify ourselves, with the forgetfulness and to the injury of our Creator.

(2.) In ascribing the glory of what we do or have to ourselves, to our own wisdom, power, virtue, &c. How flaunting is Nebuchadnezzar at the prospect of Babylon, which he had exalted to be the head of so great an empire: Dan. iv. 30, 'Is not this great Babylon that I have built? For,' &c. He struts upon the battlements of his palace, as if there were no God but himself in the world, while his eye could not but see the heavens above him to be none of his own framing; attributing his acquisitions to his own arm, and referring them to his own honour, for his own delight; not for the honour of God, as a creature ought; nor for the advantage of his subjects, as the duty of a prince. He regards Babylon as his heaven, and himself as his idol, as if he were all, and God nothing. An example of this we have in the present age; but it is often observed that God vindicates his own honour, brings the most heroical men to contempt and unfortunate ends, as a punishment of their pride, as he did here: Dan. iv. 31, 'When the word was in the king's mouth, there fell a voice from heaven,' &c.* This was Herod's crime, to suffer others to do it. He had discovered his eloquence actively, and made himself his own end passively, in approving the flatteries of the people, and offered not with one hand to God the glory he received from his people with the other, Acts xii. 22, 23. Samosatenus is reported to put down the hymns which were sung for the glory of God and Christ, and caused songs to be sung in the temple for his own honour.

When anything succeeds well, we are ready to attribute it to our own prudence and industry. If we meet with a cross, we fret against the stars and fortune and second causes, and sometimes against God, as they curse God as well as their king, Isa. viii. 21, not acknowledging any defect in themselves. The psalmist, by his repetition of 'Not unto us, not unto us, but to thy name give glory,' Ps. cxv. 1, implies the naturality of this temper, and the difficulty to cleanse our hearts from those self-reflections. If it be angelical to refuse an undue glory stolen from God's throne, Rev.

* Sanderson's Sermons.

xxii. 8, 9, it is diabolical to accept and cherish it. ' To seek our own glory is not glory,' Prov. xxv. 27. It is vile, and the dishonour of a creature, who, by the law of his creation, is referred to another end. So much as we sacrifice to our own credit, to the dexterity of our hands, or the sagacity of our wit, we detract from God.

(3.) In desires to have self-pleasing doctrines. When we cannot endure to hear anything that crosses the flesh, though the wise man tells us, ' It is better to hear the rebuke of the wise than the song of fools,' Eccles. vii. 5. If Hanani the seer reprove king Asa for not relying on the Lord, his passion shall be armed for self against the prophet, and arrest him a prisoner, 2 Chron. xvi. 10. If Micaiah declare to Ahab the evil that shall befall him, Amon the governor shall receive orders to clap him up in a dungeon. Fire doth not sooner seize upon combustible matter than fury will be kindled, if self be but pinched. This interest of lustful self barred the heart of Herodias against the entertainment of the truth, and caused her savagely to dip her hands in the blood of the Baptist, to make him a sacrifice to that inward idol, Mark vi. 18, 19, 28.

(4.) In being highly concerned for injuries done to ourselves, and little or not at all concerned for injuries done to God. How will the blood rise in us, when our honour and reputation is invaded, and scarce reflect upon the dishonour God suffers in our sight and hearing, violent passions will transform us into Boanergeses in the one case, and our unconcernedness render us Gallios in the other. We shall extenuate that which concerns God, and aggravate that which concerns ourselves. Nothing but the death of Jonathan, a firstborn and a generous son, will satisfy his father Saul, when the authority of his edict was broken by his tasting of honey, though he had recompensed his crime, committed in ignorance, by the purchase of a gallant victory. But when the authority of God was violated in saving the Amalekites' cattle against the command of a greater sovereign than himself, he can daub the business, and excuse it with a design of sacrificing. He was not so earnest in hindering the people from the breach of God's command, as he was in vindicating the honour of his own, 1 Sam. xv. 21. He could hardly admit of an excuse to salve his own honour; but in the concerns of God's honour pretends piety, to cloak his avarice.

And it is often seen, when the violation of God's authority and the stain of our own reputation are coupled together, we are more troubled for what disgraces us than for what dishonours God. When Saul had thus transgressed, he is desirous that Samuel would turn again to preserve his own honour before the elders, rather than grieved that he had broken the command of God, ver. 30.

(5.) In trusting in ourselves; when we consult with our own wit and wisdom, more than inquire of God, and ask leave of him. As the Assyrian, Isa. x. 13, ' By the strength of my hands I have done it, and by wisdom, for I am prudent.' When we attempt things in the strength of our own heads and parts, and trust in our own industry, without application to God for direction, blessing, and success, we affect the privilege of the Deity, and make gods of ourselves; the same language in reality with Ajax in Sophocles, ' Others think to overcome with the assistance of the gods, but I hope to gain honour without them.' Dependence and trust is an act due from the creature only to God. Hence God aggravates the crime of the Jews in trusting in Egypt: Isa. xxxi. 3, ' The Egyptians are men, and not gods.' Confidence in ourselves is a defection from God, Jer. xvii. 5. And when we depart from and cast off God to depend upon ourselves, which is but an arm of flesh, we choose the arm of flesh for our god; we rob God of that confidence we ought to place in him, and that adoration which is due to him, and build it upon another foundation. Not that we are to neglect the reason and parts God hath given us, or spend more time in prayer than in consulting about our own affairs, but to mix our own intentions in business, with ejaculations to heaven, and take God along with us in every motion ; but certainly it is an idolising of self when we are more diligent in our attendance on our own wit then fervent in our recourses to God.

(6.) The power of sinful self, above the efficacy of the notion of God, is evident in our workings for carnal self against the light of our own consciences. When men of sublime reason, and clear natural wisdom, are voluntary slaves to their own lusts, row against the stream of their own consciences, serve carnal self with a disgraceful and disturbing drudgery, making it their god, sacrificing natural self, all sentiments of virtue, and the quiet of their lives to the pleasure, honour, and satisfaction of carnal self,—this is a prostituting God in his deputy conscience to carnal affections, when their eyes are shut against the enlightnings of it, and their ears deaf to its voice, but open to the least breath and whisper of self ; a debt that the creature owes supremely to God.

Much more might be said, but let us see what Atheism lurks in this, and how it intrencheth upon God.

1. It is a usurping God's prerogative. It is God's prerogative to be his own end, and act for his own glory, because there is nothing superior to him in excellency and goodness to act for. He had not his being from anything without himself, whereby he should be obliged to act for anything but himself. To make ourselves, then, our last end, is to co-rival God in his being, the supreme good and blessedness to himself, as if we were our own principle, the author of our own being, and were not obliged to a higher power than ourselves for what we are and have. To direct the lines of all our motions to ourselves is to imply that they first issued only from ourselves. When we are rivals to God in his chief end, we own or desire to be rivals to him in the principle of his being. This is to set ourselves in the place of God. All things have something without them, and above them as their end. All inferior creatures act for some superior order in the rank of creation ; the lesser animals are designed for the greater, and all for man. Man therefore for something nobler than himself. To make ourselves, therefore, our own end, is to deny any superior, to whom we are to direct our actions. God alone, being the supreme being, can be his own ultimate end. For if there were anything higher and better than God, the purity and righteousness of his own nature would cause him to act for and toward that as his chiefest mark. This is the highest sacrilege, to alienate the proper good and rights of God, and employ them for our own use ; to steal from him his own honour, and put it into our own cabinets, like those birds that ravished the sacrifice from the altar and carried it to their own nests.* When we love only ourselves, and act for no other end but ourselves, we invest ourselves with the dominion which is the right of God, and take the crown from his head ; for as the crown belongs to the king, so to love his own will, to will by his own will and for himself is the property of God, because he hath no other will, no other end above him to be the rule and scope of his actions.

When therefore we are by self-love transformed wholly into ourselves, we make ourselves our own foundation, without God and against God ; when we mind our own glory and praise, we would have a royal state equal with God, who ' created all things for himself,' Prov. xvi. 4. What can man do more for God than he naturally doth for himself, since he doth all those things

* Sabunde tit. 146.

for himself which he should do for God? We own ourselves to be our own creators and benefactors, and fling off all sentiments of gratitude to him.

2. It is a vilifying of God. When we make ourselves our end, it is plain language that God is not our happiness. We postpone God to ourselves, as if he were not an object so excellent and fit for our love as ourselves are (for it is irrational to make that our end which is not God, and not the chiefest good). It is to deny him to be better than we, to make him not to be so good as ourselves, and so fit to be our chiefest good as ourselves are, that he hath not deserved any such acknowledgment at our hands by all that he hath done for us. We assert ourselves his superiors by such kind of acting, though we are infinitely more inferior to God than any creature can be to us. Man cannot dishonour God more than by referring that to his own glory which God made for his own praise, upon' account whereof he only hath a right to glory and praise, and none else. He thus ' changeth the glory of the incorruptible God into a corruptible image,' Rom. i. 23; a perishing fame and reputation, which extends but little beyond the limits of his own habitation, or, if it doth, survives but a few years, and perishes at last with the age wherein he lived.

3. It is as much as in us lies a destroying of God. By this temper we destroy that God that made us, because we destroy his intention and his honour. God cannot outlive his will and his glory, because he cannot have any other rule but his own will, or any other end but his own honour. The setting up self as our end puts a nullity upon the true Deity; by paying to ourselves that respect and honour which is due to God, we make the true God as no God. Whosoever makes himself a king of his prince's rights and territories, manifests an intent to throw him out of his government. To choose ourselves as our end is to undeify God, since to be the last end of a rational creature is a right inseparable from the nature of the Deity, and therefore not to set God but self always before us, is to acknowledge no being but ourselves to be God.

II. The second thing; man would make anything his end and happiness rather than God. An end is so necessary in all our actions, that he deserves not the name of a rational creature that proposeth not one to himself. This is the distinction between rational creatures and others; they act with a formal intention, whereas other creatures are directed to their end by a natural instinct, and moved by nature to what the others should be moved by reason. When a man therefore acts for that end, which was not intended him by the law of his creation, nor is suited to the noble faculties of his soul, he acts contrary to God, overturns his order, and merits no better a title than that of an atheist.

A man may be said two ways to make a thing his last end and chief good.

1. Formally. When he actually judges this or that thing to be his chiefest good, and orders all things to it. So man doth not formally judge sin to be good, or any object which is the incentive of sin to be his last end. This cannot be while he hath the exercise of his rational faculties.

2. Virtually and implicitly. When he loves anything against the command of God, and prefers in the stream of his actions the enjoyment of that before the fruition of God, and lays out more strength and expends more time in the gaining that than answering the true end of his creation. When he acts so as if something below God could make him happy without God, or that God could not make him happy without the addition of something else. Thus the glutton makes a god of his dainties, the ambitious man of his honours, the incontinent man of his lust, and the covetous man of his wealth, and consequently esteems them as his chiefest good, and the

most noble end to which he directs his thoughts; thus he vilifies and lessens the true God, which can make him happy, in a multitude of false gods, that can only render him miserable. He that loves pleasure more than God, says in his heart there is no god but his pleasure. He that loves his belly more than God, says in his heart there is no god but his belly. Their happiness is not accounted to lie in that God that made the world, but in the pleasure or profit they make their god.

In this, though a created object be the immediate and subordinate term to which we turn, yet principally and ultimately the affection to it terminates in self; nothing is naturally entertained by us, but as it affects our sense or mingles with some promise of advantage to us.

This is seen,

1. In the fewer thoughts we have of God than of anything else. Did we apprehend God to be our chiefest good and highest end, should we grudge him the pains of a few days' thoughts upon him? Men in their travels are frequently thinking upon their intended stage; but our thoughts run upon new acquisitions to increase our wealth, rear up our families, revenge our injuries, and support our reputation. Trifles possess us, but ' God is not in all our thoughts,' Ps. x. 4, seldom the sole object of them. We have durable thoughts of transitory things, and flitting thoughts of a durable and eternal good. The covenant of grace engageth the whole heart to God, and bars anything else from engrossing it; but what strangers are God and the souls of most men! Though we have the knowledge of him by creation, yet he is for the most part an unknown God in the relations wherein he stands to us, because a God undelighted in. Hence it is, as one observes,* that because we observe not the ways of God's wisdom, conceive not of him in his vast perfections, nor are stricken with an admiration of his goodness, that we have fewer good sacred poems than of any other kind. The wits of men hang the wing when they come to exercise their reasons and fancies about God. Parts and strength are given us, as well as corn and wine to the Israelites, for the service of God, but those are consecrated to some cursed Baal, Hosea ii. 8. Like Venus in the poet, we forsake heaven to follow some Adonis.

2. In the greedy pursuit of the world.† When we pursue worldly wealth or worldly reputation with more vehemency than the riches of grace or the favour of God. When we have a foolish imagination that our happiness consists in them, we prefer earth before heaven, broken cisterns which can hold no water before an ever springing fountain of glory and bliss, and, as though there were a defect in God, cannot be content with him as our portion without an addition of something inferior to him; when we make it our hopes to say to the wedge, Thou art my confidence, and rejoice more because it is great and because our hand hath gotten much, than in the privilege of communion with God and the promise of an everlasting fruition of him, Job xxxi. 24, 25, this is so gross, that Job joins it with the idolatry of the sun and moon, which he purgeth himself of, ver. 26. And the apostle, when he mentions covetousness or covetous men, passes it not over without the title of idolatry to the vice, and idolater to the person, Col. iii. 5, Eph. v. 5, in that it is a preferring clay and dirt as an end more desirable than the original of all goodness, in regard of affection and dependence.

3. In a strong addictedness to sensual pleasures, Philip. iii. 19. Who make their belly their God, subjecting the truths of God to the maintenance of their luxury. In debasing the higher faculties to project for the satis-

---

* Jackson, book i. cap, 14, p. 48.

† Quod quisque præ cæteris petit, summum judicat bonum.—*Boet.* lib. 3, p. 24.

faction of the sensitive appetite as their chief happiness, whereby many render themselves no better than a rout of sublimated brutes among men, and gross atheists to God. When men's thoughts run also upon inventing new methods to satisfy their bestial appetite, forsaking the pleasures which are to be had in God, which are the delights of angels, for the satisfaction of brutes; this is an open and unquestionable refusal of God for our end, when our rest is in them, as if they were the chief good, and not God.

4. In paying a service upon any success in the world to instruments, more than to God the sovereign author. When 'they sacrifice to their net, and burn incense to their drag,' Hab. i. 16. Not that the Assyrian did offer a sacrifice to his arms, but ascribed to them what was due only to God, and appropriated the victory to his forces and arms. The prophet alludes to those that worshipped their warlike instruments, whereby they had attained great victories, and those artificers who worshipped the tools by which they had purchased great wealth in the stead of God, preferring them as the causes of their happiness before God who governs the world.

And are not our affections, upon the receiving of good things, more closely fixed to the instruments of conveyance than to the chief benefactor from whose coffers they are taken ? Do we not more delight in them, and hug them with a greater endearedness, as if all our happiness depended on them, and God were no more than a bare spectator ? Just as if when a man were warmed by a beam he should adore that, and not admire the sun that darts it out upon him.

5. In paying a respect to man more than God. When in a public attendance on his service, we will not laugh or be garish, because men see us; but our hearts shall be in a ridiculous posture, playing with feathers and trifling fancies, though God see us; as though our happinesss consisted in the pleasing of men, and our misery in a respect to God. There is no fool that saith in his heart there is no God, but he sets up something in his heart as a god.

This is,

1. A debasing of God. (1.) In setting up a creature. It speaks God less amiable than the creature, short of those perfections which some silly sordid thing which hath engrossed their affections is possessed with ; as if the cause of all being could be transcended by his creature, and a vile lust could equal, yea, surmount the loveliness of God ; it is to say to God as the rich to the poor, James ii. 3, ' Stand thou there, or sit here under my footstool ;' it is to sink him below the mire of the world, to order him to come down from his glorious throne, and take his place below a contemptible creature, which in regard of its infinite distance is not to be compared with him. It strips God of the love that is due to him by the right of his nature and the greatness of his dignity, and of the trust that is due to him as the first cause and the chiefest good, as though he were too feeble and mean to be our blessedness. This is intolerable, to make that which is God's footstool, the earth, to climb up into his throne ; to set that in our heart which God hath made even below ourselves, and put under our feet; to make that which we trample upon to dispose of the right God hath to our hearts ;* it is worse than if a queen should fall in love with the little image of the prince in the palace, and slight the beauty of his person, and as if people should adore the footsteps of a king in the dirt, and turn their backs upon his presence.

(2.) It doth more debase him to set up a sin, a lust, a carnal affection, as our chief end. To steal away the honour due to God, and appropriate

* Noremberg de adorat. p. 30.

it to that which is no work of his hands, to that which is loathsome in his sight, hath disturbed his rest, and wrung out his just breath to kindle a hell for its eternal lodging, a God-dishonouring and a soul-murdering lust, is worse than to prefer Barabbas before Christ. The baser the thing, the worse is the injury to him with whom we would associate it. If it were some generous principle, a thing useful to the world, that we place in an equality with, or a superiority above him, though it were a vile usage, yet it were not altogether so criminal; but to gratify some unworthy appetite, with the displeasure of the Creator, something below the rational nature of man, much more infinitely below the excellent majesty of God, is a more unworthy usage of him. To advance one of the most virtuous nobles in a kingdom as a mark of our service and subjection, is not so dishonourable to a despised prince, as to take a scabby beggar, or a rotten carcass to place in his throne. Creeping things, abominable beasts, the Egyptian idols, cats and crocodiles, were greater abominations, and a greater despite done to God, than the image of jealousy at the gate of the altar, Ezek. viii. 5, 6, 10.

And let not any excuse themselves, that it is but one lust or one creature which is preferred as the end. Is not he an idolater that worships the sun or moon, one idol, as well as he that worships the whole host of heaven ?

The inordinancy of the heart to one lust may imply a stronger contempt of him, than if a legion of lusts did possess the heart. It argues a greater disesteem when he shall be slighted for a single vanity. The depth of Esau's profaneness in contemning his birthright, and God in it, is aggravated by his selling it for ' one morsel of meat,' Heb. xii. 16, and that none of the daintiest, none of the costliest, ' a mess of pottage,' implying, had he parted with it at a greater rate, it had been more tolerable, and his profaneness more excusable. And it is reckoned as a high aggravation of the corruption of the Israelite judges, Amos ii. 6, that ' they sold the poor for a pair of shoes ;' that is, that they would betray the cause of the poor for a bribe of no greater value than might purchase them a pair of shoes. To place any one thing as our chief end, though never so light, doth not excuse. He that will not stick to break with God for a trifle, a small pleasure, will leap the hedge upon a greater temptation.

Nay, and if wealth, riches, friends, and the best thing in the world, our own lives, be preferred before God, as our chief happiness and end but one moment, it is an infinite wrong, because the infinite goodness and excellency of God is denied. As though the creature or lust we love, or our own life which we prefer in that short moment before him, had a goodness in itself, superior to, and more desirable than the blessedness in God. And though it should be but one minute, and a man in all the periods of his days both before and after that failure, should actually and intentionally prefer God before all other things, yet he doth him an infinite wrong, because God in every moment is infinitely good, and absolutely desirable, and can never cease to be good, and cannot have the least shadow or change in him and his perfections.

2. It is a denying of God. Job. xxxi. 26-28, ' If I beheld the sun when it shined, and the moon walking in its brightness ; and my heart hath been secretly enticed, or my mouth hath kissed my hand, this also were iniquity to be punished by the judge : for I should have denied the Lord above.' This denial of God is not only the act of an open idolater, but the consequent of a secret confidence, and immoderate joy in worldly goods ; this denial of God is to be referred to, ver. 24, 25. When a man saith to gold, ' Thou art my confidence,' and rejoices because his wealth is great, he denies that God which is superior to all those, and the proper object of

trust. Both idolatries are coupled here together, that which hath wealth, and that which hath those glorious creatures in heaven for its object. And though some may think it a light sin, yet the crime being of deeper guilt, a denial of God deserves a severer punishment, and falls under the sentence of the just judge of all the earth, under that notion ; which Job intimates in those words, ' this also were an iniquity to be punished by the judge.'

The kissing the hand to the sun, moon, or any idol, was an external sign of religious worship among those and other nations. This is far less than an inward hearty confidence, and an affectionate trust. If the motion of the hand be, much more is the affection of the heart to an excrementitious creature, or a brutish pleasure, is a denial of God, and a kind of an abjuring of him, since the supreme affection of the soul is undoubtedly and solely the right of the sovereign creator, and not to be given in common to others, as the outward gesture may in a way of civil respect. Nothing that is an honour peculiar to God, can be given to a creature, without a plain exclusion of God to be God, it being a disowning the rectitude and excellency of his nature. If God should command a creature such a love, and such a confidence in anything inferior to him, he would deny himself his own glory, he would deny himself to be the most excellent being. Can the Romanists be free from this, when they call the cross *spem unicam*, and say to the virgin, *In te domina speravi*, as Bonaventura, &c.

Good reason therefore have worldlings and sensualists, persons of immoderate fondness to anything in the world, to reflect upon themselves ; since though they own the being of a God, they are guilty of so great disrespect to him, that cannot be excused from the title of an unworthy atheism. And those that are renewed by the Spirit of God, may here see ground of a daily humiliation for the frequent and too common excursions of their souls in creature confidences and affections, whereby they fall under the charge of an act of practical atheism, though they may be free from an habit of it.

III. The third thing is, man would make himself the end of all creatures. Man would sit in the seat of God, and ' set his heart as the heart of God,' as the Lord saith of Tyrus, Ezek. xxviii. 2. What is the consequence of this, but to be esteemed the chief good and end of other creatures ?—a thing that the heart of God cannot but be set upon, it being an inseparable right of the Deity, who must deny himself, if he deny this affection of the heart.

Since it is the nature of man derived from this root, to desire to be equal with God, it follows that he desires no creature should be equal with him, but subservient to his ends and his glory. He that would make himself God, would have the honour proper to God ; he that thinks himself worthy of his own supreme affection, thinks himself worthy to be the object of the supreme affection of others ; whosoever counts himself the chiefest good and last end, would have the same place in the thoughts of others. Nothing is more natural to man, than a desire to have his own judgment the rule and measure of the judgment and opinions of the rest of mankind He that sets himself in the place of the prince, doth by that act challenge all the prerogatives and dues belonging to the prince ; and apprehending himself fit to be a king, apprehends himself also worthy of the homage and fealty of the subjects. He that loves himself chiefly, and all other things and persons for himself, would make himself the end of all creatures. It hath not been once or twice only in the world, that some vain princes have assumed to themselves the title of gods, and caused divine adorations to be given to them, and altars to smoke with sacrifices for their honour. What hath been practised by one, is by nature seminally in all. We would have all pay an obedience to us, and give to us the esteem that is due to God.

This is evident ;—

1. In pride. When we entertain an high opinion of ourselves, and act for our own reputes, we dispossess God from our own hearts ; and while we would have our fame to be in every man's mouth, and be admired in the hearts of men, we would chase God out of the hearts of others, and deny his glory a residence anywhere else ; that our glory should reside more in their minds than the glory of God ; that their thoughts should be filled with our achievements, more than the works and excellency of God, with our image and not with the divine. Pride would paramount God in the affections of others, and justle God out of their souls ; and by the same reason that man doth thus in the place where he lives, he would do so in the whole world, and press the whole creation from the service of their true Lord, to his own service. Every proud man would be counted by others as he counts himself, the highest, chiefest piece of goodness, and be adored by others, as much as he adores and admires himself. No proud man in his self-love, and self-admiration, thinks himself in an error ; and if he be worthy of his own admiration, he thinks himself worthy of the highest esteem of others ; that they should value him above themselves, and value themselves only for him. What did Nebuchadnezzar intend, by setting up a golden image, and commanding all his subjects to worship it, upon the highest penalty he could inflict, but that all should aim only at the pleasing his humour ?

2. In using the creatures contrary to the end God has appointed. God created the world and all things in it, as steps whereby men might ascend to a prospect of him, and the acknowledgment of his glory ; and we would use them to dishonour God, and gratify ourselves. He appointed them to supply our necessities, and support our rational delights ; and we use them to cherish our sinful lusts. We wring groans from the creature in diverting them from their true scope, to one of our own fixing, when we use them not in his service, but purely for our own, and turn those things he created for himself to be instruments of rebellion against him to serve our turns ; and hereby endeavour to defeat the ends of God in them, to establish our own ends by them. This is a high dishonour to God, a sacrilegious undermining of his glory,* to reduce what God hath made to serve our own glory, and our own pleasure ; it perverts the whole order of the world, and directs it to another end than what God hath constituted, to another intention contrary to the intention of God ; and thus man makes himself a god by his own authority. As all things were made by God, so they are for God ; but while we aspire to the end of the creation, we deny and envy God the honour of being creator. We cannot make ourselves the chief end of the creatures against God's order, but we imply thereby that we were their first principle ; for if we lived under a sense of the Creator of them while we enjoy them for our use, we should return the glory to the right owner.

3. This is diabolical ; though the devil, for his first affecting an authority in heaven, has been hurled down from the state of an angel of light, into that of darkness, vileness, and misery, to be the most accursed creature living, yet he still aspires to mate God, contrary to the knowledge of the impossibility of success in it. Neither the terrors he feels, nor the future torments he doth expect, do a jot abate his ambition to be competitor with his Creator. How often hath he, since his first sin, arrogated to himself the honour of a God from the blind world, and attempted to make the Son of God, by a particular worship, count him as the chiefest good and benefactor of the world! Mat. iv. 9. Since all men by nature are the devil's children, the serpent's seed, they have something of this venom in their natures, as

* Sabunde Tit. 200, p. 352.

well as others of his qualities. We see that there may be, and is, a prodigious atheism lurking under the belief of a God. The devil knows there is
a God, but acts like an atheist, and so do his children.

IV. Man would make himself the end of God. This necessarily follows
upon the former. Whosoever makes himself his own law and his own end
in the place of God, would make God the subject in making himself the
sovereign. He that steps into the throne of a prince, sets the prince at his
foot-stool, and while he assumes the prince's prerogative, demands a subjection from him. The order of the creation has been inverted by the
entrance of sin.* God implanted an affection in man with a double aspect,
the one to pitch upon God, the other to respect ourselves ; but with this
proviso, that our affection to God should be infinite in regard of the object,
and centre in him, as the chiefest happiness and highest end ; our affections to ourselves should be finite, and refer ultimately to God as the
original of our being. But sin hath turned man's affections wholly to himself. Whereas he should love God first, and himself in order to God, he
now loves himself first, and God in order to himself. Love to God is lost,
and love to self hath usurped the throne. As God by creation ' put all
things under the feet' of man, Ps. viii. 6, reserving the heart for himself,
man by corruption hath dispossessed God of his heart, and put him under
his own feet. We often intend ourselves when we pretend the honour of
God, and make God and religion a stale to some designs we have in hand,
our Creator a tool for our own ends.

This is evident,

1. In our loving God because of some self-pleasing benefits distributed
by him. There is in men a kind of natural love to God ; but it is but a
secondary one, because God gives them the good things of this world,
spreads their table, fills their cup, stuffs their coffers, and doth them some
good turns by unexpected providences. This is not an affection to God for
the unbounded excellency of his own nature, but for his beneficence, as he
opens his hand for them ; an affection to themselves, and those creatures,
their gold, their honour, which their hearts are most fixed upon, without a
strong spiritual inclination that God should be glorified by them in the use
of those mercies. It is rather a disowning of God than any love to him,
because it postpones God to those things they love him for. This would
appear to be no love, if God should cease to be their benefactor, and deal
with them as a judge ; if he should change his outward smiles into afflicting
frowns, and not only shut his hand, but strip them of what he sent them.
The motive of their love being expired, the affection raised by it must cease,
for want of fuel to feed it ; so that God is beholden to sordid creatures of
no value (but as they are his creatures) for most of the love the sons of men
pretend to him. The devil spake truth of most men, though not of Job,
when he said, Job i. 10, they ' love not God for nought ;' but while he
makes a hedge about them and their families, whilst he blesseth the works
of their hands, and increaseth their honour in the land. It is like Peter's
sharp reproof of his Master, when he spake of the ill usage, even to death,
he was to meet with at Jerusalem, ' This shall not be unto thee.' It was
as much out of love to himself as zeal for his Master's interest, knowing his
Master could not be in such a storm without some drops lighting upon himself All the apostasies of men in the world are witnesses to this. They
fawn whilst they may have a prosperous profession, but will not bear one
chip of the cross for the interest of God. They would partake of his blessings, but not endure the prick of a lance for him, as those that admired the

* Pascal, Pens. sec. 30. p. 294.

miracles of our Saviour, and shrunk at his sufferings. A time of trial discovers these mercenary souls to be more lovers of themselves than their Maker. This is a pretended love of friendship to God, but a real love to a lust, only to gain by God. A good man's temper is contrary. Quench hell, burn heaven, said a holy man, I will love and fear my God.

2. It is evident, in abstinence from some sins, not because they offend God, but because they are against the interest of some other beloved corruption, or a bar to something men hunt after in the world. When temperance is cherished, not to honour God, but preserve a crazy carcass; prodigality forsaken, out of a humour of avarice; uncleanness forsaken, not out of a hatred of lust, but love to their money; declining a denial of the interest and truth of God, not out of affection to them, but an ambitious zeal for their own reputation. There is a kind of conversion from sin, when God is not made the term of it: Jer. iv. 1, 'If thou wilt return, O Israel, return unto me, saith the Lord.'* When we forbear sin as dogs do the meat they love; they forbear not out of a hatred of the carrion, but fear of the cudgel. These are as wicked in their abstaining from sin as others are in their furious committing it. Nothing of the honour of God and the end of his appointments is indeed in all this, but the conveniences self gathers from them. Again, many of the motives the generality of the world uses to their friends and relations to draw them from vices are drawn from self, and used to prop up natural or sinful self in them. Come, reform yourself, take other courses, you will smut your reputation, and be despicable; you will destroy your estate, and commence a beggar; your family will be undone, and you may rot in a prison; not laying close to them the duty they owe to God, the dishonour which accrues to him by their unworthy courses, and the ingratitude to the God of their mercies. Not that the other motives are to be laid aside and slighted. Mint and cummin may be tithed, but the weightier concerns are not to be omitted. But this shews that self is the bias not only of men in their own course, but in their dealings with others. What should be subordinate to the honour of God, and the duty we owe to him, is made superior.

3. It is evident, in performing duties merely for a selfish interest; making ourselves the end of religious actions; paying a homage to that, while we pretend to render it to God: Zech. vii. 5, 'Did you at all fast unto me, even unto me?' Things ordained by God may fall in with carnal ends affected by ourselves, and then religion is not kept up by any interest of God in the conscience, but the interest of self in the heart. We then sanctify not the name of God in the duty, but gratify ourselves. God may be the object, self is the end, and a heavenly object is made subservient to a carnal design. Hypocrisy passes a compliment on God, and is called flattery: Ps. lxxviii. 36, 'They did flatter him with their lips,' &c. They gave him a parcel of good words for their own preservation. Flattery, in the old notion among the heathens, is a vice more peculiar to serve our own turn, and purvey for the belly. They knew they could not subsist without God, and therefore gave him a parcel of good words, that he might spare them, and make provision for them: 'Israel is an empty vine,' Hos. x. 1; a vine, say some, with large branches and few clusters, but 'brings forth fruit to himself,' while they professed love to God with their lips. It was that God should promote their covetous designs, and preserve their wealth and grandeur, Ezek. xxxiii. 31; in which respect an hypocrite may be well termed a religious atheist, an atheist masked with religion. The chief arguments which prevail with many men to perform some duties, and appear

* Trap. on Gen. p. 148.

religious, are the same that Hamor and Shechem used to the people of their city to submit to circumcision, viz., the engrossing of more wealth: Gen. xxxiv. 21, 22, 'If every male among us be circumcised, as they are circumcised, shall not their cattle and their substance, and every beast of theirs, be ours?'

This is seen,

(1.) In unweildiness to religious duties where self is not concerned. With what lively thoughts will many approach to God when a revenue may be brought in to support their own ends? But when the concerns of God only are in it, the duty is not the delight but the clog; such feeble devotions that warm not the soul, unless there be something of self to give strength and heat to them. Jonah was sick of his work, and ran from God, because he thought he should get no honour by his message; God's mercy will discredit his prophecy, Jonah iv. 2. Thoughts of disadvantage cut the very sinews of service. You may as well persuade a merchant to venture all his estate upon the inconstant waves, without hopes of gain, as prevail with a natural man to be serious in duty, without expectation of some warm advantage. 'What profit should we have if we pray to him?' is the natural question, Job xxi. 15. 'What profit shall I have if I be cleansed from my sin?' Job xxxv. 3. I shall have more good by my sin than by my service. It is for God that I dance before the ark, saith David, therefore 'I will be more vile,' 2 Sam. vi. 22. It is for self that I pray, saith a natural man, therefore I will be more warm and quick. Ordinances of God are observed only as a point of interest, and prayer is often most fervent when it is least godly, and most selfish; carnal ends and affections will pour out lively expressions. If there be no delight in the means that lead to God, there is no delight in God himself, because love is *appetitus unionis*, a desire of union; and where the object is desirable, the means that brings us to it would be delightful too.

(2.) In calling upon God only in a time of necessity. How officious will men be in affliction to that God whom they neglect in their prosperity! 'When he slew them, then they sought him, and they returned and inquired after God; and they remembered that God was their rock,' Ps. lxxviii. 34. They remembered him under the scourge, and forgat him under his smiles. They visit the throne of grace, knock loud at heaven's gates, and give God no rest for their early and importunate devotions when under distress; but when their desires are answered, and the rod removed, they stand aloof from him, and rest upon their own bottom; as Jer. ii. 31, 'We are lords, we will come no more unto thee.' When we have need of him, he shall find us clients at his gate; and when we have served our turn, he hears no more of us; like Noah's dove sent out of the ark, that returned to him when she found no rest on the earth, but came not back when she found a footing elsewhere. How often do men apply themselves to God when they have some business for him to do for them! And then, too, they are loath to put it solely into his hand, to manage it for his own honour; but they presume to be his directors, that he may manage it for their glory. Self spurs men on to the throne of grace; they desire to be furnished with some mercy they want, or to have the clouds of some judgments which they fear blown over. This is not affection to God, but to ourselves; as the Romans worshipped a quartane ague as a goddess, and *Timorem et Pallorem*, fear and paleness, as gods, not out of any affection they had to the disease or the passion, but for fear to receive any hurt by them.

Again, when we have gained the mercy we need, how little do we warm our souls with the consideration of that God that gave it, or lay out the mercy in his service! We are importunate to have him our friend in our necessities, and are ungratefully careless of him, and his injuries he suffers by us or others. When he hath discharged us from the rock where we stuck, we leave him, as having no more need of him, and able to do well enough without him, as if we were petty gods ourselves, and only wanted a lift from him at first. This is not to glorify God as God, but as our servant; not an honouring of God, but a self-seeking. He would hardly beg at God's door if he could pleasure himself without him.

(3.) In begging his assistance to our own projects. When we lay the plot of our own affairs, and then come to God, not for counsel but blessing, self only shall give us counsel how to act; but because we believe there is a God that governs the world, we will desire him to contribute success. God is not consulted with till the counsel of self be fixed; then God must be the executor of our will. Self must be the principal, and God the instrument to hatch what we have contrived. It is worse when we beg of God to favour some sinful aim; the psalmist implies this, Ps. lxvi. 18, 'If I regard iniquity in my heart, the Lord will not hear me.' Iniquity regarded as the aim in prayer renders the prayer successless, and the suppliant an atheist in debasing God to back his lust by his holy providence.

The disciples had determined revenge, and because they could not act it without their master, they would have him be their second in their vindictive passion: Luke ix. 55, 'Call for fire from heaven.'

We scarce seek God till we have modelled the whole contrivance in our own brains, and resolved upon the methods of performance, as though there were not a fulness of wisdom in God to guide us in resolves, as well as power to breathe success upon them.

(4.) In impatience upon the refusal of our desires. How often do men's spirits rise against God, when he steps not in with the assistance they want! If the glory of God swayed more with them than their private interest, they would let God be judge of his own glory, and rather magnify his wisdom than complain of his want of goodness. Selfish hearts will charge God with neglect of them, if he be not as quick in their supplies as they are in their desires, like those in Isa. lviii. 3, 'Wherefore have we fasted, say they, and thou seest not? wherefore have we afflicted our souls, and thou takest no knowledge?' When we aim at God's glory in our importunities, we shall fall down in humble submissions when he denies us; whereas self riseth up in bold expostulations, as if God were our servant, and had neglected the service he owed us, not to come at our call. We over-value the satisfactions of self above the honour of God. Besides, if what we desire be a sin, our impatience at a refusal is more intolerable. It is an anger, that God will not lay aside his holiness to serve our corruption.

5. In the actual aims men have in their duties. In prayer for temporal things, when we desire health for our own ease, wealth for our own sensuality, strength for our revenge, children for the increase of our family, gifts for our applause, as Simon Magus did the Holy Ghost, or when some of those ends are aimed at, this is to desire God not to serve himself of us, but to be a servant to our worldly interest, our vain glory, the greatening of our names, &c. In spiritual mercies begged for, when pardon of sin is desired only for our own security from eternal vengeance; sanctification desired only to make us fit for everlasting blessedness; peace of conscience only that we may lead our lives more comfortably in the world; when we have not actual intentions for the glory of God, or when our thoughts of God's honour are overtopped by the aims of self-advantage. Not but that as God hath pressed us to those things by motives drawn from the blessedness

derived to ourselves by them, so we may desire them with a respect to ourselves ; but this respect must be contained within the due banks, in subordination to the glory of God, not above it, nor in an equal balance with it.*
That which is nourishing or medicinal in the first or second degree, is in the fourth or fifth degree mere destructive poison.

Let us consider it seriously ; though a duty be heavenly, doth not some base end smut us in it ?

[1.] How is it with our confessions of sin ? Are they not more to procure our pardon than to shame ourselves before God, or to be freed from the chains that hinder us from bringing him the glory for which we were created ; or more to partake of his benefits than to honour him in acknowledging the rights of his justice ? Do we not bewail sin as it hath ruined us, not as it opposed the holiness of God ? Do we not shuffle with God, and confess our † sin, while we reserve another, as if we would allure God, by declaring our dislike of one, to give us liberty to commit wantonness with another ; not to abhor ourselves, but to daub with God ?

[2.] Is it any better in our private and family worship ? Are not such assemblies frequented by some, when some upon whom they have a dependence may eye them, and have a better opinion of them and affection to them ? If God were the sole end of our hearts, would they not be as glowing under the sole eye of God as our tongues or carriages are seemingly serious under the eye of man ? Are not family duties performed by some that their voices may be heard, and their reputation supported among godly neighbours ?

[3.] Is not the charity of many men tainted with this end, self ? Mat. vi. 1, as the Pharisees were while they set the miserable object before them, but not the Lord, bestowing alms, not so much upon the necessities of the people, as the friendship we owe them for some particular respects ; or casting our bread upon those waters which stream down in the sight of the world, that our doles may be visible to them and commended by them ; or when we think to oblige God to pardon our transgressions, as if we merited it and heaven too at his hands, by bestowing a few pence upon indigent persons. And,

[4.] Is it not the same with the reproofs of men ? Is not heat and anger carried out with full sail when our worldly interest is prejudiced, and becalmed in the concerns of God ? Do not masters reprove their servants with more vehemency, for the neglect of their trade and business, than the neglect of divine duties, and that upon religious arguments, pretending the honour of God, that they may mind their own interest ? But when they are negligent in what they owe to God no noise is made, they pass without rebuke. Is not this to make God and religion a stale to their own ends ? It is a part of atheism, not to regard the injuries done to God, as Tiberius.‡ Let God's wrongs be looked to, or cared for by himself.

[5.] Is it not thus in our seeming zeal for religion ? As Demetrius and the craftsmen at Ephesus cried up aloud the greatness of Diana of the Ephesians, not out of any true zeal they had for her, but their gain, which was increased by the confluence of her worshippers, and the sale of her own shrines, Acts xix. 24, 28.

[6.] In making use of the name of God to countenance our sin. When we set up an opinion that is a friend to our lusts, and then dig deep into the Scripture to find crutches to support it, and authorise our practices ; when

---

* Gurnall, part iii. p. 337. ‡ Dei injuria Deo curæ.
† Qu. 'one '?—ED.

men will thank God for what they have got by unlawful means, fathering
the fruit of their cheating craft, and the simplicity of their chapmen upon
God; crediting their cozenage by his name, as men do brass money, with
a thin plate of silver and the stamp and image of the prince. The Jews
urge the law of God for the crucifying his Son: John xix. 7, ' We have a
law, and by that law he is to die;' and would make him a party in their
private revenge.* Thus often when we have faltered in some actions we
wipe our mouths, as if we sought God more than our own interest, prostituting the sacred name and honour of God, either to hatch or defend some
unworthy lust against his word.

Is not all this a high degree of atheism ?

1. It is a vilifying God, an abuse of the highest good. Other sins subject the creature and outward things to them; but acting in religious services
for self subjects not only the highest concernments of men's souls, but the
Creator himself to the creature, nay, to make God contribute to that which
is the pleasure of the devil; a greater slight than to cast the gifts of a
prince to a herd of nasty swine. It were more excusable to serve ourselves
of God upon the higher accounts, such that materially conduced to his glory,
but it is an intolerable wrong to make him and his ordinances caterers for
our own bellies, as they did, Hosea viii. 13.† They sacrificed the הבהבים
of which the offerer might eat, not of out of any reference to God, but love
to their gluttony; not please him, but feast themselves. The belly was truly
made the god, when God was served only in order to the belly : as though
the blessed God had his being, and his ordinances were enjoined to pleasure
their foolish and wanton appetites ; as though the work of God were only
to patronise unrighteous ends, and be as bad as themselves, and become a
pander to their corrupt affections.

2. Because it is a vilifying of God, it is an undeifying or dethroning God.
It is an acting as if we were the lords, and God our vassal ; a setting up
those secular ends in the place of God, who ought to be our ultimate end
in every action ; to whom a glory is as due as his mercy to us is utterly
unmerited by us. He that thinks to cheat and put the fool upon God by
his pretences, doth not heartily believe there is such a being. He could not
have the notion of a God without that of omniscience and justice ; an eye to
see the cheat, and an arm to punish it. The notion of the one would direct
him in the manner of his services, and the sense of the other would scare
him from the cherishing his unworthy ends. He that serves God with a
sole respect to himself is prepared for any idolatry ; his religion shall warp
with the times and his interest ; he shall deny the true God for an idol,
when his worldly interest shall advise him to it, and pay the same reverence
to the basest image which he pretends now to pay to God; as the Israelites
were as real for idolatry under their basest princes as they were pretenders
to the true religion under those that were pious.

Before I come to the use of this, give me leave to evince this practical
atheism by two other considerations.

1. Unworthy imaginations of God.

' The fool hath said in his heart, There is no God;' that is, he is not
such a God as you report him to be ; this is meant by their being corrupt,
in the second verse corrupt being taken for playing the idolaters, Exod.
xxxii. 7. We cannot comprehend God ; if we could, we should cease to be
finite ; and because we cannot comprehend him, we erect strange images of
him in our fancies and affections. And since guilt came upon us, because
we cannot root out the notions of God, we would debase the majesty and

* Sanderson's Sermons, part ii. p. 158.   † Vid. Cocc. *in locum.*

nature of God, that we may have some ease in our consciences, and lie down with some comfort in the sparks of our own kindling.

This is universal in men by nature. 'God is not in all his thoughts,' Ps. x. 4. Not in any of his thoughts, according to the excellency of his nature, and greatness of his majesty. As the heathen did not glorify God as God, so neither do they conceive of God as God. They are all infected with some one or other ill opinion of him, thinking him not so holy, powerful, just, good as he is, and as the natural force of a human understanding might arrive to. We join a new notion of God in our vain fancies, and represent him not as he is, but as we would have him to be, fit for our own use, and suited to our own pleasure. We set that active power of imagination on work, and there comes out a god (a calf), whom we own for a notion of God.

Adam cast him into so narrow a mould as to think that himself, who had newly sprouted up by his almighty power, was fit to be his corival in knowledge, and had vain hopes to grasp as much as infiniteness. If he in his first declining began to have such a conceit, it is no doubt but we have as bad under a mass of corruption. When holy Agur speaks of God, he cries out that he had not 'the understanding of a man, nor the knowledge of the holy,' Prov. xxx. 2, 3. He did not think rationally of God as man might by his strength at his first creation. There are as many carved images of God as there are minds of men, and as monstrous shapes as those corruptions into which they would transform him.

Hence sprang,

1. Idolatry. Vain imaginations first set afloat and kept up this in the world. Vain imaginations of the God 'whose glory they changed into the image of corruptible man,' Rom. i. 21, 23. They had set up vain images of him in their fancy, before they set up idolatrous representations of him in their temples; the likening him to those idols of wood and stone, and various metals, were the fruit of an idea erected in their own minds. This is a mighty debasing the divine nature, and rendering him no better than that base and stupid matter they make the visible object of their adoration, equalling him with those base creatures they think worthy to be the representations of him. Yet how far did this crime spread itself in all corners of the world, not only among the more barbarous and ignorant, but the more polished and civilized nations! Judea only, where God had placed the ark of his presence, being free from it in some intervals of time only, after some sweeping judgment. And though they vomited up their idols under some sharp scourge, they licked them up again after the heavens were cleared over their heads. The whole book of Judges makes mention of it. And though an evangelical light hath chased that idolatry away from a great part of the world, yet the principle remaining, coins more spiritual idols in the heart, which are brought before God in acts of worship.

2. Hence all superstition received its rise and growth. When we mint a God according to our own complexion, like to us in mutable and various passions, soon angry and soon appeased, it is no wonder that we invent ways of pleasing him after we have offended him, and think to expiate the sin of our souls by some melancholy devotions and self-chastisements. Superstition is nothing else but an unscriptural and unrevealed dread of God, Δεισιδαιμονία. When they imagine him a rigorous, and severe master, they cast about for ways to mitigate him whom they thought so hard to be pleased. A very mean thought of him, as if a slight and pompous devotion could as easily bribe and flatter him out of his rigours, as a few good words or babbling rattles could please and quiet little children, and whatsoever

pleased us could please a God infinitely above us. Such narrow conceits had the Philistines, when they thought to still the anger of the God of Israel, whom they thought they possessed in the ark, with the present of a few golden mice, 1 Sam. vi. 3, 4. All the superstition this day living in the world is built upon this foundation; so natural it is to man to pull God down to his own imaginations, rather than raise up his imaginations up to God. Hence doth arise also the diffidence of his mercy, though they repent, measuring God by the contracted models of their own spirits, as though his nature were as difficult to pardon their offences against him, as they are to remit wrongs done to themselves.

3. Hence springs all presumption, the common disease of the world. All the wickedness in the world, which is nothing else but presuming upon God, rises from the ill interpretations of the goodness of God, breaking out upon them in the works of creation and providence. The corruption of man's nature engendered by those notions of goodness a monstrous birth of vain imaginations, not of themselves primarily, but of God; whence arose all that folly and darkness in their minds and conversations : Rom. i. 20, 21, ' They glorified him not as God,' but according to themselves imagined him good that themselves might be bad, fancied him so indulgent as to neglect his honour for their sensuality. How doth the unclean person represent him to his own thoughts but as a goat, the murderer as a tiger, the sensual person as a swine, while they fancy a god indulgent to their crimes without their repentance ! As the image on the seal is stamped upon the wax, so the thoughts of the heart are printed upon the actions. God's patience is apprehended to be an approbation of their vices, and from the consideration of his forbearance they fashion a god that they believe will smile upon their crimes; they imagine a god that plays with them, and though he threatens, doth it only to scare, but means not as he speaks; a god they fancy like themselves, that would do as they would do, not be angry for what they count a light offence : Ps. l. 21, ' Thou thoughtest I was such a one as thyself;' that God and they were exactly alike, as two tallies. ' Our wilful misapprehensions of God are the cause of our misbehaviour in all his worship; our slovenly and lazy services tell him to his face what slight thoughts and appprehensions we have of him.'*

Compare these two together.

Superstition ariseth from terrifying misapprehensions of God; presumption from self-pleasing thoughts. One represents him only rigorous, and the other careless; one makes us over-officious in serving him by our own rules, and the other over-bold in offending him according to our humours. The want of a true notion of God's justice makes some men slight him; and the want of a true apprehension of his goodness makes others too servile in their approaches to him. One makes us careless of duties, and the other makes us look on them rather as physic than food; an unsupportable penance than a desirable privilege. In this case hell is the principle of duty performed to heaven. The superstitious man believes God hath scarce mercy to pardon; the presumptuous man believes he hath no such perfection as justice to punish. The one makes him insignificant to what he desires, kindness and goodness; the other renders him insignificant to what he fears, his vindictive justice. What between the idolater, the superstitious, the presumptuous person, God should look like no God in the world.

These unworthy imaginations of God are likewise,

A vilifying of him, debasing the Creator to be a creature of their own

* Gurnal, part ii. p. 245, 246.

fancies, putting their own stamp upon him, and fashioning him not according to that beautiful image he impressed upon them by creation, but the defaced image they inherit by their fall, and which is worse, the image of the devil which spread itself over them at their revolt and apostasy. Were it possible to see a picture of God, according to the fancies of men, it would be the most monstrous being, such a god that never was, nor ever can be.

We honour God when we have worthy opinions of him suitable to his nature ; when we conceive of him as a being of unbounded loveliness and perfection. We detract from him when we ascribe to him such qualities as would be a horrible disgrace to a wise and good man, as injustice and impurity. Thus men debase God when they invert his order, and would create him according to their image, as he first created them according to his own ; and think him not worthy to be a God, unless he fully answer the mould they would cast him into, and be what is unworthy of his nature. Men do not conceive of God as he would have them, but he must be what they would have him, one of their own shaping.

(1.) This is worse than idolatry. The grossest idolater commits not a crime so heinous, by changing his glory into the image of creeping things and senseless creatures, as the imagining God to be as one of our sinful selves, and likening him to those filthy images we erect in our fancies ; one makes him an earthly God, like an earthly creature ; the other fancies him an unjust and impure God, like a wicked creature : one sets up an image of him in the earth, which is his footstool ; the other sets up an image of him in the heart, which ought to be his throne.

(2.) It is worse than absolute atheism or a denial of God. *Dignius credimus non esse, quodcunque non ita fuerit, ut esse debebit*, was the opinion of Tertullian.* It is more commendable to think him not to be, than to think him such a one as is inconsistent with his nature. Better to deny his existence than to deny his perfection. No wise man but would rather have his memory rot than be accounted infamous, and would be more obliged to him that should deny that ever he had a being in the world, than to say he did indeed live, but he was a sot, a debauched person, and a man not to be trusted. When we apprehend God deceitful in his promises, unrighteous in his threatenings, unwilling to pardon upon repentance, or resolved to pardon notwithstanding impenitency, these are things either unworthy of the nature of God, or contrary to that revelation he hath given of himself. Better for a man never to have been born than be for ever miserable ; so better to be thought no God than represented impotent or negligent, unjust or deceitful, which are more contrary to the nature of God than hell can be to the greatest criminal. In this sense perhaps the apostle affirms the Gentiles, Eph. ii. 12, to be such as are ' without God in the world,' as being more atheists in adoring God under such notions as they commonly did, than if they had acknowledged no God at all.'

2. This is evident by our natural desire to be distant from him, and unwillingness to have any acquaintance with him. Sin set us first at a distance from God ; and every new act of gross sin estrangeth us more from him, and indisposeth us more for him : it makes us both afraid and ashamed to be near him. Sensual men were of this frame that Job discourseth of : Job xxi. 7–9, and 14, 15. Where grace reigns, the nearer to God, the more vigorous the motion ; the nearer anything approaches to us that is the object of our desires, the more eagerly do we press forward to it ; but our blood riseth at the approaches of anything to which we have an aversion. We

---

* Tertul. cont. Marcion, lib. i. cap. 2.

have naturally a loathing of God's coming to us, or our return to him; we seek not after him as our happiness; and when he offers himself, we like it not, but put a disgrace upon him in choosing other things before him. God and we are naturally at as great a distance as light and darkness, life and death, heaven and hell. The stronger impression of God anything hath, the more we fly from it. The glory of God in reflection upon Moses his face scared the Israelites; they who desired God to speak to them by Moses, when they saw a signal impression of God upon his countenance, were afraid to come near him, as they were before unwilling to come near to God, Exod. xxxiv. 30. Not that the blessed God is in his own nature a frightful object, but our own guilt renders him so to us, and ourselves indisposed to converse with him; as the light of the sun is as irksome to a distempered eye as it is in its own nature desirable to a sound one. The saints themselves have had so much frailty, that they have cried out that they were undone, if they had any more than ordinary discoveries of a God made unto them; as if they wished him more remote from them. Vileness cannot endure the splendour of majesty, nor guilt the glory of a judge.

We have naturally, (1.) No desire of remembrance of him; (2.) or converse with him; (3.) or thorough return to him; (4.) or close imitation of him: as if there were not such being as God in the world; or as if we wished there were none at all; so feeble and spiritless are our thoughts of the being of a God.

(1.) No desire for the remembrance of him. How delightful are other things in our minds! How burdensome the memorials of God, from whom we have our being! With what pleasure do we contemplate the nature of creatures, even of flies and toads; while our minds tire in the search of him who hath bestowed upon us our knowing and meditating faculties! Though God shews himself to us in every creature, in the meanest weed as well as in the highest heavens, and is more apparent in them to our reasons than themselves can be to our sense, yet though we see them, we will not behold God in them. We will view them to please our sense, to improve our reason in their natural perfections; but pass by the consideration of God's perfections so visibly beaming from them. Thus we play the beasts and atheists in the very exercise of reason, and neglect our Creator to gratify our sense; as though the pleasure of that were more desirable than the knowledge of God. The desire of our souls is not ' towards his name and the remembrance of him,' Isa. xxvi. 8, when we set not ourselves in a posture to feast our souls with deep and serious meditations of him; have a thought of him only by the by and away, as if we were afraid of too intimate acquaintance with him.

Are not the thoughts of God rather our invaders than our guests, seldom invited to reside and take up their home in our hearts? Have we not, when they have broken in upon us, bid them ' depart from us,' Job xxii. 17, and warned them to come no more upon our ground; sent them packing as soon as we could, and were glad when they were gone? And when they have departed, have we not often been afraid they should return again upon us, and therefore looked about for other inmates, things not good; or if good, infinitely below God, to possess the room of our hearts before any thoughts of him should appear again? Have we not often been glad of excuses to shake off present thoughts of him; and when we have wanted real ones, found out pretences to keep God and our hearts at a distance? Is not this a part of atheism, to be so unwilling to employ our faculties about the giver of them, to refuse to exercise them in a way of grateful remembrance of him, as though they were none of his gift, but our own acquisition;

as though the God that truly gave them had no right to them, and he that thinks on us every day in a way of providence, were not worthy to be thought on by us in a way of special remembrance?

Do not the best, that love the remembrance of him, and abhor this natural averseness, find that when they would think of God, many things tempt them and turn them to think elsewhere? Do they not find their apprehensions too feeble, their motions too dull, and the impressions too slight? This natural atheism is spread over human nature.

(2.) No desire of converse with him. The word *remember*, in the command for keeping holy the Sabbath-day, including all the duties of the day, and the choicest of our lives, implies our natural unwillingness to them, and forgetfulness of them. God's pressing this command with more reasons than the rest, manifests that man hath no heart for spiritual duties. No spiritual duty, which sets us immediately face to face with God, but in the attempts of it we find naturally a resistance from some powerful principle; so that every one may subscribe to the speech of the apostle, that ' when we would do good, evil is present with us.' No reason of this can be rendered but the natural temper of our souls, and an affecting a distance from God under any consideration; for though our guilt first made the breach, yet this aversion to a converse with him steps up without any actual reflections upon our guilt, which may render God terrible to us as an offended judge. Are we not also, in our attendance upon him, more pleased with the modes of worship which gratify our fancy, than to have our souls inwardly delighted with the object of worship himself?

This is a part of our natural atheism. To cast such duties off by total neglect, or in part, by affecting a coldness in them, is to cast off the fear of the Lord, Job xv. 4. Not to call upon God, and not to know him, are one and the same thing, Jer. x. 25. Either we think there is no such being in the world, or that he is so slight a one, that he deserves not the respect he calls for; or so impotent and poor, that he cannot supply what our necessities require.

(3.) No desire of a thorough return to him. The first man fled from him after his defection, though he had no refuge to fly to but the grace of his Creator. Cain went from his presence, would be a fugitive from God, rather than a supplicant to him; when by faith in, and application of the promised Redeemer, he might have escaped the wrath to come for his brother's blood, and mitigated the sorrows he was justly sentenced to bear in the world. Nothing will separate prodigal man from commoning with swine, and make him return to his father, but an empty trough; have we but husks to feed on, we shall never think of a father's presence. It were well if our sores and indigence would drive us to him; but when our ' strength is devoured,' we will not ' return to the Lord our God, nor seek him for all this,' Hosea vii. 10. Not his drawn sword as a God of judgment, nor his mighty power as a Lord, nor his open arms as the Lord their God, could move them to turn their eyes and their hearts towards him. The more he invites us to partake of his grace, the further we run from him to provoke his wrath: the louder God called them by his prophets, the closer they stuck to their Baal, Hosea xi. 2. We turn our backs when he stretches out his hand, stop our ears when he lifts up his voice; we fly from him when he courts us, and shelter ourselves in any bush from his merciful hand, that would lay hold upon us; nor will we set our faces towards him, till our ' way be hedged up with thorns,' and not a gap left to creep out any by-way, Hosea ii. 6, 7. Whosoever is brought to a return, puts the Holy Ghost to the pain of striving; he is not easily brought to a spiritual subjection to God, nor persuaded to a surrender at a summons, but sweetly overpowered by storm, and victoriously drawn into the arms of God. God stands ready, but the heart stands off; grace is full of entreaties, and the soul full of excuses; divine love offers, and carnal self-love rejects. Nothing so pleases us, as when we are furthest from him; as if anything were more amiable, anything more desirable than himself.

(4.) No desire of any close imitation of him. When our Saviour was to come as a refiner's fire to purify the sons of Levi, the cry is, ' Who shall abide the day of his coming?' Mal. iii. 2, 3. Since we are alienated from the life of God, we desire no more naturally to live the life of God, than a toad or any other animal desires to live the life of a man. No heart that knows God but hath a holy ambition to imitate him; no soul that refuseth him for a copy, but is ignorant of his excellency; of this temper is all mankind naturally. Man in corruption is as loath to be like God in holiness, as Adam after his creation was desirous to be like God in knowledge; his posterity are like their father, who soon turned his back upon his original copy.

What can be worse than this? Can the denial of his being be a greater injury than this contempt of him; as if he had not goodness to deserve our remembrance, nor amiableness fit for our converse; as if he were not a Lord fit for our subjection, nor had a holiness that deserved our imitation?

IV. For the use of this. It serves,

1. For information.

(1.) It gives us occasion to admire the wonderful patience and mercy of God. How many millions of practical atheists breathe every day in his air, and live upon his bounty, who deserve to be inhabitants in hell, rather than possessors of the earth! An infinite holiness is offended, an infinite justice is provoked; yet an infinite patience forbears the punishment, and an infinite goodness relieves our wants. The more we had merited his justice and forfeited his favour, the more is his affection enhanced, which makes his hand so liberal to us.

At the first invasion of his rights, he mitigates the terror of the threatening, which was set to defend his law, with the grace of a promise to relieve and recover his rebellious creature, Gen. iii. 15. Who would have looked for anything but tearing thunders, sweeping judgments, to rase up the foundations of the apostate world? But oh, how great are his bowels to his aspiring competitors! Have we not experimented his contrivances for our good, though we have refused him for our happiness? Has he not opened his arms, when we spurned with our feet; held out his alluring mercy, when we have brandished against him a rebellious sword? Has he not entreated us while we have invaded him, as if he were unwilling to lose us, who are ambitious to destroy ourselves? Has he yet denied us the care of his providence, while we have denied him the rights of his honour, and would appropriate them to ourselves? Has the sun forborne shining upon us, though we have shot our arrows against him? Have not our beings been supported by his goodness, while we have endeavoured to climb up to his throne; and his mercies continued to charm us, while we have used them as weapons to injure him? Our own necessities might excite us to own him as our happiness, but he adds his invitations to the voice of our wants. Has he not promised a kingdom to those that would strip him of his crown, and proclaimed pardon, upon repentance, to those that would take away his glory? and hath so twisted together his own end, which is his honour, and man's true end, which is his salvation, that a man cannot truly mind himself and his own salvation, but he must mind God's glory; and cannot be intent upon God's honour but by the same act he promotes himself and his own happiness; so loath is God to give any just occasion of dissatisfaction to his creature, as well as dishonour himself. All those wonders of his mercy are enhanced by the heinousness of our atheism, a multitude of gracious thoughts from him above the multitude of contempts from us, Ps. cvi. 7. What rebels in actual arms against their prince, aiming at his life, ever found that favour from him, to have all their necessaries richly afforded them, without which they would starve, and without which they would be unable to manage their attempts, as we have received from God? Had not God had ' riches of goodness, forbearance, and long-suffering,' and infinite riches too, the despite the world had done him in refusing him as their rule, happiness, and end, would have emptied him long ago, Rom. ii. 4.

(2.) It brings in a justification of the exercise of his justice. If it gives us occasion loudly to praise his patience, it also stops our mouths from accusing any acts of his vengeance. What can be too sharp a recompence for the despising and disgracing so great a being? The highest contempt merits the greatest anger, and when we will not own him for our happiness, it is equal we should feel the misery of separation from him. If he that is guilty of treason deserves to lose his life, what punishment can be thought great enough for him that is so disingenuous as to prefer himself before a God so infinitely good, and so foolish as to invade the rights of one infinitely powerful? It is no injustice for a creature to be for ever left to himself, to see what advantage he can make of that self he was so busily employed to set up in the place of his Creator. The soul of man deserves an infinite punishment for despising an infinite good. And is it not unequitable that that self, which man makes his rule and happiness above God, should become his torment and misery by the righteousness of that God whom he despised.

(3.) Hence ariseth a necessity of a new state and frame of soul, to alter an atheistical nature. We forget God, think of him with reluctancy, have no respect to God in our course and acts. This cannot be our original state. God being infinitely good, never let man come out of his hands with this actual unwillingness to acknowledge and serve him. He never intended to dethrone himself for the work of his hands, or that the creature should have any other end than that of his Creator. As the apostle saith in the case of the Galatians' error, Gal. v. 8, ' This persuasion came not of him that called you,' so this frame comes not from him that created you. How much, therefore, do we need a restoring principle in us! Instead of ordering ourselves according to the will of God, we are desirous to ' fulfil the wills of the flesh,' Eph. ii. 8. There is a necessity of some other principle in us to make us fulfil the will of God, since we were created for God, not for the flesh.

We can no more be voluntarily serviceable to God while our serpentine nature and devilish habits remain in us, than we can suppose the devil can be willing to glorify God while the nature he contracted by his fall abides powerfully in him. Our nature and will must be changed, that our actions may regard God as our end, that we may delightfully meditate on him, and draw the motives of our obedience from him. Since this atheism is seated in nature, the change must be in our nature. Since our first aspirings to the rights of God were the fruits of the serpent's breath, which tainted our nature, there must be a removal of this taint, whereby our natures may be on the side of God against Satan, as they were before on the side of Satan against God. There must be a supernatural principle before we can live a supernatural life, i.e., live to God, since we are naturally alienated from the life of God.' The aversion of our natures from God is as strong as our inclinations to evil; we are disgusted with one, and pressed with the other; we have no will, no heart to come to God in any service. This nature must be broken in pieces, and new moulded, before we can make God our rule and our end. While men's deeds are evil, they cannot comply with God, John iii. 19, 20, much less while their natures are evil. Till this be done, all the service a man performs riseth from some evil imagination of the heart, which is evil, only evil, and that continually, Gen. vi. 5, from wrong notions of God, wrong notions of duty, or corrupt motives. All the pretences of devotion to God are but the adoration of some golden image. Prayers to God for the ends of self, are like those of the devil to our Saviour, when he asked leave to go into the herd of swine. The object was right, Christ; the end was the destruction of the swine, and the satisfaction of their malice to the owners. There is a necessity, then, that depraved ends should be removed, that that which was God's end in our framing may be our end in our acting, viz., his glory, which cannot be without a change of nature. We can never honour him supremely whom we do not supremely love. Till this be, we cannot glorify God as God, though we do things by his command and order, no more than when God employed the devil in afflicting Job, chap. i. His performance cannot be said to be good, because his end was not the same with God's. He acted out of malice what God commanded out of sovereignty, and for gracious designs. Had God employed an holy angel in his design upon Job, the action had been good in the affliction, because his nature was holy, and therefore his ends holy; but bad in the devil, because his ends were base and unworthy.

(4.) We may gather from hence the difficulty of conversion, and mortification to follow thereupon. What is the reason men receive no more impression from the voice of God and the light of his truth, than a dead man in the grave doth from the roaring thunder, or a blind mole from the light of the sun? It is because our atheism is as great as the deadness of the one or the blindness of the other. The principle in the heart is strong to shut the door both of the thoughts and affections against God. If a friend oblige us, we shall act for him as for ourselves. We are won by entreaties; soft words overcome us; but our hearts are as deaf as the hardest rock at the call of God. Neither the joys of heaven proposed by him can allure us, nor the flashed terrors of hell affright us to him; as if we conceived God unable to bestow the one or execute the other. The true reason is, God and self contest for the deity. The law of sin is, God must be at the foot-stool; the law of God is, sin must be utterly deposed. Now it is difficult to leave a law beloved for a law long ago discarded. The mind of man will hunt after anything, the will of man embrace anything; upon the proposal of mean objects, the spirit of man spreads its wings, flies to catch them, becomes one with them; but attempt to bring it under the power of God, the wings flag, the creature looks lifeless, as though there were no spring of motion in it. It is as much crucified to God as the holy apostle was to the world. The sin of the heart discovers its strength the more God discovers the holiness of his will, Rom. vii. 9–12. The love of sin hath been predominant in our nature, has quashed a love to God, if not extinguished it.

Hence also is the difficulty of mortification. This is a work tending to the honour of God, the abasing of that inordinately aspiring humour in ourselves. If the nature of man be inclined to sin, as it is, it must needs be bent against anything that opposes it. It is impossible to strike any true blow at any lust, till the true sense of God be re-entertained in the soil where it ought to grow. Who can be naturally willing to crucify what is incorporated with him, his flesh; what is dearest to him, himself? Is it an easy thing for man, the competitor with God, to turn his arms against himself, that self should overthrow its own empire, lay aside all its pretensions to and designs for a godhead ; to hew off its own members and subdue its own affections ? It is the nature of man to cover his sin, to hide it in his bosom,—Job xxxi. 33, 'If I cover my transgression, as Adam,'—not to destroy it, and as unwillingly part with his carnal affections as the legion of devils were with the man that had been long possessed. And when he is forced and fired from one, he will endeavour to espouse some other lust, as those devils desired to possess swine, when they were chased from their possession of that man.

(5.) Here we see the reason of unbelief. That which hath most of God in it meets with most aversion from us; that which hath least of God finds better and stronger inclinations in us. What is the reason that the heart of man is more unwilling to embrace the gospel than acknowledge the equity of the law ? Because there is more of God's nature and perfection evident in the gospel than in the law ; besides, there is more reliance on God and distance from self commanded in the gospel. The law puts a man upon his own strength, the gospel takes him off from his own bottom. The law acknowledges him to have a power in himself, and to act for his own reward; the gospel strips him of all his proud and towering thoughts, 2 Cor. x. 5, brings him to his due place, the foot of God, orders him to deny himself as his own rule, righteousness, and end, and henceforth not to live to himself, 2 Cor. v. 15. This is the true reason why men are more against the gospel than against the law, because it doth more deify God and debase man. Hence it is easier to reduce men to some moral virtue than to faith ; to make men blush at their outward vices, but not at the inward impurity of their natures. Hence it is observed that those that assert that all happiness did arise from something in a man's self, as the Stoics and Epicureans did, and that a wise man was equal with God, were greater enemies to the truths of the gospel than others, Acts xvii. 18, because it lays the axe to the root of their principal opinion ; takes the one from their self-sufficiency, and the other from their self-gratification. It opposeth the brutish principle of the one, which placed happiness in the pleasures of the body, and the more noble principle of the other, which placed happiness in the virtue of the mind. The one was for a sensual, the other for a moral self, both disowned by the doctrine of the gospel.

(6.) It informs us, consequently, who can be the author of grace and conversion, and every other good work. No practical atheist ever yet turned to God but was turned by God ; and not to acknowledge it to God is a part of this atheism, since it is a robbing God of the honour of one of his most glorious works. If this practical atheism be natural to man ever since the first taint of nature in paradise, what can be expected from it but a resisting of the work of God, and setting up all the forces of nature against the operations of grace, till a day of power dawn and clear up upon the soul ? Ps. cx. 3. Not all the angels in heaven, or men upon earth, can be imagined to be able to persuade a man to fall out with himself; nothing can turn the tide of nature, but a power above nature. God took away the sanctifying Spirit from man, as a penalty for the first sin ; who can regain it but by his will and pleasure ? Who can restore it but he that removed it ? Since every man hath the same fundamental atheism in him by nature, and would be a rule to himself, and his own end, he is so far from dethroning himself that all the strength of his corrupted nature is alarmed up to stand to their arms, upon any attempt God makes to regain the fort. The will is so strong against God, that it is like many wills twisted together: Eph. ii. 3, 'wills of the flesh,' we translate it the 'desires of the flesh.' Like many threads twisted in a cable, never to be snapped asunder by a human arm, a power and will above ours can only untwist so many wills in a knot. Man cannot rise to an acknowledgment of God without God. Hell may as well become heaven, the devil be changed into an angel of light. The devil cannot but desire happiness, he knows the misery into which he is fallen; he cannot be desirous of that punishment he knows is reserved for him. Why doth he not sanctify God and glorify his Creator, wherein there is abundantly more pleasure than in his malicious course? Why doth he not petition to recover his ancient standing? He will not, there are chains of darkness upon his faculties; he will not be otherwise than he is. His desire to be god of the world sways him against his own interest, and out of love to his malice he will not sin at a less rate to make a diminution of his punishment. Man, if God utterly refuseth to work upon him, is no better, and to maintain his atheism would venture a hell. How is it possible for a man to turn himself to that God, against whom he hath a quarrel in his nature, the most rooted and settled habit in him being to set himself in the place of God? An atheist by nature can no more alter his own temper, and engrave in himself the divine nature, than a rock can carve itself into the statue of a man, or a serpent, that is an enemy to man, could or would raise itself to the nobility of the human nature. That soul that by nature would strip God of his rights, cannot, without a divine power, be made conformable to him, and acknowledge sincerely and cordially the rights and glory of God.

(7.) We may here see the reason why there can be no justification by the best and strongest works of nature. Can that which hath atheism at the root justify either the action or person? What strength can those works have which have neither God's law for their rule, nor his glory for their end, that are not wrought by any spiritual strength for him, nor tend with any spiritual affection to him? Can these be a foundation for the most holy God to pronounce a creature righteous? They will justify his justice in condemning, but cannot sway his justice to an absolution. Every natural man in his works picks and chooses; he owns the will of God no further than he can wring it to suit the law of his members, and minds not the honour of God, but as it justles not with his own glory and secular ends. Can he be righteous that prefers his own will and his own honour before the will and honour of the Creator? However men's actions may be beneficial to others, what reason hath God to esteem them, wherein there is no respect to him but themselves, whereby they dethrone him in their thoughts, while they seem to own him in their religious works? Every day reproves us with something different from the rule, thousands of wanderings offer themselves to our eyes. Can justification be expected from that which in itself is matter of despair?

(8.) See here the cause of all the apostasy in the world. Practical atheism was never conquered in such, they are still 'alienated from the life of God,' and will not live to God, as he lives to himself and his own honour, Eph. iv. 17, 18. They loathe his rule and distaste his glory; are loath to step out of themselves to promote the ends of another; find not the satisfaction in him as they do in themselves. They will be judges of what is good for them and righteous in itself, rather than admit of God to judge for them. When men draw back from truth to error, it is to such opinions which may serve more to foment and cherish their ambition, covetousness, or some beloved lust that disputes with God for precedency, and is designed to be served before him: John xii. 42, 43, 'They love the praise of men more than the praise of God.' A preferring man before God was the reason they would not confess Christ, and God in him.

(9.) This shews us the excellency of the gospel and Christian religion. It sets man in his due place, and gives to God what the excellency of his nature requires. It lays man in the dust from whence he was taken, and sets God upon that throne where he ought to sit. Man by nature would annihilate God and deify himself; the gospel glorifies God and annihilates man. In our first revolt we would be like him in knowledge; in the means he hath provided for our recovery he designs to make us like him in grace. The gospel shews ourselves to be an object of humiliation, and God to be a glorious object for our imitation. The light of nature tells us there is a God; the gospel gives us a more magnificent report of him. The light of nature condemns gross atheism, and that of the gospel condemns and conquers spiritual atheism in the hearts of men.

Use 2. Of exhortation.

(1.) Let us labour to be sensible of this atheism in our nature, and be humbled for it. How should we lie in the dust, and go bowing under the humbling thoughts of it all our days! Shall we not be sensible of that whereby we spill the blood of our souls, and give a stab to the heart of our own salvation? Shall we be worse than any creature, not to bewail that which tends to our destruction? He that doth not lament it cannot challenge the character of a Christian, hath nothing of the divine life and love planted in his soul. Not a man but shall one day be sensible, when the eternal God shall call him out to examination, and charge his conscience to discover every crime, which will then own the authority whereby it acted; when the heart shall be torn open, and the secrets of it brought to public view, and the world and man himself shall see what a viperous brood of corrupt principles and ends nested in his heart. Let us, therefore, be truly sensible of it, till the consideration draws tears from our eyes and sorrow from our souls. Let us urge the thoughts of it upon our hearts, till the core of that pride be eaten out, and our stubbornness changed into humility; till our heads become waters, and our eyes fountains of tears, and be a spring of prayer to God, to change the heart and mortify the atheism in it, and consider what a sad thing it is to be a practical atheist; and who is not so by nature?

Let us be sensible of it in ourselves. Have any of our hearts been a soil wherein the fear and reverence of God hath naturally grown? Have we a desire to know him, or a will to embrace him? Do we delight in his will, and love the remembrance of his name? Are our respects to him as God equal to the speculative knowledge we have of his nature? Is the heart, wherein he hath stamped his image, reserved for his residence? Is not the world more affected than the Creator of the world, as though that could contribute to us a greater happiness than the author of it? Have not creatures as much of our love, fear, trust, nay, more than God, that framed both them and thus? Have we not too often relied upon our own strength, and made a calf of our own wisdom, and said of God as the Israelites of Moses, 'As for this Moses, we wot not what is become of him,' Exod. xxxii. 1; and given oftener the glory of our good success to our drag and our net, to our craft and our industry, than to the wisdom and blessing of God? Are we then free from this sort of atheism? * It is as impossible to have two gods at one time in one heart as to have two kings at one time in full power in one kingdom. Have there not been frequent neglects of God? Have we not been deaf whilst he hath knocked at our doors, slept when he hath sounded

* Lawson, Body of Divinity, p. 153, 154.

in our ears, as if there had been no such being as a God in the world; how many strugglings have been against our approaches to him? Hath not folly often been committed with vain imaginations starting up in the time of religious service, which we would scarce vouchsafe a look to at another time, and in another business, but would have thrust them away with indignation? Had they stepped in to interrupt our worldly affairs, they would have been troublesome intruders, but while we are with God they are acceptable guests. How unwilling have our hearts been to fortify themselves with strong and influencing considerations of God before we addressed to him? Is it not too often that our lifelessness in prayer proceeds from this atheism, a neglect of seeing what arguments and pleas may be drawn from the divine perfections, to second our suit in hand, and quicken our hearts in the service? Whence are those indispositions to any spiritual duty, but because we have not due thoughts of the majesty, holiness, goodness, and excellency of God? Is there any duty which leads to a more particular inquiry after him, or a more clear vision of him, but our hearts have been ready to rise up and call it cursed rather than blessed? Are not our minds bemisted with an ignorance of him, our wills drawn by aversion from him, our affections rising in distaste of him? More willing to know anything than his nature, and more industrious to do anything than his will? Do we not all fall under some one or other of these considerations? Is it not fit then that we should have a sense of them? It is to be bewailed by us that so little of God is in our hearts, when so many evidences of the love of God are in the creatures, that God should be so little our end who hath been so much our benefactor, that he should be so little in our thoughts who sparkles in everything which presents itself to our eyes.

(2.) Let us be sensible of it in others. We ought to have a just execration of the too open iniquity in the midst of us, and imitate holy David, whose tears plentifully gushed out, 'because men kept not God's law,' Ps. cxix. 136. And is it not a time to exercise this pious lamentation? Hath the wicked atheism of any age been greater, or can you find worse in hell than we may hear of, and behold on earth? How is the excellent majesty of God adored by the angels in heaven, despised and reproached by men on earth, as if his name were published to be matter of their sport! What a gasping thing is a natural sense of God among men in the world! Is not the law of God, accompanied with such dreadful threatenings and curses, made light of, as if men would place their honour in being above or beyond any sense of that glorious majesty? How many wallow in pleasures, as if they had been made men only to turn brutes, and their souls given them only for salt to keep their bodies from putrefying? It is as well a part of atheism not to be sensible of the abuses of God's name and laws by others, as to violate them ourselves. What is the language of a stupid senselessness of them, but that there is no God in the world, whose glory is worth a vindication, and deserves our regards?

That we may be sensible of the unworthiness of neglecting God as our rule and end, consider,

1. The unreasonableness of it as it concerns God.

(1.) First, It is a high contempt of God. It is an inverting the order of things, a making God the highest to become the lowest, and self the lowest to become the highest; to be guided by every base companion, some idle vanity, some carnal interest, is to acknowledge an excellency abounding in them which is wanting in God; an equity in their orders and none in God's precepts; a goodness in their promises and a falsity in God's, as if infinite excellency were a mere vanity, and to act for God were the debasement of our reason ; to act for self, or some pitiful creature, or sordid lust, were the glory and advancement of it. To prefer any one sin before the honour of God is as if that sin had been our creator and benefactor, as if it were the original cause of our being and support. Do not men pay as great a homage to that as they do to God ? Do not their minds eagerly pursue it ? Are not the revolvings of it in their fancies as delightful to them as the remembrance of God to a holy soul ? Do any obey the commands of God with more readiness than they do the orders of their base affections ? Did Peter leap more readily into the sea to meet his master than many into the jaws of hell to meet their Delilahs ? How cheerfully did the Israelites part with their ornaments for the sake of an idol, who would not have spared a moiety for the honour of their deliverer ! Exod. xxxii. 3, ' All the people brake off the golden earrings.' If to make God our end is the principal duty in nature, then to make ourselves or anything else our end is the greatest vice in the rank of evils.

(2.) Secondly, It is a contempt of God as the most amiable object. God is infinitely excellent and desirable : Zech. ix. 17, ' How great is his goodness, and how great is his beauty ! ' There is nothing in him but what may ravish our affections ; none that knows him but finds attractives to keep them with him ; he hath nothing in him which can be a proper object of contempt, no defects or shadow of evil ; there is infinite excellency to charm us, and infinite goodness to allure us ; the author of our beings, the benefactor of our lives ; why then should man, which is his image, be so base as to slight the beautiful original which stamped it on him ! He is the most lovely object, therefore to be studied, therefore to be honoured, therefore to be followed. In regard of his perfection, he hath the highest right to our thoughts. All other beings were eminently contained in his essence, and were produced by his infinite power. The creature hath nothing but what it hath from God. And is it not unworthy to prefer the copy before the original, to fall in love with a picture instead of the beauty it represents ? The creature, which we advance to be our rule and end, can no more report to us the true amiableness of God, than a few colours mixed and suited together upon a piece of cloth can the moral and intellectual loveliness of the soul of man. To contemn God one moment is more base than if all creatures were contemned by us for ever ; because the excellency of creatures is to God like that of a drop to the sea, or a spark to the glory of unconceivable millions of suns. As much as the excellency of God is above our, conceptions, so much doth the debasing of him admit of unexpressible aggravations.

2. Consider the ingratitude in it. That we should resist that God with our hearts, who made us the work of his hands, and count him as nothing from whom we derive all the good that we are or have, there is no contempt of man but steps in here to aggravate our slighting of God, because there is no relation one man can stand in to another wherein God doth not more highly appear to man. If we abhor the unworthy carriage of a child to a tender father, a servant to an indulgent master, a man to his obliging friend, why do men daily act that towards God which they cannot speak of without abhorrency if acted by another against man ? Is God a being less to be regarded than man, and more worthy of contempt than a creature ? It would be strange if a benefactor should live in the same town, in the same house with us, and we never exchange a word with him ; yet this is our case, who have the works of God in our eyes, the goodness of God in our being, the mercy of God in our daily food, yet think so little of him, converse so little with him, serve everything before him, and prefer every-

thing above him.'* Whence have we our mercies but from his hand? Who, besides him, maintains our breath this moment? Would he call for our spirits this moment, they must depart from us to attend his command. There is not a moment wherein our unworthy carriage is not aggravated, because there is not a moment wherein he is not a guardian, and gives us not tastes of a fresh bounty. And it is no light aggravation of our crime that we injure him, without whose bounty in giving us our being, we had not been capable of casting contempt upon him; that he that hath the greatest stamp of his image, man, should deserve the character of the worst of his rebels; that he who hath only reason by the gift of God to judge of the equity of the laws of God, should swell against them as grievous, and the government of the lawgiver as burdensome. Can it lessen the crime, to use the principle wherein we excel the beasts, to the disadvantage of God, who endowed us with that principle above the beasts.

(1.) It is a debasing of God beyond what the devil doth at present. He is more excusable in his present state of acting than man is in his present refusing God for his rule and end. He strives against a God that exerciseth upon him a vindictive justice; we debase a God that loads us with his daily mercies. The despairing devils are excluded from any mercy or divine patience, but we are not only under the long-suffering of his patience, but the large expressions of his bounty. He would not be governed by him when he was only his bountiful Creator. We refuse to be guided by him after he hath given us the blessing of creation from his own hand, and the more obliging blessings of redemption by the hand and blood of his Son.

It cannot be imagined that the devils and the damned should ever make God their end, since he hath assured them he will not be their happiness, and shut up all his perfections from their experimental notice, but those of his power to preserve them, and his justice to punish them. They have no grant from God of ever having a heart to comply with his will, or ever having the honour to be actively employed for his glory. They have some plea for their present contempt of God; not in regard of his nature, for he is infinitely amiable, excellent, and lovely, but in regard of his administration towards them. But what plea can man have for his practical atheism, who lives by his power, is sustained by his bounty, and solicited by his Spirit? What an ungrateful thing is it to put off the nature of man for that of devils, and dishonour God under mercy, as the devils do under his wrathful anger!

(2.) It is an ungrateful contempt of God, who cannot be injurious to us. He cannot do us wrong, because he cannot be unjust: Gen. xviii. 25, 'Shall not the Judge of all the earth do right?' His nature doth as much abhor unrighteousness as love a communicative goodness. He never commanded anything but what was highly conducible to the happiness of man. Infinite goodness can no more injure man than it can dishonour itself. It lays out itself in additions of kindness, and whiles we debase him, he continues to benefit us. And is it not an unparalleled ingratitude to turn our backs upon an object so lovely, an object so loving, in the midst of varieties of allurements from him? God did create intellectual creatures, angels and men, that he might communicate more of himself, and his own goodness and holiness to man, than creatures of a lower rank were capable of. What do we do by rejecting him as a rule and end, but cross, as much as in us lies, God's end in our creation, and shut our souls against the communications of those perfections he was so willing to bestow? We use him as if he intended us the greatest wrong, when it is impossible for him to do any to any of his creatures.

3. Consider the misery which will attend such a temper if it continue

* Reynolds.

predominant. Those that thrust God away as their happiness and end, can expect no other but to be thrust away by him as to any relief and compassion. A distance from God here can look for nothing but a remoteness from God hereafter. When the devil, a creature of vast endowments, would advance himself above God, and instruct man to commit the same sin, he is ' cursed above all creatures,' Gen. iii. 14. When we will not acknowledge him a God of all glory, we shall be separated from him as a God of all comfort : ' All they that are afar off shall perish,' Ps. lxxiii. 27. This is the spring of all woe. What the prodigal suffered was because he would leave his father and live of himself. Whosoever is ambitious to be his own heaven, will at last find his soul to become his own hell. As it loved all things for itself, so it shall be grieved with all things for itself. As it would be its own god against the right of God, it shall then be its own tormentor by the justice of God.

2. Duty. Watch against this atheism, and be daily employed in the mortification of it. In every action we should make the inquiry, What is the rule I observe ? Is it God's will or my own ? Whether do my intentions tend to set up God or self ? As much as we destroy this, we abate the power of sin. These two things are the head of the serpent in us, which we must be bruising by the power of the cross. Sin is nothing else but a turning from God and centring in self, and most in the inferior part of self. If we bend our force against those two, self-will and self-ends, we shall intercept atheism at the spring-head, take away that which doth constitute and animate all sin. The sparks must vanish, if the fire be quenched which affords them fuel. They are but two short things to ask in every undertaking : Is God my rule in regard of his will ? Is God my end in regard of his glory ? All sin lies in the neglect of these, all grace lies in the practice of them.

Without some degree of the mortification of these, we cannot make profitable and comfortable approaches to God. When we come with idols in our hearts, we shall be answered according to the multitude and the baseness of them too, Ezek. xiv. 4. What expectation of a good look from him can we have, when we come before him with undeifying thoughts of him, a petition in our mouths, and a sword in our hearts to stab his honour !

To this purpose,

(1.) Be often in the views of the excellencies of God. When we have no intercourse with God by delightful meditations, we begin to be estranged from him, and prepare ourselves to live without God in the world. Strangeness is the mother and nurse of disaffection. We slight men sometimes because we know them not. The very beasts delight in the company of men, when being trained and familiar, they become acquainted with their disposition. A daily converse with God would discover so much of loveliness in his nature, so much of sweetness in his ways, that our injurious thoughts of God would wear off, and we should count it our honour to contemn ourselves and magnify him. By this means, a slavish fear, which is both a dishonour to God and a torment to the soul, 1 John iv. 18, and the root of atheism, will be cast out, and an ingenious* fear of him wrought in the heart. Exercised thoughts on him would issue out in affections to him, which would engage our hearts to make him both our rule and our end. This course would stifle any temptations to gross atheism wherewith good souls are sometimes haunted, by confirming us more in the belief of a God, and discourage any attempts to a deliberate practical atheism. We are not like to espouse any principle which is confuted by the delightful converse we

* That is 'ingenuous.'—ED.

daily have with him. The more we thus enter into the presence chamber
of God, the more we cling about him with our affections ; the more vigorous and lively will the true notion of God grow up in us, and be able to
prevent anything which may dishonour him and debase our souls.

Let us therefore consider him as the only happiness, set up the true God
in our understandings, possess our hearts with a deep sense of his desirable
excellency above all other things. This is the main thing we are to do in
order to our great business. All the directions in the world, with the
neglect of this, will be insignificant ciphers. The neglect of this is common,
and is the basis of all the mischiefs which happen to the souls of men.

(2.) To this purpose, prize and study the Scripture. We can have no
delight in meditation on him unless we know him, and we cannot know him
but by the means of his own revelation. When the revelation is despised,
the revealer will be of little esteem. Men do not throw off God from being
their rule, till they throw off Scripture from being their guide ; and God
must needs be cast off from being an end, when the Scripture is rejected
from being a rule. Those that do not care to know his will, that love to be
ignorant of his nature, can never be affected to his honour. Let, therefore,
the subtilties of reason veil to the doctrine of faith, and the humour of the
will to the command of the word.

(3.) Take heed of sensual pleasures, and be very watchful and cautious in
the use of those comforts God allows us. Job was afraid, when his sons
feasted, that they should ' curse God in their hearts,' Job i. 4, 5. It was
not without cause that the apostle Peter joined sobriety with watchfulness
and prayer : 1 Pet. iv. 7, ' The end of all things is at hand ; be ye therefore
sober, and watch unto prayer.' A moderate use of worldly comforts.
Prayer is the great acknowledgment of God, and too much sensuality is a
hindrance of this, and a step to atheism. Belshazzar's lifting himself up
against the Lord, and not glorifying of God, is charged upon his sensuality,
Dan. v. 23. Nothing is more apt to quench the notions of God, and root
out the conscience of him, than an addictedness to sensual pleasures. Therefore take heed of that snare.

(4.) Take heed of sins against knowledge. The more sins against knowledge are committed, the more careless we are, and the more careless we
shall be of God and his honour. We shall more fear his judicial power, and
the more we fear that, the more we shall disaffect that God in whose hand
vengeance is, and to whom it doth belong. Atheism in conversation proceeds to atheism in affection, and that will endeavour to sink into atheism in
opinion and judgment.

The sum of the whole.

And now consider, in the whole, what has been spoken.

1. Man would set himself up as his own rule. He disowns the rule of
God, is unwilling to have any acquaintance with the rule God sets him,
negligent in using the means for the knowledge of his will, and endeavours
to shake it off when any notices of it breaks in upon him. When he cannot
expel it, he hath no pleasure in the consideration of it, and the heart swells
against it. When the notions of the will of God are entertained, it is on
some other consideration, or with wavering and unsettled affections. Many
times men design to improve some lust by his truth. This unwillingness
respects truth, as it is most spiritual and holy, as it most relates and leads
to God, as it is most contrary to self. He is guilty of contempt of the will
of God, which is seen in every presumptuous breach of his law ; in the
natural aversions to the declaration of his will and mind, which way soever
he turns ; in slighting that part of his will which is most for his honour ;

in the awkwardness of the heart when it is to pay God a service; a constraint in the first engagement; slightness in the service, in regard of the matter; in regard of the frame, without a natural vigour; many distractions, much weariness; in deserting the rule of God, when our expectations are not answered upon our service; in breaking promises with God.

Man naturally owns any other rule, rather than that of God's prescribing. The rule of Satan, the will of man; in complying more with the dictates of men than the will of God; in observing that which is materially so, not because it is his will, but the injunctions of men; in obeying the will of man, when it is contrary to the will of God. This man doth, in order to the setting up himself. This is natural to man, as he is corrupted. Men are dissatisfied with their own consciences, when they contradict the desires of self. Most actions in the world are done, more because they are agreeable to self, than as they are honourable to God; as they are agreeable to natural and moral self, or sinful self. It is evident in neglects of taking God's directions upon emergent occasions; in counting the actions of others to be good or bad, as they suit with, or spurn against, our fancies and humours. Man would make himself the rule of God, and give laws to his Creator, in striving against his law, disapproving of his methods of government in the world, in impatience in our particular concerns, envying the gifts and prosperity of others, corrupt matter or ends of prayer or praise, bold interpretations of the judgments of God in the world, mixing rules in the worship of God with those which have been ordained by him, suiting interpretations of Scripture with our own minds and humours, falling off from God after some fair compliances, when his will grates upon us and crosseth ours.

2. Man would be his own end. This is natural and universal. This is seen in frequent self-applauses and inward overweening reflections; in ascribing the glory of what we do or have to ourselves; in desire of self-pleasing doctrines; in being highly concerned in injuries done to ourselves, and little or not at all concerned for injuries done to God; in trusting in ourselves; in working for carnal self, against the light of our own consciences. This is a usurping God's prerogative, vilifying God, destroying God. Man would make anything his end or happiness rather than God. This appears in the fewer thoughts we have of him than of anything else: in the greedy pursuit of the world; in the strong addictedness to sensual pleasures; in paying a service, upon any success in the world, to instruments more than to God. This is a debasing God, in setting up a creature; but more in setting up a base lust: it is a denying of God. Man would make himself the end of all creatures: in pride, using the creatures contrary to the end God hath appointed; this is to dishonour God, and it is diabolical. Man would make himself the end of God: in loving God, because of some self-pleasing benefits distributed by him; in abstinence from some sins, because they are against the interest of some other beloved corruption; in performing duties merely for a selfish interest, which is evident in unwieldiness in religious duties where self is not concerned; in calling upon God only in a time of necessity; in begging his assistance to our own projects, after we have by our own craft laid the plot; in impatience upon a refusal of our desires; in selfish aims we have in our duties. This is a vilifying God, a dethroning him. In unworthy imaginations of God, universal in man by nature. Hence springs idolatry, superstition, presumption, the common disease of the world. This is a vilifying God, worse than idolatry, worse than absolute atheism. Natural desires to be distant from him; no desires for the remembrance of him; no desires of converse with him; no desires of a thorough return to him; no desire of any close imitation of him.

A DISCOURSE UPON GOD'S BEING A SPIRIT.

God is a Spirit: and they that worship him must worship him in spirit and in truth.—JOHN IV. 24.

THE words are part of the dialogue between our Saviour and the Samaritan woman. Christ, intending to return from Judea to Galilee, passed through the country of Samaria, a place inhabited not by Jews, but a mixed company of several nations,* and some remainders of the posterity of Israel, who escaped the captivity and were returned from Assyria, and being weary with his journey, arrived about the sixth hour, or noon (according to the Jews' reckoning the time of the day), at a well that Jacob had digged, which was of great account among the inhabitants for the antiquity of it, as well as the usefulness of it, in supplying their necessities. He being thirsty, and having none to furnish him wherewith to draw water, at last comes a woman from the city, whom he desires to give him some water to drink. The woman, perceiving him by his language or habit to be a Jew, wonders at the question, since the hatred the Jews bore the Samaritans was so great, that they would not vouchsafe to have any commerce with them, not only in religious but civil affairs, and common offices belonging to mankind. Hence our Saviour takes occasion to publish to her the doctrine of the gospel, and excuseth her rude answer by her ignorance of him; and tells her, that if she had asked him a greater matter, even that which concerned her eternal salvation, he would readily have granted it, notwithstanding the rooted hatred between the Jews and Samaritans, and bestowed a water of a greater virtue, the 'water of life,' ver. 10, or 'living water.' The woman is no less astonished at his reply than she was at his first demand. It was strange to hear a man speak of giving living water to one of whom he had begged the water of that spring, and had no vessel to draw any to quench his own thirst. She therefore demands whence he could have this water that he speaks of, ver. 11, since she conceived him not greater than Jacob, who had digged that well and drunk of it. Our Saviour, desirous to make a progress in that work he had begun, extols the water he spake of above this of the well, from its particular virtue, fully to refresh those that drank of it, and be as a cooling and comforting fountain within them, of more efficacy than that without, ver. 13, 14. The woman, conceiving a good opinion of our Saviour, desires to partake of this

* Amirant, Paraph. sur Jean.

water, to save her pains in coming daily to the well, not apprehending the spirituality of Christ's discourse to her, ver. 15. Christ finding her to take some pleasure in his discourse, partly to bring her to a sense of her sin before he did communicate the excellency of his grace, bids her return back to the city and bring her husband with her to him, ver. 16. She freely acknowledges that she had no husband, whether having some check of conscience at present for the unclean life she led, or loath to lose so much time in the gaining this water so much desired by her. Our Saviour takes occasion from this to lay open her sin before her, and to make her sensible of her own wicked life, ver. 17, and the prophetic excellency of himself, and tells her that she had had five husbands, to whom she had been false, and by whom she was divorced; and the person she now dwelt with was not her lawful husband, and in living with him she violated the rights of marriage, and increased guilt upon her conscience, ver. 18. The woman, being affected with this discourse, and knowing him to be a stranger, that could not be certified of those things but in an extraordinary way, begins to have a high esteem of him as a prophet, ver. 19; and upon this opinion she esteems him able to decide a question which had been canvassed between them and the Jews about the place of worship, ver. 20, their fathers worshipping in that mountain, and the Jews affirming Jerusalem to be a place of worship. She pleads the antiquity of the worship in this place, Abraham having built an altar there, Gen. xii. 7, and Jacob upon his return from Syria. And surely, had the place been capable of an exception, such persons as they, and so well acquainted with the will of God, would not have pitched upon that place to celebrate their worship.

Antiquity hath too, too often bewitched the minds of men, and drawn them from the revealed will of God. Men are more willing to imitate the outward actions of their famous ancestors, than conform themselves to the revealed will of their Creator. The Samaritans would imitate the patriarchs in the place of worship, but not in the faith of the worshippers.

Christ answers her, that this question would quickly be resolved by a new state of the church which was near at hand, and neither Jerusalem, which had not* the precedency, nor that mountain, should be of any more value in that concern than any other place in the world, ver. 21. But yet, to make her sensible of her sin and that of her countrymen, tells her that their worship in that mountain was not according to the will of God, he having, long after the altars built in this place, fixed Jerusalem as the place of sacrifices; besides, they had not the knowledge of that God which ought to be worshipped by them, but the Jews had the true object of worship and the true manner of worship, according to the declaration God had made of himself to them, ver. 22. But all that service shall vanish, the veil of the temple shall be rent in twain, and that carnal worship give place to one more spiritual; shadows shall fly before substance, and truth advance itself above figures, and the worship of God shall be with the strength of the Spirit. Such a worship, and such worshippers, doth the Father seek: ver. 23, 'For God is a Spirit: and those that worship him must worship him in spirit and in truth.' The design of our Saviour is to declare that God is not taken with external worship invented by men, no, nor commanded by himself; and that upon this reason, because he is a spiritual essence, infinitely above gross and corporeal matter, and is not taken with that pomp which is a pleasure to our earthly imaginations.

Πνεῦμα ὁ Θεός. Some translate it just as the words lie, 'Spirit is God;'† but it is not unusual, both in the Old and New Testament languages, to put

---

* Qu. 'now'?—ED.   † Vulgar Lat. Illyric. Clav.

the predicate before the subject; as Ps. v. 9, 'Their throat is an open sepulchre,' in the Hebrew, 'A sepulchre open their throat;' so Ps. cxi. 3, 'His work is honourable and glorious;' *Hebr.*, 'Honour and glory his work.' And there wants not one example in the same evangelist: John i. 1, 'And the Word was God;' Greek, 'And God was the Word.' In all the predicate, or what is ascribed, is put before the subject to which it is ascribed.

One tells us, and he an head of a party that hath made a disturbance in the church of God,* that this place is not aptly brought to prove God to be a Spirit. And the reason of Christ runs not thus, God is of a spiritual essence, and therefore must be worshipped with a spiritual worship; for the essence of God is not the foundation of his worship, but his will; for then we were not to worship him with a corporeal worship, because he is not a body, but with an invisible and eternal worship, because he is invisible and eternal.

But the nature of God is the foundation of worship, the will of God is the rule of worship; the matter and manner is to be performed according to the will of God. But is the nature of the object of worship to be excluded? No; as the object is, so ought our devotion to be, spiritual as he is spiritual. God in his commands for worship respected the discovery of his own nature; in the law, he respected the discovery of his mercy and justice, and therefore commanded a worship by sacrifices. A spiritual worship without those institutions would not have declared those attributes, which was God's end to display to the world in Christ. And though the nature of God is to be respected in worship, yet the obligations of the creature are to be considered. God is a Spirit, therefore must have a spiritual worship. The creature hath a body as well as a soul, and both from God; and therefore ought to worship God with the one as well as the other, since one as well as the other is freely bestowed upon him.

The spirituality of God was the foundation of the change from the Judaical carnal worship to a more spiritual and evangelical.

'God is a Spirit.' That is, he hath nothing corporeal, no mixture of matter; not a visible substance, a bodily form.† He is a Spirit, not a bare spiritual substance, but an understanding, willing Spirit; holy, wise, good, and just. Before Christ spake of the Father, ver. 23, the first person in the Trinity, now he speaks of God essentially. The word *Father* is personal, the word *God* essential. So that our Saviour would render a reason, not from any one person in the blessed Trinity, but from the divine nature, why we should worship in spirit; and therefore makes use of the word God, the being a spirit being common to the other persons with the Father.

This is the reason of the proposition, ver. 23, of a spiritual worship. Every nature delights in that which is like it, and distastes that which is most different from it. If God were corporeal, he might be pleased with the victims of beasts, and the beautiful magnificence of temples, and the noise of music; but being a Spirit, he cannot be gratified with carnal things. He demands something better and greater than all those, that soul which he made, that soul which he hath endowed, a spirit of a frame suitable to his nature. He indeed appointed sacrifices and a temple, as shadows of those things which were to be most acceptable to him in the Messiah, but they were imposed only 'till the time of reformation,' Heb. ix. 10.

'Must worship him.' Not they *may*, or it would be more agreeable to God to have such a manner of worship, but they *must*. It is not exclusive

---

* Episcop. Institut. lib. iv. cap. 3.   † Melancthon.

of bodily worship, for this were to exclude all public worship in societies, which cannot be performed without reverential postures of the body.* The gestures of the body are helps to worship and declarations of spiritual acts. We can scarcely worship God with our spirits without some tincture upon the outward man. But he excludes all acts merely corporeal, all resting upon an external service and devotion, which was the crime of the Pharisees, and the general persuasion of the Jews as well as heathens, who used the outward ceremonies, not as signs of better things, but as if they did of themselves please God, and render the worshippers accepted with him, without any suitable frame of the inward man.† It is as if he had said, Now you must separate yourselves from all carnal modes to which the service of God is now tied, and render a worship chiefly consisting in the affectionate motions of the heart, and accommodated more exactly to the condition of the object, who is a Spirit.

' In spirit and truth.' The evangelical service now required has the advantage of the former, that was a shadow and figure, this the body and truth.‡ Spirit, say some,§ is here opposed to the legal ceremonies, truth to hypocritical services; or ||rather truth is opposed to shadows, and an opinion of worth in the outward action. It is principally opposed to external rites; because our Saviour saith, ver. 23, 'The hour comes, and now is,' &c. Had it been opposed to hypocrisy, Christ had said no new thing; for God always required truth in the inward parts, and all true worshippers had served him with a sincere conscience and single heart. The old patriarchs did worship God in Spirit and truth, as taken for sincerity. Such a worship was always and is perpetually due to God, because he always was and eternally will be a Spirit.¶ And it is said, 'The Father seeks such to worship him;' not *shall* seek, he always sought it, it always was performed to him by one or other in the world. And the prophets had always rebuked them for resting upon their outward solemnities, Isa. lviii. 7 and Micah vi. 8. But a worship without legal rites was proper to an evangelical state and the times of the gospel, God having then exhibited Christ, and brought into the world the substance of those shadows and the end of those institutions; there was no more need to continue them when the true reason of them was ceased. All laws do naturally expire when the true reason upon which they were first framed is changed.

Or by spirit may be meant such a worship as is kindled in the heart by the breath of the Holy Ghost. Since we are dead in sin, a spiritual light and flame in the heart, suitable to the nature of the object of our worship, cannot be raised in us without the operation of a supernatural grace. And though the fathers could not worship God without the Spirit, yet in the gospel times, there being a fuller effusion of the Spirit, the evangelical state is called 'the administration of the Spirit,' and the 'newness of the Spirit,' in opposition to the legal economy, entitled the 'oldness of the letter,' 2 Cor. iii. 8, Rom. vii. 6. The evangelical state is more suited to the nature of God than any other. Such a worship God must have, whereby he is acknowledged to be the true sanctifier and quickener of the soul. The nearer God doth approach to us, and the more full his manifestations are, the more spiritual is the worship we return to God. The gospel pares off the rugged parts of the law, and heaven shall remove what is material in the gospel, and change the ordinances of worship into that of a spiritual praise.

In the words there is,

---

* Terniti.
† Amyrald *in loc.*
‡ Amyrald *in loc.*
§ Muscul.
|| Chemnit.
¶ Muscul.

1. A proposition: 'God is a Spirit,' the foundation of all religion.

2. An inference: 'they that worship him,' &c.

As God, a worship belongs to him; as a Spirit, a spiritual worship is due to him. In the inference we have,

1. The manner of worship: 'in spirit and in truth.'

2. The necessity of such a worship: 'must.'

The proposition declares the nature of God; the inference, the duty of man.

The observations lie plain.

Obs. 1. God is a pure spiritual being; he is a Spirit.

2. The worship due from the creature to God must be agreeable to the nature of God, and purely spiritual.

8. The evangelical state is suited to the nature of God.

For the first,

Doct. God is a pure spiritual being.

It is the observation of one,* that the plain assertion of God's being a Spirit is found but once in the whole Bible, and that is in this place; which may well be wondered at, because God is so often described with hands, feet, eyes, and ears, in the form and figure of a man. The spiritual nature of God is deducible from many places; but not anywhere, as I remember, asserted *totidem verbis* but in this text. Some allege that place, 2 Cor. iii. 17, 'The Lord is that Spirit,' for the proof of it, but that seems to have a different sense. In the text, the nature of God is described; in that place, the operations of God in the gospel. 'It is not the ministry of Moses, or that old covenant, which communicates to you that Spirit it speaks of; but it is the Lord Jesus, and the doctrine of the gospel delivered by him, whereby this Spirit and liberty is dispensed to you. He opposes here the liberty of the gospel to the servitude of the law.'† It is from Christ that a divine virtue diffuseth itself by the gospel; it is by him, not by the law, that we partake of that Spirit.

The spirituality of God is as evident as his being.‡ If we grant that God is, we must necessarily grant that he cannot be corporeal, because a body is of an imperfect nature. It will appear incredible to any that acknowledge God the first being and creator of all things, that he should be a massy, heavy body, and have eyes and ears, feet and hands, as we have.

For the explication of it.

1. Spirit is taken various ways in Scripture. It signifies sometimes an aerial substance, as Ps. xi. 6, 'A horrible tempest;' *Heb.*, 'A spirit of tempest;' sometimes the breath, which is a thin substance: Gen. vi. 17, 'All flesh wherein is the breath of life;' *Heb.*, 'Spirit of life.' A thin substance, though it be material and corporeal, is called spirit; and in the bodies of living creatures, that which is the principle of their actions is called spirits, the animal and vital spirits; and the finer parts extracted from plants and minerals we call spirits, those volatile parts separated from that gross matter wherein they were immersed, because they come nearest to the nature of an incorporeal substance. And from this notion of the word, it is translated to signify those substances that are purely immaterial, as angels and the souls of men. Angels are called spirits, Ps. civ. 4; 'Who makes his angels spirits,' Heb. i. 14. And not only good angels are so called, but evil angels, Mark i. 27. Souls of men are called spirits, Eccles. xii., and the soul of Christ is called so, John xix. 30, whence God is called 'the God of the spirits of all flesh,' Numb. xvi. 22: and spirit is opposed to flesh:

---

* Episcop. Institut. l. iv. c. 8. ‡ Suarez. de Deo, vol. i. p. 9, col. 2.

† Amyrald *in loc.*

Isaiah xxxi. 3, 'The Egyptians* are flesh, and not spirit.' And our Saviour gives us the notion of a spirit to be something above the nature of a body, Luke xxiv. 39; not having flesh and bones, extended parts, loads of gross matter. It is also taken for those things which are active and efficacious, because activity is of the nature of a spirit. Caleb had 'another spirit,' Numb. xiv. 24, an active affection. The vehement motions of sin are called spirit, Hos. iv. 12, 'The spirit of whoredoms,' in that sense that Prov. xxix. 11, 'A fool utters all his mind,' 'all his spirit;' he knows not how to restrain the vehement motions of his mind. So that the notion of a spirit is, that it is a fine immaterial substance, an active being, that acts itself and other things. A mere body cannot act itself, as the body of man cannot move without the soul, no more than a ship can move itself without wind and waves.

So God is called a Spirit, as being not a body, not having the greatness, figure, thickness or length of a body, wholly separate from anything of flesh and matter. We find a principle within us nobler than that of our bodies, and therefore we conceive the nature of God according to that which is more worthy in us, and not according to that which is the vilest part of our natures. God is a most spiritual spirit, more spiritual than all angels, all souls (μονοτρόπως).† As he exceeds all in the nature of being, so he exceeds all in the nature of spirit. He hath nothing gross, heavy, material in his essence.

2. When we say God is a Spirit, it is to be understood by way of negation. There are two ways of knowing or describing God: by way of affirmation, affirming that of him in a way of eminency which is excellent in the creature, as when we say God is wise, good. The other by way of negation, when we remove from God in our conceptions what is tainted with imperfection in the creature.‡ The first ascribes to him whatsoever is excellent, the other separates from him whatsoever is imperfect. The first is like a limning, which adds one colour to another to make a comely picture; the other is like a carving, which pares and cuts away whatsoever is superfluous, to make a complete statue. This way of negation is more easy; we better understand what God *is not*, than what he *is*, and most of our knowledge of God is by this way. As when we say God is infinite, immense, immutable, they are negatives; he hath no limits, is confined to no place, admits of no change.§ When we remove from him what is inconsistent with his being, we do more strongly assert his being, and know more of him when we elevate him above all, and above our own capacity. And when we say God is a Spirit, it is a negation; he is not a body; he consists not of various parts, extended one without and beyond another. He is not a spirit so as our souls are, to be the form of any body; a spirit, not as angels and souls are, but infinitely higher. We call him so because, in regard of our weakness, we have not any other term of excellency to express or conceive him by. We transfer it to God in honour, because spirit is the highest excellency in our nature. Yet we must apprehend God above any spirit, since his nature is so great, that he cannot be declared by human speech, perceived by human sense, or conceived by human understanding.

The second thing, that God is a Spirit.

Some among the heathens‖ imagined God to have a body; some thought him to have a body of air, some a heavenly body, some a human

---

* This is not said of the Egyptians, but of their horses.—ED.
† Gerhard.   ‡ Gamacheus, tom. i. q. 3, cap. i. p. 42.
§ Coccei. Sum. Theol., cap. 8.   ‖ Thes. Sedan., part ii. p. 1000.

body ;* and many of them ascribed bodies to their gods, but bodies without
blood, without corruption; bodies made up of the finest and thinnest atoms;
such bodies, which, if compared with ours, were as no bodies. The Sadducees
also, who denied all spirits, and yet acknowledged a God, must conclude
him to be a body, and no spirit. Some among Christians have been of that
opinion. Tertullian is charged by some, and excused by others; and some
monks of Egypt were so fierce for this error, that they attempted to kill one
Theophilus, a bishop, for not being of that judgment.

But the wiser heathens† were of another mind, and esteemed it an
unholy thing (ὀυκ ὅσιον) to have such imaginations of God. And some
Christians have thought God only to be free from anything of body; because
he is omnipresent, immutable, he is only incorporeal and spiritual: all
things else, even the angels, are clothed with bodies, though of a neater
matter, and a more active frame than ours; a pure spiritual nature they
allowed to no being but God. Scripture and reason meet together to assert
the spirituality of God. Had God had the lineaments of a body, the Gentiles had not fallen under that accusation of 'changing his glory into that of
a corruptible man,' Rom. i. 23.

This is signified by the name God gives himself: Exod. iii. 14, 'I am that
I am,' a simple, pure, uncompounded being, without any created mixture;
as infinitely above the being of creatures as above the conceptions of creatures: Job xxxvii. 23, 'Touching the Almighty, we cannot find him out.'
He is so much a Spirit that he is the 'Father of spirits,' Heb. xii. 9. The
Almighty Father is not of a nature inferior to his children. The soul is a
spirit; it could not else exert actions without the assistance of the body, as
the act of understanding itself and its own nature, the act of willing, and
willing things against the incitements and interest of the body. It could
not else conceive of God, angels, and immaterial substances. It could not
else be so active as with one glance to fetch a compass from earth to heaven,
and by a sudden motion to elevate the understanding from an earthly
thought to the thinking of things as high as the highest heavens. If we
have this opinion of our souls, which in the nobleness of their acts surmount
the body, without which the body is but a dull inactive piece of clay, we
must needs have a higher 'conception of God than to clog him with any
matter, though of a finer temper than ours. We must conceive of him by
the perfections of our souls, without the vileness of our bodies. If God
made man according to his image, we must raise our thoughts of God
according to the noblest part of that image, and imagine the exemplar or
copy not to come short, but to exceed the thing copied by it. God were
not the most excellent substance if he were not a Spirit. Spiritual substances are more excellent than bodily, the soul of man more excellent than
other animals, angels more excellent than men. They contain in their own
nature whatsoever dignity there is in the inferior creatures. God must have,
therefore, an excellency above all those, and therefore is entirely remote
from the conditions of a body.

It is a gross conceit, therefore, to think that God is such a spirit as the
air is;‡ for that is to be a body as the air is, though it be a thin one; and
if God were no more a spirit than that, or than angels, he would not be the
most simple being. Yet some§ think that the spiritual Deity was represented by the air in the ark of the testament. It was unlawful to represent
him by any image that God had prohibited. Everything about the ark had

---

* Vossius Idolol., lib. ii. cap. i.   Forbes, Instrument, l. i. c. 36.
† Plutarch, incorporalis ratio; divinus spiritus, Seneca.
‡ Calov. Socin. Proflig., p. 129, 130.   § Amyrald sup., Heb. ix. p. 146, &c.

a particular signification. The gold and other ornaments about it signified something of Christ, but were unfit to represent the nature of God. A thing purely invisible, and falling under nothing of sense, could not represent him to the mind of man. The air in the ark was the fittest; it represented the invisibility of God, air being imperceptible to our eyes. Air diffuseth itself through all parts of the world, it glides through secret passages into all creatures, it fills the space between heaven and earth; there is no place wherein God is not present.

To evidence this;—

1. If God were not a Spirit, he could not be Creator. All multitude begins in, and is reduced to, unity. As above multitude there is an absolute unity, so above mixed creatures there is an absolute simplicity. You cannot conceive number without conceiving the beginning of it in that which was not number, viz., a unit. You cannot conceive any mixture but you must conceive some simple thing to be the original and basis of it. The works of art, done by rational creatures, have their foundation in something spiritual. Every artificer, watchmaker, carpenter, hath a model in his own mind of the work he designs to frame. The material and outward fabric is squared according to an inward and spiritual idea. A spiritual idea speaks a spiritual faculty as the subject of it. God could not have an idea of that vast number of creatures he brought into being if he had not a spiritual nature.* The wisdom whereby the world was created could never be the fruit of a corporeal nature; such natures are not capable of understanding and comprehending the things which are within the compass of their nature, much less of producing them; and therefore beasts, which have only corporeal faculties, move to objects by the force of their sense, and have no knowledge of things as they are comprehended by the understanding of man. All acts of wisdom speak an intelligent and spiritual agent. The effects of wisdom, goodness, power, are so great and admirable, that they bespeak him a more perfect and eminent being than can possibly be beheld under a bodily shape. Can a corporeal substance ' put wisdom in the inward parts, and give understanding to the heart'? Job xxxviii. 36.

2. If God were not a pure Spirit, he could not be one. If God had a body consisting of distinct members, as ours, or all of one nature, as the water and air are, yet he were then capable of division, and therefore could not be entirely one. Either those parts would be finite or infinite: if finite, they are not parts of God, for to be God and finite is a contradiction; if infinite, then there are as many infinites as distinct members, and therefore as many deities. Suppose this body had all parts of the same nature, as air and water hath, every little part of air is as much air as the greatest, and every little part of water is as much water as the ocean; so every little part of God would be as much God as the whole, as many particular deities to make up God as little atoms to compose a body. What can be more absurd? If God had a body like a human body, and were compounded of body and soul, of substance and quality, he could not be the most perfect unity; he would be made up of distinct parts, and those of a distinct nature, as the members of a human body are. Where there is the greatest unity, there must be the greatest simplicity; but God is one. As he is free from any change, so he is void of any multitude: Deut. vi. 4, 'The Lord our God is one Lord.'

3. If God had a body as we have, he would not be invisible. Every material thing is not visible: the air is a body, yet invisible, but it is sensible; the cooling quality of it is felt by us at every breath, and we know it by our

* Amyral. moral, tom. i. p. 282.

touch, which is the most material sense. Every body, that hath members like to bodies, is visible; but God is invisible.* The apostle reckons it amongst his other perfections : 1 Tim. i. 17, 'Now unto the King eternal, immortal, invisible.' He is invisible to our sense, which beholds nothing but material and coloured things ; and incomprehensible to our understanding, that conceives nothing but what is finite. God is therefore a Spirit incapable of being seen, and infinitely incapable of being understood. If he be invisible, he is also spiritual. If he had a body, and hid it from our eyes, he might be said not to be seen, but could not be said to be invisible. When we say a thing is visible, we understand that it hath such qualities which are the object of sense, though we may never see that which in its own nature is to be seen. God hath no such qualities as fall under the perception of our sense. His works are visible to us, but not his Godhead, Rom. i. 20. The nature of a human body is to be seen and handled ; Christ gives us such a description of it : Luke xxiv. 39, 'Handle me and see, for a spirit hath not flesh and bones, as you see me have;' but man hath been so far from seeing God, that it is impossible he can see him, 1 Tim. vi. 16. There is such a disproportion between an infinite object and a finite sense and understanding, that it is utterly impossible either to behold or comprehend him ; but if God had a body more luminous and glorious than that of the sun, he would be as well visible to us as the sun, though the immensity .of that light would dazzle our eyes, and forbid any close inspection into him by the virtue of our sense. We have seen the shape and figure of the sun, but no man hath ever seen the shape of God, John v. 37. If God had a body he were visible, though he might not perfectly and fully be seen by us ;† as we see the heavens, though we see not the extension, latitude, and greatness of them. Though God hath manifested himself in a bodily shape, Gen. xviii. 1, and elsewhere Jehovah appeared to Abraham, yet the substance of God was not seen, no more than the substance of angels was seen in their apparitions to men. A body was formed to be made visible by them, and such actions done in that body, that spake the person that did them to be of a higher eminency than a bare corporeal creature. Sometimes a representation is made to the inward sense and imagination, as to Micaiah, 1 Kings xx. 19, and to Isaiah, chap. vi. 1 ; but they saw not the essence of God, but some images and figures of him proportioned to their sense or imagination. The essence of God no man ever saw, nor can see, John i. 18.

Nor doth it follow that God hath a body,‡ because Jacob is said to 'see God face to face,' Gen. xxxii. 30; and Moses had the like privilege, Deut. xxxiv. 10. This only signifies a fuller and clearer manifestation of God, by some representations offered to the bodily sense, or rather to the inward spirit; for God tells Moses he could not see his face, Exod. xxxiii. 20; and that none ever saw the similitude of God, Deut. iv. 15. Were God a corporeal substance, he might in some measure be seen by corporeal eyes.

4. If God were not a Spirit, he could not be infinite. All bodies are of a finite nature : every body is material, and every material thing is terminated. The sun, a vast body, hath a bounded greatness : the heavens, of a mighty bulk, yet have their limits. If God had a body, he must consist of parts ; those parts would be bounded and limited, and whatsoever is limited is of a finite virtue, and therefore below an infinite nature. Reason therefore tells us, that the most excellent nature, as God is, cannot be of a corporeal condition, because of the limitation and other actions which belong

---

* Daille in Tim.   ‡ Goulart. de Dieu. p. 95, 96.
† Goulart. de Dieu, p. 94.

to every body. God is infinite, for ' the heaven of heavens cannot contain
him,' 2 Chron. ii. 6. The largest heavens, and those imaginary spaces
beyond the world, are no bounds to him. He hath an essence beyond the
bounds of the world, and cannot be included in the vastness of the heavens.
If God be infinite, then he can have no parts in him; if he had, they must
be finite, or infinite: finite parts can never make up an infinite being. A
vessel of gold of a pound weight cannot be made of the quantity of an ounce.
Infinite parts they cannot be, because then every part would be equal to
the whole, as infinite as the whole, which is contradictory. We see in all
things every part is less than the whole bulk that is composed of it. As
every member of a man is less than the whole body of man, if all the parts
were finite, then God in his essence were finite; and a finite God is not
more excellent than a creature: so that if God were not a Spirit, he could
not be infinite.

5. If God were not a Spirit, he could not be an independent being. Whatsoever is compounded of many parts, depends either essentially or integrally
upon those parts; as the essence of a man depends upon the conjunction
and union of his two main parts, his soul and body; when they are separated, the essence of a man ceaseth, and the perfection of a man depends
upon every member of the body; so that if one be wanting, the perfection
of the whole is wanting. As if a man hath lost a limb, you call him not a
perfect man, because that part is gone upon which his perfection, as an
entire man, did depend. If God, therefore, had a body, the perfection of
the Deity would depend upon every part of that body; and the more parts
he were compounded of, the more his dependency would be multiplied according to the number of those parts of the body; for that which is compounded
of many parts is more dependent than that which is compounded of fewer.

And because God would be a dependent being if he had a body, he could
not be the first being; for the compounding parts are in order of nature
before that which is compounded by them, as the soul and body are before
the man which results from the union of them. If God had parts and
bodily members as we have, or any composition, the essence of God would
result from those parts, and those parts be supposed to be before God; for
that which is a part is before that whose part it is. As in artificial things
you may conceive it, all the parts of a watch or clock are in time before
that watch, which is made by setting those parts together. In natural things,
you must suppose the members of a body framed before you can call it a
man; so that the parts of this body are before that which is constituted by
them. We can conceive no other of God, if he were not a pure, entire,
unmixed Spirit: if he had distinct parts, he would depend upon them; those
parts would be before him: his essence would be the effect of those distinct
parts, and so he would not be absolutely and entirely the first being. But
he is so: Isa. xliv. 6, ' I am the first, and I am the last.' He is the first;
nothing is before him: whereas, if he had bodily parts, and those finite, it
would follow, God is made up of those parts which are not God; and that
which is not God, is in order of nature before that which is God. So that
we see, if God were not a Spirit, he could not be independent.

6. If God were not a Spirit, he were not immutable and unchangeable.
His immutability depends upon his simplicity. He is unchangeable in his
essence, because he is a pure and unmixed spiritual being. Whatsoever is
compounded of parts, may be divided into those parts, and resolved into
those distinct parts which make up and constitute the nature. Whatsoever
is compounded, is changeable in its own nature, though it should never be
changed. Adam, who was constituted of body and soul, had he stood in

innocence, had not died; there had been no separation made between his soul and body whereof he was constituted, and his body had not resolved into those principles of dust from whence it was extracted; yet in his own nature he was dissoluble into those distinct parts whereof he was compounded. And so the glorified saints in heaven, after the resurrection, and the happy meeting of their souls and bodies in a new marriage knot, shall never be dissolved; yet in their own nature they are mutable and dissoluble, and cannot be otherwise, because they are made up of such distinct parts that may be separated in their own nature, unless sustained by the grace of God. They are immutable by will, the will of God, not by nature. God is immutable by nature as well as will; as he hath a necessary existence, so he hath a necessary unchangeableness; Mal. iii. 6, 'I the Lord change not.' He is as unchangeable in his essence, as in his veracity and faithfulnes. They are perfections belonging to his nature; but if he were not a pure Spirit, he could not be immutable by nature.

7. If God were not a pure Spirit, he could not be omnipresent. He is ' in heaven above, and the earth below,' Deut. iv. 39. He 'fills heaven and earth,' Jer. xxiii. 24. The divine essence is at once in heaven and earth; but it is impossible a body can be in two places at one and the same time. Since God is everywhere, he must be spiritual. Had he a body, he could not penetrate all things; he would be circumscribed in place. He could not be everywhere but in parts, not in the whole; one member in one place, and another in another; for to be confined to a particular place is the property of the body, but since he is diffused through the whole world, ' higher than heaven, deeper than hell, longer than the earth, broader than the sea,' Job xi. 8, he hath not any corporeal matter. If he had a body wherewith to fill heaven and earth, there could be no body besides his own. It is the nature of bodies to bound one another, and hinder the extending of one another. Two bodies cannot be in the same place, in the same point of earth : one excludes the other; and it will follow hence that we are nothing, no substances, mere illusions; there could be no place for any body else.* If his body were as big as the world, as it must be, if with that he filled heaven and earth, there would not be room for him to move a hand or a foot, or extend a finger; for there would be no place remaining for the motion.

8. If God were not a Spirit, he could not be the most perfect being. The more perfect anything is in the rank of creatures, the more spiritual and simple it is, as gold is the more pure and perfect, that hath least mixture of other metals. If God were not a Spirit, there would be creatures of a more excellent nature than God, as angels and souls, which the Scripture calls spirits, in opposition to bodies. There is more of perfection in the first notion of a spirit, than in the notion of a body. God cannot be less perfect than his creatures, and contribute an excellency of being to them which he wants himself. If angels and souls possess such an excellency, and God want that excellency, he would be less than his creatures, and excellency of the effect would exceed the excellency of the cause; but every creature, even the highest creature, is infinitely short of the perfection of God; for whatsoever excellency they have is finite and limited : it is but a spark from the sun, a drop from the ocean; but God is unboundedly perfect in the highest manner, without any limitation; and therefore above spirits, angels, the highest creatures that were made by him. An infinite sublimity, a pure act, to which nothing can be added, from which nothing can be taken. 'In him there is light and no darkness,' 1 John i. 5; spirituality without any matter, perfection without any shadow or taint of imperfection; light pierceth

* Gamacheus Theol. tom. i. quest. 3, cap. 1.

into all things, preserves its own purity, and admits of no mixture of anything else with it.

Quest. It may be said, if God be a Spirit, and it is impossible he can be otherwise than a Spirit, how comes God so often to have such members as we have in our bodies ascribed to him ; not only a soul, but particular bodily parts, as heart, arms, hands, eyes, ears, face, and back-parts ? And how is it that he is never called a Spirit in plain words, but in this text by our Saviour ?

Ans. It is true many parts of the body and natural affections of the human nature are reported of God in Scripture : head, Dan vii. 9 ; eyes and eyelids, Ps. xi. 4 ; apple of the eye, mouth, &c. ; our affections also, grief, joy, anger, &c.   But it is to be considered,

1. That this is in condescension to our weakness.* God being desirous to make himself known to man, whom he created for his glory, humbles as it were his own nature to such representations as may suit and assist the capacity of the creature.   Since by the condition of our nature nothing erects a notion of itself in our understanding, but as it is conducted in by our sense, God hath served himself of those things which are most exposed to our sense, most obvious to our understandings, to give us some acquaintance with his own nature, and those things which otherwise we were not capable of having any notion of.   As our souls are linked with our bodies, so our knowledge is linked with our sense, that we can scarce imagine anything at first but under a corporeal form and figure, till we come, by great attention to the object, to make, by the help of reason, a separation of the spiritual substance from the corporeal fancy, and consider it in its own nature.   We are not able to conceive a spirit without some kind of resemblance to something below it, nor understand the actions of a spirit without considering the operations of a human body in its several members.   As the glories of another life are signified to us by the pleasures of this, so the nature of God, by a gracious condescension to our capacities, is signified to us by a likeness to our own.   The more familiar the things are to us which God uses to this purpose, the more proper they are to teach us what he intends by them.

Ans. 2. All such representation are to signify the acts of God, as they bear some likeness to those which we perform by those members he ascribes to himself.   So that those members ascribed to him rather note his visible operations to us, than his visible nature, and signify that God doth some works like to those which men do by the assistance of those organs of their bodies.†   So the wisdom of God is called his eye, because he knows that with his mind which we see with our eyes.   The efficiency of God is called his hand and arm, because, as we act with our hands, so doth God with his power.   The divine efficacies are signified.   By his eyes and ears we understand his omniscience ; by his face, the manifestation of his favour ; by his mouth, the revelation of his will ; by his nostrils, the acceptation of our prayers ; by his bowels, the tenderness of his compassion ; by his heart, the sincerity of his affections ; by his hand, the strength of his power; by his feet, the ubiquity of his presence.   And in this he intends instruction and comfort : by his eyes, he signifies his watchfulness over us ; by his ears, his readiness to hear the cries of the oppressed, Ps. xxxiv. 15 ; by his arm his power,—an arm to destroy his enemies, and an arm to relieve his people, Isa. li. 9 ; all those attributed to God to signify divine actions, which he doth without bodily organs, as we do with them.

Ans. 3. Consider also that only those members which are the instruments

---

* Loquitur lex secundum linguam filiorum hominum.
† Amyral. de Trin. p. 218, 219.

of the noblest actions, and under that consideration, are used by him to represent a notion of him to our minds. Whatsoever is perfect and excellent is ascribed to him, but nothing that savours of imperfection.* The heart is ascribed to him, it being the principle of vital actions, to signify the life that he hath in himself. Watchful and discerning eyes, not sleepy and lazy ones; a mouth to reveal his will, not to take in food. To eat and sleep are never ascribed to him, nor those parts that belong to the preparing or transmitting nourishment to the several parts of the body, as stomach, liver, reins, nor bowels under that consideration, but as they are significant of compassion; but only those parts are ascribed to him whereby we acquire knowledge, as eyes and ears, the organs of learning and wisdom; or to communicate it to others, as the mouth, lips, tongue, as they are instruments of speaking, not of tasting. Or those parts which signify strength and power, or whereby we perform the actions of charity for the relief of others. Taste and touch, senses that extend no further than to corporeal things, and are the grossest of all the senses, are never ascribed to him.

It were worth consideration,† whether this describing God by the members of an human body were so much figuratively to be understood, as with respect to the incarnation of our Saviour, who was to assume the human nature and all the members of a human body.

Asaph, speaking in the person of God: Ps. lxxviii. 2, 'I will open my mouth in parables.' In regard of God it is to be understood figuratively, but in regard of Christ literally, to whom it is applied, Mat. xiii. 34, 35. And that apparition, Isa. vi., which was the appearance of Jehovah, is applied to Christ, John xii. 40, 41.

After the report of the creation, and the forming of man, we read of God's speaking to him, but not of God's appearing to him in any visible shape.‡ A voice might be formed in the air to give man notice of his duty; some way of information he must have what positive laws he was to observe, besides that law which was engraven in his nature, which we call the law of nature; and without a voice the knowledge of the divine will could not be so conveniently communicated to man. Though God was heard in a voice, he was not seen in a shape; but after the fall we several times read of his appearing in such a form. Though we read of his *speaking* before man's committing of sin, yet not of his *walking*, which is more corporeal, till afterwards, Gen. iii. 8. Though God would not have man believe him to be corporeal, yet he judged it expedient to give some pre-notices of that divine incarnation which he had promised.§

5. Therefore we must not conceive of the visible Deity, according to the letter of such expressions, but the true intent of them. Though the Scripture speaks of his eyes and arms, yet it denies them to be arms of flesh, Job x. 4, 2 Chron. xxxii. 8. We must not conceive of God according to the letter, but the design of the metaphor. When we hear things described by metaphorical expressions, for the clearing them up to our fancy, we conceive not of them under that garb, but remove the veil by an act of our reason. When Christ is called a sun, a vine, bread, is any so stupid as to conceive him to be a vine with material branches and clusters, or be of the same nature with a loaf? But the things designed by such metaphors are obvious to the conception of a mean understanding. If we would conceive God to have a body like a man, because he describes himself so, we may conceit him to be like a bird, because he is mentioned with wings, Ps. xxxvi. 7, or like

* Episcop. Institu. l. 4, sect. 3, cap. 8.
† It is Zanchy's observation, tom. 2, de natura Dei, lib. i. cap. 4, thes. 9.
‡ Amyrald. Moral. tom. i. p. 293, 294.   § Amyrald.

a lion or leopard, because he likens himself to them in the acts of his strength and fury, Hosea xiii. 7, 8. He is called a rock, a horn, fire, to note his strength and wrath. If any be so stupid as to think God to be really such, they would make him not only a man, but worse than a monster.

Onkelos,* the Chaldee paraphrast, upon parts of the Scripture, was so tender of expressing the notion of any corporiety in God, that, when he meets with any expressions of that nature, he translates them according to the true intent of them, as when God is said to 'descend,' Gen. xi. 5, which implies a local motion, a motion from one place to another, he translates it 'and God revealed himself.' We should conceive of God according to the design of the expressions. When we read of his eyes, we should conceive his omniscience; of his hand, his power; of his sitting, his immutability; of his throne, his majesty; and conceive of him as surmounting not only the grossness of bodies, but the spiritual excellency of the most dignified creatures, something so perfect, great, spiritual, as nothing can be conceived higher and purer.

Christ, saith one,† is truly *Deus figuratus*, and for his sake was it more easily permitted to the Jews to think of God in the shape of a man.

Use. If God be a pure spiritual being, then,

1. Man is not the image of God, according to his external bodily form and figure. The image of God in man consisted not in what is seen, but in what is not seen; not in the conformation of the members, but rather in the spiritual faculties of the soul, or, most of all, in the holy endowments of those faculties: Eph. iv. 24, 'That ye put on the new man, which, after God, is created in righteousness and true holiness,' Col. iii. 10. The image, which is restored by redeeming grace, was the image of God by original nature. The image of God cannot be in that part which is common to us with beasts, but rather in that wherein we excel all living creatures, in reason, understanding, and an immortal spirit. God expressly saith, that none 'saw a similitude' of him, Deut. iv. 15, 16, which had not been true if man in regard of his body had been the image and similitude of God, for then a figure of God had been seen every day, as often as we saw a man or beheld ourselves; nor would the apostle's argument stand good: Acts xvii. 29, that 'the Godhead is not like to stone graven by art' if we were not the offspring of God, and bore the stamp of his nature in our spirits rather than our bodies.‡ It was a fancy of Eugubinus that, when God set upon the actual creation of man, he took a bodily form for an exemplar of that which he would express in his work, and, therefore, that the words of Moses, Gen. i. 26, are to be understood of the body of man, because there was in man such a shape which God had then assumed. To let alone God's forming himself a body for that work as a groundless fancy, man can in no wise be said to be the image of God in regard of the substance of his body, but beasts may as well be said to be made in the image of God, whose bodies have the same members as the body of man for the most part, and excel men in the acuteness of the senses and swiftness of their motion, agility of body, greatness of strength, and in some kind of ingenuities also wherein man hath been a scholar to the brutes and beholden to their skill. The soul comes nearest the nature of God as being a spiritual substance, yet, considered singly in regard of its spiritual substance, cannot well be said to be the image of God. A beast, because of its corporiety, may as well be called the image of a man, for there is a greater similitude between man and a brute in the rank of bodies than there can be between God and the highest angels in the rank of spirits. If it doth not consist in the substance of the soul, much less can

---

* Maimon. More Nevoc. part i .cap. 27.   † More's Conjectura Cabalistica, p. 127.
‡ Petav. Theol. Dog. tom. i. lib. ii. cap. i. p. 104.

it in any similitude of the body. This image consisted partly in the state of man as he had dominion over the creatures, partly in the nature of man as he was an intelligent being, and thereby was capable of having a grant of that dominion, but principally in the conformity of the soul with God in the frame of his spirit and the holiness of his actions ; not at all in the figure and form of his body physically, though morally there might be, as there was a rectitude in the body, as an instrument to conform to the holy motions of the soul, as the holiness of the soul sparkled in the actions and members of the body. If man were like God because he hath a body, whatsoever hath a body hath some resemblance to God, and may be said to be in part his image; but the truth is, the essence of all creatures cannot be an image of the immense essence of God.

2. If God be a pure Spirit, it is unreasonable to frame any image or picture of God.* Some heathens have been wiser in this than some Christians. Pythagoras forbade his scholars to engrave any shape of him upon a ring, because he was not to be comprehended by sense, but conceived only in our minds ; our hands are as unable to fashion him as our own eyes to see him.† The ancient Romans worshipped their gods one hundred and seventy years before any material representations of them,‡ and the ancient idolatrous Germans thought it a wicked thing to represent God in a human shape; yet some, and those no Romanists, labour to defend the making images of God in the resemblance of man ; because he is so represented in Scripture, he may be,§ saith one, conceived so in our minds and figured so to our sense. If this were a good reason, why may he not be pictured as a lion, horn, eagle, rock, since he is under such metaphors shadowed to us ? The same ground there is for the one as for the other. What though man be a nobler creature, God hath no more the body of a man than that of an eagle, and some perfections in other creatures represent some excellencies in his nature and actions which cannot be figured by a human shape, as strength by the lion, swiftness and readiness by the wings of the bird. But God hath absolutely prohibited the making any image whatsoever of him, and that with terrible threatenings : Exod. xx. 5, 'I the Lord am a jealous God, visiting the iniquities of the fathers upon their children,' and Deut. v. 8, 9. After God had given the Israelites the commandment wherein he forbade them to have any God before him, he forbids all figuring of him by the hand of man ; not only images, but any likeness of him either by things in heaven, in the earth, or in the water. How often doth he discover his indignation by the prophets, against them that offer to mould him in a creature form ! This law was not to serve a particular dispensation, or to endure a particular time, but it was a declaration of his will, invariable in all places and all times, being founded upon the immutable nature of his being, and therefore agreeable to the law of nature ; otherwise, not chargeable upon the heathens. And, therefore, when God had declared his nature and his works in a stately and majestic eloquence, he demands of them, to whom they would liken him, or what likeness they would compare unto him, Isa. xl. 18 ; where they could find anything that would be a lively image and resemblance of his infinite excellency ? Founding it upon the infiniteness of his nature, which necessarily implies the spirituality of it. God is infinitely above any statue, and those that think to draw God by a stroke of a pencil, or form him by the engravings of art, are more stupid than the statues themselves.

To shew the unreasonableness of it, consider,

* Jamblyc. protrept, cap. 21, symb. 24.
† Austin de Civitat. Dei. lib. iv. cap. 31, out of Varro.　　‡ Tacitus.
§ Gerhard Loc. Commun. vol. iv.; Exegesis de natura Dei, cap. 8, sect. 1.

(1.) It is impossible to fashion any image of God. If our more capacious souls cannot grasp his nature, our weaker sense cannot frame his image; it is more possible of the two, to comprehend him in our minds, than to frame him in an image to our sense. He inhabits inaccessible light; as it is impossible for the eye of man to see him, it is impossible for the art of man to paint him upon walls, and carve him out of wood. None knows him but himself, none can describe him but himself.* Can we draw a figure of our own souls, and express that part of ourselves wherein we are most like to God? Can we extend this to any bodily figure, and divide it into parts? How can we deal so with the original copy, whence the first draught of our souls was taken, and which is infinitely more spiritual than men or angels? No corporeal thing can represent a spiritual substance; there is no proportion in nature between them; God is a simple, infinite, immense, eternal, invisible, incorruptible being. A statue is a compound, finite, limited, temporal, visible, and corruptible body. God is a living Spirit; but a statue nor sees, nor hears, nor perceives anything. But suppose God had a body, it is impossible to mould an image of it in the true glory of that body. Can the statue of an excellent monarch represent the majesty and air of his countenance, though made by the skilfullest workman in the world? If God had a body in some measure suited to his excellency, were it possible for man to make an exact image of him, who cannot picture the light, heat, motion, magnitude, and dazzling property of the sun? The excellency of any corporeal nature of the least creature, the temper, instinct, artifice, are beyond the power of a carving tool, much more is God.

(2.) To make any corporeal representation of God is unworthy of God. It is a disgrace to his nature. Whosoever thinks a carnal corruptible image to be fit for a representation of God, renders God no better than a carnal and corporeal being. It is a kind of debasing an angel, who is a spiritual nature, to represent him in a bodily shape, who is as far removed from any fleshliness as heaven from earth; much more to degrade the glory of the divine nature to the lineaments of a man. The whole stock of images is but a lie of God: Jer. x. 8, 14, 'A doctrine of vanities and falsehood.' It represents him in a false garb to the world, and sinks his glory into that of a corruptible creature, Rom. i. 23, 25. It impairs the reverence of God in the minds of men, and by degrees may debase men's apprehensions of God, and be a means to make them believe he is such a one as themselves, and that not being free from the figure, he is not also free from the imperfections of their bodies. Corporeal images of God were the fruits of base imaginations of him; and as they sprung from them, so they contribute to a greater corruption of the notions of the divine nature. The heathens began their first representations of him by the image of a corruptible man, then of birds, till they descended, not only to four-footed beasts, but creeping things, even serpents, as the apostle seems to intimate in his enumeration, Rom. i. 23. It had been more honourable to have continued in human representation of him, than have sunk so low as beasts and serpents, the baser images, though the first had been infinitely unworthy of him, he being more above a man, though the noblest creature, than man is above a worm, a toad, or the most despicable creeping thing upon the earth. To think we can make an image of God of a piece of marble, or an ingot of gold, is a greater debasing of him than it would be of a great prince, if you should represent him in the statue of a frog. When the Israelites represented God by a calf, it is said, 'They sinned a great sin,' Exod. xxxii. 31. And the sin of Jeroboam, who intended only a representation of God by the calves at Dan and Bethel, is

* Cocceius, Sum. Theol., cap. 9, p. 47, sec. 35.

called more emphatically, Hosea x. 15, רעת רעתכם, 'the wickedness of your wickedness,' the very scum and dregs of wickedness. As men debased God by this, so God debased men for this ; he degraded the Israelites into captivity under the worst of their enemies, and punished the heathens with spiritual judgments, as uncleanness, through the lusts of their own hearts, Rom. i. 24, which is repeated again in other expressions, ver. 26, 27, as a meet recompence for their disgracing the spiritual nature of God. Had God been like to man, they had not offended in it ; but I mention this to shew a probable reason of those base lusts which are in the midst of us, that have scarce been exceeded by any nation, viz.,. the unworthy and unspiritual conceits of God, which are as much a debasing of him as material images were when they were more rife in the world, and may be as well the cause of those spiritual judgments upon men as the worshipping molten and carved images were the cause of the same upon the heathen.

(3.) Yet this is natural to man. Wherein we may see the contrariety of man to God. Though God be a Spirit, yet there is nothing man is more prone to than to represent him under a corporeal form. The most famous guides of the heathen world have fashioned him, not only according to the more honourable images of men, but bestialised him in the form of a brute. The Egyptians, whose country was the school of learning to Greece, were notoriously guilty of this brutishness, in worshipping an ox for an image of their god ; and the Philistines their Dagon, in a figure composed of the image of a woman and a fish.* Such representations were ancient in the oriental parts. The gods of Laban, that he accuseth Jacob of stealing from him, are supposed to be little figures of men, Gen. xxxi. 30, 34. Such was the Israelites' golden calf ; their worship was not terminated on the image, but they worshipped the true God under that representation. They could not be so brutish to call a calf their deliverer, and give to him a great title, —' These be thy gods, O Israel, which brought thee up out of the land of Egypt,' Exod. xxxii. 4,—or that which they knew belonged to the true God, the God of Abraham, Isaac, and Jacob. They knew the calf to be formed of their earrings, but they had consecrated it to God as a representation of him. Though they chose the form of the Egyptian idol, yet they knew that Apis, Osiris, and Isis, the gods the Egyptians adored in that figure, had not wrought their redemption from bondage, but would have used their force, had they been possessed of any, to have kept them under the yoke, rather than have freed them from it. The feast also which they celebrated before that image is called by Aaron the feast of the Lord: ver. 5, 'A feast to Jehovah,' the incommunicable name of the Creator of the world. It is therefore evident, that both the priest and the people pretended to serve the true God, not any false divinity of Egypt ; that God who had rescued them from Egypt with a mighty hand, divided the Red Sea before them, destroyed their enemies, conducted them, fed them by miracle, spoken to them from mount Sinai, and amazed them by his thunderings and lightnings when he instructed them by his law, a God they could not so soon forget. And with this representing God by that image, they are charged by the psalmist: Ps. cvi. 19, 20, ' They made a calf in Horeb, and changed their glory into the similitude of an ox that eateth grass.' They changed their glory ; that is, God the glory of Israel ; so that they took this figure for the image of the true God of Israel, their own God, not the God of any other nation in the world. Jeroboam intended no other by his calves, but symbols of the presence of the true God, instead of the ark and the propitiatory which remained among the Jews. We see the inclinations of our natures in the

* Daille, super, Cor. i. 10, Ser. 3.

practice of the Israelites, a people chosen out the whole world to bear up God's name, and preserve his glory ; and in that the images of God were so soon set up in the Christian church, and to this day the picture of God in the shape of an old man is visible in the temples of the Romanists. It is prone to the nature of man.

(4.) To represent God by a corporeal image, and to worship him in and by that image, is idolatry. Though the Israelites did not acknowledge the calf to be God, nor intended a worship to any of the Egyptian deities by it, but worshipped that God in it who had so lately and miraculously delivered them from a cruel servitude, and could not in natural reason judge him to be clothed with a bodily shape, much less to be like an ox that eateth grass, yet the apostle brings no less a charge against them than that of idolatry, 1 Cor. x. 7. He calls them idolaters, who before that calf kept a feast to Jehovah, citing Exod. xxxii. 5. Suppose we could make such an image of God as might perfectly represent him, yet since God hath prohibited it, shall we be wiser than God ? He hath sufficiently manifested himself in his works without images ; he is seen in the creatures, more particularly in the heavens, which declare his glory. His works are more excellent representations of him, as being the works of his own hands, than anything that is the product of the art of man. His glory sparkles in the heavens, sun, moon, and stars, as being magnificent pieces of his wisdom and power, yet the kissing the hand to the sun or the heavens, as representative of the excellency and majesty of God, is idolatry in Scripture account, and a denial of God, Job xxxi. 26–28, a prostituting the glory of God to a creature. Either the worship is terminated on the image itself,* and then it is confessed by all to be idolatry, because it is a giving that worship to a creature which is the sole right of God ; or not terminated in the image, but in the object represented by it ; it is then a foolish thing ; we may as well terminate our worship on the true object, without as with an image. An erected statue is no sign or symbol of God's special presence, as the ark, tabernacle, temple were. It is no part of divine institution, has no authority of a command to support it, no cordial of a promise to encourage it ; and the image being infinitely distant from, and below the majesty and spirituality of God, cannot constitute one object of worship with him. To put a religious character upon any image formed by the corrupt imagination of man, as a representation of the invisible and spiritual Deity, is to think the Godhead to be like silver and gold, or stone graven by art and man's device, Acts xvii. 29.

3. This doctrine will direct us in our conceptions of God as a pure, perfect spirit, than which nothing can be imagined more perfect, more pure, more spiritual.

(1.) We cannot have an adequate or suitable conception of God. He dwells in inaccessible light ; inaccessible to the acuteness of our fancy, as well as the weakness of our sense. If we could have thoughts of him as high and excellent as his nature, our conceptions must be as infinite as his nature. All our imaginations of him cannot represent him, because every created species is finite ; it cannot, therefore, represent to us a full and substantial notion of an infinite being. We cannot speak or think worthily enough of him who is greater than our words, vaster than our understandings. Whatsoever we speak or think of God is handed first to us by the notice we have of some perfection in the creature, and explains to us some particular excellency of God, rather than the fulness of his essence. No creature, nor all creatures together, can furnish us with such a magnificent notion of God as can give us a clear view of him. Yet God in his word is pleased to

* Lawson, Body of Divin., p. 161.

step below his own excellency, and point us to those excellencies in his works, whereby we may ascend to the knowledge of those excellencies which are in his nature. But the creatures, whence we draw our lessons, being finite, and our understandings being finite, it is utterly impossible to have a notion of God commensurate to the immensity and spirituality of his being. ' God is not like to visible creatures, nor is there any proportion between him and the most spiritual.'* We cannot have a full notion of a spiritual nature, much less can we have of God, who is a Spirit above spirits. No spirit can clearly represent him. The angels, that are great spirits, are bounded in their extent, finite in their being, and of a mutable nature.

Yet though we cannot have a suitable conception of God, we must not content ourselves without any conception of him. It is our sin not to endeavour after a true notion of him ; it is our sin to rest in a mean and low notion of him, when our reason tells us we are capable of having higher; but if we ascend as high as we can, though we shall then come short of a suitable notion of him, this is not our sin, but our weakness. God is infinitely superior to the choicest conceptions, not only of a sinner, but of a creature. If all conceptions of God below the true nature of God were sin, there is not a holy angel in heaven free from sin, because though they are the most capacious creatures, yet they cannot have such a notion of an infinite being as is fully suitable to his nature, unless they were infinite as he himself is.

(2.) But, however, we must by no means conceive of God under a human or corporeal shape. Since we cannot have conceptions honourable enough for his nature, we must take heed we entertain not any which may debase his nature. Though we cannot comprehend him as he is, we must be careful not to fancy him to be what he is not. It is a vain thing to conceive him with human lineaments. We must think higher of him than to ascribe to him so mean a shape. We deny his spirituality when we fancy him under such a form. He is spiritual, and between that which is spiritual and that which is corporeal there is no resemblance.† Indeed, Daniel saw God in a human form : Dan. vii. 9, ' The Ancient of days did sit, whose garment was white as snow, and the hairs of his head like pure wool :' he is described as coming to judgment. It is not meant of Christ probably ; because Christ, ver. 13, is called the Son of man coming near to the Ancient of days. This is not the proper shape of God, for no man hath seen his shape. It was a vision wherein such representations were made, as were accommodated to the inward sense of Daniel. Daniel saw him in a rapture or ecstasy, wherein outward senses are of no use. God is described, not as he is in himself, of a human form, but in regard of his fitness to judge. White denotes the purity and simplicity of the divine nature ; Ancient of days, in regard of his eternity ; white hair, in regard of his prudence and wisdom, which is more eminent in age than youth, and more fit to discern causes and to distinguish between right and wrong. Visions are riddles, and must not be understood in a literal sense. We are to watch against such determinate conceptions of God. Vain-imaginations do easily infest us ; tinder will not sooner take fire, than our natures kindle into wrong notions of the divine majesty. We are very apt to fashion a god like ourselves. We must therefore look upon such representations of God as accommodated to our weakness, and no more think them to be literal descriptions of God, as he is in himself, than we will think the image of the sun in the water to be the true sun in the heavens. We may indeed conceive of Christ as man, who hath in heaven the vestment of our nature, and is *Deus figuratus*, though we cannot conceive the Godhead under a human shape.

* Amyrald, Moral., tom. i. p. 289.   † Episc. Institut., lib. iv. sec 2, c. 17.

[1.] To have such a fancy is to disparage and wrong God. A corporeal fancy of God is as ridiculous in itself, and as injurious to God, as a wooden statue. The caprices of our imagination are often more monstrous than the images which are the works of art. It is as irreligious to measure God's essence by our line, his perfections by our imperfections, as to measure his thoughts and actings by the weakness and unworthiness of our own. This is to limit an infinite essence, and pull him down to our scanty measures, and render that which is unconceivably above us equal with us. It is impossible we can conceive God after the manner of a body, but we must bring him down to the proportion of a body, which is to diminish his glory, and stoop him below the dignity of his nature. God is a pure Spirit; he hath nothing of the nature and tincture of a body. Whosoever, therefore, conceives of him as having a bodily form, though he fancy the most beautiful and comely body, instead of owning his dignity, detracts from the super-eminent excellency of his nature and blessedness. When men fancy God like themselves in their corporeal nature, they will soon make a progress, and ascribe to him their corrupt nature; and while they clothe him with their bodies, invest him also in the infirmities of them. God is a jealous God, very sensible of any disgrace, and will be as much incensed against an inward idolatry, as an outward. That command, Exod. xx. 4, which forbade corporeal images, would not indulge carnal imaginations, since the nature of God is as much wronged by unworthy images erected in the fancy, as by statues carved out of stone or metals. One, as well as the other, is a deserting of our true spouse and committing adultery, one with a material image, and the other with a carnal notion of God. Since God humbles himself to our apprehensions, we should not debase him in thinking him to be that in his nature, which he makes only a resemblance of himself to us.

[2.] To have such fancies of God, will obstruct and pollute our worship of him. How is it possible to give him a right worship, of whom we have so debasing a notion? We shall never think a corporeal deity worthy of a dedication of our spirits. The hating instruction, and casting God's word behind the back, is charged upon the imagination they had, that God was 'such a one as themselves,' Ps. l. 17, 21. Many of the wiser heathens did not judge their statues to be their gods, or their gods to be like their statues, but suited them to their politic designs, and judged them a good invention to keep people within the bounds of obedience and devotion by such visible figures of them, which might imprint a reverence and fear of those gods upon them. But these were false measures. A despised and undervalued god is not an object of petition or affection. Who would address seriously to a god he has low apprehensions of? The more raised thoughts we have of him, the viler sense we shall have of ourselves. They would make us humble and self-abhorrent in our supplications to him: Job xlii. 6, 'Wherefore I abhor myself,' &c.

(3.) Though we must not conceive of God, as of a human or corporeal shape, yet we cannot think of God without some reflection upon our own being. We cannot conceive him to be an intelligent being, but we must make some comparison between him and our own understanding nature, to come to a knowledge of him. Since we are enclosed in bodies, we apprehend nothing but what comes in by sense, and what we in some sort measure by sensible objects. And in the consideration of those things which we desire to abstract from sense, we are fain to make use of the assistances of sense and visible things. And therefore, when we frame the highest notion, there will be some similitude of some corporeal thing in our fancy; and though we would spiritualise our thoughts, and aim at a more abstracted and raised understanding, yet there will be some dregs of matter sticking to our conceptions ; yet we still judge, by argument and reasoning, what the thing is we think of under those material images. A corporeal image will follow us, as the shadow doth the body.* While we are in the body and surrounded with fleshly matter, we cannot think of things without some help from corporeal representations. Something of sense will interpose itself in our purest conceptions of spiritual things, for the faculties which serve for contemplation are either corporeal, as the sense and fancy, or so allied to them, that nothing passes into them but by the organs of the body,† so that there is a natural inclination to figure nothing but under a corporeal notion, till by an attentive application of the mind and reason to the object thought upon, we separate that which is bodily from that which is spiritual, and by degrees ascend to that true notion of that we think upon, and would have a due conception of in our mind. Therefore God tempers the declaration of himself to our weakness, and the condition of our natures. He condescends to our littleness and narrowness, when he declares himself by the similitude of bodily members ; as the light of the sun is tempered, and diffuseth itself to our sense through the air and vapours, that our weak eyes may not be too much dazzled with it. Without it we could not know or judge of the sun, because we could have no use of our sense, which we must have before we can judge of it in our understanding ; so we are not able to conceive of spiritual beings in the purity of their own nature, without such a temperament, and such shadows to usher them into our minds. And therefore we find the Spirit of God accommodates himself to our contracted and tethered capacities, and uses such expressions of God as are suited to us, in this state of flesh wherein we are ; and therefore, because we cannot apprehend God in the simplicity of his own being and his undivided essence, he draws the representations of himself from several creatures, and several actions of those creatures : as sometimes he is said to be angry, to walk, to sit, to fly. Not that we should rest in such conceptions of him, but take our rise from this foundation, and such perfections in the creatures, to mount up to a knowledge of God's nature by those several steps, and conceive of him by those divided excellencies, because we cannot conceive of him in the purity of his own essence.‡ We cannot possibly think or speak of God, unless we transfer the names of created perfections to him ; yet we are to conceive of them in a higher manner when we apply them to the divine nature, than when we consider them in the several creatures formally, exceeding those perfections and excellencies which are in the creature, and in a more excellent manner. As one§ saith : 'Though we cannot comprehend God without the help of such resemblances, yet we may, without making an image of him ; so that inability of ours excuseth those apprehensions of him from any way offending against his divine nature.' These are not notions so much suited to the nature of God as the weakness of man. They are helps to our meditations, but ought not to be formal conceptions of him. We may assist ourselves in our apprehensions of him, by considering the subtilty and spirituality of air, and considering the members of a body, without thinking him to be air or to have any corporeal member. Our reason tells us that whatsoever is a body is limited and bounded, and the notion of infiniteness and bodiliness cannot agree and consist together ; and therefore, what is offered by our fancy should be purified by our reason.

(4.) Therefore we are to elevate and refine all our notions of God, and spiritualise our conceptions of him. Every man is to have a conception of

* Nazianzen.   ‡ Lessius.
† Amyrald, Moral. tom. i. p. 180, &c.   § Towerson on the Commandments, p. 112.

God, therefore he ought to have one of the highest elevation. Since we cannot have a full notion of him, we should endeavour to make it as high and as pure as we can. Though we cannot conceive of God, but some corporeal representations or images in our minds will be conversant with us, as motes in the air when we look upon the heavens, yet our conception may and must rise higher. As when we see the draught of the heavens and earth in a globe, or a kingdom in a map, it helps our conceptions, but doth not terminate them; we conceive them to be of a vast extent, far beyond that short description of them; so we should endeavour to refine every representation of God, to rise higher and higher, and have our apprehensions still more purified; separating the perfect from the imperfect, casting away the one and greatening the other; conceive him to be a Spirit diffused through all, containing all, perceiving all. All the perfections of God are infinitely elevated above the excellencies of the creatures, above whatsoever can be conceived by the clearest and most piercing understanding. The nature of God, as a Spirit, is infinitely superior to whatsoever we can conceive perfect in the notion of a created spirit. Whatsoever God is, he is infinitely so. He is infinite wisdom, infinite goodness, infinite knowledge, infinite power, infinite spirit, infinitely distant from the weakness of creatures, infinitely mounted above the excellencies of creatures. As easy to be known that he is, as impossible to be comprehended what he is.

Conceive of him as excellent, without any imperfection. A Spirit without parts; great without quantity; perfect without quality; everywhere without place; powerful without members; understanding without ignorance; wise without reasoning; light without darkness; infinitely more excelling the beauty of all creatures, than the light in the sun pure and unviolated exceeds the splendour of the sun dispersed and divided through a cloudy and misty air. And when you have risen to the highest, conceive him yet infinitely above all you can conceive of spirit, and acknowledge the infirmity of your own minds. And whatsoever conception comes into your minds, say, This is not God, God is more than this. If I could conceive him, he were not God, for God is incomprehensibly above whatsoever I can say, whatsoever I can think and conceive of him.

Inference 4. If God be a Spirit, no corporeal thing can defile him. Some bring an argument against the omnipresence of God, that it is a disparagement to the divine essence to be everywhere, in nasty cottages as well as beautiful palaces and garnished temples. What place can defile a spirit? Is light, which approaches to the nature of spirit, polluted by shining upon a dunghill, or a sunbeam tainted by darting upon a quagmire? Doth an angel contract any soil, by stepping into a nasty prison to deliver Peter? What can steam from the most noisome body, to pollute the spiritual nature of God? As he is 'of purer eyes than to behold iniquity,' Hab. i. 13, so he is of a more spiritual substance than to contract any physical pollution from the places where he doth diffuse himself. Did our Saviour, who had a true body, derive any taint from the lepers he touched, the diseases he cured, or the devils he expelled? God is a pure Spirit, plungeth himself into no filth, is dashed with no spot by being present with all bodies. Bodies only receive defilement from bodies.

Inference 5. If God be a Spirit, he is active and communicative. He is not clogged with heavy and sluggish matter, which is cause of dulness and inactivity. The more subtle, thin, and approaching nearer the nature of a spirit anything is, the more diffusive it is. Air is a gliding substance, spreads itself through all religions,* pierceth into all bodies; it fills the

* Qu. 'regions'?—ED.

space between heaven and earth, there is nothing but partakes of the virtue of it. Light, which is an emblem of spirit, insinuates itself into all places, refresheth all things. As spirits are fuller, so they are more overflowing, more piercing, more operative than bodies. The Egyptians' horses were weak things, because they were flesh and not spirit, Isa. xxxi. 3. The soul being a spirit, conveys more to the body than the body can to it. What cannot so great a Spirit do for us! What cannot so great a Spirit work in us! God being a Spirit above all spirits, can pierce into the centre of all spirits ; make his way into the most secret recesses ; stamp what he pleases. It is no more to him to turn our spirits, than to make a wilderness become waters, and speak a chaos into a beautiful frame of heaven and earth. He can act our souls with infinite more ease than our souls can act our bodies ; he can fix in us what motions, frames, inclinations he pleases ; he can come and settle in our hearts with all his treasures. It is an encouragement to confide in him, when we petition him for spiritual blessings. As he is a Spirit, he is possessed with spiritual blessings, Eph. i. 3. A spirit delights to bestow things suitable to its nature, as bodies do to communicate what is agreeable to theirs. As he is a Father of spirits, we may go to him for the welfare of our spirits ; he being a Spirit, is as able to repair our spirits, as he was to create them.

As he is a Spirit, he is indefatigable in acting. The members of the body tire and flag ; but who ever heard of a soul wearied with being active ! Who ever heard of a weary angel ! In the purest simplicity, there is the greatest power, the most efficacious goodness, the most reaching justice to affect the spirit, that can insinuate itself everywhere to punish wickedness without weariness, as well as to comfort goodness. God is active, because he is Spirit ; and if we be like to God, the more spiritual we are, the more active we shall be.

Inference 6. God being a Spirit, is immortal. His being immortal and being invisible are joined together, 1 Tim. i. 17. Spirits are in their nature incorruptible ; they can only perish by that hand that framed them. Every compounded thing is subject to mutation ; but God being a pure and simple Spirit, is without corruption, without any shadow of change, James i. 17. Where there is composition, there is some kind of repugnancy of one part against the other ; and where there is repugnancy, there is a capability of dissolution. God, in regard of his infinite spirituality, hath nothing in his own nature contrary to it ; can have nothing in himself which is not himself. The world perishes, friends change and are dissolved, bodies moulder, because they are mutable. God is a Spirit in the highest excellency and glory of spirits ; nothing is beyond him, nothing above him, no contrariety within him. This is our comfort, if we devote ourselves to him ; this God is our God ; this Spirit is our Spirit ; this is our all, our immutable, our incorruptible support ; a Spirit that cannot die and leave us.

Inference 7. If God be a Spirit, we see how we can only converse with him ; by our spirits. Bodies and spirits are not suitable to one another ; we can only see, know, embrace a spirit with our spirits. He judges not of us by our corporeal actions, nor our external devotions, by our masks and disguises, he fixes his eye upon the frame of the heart, bends his ear to the groans of our spirits. He is not pleased with outward pomp, he is not a body ; therefore the beauty of temples, delicacy of sacrifices, fumes of incense, are not grateful to him ; by those or any external action we have no communion with him. A spirit, when broken, is his delightful sacrifice, Ps. li. 17 ; we must therefore have our spirits fitted for him, be 'renewed in the spirit of our mind,' Eph. iv. 23, that we may be in a posture to live

with him, and have an intercourse with him. We can never be united to
God but in our spirits; bodies unite with bodies, spirits with spirits. The
more spiritual anything is, the more closely doth it unite. Air hath the
closest union, nothing meets together sooner than that when the parts are
divided by the interposition of a body.

Inference 8. If God be a Spirit, he can only be the true satisfaction of
our spirits. Spirit can only be filled with a spirit. Content flows from
likeness and suitableness; as we have a resemblance to God in regard of
the spiritual nature of our soul, so we can have no satisfaction but in him.
Spirit can no more be really satisfied with that which is corporeal, than a
beast can delight in the company of an angel; corporeal things can no
more fill a hungry spirit than pure spirit can feed an hungry body; God,
the highest Spirit, can only reach out a full content to our spirits. Man is
lord of the creation; nothing below him can be fit for his converse, nothing
above him offers itself to his converse but God. We have no correspondence with angels. The influence they have upon us, the protection they
afford us, is secret and undiscerned; but God, the highest Spirit, offers
himself to us in his Son, in his ordinances, is visible in every creature,
presents himself to us in every providence; to him we must seek, in him
we must rest. God had no rest from the creation till he had made man,
and man can have no rest in the creation till he rests in God. God only
is 'our dwelling-place,' Ps. xc. 1; our souls should only long for him, Ps.
lxiii. 1; our souls should only wait upon him. The spirit of man never
riseth to its original glory, till it be carried up on the wings of faith and love
to its original copy. The face of the soul looks most beautiful when it is
turned to the face of God, the Father of spirits; when the derived spirit is
fixed upon the original Spirit, drawing from it life and glory. Spirit is only
the receptacle of spirit. God as Spirit is our principle, we must therefore
live upon him. God as Spirit hath some resemblance to us as his image,
we must therefore only satisfy ourselves in him.

Inference 9. If God be a Spirit, we should take most care of that
wherein we are like to God. Spirit is nobler than body, we must therefore
value our spirits above our bodies; the soul as spirit partakes more of the
divine nature, and deserves more of our choicest cares. If we have any
love to this Spirit, we should have a real affection to our own spirit, as
bearing a stamp of the spiritual divinity, the chiefest of all the works of
God; as it is said of Behemoth, Job xl. 19. That which is most the image
of this immense Spirit should be our darling; so David calls his soul, Ps.
xxxv. 17. Shall we take care of that wherein we partake not of God, and
not delight in the jewel which hath his own signature upon it? God was
not only the framer of spirits, and the end of spirits, but the copy and
exemplar of spirits. God partakes of no corporiety, he is pure Spirit.
But how do we act, as if we were only matter and body! We have but
little kindness for this great Spirit as well as our own, if we take no care of
his immediate offspring, since he is not only Spirit, but the Father of spirits,
Heb. xii. 9.

Inference 10. If God be a Spirit, let us take heed of those sins which are
spiritual. Paul distinguisheth between the filth of the flesh and that of the
spirit, 2 Cor. vii. 1; by the one we defile the body, by the other we defile
the spirit, which in regard of its nature is of kin to the Creator. To wrong
one who is near of kin to a prince is worse than to injure an inferior subject. When we make our spirits, which are most like to God in their
nature, and framed according to his image, a stage to act vain imaginations,
wicked desires, and unclean affections, we wrong God in the excellency of

his work, and reflect upon the nobleness of the pattern; we wrong him in that part where he hath stamped the most signal character of his own spiritual nature, we defile that whereby we have only converse with him as a Spirit, which he hath ordered more immediately to represent him in this nature, than all corporeal things in the world can, and make that Spirit with whom we desire to be joined unfit for such a knot. God's spirituality is the root of his other perfections. We have already heard he could not be infinite, omnipresent, immutable without it. Spiritual sins are the greatest root of bitterness within us; as grace in our spirits renders us more like to a spiritual God, so spiritual sins bring us into a conformity to a degraded devil, Eph. ii. 2, 3. Carnal sins change us from men to brutes, and spiritual sins divest us of the image of God for the image of Satan. We should by no means make our spirits a dunghill, which bear upon them the character of the spiritual nature of God, and were made for his residence. Let us therefore behave ourselves towards God in all those ways which the spiritual nature of God requires us.

A DISCOURSE UPON SPIRITUAL WORSHIP.

God is a Spirit: and they that worship him must worship him in spirit and in truth.—JOHN IV. 24.

HAVING thus despatched the first proposition, 'God is a Spirit,' it will not be amiss to handle the inference our Saviour makes from that proposition, which is the second observation propounded.

Doct. That the worship due from us to God ought to be spiritual, and spiritually performed.

Spirit and truth are understood variously. Either we are to worship God,

1. Not by legal ceremonies; the evangelical administration being called spirit in opposition to the legal ordinances as carnal, and truth in opposito them as typical. As the whole Judaical service is called flesh, so the whole evangelical service is called spirit. Or spirit may be opposed to the worship at Jerusalem, as it was carnal; truth, to the worship on the mount Gerizim, because it was false. They had not the true object of worship, nor the true medium of worship as those at Jerusalem had. Their worship should cease, because it was false, and the Jewish worship should cease, because it was carnal.

There is no need of a candle when the sun spreads its beams in the air; no need of those ceremonies when the Sun of righteousness appeared; they only served for a candle to instruct and direct men till the time of his coming. The shadows are chased away by the displaying the substance, so that they can be of no more use in the worship of God, since the end for which they were instituted is expired, and that is discovered to us in the gospel, which the Jews sought for in vain among the baggage and stuff of their ceremonies.

2. With a spiritual and sincere frame. 'In spirit,' *i. e.* with spirit; with the inward operations of all the faculties of our souls, and the cream and flower of them; and the reason is, because there ought to be a worship suitable to the nature of God. And as the worship was to be spiritual, so the exercise of that worship ought to be in a spiritual manner.* It shall be a worship in truth, because the true God shall be adored without those vain imaginations, and fantastic resemblances of him, which were common among the blind Gentiles, and contrary to the glorious nature of God, and unworthy ingredients in religious services. It shall be a worship in spirit, without those carnal rites the degenerated Jews rested on. Such a posture

* Lingend, tom. ii. p. 777. Taylor's Exemplar, Preface, sec. 30.

of soul, which is the life and ornament of every service, God looks for at
your hands.   There must be some proportion between the object adored,
and the manner in which we adore it.   It must not be a mere corporeal
worship, because God is not a body; but it must rise from the centre of our
soul, because God is a Spirit.   If he were a body, a bodily worship might
suit him, images might be fit to represent him; but being a Spirit, our
bodily services enter us not into communion with him.   Being a Spirit, we
must banish from our minds all carnal imaginations of him, and separate
from our wills all cold and dissembled affections to him.   We must not only
have a loud voice, but an elevated soul; not only a bended knee, but a
broken heart; not only a supplicating tone, but a groaning spirit; not only
a ready ear for the word, but a receiving heart; and this shall be of greater
value with him than the most costly outward services offered at Gerizim or
Jerusalem.

Our Saviour certainly meant not, by worshipping in spirit, only the matter
of the evangelical service as opposed to the legal administration, without
the manner wherein it was to be performed.   It is true, God always sought
a worship in spirit; he expected the heart of the worshipper should join
with his instituted rights of adoration in every exercise of them; but he
expects such a carriage more under the gospel administration, because of the
clearer discoveries of his nature made in it, and the greater assistances conveyed by it.

I shall therefore,

I. Lay down some general propositions.

II. Shew what this spiritual worship is.

III. Why we must offer to God a spiritual service.

IV. The use.

I. Some general propositions.

Prop. 1. First, The right exercise of worship is founded upon and riseth
from the spirituality of God.*   The first ground of the worship we render
to God is the infinite excellency of his nature, which is not only one
attribute, but results from all; for God as God is the object of worship, and
the notion of God consists not in thinking him wise, good, just, but all those
infinitely beyond any conception.   And hence it follows that God is an
object infinitely to be loved and honoured.   His goodness is sometimes
spoken of in Scripture as a motive of our homage: Ps. cxxx. 4, 'There is
forgiveness with thee that thou mayest be feared.'   Fear, in the Scripture
dialect, signifies the whole worship of God: Acts x. 35, 'But in every nation
he that fears him is accepted of him;' so 2 Kings xvii. 32, 33.   If God
should act towards men according to the rigours of his justice due to them
for the least of their crimes, there could be no exercise of any affection but
that of despair, which could not engender a worship of God, which ought
to be joined with love, not with hatred.   The beneficence and patience of
God, and his readiness to pardon men, is the reason of the honour they return
to him.   And this is so evident a motive, that generally the idolatrous world
ranked those creatures in the number of their gods, which they perceived
useful and beneficial to mankind, as the sun and moon, the Egyptians the
ox, &c.   And the more beneficial anything appeared to mankind, the higher
station men gave it in the rank of their deities, and bestowed a more peculiar
and solemn worship upon it.   Men worshipped God to procure or continue
his favour, which would not have been acted by them, had they not conceived it a pleasing thing to him to be merciful and gracious.

* Ames Medul. lib. ii. cap. 4, sec. 20.

Sometimes his justice is proposed to us as a motive of worship: Heb. xii. 28, 29, ' Serve God with reverence and godly fear, for our God is a consuming fire ;' which includes his holiness, whereby he doth hate sin, as well as his wrath, whereby he doth punish it. Who but a mad and totally brutish person, or one that was resolved to make war against heaven, could behold the effects of God's anger in the world, consider him in his justice as a consuming fire, and despise him, and rather be drawn out by that consideration to blasphemy and despair, than to seek all ways to appease him ? Now though the infinite power of God, his unspeakable wisdom, his incomprehensible goodness, the holiness of his nature, the vigilance of his providence, the bounty of his hand signify to man that he should love and honour him, and are the motive of worship, yet the spirituality of his nature is the rule of worship, and directs us to render our duty to him with all the powers of our soul. As his goodness beams out upon us, worship is due in justice to him ; and as he is the most excellent nature, veneration is due to him in the highest manner with the choicest affections.

So that indeed the spirituality of God comes chiefly into consideration in matter of worship. All his perfections are grounded upon this. He could not be infinite, immutable, omniscient, if he were a corporeal being.* We cannot give him a worship unless we judge him worthy, excellent, and deserving a worship at our hands ; and we cannot judge him worthy of a worship unless we have some apprehensions and admirations of his infinite virtues ; and we cannot apprehend and admire those perfections, but as we see them as causes shining in their effects. When we see, therefore, the frame of the world to be the work of his power, the order of the world to be the fruit of his wisdom, and the usefulness of the world to be the product of his goodness, we find the motives and reasons of worship ; and weighing that this power, wisdom, goodness, infinitely transcend any corporeal nature, we find a rule of worship, that it ought to be offered by us in a manner suitable to such a nature as is infinitely above any bodily being. His being a Spirit declares what he is, his other perfections declare what kind of Spirit he is. All God's perfections suppose him a Spirit ; all centre in this. His wisdom doth not suppose him merciful, or his mercy suppose him omniscient. There may be distinct notions of those, but all suppose him to be of a spiritual nature. How cold and frozen will our devotions be if we consider not his omniscience, whereby he discerns our hearts !† How carnal will our services be if we consider him not as a pure spirit ! In our offers to, and transactions with men, we deal not with them as mere animals, but as rational creatures ; and we debase their natures if we treat them otherwise. And if we have not raised apprehensions of God's spiritual nature in our treating with him, but allow him only such frames as we think fit enough for men, we debase his spirituality to the littleness of our own being. We must therefore possess our souls with this, we shall else render him no better than a fleshly service. We do not much concern ourselves in those things of which we are either utterly ignorant, or have but slight apprehensions of.

That is the first proposition ; the right exercise of worship is grounded upon the spirituality of God.

Prop. 2. This spiritual worship of God is manifest by the light of nature to be due to him. In reference to this, consider,

1. The outward means or matter of that worship which would be acceptable to God was not known by the light of nature. The law for a worship, and for a spiritual worship by the faculties of our souls, was natural, and

---

* Amyrald, Dissert. 6, disp. 1, p. 12.　　　† Amirant de Relig.

part of the law of creation, though the determination of the particular acts whereby God would have this homage testified was of positive institution, and depended not upon the law of creation. Though Adam in innocence knew God was to be worshipped, yet by nature he did not know by what outward acts he was to pay this respect, or at what time he was more solemnly to be exercised in it than at another. This depended upon the directions God, as the sovereign governor and lawgiver, should prescribe. You therefore find the positive institutions of the tree of the knowledge of good and evil, and the determination of the time of worship, Gen. ii. 3, 17. Had there been any such notion in Adam naturally, as strong as that other, that a worship was due to God, there would have been found some relics of these modes universally consented to by mankind, as well as of the other. But though all nations have by an universal consent concurred in the acknowledgment of the being of God, and his right to adoration, and the obligation of the creature to it, and that there ought to be some public rule and polity in matters of religion (for no nation hath been in the world without a worship, and without external acts and certain ceremonies to signify that worship), yet their modes and rites have been as various as their climates, unless in that common notion of sacrifices, not descending to them by nature, but tradition, from Adam; and the various ways of worship have been more provoking than pleasing. Every nation suited the kind of worship to their particular ends and polities they designed to rule by. How God was to be worshipped is more difficult to be discerned by nature with its eyes out than with its eyes clear. The pillars upon which the worship of God stands cannot be discerned without revelation,* no more than blind Samson could tell where the pillars of the Philistines' theatre stood, without one to conduct him. What Adam could not see with his sound eyes, we cannot with our dim eyes; he must be told from heaven what worship was fit for the God of heaven. It is not by nature that we can have such a full prospect of God as may content and quiet us. This is the noble effect of divine revelation, he only knows himself, and can only make himself known to us. It could not be supposed that an infinite God should have no perfections but what were visible in the works of his hands, and that these perfections should not be infinitely greater than as they were sensible in their present effects. This had been to apprehend God a limited being, meaner than he is. Now it is impossible to honour God as we ought, unless we know him as he is; and we could not know him as he is without divine revelation from himself; for none but God can acquaint us with his own nature. And therefore the nations void of this conduct heap up modes of worship from their own imaginations, unworthy of the majesty of God, and below the nature of man. A rational man would scarce have owned such for signs of honour, as the Scripture mentions in the services of Baal and Dagon, much less an infinitely wise and glorious God. And when God had signified his mind to his own people, how unwilling were they to rest satisfied with God's determination, but would be warping to their own inventions, and make gods, and ways of worship to themselves, Amos v. 26, as in the matter of the golden calf, as was lately spoken of.

2. Though the outward manner of worship acceptable to God could not be known without revelation, and those revelations might be various, yet the inward manner of worship with our spirits was manifest by nature. And not only manifest by nature to Adam in innocence, but after his fall, and the scales he had brought upon his understanding by that fall. When God gave him his positive institutions before the fall, or whatsoever additions God should

* King on Jonah, p. 63.

have made had he persisted in that state, or when he appointed him after his fall to testify his acknowledgment of him by sacrifices, there needed no command to him to make those acknowledgments by those outward ways prescribed to him with the intention and prime affection of his spirit. This nature would instruct him in without revelation. For he could not possibly have any semblance of reason to think that the offering of beasts, or the presenting the first-fruits of the increase of the ground as an acknowledgment of God's sovereignty over him, and his bounty to him, was sufficient, without devoting to him that part wherein the image of his Creator did consist. He could not but discern by a reflection upon his own being, that he was made for God as well as by God; for it is a natural principle, of which the apostle speaks Rom. xi. 36, 'For of him, and through him, and to him, are all things,' &c., that the whole whereof he did consist was due to God; and that his body, the dreggy and dusty part of his nature, was not fit to be brought alone before God, without that nobler principle which he had by creation linked with it. Nothing in the whole law of nature, as it is informed of religion, was clearer, next to the being of God, than this manner of worshipping God with the mind and spirit. And as the Gentiles never sunk so low into the mud of idolatry as to think the images they worshipped were really their gods, but the representations or habitations of their gods, so they never deserted this principle in the notion of it, that God was to be honoured with the best they were, and the best they had. As they never denied the being of a God in the notion, though they did in the practice, so they never rejected this principle in notion, though they did, and now most men do, in the inward observation of it. It was a maxim among them that God was *mens*, *animus*, mind and spirit, and therefore was to be honoured with the mind and spirit. That religion did not consist in the ceremonies of the body, but the work of the soul; whence the speech of one of them,* 'Sacrifice to the gods not so much clothed with purple garments as a pure heart.' And of another,† 'God regards not the multitude of the sacrifices, but the disposition of the sacrificer.' It is not fit we should deny God the cream and flower, and give him the slotten part and the stalks. And with what reverence and intention of mind they thought their worship was to be performed is evident by the priests' crying out often, *hoc age*, mind this, let your spirits be intent upon it.

This could not but result,

(1.) From the knowledge of ourselves. It is a natural principle, 'God hath made us, and not we ourselves,' Ps. c. 1, 2. Man knows himself to be a rational creature. As a creature, he was to serve his Creator; and as a rational creature, with the best part of that rational nature he derived from him. By the same act of reason that he knows himself to be a creature, he knows himself to have a Creator. That this Creator is more excellent than himself, and that an honour is due from him to the Creator for framing of him; and therefore this honour was to be offered to him by the most excellent part which was framed by him. Man cannot consider himself as a thinking, understanding being, but he must know that he must give God the honour of his thoughts, and worship him with those faculties whereby he thinks, wills, and acts.‡ He must know his faculties were given him to act, and to act for the glory of that God who gave him his soul and the faculties of it; and he could not in reason think they must be only active in his own service, and the service of the creature, and idle and unprofitable in the service of his Creator. With the same powers of our soul whereby we con-

* Meander, Grot. de veritat relig. lib. 4, sec. 12.   † Iamblich.
‡ Amyrald, Mor., tom. i. p. 309, 310.

template God, we must also worship God. We cannot think of him but with our minds, nor love him but with our will; and we cannot worship him without the acts of thinking and loving, and therefore cannot worship him without the exercise of our inward faculties. How is it possible, then, for any man that knows his own nature, to think that extended hands, bended knees, and lifted up eyes, were sufficient acts of worship, without a quickened and active spirit!

(2.) From the knowledge of God. As there was a knowledge of God by nature, so the same nature did dictate to man that God was to be glorified as God. The apostle implies the inference in the charge he brings against them for neglecting it, Rom. i. 21. 'We should speak of God as he is,' said one;* and the same reason would inform them that they were to act towards God as he is. The excellency of the object required a worship according to the dignity of his nature, which could not be answered but by the most serious inward affection as well as outward decency; and a want of this cannot but be judged to be unbecoming the majesty of the Creator of the world, and the excellency of religion. No nation, no person did ever assert that the vilest part of man was enough for the most excellent being, as God is; that a bodily service could be a sufficient acknowledgment of the greatness of God, or a sufficient return for the bounty of God.† Man could not but know that he was to act in religion conformably to the object of religion, and to the excellency of his own soul. The notion of a God was sufficient to fill the mind of man with admiration and reverence, and the first conclusion from it would be to honour God, and that he have all the affection placed on him that so infinite and spiritual a being did deserve. The progress then would be, that this excellent being was to be honoured with the motions of the understanding and will, with the purest and most spiritual powers in the nature of man, because he was a spiritual being, and had nothing of matter mingled with him. Such a brutish imagination to suppose that blood and fumes, beasts and incense, could please a Deity, without a spiritual frame, cannot be supposed to befall any but those that had lost their reason in the rubbish of sense. Mere rational nature could never conclude that so excellent a spirit would be put off with a mere animal service, and attendance of matter and body without spirit, when they themselves, of an inferior nature, would be loath to sit down contented with an outside service from those that belong to them; so that this instruction of our Saviour, that God is to be worshipped in spirit and truth, is conformable to the sentiments of nature, and drawn from the most undeniable principles of it. The excellency of God's nature, and the excellent constitution of human faculties, concur naturally to support this persuasion. This was as natural to be known by men, as the necessity of justice and temperance for the support of human societies and bodies. It is to be feared that if there be not among us such brutish apprehensions, there are such brutish dealings with God in our services against the light of nature, when we place all our worship of God in outward attendances and drooping countenances, with unbelieving frames and formal devotions; when prayer is muttered over in private slightly, as a parrot learns lessons by rote, not understanding what it speaks, or to what end it speaks it; not glorifying God in thought and spirit, with understanding and will.

(3.) Spiritual worship, therefore, was always required by God, and always offered to him by one or other. Man had a perpetual obligation upon him to such a worship, from the nature of God; and what is founded upon the nature of God is unvariable. This and that particular mode of worship

* Bias.   † Amyrald, ib.

may ' wax old as a garment, and as a vesture may be folded up and changed, as the expression is of the heavens, Heb. i. 11, 12, but God endures for ever. His spirituality fails not, therefore a worship of him in spirit must run through all ways and rites of worship. God must cease to be spirit, before any service but that which is spiritual can be accepted by him. The light of nature is the light of God; the light of nature being unchangeable, what was dictated by that was always, and will always be, required by God. The worshipping of God being perpetually due from the creature, the worshipping him as God is as perpetually his right, though the outward expressions of this honour were different, one way in paradise (for a worship was then due, since a solemn time for that worship was appointed), another under the law, another under the gospel. The angels also worship God in heaven, and fall down before his throne; yet though they differ in rites, they agree in this necessary ingredient,—all rites, though of a different shape, must be offered to him not as carcasses, but animated with the affections; of the soul. Abel's sacrifice had not been so excellent in God's esteem, without those gracious habits and affections working in his soul, Heb. xi. 4. Faith works by love; his heart was on fire as well as his sacrifice. Cain rested upon his present, perhaps thought he had obliged God. He depended upon the outward ceremony, but sought not for the inward purity. It was an offering brought to the Lord, Gen. iv. 5; he had the right object, but not the right manner: ver. 7, ' If thou dost well, shalt thou not be accepted?' And in the command afterwards to Abraham, ' Walk before me, and be thou perfect,' was the direction in all our religious acts and walkings with God. A sincere act of the mind and will, looking above and beyond all symbols, extending the soul to a pitch far above the body, and seeing the day of Christ through the veil of the ceremonies, was required by God. And though Moses, by God's order, had instituted a multitude of carnal ordinances, sacrifices, washings, oblations of sensible things, and recommended to the people the diligent observation of those statutes by the allurements of promises and denouncing of threatenings, as if there were nothing else to be regarded, and the true workings of grace were to be buried under a heap of ceremonies, yet sometimes he doth point them to the inward worship, and, by the command of God, requires of them the ' circumcision of the heart,' Deut. x. 16, the ' turning to God with all their heart and all their soul,' Deut. xxx. 10, whereby they might recollect that it was the engagement of the heart and the worship of the spirit that was most agreeable to God, and that he took not any pleasure in their observance of ceremonies, without true piety within, and the true purity of their thoughts.

(4.) It is therefore as much every man's duty to worship God in spirit, as it is their duty to worship him. Worship is so due to him as God, as that he that denies it disowns his Deity. And spiritual worship is so due, that he that waives it denies his spirituality. It is a debt of justice we owe to God to worship him, and it is as much a debt of justice to worship him according to his nature. Worship is nothing else but a rendering to God the honour that is due to him, and therefore the right posture of our spirits in it is as much or more due than the material worship in the modes of his own prescribing; that is grounded both upon his nature and upon his command, this only upon his command; that is perpetually due, whereas the channel wherein outward worship runs may be dried up, and the river diverted another way; such a worship wherein the mind thinks of God, feels a sense of God, has the spirit consecrated to God, the heart glowing with affections to God. It is else a mocking God with a feather. A rational

nature must worship God with that wherein the glory of God doth most
sparkle in him. God is most visible in the frame of the soul; it is there
his image glitters. He hath given us a jewel as well as a case, and the
jewel as well as the case we must return to him. The spirit is God's gift,
and must return to him, Eccles. xii. 7. It must return to him in every service
morally, as well as it must return to him at last physically. It is not fit
we should serve our Maker only with that which is the brute in us, and
withhold from him that which doth constitute us reasonable creatures. We
must give him our bodies, but 'a living sacrifice,' Rom. xii. 1. If the
spirit be absent from God when the body is before him, we present a dead
sacrifice. It is morally dead in the duty, though it be naturally alive in
the posture and action. It is not an indifferent thing whether we shall
worship God or no, nor is it an indifferent thing whether we shall worship
him with our spirits or no. As the excellency of man's knowledge consists
in knowing things as they are in truth, so the excellency of the will in
willing things as they are in goodness. As it is the excellency of man to
know God as God, so it is no less his excellency, as well as his duty, to
honour God as God. As the obligation we have to the power of God for
our being binds us to a worship of him, so the obligation we have to his
bounty, for fashioning us according to his own image, binds us to an exercise of that part wherein his image doth consist. God hath 'made all things
for himself,' Prov. xvi. 4; that is, for the evidence of his own goodness and
wisdom. We are therefore to render him a glory according to the excellency of his nature, discovered in the frame of our own. It is as much our
sin not to glorify God as God, as not to attempt the glorifying of him at all.
It is our sin not to worship God as God, as well as to omit the testifying
any respect at all to him. As the divine nature is the object of worship, so
the divine perfections are to be honoured in worship. We do not honour
God, if we honour him not as he is; we honour him not as a spirit, if we
think him not worthy of the ardours and ravishing admirations of our spirits.
If we think the devotions of the body are sufficient for him, we contract him
into the condition of our own being, and not only deny him to be a spiritual
nature, but dash out all those perfections which he could not be possessed
of were he not a spirit.

5. The ceremonial law was abolished to promote the spirituality of divine
worship. That service was gross, carnal, calculated for an infant and sensitive church. It consisted in rudiments, the circumcision of the flesh, the
blood and smoke of sacrifices, the streams of incense, observation of days,
distinction of meats, corporal purifications; every leaf of the law is clogged
with some rite to be particularly observed by them. The spirituality of
worship lay veiled under a thick cloud, that the people could not behold the
glory of the gospel, which lay covered under those shadows: 2 Cor. iii. 13,
'They could not stedfastly look to the end of that which was abolished!'
They understood not the glory and spiritual intent of the law, and therefore
came short of that spiritual frame in the worship of God, which was their
duty; and therefore, in opposition to this administration, the worship of
God under the gospel is called by our Saviour in the text, a worship in
spirit; more spiritual for the matter, more spiritual for the motives, and
more spiritual for the manner and frames of worship.

(1.) This legal service is called flesh in Scripture, in opposition to the
gospel, which is called spirit. The ordinances of the law, though of divine
institution, are dignified by the apostle with no better a title than carnal
ordinances, Heb. ix. 10, and a carnal command, Heb. vii. 16; but the
gospel is called the ministration of the spirit, as being attended with a special

and spiritual efficacy on the minds of men, 2 Cor. iii. 8. And when the degenerate Galatians, after having tasted of the pure streams of the gospel, turned about to drink of the thicker streams of the law, the apostle tells them that they ' begun in the spirit,' and would not be ' made perfect in the flesh,' Gal. iii. 3 ; they would leave the righteousness of faith for a justification by works. The moral law, which is in its own nature spiritual, Rom. vii. 14, in regard of the abuse of it in expectation of justification by the outward works of it, is called flesh. Much more may the ceremonial administration, which was never intended to run parallel with the moral, nor had any foundation in nature, as the other had.

That whole economy consisted in sensible and material things which only touched the flesh ; it is called ' the letter,' and the ' oldness of the letter,' Rom. vii. 6; as letters, which are but empty sounds in themselves, but put together and formed into words, signify something to the mind of the hearer or reader. An old letter, a thing of no efficacy upon the spirit, but as a law written upon paper. The gospel hath an efficacious spirit attending it, strongly working upon the mind and will, and moulding the soul into a spiritual frame for God ; according to the doctrine of the gospel, the one is old and decays, the other is new, and increaseth daily.

And as the law itself is called flesh, so the observers of it and resters in it are called ' Israel after the flesh,' 1 Cor. x. 18; and the evangelical worshipper is called a ' a Jew after the spirit,' Rom. ii. 29. They were Israel after the flesh as born of Jacob, not Israel after the spirit as born of God ; and therefore the apostle calls them Israel and not Israel, Rom. ix. 6 ; Israel after a carnal birth, not Israel after a spiritual ; Israel in the circumcision of the flesh, not Israel by a regeneration of the heart.

(2.) The legal ceremonies were not a fit means to bring the heart into a spiritual frame. They had a spiritual intent; the rock and manna prefigured the salvation and spiritual nourishment by the Redeemer, 1 Cor. x. 3, 4. The sacrifices were to point them to the justice of God in the punishment of sin, and the mercy of God in substituting them in their steads, as types of the Redeemer and the ransom by his blood. The circumcision of the flesh was to instruct them in the circumcision of the heart. They were flesh in regard of their matter, weakness, and cloudiness ; spiritual in regard of their intent and signification ; they did instruct, but not efficaciously work strong spiritual affections in the soul of the worshipper. They were ' weak and beggarly elements,' Gal. iv. 9, had neither wealth to enrich nor strength to nourish the soul. They could not perfect the comers to them, or put them into a frame agreeable to the nature of God, Heb. x. 1, ix. 9, nor ' purge the conscience from those dead ' and dull dispositions which were by nature in them, ver. 14; being carnal, they could not have an efficacy to purify the conscience of the offerer, and work spiritual effects. Had they continued without the exhibition of Christ, they could never have wrought any change in us, or purchased any favour for us.* At the best they were but shadows, and came unexpressibly short of the efficacy of that person and state whose shadows they were. The shadow of a man is too weak to perform what the man himself can do, because it wants the life, spirit, and activity of the substance. The whole pomp and scene was suited more to the sensitive than the intellectual nature, and, like pictures, pleased the fancy of children, rather than improved their reason. The Jewish state was a state of childhood, Gal. v. 2, and that administration a pedagogy, iv. 24. The law was a schoolmaster, fitted for their weak and childish capacity, and could no more spiritualise the heart than the teachings in a

* Burges, Vind. p. 256.

primer school can enable the mind, and make it fit for affairs of state ; and, because they could not better the spirit, they were instituted only for a time, as elements delivered to an infant age, which naturally lives a life of sense rather than a life of reason.   It was also a servile state, which doth rather debase than elevate the mind, rather carnalise than spiritualise the heart ; besides, it is a sense of mercy that both melts and elevates the heart into a spiritual frame : Ps. cxxx. 4, ' There is forgiveness with thee that thou mayest be feared.'   And they had in that state but some glimmerings of mercy in the daily bloody intimations of justice.   There was no sacrifice for some sins, but a cutting off without the least hints of pardon ; and in the yearly remembrance of sin there was as much to shiver them with fear as to possess them with hopes, and such a state which always held them under the conscience of sin could not produce a free spirit, which was necessary for a worship of God according to his nature.

(3.) In their use they rather hindered than furthered a spiritual worship. In their own nature they did not tend to the obstructing a spiritual worship, for then they had been contrary to the nature of religion and the end of God who appointed them.   Nor did God cover the evangelical doctrine under the clouds of the legal administration, to hinder the people of Israel from perceiving it, but because they were not yet capable to bear the splendour of it had it been clearly set before them.   The shining of the face of Moses was too dazzling for their weak eyes, and therefore there was a necessity of a veil, not for the things themselves, but the weakness of their eyes, 2 Cor. iii. 13, 14.   The carnal affections of that people sunk down into the things themselves, stuck in the outward pomp, and pierced not through the veil to the spiritual intent of them ; and by the use of them, without rational conceptions, they besotted their minds, and became senseless of those spiritual motions required of them.   Hence came all their expectations of a carnal Messiah ; the veil of ceremonies was so thick, and the film upon their eyes so condensed, that they could not look through the veil to the Spirit of Christ.   They beheld not the heavenly Canaan for the beauty of the earthly, nor minded the regeneration of the spirit while they rested upon the purifications of the flesh.   The prevalency of sense and sensitive affections diverted their minds from inquiring into the intent of them.   Sense and matter are often clogs to the mind, and sensible objects are the same often to spiritual motions.   Our souls are never more raised than when they are abstracted from the entanglements of them.   A pompous worship, made up of many sensible objects, weakens the spirituality of religion.   Those that are most zealous for outward are usually most cold and indifferent in inward observances, and those that overdo in carnal modes usually underdo in spiritual affections.

This was the Jewish state.*   The nature of the ceremonies being pompous and earthly, by their show and beauty meeting with their weakness and childish affections, filled their eyes with an outward lustre, allured their minds, and detained them from seeking things higher and more spiritual. The kernel of those rites lay concealed in a thick shell, the spiritual glory was little seen, and the spiritual sweetness little tasted.   Unless the Scripture be diligently searched, it seems to transfer the worship of God from true faith and the spiritual motions of the heart, and stake it down to outward observances and the *opus operatum* ; besides, the voice of the law did only declare sacrifices, and invited the worshipper to them with a promise of the atonement of sin, turning away the wrath of God.   It never plainly acquainted them that those things were types and shadows of something future, that

* Illyric. de velam. Mosis, p. 221, &c.

they were only outward purifications of the flesh. It never plainly told them at the time of appointing them that those sacrifices could not abolish sin, and reconcile them to God. Indeed, we see more of them since their death and dissection in that one Epistle to the Hebrews than can be discerned in the five books of Moses. Besides, man naturally affects a carnal life, and therefore affects a carnal worship; he designs the gratifying his sense, and would have a religion of the same nature. Most men have no mind to busy their reason above the things of sense, and are naturally unwilling to raise them up to those things which are allied to the spiritual nature of God; and therefore the more spiritual any ordinance is, the more averse is the heart of man to it. There is a ' simplicity of the gospel,' from which our minds are easily corrupted by things that pleasure the sense, as Eve was by the curiosity of her eye and the liquorishness of her palate, 2 Cor. xi. 3. From this principle hath sprung all the idolatry in the world. The Jews knew they had a God who had delivered them, but they would have a sensible God to go before them, Exod. xxxii. 1; and the papacy at this day is a witness of the truth of this natural corruption.

(4.) Upon these accounts, therefore, God never testified himself well pleased with that kind of worship. He was not displeased with them, as they were his own institution, and ordained for the representing (though in an obscure manner) the glorious things of the gospel; nor was he offended with those people's observance of them, for since he had commanded them, it was their duty to perform them, and their sin to neglect them; but he was displeased with them as they were practised by them, with souls as morally carnal in the practices, as the ceremonies were materially carnal in their substance. It was not their disobedience to observe them; but it was a disobedience, and a contempt of the end of the institution, to rest upon them, to be warm in them and cold in morals. They fed upon the bone, and neglected the marrow; pleased themselves with the shell, and sought not for the kernel. They joined not with them the internal worship of God, fear of him, with faith in the promised seed, which lay veiled under those coverings: Hos. vi. 6, ' I desired mercy and not sacrifice, and the knowledge of God more than burnt-offerings.' And therefore he seems sometimes weary of his own institutions, and calls them not his own, but *their* sacrifices, *their* feasts, Isa. i. 11, 14. They were *his* by appointment, *theirs* by abuse. The institution was from his goodness and condescension, therefore *his;* the corruption of them was from the vice of their nature, therefore *theirs.* He often blamed them for their carnality in them, shewed his dislike of placing all their religion in them, gives the sacrificers, upon that account, no better a title than that of the ' princes of Sodom and Gomorrah,' Isa. i. 10; and compares the sacrifices themselves to the ' cutting off a dog's neck,' ' swine's blood,' and the ' murder of a man,' Isa. lxvi. 3. And indeed God never valued them, or expressed any delight in them. He despised the feasts of the wicked, Amos v. 21, and had no esteem for the material offerings of the godly: Ps. l. 13, ' Will I eat the flesh of bulls, or drink the blood of goats?' which he speaks to his saints and people, before he comes to reprove the wicked, which he begins, ver. 16, ' But to the wicked, God said,' &c. So slightly he esteemed them, that he seems to disown them to be any part of his command, when he brought his people out of the land of Egypt: Jer. vii. 22, ' I spake not to your fathers, nor commanded them concerning burnt-offerings and sacrifices.' He did not value nor regard them, in comparison of that inward frame which he had required by the moral law; that being given before the law of ceremonies, obliged them, in the first place, to an observance of those precepts. They seemed to be below the nature of

God, and could not of themselves please him. None could in reason persuade themselves that the death of a beast was a proportionable offering for the sin of a man, or ever was intended for the expiation of transgression. In the same rank are all our bodily services under the gospel. A loud voice without spirit, bended bulrushes without inward affections, are no more delightful to God than the sacrifices of animals. It is but a change of one brute for another of a higher species; a mere brute, for that part of man which hath an agreement with brutes. Such a service is a mere animal service, and not spiritual.

(5.) And therefore God never intended that sort of worship to be durable, and had often mentioned the change of it for one more spiritual. It was not good or evil in itself; whatsoever goodness it had was solely derived to it by institution, and therefore it was mutable. It had no conformity with the spiritual nature of God, who was to be worshipped, nor with the rational nature of man, who was to worship. And therefore he often speaks of taking away the new moons, and feasts, and sacrifices, and all the ceremonial worship, as things he took no pleasure in, to have a worship more suited to his excellent nature. But he never speaks of removing the gospel administration, and the worship prescribed there, as being more agreeable to the nature and perfections of God, and displaying them more illustriously to the world.

The apostle tells us it was to be disannulled because of its weakness, Heb. vii. 18. A determinate time was fixed for its duration, till the accomplishment of the truth figured under that pedagogy, Gal. iv. 2. Some of the modes of that worship being only typical, must naturally expire and be insignificant in their use, upon the finishing of that by the Redeemer, which they did prefigure; and other parts of it, though God suffered them so long because of the weakness of the worshipper, yet because it became not God to be always worshipped in that manner, he would reject them, and introduce another more spiritual and elevated. 'Incense and a pure offering' should be offered everywhere unto his name, Mal. i. 11.

He often told them he would make a new covenant by the Messiah, and the old should be rejected;* that the 'former things should not be remembered, and the things of old no more considered,' when he should do 'a new thing in the earth,' Isa. xliii. 18, 19. Even the ark of the covenant, the symbol of his presence and the glory of the Lord in that nation, should not any more be remembered and visited, Jer. iii. 16; that the temple and sacrifices should be rejected, and others established; that the order of the Aaronical priesthood should be abolished, and that of Melchisedec set up in the stead of it in the person of the Messiah, to endure for ever, Ps. cx.; that Jerusalem should be changed, a new heaven and earth created, a worship more conformable to heaven, more advantageous to earth. God had proceeded in the removal of some part of it, before the time of taking down the whole furniture of this house. The pot of manna was lost, Urim and Thummim ceased, the glory of the temple was diminished, and the ignorant people wept at the sight of the one, without raising their faith and hope in the consideration of the other, which was promised to be filled with a spiritual glory. And as soon as ever the gospel was spread in the world, God thundered out his judgments upon that place in which he had fixed all those legal observances; so that the Jews, in the letter and flesh, could never practise the main part of their worship, since they were expelled from that place where it was only to be celebrated. It is one thousand six hundred years since they have been deprived of their altar, which was the foundation of all

* Pascal. Pen., 142.

the Levitical worship, and have wandered in the world ' without a sacrifice, a prince or priest, an ephod or teraphim,' Hos. iii. 4.

And God fully put an end to it in the command he gave to the apostles, and in them to us, in the presence of Moses and Elias, to hear his Son only: Mat. xvii. 5, ' Behold a voice out of the cloud, which said, This is my beloved Son, in whom I am well pleased: hear him;' and at the death of our Saviour, testified it to that whole nation and the world, by the rending in twain the vail of the temple.

The whole frame of that service, which was carnal, and by reason of the corruption of man, weakened, is nulled, and a spiritual worship is made known to the world, that we might now serve God in a more spiritual manner, and with more spiritual frames.

Prop. 6. The service and worship the gospel settles is spiritual, and the performance of it more spiritual. Spirituality is the genius of the gospel, as carnality was of the law; the gospel is therefore called spirit. We are abstracted from the employments of sense, and brought nearer to a heavenly state. The Jews had angels' bread poured upon them; we have angels' service prescribed to us: the praises of God, communion with God in spirit, through his Son Jesus Christ, and stronger foundations for spiritual affections. It is called a reasonable service, Rom. xii. 1. It is suited to a rational nature, though it finds no friendship from the corruption of reason. It prescribes a service fit for the reasonable faculties of the soul, and advanceth them while it employs them. The word *reasonable* may be translated *word service*,* as well as reasonable service; an evangelical service, in opposition to a law service. All evangelical service is reasonable, and all truly reasonable service is evangelical.

The *matter* of the worship is spiritual. It consists in love of God, faith in God, recourse to his goodness, meditation on him, and communion with him. It lays aside the ceremonial, spiritualiseth the moral. The commands that concerned our duty to God, as well as those that concerned our duty to our neighbour, were reduced by Christ to the spiritual intention.

The *motives* are spiritual. It is a state of more grace, as well as of more truth, John i. 17, supported by spiritual promises, beaming out in spiritual privileges. Heaven comes down in it to earth, to spiritualise earth for heaven.

The *manner* of worship is more spiritual. Higher flights of the soul, stronger ardours of affections, sincerer aims at his glory; mists are removed from our minds, clogs from the soul; more of love than fear; faith in Christ kindles the affections, and works by them.

The *assistances* to spiritual worship are greater. The Spirit doth not drop, but is plentifully poured out. It doth not light sometimes upon, but dwells in, the heart. Christ suited the gospel to a spiritual heart, and the Spirit changeth a carnal heart to make it fit for a spiritual gospel. He blows upon the garden, and causes the spices to flow forth; and often makes the soul in worship like the chariots of Amminadab in a quick and nimble motion. Our blessed Lord and Saviour by his death discovered to us the nature of God, and after his ascension sent his Spirit to fit us for the worship of God, and converse with him.

One spiritual evangelical believing breath is more delightful to God than millions of altars made up of the richest pearls, and smoking with the costliest oblations, because it is spiritual; and a mite of spirit is of more worth than the greatest weight of flesh. One holy angel is more excellent than a whole world of mere bodies.

* V. Hammond, *in loc.*

Prop. 7. Yet the worship of God with our bodies is not to be rejected upon the account that God requires a spiritual worship. Though we must perform the weightier duties of the law, yet we are not to omit and leave undone the lighter precepts ; since both the *magnalia* and *minutula legis,* the greater and the lesser duties of the law, have the stamp of divine authority upon them.

As God, under the ceremonial law, did not command the worship of the body, and the observation of outward rites, without the engagement of the spirit, so neither doth he command that of the spirit without the peculiar attendance of the body.

The Schwelkfendians denied bodily worship ; and the indecent postures of many in public attendance intimate no great care either of composing their bodies or spirits. A morally discomposed body intimates a tainted heart.

Our bodies as well as our spirits are to be presented to God, Rom. xii. 1. Our bodies in lieu of the sacrifices of beasts, as in the Judaical institutions : body for the whole man ; a living sacrifice, not to be slain, as the beasts were, but living a new life, in a holy posture, with crucified affections. This is the inference the apostle makes of the privileges of justification, adoption, co-heirship with Christ, which he had before discoursed of ; privileges conferred upon the person, and not upon a part of man.

1. Bodily worship is due to God. He hath a right to an adoration by our bodies as they are his by creation ; his right is not diminished but increased by the blessing of redemption : 1 Cor. vi. 20, ' For you are bought with a price ; therefore glorify God in your bodies and your spirits, which are God's.' The body as well as the spirit is redeemed, since our Saviour suffered crucifixion in his body, as well as agonies in his soul. Body is not taken here for the whole man, as it may be in Rom. xii. ; but for the material part of our nature, it being distinguished from the spirit. If we are to render to God an obedience with our bodies, we are to render him such acts of worship with our bodies as they are capable of. As God is ' the Father of spirits,' so he is ' the God of all flesh ;' therefore the flesh he hath framed of the earth, as well as the noble portion he hath breathed into us, cannot be denied him without a palpable injustice. The service of the body we must not deny to God, unless we will deny him to be the author of it, and the exercise of his providential care about it. The mercies of God are renewed every day upon our bodies as well as our souls, and therefore they ought to express a fealty to God for his bounty every day. ' Both are from God, both should be for God. Man consists of body and soul ; the service of man is the service of both. The body is to be sanctified as well as the soul, and therefore to be offered to God as well as the soul. Both are to be glorified, both are to glorify. As our Saviour's divinity was manifested in his body, so should our spirituality in ours. To give God the service of the body, and not of the soul, is hypocrisy ; to give God the service of the spirit, and not of the body, is sacrilege ; to give him neither, atheism.'* If the only part of man that is visible were exempted from the service of God, there could be no visible testimonies of piety given upon any occasion : since not a moiety of man, but the whole, is God's creature, he ought to pay a homage with the whole, and not only with a moiety of himself.

2. Worship in societies is due to God, but this cannot be without some bodily expressions. The law of nature doth as much direct men to combine together in public societies for the acknowledgment of God, as in civil communities for self-preservation and order ; and the notice of a society for religion is more ancient than the mention of civil associations for politic

* Sherman's Greek in the Temple, p. 61, 62.

government: Gen. iv. 26, 'Then began men to call upon the name of the Lord,' viz., in the time of Seth. No question but Adam had worshipped God before as well as Abel, and a family religion had been preserved; but as mankind increased in distinct families, they knit together in companies to solemnize the worship of God.* Hence, as some think, those that incorporated together for such ends were called the sons of God; sons by profession, though not sons by adoption; as those of Corinth were saints by profession, though in such a corrupted church they could not be all so by regeneration, yet saints, as being of a Christian society, and calling upon the name of Christ, that is, worshipping God in Christ, though they might not be all saints in spirit and practice. So Cain and Abel met together to worship, Gen. iv. 3, 'at the end of the days,' at a set time. God settled a public worship among the Jews, instituted synagogues for their convening together, whence called 'the synagogues of God,' Ps. lxxiv. 8. The Sabbath was instituted to acknowledge God a common benefactor. Public worship keeps up the memorials of God in a world prone to atheism, and a sense of God in a heart prone to forgetfulness. The angels sung in company, not singly, at the birth of Christ, Luke ii. 13, and praised God not only with a simple elevation of their spiritual nature, but audibly, by forming a voice in the air. Affections are more lively, spirits more raised in public than private; God will credit his own ordinance. Fire increaseth by laying together many coals in one place; so is devotion inflamed by the union of many hearts, and by a joint presence; nor can the approach of the last day of judgment, or particular judgments upon a nation, give a writ of ease from such assemblies: Heb. x. 25, 'Not forsaking the assembling ourselves together, but so much the more as you see the day approaching.' Whether it be understood of the day of judgment, or the day of the Jewish destruction and the Christian persecution, the apostle uses it as an argument to quicken them to the observance, not to encourage them to a neglect. Since, therefore, natural light informs us, and divine institution commands us, publicly to acknowledge ourselves the servants of God, it implies the service of the body. Such acknowledgments cannot be without visible testimonies, and outward exercises of devotion, as well as inward affections. This promotes God's honour, checks others' profaneness, allures men to the same expressions of duty. And though there may be hypocrisy, and an outward garb without an inward frame, yet better a moiety of worship than none at all; better acknowledge God's right in one than disown it in both.

3. Jesus Christ, the most spiritual worshipper, worshipped God with his body. He prayed orally, and kneeled, 'Father, if it be thy will,' &c., Luke xxii. 41, 42. He blessed with his mouth, 'Father, I thank thee,' Mat. xi. 26. He lifted up his eyes, as well as elevated his spirit, when he praised his Father for mercy received, or begged for the blessings his disciples wanted, John xi. 41; xvii. 1. The strength of the spirit must have vent at the outward members. The holy men of God have employed the body in significant expressions of worship; Abraham in falling on his face, Paul in kneeling, employing their tongues, lifting up their hands. Though Jacob was bed-rid, yet he would not worship God without some devout expression of reverence; it is in one place leaning upon his staff, Heb. xi. 21; in another bowing himself upon his bed's head, Gen. xlvii. 31. The reason of the diversity is in the Hebrew word, which without vowels may be read *Mittah*, a bed, or *Matteh*, a staff; howsoever, both signify a testimony of adoration by a reverent gesture of the body. Indeed, in angels and

* Stillingfleet's Irenicum, cap. i. sect. 1, p. 23.

separated souls, a worship is performed purely by the spirit; but whiles the soul is in conjunction with the body, it can hardly perform a serious act of worship without some tincture upon the outward man, and reverential composure of the body. Fire cannot be in the clothes, but it will be felt by the members; nor flames be pent up in the soul without bursting out in the body. The heart can no more restrain itself from breaking out, than Joseph could inclose his affections, without expressing them in tears to his brethren, Gen. xlv. 1, 2. 'We believe, and therefore speak,' 2 Cor. iv. 13.

To conclude; God hath appointed some parts of worship which cannot be performed without the body, as sacraments; we have need of them because we are not wholly spiritual and incorporeal creatures.

The religion which consists in externals only, is not for an intellectual nature. A worship purely intellectual is too sublime for a nature allied to sense and depending much upon it. The Christian mode of worship is proportioned to both; it makes the sense to assist the mind, and elevates the spirit above the sense. Bodily worship helps the spiritual. The members of the body reflect back upon the heart, the voice bars distractions, the tongue sets the heart on fire in good as well as in evil. It is as much against the light of nature to serve God without external significations, as to serve him only with them without the intention of the mind. As the invisible God declares himself to men by visible works and signs, so should we declare our invisible frames by visible expressions. God hath given us a soul and body in conjunction, and we are to serve him in the same manner he hath framed us.

II. The second thing I am to shew is, what spiritual worship is. In general, the whole spirit is to be employed. The name of God is not sanctified but by the engagement of our souls.

Worship is an act of the understanding, applying itself to the knowledge of the excellency of God, and actual thoughts of his majesty, recognising him as the supreme Lord and governor of the world, which is natural knowledge; beholding the glory of his attributes in the Redeemer, which is evangelical knowledge; this is the sole act of the spirit of man. The same reason is for all our worship as for our thanksgiving. This must be done with understanding: Ps. xlvii. 7, 'Sing ye praise with understanding,' with a knowledge and sense of his greatness, goodness, and wisdom. It is also an act of the will, whereby the soul adores and reverenceth his majesty, is ravished with his amiableness, embraceth his goodness, enters itself into an intimate communion with this most lovely object, and pitcheth all his affections upon him.

We must worship God understandingly; it is not else a reasonable service. The nature of God and the law of God abhor a blind offering; we must worship him heartily, else we offer him a dead sacrifice. A reasonable service is that wherein the mind doth truly act something with God. All spiritual acts must be acts of reason, otherwise they are not human acts, because they want that principle which is constitutive of man, and doth difference him from other creatures. Acts done only by sense are the acts of a brute; acts done by reason are the acts of a man; that which is only an act of sense cannot be an act of religion. The sense without the conduct of reason is not the subject of religious acts, for then beasts were capable of religion as well as men. There cannot be religion where there is not reason; and there cannot be the exercise of religion, where there is not an exercise of the rational faculties. Nothing can be a Christian act, that is not a human act. Besides, all worship must be for some end; the worship of God must be for

God ; it is by the exercise of our rational faculties, that we only can intend an end.   An ignorant and carnal worship is a brutish worship,

Particularly,

1. Spiritual worship is a worship from a spiritual nature. Not only physically spiritual, so our souls are in their frame, but morally spiritual, by a renewing principle. The heart must be first cast into the mould of the gospel, before it can perform a worship required by the gospel. Adam living in paradise might perform a spiritual worship, but Adam fallen from his rectitude could not. We being heirs of his nature, are heirs of his impotence. Restoration to a spiritual life must precede any act of spiritual worship. As no work can be good, so no worship can be spiritual, till we are created in Christ, Eph. ii. 10. ‘Christ is our life,’ Col. iii. 4. As no natural action can be performed without life in the root or heart, so no spiritual act without Christ in the soul. Our being in Christ is as necessary to every spiritual act, as the union of our soul with our body is necessary to natural action. Nothing can exceed the limits of its nature ; for then it should exceed itself in acting, and do that which it hath no principle to do. A beast cannot act like a man, without partaking of the nature of a man ; nor a man act like an angel, without partaking of the angelical nature. How can we perform spiritual acts without a spiritual principle ? Whatsoever worship proceeds from the corrupted nature, cannot deserve the title of spiritual worship, because it springs not from a spiritual habit. If those that are evil cannot speak good things, those that are carnal cannot offer a spiritual service. Poison is the fruit of a viper's nature : Mat. xii. 34, ‘O generation of vipers, how can you, being evil, speak good things ? for out of the abundance of the heart the mouth speaks.’ As the root is, so is the fruit. If the soul be habitually carnal, the worship cannot be actually spiritual. There may be an intention of spirit, but there is no spiritual principle as a root of that intention. A heart may be sensibly united with a duty, when it is not spiritually united with Christ in it. Carnal motives and carnal ends may fix the mind in an act of worship, as the sense of some pressing affliction may enlarge a man's mind in prayer. Whatsoever is agreeable to the nature of God, must have a stamp of Christ upon it ; a stamp of his grace in performance, as well as of his meditation* in the acceptance. The apostle lived not, but ‘Christ lived in him,’ Gal. ii. 20 ; the soul worships not, but Christ in him. Not that Christ performs the act of worship, but enables us spiritually to worship, after he enables us spiritually to live. As God counts not any soul living but in Christ, so he counts not any a spiritual worshipper but in Christ. The goodness and fatness of the fruit comes from the fatness of the olive wherein we are engrafted. We must find healing in Christ's wings, before God can find spirituality in our services. All worship issuing from a dead nature, is but a dead service. A living action cannot be performed without being knit to a living root.

2. Spiritual worship is done by the influence and with the assistance of the Spirit of God. A heart may be spiritual, when a particular act of worship may not be spiritual. The Spirit may dwell in the heart, when he may suspend his influence on the act. Our worship is then spiritual, when the fire that kindles our affections comes from heaven, as that fire upon the altar wherewith the sacrifices were consumed. God tastes a sweetness in no service, but as it is dressed up by the hand of the Mediator, and hath the air of his own Spirit in it ; they are but natural acts without a supernatural assistance. Without an actual influence we cannot act from spiritual motives, nor for spiritual ends, nor in a spiritual manner. We cannot

* Qu. ‘mediation’?—ED.

mortify a lust without the Spirit, Rom. viii. 13, nor quicken a service without the Spirit. Whatsoever corruption is killed, is slain by his power; whatsoever duty is spiritualised, is refined by his breath. He 'quickens our dead bodies' in our resurrection, ver. 11; he renews our dead souls in our regeneration; he quickens our carnal services in our adorations; the choicest acts of worship are but infirmities, without his auxiliary help, ver. 26. We are logs, unable to move ourselves, till he raise our faculties to a pitch agreeable to God, puts his hand to the duty, and lifts that up, and us with it. Never any great act was performed by the apostles to God, or for God, but they are said to be filled with the Holy Ghost. Christ could not have been conceived immaculate as 'that holy thing,' without the Spirit's overshadowing the virgin; nor any spiritual act conceived in our heart, without the Spirit's moving upon us, to bring forth a living religion from us. The acts of worship are said to be in the Spirit, 'supplication in the Spirit,' Eph. vi. 18; not only with the strength and affection of our own spirits, but with the mighty operation of the Holy Ghost, if Jude may be the interpreter, ver. 20,—the Holy Ghost exciting us, impelling us, and firing our souls by his divine flame, raising up the affections, and making the soul cry, with a holy importunity, 'Abba, Father.' To render our worship spiritual, we should, before every engagement in it, implore the actual presence of the Spirit, without which we are not able to send forth one spiritual breath or groan, but be wind-bound, like a ship without a gale, and our worship be no better than carnal. How doth the spouse solicit the Spirit with an 'Awake, O north wind; and come, thou south wind,' &c., Cant. iv. 16.

3. Spiritual worship is done with sincerity. When the heart stands right to God, and the soul performs what it pretends to perform; when we serve God with our spirits, as the apostle, Rom. i. 9, 'God is my witness, whom I serve with my spirit in the gospel of his Son;' this is not meant of the Holy Ghost, for the apostle would never have called the Spirit of God his own spirit; but with *my spirit*, that is, a sincere frame of heart. A carnal worship, whether under the law or gospel, is when we are busied about external rites, without an inward compliance of soul. God demands the heart: Prov. xxiii. 26, 'My son, give me thy heart;' not give me thy tongue, or thy lips, or thy hands; these may be given without the heart, but the heart can never be bestowed without these as its attendants. A heap of services can be no more welcome to God, without our spirits, than all Jacob's sons could be to Joseph without the Benjamin he desired to see. God is not taken with the cabinet, but the jewel; he first respected Abel's faith and sincerity, and then his sacrifice; he disrespected Cain's infidelity and hypocrisy, and then his offering. 'For this cause he rejected the offerings of the Jews, the prayers of the Pharisees, and the alms of Ananias and Sapphira, because their hearts and their duties were at a distance from one another. In all spiritual sacrifices our spirits are God's portion. Under the law the reins were to be consumed by the fire on the altar, because the secret intentions of the heart were signified by them: Ps. vii. 9, "The Lord trieth the heart and the reins." It was an ill omen among the heathen if a victim wanted a heart. The widow's mites, with her heart in them, were more esteemed than the richer offerings without it.'* Not the quantity of service, but the will in it, is of account with this infinite Spirit. All that was to be brought for the framing of the tabernacle was to be offered 'willingly with the heart,' Exod. xxv. 7. The more of will, the more of spirituality and acceptableness to God: Ps. cxix. 108, 'Accept the free-will-offering of my lips.' Sincerity is the salt which seasons every sacrifice. The heart is

* Moulin. Sermons, Decad. 4, Ser. 4, p. 80.

most like to the object of worship; the heart in the body is the spring of all vital actions, and a spiritual soul is the spring of all spiritual actions. How can we imagine God can delight in the mere service of the body, any more than we can delight in converse with a carcass!

Without the heart it is no worship; it is a stage-play, an acting a part without being that person really which is acted by us; a hypocrite, in the notion of the word, is a stage-player. We may as well say a man may believe with his body as worship God only with his body. Faith is a great ingredient in worship, and it is ' with the heart man believes unto righteousness,' Rom. x. 10. We may be truly said to worship God, though we want perfection, but we cannot be said to worship him if we want sincerity. A statue upon a tomb, with eyes and hands lifted up, offers as good and true a service; it wants only a voice, the gestures and postures are the same; nay, the service is better; it is not a mockery, it represents all that it can be framed to. But to worship without our spirits is a presenting God with a picture, an echo, voice, and nothing else; a compliment, a mere lie, a ' compassing him about with lies,' Hosea xi. 12. Without the heart the tongue is a liar, and the greatest zeal, dissembling with him. To present the spirit is to present that which can never naturally die; to present him only the body, is to present him that which is every day crumbling to dust, and will at last lie rotting in the grave. To offer him a few rags easily torn, a skin for a sacrifice, a thing unworthy the majesty of God, a fixed eye and elevated hands, with a sleepy heart and earthly soul, are pitiful things for an ever blessed and glorious Spirit; nay, it is so far from being spiritual, that it is blasphemy; to pretend to be a Jew outwardly, without being so inwardly, is in the judgment of Christ to blaspheme, Rev. ii. 9. And is not the same title to be given with as much reason to those that pretend a worship and perform none? Such a one is not a spiritual worshipper, but a blaspheming devil in Samuel's mantle.

4. Spiritual worship is performed with an unitedness of heart. The heart is not only now and then with God, but ' united to fear' or worship ' his name,' Ps. lxxxvi. 11. A spiritual duty must have the engagement of the Spirit, and the thoughts tied up to the spiritual object. The union of all the parts of the heart together with the body is the life of the body, and the moral union of our hearts is the life of any duty. A heart quickly flitting from God makes not God his treasure; he slights the worship, and therein affronts the object of worship. All our thoughts ought to be ravished with God, bound up in him as in a bundle of life. But when we start from him to gaze after every feather, and run after every bubble, we disown a full and affecting excellency, and a satisfying sweetness in him. When our thoughts run from God, it is a testimony we have no spiritual affection to God. Affection would stake down the thoughts to the object affected. It is but a mouth-love, as the prophet phraseth it: Ezek. xxxiii. 31, ' But their hearts go after their covetousness.' Covetous objects pipe, and the heart danceth after them, and thoughts of God are shifted off to receive a multitude of other imaginations. The heart and the service stayed a while together, and then took leave of one another. The psalmist still found his heart with God when he awaked, Ps. cxxxix. 18; still with God in spiritual affections, and fixed meditations. A carnal heart is seldom with God, either in or out of worship. If God should knock at the heart in any duty, it would be found not at home, but straying abroad. Our worship is spiritual when the door of the heart is shut against all intruders, as our Saviour commands in closet-duties, Mat. vi. 6. It was not his meaning to command the shutting the closet-door, and leave the heart-door open for every thought

that would be apt to haunt us. Worldly affections are to be laid aside, if we would have our worship spiritual. This was meant by the Jewish custom of wiping or washing off the dust of their feet before their entrance into the temple, and of not bringing money in their girdles. To be spiritual in worship is to have our souls gathered and bound up wholly in themselves, and offered to God. Our loins must be girt, as the fashion was in the eastern countries, where they wore long garments, that they might not waver with the wind, and be blown between their legs, to obstruct them in their travel. Our faculties must not hang loose about us. He is a carnal worshipper that gives God but a piece of his heart, as well as he that denies him the whole of it; that hath some thoughts pitched upon God in worship, and as many willingly upon the world. David sought God, not with a moiety of his heart, but 'with his whole heart,' with his entire frame, Ps. cxix. 10. He brought not half his heart, and left the other in the possession of another master. It was a good lesson Pythagoras gave his scholars,* not to make the observance of God a work by the by. If those guests be invited, or entertained kindly, or if they come unexpected, the spirituality of that worship is lost; the soul kicks down what is wrought before. But if they be brow-beaten by us, and our grief rather than our pleasure, they divert our spiritual intention from the work in hand, but hinder not God's acceptance of it as spiritual, because they are not the acts of our will, but offences to our wills.

5. Spiritual worship is performed with a spiritual activity and sensibleness of God, with an active understanding to meditate on his excellency, and an active will to embrace him when he drops upon the soul. If we understand the amiableness of God, our affections will be ravished; if we understand the immensity of his goodness, our spirits will be enlarged. We are to act with the highest intention, suitable to the greatness of that God with whom we have to do: Ps. cl. 2, 'Praise him according to his excellent greatness.' Not that we can worship him equally, but in some proportion the frame of the heart is to be suited to the excellency of the object; our spiritual strength is to be put out to the utmost, as creatures that act naturally do. The sun shines, and the fire burns, to the utmost of their natural power. This is so necessary that David, a spiritual worshipper, prays for it before he sets upon acts of adoration: Ps. lxxx. 18, 'Quicken us, that we may call upon thy name.' As he was loath to have a drowsy faculty, he was loath to have a drowsy instrument, and would willingly have them as lively as himself: Ps. lvii. 8, ' Awake up, my glory; awake, psaltery and harp: I myself will awake early.' How would this divine soul screw himself up to God, and be turned into nothing but a holy flame ! Our souls must be boiling hot when we serve the Lord (ζέοντες), Rom. xii. 11. The heart doth no less burn when it spiritually comes to God, than when God doth spiritually approach to it, Luke xxiv. 32. A Nabal's heart, one as cold as a stone, cannot offer up a spiritual service.

Whatsoever is enjoined us as our duty, ought to be performed with the greatest intenseness of our spirit. As it is our duty to pray, so it is our duty to pray with the most fervent importunity. It is our duty to love God, but with the purest and most sublime affections. Every command of God requires the whole strength of the creature to be employed in it. That love to God, wherein all our duty to God is summed up, is to be with all our strength, with all our might, &c.† Though in the covenant of grace he hath mitigated the severity of the law, and requires not from us such an

---

* 'Ου γάρ πάρεργον δεῖ ποιεῖσθαι τόν Θεόν.—Iamblich, l. i. c. 518, p. 87.
† Lady Falkland's Life, p. 130.

elevation of our affections as was possible in the state of innocence, yet God requires of us the utmost moral industry to raise our affections to a pitch at least equal to what they are in other things. What strength of affection we naturally have ought to be as much and more excited in acts of worship than upon other occasions and our ordinary works. As there was an activity of soul in worship, and a quickness to sin when sin had the dominion, so when the soul is spiritualised the temper is changed, there is an inactivity to sin and an ardour in duty. The more the soul is 'dead to sin,' the more it is 'alive to God,' Rom. vi. 11, and the more lively too in all that concerns God and his honour. For grace being a new strength added to our natural, determines the affections to new objects, and excites them to a greater vigour. And as the hatred of sin is more sharp, the love to everything that destroys the dominion of it is more strong. And acts of worship may be reckoned as the chiefest batteries against the power of this inbred enemy. When the Spirit is in the soul, like the rivers of waters flowing out of the belly, the soul hath the activity of a river, and makes haste to be swallowed up in God, as the streams of the river in the sea. Christ makes his people 'kings and priests to God,' Rev. i. 6. First kings, then priests; gives first a royal temper of heart, that they may offer spiritual sacrifices as priests; kings and priests to God, acting with a magnificent spirit in all their motions to him. We cannot be spiritual priests till we be spiritual kings. The Spirit appeared in the likeness of fire, and where he resides, communicates, like fire, purity and activity.

Dulness is against the light of nature. I do not remember that the heathen ever offered a snail to any of their false deities, nor an ass, but to Priapus their unclean idol; but the Persians sacrificed to the sun a horse, a swift and generous creature. God provided against those in the law, commanding an ass's firstling, the offspring of a sluggish creature, to be redeemed, or his neck broke, but by no means to be offered to him, Exod. xiii. 13. God is a Spirit infinitely active, and therefore frozen and benumbed frames are unsuitable to him: 'He rides upon a cherub, and flies,' he comes 'upon the wings of the wind,' he rides upon 'a swift cloud,' Isa. xix. 1, and therefore demands of us not a dull reason, but an active spirit. God is a living God, therefore must have a lively service. Christ is life, and slothful adorations are not fit to be offered up in the name of life. The worship of God is called wrestling in Scripture, and Paul was a striver in the service of his Master: Col. i. 29, 'in an agony' ($\dot{\alpha}\gamma\omega\nu\iota\zeta\acute{o}\mu\epsilon\nu o\varsigma$). Angels worship God spiritually with their wings on; and when God commands them to worship Christ, the next scripture quoted is that he makes them 'flames of fire,' Heb. i. 7.

If it be thus, how may we charge ourselves? What Paul said of the sensual widow, 1 Tim. v. 6, that she is 'dead while she lives,' we may say often of ourselves, we are dead while we worship. Our hearts are in duty as the Jews' were in deliverances, 'as those in a dream,' Ps. cxxvi. 1; by which unexpectedness God shewed the greatness of his care and mercy, and we attend him as men in a dream, whereby we discover our negligence and folly. This activity doth not consist in outward acts. The body may be hot and the heart may be faint, but in an inward stirring, meltings, flights. In the highest raptures, the body is most insensible. Strong spiritual affections are abstracted from outward sense.

6. Spiritual worship is performed with acting spiritual habits. When all the living springs of grace are opened, as the fountains of the deep were in the deluge, the soul and all that is within it, all the spiritual impresses of God upon it, erect themselves to bless his holy name, Ps. ciii. 1.

This is necessary to make a worship spiritual. As natural agents are determined to act suitable to their proper nature, so rational agents are to act conformable to a rational being. When there is a conformity between the act and the nature whence it flows, it is a good act in its kind; if it be rational, it is a good rational act, because suitable to its principle. As a man endowed with reason must act suitable to that endowment, and exercise his reason in his acting, so a Christian endued with grace must act suitable to that nature, and exercise his grace in his acting. Acts done by a natural inclination are no more human acts than the natural acts of a beast may be said to be human. Though they are the acts of a man as he is the efficient cause of them, yet they are not human acts, because they arise not from that principle of reason which denominates him a man. So acts of worship performed by a bare exercise of reason, are not Christian and spiritual acts, because they come not from the principle which constitutes him a Christian. Reason is not the principle, for then all rational creatures would be Christians. They ought therefore to be acts of a higher principle, exercises of that grace whereby Christians are what they are; not but that rational acts in worship are due to God, for worship is due from us as men, and we are settled in that rank of being by our reason. Grace doth not exclude reason, but ennobles it, and calls it up to another form; but we must not rest in a bare rational worship, but exert that principle whereby we are Christians. To worship God with our reason, is to worship him as men; to worship God with our grace, is to worship him as Christians, and so spiritually; but to worship him only with our bodies, is no better than brutes.

Our desires of the word are to issue from the regenerate principle: 1 Peter ii. 2, 'As new born babes, desire the sincere milk of the word.' It seems to be not a comparison, but a restriction. All worship must have the same spring, and be the exercise of that principle, otherwise we can have no communion with God. Friends that have the same habitual dispositions have a fundamental fitness for an agreeable converse with one another; but if the temper wherein their likeness consists be languishing, and the string out of tune, there is not an actual fitness, and the present indisposition breaks the converse, and renders the company troublesome. Though we may have the habitual graces which compose in us a resemblance to God, yet for want of acting those suitable dispositions, we render ourselves unfit for his converse, and make the worship, which is fundamentally spiritual, to become actually carnal. As the will cannot naturally act to any object but by the exercise of its affections, so the heart cannot spiritually act towards God but by the exercise of graces. This is God's music: Eph. v. 19, 'singing and making melody to God in your hearts.' Singing and all other acts of worship are outward, but the spiritual melody is 'by grace in the heart,' Col. iii. 16. This renders it a spiritual worship, for it is an effect of the fulness of the Spirit in the soul; as ver. 19, 'But be filled with the Spirit.' The overflowing of the Spirit in the heart, setting the soul of a believer thus on work to make a spiritual melody to God, shews that something higher than bare reason is put in tune in the heart. Then is the fruit of the garden pleasant to Christ, when the Holy Spirit, 'the north and south wind, blow upon the spices,' Cant. iv. 16, and strike out the fragrancy of them. Since God is the author of graces, and bestows them to have a glory from them, they are best employed about him and his service. It is fit he should have the cream of his own gifts. Without the exercise of grace, we perform but a work of nature, and offer him a few dry bones without marrow.

The whole set of graces must be one way or other exercised. If any treble be wanting in a lute, there will be a great defect in the music. If any one spiritual string be dull, the spiritual harmony of worship will be spoiled.

And therefore,

1. First, Faith must be acted in worship; a confidence in God. A natural worship cannot be performed without a natural confidence in the goodness of God. Whosoever comes to him must regard him as a rewarder and a faithful Creator, Heb. xi. 6; a spiritual worship cannot be performed without an evangelieal confidence in him as a gracious Redeemer. To think him a tyrant, meditating revenge, damps the soul; to regard him as a gracious king, full of tender bowels, spirits the affections to him. The mercy of God is the proper object of trust: Ps. xxxiii. 18, ' The eye of the Lord is upon them that fear him, upon them that hope in his mercy.' The worship of God in the Old Testament is most described by *fear*, in the New Testament by *faith*. Fear, or the worship of God, and hope in his mercy, are linked together. When they go hand in hand, the accepting eye of God is upon us; when we do not trust, we do not worship. Those of Judah had the temple worship among them, especially in Josiah's time, Zeph. iii. 2, the time of that prophecy; yet it was accounted no worship, because no trust in the worshippers. Interest in God cannot be improved without an exercise of faith. The gospel worship is prophesied of to be a confidence in God, as in a husband more than in a lord: Hosea ii. 16, ' Thou shalt call me Ishi, and shalt call me no more Baali.' ' Thou shalt call me;' that is, thou shalt worship me, worship being often comprehended under invocation. More confidence is to be exercised in a husband or father than in a lord or master.

If a man have not faith, he is without Christ; and though a man be in Christ by the habit of faith, he performs a duty out of Christ without an act of faith. Without the habit of faith, our persons are out of Christ; and without the exercise of faith, the duties are out of Christ. As the want of faith in a person is the death of the soul, so the want of faith in a service is the death of the offering. Though a man were at the cost of an ox, yet to kill it without bringing it to the door of the tabernacle was not a sacrifice but a murder, Lev. xvii. 3, 4. The tabernacle was a type of Christ, and a look to him is necessary in every spiritual sacrifice. As there must be faith to make any act an act of obedience, so there must be faith to make any act of worship spiritual. That service is not spiritual that is not vital, and it cannot be vital without the exercise of a vital principle; all spiritual life is ' hid in Christ,' and drawn from him by faith, Gal. ii. 20. Faith, as it hath relation to Christ, makes every act of worship a living act, and consequently a spiritual act. Habitual unbelief cuts us off from the body of Christ: Rom. xi. 20, ' Because of unbelief they were broken off;' and a want of actuated belief breaks us off from a present communion with Christ in spirit. As unbelief in us hinders Christ from doing any mighty work, so unbelief in us hinders us from doing any mighty spiritual duty.

So that the exercise of faith, and a confidence in God, is necessary to every duty.

2. Love must be acted to render a worship spiritual. Though God commanded love in the Old Testament, yet the manner of giving the law bespoke more of fear than love. The dispensation of the law was with fire, thunder, &c., proper to raise horror and benumb the spirit, which effect it had upon the Israelites, when they desired that God would speak no more to them. Grace is the genius of the gospel, proper to excite the affection of love. The

law was given ' by the disposition of angels,' with signs to amaze ; the gospel
was ushered in with the songs of angels, composed of peace and good will,
calculated to ravish the soul. Instead of the terrible voice of the law, Do this
and live ; the comfortable voice of the gospel is, Grace, grace. Upon this
account, the principle of the Old Testament was fear, and the worship often
expressed by the fear of God ; the principle of the New Testament is love.
' The mount Sinai gendereth to bondage,' Gal. iv. 24 ; mount Zion, from
whence the gospel or evangelical law goes forth, gendereth to liberty ; and,
therefore, the Spirit of bondage unto fear, as the property of the law, is
opposed to the state of adoption, the principle of love, as the property of the
gospel, Rom. viii. 15 ; and therefore the worship of God, under the gospel
or New Testament, is oftener expressed by love than fear, as proceeding
from higher principles, and acting nobler passions. In this state we are to
' serve him without fear,' Luke i. 74 ; without a bondage-fear, not without
a fear of unworthy treating him, with a fear of his goodness, as it is prophesied of, Hosea iii. 5. Goodness is not the object of terror, but reverence.
God, in the law, had more the garb of a judge ; in the gospel, of a father ;
the name of a father is sweeter, and bespeaks more of affection. As their
services were with a feeling of the thunders of the law in their consciences,
so is our worship to be with a sense of gospel grace in our spirits. Spiritual worship is that, therefore, which is exercised with a spiritual and
heavenly affection proper to the gospel. The heart should be enlarged,
according to the liberty the gospel gives of drawing near to God as a father;
as he gives us the nobler relation of children, we are to act the nobler qualities of children. Love should act according to its nature, which is desire
of union, desire of a moral union by affections, as well as a mystical union
by faith, as flame aspires to reach flame and become one with it. In every
act of worship we should endeavour to be united to God, and become one
spirit with him. This grace doth spiritualise worship. In that one word
love, God hath wrapt up all the devotion he requires of us. It is the total
sum of the first table, ' Thou shalt love the Lord thy God ;' it is to be acted
in everything we do ; but in worship our hearts should more solemnly rise
up and acknowledge him amiable and lovely, since the law is stripped of its
cursing power, and made sweet in the blood of the Redeemer. Love is a
thing acceptable of itself, but nothing acceptable without it. The gifts of
one man to another are spiritualised by it. We would not value a present
without the affection of the donor. Every man would lay claim to the love
of others, though he would not to their possessions. Love is God's right in
every service, and the noblest thing we can bestow upon him in our adorations of him. God's gifts to us are not so estimable without his love, nor our
services valuable by him without the exercise of a choice affection. Hezekiah
regarded not his deliverance without the love of the deliverer : ' In love to
my soul thou hast delivered me,' Isa. xxxviii. 17 ; so doth God say, In love
to my honour thou hast worshipped me.

So that love must be acted, to render our worship spiritual.

3. A spiritual sensibleness of our own weakness is necessary to make our
worship spiritual. Affections to God cannot be without relentings in ourselves. When the eye is spiritually fixed upon a spiritual God, the heart
will mourn that the worship is no more spiritually suitable. The more we
act love upon God, as amiable and gracious, the more we should exercise
grief in ourselves, as we are vile and offending. Spiritual worship is a
melting worship as well as an elevating worship; it exalts God, and debaseth
the creature. The publican was more spiritual in his humble address to
God, when the Pharisee was wholly carnal with his swelling language. A

spiritual love in worship will make us grieve that we have given him so little, and could give him no more. It is a part of spiritual duty to bewail our carnality mixed with it. As we receive mercies spiritually when we receive them with a sense of God's goodness and our own vileness, in the same manner we render a spiritual worship.

4. Spiritual desires for God render the service spiritual; when the soul 'follows hard after him,' Ps. lxiii. 8, pursues after God, as a God of infinite communicative goodness, with sighs and groans unutterable. A spiritual soul seems to be transformed into hunger and thirst, and becomes nothing but desire. A carnal worshipper is taken with the beauty and magnificence of the temple, a spiritual worshipper desires to see the glory of God in the sanctuary, Ps. lxiii. 2. He pants after God. As he came to worship, to find God, so he boils up in desires for God, and is loath to go from it without God, 'the living God,' Ps. xlii. 2. He would see the Urim and the Thummim, the unusual sparkling of the stones upon the high priest's breast-plate. That deserves not the title of spiritual worship, when the soul makes no longing inquiries: 'Saw you him whom my soul loves?' A spiritual worship is, when our desires are chiefly for God in the worship; as David desires to 'dwell in the house of the Lord;' but his desire is not terminated there, but 'to behold the beauty of the Lord,' Ps. xxvii. 4, and taste the ravishing sweetness of his presence. No doubt but Elijah's desires for the enjoyment of God, while he was mounting to heaven, were as fiery as the chariot wherein he was carried. Unutterable groans acted in worship are the fruit of the Spirit, and certainly render it a spiritual service, Rom. viii. 26. Strong appetites are agreeable to God, and prepare us to eat the fruit of worship. A spiritual Paul presseth forward to know Christ, and the power of his resurrection; and a spiritual worshipper actually aspires in every duty to know God, and the power of his grace. To desire worship as an end, is carnal; to desire it as a means, and act desires in it for communion with God in it, is spiritual, and the fruit of a spiritual life.

5. Thankfulness and admiration are to be exercised in spiritual services. This is a worship of spirits. Praise is the adoration of the blessed angels, Isaiah vi. 3, and of glorified spirits: Rev. iv. 11, 'Thou art worthy, O Lord, to receive glory, and honour, and power.' And Rev. v. 13, 14, they worship him, ascribing 'blessing, honour, glory, and power to him that sits upon the throne, and to the Lamb for ever and ever.' Other acts of worship are confined to this life, and leave us as soon as we have set our foot in heaven. There no notes but this of praise are warbled out. The power, wisdom, love, and grace in the dispensation of the gospel seat themselves in the thoughts and tongues of blessed souls. Can a worship on earth be spiritual, that hath no mixture of an eternal heavenly duty with it? The worship of God in innocence had been chiefly an admiration of him in the works of creation; and should not our evangelical worship be an admiration of him in the work of redemption, which is a restoration to a better state? After the petitioning for pardoning grace, Hos. xiv. 2, there is a rendering the calves or heifers of our lips, alluding to the heifers used in eucharistical sacrifices. The praise of God is the choicest sacrifice and worship, under a dispensation of redeeming grace. This is the prime and eternal part of worship under the gospel. The Psalmist, Ps. cxlix. and cl., speaking of the gospel times, spurs on to this kind of worship: 'Sing to the Lord a new song; let the children of Zion be joyful in their King; let the saints be joyful in glory, and sing aloud upon their beds; let the high praises of God be in their mouths.' He begins and ends both psalms with *Praise ye the Lord*. That cannot be a spiritual and evangelical worship that hath

nothing of the praise of God in the heart. The consideration of God's adorable perfections discovered in the gospel will make us come to him with more seriousness, beg blessings of him with more confidence, fly to him with a winged faith and love, and more spiritually glorify him in our attendances upon him.

6. Spiritual worship is performed with delight. The evangelical worship is prophetically signified by keeping the feast of tabernacles: 'They shall go up from year to year, to worship the King, the Lord of Hosts, and to keep the feast of tabernacles,' Zech. xiv. 16. Why that feast, when there were other feasts observed by the Jews? That was a feast celebrated with the greatest joy, typical of the gladness which was to be under the exhibition of the Messiah, and a thankful commemoration of the redemption wrought by him. It was to be celebrated five days after the solemn day of atonement, Lev. xxiii. 34, compared with ver. 27, wherein there was one of the solemnest types of the sacrifice of the death of Christ. In this feast they commemorated their exchange of Egypt for Canaan, the manna wherewith they were fed, the water out of the rock wherewith they were refreshed. In remembrance of this, they poured water on the ground, pronouncing those words in Isaiah, 'they shall draw waters out of the wells of salvation,' which our Saviour refers to himself, John vii. 37, inviting them to him to drink 'upon the last day, the great day of the Feast' of Tabernacles, wherein this solemn ceremony was observed. Since we are freed by the death of the Redeemer from the curses of the law, God requires of us a joy in spiritual privileges. A sad frame in worship gives the lie to all gospel liberty, to the purchase of the Redeemer's death, the triumphs of his resurrection. It is a carriage as if we were under the influences of the legal fire and lightning, and an entering a protest against the freedom of the gospel. The evangelical worship is a spiritual worship, and praise, joy, and delight are prophesied of as great ingredients in attendance on gospel ordinances, Isa. xii. 3–5. What was occasion of terror in the worship of God under the law, is the occasion of delight in the worship of God under the gospel. The justice and holiness of God, so terrible in the law, becomes comfortable under the gospel, since they have feasted themselves on the active and passive obedience of the Redeemer. The approach is to God as gracious, not to God as unpacified; as a son to a father, not as a criminal to a judge. Under the law, God was represented as a judge, remembering their sin in their sacrifices, and representing the punishment they had merited; in the gospel as a father, accepting the atonement, and publishing the reconciliation wrought by the Redeemer. Delight in God is a gospel frame, therefore the more joyful, the more spiritual. The Sabbath is to be a delight, not only in regard of the day, but in regard of the duties of it, Isaiah lviii. 13; in regard of the marvellous work he wrought on it, raising up our blessed Redeemer on that day, whereby a foundation was laid for the rendering our persons and services acceptable to God: Ps. cxviii. 24, 'This is the day which the Lord hath made, we will be glad and rejoice in it.' A lumpish frame becomes not a day and a duty that hath so noble and spiritual a mark upon it.

The angels, in the first act of worship after the creation, were highly joyful: Job xxxviii. 7, They 'shouted for joy,' &c.

The saints have particularly acted this in their worship. David would not content himself with an approach to the altar, without going to God as his 'exceeding joy,' Ps. xliii. 4, my triumphant joy. When he danced before the ark, he seems to be transformed into delight and pleasure, 2 Sam. vi. 14, 16. He had as much delight in worship as others had in their harvest and vintage. And those that took joyfully the spoiling of their goods, would as joyfully attend upon the communications of God. Where there is a fulness of the Spirit, there is a 'making melody to God in the heart,' Eph. v. 18, 19; and where there is an acting of love (as there is in all spiritual services), the proper fruit of it is joy, in a near approach to the object of the soul's affection. Love is *appetitus unionis.* The more love, the more delight in the approachings of God to the soul, or the outgoings of the soul to God. As the object of worship is amiable in a spiritual eye, so the means tending to a communion with this object are delightful in the exercise. Where there is no delight in a duty, there is no delight in the object of the duty. The more of grace, the more of pleasure in the actings of it. As the more of nature there is in any natural agent, the more of pleasure in the act, so the more heavenly the worship, the more spiritual. Delight is the frame and temper of glory. A heart filled up to the brim with joy, is a heart filled up to the brim with the Spirit. Joy is the fruit of the Holy Ghost, Gal. v. 22.

(1.) Not the joy of God's dispensation, flowing *from* God, but a gracious active joy streaming *to* God. There is a joy when the comforts of God are dropped into the soul, as oil upon the wheel, which indeed makes the faculties move with more speed and activity in his service, like the chariots of Amminadab; and a soul may serve God in the strength of this taste, and its delight terminated in the sensible comfort. This is not the joy I mean, but such a joy that hath God for its object, delighting in him as the term, in worship as the way to him. The first is God's dispensation, the other is our duty. The first is an act of God's favour to us, the second a sprout of habitual grace in us. The comforts we have from God may elevate our duties, but the grace we have within doth spiritualise our duties.

(2.) Nor is every delight an argument of a spiritual service. All the requisites to worship must be taken in. A man may invent a worship, and delight in it, as Micah in the adoration of his idol, when he was glad he had got both an ephod and a Levite, Judges xvii. As a man may have a contentment in sin, so he may have a contentment in worship; not because it is a worship of God, but the worship of his own invention, agreeable to his own humour and design, as Isaiah lviii. 2, it is said, they 'delighted in approaching to God,' but it was for carnal ends. Novelty engenders complacency; but it must be a worship wherein God will delight, and that must be a worship according to his own rule and infinite wisdom, and not our shallow fancies.

God requires a cheerfulness in his service, especially under the gospel, where he sits upon a throne of grace, discovers himself in his amiableness, and acts the covenant of grace and the sweet relation of a Father. The priests of old were not to sully themselves with any sorrow when they were in the exercise of their functions. God put a bar to the natural affections of Aaron and his sons when Nadab and Abihu had been cut off by a severe hand of God, Lev. x. 6. Every true Christian, in a higher order of priesthood, is a person dedicated to joy and peace, offering himself a lively sacrifice of praise and thanksgiving; and there is no Christian duty but is to be set off and seasoned with cheerfulness. He that loves a cheerful giver in acts of charity, requires no less a cheerful spirit in acts of worship. As this is an ingredient in worship, so it is the means to make your spirits intent in worship. When the heart triumphs in the consideration of divine excellency and goodness, it will be angry at anything that offers to jog and disturb it.

7. Spiritual worship is to be performed, though with a delight in God,

yet with a deep reverence of God. The gospel, in advancing the spirituality of worship, takes off the terror, but not the reverence of God, which is nothing else in its own nature but a due and high esteem of the excellency of a thing according to the nature of it. And therefore the gospel, presenting us with more illustrious notices of the glorious nature of God, is so far from indulging any disesteem of him, that it requires of us a greater reverence, suitable to the height of its discovery, above what could be spelled in the book of creation. The gospel worship is therefore expressed by trembling: Hos. xi. 10, 'They shall walk after the Lord; he shall roar like a lion; when he shall roar, then the children shall tremble from the west.' When the Lion of the tribe of Judah shall lift up his powerful voice in the gospel, the western Gentiles shall run trembling to walk after the Lord. God hath alway attended his greatest manifestations with remarkable characters of majesty, to create a reverence in his creature. He caused the wind to march before him, to cut the mountain, when he manifested himself to Elijah, 1 Kings xix. 11; a wind and a cloud of fire before that magnificent vision to Ezekiel, Ezek. i. 4, 5; thunders and lightnings before the giving the law, Exod. xix. 18; and a mighty wind before the giving the Spirit, Acts ii. God requires of us an awe of him in the very act of performance. The angels are pure, and cannot fear him as sinners, but in reverence they cover their faces when they stand before him, Isaiah vi. 2. His power should make us reverence him, as we are creatures; his justice, as we are sinners; his goodness, as we are restored creatures. 'God is clothed with unspeakable majesty; the glory of his face shines brighter than the lights of heaven in their beauty. Before him the angels tremble, and the heavens melt; we ought not, therefore, to come before him with the sacrifice of fools, nor tender a duty to him without falling low upon our faces, and bowing the knees of our hearts in token of reverence.'* Not a slavish fear, like that of devils, but a godly fear, like that of saints, Heb. xii. 28, joined with a sense of an unmoveable kingdom, becometh us. And this the apostle calls a grace necessary to make our service acceptable; and therefore the grace necessary to make it spiritual, since nothing finds admission to God but what is of a spiritual nature. The consideration of his glorious nature should imprint an awful respect upon our souls to him. His goodness should make his majesty more adorable to us, as his majesty makes his goodness more admirable in his condescensions to us. As God is a Spirit, our worship must be spiritual; and being he is the supreme Spirit, our worship must be reverential. We must observe the state he takes upon him in his ordinances; 'he is in heaven, we upon the earth;' we must not therefore be 'hasty to utter anything before God,' Eccles. v. 7. Consider him a Spirit in the highest heavens, and ourselves spirits dwelling in a dreggy earth. Loose and garish frames debase him to our own quality; slight postures of spirit intimate him to be a slight and mean being; our being in covenant with him must not lower our awful apprehensions of him. As he is 'the Lord thy God,' it is a 'glorious and fearful name,' or wonderful, Deut. xxviii. 58. Though he lay by his justice to believers, he doth not lay by his majesty. When we have a confidence in him, because he is the Lord our God, we must have awful thoughts of his majesty, because his name is glorious. God is terrible from his holy places, in regard of the great things he doth for his Israel, Ps. lxviii. 35. We should behave ourselves with that inward honour and respect of him as if he were present to our bodily eyes. The higher apprehensions we have of his majesty, the greater awe will be upon our hearts in his presence, and the greater spirituality in our acts.

* Daille, Sur. 3. Jean, p. 160.

We should manage our hearts so as if we had a view of God in his heavenly glory.

8. Spiritual worship is to be performed with humility in our spirits. This is to follow upon the reverence of God. As we are to have high thoughts of God, that we may not debase him, we must have low thoughts of ourselves, not to vaunt before him. When we have right notions of the divine majesty, we shall be as worms in our own thoughts, and creep as worms into his presence. We can never consider him in his glory, but we have a fit opportunity to reflect upon ourselves, and consider how basely we revolted from him, and how graciously we are restored by him. As the gospel affords us greater discoveries of God's nature, and so enhanceth our reverence of him, so it helps us to a fuller understanding of our own vileness and weakness, and therefore is proper to engender humility. The more spiritual and evangelical therefore any service is, the more humble it is. That is a spiritual service that doth most manifest the glory of God, and this cannot be manifested by us without manifesting our own emptiness and nothingness. The heathens were sensible of the necessity of humility by the light of nature;* after the name of God signified by Ἐι inscribed on the temple at Delphos, followed Γνῶθι Σεαυτον, whereby was insinuated, that when we have to do with God, who is the only Ens, we should behave ourselves with a sense of our own infirmity and infinite distance from him. As a person, so a duty, leavened with pride, hath nothing of sincerity, and therefore nothing of spirituality in it: Hab. ii. 4, 'His soul, which is lifted up, is not upright in him.' The elders that were crowned by God to be kings and priests, to offer spiritual sacrifices, uncrown themselves in their worship of him, and cast down their ornaments at his feet, Rev. iv. 10 compared with v. The Greek word to worship, προσκυνεῖν, signifies to creep like a dog upon his belly before his master, to lie low. How deep should our sense be of the privilege of God's admitting us to his worship, and affording us such a mercy under our deserts of wrath! How mean should be our thoughts, both of our persons and performances! How patiently should we wait upon God for the success of worship! How did Abraham, the father of the faithful, equal himself to the earth when he supplicated the God of heaven, and devoted himself to him under the title of very dust and ashes! Gen. xviii. 27. Isaiah did but behold an evangelical apparition of God and the angels worshipping him, and presently reflects upon his own uncleanness, Isa. vi. 5. God's presence both requires and causes humility. How lowly is David in his own opinion, after a magnificent duty performed by himself and his people: 1 Chron. xxix. 14, 'Who am I? and what is my people, that we should be able to offer so willingly?' The more spiritual the soul is in its carriage to God, the more humble it is; and the more gracious God is in his communications to the soul, the lower it lies.

God commanded not the fiercer creatures to be offered to him in sacrifices, but lambs and kids, meek and lowly creatures; none that had stings in their tails or venom in their tongues.† The meek lamb was the daily sacrifice; the doves were to be offered by pairs; God would not have honey mixed with any sacrifice, Lev. ii. 11. That breeds choler, and choler pride; but oil he commanded to be used, that supples and mollifies the parts. Swelling pride and boiling passions render our services carnal; they cannot be spiritual without an humble sweetness and an innocent sincerity; one grain of this transcends the most costly sacrifices. A contrite heart puts a gloss upon worship, Ps. li. 16, 17. The departure of men and angels from

* Plutarch, Moral. p. 844.
† Caudam aculeatam vel linguam nigram Alexand. ab Alex. l. 3, c. 12.

God began in pride ; our approaches and return to him must begin in humility ; and therefore all those graces which are bottomed on humility must be acted in worship, as faith, and a sense of our own indigence. Our blessed Saviour, the most spiritual worshipper, prostrated himself in the garden with the greatest lowliness, and offered himself upon the cross a sacrifice with the greatest humility. Melted souls in worship have the most spiritual conformity to the person of Christ in the state of humiliation, and his design in that state ; as worship without it is not suitable to God, so neither is it advantageous for us. A time of worship is a time of God's communication. The vessel must be melted to receive the mould it is designed for ; softened wax is fittest to receive a stamp, and a spiritually melted soul fittest to receive a spiritual impression. We cannot perform duty in an evangelical and spiritual strain without the meltingness and meanness in ourselves which the gospel requires.

9. Spiritual worship is to be performed with holiness. God is a holy Spirit ; a likeness to God must attend the worshipping of God, as he is ; holiness is alway in season, ' it becomes his house for ever,' Ps. xciii. 5. We can never ' serve the living God' till we have ' consciences purged from dead works,' Heb. ix. 14. Dead works in our consciences are unsuitable to God, an eternal living Spirit. The more mortified the heart, the more quickened the service. Nothing can please an infinite purity but that which is pure ; since God is in his glory in his ordinances, we must not be in our filthiness. The holiness of his Spirit doth sparkle in his ordinances ; the holiness of our spirits ought also to sparkle in our observance of them. The holiness of God is most celebrated in the worship of angels, Isa. vi. 3, Rev. iv. 8. Spiritual worship ought to be like angelical ; that cannot be with souls totally impure. As there must be perfect holiness to make a worship perfectly spiritual, so there must be some degree of holiness to make it in any measure spiritual. God would have all the utensils of the sanctuary employed about his service to be holy ; the inwards of the sacrifice were to be rinsed thrice.* The crop and feathers of sacrificed doves was to be hung† eastward towards the entrance of the temple, at a distance from the holy of holies, where the presence of God was most eminent, Lev. i. 16. When Aaron was to go into the holy of holies, he was to sanctify himself in an extraordinary manner, Lev. xvi. 4. The priests were to be barefooted in the temple in the exercise of their office ; shoes alway were to be put off upon holy ground : ' Look to thy foot when thou goest to the house of God,' saith the wise man, Eccles. v. 1. Strip the affections, the feet of the soul, of all the dirt contracted ; discard all earthly and base thoughts from the heart. A beast was not to touch the mount Sinai without losing his life ; nor can we come near the throne with brutish affections without losing the life and fruit of the worship. An unholy soul degrades himself from a spirit to a brute, and the worship from spiritual to brutish. If any unmortified sin be found in the life, as it was in the comers to the temple, it taints and pollutes the worship, Isa. i. 15, Jer. vii. 9, 10. All worship is an acknowledgment of the excellency of God as he is holy ; hence it is called a ' sanctifying God's name.' How can any person sanctify God's name that hath not a holy resemblance to his nature ? If he be not holy as he is holy, he cannot worship him according to his excellency in spirit and in truth ; no worship is spiritual wherein we have not a communion with God. But what intercourse can there be between a holy God and an impure creature, between light and darkness ? We have no fellowship with him in any service, unless we ' walk in the light,' in service and out of service, as he is

* As the Jewish doctors observe on Lev. i. 9.   † Qu. ' flung '?—ED.

light, 1 John i. 7. The heathen thought not their sacrifices agreeable to God without washing their hands, whereby they signified the preparation of their hearts before they made the oblation. Clean hands without a pure heart signify nothing; the frame of our hearts must answer the purity of the outward symbols: Ps. xxvi. 6, 'I will wash my hands in innocence, so will I compass thine altar, O Lord.' He would observe the appointed ceremonies, but not without cleansing his heart as well as his hands. Vain man is apt to rest upon outward acts and rites of worship; but this must alway be practised, the words are in the present tense, I *wash*, I *compass*. Purity in worship ought to be our continual care. If we would perform a spiritual service, wherein we would have communion with God, it must be in holiness; if we would walk with Christ, it must be in white, Rev. iii. 4, alluding to the white garments the priests put on when they went to perform their service. As without this we cannot see God in heaven, so neither can we see the beauty of God in his own ordinances.

10. Spiritual worship is performed with spiritual ends, with raised aims at the glory of God. No duty can be spiritual that hath a carnal aim. Where God is the sole object, he ought to be the principal end. In all our actions he is to be our end, as he is the principle of our being; much more in religious acts, as he is the object of our worship. The worship of God in Scripture is expressed by the 'seeking of him,' Heb. xi. 6. *Him*, not ourselves; all is to be referred to God. As we are not to live to ourselves, that being the sign of a carnal state, so we are not to worship for ourselves, Rom. xiv. 7, 8. As all actions are denominated good from their end as well as their object, so upon the same account they are denominated spiritual. The end spiritualiseth our natural actions, much more our religious. Then are our faculties devoted to him when they centre in him. If the intention be evil, there is nothing but darkness in the whole service, Luke xi. 34. The first institution of the Sabbath, the solemn day for worship, was to contemplate the glory of God in his stupendous works of creation, and render him a homage for them: Rev. iv. 11, 'Thou art worthy, O Lord, to receive honour, glory, and power: for thou hast created all things, and for thy pleasure they are and were created.' No worship can be returned without a glorifying of God; and we cannot actually glorify him without direct aims at the promoting his honour. As we have immediately to do with God, so we are immediately to mind the praise of God. As we are not to content ourselves with habitual grace, but be rich in the exercise of it in worship, so we are not to acquiesce in habitual aims at the glory of God, without the actual overflowings of our hearts in those aims.

It is natural for man to worship God for self. Self-righteousness is the rooted aim of man in his worship since his revolt from God; and being sensible it is not to be found in his natural actions, he seeks for it in his moral and religious. By the first pride we flung God off from being our sovereign, and from being our end; since a pharisaical spirit struts it in nature, not only to do things to be seen of men, but to be admired by God: Isa. lviii. 3, 'Wherefore have we fasted, and thou takest no knowledge?' This is to have God worship them instead of being worshipped by them. Cain's carriage, after his sacrifice, testifieth some base end in his worship; he came not to God as a subject to a sovereign, but as if he had been the sovereign, and God the subject; and when his design is not answered, and his desire not gratified, he proves more a rebel to God, and a murderer of his brother. Such base scents will rise up in our worship from the body of death, which cleaves to us, and mix themselves with our services, as weeds with the fish in the net. David therefore, after his people had offered willingly to the temple, begs of God that their 'hearts might be prepared to him,' 1 Chron. xxix. 18; that their hearts might stand right to God, without any squinting to self-ends.

Some present themselves to God, as poor men offer a present to a great person, not to honour them, but to gain for themselves a reward richer than their gift. 'What profit is it that we have kept his ordinances?' &c., Mal. iii. 14. Some worship him, intending thereby to make him amends for the wrong they have done him, wipe off their scores, and satisfy their debts; as though a spiritual wrong could be recompensed with a bodily service, and an infinite Spirit be outwitted and appeased by a carnal flattery. Self is the spirit of carnality. To pretend a homage to God, and intend only the advantage of self, is rather to mock him than worship him. When we believe that we ought to be satisfied rather than God glorified; we set God below ourselves, imagine that he should submit his own honour to our advantage. We make ourselves more glorious than God, as though we were not made for him, but he hath a being only for us; this is to have a very low esteem of the majesty of God. Whatsoever any man aims at in worship above the glory of God, that he forms as an idol to himself instead of God, and sets up a golden image. God counts not this as a worship. The offerings made in the wilderness for forty years together, God esteemed as not offered to him: Amos v. 25, 'Have you offered to me sacrifices and offerings in the wilderness forty years, O house of Israel?' They did it not to God, but to themselves; for their own security, and the attainment of the possession of the promised land. A spiritual worshipper performs not worship for some hopes of carnal advantage; he uses ordinances as means to bring God and his soul together, to be more fitted to honour God in the world in his particular place. When he hath been inflamed and humble in any address or duty, he gives God the glory; his heart suits the doxology at the end of the Lord's prayer, ascribes the kingdom, power, and glory to God alone; and if any viper of pride starts out upon him, he endeavours presently to shake it off. That which was the first end of our framing ought to be the chief end of our acting towards God. But when men have the same ends in worship as brutes, the satisfaction of a sensitive part, the service is no more than brutish. The acting for a sensitive end is unworthy of the majesty of God to whom we address, and unbecoming a rational creature. The acting for a sensitive end is not rational, much less can it be a spiritual service; though the acting may be good in itself, yet not good in the agent, because he wants a due end. We are then spiritual, when we have the same end in our redeemed services as God had in his redeeming love, viz., his own glory.

11. Spiritual service is offered to God in the name of Christ. Those are only 'spiritual sacrifices' that are 'offered up to God by Jesus Christ,' 1 Peter ii. 5; that are the fruits of the sanctification of the Spirit, and offered in the mediation of the Son. As the altar sanctifies the gift, so doth Christ spiritualise our services for God's acceptation; as the fire upon the altar separated the airy and finer parts of the sacrifice from the terrene and earthly. This is the golden altar upon which the prayers of the saints are offered up before the throne, Rev. viii. 3. As all that we have from God streams through his blood, so all that we give to God ascends by virtue of his merits. All the blessings God gave to the Israelites came out of Zion,— Ps. cxxxiv. 3, 'The Lord bless thee out of Zion,'—that is, from the gospel hid under the law; all the duties we present to God, are to be presented in Zion, in an evangelical manner. All our worship must be bottomed on Christ. God hath intended that we should 'honour the Son as we honour

the Father.' As we honour the Father by offering our service only to him, so we are to honour the Son by offering it only in his name. In him alone God is well pleased, because in him alone he finds our services spiritual and worthy of acceptation. We must therefore take fast hold of him with our spirits, and the faster we hold him, the more spiritual is our worship. To do anything in the name of Christ, is not to believe the worship shall be accepted for itself, but to have our eye fixed upon Christ for the acceptance of it, and not to rest upon the work done, as carnal people are apt to do. The creatures present their acknowledgments to God by man, and man can only present his by Christ. It was utterly unlawful, after the building of the temple, to sacrifice anywhere else. The temple being a type of Christ, it is utterly unlawful for us to present our services in any other name than his.

This is the way to be spiritual. If we consider God out of Christ, we can have no other notions but those of horror and bondage. We behold him a Spirit, but environed with justice and wrath for sinners; but the consideration of him in Christ veils his justice, draws forth his mercy, represents him more a Father than a Judge. In Christ, the aspect of justice is changed, and by that the temper of the creature; so that in and by this mediator we can have a spiritual 'boldness, and access to God with confidence,' Eph. iii. 12, whereby the spirit is kept from benumbedness and distraction, and our souls quickened and refined. The thoughts kept upon Christ, in a duty of worship, quickly elevates the soul, and spiritualizeth the whole service. Sin makes our services black, and the blood of Christ makes both our persons and services white.

To conclude this head.

God is a Spirit infinitely happy, therefore we must approach to him with cheerfulness; he is a Spirit of infinite majesty, therefore we must come before him with reverence; he is a Spirit infinitely high, therefore we must offer up our sacrifices with the deepest humility; he is a Spirit infinitely holy, therefore we must address with purity; he is a Spirit infinitely glorious, we must therefore acknowledge his excellency in all that we do, and in our measures contribute to his glory, by having the highest aims in his worship; he is a Spirit infinitely provoked by us, therefore we must offer up our worship in the name of a pacifying mediator and intercessor.

III. The third general is, Why a spiritual worship is due to God, and to be offered to him. We must consider the object of worship, and the subject of worship; the worshipper and the worshipped. God is a spiritual being, man is a reasonable creature. The nature of God informs us what is fit to be presented to him; our own nature informs us what is fit to be presented by us.

Reason 1. The best we have is to be presented to God in worship. For,

1. Since God is the most excellent being, he is to be served by us with the most excellent thing we have, and with the choicest veneration. God is so incomprehensibly excellent, that we cannot render him what he deserves. We must render him what we are able to offer: the best of our affections, the flower of our strength, the cream and top of our spirits. By the same reason that we are bound to give to God the best worship, we must offer it to him in the best manner. We cannot give to God anything too good for so blessed a being. God being a great King, slight services become not his majesty, Mal. i. 13, 14. It is unbecoming the majesty of God, and the reason of a creature, to give him a trivial thing. It is unworthy to bestow the best of our strength on our lust, and the worst and weakest in the service of God. An infinite Spirit should have affections as near to infinite

as we can. As he is a Spirit without bounds, so he should have a service
without limits : when we have given him all, we ' cannot serve him' according to the excellency of his nature, Joshua xxiv. 19 ; and shall we give him
less than all ? His infinite excellency, and our dependence on him as creatures, demands the choicest adoration. Our spirits being the noblest part
of our nature, are as due to him as the service of our bodies, which are the
vilest. To serve him with the worst only is to diminish his honour.

2. Under the law God commanded the best to be offered him. He would
have the males, the best of the kind ; the fat, the best of the creature,
Exod. xxix. 13, the inward fat, not the offals. He commanded them to
offer him the firstlings of the flock ; not the firstlings of the womb, but the
firstlings of the year, the Jewish cattle having two breeding times, in the
beginning of the spring and the beginning of September ; the latter breed was
the weaker, which Jacob knew, Gen. xxx., when he laid the rods before
the cattle when they were strong in the spring, and withheld them when
they were feeble in the autumn. One reason, as the Jews say, why God
accepted not the offerings of Cain was, because he brought the meanest, not
the best of the fruit ; and therefore it is said only that he brought of
the fruit of the ground, Gen. iv. 3, not the first of the fruit, or the best of
the fruit, as Abel, who brought the firstling of his flock, and the fat
thereof, ver. 4.

3. And this the heathen practised by the light of nature. They for the
most part offered males, as being more worthy ; and burnt the male, not
the female, frankincense, as it is divided into those two kinds. They offered
the best when they offered their children to Moloch. Nothing more excellent than man, and nothing dearer to parents than their children, which
are parts of themselves. When the Israelites would have a golden calf
for a representation of God, they would dedicate their jewels, and strip
their wives and children of their richest ornaments, to shew their devotion.
Shall men serve their dumb idols with the best of their substance, and the
strength of their souls ; and shall the living God have a duller service from
us than idols had from them ? God requires no such hard but delightful
worship from us, our spirits.

4. All creatures serve man, by the providential order of God, with the
best they have. As we, by God's appointment, receive from creatures the
best they can give, ought we not with a free will render to God the best we
can offer ? The beasts give us their best fat, the trees their best fruit, the
sun its best light, the fountains their best streams : shall God order us
the best from creatures, and we put him off with the worst from ourselves ?

5. God hath given us the choicest thing he had : a Redeemer that was
' the power of God, and the wisdom of God ;' the best he had in heaven,
his own Son, and in himself a sacrifice for us, that we might be enabled to
present ourselves a sacrifice to him. And Christ offered himself for us, the
best he had, and that with the strength of the Deity ' through the eternal
Spirit ;' and shall we grudge God the best part of ourselves ? As God would
have a worship from his creature, so it must be with the best part of his creature.
If we have ' given ourselves to the Lord,' 2 Cor. viii. 5, we can worship
with no less than ourselves. What is the man without his spirit ? If we
are to worship God with all that we have received from him, we must worship
him with the best part we have received from him. It is but a small glory
we can give him with the best, and shall we deprive him of his right by
giving him the worst ? As what we are is from God, so what we are
ought to be for God. Creation is the foundation of worship : Ps. c. 2, 3,
' Serve the Lord with gladness : know ye that the Lord he is God ; it is he

that made us.' He hath ennobled us with spiritual affections ; where is it fittest for us to employ them, but upon him? and at what time, but when we come solemnly to converse with him ? Is it justice to deny him the honour of his best gift to us ? Our souls are more his gift to us than anything in the world. Other things are so given, that they are often taken from us, but our spirits are the most durable gift. Rational faculties cannot be removed without a dissolution of nature.

Well, then ;* as he is God, he is to be honoured with all the propensions and ardour that the infiniteness and excellency of such a Being requires, and the incomparable obligations he hath laid upon us in this state deserve at our hands. In all our worship, therefore, our minds ought to be filled with the highest admiration, love, and reverence. Since our end was to glorify God, we answer not our end, and honour him not, unless we give him the choicest we have.

Reason 2. We cannot else act towards God according to the nature of rational creatures. Spiritual worship is due to God, because of his nature ; and due from us, because of our nature. As we are to adore God, so we are to adore him as men. The nature of a rational creature makes this impression upon him : he cannot view his own nature without having this duty striking upon his mind. As he knows by inspection into himself, that there was a God that made him, so that he is made to be in subjection to God, subjection to him in his spirit as well as his body, and ought morally to testify this natural dependence on him. His constitution informs him that he hath a capacity to converse with God; that he cannot converse with him but by those inward faculties. If it could be managed by his body without his spirit, beasts might as well converse with God as men. It can never be a ' reasonable service' as it ought to be, Rom. xii. 1, unless the reasonable faculties be employed in the management of it. It must be a worship prodigiously lame, without the concurrence of the chiefest part of man with it. As we are to act conformably to the nature of the object, so also to the nature of our own faculties. Our faculties in the very gift of them to us were destined to be exercised ; about what? What? All other things but the author of them ? It is a conceit cannot enter into the heart of a rational creature, that he should act as such a creature in other things, and as a stone in things relating to the donor of them ; as a man with his mind about him in the affairs of the world, as a beast without reason in his acts towards God. If a man did not employ his reason in other things, he would be an unprofitable creature in the world. If he do not employ his spiritual faculties in worship, he denies them the proper end and use for which they were given him ; it is a practical denial that God hath given him a soul, and that God hath any right to the exercise of it. If there were no worship appointed by God in the world, the natural inclination of man to some kind of religion would be in vain ; and if our inward faculties were not employed in the duties of religion, they would be in vain. The true end of God in the endowment of us with them would be defeated by us, as much as lies in us, if we did not serve him with that which we have from him solely at his own cost. As no man can with reason conclude that the rest commanded on the Sabbath, and the sanctification of it, was only a rest of the body,—that had been performed by the beasts as well as men ; but some higher end was aimed at for the rational creature,—so no man can think that the command for worship terminated only in the presence of the body ; that God should give the command to man as a reasonable creature, and expect no other service from him than that of a brute.

* Amyrald, Mor., tom. ii. p. 811.

God did not require a worship from man for any want he had, or any essential honour that could accrue to him, but that men might testify their gratitude to him, and dependence on him. It is the most horrid ingratitude not to have lively and deep sentiments of gratitude after such obligations, and not to make those due acknowledgments that are proper for a rational creature. Religion is the highest and choicest act of a reasonable creature. No creature under heaven is capable of it that wants reason. As it is a violation of reason not to worship God, so it is no less a violation of reason not to worship him with the heart and spirit. It is a high dishonour to God, and defeats him not only of the service due to him from man, but that which is due to him from all the creatures. Every creature, as it is an effect of God's power and wisdom, doth passively worship God; that is, it doth afford matter of adoration to man, that hath reason to collect it and return it where it is due. Without the exercise of the soul, we can no more hand it to God, than without such an exercise we can gather it from the creature; so that by this neglect the creatures are restrained from answering their chief end; they cannot pay any service to God without man; nor can man without the employment of his rational faculties render a homage to God, any more than beasts can. This engagement of our inward power stands firm and unviolable, let the modes of worship be what they will, or the changes of them by the sovereign authority of God never so frequent, this could not expire or be changed as long as the nature of man endured. As man had not been capable of a command for worship, unless he had been endued with spiritual faculties, so he is not active in a true practice of worship, unless they be employed by him in it. The constitution of man makes this manner of worship perpetually obligatory, and the obligation can never cease till man cease to be a creature furnished with such faculties. In our worship, therefore, if we would act like rational creatures, we should extend all the powers of our souls to the utmost pitch, and essay to have apprehensions of God equal to the excellency of his nature, which though we may attempt, we can never attain.

Reason 3. Without this engagement of our spirits, no act is an act of worship. True worship being an acknowledgment of God and the perfections of his nature, results only from the soul, that being only capable of knowing God, and those perfections, which are the object and motive of worship. The posture of the body is but to testify the inward temper and affection of the mind. If therefore it testifies what it is not, it is a lie and no worship. The cringes a beast may be taught to make to an altar may as well be called worship, since a man thinks as little of that God he pretends to honour, as the beast doth of the altar to which he bows. Worship is a reverent remembrance of God, and giving some honour to him with the intention of the soul. It cannot justly have the name of worship that wants the essential part of it. It is an ascribing to God the glory of his nature, an owning subjection and obedience to him as our sovereign Lord. This is as impossible to be performed without the spirit as that there can be life and motion in a body without a soul. It is a drawing near to God, not in regard of his essential presence,—so all things are near to God,—but in acknowledgment of his excellency, which is an act of the spirit; without this, the worst of men in a place of worship are as near to God as the best. The necessity of the conjunction of our soul ariseth from the nature of worship, which being the most serious thing we can be employed in, the highest converse with the highest object requires the choicest temper of spirit in the performance. That cannot be an act of worship which is not an act of piety and virtue, but there is no act of virtue done by the members of the body without the concurrence of the powers of the soul. We may as well call the presence of a dead carcass in a place of worship an act of religion, as the presence of a living body without an intent spirit. The separation of the soul from one is natural, the other moral; that renders the body lifeless, but this renders the act loathsome to God. As the being of the soul gives life to the body, so the operation of the soul gives life to the actions. As he cannot be a man that wants the form of a man, a rational soul, so that cannot be a worship that wants an essential part, the act of the spirit. God will not vouchsafe any acts of man so noble a title, without the requisite qualifications: Hosea v. 6, ' They shall go with their flocks and their herds to seek the Lord,' &c. A multitude of lambs and bullocks for sacrifice to appease God's anger, God would not give it the title of worship, though instituted by himself, when it wanted the qualities of such a service. The spirit of whoredom was in the midst of them, ver. 4. In the judgment of our Saviour it is a vain worship, when the traditions of men are taught for the doctrines of God, Mat. xv. 9; and no less vain must it be, when the bodies of men are presented to supply the place of their spirits. As an omission of duty is a contempt of God's sovereign authority, so the omission of the manner of it is a contempt of it, and of his amiable excellency; and that which is a contempt and mockery can lay no just claim to the title of worship.

Reason 4. There is in worship an approach of God to man. It was instituted to this purpose, that God might give out his blessings to man. And ought not our spirits to be prepared and ready to receive his communications? We are in such acts more peculiarly in his presence. In the Israelites' hearing the law, it said God was to ' come among them,' Exod. xix. 10, 11. Then, men are said to stand before the Lord: Deut. x. 8, ' God before whom I stand;' that is, whom I worship. And therefore when Cain forsook the worship of God, settled in his father's family, he is said to ' go out from the presence of the Lord,' Gen. iv. 16. God is essentially present in the world, graciously present in his church. The name of the evangelical city is *Jehovah Shammah:* Ezek. xlviii. 35, ' The Lord is there.' God is more graciously present in the evangelical institutions than in the legal; he ' loves the gates of Zion, more than all the dwellings of Jacob,' Ps. lxxxvii. 2. His evangelical law and worship which was to go forth from Zion, as the other did from Sinai, Micah iv. 2. God delights to approach to men, and converse with them in the worship instituted in the gospel, more than in all the dwellings of Jacob. If God be graciously present, ought not we to be spiritually present? A lifeless carcass service becomes not so high and delectable a presence as this; it is to thrust him from us, not invite him to us; it is to practise in the ordinances what the prophet predicts concerning men's usage of our Saviour: Isa. liii. 2, ' There is no form, no comeliness, nor beauty that we should desire him.' A slightness in worship reflects upon the excellency of the object of worship. God and his worship are so linked together, that whosoever thinks the one not worth his inward care, esteems the other not worth his inward affection. How unworthy a slight is it of God, who proffers the opening his treasure, the re-impressing his image, conferring his blessings, admits us into his presence, when he hath no need for us, who hath millions of angels to attend him in his court, and celebrate his praise! He that worships not God with his spirit, regards not God's presence in his ordinances, and slights the great end of God in them, and that perfection he may attain by them. We can only expect what God hath promised to give, when we render to him what he hath commanded us to present. If we put off God with a shell, he will put us off with a husk. How can we expect his heart, when we do not not give him ours ? or hope for the blessing needful for us, when we render not the glory due to him ? It cannot be an advantageous worship without spiritual graces ; for those are uniting, and union is the ground of all communion.

Reason 5. To have a spiritual worship is God's end in the restoration of the creature, both in redemption by his Son, and sanctification by his Spirit. A fitness for spiritual offerings was the end of the coming of Christ, Mal. iii. 3. He should purge them, as gold and silver by fire, a spirit burning up their dross, melting them into a holy compliance with, and submission to, God. To what purpose ? That they may ' offer to the Lord an offering in righteousness,' a pure offering from a purified spirit. He came to ' bring us to God,' 1 Peter iii. 18, in such a garb as that we might be fit to converse with him. Can we be thus without a fixedness of our spirits on him ?

The ' offering of spiritual sacrifices' is the end of making any ' a spiritual habitation, and a holy priesthood,' 1 Peter ii. 5. We can no more be worshippers of God, without a worshipper's nature, than a man be a man without human nature. As man was at first created for the honour and worship of God, so the design of restoring that image, which was defaced by sin, tends to the same end. We are not brought to God by Christ, nor are our services presented to him, if they be without our spirits. Would any man, that undertakes to bring another to a prince, introduce him in a slovenly and sordid habit, such a garb that he knows hateful to him ? or bring the clothes or skin of a man stuffed with straw, instead of the person ? To come with our skins before God, without our spirits, is contrary to the design of God in redemption and regeneration.

If a carnal worship would have pleased God, a carnal heart would have served his turn, without the expense of his Spirit in sanctification. He bestows upon man a spiritual nature, that he may return to him a spiritual service. He enlightens the understanding, that he may have a rational service, and new moulds the will, that he may have a voluntary service. As it is the milk of the word wherewith he feeds us, so it is the service of the word wherewith we must glorify him. So much as there is of confusedness in our understanding, so much of starting and levity in our wills, so much of slipperiness and skipping in our affections, so much is abated of the due qualities of the worship of God, and so much we fall short of the end of redemption and sanctification.

Reason 6. A spiritual worship is to be offered to God, because no worship but that can be acceptable. We can never be secured of acceptance without it. He being a Spirit, nothing but the worship in spirit can be suitable to him. What is unsuitable cannot be acceptable. There must be something in us, to make our services capable of being presented by Christ for an actual acceptation. No service is ' acceptable to God by Jesus Christ,' but as it is a ' spiritual sacrifice,' and offered by a spiritual heart, 1 Pet. ii. 5. The sacrifice is first spiritual, before it be acceptable to God by Christ. When it is ' an offering in righteousness,' it is then, and only then, pleasant to the Lord, Mal. iii. 3, 4. No prince would accept a gift that is unsuitable to his majesty, and below the condition of the person that presents it. Would he be pleased with a bottle of water for drink, from one that hath his cellar full of wine ? How unacceptable must that be that is unsuitable to the divine majesty ! And what can be more unsuitable, than a withdrawing the opera-tions of our souls from him, in the oblation of our bodies ? We as little ' glorify God as God' when we give him only a corporeal worship, as the heathen did when they represented him in a corporeal shape, Rom. i. 21 ; one as well as the other denies his spiritual nature. This is worse, for had it been lawful to represent God to the eye, it could not have been done but by a bodily figure suited to the sense ; but since it is necessary to worship him, it cannot be by a corporeal attendance, without the operation of the spirit. A spiritual frame is more pleasing to God than the highest exterior adornments, than the greatest gifts and the highest prophetical illumination. The glory of the second temple exceeded the glory of the first, Hag. ii. 8, 9. As God accounts the spiritual glory of ordinances most beneficial for us, so our spiritual attendance upon ordinances is most pleasing to him. He that offers the greatest services without it, offers but flesh : Hos. viii. 13, ' They sacrifice flesh for the sacrifices of my offerings, but the Lord accepts them not.' Spiritual frames are the soul of religious services ; all other carriages without them, are contemptible to this spirit. We can never lay claim to that promise of God, none shall ' seek my face in vain.' We affect a vain seeking of him, when we want a due temper of spirit for him ; and vain spirits shall have vain returns. It is more contrary to the nature of God's holiness to have communion with such, than it is contrary to the nature of light to have communion with darkness.

IV. To make use of this :
Use 1. First, it serves for information.
1. If spiritual worship be required by God, how sad is it for them that are so far from giving God a spiritual worship, that they render him no worship at all ! I speak not of the neglect of public, but of private ; when men present not a devotion to God from one year's end to the other. The speech of our Saviour, that we must worship God in spirit and in truth, implies that a worship is due to him from every one. That is the common impression upon the consciences of all men in the world, if they have not, by some constant course in gross sins, hardened their souls, and stifled those natural sentiments. There was never a nation in the world without some kind of religion, and no religion was ever without some modes to testify a devotion. The heathens had their sacrifices and purifications ; and the Jews, by God's order, had their rites whereby they were to express their allegiance to God.
Consider,
(1.) Worship is a duty incumbent upon all men. It is a homage mankind owes to God, under the relation wherein he stands obliged to him. It is a prime and immutable justice to own our allegiance to him. It is as unchangeable a truth that God is to be worshipped, as that God is. He is to be worshipped as God, as Creator, and therefore by all, since he is the Creator of all, the Lord of all, and all are his creatures, and all are his subjects. Worship is founded upon creation, Ps. c. 2, 3. It is due to God for himself and his own essential excellency, and therefore due from all. It is due upon the account of man's nature. The human rational nature is the same in all. Whatsoever is due to God upon the account of man's nature, and the natural obligations he hath laid upon man, is due from all men, because they all enjoy the benefits which are proper to their nature.
Man in no state was exempted, nor can be exempted from it. In paradise he had his Sabbaths and sacraments. Man therefore dissolves the obligation of a reasonable nature, by neglecting the worship of God.
Religion is in the first place to be minded. As soon as Noah came out of the ark, he contrived not a habitation for himself, but an altar for the Lord, to acknowledge him the author of his preservation from the deluge, Gen.

viii. 20 ; and wheresoever Abraham came, his first business was to erect an altar, and pay his arrears of gratitude to God, before he ran upon the score for new mercies, Gen. xii. 7, xiii. 4, 18. He left a testimony of worship wherever he came.

(2.) Wholly therefore to neglect it, is a high degree of atheism. He that ' calls not upon God,' ' saith in his heart, There is no God,' and seems to have the sentiments of natural conscience as to God stifled in him, Ps. xiv. 1, 4. It must arise from a conceit that there is no God, or that we are equal to him (adoration not being due from persons of an equal state), or that God is unable or unwilling to take notice of the adoring acts of his creatures. What is any of these but an undeifying the supreme Majesty ? When we lay aside all thoughts of paying any homage to him, we are in a fair way opinionatively to deny him, as much as we practically disown him. Where there is no knowledge of God, that is, no acknowledgment of God, a gap is opened to all licentiousness, Hos. iv. 1, 2 ; and that by degrees brawns the conscience, and razeth out the sense of God. Those forsake God that ' forget his holy mountain,' Isa. lxv. 11. They do not practically own him as the Creator of their souls or bodies. It is the sin of Cain, who, turning his back upon worship, is said to ' go out from the presence of the Lord,' Gen. iv. 16. Not to worship him with our spirits, is against his law of creation ; not to worship him at all, is against his act of creation ; not to worship him in truth is hypocrisy ; not to worship him at all is atheism, whereby we render ourselves worse than the worms in the earth, or a toad in a ditch.

(3.) To perform a worship to a false God, or to the true God in a false manner, seems to be less a sin than to live in perpetual neglect of it. Though it be directed to a false object instead of God, yet it is under the notion of a God, and so is an acknowledgment of such a being as God in the world ; whereas the total neglect of any worship is a practical denying of the exist- ence of any supreme Majesty.

Whosoever constantly omits a public and private worship, transgresses against an universally-received dictate, for all nations have agreed in the common notion of worshipping God, though they have disagreed in the several modes and rites whereby they would testify that adoration. By a worship of God, though superstitious, a veneration and reverence of such a being is maintained in the world ; whereas by a total neglect of worship, he is virtually disowned and discarded, if not from his existence, yet from his providence and government of the world. All the mercies we breathe in are denied to flow from him. A foolish worship owns religion, though it be- spatters it. As if a stranger coming into a country mistakes a subject for the prince, and pays that reverence to the subject which is due to the prince, though he mistakes the object, yet he owns an authority ; or if he pays any respect to the true prince of that country after the mode of his own, though appearing ridiculous in the place where he is, he owns the authority of the prince ; whereas the omission of all respect would be a contempt of majesty. And therefore, the judgments of God have been more signal upon the sacri- legious contemners of worship among the heathens, than upon those that were diligent and devout in their false worship ; and they generally owned the blessings received, to the preservation of a sense and worship of a deity among them. Though such a worship be not acceptable to God, and every man is bound to offer to God a devotion agreeable to his own mind, yet it is commendable, not as worship, but as it speaks an acknowledgment of such a being as God, in his power in creation, and his beneficence in his providence.

Well, then, omissions of worship are to be avoided. Let no man execute that upon himself, which God will pronounce at last as the greatest misery, and bid God depart from him, who will at last be loath to hear God bid him depart from him. Though man hath natural sentiments that God is to be worshipped, yet having an hostility in his nature, he is apt to neglect, or give it him in a slight manner. He therefore sets a particular mark and notice of attention upon the fourth command, 'Remember thou keep holy the Sabbath day.' Corrupt nature is apt to neglect the worship of God, and flag in it. This command therefore, which concerns his worship, he fortifies with several reasons.

Nor let any neglect worship, because they cannot find their hearts spiritual in it. The further we are from God, the more carnal shall we be. No man can expect heat by a distance from the sunbeams, or other means of warmth. Though God commanded a circumcised heart in the Jewish services, yet he did not warrant a neglect of the outward testimonies of religion he had then appointed; he expected according to his command, that they should offer the sacrifices, and practise the legal purifications he had commanded; he would have them diligently observed, though he had declared that he imposed them only for a time. And our Saviour ordered the practice of those positive rights as long as the law remained unrepealed, as in the case of the leper, Mark xiv. 4. It is an injustice to refuse the offering ourselves to God, according to the manner he hath in his wisdom prescribed and required.

If spiritual worship be required by God, then

2. It informs us, that diligence in outward worship is not to be rested in. Men* may attend all their days on worship, with a juiceless heart and unquickened frame, and think to compensate the neglect of the manner, with abundance of the matter of service. Outward expressions are but the badges and liveries of service, not the service itself. As the strength of sin lies in the inward frame of the heart, so the strength of worship in the inward complexion and temper of the soul. What do a thousand services avail, without cutting the throat of our carnal affections! What are loud prayers, but as sounding brass and tinkling cymbals, without divine charity! A pharisaical diligence in outward forms, without inward spirit, had no better a title vouchsafed by our Saviour, than that of hypocritical. God desires not sacrifices, nor delights in burnt offerings. Shadows are not to be offered instead of substance. God required the heart of man for itself; but commanded outward ceremonies, as subservient to inward worship, and goads and spurs unto it. They were never appointed as the substance of religion, but auxiliaries to it. What value had the offering of the human nature of Christ been of, if he had not had a divine nature to qualify him to be the priest! And what is the oblation of our bodies, without a priestly act of the spirit in the presentation of it! Could the Israelites have called themselves worshippers of God according to his order, if they had brought a thousand lambs that had died in a ditch, or been killed at home? They were to be brought living to the altar, the blood shed at the foot of it. A thousand sacrifices killed without, had not been so valuable as one brought alive to the place of offering. One sound sacrifice is better than a thousand rotten ones. As God took no pleasure in the blood of beasts without its relation to the antitype, so he takes no pleasure in the outward rites of worship, without faith in the Redeemer. To offer a body with a sapless spirit, is a sacrilege of the same nature with that of the Israelites when they offered dead beasts. A man without spiritual worship is dead whiles he worships, though by his diligence in the externals of it, he may, like the angel of the church of Sardis, 'have a name to live,' Rev. iii. 1. What

* Daille, Melange des Sermons, Ser. ii.

security can we expect from a multitude of dead services! What weak shields are they against the holy eye and revenging wrath of God! What man, but one out of his wits, would solicit a dead man to be his advocate or champion? Diligence in outward worship is not to be rested in.

Use 2. Shall be for examination. Let us try ourselves concerning the manner of our worship. We are now in the end of the world, and the dregs of time; wherein the apostle predicts, there may be much of a 'form, and little of the power of godliness,' 2 Tim. iii. 1, 5. And therefore it stands us in hand to search into ourselves, whether it be not thus with us; whether there be as much reverence in our spirits, as there may be devotion in our countenances and outward carriages.

1. How therefore are our hearts prepared to worship? Is our diligence greater to put our hearts in an adoring posture, than our bodies in a decent garb? Or are we content to have a muddy heart, so we may have a dressed carcass? To have a spirit a cage of unclean birds, while we wipe the filth from the outside of the platter, is no better than a pharisaical devotion, and deserves no better a name than that of a whited sepulchre.

Do we take opportunities to excite and quicken our spirits to the performance, and cry aloud with David, 'Awake, awake, my glory'? Are not our hearts asleep when Christ knocks? When we hear the voice of God, 'Seek my face,' do we answer him with warm resolutions, 'Thy face, Lord, we will seek'? Ps. xxvii. 8. Do we comply with spiritual motions, and strike whiles the iron is hot? Is there not more of reluctancy than readiness? Is there a quick rising of the soul in reverence to the motion, as Eglon to Ehud, or a sullen hanging the head at the first approach of it? Or if our hearts seem to be engaged and on fire, what are the motives that quicken that fire? Is it only the blast of a natural conscience, fear of hell, desires of heaven as abstracted from God? Or is it an affection to God, an obedient will to please him, longings to enjoy him, as a holy and sanctifying God in his ordinances, as well as a blessed and glorified God in heaven?

What do we expect in our approaches from him? That which may make divine impressions upon us, and more exactly conform us to the divine nature? Or do we design nothing but an empty formality, a rolling eye, and a filling the air with a few words, without any openings of heart to receive the incomes, which according to the nature of the duty might be conveyed to us? Can this be a spiritual worship? The soul then 'closely waits' upon him, when its 'expectation is only from him,' Ps. lxii. 6. Are our hearts seasoned with a sense of sin, a sight of our spiritual wants, raised notions of God, glowing affections to him, strong appetite after a spiritual fulness? Do we rouse up our sleepy spirits, and make a covenant with all that is within us to attend upon him? So much as we want of this, so much we come short of a spiritual worship. In Ps. lvii. 7, 'My heart is fixed, O God, my heart is fixed.' David would fix his heart, before he would engage in a praising act of worship. He appeals to God about it, and that with doubling the expression, as being certain of an inward preparedness. Can we make the same appeals in a fixation of spirit?

2. How are our hearts fixed upon him, how do they cleave to him in the duty? Do we resign our spirits to God, and make them an entire holocaust, a whole burnt-offering in his worship? Oh, do we not willingly admit carnal thoughts to mix themselves with spiritual duties, and fasten our minds to the creature, under pretences of directing them to the Creator? Do we not pass a mere compliment on God, by some superficial act of devotion, while some covetous, envious, ambitious, voluptuous imagination may possess our minds? Do we not invert God's order, and worship a lust instead of God

with our spirit, that should not have the least service, either from our souls or bodies, but with a spiritual disdain be sacrificed to the just indignation of God? How often do we fight against his will, while we cry 'Hail, master;' instead of crucifying our own thoughts, crucifying the Lord of our lives; our outward carriage plausible, and our inward stark naught! Do we not often regard iniquity more than God in our hearts, in a time of worship, roll some filthy imagination as a sweet morsel under our tongues, and taste more sweetness in that than in God? Do not our spirits smell rank of earth while we offer to heaven? and have we not hearts full of thick clay, as their 'hands were full of blood'? Isa. i. 15. When we sacrifice, do we not wrap up our souls in communion with some sordid fancy, when we should entwine our spirits about an amiable God? While we have some fear of him, may we not have a love to something else above him? This is to worship, or swear by the Lord, and by Malcham, Zeph. i. 5. How often doth an apish fancy render a service inwardly ridiculous, under a grave outward posture, skipping to the shop, warehouse, counting-house, in the space of a short prayer! And we are before God as a Babel, a confusion of internal languages; and this in those parts of worship which are in the right use most agreeable to God, profitable for ourselves, ruinous to the kingdom of sin and Satan, and means to bring us into a closer communion with the divine majesty. Can this be a spiritual worship?

3. How do we act our graces in worship? Though the instrument be strung, if the strings be not wound up, what melody can be the issue? All readiness and alacrity discover a strength of nature, and a readiness in spirituals discovers a spirituality in the heart. As unaffecting thoughts of God are not spiritual thoughts, so unaffecting addresses to God are not spiritual addresses. Well then, what awakenings and elevations of faith and love have we? what strong outflowings of our souls to him? what indignation against sin? what admirations of redeeming grace? How low have we brought our corruptions to the footstool of Christ, to be made his conquered enemies? how straitly have we clasped our faith about the cross and the throne of Christ, to become his intimate spouse? Do we in hearing hang upon the lips of Christ; in prayer, take hold of God and will not let him go; in confession, rend the caul of our hearts, and indict our souls before him with a deep humility? Do we act more by a soaring love than a drooping fear? So far as our spirits are servile, so far they are legal and carnal; so much as they are free and spontaneous, so much they are evangelical and spiritual. As men under the law are subject to the constraint of bondage, Heb. ii. 15, 'all their lifetime,' in all their worship, so under the gospel they are under a constraint of love, 2 Cor. v. 14. How then are believing affections exercised, which are always accompanied with holy fear, a fear of his goodness that admits us into his presence, and a fear to offend him in our act of worship? So much as we have of forced or feeble affection, so much we have of carnality.

4. How do we find our hearts after worship? By our after-carriage we may judge of the spirituality of it.

(1.) How are we as to inward strength? When a worship is spiritually performed, grace is more strengthened, corruption more mortified. The soul, like Samson after his awakening, goes out with a renewed strength. As the inward man is renewed day by day, that is, every day, so it is renewed in every worship. Every shower makes the grass and fruit grow in good ground where the root is good, and the weeds where the ground is naught. The more prepared the heart is to obedience in other duties after worship, the more evidence there is that it hath been spiritual in the exercise of it. It is the end of God in every dispensation, as in that of John Baptist, to 'make ready a people prepared for the Lord,' Luke i. 17 ; when the heart is by worship prepared for fresh acts of obedience, and hath a more exact watchfulness against the encroachments of sin. As carnal men, after worship, sprout up in spiritual wickedness, so do spiritual worshippers in spiritual graces. Spiritual fruits are a sign of a spiritual frame. When men are more prone to sin after duty, it is a sign there was but little communion with God in it, and a greater strength of sin, because such an act is contrary to the end of worship, which is the subduing of sin. It is a sign the physic hath wrought well, when the stomach hath a better appetite to its appointed food; and worship hath been well performed when we have a stronger inclination to other acts well pleasing to God, and a more sensible distaste of those temptations we too much relished before. It is a sign of a good concoction, when there is a greater strength in the vitals of religion, a more eager desire to know God. When Moses had been praying to God, and prevailed with him, he puts up a higher request, to behold his glory, Exod. xxxiii. 13, 18. When the appetite stands strong to fuller discoveries of God, it is a sign there hath been a spiritual converse with him.

(2.) How is it especially as to humility. The Pharisees' worship was, without dispute, carnal ; and we find them not more humble after all their devotions, but over-grown with more weeds of spiritual pride ; they performed them as their righteousness. What men dare plead before God in his day, they plead before them in their hearts in their day ; but this men will do at the day of judgment, 'we have prophesied in thy name,' &c., Mat. vii. 11. They shew what tincture their services left upon their spirits. That which excludes them from any acceptation at the last day, excludes them from any estimation of being spiritual in this day. The carnal worshippers charge God with injustice in not rewarding them, and claim an acceptation as a compensation due to them: Isa. lviii. 3, 'Wherefore have we afflicted our souls, and thou takest no knowledge ?' A spiritual worshipper looks upon his duties with shame, as well as he doth upon his sins with confusion, and implores the mercy of God for the one as well as the other. In Psalm cxliii. 2, the prophet David, after his supplications, begs of God not to enter into judgment with him, and acknowledges any answer that God should give him, as a fruit of his faithfulness to his promise, and not the merit of his worship. 'In thy faithfulness answer me,' &c. Whatsoever springs from a gracious principle, and is the breath of the Spirit, leaves a man more humble ; whereas that which proceeds from a stock of nature, hath the true blood of nature running in the veins of it, viz., that pride which is naturally derived from Adam. The breathing of the divine Spirit is in everything to conform us to our Redeemer ; that being the main work of his office is his work in every particular Christian act influenced by him. Now Jesus Christ in all his actions was an exact pattern of humility. After the institution and celebration of the Supper, a special act of worship in the church, though he had a sense of all the authority his Father had given him, yet he humbles himself to wash his disciples' feet, John xiii. 2–4. And after his sublime prayer, John xvii., he humbles himself to the death, and offers himself to his murderers, because of his Father's pleasure: John xviii. 1, 'When he had spoken those words, he went over the brook Kedron' into the garden. What is the end of God in appointing worship is the end of a spiritual heart in offering it, not his own exaltation, but God's glory. Glorifying the name of God is the fruit of that evangelical worship the Gentiles were in time to give to God: Ps. lxxxvi. 9, 'All nations which thou hast made shall come and worship before thee, O Lord ; and shall glorify thy name.' Let us examine, then, what debasing ourselves there is in a sense of our own vileness and distance from so glorious a Spirit. Self-denial is the heart of all gospel grace. Evangelical spiritual worship cannot be without the ingredient of the main evangelical principle.

(3.) What delight is there after it? What pleasure is there, and what is the object of that pleasure? Is it communion we have had with God, or a fluency in ourselves? Is it something which hath touched our hearts or tickled our fancies? As the strength of sin is known by the delightful thoughts of it after the commission, so is the spirituality of duty by the object of our delightful remembrance after the performance. It was a sign David was spiritual in the worship of God in the tabernacle when he enjoyed it, because he longed for the spiritual part of it when he was exiled from it. His desires were not only for liberty to revisit the tabernacle, but to see the 'power and glory of God in the sanctuary,' as he had seen it before, Ps. lxiii. 2. His desires for it could not have been so ardent, if his reflection upon what had passed had not been delightful; nor could his soul be poured out in him for the want of such opportunities, if the remembrance of the converse he had had with God had not been accompanied with a delightful relish, Ps. xlii. 4. Let us examine what delight we find in our spirits after worship.

Use 3 is of comfort. And it is very comfortable to consider that the smallest worship with the heart and spirit, flowing from a principle of grace, is more acceptable than the most pompous veneration, yea, if the oblation were as precious as the whole circuit of heaven and earth, without it. That God, that values a cup of cold water given to any as his disciple, will value a sincere service above a costly sacrifice. God hath his eye upon them that honour his nature. He would not 'seek such to worship him' if he did not intend to accept such a worship from them. When we therefore invoke him, and praise him, which are the prime parts of religion, he will receive it as a sweet savour from us, and overlook infirmities mixed with the graces.

The great matter of discomfort, and that which makes us question the spirituality of worship, is the many starts of our spirits and rovings to other things.

For answer to which,

1. It is to be confessed that these starts are natural to us. Who is free from them? We bear in our own bosom a nest of turbulent thoughts, which, like busy gnats, will be buzzing about us while we are in our most inward and spiritual converses. Many wild beasts lurk in a man's heart, as in a close and covert wood, and scarce discover themselves but at our solemn worship. No duty so holy, no worship so spiritual, that can wholly privilege us from them. They will jog us in our most weighty employments, that, as God said to Cain, sin lies at the door, and enters in, and makes a riot in our souls. As it is said of wicked men, they cannot sleep for multitude of thoughts, Eccles. v. 12, so it may be of many a good man, he cannot worship for multitude of thoughts. There will be starts, and more in our religious than natural employments; it is natural to man. Some therefore think the bells tied to Aaron's garments between the pomegranates were to warn the people, and recall their fugitive minds to the present service, when they heard the sound of them, upon the least motion of the high priest. The sacrifice of Abraham, the father of the faithful, was not exempt from the fowls picking at it, Gen. xv. 11. Zechariah himself was drowsy in the midst of his vision, which being more amazing, might cause a heavenly intentness: Zech. iv. 1, 'The angel that talked with me came again, and awaked me, as a man is awaked out of sleep.' He had been roused up before, but he was ready to drop down again; his heart was gone till the

angel jogged him. We may complain of such imaginations, as Jeremiah doth of the enemies of the Jews: Lam. iv. 19, ' Our persecutors are swifter than eagles;' they light upon us with as much speed as eagles upon a carcass; they pursue us upon the mountain of divine institution, and they lay wait for us in the wilderness, in our retired addresses to God.

And this will be so while,

(1.) There is natural corruption in us. There are in a godly man two contrary principles, flesh and spirit, which endeavour to hinder one another's acts, and are always stirring upon the offensive or defensive part, Gal. v. 17. There is a body of death continually exhaling its noisome vapours. It is a body of death in our worship as well as in our natures; it snaps our resolutions asunder, Rom. vii. 19; it hinders us in the doing good, and contradicts our wills in the stirring up evil. This corruption being seated in all the faculties, and a constant domestic in them, has the greater opportunity to trouble us, since it is by those faculties that we spiritually transact with God; and it stirs more in the time of religious exercises, though it be in part mortified; as a wounded beast, though tired, will rage and strive to its utmost, when the enemy is about to fetch a blow at it. All duties of worship tend to the wounding of corruption; and it is no wonder to feel the striving of sin to defend itself and offend us, when we have our arms in our hands to mortify it, that the blow may be diverted which is directed against it.

The apostles had aspiring thoughts, and being persuaded of an earthly kingdom, expected a grandeur in it. And though we find some appearance of it at other times,—as when they were casting out devils, and gave an account of it to their Master, he gives them a kind of a check, Luke x. 20, intimating that there was some kind of evil in their rejoicing upon that account,—yet this never swelled so high as to break out into a quarrel who should be greatest, until they had the most solemn ordinance, the Lord's supper, to quell it, Luke xxii. 24. Our corruption is like lime, which discovers not its fire by any smoke or heat till you cast water, the enemy of fire, upon it; neither doth our natural corruption rage so much as when we are using means to quench and destroy it.

(2.) While there is a devil, and we in his precinct. As he accuseth us to God, so he disturbs us in ourselves; he is a bold spirit, and loves to intrude himself when we are conversing with God. We read that when the angels presented themselves before God, Satan comes among them, Job i. 6. Motions from Satan will thrust themselves in with our most raised and angelical frames. He loves to take off the edge of our spirits from God; he acts but after the old rate; he from the first envied God an obedience from man, and envied man the felicity of communion with God; he is unwilling God should have the honour of worship, and that we should have the fruit of it; he hath himself lost it, and therefore is unwilling we should enjoy it; and being subtle, he knows how to make impressions upon us suitable to our inbred corruptions, and assaults us in the weakest part; he knows all the avenues to get within us (as he did in the temptation of Eve), and being a spirit, he wants not a power to dart them immediately upon our fancy; and being a spirit, and therefore active and nimble, he can shoot those darts faster than our weakness can beat them off. He is diligent also, and watcheth for his prey, and seeks to devour our services as well as our souls, and snatch our best morsels from us. We know he mixed himself with our Saviour's retirements in the wilderness, and endeavoured to fly-blow his holy converse with his Father in the preparation to his mediatory work.

Satan is God's ape, and imitates the Spirit in the office of a remembrancer. As the Spirit brings good thoughts and divine promises to mind, to quicken our worship, so the devil brings evil things to mind, and endeavours to fasten them in our souls to disturb us. And though all the foolish starts we have in worship are not purely his issue, yet being of kin to him, he claps his hands, and sets them on like so many mastiffs to tear the service in pieces.

And both those distractions, which arise from our own corruption and from Satan, are most rife in worship when we are under some pressing affliction. This seems to be David's case, Ps. lxxxvi. When, in verse 11, he prays God to 'unite his heart to fear and worship his name,' he seems to be under some affliction, or fear of his enemies: Oh free me from those distractions of spirit, and those passions which arise in my soul upon considering the designs of my enemies against me, and press upon me in my addresses to thee and attendance on thee. Job also in his affliction complains, Job xvii. 11, that his purposes were broken off. He could not make an even thread of thoughts and resolutions; they were frequently snapped asunder, like rotten yarn when one is winding up.

Good men and spiritual worshippers have lain under this trouble. Though they are a sign of weakness of grace, or some obstructions in the acting of strong grace, yet they are not alway evidences of a want of grace. What ariseth from our own corruption, is to be matter of humiliation and resistance; what ariseth from Satan, should edge our minds to a noble conquest of them. If the apostle did comfort himself with his disapproving of what rose from the natural spring of sin within him, with his consent to the law and dissent from his lust, and charges it not upon himself, but upon the sin that dwelt in him, with which he had broken off the former league, and was resolved never to enter into amity with it, by the same reason we may comfort ourselves, if such thoughts are undelighted in, and alienate not our hearts from the worship of God by all their busy intrusions to interrupt us.

2. These distractions (not allowed) may be occasions, by an holy improvement, to make our hearts more spiritual after worship, though they disturb us in it, by answering those ends for which we may suppose God permits them to invade us. And that is,

(1.) When they are occasions to humble us.

[1.] For our carriage in the particular worship. There is nothing so dangerous as spiritual pride; it deprived devils and men of the presence of God, and will hinder us of the influence of God. If we had had raised and uninterrupted motions in worship, we should be apt to be lifted up; and the devil stands ready to tempt us to self-confidence. You know how it was with Paul, 2 Cor. xii. 1–7, his buffetings were occasions to render him more spiritual than his raptures, because more humble. God suffers those wanderings, starts, and distractions to prevent our spiritual pride, which is as a worm at the root of spiritual worship, and minds us of the dusty frame of our spirits, how easily they are blown away, as he sends sickness to put us in mind of the shortness of our breath and the easiness to lose it. God would make us ashamed of ourselves in his presence, that we may own that what is good in any duty is merely from his grace and Spirit, and not from ourselves; that with Paul we may cry out, 'By grace we are what we are,' and by grace we do what we do. We may be hereby made sensible that God can alway find something in our exactest worship, as a ground of denying us the successful fruit of it. If we cannot stand upon our duties for salvation, what can we bottom upon in ourselves? If, therefore, they are occasions to make us out of love with any righteousness of our own, to make us break our hearts for them because we cannot keep them out, if we mourn for them as our sins, and count them our great afflictions, we have attained that brokenness which is a choice ingredient in a spiritual sacrifice. Though we have been disturbed by them, yet we are not robbed of the success; we may behold an answer of our worship in our humiliation in spite of all of them.

[2.] For the baseness of our nature. These unsteady motions help us to discern that heap of vermin that breeds in our nature. Would any man think he had such an averseness to his Creator and benefactor, such an unsuitableness to him, such an estrangedness from him, were it not for his inspection into his distracted frames? God suffers this to hang over us as a rod of correction, to discover and fetch out the folly of our hearts. Could we imagine our natures so highly contrary to that God who is so infinitely amiable, so desirable an object, or that there should be so much folly and madness in the heart, as to draw back from God in those services which God hath appointed as pipes through which to communicate his grace, to convey himself, his love, and goodness to the creature? If, therefore, we have a deep sense of, and strong reflections upon, our base nature, and bewail that mass of averseness which lies there, and that fulness of irreverence towards the God of our mercies, the object of our worship, it is a blessed improvement of our wanderings and diversions. Certainly if any Israelite had brought a lame and rotten lamb to be sacrificed to God, and afterward had bewailed it, and laid open his heart to God in a sensible and humble confession of it, that repentance had been a better sacrifice, and more acceptable in the sight of God, than if he had brought a sound and a living offering.

(2.) When they are occasions to make us prize duties of worship. When we argue, as rationally we may, that they are of singular use, since our corrupt hearts and a malicious devil doth chiefly endeavour to hinder us from them, and that we find we have not those gadding thoughts when we are upon worldly business, or upon any sinful design which may dishonour God and wound our souls, this is a sign sin and Satan dislike worship, for he is too subtile a spirit to oppose that which would further his kingdom. As it is an argument the Scripture is the word of God, because the wickedness of the world doth so much oppose it, so it is a ground to believe the profitableness and excellency of worship because Satan and our own unruly hearts do so much interrupt us in it. If, therefore, we make this use of our cross-steps in worship, to have a greater value for such duties, more affections to them and desires to be frequent in them, our hearts are growing spiritual, under the weights that would depress them to carnality.

(3.) When we take a rise from hence, to have heavenly admirations of the graciousness of God; that he should pity and pardon so many slight addresses to him, and give any gracious returns to us. Though men have foolish ranging every day, and in every duty, yet free grace is so tender as not to punish them: Gen. viii. 21, 'And the Lord smelt a sweet savour; and the Lord said in his heart, I will not curse the ground for man's sake; for the imagination of man's heart is evil from his youth.' It is observable that this was just after a sacrifice which Noah offered to God, ver. 20; but probably not without infirmities common to human nature, which may be grounded upon the reason God gives, that though he had destroyed the earth before, because of the evil of man's imaginations, Gen. vi. 5, he still found evil imaginations; he doth not say in the heart of Shem, or others of Noah's family, but in man's heart, including Noah also, who had both the judgments of God upon the former world, and the mercy of God in his own preservation before his eyes; yet God saw evil imaginations rooted in the nature of man, and though it were so, yet he would be merciful. If therefore we can, after finding our hearts so vagrant in worship, have real frames of thankfulness that God hath spared us, and be heightened in our admirations at God's giving us any fruit of such a distracted worship, we take advantage from them to be raised into an evangelical frame, which consists in the humble acknowledgments of the grace of God. When David takes a review of those tumultuous passions which had ruffled his mind, and possessed him with unbelieving notions of God in the persons of his prophets, Ps. cxvi. 11, how high doth his soul mount in astonishment and thankfulness to God for his mercy, ver. 12. Notwithstanding his distrust, God did graciously perform his promise, and answer his desire; then it is, ' What shall I render to the Lord?' His heart was more affected for it, because it had been so passionate in former distrusts. It is indeed a ground of wondering at the patience of the Spirit of God, that he should guide our hearts when they are so apt to start out; as it is the patience of a master to guide the hand of his scholar, while he mixes his writing with many blots. It is not one or two infirmities the Spirit helps us in, and helps over, but many, Rom. viii. 26. It is a sign of a spiritual heart when he can take a rise to bless God for the renewing and blowing up his affections, in the midst of so many incursions from Satan to the contrary, and the readiness of the heart too much to comply with them.

(4.) When we take occasion from thence to prize the mediation of Christ. The more distractions jog us, the more need we should see of going out to a Saviour by faith. One part of our Saviour's office is to stand between us and the infirmities of our worship. As he is an advocate, he presents our services, and pleads for them and us, 1 John ii. 1; for the sins of our duties, as well as for our other sins. Jesus Christ is an high priest, appointed by God to take away the iniquities of our holy things, which was typified by Aaron's plate upon his mitre, Exod. xxviii. 36, 38. Were there no imperfections, were there no creeping up of those frogs into our minds, we would think our worship would merit acceptance with God upon its own account; but if we behold our own weakness, that not a tear, a groan, a sigh is so pure, but must have Christ to make it entertainable; that there is no worship without those blemishes; and upon this, throw all our services into the arms of Christ for acceptance, and solicit him to put his merits in the front to make our ciphers appear valuable: it is a spiritual act, the design of God in the gospel being to advance the honour and mediation of his Son. That is a spiritual and evangelical act, which answers the evangelical design. The design of Satan and our own corruption is defeated, when those interruptions make us run swifter, and take faster hold on the high priest, who is to present our worship to God, and our own souls receive comfort thereby. Christ had temptations offered to him by the devil in his wilderness retirement, that from an experimental knowledge he might be able more compassionately to succour us, Heb. ii. 18: we have such assaults in our retired worship especially, that we may be able more highly to value him and his mediation.

3. Let us not therefore be discouraged by those interruptions and starts of our hearts.

(1.) If we find in ourselves a strong resistance of them. The flesh will be lusting: that cannot be hindered; yet if we do not fulfil the lusts of it, rise up at its command and go about its work, we may be said to walk in the Spirit: Gal. v. 16, 17, we ' walk in the Spirit,' if we ' fulfil not the lusts of the flesh,' though there be a lusting of the flesh against the spirit. So we worship in the Spirit, though there be carnal thoughts arising, if we do not fulfil them; though the stirring of them discovers some contrariety in us to God, yet the resistance manifests that there is a principle of contrariety in us to them; that as there is something of flesh that lusts against the spirit, so there is something of spirit in worship which lusts against the flesh. We must take heed of omitting worship, because of such inroads, and lying down in the mire of a total neglect. If our spirits are made more lively and vigorous against them; if those cold vapours which have risen from our hearts, make us like a spring in the midst of the cold earth more warm, there is in this case more reason for us to bless God than to be discouraged. God looks upon it as the disease, not the wilfulness of our nature; as the weakness of the flesh, not the wilfulness of the spirit. If we would shut the door upon them, it seems they are unwelcome company; men do not use to lock their doors upon those they love: if they break in and disturb us with their impertinencies, we need not be discomforted, unless we give them a share in our affections, and turn our back upon God to entertain them. If their presence makes us sad, their flight would make us joyful.

(2.) If we find ourselves excited to a stricter watch over our hearts against them; as travellers will be careful when they come to places where they have been robbed before, that they be not so easily surprised again. We should not only lament when we have had such foolish imaginations in worship breaking in upon us, but also bless God that we have had no more, since we have hearts so fruitful of weeds. We should give God the glory when we find our hearts preserved from these intruders, and not boast of ourselves, but return him our praise for the watch and guard he kept over us to preserve us from such thieves.

Let us not be discomforted; for as the greatness of our sins upon our turning to God is no hindrance to our justification, because it doth not depend upon our conversion as the meritorious cause, but upon the infinite value of our Saviour's satisfaction, which reaches the greatest sins as well as the least, so the multitude of our bewailed distractions in worship are not a hindrance to our acceptation, because of the uncontrollable power of Christ's intercession.

Use 4 is for exhortation. Since spiritual worship is due to God, and the Father seeks such to worship him, how much should we endeavour to satisfy the desire and order of God, and act conformable to the law of our creation and the love of redemption! Our end must be the same in worship which was God's end in creation and redemption: to glorify his name, set forth his perfections, and be rendered fit, as creatures and redeemed ones, to partake of that grace which is the fruit of worship. An evangelical dispensation requires a spiritual homage; to neglect, therefore, either the matter or manner of gospel duties, is to put a slight upon gospel privileges. The manner of duty is ever of more value than the matter; the scarlet dye is more precious than the cloth tinctured with it. God respects more the disposition of the sacrificer than the multitude of the sacrifices.* The solemn feasts appointed by God were but dung, as managed by the Jews, Mal. ii. 3. The heart is often welcome without the body, but the body never grateful without the heart. The inward acts of the Spirit require nothing from without to constitute them good in themselves; but the outward acts of devotion require inward acts to render them savoury to God. As the goodness of outward acts consists not in the acts themselves, so the acceptableness of them

---

* Μᾶλλον τὸ δαιμόνιον πρὸς τὸ τῶν φυόντων ἦθος ἢ τῶν θυομένων πλῆθος.—
Porphyr. de Abstinentia.

results not from the acts themselves, but from the inward frame animating and quickening those acts, as blood and spirits running through the veins of a duty to make it a living service in the sight of God. Imperfections in worship hinder not God's acceptation of it, if the heart spirited by grace be there to make it a sweet savour. The stench of burning flesh and fat in the legal sacrifices might render them noisome to the outward senses, but God smelt a sweet savour in them as they respected Christ. When the heart and spirit are offered up to God, it may be a savoury duty, though attended with unsavoury imperfections; but a thousand sacrifices without a stamp of faith, a thousand spiritual duties with an habitual carnality, are no better than stench with God.

The heart must be purged, as well as the temple was by our Saviour, of the thieves that would rob God of his due worship. Antiquity had some temples, wherein it was a crime to bring any gold; therefore those that came to worship laid their gold aside before they went into the temple. We should lay aside our worldly and trading thoughts before we address to worship: Isa. xxvi. 9, 'With my spirit within me will I seek thee early.' Let not our minds be gadding abroad, and exiled from God and themselves. It will be thus when ' the desire of our soul is to his name, and the remembrance of him,' ver. 8. When he hath given so great and admirable a gift, as that of his Son, in whom are all things necessary to salvation, righteousness, peace, and pardon of sin, we should manage the remembrance of his name in worship with the closest unitedness of heart, and the most spiritual affections. The motion of the spirit is the first act in religion; to this we are obliged in every act. The devil requires the spirit of his votaries: should God have a less dedication than the devil?

Motives to back this exhortation:

1. Not to give God our spirit is a great sin. It is a mockery of God, not worship; contempt, not adoration, whatever our outward fervency or protestations may be.* Every alienation of our hearts from him is a real scorn put upon him. The acts of the soul are real, and more the acts of the man than the acts of the body, because they are the acts of the choicest part of man, and of that which is the first spring of all bodily motions; it is the λόγος ἐνδιαθετος, the internal speech, whereby we must speak with God. To give him, therefore, only an external form of worship, without the life of it, is a taking his name in vain. We mock him, when we mind not what we are speaking to him, or what he is speaking to us; when the motions of our hearts are contrary to the motions of our tongues; when we do anything before him slovenly, impudently, or rashly. As in a lutinist it is absurd to sing one tune and play another, so it is a foul thing to tell God one thing with our lips, and think another thing with our hearts. It is a sin like that the apostle chargeth the heathens with: Rom. i. 28, ' They like not to retain God in their knowledge;' their stomachs are sick while they are upon any duty, and never leave working, till they have thrown up all the spiritual part of worship, and rid themselves of the thoughts of God, which are as unwelcome and troublesome guests to them. When men behave themselves in the sight of God as if God were not God, they do not only defame him, but deny him, and violate the unchangeable perfections of the divine nature.

(1.) It is against the majesty of God, when we have not awful thoughts of that great majesty to whom we address; when our souls cleave not to him when we petition him in prayer, or when he gives out his orders in his word. It is a contempt of the majesty of a prince, if, whiles he is speaking to us, we listen not to him with reverence and attention, but turn our backs on

* *Non valet protestatio contra factum*, is a rule in the civil law.

him to play with one of his hounds or talk with a beggar, or while we speak
to him to rake in a dunghill. Solomon adviseth us to 'keep our foot when
we go to the house of God,' Eccles. v. 1. Our affections should be steady,
and not slip away again ; why ? ver. 2. Because 'God is in heaven,' &c.
He is a God of majesty, earthly dirty frames are unsuitable to the God of
heaven, low spirits are unsuitable to the Most High. We would not bring
our mean servants or dirty dogs in a prince's presence chamber ; yet we
bring not only our worldly but our profane affections into God's presence.
We give in this case those services to God which our governor would think
unworthy of him, Mal. i. 8. The more excellent and glorious God is, the
greater contempt of him it is to suffer such foolish affections to be competitors with him for our hearts. It is a scorn put upon him to converse with
a creature while we are dealing with him ; but a greater to converse in our
thoughts and fancies with some sordid lust which is most hateful to him.
And the more aggravation it attracts, in that we are to apprehend him, the
most glorious object, sitting upon his throne in time of worship, and ourselves standing as vile creatures before him, supplicating for our lives, and
the conveyances of grace and mercy to our souls. As if a grand mutineer,
instead of humble begging the pardon of his offending prince, should present
his petition not only scribbled and blotted, but besmeared with some loathsome excrement. It is unbecoming the majesty both of God and the worship
itself, to present him with a picture instead of substance, and bring a world
of nasty affections in our hearts, and ridiculous toys in our heads before
him, and worship with indisposed and heedless souls. Mal. i. 14, He is a
great king, therefore address to him with fear and reverence.

(2.) It is against the life of God. Is a dead worship proportioned to a
living God ? The separation of heavenly affections from our souls before
God, makes them as much a carcass in his sight as the divorce of the soul
makes the body a carcass. When the affections are separated, worship is
no longer worship but a dead offering, a lifeless bulk ; for the essence and
spirit of worship is departed. Though the soul be present with the body in
a way of information, yet it is not present in a way of affection, and this is
the worst ; for it is not the separation of the soul from informing that doth
separate a man from God, but the removal of our affections from him. If
a man pretend an application to God, and sleep and snore all the time,
without question such a one did not worship. In a careless worship the
heart is morally dead while the eyes are open. The heart of the spouse
awaked whiles her eyes slept, Cant. v. 2, and our hearts on the contrary
sleep while our eyes awake.

Our blessed Saviour hath died to 'purge our consciences from dead works'
and frames, that we may 'serve the living God,' Heb. ix. 14; to serve God
as a God of life. David's soul cried and fainted for God under this consideration, Ps. xlii. 2. But to present our bodies without our spirits is such
a usage of God that implies he is a dead image, not worthy of any but a
dead and heartless service, like one of those idols the psalmist speaks of,
Ps. cxv. 5, that 'have eyes and see not, ears and hear not,' no life in it.
Though it be not an objective idolatry, because the worship is directed to
the true God, yet I may call it a subjective idolatry, in regard of the frame,
fit only to be presented to some senseless stock. We intimate God to be
no better than an idol, and to have no more knowledge of us and insight
into us than an idol can have. If we did believe him to be the living God,
we durst not come before him with services so unsuitable to him, and
reproaches of him.

(3.) It is against the infiniteness of God. We should worship God with those boundless affections which bear upon them a shadow or image of his infiniteness, such as the desires of the soul, which know no limits, but start out beyond whatsoever enjoyment the heart of man possesses. No creeping creature was to be offered to God in sacrifice, but such as had legs to run or wings to fly. For us to come before God with a light creeping frame is to worship him with the lowest finite affections; as though anything, though never so mean or torn, might satisfy an infinite being; as though a poor shallow creature could give enough to God without giving him the heart, when indeed we cannot give him a worship proportionable to his infiniteness, did our hearts swell as large as heaven in our desires for him in every act of our duties.

(4.) It is against the spirituality of God. God being a Spirit, calls for a worship in spirit: to withhold this from him, implies him to be some gross corporeal matter. As a Spirit, he looks for the heart, a wrestling heart in prayer, a trembling heart in the word, Isa. lxvi. 2. To bring nothing but the body when we come to a spiritual God to beg spiritual benefits, to wait for spiritual communications, which can only be dispensed to us in a spiritual manner, is unsuitable to the spiritual nature of God. A mere carnal service implicitly denies his spirituality, which requires of us higher engagements than mere corporeal ones.

Worship should be rational, not an imaginative service, wherein is required the activity of our noblest faculties; and our fancy ought to have no share in it, but in subserviency to the more spiritual part of our soul.

(5.) It is against the supremacy of God. As God is one, the only sovereign, so our hearts should be one, cleaving wholly to him, and undivided from him. In pretending to deal with him, we acknowledge his Deity and sovereignty; but in withholding our choicest faculties and affections from him, and the starting of our minds to vain objects, we intimate their equality with God, and their right as well as his to our hearts and affections. It is as if a princess should commit adultery with some base scullion while she is before her husband, which would be a plain denial of his sole right to her. It intimates that other things are superior to God; they are true sovereigns that engross our hearts. If a man were addressing himself to a prince, and should in an instant turn his back upon him upon a beck or nod from some inconsiderable person, is it not an evidence that that person that invited him away hath a greater sovereignty over him than that prince to whom he was applying himself? And do we not discard God's absolute dominion over us, when, at the least beck of a corrupt inclination, we can dispose of our hearts to it, and alienate them from God? As they in Ezek. xxxiii. 32, left the service of God for the service of their covetousness, which evidenced that they owned the authority of sin more than the authority of God. This is not to serve God as our Lord and absolute master, but to make God serve our turn, and submit his sovereignty to the supremacy of some unworthy affection. The creature is preferred before the Creator, when the heart runs most upon it in time of religious worship, and our own carnal interest swallows up the affections that are due to God: it is 'an idol set up in the heart,' Ezek. xiv. 4, in his solemn presence, and attracts that devotion to itself which we only owe to our sovereign Lord; and the more base and contemptible that is to which the spirit is devoted, the more contempt there is of God's dominion. Judas his kiss, with a Hail, Master, was no act of worship, or an owning his Master's authority, but a designing the satisfaction of his covetousness in the betraying of him.

(6.) It is against the wisdom of God. God, as a God of order, has put earthly things in subordination to heavenly, and we by this unworthy

carriage invert this order, and put heavenly things in subordination to
earthly, in placing mean and low things in our hearts, and bringing them
so placed into God's presence, which his wisdom at the creation put under
our feet.   A service without spiritual affections is a 'sacrifice of fools,'
Eccles. v. 1, which have lost their brains and understandings ; a foolish
spirit is very unsuitable to an infinitely wise God.   Well may God say of
such a one, as Achish of David, who seemed mad, 'Why have you brought
this fellow to play the madman in my presence ? shall this fellow come into
my house ?' 1 Sam. xxi. 15.

(7.) It is against the omnisciency of God.   To carry it fair without and
impertinently within, is as though God had not an all-seeing eye that could
pierce into the heart, and understand every motion of the inward faculties ;
as though God were easily cheated with an outward fawning service, like an
apothecary's box with a gilded title, that may be full of cobwebs within.
What is such a carriage, but a design to deceive God, when with Herod
we pretend to worship Christ, and intend to murder all the motions of
Christ in our souls !   A heedless spirit, an estrangement of our souls, a
giving the reins to them to run out from the presence of God to see every
reed shaken with the wind, is to deny him to be searcher of hearts, and the
discerner of secret thoughts ; as though he could not look through us to the
darkness and remoteness of our minds, but were an ignorant God, who
might be put off with the worst as well as the best in our flock.   If we did
really believe there were a God of infinite knowledge, who saw our frames,
and whether we came dressed with wedding-garments suitable to the duties
we are about to perform, should we be so garish, and put him off with such
trivial stuff, without any reverence of his majesty ?

(8.) It is against the holiness of God.   To alienate our spirits is to offend
him while we pretend to worship him ; though we may be mighty officious
in the external part, yet our base and carnal affections make all our worship
but as a heap of dung; and who would not look upon it as an affront to lay
dung before a prince's throne ?   Prov. xxi. 27, 'The sacrifice of the wicked
is an abomination : how much more when he brings it with a wicked mind?'
A putrified carcass under the law had not been so great an affront to the
holiness of God as a frothy, unmelted heart, and a wanton fancy in a time of
worship.   God is so holy, that if we could offer the worship of angels, and
the quintessence of our souls in his service, it would be beneath his infinite
purity.   How unworthy then are they of him, when they are presented not
only without the sense of our uncleanness, but sullied with the fumes and
exhalations of our corrupt affections, which are so many plague-spots upon
our duties, contrary to the unspotted purity of the divine nature !   Is not
this an unworthy conceit of God, and injurious to his infinite holiness ?

(9.) It is against the love and kindness of God.   It is a condescension in
God to admit a piece of earth to offer up a duty to him, when he hath
myriads of angels to attend him in his court and celebrate his praise ; to
admit man to be an attendant on him, and a partner with angels, is a high
favour.   It is not a single mercy, but a heap of mercies to be admitted into
the presence of God: Ps. v. 7, 'I will come into thy house in the multitude
of thy mercies.'   When the blessed God is so kind as to give us access to
his majesty, do we not undervalue his kindness when we deal uncivilly with
him, and deny him the choicest part of ourselves ?   It is a contempt of his
sovereignty, as our spirits are due to him by nature ; a contempt of his
goodness, as our spirits are due to him by gratitude !   How abusive a
carriage is it to make use of his mercy to encourage our impudence, that
should excite our fear and reverence !   How unworthy would it be for an

indigent debtor to bring to his indulgent creditor an empty purse instead of payment! When God holds out his golden sceptre to encourage our approaches to him, stands ready to give us the pardon of sin and full felicity, the best things he hath, is it a fit requital of his kindness to give him a formal outside only, a shadow of religion, to have the heart overswayed with other thoughts and affections, as if all his proffers were so contemptible as to deserve only a slight at our hands? It is a contempt of the love and kindness of God.

(10.) It is against the sufficiency and fulness of God. When we give God our bodies and the creature our spirits, it intimates a conceit that there is more content to be had in the creature than in God blessed for ever, that the waters in the cistern are sweeter than those in the fountain. Is not this a practical giving God the lie, and denying those promises wherein he hath declared the satisfaction he can give to the spirit, as he is the God of the spirits of all flesh?

If we did imagine the excellency and loveliness of God were worthy to be the ultimate object of our affections, the heart would attend more closely upon him, and be terminated in him; did we believe God to be all-sufficient, full of grace and goodness, a tender Father, not willing to forsake his own, willing as well as able to supply their wants, the heart would not so lamely attend upon him, and would not upon every impertinency be diverted from him. There is much of a wrong notion of God, and a predominancy of the world above him in the heart, when we can more savourly relish the thoughts of low inferior things than heavenly, and let our spirits upon every trifling occasion be fugitives from him. It is a testimony that we make not God our chiefest good. If apprehensions of his excellency did possess our souls, they would be fastened on him, glued to him; we should not listen to that rabble of foolish thoughts that steal our hearts so often from him. Were our breathings after God as strong as the pantings of the hart after the water brooks, we should be like that creature, not diverted in our course by every puddle. Were God the predominant satisfactory object in our eye, he would carry our whole soul along with him.

When our spirits readily retreat from God in worship upon every giddy motion, it is a kind of repentance that ever we did come near him, and implies that there is a fuller satisfaction, and more attractive excellency, in that which doth so easily divert us, than in that God to whose worship we did pretend to address ourselves; it is as if, when we were petitioning a prince, we should immediately turn about, and make request to one of his guard, as though so mean a person were more able to give us the boon we want, than the sovereign is.

2. Consideration by way of motive. To have our spirits off from God in worship is a bad sign. It was not so in innocence. The heart of Adam could cleave to God; the law of God was engraven upon him; he could apply himself to the fulfilling of it without any twinkling; there was no folly and vanity in his mind, no independency in his thoughts, no duty was his burden; for there was in him a proneness to, and delight in, all the duties of worship. It is the fall hath distempered us, and the more unwieldiness there is in our spirits, the more carnal our affections are in worship, the more evidence there is of the strength of that revolted state.

(1.) It argues much corruption in the heart. As by the eructations of the stomach we may judge of the windiness and foulness of it, so by the inordinate motions of our minds and hearts we may judge of the weakness of its complexion. A strength of sin is evidenced by the eruptions and ebullitions of it in worship, when they are more sudden, numerous, and

vigorous than the motions of grace. When the heart is apt like tinder to
catch fire from Satan, it is a sign of much combustible matter suitable to
his temptation. Were not corruption strong, the soul could not turn so
easily from God when it is in his presence, and hath advantageous opportunity to create a fear and awe of God in it; such base fruit could not
sprout up so suddenly were there not much sap and juice in the root of sin.

What communion with a living root can be evidenced without exercises
of an inward life! That Spirit, which is a well of living waters in a gracious
heart, will be especially springing up when it is before God.

(2.) It shews much affection to earthly things, and little to heavenly.
There must needs be an inordinate affection to earthly things, when upon every
slight solicitation we can part with God, and turn the back upon a service
glorious for him, and advantageous for ourselves, to wed our hearts to some
idle fancy that signifies nothing. How can we be said to entertain God in
our affections, when we give him not the precedency in our understandings,
but let every trifle jostle the sense of God out of our minds? Were our
hearts fully determined to spiritual things, such vanities could not seat
themselves in our understandings, and divide our spirits from God. Were
our hearts balanced with a love to God, the world could never steal our
hearts so much from his worship, but his worship would draw our hearts to it.

It shews a base neutrality in the greatest concernments, a halting between
God and Baal, a contrariety between affection and conscience, when natural
conscience presses a man to duties of worship, and his other affections pull
him back, draw him to carnal objects, and make him slight that whereby
he may honour God. God argues the profaneness of the Jews' hearts from
the wickedness they brought into his house and acted there: Jer. xxiii.,
'Yea, in my house,' that is, my worship, 'I found their wickedness,' saith
the Lord. Carnality in worship is a kind of an idolatrous frame; when the
heart is renewed, idols are cast to the moles and the bats, Isa. ii. 20.

(3.) It shews much hypocrisy to have our spirits off from God. The
mouth speaks, and the carriage pretends, what the heart doth not think;
there is a dissent of the heart from the pretence of the body.

Instability is a sure sign of hypocrisy. Double thoughts argue a double
heart. The wicked are compared to chaff, Ps. i. 4, for the uncertain and
various motions of their minds by the least wind of fancy. The least motion
of a carnal object diverts the spirit from God, as the scent of carrion doth
the raven from the flight it was set upon.

The people of God are called God's spouse, and God calls himself their
husband; whereby is noted the most intimate union of the soul with God,
and that there ought to be the highest love and affection to him, and faithfulness in his worship; but when the heart doth start from him in worship,
it is a sign of the unstedfastness of it with God, and a disrelish of any
communion with him. It is as God complains of the Israelites, a going
a-whoring after our own imaginations.

As grace respects God as the object of worship, so it looks most upon
God in approaching to him. Where there is a likeness and love, there is a
desire of converse and intimacy; if there be no spiritual entwining about
God in our worship, it is a sign there is no likeness to him, no true sense of
him, no renewed image of God in us. Every living image will move strongly
to join itself with its original copy, and be glad, with Jacob, to sit steadily in
those chariots that shall convey him to his beloved Joseph.

Motive 3. Consider the danger of a carnal worship.

(1.) We lose the comfort of worship. The soul is a great gainer when it
offers a spiritual worship, and as great a loser when it is unfaithful with God.

Treachery and perfidiousness hinder commerce among men, so doth hypocrisy in its own nature communion with God. God never promised anything to the carcass, but to the spirit of worship. God hath no obligation upon him by any word of his, to reward us with himself, when we perform it not to himself. When we give an outside worship, we have only the outside of an ordinance. We can expect no kernel, when we give God only the shell. He that only licks the outside of the glass can never be refreshed with the rich cordial enclosed within. A cold and lazy formality will make God to withdraw the light of his countenance, and not shine with any delightful communications upon our souls; but if we come before him with a liveliness of affections, and steadiness of heart, he will draw the veil, and cause his glory to display itself before us. An humble praying Christian, and a warm affectionate Christian in worship, will soon find a God who is delighted with such frames, and cannot long withhold himself from the soul. When our hearts are inflamed with love to him in worship, it is a preparation for some act of love on his part, whereby he intends further to gratify us. When John was ' in the Spirit on the Lord's day,'—that is, in spiritual employment, and meditation, and other duties,—he had that great revelation of what should happen to the church in all ages, Rev. i. 10. His being in the Spirit, intimates his ordinary course on that day, and not any extraordinary act in him, though it was followed with an extraordinary discovery of God to him. When he was thus engaged, he ' heard a voice behind him.'

God doth not require of us spirituality in worship to advantage himself, but that we might be prepared to be advantaged by him. If we have a clear and well disposed eye, it is not a benefit to the sun, but fits us to receive benefits from his beams. Worship is an act that perfects our own souls; they are then most widened by spiritual frames, to receive the influence of divine blessings, as an eye most opened receives the fruit of the sun's light better than the eye that is shut. The communications of God are more or less, according as our spiritual frames are more or less in our worship. God will not give his blessings to unsuitable hearts. What a nasty vessel is a carnal heart for a spiritual communication! The chief end of every duty enjoined by God is to have communion with him; and therefore it is called a drawing near to God. It is impossible, therefore, that the outward part of any duty can answer the end of God in his institution. It is not a bodily appearance or gesture whereby men can have communion with God, but by the impressions of the heart and reflections of the heart upon God. Without this, all the rich streams of grace will run beside us, and the growth of the soul be hindered and impaired. ' A diligent hand makes rich,' saith the wise man; a diligent heart in spiritual worship brings in rich incomes to the humble and spiritual soul.

(2.) It renders the worship not only unacceptable, but abominable to God. It makes our gold to become dross, it soils our duties, and bespots our souls. A carnal and unsteady frame shews an indifference of spirit at best; and lukewarmness is as ungrateful to God as heavy and nauseous meat is to the stomach; he ' spues them out of his mouth,' Rev. iii. 16. As our gracious God doth overlook infirmities where intentions are good, and endeavours serious and strong, so he loathes the services where the frames are stark naught: Ps. lxvi. 18, ' If I regard iniquity in my heart, the Lord will not hear my prayer.' Lukewarm and indifferent services stink in the nostrils of God. The heart seems to loathe God, when it starts from him upon every occasion, when it is unwilling to employ itself about and stick close to him; and can God be pleased with such a frame? The more of the heart and spirit is in any service, the more real goodness there is in it, and the more savoury it is to God; the less of the heart and spirit, the less of goodness, and the more nauseous to God, who loves righteousness and 'truth in the inward parts,' Ps. li. 9. And therefore infinite goodness and holiness cannot but hate worship presented to him with deceitful, carnal, and flitting affections. They must be more nauseous to God than a putrified carcass can be to man; they are the profanings of that which should be the habitation of the spirit; they make the spirit, the seat of duty, a filthy dunghill, and are as loathsome to God as money-changers in the temple were to our Saviour.

We see the evil of carnal frames, and the necessity and benefit of spiritual frames. For further help in this last, let us practise these following directions:

Direct. 1. Keep up spiritual frames out of worship. To avoid low affections, we must keep our hearts as much as we can in a settled elevation. If we admit unworthy dispositions at one time, we shall not easily be rid of them at another. * As he that would not be bitten with gnats in the night, must keep his windows shut in the day: when they are once entered, it is not easy to expel them; in which respect, one adviseth, to be such out of worship as we would be in worship. If we mix spiritual affections with our worldly employments, worldly affections will not mingle themselves so easily with our heavenly engagements. If our hearts be spiritual in our outward calling, they will scarce be carnal in our religious service. If we 'walk in the Spirit, we shall not fulfil the lusts of the flesh,' Gal. v. 16. A spiritual walk in the day will hinder carnal lustings in worship. The fire was to be kept alive upon the altar when sacrifices were not offered, from morning till night, from night till morning, as well as in the very time of sacrifice. A spiritual life and vigour out of worship, would render it at its season sweet and easy, and preserve a spontaneity and preparedness to it, and make it both natural and pleasant to us.

Anything that doth unhinge and discompose our spirits, is inconsistent with religious services, which are to be performed with the greatest sedateness and gravity. All irregular passions disturb the serenity of the spirit, and open the door for Satan. Saith the apostle, 'Let not the sun go down upon your wrath, neither give place to the devil,' Eph. iv. 26, 27. Where wrath breaks the lock, the devil will quickly be over the threshold; and though they be allayed, yet they leave the heart some time after, like the sea, rolling and swelling after the storm is ceased.

Mixture with ill company leaves a tincture upon us in worship. Ephraim's allying himself with the Gentiles, bred an indifferency in religion: Hosea vii. 8, Ephraim 'hath mixed with the people;' 'Ephraim is a cake not turned.' It will make our hearts, and consequently our services, half dough, as well as half baked. These and the like make the Holy Spirit withdraw himself, and then the soul lies like a wind-bound vessel, and can make no way. When the sun departs from us, it carries its beams away with it; then doth 'darkness spread itself over the earth, and the beasts of the forests creep out,' Ps. civ. 20. When the Spirit withdraws a while from a good man, it carries away (though not habitual, yet) much of the exciting and assisting grace; and then carnal dispositions perk up themselves from the bosom of natural corruption. To be spiritual in worship, we must bar the door at other times against that which is contrary to it. As he that would not be infected with a contagious disease, carries some preservative about with him, and inures himself to good scents.

To this end, be much in secret ejaculations to God; these are the purest

---

* Fitzherbert, Pol. in Relig., part ii. cap. 19, sect. 12.

flights of the soul, that have more of fervour and less of carnality; they preserve a liveliness in the spirit, and make it more fit to perform solemn stated worship with greater freedom and activity. A constant use of this would make our whole lives, lives of worship. As frequent sinful acts strengthen habits of sin, so frequent religious acts strengthen habits of grace.

Direct. 2. Excite and exercise particularly a love to God, and dependence on him.

Love is a commanding affection, a uniting grace; it draws all the faculties of the soul to one centre. The soul that loves God, when it hath to do with him, is bound to the beloved object: it can mind nothing else during such impressions. When the affection is set to the worship of God, everything the soul hath will be bestowed upon it; as David's disposition was to the temple, 1 Chron. xxix. 3. Carnal frames, like the fowls, will be lighting upon the sacrifice, but not when it is inflamed. Though the scent of the flesh invite them, yet the heat of the fire drives them to their distance. A flaming love will singe the flies that endeavour to interrupt and disturb us. The happiness of heaven consists in a full attraction of the soul to God, by his glorious influence upon it. There will be such a diffusion of his goodness throughout the souls of the blessed, as will unite the affections perfectly to him. These affections, which are scattered here, will be there gathered into one flame, moving to him, and centering in him. Therefore the more of a heavenly frame possesses our affections here, the more settled and uniform will our hearts be in all their motions to God, and operations about him.

Excite a dependence on him: Prov. xvi. 3, ' Commit thy works to the Lord, and thy thoughts shall be established.' Let us go out in God's strength, and not in our own; vain is the help of man in anything, and vain is the help of the heart. It is through God only we can do valiantly in spiritual concerns as well as temporal; the want of this makes but slight impressions upon the spirit.

Direct. 3. Nourish right conceptions of the majesty of God in your minds. Let us consider, that we are drawing to God, the most amiable object, the best of beings, worthy of infinite honour, and highly meriting the highest affections we can give; a God that made the world by a word; that upholds the great frame of heaven and earth; a majesty above the conceptions of angels; who uses not his power to strike us to our deserved punishment, but his love and bounty to allure us; a God that gave all the creatures to serve us, and can in a trice make them as much our enemies as he hath now made them our servants. Let us view him in his greatness, and in his goodness, that our hearts may have a true value of the worship of so great a majesty, and count it the most worthy employment with all diligence to attend upon him. When we have a fear of God, it will make our worship serious; when we have a joy in God, it will make our worship durable. Our affections will be raised, when we represent God in the most reverential, endearing, and obliging circumstances. We honour the majesty of God, when we consider him with due reverence, according to the greatness and perfection of his works; and in this reverence of his majesty doth worship chiefly consist. Low thoughts of God will make low frames in us before him. If we thought God an infinite glorious Spirit, how would our hearts be lower than our knees in his presence! How humbly, how believingly pleading is the psalmist, when he considers God to be without comparison in the heavens; to whom none of the sons of the mighty can be likened; when there was none like to him in strength or faithfulness round about, Ps. lxxxix. 6–8. We should have also deep impressions of the omniscience

of God; and remember we have to deal with a God that searcheth the
heart and trieth the reins; to whom the most secret temper is as visible as
the loudest words are audible; that though man judges by outward expressions, God judges by inward affections. As the law of God regulates the
inward frames of the heart, so the eye of God pitches upon the inward intentions of the soul. If God were visibly present with us, should we not
approach to him with strong affections, summon our spirits to attend upon
him, behave ourselves modestly before him? Let us consider, he is as
really present with us, as if he were visible to us; let us therefore preserve
a strong sense of the presence of God. No man but one out of his wits,
when he were in the presence of a prince, and making a speech to him,
would break off at every period, and run after the catching of butterflies.
Remember in all worship you are before the Lord, to whom all things are
open and naked.

Direct. 4. Let us take heed of inordinate desires after the world. As the
world steals away a man's heart from the word, so it doth from all other
worship; 'it chokes the word,' Mat. xiii. 27; it stifles all the spiritual
breathings after God in every duty. The edge of the soul is blunted by it,
and made too dull for such sublime exercises. The apostle's rule in prayer,
1 Peter iv. 7, when he joins 'sobriety' with 'watching unto prayer,' is of
concern in all worship, sobriety in the pursuit and use of all worldly things.
A man drunk with worldly fumes cannot watch, cannot be heavenly, affectionate, spiritual in service. There is a magnetic force in the earth, to
hinder our flights to heaven. Birds, when they take their first flights from
the earth, have more flutterings of their wings, than when they are mounted
further in the air, and got more without the sphere of the earth's attractive-
ness; the motion of their wings is more steady, that you can scarce perceive
them stir; they move like a ship with a full gale. The world is a clog
upon the soul, and a bar to spiritual frames. It is as hard to elevate the
heart to God in the midst of a hurry of worldly affairs, as it is difficult to
meditate when we are near a great noise of waters falling from a precipice,
or in the midst of a volley of muskets. Their clayey affections bemire the
heart, and make it unfit for such high flights it is to take in worship. Therefore get your hearts clear from worldly thoughts and desires, if you would
be more spiritual in worship.

Direct. 5. Let us be deeply sensible of our present wants, and the supplies we may meet with in worship. Cold affections to the things we would
have, will grow cooler. Weakness of desire for the communications in
worship, will freeze our hearts at the time of worship, and make way for vain
and foolish diversions. A beggar that is ready to perish, and knows he is
next door to ruin, will not slightly and dully beg an alms, and will not be
diverted from his importunity by every slight call, or the moving of an atom
in the air. Is it pardon we would have? Let us apprehend the blackness
of sin, with the aggravations of it as it respects God; let us be deeply sensible of the want of pardon and worth of mercy, and get our affections into
such a frame as a condemned man would do. Let us consider, that as we
are now at the throne of God's grace, we shall shortly be at the bar of God's
justice; and if the soul should be forlorn there, how fixedly and earnestly
would it plead for mercy! Let us endeavour to stir up the same affections
now, which we have seen some dying men have, and which we suppose despairing souls would have done at God's tribunal.* We must be sensible
that the life or death of our souls depends upon worship. Would we not
be ashamed to be ridiculous in our carriage while we are eating? and shall

* Guliel. Paris, Rhetor. Divin. cap. xxvi. p. 350, col. i.

we not be ashamed to be cold or garish before God, when the salvation of our souls, as well as the honour of God, is concerned? If we did see the heaps of sins, the eternity of punishment due to them; if we did see an angry and offended judge; if we did see the riches of mercy, the glorious outgoings of God in the sanctuary, the blessed doles he gives out to men when they spiritually attend upon him: both the one and the other would make us perform our duties humbly, sincerely, earnestly, and affectionately, and wait upon him with our whole souls, to have misery averted and mercy bestowed. Let our sense of this be encouraged by the consideration of our Saviour presenting his merits. With what affection doth he present his merits, his blood shed upon the cross now in heaven! And shall our hearts be cold and frozen, flitting and unsteady, when his affections are so much concerned? Christ doth not present any man's case and duties without a sense of his wants, and shall we have none of our own?

Let me add this: let us affect our hearts with a sense of what supplies we have met with in former worship. The delightful remembrance of what converse we have had with God in former worship, would spiritualise our hearts for the present worship. Had Peter a view of Christ's glory in the mount fresh in his thoughts, he would not so easily have turned his back upon his master. Nor would the Israelites have been at leisure for their idolatry, had they preserved the sense of the majesty of God discovered in his late thunders from mount Sinai.

Direct. 6. If anything intrudes that may choke the worship, cast it speedily out. We cannot hinder Satan and our own corruption from presenting coolers to us, but we may hinder the success of them. We cannot hinder the gnats from buzzing about us when we are in our business, but we may prevent them from settling upon us. A man that is running on a considerable errand, will shun all unnecessary discourse that may make him forget or loiter in his business. What though there may be something offered that is good in itself; yet if it hath a tendency to despoil God of his honour, and ourselves of the spiritual intentness in worship, send it away. Those that weed a field of corn, examine not the nature and particular virtues of the weeds, but consider only how they choke the corn, to which the native juice of the soil is designed. Consider what you are about; and if anything interpose that may divert you, or cool your affections in your present worship, cast it out.

Direct. 7. As to private worship, let us lay hold of the most melting opportunities and frames. When we find our hearts in a more than ordinary spiritual frame, let us look upon it as a call from God to attend him. Such impressions and motions are God's voice, inviting us into communion with him in some particular act of worship, and promising us some success in it. When the psalmist had a secret motion to seek God's face, and complied with it, Ps. xxvii. 8, the issue is the encouragement of his heart, which breaks out into an exhortation to others to be of good courage, and wait on the Lord, ver. 13, 14, 'Wait on the Lord, be of good courage, and he shall strengthen thy heart; wait, I say, on the Lord.'

One blow will do more on the iron when it is hot, than a hundred when it is cold. Melted metals may be stamped with any impression; but once hardened, will with difficulty be brought into the figure we intend.*

Direct. 8. Let us examine ourselves at the end of every act of worship, and chide ourselves for any carnality we perceive in them. Let us take a review of them, and examine the reason, Why art thou so low and carnal, O my soul? as David did of his disquietedness: Ps. xlii. 5, 'Why art

* Reynolds.

thou cast down, O my soul? and why art thou disquieted within me?' If
any unworthy frames have surprised us in worship, let us seek them out
after worship; call them to the bar; make an exact scrutiny into the causes
of them, that we may prevent their incursions another time; let our pulses
beat quick, by way of anger and indignation, against them. This would be
a repairing what hath been amiss; otherwise they may grow, and clog an
after worship more than they did a former. Daily examination is an anti-
dote against the temptations of the following day, and constant examination
of ourselves after duty is a preservative against vain encroachments in following duties; and upon the finding them out, let us apply the blood of
Christ by faith for our cure, and draw strength from the death of Christ for
the conquest of them, and let us also be humbled for them. God lifts up
the humble. When we are humbled for our carnal frames in one duty, we
shall find ourselves by the grace of God more elevated in the next.

A DISCOURSE UPON THE ETERNITY OF GOD.

Before the mountains were brought forth, or ever thou hadst formed the earth and the world, even from everlasting to everlasting, thou art God.— PSALM XC. 2.

THE title of this psalm is a prayer; the author, Moses. Some think not only this, but the ten following psalms were composed by him. The title wherewith he is dignified is 'the man of God,' as also in Deut. xxxiii. 1: one inspired by him, to be his interpreter, and deliver his oracles; one particularly directed by him; one who, as a servant, did diligently employ himself in his Master's business, and acted for the glory of God.* He was the minister of the Old Testament, and the prophet of the New.†

There are two parts of this psalm.

1. A complaint of the frailty of man's life in general, ver. 3–6; and then a particular complaint of the condition of the church, ver. 8–10.‡

2. A prayer, ver. 12.

But before he speaks of the shortness of human life, he fortifies them by the consideration of the refuge they had and should find in God: ver. 1, 'Lord, thou hast been our dwelling-place in all generations.'

We have had no settled abode in the earth since the time of Abraham's being called out from Ur of the Chaldees. We have had Canaan in a promise, we have it not yet in possession; we have been exposed to the cruelties of an oppressing enemy, and the incommodities of a desert wilderness; we have wanted the fruits of the earth, but not the dews of heaven. 'Thou hast been our dwelling-place in all generations.' Abraham was under thy conduct, Isaac and Jacob under thy care. Their posterity were multiplied by thee, and that under their oppressions. Thou hast been our shield against dangers, our security in the times of trouble. When we were pursued to the Red sea, it was not a creature delivered us; and when we feared the pinching of our bowels in the desert, it was not a creature rained manna upon us. Thou hast been our dwelling-place; thou hast kept open house for us, sheltered us against storms, and preserved us from mischief, as a house doth an inhabitant from wind and weather, and that not in one or two, but in all generations. Some think an allusion is here made to the ark, to which they were to have recourse in all emergencies. Our refuge and defence have not been from created things; not from the ark, but from the God of the ark.

* Coccei *in loc.*　　　　† Austin *in loc.*　　　　‡ Pareus *in loc.*

Observe,

1. God is a perpetual refuge and security to his people. His providence is not confined to one generation; it is not one age only that tastes of his bounty and compassion. His eye never yet slept, nor hath he suffered the little ship of his church to be swallowed up, though it hath been tossed upon the waves. He hath always been an haven to preserve us, a house to secure us. He hath always had compassions to pity us, and power to protect us. He hath had a face to shine, when the world hath had an angry countenance to frown.* He brought Enoch home by an extraordinary translation from a brutish world; and when he was resolved to reckon with men for their brutish lives, he lodged Noah, the Phœnix of the world, in an ark, and kept him alive as a spark in the midst of many waters, whereby to rekindle a church in the world. In all generations he is a dwelling-place, to secure his people here, or entertain them above.

His providence is not wearied, nor his care fainting. He never wanted will to relieve us, for ' he hath been our refuge;' nor ever can want power to support us, for he is a God ' from everlasting to everlasting.' The church never wanted a pilot to steer her, and a rock to shelter her, and dash in pieces the waves which threaten her.

2. How worthy is it to remember former benefits, when we come to beg for new! Never were the records of God's mercies so exactly revised as when his people have stood in need of new editions of his power. How necessary are our wants to stir us up to pay the rent of thankfulness in arrear! He renders himself doubly unworthy of the mercies he wants, that doth not gratefully acknowledge the mercies he hath received. God scarce promised any deliverance to the Israelites, and they in their distress scarce prayed for any deliverance, but that from Egypt was mentioned on both sides: by God to encourage them, and by them to acknowledge their confidence in him. The greater our dangers, the more we should call to mind God's former kindness. We are not only thankfully to acknowledge the mercies bestowed upon our persons, or in our age, but those of former times. Thou hast been our dwelling-place in all generations.

Moses was not living in the former generations, yet he appropriates the former mercies to the present age. Mercies as well as generations proceed out of the loins of those that have gone before. All mankind are but one Adam, the whole church but one body.

In the second verse he backs his former consideration.

1. By the greatness of his power in forming the world.

2. By the boundlessness of his duration; ' from everlasting to everlasting.' As thou hast been our dwelling-place, and expended upon us the strength of thy power and riches of thy love, so we have no reason to doubt the continuance on thy part, if we be not wanting on our parts; for the vast mountains and fruitful earth are the works of thy hands, and there is less power requisite for our relief than there was for their creation; and though so much strength hath been upon various occasions manifested, yet thy arm is not weakened; for ' from everlasting to everlasting thou art God.'†

Thou hast always been God, and no time can be assigned as the beginning of thy being.‡ The mountains are not of so long a standing as thyself; they are the effects of thy power, and therefore cannot be equal to thy duration. Since they are effects, they suppose a precedency of their cause. If we would look back, we can reach no further than the beginning of the creation, and account the years from the first foundation of the world; but after that we must lose ourselves in the abyss of eternity. We have no

* Theodoret *in loc.*   † אֵל, *strong.*   ‡ Amyrald. *in loc.*

clue to guide our thoughts; we can see no bounds in thy eternity; but as for man, he traverseth the world a few days, and by thy order, pronounced concerning all men, returns to the dust, and moulders into the grave.

By mountains some understand angels, as being creatures of a more elevated nature; by earth they understand human nature, the earth being the habitation of men. There is no need to divert in this place from the letter to such a sense. The description seems to be poetical, and amounts to this: he neither began with the beginning of time, nor will expire with the end of it.* He did not begin when he made himself known to our fathers, but his being did precede the creation of the world, before any created being was formed, and any time settled.

' Before the mountains were brought forth,' or before they were begotten or born, the word being used in those senses in Scripture; before they stood up higher than the rest of the earthly mass God had created. It seems that mountains were not casually cast up by the force of the deluge softening the ground, and driving several parcels of it together, to grow up into a massy body, as the sea doth the sand in several places, but they were at first formed by God.

The eternity of God is here described.

1. In his priority ' before the world.'

2. In the extension of his duration: 'From everlasting to everlasting thou art God.' He was before the world, yet he neither began nor ends. He is not a temporary, but an eternal God. It takes in both parts of eternity, what was before the creation of the world, and what is after. Though the eternity of God be one permanent state without succession, yet the Spirit of God, suiting himself to the weakness of our conception, divides it into two parts, one past before the foundation of the world, another to come after the destruction of the world; as he did exist before all ages, and as he will exist after all ages.

Many truths lie couched in the verse.

1. The world had a beginning of being. It was not from eternity; it was once nothing. Had it been of a very long duration, some records would have remained of some memorable actions done of a longer date than any extant.

2. The world owes its being to the creating power of God. ' Thou hadst formed it' out of nothing into being. *Thou*, that is, God. It could not spring into being of itself: it was nothing; it must have a former.

3. God was in being before the world. The cause must be before the effect; that Word which gives being must be before that which receives being.

4. This Being was from eternity: ' from everlasting.'

5. This Being shall endure to eternity: ' to everlasting.'

6. There is but one God, one Eternal: ' From everlasting to everlasting thou art God.' None else but one hath the property of eternity; the gods of the heathen cannot lay claim to it.

Doct. God is of an eternal duration. The eternity of God is the foundation of the stability of the covenant, the great comfort of a Christian. The design of God in Scripture is to set forth his dealing with men in the way of a covenant. The priority of God before all things begins the Bible: ' In the beginning God created,' Gen. i. 1. His covenant can have no foundation but in his duration before and after the world.† And Moses here mentions his eternity, not only with respect to the essence of God, but to his federal providence; as he is the dwelling-place of his people in all

* ἄναρχος καὶ ἀτελεύτητος, Theodoret *in loc.*　　　　† Calv. *in loc.*

generations. The duration of God for ever is more spoken of in Scripture than his eternity *à parte ante*, though that is the foundation of all the comfort we can take from his immortality. If he had a beginning, he might have an end, and so all our happiness, hope, and being would expire with him; but the Scripture sometimes takes notice of his being without beginning as well as without end: 'Thou art from everlasting,' Ps. xciii. 2; 'Blessed be God from everlasting to everlasting,' Ps. xli. 13; 'I was set up from everlasting,' Prov. viii. 23. If his wisdom were from everlasting, himself was from everlasting. Whether we understand it of Christ the Son of God, or of the essential wisdom of God, it is all one to the present purpose. The wisdom of God supposeth the essence of God, as habits in creatures suppose the being of some power or faculty as their subject. The wisdom of God supposeth mind and understanding, essence and substance.

The notion of eternity is difficult, as Austin said of time:* If no man will ask me the question what time is, I know well enough what it is; but if any ask me what it is, I know not how to explain it. So may I say of eternity; it is easy in the word pronounced, but hardly understood, and more hardly expressed; it is better expressed by negative than positive words.

Though we cannot comprehend eternity, yet we may comprehend that there is an eternity; as though we cannot comprehend the essence of God, what he is, yet we may comprehend that he is; we may understand the notion of his existence, though we cannot understand the infiniteness of his nature. Yet we may better understand eternity than infiniteness; we can better conceive a time with the addition of numberless days and years, than imagine a being without bounds; whence the apostle joins his eternity with his power: 'His eternal power and Godhead,' Rom. i. 20; because, next to the power of God apprehended in the creature, we come necessarily, by reasoning, to acknowledge the eternity of God. He that hath an incomprehensible power, must needs have an eternity of nature. His power is most sensible in the creatures to the eye of man, and his eternity easily from thence deducible by the reason of man.

1. Eternity is a perpetual duration, which hath neither beginning nor end. Time hath both. Those things we say are in time, that have beginning, grow up by degrees, have succession of parts. Eternity is contrary to time, and is therefore a permanent and immutable state, a perfect possession of life without any variation. It comprehends in itself all years, all ages, all periods of ages. It never begins! It endures after every duration of time, and never ceaseth. It doth as much outrun time as it went before the beginning of it. Time supposeth something before it, but there can be nothing before eternity; it were not then eternity. Time hath a continual succession; the former time passeth away, and another succeeds; the last year is not this year, nor this year the next. We must conceive of eternity contrary to the notion of time. As the nature of time consists in the succession of parts, so the nature of eternity in an infinite immutable duration.† Eternity and time differ as the sea and rivers; the sea never changes place, and is always one water, but the rivers glide along, and are swallowed up in the sea; so is time by eternity.

A thing is said to be eternal, or everlasting rather, in Scripture,

2. When it is of a long duration, though it will have an end; when it hath no measures of time determined to it. So circumcision is said to be in the flesh 'for an everlasting covenant,' Gen. xvii. 14; not purely everlasting, but so long as that administration of the covenant should endure. And so when a servant would not leave his master, but would have his

* Consul. lib. ii. Confes. 15.   † Moulin. Cor. i., Ser. 2, p. 52.

ear bored, it is said he should be a servant 'for ever,' Deut. xv. 17; *i. e.*, till the jubilee, which was every fiftieth year. So the meat-offering they were to offer is said to be perpetual, Lev. vi. 20. Canaan is said to be given to Abraham for an everlasting possession, Gen. xvii. 8, whenas the Jews are expelled from Canaan, which is given a prey to the barbarous nations. Indeed, circumcision was not everlasting, yet the substance of the covenant, whereof this was a sign, viz., that God would be the God of believers, endures for ever; and that circumcision of the heart which was signified by circumcision of the flesh, shall remain for ever in the kingdom of glory. It was not so much the lasting of the sign, as of the thing signified by it, and the covenant sealed by it. The sign had its abolition, so that the apostle is so peremptory in it, that he asserts that if any went about to establish it, he excluded himself from a participation of Christ, Gal. v. 2. The sacrifices were to be perpetual in regard of the thing signified by them, viz., the death of Christ, which was to endure in the efficacy of it. And the passover was to be for ever, Exod. xii. 24, in regard of the redemption signified by it, which was to be of everlasting remembrance. Canaan was to be an everlasting possession in regard of the glory of heaven typified, to be for ever conferred upon the spiritual seed of Abraham.

3. When a thing hath no end, though it hath a beginning. So angels and souls are everlasting; though their being shall never cease, yet there was a time when their being began. They were nothing before they were something, though they shall never be nothing again, but shall live in endless happiness or misery.

But that properly is eternal that hath neither beginning nor end; and thus eternity is a property of God. In this doctrine I shall shew,

I. How God is eternal, or in what respects eternity is his property.

II. That he is eternal, and must needs be so.

III. That eternity is only proper to God, and not common to him with any creature.

IV. The use.

I. How God is eternal, or in what respects he is so. Eternity is a negative attribute, and is a denying of God any measures of time, as immensity is a denying of him any bounds of place; as immensity is the diffusion of his essence, so eternity is the duration of his essence; and when we say God is eternal, we exclude from him all possibility of beginning and ending, all flux and change. As the essence of God cannot be bounded by any place, so it is not to be limited by any time; as it is his immensity to be everywhere, so it is his eternity to be always. As created things are said to be somewhere in regard of place, and to be present, past, or future in regard of time, so the Creator in regard of place is everywhere, in regard of time is *semper*.* His duration is as endless as his essence is boundless; he always was and always will be, and will no more have an end than he had a beginning; and this is an excellency belonging to the Supreme Being.† As his essence comprehends all beings and exceeds them, and his immensity surmounts all places, so his eternity comprehends all times, all durations, and infinitely excels them.‡

1. God is without beginning.

'In the beginning God created' the world,' Gen. i. 1. God was then before the beginning of it; and what point can be set wherein God began, if he were before the beginning of created things? God was without beginning, though all other things had time and beginning from him. As

_____
* Gassend.　　† Crellius, de Deo, cap. xviii. p. 41.　　‡ Lingend, tom. ii. p. 496.

unity is before all numbers, so is God before all his creatures. Abraham called upon the name of the 'everlasting God,' אֵל עוֹלָם, Gen. xxi. 33, the eternal God. It is opposed to heathen gods, which were but of yester-day, new coined, and so new; but the eternal God was before the world was made. In that sense it is to be understood: Rom. xvi. 26, 'The mystery which was kept secret since the world began, but now is made manifest, and by the scriptures of the prophets, according to the command of the everlasting God, made known to all nations for the obedience of faith.' The gospel is not preached by the command of a new and tem-porary God, but of that God that was before all ages. Though the mani-festation of it be in time, yet the purpose and resolve of it was from eternity.

If there were decrees before the foundation of the world, there was a decreer before the foundation of the world. Before the foundation of the world he loved Christ as a mediator, John xvii. 24; a foreordination of him was before the foundation of the world, Eph. i. 4. A choice of men, and therefore a chooser before the foundation of the world; a 'grace given in Christ before the world began,' 2 Tim. i. 9, and therefore a donor of that grace. From those places, saith Crellius, it appears that God was before the foundation of the world; but they do not assert an absolute eternity. But to be before all creatures, is equivalent to his being from eternity.* Time began with the foundation of the world, but God being before time, could have no beginning in time; before the beginning of the creation and the beginning of time, there could be nothing but eternity, nothing but what was uncreated, that is, nothing but what was without beginning. To be in time, is to have a beginning; to be before all time, is never to have a beginning, but always to be; for as between the Creator and creatures there is no medium, so between time and eternity there is no medium. It is as easily deduced that he that was before all creatures is eternal, as he that made all creatures is God; if he had a beginning, he must have it from another, or from himself. If from another, that from whom he received his being would be better than he, so more a God than he. He cannot be God that is not supreme, he cannot be supreme that owes his being to the power of another. He would not be said 'only to have immortality' as he is, 1 Tim. vi. 16, if he had it dependent upon another; nor could he have a beginning from himself. If he had given beginning to himself, then he was once nothing, there was a time when he was not; if he was not, how could he be the cause of himself? It is impossible for any to give a beginning and being to itself; if it acts, it must exist, and so exist before it existed. A thing would exist as a cause before it existed as an effect. He that is not cannot be the cause that he is. If therefore God doth exist, and hath not his being from another, he must exist from eternity. There-fore when we say God is of and from himself, we mean not that God gave being to himself; but it is negatively to be understood, that he hath no cause of existence without himself.

Whatsoever number of millions of millions of years we can imagine before the creation of the world, yet God was infinitely before those; he is there-fore called 'the Ancient of days,' Dan. vii. 9, as being before all days and time, and eminently containing in himself all times and ages. Though indeed God cannot properly be called ancient, that will testify that he is decaying, and shortly will not be; no more than he can be called young, which would signify that he was not long before. All created things are new and fresh, but no creature can find out any beginning of God. It is impossible there should be any beginning of him.

* Coccei, Sum. Theol. p. 48; Gerhard, Exeges. cap. lxxxvi. 4, p. 266.

2. God is without end. He always was, always is, and always will be what he is. He remains always the same in being; so far from any change, that no shadow of it can touch him, James i. 17. He will continue in being as long as he hath already enjoyed it; and if we could add never so many millions of years together, we are still as far from an end as from a beginning, for 'the Lord shall endure for ever,' Ps. ix. 7. As it is impossible he should not be, being from all eternity, so it is impossible that he should not be to all eternity. The Scripture is most plentiful in testimonies of this eternity of God, *à parte post*, or after the creation of the world. He is said to 'live for ever,' Rev. iv. 9, 10. The earth shall perish, but God shall endure for ever, and his years shall have no end, Ps. cii. 27. Plants and animals grow up from small beginnings, arrive to their full growth and decline again, and have always remarkable alterations in their nature; but there is no declination in God by all the revolutions of time. Hence some think the incorruptibility of the Deity was signified by the Shittim or cedar wood, whereof the ark was made, it being of an incorruptible nature, Exod. xxv. 10.

That which had no beginning of duration can never have an end, or any interruptions in it. Since God never depended upon any, what should make him cease to be what eternally he hath been, or put a stop to the continuance of his perfections? He cannot will his own destruction; that is against universal nature in all things to cease from being, if they can preserve themselves. He cannot desert his own being, because he cannot but love himself as the best and chiefest good. The reason that anything decays, is either its own native weakness, or superior power of something contrary to it.* There is no weakness in the nature of God that can introduce any corruption, because he is infinitely simple, without any mixture. Nor can he be overpowered by anything else; a weaker cannot hurt him, and a stronger than he there cannot be. Nor can he be outwitted or circumvented, because of his infinite wisdom. As he received his being from none, so he cannot be deprived of it by any. As he doth necessarily exist, so he doth necessarily always exist. This indeed is the property of God; nothing so proper to him as always to be. Whatsoever perfection any being hath, if it be not eternal it is not divine. God only is immortal,† 1 Tim. vi. 16; he only is so by a necessity of nature. Angels, souls, and bodies too, after the resurrection, shall be immortal; not by nature but grant; they are subject to return to nothing, if that word that raised them from nothing should speak them into nothing again. It is as easy with God to strip them of it as to invest them with it; nay, it is impossible but that they should perish, if God should withdraw his power from preserving them, which he exerted in creating them. But God is immovably fixed in his own being, that as none gave him his life, so none can deprive him of his life, or the least particle of it. Not a jot of the happiness and life which God infinitely possesses can be lost; it will be as durable to everlasting as it hath been possessed from everlasting.

8. There is no succession in God. God is without succession or change; it is a part of eternity: 'From everlasting to everlasting he is God,' *i.e.* the same. God doth not only always remain in being, but he always remains the same in that being: 'Thou art the same,' Ps. cii. 27. The being of creatures is successive, the being of God is permanent, and remains entire with all its perfections, unchanged in an infinite duration. Indeed, the first notion of eternity is to be without beginning and end, which notes to us the duration of a being in regard of its existence; but to have no succession,

_____

* Crellius, de Deo, cap. xviii. p. 41.   † Daille *in loc.*

nothing first or last, notes rather the perfection of a being in regard of its essence.

The creatures are in a perpetual flux; something is acquired, or something lost, every day. A man is the same in regard of existence when he is a man as he was when he was a child, but there is a new succession of quantities and qualities in him. Every day he acquires something till he comes to his maturity, every day he loseth something till he comes to his period. A man is not the same at night that he was in the morning, something is expired and something is added; every day there is a change in his age, a change in his substance, a change in his accidents; but God hath his whole being in one and the same point or moment of eternity. He receives nothing as an addition to what he was before, he loseth nothing of what he was before; he is always the same excellency and perfection in the same infiniteness as ever. His 'years do not fail,' Heb. i. 12; his years do not come and go as others do, there is not this day, to-morrow, or yesterday with him. As nothing is past or future with him in regard of knowledge, but all things are present, so nothing is past or future in regard of his essence. He is not in his essence this day what he was not before, or will be the next day and year what he is not now.* All his perfections are most perfect in him every moment, before all ages, after all ages. As he hath his whole essence undivided in every place, as well as in immense space, so he hath all his being in one moment of time, as well as in infinite intervals of time.† Some illustrate the difference between eternity and time by the similitude of a tree or a rock standing upon the side of a river or shore of the sea; the tree stands, always the same and unmoved, while the waters of the river glide along at the foot. The flux is in the river, but the tree acquires nothing but a diverse respect and relation of presence to the various parts of the river as they flow. The waters of the river press on, and push forward one another, and what the river hath this minute it hath not the same the next; so are all sublunary things in a continual flux. And though the angels have no substantial change, yet they have an accidental, for the actions of the angels this day are not the same individual actions which they performed yesterday; but in God there is no change, he always remains the same.

Of a creature it may be said, he was, or he is, or he shall be.‡ Of God it cannot be said but only he is; he is what he always was, and he is what he always will be; whereas a creature is what he was not, and will be what he is not now. As it may be said of the flame of a candle, it is flame, but it is not the same individual flame as was before, nor is it the same that will be presently after; there is a continual dissolution of it into air, and a continual supply for the generation of more; while it continues it may be said there is a flame, yet not entirely one, but in a succession of parts: so of a man it may be said, he is in a succession of parts; but he is not the same that he was, and will not be the same that he is. But God is the same without any succession of parts, and of time; of him it may be said, he is; he is no more now than he was, and he shall be no more hereafter than he is. God possesses a firm and absolute being, always constant to himself; § he sees all things sliding under him in a continual variation; he beholds the revolutions in the world without any change of his most glorious and immoveable nature. All other things pass from one state to

* Lessius, de perfect. divin. lib. iv. cap. 1.
† Gamacheus in Aquin. part i. qu. 10, cap. 1.
‡ Gassend, tom. i.; Physic. sec. i. l. 2, c. 7, p. 223.
§ Daille, Melange de Sermons, p. 252.

another, from their original to their eclipse and destruction; but God possesses his being in one indivisible point, having neither beginning, end, nor middle.

(1.) There is no succession in the knowledge of God. The variety of successions and changes in the world make no succession or new objects in the divine mind, for all things are present to him from eternity in regard of his knowledge, though they are not actually present in the world in regard of their existence. He doth not know one thing now and another anon, he sees all things at once: 'Known unto God are all things from the beginning of the world,' Acts xv. 18, but in their true order of succession, as they lie in the eternal counsel of God, to be brought forth in time. Though there be a succession and order of things as they are wrought, yet there is no succession in God in regard of his knowledge of them. God knows the things that shall be wrought, and the order of them in their being brought upon the stage of the world; yet both the things and the order he knows by one act. Though all things be present with God, yet they are present in him in the order of their appearance in the world, and not so present with him as if they should be wrought at once. The death of Christ was to precede his resurrection in order of time; there is a succession in this; both at once are known by God, yet the act of his knowledge is not exercised about Christ as dying and rising at the same time, so that there is succession in things when there is no succession in God's knowledge of them. Since God knows time, he knows all things as they are in time; he doth not know all things to be at once, though he knows at once what is, has been, and will be. All things are past, present, and to come in regard of their existence; but there is not past, present, and to come in regard of God's knowledge of them,* because he sees and knows not by any other but by himself; he is his own light by which he sees, his own glass wherein he sees; beholding himself, he beholds all things.

(2.) There is no succession in the decrees of God. He doth not decree this now which he decreed not before, for as his works were known from the beginning of the world, so his works were decreed from the beginning of the world; as they are known at once, so they are decreed at once; there is a succession in the execution of them, first grace, then glory; but the purpose of God for the bestowing of both was in one and the same moment of eternity: Eph. i. 4, 'He chose us in him before the foundation of the world, that we should be holy;' the choice of Christ, and the choice of some in him to be holy, and to be happy, were before the foundation of the world. It is by the eternal counsel of God all things appear in time; they appear in their order, according to the counsel and will of God, from eternity. The redemption of the world is after the creation of the world, but the decree whereby the world was created, and whereby it was redeemed, was from eternity.

(3.) God is his own eternity. He is not eternal by grant, and the disposal of any other, but by nature and essence. The eternity of God is nothing else but the duration of God, and the duration of God is nothing else but his existence enduring, *existentia durans*.* If eternity were anything distinct from God, and not of the essence of God, then there would be something which was not God necessary to perfect God. As immortality is the great perfection of a rational creature, so eternity is the choice perfection of God, yea, the gloss and lustre of all others. Every perfection would be imperfect if it were not always a perfection.

God is essentially whatsoever he is, and there is nothing in God but his

* Parisiensis.   † Calov. Socinian.

essence. Duration or continuance in being in creatures differs from their being, for they might exist but for one instant, in which case they may be said to have being, but not duration, because all duration includes *prius et posterius.* All creatures may cease from being, if it be the pleasure of God; they are not therefore durable by their essence, and therefore are not their own duration, no more than they are their own existence; and though some creatures, as angels and souls, may be called everlasting, as a perpetual life is communicated to them by God, yet they can never be called their own eternity, because such a duration is not simply necessary nor essential to them, but accidental, depending upon the pleasure of another; there is nothing in their nature that can hinder them from losing it, if God, from whom they received it, should design to take it away; but as God is his own necessity of existing, so he is in his own duration in existing.* As he doth necessarily exist by himself, so he will always necessarily exist by himself.

(4.) Hence all the perfections of God are eternal. In regard of the divine eternity, all things in God are eternal: his power, mercy, wisdom, justice, knowledge. God himself were not eternal if any of his perfections, which are essential to him, were not eternal also; he had not else been a perfect God from all eternity, and so his whole self had not been eternal. If anything belonging to the nature of a thing be wanting, it cannot be said to be that thing which it ought to be; if anything requisite to the nature of God had been wanting one moment, he could not have been said to be an eternal God.

II. The second thing, God is eternal. The Spirit of God in Scripture condescends to our capacities in signifying the eternity of God by days and years, which are terms belonging to time, whereby we measure it, Ps. cii. 27; but we must no more conceive that God is bounded or measured by time, and hath succession of days because of those expressions, than we can conclude him to have a body because members are ascribed to him in Scripture, to help our conceptions of his glorious nature and operations.

Though years are ascribed to him, yet they are such as cannot be numbered, cannot be finished, since there is no proportion between the duration of God and the years of men: 'The number of his years cannot be searched out, for he makes small the drops of water, they pour down rain according to the vapour thereof,' Job xxxvi. 26, 27. The numbers of the drops of rain which have fallen in all parts of the earth since the creation of the world, if subtracted from the number of the years of God, would be found a small quantity, a mere nothing to the years of God. As all the nations in the world compared with God are but as the 'drop of a bucket, worse than nothing, than vanity,' Isa. xl. 15, so all the ages of the world, if compared with God, amount not to so much as the one hundred thousandth part of a minute. The minutes from the creation may be numbered, but the years of the duration of God, being infinite, are without measure.

As one day is to the life of man, so are a thousand years to the life of God, Ps. xc. 4. The Holy Ghost expresseth himself to the capacity of man, to give us some notion of an infinite duration, by a resemblance suited to the capacity of man.† If a thousand years be but as a day to the life of God, then as a year is to the life of man, so are three hundred sixty-five thousand years to the life of God; and as seventy years are to the life of man, so are twenty-five millions four ‡ hundred and fifty thousand years to the life of God. Yet still, since there is no proportion between time and eternity, we

* Gassend.　　　　† Amyrald, Trin. p. 44.　　　　‡ 'five.'—ED.

must dart our thoughts beyond all those,* for years and days measure only the duration of created things, and of those only that are material and corporeal, subject to the motion of the heavens, which makes days and years.

Sometimes this eternity is expressed by parts, as looking backward and forward, by the differences of time past, present, and to come, ' which was, and is, and is to come.'† Though this might be spoken of anything in being, though but for an hour, it was the last minute, it is now, and it will be the next minute, yet the Holy Ghost would declare something proper to God, as including all parts of time ; he always was, is now, and always shall be ; it might always be said of him he was, and it may always be said of him ·he will be. There is no time when he began, no time when he shall cease. It cannot be said of a creature he always was, he always is what he was, and he always will be what he is ; but God always is what he was, and always will be what he is, so that it is a very significant expression of the eternity of God, as can be suited to our capacities.

1. His eternity is evident, by the name God gives himself: Exod. iii. 14, ' And God said unto Moses, I AM THAT I AM ; thus 'shalt thou say to the children of Israel, I AM hath sent me unto you.' This is the name whereby he is distinguished from all creatures. I AM is his proper name. This description being in the present tense, shews that his essence knows no past nor future. If it were *he was*, it would intimate he were not now what he once was ; if it were *he will be*, it would intimate he were not yet what he will be ; but *I am;* I am the only being, the root of all beings ; he is therefore at the greatest distance from not being, and that is eternal ; so that *is* signifies his eternity, as well as his perfection and immutability. As *I am* speaks the want of no blessedness, so it speaks the want of no duration ; and therefore the French, wherever they find this word *Jehovah* in the Scripture, which we translate *Lord*, and *Lord eternal*, render it the *Eternal,*— I am always and immutably the same. The eternity of God is opposed to the volubility of time, which is extended into past, present, and to come. Our time is but a small drop, as sand to all the atoms and small particles of which the world is made ; but God is an unbounded sea of being,—' I am that I am,' *i.e.* am infinite life. I have not that now which I had not formerly ; I shall not afterwards have that which I have not now. *I am* that in every moment which I was, and will be in all moments of time. Nothing can be added to me, nothing can be detracted from me. There is nothing superior to him which can detract from him, nothing desirable that can be added to him. Now if there were any beginning and end of God, any succession in him, he could not be *I am ;*‡ for in regard of what was past he would not be, in regard of what was to come he is not yet. And upon this account a heathen § argues well, of all creatures it may be said they were, or they will be, but of God it cannot be said anything else but *Est*, God *is*, because he fills an eternal duration. A creature cannot be said to be if it be not yet, nor if it be not now, but hath been. ||

God only can be called *I am ;* all creatures have more of not being than being ; for every creature was nothing from eternity, before it was made something in time ; and if it be corruptible in its whole nature, it will be nothing to eternity after it hath been something in time ; and if it be not corruptible in its nature, as the angels, or in every part of its nature, as man in regard of his soul, yet it hath not properly a being, because it is depen-

* Daille, Vent. Sermons, Ser. 1. sur. Ps. cll. 27, p. 21.

† Rev. i. 8 iv. 8. Crellius weakens this argument, de Deo, cap. 18, p. 42.

‡ Thes. Salmur., p. i. p. 145. Thes. 14.   § Plutarch, de 'E, i. p. 462.

|| Perer. in Exod. iii. Disput. 18.

dent upon the pleasure of God to continue it, or deprive it of it; and while
it is, it is mutable, and all mutability is a mixture of not being. If God,
therefore, be properly *I am*, *i. e. being*, it follows that he always was; for if
he were not always, he must, as was argued before, be produced by some
other, or by himself. By another he could not, then he had not been God,
but a creature; nor by himself, for then, as producing, he must be before
himself, as produced; he had been before he was. And he always will be,
for being *I am*, having all being in himself, and the fountain of all being to
everything else, how can he ever have his name changed to *I am not?*

2. God hath life in himself: John v. 26, 'The Father hath life in himself.' He is the 'living God,' therefore 'stedfast' for ever,' Dan. vi. 26.
He hath life by his essence, not by participation. He is a sun to give light
and life to all creatures, but receives not light or life from anything, and
therefore he hath an unlimited life; not a drop of life, but a fountain; not
a spark of a limited life, but a life transcending all bounds. He hath life in
himself; all creatures have their life in him, and from him. He that hath
life in himself doth necessarily exist, and could never be made to exist, for
then he had not life in himself, but in that which made him to exist, and
gave him life. What doth necessarily exist, therefore, exists from eternity;
what hath being of itself could never be produced in time, could not want
being one moment, because it hath being from its essence, without influence
of any efficient cause. When God pronounced his name, *I am that I am*,
angels and men were in being; the world had been created above two thousand four hundred years.* Moses, to whom he then speaks, was in being;
yet God only *is*, because he only hath the fountain of being in himself, but
all that they were was a rivulet from him. He hath from nothing else that
he doth subsist; everything else hath its subsistence from him as their root,
as the beam from the sun, as the rivers and fountains from the sea. All
life is seated in God, as in its proper throne, in its most perfect purity.
God is life; it is in him originally, radically, therefore eternally. He is a
pure act, nothing but vigour and act. He hath by his nature that life which
others have by his grant; whence the apostle saith, 1 Tim. vi. 16, not only
that he is immortal, but he 'hath immortality' in a full possession, fee-
simple, not depending upon the will of another, but containing all things
within himself. He that hath life in himself, and is from himself, cannot
but be. He always was, because he received his being from no other, and
none can take away that being which was not given by another.† If there
were any space before he did exist, then there were something which made
him to exist; life would not then be in him, but in that which produced him
into being. He could not then be God, but that other which gave him
being would be God. And to say God sprung into being by chance, when
we see nothing in the world that is brought forth by chance, but hath
some cause of its existence, would be vain; for since God is a being, chance,
which is nothing, could not bring forth something; and by the same reason
that he sprung up by chance, he might totally vanish by chance. What a
strange notion of a God would this be, such a God that had no life in himself, but from chance.

Since he had life in himself, and that there was no cause of his existence,
he can have no cause of his limitation, and can no more be determined to
a time than he can to a place. What hath life in itself hath life without
bounds, and can never desert it, nor be deprived of it; so that he lives
necessarily, and it is absolutely impossible that he should not live; whereas

---

* Petav. Theol. Dogm., tom. i. lib. i. c. 6, sec. 6, 7.
† Amyrald, de Trinit., p. 48.

all other things ' live, and move, and have their being in him,' Acts xvii. 28 ; and as they live by his will, so they can return to nothing at his word.

3. If God were not eternal, he were not immutable in his nature. It is contrary to the nature of immutability to be without eternity ; for whatsoever begins, is changed, in its passing from not being to being. It began to be what it was not, and if it ends, it ceaseth to be what it was. It cannot, therefore, be said to be God, if there were either beginning or ending or succession in it : Mal. iii. 6, ' I am the Lord, I change not ;' Job xxxvii. 23, ' Touching the Almighty, we cannot find him out.' God argues here, saith Calvin, from his unchangeable nature as Jehovah, to his immutability in his purpose. Had he not been eternal, there had been the greatest change, from nothing to something. A change of the essence is greater than a change of purpose. God is a sun, glittering always in the same glory ; no growing up in youth, no passing on to age. If he were not without succession, standing in one point of eternity, there would be a change from past to present, from present to future. The eternity of God is a shield against all kind of mutability. If anything sprang up in the essence of God that was not there before, he could not be said to be either an eternal or an unchanged substance.

4. God could not be an infinitely perfect being, if he were not eternal. A finite duration is inconsistent with infinite perfection. Whatsoever is contracted within the limits of time, cannot swallow up all perfections in itself. God hath an unsearchable perfection : ' Canst thou by searching find out God ? canst thou find out the Almighty unto perfection ?' Job xi. 7. He cannot be found out, he is infinite, because he is incomprehensible. Incomprehensibility ariseth from an infinite perfection, which cannot be fathomed by the short lines of man's understanding. His essence, in regard of its diffusion and in regard of its duration, is incomprehensible, as well as his action. If God, therefore, had beginning, he could not be infinite ; if not infinite, he did not possess the highest perfection, because a perfection might be conceived beyond it. If his being could fail, he were not perfect. Can that deserve the name of the highest perfection, which is capable of corruption and dissolution ? To be finite and limited is the greatest imperfection, for it consists in a denial of being. He could not be the most blessed being if he were not always so, and should not for ever remain to be so ; and whatsoever perfections he had, would be soured by the thoughts that in time they would cease, and so could not be pure perfections, because not permanent ; but he is ' blessed from everlasting to everlasting,' Ps. xli. 13. Had he a beginning, he could not have all perfection without limitation ; he would have been limited by that which gave him beginning ; that which gave him being would be God and not himself, and so more perfect than he. But since God is the most sovereign perfection, than which nothing can be imagined perfecter by the most capacious understanding, he is certainly eternal ; being infinite, nothing can be added to him, nothing detracted from him.

5. God could not be omnipotent, almighty, if he were not eternal. The title of *Almighty* agrees not with a nature that had a beginning ; whatsoever hath a beginning was once nothing, and when it was nothing, could act nothing. Where there is no being, there is no power ; neither doth the title of *Almighty* agree with a perishing nature. He can do nothing to purpose, that cannot preserve himself against the outward force and violence of enemies, or against the inward causes of corruption and dissolution. No account is to be made of man, because ' his breath is in his nostrils,' Isa. ii. 22. Could a better account be made of God, if he were of the like condition ? He could not properly be *almighty*, that were not *always mighty*. If he be

omnipotent, nothing can impair him ; he that hath all power can have no hurt.* If he doth whatsoever he pleaseth, nothing can make him miserable, since misery consists in those things which happen against our will. The almightiness and eternity of God are linked together : ' I am Alpha and Omega, the beginning and the ending, saith the Lord, which was, and which is, and which is to come, the Almighty,' Rev. i. 8. Almighty because eternal, and eternal because almighty.

6. God would not be the first cause of all, if he were not eternal. But he is ' the first and the last,' Rev. i. 8 ; the first cause of all things, the last end of all things.† That which is the first cannot begin to be : it were not then the first. It cannot cease to be : whatsoever is dissolved, is dissolved into that whereof it doth consist, which was before it, and then it was not the first.‡ The world might not have been ; it was once nothing : it must have some cause to call it out of nothing. Nothing hath no power to make itself something ; there is a superior cause, by whose will and power it comes into being, and so gives all the creatures their distinct forms.

This power cannot but be eternal, it must be before the world ; the founder must be before the foundation,§ and his existence must be from eternity, or we must say nothing did exist from eternity. And if there were no being from eternity, there could not now be any being in time. What we see, and what we are, must arise from itself or some other. It cannot from itself. If anything made itself, it had a power to make itself ; it then had an active power before it had a being. It was something in regard of power, and was nothing in regard of existence, at the same time. Suppose it had a power to produce itself, this power must be conferred upon it by another ; and so the power of producing itself was not from itself, but from another. But if the power of being was from itself, why did it not produce itself before ? Why was it one moment out of being ? If there be any existence of things, it is necessary that that which was the first cause should exist from eternity. || Whatsoever was the immediate cause of the world, yet the first and chief cause, wherein we must rest, must have nothing before it ; if it had anything before it, it were not the first. He therefore that is the first cause must be without beginning, nothing must be before him. If he had a beginning from some other, he could not be the first principle and author of all things. If he be the first cause of all things, he must give himself a beginning, or to be from eternity. He could not give himself a beginning : whatsoever begins in time was nothing before, and when it was nothing, it could do nothing ; it could not give itself anything, for then it gave what it had not, and did what it could not. If he made himself in time, why did he not make himself before ? What hindered him ? It was either because he could not, or because he would not. If he could not, he always wanted power, and always would, unless it were bestowed upon him, and then he could not be said to be from himself. If he would not make himself before, then he might have made himself when he would : how had he the power of willing and nilling without a being ? Nothing cannot will or nill ; nothing hath no faculties. So that it is necessary to grant some eternal being, or run into inextricable labyrinths and mazes. If we deny some eternal being, we must deny all being : our own being, the being of everything about us ; unconceivable absurdities will arise.

So then, if God were the cause of all things, he did exist before all things, and that from eternity.

<hr/>

* Voet. Natural. Theol., p. 310.   § Crellius de Deo, cap. 18, p. 43.
† Ficin. de Immort., lib. ii. cap. 5. || Petav. Theol. Dogmat., tom. i. l. i. c. 10, 11.
‡ Coccei Sum. Theol.

III. The third thing is, eternity is only proper to God, and not communicable. It is as great a madness to ascribe eternity to the creature, as to deprive the Lord of the creature of eternity.* It is so proper to God, that when the apostle would prove the deity of Christ, he proves it by his immutability and eternity, as well as his creating power: ' Thou art the same, and thy years shall not fail,' Heb. i. 10–12. The argument had no strength, if eternity belonged essentially to any but God ; and therefore he is said ' only to have immortality,' 1 Tim. vi. 16. All other things receive their being from him, and can be deprived of their being by him. All things depend on him, he of none. All other things are like clothes, which would consume if God preserved them not. Immortality is appropriated to God, *i. e.* an independent immortality. Angels and souls have an immortality, but by donation from God, not by their own essence ; dependent upon their Creator, not necessary in their own nature. God might have annihilated them after he had created them ; so that their duration cannot properly be called an eternity, it being extrinsecal to them, and depending upon the will of their Creator, by whom they may be extinguished. It is not an absolute and necessary, but a precarious, immortality. Whatsoever is not God, is temporary ; whatsoever is eternal, is God.

It is a contradiction to say a creature can be eternal : as nothing eternal is created, so nothing created is eternal. What is distinct from the nature of God cannot be eternal, eternity being the essence of God. Every creature, in the notion of a creature, speaks a dependence on some cause, and therefore cannot be eternal. As it is repugnant to the nature of God not to be eternal, so it is repugnant to the nature of a creature to be eternal ; for then a creature would be equal to the Creator, and the Creator, or the cause, would not be before the creature, or effect. †

It would be all one to admit many gods, as many eternals ; and all one to say God can be created, as to say a creature can be uncreated, which is to be eternal.

1. Creation is a producing something from nothing. What was once nothing, cannot therefore be eternal : [its] not being was eternal ; therefore its being could not be eternal, for it should be then before it was, and would be something when it was nothing. It is the nature of a creature to be nothing before it was created ; what was nothing before it was, cannot be equal with God in an eternity of duration.

2. There is no creature but is mutable, therefore not eternal. As it had a change from nothing to something, so it may be changed from being to not being. If the creature were not mutable, it would be most perfect, and so would not be a creature, but God, for God only is most perfect. It is as much the essence of a creature to be mutable, as it is the essence of God to be immutable. Mutability and eternity are utterly inconsistent.

3. No creature is infinite, therefore not eternal. To be infinite in duration, is all one as to be infinite in essence. It is as reasonable to conceive a creature immense, filling all places at once, as eternal, extended to all ages; because neither can be without infiniteness, which is the property of the Deity.‡ A creature may as well be without bounds of place, as limitations of time.

4. No effect of an intellectual free agent, can be equal in duration to its cause. The production of natural agents are as ancient often as themselves : the sun produceth a beam as old in time as itself ; but who ever heard of a piece of wise workmanship as old as the wise artificer ? God produced a creature, not necessarily and naturally, as the sun doth a beam, but freely,

* Bapt.   † Lessius de Perfect., lib. iv. cap. 2.   ‡ Ibid.

as an intelligent agent. The sun was not necessary; it might be or not be, according to the pleasure of God. A free act of the will is necessary to precede in order of time, as the cause of such effects as are purely voluntary.* Those causes that act as soon as they exist, act naturally, necessarily, not freely, and cannot cease from acting.

But suppose a creature might have existed by the will of God from eternity: yet, as some think, it could not be said, absolutely and in its own nature, to be eternal, because eternity was not of the essence of it. The creature could not be its own duration; for though it were from eternity, it might not have been from eternity, because its existence depended upon the free will of God, who might have chose whether he would have created it or no.

God only is eternal, 'the first and the last, the beginning and the end,' who, as he subsisted before any creature had a being, so he will eternally subsist, if all creatures were reduced to nothing.

IV. *Use.* 1. Information.

. (1.) If God be of an eternal duration, then Christ is God. Eternity is the property of God, but it is ascribed to Christ: 'He is before all things,' Col. i. 17, *i. e.* all created things. He is therefore no creature; and if no creature, eternal. 'All things were created by him,' both in heaven and in earth, angels as well as men, 'whether they be thrones or dominions,' Col. i. 16. If all things were his creatures, then he is no creature; if he were, all things were not created by him, or he must create himself.

He hath no difference of time, for he is 'the same yesterday, to-day, and for ever,' Heb. xiii. 8; Rev. i. 8, 'He which is, and which was, and which is to come:' the same with the name of God, *I am*, which signifies his eternity. He is no more to-day than he was yesterday, nor will be any other to-morrow than he is to-day; and therefore Melchisedec, whose descent, birth and death, father and mother, beginning and end of days, are not upon record, was a type of the existence of Christ, without difference of time: 'Having neither beginning of days nor end of life, but made like the Son of God,' Heb. vii. 3. The suppression of his birth and death was intended by the Holy Ghost as a type of the excellency of Christ's person in regard of his eternity, and the duration of his charge in regard of his priesthood. As there was an appearance of an eternity in the suppression of the race of Melchisedec, so there is a true eternity in the Son of God. How could the eternity of the Son of God be expressed by any resemblance so well, as by such a suppression of the beginning and end of this great person, different from the custom of the Spirit of God in the Old Testament, who often records the generations and ends of holy men; and why might not this, which was a kind of a shadow of eternity, be a representation of the true eternity of Christ, as well as the restoration of Isaac to his father without death, is said to be a figure of the resurrection of Christ after a real death.† Melchisedec is only mentioned once (without any record of his extraction), in his appearance to Abraham after his victory, as if he came from heaven only for that action, and instantly disappeared again, as if he had been an eternal person.

And Christ himself hints his own eternity: 'I came forth from the Father, and am come into the world; again I leave the world, and go to the Father,' John xvi. 28. He goes to the Father as he came from the Father; he goes to the Father for everlasting, so he came from the Father from everlasting; there is the same duration in coming forth from the Father as in returning to the Father. But more plainly, John xvii. 5, he speaks of a glory that he 'had with the Father before the world was,' when there was no creature

* Crellius de Deo, cap. 18, p. 43.   † Mestræzat. *in loc.*

in being; this is an actual glory, and not only in decree; for a decreed glory believers had, and why may not every one of them say the same words, 'Father, glorify me with that glory which I had with thee before the world was,' if it were only a glory in decree? Nay, it may be said of every man, he was before the world was, because he was so in decree. Christ speaks of something peculiar to him, a glory in actual possession before the world was; glorify me, embrace, honour me as thy Son, whereas I have now been in the eyes of the world handled disgracefully as a servant. If it were only in decree, why is not the like expression used of others in Scripture, as well as of Christ? Why did he not use the same words for his disciples that were then with him, who had a glory in decree? His eternity is also mentioned in the Old Testament; 'The Lord possessed me in the beginning of his way, before his works of old,' Prov. viii. 22. If he were the work of God, he existed before himself if he existed before all the works of God; it is not so properly meant of the essential wisdom of God, since the discourse runs in the name of a person, and several passages there are which belong not so much to the essential wisdom of God, as ver. 13, 'The evil way and the froward mouth do I hate;' which belongs rather to the holiness of God than to the essential wisdom of God; besides, it is distinguished from Jehovah, as possessed by him and rejoicing before him. Yet plainer, Micah v. 2, 'Out of thee,' i. e. Bethlehem, 'shall he come forth to be ruler in Israel, whose goings forth have been from of old, from everlasting,' מִימֵי עוֹלָם, 'from the ways* of eternity.' There are two goings forth of Christ described, one from Bethlehem in the days of his incarnation, and another from eternity. The Holy Ghost adds after his prediction of his incarnation, his going out from everlasting, that none should doubt of his deity. If this going out from everlasting were only in the purpose of God, it might be said of David and of every creature. And in Isa. ix. he is particularly called the Everlasting, or eternal Father; not the Father in the Trinity, but a father to us; yet eternal, the Father of eternity. As he is 'the mighty God,' so he is 'the everlasting Father.' Can such a title be ascribed to any whose being depends upon the will of another, and may be dashed out at the pleasure of a superior?

As the eternity of God is the ground of all religion, so the eternity of Christ is the ground of the Christian religion. Could our sins be perfectly expiated had he not an eternal divinity to answer for the offences committed against an eternal God? Temporary sufferings had been of little validity, without an infiniteness and eternity in his person to add weight to his passion.

(2.) If God be eternal, he knows all things as present.† All things are present to him in his eternity; for this is the notion of eternity, to be without succession. If eternity be one indivisible point, and is not diffused into preceding and succeeding parts, then that which is known in it or by it is perceived without any succession, for knowledge is as the substance of the person knowing; if that hath various actions and distinct from itself, then it understands things in differences of time as time presents them to view; but since God's being depends not upon the revolutions of time, so neither doth this knowledge; it exceeds all motions of years and days, comprehends infinite spaces of past and future. God considers all things in his eternity in one simple knowledge, as if they were now acted before him: Acts xv. 18, 'Known unto God are all his works from the beginning of the world;' ἀπ' αἰῶνος, à seculo, from eternity. God's knowledge is co-eternal with him. If he knows that in time which he did not know from eternity, he would not be eternally perfect, since knowledge is the perfection of an intelligent nature.

* Qu. 'days'?—ED.   † Petav.

(3.) How bold and foolish is it for a mortal creature to censure the counsels and actions of an eternal God, or be too curious in his inquisitions? It is by the consideration of the unsearchable number of the years of God that Elihu checks too bold inquiries: 'Who hath enjoined him his way, or who can say thou hast wrought iniquity? Behold, God is great, and we know him not, neither can the number of his years be searched out,' Job xxxvi. 26 compared with ver. 23. Eternity sets God above our inquiries and censures. Infants of a day old are not able to understand the acts of wise and grey heads. Shall we, that are of so short a being and understanding as yesterday, presume to measure the motions of eternity by our scanty intellects? we that cannot foresee an unexpected accident which falls in to blast a well laid design, and run a ship many leagues back from the intended harbour? We cannot understand the reason of things we see done in time, the motions of the sea, the generation of rain, the nature of light, the sympathies and antipathies of the creatures; and shall we dare to censure the actions of an eternal God, so infinitely beyond our reach? The counsels of a boundless being are not to be scanned by the brain of a silly worm, that hath breathed but a few minutes in the world. Since eternity cannot be comprehended in time, it is not to be judged by a creature of time. 'Let us remember to magnify his works which we behold,' because he is eternal, which is the exhortation of Elihu backed by this doctrine of God's eternity, Job xxxvi. 24, and not accuse any work of him who is the ancient of days, or presume to direct him of whose eternity we come infinitely short. Whenever therefore any unworthy notion of the counsels and works of God is suggested to us by Satan or our own corrupt hearts, let us look backward to God's eternal and our own short duration, and silence ourselves with the same question wherewith God put a stop to the reasoning of Job, chap. xxxviii. 4, 'Where wast thou when I laid the foundations of the earth?' and reprove ourselves for our curiosity, since we are of so short a standing, and were nothing when the eternal God laid the first stone of the world.

(4.) What a folly and boldness is there in sin, since an eternal God is offended thereby! All sin is aggravated by God's eternity. The blackness of the heathen idolatry was in changing 'the glory of the *incorruptible* God,' Rom. i. 23, erecting resemblances of him contrary to his immortal nature; as if the eternal God, whose life is as unlimited as eternity, were like those creatures whose beings are measured by the short ell of time, which are of a corruptible nature, and daily passing on to corruption. They could not really deprive God of his glory and immortality, but they did in estimation. There is in the nature of every sin a tendency to reduce God to a not being. He that thinks unworthily of God, or acts unworthily towards him, doth (as much as in him lies) sully and destroy these two perfections of his, immutability and eternity. It is a carriage as if he were as contemptible as a creature that were but of yesterday, and shall not remain in being to-morrow. He that would put an end to God's glory by darkening it, would put an end to God's life by destroying it. He that should love a beast with as great an affection as he loves a man, contemns a rational creature, and he that loves a perishing thing with the same affection he should love an everlasting God, contemns his eternity; he debaseth the duration of God below that of the world; the low valuation of God speaks him, in his esteem, no better than withering grass, or a gourd, which lasts for a night; and the creature, which possesses his affection, to be a good that lasts for ever. How foolish then is every sin, that tends to destroy a being that cannot destroy or desert himself; a being, without whose eternity the sinner himself could not have had the capacity of a being, to affront him! How base is that which would not let the works of God remain in their established posture ! How much more base in not enduring the fountain and glory of all beings, that would not only put an end to the beauty of the world, but the eternity of God !

(5.) How dreadful is it to lie under the stroke of an eternal God ! His eternity is as great a terror to him that hates him, as it is a comfort to him that loves him, because he is the ' living God, an everlasting king, the nations shall not be able to abide his indignation,' Jer. x. 10. Though God be least in their thoughts, and is made light of in the world, yet the thoughts of God's eternity, when he comes to judge the world, shall make the slighters of him tremble. That the judge and punisher lives for ever is the greatest grievance to a soul in misery, and adds an unconceivable weight to it, above what the infiniteness of God's executive power could do without that duration ; his eternity makes the punishment more dreadful than his power ; his power makes it sharp, but his eternity renders it perpetual ; ever to endure is the sting at the end of every lash.

And how sad is it to think that God lays his eternity to pawn for the punishment of obstinate sinners, and engageth it by an oath, that he will ' whet his glittering sword,' that his ' hand shall take hold of judgment,' that he will ' render vengeance to his enemies, and a reward to them that hate him,' a reward proportioned to the greatness of their offences, and the glory of an eternal God ! Deut. xxxii. 40, 41, ' I lift up my hand to heaven, and say, I live for ever ;' *i. e.* as surely as I live for ever, I will whet my glittering sword. As none can convey good with a perpetuity, so none can convey evil with such a lastingness as God. It is a great loss to lose a ship richly fraught in the bottom of the sea, never to be cast upon the shore ; but how much greater is it to lose eternally a sovereign God,* which we were capable of eternally enjoying, and undergo an evil as durable as that God we slighted, and were in a possibility of avoiding ? The miseries of men after this life are not eased, but sharpened by the life and eternity of God.

Use 2. The second use is of comfort. What foundation of comfort can we have in any of God's attributes, were it not for his infiniteness and eternity, though he be merciful, good, wise, faithful. What support could there be if they were perfections belonging to a corruptible God ? What hopes of a resurrection to happiness can we have, or of the duration of it, if that God that promised it were not immortal to continue it, as well as powerful to effect it ? His power were not almighty, if his duration were not eternal.

1. If God be eternal, his covenant will be so. It is founded upon the eternity of God ; the oath whereby he confirms it, is by his life. Since there is none greater than himself, he swears by himself, Heb. vi. 13, or by his own life, which he engageth, together with his eternity, for the full performance, so that if he lives for ever, the covenant shall not be disannulled, it is an immutable counsel, ver. 16, 17. The immutability of his counsel follows the immutability of his nature. Immutability and eternity go hand in hand together. The promise of eternal life is as ancient as God himself in regard of the purpose of the promise, or in regard of the promise made to Christ for us : Titus i. 2, ' Eternal life, which God promised before the world began.' As it hath an ante-eternity, so it hath a post-eternity ; therefore the gospel, which is the new covenant published, is termed ' the everlasting gospel,' Rev. xiv. 6, which can no more be altered and perish than God can change and vanish into nothing. He can as little morally deny his truth as he can naturally desert his life. The covenant is there represented in a green colour, to note its perpetual verdure. ' The rainbow,' the

* Qu. ' good'?—Ed.

emblem of the covenant ' about the throne, was like to an emerald,' a stone of a green colour, Rev. iv. 3; whereas the natural rainbow hath many colours, but this but one, to signify its eternity.

2. If God be eternal, he being our God in covenant, is an eternal good and possession. 'This God is our God for ever and ever,' Ps. xlviii. 14; he is a ' dwelling place in all generations.' We shall traverse the world a while, and then arrive at the blessings Jacob wished for Joseph : ' The blessings of the everlasting hills,' Gen. xlix. 26. If an estate of a thousand pound per annum render a man's life comfortable for a short time, how much more may the soul be swallowed up with joy in the enjoyment of the Creator, whose years never fail, who lives for ever to be enjoyed, and can keep us in life for ever to enjoy him! Death indeed will seize upon us by God's irreversible order, but the immortal Creator will make him disgorge his morsel, and land us in a glorious immortality, our souls at their dissolution, and our bodies at the resurrection ; after which they shall remain for ever, and employ the extent of that boundless eternity in the fruition of the sovereign and eternal God ; for it is impossible that the believer, who is united to the immortal God, that is from everlasting to everlasting, can ever perish ; for being in conjunction with him who is an ever flowing fountain of life, he cannot suffer him to remain in the jaws of death. While God is eternal, and always the same, it is not possible that those that partake of his spiritual life should not also partake of his eternal ; it is from the considera- tion of the endlessness of the years of God that the church comforts herself, that her ' children shall continue,' and ' their seed be established for ever,' Ps. cii. 27, 28. And from the eternity of God, Habakkuk, chap. i. ver. 12, concludes the eternity of believers, ' Art thou not from everlasting, O Lord my God, my Holy One ? we shall not die, O Lord.' After they are retired from this world, they shall live for ever with God, without any change by the multitude of those imaginable years and ages that shall run for ever. It is that God that hath neither beginning nor end, that is our God, who hath not only immortality in himself, but immortality to give out to others. As he hath abundance of Spirit to quicken them, Mal. ii. 15, so he hath abundance of immortality to continue them. It is only in the consideration of this a man can with wisdom say, ' Soul, take thy ease, thou hast goods laid up for many years;' to say it of any other possession, is the greatest folly in the judgment of our Saviour, Luke xii. 19, 20. Mortality shall be swallowed up of immortality ; rivers of pleasure shall be for evermore. Death is a word never spoken there by any, never heard by any in that possession of eternity ; it is for ever put out, as one of Christ's conquered enemies.

The happiness depends upon the presence of God, with whom believers shall be for ever present. Happiness cannot perish as long as God lives : he is the first and the last ; the first of all delights, nothing before him; the last of all pleasures, nothing beyond him : a paradise of delights in every point, without a flaming sword.

3. The enjoyment of God will be as fresh and glorious after many ages as it was at first. God is eternal, and eternity knows no change ; there will then be the fullest possession, without any decay in the object enjoyed. There can be nothing past, nothing future ; time neither adds to it, nor detracts from it ; that infinite fulness of perfection which flourisheth in him now, will flourish eternally, without any discolouring of it in the least by those innumerable ages that shall run to eternity, much less any despoiling him of them. He is the same in his endless duration, Ps. cii. 27. As God is, so will the eternity of him be, without succession, without division.

The fulness of joy will be always present; without past to be thought of with regret for being gone, without future to be expected with tormenting desires. When we enjoy God, we enjoy him in his eternity without any flux, an entire possession of all together, without the passing away of pleasures that may be wished to return, or expectation of future joys which might be desired to hasten. Time is fluid, but eternity is stable; and after many ages, the joys will be as savoury and satisfying as if they had been but that moment first tasted by our hungry appetites. When the glory of the Lord shall rise upon you, it shall be so far from ever setting, that after millions of years are expired, as numerous as the sands on the sea shore, the Sun, in the light of whose countenance you shall live, shall be as bright as at the first appearance. He will be so far from ceasing to flow, that he will flow as strong, as full as at the first communication of himself in glory to the creature. God therefore, as sitting upon his throne of grace, and acting according to his covenant, is like a jasper stone, which is of a green colour, a colour always delightful, Rev. iv. 3; because God is always vigorous and flourishing, a pure act of life, sparkling new and fresh rays of life and light to the creature, flourishing with a perpetual spring, and contenting the most capacious desire; forming your interest, pleasure, and satisfaction with an infinite variety, without any change or succession. He will have variety to increase delights, and eternity to perpetuate them; this will be the fruit of the enjoyment of an infinite, an eternal God. He is not a cistern, but a fountain, wherein water is always living, and never putrifies.

4. If God be eternal, here is a strong ground of comfort against all the distresses of the church, and the threats of the church's enemies. God's abiding for ever is the plea Jeremiah makes for his return to his forsaken church: Lament. v. 19, ' Thou, O Lord, remainest for ever; thy throne from generation to generation.' The church is weak; created things are easily cut off. What prop is there but that God that lives for ever? What though Jerusalem lost its bulwarks, the temple were defaced, the land wasted, yet the God of Jerusalem sits upon an eternal throne, and from everlasting to everlasting there is no diminution of his power. The prophet intimates in this complaint that it is not agreeable to God's eternity to forget his people, to whom he hath from eternity bore good will. In the greatest confusions, the church's eyes are to be fixed upon the eternity of God's throne, where he sits as governor of the world. No creature can take any comfort in this perfection but the church; other creatures depend upon God, but the church is united to him.

The first discovery of the name I AM, which signifies the divine eternity as well as immutability, was for the comfort of the oppressed Israelites in Egypt, Exod. iii. 14, 15; it was then published from the secret place of the Almighty, as the only strong cordial to refresh them. It hath not yet, it shall not ever lose its virtue in any of the miseries that have or shall successively befall the church; it is a comfort as durable as the God whose name it is. He is still I AM, and the same to the church as he was then to his Israel. His spiritual Israel have a greater right to the glories of it than the carnal Israel could have. No oppression can be greater than theirs; what was a comfort suited to that distress hath the same suitableness to every other oppression. It was not a temporary name, but a name for ever, his ' memorial to all generations,' ver. 15, and reacheth to the church of the Gentiles, with whom he treats as the God of Abraham, ratifying that covenant by the Messiah, which he made with Abraham the father of the faithful.

The church's enemies are not to be feared; they may ' spring as the grass,' but soon after do wither by their own inward principles of decay, or are cut down by the hand of God, Ps. xcii. 7–9. They may be instruments of the anger of God, but they shall be scattered as the workers of iniquity, by the hand of the Lord ' that is high for evermore,' ver. 8, and is engaged by his promise to preserve a church in the world. They may threaten, but their breath may vanish as soon as their threatenings are pronounced, for they carry their breath in no surer a place than their own nostrils, upon which the eternal God can put his hand, and sink them with all their rage. 'Do the prophets' and the instructors of the church ' live for ever ? ' Zech. i. 15. No. Shall, then, the adversaries and disturbers of the church live for ever ? They shall vanish as a shadow ; their being depends upon the eternal God of the faithful, and the everlasting judge of the wicked. He that inhabits eternity is above them that inhabit mortality, and must, whether they will or no, ' say to corruption, Thou art my father ; and to the worm, Thou art my mother, and my sister,' Job. xvii. 14. When they will act with a confidence as if they were living gods, he will not be mated, but evidence himself to be a living God above them. Why then should mortal men be feared in their frowns, when an immortal God hath promised protection in his word, and lives for ever to perform it ?

5. Hence follows another comfort ; since God is eternal, he hath as much power as will to be as good as his word. His promises are established upon his eternity, and this perfection is a main ground of trust : Isa. xxvi. 4, ' Trust in the Lord for ever, for in the Lord Jehovah is everlasting strength,' ביה יהוה צור עולמים. His name is doubled, that name Jah and Jehovah, which was always the strength of his people, and not a single one, but the strength or rock of eternities ; not a failing, but an eternal truth and power ; that as his strength is eternal, so our trust in him should imitate his eternity in its perpetuity ; and therefore in the despondency of his people, as if God had forgot his promises and made no account of them, or his word, and were weary of doing good, he calls them to reflect on what they had heard of his eternity, which is attended with immutability, who hath an infiniteness of power to perform his will, and an infiniteness of understanding to judge of the right seasons of it, Isa. xl. 27, 28 ; his wisdom, will, truth, have always been, and will to eternity be, the same. He wants not life any more than love for ever to help us ; since his word is past, he will never fail us ; since his life continues, he can never be out of a capacity to relieve us ; and therefore, whenever we foolishly charge him by our distrustful thoughts, we forget his love, which made the promise, and his eternal life, which can accomplish it. As his word is the bottom of our trust, and his truth is the assurance of his sincerity, so his eternity is the assurance, of his ability to perform. His ' word stands for ever,' Isa. xl. 8. A man may be my friend this day, and be in another world to-morrow ; and though he be never so sincere in his word, yet death snaps his life asunder, and forbids the execution. But as God cannot die, so he cannot lie, because he is the eternity of Israel : 1 Sam. xv. 29, ' The strength of Israel will not lie nor repent,' נצח, perpetuity or eternity of Israel. Eternity implies immutability ; we could have no ground for our hopes if we knew him not to be longer lived than ourselves. The psalmist beats off our hands from trust in men, because ' their breath goes forth, they return to their earth, and in that day their thoughts perish,' Ps. cxlvi. 3, 4. And if the God of Jacob were like them, what happiness could we have in making him our help ? As his sovereignty in giving precepts had not been a strong ground of obedience, without considering him as an eternal lawgiver, who could maintain his rights ; so his kindness in making the promises had not been a strong ground

of confidence, without considering him as an eternal promiser, whose thoughts and whose life can never perish.* And this may be one reason why the Holy Ghost mentions so often the post-eternity of God, and so little his ante-eternity; because that is the strongest foundation of our faith and hope, which respects chiefly that which is future, and not that which is past, yet, indeed, no assurance of his after-eternity can be had if his ante-eternity be not certain. If he had a beginning, he may have an end; and if he had a change in his nature, he might have in his counsels; but since all the resolves of God are as himself is, eternal, and all the promises of God are the fruits of his counsel, therefore they cannot be changed. If he should change them for the better, he would not have been eternally wise, to know what was best; if for the worse, he had not been eternally good or just. Men may break their promises, because they are made without foresight; but God, that inhabits eternity, foreknows all things that shall be done under the sun, as if they had been then acting before him; and nothing can intervene, or work a change in his resolves, because the least circumstances were eternally foreseen by him. Though there may be variations and changes to our sight, the winds may tack about, and every hour new and cross accidents happen, yet the eternal God, who is eternally true to his word, sits at the helm, and the winds and the waves obey him. And though he should defer his promise a thousand years, yet he is 'not slack,' 2 Peter iii. 8, 9, for he defers it but a day to his eternity; and who would not with comfort stay a day in expectation of a considerable advantage?

Use 8 is for exhortation.

1. To something which concerns us in ourselves.

2. To something which concerns us with respect to God.

1. To something which concerns us in ourselves.

(1.) Let us be deeply affected with our sins long since committed. Though they are past with us, they are in regard of God's eternity present with him; there is no succession in eternity as there is in time. All things are before God at once; our sins are before him, as if committed this moment, though committed long ago. As he is what he is in regard of duration, so he knows what he knows in regard of knowledge; as he is not more than he was, nor shall not be any more than he is, so he always knew what he knows, and shall not cease to know what he now knows; as himself, so his knowledge is one indivisible point of eternity. He knows nothing but what he did know from eternity; he shall know no more for the future than he now knows. Our sins being present with him in his eternity, should be present with us in regard of our remembrance of them, and sorrow for them. What though many years are lapsed, much time run out, and our iniquities almost blotted out of our memory! yet since a thousand years are in God's sight, and in regard of his eternity, but as a day,—Ps. xc. 4, 'A thousand years in thy sight are but as yesterday when it is past, and as a watch in the night,'— they are before him; for, suppose a man were as old as the world, above five thousand six hundred years, the sins committed five thousand years ago are, according to that rule, but as if they were committed five days ago, so that sixty-two years are but as an hour and a-half, and the sins committed forty years since are as if they were committed but this present hour. But if we will go further, and consider them but as a watch of the night, about three hours (for the night, consisting of twelve hours, was divided into set watches), then a thousand years are but as three hours in the sight of God, and then sins committed sixty years ago are but as if they were committed within this five minutes.

* Crellius de Deo. cap. 18, p. 44, 45.

Let none of us set light by the iniquities committed many years ago, and imagine that length of time can wipe out their guilt. No; let us consider them in relation to God's eternity, and excite an inward remorse, as if they had been but the birth of this moment.

(2.) Let the consideration of God's eternity abate our pride. This is the design of the verses following the text, the eternity of God being so sufficient to make us understand our own nothingness, which ought to be one great end of man, especially as fallen. The eternity of God should make us as much disesteem ourselves, as the excellency of God made Job abhor himself, Job xlii. 5, 6. His excellency should humble us under a sense of our vanity, and his eternity under a sense of the shortness of our duration. If man compares himself with other creatures, he may be too sensible of his greatness; but if he compares himself with God, he cannot but be sensible of his baseness.

[1.] In regard of our impotence to comprehend this eternity of God. How little do we know, how little can we know, of God's eternity! We cannot fully conceive it, much less express it: we have a brutish understanding in all those things, as Agur said of himself, Prov. xxx. 7.

What is infinite and eternal cannot be comprehended by finite and temporary creatures. If it could, it would not be infinite and eternal; for to know a thing, is to know the extent and cause of it. It is repugnant to eternity to be known, because it hath no limits, no causes; the most soaring understanding cannot have a proportionable understanding of it.* What disproportion is there between a drop of water and the sea, in their greatness and motion! Yet by a drop we may arrive to a knowledge of the nature of the sea, which is a mass of drops joined together; but the longest duration of times cannot make us know what eternity is, because there is no proportion between time and eternity. The years of God are as numberless as his thoughts, Ps. xl. 5, and our minds as far from reckoning the one as the other. If our understandings are too gross to comprehend the majesty of his infinite works, they are much more too short to comprehend the infiniteness of his eternity.

[2.] In regard of the vast disproportion of our duration to this duration of God.

First, We have more of not being than being. We were nothing from an unbegun eternity, and we might have been nothing to an endless eternity, had not God called us unto being; and if he please, we may be nothing by a short annihilating word, as we were something by a creating word. As it is the prerogative of God to be ' *I am that I am*,' so it is the property of a creature to be *I am not what I am;* I am not by myself what I am, but by the indulgence of another. I was nothing formerly, I may be nothing again, unless he that is *I am* make me to subsist what I now am. Nothing is as much the title of the creature, as being is the title of God. Nothing is so holy as God, because nothing hath being as God: 1 Sam. ii. 2, ' There is none holy as the Lord; for there is none besides thee.' Man's life is an image, a dream, which are next to nothing; and if compared with God, worse than nothing, a nullity as well as a vanity; because ' with God only is the fountain of life,' Ps. xxxvi. 9. The creature is but a drop of life from him, dependent on him. A drop of water is a nothing, if compared with the vast conflux of waters, and numberless drops in the ocean.

How unworthy is it for dust and ashes, kneaded together in time, to strut against the Father of eternity! Much more unworthy for that which is

* Charron. Vent. liv. i. chap. 5, p. 17, &c.

nothing, worse than nothing, to quarrel with that which is only being, and equal himself with him that inhabits eternity.

Secondly, What being we have, had a beginning. After an unaccountable eternity was run out, in the very dregs of time, a few years ago we were created, and made of the basest and vilest dross of the world, the slime and dust of the earth; made of that wherewith birds build their nests; made of that which creeping things make their habitation, and beasts trample upon. How monstrous is pride in such a creature, to aspire, as if he were the Father of eternity, and as eternal as God, and so his own eternity!

Thirdly, What being we have, is but of a short duration in regard of our life in this world. Our life is a constant change and flux: we remain not the same an entire day; youth quickly succeeds childhood, and age as speedily treads upon the heels of youth; there is a continual defluxion of minutes, as there is of sands in a glass. He is as a watch wound up at the beginning of his life, and from that time is running down till he comes to the bottom: some part of our lives is cut off every day, every minute. Life is but a moment, what is past cannot be recalled; what is future cannot be insured. If we enjoy this moment, we have lost that which is past, and shall presently lose this by the next that is to come.

The short duration of men is set out in Scripture by such creatures as soon disappear: a worm, Job xxv. 6, that can scarce live a winter; grass, that withers by the summer sun. Life is a flower soon withering, Job xiv. 2; a vapour soon vanishing, James iv. 14; a smoke soon disappearing, Ps. cii. 3. The strongest man is but compacted dust, the fabric must moulder, the highest mountain falls and comes to nought. Time gives place to eternity; we live now, and die to-morrow. Not a man, since the world began, ever lived a day in God's sight; for no man ever lived a thousand years. The longest day of any man's life never amounted to twenty-four hours in the account of divine eternity. A life of so many hundred years, with the addition 'he died,' makes up the greatest part of the history of the patriarchs, Gen. v.; and since the life of man hath been curtailed, if any be in the world eighty years, he scarce properly lives sixty of them, since the fourth part of time is at least consumed in sleep.

A greater difference there is between the duration of God and that of a creature, than between the life of one for a minute, and the life of one that should live as many years as the whole globe of heaven and earth, if changed into papers, could contain figures. And this life, though but of short duration according to the period God hath determined, is easily cut off; the treasure of life is deposited in a brittle vessel. A small stone hitting against Nebuchadnezzar's statue will tumble it down into a poor and nasty grave; a grape-stone, the bone of a fish, a small fly in the throat, a moist damp, are enough to destroy an earthly eternity, and reduce it to nothing.

What a nothing then is our shortness, if compared with God's eternity! our frailty, with God's duration! How humble then should perishing creatures be before an eternal God, with whom 'our days are as a hand's-breadth, and our age as nothing'! Ps. xxxix. 5. The angels, that have been of as long a duration as heaven and earth, tremble before him, the heavens melt at his presence; and shall we, that are but of yesterday, approach a divine eternity with unhumbled souls, and offer the calves of our lips with the pride of devils, and stand upon our terms with him, without falling upon our faces, with a sense that we are but dust and ashes, and creatures of time? How easily it is to reason out man's humility, but how hard is it to reason man into it!

(3.) Let the consideration of God's eternity take off our love and confidence from the world, and the things thereof. The eternity of God reproaches a pursuit of the world, as preferring a momentary pleasure before an everlasting God; as though a temporal world could be a better supply than a God whose years never fail. Alas, what is this earth men are so greedy of, and will get, though by blood and sweat! What is this whole earth, if we had the entire possession of it, if compared with the vast heavens, the seat of angels and blessed spirits! It is but as an atom to the greatest mountain, or a drop of dew to the immense ocean. How foolish is it to prefer a drop before the sea, or an atom before the world! The earth is but a point to the sun, the sun with its whole orb but a little part of the heavens, compared with the whole fabric. If a man had the possession of all those, there could be no comparison between those that have had a beginning, and shall have an end, and God, who is without either of them. Yet how many are there that make nothing of the divine eternity, and imagine an eternity of nothing!

[1.] The world hath been but of a short standing. It is not yet six thousand years since the foundations of it were laid, and therefore it cannot have a boundless excellency, as that God, who hath been from everlasting, doth possess. If Adam had lived to this day, and been as absolute lord of his posterity as he was of the other creatures, had it been a competent object to take up his heart, had he not been a madman to have preferred this little created pleasure before an everlasting, uncreated God; a thing that had a dependent beginning, before that which had an independent eternity!

[2.] The beauties of the world are transitory and perishing. The whole world is nothing else but a fluid thing, the fashion of it is a pageantry 'passing away,' 1 Cor. vii. 31. Though the glories of it might be conceived greater than they are, yet they are not consistent, but transient. There cannot be an entire enjoyment of them, because they grow up and expire every moment, and slip away between our fingers while we are using them. Have we not heard of God's dispersing the greatest empires like 'chaff before a whirlwind, or as smoke out of a chimney,' Hosea xiii. 3, which, though it appears as a compacted cloud, as if it would choke the sun, is quickly scattered into several parts of the air, and becomes invisible? Nettles have often been heirs to stately palaces, as God threatens Israel, Hosea ix. 6. We cannot promise ourselves over night anything the next day. A kingdom with the glory of a throne may be cut off in a morning, Hosea x. 15. The new wine may be taken from the mouth when the vintage is ripe, the devouring locust may snatch away both the hopes of that and the harvest, Joel i. 15; they are therefore things which are not, and nothing cannot be a fit object for confidence or affection: Prov. xxiii. 5, 'Wilt thou set thy eyes upon that which is not? for riches certainly make themselves wings.' They are not properly beings, because they are not stable, but flitting. They are not, because they may not be the next moment to us what they are this; they are but cisterns, not springs; and 'broken cisterns,' not sound and stable; no solidity in their substance, nor stability in their duration. What a foolish thing is it then to prefer a transient felicity, a mere nullity, before an eternal God! What a senseless thing would it be in a man to prefer the map of a kingdom, which the hand of a child can tear in pieces, before the kingdom shadowed by it! How much more inexcusable is it to value things that are so far from being eternal, that they are not so much as dusky resemblances of an eternity! Were the things of the world more glorious than they are, yet they are but as a counterfeit sun in a cloud, which comes short of the true sun in the heavens both in glory and duration; and to esteem them before God is inconceivably baser than if a man should value a parti-coloured bubble in the air before a durable rock of diamonds. The comforts of this world are as candles that will end in a snuff, whereas the felicity that flows from an eternal God is like the sun, that shines more and more to a perfect day.

[3.] They cannot therefore be fit for a soul which was made to have an interest in God's eternity. The soul being of a perpetual nature, was made for the fruition of an eternal good; without such a good, it can never be perfect. Perfection, that noble thing, riseth not from anything in this world, nor is it a title due to a soul while in this world. It is then they are said to be 'made perfect,' when they arrive at that entire conjunction with the eternal God in another life, Heb. xii. 23. The soul cannot be ennobled by an acquaintance with these things, or established by a dependence on them; they cannot confer what a rational nature should desire, or supply it with what it wants.

The soul hath a resemblance to God in a post-eternity. Why should it be drawn aside by the blandishments of earthly things, to neglect its true establishment, and lacquey after the body, which is but a shadow of the soul, and was made to follow it and serve it! But while it busieth itself altogether in the concerns of a perishing body, and seeks satisfaction in things that glide away, it becomes rather a body than soul, descends below its nature, reproacheth that God who hath imprinted upon it an image of his own eternity, and loseth the comfort of the everlastingness of its Creator. How shall the whole world, if our lives were as durable as that, be an happy eternity to us, who have souls that shall survive all the delights of it, which must fry in those flames that shall fire the whole frame of nature at the general conflagration of the world? 2 Peter iii. 10.

[4.] Therefore let us provide for an happy interest in the eternity of God. Man is made for an eternal state. The soul hath such a perfection in its nature, that it is fit for eternity, and cannot display all its operations but in eternity; to an eternity it must go, and live as long as God himself lives. Things of a short duration are not proportioned to a soul made for an eternal continuance; to see that it be a comfortable eternity, is worth all our care. Man is a forecasting creature, considers not only the present, but the future too, in his provisions for his family; and shall he disgrace his nature in casting off all consideration of a future eternity? Get possession therefore of the eternal God. A 'portion in this life' is the lot of those who shall be for ever miserable, Ps. xvii. 14; but God, an 'everlasting portion,' is the lot of them that are designed for happiness: 'God is my portion for ever,' Ps. lxxiii. 26.

Time is short, 1 Cor. vii. 29. The whole time for which God designed this building of the world is of a little compass; it is a stage erected for rational creatures to act their parts upon for a few thousand years, the greatest part of which time is run out, and then shall time like a rivulet fall into the sea of eternity, from whence it sprung. As time is but a slip of eternity, so it will end in eternity. Our advantages consist in the present instant; what is past never promised a return, and cannot be fetched back by all our vows; what is future we cannot promise ourselves to enjoy, we may be snatched away before it comes. Every minute that passeth speaks the fewer remaining till the time of death; and as we are every hour further from our beginning, we are nearer our end. The child born this day grows up, to grow nothing at last. In all ages 'there is but a step between us and death,' as David said of himself, 1 Sam. xx. 3. The little time that remains for the devil till the day of judgment, envenoms his wrath; he rageth, because 'his time is short,' Rev. xii. 12. The little time that remains between this moment and our death, should quicken our diligence to inherit the endless and unchangeable eternity of God.

[5.] Often meditate on the eternity of God. The holiness, power, and eternity of God are the fundamental articles of all religion, upon which the whole body of it leans: his holiness for conformity to him, his power and eternity for the support of faith and hope. The strong and incessant cries of the four beasts, representing that Christian church, are 'Holy, holy, holy, Lord God Almighty, which was, and is, and is to come,' Rev. iv. 8. Though his power is intimated, yet the chiefest are his holiness, three times expressed; and his eternity, which is repeated, ver. 9, 'who lives for ever and ever.' This ought to be the constant practice in the church of the Gentiles, which this book chiefly respects. The meditation of his converting grace manifested to Paul ravished the apostle's heart, but not without the triumphant consideration of his immortality and eternity, which are the principal parts of the doxology: 1 Tim. i. 15–17, 'Now unto the King eternal, immortal, invisible, only wise God, be honour and glory for ever and ever.' It could be no great transport to the spirit to consider him glorious, without considering him immortal; the unconfinedness of his perfections in regard of time presents the soul with matter of the greatest complacency. The happiness of our souls depends upon his other attributes, but the perpetuity of it upon his eternity. Is it a comfort to view his immense wisdom, his overflowing goodness, his tender mercy, his unerring truth? What comfort were there in any of those, if it were a wisdom that could be baffled, a goodness that could be damped, a mercy that can expire, and a truth that can perish with the subject of it! Without eternity, what were all his other perfections but as glorious yet withering flowers, a great but a decaying beauty! By a frequent meditation of God's eternity, we should become more sensible of our own vanity and the world's triflingness. How nothing should ourselves, how nothing would all other things appear in our eyes! how coldly should we desire them! how feebly should we place any trust in them! Should we not think ourselves worthy of contempt to doat upon a perishing glory, to expect support from an arm of flesh, when there is an eternal beauty to ravish us, an eternal arm to protect us? Asaph, when he considered God a 'portion for ever,' thought nothing of the glories of the earth, or the beauties of the created heavens worth his appetite or complacency, but God, Ps. lxxiii. 25, 26. Besides, an elevating frame of heart at the consideration of God's eternity, would batter down the strongholds and engines of any temptation. A slight temptation will not know where to find and catch hold of a soul high and hid in a meditation of it; and if he doth, there will not be wanting from hence preservatives to resist and conquer it. What transitory pleasures will not the thoughts of God's eternity stifle! When this work busieth a soul, it is too great to suffer it to descend, to listen to a sleeveless errand from hell or the world. The wanton allurements of the flesh will be put off with indignation. The proffers of the world will be ridiculous when they are cast into the balance with the eternity of God, which sticking in our thoughts, we shall not be so easy a prey for the fowler's gin.

Let us therefore often meditate upon this, but not in a bare speculation, without engaging our affections, and making every notion of the divine eternity end in a suitable impression upon our hearts. This would be much like the disciples gazing upon the heavens at the ascension of their Master, while they forgat the practice of his orders, Acts i. 11. We may else find something of the nature of God, and lose ourselves, not only in eternity, but to eternity.

2. And hence the second part of the exhortation is to something which concerns us with a respect to God.

(1.) If God be eternal, how worthy is he of our choicest affections, and strongest desires of communion with him! Is not everything to be valued according to the greatness of its being? How then should we love him, who is not only lovely in his nature,' but eternally lovely, having from ever-lasting all those perfections centred in himself, which appear in time! If everything be lovely, by how much the more it partakes of the nature of God, who is the chief good, how much more infinitely lovely is God, who is superior to all other goods, and eternally so! Not a God of a few minutes, months, years, or millions of years; not of the dregs of time or the top of time, but of eternity; above time, unconceivably immense beyond time. The loving him infinitely, perpetually, is an act of homage due to him for his eternal excellency. We may give him the one, since our souls are immortal, though we cannot the other, because they are finite. Since he encloseth in himself all the excellencies of heaven and earth for ever, he should have an affection, not only of time in this world, but of eternity in the future; and if we did not owe him a love for what we are by him, we owe him a love for what he is in himself; and more for what he is, than for what he is to us. He is more worthy of our affections because he is the eternal God, than because he is our Creator; because he is more excellent in his nature than in his transient actions. The beams of his goodness to us, are to direct our thoughts and affections to him; but his own eternal excellency ought to be the ground and foundation of our affections to him. And truly, since nothing but God is eternal, nothing but God is worth the loving; and we do but a just right to our love, to pitch it upon that which can always possess us and be possessed by us, upon an object that cannot deceive our affection, and put it out of countenance by a dissolution.

And if our happiness consists in being like to God, we should imitate him in loving him as he loves himself, and as long as he loves himself. God cannot do more to himself than love himself; he can make no addition to his essence, nor diminution from it. What should we do less to an eternal being, than to bestow affections upon him, like his own to himself, since we can find nothing so durable as himself, for which we should love it!

(2.) He only is worthy of our best service. The ' Ancient of days' is to be served before all that are younger than himself; our best obedience is due to him as a God of unconfined excellency. Every thing that is excellent deserves a veneration suitable to its excellency. As God is infinite, he hath right to a boundless service; as he is eternal, he hath right to a perpetual service. As service is a debt of justice upon the account of the excellency of his nature, so a perpetual service is as much a debt of justice upon the account of his eternity. If God be infinite and eternal, he merits an honour and comportment from his creatures suited to the unlimited perfection of his nature, and the duration of his being. How worthy is the psalmist's resolution, ' I will sing unto the Lord as long as I live; I will sing praises to my God while I have any being,' Ps. civ. 33. It is the use he makes of the endless duration of the glory of God, and will extend to all other service as well as praise. To serve other things, or to serve ourselves, is to waste a service upon that which is nothing. In devoting ourselves to God, we serve him that is; that was, so as that he never began; is to come, so as that he never shall end; by whom all things are what they are; who hath both eternal knowledge to remember our service, and eternal goodness to reward it.

A DISCOURSE UPON THE IMMUTABILITY
OF GOD.

They shall perish, but thou shalt endure; yea, all of them shall wax old as a
garment: as a vesture shalt thou change them, and they shall be changed:
but thou art the same, and thy years shall have no end.—Ps. CII. 26, 27.

THIS psalm contains a complaint of a people pressed with a great calamity;
some think of the Jewish church in Babylon, others think the psalmist doth
here personate mankind lying under a state of corruption, because he wishes
for the coming of the Messiah, to accomplish that redemption promised by
God, and needed by them. Indeed, the title of the psalm is 'A prayer of
the afflicted, when he is overwhelmed, and pours out his complaint before
the Lord:' whether afflicted with the sense of corruption, or with the sense
of oppression. And the redemption by the Messiah, which the ancient
church looked upon as the fountain of their deliverance from a sinful or a
servile bondage, is in this psalm spoken of: a set time appointed for the
discovery of his mercy to Sion, ver. 13; an appearance in glory to build up
Sion, ver. 16; the loosening of the prisoner by redemption, and them
that are appointed to death, ver. 20; the calling of the Gentiles, ver. 22;
and the latter part of the psalm, wherein are the verses I have read, are
applied to Christ, Heb. i. Whatsoever the design of the psalm might be,
many things are intermingled that concern the kingdom of the Messiah, and
redemption by Christ.

Some make three parts of the psalm.

1. A petition plainly delivered: ver. 1, 2, 'Hear my prayer, O Lord, and
let my cry come unto thee,' &c.

2. The petition strongly and argumentatively enforced and pleaded,
ver. 3, from the misery of the petitioner in himself, and his reproach from
his enemies.

3. An acting of faith, in the expectation of an answer in the general
redemption promised: ver. 12, 13, 'But thou, O Lord, shalt endure for
ever; thou shalt arise and have mercy upon Sion: the heathen shall fear
thy name.'

The first part is the petition pleaded, the second part is the petition
answered in an assurance that there should in time be a full deliverance.*

* Pareus.

The design of the penman is to confirm the church in the truth of the divine promises, that though the foundations of the world should be ripped up, and the heavens clatter together, and the whole fabric of them be unpinned and fall to pieces, the firmest parts of it dissolved, yet the church should continue in its stability, because it stands not upon the changeableness of creatures, but is built upon the immutable rock of the truth of God, which is as little subject to change as his essence.

They shall perish, thou shalt change them. As he had before ascribed to God the foundation of heaven and earth, ver. 25, so he ascribes to God here the destruction of them. Both the beginning and end of the world are here ascertained. There is nothing indeed from the present appearance of things that can demonstrate the cessation of the world. The heaven and earth stand firm; the motions of the heavenly bodies are the same, their beauty is not decayed; individuals corrupt, but the species and kinds remain; the successions of the year observe their due order, but the sin of man renders the change of the present appearance of the world necessary to accomplish the design of God for the glory of his elect. The heavens do not naturally perish, as some fancied an old age of the world, wherein it must necessarily decay, as the bodies of animals do; or that the parts of the heavens are broken off by their rubbing one against another in their motion, and falling to the earth, are the seeds of those things that grow up among us.*

The earth and heavens. He names here the most stable parts of the world, and the most beautiful parts of the creation, those that are freest from corruptibility and change, to illustrate thereby the immutability of God, that though the heavens and earth have a prerogative of fixedness above other parts of the world, and the creatures that reside below, the heavens remain the same as they were created, and the centre of the earth retains its fixedness, and are as beautiful and fresh in their age as they were in their youth many years ago, notwithstanding the change of the elements, fire and water being often turned into air, so that there may remain but little of that air which was first created by reason of the continual transmutation; yet this firmness of the earth and heavens is not to be regarded in comparison of the unmoveablenes and fixedness of the being of God. As their beauty comes short of the glory of his being, so doth their firmness come short of his stability.

Some by heavens and earth understand the creatures which reside in the earth, and those which are in the air, which is called heaven often in Scripture; but the ruin and fall of these being seen every day, had been no fit illustration of the unchangeableness of God.

'They shall perish, they shall be changed.'

1. They *may* perish, say some; they have it not from themselves that they do not perish, but from thee, who didst endue them with an incorruptible nature; they shall perish if thou speakest the word; thou canst with as much ease destroy them as thou canst create them. But the psalmist speaks not of their possibility, but the certainty of their perishing.

2. They *shall* perish in their qualities and motion, not in their substance, say others. They shall cease from that motion which is designed properly for the generation and corruption of things in the earth, but in regard of their substance and beauty they shall remain. As when the strings or wheels of a clock or watch are taken off, the material parts remain, though the motion of it, and the use for discovering the time of the day, ceaseth.†
To perish doth not signify always a falling into nothing, an annihilation, by

---

* Plin. Hist. lib. 2, cap. 3.   † Coccei. *in loc.*

which both the matter and the form are destroyed, but a ceasing of the present appearance of them; a ceasing to be what they now are, as a man is said to perish when he dies, whereas the better part of man doth not cease to be. The figure of the body moulders away, and the matter of it returns to dust; but the soul, being immortal, ceaseth not to act, when the body, by reason of the absence of the soul, is incapable of acting. So the heavens shall perish. The appearance they now have shall vanish, and a more glorious and incorruptible frame be erected by the power and goodness of God. The dissolution of heaven and earth is meant by the word *perish*; the raising a new frame is signified by the word *changed*; as if the Spirit of God would prevent any wrong meaning of the word *perish* by alleviating the sense of that by another which signifies only a mutation and change; as when we change a habit and garment, we quit the old to receive the new.

'As a garment, as a vesture.' Thou shalt change them;—Septuagint, ἀλίξεις, 'Thou shalt fold them up.' The heavens are compared to a curtain, Ps. civ. 2, and shall in due time be folded up as cloths and curtains are. As a garment encompasseth the whole body, so do the heavens encircle the earth.* Some say, as a garment is folded up to be laid aside, that when there is need it may be taken again for use, so shalt thou fold up the heavens like a garment, that when they are repaired, thou mayest again stretch them out about the earth; thou shalt fold them up, so that what did appear shall not now appear. It may be illustrated by the metaphor of a scroll or book, which the Spirit of God useth, Isa. xxxiv. 4, Rev. vi. 14, 'The heavens departed as a scroll when it is rolled together.' When a book is rolled up or shut, nothing can be read in it till it be opened again; so the face of the heavens, wherein the stars are as letters declaring the glory of God, shall be shut or rolled together, so that nothing shall appear till by its renovation it be opened again. As a garment it shall be changed, not to be used in the same fashion and for the same use again. It seems indeed to be for the worse; an old garment is not changed but into rags, to be put to other uses, and afterwards thrown upon the dunghill. But similitudes are not to be pressed too far; and this will not agree with the new heavens and new earth, physically so as well as metaphorically so. It is not likely the heavens will be put to a worse use than God designed them for in creation. However, a change as a garment speaks not a total corruption, but an alteration of qualities, as a garment, not to be used in the same fashion as before. We may observe,

1. That it is probable the world shall not be annihilated, but refined. It shall lose its present form and fashion, but not its foundation. Indeed, as God raised it from nothing, so he can reduce it into nothing; yet it doth not appear that God will annihilate it, and utterly destroy both the matter and form of it; part shall be consumed, and part purified: 2 Peter iii. 12, 13, 'The heavens shall be on fire, and dissolved. Nevertheless we, according to his promise, look for a new heaven and a new earth.' They shall be melted down, as gold by the artificer, to be refined from its dross, and wrought into a more beautiful fashion, that they may serve the design of God for those that shall reside therein; a new world, wherein righteousness shall dwell, the apostle opposing it thereby to the old world, wherein wickedness did reside. The heavens are to be purged, as the vessels that held the sin-offering were to be purified by the fire of the sanctuary.

God indeed will take down this scaffold, which he hath built to publish his glory. As every individual hath a certain term of its duration, so an

---

* Estius in Heb. i.

end is appointed for the universal nature of heaven and earth: Isa. li. 6, 'The heavens shall vanish like smoke' which disappears. As smoke is resolved and attenuated into air, not annihilated, so shall the world assume a new face, and have a greater clearness and splendour. As the bodies of men dissolved into dust shall have more glorious qualities at their resurrection ; as a vessel of gold is melted down to remove the batterings in it, and receive a more comely form by the skill of the workman.

(1.) The world was not destroyed by the deluge ; it was rather washed by water than consumed ; so it shall be rather refined by the last fire than lie under an irrecoverable ruin.

(2.) It is not likely God would liken the everlastingness of his covenant, and the perpetuity of his spiritual Israel, to the duration of the ordinances of the heavens (as he doth in Jer. xxxi. 35, 36) if they were wholly to depart from before him. Though that place may only tend to an assurance of a church in the world while the world endures, yet it would be but small comfort if the happiness of believers should endure no longer than the heavens and earth, if they were to have a total period.

(3.) Besides, the bodies of the saints must have place for their support to move in, and glorious objects fitted to those glorious senses which shall be restored to them. Not in any carnal way, which our Saviour rejects, when he saith there is no eating, or drinking, or marrying, &c., in the other world, but whereby they may glorify God ; though how or in what manner their senses shall be used would be rashness to determine ; only something is necessary for the corporeal state of men, that there may be an employment for their senses as well as their souls.

(4.) Again, How could the creature, the world, or any part of it, be said to be delivered from the bondage of corruption into the glorious liberty of the sons of God, if the whole frame of heaven and earth were to be annihilated ? Rom. viii. 21. The apostle also saith that ' the creature waits with an earnest expectation for this manifestation of the sons of God,' ver. 19, which would have no foundation if the whole frame should be reduced to nothing. What joyful expectation can there be in any of a total ruin ? How should the creature be capable of partaking in this glorious liberty of the sons of God ? * As the world, for the sin of man, lost its first dignity, and was cursed after the fall, and the beauty bestowed upon it by creation defaced, so it shall recover that ancient glory, when he shall be fully restored by the resurrection to that dignity he lost by his first sin. As man shall be freed from his corruptibility, to receive that glory which is prepared for him, so shall the creatures be freed from that imperfection or corruptibility, those stains and spots upon the face of them, to receive a new glory suited to their nature, and answerable to the design of God, when the glorious liberty of the saints shall be accomplished.† As, when a prince's nuptials are solemnised, the whole country echoes with joy, so the inanimate creatures, when the time of the marriage of the Lamb is come, shall have a delight and pleasure from that renovation. The apostle sets forth the whole world as a person groaning, and the Scripture is frequent in such metaphors, as when the creatures are said to wait upon God, and to be troubled, Ps. civ. 27, 29; the hills are said to leap, and the mountains to rejoice. The creature is said to groan, as the heavens are said to declare the glory of God, passively, naturally, not rationally. It is not likely angels are here meant, though they cannot but desire it : since they are affected with the dishonour and reproach God hath in the world, they cannot but long for the restoration of his honour, in the restoration of the creature to its true end. And indeed

* Hyper. in Heb. i.   † Mestræzat sur Heb. i.

the angels are employed to serve man in this sinful state, and cannot but in holiness wish the creature freed from his corruption. Nor is it meant of the new creatures, which have the first fruits of the Spirit, those he brings in afterwards, ver. 23, ' groaning,' and ' waiting for the adoption,' where he distinguisheth the rational creature from the creature he had spoken of before. If he had meant the believing creature by that creature that desired the liberty of the sons of God, what need had there been of that additional distinction, ' and not only they, but we also, who have the first fruits of the Spirit, groan within ourselves'? whereby it seems he means some crea- tures below rational creatures, since neither angels nor blessed souls can be said to travail in pain with that distress as a woman in travail hath, as the word signifies, who perform the work joyfully which God sets them upon.* If the creatures be subject to vanity by the sin of man, they shall also par- take of a happiness by the restoration of man. The earth hath both thorns and thistles and venomous beasts, the air hath had its tempests and infec- tious qualities, the water hath caused its floods and deluges. The creature hath been abused to luxury and intemperance, and been tyrannised over by man, contrary to the end of its creation. It is convenient that some time should be allotted for the creature's attaining its true end, and that it may partake of the peace of man, as it hath done of the fruits of his sin; other- wise it would seem that sin had prevailed more than grace, and would have had more power to deface, than grace to restore things into their due order.

(5.) Again, upon what account should the psalmist exhort the heavens to rejoice and the earth to be glad, when God comes to judge the world with righteousness, Ps. xcvi. 11–13, if they should be annihilated, and sunk for ever into nothing? It would seem, saith Daille, to be an impertinent figure if the Judge of the world brought them to a total destruction. An entire ruin could not be matter of triumph to creatures, who naturally have that instinct or inclination put into them by their Creator to preserve themselves, and to effect their own preservation.

(6.) Again, the Lord is to rejoice in his works, Ps. civ. 31: ' The glory of the Lord shall endure for ever; the Lord shall rejoice in his works;' not hath, but shall rejoice in his works; in the works of creation, which the psalmist had enumerated, and which is the whole scope of the psalm. And he intimates that it is part of the glory of the Lord which endures for ever; that is, his manifestative glory, to rejoice in his works. The glory of the Lord must be understood with reference to the creation he had spoken of before. How short was that joy God had in his works, after he had sent them beautified out of his hand! How soon did he ' repent' not only ' that he had made man,' but ' was grieved at the heart' also that he made the other creatures which man's sin had disordered! Gen. vi. 7. What joy can God have in them, since the curse upon the entrance of sin into the world remains upon them? If they are to be annihilated upon the full restoration of his holiness, what time will God have to rejoice in the other works of creation? It is the joy of God to see all his works in their due order, every one pointing to their true end, marching together in their excellency, accord- ing to his first intendment in their creation. Did God create the world to perform its end only for one day? Scarce so much, if Adam fell the very first day of his creation. What would have been their end if Adam had been confirmed in a state of happiness as the angels were, it is likely will be answered and performed upon the complete restoration of man to that happy state from whence he fell. What artificer compiles a work by his skill but to rejoice in it? and shall God have no joy from the works of his hands?

* Mestræzat sur. Heb. i.

Since God can only rejoice in goodness, the creatures must have that goodness restored to them which God pronounced them to have at the first creation, and which he ordained them for, before he can again rejoice in his works. The goodness of the creatures is the glory and joy of God.

Inf. 1. We may infer from hence, what a base and vile thing sin is, which lays the foundation of the world's change. Sin brings it to decrepit age ; sin overturned the whole work of God, Gen. iii. 17 ; so that to render it useful to its proper end, there is a necessity of a kind of a new creating it. This causes God to fire the earth, for a purification of it from that infection and contagion brought upon it by the apostasy and corruption of man. It hath served sinful man, and therefore must undergo a purging flame to be fit to serve the holy and righteous Creator. As sin is so riveted in the body of man, that there is need of a change by death to rase it out, so hath the curse for sin got so deep into the bowels of the world, that there is need of a change by fire to refine it for its Master's use. Let us look upon sin with no other notion than as the object of God's hatred, the cause of his grief in the creatures, and the spring of the pain and ruin of the world.

Inf. 2. How foolish a thing is it to set our hearts upon that which shall perish, and be no more what it is now ! The heavens and earth, the solidest and firmest parts of the creation, shall not continue in the posture they are, they must perish and undergo a refining change. How feeble and weak are the other parts of the creation, the little creatures walking upon and fluttering about the world, that are perishing and dying every day ; and we scarce see them clothed with life and beauty this day, but they wither and are despoiled of all the next ; and are such frail things fit objects for our everlasting spirits and affections ? Though the daily employment of the heavens is the declaration of the glory of God, Ps. xix. 1, yet neither this, nor their harmony, order, beauty, amazing greatness and glory of them, shall preserve them from a dissolution and melting at the presence of the Lord. Though they have remained in the same posture from the creation till this day, and are of so great antiquity, yet they must bow down to a change before the will and word of their Creator ; and shall we rest upon that which shall vanish like smoke ? Shall we take any creature for our support, like ice, that will crack under our feet, and must by the order of their Lord Creator deceive our hopes ? Perishing things can be no support to the soul ; if we would have rest, we must run to God and rest in God. How contemptible should that be to us, whose fashion shall pass away, which shall not endure long in its present form and appearance ; contemptible as a rest, not contemptible as the work of God ; contemptible as an end, not contemptible as a means to attain our end. If these must be changed, how unworthy are other things to be the centre of our souls, that change in our very using of them, and slide away in our very enjoyment of them.

' Thou art the same.' The essence of God, with all the perfections of his nature, are pronounced the same, without any variation from eternity to eternity. So that the text doth not only assert the eternal duration of God, but his immutability in that duration ; his eternity is signified in that expression ' thou shalt endure ;' his immutability in this, ' thou art the same.'* To endure, argues indeed this immutability as well as eternity ; for what endures is not changed, and what is changed doth not endure. But thou art the same ; אתה הוא, doth more fully signify it. He could not be the same if he could be changed into any other thing than what he is. The psalmist therefore puts, not thou *hast been* or *shall be*, but *thou art* the same, without any alteration ; thou art the same, that is, the same God, the same

* Estius in Heb. i.

in essence and nature, the same in will and purpose, thou dost change all other things as thou pleasest; but thou art immutable in every respect, and receivest no shadow of change, though never so light and small. The psalmist here alludes to the name *Jehovah, I am,** and doth not only ascribe immutability to God, but exclude everything else from partaking in that perfection. All things else are tottering; God sees all other things in continual motion under his feet, like water passing away and no more seen, while he remains fixed and immoveable. His wisdom and power, his knowledge and will, are always the same. His essence can receive no alteration, neither by itself nor by any external cause; whereas other things either naturally decline to destruction, pass from one term to another till they come to their period; or shall at the last day be wrapped up, after God hath completed his will in them and by them; as a man doth a garment he intends to repair and transform to another use.

So that in the text God, as immutable, is opposed to all creatures, as perishing and changeable.

Doct. God is unchangeable in his essence, nature, and perfections. Immutability and eternity are linked together; and indeed true eternity is true immutability, whence eternity is defined the possession of an immutable life. Yet immutability differs from eternity in our conception. Immutability respects the essence or existence of a thing, eternity respects the duration of a being in that state; or rather, immutability is the state itself,† eternity is the measure of that state. A thing is said to be changed, when it is otherwise now in regard of nature, state, will, or any quality than it was before; when either something is added to it or taken from it; when it either loses or acquires. But now it is the essential property of God, not to have any accession to, or diminution of, his essence or attributes, but to remain entirely the same. He wants nothing, he loses nothing, but doth uniformly exist by himself, without any new nature, new thought, new will, new purpose, or new place.

This unchangeableness of God was anciently represented by the figure of a cube,‡ a piece of metal or wood framed four square; when every side is exactly of the same equality, cast it which way you will, it will always be in the same posture, because it is equal to itself in all its dimensions. He was therefore said to be the centre of all things, and other things the circumference; the centre is never moved while the circumference is; it remains immoveable in the midst of the circle. ' There is no variableness nor shadow of turning with him,' James i. 17. The moon hath her spots, so hath the sun; there is a mixture of light and darkness; it hath its changes; sometimes it is in the increase, sometimes in the wane; it is always either gaining or losing, and by the turnings and motions, either of the heavenly bodies or of the earth, it is in its eclipse, by the interposition of the earth between that and the sun. The sun also hath its diurnal and annual motion; it riseth and sets, and puts on a different face. It doth not alway shine with a noonday light; it is sometimes vailed with clouds and vapours; it is always going from one tropic to another, whereby it makes various shadows on the earth, and produceth the various seasons of the year; it is not always in our hemisphere, nor doth it always shine with an equal force and brightness in it. Such shadows and variations have no place in the eternal Father of lights; he hath not the least spot or diminution of brightness; nothing can cloud him or eclipse him. For the better understanding this perfection of God,

---

* Ἀλλοιώσεως κρείττων, *above all change*, Theodor.
† Gamacheus.　　　　　‡ Amyrant sur Heb. ix. p. 153.

I shall premise three things.

1. The immutability of God is a perfection. Immutability considered in itself, without relation to other things, is not a perfection. It is the greatest misery and imperfection of the evil angels, that they are immutable in malice against God. But as God is infinite in essence, infinitely good, wise, holy; so it is a perfection necessary to his nature, that he should be immutably all this; all excellency, goodness, wisdom, immutably all that he is; without this he would be an imperfect being. Are not the angels in heaven, who are confirmed in a holy and happy state, more perfect than when they were in a possibility of committing evil and becoming miserable? Are not the saints in heaven, whose wills by grace do unalterably cleave to God and goodness, more perfect than if they were as Adam in paradise, capable of losing their felicity as well as preserving it? We count a rock, in regard of its stability, more excellent than the dust of the ground, or a feather that is tossed about with every wind. Is it not also the perfection of the body to have a constant tenor of health, and the glory of a man not to warp aside from what is just and right, by the persuasions of any temptations?

2. Immutability is a glory belonging to all the attributes of God. It is not a single perfection of the divine nature, nor is it limited to particular objects thus and thus disposed. Mercy and justice have their distinct objects and distinct acts; mercy is conversant about a penitent, justice conversant about an obstinate, sinner. In our notion and conception of the divine perfections, his perfections are different; the wisdom of God is not his power, nor his power his holiness, but immutability is the centre wherein they all unite. There is not one perfection but may be said to be, and truly is, immutable; none of them will appear so glorious without this beam, the sun of immutability, which renders them highly excellent without the least shadow of imperfection. How cloudy would his blessedness be if it were changeable; how dim his wisdom if it might be obscured; how feeble his power if it were capable to be sickly and languish; how would mercy lose much of its lustre if it could change into wrath, and justice much of its dread if it could be turned into mercy, while the object of justice remains unfit for mercy, and one that hath need of mercy continues only fit for the divine fury? But unchangeableness is a thread that runs through the whole web, it is the enamel of all the rest; none of them without it could look with a triumphant aspect. His power is unchangeable: Isa. xxvi. 4, 'In the Lord Jehovah is everlasting strength;' his mercy and his holiness endure for ever; he never could, nor ever can, look upon iniquity, Hab. i. 13: he is a rock in the righteousness of his ways, the truth of his word, the holiness of his proceedings, and the rectitude of his nature. All are expressed: Deut. xxxii. 4, 'He is a rock, his work is perfect, for all his ways are judgment; a God of truth and without iniquity, just and right he is.' All that we consider in God is unchangeable, for his essence and his properties are the same, and therefore what is necessarily belonging to the essence of God belongs also to every perfection of the nature of God; none of them can receive any addition or diminution. From the unchangeableness of his nature the apostle James, chap. i. 17, infers the unchangeableness of his holiness, and himself in Mal. iii. 6, the unchangeableness of his counsel.

3. Unchangeableness doth necessarily pertain to the nature of God. It is of the same necessity with the rectitude of his nature; he can no more be changeable in his essence than he can be unrighteous in his actions. God is a necessary being; he is necessarily what he is, and therefore is unchangeably what he is. Mutability belongs to contingency; if any perfection of his nature could be separated from him, he would cease to be God; what

did not possess the whole nature of God could not have the essence of God; it is reciprocated with the nature of God. Whatsoever is immutable by nature, is God; whatsoever is God, is immutable by nature. Some creatures are immutable by his grace and power;* God is holy, happy, wise, good by his essence; angels and men are made holy, wise, happy, strong, and good by qualities and graces. The holiness, happiness, and wisdom of saints and angels, as they had a beginning, so they are capable of increase and diminution, and of an end also; for their standing is not from themselves, or from the nature of created strength, holiness, or wisdom, which in themselves are apt to fail and finally to decay, but from the stability and confirmation they have by the gift and grace of God. The heaven and earth shall be changed, and after that renewal and reparation they shall not be changed. Our bodies after the resurrection shall not be changed, but for ever be 'made conformable to the glorious body of Christ,' Philip. iii. 21; but this is by the powerful grace of God: so that, indeed, those things may be said afterwards rather to be unchanged than unchangeable, because they are not so by nature, but by sovereign dispensation; as creatures have not necessary beings, so they have not necessary immutability. Necessity of being, and, therefore, immutability of being, belongs by nature to God; otherwise, if there were any change in God, he would be sometimes what he was not, and would cease to be what he was, which is against the nature, and, indeed, against the natural notion of a Deity. Let us see then,

I. In what regards God is immutable.

II. Prove that God is immutable.

III. That this is proper to God and incommunicable to any creature.

IV. Some propositions to clear the unchangeableness of God from anything that seems contrary to it.

V. The use.

I. First, In what respects God is unchangeable.

1. God is unchangeable in his essence. He is unalterably fixed in his being, that not a particle of it can be lost from it, nor a mite added to it. If a man continue in being as long as Methuselah, nine hundred and sixty-nine years, yet there is not a day, nay, an hour, wherein there is not some alteration in his substance; though no substantial part is wanting, yet there is an addition to him by his food, a diminution of something by his labour; he is always making some acquisition or suffering some loss; but in God there can be no alteration by the accession of anything to make his substance greater or better, or by diminution to make it less or worse; he who hath no being from another cannot but be always what he is. God is the first being, an independent being; he was not produced of himself, or of any other, but by nature always hath been, and therefore cannot by himself, or by any other, be changed from what he is in his own nature: that which is not may as well assume to itself a being, as he, who hath and is all being, have the least change from what he is. Again, because he is a Spirit, he is not subject to those mutations which are found in corporeal and bodily natures; because he is an absolutely simple Spirit, not having the least particle of composition, he is not capable of those changes which may be in created spirits.

(1.) If his essence were mutable, God would not truly be. It could not be truly said by himself, *I am that I am*, Exod. iii. 14, if he were such a thing or being at this time, and a different being at another time. Whatsoever is changed properly is not, because it doth not remain to be what it

* Archbold. Serm.

was; that which is changed was something, is something, and will be something; a being remains to that thing which is changed, yet, though it may be said such a thing is, yet it may be also said such a thing is not; because it is not what it was in its first being; it is not now what it was, it is now what it was not; it is another thing than it was, it was another thing than it is; it will be another thing than what it is or was; it is indeed a being, but a different being from what it was before. But if God were changed, it could not be said of him that *he is*, but it might also be said of him that *he is not*; or, if he were changeable or could be changed, it might be said of him he is, but he will not be what he is; or he may not be what he is, but there will be or may be some difference in his being, and so God would not be *I am that I am*; for though he would not cease utterly to be, yet he would cease to be what he was before.

(2.) Again, If his essence were mutable, he could not be perfectly blessed, and fully rejoice in himself. If he changed for the better, he could not have an infinite pleasure in what he was before the change, because he was not infinitely blessed, and the pleasure of that state could not be of a higher kind than the state itself, or at least the apprehension of a happiness in it; if he changed for the worse, he could not have a pleasure in it after the change; for according to the diminution of his state would be the decrease of his pleasure. His pleasure could not be infinite before the change if he changed for the better; it could not be infinite after the change if he changed for the worse. If he changed for the better, he would not have had an infinite goodness of being before; and not having an infinite goodness of being, he would have a finite goodness of being; for there is no medium between finite and infinite. Then though the change were for the better, yet being finite before, something would be still wanting to make him infinitely blessed; because being finite, he could not change to that which is infinite; for finite and infinite are extremes so distant, that they can never pass into one another; that is, that that which is finite should become infinite, or that which is infinite should become finite; so that supposing him mutable, his essence in no state of change could furnish him with an infinite peace and blessedness.

(3.) Again, if God's essence be changed, he either increaseth or diminisheth.* Whatsoever is changed doth either gain by receiving something larger and greater than it had in itself before, or gains nothing by being changed. If the former, then it receives more than itself, more than it had in itself before. The divine nature cannot be increased; for whatsoever receives anything than what it had in itself before, must necessarily receive it from another, because nothing can give to itself that which it hath not; but God cannot receive from another what he hath not already, because whatsoever other things possess is derived from him, and therefore contained in him, as the fountain contains the virtue in itself which it conveys to the streams, so that God cannot gain anything. If a thing that is changed gain nothing by that change, it loseth something of what it had before in itself, and this loss must be by itself or some other. God cannot receive any loss from anything in himself; he cannot will his own diminution; that is repugnant to every nature. He may as well will his own destruction as his own decrease; every decrease is a partial destruction; but it is impossible for God to die any kind of death, to have any resemblance of death, for he is immortal, and ' only hath immortality,' 1 Tim. vi. 16, therefore impossible to be diminished in any particle of his essence; nor can he be diminished by anything in his own nature, because his infinite simplicity admits of

* Hugo Victorin. in Petavio.

nothing distinct from himself, or contrary to himself. All decreases come. from something contrary to the nature of that thing which doth decrease. Whatsoever is made less than itself was not truly *unum*, one and simple, because that which divides itself in separation was not the same in conjunction. Nor can he be diminished by any other without himself, because nothing is superior to God, nothing stronger than God which can oppress him ; but whatsoever is changed, is weaker than that which changeth it, and sinks under a power it cannot successfully resist; weakness belongs not to the Deity.* Nor, lastly, can God change from a state wherein he is to another state equal to the former, as men in some cases may do ; for in passing from one state to another equal to it, something must be parted with which he had before, that some other thing may accrue to him as a recompence for that loss, to make him equal to what he was. This recompence then he had not before, though he had something equal to it ; and in this case it could not be said by God, *I am that I am*, but I am equal to what I was ; for in this case there would be a diminution and increase which (as was shewed) cannot be in God.

(4.) Again, God is of himself, from no other.† Natures, which are made by God, may increase, because they began to be ; they may decrease, because they were made of nothing, and so tend to nothing ; the condition of their originals leads them to defect, and the power of their Creator brings them to increase. But God hath no original, he hath no defect, because he was not made of nothing; he hath no increase, because he had no beginning ; he was before all things, and therefore depends upon no other thing which by its own change can bring any change upon him.‡ That which is from itself cannot be changed, because it hath nothing before it, nothing more excellent than itself; but that which is from another, as its first cause and chief good, may be changed by that which was its efficient cause and last end.

2. God is immutable in regard of knowledge. God hath known from all eternity all that which he can know, so that nothing is hid from him ; he knows not at present any more than he hath known from eternity, and that which he knows now, he always knows: ' All things are open and naked before him,' Heb. iv. 13. A man is said to be changed in regard of knowledge, when he knows that now which he did not know before, or knows that to be false now which he thought true before, or hath something for the object of his understanding now, which he had not before ; but

(1.) This would be repugnant to the wisdom and omniscience which belongs to the notion of a Deity. That cannot be God that is not infinitely wise ; that cannot be infinitely wise that is either ignorant of or mistaken in his apprehension of any one thing. If God be changed in knowledge, it must be for want of wisdom: all change of this nature in creatures implies this defect preceding or accompanying it. Such a thought of God would have been unworthy of him that is ' only wise,' that hath no mate for wisdom, 1 Tim. i. 17, none wise besides himself. If he knew that thing this day which he knew not before, he would not be an only wise being, for a being that did know everything at once might be conceived, and so a wiser being be apprehended by the mind of man. If God understood a thing at one time which he did not at another, he would be changed from ignorance to knowledge ; as, if he could not do that this day which he could do to-morrow, he would be changed from impotence to power. He could not be always omniscient, because there might be yet something still to come which

---

* Victorinus in Petavio.   ‡ Petav. tom. i. p. 817.
† Austin. Fulgen in Petavio.

he yet knows not, though he may know all things that are past. What way soever you suppose a change, you must suppose a present or a past ignorance. If he be changed in his knowledge for the perfection of his understanding, he was ignorant before; if his understanding be impaired by the change, he is ignorant after it.

(2.) If God were changeable in his knowledge, it would make him unfit to be an object of trust to any rational creature. His revelations would want the due ground for entertainment if his understanding were changeable, for that might be revealed as truth now which might prove false hereafter, and that as false now which hereafter might prove true; and so God would be an unfit object of obedience in regard of his precepts, and an unfit object of confidence in regard of his promises; for if he be changeable in knowledge, he is defective in knowledge, and might promise that now which he would know afterwards was unfit to be promised, and therefore unfit to be performed. It would make him an incompetent object of dread in regard of his threatenings, for he might threaten that now which he might know hereafter were not fit or just to be inflicted. A changeable mind and understanding cannot make a due and right judgment of things to be done and things to be avoided. No wise man would judge it reasonable to trust a weak and flitting person.

God must needs be unchangeable in his knowledge; but, as the schoolmen say, that as the sun always shines, so God always knows; as the sun never ceaseth to shine, so God never ceaseth to know. Nothing can be hid from the vast compass of his understanding, no more than anything can shelter itself without the verge of his power. This farther appears in that,

(1.) God knows by his own essence. He doth not know as we do, by habits, qualities, species, whereby we may be mistaken at one time and rectified at another. He hath not an understanding distinct from his essence, as we have; but being the most simple being, his understanding is his essence; and as from the infiniteness of his essence we conclude the infiniteness of his understanding, so from the unchangeableness of his essence we may justly conclude the unchangeableness of his knowledge. Since, therefore, God is without all composition, and his understanding is not distinct from his essence, what he knows he knows by his essence; and there can then be no more mutability in his knowledge than there can be in his essence; and if there were any in that, he could not be God, because he would have the property of a creature. If his understanding then be his essence, his knowledge is as necessary, as unchangeable, as his essence. As his essence eminently contains all perfections in itself, so his understanding comprehends all things past, present, and future in itself. If his understanding and his essence were not one and the same, he were not simple, but compounded; if compounded, he would consist of parts; if he consisted of parts, he would not be an independent being, and so would not be God.

(2.) God knows all things by one intuitive act. As there is no succession in his being, so that he is one thing now and another thing hereafter, so there is no succession in his knowledge. He knows things that are successive, before their existence and succession, by one single act of intuition. By one cast of his eye, all things future are present to him in regard of his eternity and omnipresence; so that though there is a change and variation in the things known, yet his knowledge of them and their several changes in nature is invariable and unalterable. As imagine a creature that could see with his eye at one glance the whole compass of the heavens; by sending out beams from his eye, without receiving any species from them, he would see the whole heavens uniformly; this part now in the east, then in the west, without any change in his eye; for he sees every part and every motion together; and though that great body varies and whirls about, and is in continual agitation, his eye remains stedfast, suffers no change, beholds all their motions at once, and by one glance.* God knows all things from eternity, and therefore perpetually knows them; the reason is, because the divine knowledge is infinite: Ps. cxlvii. 5, 'His understanding is infinite;' and therefore comprehends all knowable truths at once. An eternal knowledge comprehends in itself all time, and beholds past and present in the same manner, and therefore his knowledge is immutable. By one simple knowledge he considers the infinite spaces of past and future.

(3.) God's knowledge and will is the cause of all things and their successions. There can be no pretence of any changeableness of knowledge in God, but in this case, before things come to pass, he knows that they will come to pass; after they are come to pass, he knows that they are past and slid away.† This would be something, if the succession of things were the cause of the divine knowledge, as it is of our knowledge; but on the contrary, the divine knowledge and will is the cause of the succession of them. God doth not know creatures because they are, but they are because he knows them: 'All his works were known to him from the beginning of the world,' Acts xv. 18. All his works were not known to him, if the events of all those works were not also known to him. If they were not known to him, how should he make them? He could not do anything ignorantly. He made them then after he knew them, and did not know them after he made them. His knowledge of them made a change in them; their existence made no change in his knowledge. He knew them when they were to be created, in the same manner that he knew them after they were created; before they were brought into act, as well as after they were brought into act; before they were made, they were, and were not; they were in the knowledge of God when they were not in their own nature. God did not receive his knowledge from their existence, but his knowledge and will acted upon them to bring them into being.

(4.) Therefore the distinction of past and future makes no change in the knowledge of God. When a thing is past, God hath no more distinct knowledge of it after it is past than he had when it was to come; all things were all in their circumstances of past, present, and to come, seen by his understanding as they were determined by his will;‡ besides, to know a day to be past or future is only to know the state of that day in itself, and to know its relation to that which follows and that which went before. This day wherein we are, if we consider it in the state wherein it was yesterday, it was to come, it was future; but, if we consider it in that state wherein it will be to-morrow, we understand it as past. This in man cannot be said to be a different knowledge of the thing itself, but only of the circumstance attending a thing, and the different relation of it; as I see the sun this day, I know it was up yesterday, I know it will be up to-morrow, my knowledge of the sun is the same; if there be any change, it is in the sun, not in my knowledge, only I apply my knowledge to such particular circumstances. How much more must the knowledge of those things in God be unchangeable, who knows all those states, conditions, and circumstances most perfectly from eternity, wherein there is no succession, no past or future, and therefore will know them for ever! He always beholds the same thing; he sees, indeed, succession in things, and he sees a thing to be past which before was future; as from eternity he saw Adam as existing

---

* Suarez. vol. i. p. 137.   † Austin. Bradwardine.
‡ Gamach. in Aquin. Qu. 9, cap. i. p. 73.

in such a time; in the first time he saw that he would be, in the following time he saw that he had been; but this he knew from eternity, this he knew in the same manner; though there was a variation in Adam, yet there was no variation in God's knowledge of him in all his states; though Adam was not present to himself, yet in all his states he was present to God's eternity.

(5.) Consider that the knowledge of God, in regard of the manner of it, as well as the objects, is incomprehensible to a finite creature. So that, though we cannot arrive to a full understanding of the manner of God's knowledge, yet we must conceive so of it, as to remove all imperfection from him in it; and since it is an imperfection to be changeable, we must remove that from God; the knowledge of God about things past, present, and future, must be inconceivably above ours: 'His understanding is infinite,' Ps. cxlvii. 5. There is no number of it; it can no more be calculated or drawn into an account by us, than infinite spaces, which have no bounds and limits, can be measured by us. We can no more arrive, even in heaven, to a comprehensive understanding of the manner of his knowledge, than of the infinite glory of his essence; we may as well comprehend one as the other. This we must conclude, that God being not a body, doth not see one thing with eyes and another thing with mind, as we do; but being a Spirit, he sees and knows only with mind, and his mind is himself, and is as unchangeable as himself; and therefore, as he is not now another thing than what he was, so he knows not anything now in another manner than as he knew it from eternity. He sees all things in the glass of his own essence; as therefore the glass doth not vary, so neither doth his vision.

3. God is unchangeable in regard of his will and purpose. A change in purpose is, when a man determines to do that now which before he determined not to do, or to do the contrary; when a man hates that thing which he loved, or begins to love that which he before hated. When the will is changed, a man begins to will that which he willed not before, and ceaseth to will that which he willed before. But whatsoever God hath decreed, is immutable; whatsoever God hath promised, shall be accomplished: 'The word that goes forth of his mouth shall not return to him void, but it shall accomplish that which he pleaseth,' Isa. lv. 11; whatsoever 'he purposeth he will do,' Isa. xlvi. 11, Num. xxiii. 19. His decrees are therefore called 'mountains of brass,' Zech. vi. 1: brass, as having substance and solidity; mountains, as being immoveable, not only by any creature, but by himself, because they stand upon the basis of infallible wisdom, and are supported by uncontrollable power. From this immutability of his will published to man, there could be no release from the severity of the law, without satisfaction made by the death of a mediator, since it was the unalterable will of God that death should be the wages of sin; and from this immutable will it was, that the length of time from the first promise of the Redeemer to his mission, and the daily provocations of men, altered not his purpose for the accomplishment of it in the fulness of that time he had resolved upon; nor did the wickedness of former ages hinder the addition of several promises as buttresses to the first.

To make this out, consider,

(1.) The will of God is the same with his essence. If God had a will distinct from his essence, he would not be the most simple being. God hath not a faculty of will distinct from himself. As his understanding is nothing else but *Deus intelligens*, God understanding, so his will is nothing else but *Deus volens*, God willing; being therefore the essence of God, though it is considered according to our weakness as a faculty, it is as his understanding and wisdom, eternal and immutable, and can no more be changed than his essence. The immutability of the divine counsel depends upon that of his essence. He is the Lord Jehovah, therefore he is true to his word: Mal. iii. 6, Isa. xliii. 13, 'Yea, before the day was, I am he, and there is none that can deliver out of my hand.' He is the same, immutable in his essence, therefore irresistible in his power.

(2.) There is a concurrence of God's will and understanding in everything. As his knowledge is eternal, so is his purpose. Things created had not been known to be, had not God resolved them to be [by] the act of his will. The existence of anything supposeth an act of his will. Again, as God knows all things by one simple vision of his understanding, so he wills all things by one act of volition; therefore the purpose of God in the Scripture is not expressed by counsels, in the plural number, but counsel, shewing that all the purposes of God are not various, but as one will, branching itself out into many acts towards the creature, but all knit in one root,* all links of one chain. Whatsoever is eternal is immutable. As his knowledge is eternal, and therefore immutable, so is his will. He wills or nills nothing to be in time, but what he willed and nilled from eternity. If he willed in time that to be that he willed not from eternity, then he would know that in time which he knew not from eternity; for God knows nothing future but as his will orders it to be future, and in time to be brought into being.

(3.) There can be no reason for any change in the will of God. When men change in their minds, it must be for want of foresight, because they could not foresee all the rubs and bars which might suddenly offer them-selves; which, if they had foreseen, they would not have taken such mea-sures. Hence men often will that which they afterwards wish they had not willed, when they come to understand it clearer, and see that to be injurious to them which they thought to be good for them; or else the change pro-ceeds from a natural instability without any just cause, and an easiness to be drawn into that which is unrighteous; or else it proceeds from a want of power, when men take new counsels, because they are invincibly hindered from executing the old. But none of those can be in God.

[1.] It cannot be for want of foresight. What can be wanting to an in-finite understanding? How can any unknown event defeat his purpose, since nothing happens in the world but what he wills to effect, or wills to permit, and therefore all future events are present with him? Besides, it doth not consist with God's wisdom to resolve anything but upon the highest reason; and what is the highest and infinite reason cannot but be unalterable in itself, for there can be no reason and wisdom higher than the highest. All God's purposes are not bare acts of will, but acts of counsel: Eph. i. 11, 'He works all things according to the counsel of his own will;' and he doth not say so much that his will as that his 'counsel shall stand,' Isa. xlvi. 10. It stands because it is counsel. And the immutability of a promise is called the 'immutability of his counsel,' Heb. vi. 17, as being introduced and settled by the most perfect wisdom, and therefore to be carried on to a full and complete execution. His purpose then cannot be changed for want of foresight, for this would be a charge of weakness.

[2.] Nor can it proceed from a natural instability of his will, or an easi-ness to be drawn to that which is unrighteous. If his will should not adhere to his counsel, it is because it is not fit to be followed, or because it will not follow it. If not fit to be followed, it is a reflection upon his wisdom; if it be established, and he will not follow it, there is a contrariety in God, as there is in a fallen creature, will against wisdom. That cannot

* Qu. 'knot'?—Ed.

be in God which he hates in a creature, viz., the disorder of faculties, and being out of their due place. The righteousness of God is like a great mountain, Ps. xxxvi. 6. The rectitude of his nature is as immovable in itself as all the great mountains in the world [are by the strength of man: 'He is not as a man that he should repent or lie,' Num. xxiii. 19, who often changes out of a perversity of will, as well as want of wisdom to foresee, or want of ability to perform. His eternal purpose must either be righteous or unrighteous; if righteous and holy, he would become unholy by the change; if not righteous nor holy, then he was unrighteous before the change; which way soever it falls, it would reflect upon the righteousness of God, which is a blasphemous imagination.* If God did change his purpose, it must be either for the better, then the counsel of God was bad before; or for the worse, then he was not wise and good before.

[3.] Nor can it be for want of strength. Who hath power to control him? Not all the combined devices and endeavours of men can make the counsel of God to totter: Prov. xix. 21, 'There are many devices in a man's heart, nevertheless the counsel of the Lord, that shall stand;' that, and that only, shall stand. Man hath a power to devise and imagine, but no power to effect and execute of himself. God wants no more power to effect what he will, than he wants understanding to know what is fit.

Well, then, since God wanted not wisdom to frame his decrees, nor holiness to regulate them, nor power to effect them, what should make him change them, since there can be no reason superior to his, no event unforeseen by him, no holiness comparable to his, no unrighteousness found in him, no power equal to his to put a rub in his way?

(4.) Though the will of God be immutable, yet it is not to be understood so as that the things themselves so willed are immutable. Nor will the immutability of the things willed by him follow upon the unchangeableness of his will in willing them; though God be firm in willing them, yet he doth not will that they should alway be. God did not perpetually will the doing† those things which he once decreed to be done. He decreed that Christ should suffer, but he did not decree that Christ should alway suffer; so he willed the Mosaical rites for a time, but he did not will that they should alway continue; he willed that they should endure only for a time, and when the time came for their ceasing, God had been mutable if he had not put an end to them, because his will had fixed such a period. So that the changing of those things which he had once appointed to be practised, is so far from charging God with changeableness, that God would be mutable if he did not take them away, since he decreed as well their abolition at such a time as their continuance till such a time, so that the removal of them was pursuant to his unchangeable will and decree. If God had decreed that such laws should alway continue, and afterwards changed that decree, and resolved the abrogation of them, then indeed God had been mutable; he had rescinded one decree by another, he had then seen an error in his first resolve, and there must be some weakness in the reason and wisdom whereon it was grounded.‡ But it was not so here, for the change of those laws is so far from slurring God with any mutability, that the very change of them is no other than the issue of his eternal decree; for from eternity he purposed in himself to change this or that dispensation, though he did decree to bring such a dispensation into the world. The decree itself was eternal and immutable, but the thing decreed was temporary and mutable. As a decree from eternity doth not make the thing decreed to be eternal, so neither doth the immutability of the decree render

* Max. Tyr. diss. iii.   † Qu. 'will the perpetual doing'?—ED.   ‡ Turret., de satisf.

the thing so decreed to be immutable. As, for example, God decreed from all eternity to create the world, the eternity of this decree did not make the world to be in being and actually created from eternity; so God decreed immutably that the world so created should continue for such a time; the decree is immutable if the world perish at that time, and would not be immutable if the world did endure beyond that time that God hath fixed for the duration of it. As when a prince orders a man's remaining in prison for so many days, if he be prevailed with to give him a delivery before those days, or to continue him in custody for the same crime after those days, his order is changed; but if he orders the delivery of him just at that time till which he had before decreed that he should continue in prison, the purpose and order of the prince remains firm, and the change in the state of the prisoner is the fruit of that firm and fixed resolution; so that we must distinguish between the person decreeing, the decree itself, and the thing decreed. The person decreeing, viz., God, is in himself immutable, and the decree is immutable, but the thing decreed may be mutable; and if it were not changed according to the first purpose, it would argue the decree itself to be changed; for whiles a man wills that this may be done now and another thing done afterwards, the same will remains, and though there be a change in the effect, there is no change in the will.

(5.) The immutability of God's will doth not infringe the liberty of it. The liberty of God's will consists with the necessity of continuing his purpose. God is necessarily good, immutably good; yet he is freely so, and would not be otherwise than what he is. God was free in his first purpose; and purposing this or that by an infallible and unerring wisdom, it would be a weakness to change the purpose. But indeed the liberty of God's will doth not seem so much to consist in an indifferency to this or that, as in an independency on anything without himself. His will was free, because it did not depend upon the objects about which his will was conversant. To be immutably good, is no point of imperfection, but the height of perfection.

4. As God is unchangeable in regard of essence, knowledge, purpose, so he is unchangeable in regard of place. He cannot be changed in time, because he is eternity; so he cannot be changed in place, because he hath ubiquity. He is eternal, therefore cannot be changed in time; he is omnipresent, therefore cannot be changed in place; he doth not begin to be in one place wherein he was not before, or cease to be in a place wherein he was before. He that fills every place in heaven and earth, cannot change place; he cannot leave one to possess another, that is equally in regard of his essence in all: 'He fills heaven and earth,' Jer. xxiii. 24. The heavens, that are not subject to those changes to which sublunary bodies are subject, that are not diminished in quantity or quality, yet they are alway changing place in regard of their motion; no part of them doth alway continue in the same point. But God hath no change of his nature, because he is most inward in everything. He is substantially in all space, real and imaginary; there is no part of the world which he doth not fill; no place can be imagined wherein he doth not exist. Suppose a million of worlds above and about this, encircling one another, his essence would be in every part and point of those worlds, because it is indivisible, it cannot be divided; nor can it be contained within those created limits of millions of worlds, when the most soaring and best coining fancy hath run through all creatures, to the highest sphere of the heavens, and imagined one world after another, till it can fancy no more. None of these, nor all of these, can contain God; for 'the heaven of heavens cannot contain him,' 1 Kings viii. 27. He is 'higher than heaven, deeper than hell,' Job xi. 8, and

possesses infinite imaginary spaces beyond created limits. He who hath no cause of being, can have no limits of being.* And though by creation he began to be in the world, yet he did not begin to be where the world is, but was in the same imaginary space from all eternity; for he was alway in himself by his own eternal *ubi*.

Therefore observe, that when God is said to ' draw near to us ' when ' we draw near to him,' James iv. 8, it is not by local motion or change of place, but by special and spiritual influences, by exciting and supporting grace. As we ordinarily say, the sun is come into the house, when yet it remains in its place and order in the heavens, because the beams pierce through the windows and enlighten the room, so when God is said to come down or descend, Gen. xi. 5, Exod. xxxiv. 5, it is not by a change of place, but a change of outward acts, when he puts forth himself in ways of fresh mercy or new judgments, in the effluxes of his love or the flames of his wrath. When good men feel the warm beams of his grace refreshing them, or wicked men feel the hot coals of his anger scorching them. God's drawing near to us is not so much his coming to us, but his drawing us to him;† as when watermen pull a rope that is in one end fastened to the shore and the other end to the vessel, the shore is immoveable, yet it seems to the eye to come to them, but they really move to the shore. God is an immoveable rock, we are floating and uncertain creatures; while he seems to approach to us, he doth really make us to approach to him. He comes not to us by any change of place himself, but draws us to him by a change of mind, will, and affections in us.

II. The second thing propounded is the reasons to prove God immutable. The heathens‡ acknowledged God to be so; Plato and the Pythagoreans called God, or the stable good principle, αὐτόν, *idem;* the evil principle ἕτερον, another thing, changeable; one thing one time and another thing another time:§ Daniel vi. 26, ' He is the living God, and stedfast for ever.'

1. The name Jehovah signifies this attribute : Exod. iii. 14, ' I am that I am ; I am hath sent me to you.' It signifies his immutability as well as eternity.‖ *I am* signifies his eternity ; *that* or *the same that I am*, his immutability. As it respects the essence of God, it signifies his unchangeable being from eternity to eternity ;¶ as it respects the creature, it signifies his constancy in his counsels and promises, which spring from no other cause but the unchangeableness of his nature. The reason why men stand not to their covenant, is because they are not always the same. *I am*, that is, I am the same, before the creation of the world, and since the creation of the world ; before the entrance of sin, and since the entrance of sin ; before their going into Egypt, and whiles they remain in Egypt. The very name *Jehovah* bears, according to the grammatical order, a mark of God's unchangeableness.** It never hath anything added to it, nor anything taken from it ; it hath no plural number, no affixes, a custom peculiar to the eastern languages ; it never changes its letters as other words do. That only is a true being, which hath not only an eternal existence, but stability in it : that is not truly a being that never remains in the same state.†† All things

* Gamacheus, *ut supra*.
† The ancients, as Dionysius, expressed it by this similitude.
‡ Plato calls God οὐσίαν ʼαεὶ ἐχομένον, lib. i. de Be.
§ Stabilisque manens dat cuncta moveri.—*Boet.*, Consolat. lib. iii.
‖ Trap. on Exod.   ¶ Amyrald. de Trinitat. p. 433.
** Spanheim, Syntag, part i. p. 39.
†† Petav. Theol. Dogmat. tom. i. cap. 6, sect. 6, 7, 8.

that are changed cease to be what they were, and begin to be what they were not, and therefore cannot have the title truly applied to them *they are;* they are indeed, but like a river in a continual flux, that no man ever sees the same; let his eye be fixed upon one place of it, the water he sees slides away, and that which he saw not succeeds in its place; let him take his eye off but for the least moment, and fix it there again, and he sees not the same that he saw before. All sensible things are in a perpetual stream; that which is sometimes this and sometimes that, is not, because it is not always the same; whatsoever is changed, is something now which it was not alway; but of God it is said *I am,* which could not be if he were changeable; for it may be said of him he is not, as well as he is, because he is not what he was. If we say not of him he was, nor he will be, but only he is, whence should any change arrive? He must invincibly remain the same, of whose nature, perfections, knowledge, and will, it cannot be said *it was,* as if it were not now in him; or *it shall be,* as if it were not yet in him; but *he is,* because he doth not only exist, but doth alway exist the same. *I am,* that is, I receive from no other what I am in myself. He depends upon no other in his essence, knowledge, purposes, and therefore hath no changing power over him.

2. If God were changeable, he could not be the most perfect being. God is the most perfect being, and possesses in himself infinite and essential goodness: Mat. v. 48, 'Your heavenly Father is perfect.' If he could change from that perfection, he were not the highest exemplar and copy for us to write after. If God doth change, it must be either to a greater perfection than he had before, or to a less, *mutatio perfectiva vel amissiva;* if he changes to acquire a perfection he had not, then he was not before the most excellent being necessarily; he was not what he might be; there was a defect in him, and a privation of that which is better than what he had and was, and then he was not alway the best, and so was not alway God; and being not alway God, could never be God; for to begin to be God is against the notion of God. Not to a less perfection than he had; that were to change to imperfection, and to lose a perfection which he possessed before, and cease to be the best being; for he would lose some good which he had, and acquire some evil which he was free from before. So that the sovereign perfection of God is an invincible bar to any change in him; for which way soever you cast it for a change, his supreme excellency is impaired and nulled by it; for in all change there is something from which a thing is changed, and something to which it is changed: so that on the one part there is a loss of what it had, and on the other part there is an acquisition of what it had not. If to the better, he was not perfect, and so was not God; if to the worse, he will not be perfect, and so be no longer God after that change.

If God be changed, his change must be voluntary or necessary; if voluntary, he then intends the change for the better, and chose it to acquire a perfection by it. The will must be carried out to anything under the notion of some goodness in that which it desires. Since good is the object of the desire and will of the creature, evil cannot be the object of the desire and will of the Creator. And if he should be changed for the worse when he did really intend the better, it would speak a defect of wisdom, and a mistake of that for good which was evil and imperfect in itself; and if it be for the better, it must be a motion or change for something without himself; that which he desireth is not possessed by himself but by some other. There is then some good without him and above him, which is the end in this change; for nothing acts but for some end, and that end is within itself or without itself. If the end for which God changes be without himself, then there is something better than himself. Besides, if he were voluntarily changed for the better, why did he not change before? If it were for want of power, he had the imperfection of weakness; if for want of knowledge of what was the best good, he had the imperfection of wisdom, he was ignorant of his own happiness; if he had both wisdom to know it, and power to effect it, it must be for want of will. He then wanted that love to himself and his own glory, which is necessary in the supreme being. Voluntarily he could not be changed for the worse, he could not be such an enemy to his own glory; there is nothing but would hinder its own imperfection and becoming worse. Necessarily he could not be changed, for that necessity must arise from himself, and then the difficulties spoken of before will recur; or it must arise from another. He cannot be bettered by another, because nothing hath any good but what it hath received from the hands of his bounty, and that without loss to himself: nor made worse. If anything made him worse, it would be sin, but that cannot touch his essence or obscure his glory, but in the design and nature of the sin itself: Job xxxv. 6, 7, 'If thou sinnest, what dost thou against him? or if thy transgressions be multiplied, what dost thou unto him? If thou be righteous, what givest thou him? or what receives he at thy hand?' He hath no addition by the service of man, no more than the sun hath of light by a multitude of torches kindled on the earth; nor any more impair by the sins of men, than the light of the sun hath by men's shooting arrows against it.

3. God were not the most simple being if he were not immutable.* There is in everything that is mutable a composition, either essential or accidental; and in all changes something of the thing changed remains, and something of it ceaseth and is done away; as, for example, in an accidental change, if a white wall be made black, it loses its white colour; but the wall itself, which was the subject of that colour, remains, and loses nothing of its substance. Likewise, in a substantial change, as when wood is burnt, the substantial part of wood is lost, the earthly part is changed into ashes, the airy part ascends in smoke, the watery part is changed into air by the fire. There is not an annihilation of it, but a resolution of it into those parts whereof it was compounded; and this change doth evidence that it was compounded of several parts distinct from one another. If there were any change in God, it is by separating something from him, or adding something to him: if by separating something from him, then he was compounded of something distinct from himself; for if it were not distinct from himself, it could not be separated from him without loss of his being; if by adding anything to him, then it is a compounding of him, either substantially or accidentally.

Mutability is absolutely inconsistent with simplicity, whether the change come from an internal or external principle. If a change be wrought by something without, it supposeth either contrary or various parts in the thing so changed, whereof it doth consist; if it be wrought by anything within, it supposeth that the thing so changed doth consist of one part that doth change it, and another part that is changed, and so it would not be a simple being. If God could be changed by anything within himself, all in God would not be God; his essence would depend upon some parts, whereof some would be superior to others. If one part were able to change or destroy another, that which doth change would be God, that which is changed would not be God; so God would be made up of a deity and a non-deity, and part of God would depend upon God; part would be dependent, and part would be independent; part would be mutable, part immutable; so that mutability

* Gamach. in Prim. Part. Aquin. quest. 9, cap. 1, part. 72.

is against the notion of God's independency as well as his simplicity.* God is the most simple being; for that which is first in nature, having nothing beyond it, cannot by any means be thought to be compounded; for whatsoever is so depends upon the parts whereof it is compounded, and so is not the first being. Now God being infinitely simple, hath nothing in himself which is not himself, and therefore cannot will any change in himself, he being his own essence and existence.

4. God were not eternal if he were mutable. In all change there is something that perishes, either substantially or accidentally. All change is a kind of death, or imitation of death; that which was, dies, and begins to be what it was not. The soul of man, though it ceaseth not to be and exist, yet when it ceaseth to be in quality what it was, it is said to die. Adam died when he changed from integrity to corruption, though both his soul and body were in being, Gen. ii. 17; and the soul of a regenerate man is said to 'die to sin,' Rom. vi. 11, when it is changed from sin to grace. In all change there is a resemblance of death: so the notion of mutability is against the eternity of God. If anything be acquired by a change, then that which is acquired was not from eternity, and so he was not wholly eternal; if anything be lost which was from eternity, he is not wholly everlasting; if he did decrease by the change, something in him which had no beginning would have an end; if he did increase by that change, something in him would have a beginning that might have no end.† What is changed doth not remain, and what doth not remain is not eternal. Though God alway remains in regard of existence, he would be immortal and live alway; yet if he should suffer any change he could not properly be eternal, because he would not alway be the same, and would not in every part be eternal; for all change is finished in time, one moment preceding, another moment following, but that which is before time cannot be changed by time. God cannot be eternally what he was; that is, he cannot have a true eternity, if he had a new knowledge, new purpose, a new essence; if he were sometimes this and sometimes that, sometimes know this and sometimes know that, sometimes purpose this and afterwards hath a new purpose, he would be partly temporary and partly eternal, not truly and universally eternal. He that hath anything of newness, hath not properly and truly an entire eternity. Again, by the same reason that God could in the least cease to be what he was, he might also cease wholly to be, and no reason can be rendered why God might not cease wholly to be, as well as cease to be entirely and uniformly what he was. All changeableness implies a corruptibility.

5. If God were changeable, he were not infinite and almighty. All change ends in addition or diminution; if anything be added, he was not infinite before; if anything be diminished, he is not infinite after. All change implies bounds and limits to that which is changed; but God is infinite, 'his greatness is unsearchable,' Ps. cxlv. 3, אֵין חֵקֶר, no end, no term. We can add number to number without any end, and can conceive an infinite number, yet the greatness of God is beyond all our conceptions. But if there could be any change in his greatness for the better, it would not be unsearchable before that change; if for the worse, it would not be unsearchable after that change. Whatsoever hath limits and is changeable, is conceivable and searchable; but God is not only not known, but impossible in his own nature to be known and searched out, and therefore impossible to have any

---

* Ficinus Zachar. Mitylen. in Peta, tom. i. p. 169.
† Austin in Pet., tom. i. p. 201.

diminution in his nature. All that which is changed arrives to something which it was not before, or ceaseth in part to be what it was before.

He would not also be almighty. What is omnipotent cannot be made worse; for to be made worse, is in part to be corrupted. If he be made better, he was not almighty before; something of power was wanting to him. If there should be any change, it must proceed from himself or from another: if from himself, it would be an inability to preserve himself in the perfection of his nature; if from another, he would be inferior in strength, knowledge, and power to that which changes him, either in his nature, knowledge, or will; in both an inability; an inability in him to continue the same, or an inability in him to resist the power of another.

6. The world could not be ordered and governed but by some principle or being which were immutable. Principles are alway more fixed and stable than things which proceed from those principles, and this is true both in morals and naturals. Principles in conscience, whereby men are governed, remain firmly engraven in their minds. The root lies firmly in the earth, while branches are shaken with the wind. The heavens, the cause of generation, are more firm and stable than those things which are wrought by their influence. All things in the world are moved by some power and virtue which is stable; and unless it were so, no order would be observed in motion, no motion could be regularly continued. He could not be a full satisfaction to the infinite desire of the souls of his people. Nothing can truly satisfy the soul of man but rest, and nothing can give it rest but that which is perfect, and immutably perfect; for else it would be subject to those agitations and variation which the being [it] depends upon is subject to.

The principle of all things must be immutable,* which is described by some by a unit, the principle of number, wherein there is a resemblance of God's unchangeableness. A unit is not variable, it continues in its own nature immutably an unit; it never varies from itself, it cannot be changed from itself, but is as it were so omnipotent towards others, that it changes all numbers; if you add any number, it is the beginning of that number, but the unit is not increased by it; a new number ariseth from that addition, but the unit still remains the same, and adds a value to other figures, but receives none from them.

III. The third thing to speak to is,

That immutability is proper to God, and incommunicable to any creature. Mutability is natural to every creature as a creature, and immutability is the sole perfection of God. He only is infinite wisdom, able to foreknow future events; he only is infinitely powerful, able to call forth all means to effect; so that wanting neither wisdom to contrive, nor strength to execute, he cannot alter his counsel. None being above him, nothing in him contrary to him, and being defective in no blessedness and perfection, he cannot vary in his essence and nature. Had not immutability as well as eternity been a property solely pertaining to the divine nature, as well as creative power and eternal duration, the apostle's argument to prove Christ to be God from this perpetual sameness, had come short of any convincing strength. These words of the text he applies to Christ: Heb. i. 10–12, ' They shall be changed, but thou art the same.' There had been no strength in the reason, if immutability by nature did belong to any creature.

The changeableness of all creatures is evident.

1. Of corporeal creatures it is evident to sense. All plants and animals, as they have their duration bounded in certain limits, so while they do exist

* Fotherby, Atheomastix., p. 308; Gerhard. *loc. com.*

they proceed from their rise to their fall ; they pass through many sensible alterations, from one degree of growth to another, from buds to blossoms, from blossoms to flowers and fruits ; they come to their pitch that nature hath set them, and return back to the state from whence they sprung; there is not a day but they make some acquisition, or suffer some loss ; they die and spring up every day ; nothing in them more certain than their inconstancy : ' The creature is subject to vanity,' Rom. viii. 20. The heavenly bodies are changing their place ; the sun every day is running his race, and stays not in the same point ; and though they are not changed in their essence, yet they are in their place ; some indeed say there is a continual generation of light in the sun, as there is a loss of light by the casting out its beams, as in a fountain there is a flowing out of the streams, and a continual generation of supply. And though these heavenly bodies have kept their standing and motion from the time of their creation, yet both the sun's standing still in Joshua's time, and its going back in Hezekiah's time, shew that they are changeable at the pleasure of God.

But in man the change is perpetually visible; every day there is a change from ignorance to knowledge, from one will to another, from passion to passion, sometimes sad, and sometimes cheerful, sometimes craving this and presently nauseating it. His body changes from health to sickness, or from weakness to strength ; some alteration there is either in body or mind. Man, who is the noblest creature, the subordinate end of the creation of other things, cannot assure himself of a consistency and fixedness in anything the short space of a day, no, not of a minute; all his months are ' months of vanity,' Job vii. 3 ; whence the psalmist calls man, ' at the best estate, altogether vanity,' Ps. xxxix. 5, a mere heap of vanity. As he contains in his nature the nature of all creatures, so he inherits in his nature the vanity of all creatures. A little world, the centre of the world, and of the vanity of the world ; yea, ' lighter than vanity,' Ps. lxii. 9 ; more moveable than a feather ; tossed between passion and passion ; daily changing his end, and changing the means ; an image of nothing.

2. Spiritual natures, as angels. They change not in their being, but that is from the indulgence of God ; they change not in their goodness, but that is not from their nature, but divine grace in their confirmation ; but they change in their knowledge, they know more by Christ than they did by creation, 1 Tim. iii. 16. They have an addition of knowledge every day, by the providential dispensations of God to his church, Eph. iii. 10, and the increase of their astonishment and love is according to the increase of their knowledge and insight. They cannot have a new discovery without new admirations of what is discovered to them. There is a change in their joy when there is a change in a sinner, Luke xv. 10. They were changed in their essence when they were made such glorious spirits of nothing. Some of them were changed in their will, when of holy they became impure. The good angels were changed in their understandings when the glories of God in Christ were presented to their view ; and all can be changed in their essence again ; and as they were made of nothing, so, by the power of God, may be reduced to nothing again. So glorified souls shall have an unchanged operation about God, for they shall behold his face without any grief or fear of loss, without vagrant thoughts ; but they can never be unchangeable in their nature, because they can never pass from finite to infinite.

No creature can be unchangeable in its nature.

(1.) Because every creature rose from nothing. As they rose from nothing, so they tend to nothing, unless they are preserved by God. The notion of a creature speaks changeableness, because, to be a creature, is to be made something of nothing, and therefore creation is a change of nothing into something. The being of a creature begins from change, and therefore the essence of a creature is subject to change. God only is uncreated, and therefore unchangeable. If he were made, he could not be immutable, for the very making is a change of not being into being. All creatures were made good, as they were the fruits of God's goodness and power, but must needs be mutable, because they were the extracts of nothing.

(2.) Because every creature depends purely upon the will of God. They depend not upon themselves, but upon another for their being. As they received their being from the word of his mouth and the arm of his power, so by the same word they can be cancelled into nothing, and return into as little significancy as when they were nothing. He that created them by a word, can by a word destroy them, Ps. civ. 29. If God should ' take away their breath, they die, and return into their dust.' As it was in the power of the Creator that things might be before they actually were, so it is in the power of the Creator that things, after they are, may cease to be what they are, and they are in their own nature as reducible to nothing as they were producible by the power of God from nothing; for there needs no more than an act of God's will to null them, as there needed only an act of God's will to make them. Creatures are all subject to a higher cause. They are all ' reputed as nothing. He doth according to his will in the armies of heaven, and among the inhabitants of the earth, and none can stay his hand, or say unto him what doest thou' ? Dan. iv. 35. But God is unchangeable, because he is the highest God; none above him, all below him; all dependent on him, himself upon none.

(3.) No creature is absolutely perfect. No creature can be so perfect, or can ever be, but something by the infinite power of God may be added to it; for whatsoever is finite may receive greater additions, and therefore a change. No creature you can imagine, but in your thoughts you may fancy him capable of greater perfections than you know he hath, or than really he hath. The perfections of all creatures are searchable, the perfection of God is only unsearchable, Job xi. 6, and therefore he only immutable.

God only is always the same. Time makes no addition to him, nor diminisheth anything of him. His nature and essence, his wisdom and will, have always been the same from eternity, and shall be the same to eternity, without any variation.

IV. The fourth thing propounded, is some propositions to clear this unchangeableness of God from anything that seems contrary to it.

1. There was no change in God when he began to create the world in time. The creation was a real change, but the change was not subjectively in God, but in the creature; the creature began to be what it was not before. Creation is considered as active or passive;* active creation is the will and power of God to create; this is from eternity, because God willed from eternity to create in time. This never had beginning, for God never began in time to understand anything, to will anything, or to be able to do anything; but he alway understood, and alway willed, those things which he determined from eternity to produce in time. The decree of God may be taken for the act decreeing, that is eternal and the same; or for the object decreed, that is in time; so that there may be a change in the object, but not in the will whereby the object doth exist.

(1.) There was no change in God by the act of creation, because there

* Gamach. in part i. Aquin. Qu. 9, cap. i. p. 72.

was no new will in him.   There was no new act of his will which was not
before.   The creation begun in time, but the will of creating was from eternity.   The work was new, but the decree whence that new work sprung was
as ancient as the Ancient of days.   When the time of creating came, God
was not made *ex nolente volens*, as we are; for whatsoever God willed to be
now done, he willed from eternity to be done; but he willed also that it
should not be done till such an instant of time, and that it should not exist
before such a time.   If God had willed the creation of the world only at that
time when the world was produced, and not before, then, indeed, God had
been changeable.   But though God spake that word which he had not spoke
before, whereby the world was brought into act, yet he did not will that will
he willed not before.   God did not create by a new counsel or new will, but
by that which was from eternity, Eph. i. 9.   All things are wrought according to that ' purpose in himself,' and ' according to the counsel of his will,'
ver. 11; and as the holiness of the elect is the fruit of his eternal will ' before
the foundation of the world,' ver. 4, so likewise is the existence of things,
and of those persons whom he did elect.   As when an artificer frames a
house or a temple according to that model he had in his mind some years
before, there is no change in the model in his mind, the artificer is the
same, though the work is produced by him some time after he had framed
that copy of it in his own mind; but there is a change of the thing produced
by him according to that model.   Or when a rich man intends, four or five
years hence, if he lives, to build an hospital, is there any change in his will
when, after the expiration of that time, he builds and endows it?   Though
it be after his will, yet it is the fruit of his precedent will; so God from all
eternity did will and command that the creatures should exist in such a part
of time; and by this eternal will all things, whether past, present, or to
come, did, do, and shall exist at that point of time which that will did appoint for them.   Not as though God had a new will when things stood up
in being, but only that which was prepared in his immutable counsel and
will from eternity doth then appear.   There can be no instant fixed from
eternity wherein it can be said God did not will the creation of the world;
for had the will of God for the shortest moment been undetermined to the
creation of the world, and afterwards resolved upon it, there had been a
moral change in God from not willing to willing; but this there was not, for
God executes nothing in time which he had not ordained from eternity, and
appointed all the means and circumstances whereby it should be brought
about; as the determination of our Saviour to suffer was not a new will, but
an eternal counsel, and wrought no change in God, Acts ii. 23.

(2.) There is no change in God by the act of creation, because there was
no new power in God.   Had God had a will at the time of the creation,
which he had not before, there had been a moral change in him; so had
there been in him a power only to create then and not before; there had
been a physical change in him from weakness to ability.   There can be no
more new power in God than there can be a new will in God; for his will
is his power, and what he willeth to effect that he doth effect.   As he was
unchangeably holy, so he was unchangeably almighty, ' which was, and is, and
is to come,' Rev. iv. 8; which was almighty, and is almighty, and ever will
be almighty.   The work, therefore, makes no change in God, but there is a
change in the thing wrought by that power of God.   Suppose you had a
seal engraven upon some metal a hundred years old, or as old as the creation, and you should this day, so many ages after the engraving of it, make
an impression of that seal upon wax, would you say the engravement upon
the seal were changed because it produced that stamp upon the wax now

which it did not before? No; the change is purely in the wax, which receives a new figure or form by the impression; not in the seal, that was capable of imprinting the same long before. God was the same from eternity as he was when he made a signature of himself upon the creatures by creation, and is no more changed by stamping them into several forms, than the seal is changed by making impression upon the wax. As when a house is enlightened by the sun, or that which was cold is heated by it, there is a change in the house from darkness to light, from coldness to heat, but is there any change in the light and heat of the sun? There is a change in the thing enlightened or warmed by that light and heat which remains fixed and constant in the sun, which was as capable in itself to produce the same effects before as at that instant when it works them. So when God is the author of a new work, he is not changed, because he works it by an eternal will and an eternal power.

(3.) Nor is there any new relation acquired by God by the creation of the world. There was a new relation acquired by the creature; as when a man sins, he hath another relation to God than he had before; he hath relation to God as a criminal to a judge; but there is no change in God, but in the malefactor. The being of men makes no more change in God than the sins of men. As a tree is now on our right hand, and by our turning about it is on our left hand, sometimes before us, sometimes behind us, according to our motion near it or about it, and the turning of the body. There is no change in the tree, which remains firm and fixed in the earth; but the change is wholly in the posture of the body, whereby the tree may be said to be before us or behind us, or on the right hand or on the left hand.* God gained no new relation of Lord or Creator by the creation; for though he had created nothing to rule over, yet he had the power to create and rule though he did not create and rule. As a man may be called a skilful writer though he does not write, because he is able to do it when he pleases; or a man skilful in physic is called a physician though he doth not practise that skill, or discover his art in the distribution of medicines, because he may do it when he pleases, it depends upon his own will to shew his art when he has a mind to it, so the name Creator and Lord belongs to God from eternity, because he could create and rule though he did not create and rule. But howsoever, if there were any such change of relation, that God may be called Creator and Lord after the creation and not before, it is not a change in essence, nor in knowledge, nor in will; God gains no perfection nor diminution by it, his knowledge is not increased by it; he is no more by it than he was and will be if all those things ceased; and therefore Austin illustrates it by this similitude: as a piece of money, when it is given as the price of a thing, or deposited only as a pledge for the security of a thing borrowed, the coin is the same and is not changed, though the relation it had as a pledge and as a price be different from one another, so that suppose any new relation be added, yet there is nothing happens to the nature of God which may infer any change.

2. The second proposition. There was no change in the divine nature of the Son when he assumed human nature. There was an union of the two natures, but no change of the Deity into the humanity, or of the humanity into the Deity, both preserved their peculiar properties. The humanity was changed by a communication of excellent gifts from the divine nature, not by being brought into an equality with it; for that was impossible that a creature should become equal to the Creator. He 'took the form of a servant,' but he lost not the form of God, he despoiled not himself of the per-

* Petav. Theol. Dogmat., tom. i. lib.

fections of the Deity; he was indeed 'emptied, and became of no reputation,' Philip. ii. 7, but he did not cease to be God, though he was reputed to be only a man, and a very mean one too. The glory of his divinity was not extinguished nor diminished, though it was obscured and darkened under the veil of our infirmities; but there was no more change in the hiding of it than there is in the body of the sun when it is shadowed by the inter-position of a cloud. His blood, while it was pouring out from his veins, was the blood of God, Acts xx. 28; and therefore, when he was bowing the head of his humanity upon the cross, he had the nature and perfections of God; for had he ceased to be God, he had been a mere creature, and his sufferings would have been of as little value and satisfaction as the suffer-ings of a creature.

He could not have been a sufficient mediator had he ceased to be God; and he had ceased to be God had he lost any one perfection proper to the divine nature; and losing none, he lost not this of unchangeableness, which is none of the meanest belonging to the Deity. Why, by his union with the human nature, should he lose this any more than he lost his omniscience, which he discovered by his knowledge of the thoughts of men; or his mercy, which he manifested to the height in the time of his suffering? That is truly a change, when a thing ceaseth to be what it was before. This was not in Christ. He assumed our nature without laying aside his own.* When the soul is united to the body, doth it lose any of those perfections that are proper to its nature? Is there any change either in the substance or qualities of it? No; but it makes a change in the body; and of a dull lump it makes it a living mass, conveys vigour and strength to it, and by its power quickens it to sense and motion. So did the divine nature and human nature remain entire, there was no change of the one into the other, as Christ by a miracle changed water into wine, or men by art change sand or ashes into glass. And when he prays for 'the glory he had with God before the world was,' John xvii. 5, he prays that a glory he had in his Deity might shine forth in his person as Mediator, and be evinced in that height and splendour suitable to his dignity, which had been so lately darkened by his abasement; that as he had appeared to be the Son of man in the infirmity of the flesh, he might appear to be the Son of God in the glory of his per-son, that he might appear to be the Son of God and the Son of man in one person.

Again, there could be no change in this union†; for in a real change something is acquired which was not possessed before, neither formally nor eminently; but the divinity had from eternity before the incarnation, all the perfections of the human nature eminently in a nobler manner than they are in themselves, and therefore could not be changed by a real union.

3. The third proposition. Repentance and other affections ascribed to God in Scripture argue no change in God. We often read of God's repent-ing, repenting of the good he promised, Jer. xviii. 10, and of the evil he threatened, Exod. xxxii. 14, or of the work he hath wrought, Gen. vi. 6.

We must observe therefore that

(1.) Repentance is not properly in God. He is a pure Spirit, and is not capable of those passions which are signs of weakness and impotency, or subject to those regrets we are subject to. Where there is a proper repent-ance, there is a want of foresight, an ignorance of what would succeed, or a defect in the examination of the occurrences which might fall within con-sideration. All repentance of a fact is grounded upon a mistake in the

* Zanch. de Immutab. Dei. Goulart Immutab. de Dieu.
† Gamach. in part. 1, Aquin. qu. 9, cap. 1.

event which was not foreseen, or upon an after knowledge of the evil of the thing which was acted by the person repenting. But God is so wise that he cannot err, so holy he cannot do evil, and his certain prescience or foreknowledge secures him against any unexpected events. God doth not act but upon clear and infallible reason. And a change upon passion is accounted by all so great a weakness in man, that none can entertain so unworthy a conceit of God. Where he is said to repent, Gen. vi. 6, he is also said to grieve; now no proper grief can be imagined to be in God. As repentance is inconsistent with infallible foresight, so is grief no less inconsistent with undefiled blessedness: 'God is blessed for ever,' Rom. ix. 8, and therefore nothing can befall him that can stain that blessedness; his blessedness would be impaired and interrupted, while he is repenting, though he did soon rectify that which is the cause of his repentance: 'God is of one mind, and who can turn him? what his soul desires, that he doth,' Job xxiii. 13.

2. But God accommodates himself in the Scripture to our weak capacity. God hath no more of a proper repentance than he hath of a real body: though he, in accommodation to our weakness, ascribes to himself the members of our bodies to set out to our understanding the greatness of his perfections, we must not conclude him a body like us; so, because he is said to have anger and repentance, we must not conclude him to have passions like us. When we cannot fully comprehend him as he is, he clothes himself with our nature in his expressions, that we may apprehend him as we are able, and, by an inspection into ourselves, learn something of the nature of God; yet those human ways of speaking ought to be understood in a manner agreeable to the infinite excellency and majesty of God, and are only designed to mark out something in God which hath a resemblance with something in us. As we cannot speak to God as gods, but as men, so we cannot understand him speaking to us as a God, unless he condescends to speak to us like a man. God therefore frames his language to our dulness, not to his own state, and informs us, by our own phrases, what he would have us learn of his nature, as nurses talk broken language to young children. In all such expressions, therefore, we must ascribe the perfection we conceive in them to God, and lay the imperfection at the door of the creature.

3. Therefore repentance in God is only a change of his outward conduct, according to his infallible foresight and immutable will. He changes the way of his providential proceeding according to the carriage of the creature, without changing his will, which is the rule of his providence. When God speaks of his repenting that he had made man, Gen. vi. 6, it is only his changing his conduct from a way of kindness to a way of severity, and is a word suited to our capacities, to signify his detestation of sin and his resolution to punish it, after man had made himself quite another thing than God had made him. 'It repents me,' that is, I am purposed to destroy the world, as he that repents of his work throws it away;* as if a potter cast away the vessel he had framed, it were a testimony that he repented that ever he took pains about it; so the destruction of them seems to be a repentance in God that ever he made them, it is a change of events, not of counsels. Repentance in us is a grief for a former fact, and a changing of our course in it. Grief is not in God,† but his repentance is a willing a thing should not be as it was, which will was fixed from eternity; for, God foreseeing man would fall, and decreeing to permit it, he could not be said to repent in time of what he did not repent from eternity; and, therefore, if there were no repentance in God from eternity, there could be none in time; but

* Mercer *in loc.*   † Petavius Theol. Dogmat

God is said to repent when he changes the disposition of affairs without himself; as men when they repent alter the course of their actions, so God alters things *extra se*, or without himself, but changes nothing of his own purpose within himself; it rather notes the action he is about to do than anything in his own nature, or any change in his eternal purpose. God's repenting of his kindness is nothing but an inflicting of punishment, which the creature, by the change of his carriage, hath merited; as his repenting of the evil threatened is the withholding the punishment denounced, when the creature hath humbly submitted to his authority and acknowledged his crime.

Or else we may understand those expressions of joy, and grief, and re-pentance to signify thus much,* that the things declared to be the objects of joy, and grief, and repentance are of that nature that if God were capable of our passions he would discover himself in such cases as we do; as when the prophets mention the joys and applaudings of heaven, earth, and the sea, they only signify that the things they speak of are so good, that, if the heavens and the sea had natures capable of joy, they would express it upon that occasion in such a manner as we do; so would God have joy at the obedience of men, and grief at the unworthy carriage of men, and repent of his kindness when men abuse it, and repent of his punishment when men reform under his rod, were the majesty of his nature capable of such affections.

Prop. 4. The not fulfilling of some predictions in Scripture, which seem to imply a changeableness of the divine will, do not argue any change in it. As when he reprieved Hezekiah from death, after a message sent by the prophet Isaiah that he should die, 2 Kings xx. 1, 5, Isa. xxxviii. 1, 5, and when he made an arrest of that judgment he had threatened by Jonah against Nineveh, Jonah iii. 4, 10.

There is not, indeed, the same reason of promises and threatenings alto-gether, for in promising the obligation lies upon God, and the right to de-mand is in the party that performs the condition of the promise; but in threatenings the obligation lies upon the sinner, and God's right to punish is declared thereby; so that, though God doth not punish, his will is not changed, because his will was to declare the demerit of sin, and his right to punish upon the commission of it, though he may not punish, according to the strict letter of the threatening, the person sinning, but relax his own law for the honour of his attributes, and transfer the punishment from the offender to a person substituted in his room; this was the case in the first threatening against man, and the substituting a surety in the place of the malefactor.

But the answer to these cases is this,† that where we find predictions in Scripture declared and yet not executed, we must consider them not as absolute, but conditional, or, as the civil law calls it, an interlocutory sentence. God declared what would follow by natural causes, or by the de-merit of man, not what he would absolutely himself do; and in many of those predictions, though the condition be not expressed, yet it is to be understood; so the promises of God are to be understood with the condi-tion of perseverance in well-doing, and threatenings with a clause of revoca-tion annexed to them, provided that men repent. And this God lays down as a general case, alway to be remembered as a rule for the interpreting his threatenings against a nation, and the same reason will hold in threaten-ings against a particular person: Jer. xviii. 7–10, 'At what instant I shall speak concerning a nation, and concerning a kingdom, to pluck up,

* Daillé, in Sermon on 2 Peter iii. 9, p. 60.   † Rivet in Genes. exercita. 51, p. 213.

and pull down, and destroy it; if that nation against whom I have pronounced turn from their evil, I will repent of the evil that I thought to do unto them;' and so, when he speaks of planting a nation, if they do evil he will repent of the good, &c.   It is a universal rule by which all particular cases of this nature are to be tried, so that when man's repentance arrives, God remains firm in his first will, always equal to himself, and it is not he that changes, but man ; for since the interposition of the mediator, with an eye to whom God governed the world after the fall, the right of punishing was taken off if men repented, and mercy was to flow out, if, by a conversion, men returned to their duty, Ezek. xviii. 20, 21.   This I say is grounded upon God's entertaining the mediator, for the covenant of works discovered no such thing as repentance or pardon.   Now these general rules are to be the interpreters of particular cases, so that predictions of good are not to be counted absolute, if men return to evil; nor predictions of evil, if men be thereby reduced to a repentance of their crimes.

So Nineveh shall be destroyed, that is, according to the general rule, unless the inhabitants repent, which they did ; they manifested a belief of the threatening, and gave glory to God by giving credit to the prophet; and they had a notion of this rule God lays down in the other prophets, for they had an apprehension that, upon their humbling themselves, they might escape the threatened vengeance, and stop the shooting those arrows that were ready in the bow.*   Though Jonah proclaimed destruction without declaring any hopes of an arrest of judgment, yet their natural notions of God afforded some natural hopes of relief, if they did their duty, and spurned not against the prophet's message ; and therefore, saith one, God did not always express this condition, because it was needless ; his own rule revealed in Scripture was sufficient to some, and the natural notion all men had of God's goodness upon their repentance made it not absolutely necessary to declare it ; and, besides, saith he, it is bootless, the expressing it can do but little good ; secure ones will repent never the sooner, but rather presume upon their hopes of God's forbearance, and linger out their repentance till it be too late ; and to work men to repentance, whom he hath purposed to spare, he threatens them with terrible judgments, which, by how much the more terrible and peremptory they are, are likely to be more effectual for the end God in his purpose designs them, viz. to humble them under a sense of their demerit, and an acknowledgment of his righteous justice, and therefore, though they be absolutely denounced, yet they are to be conditionally interpreted, with a reservation of repentance.   As for that answer which one gives, that by forty days was not meant forty natural days, but forty prophetical days, that is, years, a day for year ; and that the city was destroyed forty years after by the Medes ; the expression of God's repenting upon their humiliation puts a bar to that interpretation.   God repented, that is, he did not bring the punishment upon them according to those days the prophet had expressed, and therefore forty days are to be understood ; and if it were meant of forty years, and they were destroyed at the end of that term, how could God be said to repent, since, according to that, the punishment threatened was, according to the time fixed, brought upon them ?   And the destruction of it forty years after will not be easily evinced, if Jonah lived in the time of Jeroboam the Second, king of Israel, as he did, 2 Kings xiv. 25 ; and Nineveh was destroyed in the time of Josiah, king of Judah. But the other answer is plain : God did not fulfil what he had threatened, because they reformed what they had committed. When the threatening was made, they were a fit object for justice ; but when they repented, they

* Sanderson's Sermon, part. ii. p. 157, 158.

were a fit object for a merciful respite. To threaten when sins are high, is a part of God's justice; not to execute when sins are revoked by repentance, is a part of God's goodness. And in the case of Hezekiah, 2 Kings xx. 1, 5, Isa. xxxviii. 1, 5, Isaiah comes with a message from God, that he should 'set his house in order, for he shall die;' that is, the disease was mortal, and no outward applications could in their own nature resist the distemper. 'Behold I will add to thy days fifteen years; I will heal thee.' It seems to me to be one entire message, because the latter part of it was so suddenly after the other committed to Isaiah, to be delivered to Hezekiah; for he was not gone out of the king's house before he was ordered to return with the news of his health, by an extraordinary indulgence of God against the power of nature and force of the disease: 'Behold, I will add to thy life,' noting it an extraordinary thing. He was in the second court of the king's house when this word came to him, 2 Kings xx. 4; the king's house having three courts, so that he was not gone above half-way out the palace. God might send this message of death, to prevent the pride Hezekiah might swell with for his deliverance from Sennacherib: as Paul had a messenger of Satan to buffet him, to prevent his lifting up, 2 Cor. xii. 7; and this good man was subject to this sin, as we find afterwards in the case of the Babylonish ambassadors; and God delayed this other part of the message to humble him, and draw out his prayer; and, as soon as ever he found Hezekiah in this temper, he sent Isaiah with a comfortable message of recovery, so that the will of God was to signify to him the mortality of his distemper, and afterwards to relieve him by a message of an extraordinary recovery.

Prop. 5. God is not changed, when of loving to any creatures he becomes angry with them, or of angry he becomes appeased. The change in these cases is in the creature; according to the alteration in the creature, it stands in a various relation to God; an innocent creature is the object of his kindness, an offending creature is the object of his anger; there is a change in the dispensation of God, as there is a change in the creature, making himself capable of such dispensations. God always acts according to the immutable nature of his holiness, and can no more change in his affections to good and evil, than he can in his essence. When the devils now fallen stood as glorious angels, they were the objects of God's love, because holy. When they fell, they were the objects of God's hatred, because impure; the same reason which made him love them while they were pure, made him hate them when they were criminal. The reason of his various dispensations to them was the same in both, as considered in God, his immutable holiness, but as respecting the creature different; the nature of the creature was changed, but the divine holy nature of God remained the same. 'With the pure thou wilt shew thyself pure, and with the froward thou wilt shew thyself froward,' Ps. xviii. 26. He is a refreshing light to those that obey him, and a consuming fire to those that resist him. Though the same angels were not always loved, yet the same reason that moved him to love them, moved him to hate them. It had argued a change in God, if he had loved them alway, in whatsoever posture they were towards him. It could not be counted love, but a weakness and impotent fondness; the change is in the object, not in the affection of God. For the object loved before is not beloved now, because that which was the motive of love, is not now in it. So that the creature having a different state from what it had, falls under a different affection or dispensation.

It had been a mutable affection in God, to love that which was not worthy of love, with the same love wherewith he loved that which had the greatest resemblance to himself. Had God loved the fallen angels in that state and for that state, he had hated himself, because he had loved that which was contrary to himself and the image of his own holiness, which made them appear before good in his sight. The will of God is unchangeably set to love righteousness and hate iniquity, and from this hatred to punish it. And if a righteous creature contracts the wrath of God, or a sinful creature hath the communications of God's love, it must be by a change in themselves. Is the sun changed when it hardens one thing and softens another, according to the disposition of the several subjects? or when the sun makes a flower more fragrant, and a dead carcass more noisome? There are diverse effects, but the reason of that diversity is not in the sun, but in the subject; the sun is the same, and produceth those different effects, by the same quality of heat. So if an unholy soul approach to God, God looks angrily upon him; if a holy soul come before him, the same immutable perfection in God draws out his kindness towards him. As some think, the sun would rather refresh than scorch us, if our bodies were of the same nature and substance with that luminary.

As the will of God for creating the world was no new, but an eternal will, though it manifested itself in time, so the will of God for the punishment of sin, or the reconciliation of the sinner, was no new will, though his wrath in time break out in the effects of it upon sinners, and his love flows out in the effects of it upon penitents. Christ by his death reconciling God to man, did not alter the will of God, but did what was consonant to his eternal will. He came not to change his will, but to execute his will: ' Lo I come to do thy will, O God,' Heb. x. 7. And the grace of God in Christ was not a new grace, but an old grace in a new appearance; ' the grace of God hath appeared,' Titus ii. 11.

Prop. 6. A change of laws by God argues no change in God, when God abrogates some laws which he had settled in the church, and enacts others. I spake of this something the last day; I shall only add this, God commanded one thing to the Jews, when the church was in an infant state, and removed those laws when the church came to growth. The elements of the world were suited to the state of children, Gal. iv. 3. A mother feeds not the infant with the same diet as she doth when it is grown up. Our Saviour acquainted not his disciples with some things at one time which he did at another, because they were not able to bear them. Where was the change, in Christ's will, or in their growth from a state of weakness to that of strength? A physician prescribes not the same thing to a person in health, as he doth to one conflicting with a distemper; nor the same thing in the beginning, as he doth in the state or declination of the disease. The physician's will and skill are the same, but the capacity and necessity of the patient for this ¡or that medicine or method of proceeding are [not] the same.

When God changed the ceremonial law, there was no change in the divine will, but an execution of his will. For when God commanded the observance of the law, he intended not the perpetuity of it; nay, in the prophet he declares the cessation of it; he decreed to command it, but he decreed to command it only for such a time; so that the abrogation of it was no less an execution of his decree, than the establishment of it for a season was. The commanding of it was pursuant to his decree for the appointing of it, and the nulling of it was pursuant to his decree of continuing it only for such a season. So that in all this there was no change in the will of God.

The counsel of God stands sure; what changes soever there are in the world, are not in God or his will, but in the events of things, and the different relations of things to God; it is in the creature, not in the Creator. The sun alway remains of the same hue, and is not discoloured in itself, because it shines green through a green glass, and blue through a blue glass; the different colours come from the glass, not from the sun. The change is alway in the disposition of the creature, not in the nature of God or his will.

V. *Use* 1. For information.

1. If God be unchangeable in his nature, and immutability be a property of God, then Christ hath a divine nature. This in the psalm is applied to Christ in the Hebrews, Heb. i. 11, where he joins the citation out of this psalm with that out of Ps. xlv. 6, 7, 'Thy throne, O God, is for ever and ever: thou hast loved righteousness and hated iniquity: therefore God, even thy God, hath anointed thee with the oil of gladness above thy fellows; and thou, Lord, in the beginning hast laid the foundation of the earth,' &c. As the first must necessarily be meant of Christ the mediator,—and therein he is distinguished from God, as one anointed by him,—so the other must be meant of Christ, whereby he is made one with God in regard of the creation and dissolution of the world, in regard of eternity and immutability. Both the testimonies are linked together by the copulative *and:* 'AND thou Lord,' declaring thereby that they are both to be understood of the same person, the Son of God. The design of the chapter is to prove Christ to be God; and such things are spoken of him as could not belong to any creature, no, not to the most excellent of angels. The same person that is said to be anointed above his fellows, and is said to lay the foundation of the earth and heavens, is said to be 'the same,' that is, the same in himself. The prerogative of sameness belongs to that person, as well as creation of heaven and earth.

The Socinians say it is spoken of God, and that God shall destroy the heavens by Christ; if so, Christ is not a mere creature, not created when he was incarnate; for the same person that shall change the world, did create the world. If God shall change the world by him, God also created the world by him. He was then before the world was; for how could God create the world by one that was not? that was not in being till after the creation of the world? The heavens shall be changed, but the person who is to change the heavens is said to be the same, or unchangeable, in the creation as well as the dissolution of the world. This sameness refers to the whole sentence.

The psalm wherein the text is,* and whence this in the Hebrews is cited, is properly meant of Christ, and redemption by him, and the completing of it at the last day, and not of the Babylonish captivity. That captivity was not so deplorable as the state the psalmist describes. Daniel and his companions flourished in that captivity. It could not reasonably be said of them, 'that their days were consumed like smoke,' their 'heart withered like grass;' that they 'forgot to eat their bread,' as it is, ver. 3, 4; besides, he complains of shortness of life, ver. 11. But none had any more reason to complain of that in the time of the captivity, than before and after it, than at any other time. Their deliverance would contribute nothing to the natural length of their lives; besides, when Sion should be built, the 'heathen should fear the name of the Lord' (that is, worship God), 'and all the kings of the earth his glory,' ver. 15. The rearing the second temple after the deliverance did not proselyte the nations; nor did the kings of the earth worship the glory of God; nor did God appear in such glory at the erecting the

* Placeus de Deitate Christi.

second temple. The second temple was less glorious than the first, for it wanted some of the ornaments which were the glory of the first. But it is said of this state, that 'when the Lord should build up Sion, he should appear in his glory,' ver. 16, his proper glory, and extraordinary glory. Now that God, who shall appear in glory and build up Sion, is the Son of God, the Redeemer of the world; he builds up the church, he causes the nations to fear the Lord, and the kings of the earth his glory. He broke down the partition wall, and opened a door for the entrance of the Gentiles. He struck the chains from off the prisoners, and 'loosed those that were appointed to death' by the curse of the law, ver. 20. And to this person is ascribed the creation of the world; and he is pronounced to remain the same in the midst of an infinite number of changes in inferior things. And it is likely the psalmist considers not only the beginning of redemption, but the completing of it at the second coming of Christ; for he complains of those evils which shall be removed by his second coming, viz., the shortness of life, persecutions, and reproaches, wherewith the church is afflicted in this world; and comforts not himself with those attributes which are directly opposed to sin, as the mercy of God, the covenant of God, but with those that are opposed to mortality and calamities, as the unchangeableness and eternity of God; and from thence infers a perpetual establishment of believers: 'The children of thy servants shall continue, and their seed shall be established before thee,' ver. 28; so that the psalm itself seems to aim in the whole discourse at Christ, and asserts his divinity, which the apostle, as an interpreter, doth fully evidence; applying it to him, and manifesting his deity by his immutability as well as eternity. While all other things lose their forms, and pass through multitudes of variations, he constantly remains the same, and shall be the same, when all the empires of the world shall slide away, and a period be put to the present motions of the creation.* And as there was no change made in his being by the creation of things, so neither shall there be by the final alteration of things; he shall see them finish, as he saw them rise up into being, and be the same after their reign as he was before their original; he is 'the first and the last,' Rev. i. 17.

2. Here is ground and encouragement for worship. An atheist will make another use of this. If God be immutable, why should we worship him, why should we pray to him? Good will come if he wills it, evil cannot be averted by all our supplications, if he hath ordered it to fall upon us.

But certainly, since unchangeableness in knowing, and willing goodness is a perfection, an adoration and admiration is due to God, upon the account of this excellence. If he be God, he is to be reverenced, and the more highly reverenced, because he cannot but be God.

Again, what comfort could it be to pray to a god, that, like the chameleon, changed colours every day, every moment? What encouragement could there be to lift up our eyes to one that were of one mind this day, and of another mind to-morrow? Who would put up a petition to an earthly prince that were so mutable as to grant a petition one day, and deny it another, and change his own act? But if a prince promise this or that thing upon such or such a condition, and you know his promise to be as unchangeable as the laws of the Medes and Persians, would any man reason thus;—because it is unchangeable, we will not seek to him, we will not perform the condition upon which the fruit of the proclamation is to be enjoyed?—Who would not count such an inference ridiculous? What blessings hath not God promised upon the condition of seeking him? Were he of an unrighteous nature, or changeable in his mind, this would be a bar to our seeking him,

* Daille, Melang. des Sermons, part ii. sect. i. p. 8–10, &c.

and frustrate our hopes.   But since it is otherwise, is not this excellency of his nature the highest encouragement to ask of him the blessings he hath promised, and a beam from heaven to fire our zeal in asking ?   If you desire things against his will, which he hath declared he will not grant, prayer then would be an act of disobedience, an injury to him, as well as an act of folly in itself ; his unchangeableness then might stifle such desires. But if we ask according to his will, and according to our reasonable wants, what ground have we to make such a ridiculous argument ?   He hath willed everything that may be for our good, if we perform the condition he hath required ; and hath put it upon record, that we may know it and regulate our desires and supplications according to it.   If we will not seek him, his immutability cannot be a bar, but our own folly is the cause ; and by our neglect we despoil him of this perfection as to us, and either imply that he is not sincere, and means not as he speaks ; or that he is as changeable as the wind, sometimes this thing, sometimes that, and not at all to be con- fided in.   If we ask according to his revealed will, the unchangeableness of his nature will assure us of the grant ; and what a presumption would it be in a creature dependent upon his sovereign, to ask that which he knows he has declared his will against, since there is no good we can want but he hath promised to give, upon our sincere and ardent desire for it.

God hath decreed to give this or that to man, but conditionally, and by the means of inquiring after him, and asking for it : Ezek. xxxvi. 37, Mat. vii. 7, ' Ask, and you shall receive ;' as much as to say, You shall not receive unless you ask.   When the highest promises are made, God expects they shall be put in suit.   Our Saviour joins the promise and the petition together, the promise to encourage the petition, and the petition to enjoy the promise.   He doth not say, perhaps it shall be given, but it shall, that is, it certainly shall ; your heavenly Father is unchangeably willing to give you those things.   We must depend upon his immutability for the thing, and submit to his wisdom for the time.   Prayer is an acknowledgment of our dependence upon God, which dependence could have no firm foundation without unchangeableness.   Prayer doth not desire any change in God, but is offered to God that he would confer those things which he hath immu- tably willed to communicate ; but he willed them not without prayer as the means of bestowing them.   The light of the sun is ordered for our comfort, for the discovery of visible things, for the ripening the fruits of the earth ; but withal it is required that we use our faculty of seeing, that we employ our industry in sowing and planting, and expose our fruits to the view of the sun, that they may receive the influence of it.   If a man shuts his eyes, and complains that the sun has changed into darkness, it would be ridiculous ; the sun is not changed, but we alter ourselves.   Nor is God changed in not giving us the blessings he hath promised, because he hath promised in the way of a due address to him, and opening our souls to receive his influence ; and to this, his immutability is the greatest encouragement.

3. This shews how contrary man is to God, in regard of his inconstancy. What an infinite distance is there between the immutable God and mutable man, and how should we bewail this flittingness in our nature !

There is a mutability in us as creatures, and a creature cannot but be mutable by nature, otherwise it were not a creature, but God.   The establish- ment of any creature is from grace and gift.   Naturally we tend to nothing, as we come from nothing.   This creature-mutability is not our sin, yet it should cause us to lie down under a sense of our own nothingness in the presence of the Creator.   The angels, as creatures, though not corrupt, cover their faces before him.   And the arguments God uses to humble Job, though a fallen creature, are not from his corruption, for I do not remember that he taxed him with that, but from the greatness of his majesty, and excellency of his nature declared in his works, Job xxxviii.-xli. And therefore men that have no sense of God, and humility before him, forget that they are creatures, as well as corrupt ones.

How great is the distance between God and us in regard of our inconstancy in good, which is not natural to us by creation! For the mind and affections were regular, and by the great Artificer were pointed to God as the object of knowledge and love. We have the same faculties of understanding, will, and affection as Adam had in innocence; but not with the same light, the same bias, and the same ballast. Man, by his fall, wounded his head and heart; the wound in his head made him unstable in the truth, and that in his heart unstedfast in his affections. He changed himself from the image of God to that of the devil, from innocence to corruption, and from an ability to be stedfast to a perpetual inconstancy. His 'silver became dross, and his wine was mixed with water,' Isa. i. 22. He changed,

(1.) To inconstancy in truth, opposed to the immutability of knowledge in God. How are our minds floating between ignorance and knowledge! Truth in us is like those *ephemera*, creatures of a day's continuance, springs up in the morning and expires at night. How soon doth that fly away from us which we have had, not only some weak flashes of, but which we have learned and had some relish of! The devil 'stood not in the truth,' John viii. 44, and therefore manages his engines to make us as unstable as himself. Our minds reel, and corrupt reasonings oversway us; like sponges we suck up water, and a light compression makes us spout it out again. Truths are not engraven upon our hearts, but writ as in dust, defaced by the next puff of wind: 'carried about with every wind of doctrine,' Eph. iv. 14, like a ship without a pilot and sails, at the courtesy of the next storm; or like clouds, that are tenants to the wind and sun, moved by the wind, and melted by the sun. The Galatians were no sooner called into the grace of God, but they were removed from it, Gal. i. 6. Some have been reported to have *menstruam fidem*, kept an opinion for a month, and many are like him that believed the soul's immortality no longer than he had Plato's book of that subject in his hand.* One likens such to children; they play with truths as children do with babies, one while embrace them, and a little after throw them into the dirt. How soon do we forget what the truth is delivered to us, and what it represented us to be! James i. 23, 24. Is it not a thing to be bewailed, that man should be such a weather-cock, turned about with every breath of wind, and shifting aspects as the wind shifts points?

(2.) Inconstancy in will and affections, opposed to the immutability of will in God. We waver between God and Baal; and while we are not only resolving, but upon motion a little way, look back with a hankering after Sodom; sometimes lifted up with heavenly intentions, and presently cast down with earthly cares; like a ship that by an advancing wave seems to aspire to heaven, and the next fall of the wave makes it sink down to the depths. We change purposes oftener than fashions, and our resolutions are like letters in water, whereof no mark remains. We will be as John to-day to love Christ, and as Judas to-morrow to betray him, and by an unworthy levity pass into the camp of the enemies of God; resolved to be as holy as angels in the morning, when the evening beholds us as impure as devils How often do we hate what before we loved, and shun what before we longed for! And our resolutions are like vessels of crystal, which break at the

* Sedgwick, Christ's Counsel, p. 230.

first knock, are dashed in pieces by the next temptation. Saul resolved not to persecute David any more, but you soon find him upon his old game. Pharaoh more than once promised, and probably resolved, to let Israel go ; but at the end of the storm his purposes vanish, Exod. viii. 27, 32. When an affliction pincheth men, they intend to change their course, and the next news of ease changes their intentions ; like a bow, not fully bent in their inclinations, they cannot reach the mark, but live many years between resolutions of obedience and affections to rebellion, Ps. lxxviii. 17 ; and what promises men make to God are often the fruit of their passion, their fear, not of their will. The Israelites were startled at the terrors wherewith the law was delivered, and promised obedience, Exod. xx. 19 ; but a month after forgat them, and made a golden calf, and in the sight of Sinai call for and dance before their gods, Exod. xxxii. Never people more inconstant. Peter, who vowed an allegiance to his Master, and a courage to stick to him, forswears him almost with the same breath. Those that cry out with a zeal, ' The Lord he is God,' shortly after return to the service of their idols, 1 Kings xviii. 39. That which seems to be our pleasure this day, is our vexation to-morrow. A fear of a judgment puts us into a religious pang, and a love to our lusts reduceth us to a rebellious inclination ; as soon as the danger is over, the saint is forgotten. Salvation and damnation present themselves to us, touch us, and engender some weak wishes, which are dissolved by the next allurements of a carnal interest. No hold can be taken of our promises, no credit is to be given to our resolutions.

(3.) Inconstancy in practice. How much beginning in the Spirit and ending in the flesh ; one day in the sanctuary, another in the stews ; clear in the morning as the sun, and clouded before noon ; in heaven by an excellency of gifts, in hell by a course of profaneness ! Like a flower, which some mention, that changes its colour three times a day, one part white, then purple, then yellow. The spirit lusts against the flesh, and the flesh quickly triumphs over the spirit. In a good man, how often is there a spiritual lethargy ! Though he doth not openly defame God, yet he doth not always glorify him ; he doth not forsake the truth, but he doth not always make the attainment of it, and settlement in it, his business. This levity discovers itself in religious duties : ' When I would do good, evil is present with me,' Rom. vii. 21. Never more present than when we have a mind to do good, and never more present than when we have a mind to do the best and greatest good. How hard is it to make our thoughts and affections keep their stand ! Place them upon a good object, and they will be frisking from it, as a bird from one bough, one fruit to another. We vary postures according to the various objects we meet with. The course of the world is a very airy thing, suited to the uncertain motions of that prince of the power of the air which works in it, Eph. ii. 2.

This ought to be bewailed by us. Though we may stand fast in the truth, though we may spin our resolutions into a firm web, though the spirit may triumph over the flesh in our practice, yet we ought to bewail it, because inconstancy is our nature, and what fixedness we have in good is from grace. What we find practised by most men, is natural to all.* ' As face answers to face in a glass, so doth heart to heart,' Prov. xxvii. 19 ; a face in the glass is not more like a natural face, whose image it is, than one man's heart is naturally like another.

First, It is natural to those out of the church. Nebuchadnezzar is so affected with Daniel's prophetic spirit, that he would have none accounted the true God, but the God of Daniel, Dan. ii. 47. How soon doth this

---

* Lawrence of Faith, p. 262.

notion slip from him, and an image must be set up for all to worship, upon pain of a most cruel, painful death! Daniel's God is quite forgotten. The miraculous deliverance of the three children for not worshipping his image, makes him settle a decree to secure the honour of God from the reproach of his subjects, Dan. iii. 29; yet a little while after, you have him strutting in his palace, as if there were no God but himself.

Secondly, It is natural to those in the church. The Israelites were the only church God had in the world, and a notable example of inconstancy. After the miracles of Egypt, they murmured against God, when they saw Pharaoh marching with an army at their heels. They desired food, and soon nauseated the manna they were before fond of. When they came into Canaan, they sometimes worshipped God, and sometimes idols, not only the idols of one nation, but of all their neighbours. In which regard God calls this his heritage a speckled bird, Jer. xii. 9, a peacock, saith Jerome, inconstant, made up of varieties of idolatrous colours and ceremonies.

This levity of spirit is the root of all mischief: it scatters our thoughts in the service of God; it is the cause of all revolts and apostasies from him; it makes us unfit to receive the communications of God; whatsoever we hear is like words writ in sand, ruffled out by the next gale; whatsoever is put into us is like precious liquour in a palsy hand, soon spilt. It breeds distrust of God; when we have an uncertain judgment of him, we are not like to confide in him. An uncertain judgment will be followed with a distrustful heart. In fine, where it is prevalent, it is a certain sign of ungodliness; to be driven with the wind like chaff, and to be ungodly, is all one in the judgment of the Holy Ghost: Ps. i. 4, ' The ungodly are like the chaff which the wind drives away,' which signifies not their destruction, but their disposition, for their destruction is inferred from it, ver. 5, ' Therefore the ungodly shall not stand in judgment.'

How contrary is this to the unchangeable God, who is always the same, and would have us the same, in our religious promises and resolutions for good!

4. If God be immutable, it is sad news to those that are resolved in wickedness, or careless of returning to that duty he requires. Sinners must not expect that God will alter his will, make a breach upon his nature, and violate his own word, to gratify their lusts. No; it is not reasonable God should dishonour himself to secure them, and cease to be God, that they may continue to be wicked, by changing his own nature, that they may be unchanged in their vanity. God is the same; goodness is as amiable in his sight, and sin as abominable in his eyes now, as it was at the beginning of the world. Being the same God, he is the same enemy to the wicked, as the same friend to the righteous; he is the same in knowledge, and cannot forget sinful acts; he is the same in will, and cannot approve of unrighteous practices; goodness cannot but be alway the object of his love, and wickedness cannot but be alway the object of his hatred; and as his aversion to sin is alway the same, so as he hath been in his judgments upon sinners, the same he will be still; for the same perfection of immutability belongs to his justice for the punishment of sin, as to his holiness for his disaffection to sin. Though the covenant of works was changeable by the crime of man violating it, yet it was unchangeable in regard of God's justice vindicating it, which is inflexible in the punishment of the breaches of his law. The law had a preceptive part, and a minatory part; when man changed the observation of the precept, the righteous nature of God could not null the execution of the threatening; he could not upon the account of this perfection neglect his just word, and countenance the unrighteous transgression. Though there were no more rational creatures in being but

Adam and Eve, yet God subjected them to that death he had assured them of; and from this immutability of his will ariseth the necessity of the suffering of the Son of God for the relief of the apostate creature. His will in the second covenant is as unchangeable as that in the first, only repentance is settled as the condition of the second, which was not indulged in the first; and without repentance the sinner must irrevocably perish, or God must change his nature. There must be a change in man, there can be none in God: 'His bow is bent, his arrows are ready, if the wicked do not turn,' Ps. vii. 12. There is not an atheist, an hypocrite, a profane person, that ever was upon the earth, but God's soul abhorred him as such, and the like he will abhor for ever. While any therefore continue so, they may sooner expect the heavens should roll as they please, the sun stand still at their order, the stars change their course at their beck, than that God should change his nature, which is opposite to profaneness and vanity: 'Who hath hardened himself against him, and hath prospered?' Job ix. 4.

Use 2. Of comfort.

The immutability of a good God is a strong ground of consolation. Subjects wish a good prince to live for ever, as being loath to change him, but care not how soon they are rid of an oppressor. This unchangeableness of God's will shews him as ready to accept any that come to him as ever he was, so that we may with confidence make our addresses to him, since he cannot change his affections to goodness. The fear of change in a friend hinders a full reliance upon him; an assurance of stability encourages hope and confidence. This attribute is the strongest prop for faith in all our addresses; it is not a single perfection, but the glory of all those that belong to his nature; for he is 'unchangeable in his love,' Jer. xxxi. 3; 'in his truth,' Ps. cxvii. 2. The more solemn revelation of himself in this name *Jehovah*, which signifies chiefly his eternity and immutability, was to support the Israelites' faith, in expectation of a deliverance from Egypt, that he had not retracted his purpose, and his promise made to Abraham for giving Canaan to his posterity. Exod. iii. 14–17. Herein is the basis and strength of all his promises; therefore saith the psalmist, 'Those that know thy name will put their trust in thee,' Ps. ix. 10; those that are spiritually acquainted with thy name *Jehovah*, and have a true sense of it upon their hearts, will put their trust in thee. His goodness could not be distrusted, if his unchangeableness were well apprehended and considered. All distrust would fly before it as darkness before the sun; it only gets advantage of us when we are not well grounded in his name; and if ever we trusted God, we have the same reason to trust him for ever: Isa. xxvi. 4, 'Trust in the Lord for ever, for in the Lord Jehovah is everlasting strength,' or as it is in the Hebrew, 'a rock of ages;' that is, perpetually unchangeable. We find the traces of God's immutability in the creatures; he has by his peremptory decree set bounds to the sea: 'Hitherto shalt thou come, but no further; and here shall thy proud waves be stayed,' Job xxxviii. 11. Do we fear the sea overflowing us in this island? No, because of his fixed decree. And is not his promise in his word as unchangeable as his word concerning inanimate things, as good a ground to rest upon?

1. The covenant stands unchangeable. Mutable creatures break their leagues and covenants, and snap them asunder like Samson's cords, when they are not accommodated to their interests. But an unchangeable God keeps his: 'The mountains shall depart, and the hills be removed; but my kindness shall not depart from thee, nor shall the covenant of my peace be removed,' Isa. liv. 10. The heaven and earth shall sooner fall asunder, and the strongest and firmest parts of the creation crumble to dust,

sooner than one iota of my covenant shall fail. It depends upon the unchangeableness of his will, and the unchangeableness of his word, and therefore is called ' the immutability of his counsel,' Heb. vi. 17. It is the fruit of the everlasting purpose of God, whence the apostle links purpose and grace together, 2 Tim. i. 9. A covenant with a nation may be changeable, because it may not be built upon the eternal purpose of God to put his fear in the heart, but with respect to the creature's obedience. Thus God chose Jerusalem as the place wherein he would dwell for ever, Ps. cxxxii. 14, yet he threatens to depart from them, when they had broken covenant with him, and ' the glory of the Lord went up from the midst of the city to the mountain on the east side,' Ezek. xi. 23. The covenant of grace doth not run, ' I will be your God, *if* you will be my people;' but ' I will be their God, *and* they shall be my people.' Hosea ii. 19, &c., ' I will betroth thee to me for ever; I will say, Thou art my people; and they shall say, Thou art my God.' His everlasting purpose is to write his laws in the hearts of the elect. He puts a condition to his covenant of grace, the condition of faith, and he resolves to work that condition in the hearts of the elect; and therefore believers have two immutable pillars for their support, stronger than those erected by Solomon at the porch of the temple, 1 Kings vii. 21, called Jachin and Boaz, to note the firmness of that building dedicated to God : these are *election*, or the standing counsel of God, and the *covenant of grace*. He will not revoke the covenant, and blot the names of his elect out of the book of life.

2. Perseverance is ascertained. It consists not with the majesty of God to call a person effectually to himself to-day, to make him fit for his eternal love, to give him faith, and take away that faith to-morrow; his effectual call is the fruit of his eternal election, and that counsel hath no other foundation but his constant and unchangeable will; a foundation that stands sure, and therefore called the foundation of God, and not of the creature; ' the foundation of God stands sure, the Lord knows who are his,' 2 Tim. ii. 19. It is not founded upon our own natural strength, it may be then subject to change, as all the products of nature are; the fallen angels had created grace in their innocency, but lost it by their fall.* Were this the foundation of the creature, it might soon be shaken, since man after his revolt can ascribe nothing constant to himself but his own inconstancy; but the foundation is not in the infirmity of nature, but the strength of grace, and of the grace of God who is immutable, who wants not virtue to be able, nor kindness to be willing, to preserve his own foundation. To what purpose doth our Saviour tell his disciples their ' names were written in heaven,' Luke x. 20, but to mark the infallible certainty of their salvation by an opposition to those things which perish and have their names written in the earth, Jer. xvii. 13, or upon the sand, where they may be defaced? And why should Christ order his disciples to rejoice that their names were written in heaven, if God were changeable to blot them out again? Or why should the apostle assure us that though God had rejected the greatest part of the Jews, he had not therefore rejected his people elected according to his purpose and immutable counsel, because there are none of the elect of God but will come to salvation; for, saith he, ' the election hath obtained it,' Rom. xi. 7; that is, all those that are of the election have obtained it, and the others are hardened. Where the seal of sanctification is stamped it is a testimony of God's election, and that foundation shall stand true. ' The foundation of the Lord stands sure, having this seal, the Lord knows who are his;' that is, the foundation, the ' naming the name of Christ,' or believ-

* Turretine, Ser. p. 322.

ing in Christ and ‘ departing from iniquity,’ is the seal.* As it is impossible when God calls those things that are not, but that they should spring
up into being and appear before him, so it is impossible but that the seed
of God by his eternal purpose should be brought to a spiritual life ; and that
calling cannot be retracted, for that ‘ gift and calling is without repentance,’
Rom. xi. 29. And when repentance is removed from God in regard of some
works, the immutability of those works is declared ; and the reason of that
immutability is their pure dependence on the eternal favour and unchangeable grace of God, ‘ purposed in himself,’ Eph. i. 9, 11, and not upon the
mutability of the creature. Hence their happiness is not as patents among
men, *quamdiu bene se gesserint*, so long as they behave themselves well, but
they have a promise, that they shall behave themselves so as never wholly
to depart from God : Jer. xxxii. 40, ‘ I will make an everlasting covenant
with them, that I will not turn away from them, to do them good ; but I
will put my fear in their hearts, that they shall not depart from me.’ God
will not turn from them, to do them good, and promiseth that they shall
not turn from him for ever or forsake him. And the bottom of it is the
everlasting covenant, and therefore believing and sealing, for security, are
linked together, Eph. i. 13. And when God doth inwardly teach us his
law, he puts in a will not to depart from it : Ps. cxix. 102, ‘ I have not
departed from thy judgments.’ What is the reason ?   ‘ For thou hast
taught me.’
    3. By this, eternal happiness is ensured. This is the inference made
from the eternity and unchangeableness of God in the verse following the
text : ver. 28, ‘ The children of thy servants shall continue, and their seed
shall be established before thee.’ This is the sole conclusion drawn from
those perfections of God solemnly asserted before. The children which the
prophets and apostles have begotten to thee, shall be totally delivered from
the relics of their apostasy and the punishment due to them, and rendered
partakers of immortality with thee, as sons to dwell in their Father's house
for ever. The Spirit begins a spiritual life here, to fit for an immutable life
in glory hereafter, where believers shall be placed upon a throne that cannot
be shaken, and possess a crown that shall not be taken off their heads for
ever.
    Use 3. Of exhortation.
    1. Let a sense of the changeableness and uncertainty of all other things
beside God be upon us. There are as many changes as there are figures in
the world. The whole fashion of the world is a transient thing ; every man
may say as Job, ‘ Changes and war are against me,’ Job x. 17. Lot chose
the plain of Sodom, because it was the richer soil ; he was but a little time
there before he was taken prisoner, and his substance made the spoil of his
enemy. That is again restored ; but a while after, fire from heaven devours
his wealth, though his person was secured from the judgment by a special
providence. We burn with a desire to settle ourselves, but mistake the way,
and build castles in the air, which vanish like bubbles of soap in water.
    And therefore,
    (1.) Let not our thoughts dwell much upon them. Do but consider those
souls that are in the possession of an unchangeable God, that behold his
never-fading glory. Would it not be a kind of hell to them, to have their
thoughts starting out to these things, or find any desire in themselves to the
changeable trifles of the earth ? Nay, have we not reason to think that they
cover their faces with shame, that ever they should have such a weakness of
spirit when they were here below, as to spend more thoughts upon them than

* Cocceius.

were necessary for this present life, much more that they should, at any time, value and court them above an unchangeable good ? Do they not disdain themselves, that they should ever debase the immutable perfections of God, as to have neglecting thoughts of him at any time, for the entertainment of such a mean and inconstant rival ?

(2.) Much less should we trust in them or rejoice in them. The best things are mutable, and things of such a nature are not fit objects of confidence. Trust not in riches ; they have their wanes as well as increases. They rise sometimes like a torrent, and flow in upon men ; but resemble also a torrent in as sudden a fall and departure, and leave nothing but slime behind them. Trust not in honour ; all the honour and applause in the world is no better than an inheritance of wind, which the pilot is not sure of, but shifts from one corner to another, and stands not perpetually in the same point of the heavens. How in a few ages did the house of David, a great monarch, and a man after God's own heart, descend to a mean condition, and all the glory of that house shut up in the stock of a carpenter ! David's sheep-hook was turned into a sceptre, and the sceptre, by the same hand of providence, turned into a hatchet in Joseph his descendant.

Rejoice not immoderately in wisdom ; that and learning languish with age. A wound in the head may impair that which is the glory of a man. If an organ be out of frame, folly may succeed, and all a man's prudence be wound up in an irrecoverable dotage. Nebuchadnezzar was no fool, yet by a sudden hand of God he became, not only a fool or a madman, but a kind of brute. Rejoice not in strength ; that decays, and a mighty man may live to see his strong arm withered, and a ' grasshopper to become a burden,' Eccles. xii. 5. ' The strong men shall bow themselves, and the grinders shall cease because they are few,' ver. 3. Nor rejoice in children ; they are like birds upon a tree, that make a little chirping music, and presently fall into the fowler's net. Little did Job expect such sad news as the loss of all his progeny at a blow, when the messenger knocked at his gate. And such changes happen oftentimes, when our expectations of comfort, and a contentment in them, are at the highest. How often doth a string crack when the musician hath wound it up to a just height for a tune, and all his pains and delight marred in a moment ! Nay, all these things change while we are using them, like ice that melts between our fingers, and flowers that wither while we are smelling to them. The apostle gave them a good title, when he called them ' uncertain riches,' and thought it a strong argument to dissuade them from trusting in them, 1 Tim. vi. 17. The wealth of the merchant depends upon the winds and waves, and the revenue of the husbandman upon the clouds ; and since they depend upon those things which are used to express the most changeableness, they can be no fit object for trust. Besides, God sometimes ' kindles a fire under all a man's glory,' Isa. x. 16, which doth insensibly consume it ; and while we have them, the fear of losing them renders us not very happy in the fruition of them. We can scarce tell whether they are contentments or no, because sorrow follows them so close at the heels. It is not an unnecessary exhortation for good men ; the best men have been apt to place too much trust in them. David thought himself immutable in his prosperity ; and such thoughts could not be without some immoderate outlets of the heart to them, and confidences in them. And Job promised himself to ' die in his nest,' and ' multiply his days as the sand,' without any interruption, Job xxix. 18, 19, &c. ; but he was mistaken and disappointed.

Let me add this : trust not in men, who are as inconstant as anything else, and often change their most ardent affections into implacable hatred ; and though their affections may not be changed, their power to help you may.

Haman's friends, that depended on him one day, were crest-fallen the next, when their patron was to exchange his chariot of state for an ignominious gallows.

(3.) Prefer an immutable God before mutable creatures. Is it not a horrible thing to see what we are, and what we possess, daily crumbling to dust, and in a continual flux from us, and not seek out something that is permanent, and always abides the same, for our portion? In God, or Wisdom, which is Christ, there is substance, Prov. viii. 21, in which respect he is opposed to all the things in the world, that are but shadows, that are shorter or longer, according to the motion of the sun; mutable also, by every little body that intervenes. God is subject to no decay within, to no force without; nothing in his own nature can change him from what he is, and there is no power above can hinder him from being what he will to the soul. He is an ocean of all perfection. He wants nothing without himself to render him blessed, which may allure him to a change. His creatures can want nothing out of him to make them happy, whereby they may be enticed to prefer anything before him. If we enjoy other things, it is by God's donation, who can as well withdraw them as bestow them; and it is but a reasonable as well as a necessary thing to endeavour the enjoyment of the immutable Benefactor rather than his revocable gifts.

If the creatures had a sufficient virtue in themselves to ravish our thoughts and engross our souls, yet when we take a prospect of a fixed and unchangeable being, what beauty, what strength have any of those things to vie with him? How can they bear up and maintain their interest against a lively thought and sense of God? All the glory of them would fly before him like that of the stars before the sun. They were once nothing, they may be nothing again. As their own nature brought them not out of nothing, so their nature secures them not from being reduced to nothing. What an unhappiness is it to have our affections set upon that which retains something of its *non esse* with its *esse*, its not being with its being; that lives indeed, but in a continual flux, and may lose that pleasureableness to-morrow which charms us to-day!

2. This doctrine will teach us patience under such providences as declare his unchangeable will. The rectitude of our wills consists in conformity to the divine, as discovered in his words and manifested in his providence, which are the effluxes of his immutable will. The time of trial is appointed by his immutable will, Dan. xi. 35; it is not in the power of the sufferer's will to shorten it, nor in the power of the enemy's will to lengthen it. Whatsoever doth happen hath been decreed by God: Eccles. vi. 10, 'That which hath been is named already;' therefore to murmur, or be discontented, is to contend with God, who is mightier than we to maintain his own purposes. God doth act all things conveniently for that immutable end intended by himself, and according to the reason of his own divine will, in the true point of time most proper for it and for us, not too soon or too slow, because he is unchangeable in knowledge and wisdom. God doth not act anything barely by an immutable will, but by an immutable wisdom and an unchangeable rule of goodness; and therefore we should not only acquiesce in what he works, but have a complacency in it; and by having our wills thus knitting themselves with the immutable will of God, we attain some degree of likeness to him in his own unchangeableness. When, therefore, God hath manifested his will in opening his decree to the world by his work of providence, we must cease all disputes against it, and with Aaron hold our peace, though the affliction be very smart, Lev. x. 3: 'All flesh must be silent before God,' Zech. ii. 13; for whatsoever is his counsel shall stand,

and cannot be recalled; all struggling against it, is like a brittle glass contending with a rock; for 'if he cut off and shut up, or gather together, then who can hinder him?' Job xi. 10. Nothing can help us, if he hath determined to afflict us, as nothing can hurt us, if he hath determined to secure us. The more clearly God hath evidenced this or that to be his will, the more sinful is our struggling against it. Pharaoh's sin was the greater in keeping Israel, by how much the more God's miracles had been demonstrations of his settled will to deliver them. Let nothing snatch our hearts to a contradiction to him, but let us fear, and give glory to him, when the hour of judgment which he hath appointed is come, Rev. xiv. 7; that is, comply with the unchangeable will of his precept, the more he declares the immutable will of his providence. We must not think God must disgrace his nature and change his proceedings for us. Better the creature should suffer, than God be impaired in any of his perfections. If God changed his purpose, he would change his nature. Patience is the way to perform the immutable will of God, and a means to attain a gracious immutability for ourselves by receiving the promise: Heb. x. 36, 'Ye have need of patience, that after ye have done the will of God, ye might receive the promise.'

3. This doctrine will teach us to imitate God in this perfection, by striving to be immoveable in goodness. God never goes back from himself; he finds nothing better than himself for which he should change; and can we find anything better than God, to allure our hearts to a change from him? The sun never declines from the ecliptic line, nor should we from the paths of holiness. A stedfast obedience is encouraged by an unchangeable God to reward it: 1 Cor. xv. 58, 'Be stedfast and immoveable, always abounding in the work of the Lord, knowing that your labour shall not be in vain in the Lord.' Unstedfastness is the note of an hypocrite, Ps. lxxviii. 37; stedfastness in that which is good is the mark of a saint; it is the character of a righteous person to 'keep the truth,' Isa. xxvi. 2; and it is as positively said that 'he that abides not in the doctrine of Christ hath not God,' 2 John 9; but he that doth, 'hath both the Father and the Son.' So much of uncertainty, so much of nature; so much of firmness in duty, so much of grace. We can never honour God unless we finish his work, as Christ did not glorify God but in 'finishing the work God gave him to do,' John xvii. 4. The nearer the world comes to an end, the more is God's immutability seen in his promises and predictions, and the more must our unchangeableness be seen in our obedience: Heb. x. 23, 25, 'Let us hold fast the profession of our faith without wavering, and so much the more as you see the day approaching.' The Christian Jews were to be the more tenacious of their faith the nearer they saw the day approaching, the day of Jerusalem's destruction prophesied of by Daniel, chap. ix. 26; which accomplishment must be a great argument to establish the Christian Jews in the profession of Christ to be the Messiah, because the destruction of the city was not to be before the cutting off the Messiah. Let us be therefore constant in our profession and service of God, and not suffer ourselves to be driven from him by the ill usage, or flattered from him by the caresses of the world.

(1.) It is reasonable. If God be unchangeable in doing us good, it is reason we should be unchangeable in doing him service. If he assure us that he is our God, our I AM, he would also that we should be his people. His we are. If he declare himself constant in his promises, he expects we should be so in our obedience. As a spouse, we should be unchangeably faithful to him as a husband; as subjects, have an unchangeable allegiance to him as our prince, He would not have us faithful to him for an hour or a day, but to the death, Rev. ii. 10. And it is reason we should be his; and if we be his children, imitate him in his constancy of his holy purposes.

(2.) It is our glory and interest. To be a reed shaken with every wind is no commendation among men, and it is less a ground of praise with God. It was Job's glory that he held fast in his integrity: 'In all this Job sinned not,' Job i. 22,—in all this, which whole cities and kingdoms would have thought ground enough of high exclamations against God. And also against the temptation of his wife he retained his integrity: chap. ii. 9, 'Dost thou still retain thy integrity?' The devil, who, by God's permission, stripped him of his goods and health, yet could not strip him of his grace; as a traveller, when the wind and snow beats in his face, wraps his cloak more closely about him, to preserve that and himself. Better we had never made profession, than afterwards to abandon it; such a withering profession serves for no other use than to aggravate the crime, if any of us fly like a coward or revolt like a traitor. What profit will it be to a soldier if he hath withstood many assaults, and turn his back at last? If we would have God crown us with an immutable glory, we must crown our beginnings with a happy perseverance: Rev. ii. 10, 'Be faithful to the death, and I will give thee a crown of life.' Not as though this were the cause to merit it, but a necessary condition to possess it. Constancy in good is accompanied with an immutability of glory.

(3.) By an unchangeable disposition to good we should begin the happiness of heaven upon earth. This is the perfection of blessed spirits, those that are nearest to God, as angels and glorified souls, they are immutable; not, indeed, by nature, but by grace; yet not only by a necessity of grace, but a liberty of will. Grace will not let them change, and that grace doth animate their wills, that they would not change; an immutable God fills their understandings and affections, and gives satisfaction to their desires. The saints, when they were below, tried other things and found them deficient; but now they are so fully satisfied with the beatific vision, that, if Satan should have entrance among the angels and sons of God, it is not likely he should have any influence upon them, he could not present to their understandings anything that could, either at the first glance or upon a deliberate view, be preferable to what they enjoy and are fixed in.

Well then, let us be immoveable in the knowledge and love of God. It is the delight of God to see his creatures resemble him in what they are able. Let not our affections to him be as Jonah's gourd, growing up in one night and withering the next. Let us not only fight a good fight, but do so till we have finished our course, and imitate God in an unchangeableness of holy purposes; and to that purpose examine ourselves daily what fixedness we have arrived unto; and, to prevent any temptation to a revolt, let us often possess our minds with thoughts of the immutability of God's nature and will, which, like fire under water, will keep a good matter boiling up in us, and make it both retain and increase its heat.

4. Let this doctrine teach us to have recourse to God, and aim at a near conjunction with him. When our spirits begin to flag, and a cold aguish temper is drawing upon us, let us go to him who can only fix our hearts, and furnish us with a ballast to render them stedfast; as he is only immutable in his nature, so he is the only principle of immutability as well as being in the creature. Without his grace we shall be as changeable in our appearances as a chameleon, and in our turnings as the wind. When Peter trusted in himself, he changed to the worse; it was his master's recourse to God for him that preserved in him a reducing principle, which changed him again for the better and fixed him in it, Luke xxii. 32.

It will be our interest to be in conjunction with him that moves not about with the heavens, nor is turned by the force of nature, nor changed by the accidents in the world, but sits in the heavens, moving all things by his powerful arm, according to his infinite skill; while we have him for our God, we have his immutability, as well as any other perfection of his nature, for our advantage; the nearer we come to him, the more stability we shall have in ourselves; the further from him, the more liable to change. The line that is nearest to the place where it is first fixed is least subject to motion; the further it is stretched from it, the weaker it is, and more liable to be shaken. Let us also affect those things which are nearest to him in this perfection : the righteousness of Christ, that shall never wear out; and the graces of the Spirit, that shall never burn out. By this means, what God is infinitely by nature, we shall come to be finitely, immutable by grace, as much as the capacity of a creature can obtain.

A DISCOURSE UPON GOD'S OMNIPRESENCE.

*Can any hide himself in secret places that I shall not see him? saith the Lord:
do not I fill heaven and earth? saith the Lord.*—JER. XXIII. 24.

THE occasion of this discourse begins, ver. 16, where God admonisheth the people not to hearken to the words of the false prophets, which spake a vision of their own heart, and not out of the mouth of the Lord. They made the people vain by their insinuations of peace, when God had proclaimed war and calamity; and uttered the dreams of their fancies, and not the visions of the Lord; and so turned the people from the expectation of the evil day which God had threatened: ver. 17, 'They say still unto them that despise me, The Lord hath said, Ye shall have peace; and they say unto every one that walks after the imagination of his own heart, No evil shall come upon you.' And they invalidate the prophecies of those whom God had sent: ver. 18, 'Who hath stood in the counsel of the Lord, and hath perceived and heard his word? who hath marked his word and heard it?' 'Who hath stood in the counsel of the Lord?' Are they acquainted with the secrets of God more than we? Who have the word of the Lord, if we have not? Or it may be a continuation of God's admonition. Believe not those prophets; for who of them have been acquainted with the secrets of God? or by what means should they learn his counsel? No; assure yourselves, 'a whirlwind of the Lord is gone forth in fury, even a grievous whirlwind: it shall fall grievously upon the head of the wicked,' ver. 19. A whirlwind shall come from Babylon; it is just at the door, and shall not be blown over; it shall fall with a witness upon the wicked people, and the deceiving prophets, and sweep them together into captivity. For, ver. 20, 'the anger of the Lord shall not return, until he have executed, and till he have performed the thoughts of his heart.' My fury shall not be a childish fury, that quickly languisheth, but shall accomplish whatsoever I threaten, and burn so hot, as not to be cool till I have satisfied my vengeance; 'in the latter days ye shall consider it perfectly,' ver. 20, when the storm shall beat upon you; you shall then know, that the calamities shall answer the words you have heard. When the conqueror shall waste your grounds, demolish your houses, and manacle your hands, then shall you consider it, and have the wishes of fools, that you had had your eyes in your heads before; you shall then know the falseness of your guides, and the truth of my prophets, and discern who stood in the counsel of the Lord, and subscribe to the messages I have sent you.

Some understand this not only of the Babylonish captivity, but refer it to the time of Christ, and the false doctrine of men's own righteousness in opposition to the righteousness of God, understanding this verse to be partly a threatening of wrath, which shall end in an advantage to the Jews, who shall in the latter time consider the falseness of their notions about a legal righteousness, and so make it a promise ; they shall then know the intent of the Scripture, and in the latter days, the latter end of the world, when time shall be near the rolling up, they shall reflect upon themselves, ' they shall look upon him whom they have pierced :' and till these latter days, they shall be hardened, and believe nothing of evangelical truths.

Now God denieth that he sent those prophets : ver. 21, ' I have not sent these prophets, yet they ran ; I have not spoken to them, yet they prophesied.'   They have intruded themselves without a commission from me, whatsoever their brags are.   The reason to prove it is ver. 22, ' If they had stood in my counsel,' if they had been instructed and inspired by me, ' they would have caused my people to hear my words ;' they would have regulated themselves according to my word, ' and have turned them from their evil way ;' i. e., endeavoured to shake down their false confidences of peace, and make them sensible of their false notions of me and my ways.   Now, because those false prophets could not be so impudent as to boast, that they prophesied in the name of God, when they had not commission from him, unless they had some secret sentiment that they and their intentions were hid from the knowledge and eye of God, he adds, ver. 23, ' Am I a God at hand, and not a God afar off ? Can any hide himself in secret places, that I shall not see him ?'   Have I not the power of seeing and knowing what they do, what they design, what they think ?   Why should I not have such a power, since ' I fill heaven and earth' by my essence ?   ' Am I a God at hand, and not a God afar off ?'   He excludes here the doctrine of those that excluded the providence of God from extending itself to the inferior things of the earth ; which error was ancient, as ancient as the time of Job, as appears by their opinion, that' God's eyes were hood-winked and muffled by the thickness of the clouds, and could not pierce through their dark and dense body : ' Thick clouds are a covering to him, that he seeth not,' Job xxii. 14.

Some* refer it to time.   Do you imagine me a God new framed like your idols, beginning a little time ago, and not existing before the foundation of the world, yea, from eternity ? ' a God afar off,' further than your acutest understandings can reach ?   I am of a longer standing, and you ought to know my majesty.   But it rather refers to place than time.   Do you think I do not behold everything in the earth as well as in heaven.   Am I locked up within the walls of my palace, and cannot peep out to behold the things done in the world ? or that I am so linked to pleasure in the place of my glory, as earthly kings are in their courts, that I have no mind or leisure to take notice of the carriages of men upon earth ?   God doth not say he was afar off, but only gives an account of the inward thoughts of their minds, or at least of the language expressed by their actions.

The interrogation carries in it a strong affirmation, and assures us more of God's care, and the folly of men in not considering it : ' Am I a God at hand, and not a God afar off ? Can any hide himself in secret places ?' Heb., ' in hiddenness,' in the deepest cells.   What ! are you besotted by your base lusts, that you think me a God careless, ignorant, blind, that I can see nothing but as a purblind man what is very near my eye ?   Are you so out of your wits, that you imagine you can deceive me ?   Do not all your behaviours speak such a sentiment to lie secret in your heart, though

* Munster, Vatablus, Castalio, Œcolamp.

not formed into a full conception, yet testified by your actions? No, you are much mistaken; it is impossible but that I should see and know all things, since I am present with all things, and am not at a greater distance from the things on earth than from the things in heaven, for I fill all that vast fabric which is divided into those two parts of heaven and earth; and he that hath such an infinite essence cannot be distant, cannot be ignorant; nothing can be far from his eyes, since everything is so near to his essence.

So that it is an elegant expression of the omniscience of God, and a strong argument for it. He asserts, first, the universality of his knowledge; but lest they should mistake, and confine his presence only to heaven, he adds, that he 'fills heaven and earth.' I do not see things so, as if I were in one place and the things seen in another, as it is with man; but whatsoever I see, I see not without myself, because every corner of heaven and earth is filled by me. He that fills all must needs see and know all.

And indeed men that question the knowledge of God would be more convinced by the doctrine of his immediate presence with them. And this seems to be the design and manner of arguing in this place. Nothing is remote from my knowledge, because nothing is distant from my presence.

'I fill heaven and earth.' He doth not say, I am in heaven and earth, but I fill heaven and earth; *i. e.*, say some,* with my knowledge, others with my authority or my power. But,

1. The word *filling* cannot properly be referred to the act of understanding and will. A presence by knowledge is to be granted, but to say such a presence fills a place, is an improper speech. Knowledge is not enough to constitute a presence.

A man at London knows there is such a city as Paris, and knows many things in it; can he be concluded therefore to be present in Paris, or fill any place there, or be present with the things he knows there? If I know anything to be distant from me, how can it be present with me? for by knowing it to be distant I know it not to be present. Besides, filling heaven and earth is distinguished here from knowing or seeing. His presence is rendered as an argument to prove his knowledge. Now, a proposition, and the proof of that proposition, are distinct, and not the same.

It cannot be imagined that God should prove *idem per idem*, as we say; for what would be the import of the speech then, I know all things, I see all things, because I know and see all things?† The Holy Ghost here accommodates himself to the capacity of men, because we know that a man sees and knows that which is done where he is corporally present; so he proves that God knows all things that are done in the most secret caverns of the heart, because he is everywhere in heaven and earth, as light is everywhere in the air, and air everywhere in the world. Hence the schools use the term *repletive* for the presence of God.

2. Nor by filling of heaven and earth is meant his authority and power. It would be improperly said of a king, that in regard of the government of his kingdom, is everywhere by his authority, that he fills all the cities and countries of his dominions. 'I, do not I fill?'‡ That *I* notes the essence of God, as distinguished according to our capacity, from the perfections pertaining to his essence, and is in reason better referred to the substance of God than to those things we conceive as attributes in him. Besides, were it meant only of his authority or power, the argument would not run well. I see all things, because my authority and power fills heaven and earth. Power doth not always rightly infer knowledge, no, not in a rational

* Tum perspicacia, tum efficacia.—*Grot.*   ‡ Amyrald, de Trinitate, p. 87.
† Suarez.

agent. Many things in a kingdom are done by the authority of the king, that never arrive to the knowledge of the king; many things in us are done by the power of our souls, which yet we have not a distinct knowledge of in our understandings. There are many motions in sleep, by virtue of the soul informing the body, that we have not so much as a simple knowledge of in our minds. Knowledge is not rightly inferred from power, or power from knowledge.

By filling heaven and earth is meant therefore a filling it with his essence. No place can be imagined that is deprived of the presence of God, and therefore when the Scripture anywhere speaks of the presence of God, it joins heaven and earth together. He so fills them, that there is no place without him. We do not say a vessel is full so long as there is any space to contain more. Not a part of heaven nor a part of earth, but the whole heaven, the whole earth, at one and the same time. If he were only in one part of heaven, or one part of earth, nay, if there were any part of heaven or any part of earth void of him, he could not be said to fill them. I fill heaven and earth; not a part of me fills one place and another part of me fills another, but I, God, fill heaven and earth, I am whole God filling the heaven and whole God filling the earth. I fill heaven, and yet fill earth; I fill earth and yet fill heaven, and fill heaven and earth at one and the same time. God fills his own works, a heathen philosopher saith.*

Here is then a description of God's presence.

1. By power: Am I not a God afar off? a God in the extension of his arm.

2. By knowledge: Shall I not see them?

3. By essence: as an undeniable ground for inferring the two former, I fill heaven and earth.

Doct. God is essentially everywhere present in heaven and earth.

If God be, he must be somewhere; that which is nowhere is nothing. Since God is, he is in the world; not in one part of it, for then he were circumscribed by it. If in the world, and only there, though it be a great space, he were also limited. Some† therefore said, God was everywhere, and nowhere. Nowhere; *i.e.* not bounded by any place, nor receiving from any place anything for his preservation or sustainment. He is everywhere, because no creature, either body or spirit, can exclude the presence of his essence; for he is not only near, but in everything: Acts xvii. 28, 'In him we live, and move, and have our being.' Not absent from anything, but so present with them, that they live and move in him, and move more in God than in the air or earth wherein they are; nearer to us than our flesh to our bones, than the air to our breath. He cannot be far from them that live and have every motion in him. The apostle doth not say *by him*, but *in him*, to shew the inwardness of his presence.

As eternity is the perfection whereby he hath neither beginning nor end, immutability is the perfection whereby he hath neither increase nor diminution, so immensity or omnipresence is that whereby he hath neither bounds nor limitation. As he is in all time, yet so as to be above time, so is he in all places, yet so as to be above limitation by any place. It was a good expression of a heathen to illustrate this, that God is a sphere or circle, whose centre is everywhere and circumference nowhere. His meaning was, that the essence of God was indivisible, *i.e.* could not be divided. It cannot be said, here and there the lines of it terminate; it is like a line drawn out in infinite spaces, that no point can be conceived where its length and breadth ends. The sea is a vast mass of waters, yet to that it is said,

* Seneca, de Benefic. lib. iv. cap. 8, *Ipse opus suum implet.*   † Chrysostom.

'Hitherto shalt thou go, and no further.' But it cannot be said of God's essence, Hitherto it reaches, and no further; here it is, and there it is not. It is plain that God is thus immense, because he is infinite; we have reason and Scripture to assent to it, though we cannot conceive it. We know that God is eternal, though eternity is too great to be measured by the short line of a created understanding. We cannot conceive the vastness and glory of the heavens, much less that which is so great as to fill heaven and earth; yea, 'not to be contained in the heaven of heavens,' 1 Kings viii. 27.

Things are said to be present, or in a place.

1. *Circumscriptivè*, as circumscribed. This belongs to things that have quantity, as bodies that are encompassed by that place wherein they are; and a body fills but one particular space wherein it is, and the space is commensurate to every part of it, and every member hath a distinct place. The hand is not in the same particular space that the foot or head is.

2. *Definitivè*, which belongs to angels and spirits, which are said to be in a point, yet so as that they cannot be said to be in another at the same time.

3. *Repletivè*, filling all places; this belongs only to God. As he is not measured by time, so he is not limited by place. A body or spirit, because finite, fills but one space; God, because infinite, fills all, yet so as not to be contained in them, as wine and water is in a vessel. He is from the height of the heaven to the bottom of the deeps, in every point of the world, and in the whole circle of it, yet not limited by it, but beyond it.

Now this hath been acknowledged by the wisest in the world.

Some indeed had other notions of God. The more ignorant sort of the Jews confined him to the temple.* And God intimates that they had such a thought, when he asserts his presence in heaven and earth, in opposition to the temple they built as his house and 'the place of his rest.'† And the idolaters among them thought their gods might be at a distance from them, which Elias intimates in the scoff he puts upon them: 1 Kings xviii. 27, 'Cry aloud, for he is a god,' meaning Baal; 'either he is talking, or he is pursuing, or he is in a journey;' and they follow his advice, and cried 'louder,' ver. 28, whereby it is evident they looked not on it as a mock, but as a truth. And the Syrians called the God of Israel the god of the hills, as though his presence were fixed there, and not in the valleys, 1 Kings xx. 23; and their own gods in the valleys, and not in the mountains. They fancied every god to have a particular dominion and presence in one place, and not in another, and bounded the territories of their gods as they did those of their princes.‡ And some thought him tied to, and shut up in, their temples and groves wherein they worshipped him.§ Some of them thought God to be confined to heaven, and therefore sacrificed upon the highest mountains, that the steam might ascend nearer heaven, and their praises be heard better in those places which were nearest to the habitation of God. But the wiser Jews acknowledged it, and therefore called God place,‖ whereby they denoted his immensity; he was not contained in any place; every part of the world subsists by him. He was a place to himself, greater than anything made by him. And the wiser heathens acknowledged it also.

One ¶ calls God a mind passing through the universal nature of things; another, that he was an infinite and immense air;** another, that it is as

* Jerome on Isa. lxvi. 1.   † Med. Diatrib., vol. i. p. 71, 72.
† Hammond on Mat. vi. 7.   § Dought Analec. excurs. 61. 118.
‖ םוקמ. Grot. upon Matt. v. 16. Mares. contra Volk. lib. i. cap. 27, p. 494.
¶ Vide Minut. Fel. p. 20.   ** Plotin. Enead vi. lib. v. cap. 4.

natural to think God is everywhere, as to think that God is. Hence they called God the soul of the world; that as the soul is in every part of the body to quicken it, so is God in every part of the world to support it.

And there are some resemblances of this in the world, though no creature can fully resemble God in any one perfection; for then it would not be a creature, but God. But air and light are some weak resemblances of it. Air is in all the spaces of the world, in the pores of all bodies, in the bowels of the earth, and extends itself from the lowest earth to the highest regions, and the heavens themselves are probably nothing else but a refined kind of air; and light diffuseth itself through the whole air, and every part of it is truly light, as every part of the air is truly air; and though they seem to be mingled together, yet they are distinct things, and not of the same essence. So is the essence of God in the whole world, not by diffusion as air or light, not mixed with any creature, but remaining distinct from the essence of any created being. Now when this hath been owned by men instructed only in the school of nature, it is a greater shame to any acquainted with the Scripture to deny it. For the understanding of this, there shall be some propositions premised in general.

Prop. 1. This is negatively to be understood. Our knowledge of God is most by withdrawing from him, or denying to him, in our conception, any weaknesses or imperfections in the creature. As the infiniteness of God is a denial of limitation of being, so immensity, or omnipresence, is a denial of limitation of place. And when we say God is *totus* in every place, we must understand it thus, that he is not everywhere by parts, as bodies are, as air and light are. He is everywhere, *i.e.* his nature hath no bounds; he is not tied to any place as the creature is, who, when he is present in one place, is absent from another. As no place can be without God, so no place can compass and contain him.

Prop. 2. There is an influential omnipresence of God.

(1.) Universal, with all creatures. He is present with all things by his authority, because all things are subject to him; by his power, because all things are sustained by him; by his knowledge, because all things are naked before him. He is present in the world, as a king is in all parts of his kingdom regally present; providentially present with all, since his care extends to the meanest of his creatures. His power reacheth all, and his knowledge pierceth all.

As everything in the world was created by God, so everything in the world is preserved by God; and since preservation is not wholly distinct from creation, it is necessary God should be present with everything while he preserves it, as well as present with it when he created it: 'Thou preservest man and beast,' Ps. xxxvi. 6; he 'upholds all things by the word of his power,' Heb. i. 8. There is a virtue sustaining every creature, that it may not fall back into that nothing from whence it was elevated by the power of God. All those natural virtues we call the principles of operation, are fountains springing from his goodness and power, all things are acted and managed by him, as well as preserved by him; and in this sense God is present with all creatures, for whatsoever acts another is present with that which it acts, by sending forth some virtue and influence whereby it acts. If free agents do not only 'live,' but 'move in him,' and by him, Acts xvii. 28, much more are the motions of other natural agents, by a virtue communicated to them, and upheld in them in the time of their acting. This virtual presence of God is evident to our sense, a presence we feel; his essential presence is evident in our reason. This influential presence may be compared to that of the sun, which, though at so great a distance from the earth, is present in the air and

earth by its light, and within the earth by its influence in concocting those
metals which are in the bowels of it, without being substantially either of
them.   God is thus so intimate with every creature, that there is not the
least particle of any creature, but the marks of his power and goodness are
seen in it, and his goodness doth attend them, and is more swift in its effluxes
than the breaking out of light from the sun, which yet are more swift than
can be declared ; but to say he is in the world only by his virtue, is to
acknowledge only the effects of his power and wisdom in the world, that his
eye sees all, his arm supports all, his goodness nourisheth all, but himself
and his essence at a distance from them.*   And so the soul of man, according to its measure, would have in some kind a more excellent manner of
presence in the body than God, according to the infiniteness of his being
with his creatures ; for that doth not only communicate life to the body, but
is actually present with it, and spreads its whole essence through the body
and every member of it.   All grant that God is efficaciously in every creek
of the world, but some say he is only substantially in heaven.

(2.) Limited to such subjects that are capacitated for this or that kind of
presence.   Yet it is an omnipresence, because it is a presence in all the
subjects capacitated for it : thus there is a special providential presence of
God with some, in assisting them when he sets them on work as his instruments for some special service in the world.   As with Cyrus : Isa. xlv. 2,
' I will go before thee ;' and with Nebuchadnezzar and Alexander, whom he
protected and directed to execute his counsels in the world ; such a presence
Judas and others, that shall not enjoy his glorious presence, had in the working of miracles in the world : Mat. vii. 22, ' In thy name we have done many
wonderful works.'   Besides, as there is an *effective* presence of God with all
creatures, because he produced them, and preserves them, so there is an
objective presence of God with rational creatures, because he offers himself
to them, to be known and loved by them.†   He is near to wicked men in
the offers of grace : Isa. lv. 6, ' Call ye upon him while he is near ;' besides,
there is a gracious presence of God with his people in whom he dwells, and
makes his abode, as in a temple consecrated to him by the graces of the
Spirit.   ' We will come,' *i. e.* the Father and the Son, ' and make our abode
with him,' John xiv. 23.   He is present with all by the presence of his
divinity, but only in his saints by the presence of a gracious efficacy ; he
walks in the midst of the golden candlesticks, and hath dignified the congregation of his people with the title of *Jehovah Shammah*, ' the Lord is
there,' Ezek. xlviii. 35 ; ' In Salem is his tabernacle, and his dwelling-
place in Sion,' Ps. lxxvi. 2.   As he filled the tabernacle, so he doth the
church, with the signs of his presence ; this is not the presence wherewith
he fills heaven and earth.   His Spirit is not bestowed upon all, to reside in
their hearts, enlighten their minds, and bedew them with refreshing comforts.   When the apostle speaks of God's being ' above all, and through all,'
Eph. iv. 6,—above all in his majesty, through all in his providence,—he doth
not appropriate that, as he doth what follows, and ' in you all ;' in you all by
a special grace ; as God was specially present with Christ by the grace of
union, so he is specially present with his people by the grace of regeneration.   So there are several manifestations of his presence : he hath a presence of glory in heaven, whereby he comforts the saints ; a presence of
wrath in hell, whereby he torments the damned ; in heaven he is a God
spreading his beam of light ; in hell, a God distributing his strokes of justice ; by the one he fills heaven, by the other he fills hell ; by his providence
and essence he fills both heaven and earth.

          * Zanch.   † Cajetan in Aquin. part i. qu. 8, artic. 3.

Prop. 3. There is an essential presence of God in the world. He is not only everywhere, by his power upholding the creatures, by his wisdom understanding them, but by his essence containing them. That anything is essentially present anywhere, it hath from God: God is therefore much more present everywhere, for he cannot give that which he hath not.

(1.) He is essentially present in all places.* It is as reasonable to think the essence of God to be everywhere, as to be always; immensity is as rational as eternity. That indivisible essence which reaches through all times, may as well reach through all places. It is more excellent to be always, than to be everywhere; for to be always in duration is intrinsecal, to be everywhere is extrinsic: if the greater belongs to God, why not the less? As all times are a moment to his eternity, so all places are as a point to his essence. As he is larger than all time, so he is vaster than all place. The nations of the world are to him 'as the dust of the balance, or drop of a bucket: the nations are accounted as the small dust,' Isa. xl. 15. The essence of God may well be thought to be present everywhere with that which is no more than a grain of dust to him, and in all those isles, which, if put together, are 'a very little thing' in his hand. Therefore, saith a learned Jew,† If a man were set in the highest heavens, he would not be nearer to the essence of God than if he were in the centre of the earth. Why may not the presence of God in the world be as noble as that of the soul in the body, which is generally granted to be essentially in every part of the body of man, which is but a little world; and animates every member by its actual presence, though it exerts not the same operation in every part?‡ The world is less to the Creator than the body to the soul, and needs more the presence of God than the body needs the presence of the soul. That glorious body of the sun visits every part of the habitable earth in twenty-four hours by its beams; which reaches the troughs of the lowest valleys, as well as the pinnacles of the highest mountains: must we not acknowledge in the Creator of this sun an infinite greater proportion of presence? Is it not as easy with the essence of God to overspread the whole body of heaven and earth, as it is for the sun to pierce and diffuse itself through the whole air between it and the earth, and send up its light also as far to the regions above? Do we not see something like it in sounds and voices? Is not the same sound of a trumpet, or any other musical instrument, at the first breaking out of a blast, in several places within such a compass at the same time? Doth not every ear that hears it receive alike the whole sound of it? And fragrant odours scented in several places at the same time, in the same manner, and the organ proper for smelling takes in the same in every person within the compass of it. How far is the noise of thunder heard alike to every ear, in places something distant from one another? And do we daily find such a manner of presence in those things of so low a concern, and not imagine a kind of presence of God greater than all those? Is the sound of thunder, the voice of God, as it is called, everywhere in such a compass, and shall not the essence of an infinite God be much more everywhere? Those that would confine the essence of God only to heaven, and exclude it from the earth, run into great inconveniences. It may be demanded whether he be in one part of the heavens, or in the whole vast body of them? If in one part of them, his essence is bounded; if he moves from that part, he is mutable, for he changes a place wherein he was, for another wherein he was not. If he be always fixed in one part of the heavens, such a notion would render him little better than a living statue.§

* Ficin.   ‡ Ficin.
† Maimonid.   § Hornbeck, Soun. part i. p. 303.

If he be in the whole heaven, why cannot his essence possess a greater space than the whole heavens, which are so vast? How comes he to be confined within the compass of that, since the whole heaven compasseth the earth? If he be in the whole heaven, he is in places farther distant one from another, than any part of the earth can be from the heavens; since the earth is like a centre in the midst of a circle, it must be nearer to every part of the circle than some parts of the circle can be to one another. If, therefore, his essence possesses the whole heavens, no reason can be rendered why he doth not also possess the earth, since also the earth is but a little point in comparison of the vastness of the heavens. If, therefore, he be in every part of the heavens, why not in every part of the earth?

The Scripture is plain: Ps. cxxxix. 7–9, 'Whither shall I go from thy Spirit? or whither shall I fly from thy presence? If I ascend up to heaven, thou art there: if I make my bed in hell, behold, thou art there. If I take the wings of the morning, and dwell in the uttermost parts of the sea, even there shall thy hand lead me, and thy right hand shall uphold me.' If he be in heaven, earth, hell, sea, he fills all places with his presence: his presence is here asserted in places the most distant from one another; all the places, then, between heaven and earth are possessed by his presence. It is not meant of his knowledge, for that the psalmist had spoken of before: ver. 2, 3, 'Thou understandeth my thoughts afar off: thou art acquainted with all my ways.' Besides, 'thou art there,' not thy wisdom or knowledge; but *thou*, thy essence, not only thy virtue. For having before spoken of his omniscience, he proves that such knowledge could not be in God, unless he were present in his essence in all places, so as to be excluded from none. He fills the depths of hell, the extension of the earth, and the heights of the heavens. When the Scripture mentions the power of God only, it expresseth it by hand or arm; but when it mentions the Spirit of God, and doth not intend the third person in the Trinity, it signifies the nature and essence of God; and so here, when he saith, 'Whither shall I go from thy Spirit?' he adds exegetically, 'whither shall I fly from thy presence,' or *Heb.* 'face?' and the face of God in Scripture signifies the essence of God: Exod. xxxiii. 20, 23, 'Thou canst not see my face,' and 'my face shall not be seen;' the effects of his power, wisdom, providence, are seen, which are his back-parts, but not his face. The effects of his power and wisdom are seen in the world, but his essence is invisible, and this the psalmist elegantly expresseth. Had I wings endued with as much quickness as the first dawnings of the morning light, or the first darts of any sunbeam that spreads itself through the hemisphere, and passes many miles in as short a space as I can think a thought, I should find thy presence in all places before me, and could not fly out of the infinite compass of thy essence.

(2.) He is essentially present with all creatures. If he be in all places, it follows that he is with all creatures in those places; as he is in heaven, so he is with all angels; as he is in hell, so is he with all devils; as he is in the earth and sea, he is with all creatures inhabiting those elements. As his essential presence was the ground of the first being of things by creation, so it is the ground of the continued being of things by conservation. As his essential presence was the original, so it is the support of the existence of all the creatures. What are all those magnificent expressions of his creative virtue, but testimonies of his essential presence at the laying the foundation of the world? 'When he measured the waters in the hollow of his hand, meted out heaven with the span, and comprehended the dust of the earth in a measure, and weighed the mountains in scales, and the hills in a balance,' Isa. xl. 12; he sets forth the power and majesty of God in the creation and preservation of things, and every expression testifies his presence with them. The waters that were upon the face of the earth at first were no more than a drop in the palm of a man's hand, which in every part is touched by his hand. And thus he is equally present with the blackest devils, as well as the brightest angels; with the lowest dust, as well as with the most sparkling sun. He is equally present with the damned and the blessed, as he is an infinite being, but not in regard of his goodness and grace; he is equally present with the good and the bad, with the scoffing Athenians, as well as the believing apostles, in regard of his essence, but not in regard of the breathing of his divine virtue upon them to make them like himself: Acts xvii. 27, ' He is not far from every one of us : for in him we live, and move, and have our being.' The apostle includes all; he tells them they should seek the Lord; the Lord that they were to seek is God essentially considered. We are indeed to seek the perfections of God, that glitter in his works, but to the end that they should direct us to the seeking of God himself in his own nature and essence.* And therefore what follows, ' in him we live,' is to be understood not of his power and goodness, perfections of his nature, distinguished according to our manner of conception from his essence, but of the essential presence of God with his creatures. If he had meant it of his efficacy in preserving us, it had not been any proof of his nearness to us. Who would go about to prove the body or substance of the sun to be near us, because it doth warm and enlighten us, when our sense evidenceth the distance of it ? We live in the beams of the sun, but we cannot be said to live in the sun, which is so far distant from us. The expression seems to be more emphatical than to intend any less than his essential presence ; but we live in him not only as the efficient cause of our life, but as the foundation, sustaining our lives and motions, as if he were like air, diffused round about us. And we move in him, as Austin saith, as a sponge in the sea, not containing him, but being contained by him. He compasseth all, is encompassed by none ; he fills all, is comprehended by none. The Creator contains the world, the world contains not the Creator; as the hollow of the hand contains the water, the water in the hollow of the hand contains not the hand, and therefore some have chose to say rather, that the world is in God, it lives and moves in him, than that God is in the world. If all things thus live and move in him, then he is present with everything that hath life and motion ; and as long as the devils and damned have life, and motion, and being, so long is he with them, for whatsoever lives and moves, lives and moves in him.

But now this essential presence is,

(1.) Without any mixture. ' I fill heaven and earth,' not, I am mixed with heaven and earth; his essence is not mixed with the creatures, it remains entire in itself. The sponge retains the nature of a sponge, though encompassed by the sea, and moving in it, and the sea still retains its own nature. God is most simple, his essence therefore it is not mixed with anything. The light of the sun is present with the air, but not mixed with it, it remains light, and the air remains air; the light of the sun is diffused through all the hemisphere, it pierceth all transparent bodies, it seems to mix itself with all things, yet remains unmixed and undivided ; the light remains light, and the air remains air; the air is not light though it be enlightened. Or, take this similitude: when many candles are lighted up in a room, the light is altogether, yet not mixed with one another; every

* Amyrald. de Trinit.

candle hath a particular light belonging to it, which may be separated in a moment by removing one candle from another; but if they were mixed they could not be separated, at least so easily. God is not formally one with the world, or with any creature in the world by his presence in it; nor can any creature in the world, no, not the soul of man or an angel, come to be essentially one with God, though God be essentially present with it.

(2.) The essential presence is without any division of himself. 'I fill heaven and earth,' not part in heaven, and part in earth; I fill one as well as the other. One part of his essence is not in one place, and another part of his essence in another place; he would then be changeable; for that part of his essence which were now in this place, he might alter it to another, and place that part of his essence which were in another place to this; but he is undivided everywhere. As his eternity is one indivisible point, though in our conception we divide it into past, present, and to come, so the whole world is as a point to him in regard of place, as before was said; it is as a small dust, and grain of dust; it is impossible that one part of his essence can be separated from another, for he is not a body, to have one part separable from another. The light of the sun cannot be cut into parts, it cannot be shut into any place and kept there, it is entire in every place. Shall not God, who gives the light that power, be much more present himself? Whatsoever hath parts is finite, but God is infinite, therefore hath no parts of his essence. Besides, if there were such a division of his being, he would not be the most simple and uncompounded being, but would be made up of various parts; he would not be a Spirit; for parts are evidences of composition, and it could not be said that God is here or there, but only a part of God here, and a part of God there. But he fills heaven and earth, he is as much a God 'in the earth beneath' as 'in heaven above,' Deut. iv. 39; entirely in all places, not by scraps and fragments of his essence.

(3.) This essential presence is not by multiplication. For that which is infinite cannot multiply itself, or make itself more or greater than it was.

(4.) This essential presence is not by extension or diffusion; as a piece of gold may be beaten out to cover a large compass of ground. No; if God should create millions of worlds, he would be in them all, not by stretching out his being, but by the infiniteness of his being; not by a new growth of his being, but by the same essence he had from eternity; upon the same reasons mentioned before, his simplicity and indivisibility.

(5.) But, totally; there is no space, not the least, wherein God is not wholly according to his essence, and wherein his whole substance doth not exist; not a part of heaven can be designed wherein the Creator is not wholly; as he is in one part of heaven, he is in every part of heaven. Some kind of resemblance we may have from the water of the sea, which fills the great space of the world, and is diffused through all; yet the essence of water is in every drop of water in the sea, as much as the whole, and the same quality of water, though it comes short in quantity; and why shall we not allow God a nobler way of presence, without diffusion, as is in that? Or take this resemblance, since God likens himself to the light in the Scripture: 'He covereth himself with light,' Ps. civ. 2; 1 John i. 5, 'God is light, and in him is no darkness at all.' A crystal globe hung up in the air hath light all about it, all within it, every part is pierced by it; wherever you see the crystal, you see the light; the light in one part of the crystal cannot be distinguished from the light in the other part, and the whole essence of light is in every part; and shall not God be as much present with his creatures as one creature can be with another?* God is totally everywhere by his own simple substance.

Prop. 4. God is present beyond the world. He is within and above all places, though places should be infinite in number. As he was before and beyond all time, so he is above and beyond all place; being from eternity before any real time, he must also be without as well as within any real space; if God were only confined to the world, ho would be no more infinite in his essence than the world is in quantity; as a moment cannot be conceived from eternity, wherein God was not in being, so a space cannot be conceived in the mind of man wherein God is not present; he is not contained in the world nor in the heavens: 1 Kings viii. 27, 'But will God, indeed, dwell on the earth? Behold, the heaven of heavens cannot contain thee.' Solomon wonders that God should appoint a temple to be erected to him upon the earth, when he is not contained in the vast circuit of the heavens; his essence is not straitened in the limits of any created work, he is not contained in the heavens, *i. e.* in the manner that he is there; but he is there in his essence, and therefore cannot be contained there in his essence. If it should be meant only of his power and providence, it would conclude also for his essence; if his power and providence were infinite, his essence must be so too, for the infiniteness of his essence is the ground of the infiniteness of his power. It can never enter into any thought that a finite essence can have an infinite power, and that an infinite power can be without an infinite essence; it cannot be meant of his providence, as if Solomon should say, the heaven of heaven cannot contain thy providence, for, naming the heaven of heavens, that which encircles and bounds the other parts of the world, he could not suppose a providence to be exercised where there was no object to exercise it about, as no creature is mentioned to be beyond the uttermost heaven, which he calls here the heaven of heavens; besides, to understand it of his providence doth not consist with Solomon's admiration. He wonders that God, that hath so immense an essence, should dwell in a temple made with hands; he could not so much wonder at his providence in those things that immediately concern his worship. Solomon plainly asserts this?of God, that he was so far from being bounded within the rich wall of the temple, which, with so much cost, he had framed for the glory of his name, that the richer palace of the heaven of heavens could not contain him. It is true, it could not contain his power and wisdom, because his wisdom could contrive other kind of worlds, and his power erect them. But doth the meaning of that wise king reach no farther than this? Will the power and wisdom of God reside on the earth? He was too wise to ask such a question, since every object that his eyes met with in the world resolved him that the wisdom and power of God dwelt upon the earth, and glittered in everything he had created; and reason would assure him that the power that had framed this world was able to frame many more. But Solomon, considering the immensity of God's essence, wonders that God should order a house to be built for him, as if he wanted roofs, and coverings, and habitation, as bodily creatures do. Will God, indeed, dwell in a temple, who hath an essence so immense as not to be contained in the heaven of heavens? It is not the heaven of heavens that can contain Him, his substance. Here he asserts the immensity of his essence and his presence, not only in the heaven, but beyond the heavens; he that is not contained in the heavens, as a man is in a chamber, is without, and above, and beyond the heavens; it is not said they do not contain him, but it is impossible they should contain him, they

* Bernard.

'cannot contain him.' It is impossible then but that he should be above them; he that is without the compass of the world is not bounded by the limits of the world. As his power is not limited by the things he hath made, but can create innumerable worlds, so can his essence be in innumerable spaces; for as he hath power enough to make more worlds, so he hath essence enough to fill them, and therefore cannot be confined to what he hath already created. Innumerable worlds cannot be a sufficient place to contain God; he can only be a sufficient place to himself;* he that was before the world, and place, and all things, was to himself a world, a place, and everything.† He is really out of the world in himself, as he was in himself before the creation of the world; as, because God was before the foundation of the world, we conclude his eternity, so, because he is without the bounds of the world, we conclude his immensity, and from thence his omnipresence. The world cannot be said to contain him, since it was created by him; it cannot contain him now, who was contained by nothing before the world was. As there was no place to contain him before the world was, there can be no place to contain him since the world was.

God might create more worlds circular and round as this, and those could not be so contiguous, but some spaces would be left between; as, take three round balls, lay them as close as you can to one another, there will be some spaces between, none would say but God would be in these spaces, as well as in the world he had created, though there were nothing real and positive in those spaces. Why should we then exclude God from those imaginary spaces without the world? God might also create many worlds, and separate them by distances, that they might not touch one another, but be at a great distance from one another, and would not God fill them as well as he doth this? If so, he must also fill the spaces between them, for if he were in all those worlds, and not in the spaces between those worlds, his essence would be divided; there would be gaps in it, his essence would be cut into parts, and the distance between every part of his essence would be as great as the space between each world. The essence of God may be conceived then well enough to be in all those infinite spaces where he can erect new worlds.

I shall give one place more to prove both these propositions, viz. that God is essentially in every part of the world, and essentially above ours without the world: Isa. lxvi. 1, 'The heaven is my throne, and the earth is my footstool.' He is essentially in every part of the world; he is in heaven and earth at the same time, as a man is upon his throne and his footstool. God describes himself in a human shape, accommodated to our capacity, as if he had his head in heaven and his feet on earth; doth not his essence then fill all intermediate spaces between heaven and earth? As when the head of a man is in the upper part of a room, and his feet upon the floor, his body fills up the space between the head and his feet, this is meant of the essence of God; it is a similitude drawn from kings sitting upon the throne, and not their power and authority, but the feet of their persons, are supported by the footstool; so here it is not meant only of the perfections of God, but the essence of God. Besides, God seems to tax them with an erroneous conceit they had, as though his essence were in the temple, and not in any part of the world, therefore God makes an opposition between heaven, and earth, and the temple: 'Where is the house that you built unto me? and where is the place of my rest?' Had he understood it only of his providence, it had not been anything against their mistake, for they granted his providence to be not only in the temple, but in all parts of the

---

* Petav.   † Maccor. loc. commun. cap. xix. p. 153.

world. ' Where is the house that you build to me?' to ME, not to my power or providence, but think to include *me* within those walls?

Again, it shews God to be above the heavens, if the heavens be his throne; he sits upon them, and is above them as kings are above the thrones on which they sit; so it cannot be meant of his providence, because, no creature being without the sphere of the heavens, there is nothing of the power and the providence of God visible there, for there is nothing for him to employ his providence about; for providence supposeth a creature in actual being; it must be therefore meant of his essence, which is above the world, and in the world.

And the like proof you may see, Job xi. 7, 8, ' It is as high as heaven, what canst thou do? deeper than hell, what canst thou know? the measure thereof is longer than the earth, and broader than the sea;' where he intends the unsearchableness of God's wisdom, but proves it by the infiniteness of his essence; *Heb.* ' He is the height of the heavens,' he is the top of all the heavens; so that when you have begun at the lowest part, and traced him through all the creatures, you will find his essence filling all the creatures to be at the top of the world, and infinitely beyond it.

Prop. 5. This is the property of God, incommunicable to any creature. As no creature can be eternal and immutable, so no creature can be immense, because it cannot be infinite; nothing can be of an infinite nature, and therefore nothing of an immense presence but God. It cannot be communicated to the human nature of Christ, though in union with the divine.* Some indeed argue that Christ, in regard of his human nature, is everywhere, because he sits at the right hand of God, and the right hand of God is everywhere. His sitting at the right hand of God signifies his exaltation, and cannot with any reason be extended to such a kind of arguing. ' The hearts of kings are in the hand of God:' are the hearts of kings everywhere, because God's hand is everywhere? The souls of the righteous are in the hand of God; is the soul therefore of every righteous man everywhere in the world? The right hand of God is from eternity; is the humanity of Christ therefore from eternity, because it sits at the right hand of God? The right hand of God made the world; did the humanity of Christ therefore make heaven and earth? The humanity of Christ must then be confounded with his divinity, be the same with it, not united to it. All creatures are distinct from their Creator, and cannot inherit the properties essential to his nature, as eternity, immensity, immutability, omnipresence, omniscience. No angel, no soul, no creature can be in all places at once; before they can be so, they must be immense, and so must cease to be creatures, and commence God. This is impossible.

II. Reasons to prove God's essential presence.

Reason 1. Because he is infinite. As he is infinite, he is everywhere; as he is simple, his whole essence is everywhere; for in regard of his infiniteness, he hath no bounds; in regard of his simplicity, he hath no parts; and therefore those that deny God's omnipresence, though they pretend to own him infinite, must really conceive him finite.

1. God is infinite in his perfections. None can set bounds to terminate the greatness and excellency of God: 'his greatness is unsearchable,' Ps. cxlv. 3; Sept., οὐκ ἐστι πέρας, there is no end, no limitation. What hath no end is infinite; his power is infinite: Job v. 9, ' Which doth great things and unsearchable,' no end of those things he is able to do. His wisdom infinite, Ps. cxlvii. 5; he understands all things, past, present, and to come,

* Rivet, Ps. cx. p. 301, col. 2.

what is already made, what is possible to be made; his duration infinite: Job xxxvi. 26, ' The number of his years cannot be searched out,' ἀπέραντος. To make a finite thing of nothing is an argument of an infinite virtue. Infinite power can only extract something out of the barren womb of nothing, but all things were drawn forth by the word of God, the heavens and all the host of them. The sun, moon, stars, the rich embellishments of the world, appeared in being ' at the breath of his mouth,' Ps. xxxiii. 6. The author therefore must be infinite. And since nothing is the cause of God, or of any perfection in him, since he derives not his being, or the least spark of his glorious nature, from anything without him, he cannot be limited in any part of his nature by anything without him; and indeed the infiniteness of his power and his other perfections is asserted by the prophet, when he tells us that ' the nations are as a drop of a bucket, or the dust of the balance, and less than nothing, and vanity,' Isa. xl. 15, 17. They are all so in regard of his power, wisdom, &c. Conceive what a little thing a grain of dust or sand is to all the dust that may be made by the rubbish of a house; what a little thing the heap of the rubbish of a house is to the vast heap of the rubbish of a whole city, such a one as London; how little that also would be to the dust of a whole empire; how inconsiderable that also to the dust of one quarter of the world, Europe or Asia; how much less that still to the dust of the whole world. The whole world is composed of an unconceivable number of atoms, and the sea of an unconceivable number of drops; now what a little grain of dust is in comparison of the dust of the whole world, a drop of water from the sea to all the drops remaining in the sea, that is the whole world to God. Conceive it still less, a mere nothing, yet is it all less than this in comparison of God. There can be nothing more magnificently expressive of the infiniteness of God to a human conception than this expression of God himself in the prophet.

In the perfection of a creature, something still may be thought greater to be added to it, but God containing all perfections in himself formally, if they be mere perfections, and eminently, if they be but perfections in the creature mixed with imperfection, nothing can be thought greater, and therefore every one of them is infinite.

2. If his perfections be infinite, his essence must be so. How God can have infinite perfections and a finite essence is unconceivable by a human or angelical understanding. An infinite power, an infinite wisdom, an infinite duration, must needs speak an infinite essence, since the infiniteness of his attributes is grounded upon the infiniteness of his essence. To own infinite perfections in a finite subject is contradictory. The manner of acting by his power, and knowing by his wisdom, cannot exceed the manner of being by his essence. His perfections flow from his essence, and the principle must be of the same rank with what flows from it; and if we conceive his essence to be the cause of his perfections, it is utterly impossible that an infinite effect should arise from a finite cause; but indeed his perfections are his essence; for though we conceive the essence of God as the subject, and the attributes of God as faculties and qualities in that subject, according to our weak model, who cannot conceive of an infinite God without some manner of likeness to ourselves; who find understanding, and will, and power in us distinct from our substance, yet truly and really there is no distinction between his essence and attributes; one is inseparable from the other. His power and wisdom are his essence; and therefore to maintain God infinite in the one and finite in the other, is to make a monstrous God, and have an unreasonable notion of the Deity; for there would be the greatest disproportion in his nature, since there is no greater disproportion

can possibly be between one thing and another than there is between finite and infinite. God must not only then be compounded, but have parts of the greatest distance from one another in nature; but God being the most simple being, without the least composition, both must be equally infinite. If, then, his essence be not infinite, his power and wisdom cannot be infinite, which is both against Scripture and reason.

Again, how should his essence be finite and his perfections be infinite, since nothing out of himself gave them, either the one or the other?

Again, either the essence can be infinite, or it cannot;* if it cannot, there must be some cause of that impossibility. That can be nothing without him, because nothing without him can be as powerful as himself, much less too powerful for him. Nothing within him can be an enemy to his highest perfection; since he is necessarily what he is, he must be necessarily the most perfect being, and therefore necessarily infinite; since to be something infinitely is a greater perfection than to be something finitely.† If he can be infinite, he is infinite, otherwise he could be greater than he is, and so more blessed and more perfect than he is, which is impossible; for being the most perfect being, to whom nothing can be added, he must needs be infinite.

If, therefore, God have an infinite essence, he hath an infinite presence. An infinite essence cannot be contained in a finite place; as those things which are finite have a bounded space wherein they are, so that which is infinite hath an unbounded space; for as finiteness speaks limitedness, so infiniteness speaks unboundedness. And if we grant to God an infinite duration, there is no difficulty in acknowledging an infinite presence. Indeed, the infiniteness of God is a property belonging to him in regard of time and place; he is bounded by no place, and limited to no time.

Again, infinite essence may as well be everywhere, as infinite power reach everything; it may as well be present with every being, as infinite power in its working may be present with nothing to bring it into being. Where God works by his power, he is present in his essence, because his power and his essence cannot be separated, and therefore his power, wisdom, goodness, cannot be anywhere where his essence is not. His essence cannot be severed from his power, nor his power from his essence; for the power of God is nothing but God acting, and the wisdom of God nothing but God knowing. As the power of God is always, so is his essence; as the power of God is everywhere, so is his essence. Whatsoever God is, he is alway, and everywhere. To confine him to a place is to measure his essence, as to confine his actions is to limit his power. His essence being no less infinite than his power and his wisdom, can be no more bounded than his power and wisdom; but they are not separable from his essence, yea, they are his essence. If God did not fill the whole world, he would be determined to some place, and excluded from others, and so his substance would have bounds and limits, and then something might be conceived greater than God; for we may conceive that a creature may be made by God of so vast a greatness as to fill the whole world; for the power of God is able to make a body that should take up the whole space between heaven and earth, and reach to every corner of it. But nothing can be conceived by any creature greater than God; he exceeds all things, and is exceeded by none. God therefore cannot be included in heaven, nor included in the earth; cannot be contained in either of them; for if we should imagine them vaster than they are, yet still they would be finite; and if his essence were contained

---

* Amyrald de Trinitat., p. 89.

† *Deus est actus purus et nullam habet potentiam passivam.*

in them, it could be no more infinite than the world which contains it, as water is not of a larger compass than the vessel which contains it. If the essence of God were limited either in the heavens or earth, it must needs be finite, as the heavens and earth are; but there is no proportion between finite and infinite; God therefore cannot be contained in them. If there were an infinite body, that must be everywhere; certainly, then, an infinite spirit must be everywhere. Unless we will account him finite, we can render no reason why he should not be in one creature as well as in another. If he be in heaven, which is his creature, why can he not be in the earth, which is as well his creature as the heavens?

Reason 2. Because of the continual operation of God in the world. This was one reason made the heathen believe that there was an infinite spirit in the vast body of the world, acting in everything, and producing those admirable motions which we see everywhere in nature. The cause which acts in the most perfect manner, is also in the most perfect manner present with its effects.

God preserves all, and therefore is in all. The apostle thought it a good induction, 'He is not far from us: for in him we live,' Acts xvii. 27. *For* being as much as *because*, shews that from his operation he concluded his real presence with all. It is not his virtue is not far from every one of us, but *he*, his substance, himself; for none that acknowledge a God will deny the absence of the virtue of God from any part of the world. He works in everything, everything works and lives in him; therefore he is present with all,* or rather, if things live, they are in God, who gives them life. If things live, God is in them, and gives them life; if things move, God is in them, and gives them motion; if things have any being, God is in them, and gives them being; if God withdraws himself, they presently lose their being; and therefore some have compared the creature to the impression of a seal upon the wafer,† that cannot be preserved but by the presence of the seal. As his presence was actual with what he created, so his presence is actual with what he preserves, since creation and preservation do so little differ; if God creates things by his essential presence, by the same he supports them. If his substance cannot be disjoined from his preserving power, his power and wisdom cannot be separated from his essence; where there are the marks of the one, there is the presence of the other; for it is by his essence that he is powerful and wise; no man can distinguish the one from the other in a simple being. God doth not preserve and act things by a virtue diffused from him.

It may be demanded whether that virtue be distinct from God? If it be not, it is then the essence of God; if it be distinct, it is a creature, and then it may be asked how that virtue which preserves other things is preserved itself? It must be ultimately resolved into the essence of God, or else there must be a running *in infinitum;* or else,‡ is that virtue of God a substance or not? Is it endued with understanding or not? If it hath understanding, how doth it differ from God? If it wants understanding, can any imagine that the support of the world, the guidance of all creatures, the wonders of nature, can be wrought, preserved, managed, by a virtue that hath nothing of understanding in it? If it be not a substance, it can much less be able to produce such excellent operations as the preserving all the kinds of things in the world, and ordering them to perform such excellent ends; this virtue is therefore God himself, the infinite power and wisdom of God; and therefore wheresoever the effects of these are seen in the world, God is essentially present. Some creatures, indeed, act at a distance by a

* Pont.   † Qu. 'water'?—ED.   ‡ Amyrald de Trinitat., p. 106, 107.

virtue diffused; but such a manner of acting comes from a limitedness of nature, that such a nature cannot be everywhere present, and extend its substance to all parts. To act by a virtue, speaks the subject finite, and it is a part of indigence. Kings act in their kingdoms by ministers and messengers, because they cannot act otherwise; but God, being infinitely perfect, 'works all things in all' immediately, 1 Cor. xii. 6. Illumination, sanctification, grace, &c., are the immediate works of God in the heart, and immediate agents are present with what they do; it is an argument of the greater perfection of a being to know things immediately which are done in several places, than to know them at the second hand by instruments. It is no less a perfection to be everywhere, rather than to be tied to one place of action, and to act in other places by instruments for want of a power to act immediately itself. God indeed acts by means and second causes in his providential dispensations in the world, but this is not out of any defect of power to work all immediately himself; but he thereby accomodates his way of acting to the nature of the creature, and the order of things which he hath settled in the world. And when he works by means, he acts with those means, in those means, sustains their faculties and virtues in them, concurs with them by his power, so that God's acting by means doth rather strengthen his essential presence than weaken it; since there is a necessary dependence of the creatures upon the Creator in their being and acting; and what they are, they are by the power of God; what they act, they act in the power of God concurring with them. They have their motion in him as well as their being; and where the power of God is, his essence is, because they are inseparable; and so this omnipresence ariseth from the simplicity of the nature of God. The more vast anything is, the less confined. All that will acknowledge God so great as to be able to work all things by his will without an essential presence, cannot imagine him upon the same reason, so little as to be contained in and bounded by any place.

Reason 3. Because of his supreme perfection.

No perfection is wanting to God; but an unbounded essence is a perfection, a limited one is an imperfection. Though it be a perfection in a man to be wise, yet it is an imperfection that his wisdom cannot rule all the things that concern him; though it be a perfection to be present in a place where his affairs lie, yet. is it his imperfection that he cannot be present everywhere in the midst of all his concerns. If any man could be so, it would be universally owned as a prime perfection in him above others. Is that which would be a perfection in man to be denied to God? * As that which hath life is more perfect than that which hath not life, and that which hath sense is more perfect than that which hath only life, as the plants have, and what hath reason is more perfect than that which hath only life and sense as the beasts have, so what is everywhere is more perfect than that which is bounded in some narrow confines. If a power of motion be more excellent than to be bed-rid, and swiftness in a creature be a more excellent endowment than to be slow and snail-like, then to be everywhere without motion is unconceivably a greater excellency than to be everywhere successively by motion. God sets forth his readiness to help his people and punish his enemies; or his omnipresence, by swiftness, or 'flying upon the wings of the wind,' Ps. xviii. 10. The wind is in every part of the air where it blows; it cannot be said that it is in this or that point of the air where you feel it, so as to exclude it from another part of the air where you are not; it seems to possess all at once.

If the divine essence had any bounds of place, it would be imperfect, as

* Amyrald de Trinitat., p. 74, 75.

well as if it had bounds of time; where anything hath limitation, it hath
some defect in being; and therefore, if God were confined or concluded, he
would be as good as nothing in regard of infiniteness. Whence should this
restraint arise? There is no power above him to restrain him to a certain
space; if so, then he would not be God, but that power which restrained
him would be God. Not from his own nature, for the being everywhere
implies no contradiction to his nature; if his own nature determined him to
a certain place, then if he removed from that place, he would act against his
nature. To conceive any such thing of God is highly absurd. It cannot
be thought God should voluntarily impose any such restraint or confinement
upon himself; this would be to deny himself a perfection he might have.
If God have not this perfection, it is either because it is inconsistent with
his nature, or because he cannot have it, or because he will not. The
former cannot be; for if he hath impressed upon air and light a resemblance
of his excellency to diffuse themselves and fill so vast a space, is such an
excellency inconsistent with the Creator more than the creature? Whatsoever perfection the creature hath is eminently in God. Ps. xciv. 8, 9,
'Understand, O ye brutish among the people: and ye fools, when will you
be wise? He that planted the ear, shall he not hear? he that formed the
eye, shall he not see? he that teacheth man knowledge, shall not he know?'
By the same reason he that hath given such a power to those creatures, air
and light, shall not he be much more filling all spaces of the world? It is
so clear a rule, that the psalmist fixes a folly and brutishness upon those
that deny it. It is not therefore inconsistent with his nature; it were not
then a perfection, but an imperfection; but whatsoever is an excellency in
creatures, cannot in a way of eminency be an imperfection in God. If it be
then a perfection, and God want it, it is because he cannot have it. Where,
then, is his power? How can he be then the fountain of his own being?
If he will not, where is his love to his own nature and glory? since no
creature would deny that to itself which it can have and is an excellency to
it. God therefore hath not only a power or fitness to be everywhere, but
he is actually everywhere.

Reason 4. Because of his immutability.

If God did not fill all the spaces of heaven and earth, but only possess
one, yet it must be acknowledged that God hath a power to move himself
to another. It were absurd to fix God in a part of the heavens, like a star
in an orb, without a power of motion to another place. If he be, therefore,
essentially in heaven, may he not be upon the earth if he please, and transfer his substance from one place to another? To say he cannot is to deny
him a perfection, which he hath bestowed upon his creatures; the angels,
his messengers, are sometimes in heaven, sometimes on earth; the eagles,
meaner creatures, are sometimes in the air out of sight, sometimes upon
the earth. If he doth move, therefore, and recede from one place and settle
in another, doth he not declare himself mutable by changing places, by
being where he was not before, and in not being where he was before? He
would not fill heaven and earth at once, but successively; no man can be
said to fill a room that moves from one part of a room to another; if, therefore, any in their imaginations stake God to the heavens, they render him
less than his creatures; if they allow him a power of motion from one place
to another, they conceive him changeable; and, in either of them, they own
him no greater than a finite and limited being; limited to heaven, if they
fix him there; limited to that space, to which they imagine him to move.

Reason 5. Because of his omnipotency.

The Almightiness of God is a notion settled in the minds of all, that God can do whatsoever he pleases, everything that is not against the purity of his nature, and doth not imply a contradiction in itself; he can therefore create millions of worlds greater than this, and millions of heavens greater than this heaven he hath already created; if so, he is then in unconceivable spaces beyond this world, for his essence is not less and narrower than his power, and his power is not to be thought of a further extent than his essence; he cannot be excluded therefore from those vast spaces where his power may fix those worlds if he please; if so, it is no wonder that he should fill this world, and there is no reason to exclude God from the narrow space of this world, that is not contained in infinite spaces beyond the world. God is wheresoever he hath a power to act, but he hath a power to act everywhere in the world, everywhere out of the world; he is therefore everywhere in the world, everywhere out of the world. Before this world was made, he had a power to make it in the space where now it stands. Was he not then unlimitedly where the world now is, before the world received a being by his powerful word? Why should he not then be in every part of the world now? Can it be thought that God, who was immense before, should, after he had created the world, contract himself to the limits of one of his creatures, and tie himself to a particular place of his own creation, and be less after his creation than he was before?

This might also be prosecuted by an argument from his eternity. What is eternal in duration is immense in essence; the same reason which renders him eternal renders him immense; that which proves him to be always will prove him to be everywhere.

III. The third thing is, propositions for the further clearing this doctrine from any exceptions.

1. This truth is not weakened by the expressions in Scripture, where God is said to dwell in heaven, and in the temple.

(1.) He is, indeed, said to 'sit in heaven,' Ps. ii. 4, and to 'dwell on high,' Ps. cxiii. 5; but he is nowhere said to dwell only in the heavens, as confined to them. It is the court of his majestical presence, but not the prison of his essence; for when we are told that the 'heaven is his throne,' Isa. lxvi. 1, we are told with the same breath that the 'earth is his footstool. He dwells on high in regard of the excellency of his nature, but he is in all places in regard of the diffusion of his presence. The soul is essentially in all parts of the body, but it doth not exert the same operations in all; the more noble discoveries of it are in the head and heart: in the head, where it exerciseth the chiefest senses for the enriching the understanding; in the heart, where it vitally resides, and communicates life and motion to the rest of the body. It doth not understand with the foot or toe, though it be in all parts of the body it forms. And so God may be said to dwell in heaven, in regard of the more excellent and majestic representation of himself, both to the creatures that inhabit the place, as angels and blessed spirits, and also in those marks of his greatness which he hath planted there, those spiritual natures which have a nobler stamp of God upon them, and those excellent bodies, as sun and stars, which as so many tapers light us to behold his glory, Ps. xix. 1, and astonish the minds of men when they gaze upon them. It is his court, where he hath the most solemn worship from his creatures, all his courtiers attending there with a pure love and glowing zeal. He reigns there in a special manner, without any opposition to his government; it is therefore called his 'holy dwelling-place,' 2 Chron. iii. 27. The earth hath not that title, since sin cast a stain and a ruining curse upon it; the earth is not his throne, because his government is opposed; but heaven is none of Satan's precinct, and the rule of God is uncontradicted by the inhabitants of it. It is from thence also he hath given the greatest discoveries of himself; thence he sends the angels his messengers, his Son upon redemption, his Spirit for sanctification. From heaven his gifts drop down upon our heads, and his grace upon our hearts, James iii. 17; from thence the chiefest blessings of earth descend. The motions of the heavens fatten the earth, and the heavenly bodies are but stewards to the earthly comforts for man by their influence. Heaven is the richest, vastest, most stedfast and majestic part of the visible creation. It is there where he will at last manifest himself to his people in a full conjunction of grace and glory, and be for ever open to his people in uninterrupted expressions of goodness, and discoveries of his presence, as a reward of their labour and service; and, in these respects, it may peculiarly be called his throne. And this doth no more hinder his essential presence in all parts of the earth, than it doth his gracious presence in all the hearts of his people. God is in heaven, in regard of the manifestation of his glory; in hell, by the expression of his justice; in the earth, by the discoveries of his wisdom, power, patience, and compassion; in his people, by the monuments of his grace; and in all, in regard of his substance.

(2.) He is said also to dwell in the ark and temple. It is called, Ps. xxvi. 8, 'the habitation of his house, and the place where his honour dwells;' and to dwell in Jerusalem, as in his holy mountain, 'the mountain of the Lord of hosts,' Zech. viii. 3; in regard of publishing his oracles, answering their prayers, manifesting more of his goodness to the Israelites than to any other nation in the world; erecting his true worship among them, which was not settled in any part of the world besides; and his worship is principally intended in that psalm. The ark is the place where his honour dwells; the worship of God is called the glory of God: 'They changed the glory of God into an image made like to corruptible men,' Rom. i. 23, *i. e.* they changed the worship of God into idolatry; and to that also doth the place in Zechariah refer.

Now, because he is said to dwell in heaven, is he essentially only there? Is he not as essentially in the temple and ark as he is in heaven, since there are as high expressions of his habitation there, as of his dwelling in heaven? If he dwell only in heaven, how came he to dwell in the temple? Both are asserted in Scripture, one as much as the other. If his dwelling in heaven did not hinder his dwelling in the ark, it could as little hinder the presence of his essence on the earth. To dwell in heaven and in one part of the earth at the same time, is all one as to dwell in all parts of heaven and all parts of earth. If he were in heaven, and in the ark and temple, it was the same essence in both, though not the same kind of manifestation of himself. If by his dwelling in heaven he meant his whole essence, why is it not also to be meant by his dwelling in the ark? It was not sure part of his essence that was in heaven, and part of his essence that was on earth; his essence would then be divided; and can it be imagined that he would be in heaven and the ark at the same time, and not in the spaces between? Could his essence be split into fragments, and a gap made in it, that two distinct spaces should be filled by him, and all between be empty of him? So that God's being, said to dwell in heaven, and in the temple, is so far from impairing the truth of his doctrine, that it more confirms and evidences it.

2. Nor do the expressions of God's coming to us, or departing from us, impair this doctrine of his omnipresence.

God is said to 'hide his face' from his people, Ps. x. 1, to be 'far from the wicked,' Prov. xv. 29; and the Gentiles are said to be 'afar off,' viz., from God, Eph. ii. 17, and upon the manifestation of Christ, 'made near.' These must not be understood of any distance or nearness of his essence, for that is equally near to all persons and things, but of some other special way and manifestation of his presence. Thus God is said to be in believers by love, as they are in him: 1 John iv. 15, 'He that abides in love abides in God, and God in him.' He that loves is in the thing beloved; and when two love one another, they are in one another. God is in a righteous man by a special grace, and far from the wicked in regard of such special works; and God is said to be in a place by a special manifestation, as when he was in the bush, Exod. iii., or manifesting his glory upon mount Sinai: Exod. xxiv. 16, 'The glory of the Lord abode upon mount Sinai.' God is said to hide his face when he withdraws his comforting presence, disturbs the repose of our hearts, flasheth terror into our consciences, when he puts men under the smart of the cross, as though he had ordered his mercy utterly to depart from them, or when he doth withdraw his special assisting providence from us in our affairs. So he departed from Saul, when he withdrew his direction and protection from him in the concerns of his government: 1 Sam. xvi. 14, 'The Spirit of the Lord departed from Saul,' *i.e.* the spirit of government. God may be far from us in one respect, and near to us in another; far from us in regard of comfort, yet near to us in regard of support, when his essential presence continues the same. This is a necessary consequent upon the infiniteness of God, the other is an act of the will of God; so he was said to forsake Christ in regard of his obscuring his glory from his human nature and inflicting his wrath, though he was near to him in regard of his grace, and preserved him from contracting any spot in his sufferings. We do not say the sun is departed out of the heavens when it is bemisted; it remains in the same part of the heavens, passes on its course, though its beams do not reach us by reason of the bar between us and it. The soul is in every part of the body in regard of its substance, and constantly in it, though it doth not act so sprightly and vigorously at one time as at another in one and the same member, and discover itself so sensibly in its operations; so all the various effects of God towards the sons of men are but diverse operations of one and the same essence. He is far from us or near to us, as he is a judge or a benefactor. When he comes to punish, it notes, not the approach of his essence, but the stroke of his justice; when he comes to benefit, it is not by a new access of his essence, but an efflux of his grace. He departs from us when he leaves us to the frowns of his justice, he comes to us when he encircles us in the arms of his mercy; but he was equally present with us in both dispensations in regard of his essence. And likewise God is said to come down—Gen. xi. 5, 'And the Lord came down to see the city'—when he doth some signal and wonderful works which attract the minds of men to the acknowledgment of a supreme power and providence in the world, who judged God absent and careless before.

8. Nor is the essential presence of God with all creatures any disparagement to him. Since it was no disparagement to create the heaven and the earth, it is no disparagement to him to fill them. If he were essentially present with them when he created them, it is no dishonour to him to be essentially present with them to support them. If it were his glory to create them by his essence when they were nothing, can it be his disgrace to be present by his essence, since they are something, and something good, and very good in his eye? Gen. i. 31, 'God saw everything, and behold it was very good,' or 'mighty good;' all ordered to declare his goodness, wisdom, power, and to make him adorable to man, and therefore took com-

placency in them. There is a harmony in all things, a combination in them for those glorious ends for which God created them; and is it a disgrace for God to be present with his own harmonious composition? Is it not a musician's glory to touch with his fingers the treble, the least and tenderest string, as well as the strongest and greatest bass? Hath not everything some stamp of God's own being upon it, since he eminently contains in himself the perfections of all his works? Whatsoever hath being hath a footstep of God upon it, who is all being. Everything in the earth is his footstool, having a mark of his foot upon it. All declare the being of God, because they had their being from God; and will God account it any disparagement to him to be present with that which confirms his being, and the glorious perfections of his nature to his intelligent creatures? The meanest things are not without their virtues, which may boast God's being the Creator of them, and rank them in the midst of his works of wisdom as well as power. Doth God debase himself to be present by his essence with the things he hath made, more than he doth to know them by his essence? Is not the least thing known by him? How? Not by a faculty or act distinct from his essence, but by his essence itself. How is anything disgraceful to the essential presence of God, that is not disgraceful to his knowledge by his essence? Besides, would God make anything that should be an invincible reason to him to part with his own infiniteness, by a contraction of his own essence into a less compass than before? It was immense before, it had no bounds; and would God make a world that he would be ashamed to be present with, and continue it to the diminution and lessening of himself, rather than annihilate it to avoid the disparagement? This were to impeach the wisdom of God, and cast a blemish upon his infinite understanding, that he knows not the consequences of his work, or is well contented to be impaired in the immensity of his own essence by it. No man thinks it a dishonour to light, a most excellent creature, to be present with a toad or serpent; and though there be an infinite disproportion between light, a creature, and the Father of lights, the Creator, yet* God, being a Spirit, knows how to be with bodies as if they were not bodies. And being jealous of his own honour, would not, could not, do anything that might impair it.

4. Nor will it follow, that because God is essentially everywhere, that everything is God. God is not everywhere by any conjunction, composition, or mixture with anything on earth. When light is in every part of a crystal globe, and encircles it close on every side, do they become one? No; the crystal remains what it is, and the light retains its own nature. God is not in us as a part of us, but as an efficient and preserving cause. It is not by his essential presence, but his efficacious presence, that he brings any person into a likeness to his own nature. God is so in his essence with things as to be distinct from them, as a cause from the effect, as a Creator different from the creature, preserving their nature, not communicating his own. His essence touches all, is in conjunction with none. *Finite* and *infinite* cannot be joined. He is not far from us, therefore near to us; so near, that we 'live and move in him,' Acts xvii. 28. Nothing is God because it moves in him, any more than a fish in the sea is the sea, or a part of the sea, because it moves in it.† Doth a man that holds a thing in the hollow of his hand transform it by that action, and make it like his hand? The soul and body are more straitly united than the essence of God is by his presence with any creature. The soul is in the body as a form in matter, and from their union doth arise a man; yet in this near conjunc-

---

     * Gassend.   † Amyrald de Trinit., p. 99, 100.

tion both body and soul remain distinct. The soul is not the body, nor the body the soul; they both have distinct natures and essences. The body can never be changed into a soul, nor the soul into a body; no more can God into the creature, or the creature into God. Fire is in heated iron, in every part of it, so that it seems to be nothing but fire; yet is not fire and iron the same thing? But such a kind of arguing against God's omnipresence, that if God were essentially present everything would be God, would exclude him from heaven as well as from earth. By the same reason, since they acknowledge God essentially in heaven, the heaven where he is should be changed into the nature of God; and by arguing against his presence in earth upon this ground, they run such an inconvenience, that they must own him to be nowhere, and that which is nowhere is nothing! Doth the earth become God because God is essentially there, any more than the heavens, where God is acknowledged by all to be essentially present?

Again, if where God is essentially, that must be God, then if they place God in a point of the heavens, not only that point must be God, but all the world, because if that point be God, because God is there, then the point touched by that point must be God, and so consequently as far as there are any points touched by one another. We live and move in God, so we live and move in the air; we are no more God by that than we are mere air, because we breathe in it, and it enters into all the pores of our body; nay, where there was a straiter union of the divine nature to the human in our Saviour, yet the nature of both was distinct, and the humanity was not changed into the divinity, nor the divinity into the humanity.

5. Nor doth it follow, that because God is everywhere, therefore a creature may be worshipped without idolatry. Some of the heathens, who acknowledged God's omnipresence, abused it to the countenancing idolatry; because God was resident in everything, they thought everything might be worshipped, and some have used it as an argument against this doctrine; the best doctrines may by men's corruption be drawn out into unreasonable and pernicious conclusions. Have you not met with any, that from the doctrine of God's free mercy, and our Saviour's satisfactory death, have drawn poison to feed their lusts, and consume their souls; a poison composed by their own corruption, and not offered by those truths? The apostle intimates to us, that some did, or at least were ready to be more lavish in sinning, because God was abundant in grace: Rom. vi. 1, 2, ' Shall we continue in sin, that grace may abound?' ver. 1, ' Shall we sin, because we are not under the law but under grace?' when he prevents an objection that he thought might be made by some; but as to this case, since, though God be present in everything, yet everything retains its nature, distinct from the nature of God, therefore it is not to have a worship due to the excellency of God. As long as anything remains a creature, it is only to have the respect from us which is due to it in the rank of creatures. When a prince is present with his guard, or if he should go arm in arm with a peasant, is therefore the veneration and honour due to the prince to be paid to the peasant, or any of his guard? Would the presence of the prince excuse it, or would it not rather aggravate it? He acknowledged such a person equal to me, by giving him my rights, even in my sight. Though God dwelt in the temple, would not the Israelites have been accounted guilty of idolatry had they worshipped the images of the cherubims, or the ark, or the altar, as objects of worship, which were erected only as a means for his service? Is there not as much reason to think God was as essentially present in the temple as in heaven, since the same expressions are used of the one and the other? The sanctuary is called

the ' glorious high throne,' Jer. xvii. 12 ; and he is said to ' dwell between the cherubims,' Ps. lxxx. 1, *i. e.* the two cherubims that were at the two ends of the mercy-seat, appointed by God as the two sides of his throne in the sanctuary, Exod. xxv. 18, where he was to ' dwell,' ver. 8, and meet and ' commune with his people,' ver. 22. Could this excuse Manasseh's idolatry in bringing in a carved image into the house of God ? 2 Chron. xxxiii. 7. Had it been a good answer to the charge, God is present here, and therefore everything may be worshipped as God. If he be only essentially in heaven, would it not be idolatry to direct a worship to the heavens, o· any part of it as a due object, because of the presence of God there ? Though we look up to the heavens, where we pray and worship God, yet heaven is not the object of worship, the soul abstracts God from the creature.

6. Nor is God defiled by being present with those creatures which seem filthy to us. Nothing is filthy in the eye of God as his creature ; he could never else have pronounced all good ; whatsoever is filthy to us, yet as it is a creature, it owes itself to the power of·God. His essence is no more defiled by being present with it, than his power by producing it. No creature is foul in itself, though it may seem so to us. Doth not an infant lie in a womb of filthiness and rottenness ? Yet is not the power of God present with it, in ' working it curiously in the lower parts of the earth?' Are his eyes defiled by ' seeing the substance when it is yet imperfect' ? Or his hand defiled by ' writing every member in his book' ? Ps. cxxxix. 15, 16, Have not the vilest and most noisome things excellent medicinal virtues ? How are they endued with them ? How are those qualities preserved in them ? By anything without God or no ? Every artificer looks with pleasure upon the work he hath wrought with art and skill ; can his essence be defiled by being present with them, any more than it was in giving them such virtues, and preserving them in them ? God measures the heaven and the earth with his hand ; is his hand defiled by the evil influences of the planets, or the corporeal impurities of the earth? Nothing can be filthy in the eye of God but sin, since everything else owes its being to him. What may appear deformed and unworthy to us, is not so to the Creator ; he sees beauty where we see deformity ; finds goodness where we behold what is nauseous to us. All creatures, being the effects of his power, may be the objects of his presence ; can any place be more foul than hell, if you take it either for the hell of the damned, or for the grave, where there is rottenness ? yet there he is, Ps. cxxxix. 8. When Satan appeared before God, and spake with him, Job i. 7, could God contract any impurity by being present where that filthy spirit was, more impure than any corporeal, noisome, and defiling thing can be ? No ; God is purity to himself in the midst of noisomeness ; a heaven to himself in the midst of hell. Who ever heard of a sunbeam stained by shining upon a quagmire, any more than sweetened by breaking into a perfumed room !* Though the light shines upon pure and impure things, yet it mixes not itself with either of them ; so, though God be present with devils and wicked men, yet without any mixture, he is present with their essence to sustain and support it, not in their defection, wherein lies their defilement, and which is not a physical but a moral evil ; bodily filth can never touch an incorporeal substance. Spirits are not present with us in the same manner that one body is present with another ; bodies can, by a touch only, defile bodies. Is the glory of an angel stained by being in a coal mine ? or could the angel that came into the lions' den, to deliver Daniel, chap. vi. 22, be any more disturbed by the stench of the place, than he could be scratched by the paws or torn by

* Shelford of the Attributes, p. 170.

the teeth of the beasts? Their spiritual nature secures them against any infection, when they are ' ministering spirits' to persecuted believers in their nasty prisons, Acts xii. 7. The soul is straitly united with the body, but it is not made white or black by the whiteness or blackness of its habitation; is it infected by the corporeal impurities of the body, while it continually dwells in a sea of filthy pollution ? If the body be cast into a common sewer, is the soul defiled by it ? Can a diseased body derive a contagion to the spirit that animates it ? Is it not often the purer by grace, the more the body is infected by nature. Hezekiah's spirit was scarce ever more fervent with God than when the sore, which some think to be a plague-sore, was upon him, Isa. xxxviii. 3. How can any corporeal filth impair the purity of the divine essence ? It may as well be said, that God is not present in battles and fights for his people, Joshua xxiii. 10, because he would not be disturbed by the noise of cannons and clashing of swords, as that he is not present in the world, because of the ill scents. Let us therefore conclude this with the expression of a learned man of our own :* ' To deny the omnipresence of God, because of ill scented places, is to measure God rather by the nicety of sense than by the sagacity of reason.'

IV. Use.
1. Of information.
(1.) Christ hath a divine nature. As eternity and immutability, two incommunicable properties of the divine nature, are ascribed to Christ, so also is this of omnipresence or immensity. John iii. 13, ' No man hath ascended up to heaven, but he that came down from heaven, even the Son of man which is in heaven.' Not which *was*, but which *is ;* he comes from heaven by incarnation, and remains in heaven by his divinity. He was, while he spake to Nicodemus, locally on earth, in regard of his humanity, but in heaven according to his deity, as well as upon earth in the union of his divine and human nature. He descended upon earth, but he left not heaven; he was in the world before he came in the flesh. John i. 10, ' He was in the world, and the world was made by him.' He was in the world, as the ' light that enlightens every man that comes into the world ;' in the world as God, before he was in the world as man. He was then in the world as a man, while he discoursed with Nicodemus, yet so that he was also in heaven as God. No creature but is bounded in place, either circumscribed as body or determined as spirit to be in one space, so as not to be in another at the same time ; to leave a place where they were, and possess a place where they were not. But Christ is so on earth, that at the same time he is in heaven ; he is therefore infinite. To be in heaven and earth at the same moment of time, is a property solely belonging to the Deity, wherein no creature can be a partner with him. ' He was in the world' before he came to the world, ' and the world was made by him,' John i. 10. His coming was not as the coming of angels, that leave heaven and begin to be on earth, where they were not before, but such a presence as can be ascribed only to God, who fills heaven and earth. Again, if all things were made by him, then he was present with all things which were made, for where there is a presence of power, there is also a presence of essence, and therefore he is still present ; for the right and power of conservation follows the power of creation. And according to this divine nature he promiseth his presence with his church: ' There am I in the midst of them,' Mat. xviii. 20. And ' I am with you alway, even to the end of the world,' chap. xxviii. 20, *i. e.* by his divinity ; for he had before

* Dr More.

told them that they were not to have him alway with them, chap. xxvi. 11,
i. e., according to his humanity; but in his divine nature he is present with,
and 'walks in the midst of the golden candlesticks.' If we understand it
of a presence by his Spirit in the midst of the church, doth it invalidate his
essential presence? No; he is no less than the Spirit whom he sends, and
therefore as little confined as the Spirit is, who dwells in every believer; and
this may also be inferred from John x. 30, 'My Father and I are one;' not
one by consent, though that be included, but one in power; for he speaks
not of their consent, but of their joint power in keeping his people. Where
there is a unity of essence there is a unity of presence.

(2.) Here is a confirmation of the spiritual nature of God. If he were
an infinite body, he could not fill heaven and earth, but with the exclusion
of all creatures. Two bodies cannot be in the same space; they may be
near one another, but not in any of the same points together. A body
bounded he hath not, for that would destroy his immensity; he could not
then fill heaven and earth, because a body cannot be at one and the same
time in two different spaces; but God doth not fill heaven at one time, and
the earth at another, but both at the same time. Besides, a limited body
cannot be said to fill the whole earth, but one particular space in the earth
at a time. A body may fill the earth with its virtue, as the sun, but not
with its substance. Nothing can be everywhere with a corporeal weight and
mass; but God being infinite, is not tied to any part of the world, but pene-
trates all, and equally acts by his infinite power in all.

(3.) Here is an argument for providence. His presence is mentioned in
the text, in order to his government of the affairs of the world. Is he everywhere, to be unconcerned with every thing? Before the world had a being,
God was present with himself; since the world hath a being, he is present
with his creatures, to exercise his wisdom in the ordering, as he did his
power in the production of them. As the knowledge of God is not a bare
contemplation of a thing, so his presence is not a bare inspection into a
thing. Were it an idle, careless, presence, it were a presence to no purpose,
which cannot be imagined of God. Infinite power, goodness, and wisdom,
being everywhere present with his essence, are never without their exercise.
He never manifests any of his perfections, but the manifestation is full of
some indulgence and benefit to his creatures. It cannot be supposed God
should neglect those things, wherewith he is constantly present in a way of
efficiency and operation.* He is not everywhere without acting everywhere.
Wherever his essence is, there is a power and virtue worthy of God everywhere dispensed. He governs by his presence what he made by his power,
and is present as an agent with all his works. His power and essence are
together, to preserve them while he pleases, as his power and his essence
are together to create them when he saw good to do it. Every creature hath
a stamp of God, and his presence is necessary to keep the impression standing upon the creature. As all things are his works, they are the objects of
his care; and the wisdom he employed in framing them, will not suffer him
to be careless of them. His presence with them, engageth him in honour
not to be a negligent governor. His immensity fits him for government;
and where there is a fitness, there is an exercise of government, where there
are objects for the exercise of it. He is worthy to have the universal rule
of the world, he can be present in all places of his empire, there is nothing
can be done by any of his subjects, but in his sight. As his eternity renders
him king alway, so his immensity renders him king everywhere. If he were
only present in heaven, it might occasion a suspicion that he minded only

* Cyril.

the things of heaven, and had no concern for things below that vast body; but if he be present here, his presence hath a tendency to the government of those things with which he is present. We are all in him as fish in the sea; and he bears all creatures in the womb of his providence, and the arms of his goodness. It is most certain that his presence with his people is far from being an idle one; for when he promises to be with them, he adds some special cordial, as, ' I will be with thee, and bless thee,' Gen. xxvi. 3, Jer. xv. 20. ' I am with thee, and I will strengthen thee; I will help thee, I will uphold thee,' Isa. xli. 10, 14. Infinite goodness will never countenance a negligent presence.

(4.) The omniscience of God is inferred from hence. If God be present everywhere, he must needs know what is done everywhere. It is for this end he proclaims himself a God filling heaven and earth, in the text. ' Can any hide himself in secret places that I shall not see him, saith the Lord ?' I have heard what the prophets say, that prophesy lies in my name. If I fill heaven and earth, the most secret thing cannot be hid from my sight. An intelligent being cannot be everywhere present, and more intimate in everything, than it can be in itself; but he must know what is done without, what is thought within. Nothing can be obscure to him, who is in every part of the world, in every part of his creatures. Not a thought can start up but in his sight, who is present in the souls and minds of everything. How easy is it with him, to whose essence the world is but a point, to know and observe everything done in this world, as any of us can know what is done in one point of place where we are present ? If light were an understanding being, it would behold and know everything done, where it diffuseth itself. God is light (as light in a crystal glass, all within it, all without it), and is not ignorant of what is done within and without; no ignorance can be fastened upon him who hath an universal presence.

Hence by the way we may take notice of the wonderful patience of God, who bears with so many provocations, not from a principle of ignorance, for he bears with sins that are committed near him, in his sight, sins that he sees, and cannot but see.

(5.) Hence may be inferred the incomprehensibility of God. He that fills heaven and earth, cannot be contained in anything; he fills the understandings of men, the understandings of angels, but is comprehended by neither; it is a rashness to think to find out any bounds of God ; there is no measuring of an infinite being; if it were to be measured, it were not infinite ; but because it is infinite, it is not to be measured. God sits above the cherubims, Ezek. x. 1, above the fulness, above the brightness, not only of a human, but a created understanding. Nothing is more present than God, yet nothing more hid ; he is light, and yet obscurity ;* his perfections are visible, yet unsearchable ; we know there is an infinite God, but it surpasseth the compass of our minds ; we know there is no number so great, but another may be added to it; but no man can put it in practice without losing himself in a maze of figures. What is the reason we comprehend not many, nay, most things in the world ? Partly from the excellency of the object, and partly from the imperfection of our understanding. How can we then comprehend God, who exceeds all, and is exceeded by none ; contains all, and is contained by none; is above our understanding, as well as above our sense ; as considered in himself, infinite ; as considered in comparison with our understandings, incomprehensible ; who can with his eye measure the breadth, length, and depth of the sea, and at one cast view every dimension of the heavens ! God is greater, and ' we cannot know him,' Job xxxvi. 25 ;

* Κρυφιότης, Dionysius called God.

he fills the understanding as he fills heaven and earth : yet is above the understanding as he is above heaven and earth. He is known by faith, enjoyed by love, but comprehended by no mind. God is not contained in that one syllable, *God;* by it we apprehend an excellent and unlimited nature ; himself only understands himself, and can unveil himself.

(6.) How wonderful is God, and how nothing are creatures ! ' Ascribe the greatness to our God,' Deut. xxxii. 8. He is admirable in the consideration of his power, in the extent of his understanding, and no less wonderful in the immensity of his essence ; that as Austin saith, he is in the world, yet not confined to it ; he is out of the world, yet not debarred from it ; he is above the world, yet not elevated by it ; he is below the world, yet not depressed by it ; he is above all, equalled by none ; he is in all, not because he needs them, but they stand in need of him ; this, as well as eternity, makes a vast disproportion between God and the creature. The creature is bounded by a little space, and no space is so great as to bound the Creator. By this we may take a prospect of our own nothingness ; as in the consideration of God's holiness we are minded of our own impurity ; and in the thoughts of his wisdom have a view of our own folly ; and in the meditation of his power, have a sense of our weakness ; so his immensity should make us, according to our own nature, appear little in our own eyes. What little, little, little things are we to God ! Less than an atom in the beams of the sun ; poor drops to a God that fills heaven and earth ; and yet dare we to strut against him, and dash ourselves against a rock. If the consideration of ourselves, in comparison with others, be apt to puff us up, the consideration of ourselves, in comparison with God, will be sufficient to pull us down. If we consider him in the greatness of his essence, there is but little more proportion between him and us, than between being and not being, than between a drop and the ocean. How should we never think of God without a holy admiration of his greatness, and a deep sense of our own littleness ! and as the angels cover their faces before him, with what awe should creeping worms come into his sight ! and since God fills heaven and earth with his presence, we should fill heaven and earth with his glory ; for this end he created angels to praise him in heaven, and men to worship him on earth, that the places he fills with his presence may be filled with his praise. We should be swallowed up in admiration of the immensity of God, as men are at the first sight of the sea, when they behold a mass of waters, without beholding the bounds, and immense depth of it.

(7.) How much is this attribute of God forgotten or contemned ! We pretend to believe him to be present everywhere, and yet many live as if he were present nowhere.

[1.] It is commonly forgotten, or not believed. All the extravagancies of men may be traced to the forgetfulness of this attribute as their spring. The first speech Adam spake in paradise after his fall, testified his unbelief of this : Gen. iii. 10, ' I heard thy voice in the garden, and I hid myself ;' his ear understood the voice of God, but his mind did not conclude the presence of God ; he thought the trees could shelter him from him, whose eye was present in the minutest parts of the earth ; he that thought after his sin, that he could hide himself from the presence of his justice, thought before that he could hide himself from the presence of his knowledge ; and being deceived in the one, he would try what would be the fruit of the other. In both he forgets, if not denies, this attribute ; either corrupt notions of God, or a slight belief of what in general men assent unto, gives birth to every sin. In all transgressions there is something of atheism : either denying the being of God, or a dash upon some perfection of God ; a not believing his holiness to hate it, his truth that threatens, his justice to punish it, and his presence to observe it. Though God be not afar off in his essence, he is afar off in the apprehension of the sinner.* There is no wicked man, but if he be† an atheist, he is a heretic; and to gratify his lust, will fancy himself to be out of the presence of his Judge. His reason tells him, God is present with him; his lust presseth him to embrace the season of a sensual pleasure. He will forsake his reason, and prove a heretic, that he may be an undisturbed sinner; and sins doubly both in the error of his mind and the vileness of his practice; he will conceit God with those in Job, chap xxii. 14, 'veiled with thick clouds,' and not able to pierce into the lower world; as if his presence and cares were confined to celestial things, and the earth were too low a sphere for his essence to reach, at least with any credit. It is forgotten by good men, when they fear too much the designs of their enemies; 'Fear not, for I am with thee,' Isa. xliii. 5. If the presence of God be enough to strengthen against fear, then the prevailing of fear issues from our forgetfulness of it.

[2.] This attribute of God's omnipresence is for the most part contemned. When men will commit that in the presence of God, which they would be afraid or ashamed to do before the eye of man. Men do not practise that modesty before God, as before men. He that would restrain his tongue out of fear of men's eye, will not restrain either his tongue or hands out of fear of God's. What is the language of this, but that God is not present with us, or his presence ought to be of less regard with us, and influence upon us, than that of a creature? Ask the thief why he dares to steal? Will he not answer, No eye sees him? Ask the adulterer why he strips himself of his chastity, and invades the rights of another? Will he not answer, No eye sees me? Job xxiv. 15. He disguiseth himself to be unseen by man, but slights the all-seeing eye of God.‡ If only a man know them, they are in terror of the shadow of death, Job xxiv. 17; they are planet-struck, but stand unshaken at the presence of God. Is not this to account God as limited as man, as ignorant, as absenting, as if God were something less than those things which restrain us? It is a debasing God below a creature. If we can forbear sin from any awe of the presence of man, to whom we are equal in regard of nature; or from the presence of a very mean man, to whom we are superior in regard of condition; and not forbear it because we are within the ken of God, we respect him not only as our inferior, but inferior to the meanest man or child of his creation, in whose sight we would not commit the like action. It is to represent him as a sleepy, negligent, or careless God; as though anything might be concealed from him, before whom the least fibres of the heart are anatomized and open, Heb. iv. 13, who sees as plainly midnight as noonday sins. Now this is a high aggravation of sin. To break a king's laws in his sight is more bold than to violate them behind his back; as it was Haman's offence when he lay upon Esther's bed, to force the queen before the king's face. The least iniquity receives a high tincture from this; and no sin can be little that is an affront in the face of God, and casting the filth of the creature before the eyes of his holiness,—as if a wife should commit adultery before her husband's face, or a slave dishonour his master, and disobey his commands in his presence. And hath it not often been thus with us? Have we not been disloyal to God in his sight, before his eyes, those pure eyes, that cannot behold iniquity without anger and grief? Isa. lxv. 12, 'Ye did evil before my eyes.' Nathan chargeth this home upon David: 2 Sam. xii. 9,

* Drexel. Nicet. lib. ii. cap. 10.   ‡ Drexel. Nicet. lib. ii. cap. 10.
† Qu. 'be not?'—ED.

'Thou hast despised the commandment of the Lord, to do evil in his sight.' And David, in his repentance, reflects upon himself for it: Ps. li. 4, 'Against thee, thee only have I sinned, and done this evil in thy sight.' I observed not thy presence; I neglected thee while thy eye was upon me. And this consideration should sting our hearts in all our confessions of our crimes. Men will be afraid of the presence of others, whatsoever they think in their heart. How unworthily do we deal with God, in not giving him so much as an eye-service, which we do man?

(8.) How terrible should the thoughts of this attribute be to sinners! How foolish is it to imagine any hiding-place from the incomprehensible God, who fills and contains all things, and is present in every point of the world.* When men have shut the door, and made all darkness within, to meditate or commit a crime, they cannot in the most intricate recesses be sheltered from the presence of God. If they could separate themselves from their own shadows, they could not avoid his company, or be obscured from his sight: Ps. cxxxix. 12, 'The darkness and light are both alike to him.' Hypocrites cannot disguise their sentiments from him; he is in the most secret nook of their hearts. No thought is hid, no lust is secret, but the eye of God beholds this, and that, and the other. He is present with our heart when we imagine, with our hands when we act. We may exclude the sun from peeping into our solitudes, but not the eyes of God from beholding our actions. 'The eyes of the Lord are in every place, beholding the evil and good,' Prov. xv. 3. He lies in the depths of our souls, and sees afar off our designs before we have conceived them. He is in the greatest darkness, as well as the clearest light; in the closest thought of the mind, as well as the openest expressions. Nothing can be hid from him; no, not in the darkest cells or thickest walls. 'He compasseth our path' wherever we are, and 'is acquainted with all our ways,' Ps. cxxxix. 3. He is as much present with wicked men to observe their sins, as he is to detest them. Where he is present in his essence, he is present in his attributes: his holiness to hate, and his justice to punish, if he please to speak the word. It is strange men should not be mindful of this, when their very sins themselves might put them in mind of his presence. Whence hast thou the power to act? Who preserves thy being, whereby thou art capable of committing that evil? Is it not his essential presence that sustains us, and his arm that supports us? And where can any man fly from his presence? Not the vast regions of heaven could shelter a sinning angel from his eye. How was Adam ferreted out of his hiding-places in paradise? Nor can we find the depths of the sea a sufficient covering to us. If we were with Jonah, closeted up in the belly of a whale; if we had the wings of the morning, as quick a motion as the light at the dawning of the day, that doth in an instant surprise and overpower the regions of darkness, and could pass to the utmost parts of the earth or hell, there we should find him; there his eye would be upon us, there would his hand lay hold of us, and lead us as a conqueror triumphing over a captive, Ps. cxxxix. 8–10. Nay, if we could leap out of the compass of heaven and earth, we should find as little reserves from him. He is without the world in those infinite spaces which the mind of man can imagine. In regard of his immensity, nothing in being can be distant from him, wheresoever it is.

Use 2 is for comfort. That God is present everywhere, is as much a comfort to a good man as it is a terror to a wicked one. He is everywhere for his people, not only by a necessary perfection of his nature, but an immense diffusion of his goodness. He is in all creatures as their preserver,

---

* Quo fugis, Encelade? Quascunque accesseris oras,
  Sub Jove semper eris.

in the damned as their terror, in his people as their protector. He fills hell with his severity, heaven with his glory, his people with his grace. He is with his people as light in darkness, a fountain in a garden, as manna in the ark. God is in the world as a spring of preservation, in the church as his cabinet, a spring of grace and consolation. A man is present sometimes in his field, but more delightfully in his garden. A vineyard, as it hath more of cost, so more of care, and a watchful presence of the owner: Isa. xxvii. 3, ' I the Lord do keep it,' viz., his vineyard; ' I will water it every moment: lest any hurt it, I will keep it night and day.' As there is a presence of essence, which is natural, so there is a presence of grace, which is federal,—a presence by covenant, ' I will not leave thee,' I will be with thee ;' this latter depends upon the former. For take away the immensity of God, and you leave no foundation for his universal gracious presence with his people in all their emergencies, in all their hearts ; and, therefore, where he is present in his essence, he cannot be absent in his grace from them that fear him. It is from his filling heaven and earth he proves his knowledge of the designs of the false prophets ; and from the same topic may as well be inferred the employment of his power and grace for his people.

1. The omnipresence of God is comfort in all violent temptations. No fiery dart can be so present with us, as God is present both with that and the marksman. The most raging devils cannot be so near us as God is to us and them. He is present with his people, to relieve them ; and present with the devil, to manage him to his own holy purposes. So he was with Job, defeating his enemies, and bringing him triumphantly out of those pressing trials. This presence is such a terror that, whatsoever the devil can despoil us of, he must leave this untouched. He might scratch the apostle with a thorn, 2 Cor. xvii. 7, 9, but he could not rifle him of the presence of divine grace, which God promised him. He must prevail so far as to make God cease to be God, before he can make him to be distant from us ; and, while this cannot be, the devils and men can no more hinder the emanations of God to the soul, than a child can cut off the rays of the sun from embellishing the earth ; it is no mean support for a good man, at any time buffeted by a messenger of Satan, to think God stands near him, and beholds how ill he is used. It would be a satisfaction to a king's favourite, in the midst of the violence some enemies might use to him upon a surprise, to understand that the king who loves him, stands behind a curtain, and through a hole sees the injuries he suffers ; and were the devil as considering as he is malicious, he could not but be in great fear at God's being in the generation of the righteous, as his serpentine seed is: Ps. xiv. 5, ' There were they in great fear, for God is in the generation of the righteous.'

2. The omnipresence of God is a comfort in sharp afflictions. Good men have a comfort in this presence in their nasty prisons, oppressing tribunals ; in the overflowing waters or scorching flames, he is still with them, Isa. xliii. 2 ; and many times, by his presence, keeps the bush from consuming, when it seems to be all in a flame. In afflictions, God shews himself most present when friends are most absent: ' When my father and mother forsake me, then the Lord shall take me up,' Ps. xxvii. 10 ; then God will stoop and gather me into his protection ; *Heb.* ' shall gather me,' alluding to those tribes that were to bring up the rear in the Israelites' march, to take care that none were left behind, and exposed to famine or wild beasts, by reason of some disease that disenabled them to keep pace with their brethren. He that is the sanctuary of his people in all calamities, is more present with them, to support them, than their adversaries can be present with them, to afflict them: Ps. xlvi. 2, ' A present help in the time of

trouble.' He is present with all things for this end; though his presence be a necessary presence, in regard of the immensity of his nature, yet the end of this presence, in regard that it is for the good of his people, is a voluntary presence. It is for the good of man he is present in the lower world, and principally for the good of his people, for whose sake he keeps up the world: 2 Chron. xvi. 9, 'His eyes run to and fro throughout the whole earth, to shew himself strong in the behalf of them whose heart is perfect towards him.' If he doth not deliver good men from afflictions, he will be so present as to manage them in them, as that his glory shall issue from them, and their grace be brightened by them.*

What a man was Paul, when he was lodged in a prison, or dragged to the courts of judicature; when he was torn with rods, or laden with chains! Then did he shew the greatest miracles, made the judge tremble upon the bench, and break the heart, though not the prison, of the jailor,—so powerful is the presence of God in the pressures of his people. This presence outweighs all other comforts, and is more valuable to a Christian than barns of corn or cellars of wine can be to a covetous man, Ps. iv. 7. It was this presence was David's cordial in the mutinying of his soldiers, 1 Sam. xxx. 6. What a comfort is this in exile, or a forced desertion of our habitations! Good men may be banished from their country, but never from the presence of their protector; ye cannot say of any corner of the earth, or of any dungeon in a prison, God is not here. If you were cast out of your country a thousand miles off, you are not out of God's precinct, his arm is there to cherish the good, as well as to drag out the wicked; it is the same God, the same presence in every country, as well as the same sun, moon, and stars; and were not God everywhere, yet he could not be meaner than his creature, the sun in the firmament, which visits every part of the habitable world in twenty-four hours.

3. The omnipotence † of God is a comfort in all duties of worship. He is present to observe, and present to accept our petitions, and answer our suits. Good men have not only the essential presence, which is common to all, but his gracious presence; not only the presence that flows from his nature, but that which flows from his promise; his essential presence makes no difference between this and that man in regard of spirituals, without this in conjunction with it; his nature is the cause of the presence of his essence; his will, engaged by his truth, is the cause of the presence of his grace. He promised to meet the Israelites in the place where he should set his name, and in all places where he doth record it: Exod. xx. 24, 'In all places where I record my name, I will come unto thee, and I will bless thee;' in every place where I shall manifest the special presence of my divinity. In all places hands may be lifted up, without doubting of his ability to hear; he dwells in the 'contrite hearts,' Isa. lvii. 15, wherever it is most in the exercise of contrition, which is usually in times of special worship; and that to revive and refresh them. Habitation notes a special presence; though he dwell in the highest heavens, in the sparklings of his glory, he dwells also in the lowest hearts in the beams of his grace; as none can expel him from his dwelling in heaven, so none can reject him from his residence in the heart. The tabernacle had his peculiar presence fixed to it, Levit. xxvi. 11; his soul should not abhor them as they are washed by Christ, though they are loathsome by sin. In a greater dispensation there cannot be a less presence, since the church, under the New Testament, is called the temple of the Lord, wherein he will both dwell and walk: 2 Cor. vi. 16, or, 'I will indwell them;' as if he should say, I will dwell in and in them;

* Chrysostom.   † Qu. 'omnipresence?'—ED.

I will dwell in them by grace, and walk in them by exciting their graces; he will be more intimate with them than their own souls, and converse with them as the living God, *i. e.* as a God that hath life in himself, and life to convey to them in their converse with him; and shew his spiritual glory among them in a greater measure than in the temple, since that was but a heap of stones, and the figure of the Christian church, the mystical body of his Son. His presence is not less in the substance than it was in the shadow; this presence of God, in his ordinances, is the glory of a church, as the presence of a king is the glory of a court; the defence of it, too, as a wall of fire, Zech. ii. 5, alluding to the fire travellers in a wilderness made to fright away wild beasts. It is not the meanness of the place of worship can exclude him; the second temple was not so magnificent as the first, of Solomon's erecting; and the Jews seem to despond of so glorious a presence of God in the second, as they had in the first, because they thought it not so good for the entertainment of him that inhabits eternity; but God comforts them against this conceit again and again: Hag. ii. 3, 4, 'Be strong, be strong, be strong, I am with you;' the meanness of the place shall not hinder the grandeur of my presence. No matter what the room is, so it be the presence-chamber of the King, wherein he will favour our suits, he can everywhere slide into our souls with a perpetual sweetness, since he is everywhere, and so intimate with every one that fears him. If we should see God on earth in his amiableness, as Moses did, should we not be encouraged by his presence, to present our requests to him, to echo out our praises of him? And have we not as great a ground now to do it, since he is as really present with us, as if he were visible to us? He is in the same room with us, as near to us as our souls to our bodies; not a word but he hears, not a motion but he sees, not a breath but he perceives; he is through all, he is in all.

4. The omnipresence of God is a comfort in all special services. God never puts any upon a hard task, but he makes promises to encourage them and assist them; and the matter of the promise is that of his presence. So he did assure the prophets of old when he set them difficult tasks; and strengthened Moses against the face of Pharaoh, by assuring him he would ' be with his mouth,' Exod. iv. 12; and when Christ put his apostles upon a contest with the whole world, to preach a gospel that would be foolishness to the Greeks, and a stumbling-block to the Jews, he gives them a cordial only composed of his presence: Mat. xxviii. 20, ' I will be with you.' It is this presence scatters, by its light, the darkness of our spirits; it is this that is the cause of what is done for his glory in the world; it is this that mingles itself with all that is done for his honour; it is this from whence springs all the assistance of his creatures, marked out for special purposes.

5. This presence is not without the special presence of all his attributes. Where his essence is, his perfections are, because they are one with his essence; yea, they are his essence, though they have their several degrees of manifestation. As in the covenant, he makes over himself as our God, not a part of himself, but his whole deity; so, in promising of his presence, he means not a part of it, but the whole, the presence of all the excellencies of his nature to be manifested for our good. It is not a piece of God is here, and another parcel there, but God in his whole essence and perfections; in his wisdom to guide us, his power to protect and support us, his mercy to pity us, his fulness to refresh us, and his goodness to relieve us. He is ready to sparkle out in this or that perfection, as the necessities of his people require, and his own wisdom directs for his own honour; so that being not far from us in any excellency of his nature, we can quickly have recourse to him upon any emergency; so that if we are miserable, we have the presence of

his goodness; if we want direction, we have the presence of his wisdom; if we are weak, we have the presence of his power; and should we not rejoice in it, as a man doth in the presence of a powerful, wealthy, and compassionate friend?

Use 3. Of exhortation.

1. Let us be much in the actual thoughts of his truth. How should we enrich our understandings with the knowledge of the excellency of God, whereof this is none of the least; nor hath less of honey in its bowels, though it be more terrible to the wicked than the presence of a lion! It is this that makes all other excellencies of the divine nature sweet. What would grace, wisdom, power, signify at a distance from us? Let us frame in our minds a strong idea of it; it is this makes so great a difference between the actions of one man and another; one maintains actual thoughts of it, another doth not, though all believe it as a perfection pertaining to the infiniteness of his essence. David, or rather a greater than David, had God 'always before him;' there was no time, no occasion, wherein he did not stir up some lively thoughts of him, Ps. xvi. 8. Let us have right notions of it: imagine not God as a great king, sitting only in his majesty in heaven, acting all by his servants and ministers. This, saith one,* is a childish and unworthy conceit of God, and may in time bring such a conceiver by degrees to deny his providence. The denial of this perfection is an axe at the root of religion; if it be not deeply imprinted in the mind, personal religion grows faint and feeble. Who would fear that God that is not imagined to be a witness of his actions? Who would worship a God at a distance both from the worship and worshipper?† Let us believe this truth, but not with an idle faith, as if we did not believe it. Let us know that as wheresoever the fish moves, it is in the water; wheresoever the bird moves, it is in the air; so wheresoever we move, we are in God. As there is not a moment but we are under his mercy, so there is not a moment that we are out of his presence. Let us therefore look upon nothing without thinking who stands by, without reflecting upon him in whom it lives, moves, and hath its being. When you view a man, you fix your eyes upon his body, but your mind upon that invisible part that acts every member by life and motion, and makes them fit for your converse. Let us not bound our thoughts to the creatures we see, but pierce through the creature to that boundless God we do not see. We have continual remembrancers of his presence; the light whereby we see, and the air whereby we live, give us perpetual notices of it, and some weak resemblance. Why should we forget it? Yea, what a shame is our unmindfulness of it, when every cast of our eye, every motion of our lungs, jogs us to remember it. Light is in every part of the air, in every part of the world, yet not mixed with any; both remain entire in their own substance. Let us not be worse than some of the heathens, who pressed this notion upon themselves for the spiriting their actions with virtue, that all places were full of God.‡ This was the means Basil used to prescribe. Upon a question was asked him, How shall we do to be serious? Mind God's presence. How shall we avoid distractions in service? Think of God's presence. How shall we resist temptations? Oppose to them the presence of God.

(1.) This will be a shield against all temptations. *God is present*, is enough to blunt the weapons of hell; this will secure us from a ready compliance with any base and vile attractives, and curb that head-strong principle in our nature that would join hands with them. The thoughts of this would, like the powerful presence of God with the Israelites, take off the wheels from the chariots of our sensitive appetites, and make them perhaps

* Musculus.   † Drexel.   ‡ Omnia Diis plena.

move slower at least towards a temptation. How did Peter fling off the temptation which had worsted him? Upon a look from Christ. The actuated faith of this would stifle the darts of Satan, and fire us with an anger against his solicitations as strong as the fire that inflames the darts. Moses his sight of 'him that was invisible' strengthened him against the costly pleasures and luxuries of a prince's court, Heb. xi. 27. We are utterly senseless of a Deity if we are not moved with this *item* from our consciences, *God is present.* Had our first parents actually considered the nearness of God to them when they were tempted to eat of the forbidden fruit, they had not probably so easily been overcome by the temptation. What soldier would be so base as to revolt under the eye of a tender and obliging general? or what man so negligent of himself as to rob a house in the sight of a judge? Let us consider that God is as near to observe us as the devil to solicit us; yea, nearer. The devil stands by us, but God is in us. We may have a thought the devil knows not, but not a thought but God is actually present with, as our souls are with the thoughts they think; nor can any creature attract our heart, if our minds were fixed on that invisible presence that contributes to that excellency, and sustains it, and considered that no creature could be so present with us as the Creator is.

(2.) It will be a spur to holy actions. What man would do an unworthy action, or speak an unhandsome word in the presence of his prince? The eye of the general inflames the spirit of a soldier. Why did David 'keep God's testimonies?' Because he considered that 'all his ways were before him,' Ps. cxix. 168; because he was persuaded his ways were present with God, God's precepts should be present with him. The same was the cause of Job's integrity; 'doth he not see my ways?' Job xxxi. 4; to have God in our eye is the way to be sincere, 'walk before me,' as in my sight, 'and be thou perfect,' Gen. xvii. 1. Communion with God consists chiefly in an ordering our ways as in the presence of him that is invisible. This would make us spiritual, raised and watchful in all our passions, if we considered that God is present with us in our shops, in our chambers, in our walks, and in our meetings, as present with us as with the angels in heaven; who though they have a presence of glory above us, yet have not a greater measure of his essential presence than we have. What an awe had Jacob upon him when he considered God was present in Bethel, Gen. xxviii. 16, 17. If God should appear visibly to us when we were alone, should we not be reverent and serious before him? God is everywhere about us, he doth encompass us with his presence; should not God's seeing have the same influence upon us as our seeing God? He is not more essentially present if he should so manifest himself to us, than when he doth not; who would appear besmeared in the presence of a great person? or not be ashamed to be found in his chamber in a nasty posture, by some visitant? Would not a man blush to be catched about some mean action, though it were not an immoral crime? If this truth were impressed upon our spirits, we should more blush to have our souls daubed with some loathsome lust, swarms of sin, like Egyptian lice and frogs, creeping about our heart in his sight. If the most sensual man be ashamed to do a dishonest action in the sight of a grave and holy man, one of great reputation for wisdom and integrity, how much more should we lift up ourselves in the ways of God, who is infinite and immense, is everywhere, and infinitely superior to man, and more to be regarded! We could not seriously think of his presence, but there would pass some intercourse between us; we should be putting up some petition upon the sense of our indigence, or sending up our praises to him upon the sense of his bounty. The actual thoughts of the presence of

God is the 'life and spirit of all religion ; we could not have sluggish spirits and a careless watch if we considered that his eye is upon us all the day.

(8.) It will quell distractions in worship. The actual thoughts of this would establish our thoughts, and pull them back when they begin to rove ; the mind could not boldly give God the slip if it had lively thoughts of it ; the consideration of this would blow off all the froth that lies on the top of our spirits. An eye taken up with the presence of one object is not at leisure to be filled with another ; he that looks intently upon the sun shall have nothing for a while but the sun in his eye. Oppose to every intruding thought the idea of the divine omnipresence, and put it to silence by the awe of his majesty. When the master is present, scholars mind their books, keep their places, and run not over the forms to play with one another ; the master's eye keeps an idle servant to his work, that otherwise would be gazing at every straw, and prating to every passenger. How soon would the remembrance of this dash all extravagant fancies out of countenance, just as the news of the approach of a prince would make the courtiers bustle up themselves, huddle up their vain sports, and prepare themselves for a reverent behaviour in his sight. We should not dare to give God a piece of our heart, when we apprehend him present with the whole ; we should not dare to mock one that we knew were more inwards with us than we are with our-selves, and that beheld every motion of our mind as well as action of our body.

Let us endeavour for the more special and influential presence of God. Let the essential presence of God be the ground of our awe, and his gracious influential presence the object of our desire. The heathen thought them-selves secure if they had their little petty household gods with them in their journeys ; such seem to be the images Rachel stole from her father, Gen. xxxi. 19, to accompany her travel with their blessings ; she might not at that time have cast off all respect to those idols, in the acknowledgment of which she had been educated from her infancy ; and they seem to be kept by her till God called Jacob to Bethel, after the rape of Dinah, Gen. xxxv. 4, when Jacob called for the strange gods, and hid them under the oak. The gracious presence of God we should look after in our actions, as travellers that have a charge of money or jewels, desire to keep themselves in company that may protect them from highwaymen that would rifle them. Since we have the concerns of the eternal happiness of our souls upon our hands, we should endeavour to have God's merciful and powerful presence with us in all our ways : Prov. iii. 6, 'In all thy ways acknowledge him, and he shall direct thy paths ;' acknowledge him before any action by imploring ; acknowledge him after, by rendering him the glory ; acknow-ledge his presence before worship, in worship, after worship. It is this presence makes a kind of heaven upon earth, causeth affliction to put off the nature of misery. How much will the presence of the sun outshine the stars of lesser comforts, and fully answer the want of them ! The ark of God going before us can only make all things successful. It was this led the Israelites over Jordan, and settled them in Canaan. Without this, we signify nothing ; though we live without this, we cannot be distinguished for ever from devils ; his essential presence they have, and if we have no more, we shall be no better. It is the enlivening, fructifying presence of the sun that revives the languishing earth, and this only can repair our ruined soul. Let it be therefore our desire, that as he fills heaven and earth by his essence, he may fill our understandings and wills by his grace ; that we may have another kind of presence with us than animals have in their brutish state, or devils in their chains ; his essential presence maintains our beings, but his gracious presence confers and continues a happiness.

A DISCOURSE UPON GOD'S KNOWLEDGE.

Great is our Lord, and of great power: his understanding is infinite.—
PSALM CXLVII. 5.

IT is uncertain who was the author of this psalm, and when it was penned; some think after the return from the Babylonish captivity. It is a psalm of praise, and is made up of matter of praise from the beginning to the end: God's benefits to the church, his providence over his creatures, the essential excellency of his nature.

The psalmist doubles his exhortation to praise God: ver. 1, 'Praise ye the Lord, sing praise to our God:' to praise him from his dominion as *Lord;* from his grace and mercy as *our God;* from the excellency of the duty itself, 'it is good, it is comely.' Some read it *comely,* some *lovely* or desirable, from the various derivation of the word.

Nothing doth so much delight a gracious soul, as an opportunity of celebrating the perfections and goodness of the Creator.

The highest duties a creature can render to the Creator, are pleasant and delightful in themselves, 'it is comely.' Praise is a duty that affects the whole soul.

The praise of God is a decent thing, the excellency of God's nature deserves it, and the benefits of God's grace requires it.

It is comely when done as it ought to be, with the heart as well as with the voice; a sinner sings ill though his voice be good, the soul in it is to be elevated above earthly things.

The first matter of praise is God's erecting and preserving his church: ver. 2, 'The Lord doth build up Jerusalem; he gathers together the outcasts of Israel.' The walls of demolished Jerusalem are now re-edified; God hath brought back the captivity of Jacob, and reduced his people from their Babylonish exile; and those that were dispersed into strange regions, he hath restored to their habitations. Or it may be prophetic of the calling of the Gentiles, and the gathering the outcasts of the spiritual Israel, that were before as without God in the world, and strangers to the covenant of promise. Let God be praised, but especially for building up his church and gathering the Gentiles, before counted as outcasts, Isa. xi. 12; he gathers them in this world to the faith, and hereafter to glory.

Obs. 1. From the two first verses, observe,

1. All people are under God's care; but he has a particular regard to his

church. This is the signet on his hand, as a bracelet upon his arm; this is his garden, which he delights to dress; if he prunes it, it is to purge it; if he digs about his vine and wounds the branches, it is to make it more beautiful with new clusters, and restore it to a fruitful vigour.

2. All great deliverances are to be ascribed to God, as the principal author, whosoever are the instruments. The Lord doth build up Jerusalem, he gathers together the outcasts of Israel. This great deliverance from Babylon is not to be ascribed to Cyrus or Darius, or the rest of our favourers; it is the Lord that doth it, we had his promise for it, we have now his performance. Let us not ascribe that which is the effect of his truth, only to the good-will of men; it is God's act, 'not by might, nor by power,' nor by weapons of war, or strength of horses, 'but by the Spirit of the Lord.' He sent prophets to comfort us while we were exiles, and now he hath stretched out his own arm to work our deliverance according to his word; blind man looks so much upon instruments, that he hardly takes notice of God, either in afflictions or mercies; and this is the cause that robs God of so much prayer and praise in the world.

Verse 3, 'He heals the broken in heart, and binds up their wounds.' He hath now restored those who had no hope but in his word; he hath dealt with them as a tender and skilful chirurgeon, he hath applied his curing plasters, and dropped in his sovereign balsams; he hath now furnished our fainting hearts with refreshing cordials, and comforted our wounds with strengthening ligatures.

How gracious is God, that restores liberty to the captives, and righteousness to the penitent! Man's misery is the fittest opportunity for God to make his mercy illustrious in itself, and most welcome to the patient.

He proceeds, verse 4. Wonder not that God calls together the outcasts, and singles them out from every corner for a return; why can he not do this, as well as 'tell the number of the stars, and call them all by their names'?

There are none of his people so despicable in the eye of man, but they are known and regarded by God. Though they are clouded in the world, yet they are the stars of the world; and shall God number the inanimate stars in the heavens, and make no account of his living stars on the earth? No; wherever they are dispersed, he will not forget them; however they are afflicted, he will not despise them. The stars are so numerous that they are innumerable by man; some are visible and known by men, others lie more hid and undiscovered in a confused light, as those in the milky way; man cannot see one of them distinctly.

God knows all his people. As he can do what is above the power of man to perform, so he understands what is above the skill of man to discover. Shall man measure God by his scantiness? Proud man must not equal himself to God, nor cut God as short as his own line.

'He tells the number of the stars; and calls them all by their names.' He hath them all in his list, as generals the names of their soldiers in their muster-roll, for they are his host, which he marshals in the heavens, as Isa. xl. 26, where you have the like expression; he knows them more distinctly than man can know anything, and so distinctly as to 'call them all by their names.' He knows their names, that is, their natural offices, influences, the different degrees of heat and light, their order and motion; and *all* of them, the least glimmering star as well as the most glaring planet, this man cannot do: 'Tell the stars if thou be able to number them,' Gen. xv. 5, saith God to Abraham (whom Josephus represents as a great astronomer); yea, they cannot be numbered, Jer. xxxiii. 22, and the uncertainty of the opinions of men evidenceth their ignorance of their number, some reckoning 1022, others 1025, others 1098, others 7000, besides those that, by reason of their mixture of light with one another, cannot be distinctly discerned, and others perhaps so high as not to be reached by the eye of man. To impose names on things, and names according to their natures, is both an argument of power and dominion, and of wisdom and understanding; from the imposition of names upon the creatures by Adam, the knowledge of Adam is generally concluded, and it was also a fruit of that dominion God allowed him over the creatures. Now he that numbers and names the stars, that seem to lie confused among one another, as well as those that appear to us in an unclouded night, may well be supposed accurately to know his people, though lurking in secret caverns, and know those that are fit to be instruments of their deliverance; the one is as easy to him as the other, and the number of the one as distinctly known by him as the multitude of the other.

Verse 5, 'For great is our Lord, and of great power : his understanding is infinite.' He wants not knowledge to know the objects, nor power to effect his will concerning them. Of great power, רב כח. Much power, plenteous in power; so the word רב is rendered, Ps. lxxxvi. 5. 15, רב חסר. A multitude of power, as well as a multitude of mercy; a power that exceeds all created power and understanding.

'His understanding is infinite.' You may not imagine how he can call all the stars by name, the multitude of visible being so great, and the multitude of the invisible being greater; but you must know that as God is almighty, so he is omniscient; and as there is no end of his power, so no account can exactly be given of his understanding: 'his understanding is infinite,' אין מספר. No number or account of it; and so the same words are rendered, Joel i. 6, 'A nation strong, and without number.' No end of his understanding; *Syriac*, no measure, no bounds. His essence is infinite, and so is his power and understanding; and vast is his knowledge, that we can no more comprehend it, than we can measure spaces that are without limits, or tell the minutes or hours of eternity. Who then can fathom that whereof there is no number, but which exceeds all, so that there is no searching of it out ? He knows universals, he knows particulars. We must not take understanding, תבונה, here, as noting a faculty, but the use of the understanding in the knowledge of things, and the judgment in the consideration of them, and so it is often used.

In the verse there is a description of God.

1. In his essence : 'great is our Lord.'

2. In his power : 'of great power.'

8. In his knowledge: 'his understanding is infinite ;' his understanding is his eye, and his power is his arm. Of his infinite understanding I am to discourse.

Doct. God hath an infinite knowledge and understanding ; all knowledge. Omnipresence, which before we spake of, respects his essence ; omniscience respects his understanding, according to our manner of conception.

This is clear in Scripture ; hence God is called a God of knowledge : 1 Sam. ii. 3, 'The Lord is a God of knowledge ;' *Heb.* 'knowledges,' in the plural number, of all kind of knowledge. It is spoken there to quell man's pride in his own reason and parts. What is the knowledge of man but a spark to the whole element of fire, a grain of dust, and worse than nothing, in comparison of the knowledge of God, as his essence is in comparison of the essence of God ? All kind of knowledge. He knows what angels know, what man knows, and infinitely more ; he knows himself, his own operations, all his creatures, the notions and thoughts of them ; he is understanding above understanding, mind above mind, the mind of minds, the light of lights; this the Greek word Θεὸς signifies in the etymology of it, of Θειᾶϑαι* to *see*, to contemplate; and δαίμων of δαίω *scio*. The names of God signify a nature viewing and piercing all things; and the attribution of our senses to God in Scripture, as hearing and seeing, which are the senses whereby knowledge enters into us, signifies God's knowledge.

1. The notion of God's knowledge of all things lies above the ruins of nature : it was not obliterated by the fall of man. It was necessary offending man was to know that he had a Creator whom he had injured, that he had a Judge to try and punish him; since God thought fit to keep up the world, it had been kept up to no purpose, had not this notion been continued alive in the minds of men; there would not have been any practice of his laws, no bar to the worst of crimes. If men had thought they had to deal with an ignorant Deity, there could be no practice of religion. Who would lift up his eyes, or spread his hand towards heaven, if he imagined his devotion were directed to a God as blind as the heathens imagined fortune ? To what boot would it be for them to make heaven and earth resound with their cries, if they had not thought God had an eye to see them and an ear to hear them ? And indeed the very notion of a God at the first blush speaks him a being endued with understanding; no man can imagine a Creator void of one of the noblest perfections belonging to those creatures that are the flower and cream of his works.

2. Therefore all nations acknowledge this, as well as the existence and being of God. No nation but had their temples, particular ceremonies of worship, and presented their sacrifices, which they could not have been so vain as to do, without an acknowledgement of this attribute. This notion of God's knowledge owed not its rise to tradition, but to natural implantation; it was born and grew up with every rational creature. Though the several nations and men of the world agreed not in one kind of Deity, or in their sentiments of his nature or other perfections, some judging him clothed with a fine and pure body, others judging him an uncompounded spirit, some fixing him to a seat in the heavens, others owning his universal presence in all parts of the world, yet they all agreed in the universality of his knowledge; and their own consciences reflecting their crimes, unknown to any but themselves, would keep this notion in some vigour whether they would or no. Now this being implanted in the minds of all men by nature, cannot be false, for nature imprints not in the minds of all men an assent to a falsity. Nature would not pervert the reason and minds of men. Universal notions of God are from original, not lapsed nature, and preserved in mankind in order to a restoration from a lapsed state. The heathens did acknowledge this; in all the solemn covenants, solemnised with oaths and the invocation of the name of God, this attribute was supposed.† They confessed knowledge to be peculiar to the Deity; *Scientia Deorum vita*, saith Cicero. Some called him Νοῦς, *mens*, mind, pure understanding, without any mote ; 'Επόπτης, the inspector of all. As they called him Life, because he was the author of life, so they called him *Intellectus*, because he was the author of all knowledge and understanding in his creatures. And one being asked, Whether any man could be hid from God? No, saith he, not so much as thinking. Some call him the Eye of the world,‡ and the

---

* Qu 'Θεᾶσθαι' ?—ED.

† Agamemnon (Homer Il. 3. v. 277), making a covenant with Priam, invocates the sun :— ƒ

     'Ηέλιος ϑ' ὅς πάντ' ἐφορᾷς καὶ πάντ' ἐπακούεις.

‡ Gamach in 1 Pa. Aquin. q. 14. cap. i. p. 119.

event which was not foreseen, or upon an after knowledge of the evil of the thing which was acted by the person repenting. But God is so wise that he cannot err, so holy he cannot do evil, and his certain prescience or foreknowledge secures him against any unexpected events. God doth not act but upon clear and infallible reason. And a change upon passion is accounted by all so great a weakness in man, that none can entertain so unworthy a conceit of God. Where he is said to repent, Gen. vi. 6, he is also said to grieve; now no proper grief can be imagined to be in God. As repentance is inconsistent with infallible foresight, so is grief no less inconsistent with undefiled blessedness: 'God is blessed for ever,' Rom. ix. 8, and therefore nothing can befall him that can stain that blessedness; his blessedness would be impaired and interrupted, while he is repenting, though he did soon rectify that which is the cause of his repentance: 'God is of one mind, and who can turn him? what his soul desires, that he doth,' Job xxiii. 13.

2. But God accommodates himself in the Scripture to our weak capacity. God hath no more of a proper repentance than he hath of a real body: though he, in accommodation to our weakness, ascribes to himself the members of our bodies to set out to our understanding the greatness of his perfections, we must not conclude him a body like us; so, because he is said to have anger and repentance, we must not conclude him to have passions like us. When we cannot fully comprehend him as he is, he clothes himself with our nature in his expressions, that we may apprehend him as we are able, and, by an inspection into ourselves, learn something of the nature of God; yet those human ways of speaking ought to be understood in a manner agreeable to the infinite excellency and majesty of God, and are only designed to mark out something in God which hath a resemblance with something in us. As we cannot speak to God as gods, but as men, so we cannot understand him speaking to us as a God, unless he condescends to speak to us like a man. God therefore frames his language to our dulness, not to his own state, and informs us, by our own phrases, what he would have us learn of his nature, as nurses talk broken language to young children. In all such expressions, therefore, we must ascribe the perfection we conceive in them to God, and lay the imperfection at the door of the creature.

3. Therefore repentance in God is only a change of his outward conduct, according to his infallible foresight and immutable will. He changes the way of his providential proceeding according to the carriage of the creature, without changing his will, which is the rule of his providence. When God speaks of his repenting that he had made man, Gen. vi. 6, it is only his changing his conduct from a way of kindness to a way of severity, and is a word suited to our capacities, to signify his detestation of sin and his resolution to punish it, after man had made himself quite another thing than God had made him. 'It repents me,' that is, I am purposed to destroy the world, as he that repents of his work throws it away;* as if a potter cast away the vessel he had framed, it were a testimony that he repented that ever he took pains about it; so the destruction of them seems to be a repentance in God that ever he made them, it is a change of events, not of counsels. Repentance in us is a grief for a former fact, and a changing of our course in it. Grief is not in God,† but his repentance is a willing a thing should not be as it was, which will was fixed from eternity; for, God foreseeing man would fall, and decreeing to permit it, he could not be said to repent in time of what he did not repent from eternity; and, therefore, if there were no repentance in God from eternity, there could be none in time; but

---

* Mercer *in loc.*　　　　　† Petavius Theol. Dogmat

power of God, though they shall never in the least peep up into being, but lie for ever wrapt up in darkness and nothing.* This also is a necessary knowledge to be allowed to God, because the object of this knowledge is necessary. The possibility of more creatures than ever were or shall be, is a conclusion that hath a necessary truth in it, as it is necessary that the power of God can produce more creatures, though it be not necessary that it should produce more creatures; so it is necessary that whatsoever the power of God can work, is possible to be. And as God knows this possibility, so he knows all the objects that are thus possible; and herein doth much consist the infiniteness of his knowledge, as shall be shewn presently.

These two kinds of knowledge differ. That of *vision* is of things which God hath decreed to be, though they are not yet. That of *intelligence* is of things which never shall be, yet they may be, or are possible to be, if God please to will and order their being; one respects things that shall be, the other, things that may be, and are not repugnant to the nature of God to be. The knowledge of vision follows the act of God's will, and supposeth an act of God's will before, decreeing things to be. (If we could suppose any first or second in God's decree, we might say God knew them as possible *before* he decreed them; he knew them as future *because* he decreed them.) For without the will of God decreeing a thing to come to pass, God cannot know that it will infallibly come to pass. But the knowledge of intelligence stands without any act of his will, in order to the being of those things he knows. He knows possible things only in his power; he knows other things both in his power, as able to effect them, and in his will, as determining the being of them. Such knowledge we must grant to be in God, for there is such a kind of knowledge in man; for man doth not only know and see what is before his eyes in this world, but he may have a conception of many more worlds, and many more creatures, which he knows are possible to the power of God.

2. Secondly, There is a speculative and practical knowledge in God.

(1). A speculative knowledge is, when the truth of a thing is known without a respect to any working or practical operation. The knowledge of things possible is in God only speculative,† and some say God's knowledge of himself is only speculative, because there is nothing for God to work in himself. And, though he knows himself, yet this knowledge of himself doth not terminate there, but flowers into a love of himself, and delight in himself; yet this love of himself, and delight in himself, is not enough to make it a practical knowledge, because it is natural, and naturally and necessarily flows from the knowledge of himself and his own goodness. He cannot but love himself, and delight in himself, upon the knowledge of himself. But that which is properly practice is where there is a dominion over the action, and it is wrought, not naturally and necessarily, but in a way of freedom and counsel. As when we see a beautiful flower or other thing, there ariseth a delight in the mind; this no man will call practice, because it is a natural affection of the will, arising from the virtue of the object, without any consideration of the understanding in a practical manner, by counselling, commanding, &c.

(2.) A practical knowledge, which tends to operation and practice, and is the principle of working about things that are known, as the knowledge an artificer hath in an art or mystery. This knowledge is in God. The knowledge he hath of the things he hath decreed, is such a kind of knowledge, for it terminates in the act of creation, which is not a natural and necessary act, as the loving himself and delighting in himself is, but wholly free; for

* Suarez de Deo, lib. iii. cap. iv. p. 280.   † Ibid. p. 138.

it was at his liberty whether he would create them or no. This is called discretion : Jer. x. 12, 'He hath stretched out the heavens by his discretion.' Such also is his knowledge of the things he hath created, and which are in being, for it terminates in the government of them for his own glorious ends. It is by this knowledge 'the depths are broken up, and the clouds drop down their dew,' Prov. iii. 20. This is a knowledge whereby he knows the essence, qualities, and properties of what he creates, and governs in order to his own glory, and the common good of the world over which he [p]resides ; so that speculative knowledge is God's knowledge of himself and things possible ; practical knowledge is his knowledge of his creatures and things governable ; yet in some sort, this practical knowledge is not only of things that are made, but of things which are possible, which God might make, though he will not. For as he knows that they can be created, so he knows how they are to be created, and how to be governed, though he never will create them. This is a practical knowledge ; for it is not requisite to constitute a knowledge practical, actually to act, but that the knowledge in itself be referrible to action.*

8. There is a knowledge of approbation, as well as apprehension. This the Scripture often mentions. Words of understanding are used to signify the acts of affection. This knowledge adds to the simple act of the understanding, the complacency and pleasure of the will, and is improperly knowledge, because it belongs to the will, and not to the understanding ; only it is radically in the understanding, because affection implies knowledge : men cannot approve of that which they are ignorant of. Thus knowledge is taken : Amos iii. 2, 'You only have I known of all the families of the earth ;' and 2 Tim. ii. 19, 'The Lord knows who are his,' that is, he loves them : he doth not only know them, but acknowledge them for his own. It notes not only an exact understanding, but a special care of them ; and so is that to be understood, Gen. i. 31, 'God saw everything that he had made, and behold it was very good ;' that is, he saw it with an eye of approbation, as well as apprehension. This is grounded upon God's knowledge of vision, his sight of his creatures ; for God doth not love or delight in anything but what is actually in being, or what he hath decreed to bring into being. On the contrary also, when God doth not approve, he is said not to know: Mat. xxv. 12, 'I know you not ;' and Mat. vii. 23, 'I never knew you.' He doth not approve of their works. It is not an ignorance of understanding, but an ignorance of will ; for whiles he saith he never knew them, he testifies that he did know them, in rendering the reason of his disapproving them, because he knows all their works. So he knows them, and doth not know them, in a different manner ; he knows them so as to understand them, but he doth not know them so as to love them.

We must then ascribe an universal knowledge to God. If we deny him a speculative knowledge, or knowledge of intelligence, we destroy his deity, we make him ignorant of his own power. If we deny him practical knowledge, we deny ourselves to be his creatures ; for as his creatures, we are the fruits of this his discretion discovered in creation. If we deny his knowledge of vision, we deny his governing dominion. How can he exercise a sovereign and uncontrollable dominion, that is ignorant of the nature and qualities of the things he is to govern ? If he had not knowledge, he could make no revelation ; he that knows not, cannot dictate : we could then have no Scripture. To deny God knowledge, is to dash out the Scripture and demolish the Deity.

God is described in Zech. ii. 9, with 'seven eyes,' to shew his perfect

* Suarez de Deo, l. iii. c. iv. p. 140.

knowledge of all things, all occurrences in the world; and the cherubims, or whatsoever is meant by the wings, are described to be 'full of eyes both before and behind,' Ezek. i. 18, round about them; much more is God all eye, all ear, all understanding. The sun is a natural image of God. If the sun had an eye, it would see; if it had an understanding, it would know all visible things; it would see what it shines upon, and understand what it influenceth in the most obscure bowels of the earth. Doth God excel his creature the sun in excellency and beauty, and not in light and understanding? Certainly more than the sun excels an atom or grain of dust.

We may yet make some representation of this knowledge of God by a lower thing, a picture, which seems to look upon every one, though there be never so great a multitude in the room where it hangs. No man can cast his eye upon it, but it seems to behold him in particular, and so exactly, as if there were none but him upon whom the eye of it were fixed; and every man finds the same cast of it. Shall art frame a thing of that nature, and shall not the God of art and all knowledge be much more in reality than that is in imagination? Shall not God have a far greater capacity to behold everything in the world, which is infinitely less to him than a wide room to a picture?

II. The second thing, What God knows; how far his understanding reaches.

1. God knows himself, and only knows himself. This is the first and original knowledge wherein he excels all creatures. No man doth exactly know himself, much less doth he understand the full nature of a spirit, much less still the nature and perfections of God; for what proportion can there be between a finite faculty and an infinite object? Herein consists the infiniteness of God's knowledge, that he knows his own essence, that he knows that which is unknowable to any else. It doth not so much consist in knowing the creature which he hath made, as in knowing himself who was never made. It is not so much infinite, because he knows all things which are in the world, or that shall be, or things that he can make, because the number of them is finite; but because he hath a perfect and comprehensive knowledge of his own infinite perfections.* Though it be said that 'angels see his face,' Mat. xviii. 10, that sight notes rather their immediate attendance than their exact knowledge. They see some signs of his presence and majesty, more illustrious and express than ever appeared to man in this life; but the essence of God is invisible to them, hid from them in the secret place of eternity. None knows God but himself: 1 Cor. ii. 11, 'What man knows the things of a man save the spirit of a man? so the things of God knows no man, but the Spirit of God; the Spirit of God searches the deep things of God.' Searcheth, that is, exactly knows, thoroughly understands, as those who have their eyes in every chink and crevice, to see what lies hid there. The word *search* notes not an inquiry, but an exact knowledge, such as men have of things upon a diligent scrutiny; as when God is said to search the heart and the reins, it doth not signify a precedent ignorance, but an exact knowledge of the most intimate corners of the hearts of men. As the conceptions of men are unknown to any but themselves, so the depths of the divine essence, perfections, and decrees are unknown to any but to God himself; he only knows what he is, and what he knows, what he can do, and what he hath decreed to do.

(1.) For, first, if God did not know himself, he would not be perfect. It is the perfection of a creature to know itself, much more a perfection belonging to God. If God did not comprehend himself, he would want an infinite

* Moulin.

perfection, and so would cease to be God, in being defective in that which intellectual creatures in some measure possess. As God is the most perfect being, so he must have the most perfect understanding. If he did not understand himself, he would be under the greatest ignorance, because he would be ignorant of the most excellent object. Ignorance is the imperfection of the understanding, and ignorance of one's self is a greater imperfection than ignorance of things without. If God should know all things without himself, and not know himself, he would not have the most perfect knowledge, because he would not have the knowledge of the best of objects.

(2.) Without the knowledge of himself he could not be blessed. Nothing can have any complacency in itself without the knowledge of itself. Nothing can in a rational manner enjoy itself without understanding itself. The blessedness of God consists not in the knowledge of anything without him, but in the knowledge of himself and his own excellency as the principle of all things. If, therefore, he did not perfectly know himself and his own happiness, he could not enjoy a happiness; for to be, and not to know to be, is as if a thing were not. He is 'God blessed for ever,' Rom. ix. 5, and therefore for ever had a knowledge of himself.

(3.) Without the knowledge of himself he could create nothing. For he would be ignorant of his own power and his own ability; and he that doth not know how far his power extends could not act. If he did not know himself, he could know nothing; and he that knows nothing can do nothing. He could not know an effect to be possible to him unless he knew his own power as a cause.

(4.) Without the knowledge of himself he could govern nothing. He could not without the knowledge of his own holiness and righteousness prescribe laws to men, nor without a knowledge of his own nature order himself a manner of worship suitable to it.

All worship must be congruous to the dignity and nature of the object worshipped; he must therefore know his own authority, whereby worship was to be enacted; his own excellency, to which worship was to be suited; his own glory, to which worship was to be directed. If he did not know himself, he did not know what to punish, because he could not know what was contrary to himself. Not knowing himself, he would not know what was a contempt of him, and what an adoration of him; what was worthy of God, and what was unworthy of him. In fine, he could not know other things unless he knew himself. Unless he knew his own power, he could not know how he created things; unless he knew his own wisdom, he could not know the beauty of his works; unless he knew his own glory, he could not know the end of his works; unless he knew his own holiness, he could not know what was evil; and unless he knew his own justice, he could not know how to punish the crimes of his offending creatures. And therefore,

[1.] God knows himself, because his knowledge with his will is the cause of all other things that can fall under his cognizance. He knows himself first before he can know any other thing, that is, first according to our conceptions; for indeed God knows himself and all other things at once. He is the first truth, and therefore is the first object of his own understanding. There is nothing more excellent than himself, and therefore nothing more known to him than himself. As he is all knowledge, so he hath in himself the most excellent object of knowledge. To understand is properly to know one's self. No object is so intelligible to God as God is to himself, nor so intimately and immediately joined with his understanding as himself. For his understanding is his essence, himself.

[2.] He knows himself by his own essence. He knows not himself and his own power by the effect, because he knows himself from eternity, before there was a world, or any effect of his power extant. It is not a knowledge by the cause, for God hath no cause, nor a knowledge of himself by any species or anything from without. If it were anything from without himself, that must be created or uncreated: if uncreated, it would be God, and so we must either own many gods, or own it to be his essence, and so not distinct from himself; if created, then his knowledge of himself would depend upon a creature. He could not then know himself from eternity, but in time, because nothing can be created from eternity but in time. God knows not himself by any faculty, for there is no composition in God, he is not made up of parts, but is a simple being. Some therefore have called God, not *intellectus*, understanding, because that savours of a faculty, but *intellectio*, intellection. God is all act in the knowledge of himself, and his knowledge of other things.

[3.] God therefore knows himself perfectly, comprehensively. Nothing in his own nature is concealed from him, he reflects upon everything that he is.* There is a positive comprehension, so God doth not comprehend himself; for what is comprehended hath bounds, and what is comprehended by itself is finite to itself. And there is a negative comprehension, God so comprehends himself; nothing in his own nature is obscure to him, unknown by him. For there is as great a perfection in the understanding of God to know, as there is in the divine nature to be known. The understanding of God and the nature of God are both infinite, and so equal to one another. His understanding is equal to himself; he knows himself so well, that nothing can be known by him more perfectly than himself is known to himself. He knows himself in the highest manner, because nothing is so proportioned to the understanding of God as himself. He knows his own essence, goodness, power, all his perfections, decrees, intentions, acts, the infinite capacity of his own understanding, so that nothing of himself is in the dark to himself. And in this respect, some use this expression, that the infiniteness of God is in a manner finite to himself, because it is comprehended by himself.

Thus God transcends all creatures. Thus his understanding is truly infinite, because nothing but himself is an infinite object for it. What angels may understand of themselves perfectly I know not, but no creature in the world understands himself. Man understands not fully the excellency and parts of his own nature; upon God's knowledge of himself depends the comfort of his people and the terror of the wicked. This is also a clear argument for his knowledge of all other things without himself; he that knows himself must needs know all other things less than himself, and which were made by himself. When the knowledge of his own immensity and infiniteness is not an object too difficult for him, the knowledge of a finite and limited creature in all his actions, thoughts, circumstances, cannot be too hard for him. Since he knows himself who is infinite, he cannot but know whatsoever is finite. This is the foundation of all his other knowledge. The knowledge of everything present, past, and to come is far less than the knowledge of himself. He is more incomprehensible in his own nature than all things created, or that can be created, put together can be. If he then have a perfect comprehensive knowledge of his own nature, any knowledge of all other things is less than the knowledge of himself. This ought to be well considered by us, as the fountain whence all his other knowledge flows.

2. Therefore God knows all other things, whether they be possible, past, present, or future.

---

* Magalaneus.

Whether they be things that he can do, but will never do; or whether they be things that he hath done, but are not now; things that are now in being, or things that are not now existing, that lie in the womb of their proper and immediate causes,[*] if his understanding be infinite, he then knows all things whatsoever that can be known, else his understanding would have bounds; and what hath limits is not infinite, but finite. If he be ignorant of any one thing that is knowable, that is a bound to him, it comes with an exception, a *but;* God knows all things but this, a bar is then set to his knowledge. If there were anything, any particular circumstance in the whole creation, or non-creation, and possible to be known by him, and yet were unknown to him, he could not be said to be omniscient, as he would not be almighty if any one thing that implied not a repugnancy to his nature did transcend his power.

(1.) First, all things possible. No question but God knows what he could create as well as what he hath created, what he would not create as well as what he resolved to create; he knew that he would not do before he willed to do it. This is the next thing which declares the infiniteness of his understanding; for as his power is infinite, and can create innumerable worlds and creatures, so is his knowledge infinite, in knowing innumerable things possible to his power. Possibles are infinite, that is, there is no end of what God can do, and therefore no end of what God doth know, otherwise his power would be more infinite than his knowledge. If he knew only what is created, there would be an end of his understanding, because all creatures may be numbered, but possible things cannot be reckoned up by any creature. There is the same reason of this in eternity. When never so many numbers of years are run out, there is still more to come, there still wants an end; and when millions of worlds are created, there is no more an end of God's power than of eternity. Thus there is no end of his understanding; that is, his knowledge is not terminated by anything.

This the Scripture gives us some account of. God knows things that are not, for 'he calls things that are not as if they were,' Rom. iv. 17. He calls things that are not as if they were in being; what he calls is not unknown to him. If he knows things that are not, he knows things that may never be, as he knows things that shall be because he wills them, so he knows things that might be, because he is able to effect them. He knew that the inhabitants of Keilah would betray David to Saul if he remained in that place, 1 Sam. xxiii. 11; he knew what they would do upon that occasion, though it was never done. As he knew what was in their power and in their wills, so he must needs know what is within the compass of his own power. As he can permit more than he doth permit, so he knows what he can permit, and what upon that permission would be done by his creatures; so God knew the possibility of the Tyrians' repentance, if they had the same means, heard the same truths, and beheld the same miracles which were offered to the ears and presented to the eyes of the Jews, Mat. xi. 21.

This must needs be so, because,

[1.] Man knows things that are possible to him, though he will never effect them. A carpenter knows a house in the model he hath of it in his head, though he never build a house according to that model. A watchmaker hath the frame of a watch in his mind, which he will never work with his instruments. Man knows what he could do, though he never intends to do it.[†] As the understanding of man hath a virtue, that where it sees one man it may imagine thousands of men of the same shape, stature, form, parts, yea, taller, more vigorous, sprightly, intelligent than

* Petáv, Theol. Dogm., lib. ix. 257.　　† Ficin. de immort, lib. ii. cap. 10.

the man he sees, because it is possible such a number may be ; shall not
the understanding of God much more know what he is able to effect, since
the understanding of man can know what he is never able to produce, yet
may be produced by God, viz. that he who produced this man which I see,
can produce a thousand exactly like him ? If the divine understanding did
not know infinite things, but were confined to a certain number, it may be
demanded whether God can understand anything further than that number,
or whether he cannot ? If he can, then he doth actually understand all
those things which he hath a power to understand, otherwise there would
be an increase of God's knowledge, if it were actually now and not before,
and so he would be more perfect than he was before. If he cannot understand them, then he cannot understand what a human mind can understand; for our understandings can multiply numbers *in infinitum*, and there
is no number so great but a man can still add to it. We must suppose the
divine understanding more excellent in knowledge. God knows all that a
man can imagine, though it never were nor never shall be. He must needs
know whatsoever is in the power of man to imagine or think, because God
concurs to the support of the faculty in that imagination ; and though it
may be replied, an atheist may imagine that there is no God, a man may
imagine that God can lie, or that he can be destroyed, doth God know
therefore that he is not, or that he can lie, or cease to be ? No, he knows
he cannot ; his knowledge extends to things possible, not to things impossible
to himself. He knows it as imaginable by man, not as possible in itself,
because it is utterly impossible* and repugnant to the nature of God, since
he eminently contains in himself all things possible, past, present, and to
come. He cannot know himself without knowing them.

[2.] God knowing his own power, knows whatsoever is in his power to
effect. If he knows not all things possible, he could not know the extent of
his own power, and so would not know himself as a cause sufficient for more
things than he hath created. How can he comprehend himself, who comprehends not all effluxes of things possible that may come from him, and be
wrought by him ? How can he know himself as a cause, if he know not
the objects and works which he is able to produce ? † Since the power of
God extends to numberless things, his knowledge also extends to numberless objects ; as if a unit could see the numbers it could produce, it would
see infinite numbers, for a unit is as it were all number. God, knowing
the fruitfulness of his own virtue, knows a numberless multitude of things
which he can do more than have been done or shall be done by him ; he
therefore knows innumerable worlds, innumerable angels, with higher perfections than any of them which he hath created have. So that if the world
should last many millions of years, God knows that he can every day create
another world more capacious than this ; and having created an inconceivable number, he knows he could still create more. So that he beholds
infinite worlds, infinite numbers of men and other creatures in himself,
infinite kinds of things, infinite species and individuals under those kinds,
even as many as he can create, if his will did order and determine it ; for
not being ignorant of his own power, he cannot be ignorant of the effects
wherein it may display and discover itself. A comprehensive knowledge of
his own power doth necessarily include the objects of that power; so he
knows whatsoever he could effect, and whatsoever he could permit, if he
pleased to do it.

If God could not understand more than he hath created, he could not
create more than he hath created ; for it cannot be conceived how he can

* Gamach.   † Ficin. de immort, lib. ii. cap. x.

create anything that he is ignorant of; what he doth not know, he cannot do; he must know also the extent of his own goodness, and how far anything is capable to partake of it. So much therefore as any detract from the knowledge of God, they detract from his power.

[3.] It is further evident that God knows all possible things, because he knew those things which he has created before they were created, when they were yet in a possibility. If God knew things before they were created, he knew them when they were in a possibility, and not in actual reality. It is absurd to imagine that his understanding did lacquey after the creatures, and draw knowledge from them after they were created. It is absurd to think that God did create, before he knew what he could or would create. If he knew those things he did create when they were possible, he must know all things which he can create, and therefore all things that are possible.

To conclude this, we must consider that this knowledge is of another kind than his knowledge of things that are or shall be. He sees possible things as possible, not as things that ever are or shall be. If he saw them as existing or future, and they shall never be, this knowledge would be false, there would be a deceit in it, which cannot be. He knows those things not in themselves, because they are not, nor in their causes, because they shall never be; he knows them in his own power, not in his will; he understands them as able to produce them, not as willing to effect them. Things possible he knows only in his power, things future he knows both in his power and his will, as he is both able and determined in his own good pleasure to give being to them. Those that shall never come to pass, he knows only in himself, as a sufficient cause; those things that shall come into being he knows in himself as the efficient cause, and also in their immediate second causes.

This should teach us to spend our thoughts in the admiration of the excellency of God and the divine knowledge; his understanding is infinite.

(2.) God knows all things past. This is an argument used by God himself to elevate his excellency above all the commonly adored idols: Isa. xli. 22, 'Let them shew the former things, what they be, that we may consider them, and know the latter end of them.' He knows them as if they were now present, and not past; for indeed in his eternity there is nothing past or future to his knowledge. This is called remembrance in Scripture, as when God remembered Rachel's prayer for a child, Gen. xxx. 22; and he is said to put tears into his bottle, and write them into his book of accounts, which signifies the exact and unerring knowledge in God of the minute circumstances past in the world; and this knowledge is called a 'book of remembrance,' Mal. iii. 16, signifying the perpetual presence of things past before him. There are two elegant expressions signifying the certainty and perpetuity of God's knowledge of sins past: Job xiv. 17, 'My transgression is sealed up in a bag, and thou sewest up my iniquity!' A metaphor taken from men, that put up in a bag the money they would charily keep, tie the bag, sew up the holes, and bind it hard that nothing may fall out; or a vessel wherein they reserve liquors, and daub it with pitch and glutinous stuff, that nothing may leak out, but be safely kept till the time of use. Or else, as some think, from the bags attorneys carry with them full of writings, when they are to manage a cause against a person. Thus we find God often in Scripture calling to men's minds their past actions, upbraiding them with their ingratitude; wherein he testifies his remembrance of his own past benefits, and their crimes. His knowledge in this regard has something of infinity in it, since though the sins of all men that have been in the world are finite in regard of number, yet when the sins of one man in thoughts, words, and deeds, are numberless in his own account, and perhaps in the account of any creature, the sins of all the vast numbers of men that have been, or shall be, are much more numberless, it cannot be less than infinite knowledge that can make a collection of them, and take a survey of them all at once.

If past things had not been known by God, how could Moses have been acquainted with the original of things? How could he have declared the former transactions, wherein all histories are silent but the Scripture? How could he know the cause of man's present misery so many ages after, wherewith all philosophy was unacquainted? How could he have writ the order of the creation, the particulars of the sin of Adam, the circumstances of Cain's murder, the private speech of Lamech to his wives, if God had not revealed them? And how could a revelation be made, if things past were forgotten by him? Do we not remember many things done among men, as well as by ourselves, and reserve the forms of divers things in our minds, which rise as occasions are presented to draw them forth? And shall not God much more, who hath no cloud of darkness upon his understanding? A man that makes a curious picture, hath the form of it in his mind before he made it; and if the fire burn it, the form of it in his mind is not destroyed by the fire, but retained in it. God's memory is no less perfect than his understanding. If he did not know things past, he could not be a righteous governor, or exercise any judicial act in a righteous manner; he could not dispense rewards and punishments according to his promises and threatenings, if things that were past could be forgotten by him; he could not require that which is past, Eccles. iii. 15, if he did not remember that which is past.

And though God be said to forget in Scripture, and not to know his people, and his people pray to him to remember them, as if he had forgotten them, Ps. cxix. 49, this is improperly ascribed to God.* As God is said to repent, when he changes things according to his counsel beyond the expectation of men, so he is said to forget, when he defers the making good his promise to the godly, or his threatenings to the wicked. This is not a defect of memory belonging to his mind, but an act of his will. When he is said to remember his covenant, it is to will grace according to his covenant; when he is said to forget his covenant, it is to intercept the influences of it, whereby to punish the sin of his people; and when he is said not to know his people, it is not an absolute forgetfulness of them, but withdrawing from them the testimonies of his kindness, and clouding the signs of his favour; so God in pardoning is said to forget sin, not that he ceaseth to know it, but ceaseth to punish it. It is not to be meant of a simple forgetfulness, or a lapse of his memory, but of a judicial forgetfulness; so when his people in Scripture pray, 'Lord, remember thy word unto thy servant,' no more is to be understood, but, Lord, fulfil thy word and promise to thy servant.

(3.) He knows things present. Heb. iv. 13, 'All things are naked and opened unto the eyes of him with whom we have to do.' This is grounded upon the knowledge of himself; it is not so difficult to know all creatures exactly, as to know himself, because they are finite, but himself is infinite; he knows his own power, and therefore everything through which his omnipotence is diffused, all the acts and objects of it; not the least thing that is the birth of his power can be concealed from him; he knows his own goodness, and therefore every object upon which the warm beams of his goodness strike; he therefore knows distinctly the properties of every creature, because every property in them is a ray of his goodness; he is not only the

* Bradward.

efficient, but the exemplary cause; therefore, as he knows all that his power hath wrought, as he is the efficient, so he knows them in himself as the pattern, as a carpenter can give account of every part and passage in a house he hath built, by consulting the model in his own mind, whereby he built it. 'He looked upon all things after he had made them, and pronounced them good,' Gen. i. 31; full of a natural goodness he had endowed them with; he did not ignorantly pronounce them so, and call them good, whether he knew them or not; and therefore he knows them in particular, as he knew them all in their first presence. Is there any reason he should be ignorant of everything now present in the world, or that anything that derives an existence from him as a free cause, should be concealed from him? If he did not know things present in their particularities, many things would be known by man, yea, by beasts, which the infinite God were ignorant of; and if he did not know all things present, but only some, it is possible for the most blessed God to be deceived and be miserable. Ignorance is a calamity to the understanding. He could not prescribe laws to his creatures, unless he knew their natures, to which those laws were to be suited; no, not natural ordinances to the sun, moon, and heavenly bodies, and inanimate creatures, unless he knew the vigour and virtue in them, to execute those ordinances; for to prescribe laws above the nature of things, is inconsistent with the wisdom of government; he must know how far they were able to obey, whether the laws were suited to their ability; and for his rational creatures, whether the punishment annexed to the law were proper, and suited to the transgression of the creature.

[1.] First, He knows all creatures, from the highest to the lowest, the least as well as the greatest. He knows the ravens and their young ones, Job xxxviii. 41; the drops of rain and dew which he hath begotten, ver. 29, every bird in the air, as well as any man doth what he hath in a cage at home: Ps. l. 11, 'I know all the fowls in the mountains, and the wild beasts in the field,' which some read creeping things. The clouds are numbered in his wisdom, Job xxxviii. 37, every worm in the earth, every drop of rain that falls upon the ground, the flakes of snow, and the knots of hail, the sands upon the sea shore, the hairs upon the head; it is no more absurd to imagine that God knows them, than that God made them; they are all the effects of his power, as well as the stars, which he calls by their names, as well as the most glorious angel and blessed spirit; he knows them as well as if there were none but them in particular for him to know; the least things were framed by his art as well as the greatest; the least things partake of his goodness as well as the greatest; he knows his own arts, and his own goodness, and therefore all the stamps and impressions of them upon all his creatures; he knows the immediate causes of the least, and therefore the effects of those causes. Since his knowledge is infinite, it must extend to those things which are at the greatest distance from him, to those which approach nearest to not being; since he did not want power to create, he cannot want understanding to know everything he hath created, the dispositions, qualities, and virtues of the minutest creature.

Nor is the understanding of God imbased, and suffers a diminution by the knowledge of the vilest and most inconsiderable things. Is it not an imperfection to be ignorant of the nature of anything? and can God have such a defect in his most perfect understanding? Is the understanding of man of an impurer alloy by knowing the nature of the rankest poisons? by understanding a fly, or a small insect, or by considering the deformity of a toad? Is it not generally counted a note of a dignified mind to be able to discourse of the nature of them? Was Solomon, who knew all from the cedar to the hyssop, debased by so rich a present of wisdom from his Creator? Is any glass defiled by presenting a deformed image? Is there anything more vile than the imagination, 'which are only evil, and continually'? Doth not the mind of man descend to the mud of the earth, play the adulterer or idolater with mean objects, suck in the most unclean things? Yet God knows these in all their circumstances, in every appearance, inside and outside. Is there anything viler than some thoughts of men, than some actions of men, their unclean beds, and gluttonous vomiting, and Luciferian pride? Yet do not these fall under the eye of God in all their nakedness!

The second person's taking human nature, though it obscured, yet it did not disparage the Deity, or bring any disgrace to it. Is gold the worse for being formed into the image of a fly? Doth it not still retain the nobleness of the metal? When men are despised for descending to the knowledge of mean and vile things, it is because they neglect the knowledge of the greater, and sin in their inquiries after lesser things, with a neglect of that which concerns more the honour of God and the happiness of themselves; to be ambitious of such a knowledge, and careless of that of more concern, is criminal and contemptible. But God knows the greatest as well as the least; mean things are not known by him to exclude the knowledge of the greater, nor are vile things governed by him to exclude the order of the better. The deformity of objects known by God doth not deform him, nor defile him; he doth not view them without himself, but within himself, wherein all things in their ideas are beautiful and comely. Our knowledge of a deformed thing is not a deforming of our understanding, but is beautiful in the knowledge, though it be not in the object; nor is there any fear that the understanding of God should become material by knowing material things, any more than our understandings lose their spirituality by knowing the nature of bodies; it is to be observed therefore that only those senses of men, as seeing, hearing, smelling, which have those qualities for their objects that come nearest the nature of spiritual things, as light, sounds, fragrant odours, are ascribed to God in Scripture; not touching or tasting, which are senses that are not exercised without a more immediate commerce with gross matter; and the reason may be, because we should have no gross thoughts of God, as if he were a body, and made of matter like the things he knows.

[2.] As he knows all creatures, so God knows all the actions of creatures. He counts in particular all the ways of men: 'Doth he not see all my ways, and count all my steps?' Job xxxi. 4. He 'tells their wanderings,' as if one by one, Ps. lvi. 8; 'His eyes are upon all the ways of man, and he sees all his goings,' Job xxxiv. 21, a metaphor taken from men when they look wistly, with fixed eyes upon a thing, to view it in every circumstance, whence it comes, whither it goes, to observe every little motion of it. God's eye is not a wandering, but a fixed eye, and the ways of man are not only 'before his eyes,' but he doth exactly 'ponder' them, Prov. v. 21; as one that will not be ignorant of the least mite in them, but weigh and examine them by the standard of his law; he may as well know the motions of our members as the hairs of our heads; the smallest actions before they be, whether civil, natural, or religious, fall under his cognisance. What meaner than a man carrying a pitcher? yet our Saviour foretells it, Luke xxii. 10. God knows not only what men do, but what they would have done had he not restrained them; what Abimelech would have done to Sarah had not God put a bar in his way, Gen. xx. 6; what a man that is taken away in his youth would have done, had he lived to a riper age; yea, he knows the most secret words as well as actions; the words spoken by the king of

Israel in his bed-chamber were revealed to Elisha, 2 Kings vi. 12; and indeed how can any action of man be concealed from God ? Can we view the various actions of a heap of ants or a hive of bees in a glass, without turning our eyes ; and shall not God behold the actions of all men in the world, which are less than bees or ants in his sight, and more visible to him than an ant-hill or bee-hive can be to the acutest eye of man ?

[3.] As God knows all the actions of creatures, so he knows all the thoughts of creatures. The thoughts are the most closeted acts of man, hid from men and angels, unless disclosed by some outward expressions ; but God descends into the depths and abysses of the soul, discerns the most inward contrivances ; nothing is impenetrable to him ; the sun doth not so much enlighten the earth as God understands the heart; all thoughts are as visible to him as flies and motes enclosed in a body of transparent crystal. This man naturally allows to God. Men often speak to God by the motions of their minds and secret ejaculations, which they would not do if it were not naturally implanted in them, that God knows all their inward motions. The Scripture is plain and positive in this: ' He tries the heart and reins,' Ps. vii. 9, as men by the use of fire discern the drossy and purer parts of metals. The secret intentions and aims, the most lurking affections seated in the reins, he knows that which no man, no angel is able to know, which a man himself knows not, nor makes any particular reflection upon ; yea, he ' weighs the spirit,' Prov. xvi. 2, he exactly numbers all the devices and inclinations of men, as men do every piece of coin they tell out of a heap. He ' discerns the thoughts and intents of the heart,' Heb. iv. 12, all that is in the mind, all that is in the affections, every stirring and purpose, so that not one thought can be withheld from him, Job xlii. 2 ; yea, ' hell and destruction are before him, much more then the hearts of the children of men,' Prov. xv. 11. He works all things in the bowels of the earth, and brings forth all things out of that treasure, say some; but more naturally, God knows the whole state of the dead, all the receptacles and graves of their bodies, all the bodies of men consumed by the earth, or devoured by living creatures, things that seem to be out of all being; he knows the thoughts of the devils and damned creatures, whom he hath cast out of his care for ever into the arms of his justice, never more to cast a delightful glance towards them ; not a secret in any soul in hell (which he hath no need to know, because he shall not judge them by any of the thoughts they now have, since they were condemned to punishment) is hid from him, much more is he acquainted with the thoughts of living men, the counsels of whose hearts are yet to be manifested in order to their trial and censure ; yea, he knows them before they spring up into actual being: Ps. cxxxix. 2, ' Thou understandest my thoughts afar off;' my thoughts, that is, every thought, though innumerable thoughts pass through me in a day, and that in the source and fountain when it is yet in the womb, before it is our thought. If he knows them before their existence, before they can be properly called ours, much more doth he know them when they actually spring up in us ; he knows the tendency of them, where the bird will light when it is in flight ; he knows them exactly, he is therefore called a ' discerner' or criticiser ' of the heart,' Heb. iv. 12. As a critic discerns every letter, point, and stop, he is more intimate with us than our soul with our bodies, and hath more the possession of us than we have of ourselves ; he knows them by an inspection into the heart, not by the mediation of second causes, by the looks or gestures of men, as men may discern the thoughts of one another.

First, God discerns all good motions of the mind and will. These he puts into men, and needs must God know his own act: he knew the son of

Jeroboam to have 'some good thing in him towards the Lord God of Israel,' 1 Kings xiv. 13, and the integrity of David and Hezekiah, the freest motions of the will and affections to him. 'Lord, thou knowest that I love thee,' saith Peter, John xxi. 17. Love can be no more restrained than the will itself can. A man may make another to grieve and desire, but none can force another to love.

Secondly, God discerns all the evil motions of the mind and will; every imagination of the heart,' Gen. vi. 5; the vanity of men's thoughts, Ps. xciv. 11; their inward darkness and deceitful disguises. No wonder that God, who fashioned the heart, should understand the motions of it: Ps. xxxiii. 13, 15, 'He looks from heaven, and beholds all the children of men: he fashioneth their hearts alike, and considers all their works.' Doth any man make a watch, and yet be ignorant of its motion? Did God fling away the key to this secret cabinet, when he framed it, and put off the power of unlocking it when he pleased? He did not surely frame it in such a posture as that anything in it should be hid from his eye; he did not fashion it to be privileged from his government; which would follow if he were ignorant of what was minted and coined in it.

He could not be a judge to punish men, if the inward frames and principles of men's actions were concealed from him; an outward action may glitter to an outward eye, yet the secret spring be a desire of applause, and not the fear and love of God. If the inward frames of the heart did lie covered from him in the secret recesses of the heart, those plausible acts, which in regard of their principles would merit a punishment, would meet with a reward, and God should bestow happiness where he had denounced misery. As without the knowledge of what is just, he would not be a wise lawgiver, so without the knowledge of what is inwardly committed, he could not be a righteous judge; acts that are rotten in the spring, might be judged good by the fair colour and appearance.

This is the glory of God at the last day, to 'manifest the secrets of all hearts,' 1 Cor. iv. 5; and the prophet Jeremiah links the power of judging, and the prerogative of trying the hearts together: Jer. xi. 20, 'But thou, O Lord of Hosts, that judgest righteously, that triest the reins and the heart;' and chap. xvii. 10, 'I the Lord search the heart; I try the reins;' To what end? Even ' to give every man according to his way, and according to the fruit of his doings.' And indeed his binding up the whole law with that command of not coveting, evidenceth that he will judge men by the inward affections and frames of their hearts. Again, God sustains the mind of man in every act of thinking. In him we have not only the principle of life, but every motion, the motion of our minds as well as of our members. 'In him we live and move,' &c., Acts xvii. 28. Since he supports the vigour of the faculty in every act, can he be ignorant of those acts which spring from the faculty, to which he doth at that instant communicate power and ability?

Now this knowledge of the thoughts of men is,

First, An incommunicable property, belonging only to the divine understanding. Creatures indeed may know the thoughts of others by divine revelation, but not by themselves; no creature hath a key immediately to open the minds of men, and see all that lodgeth there; no creature can fathom the heart by the line of created knowledge.* Devils may have a conjectural knowledge, and may guess at them, by the acquaintance they have with the disposition and constitution of men, and the images they behold in their fancies; and by some marks which an inward imagination

* Daille, Serm. part i. p. 280.

may stamp upon the brain, blood, animal spirits, face, &c.; but the knowing the thoughts merely as thought, without any impression by it, is a royalty God appropriates to himself, as the main secret of his government, and a perfection declarative of his Deity as much as any else: Jer. xvii. 9, 10, ' The heart of man is desperately wicked, who can know it?' Yes, there is one, and but one; ' I the Lord search the heart; I try the reins.' ' Man looks on the outward appearance, but the Lord looks upon the heart,' 1 Sam. xvi. 7, where God is distinguished by this perfection from all men whatsoever; others may know by revelation, as Elisha did, what was in Gehazi's heart, 2 Kings v. 26; but God knows a man more than any man knows himself. What person upon earth understands the windings and turnings of his own heart, what reserves it will have, what contrivances, what inclinations? all which God knows exactly.

Secondly, God acquires no new knowledge of the thoughts and heart, by the discovery of them in the actions. He would then be but equal in this part of knowledge to his creature; no man or angel but may thus arrive to the knowledge of them. God were then excluded from an absolute dominion over the prime work of his lower creation; he would have made a creature superior in this respect to himself, upon whose will to discover, his knowledge of their inward intentions should depend; and, therefore, when God is said to search the heart, we must not understand it as if God were ignorant before, and was fain to make an exact scrutiny and inquiry, before he attained what he desired to know; but God condescends to our capacity in the expression of his own knowledge, signifying that his knowledge is as complete as any man's knowledge can be, of the designs of others, after he hath sifted them by a strict and thorough examination, and wrung out a discovery of their intentions; that he knows them as perfectly as if he had put them upon the rack, and forced them to make a discovery of their secret plottings. Nor must we understand that in Gen. xxii. 12, where God saith, after Abraham had stretched out his hand to sacrifice his son, ' Now I know that thou fearest God,' as though God was ignorant of Abraham's gracious disposition to him. Did Abraham's drawing his knife furnish God with a new knowledge? No; God knew Abraham's pious inclinations before: Gen. xviii. 19, ' I know him that he will command his children after him,' &c. Knowledge is sometimes taken for approbation; then the sense will be, Now I approve this fact as a testimony of thy fear of me; since thy affection to thy Isaac is extinguished by the more powerful flame of affection to my will and command, I now accept thee, and count thee a meet subject of my choicest benefits; or now I know, that is, I have made known and manifested, the faith of Abraham to himself and to the world. Thus Paul uses the word know: 1 Cor. ii. 2, ' I have determined to know nothing;' that is, to declare and teach nothing, to make known nothing ' but Christ crucified;' or else, now I know, that is, I have an evidence and experiment in this noble fact, that thou fearest me. God often condescends to our capacity in speaking of himself after the manner of men, as if he had (as men do) known the inward affections of others by their outward actions.

[4.] God knows all the evils and sins of creatures.

First, God knows all sin. This follows upon the other. If he knows all the actions and thoughts of creatures, he knows also all the sinfulness in those acts and thoughts. This Zophar infers from God's punishing men: Job xi. 11, ' For he knows vain man; he sees his wickedness also;' he knows every man, and sees the wickedness of every man. ' He looks down from heaven,' and beholds not only the filthy persons, but what is filthy in them, Ps. xiv. 2, 3, all nations in the world, and every man of every nation;

none of their iniquity is hid from his eyes. 'He searches Jerusalem with candles,' Zeph. i. 22. God follows sinners step by step with his eye, and will not leave searching out till he hath taken them; a metaphor taken from one that searches all chinks with a candle, that nothing can be hid from him. He knows it distinctly in all the parts of it, how an adulterer rises out of his bed to commit uncleanness; what contrivances he had, what steps he took, every circumstance in the whole progress; not only evil in the bulk, but every one of the blacker spots upon it, which may most aggravate it. If he did not know evil, how could he permit it, order it, punish it, or pardon it? Doth he permit he knows not what? order ¦to his own holy ends what he is ignorant of? punish or pardon that which he is uncertain whether it be a crime or no? 'Cleanse me,' saith David, 'from my secret faults,' Ps. xix. 12, secret in regard of others, secret in regard of himself; how could God cleanse him from that whereof he was ignorant? He knows sins before they are committed, much more when they are in act; he foreknew the idolatry and apostasy of the Jews; what gods they would serve, in what measure they would provoke him, and violate his covenant, Deut. xxxi. 20, 21; he knew Judas his sin long before Judas his actual existence, foretelling it in the Psalms; and Christ predicts it before he acted it. He sees sins future in his own permitting will; he sees sins present in his own supporting act. As he knows things possible to himself, because he knows his own power; so he knows things practicable by the creature, because he knows the power and principles of the creature.* This sentiment of God is naturally writ in the fear of sinners, upon lightning, thunder, or some prodigious operation of God in the world; what is the language of them, but that he sees their deeds, hears their words, knows the inward sinfulness of their hearts; that he doth not only behold them as a mere spectator, but considers them as a just judge? And the poets say, that the sins of men leaped into heaven, and were writ in parchments of Jupiter, *scelus in terrâ geritur, in cœlo scribitur*, sin is acted on earth, and recorded in heaven. God, indeed, doth not behold evil with the approving eye; he knows it not with a practical knowledge to be the author of it, but with a speculative knowledge, so as to understand the fulness of it; or a knowledge *simplicis intelligentiæ*, of simple intelligence, as he permits them, not positively wills them; he knows them not with a knowledge of assent to them, but dissent from them. Evil pertains to a dissenting act of the mind, and an aversive act of the will; and what though evil formally taken hath no distinct conception, because it is a privation, a defect hath no being, and all knowledge is by the apprehension of some being, would not this lie as strongly against our own knowledge of sin? Sin is the privation of the rectitude due to an act; and who doubts man's knowledge of sin? By his knowing the act, he knows the deficiency of the act; the subject of evil hath a being, and so hath a conception in the mind; that which hath no being cannot be known by itself, or in itself, but will it follow that it cannot be known by its contrary? as we know darkness to be a privation of light, and folly to be a privation of wisdom. God knows all good by himself, because he is the sovereign good. Is it strange, then, that he should know all evil, since all evil is in some natural good?

Secondly, The manner of God's knowing evil is not so easily known; and, indeed, as we cannot comprehend the essence of God, though it is easily intelligible that there is such a being, so we can as little comprehend the manner of God's knowledge, though we cannot but conclude him to be an intelligent being, a pure understanding, knowing all things. As God hath a higher manner of being than his creatures, so he hath another and higher

* Fotherby, Atheoma, p. 132.

manner of knowing; and we can as little comprehend the manner of his knowing, as we can the manner of his being. But as to the manner.

Doth not God know his own law? and shall he not know how much any action comes short of his rule? He cannot know his own rule without knowing all the deviations from it. He knows his own holiness, and shall he not see how any action is contrary to the holiness of his own nature? Doth not God know everything that is true, and is it not true that this or that is evil? and shall God be ignorant of any truth? How doth God know that he cannot lie, but by knowing his own veracity? How doth God know that he cannot die, but by knowing his own immutability? And, by knowing those, he knows what a lie is, he knows what death is; so, if sin never had been, if no creature had ever been, God would have known what sin was, because he knows his own holiness, because he knew what law was fit to be appointed to his creatures, if he should create them, and that that law might be transgressed by them. God knows all good, all goodness in himself; he therefore hath a foundation in himself, to know all that comes short of that goodness, that is opposite to that holiness. As if light were capable of understanding, it would know darkness only by knowing itself; by knowing itself, it would know what is contrary to itself. God knows all created goodness which he hath planted in the creature; he knows then all defects from this goodness, what perfection an act is deprived of, what is opposite to that goodness, and that is evil. As we know sickness by health, discord by harmony, blindness by sight, because it is a privation of sight; whosoever knows one contrary knows the other. God knows unrighteousness by the idea which he hath of righteousness, and sees an act deprived of that rectitude and goodness which ought to be in it; he knows evil because he knows the causes whence evil proceeds.* A painter knows a picture of his own framing; and if any one dashes any base colour upon it, shall not he also know that? God by his hand painted all creatures, impressed upon man the fair stamp and colour of his own image; the devil defiles it, man daubs it. Doth not God, that knows his own work, know how this piece is become different from his work? Doth not God, that knows his creatures' goodness, which himself was the fountain of, know the change of this goodness? Yea, he knew before, that the devil would sow tares where he had sown wheat; and, therefore, that controversy of some in the schools, whether God knew evil by its opposition to created or uncreated goodness, is needless. We may say God knows sin as it is opposite to created goodness, yet he knows it radically by his own goodness, because he knows the goodness he hath communicated to the creature by his own essential goodness in himself. To conclude this head:

The knowledge of sin doth not bespot the holiness of God's nature, for the bare knowledge of a crime doth not infect the mind of man with the filth and pollution of that crime, for then every man that knows an act of murder committed by another, would, by that bare knowledge, be tainted with his sin; yea, and a judge that condemns a malefactor, may as well condemn himself, if this were so. The knowledge of sins infects not the understanding that knows them, but only the will that approves them. It is no discredit to us to know evil, in order to pass a right judgment upon it; so neither can it be to God.

(4.) God knows all future things, all things to come. The differences of time cannot hinder a knowledge of all things by him who is before time, above time, that is not measured by hours, or days, or years; if God did not know them, the hindrance must be in himself, or in the things them-

* Cusan, p. 245.

selves, because they are things to come. Not in himself: if it did, it must
arise from some impotency in his own nature, and so we render him weak;
or from an unwillingness to know, and so we render him lazy, and an enemy
to his own perfection; for, simply considered, the knowledge of more things
is a greater perfection than the knowledge of a few; and if the knowledge
of a thing includes something of perfection, the ignorance of a thing includes
something of imperfection. The knowledge of future things is a greater
perfection than not to know them, and is accounted among men a great part
of wisdom, which they call foresight; it is then surely a greater perfection
in God to know future things, than to be ignorant of them. And would
God rather have something of imperfection than be possessor of all perfection?
Nor doth the hindrance lie in the things themselves, because their futurition
depends upon his will; for as nothing can actually be without his will,
giving it existence, so nothing can be future without his will, designing the
futurity of it. Certainly, if God knows all things possible, which he will
not do, he must know all things future, which he is not only able, but resolved to do, or resolved to permit. God's perfect knowledge of himself,
that is, of his own infinite power and concluding will, necessarily includes a
foreknowledge of what he is able to do, and what he will do.

Again, if God doth not know future things, there was a time when God
was ignorant of most things in the world, for, before the deluge, he was
more ignorant than after; the more things were done in the world, the more
knowledge did accrue to God, and so the more perfection; then, the understanding of God was not perfect from eternity, but in time; nay, is not
perfect yet, if he be ignorant of those things which are still to come to pass;
he must tarry for a perfection he wants, till those futurities come to be in
act, till those things which are to come cease to be future, and begin to be
present. Either God knows them, or desires to know them; if he desires
to know them and doth not, there is something wanting to him; all desire
speaks an absence of the object desired, and a sentiment of want in the
person desiring. If he doth not desire to know them, nay, if he doth not
actually know them, it destroys all providence, all his government of affairs,
for his providence hath a concatenation of means with a prospect of something that is future; as in Joseph's case, who was put into the pit,
and sold to the Egyptians, in order to his future advancement, and the preservation both of his father and his envious brethren. If God did not know
all the future inclinations and actions of men, something might have been
done by the will of Potiphar, or by the free will of Pharaoh, whereby
Joseph might have been cut short of his advancement, and so God have been
interrupted in the track and method of his designed providences. He that
hath decreed to govern man for that end he hath designed him, knows all
the means before whereby he will govern him, and therefore hath a distinct
and certain knowledge of all things, for a confused knowledge is an imperfection in government; it is in this the infiniteness of his understanding is
more seen than in knowing things past or present; 'his eyes are as a flame
of fire,' Rev. i. 14, in regard of the penetrating virtue of them into things
impenetrable by any else.

To make it further appear that God knows all things future, consider,

1. First, everything which is the object of God's knowledge without himself was once only future. There was a moment when nothing was in being
but himself; he knew nothing actually past, because nothing was past; nothing actually present, because nothing had any existence but himself;
therefore only what was future, and why not everything that is future now,
as well as only what was future and to come to pass just at the beginning of

the creation? God, indeed, knows everything as present, but the things themselves known by him were not present, but future. The whole creation was once future, or else it was from eternity; if it begun in time, it was once future in itself, else it could never have begun to be. Did not God know what would be created by him before it was created by him?* Did he create he knew not what, and knew not before what he should create? Was he ignorant before he acted, and in his acting, what his operation would tend to? Or did he not know the nature of things, and the ends of them, till he had produced them, and saw them in being? Creatures then did not arise from his knowledge, but his knowledge from them; he did not then will that his creatures should be, or he had then willed what he knew not, and knew not what he willed; they, therefore, must be known before they were made, and not known because they were made; he knew them to make them, and he did not make them to know them. By the same reason he knew what creatures should be before they were, he knows still what creatures shall be before they are;† for all things that are were in God, not really in their own nature, but in him as a cause; so the earth and heavens were in him, as a model in the mind of a workman, which is in his mind and soul before it be brought forth into outward act.

2. The predictions of future things evidence this. There is not a prophecy of anything to come but is a spark of his foreknowledge, and bears witness to the truth of this assertion in the punctual accomplishment of it. This is a thing challenged by God as his own peculiar, wherein he surmounts all the idols that man's inventions have goded in the world: Isa. xli. 21, 22, 'Let them bring forth' (speaking of the idols), 'and shew us what shall happen, or declare us things to come: shew the things that are to come hereafter, that we may know that you are gods.' Such a foreknowledge of things to come is here ascribed to God by God himself, as a distinction of him from all false gods. Such a knowledge that, if any could prove that they were possessors of, he would acknowledge them gods as well as himself; 'that we may know that you are gods.' He puts his Deity to stand or fall upon this account, and this should be the point which should decide the controversy whether he or the heathen idols were the true God. The dispute is managed by this medium: he that knows things to come is God; I know things to come, *ergo* I am God: the idols know not things to come, therefore they are not gods. God submits the being of his Deity to this trial. If God know things to come no more than the heathen idols, which were either devils or men, he would be, in his own account, no more a God than devils or men; no more a God than the pagan idols he doth scoff at for this defect. If the heathen idols were to be stripped of their deity for want of this foreknowledge of things to come, would not the true God also fall from the same excellency if he were defective in knowledge? He would, in his own judgment, no more deserve the title and character of a God than they. How could he reproach them for that, if it were wanting in himself? It cannot be understood of future things in their causes, when the effects necessarily arise from such causes, as light from the sun and heat from the fire. Many of these men know; more of them, angels and devils know; if God, therefore, had not a higher and farther knowledge than this, he would not by this be proved to be God, any more than angels and devils, who know necessary effects in their causes. The devils, indeed, did predict some things in the heathen oracles, but God is differenced from them here by the infiniteness of his knowledge, in being able to predict things to come that they knew not, or things in their particularities, things that depended on the

* Petavius *changed*.   † Bradward, lib. iii. cap. 14.

liberty of man's will, which the devils could 'lay no claim to a certain knowledge of. Were it only a conjectural knowledge that is here meant, the
devils might answer they can conjecture, and so their.deity were as good as
God's; for though God might know more things, and conjecture nearer to
what would be, yet still it would be but. conjectural, and therefore not a
higher kind of knowledge than what the devils might challenge. How much,
then, is God beholden to the Socinians for denying the knowledge of all
future things to him, upon which here he puts the trial of his deity? God
asserts his knowledge of things to come as a manifest evidence of his Godhead; those that deny, therefore, the argument that proves it, deny the
conclusion too; for this will necessarily follow, that if he be God because
he knows future things, then he that doth not know future things is not
God; and if God knows not future things but only by conjecture, then there
is no God, because a certain knowledge, so as infallibly to predict things
to come, is an inseparable perfection of the Deity. It was therefore well
said of Austin, that it was as high a madness to deny God to be as* to deny
him the foreknowledge of things to come.

The whole prophetic part of Scripture declares this perfection of God.
Every prophet's candle was lighted at this torch; they could not have this
foreknowledge of themselves. Why might not many other men have the
same insight, if it were by nature?† It must be from some superior agent;
and all nations owned prophecy as a beam from God, a fruit of divine illumination. Prophecy must be totally expunged if this be denied, for the
subjects of prophecy are things future, and no man is properly a prophet
but in prediction. Now prediction is nothing but foretelling, and things
foretold are not yet come; and the foretelling of them supposeth them not
to be yet, but that they shall be in time. Several such predictions we have
in Scripture, the event whereof hath been certain. The years of famine in
Egypt foretold that he would order second causes for bringing that judgment
upon them; the captivity of his people in Babylon; the calling of the Gentiles; the rejection of the Jews. Daniel's revelation of Nebuchadnezzar's
dream, that prince refers to God as the revealer of secrets, Dan. ii. 47. By
the same reason that he knows one thing future by himself, and by the
infiniteness of his knowledge, before any causes of them appear, he doth
know all things future.

8. Some future things are known by men, and we must allow God a
greater knowledge than any creature. Future things in their causes may be
known by angels and men, as I said before; whosoever knows necessary
causes, and the efficacy of them, may foretell the effects; and when he sees
the meeting and concurrence of several causes together, he may presage
what the consequent effect will be of such a concurrence. So physicians
foretell the progress of a disease, the increase or diminution of it by natural
signs; and astronomers foretell eclipses by their observation of the motion
of heavenly bodies many years before they happen.‡ Can they be hid from
God, with whom are the reasons of all things?§ An expert gardener, by
knowing the root in the depth of winter, can tell what flowers and what fruit
it will bear, and the month when they will peep out their heads; and shall
not God much more, that knows the principles of all his creatures, and is
exactly privy to all their natures and qualities, know what they will be, and
what operations shall be from those principles? Now if God did know
things only in their causes, his knowledge would not be more excellent than

---

* Qu. 'no higher . . . than'?—ED.
† Pacuvius said, *Siqui quæ eventura sunt provident, æquiparent.*
‡ Cusanus.   § Fuller's Pisgah, l. ii. p. 281.

the knowledge of angels and men, though he might know more than they of the things that will come to pass from every cause singly, and from the concurrence of many. Now as God is more excellent in being than his creature, so he is more excellent in the objects of his knowledge and the manner of his knowledge : well, then, shall a certain knowledge of something future, and a conjectural knowledge of many things, be found among men, and shall a determinate and infallible knowledge of things to come be found nowhere, in no being? If the conjecture of future things savours of ignorance, and God knows them only by conjecture, there is then no such thing in being as a perfect intelligent being, and so no God.

4. God knows his own decree and will, and therefore must needs know all future things. If anything be future, or to come to pass, it must be from itself or from God ; not from itself, then it would be independent and absolute. If it hath its futurity from God, then God must know what he hath decreed to come to pass. Those things that are future in necessary causes God must know, because he willed them to be causes of such effects ; he therefore knows them, because he knows what he willed. The knowledge of God cannot arise from the things themselves, for then the knowledge of God would have a cause without him ; and knowledge, which is an eminent perfection, would be conferred upon him by his creatures. But as God sees things possible in the glass of his own power, so he sees things future in the glass of his own will : in his effecting will, if he hath decreed to produce them ; in his permitting will, as he hath decreed to suffer them and dispose of them. Nothing can pass out of the rank of things merely possible into the order of things future, before some act of God's will hath passed for its futurition.*

It is not from the infiniteness of his own nature, simply considered, that God knows things to be future ; for as things are not future because God is infinite (for then all possible things should be future), so neither is anything known to be future only because God is infinite, but because God hath decreed it ; his declaration of things to come is founded upon his appointment of things to come.† In Isa. xliv. 7, it is said, 'And who, as I, shall call, and declare it, since I appointed the ancient people, and the things that are coming?'‡ Nothing is created and ordered in the world but what God decreed to be created and ordered. God knows his own decree, and therefore all things which he hath decreed to exist in time, not the minutest part of the world, could have existed without his will, not an action can be done without his will. As life, the principle, so motion, the fruit of that life, is by and from God. As he decreed life to this or that thing, so he decreed motion as the effect of life, and decreed to exert his power in concurring with them, for producing effects natural from such causes ; for without such a concourse they could not have acted anything, or produced anything. And therefore, as for natural things, which we call necessary causes, God foreseeing them all particularly in his own decree, foresaw also all effects which must necessarily flow from them, because such causes cannot but act when they are furnished with all things necessary for action. He knows his own decrees, and therefore necessarily knows what he hath decreed, or else we must say things come to pass whether God will or no ; or, that he wills he knows not what. But this cannot be ; for 'known unto God are all his works from the beginning of the world,' Acts xv. 18. Now this necessarily flows from that principle first laid down, that God knows himself, since nothing is future without God's will. If God did not know future things, he would not know his own will ; for as things possible could not be

* Chequell.   † Coccei Sum. Theol., p. 50.
‡ Gamach in Aquin., part i. qu. 24, cap. 3, p. 124.

known by him unless he knew the fulness of his own power, so things future could not be known by his understanding unless he knew the resolves of his own will.

Thus the knowledge of God differs from the knowledge of men. God's knowledge of his works precedes his works,* man's knowledge of God's works follows his works. Just as an artificer's knowledge of a watch, instrument, or engine which he would make, is before his making of it; he knows the motions of it, and the reasons of those motions before it is made, because he knows what he hath determined to work; he knows not those motions from the consideration of them after they were made, as the spectator doth, who by viewing the instrument after it is made, gains a knowledge from the sight and consideration of it, till he understands the reason of the whole; so we know things from the consideration of them after we see them in being, and therefore we know not future things. But God's knowledge doth not arise from things because they are, but because he wills them to be; and therefore he knows everything that shall be, because it cannot be without his will, as the creator and maintainer of all things; knowing his own substance, he knows all his works.

5. If God did not know all future things, he would be mutable in his knowledge.

If he did not know all things that ever were or are to be, there would be upon the appearance of every new object an addition of light to his understanding, and therefore such a change in him as every new knowledge causes in the mind of a man, or as the sun works in the world upon its rising every morning, scattering the darkness that was upon the face of the earth. If he did not know them before they came, he would gain a knowledge by them when they came to pass, which he had not before they were effected; his knowledge would be new according to the newness of the objects, and multiplied according to the multitude of the objects. If God did not know things to come as perfectly as he knew things present and past, but knew those certainly, and the others doubtfully and conjecturally, he would suffer some change, and acquire some perfection in his knowledge, when those future things should cease to be future, and become present; for he would know it more perfectly when it were present than he did when it was future, and so there would be a change from imperfection to a perfection; but God is every way immutable.

Besides, that perfection would not arise from the nature of God, but from the existence and presence of the thing. But who will affirm that God acquires any perfection of knowledge from his creatures, any more than he doth of being? He would not then have had that knowledge, and consequently that perfection from eternity, as he had when he created the world, and will not have a full perfection of the knowledge of his creature till the end of the world, nor of immortal souls, which will certainly act as well as live to eternity. And so God never was, nor ever will be perfect in knowledge; for when you have conceived millions of years, wherein angels and souls live and act, there is still more coming than you can conceive, wherein they will act. And if God be always changing to eternity from ignorance to knowledge, as those acts come to be exerted by his creatures, he will not be perfect in knowledge, no, not to eternity, but will always be changing from one degree of knowledge to another; a very unworthy conceit to entertain of the most blessed, perfect, and infinite God.

Hence then it follows, that,

(1.) God foreknows all his creatures; all kinds which he determined to

* Maimonid. More Nevoch., part iii. cap. 21, p. 393, 394.

make, all particulars that should spring out of every species, the time when they should come forth of the womb, the manner how: 'In thy book all members were written,' Ps. cxxxix. 16. *Members* is not in the Hebrew, whence some refer *all* to all living creatures whatsoever, and all the parts of them which God did foresee. He knew the numbers of creatures, with all their parts; they were written in the book of his foreknowledge; the duration of them, how long they shall remain in being and act upon the stage; he knows their strength, the links of one cause with another, and what will follow in all their circumstances, and the series and combination of effects with their causes.

The duration of everything is foreknown, because determined: Job xiv. 5, ' Seeing his days are determined, the number of his months are with thee; thou hast appointed his bounds that he cannot pass.' Bounds are fixed, beyond which none shall reach; he speaks of days and months, not of years, to give us notice of God's particular foreknowledge of everything, of every day, month, year, hour of a man's life.

(2.) All the acts of his creatures are foreknown by him. All natural acts, because he knows their causes; voluntary acts I shall speak of afterwards.

(3.) This foreknowledge was certain. For it is an unworthy notion of God to ascribe to him a conjectural knowledge; if there were only a conjectural knowledge, he could but conjecturally foretell anything; and then it is possible the events of things might be contrary to his predictions. It would appear then that God were deceived and mistaken, and then there could be no rule of trying things whether they were from God or no; for the rule God sets down to discern his words from the words of false prophets is the event and certain accomplishment of what is predicted. Deut. xviii. 21, to that question, ' How shall we know whether God hath spoken or no?' he answers, that 'If the thing doth not come to pass, the Lord hath not spoken.' If his knowledge of future things were not certain, there were no stability in this rule, it would fall to the ground. We never yet find God deceived in any prediction; but the event did answer his forerevelation; his foreknowledge therefore is certain and infallible. We cannot make God uncertain in his knowledge, but we must conceive him fluctuating and wavering in his will; but if his will be not ' yea and nay,' but ' yea,' his knowledge is certain, because he doth certainly will and resolve.

(4.) This foreknowledge was from eternity. Seeing he knows things possible in his power, and things future in his will, if his power and resolves were from eternity, his knowledge must be so too, or else we must make him ignorant of his own power, and ignorant of his own will from eternity, and consequently not from eternity blessed and perfect. His knowledge of possible things must run parallel with his power, and his knowledge of future things run parallel with his will. If he willed from eternity, he knew from eternity what he willed; but that he did will from eternity we must grant, unless we would render him changeable, and conceive him to be made in time of not willing, willing. The knowledge God hath in time was alway one and the same, because his understanding is his proper essence, as perfect as his essence, and of an immutable nature.

And indeed the actual existence of a thing is not simply necessary to its being perfectly known.* We may see a thing that is passed out of being when it doth not actually exist, and a carpenter may know the house he is to build before it be built, by the model of it in his own mind; much more we may conceive the same of God, whose decrees were before the foundation

* Gamach in Aquin., part i. q. xiv. c. iii. p. 124.

of the world, Eph. i. 5, and in other places ; and to be before time was, and to be from eternity, hath no difference. As God in his being exceeds all beginning of time, so doth his knowledge all motions of time.

(5.) God foreknows all things, as present with him from eternity.* As he knows mutable things with an immutable and firm knowledge, so he knows future things with a present knowledge. Not that the things which are produced in time were actually and really present with him in their own beings from eternity, for then they could not be produced in time ; had they a real existence, then they would not be creatures, but God ; and had they actual being, then they could not be future, for future speaks a thing to come that is not yet ; if things had been actually present with him, and yet future, they had been made before they were made, and had a being before they had a being ; but they were all present to his knowledge, as if they were in actual being, because the reason of all things that were to be made was present with him.

The reason of the will of God that they shall be, was equally eternal with him,† wherein he saw what, and when, and how he would create things, how he would govern them, to what ends he would direct them. Thus all things are present to God's knowledge, though in their own nature they may be past or future, not *in esse reali*, but *in esse intelligibili*, objectively, not actually present ;‡ for as the unchangeableness and infiniteness of God's knowledge of changeable and finite things doth not make the things he knows immutable and infinite, so neither doth the eternity of his knowledge make them actually present with him from eternity, but all things are present to his understanding, because he hath at once a view of all successions of times, and his knowledge of future things is as perfect as of present things, or what is past. It is not a certain knowledge of present things, and an uncertain knowledge of future ; but his knowledge of one is as certain and unerring as his knowledge of the other.§ As a man that beholds a circle with several lines from the centre, beholds the lines as they are joined in the centre, beholds them also as they are distant and severed from one another, beholds them in their extent and in their point all at once, though they may have a great distance from one another. He saw from the beginning of time to the last minute of it, all things coming out of their causes, marching in their order according to his own appointment, as a man may see a multitude of ants, some creeping one way, some another, employed in several businesses for their winter provision. The eye of God at once runs through the whole circle of time, as the eye of man upon a tower sees all the passengers at once, though some be past, some under the tower, some coming at a farther distance. God, saith Job, 'looks to the end of the earth, and sees under the whole heaven,' Job xxviii. 24. The knowledge of God is expressed by sight in Scripture, and futurity to God is the same thing as distance to us. We can, with a perspective glass, make things that are afar off appear as if they were near, and the sun, so many thousand miles distant from us, to appear as if it were at the end of the glass. Why should then future things be at so great a distance from God's knowledge, when things so far from us may be made to approach so near to us ?

God considers all things, in his own simple knowledge, as if they were now acted ; and therefore some have chosen to call the knowledge of things to come not prescience or foreknowledge, but knowledge, because God sees all things in one instant, *scientiâ nunquam deficientis instantiæ.*|| Upon this

* Gerhard Exeges, ch. viii., de Deo, sect. xiii. p. 303.
† Bradward, l. iii. c. 14.
‡ Hornbeck.
§ Pugio Fidei, part i. ch. 19.
|| Boet. Consolat., lib. v. prof. 6.

account things that are to come are set down in Scripture as present, and sometimes as past : Isa. ix. 6, ' Unto us a Child *is* born,' though not yet born ; so of the sufferings of Christ : Isa. liii. 4, &c., ' He *hath* borne our griefs, he *was* wounded for our transgressions, he *was* taken from prison,' &c., not *shall be ;* and Ps. xxii. 18, ' They *part* my garments among them,' as if it were present ; all to express the certainty of God's foreknowledge, as if things were actually present before him.

(6.) This is proper to God, and incommunicable to any creature. Nothing but what is eternal can know all things that are to come. Suppose a creature might know things that are to come after he is in being, he cannot know things simply as future, because there were things future before he was in being. The devils know not men's hearts, therefore cannot foretell their actions with any certainty. They may indeed have a knowledge of some things to come, but it is only conjectural, and often mistaken, as the devil was in his predictions among the heathen, and in his presage of Job's cursing God to his face upon his pressing calamities, Job i. 11. Sometimes indeed they have a certain knowledge of something future by the revelation of God, when he uses them as instruments of his vengeance, or for the trial of his people, as in the case of Job, when he gave him a commission to strip him of his goods, or as the angels have, when he uses them as instruments of the deliverance of his people.

(7.) Though this be certain, that God foreknows all things and actions, yet the manner of his knowing all things before they come, is not so easily resolved. We must not, therefore, deny this perfection in God, because we understand not the manner how he hath the knowledge of all things. It were unworthy for us to own no more of God than we can perfectly conceive of him ; we should then own no more of him than that he doth exist. ' Canst thou,' saith Job, ' by searching find out God ? canst thou find out the Almighty unto perfection ?' Job xi. 7. Do we not see things, unknown to inferior creatures, to be known to ourselves ? Irrational creatures do not apprehend the nature of a man, nor what we conceive of them when we look upon them, nor do we know what they fancy of us when they look wistly upon us ; for aught as I know, we understand as little the manner of their imaginations as they do of ours ; and shall we ascribe a darkness in God as to future things, because we are ignorant of them, and of the manner how he should know them ?* Shall we doubt whether God doth certainly know those things which we only conjecture ? As our power is not the measure of the power of God, so neither is our knowledge the judge of the knowledge of God, no better, nor so well, as an irrational creature can be the judge of our reason. Do we perfectly know the manner how we know ? Shall we therefore deny that we know anything ? We know we have such a faculty which we call understanding, but doth any man certainly know what it is ? And because he doth not, shall he deny that which is plain and evident to him ? Because we cannot ascertain ourselves of the causes of the ebbing and flowing of the sea, of the manner how minerals are engendered in the earth, shall we therefore deny that which our eyes convince us of ?

And this will be a preparation to the last thing.

C. God knows all future contingencies ; that is, God knows all things that shall accidentally happen, or, as we say, by chance ; and he knows all the free motions of men's wills that shall be to the end of the world.

If ' all things be open to him,' Heb. iv. 13, then all contingencies are, for they are in the number of things ; and as, according to Christ's speech, those things that are impossible to man, are possible to God, so those

* Ficinus in Procl., cap 19.

things which are unknown to man, are known to God, because of the infinite fulness and perfection of the divine understanding.

Let us see what a contingent is.

That is contingent which we commonly call accidental, as when a tile falls suddenly upon a man's head as he is walking in the street, or when one letting off a musket at random shoots another he did not intend to hit; such was that arrow whereby Ahab was killed, shot by a soldier at a venture, 1 Kings xxii. 34. This some call a mixed contingent, made up partly of necessity, and partly of accident; it is necessary the bullet, when sent out of the gun, or arrow out of the bow, should fly and light somewhere, but it is an accident that it hits this or that man, that was never intended by the archer. Other things, as voluntary actions, are purely contingents, and have nothing of necessity in them; all free actions that depend upon the will of man, whether to do or not to do, are of this nature, because they depend not upon a necessary cause, as burning doth upon the fire, moistening upon water, or as descent or falling down is necessary to a heavy body, for those cannot in their own nature do otherwise; but the other actions depend upon a free agent, able to turn to this or that point, and determine himself as he pleases.

Now we must know that what is accidental in regard of the creature, is not so in regard of God. The manner of Ahab's death was accidental in regard of the hand by which he was slain, but not in regard of God, who foretold his death, and foreknew the shot, and directed the arrow. God was not uncertain before of the manner of his fall, nor hovered over the battle to watch for an opportunity to accomplish his own prediction; what may be or not be in regard of us, is certain in regard of God. To imagine that what is accidental to us is so to God, is to measure God by our short line. How many events, following upon the results of princes in their counsels, seem to persons ignorant of those counsels to be a hap-hazard, yet were not contingencies to the prince and his assistants, but foreseen by him as certainly to issue so as they do, which they knew before would be the fruit of such causes and instruments they would knit together! That may be necessary in regard of God's foreknowledge, which is merely accidental in regard of the natural disposition of the immediate causes which do actually produce it; contingent in its own nature and in regard of us, but fixed in the knowledge of God. One illustrates it by this similitude:* A master sends two servants to one and the same place, two several ways, unknown to one another; they meet at the place which their master had appointed them; their meeting is accidental to them, one knows not of the other, but it was foreseen by the master that they should so meet, and that in regard of them it would seem a mere accident till they came to explain the business to one another; both the necessity of their meeting in regard of their master's order, and the accidentalness of it in regard of themselves, were in both their circumstances foreknown by the master that employed them.

For the clearing of this, take it in this method.

(1.) It is an unworthy conceit of God, in any, to exclude him from the knowledge of these things.

[1.] It will be a strange contracting of him, to allow him no greater a knowledge than we have ourselves. Contingencies are known to us when they come into act, and pass from futurity to reality; and when they are present to us, we can order our affairs accordingly; shall we allow God no greater a measure of knowledge than we have, and make him as blind as ourselves, not to see things of that nature before they come to pass? Shall

* Zanch.

God know them no more; shall we imagine God knows no otherwise than we know, and that he doth, like us, stand gazing with admiration at events? Man can conjecture many things; is it fit to ascribe the same uncertainty to God, as though he as well as we could have no assurance till the issue appear in the view of all? If God doth not certainly foreknow them, he doth but conjecture them; but a conjectural knowledge is by no means to be fastened on God, for that is not knowledge but guess, and destroys a deity by making him subject to mistake; for he that only guesseth, may guess wrong, so that this is to make God like ourselves, and strip him of an universally acknowledged perfection of omniscience. A conjectural knowledge, saith one,† is as unworthy of God, as the creature is unworthy of omniscience. It is certain man hath a liberty to act many things this or that way as he pleases, to walk to this or that quarter, to speak or not to speak, to do this or that thing or not to do it; which way a man will certainly determine himself, is unknown before to any creature, yea, often at the present to himself, for he may be in suspense; but shall we imagine this future determination of himself is concealed from God. Those that deny God's foreknowledge in such cases, must either say that God hath an opinion that a man will resolve rather this way than that;—but then if a man by his liberty determine himself contrary to the opinion of God, is not God then deceived? and what rational creature can own him for a God that can be deceived in anything?—or else they must say that God is at uncertainty, and suspends his opinion without determining it any way; then he cannot know free acts till they are done, he would then depend upon the creature for his information, his knowledge would be every instant increased, as things he knew not before came into act; and since there are every minute an innumerable multitude of various imaginations in the minds of men, there would be every minute an accession of new knowledge to God, which he had not before; besides, this knowledge would be mutable, according to the wavering and weather-cock resolutions of men, one while standing to this point, another while to that, if he depended upon the creatures' determination for his knowledge.

[2.] If the free acts of men were unknown before to God, no man can see how there can be any government of the world by him. Such contingencies may happen, and such resolves of men's free wills unknown to God, as may perplex his affairs, and put him upon new counsels and methods for attaining those ends which he settled at the first creation of things; if things happen which God knows not of before, this must be the consequence, where there is no foresight, there is no providence; things may happen so sudden, if God be ignorant of them, that they may give a check to his intentions and scheme of government, and put him upon changing the model of it. How often doth a small intervening circumstance, unforeseen by man, dash in pieces a long meditated and well-formed design. To govern necessary causes, as sun and stars, whose effects are natural and constant in themselves, is easy to be imagined; but how to govern the world, that consists of so many men of free will, able to determine themselves to this or that, and which have no constancy in themselves, as the sun and stars have, cannot be imagined, unless we will allow in God as great a certainty of foreknowledge of the designs and actions of men, as there is inconstancy in their resolves. God must be altering the methods of his government every day, every hour, every minute, according to the determinations of men, which are so various and changeable in the whole compass of the world in the space of one minute; he must wait to see what the counsels

† Scrivener.

of men will be, before he could settle his own methods of government ; and so must govern the world according to their mutability, and not according to any certainty in himself. But his 'counsel is stable' in the midst of multitudes of free 'devices' in the heart of man, Prov. xix. 21, and knowing them all before, orders them to be subservient to his own stable counsel. If he cannot know what to-morrow will bring forth in the mind of a man, how can he certainly settle his own determination of governing him ; his degrees and resolves must be temporal, and arise *pro re natá*, and he must alway be in counsel what he should do upon every change of men's minds. This is an unworthy conceit of the infinite majesty of heaven, to make his government depend upon the resolves of men, rather than their resolves upon the design of God.

(2.) It is therefore certain that God doth foreknow the free and voluntary acts of man. How could he else order his people to ask of him 'things to come,' in order to their deliverance, such things as depend upon the will of man, if he foreknew not the motions of their will, Isa. xlv. 11.

[1.] Actions good or indifferent depending upon the liberty of man's will as much as any whatsoever. Several of these he hath foretold ; not only a person to build up Jerusalem was predicted by him, but the name of that person, Cyrus, Isa. xliv. 28. What is more contingent, or is more the effect of the liberty of man's will, than the names of their children ? Was not the destruction of the Babylonish empire foretold, which Cyrus undertook, not by any compulsion, but by a free inclination and resolve of his own will ? And was not the dismission of the Jews into their own country a voluntary act in that conquerer ? If you consider the liberty of man's will, might not Cyrus as well have continued their yoke as have struck off their chains, and kept them captive as well as dismissed them ? Had it not been for his own interest rather to have strengthened the fetters of so turbulent a people, who, being tenacious of their religion and laws, different from that professed by the whole world, were like to make disturbances more when they were linked in a body in their own country, than when they were transplanted and scattered into the several parts of his empire ? It was in the power of Cyrus (take him as a man) to choose one or the other. His interest invited him to continue their captivity rather than grant their deliverance, yet God knew that he would willingly do this rather than the other ; he knew this which depended upon the will of Cyrus ; and why may not an infinite God foreknow the free acts of all men, as well as of one ? If the liberty of Cyrus's will was no hindrance to God's certain and infallible foreknowledge of it, how can the contingency of any other thing be a hindrance to him ? for there is the same reason of one and all ; and his government extends to every village, every family, every person, as well as to kingdoms and nations.

So God foretold by his prophet, not only the destruction of Jeroboam's altar, but the name of the person that should be the instrument of it, 1 Kings xiii. 2, and this about three hundred years before Josiah's birth. It is a wonder that none of the pious kings of Judah, in detestation of idolatry, and hopes to recover again the kingdom of Israel, had in all that space named one of their sons by that name of Josiah, in hopes that that prophecy should be accomplished by him ; that Manasseh only should do this, who was the greatest imitator of Jeroboam's idolatry among all the Jewish kings, and indeed went beyond them, and had no mind to destroy in another kingdom what he propagated in his own. What is freer than the imposition of a name ? Yet this he foreknew, and this Josiah was Manasseh's son, 2 Kings xxi. 26. Was there anything more voluntary than for

Pharaoh to honour the butler by restoring him to his place, and punish the baker by hanging him on a gibbet? Yet this was foretold, Gen. xl. 8. And were not all the voluntary acts of men, which were the means of Joseph's advancement, foreknown by God, as well as his exaltation, which was the end he aimed at by those means? Many of these may be reckoned up.

Can all the free acts of man surmount the infinite capacity of the divine understanding? If God singles out one voluntary action in man as contingent as any, and lying among a vast number of other designs and resolutions, both antecedent and subsequent, why should he not know the whole mass of men's thoughts and actions, and pierce into all that the liberty of man's will can effect? Why should he not know every grain, as well as one that lies in the midst of many of the same kind?

And since the Scripture gives so large an account of contingents predicted by God, no man can certainly prove that anything is unforeknown to him. It is as reasonable to think he knows every contingent, as that he knows some that lie as much hid from the eye of any creature, since there is no more difficulty to an infinite understanding to know all, than to know some.* Indeed, if we deny God's foreknowledge of the voluntary actions of men, we must strike ourselves off from the belief of Scripture predictions that yet remain unaccomplished, and will be brought about by the voluntary engagements of men, as the ruin of antichrist, &c. If God foreknows not the secret motions of man's will, how can he foretell them? If we strip him of this perfection of prescience, why should we believe a word of Scripture predictions? All the credit of the word of God is torn up by the roots. If God were uncertain of such events, how can we reconcile God's declaration of them to his truth, and his demanding our belief of them to his goodness? Were it good and righteous in God to urge us to the belief of that he were uncertain of himself? How could he be true in predicting things he were not sure of? Or good in requiring credit to be given to that which might be false? This would necessarily follow, if God did not foreknow the motions of men's wills, whereby many of his predictions were fulfilled, and some remain yet to be accomplished.

[2.] God foreknows the voluntary sinful motions of men's wills.

First, God hath foretold several of them. Were not all the minute sinful circumstances about the death of our blessed Redeemer, as the piercing him, giving him gall to drink, foretold, as well as the not breaking his bones, and parting his garments? What were those but the free actions of men, which they did willingly, without any constraint? And those foretold by David, Isaiah, and other prophets, some above a thousand, some above eight hundred, and some more, some fewer years, before they came to pass; and events punctually answered the prophecies. Many sinful acts of men, which depended upon their free will, have been foretold: the Egyptians' voluntary oppressing Israel, Gen. xv. 13; Pharaoh's hardening his heart against the voice of Moses, Exod. iii. 19; that Isaiah's message would be in vain to the people, Isa. vi. 19; that the Israelites would be rebellious after Moses his death, and turn idolaters, Deut. xxxi. 16; Judas his betraying of our Saviour, a voluntary action, John vi. 71; he was not forced to do what he did, for he had some kind of repentance for it; and not violence, but voluntariness, falls under repentance.

Secondly, His truth hath depended upon this foresight. Let us consider

* The stoics, that thought their souls to be some particle of God, Ἀποσπάσματα, pieces pulled off from him, did conclude from thence that he knew all the motions of their souls as his own movements, as things coherent with him.—*Arrian Epictet.*, lib. i. chap. xiv. p. 60.

that in Gen. xv. 16, but 'the fourth generation, they shall come hither again;' that is, the posterity of Abraham shall come into Canaan; 'for the iniquity of the Amorites is not yet full.'* God makes a promise to Abraham of giving his posterity the land of Canaan, not presently, but in the fourth generation. If the truth of God be infallible in the performance of his promise, his understanding is as infallible in the foresight of the Amorites' sin : the fulness of their iniquity was to precede the Israelites' possession. Did the truth of God depend upon an uncertainty? Did he make the promise hand over head, as we say? How could he with any wisdom and truth assure Israel of the possession of the land in the fourth generation, if he had not been sure that the Amorites would fill up the measure of their iniquities by that time? If Abraham had been a Socinian, to deny God's knowledge of the free acts of men, had he not had a fine excuse for unbelief? What would his reply have been to God? Alas, Lord, this is not a promise to be relied upon; the Amorites' iniquity depends upon the acts of their free will, and such thou canst have no knowledge of. Thou canst see no more than a likelihood of their iniquity being full, and therefore there is but a likelihood of thy performing thy promise, and not a certainty. Would not this be judged not only a saucy, but a blasphemous answer? And upon these principles the truth of the most faithful God had been dashed to uncertainty and a peradventure.

Thirdly, God provided a remedy for man's sin, and therefore foresaw the entrance of it into the world by the fall of Adam. He had a decree before the foundation of the world, to manifest his wisdom in the gospel by Jesus Christ, an 'eternal purpose in Jesus Christ,' Eph. iii. 11. And a decree of election passed before the foundation of the world, a separation of some to redemption and forgiveness of sin in the blood of Christ, in whom they were from eternity chosen, as well as in time accepted in Christ, Eph. i. 4, 6, 7, which is called a 'purpose in himself,' ver. 9. Had not sin entered, there had been no occasion for the death of the Son of God, it being everywhere in Scripture laid upon that score. A decree for the shedding of blood supposed a decree for the permission of sin, and a certain foreknowledge of God, that it would be committed by man. An uncertainty of foreknowledge, and a fixedness of purpose, are not consistent in a wise man, much less in the only wise God. God's purpose to manifest his wisdom to men and angels in this way might have been defeated, had God had only a conjectural foreknowledge of the fall of man; and all those solemn purposes of displaying his perfections in those methods had been to no purpose.† The provision of a remedy supposed a certainty of the disease. If a sparrow fall not to ground without the will of God, how much less could such a deplorable ruin fall upon mankind, without God's will permitting it, and his knowledge foreseeing it!

It is not hard to conceive how God might foreknow it.‡ He indeed decreed to create man in an excellent state. The goodness of God could not but furnish him with a power to stand. Yet in his wisdom he might foresee that the devil would be envious to man's happiness, and would, out of envy, attempt his subversion. As God knew of what temper the faculties were he had endued man with, and how far they were able to endure the assaults of a temptation, so he also foreknew the grand subtilty of Satan, how he would lay his mine, and to what point he would drive his temptation : how he would propose and manage it, and direct his battery against the sensitive appetite, and assault the weakest part of the fort; might he not foresee that

* Vid. Rivet. *in loc.* exerci. 86, p, 329.
† Mares. cont. Volkel. lib. i. cap. 24, p. 343.   ‡ Amyrald. de Prædestin. cap. 6.

the efficacy of the temptation would exceed the measure of the resistance? Cannot God know how far the malice of Satan would extend; what shots he would, according to his nature, use; how high he would charge his temptation without his powerful restraint, as well as an engineer judge how many shots of a cannon will make a breach in a town, and how many casks of powder will blow up a fortress, who never yet built the one nor founded the other? We may easily conclude God could not be deceived in the judgment of the issue and event, since he knew how far he would let Satan loose, how far he would permit man to act; and since he dives to the bottom of the nature of all things, he foresaw that Adam was endued with an ability to stand, as he foresaw that Benhadad might naturally recover of his disease; but he foresaw also that Adam would sink under the allurements of the temptation, as he foresaw that Hazael would not let Benhadad live, 2 Kings viii. 10.

Now since the whole race of mankind lies in corruption, and is subject to the power of the devil, 1 John v. 19, may not God, that knows that corruption in every man's nature, and the force of every man's spirit, and what every particular nature will incline him to upon such objects proposed to him, and what the reasons of the temptation will be, know also the issues? Is there any difficulty in God's foreknowing this, since man, knowing the nature of one he is well acquainted with, can conclude what sentiments he will have, and how he will behave himself, upon presenting this or that object to him?

If a man that understands the disposition of his child or servant, knows before what he will do upon such an occasion, may not God much more, who knows the inclination of all his creatures, and from eternity run with his eyes over all the works he intended? Our wills are in the number of causes, and since God knows our wills, as causes, better than we do ourselves, why should he be ignorant of the effects?

God determines to give grace to such a man; not to give it to another, but leave him to himself, and suffer such temptations to assault him. Now God, knowing the corruption of man in the whole mass, and in every part of it, is it not easy for him to foreknow what the future actions of the will will be, when the tinder and fire meet together, and how such a man will determine himself, both as to the substance and manner of the action? Is it not easy for him to know how a corrupted temper and a temptation will suit? God is exactly privy to all the gall in the hearts of men, and what principles they will have before they have a being. He 'knows their thoughts afar off,' Ps. cxxxix. 2, as far off as eternity, as some explain the words, and thoughts are as voluntary as anything; he knows the power and inclinations of men in the order of second causes; he understands the corruption of men, as well as the poison of dragons and the venom of asps. This is 'laid up in store with him, and sealed among his treasures,' Deut. xxxii. 33, 34; among the treasures of his foreknowledge, say some.

What was the cruelty of Hazael but a free act? Yet God knew the frame of his heart, and what acts of murder and oppression would spring from that bitter fountain, before Hazael had conceived them in himself, 2 Kings viii. 12. As a man that knows the mineral through which waters pass may know what relish they will have before they appear above the earth, so our Saviour knew how Peter would deny him; he knew what quantity of powder would serve for such a battery, in what measure he would let loose Satan, how far he would leave the reins in Peter's hands, and then the issue might easily be known; and so, in every act of man, God knows in his own will what measure of grace he will give to determine the will to good, and what measure of grace he will withdraw from such a person, or not give to him, and consequently, how far such a person will fall or not. God knows the inclinations of the creature ; he knows his own permissions, what degrees of grace he will either allow him or keep from him, according to which will be the degree of his sin. This may in some measure help our conceptions in this, though, as was said before, the manner of God's foreknowledge is not so easily explicable.

(3). God's foreknowledge of man's voluntary actions doth not necessitate the will of man. The foreknowledge of God is not deceived, nor the liberty of man's will diminished. I shall not trouble you with any school distinctions, but be as plain as I can, laying down several propositions in this case.

Prop. 1. It is certain all necessity doth not take away liberty. Indeed, a compulsive necessity takes away liberty, but a necessity of immutability removes not liberty from God ; why should then a necessity of infallibility in God remove liberty from the creature ? God did not necessarily create the world, because he decreed it ; yet freely, because his will from eternity stood to it : he freely decreed it, and freely created it. As the apostle saith, in regard of God's decrees, 'Who hath been his counsellor ?' Rom. xi. 34, so, in regard of his actions, I may say, Who hath been his compeller ? He freely decreed, and he freely created. Jesus Christ necessarily took our flesh, because he had covenanted with God so to do, yet he acted freely and voluntar[il]y according to that covenant, otherwise his death had not been efficacious for us. A good man doth naturally necessarily love his children, yet voluntary. It is part of the happiness of the blessed to love God unchangeably, yet freely, for it would not be their happiness if it were done by compulsion. What is done by force cannot be called felicity, because there is no delight or complacency in it ; and though the blessed love God freely, yet, if there were a possibility of change, it would not be their happiness ; their blessedness would be damped by their fear of falling from this love, and consequently from their nearness to God, in whom their happiness consists. God foreknows that they will love him for ever, but are they therefore compelled for ever to love him ? If there were such a kind of constraint, heaven would be rendered burdensome to them, and so no heaven.

Again, God's foreknowledge of what he will do doth not necessitate him to do ; he foreknew that he would create a world, yet he freely created a world. God's foreknowledge doth not necessitate himself, why should it necessitate us more than himself ? We may instance in ourselves : when we will a thing, we necessar[il]y use our faculty of will ; and when we freely will anything, it is necessary that we freely will ; but this necessity doth not exclude but include liberty ; or more plainly, when a man writes or speaks, whilst he writes or speaks, those actions are necessary, because to speak and be silent, to write and not to write, at the same time, are impossible ; yet our writing or speaking doth not take away the power not to write or to be silent at that time, if a man would be so, for he might have chose whether he would have spoke or writ. So there is a necessity of such actions of man which God foresees ; that is, a necessity of infallibility, because God cannot be deceived, but not a coactive necessity, as if they were compelled by God to act thus or thus.

Prop. 2. No man can say in any of his voluntary actions that he ever found any force upon him. When any of us have done anything according to our wills, can we say we could not have done the contrary to it ? Were we determined to it in our own intrinsic nature, or did we not determine ourselves ? Did we not act either according to our reason, or according to outward allurements ; did we find anything without us or within us that did force our wills to the embracing this or that ? Whatever action you do, you do it because you judge it fit to be done, or because you will do it. What though God foresaw that you would do so, and that you would do this or that, did you feel any force upon you ? Did you not act according to your nature ? God foresees that you will eat or walk at such a time; do you find anything that moves you to eat but your own appetite, or to walk but your own reason and will ? If prescience had imposed any necessity upon man, should we not probably have found some kind of plea from it in the mouth of Adam ? He knew as much as any man ever since knew of the nature of God, as discoverable in creation; he could not in innocence fancy an ignorant God, a God that knew nothing of future things ; he could not be so ignorant of his own action but he must have perceived a force upon his will, had there been any; had he thought that God's prescience imposed any necessity upon him, he would not have omitted the plea, especially when he was so daring as to charge the providence of God, in the gift of the woman to him, to be the cause of his crime, Gen. iii. 12. How came his posterity to invent new charges against God, which their father Adam never thought of, who had more knowledge than all of them? He could find no cause of his sin but the liberty of his own will. He charges it not upon any necessity from the devil, or any necessity from God ; nor doth he allege the gift of the woman as a necessary cause of his sin, but an occasion of it, by giving the fruit to him. Judas knew that our Saviour did foreknow his treachery, for he had told him of it in the hearing of his disciples, John xiii. 21, 26, yet he never charged the necessity of his crime upon the foreknowledge of his Master. If Judas had not done it freely, he had had no reason to repent of it ; his repentance justifies Christ from imposing any necessity upon him by that foreknowledge. No man acts anything but he can give an account of the motives of his action ; he cannot father it upon a blind necessity ; the will cannot be compelled, for then it would cease to be will. God doth not root up the foundations of nature, or change the order of it, and make men unable to act like men, that is, as free agents. God foreknows the actions of irrational creatures; this concludes no violence upon their nature, for we find their actions to be according to their nature, and spontaneous.

Prop. 3. God's foreknowledge is not, simply considered, the cause of anything. It puts nothing into things, but only beholds them as present, and arising from their proper causes. The knowledge of God is not the principle of things, or the cause of their existence, but directive of the action. Nothing is because God knows it, but because God wills it, either positively or permissively. God knows all things possible ; yet because God knows them, they are not brought into actual existence, but remain still only as things possible. Knowledge only apprehends a thing, but acts nothing; it is the rule of acting, but not the cause of acting ; the will is the immediate principle, and the power the immediate cause. To know a thing is not to do a thing ; for then we may be said to do everything that we know. But every man knows those things which he never did, nor never will do. Knowledge in itself is an apprehension of a thing, and is not the cause of it. A spectator of a thing is not the cause of that thing which he sees ; that is, he is not the cause of it as he beholds it. We see a man write ; we know before that he will write at such a time; but this foreknowledge is not the cause of his writing. We see a man walk; but our vision of him brings no necessity of walking upon him; he was free to walk, or not to walk.* We foreknow that death will seize upon all men ; we foreknow that the seasons of the year will succeed one another; yet is not our foreknowledge the cause

* Raleigh, of the World, lib i. cap. i. sec. 12.

of this succession of spring after winter, or of the death of all men, or any man. We see one man fighting with another; our sight is not the cause of that contest, but some quarrel among themselves exciting their own passions. As the knowledge of present things imposeth no necessity upon them while they are acting and present, so the knowledge of future things imposeth no necessity upon them while they are coming. We are certain there will be men in the world to-morrow, and that the sea will ebb and flow; but is this knowledge of ours the cause that those things will be so? I know that the sun will rise to-morrow; it is true that he shall rise; but it is not true that my foreknowledge makes it to rise. If a physician prognosticates, upon seeing the intemperances and debaucheries of men, that they will fall into such a distemper, is his prognostication any cause of their disease, or of the sharpness of any symptoms attending it? The prophet foretold the cruelty of Hazael before he committed it; but who will say that the prophet was the cause of his commission of that evil? And thus the foreknowledge of God takes not away the liberty of man's will, no more than a foreknowledge that we have of any man's actions takes away his liberty. We may, upon our knowledge of the temper of a man, certainly foreknow that if he falls into such company, and get among his cups, he will be drunk; but is this foreknowledge the cause that he is drunk? No; the cause is the liberty of his own will, and not resisting the temptation. God purposes to leave such a man to himself and his own ways; and man being so left, God foreknows what will be done by him according to that corrupt nature which is in him. Though the decree of God, of leaving a man to the liberty of his own will, be certain, yet the liberty of man's will, as thus left, is the cause of all the extravagancies he doth commit. Suppose Adam had stood; would not God certainly have foreseen that he would have stood? Yet it would have been concluded that Adam had stood, not by any necessity of God's foreknowledge, but by the liberty of his own will. Why should, then, the foreknowledge of God add more necessity to his falling than to his standing?* And though it be said sometimes in Scripture that such a thing was done, 'that the Scripture might be fulfilled,' as John xii. 38, 'that the saying of Esaias might be fulfilled, Lord, who hath believed our report?' the word *that* doth not infer that the prediction of the prophet was the cause of the Jews' unbelief; but infers this, that the prediction was manifested to be true by their unbelief, and the event answered the prediction. This prediction was not the cause of their sin; but their foreseen sin was the cause of this prediction. And so the particle *that* is taken, Ps. li. 4, 'Against thee, thee only have I sinned, that thou mightest be justified,' &c. The justifying God was not the end and intent of the sin, but the event of it upon his acknowledgment.

Prop. 4. God foreknows things because they will come to pass; but things are not future because God knows them. Foreknowledge presupposeth the object which is foreknown. A thing that is to come to pass is the object of the divine knowledge, but not the cause of the act of divine knowledge; and though the foreknowledge of God doth in eternity precede the actual presence of a thing which is foreseen as future, yet the future thing, in regard of its futurity, is as eternal as the foreknowledge of God. As the voice is uttered before it be heard, and a thing is visible before it be seen, and a thing knowable before it be known; but how comes it to be knowable to God? It must be answered, either in the power of God as a thing possible, or in the will of God as a thing future. He first willed, and then knew what he willed; he knew what he willed to effect, and he knew what he willed to

* Rivet in Isa. liii. 1, p. 16.

permit; as he willed the death of Christ by a determinate counsel, and willed the permission of the Jews' sin, and the ordering of the malice of their nature to that end, Acts ii. 23. God decrees to make a rational creature, and to govern him by a law; God decrees not to hinder this rational creature from transgressing his law; and God foresees that what he would not hinder would come to pass. Man did not sin because God foresaw him; but God foresaw him to sin, because man would sin. If Adam and other men would have acted otherwise, God would have foreknown that they would have acted well. God foresaw our actions because they would so come to pass by the motion of our free-will, which he would permit, which he would concur with, which he would order to his own holy and glorious ends for the manifestation of the perfection of his nature. If I see a man lie in a sink, no necessity is inferred upon him from my sight to lie in that filthy place; but there is a necessity inferred by him that lies there, that I should see him in that condition if I pass by and cast my eye that way.

Prop. 5. God did not only foreknow our actions, but the manner of our actions; that is, he did not only know that we would do such actions, but that we would do them freely. He foresaw that the will would freely determine itself to this or that. The knowledge of God takes not away the nature of things. Though God knows possible things, yet they remain in the nature of possibility; and though God knows contingent things, yet they remain in the nature of contingencies; and though God knows free agents, yet they remain in the nature of liberty. God did not foreknow the actions of man as necessary, but as free; so that liberty is rather established by this foreknowledge than removed. God did not foreknow that Adam had not a power to stand, or that any man hath not a power to omit such a sinful action, but that he would not omit it. Man hath a power to do otherwise than that which God foreknows he will do. Adam was not determined by any inward necessity to fall, nor any man by any inward necessity to commit this or that particular sin; but God foresaw that he would fall, and fall freely; for he saw the whole circle of means and causes whereby such and such actions should be produced, and can be no more ignorant of the motions of our wills, and the manner of them, than an artificer can be ignorant of the motions of his watch, and how far the spring will let down the string in the space of an hour. He sees all causes leading to such events in their whole order, and how the free-will of man will comply with this, or refuse that; he changes not the manner of the creature's operation, whatsoever it be.

Prop. 6. But what if the foreknowledge of God, and the liberty of the will, cannot be fully reconciled by man? Shall we therefore deny a perfection in God, to support a liberty in ourselves? Shall we rather fasten ignorance upon God, and accuse him of blindness, to maintain our liberty? That God doth foreknow everything, and yet that there is liberty in the rational creature, are both certain; but how fully to reconcile them, may surmount the understanding of man. Some truths the disciples were not capable of bearing in the days of Christ; and several truths our understandings cannot reach as long as the world doth last; yet in the mean time we must on the one hand take heed of conceiving God ignorant, and on the other hand of imagining the creature necessitated: the one will render God imperfect, and the other will seem to render him unjust, in punishing man for that sin which he could not avoid, but was brought into by a fatal necessity. God is sufficient to render a reason of his own proceedings, and clear up all at the day of judgment; it is a part of man's curiosity, since the fall, to be prying into God's secrets, things too high for him, whereby he singes his own wings, and confounds his own understanding. It is a cursed affectation that runs in the blood of Adam's posterity, to know as God, though our first father smarted and ruined his posterity in that attempt; the ways and knowledge of God are as much ' above our thoughts' and conceptions, as ' the heavens are above the earth,' Isa. lv. 9, and so sublime, that we cannot comprehend them in their true and just greatness;* his designs are so mysterious, and the ways of his conduct so profound, that it is not possible to dive into them. The force of our understandings is below his infinite wisdom, and therefore we should adore him with an humble astonishment, and cry out with the apostle; Rom. xi. 33, ' Oh the depth of the riches of the wisdom and knowledge of God! how unsearchable are his judgments, and his ways past finding out!' Whenever we meet with depths that we cannot fathom, let us remember that he is God, and we his creatures; and not be guilty of so great extravagance, as to think that a subject can pierce into all the secrets of a prince, or a work understand all the operations of the artificer. Let us only resolve not to fasten any thing on God that is unworthy of the perfection of his nature, and dishonourable to the glory of his majesty; nor imagine that we can ever step out of the rank of creatures to the glory of the Deity, to understand fully everything in his nature.

So much for the second general, what God knows.

III. The third is, How God knows all things? As it is necessary we should conceive God to be an understanding being, else he could not be God, so we must conceive his understanding to be infinitely more pure and perfect than ours in the act of it, else we liken him to ourselves, and debase him as low as his footstool. As among creatures there are degrees of being and perfection; plants above earth and sand, because they have a power of growth; beasts above plants, because to their power of growth, there is an addition of excellency of sense; rational creatures above beasts, because to sense there is added the dignity of reason; the understanding of man is more noble than all the vegetative power of plants, or the sensitive power of beasts: God therefore must be infinitely more excellent in his understanding, and therefore in the manner of it.† As man differs from a beast in regard of his knowledge, so doth God also from man in regard of his knowledge. As God therefore is, in being and perfection, infinitely more above a man than a man is above a beast, the manner of his knowledge must be infinitely more above a man's knowledge, than the knowledge of a man is above that of a beast; our understandings can clasp an object in a moment, that is at a great distance from our sense; our eye by one elevated motion can view the heavens; the manner of God's understanding must be unconceivably above our glimmerings; as the manner of his being is infinitely more perfect than all beings, so must the manner of his understanding be infinitely more perfect than all created understandings. Indeed, the manner of God's knowledge can no more be known by us, than his essence can be known by us; and the same incapacity in man, which renders him unable to comprehend the being of God, renders him as unable to comprehend the manner of God's understanding.‡ As there is a vast distance between the essence of God, and our beings, so there is between the thoughts of God and our thoughts. The heavens are not so much higher than the earth, as the thoughts of God are above the thoughts of men, yea, and of the highest

* Daille, Melang. part i. p. 712, 725.
† Maxim. Tyrius Dissert. i. p. 9, 10.
‡ Maimonides More Nevochim. part iii. c. xx. p. 391–393.

angel, Isa. lv. 8, 9 ; yet though we know not the manner of God's knowledge, we know that he knows ; as though we know not the infiniteness of God, yet we know that he is infinite. It is God's sole prerogative to know himself what he is ; and it is equally his prerogative to know how he knows ; the manner of God's knowledge therefore must be considered by us, as free from those imperfections our knowledge is encumbered with.

In general, God doth necessarily know all things ; he is necessarily omnipresent, because of the immensity of his essence ; so he is necessarily omniscient, because of the infiniteness of his understanding. It is no more at the liberty of his will, whether he will know all things, than whether he will be able to create all things ; it is no more at the liberty of his will, whether he will be omniscient, than whether he will be holy ; he can as little be ignorant, as he can be impure ; he knows not all things because he *will* know them, but because it is essential to his nature to know them.

In particular.

Prop. 1. God knows by his own essence ; that is, he sees the nature of things in the ideas of his own mind, and the events of things in the decrees of his own will ; he knows them not by viewing the things, but by viewing himself ; his own essence is the mirror and book, wherein he beholds all things that he doth ordain, dispose, and execute ; and so he knows all things in the first and original cause, which is no other than his own essence willing, and his own essence executing what he wills ; he knows them in his power as the physical principle, in his will as the moral principle of things, as some speak.

He borrows not the knowledge of creatures from the creatures, nor depends upon them for means of understanding, as we poor worms do, who are beholden to the objects abroad to assist us with images of things, and to our senses to convey them into our minds ; God would then acquire a perfection from those things which are below himself, and an excellency from those things that are vile ; his knowledge would not precede the being of the creatures, but the creatures would be before the act of his knowledge. If he understood by images drawn from the creatures, as we do, there would be something in God which is not God, viz., the images of things drawn from outward objects. God would then depend upon creatures for that which is more noble than a bare being ; for to be understanding, is more excellent than barely to be. Besides, if God's knowledge of his creatures were derived from the creatures by the impression of anything upon him, as there is upon us, he could not know from eternity, because from eternity there was no actual existence of anything but himself ; and therefore there could not be any images shot out from any thing, because there was not anything in being but God ; as there is no principle of being to anything but by his essence, so there is no principle of the knowledge of anything by himself but his essence. If the knowledge of God were distinct from his essence, his knowledge were not eternal, because there is nothing eternal but his essence.

His understanding is not a faculty in him as it is in us, but the same with his essence, because of the simplicity of his nature ; God is not made up of various parts, one distinct from another, as we are, and therefore doth not understand by a part of himself, but by himself ; so that to be and to understand is the same with God ; his essence is not one thing, and the power whereby he understands another ; he would then be compounded, and not be the most simple being. This also is necessary for the perfection of God ; for the more perfect and noble the way and manner of knowing is, the more perfect and noble is the knowledge. The perfection of knowledge depends upon the excellency of the medium whereby we know. As a knowledge by reason is a more noble way of knowing than knowledge by sense, so it is more excellent for God to know by his essence, than by anything without him, anything mixed with him ; the first would render him dependent, and the other would demolish his simplicity.

Again, the natures of all things are contained in God,—not formally, for then the nature of the creatures would be God ;*—but eminently, ' he that planted the ear, shall he not hear ? he that formed the eye, shall he not see ?' Ps. xciv. 9. He hath in himself eminently the beauty, perfection, life and vigour of all creatures; he created nothing contrary to himself, but every-thing with some footsteps of himself in them ; he could not have pronounced them good, as he did, had there been anything in them contrary to his own goodness ; and therefore as his essence primarily represents itself, so it re-presents the creatures, and makes them known to him. As the essence of God is eminently all things, so by understanding his essence, he eminently understands all things. And therefore he hath not one knowledge of him-self, and another knowledge of the creatures ; but by knowing himself, as the original and exemplary cause of all things, he cannot be ignorant of any creature which he is the cause of; so that he knows all things, not by an understanding of them, but by an understanding of himself; by understand-ing his own power as the efficient of them, his own will as the order† of them, his own goodness as the adorner and beautifier of them, his own wisdom as the disposer of them, and his own holiness, to which many of their actions are contrary.

As he sees all things possible in his own power,‡ because he is able to produce them, so he sees all things future in his own will ; decreeing to effect them, if they be good ; or decreeing to permit them, if they be evil. In this glass he sees what he will give being to, and what he will suffer to fall into a deficiency, without looking out of himself, or borrowing knowledge from his creatures ; he knows all things in himself. And thus his know-ledge is more noble, and of a higher elevation than ours, or the knowledge of any creature can be ; he knows all things by one comprehension of the causes in himself.

Prop. 2. God knows all things by one act of intuition. This the schools call an intuitive knowledge. This follows upon the other; for if he know by his own essence, he knows all things by one act; there would be other-wise a division in his essence, a first and a last, a nearness and a distance. As what he made, he made by one word, so what he sees, he pierceth into by one glance from eternity to eternity; as he wills all things by one act of his will, so he knows all things by one act of his understanding. He knows not some things discursively from other things, nor knows one thing suc-cessively after another. As by one act he imparts essence to things, so by one act he knows the nature of things.

1. He doth not know by discourse as we do ; that is, by deducing one thing from another, and from common notions drawing out other rational conclusions, and arguing one thing from another, and springing up various consequences from some principle assented to; but God stands in no need of reasonings : the making inferences and abstracting things would be stains in the infinite perfection of God. Here would be a mixture of knowledge and ignorance; while he knew the principle, he would not know the con-sequence and conclusion till he had actually deduced it; one thing would be known after another, and so he would have an ignorance and then a knowledge, and there would be different conceptions in God, and knowledge

* Dionys.　† Qu. ' orderer '?—Ed.　‡ Kendal against Goodwin of Foreknowledge.

would be multiplied according to the multitude of objects, as it is in human understandings. But God knows all things before they did exist, and never was ignorant of them: Acts xv. 18, 'Known unto God are all his works, from the beginning of the world.' He therefore knows them all at once; the knowledge of one thing was not before another, nor depended upon another, as it doth in the way of human reasoning. Though indeed some* make a virtual discourse in God, that is, though God hath a simple knowledge, yet it doth virtually contain a discourse by the flowing of one knowledge from another; as from the knowledge of his own power he knows what things are possible to be made by him, and from the knowledge of himself he passes to the knowledge of the creatures; but this is only according to our conception, and because of our weakness they are apprehended as two distinct acts in God, one of which is the reason of another. As we say that one attribute is the reason of another; as his mercy may be said to be the reason of his patience, and his omnipresence to be the reason of the knowledge of present things done in the world. God indeed by one simple act knows himself and the creatures, but when that act whereby he knows himself is conceived by us to pass to the knowledge of the creatures, we must not understand it to be a new act distinct from the other, but the same act upon different terms or objects. Such an order is in our understanding and conceptions, not in God's.

2. Nor doth he know successively as we do; that is, not by drops, one thing after another. This follows from the former, a knowledge of all things without discourse is a knowledge without succession.† The knowledge of one thing is not in God before another, one act of knowledge doth not forget‡ another. In regard of the objects, one thing is before another, one year before another, one generation of men before another; one is the cause, the other is the effect. In the creatures there is such a succession, and God knows there will be such a succession; but there is no such order in God's knowledge, for he knows all those successions by one glance, without any succession of knowledge in himself.

Man in his view of things must turn sometimes his body, sometimes only his eyes. He cannot see all the contents of a letter at once; and though he beholds all the lines in the page of a book at once, and a whole country in a map, yet to know what is contained in them, he must turn his eye from word to word, and line to line, and so spin out one thing after another by several acts and motions. We behold a great part of the sea at once, saith Epiphanius, but not all the dimensions of it; for to know the length of the sea we move our eyes one way; to see the breadth of it, we turn our eyes another way; to behold the depth of it, we hath another motion of them. And when we cast our eyes up to heaven, we seem to receive in at an instant the whole extent of the hemisphere; yet there is but one object the eye can attentively pitch upon, and we cannot distinctly view what we see in a lump without various motions of our eyes, which is not done without succession of time.§ And certainly the understanding of angels is bounded according to the measure of their beings, so that it cannot extend itself at one time to a quantity of objects, to make a distinct application of them, but the objects must present themselves one by one. But God is all eye, all understanding; as there is no succession in his essence, so there is none in his knowledge; 'his understanding,' in the nature and in the act, 'is infinite,' as it is in the text. He therefore sees eternally and universally all

---

* Suarez. vol. i. de Deo, lib. iii cap. ii. p. 133, 134.
† Gamach. in Aquin. q. xiv. cap. i. p. 119.   ‡ Qu. 'beget' or 'forego'?—ED.
§ Amyrant, Morale Chresti, tom. iii. p. 137.

things by one act, without any motion, much less various motions. The various changes of things in their substance, qualities, places, and relations, withdraw not anything from his eye, nor bring any new thing to his knowledge. He doth not, upon consideration of present things, turn his mind from past, or when he beholds future things, turn his mind from present; but he sees them not one after another, but all at once and altogether, the whole circle of his own counsels, and all the various lines drawn forth from the centre of his will to the circumference of his creatures. Just as if a man were able in one moment to read a whole library; or as if you should imagine a transparent crystal globe, hung up in the midst of a room, and so framed as to take in the images of all things in the room, the fretwork in the ceiling, the inlaid parts of the floor, and the particular parts of the tapestry about it, the eye of a man would behold all the beauty of the room at once in it. As the sun by one light and heat frames sensible things, so God by one simple act knows all things. As he knows mutable things by an immutable knowledge, bodily things by a spiritual knowledge, so he knows many things by one knowledge: Heb. iv. 13, 'All things are open and naked to him,' more than any one thing can be to us, and therefore he views all things at once as well as we can behold and contemplate one thing alone. As he is the 'Father of lights,' a God of infinite understanding, there is 'no variableness' in his mind, 'nor any shadow of turning' of his eye as there is of ours, to behold various things, James i. 17. His knowledge being eternal, includes all times; there is nothing past or future with him, and therefore he beholds all things by one and the same manner of knowledge, and comprehends all knowable things by one act, and in one moment.

This must needs be so,

(1.) Because of the eminency of God. God is above all, and therefore cannot but see the motions of all. He that sits in a theatre, or at the top of a place, sees all things, all persons; by one aspect he comprehends the whole circle of the place; whereas he that sits below, when he looks before, he cannot see things behind. God being above all, about all, in all, sees at once the motions of all. The whole world in the eye of God is less than a point that divides one sentence from another in a book; as a cipher, 'a grain of dust,' Isa. xl. 15. So little a thing can be seen by man at once, and all things being as little in the eye of God, are seen at once by him. As all time is but a moment to his eternity, so all things are but as a point to the immensity of his knowledge, which he can behold with more ease than we can move or turn our eye.

(2.) Because all the perfections of knowing are united in God. As particular senses are divided in man,*—by one he sees, by another he hears, by another he smells, yet all those are united in one common sense, and this common sense apprehends all,—so the various and distinct ways of knowledge in the creatures, are all eminently united in God. A man, when he sees a grain of wheat, understands at once all things that can in time proceed from that seed; so God, by beholding his own virtue and power, beholds all things which shall in time be unfolded by him. We have a shadow of this way of knowledge in our own understanding: the sense only perceives a thing present, and one object only proper and suitable to it; as the eye sees colour, the ear hears sounds, we see this and that man, one time this, another minute that; but the understanding abstracts a notion of the common nature of man, and frames a conception of that nature wherein all men agree, and so in a manner beholds and understands all men at once,

* Cusan. p. 646.

by understanding the common nature of man, which is a degree of knowledge above the sense and fancy; we may then conceive an infinite vaster perfection in the understanding of God. As to know is simply better than not to know at all, so to know by one act comprehensive is a greater perfection than to know by divided acts, by succession to receive information, and to have an increase or decrease of knowledge, to be like a bucket, alway descending into the well and fetching water from thence. It is a man's weakness that he is fixed on one object only at a time; it is God's perfection that he can behold all at once, and is fixed upon one no more than upon another.

Prop. 3. God knows all things independently. This is essential to an infinite understanding. He receives not his knowledge from anything without him, he hath no tutor to instruct him, or book to inform him; ' Who hath been his counsellor?' saith the prophet, Isa. xl. 13. He hath no need of the counsels of others, nor of the instructions of others. This follows upon the first and second propositions; if he knows things by his essence, then as his essence is independent from the creatures, so is his knowledge; he borrows not any images from the creature, hath no species or pictures of things in his understanding, as we have; no beams from the creature strike upon him to enlighten him, but beams from him upon the world; the earth sends not light to the sun, but the sun to the earth.

Our knowledge indeed depends upon the object, but all created objects depend upon God's knowledge and will. We could not know creatures unless they were, but creatures could not be unless God knew them. As nothing that he wills is the cause of his will, so nothing that he knows is the cause of his knowledge; he did not make things to know them, but he knows them to make them. Who will imagine that the mark of the foot in the dust is the cause that the foot stands in this or that particular place?

If his knowledge did depend upon the things, then the existence of things did precede God's knowledge of them; to say that they are the cause of God's knowledge is to say, that God was not the cause of their being; and if he did create them, it was effected by a blind and ignorant power, he created he knew not what till he had produced it. If he be beholden for his knowledge to the creatures he hath made, he had then no knowledge of them before he made them. If his knowledge were dependent upon them, it could not be eternal, but must have a beginning when the creatures had a beginning, and be of no longer a date than since the nature of things was in actual existence; for whatsoever is a cause of knowledge doth precede the knowledge it causes, either in order of time or order of nature; temporal things therefore cannot be the cause of that knowledge which is eternal. His works could not be foreknown to him, Acts xv. 18, if his knowledge commenced with the existence of his works; if he knew them before he made them, he could not derive a knowledge from them after they were made. He made all things in wisdom, Ps. civ. 24. How can this be imagined, if the things known were the cause of his knowledge, and so before his knowledge, and therefore before his action?* God would not then be the first in the order of knowing agents, because he would not act by knowledge, but act before he knew, and know after he had acted, and so the creature which he made would be before the act of his understanding, whereby he knew what he made.

Again, since knowledge is a perfection, if God's knowledge of the creatures depended upon the creatures, he would derive an excellency from them, they would derive no excellency from any *idea* in the divine mind; he would

* Bradward. lib. i. cap. 15.

not be infinitely perfect in himself. If his perfection in knowledge were gained from anything without himself and below himself, he would not be sufficient of himself, but be under an indigence which wanted a supply from the things he had made, and could not be eternally perfect till he had created, and seen the effects of his own power, goodness, and wisdom to render him more wise and knowing in time than he was from eternity. Who can fancy such a God as this, without destroying the Deity he pretends to adore? For if his understanding be perfected by something without him, why may not his essence be perfected by something without him? that as he was made knowing by something without him, he might be made God by something without him?

How could his understanding be infinite, if it depended upon a finite object, as upon a cause? Is the majesty of God to be debased to a mendicant condition, to seek for a supply from things inferior to himself? Is it to be imagined that a fool, a toad, a fly should be assistant to the knowledge of God? that the most noble being should be perfected by things so vile, that the supreme cause of all things should receive any addition of knowledge, and be determined in his understanding by the notion of things so mean? To conclude this particular; all things depend upon his knowledge, his knowledge depends upon nothing, but is as independent as himself, and his own essence.

Prop. 4. God knows all things distinctly. His understanding is infinite in regard of clearness: 'God is light, and in him is no darkness at all,' 1 John i. 5. He sees not through a mist or cloud; there is no blemish in his understanding, no mote or beam in his eye to render anything obscure to him. Man discerns the surface and outside of things, little or nothing of the essence of things; we see the noblest things, but 'as in a glass darkly,' 1 Cor. xiii. 12. The too great nearness, as well as the too great distance of a thing, hinders our sight; the smallness of a mote escapes our eye, and so our knowledge; also the weakness of our understanding is troubled with the multitude of things, and cannot know many things but confusedly. But God knows the forms and essence of things, every circumstance; nothing is so deep but he sees to the bottom; he sees the mass, and sees the motes of beings. His understanding being infinite, is not offended with a multitude of things, or distracted with the variety of them; he discerns everything infinitely more clearly and perfectly than Adam or Solomon could any one thing in the circle of their knowledge. What knowledge they had was from him; he hath therefore infinitely a more perfect knowledge than they were capable in their natures to receive a communication of. 'All things are open to him,' Heb. iv. 13. The least fibre in its nakedness and distinct frame is transparent to him; as by the help of glasses, the mouth, feet, hands of a small insect are visible to a man, which seem to the eye, without that assistance, one entire piece, not diversified into parts. All the causes, qualities, natures, properties of things are open to him: 'He brings out the host of heaven by number, and calleth them by names,' Isa. xl. 26. He numbers the hairs of our heads; what more distinct than number? Thus God beholds things in every unity, which makes up the heap. He knows, and none else can, everything in its true and intimate causes, in its original and intermediate causes; in himself as the cause of every particular of their being, every property in their being.

Knowledge by the causes is the most noble and perfect knowledge, and most suited to the infinite excellency of the divine being; he created all things, and ordered them to a universal and particular end; he therefore knows the essential properties of everything, every activity of their nature, all their fitness for those distinct ends to which he orders them, and for which he governs and disposeth them, and understands their darkest and most hidden qualities, infinitely clearer than any eye can behold the clear beams of the sun. He knows all things as he made them; he made them distinctly, and therefore knows them distinctly, and that every individual; therefore God is said, Gen. i. 31, to ' see everything that he 'hath made;' he took a review of every particular creature he had made, and upon his view pronounced it good. To pronounce that good, which was not exactly known in every creek, in every mite of its nature, had not consisted with his veracity; for every one that speaks truth ignorantly, that knows not that he speaks truth, is a liar in speaking that'which is true. God knows every act of his own will, whether it be positive or permissive, and therefore every effect of his will. We must needs ascribe to God a perfect knowledge, but a confused knowledge cannot challenge that title. To know things only in a heap is unworthy of the divine perfection; for if God knows his own ends in the creation of things, he knows distinctly the means whereby he will bring them to those ends for which he hath appointed them. No wise man intends an end without a knowledge of the means conducing to that end; an ignorance then of anything in the world, which falls under the nature of a means to a divine end (and there is nothing in the world but doth), would be inconsistent with the perfection of God; it would ascribe to him a blind providence in the world. As there can be nothing imperfect in his being and essence, so there can be nothing imperfect in his understanding and knowledge, and therefore not a confused knowledge, which is an imperfection: ' Darkness and light are both alike to him,' Ps. cxxxix. 12. He sees distinctly into the one as well as the other; what is darkness to us is not so to him.

Prop. 5. God knows all things infallibly. His understanding is infinite in regard of certainty. Every tittle of what he knows is as far from failing, as what he speaks; our Saviour affirms the one, Mat. v. 18. And there is the same reason of the certainty of one as well as the other. His essence is the measure of his knowledge; whence it is as impossible that God should be mistaken in the knowledge of the least thing in the world, as it is that he should be mistaken in his own essence; for, knowing himself comprehensively, he must know all other things infallibly. Since he is essentially omniscient, he is no more capable of error in his understanding, than of imperfection in his essence; his counsels are as unerring as his essence is perfect, and his knowledge as infallible as his essence is free from defect.

Again, since God knows all things with a knowledge of vision, because he wills them, his knowledge must be as infallible as his purpose; now his purpose will certainly be effected: ' What he hath thought shall come to pass, and what he hath purposed shall stand,' Isa. xiv. 24; ' His counsel shall stand, and he will do all his pleasure,' chap. xlvi. 10. There may be interruptions of nature, the foundations of it may be out of course, but there can be no bar upon the author of nature. He hath an infinite power to carry on and perfect the resolves of his own will, he can effect what he pleases by a word. Speech is one of the least motions; yet when God said, ' Let there be light,' ' there was light,' arising from darkness. No reason can be given why God knows a thing to be, but because he infallibly wills it to be.

Again, the schools make this difference between the knowledge of the good and bad angels, that the good are never deceived,* for that is repugnant to their blessed state, for deceit is an evil and an imperfection, inconsistent with that perfect blessedness the good angels are possessed of; and would it

* Suarez, vol. ii. p. 228.

not much more be a stain upon the blessedness of that God, that is blessed for ever, to be subject to deceit? His knowledge, therefore, is not an opinion, for an opinion is uncertain; a man knows not what to think, but leans to one part of the question proposed, rather than to the other. If things did not come to pass, therefore, as God knows them, his knowledge would be imperfect; and since he knows by his essence, his essence also would be imperfect, if God were exposed to any deceit in his knowledge. He knows by himself, who is the highest truth; and therefore it is impossible he should err in his understanding.

Prop. 6. God knows immutably. His understanding else could not be infinite. Every thing and every act that is mutable is finite, it hath its bounds; for there is a term from which it changeth, and a term to which it changes. There is a change in the understanding, when we gain the knowledge of a thing which was unknown to us before, or when we actually consider a thing which we did not know before, though we had the principles of the knowledge of it, or when we know that distinctly which we before knew confusedly.* None of these can be ascribed to God, without a manifest disparagement of his infiniteness. Our knowledge, indeed, is alway arriving to us or flowing from us; we pass from one degree to another, from worse to better, or from better to worse; but God loses nothing by the ages that are run, nor will gain anything by the ages that are to come. If there were a variation in the knowledge of God, by the daily and hourly changes in the world, he would grow wiser than he was; he was not then perfectly wise before. A change in the objects known, infers not any change in the understanding exercised about them. The wheel moves round: the spokes that are lowest are presently highest, and presently return to be low again; but the eye that beholds them changes not with the motion of the wheels. God's knowledge admits no more of increase or decrease than his essence doth. Since God knows by his essence, and the essence of God is God himself, his knowledge must be void of any change. The knowledge of possible things, arising from the knowledge of his own power, cannot be changed unless his power be changed, and God become weak and impotent. The knowledge of future things cannot be changed, because that knowledge ariseth from his will, which is irreversible: 'The counsel of the Lord, that shall stand,' Prov. xix. 21. So that if God can never decay into weakness, and never turn to inconstancy, there can be no variation of his knowledge. He knows what he can do, and he knows what he will do, and both these being immutable, his knowledge must consequently be so too. It was not necessary that this or that creature should be, and therefore it was not necessary that God should know this or that creature with a knowledge of vision; but after the will of God had determined the existence of this or that creature, his knowledge being then determined to this or that object, did necessarily continue unchangeable. God therefore knows no more now than he did before; and at the end of the world, he shall know no more than he doth now; and from eternity he knows no less than he doth now, and shall do to eternity. Though things pass into being and out of being, the knowledge of God doth not vary with them, for he knows them as well before they were as when they are, and knows them as well when they are past, as when they are present.

Prop. 7. God knows all things perpetually, *i. e.* in act. Since he knows by his essence, he always knows, because his essence never ceaseth, but is a pure act; so that he doth not know only in habit, but in act. Men that have the knowledge of some art or science, have it always in habit, though,

---

* Tileni Syntagma, part. i. disp. xiii. thes. 13.

when they are asleep, they have it not in act. A musician hath the habit of music, but doth not so much as think of it when his senses are bound up. But God is an unsleepy eye,* he never slumbers nor sleeps; he never slumbers in regard of his providence, and therefore never slumbers in regard of his knowledge. He knows not himself, nor any other creature, more perfectly at one time than at another; he is perpetually in the act of knowing, as the sun is in the act of shining. The sun never ceased to shine, in one or other part of the world, since it was first fixed in the heavens, nor God to be in the act of knowledge, since he was God; and therefore, since he always was, and always will be God, he always was, and always will be, in the act of knowledge. Always knowing his own essence, he must always actually know what hath been gone and ceased from being, and what shall come and arise into being. As a watchmaker knows what watch he intends to make, and after he hath made it, though it be broken to pieces or consumed by the fire, he still knows it, because he knows the copy of it in his own mind. Some, therefore, in regard of this perpetual act of the divine knowledge, have called God not *intellectus*, but 'the intellection of intellections' (we have no proper English word to express the act of the understanding). As his power is co-eternal with him, so his knowledge; all times past, present, and to come, are embraced in the bosom of his understanding; he fixed all things in their seasons, that nothing new comes to him, nothing old passes from him.† What is done in a thousand years, is as actually present with his knowledge, as what is done in one day, or in one watch in the night, is with ours, since 'a thousand years are no more to God than a day, or a watch in the night' is to us, Ps. xc. 4. God is in the highest degree of being, and therefore in the highest degree of understanding. Knowledge is one of the most perfect acts in any creature. God therefore hath all actual, as well as essential and habitual, knowledge: 'His understanding is infinite.'

IV. The fourth general is, reasons to prove this.

Reas. 1. God must know what any creature knows, and more than any creature knows. There is nothing done in the world, but is known by some creature or other; every action is at least known by the person that acts, and therefore known by the Creator, who cannot be exceeded by any of the creatures, or all of them together; and every creature is known by him, since every creature is made by him. And as God works all things by an infinite power, so he knows all things by an infinite understanding.‡

The perfection of God requires this.§ All perfections that include no essential defect are formally in God; but knowledge includes no essential defect in itself, therefore it is in God. Knowledge in itself is desirable, and an excellency; ignorance is a defect. It is impossible that the least grain of defect can be found in the most perfect being. Since God is wise, he must be knowing, for wisdom must have knowledge for the basis of it. A creature can no more be wise without knowledge, than he can be active without strength. Now God is 'only wise,' Rom. xvi. 27, and therefore only knowing in the highest degree of knowledge, incomprehensibly beyond all degrees of knowledge, because infinite.

Again, the more spiritual anything is, the more understanding it is. The dull body understands nothing: sense perceives, but the understanding faculty is seated in the soul, which is of a spiritual nature, which knows things that are present, remembers things that are past, foresees many things to come. What is the property of a spiritual nature, must be in a most

---

* Plato, ἀκοίμητος ὀφθαλμός.   † Damianus.   ‡ Gerhard.
§ Gamach. in part i. Aquin. qu. xiv. cap. i. p. 118, 119.

eminent manner in the supreme Spirit of the world; that is, in the highest degree of spirituality, and most remote from any matter.

Again, nothing can enjoy other things but by some kind of understanding them. God hath the highest enjoyment of himself, of all things he hath created, of all the glory that accrues to him by them; nothing of perfection and blessedness can be wanting to him. Felicity doth not consist with ignorance, and all imperfect knowledge is a degree of ignorance. God therefore doth perfectly know himself, and all things from whence he designs any glory to himself. The most noble manner of acting must be ascribed to God, as being the most noble and excellent being. To act by knowledge is the most excellent manner of acting; God hath therefore not only knowledge, but the most excellent manner of knowledge; for as it is better to know than to be ignorant, so it is better to know in the most excellent manner than to have a mean and low kind of knowledge. His knowledge, therefore, must be every way as perfect as his essence, infinite as well as that. An infinite nature must have an infinite knowledge. A God ignorant of anything cannot be counted infinite, for he is not infinite to whom any degree of perfection is wanting.

2. All the knowledge in any creature is from God; and you must allow God a greater and more perfect knowledge than any creature hath, yea, than all creatures have. All the drops of knowledge any creature hath come from God, and all the knowledge in every creature that ever was, is, or shall be in the whole mass, was derived from him. If all those several drops in particular creatures were collected into one spirit, into one creature, it would be an unconceivable knowledge, yet still lower than what the author of all that knowledge hath; for God cannot give more knowledge than he hath himself, nor is the creature capable of receiving so much knowledge as God hath. As the creature is uncapable of receiving so much power as God hath, for then it would be almighty, so it is uncapable of receiving so much knowledge as God hath, for then it would be God. Nothing can be made by God equal to him in anything; if anything could be made as knowing as God, it would be eternal as God, it would be the cause of all things as God. The knowledge that we poor worms have is an argument God uses for the asserting the greatness of his own knowledge: Ps. xciv. 10, 'He that teaches man knowledge, shall not he know?' Man hath here knowledge ascribed to him; the author of this knowledge is God; he furnished him with it, and therefore doth in a higher manner possess it, and much more than can fall under the comprehension of any creature; as the sun enlightens all things, but hath more light in itself than it darts upon the earth or the heavens; and shall not God eminently contain all that knowledge he imparts to the creatures, and infinitely more exact and comprehensive?

3. The accusations of conscience evidence God's knowledge of all actions of all his creatures. Doth not conscience check for the most secret sins, to which none are privy but a man's self, the whole world beside being ignorant of his crime? Do not the fears of another judge gall the heart? If a judgment above him be feared, an understanding above him discerning their secrets is confessed by those fears. Whence can those horrors arise, if there be not a Superior that understands and records the crime? What perfection of the divine Being can this relate unto but omniscience? What other attribute is to be feared, if God were defective in this?

The condemnation of us by our own hearts, when none in the world can condemn us, renders it legible that there is one 'greater than our hearts' in respect of knowledge, who 'knows all things,' 1 John iii. 20. Conscience would be a vain principle, and stingless without this. It would be an easy matter to silence all its accusations, and mockingly laugh in the face of its severest frowns. What need any trouble themselves, if none knows their crimes but themselves ? Concealed sins, gnawing the conscience, are arguments of God's omniscience of all present and past actions.

4. God is the first cause of everything; every creature is his production. Since all creatures, from the highest angel to the lowest worm, exist by the power of God, if God understands his own power and excellency, nothing can be hid from him that was brought forth by that power, as well as nothing can be unknown to him that that power is able to produce.* If God knows nothing besides himself, he may then believe there is nothing besides himself. We shall then fancy a God miserably mistaken. If he knows nothing besides himself, then things were not created by him, or not understandingly and voluntarily created, but dropped from him before he was aware. To think that the first cause of all should be ignorant of those things he is the cause of, is to make him not a voluntary, but natural agent, and therefore necessary; and then that the creature came from him as light from the sun and moisture from the water ; this would be an absurd opinion of the world's creation. If God be a voluntary agent, as he is, he must be an intelligent agent. The faculty of will is not in any creature without that of understanding also. If God be an intelligent agent, his knowledge must extend as far as his operation, and every object of his operation, unless we imagine God hath lost his memory in that long tract of time since the first creation of them. An artificer cannot be ignorant of his own work. If God knows himself, he knows himself to be a cause. How can he know himself to be a cause, unless he know the effects he is the cause of ? One relation implies another. A man cannot know himself to be a father unless he hath a child, because it is a name of relation, and in the notion of it refers to another. The name of cause is a name of relation, and implies an effect. If God, therefore, know himself in all his perfections as the cause of things, he must know all his acts, what his wisdom contrived, what his counsel determined, and what his power effected. The knowledge of God is to be supposed in a free determination of himself; and that knowledge must be perfect both of the object, act, and all the circumstances of it. How can his will freely produce anything that was not first known in his understanding ? From this the prophet argues the understanding of God, and the unsearchableness of it, because he is the ' Creator of the ends of the earth,' Isa. xl. 28 ; and the same reason David gives of God's knowledge of him, and of everything he did, and that afar off, because he was formed by him, Ps. cxxxix. 2, 15, 16. As the perfect making of things only belongs to God, so doth the perfect knowledge of things. It is absurd to think that God should be ignorant of what he hath given being to ; that he should not know all the creatures and their qualities, the plants and their virtues, as that a man should not know the letters that are formed by him in writing. Everything bears in itself the mark of God's perfections, and shall not God know the representation of his own virtue ?

5. Without this knowledge God could no more be the governor than he could be the creator of the world. Knowledge is the basis of providence ; to know things is before the government of things ; a practical knowledge cannot be without a theoretical knowledge. Nothing could be directed to its proper end without the knowledge of the nature of it, and its suitableness to answer that end for which it is intended. As everything, even the minutest, falls under the conduct of God, so everything falls under the knowledge of God. A blind coachman is not able to hold the reins of his horses, and

* Bradwardine, p. 6.

direct them in right paths. Since the providence of God is about particulars, his knowledge must be about particulars; he could not else govern them in particular, nor could all things be said to depend upon him in their being and operations. Providence depends upon the knowledge of God, and the exercise of it upon the goodness of God; it cannot be without understanding and will: understanding to know what is convenient, and will to perform it. When our Saviour therefore speaks of providence, he intimates these two, in a special manner, 'Your heavenly Father knows that you have need of these things,' Mat. vi. 32, and goodness, in Luke xi. 13. The reason of providence is so joined with omniscience that they cannot be separated. What a kind of God would he be that were ignorant of those things that were governed by him! The ascribing this perfection to him asserts his providence, for it is as easy for one that knows all things to look over the whole world, if writ with monosyllables in every little particular of it, as it is with a man to take a view of one letter in an alphabet.

Again,* if God were not omniscient, how could he reward the good, and punish the evil? The works of men are either rewardable or punishable, not only according to their outward circumstances, but inward principles and ends, and the degrees of venom lurking in the heart. The exact discerning of these, without a possibility to be deceived, is necessary to pass a right and infallible judgment upon them, and proportion the censure and punishment to the crime. Without such a knowledge and discerning men would not have their due; nay, a judgment, just for the matter, would be unjust in the manner, because unjustly past, without an understanding of the merit of the cause. It is necessary therefore that the supreme Judge of the world should not be thought to be blindfold when he distributes his rewards and punishments, and muffle his face when he passes his sentence. It is necessary to ascribe to him the knowledge of men's thoughts and intentions, the secret wills and aims, the hidden works of darkness in every man's conscience, because every man's work is to be measured by the will and inward frame. It is necessary that he should perpetually retain all those things in the indelible and plain records of his memory, that there may not be any work without a just proportion of what is due to it. This is the glory of God, to discover the secrets of all hearts at last; as, 1 Cor. iv. 5, 'The Lord shall bring to light the hidden things of darkness, and will make manifest the counsels of all hearts, and then shall every man have praise of God.' This knowledge fits him to be a judge; the reason why 'the ungodly shall not stand in judgment' is because God knows their ways, which is implied in his 'knowing the way of the righteous,' Ps. i. 5, 6.

V. I now proceed to the use.

Use 1. is of information or instruction. If God hath all knowledge, then,

1. Jesus Christ is not a mere creature. The two titles of 'wonderful Counsellor' and 'mighty God' are given him in conjunction, Isa. ix. 6; not only the 'angel of the covenant,' as he is called, Mal. iii. 1, or the executor of his counsels, but a counsellor, in conjunction with him in counsel, as well as power. This title is superior to any title given to any of the prophets in regard of their predictions, and therefore I should take it rather as the note of his perfect understanding than of his perfect teaching and discovering, as Calvin doth. He is not only the revealer of what he knows,—so were the prophets according to their measures,—but the counsellor of what he revealed, having a perfect understanding of all the counsels of God, as being interested in them as the mighty God. He calls himself by the peculiar

* Sabund, tit. 84, much changed.

title of God, and declares that he will manifest himself by this prerogative to all the churches : Rev. ii. 23, 'And all the churches shall know that I am he which searches the reins and hearts,' the most hidden operations of the minds of men that lie locked up from the view of all the world besides. And this was no new thing to him after his ascension, for the same perfection he had in the time of his earthly flesh : Luke vi. 8, 'he knew their thoughts ;' his eyes are therefore compared, Cant. v. 12, to 'doves' eyes,' which are clear and quick, and to 'a flame of fire,' Rev. i. 14, not only heat to consume his enemies, but light to discern their contrivances against the church.   He pierceth, by his knowledge, into all parts, as fire pierceth into the closest particle of iron, and separates between the most united parts of metals ; and some tell us he is called a roe, from the perspicacity of his sight, as well as from the swiftness of his motion.

(1.) He hath a perfect knowledge of the Father ; he knows the Father, and none else knows the Father ; angels know God, men know God, but Christ in a peculiar manner knows the Father : 'No man knows the Son but the Father, neither knows any man the Father save the Son,' Mat. xi. 27.   He knows, so as that he learns not from any other ; he doth perfectly comprehend him, which is beyond the reach of any creature, with the addition of all the divine virtue ; not because of any incapacity in God, but the incapacity of the creature to receive.   Finite is uncapable of being made infinite, and therefore incapable of comprehending infinite, so that Christ cannot be *deus factus*, made of a creature a god, to comprehend God, for then of finite he would become infinite, which is a contradiction.   As the Spirit is God, because he 'searches the deep things of God,' 1 Cor. ii. 10, that is, comprehends them ;* as the spirit of a man doth the things of a man (now the spirit of man understands what it thinks, and what it wills), so the Spirit of God understands what is in the understanding of God, and what is in the will of God.   He hath an absolute knowledge ascribed to him, and such as could not be ascribed to anything but a divinity.   Now, if the Spirit knows the deep things of God, and takes from Christ what he shews to us of him, John xvi. 15, he cannot be ignorant of those things himself, he must know the depths of God that affords us that Spirit, that is not ignorant of any of the counsels of the Father's will ; since he comprehends the Father, and the Father him, he is in himself infinite, for God, whose essence is infinite, is infinitely knowable, but no created understanding can infinitely know God. The infiniteness of the object hinders it from being understood by anything that is not infinite.   Though a creature should understand all the works of God, yet it cannot be therefore said to understand God himself.   As though I may understand all the volitions and motions of my soul, yet it doth not follow that therefore I understand the whole nature and substance of my soul ; or, if a man understood all the effects of the sun, that therefore he understands fully the nature of the sun.   But Christ knows the Father, he lay 'in the bosom of the Father,' was in the greatest intimacy with him, John i. 18, and, from this intimacy with him, he saw him and knew him ; so he knows God as much as he is knowable, and therefore knows him perfectly, as the Father knows himself by a comprehensive vision.   This is the knowledge of God wherein properly the infiniteness of his understanding appears.   And our Saviour uses such expressions which manifest his knowledge to be above all created knowledge, and such a manner of knowledge of the Father as the Father hath of him.

(2.) Christ knows all creatures.   That knowledge which comprehends God comprehends all created things as they are in God ; it is a knowledge

* Petav. Theol. Dogmat., tom. i. p. 467, &c.

that sinks to the depths of his will, and therefore extends to all the acts of his will in creation and providence. By knowing the Father, he knows all things that are contained in the virtue, power, and will of God; 'whatsoever the Father doth, that the Son doth,' John v. 19. As the Father therefore knows all things he is the cause of, so doth the Son know all things he is the worker of; as the perfect making of all things belongs to both, so doth the perfect knowledge of all things belong to both; where the action is the same, the knowledge is the same. Now, the Father did not create one thing, and Christ another, but 'all things were created by him, and for him,'—all things, 'both in heaven and earth,' Col. i. 16. As he knows himself, the cause of all things, and the end of all things, he cannot be ignorant of all things that were effected by him, and are referred to him. He knows all creatures in God, as he knows the essence of God; and knows all creatures in themselves, as he knows his own acts and the fruits of his power. Those things must be in his knowledge that were in his power; 'all the treasures of the wisdom and knowledge' of God are 'hid in him,' Col. ii. 3. Now it is not the wisdom of God to know in part, and be in part ignorant. He cannot be ignorant of anything, since there is nothing but what was made by him, John i. 3, and since it is less to know than create; for we know many things which we cannot make. If he be the creator, he cannot but be the discerner of what he made; this is a part of wisdom belonging to an artificer, to know the nature and quality of what he makes.* Since he cannot be ignorant of what he furnished with being, and with various endowments, he must know them not only universally, but particularly. .

(3.) Christ knows the hearts and affections of men. Peter scruples not to ascribe to him this knowledge among the knowledge of all other things : John xxi. 17, 'Lord, thou knowest all things; thou knowest that I love thee.' From Christ's knowledge of all things, he concludes his knowledge of the inward frames and dispositions of men. To search the heart is the sole prerogative of God: 1 Kings viii. 39, 'For thou, even thou only, knowest the hearts of all the children of men.' Shall we take *only* here with a limitation, as some that are no friends to the deity of Christ would, and say, God only knows the hearts of men from himself and by his own infinite virtue? Why may we not take *only* in other places with a limitation, and make nonsense of it, as Ps. lxxxvi. 10, 'thou art God alone'? Is it to be understood that God is God alone from himself, but other gods may be made by him, and so there may be numberless infinities? As God is God alone, so that none can be God but himself, so he alone knows all the hearts of all the children of men, and none but he can know them; this knowledge is from his nature.† The reason why God knows the hearts of men is rendered in the Scripture double, because he created them, and because he is present everywhere, Ps. xxxiii. 13, 15. These two are by the confession of Christians and pagans universally received as the proper characters of divinity, whereby the Deity is distinguished from all creatures. Now when Christ ascribes this to himself, and that with such an emphasis, that nothing greater than that could be urged, as he doth Rev. ii. 23, we must conclude that he is of the same essence with God, one with him in his nature, as well as one with him in his attributes. God only knows the hearts of the children of men: there is the unity of God; Christ searches the hearts and reins; there is a distinction of persons in an oneness of essence. He knows the hearts of all men, not only of those that were with him in the time of the flesh, that have been and shall be since his ascension, but of those that

* Petav. Theol. Dogmat., tom. i. p. 467.   † Placeus de deitate Christi.

lived and died before his coming, because he is to be the judge of all that lived before his humiliation on earth as well as after his exaltation in heaven. It pertains to him as a judge to know distinctly the merits of the cause of which he is to judge; and this excellency of searching the hearts is mentioned by himself with relation to his judicial proceeding, I will 'give to every one of you according to your works.' And though a creature may know what is in a man's heart if it be revealed to him, yet such a knowledge is a knowledge only by report, not by inspection; yet this latter is ascribed to Christ: John ii. 24, 25, 'He knew all men, and needed not that any should testify of man: for he knew what was in man;' he looked into their hearts. The evangelist, to allay the amazement of men at his relation of our Saviour's knowledge of the inward falsity of those that made a splendid profession of him, doth not say the Father revealed it to him, but intimates it to be an inseparable property of his nature. No covering was so thick as to bound his eye, no pretence so glittering as to impose upon his understanding. Those that made a profession of him, and could not be discerned by the eye of man from his faithfullest attendants, were in their inside known to him plainer than their outside was to others; and therefore he committed not himself to them, though they seemed to be persuaded to a real belief in his name because of the power of his miracles, and were touched with an admiration of him as some great prophet, and perhaps declared him to be the Messiah, ver. 23.

(4.) He had a foreknowledge of the particular inclinations of men before those distinct inclinations were in actual being in them. This is plainly asserted, John vi. 64, 'But there are some of you that believe not. For Jesus knew from the beginning who they were that believed not, and who should betray him.' When Christ assured them from the knowledge of the hearts of his followers, that some of them were void of that faith they professed, the evangelist, to stop their amazement that Christ should have such a power and virtue, adds, that 'he knew from the beginning;' that he had not only a present knowledge, but a foreknowledge of every one's inclination; he knew not only now and then what was in the hearts of his disciples, but from the beginning of any one's giving up their names to him; he knew whether it were a pretence or sincere, he knew who should betray him, and there was no man's inward affection but was foreseen by him. 'From the beginning,' 'Εξ ἀρχῆς, whether we understand it from the beginning of the world, as when Christ saith concerning divorces, 'from the beginning it was not so;' that is, from the beginning of the world, from the beginning of the law of nature; or from the beginning of their attending him; as it is taken, Luke i. 2, he had a certain prescience of the inward dispositions of men's hearts and their succeeding sentiments. He foreknew the treacherous heart of Judas in the midst of his splendid profession, and discerned his resolution in the root, and his thought in the confused chaos of his natural corruption; he knew how it would spring up before it did spring up, before Judas had any distinct and formal conception of it himself, or before there was any actual preparation to a resolve. Peter's denial was not unknown to him when Peter had a present resolution, and no question spake it in the present sincerity of his soul, never to forsake him; he foreknew what would be the result of that poison which lurked in Peter's nature before Peter himself imagined anything of it; he discerned Peter's apostatising heart when Peter resolved the contrary; our Saviour's prediction was accomplished, and Peter's valiant resolution languished into cowardice.

Shall we then conclude our blessed Saviour a creature, who perfectly and only knew the Father, who knew all creatures, who had all the treasures of wisdom and knowledge, who knew the inward motions of men's hearts by his own virtue, and had not only a present knowledge, but a prescience of them.

2. The second instruction from this position, that God hath an infinite knowledge and understanding. Then there is a providence exercised by God in the world, and that about everything. As providence infers omniscience as the guide of it, so omniscience infers providence as the end of it. What exercise would there be of this attribute but in the government of the world? To this infinite perfection [he] refers, Jer. xvii. 10, 'I the Lord search the heart, I try the reins, to give every man according to his ways, and according to the fruit of his doings.' He searches the heart to reward, he rewards every man according to the rewardableness of his actions. His government therefore extends to every man in the world; there is no heart but he searches, therefore no heart but he governs. To what purpose else would be this knowledge of all his creatures? For a mere contemplation of them? No. What pleasure can that be to God, who knows himself, who is infinitely more excellent than all his creatures? Doth he know them to neglect all care of them? This must be either out of sloth, but how incompatible is laziness to a pure and infinite activity! or out of majesty, but it is no less for the glory of his majesty to conduct them than it was for the glory of his power to erect them into being. He that counts nothing unworthy of his arms to make, nothing unworthy of his understanding to know, why should he count anything unworthy of his wisdom to govern? If he knows them to neglect them, it must be because he hath no will to it, or no goodness for it. Either of these would be a stain upon God; to want goodness is to be evil, and to want will is to be negligent and scornful, which are inconsistent with an infinite active goodness. Doth a father neglect providing for the wants of the family which he knows? or a physician the cure of that disease he understands? God is omniscient, he therefore sees all things; he is good, he doth not therefore neglect anything, but conducts it to the end he appointed it. There is nothing so little that can escape his knowledge, and therefore nothing so little but falls under his providence; nothing so sublime as to be above his understanding, and therefore nothing can be without the compass of his conduct; nothing can escape his eye, and therefore nothing can escape his care; nothing is known by him in vain, as nothing was made by him in vain; there must be acknowledged therefore some end of this knowledge of all his creatures.

3. Hence, then, will follow the certainty of a day of judgment. To what purpose can we imagine this attribute of omniscience, so often declared and urged in Scripture to our consideration, but in order to a government of our practice, and a future trial? Every perfection of the divine nature hath sent out brighter rays in the world than this of his infinite knowledge; his power hath been seen in the being of the world, and his wisdom in the order and harmony of the creatures; his grace and mercy hath been plentifully poured out in the mission of a Redeemer; and his justice hath been elevated by the dying groans of the Son of God upon the cross. But hath his omniscience yet met with a glory proportionable to that of his other perfections? All the attributes of God that have appeared in some beautiful glimmerings in the world, wait for a more full manifestation in glory, as the creatures do for 'the manifestation of the sons of God,' Rom. viii. 19; but especially this, since it hath been less evidenced than others, and as much or more abused than any; it expects, therefore, a public righting in the eye of the world. There have been indeed some few sparks of this perfection sensibly struck out now and then in the world, in some horrors of con-

science, which have made men become their own accusers of unknown crimes, in bringing out hidden wickedness to a public view by various providences. This hath also been the design of sprinklings of judgments upon several generations, as Ps. xc. 7, 8, ' We are consumed by thy anger, and by thy wrath we are troubled. Thou hast set our iniquities before thee, and our secret sins in the light of thy countenance.' The word עֲלֻמֵנוּ signifies youth, as well as secret, *i. e.* sins committed long ago, and that with secresy. By this he hath manifested that secret sins are not hid from his eye. Though inward terrors and outward judgments have been let loose to worry men into a belief of this, yet the corruptions of men would still keep a contrary notion in their minds, that ' God hath forgotten : that he hides his face from transgression, and will not regard their impiety,' Ps. x. 11. There must therefore be a time of trial for the public demonstration of this excellency, that it may receive its due honour by a full testimony, that no secresy can be a shelter from it. As his justice, which consists in giving every one his due, could not be glorified, unless men were called to an account for their actions, so neither would his omniscience appear in its illustrious colours, without such a manifestation of the secret motions of men's hearts, and of villanies done under lock and key, when none were conscious to them but the committers of them. Now the last judgment is the time appointed for the opening of the books, Dan. vii. 10. The book of God's records, and conscience the counterpart, were never fully opened and read before, only now and then some pages turned to in particular judgments ; and out of those books shall men be ' judged according to their works,' Rev. xx. 12. Then shall the defaced sins be brought with all their circumstances to every man's memory ; the counsels of men's hearts fled afar from their present remembrance ; all the habitual knowledge they had of their own actions, shall by God's knowledge of them be excited to an actual review ; and their works not only made manifest to themselves, but notorious to all the world. All the words, thoughts, deeds of men shall be brought forth into the light of their own minds, by the infinite light of God's understanding reflecting on them. His knowledge renders him an unerring witness, as well as his justice a ' swift witness,' Mal. iii. 5 ; a swift witness, because he shall without any circuit, or length of speech, convince their consciences by an inward illumination of them, to take notice of the blackness and deformity of their hearts and works. In all judgments God is somewhat known to be the searcher of hearts ; the time of judgment is the time of his remembrance : Hosea viii. 13, ' Now will he remember their iniquity, and visit their sins ;' but the great instant, or *now*, of the full glorifying it, is the grand day of account. This attribute must have a time for its full discovery ; and no time can be fit for it but a time of a general reckoning. Justice cannot be exercised without omniscience ; for as justice is a giving to every one his due, so there must be knowledge to discern what is due to every man ; the searching the heart is in order to the rewarding the works.

4. This perfection in God gives us ground to believe a resurrection. Who can think this too hard for his power, since not the least atom of the dust of our bodies can escape his knowledge ? An infinite understanding comprehends every mite of a departed carcass ; this will not appear impossible nor irrational to any, upon a serious consideration of this excellency in God. The body is perished, the matter of it hath been since clothed with different forms and figures ; part of it hath been made the body of a worm, part of it returned to the dust that hath been blown away by the wind ; part of it hath been concocted in the bodies of cannibals, fish, ravenous beasts ; the

spirits have evaporated into air, part of the blood melted into water; what then, is the matter of the body annihilated? Is that wholly perished? No; the foundation remains, though it hath put on variety of forms; the body of Abel, the first man that died, nor the body of Adam, are not to this day reduced to nothing. Indeed, the quantity and the quality of those bodies have been lost by various changes they have passed through since their dissolution; but the matter or substance of them remains entire, and is not capable to be destroyed by all those transforming alterations, in so long a revolution of time.

The body of a man in his infancy and his old age, if it were Methuselah's, is the same in the foundation in those multitude of years; though the quantity of it be altered, the quality different, though the colour and other things be changed in it, the matter of this body remains the same among all the alterations after death. And can it be so mixed with other natures and creatures, as that it is past finding out by an infinite understanding? Can any particle of this matter escape the eye of him that makes and beholds all those various alterations, and where every mite of the substance of those bodies is particularly lodged, so as that he cannot compact it together again for a habitation of that soul, that many a year before fled from it? Since the knowledge of God is infinite, and his providence extensive over the least as well as the greatest parts of the world, he must needs know the least as well as the greatest of his creatures in their beginning, progress, and dissolution; all the forms through which the bodies of all creatures roll, the particular instants of time, and the particular place when and where those changes are made, they are all present with him; and therefore when the revolution of time allotted by him for the reunion of souls and deceased bodies is come, it cannot be doubted but out of the treasures of his knowledge he can call forth every part of the matter of the bodies of men, from the first to the last man that expired, and strip it of all those forms and figures which it shall then have, to compact it to be a lodging for that soul which before it entertained; and though the bodies of men have been devoured by wild beasts in the earth, and fish in the sea, and been lodged in the stomachs of barbarous men-eaters, the matter is not lost.* There is but little of the food we take that is turned into the substance of our own bodies; that which is not proper for nourishment, which is the greatest part, is separated and concocted, and rejected; whatsoever objections are made, are answered by this attribute. Nothing hinders a God of infinite knowledge from discerning every particle of the matter, wheresoever it is disposed; and since he hath an eye to discern, and a hand to re-collect and unite, what difficulty is there in believing this article of the Christian faith? He that questions this revealed truth of the resurrection of the body, must question God's omniscience, as well as his omnipotence and power.

5. What semblance of reason is there to expect a justification in the sight of God by anything in ourselves? Is there any action done by any of us, but upon a scrutiny we may find flaws and deficiency in it? What then? Shall not this perfection of God discern them? The motes that escape our eyes cannot escape his: 1 John iii. 20, 'God is greater than our hearts, and knows all things;' so that it is in vain for any man to flatter himself with the rectitude of any work, or enter into any debate with him who can bring a thousand articles against us, out of his own infinite records, unknown to us, and unanswerable by us. If conscience, a representative or counterpart of God's omniscience in our own bosoms, find nothing done by us but in a copy short of the original, and beholds, if not blurs, yet imperfections in

* Daille, Serm. xv. p. 21–24.

the best actions, God must much more discern them. We never knew a copy equally exact with the original. If our own conscience be as a thousand witnesses, the knowledge of God is as millions of witnesses against us. If our corruption be so great, and our holiness so low in our own eyes, how much greater must the one, and how much meaner must the other, appear in the eyes of God! God hath an unerring eye to see, as well as an unspotted holiness to hate, and an unbribable justice to punish; he wants no more understanding to know the shortness of our actions, than he doth holiness to enact, and power to execute his laws. Nay, suppose we could recollect many actions wherein there were no spot visible to us, the consideration of this attribute should scare us from resting upon any or all of them, since it is the Lord that, by a piercing eye, sees and judges according to the heart, and not according to appearance. The least crookedness of a stick, not sensible to an acute eye, yet will appear when laid to the line, and the impurity of a counterfeit metal be manifest when applied to the touchstone; so will the best action of any mere man in the world, when it comes to be measured in God's knowledge by the straight line of his law.

Let every man therefore, as Paul, though he should 'know nothing by himself, think not himself therefore justified;' since it is the Lord, who is of an infinite understanding, that judgeth, 1 Cor. iv. 4. A man may be justified in his own sight, but 'not any living man can be justified in the sight of God,' Ps. cxliii. 2, in his sight, whose eye pierceth into our unknown secrets and frames. It was therefore well answered of a good man upon his death-bed, being asked what he was afraid of: I have laboured, saith he, with all my strength to observe the commands of God; but since I am a man, I am ignorant whether my works are acceptable to God, since God judges in one manner, and I in another manner. Let the consideration therefore of this attribute make us join with Job in his resolution: Job ix. 21, 'Though we were perfect,' yet would we not 'know our own souls.' I would not stand up to plead any of my virtues before God. Let us therefore look after another righteousness, wherein the exact eye of the divine Omniscience, we are sure, can discern no stain or crookedness.

6. What honourable and adoring thoughts ought we to have of God for this perfection! Do we not honour a man that is able to predict? do we not think it a great part of wisdom? Have not all nations regarded such a faculty as a character and a mark of divinity? There is something more ravishing in the knowledge of future things, both to the person that knows them and the person that hears them, than there is in any other kind of knowledge; whence the greatest prophets have been accounted in the greatest veneration, and men have thought it a way to glory to divine and predict. Hence it was that the devils and pagan oracles gained so much credit; upon this foundation were they established, and the enemies of mankind owned for a true god. I say from the prediction of future things, though their oracles were often ambiguous, many times false. Yet those poor heathens framed many ingenious excuses to free their adored gods from the charge of falsity and imposture. And shall we not adore the true God, the God of Israel, the God blessed for ever, for this incommunicable property, whereby he flies above the wings of the wind, the understandings of men and cherubims?

Consider how great it is to know the thoughts, and intentions, and works of one man from the beginning to the end of his life;* to foreknow all these before the being of this man, when he was lodged afar off in the loins of his ancestors, yea, of Adam. How much greater is it to foreknow and know the

* Sabund, Theol. Natural. tit. 84, somewhat changed.

thoughts and works of three or four men, of a whole village or neighbour-hood! It is greater still to know the imaginations and actions of such a multitude of men as are contained in London, Paris, or Constantinople; how much greater still to know the intentions and practices, the clandestine contrivances of so many millions, that have, do, or shall swarm in all quar-ters of the world, every person of them having millions of thoughts, desires, designs, affections, and actions!

Let this attribute, then, make the blessed God honourable in our eyes and adorable in all our affections, specially since it is an excellency which hath so lately discovered itself, in bringing to light the hidden things of darkness, in opening and in part confounding the wicked devices of bloody men. Especially let us adore God for it, and admire it in God, since it is so necessary a perfection, that, without it, the goodness of God had been impotent, and could not have relieved us; for what help can a distressed person expect from a man of the sweetest disposition and the strongest arm, if the eyes which should discover the danger, and direct the defence and rescue, were closed up by blindness and darkness? Adore God for this wonderful perfection.

7. In the consideration of this excellent attribute, what low thoughts should we have of our own knowledge, and how humble ought we to be before God! There is nothing man is more apt to be proud of than his knowledge; it is a perfection he glories in; but if our own knowledge of the little outside and barks of things puffs us up, the consideration of the in-finiteness of God's knowledge should abate the tumour. As our beings are nothing in regard to the infiniteness of his essence, so our knowledge is nothing in regard of the vastness of his understanding. We have a spark of being, but nothing to the heat of the sun; we have a drop of knowledge, but nothing to the divine ocean. What a vain thing is it for a shallow brook to boast of its streams, before a sea whose depths are unfathomable! As it is a vanity to brag of our strength when we remember the power of God, and of our prudence when we glance upon the wisdom of God, so it is no less a vanity to boast of our knowledge when we think of the under-standing and knowledge of God.

How hard is it for us to know anything!* Too much noise deafs us, and too much light dazzles us; too much distance alienates the object from us, and too much nearness bars up our sight from beholding it. When we think ourselves to be near the knowledge of a thing, as a ship to the haven, a puff of wind blows us away, and the object which we desired to know eternally flies from us. We burn with a desire of knowledge, and yet are oppressed with the darkness of ignorance; we spend our days more in dark Egypt than in enlightened Goshen. In what narrow bounds is all the know-ledge of the most intelligent persons included!† How few understand the exact harmony of their own bodies, the nature of the life they have in com-mon with other animals! Who understands the nature of his own faculties, how he knows, and how he wills, how the understanding proposeth, and how the will embraceth, how his spiritual soul is united to his material body, what the nature is of the operation of our spirits? Nay, who understands the nature of his own body, the offices of his senses, the motion of his members, how they come to obey the command of the will, and a thousand other things? What a vain, weak, and ignorant thing is man, when com-pared with God! Yet there is not a greater pride to be found among devils than among ignorant men, with a little, very little, flashy knowledge. Igno-rant man is as proud as if he knew as God!

* Pascal, p 170.   † Amyraut, de Prædest., p. 116, 117, somewhat changed.

As the consideration of God's omniscience should render him honourable in our eyes, so it should render us vile in our own. God, because of his knowledge, is so far from disdaining his creatures, that his omniscience is a minister to his goodness. No knowledge that we are possessed of should make us swell with too high a conceit of ourselves and a disdain of others. We have infinitely more of ignorance than knowledge; let us therefore remember, in all our thoughts of God, that he is God, and we are men, and therefore ought to be humble, as becomes men, and ignorant and foolish men, to be. As weak creatures should lie low before an almighty God, and impure creatures before a holy God, false creatures before a faithful God, finite creatures before an infinite God, so should ignorant creatures before an all-knowing God. All God's attributes teach admiring thoughts of God, and low thoughts of ourselves.

8. It may inform us how much this attribute is injured in the world. The first error after Adam's eating the forbidden fruit was the denial of this, as well as the omnipresence of God: Gen. iii. 10, 'I heard thy voice in the garden, and I hid myself,' as if the thickness of the trees could screen him from the eye of his Creator. And, after Cain's murder, this is the first perfection he affronts: Gen. iv. 9, ' Where is Abel, thy brother ? ' saith God. How roundly doth he answer, ' I know not ! ' as if God were as weak as man, to be put off with a lie. Man doth as naturally hate this perfection as much as he cannot naturally but acknowledge it; he wishes God stripped of this eminency, that he might be incapable to be an inspector of his crimes, and a searcher of the closets of his heart. In wishing him deprived of this, there is a hatred of God himself, for it is a loathing an essential property of God, without which he would be a pitiful governor of the world. What a kind of God should that be, of a sinner's wishing, that had wanted eyes to see a crime, and righteousness to punish it ? The want of the consideration of this attribute is the cause of all sin in the world : Hos. vii. 2, ' They consider not in their hearts that I remember all their wickedness.' They speak not to their hearts, nor make any reflection upon the infiniteness of my knowledge; it is a high contempt of God, as if he were an idol, a senseless stock or stone; in all evil practices this is denied. We know God sees all things, yet we live and walk as if he knew nothing; we call him omniscient, and live as if he were ignorant; we say he is all eye, yet act as if he were wholly blind.

In particular, this attribute is injured, by invading the peculiar rights of it, by presuming on it, and by a practical denial of it.

(1.) By invading the peculiar rights of it.

[1.] By invocation of creatures. Praying to saints, by the Romanists, is a disparagement to this divine excellency; he that knows all things is only fit to have the petitions of men presented to him. Prayer supposeth an omniscient being as the object of it; no other being but God ought to have that honour acknowledged to it, no understanding but his is infinite, no other presence but his is everywhere. To implore any deceased creature for a supply of our wants, is to own in them a property of the Deity, and make them deities that were but men, and increase their glory by a diminution of God's honour, in ascribing that perfection to creatures which belongs only to God. Alas! they are so far from understanding the desires of our souls, that they know not the words of our lips. It is against reason to address our supplications to them that neither understand us nor discern us : Isa. lxiii. 16, ' Abraham is ignorant of us, and Israel acknowledges us not.' The Jews never called upon Abraham, though the covenant was made with him for the whole seed; not one departed saint, for the whole four thousand

years between the creation of the world and the coming of Christ, was ever
prayed to by the Israelites, or ever imagined to have a share in God's
omniscience, so that to pray to St Peter, St Paul, much less to St Roch,
St Swithin, St Martin, St Francis, &c., is such a superstition that hath no
footing in the Scripture.

To desire the prayers of the living, with whom we have a communion,
who can understand and grant our desires, is founded upon a mutual charity;
but to implore persons that are absent, at a great distance from us, with
whom we have not, nor know how to have any commerce, supposeth them
in their departure to have put off humanity, and commenced gods, and endued with some part of the divinity to understand our petitions;* we are,
indeed, to cherish their memories, consider their examples, imitate their
graces, and observe their doctrines; we are to follow them as saints, but
not elevate them as gods, in ascribing to them such a knowledge which is
only the necessary right of their and our common Creator. As the invocation of saints mingles them with Christ in the exercise of his office, so it sets
them equal with God in the throne of his omniscience, as if they had as
much credit with God as Christ in a way of mediation, and as much knowledge of men's affairs as God himself. Omniscience is peculiar to God, and
incommunicable to any creature; it is the foundation of all religion, and
therefore one of the choicest acts of it, viz. prayer and invocation. To
direct our vows and petitions to any else is to invade the peculiarity of this
perfection in God, and to rank some creatures in a partnership with him
in it.

[2.] This attribute is injured by curiosity of knowledge, especially of
future things, which God hath not discovered in natural causes, or supernatural revelation. It is a common error of men's spirits to aspire to know
what God would have hidden, and to pry into divine secrets; and many
men are more willing to remain without the knowledge of those things which
may, with a little industry, be attained, than be divested of the curiosity of
inquiring into those things which are above their reach. It is hence that
some have laid aside the study of the common remedies of nature, to find
out the philosopher's stone, which scarce any ever yet attempted but sunk
in the enterprise. From this inclination to know the most abstruse and
difficult things, it is that the horrors of magic and the vanities of astrology
have sprung, whereby men have thought to find, in a commerce with devils
and the jurisdiction of the stars, the events of their lives, and the disposal
of states and kingdoms.† Hence also arose those multitudes of ways of divi-
nation invented among the heathen, and practised too commonly in these
ages of the world. This is an invasion of God's prerogative, to whom secret
things belong: Deut. xxix. 29, 'Secret things belong unto the Lord our
God, but revealed things belong to us and our children.' It is an intolerable boldness to attempt to fathom those, the knowledge whereof God hath
reserved to himself, and to search that which God will have to surpass our
understandings, whereby we more truly envy God a knowledge superior to
our own, than we in Adam imagined that he envied us. Ambition is the
greatest cause of this, ambition to be accounted some great thing among
men, by reason of a knowledge estranged from the common mass of mankind, but more especially that soaring pride to be equal with God, which
lurks in our nature ever since the fall of our first parents. This is not yet
laid aside by man, though it was the first thing that embroiled the world
with the wrath of God. Some think a curiosity of knowledge was the cause
of the fall of the devils; I am sure it was the foil of Adam, and is yet the

* Daille, Melang. part ii. p. 560, 561.   † Amyraut, Moral. tom. iii. p. 75, &c.

crime of his posterity ; had he been contented to know what God had furnished him with, neither he nor his posterity had smarted under the venom of the serpent's breath.

All curious and bold inquiries into things not revealed are an attempt upon the throne of God, and are both sinful and pernicious, like to glaring upon the sun, where, instead of a greater acuteness, we meet with blindness, and too dearly by * our ignorance in attempting a superfluous knowledge. As God's knowledge is destined to the government of the world, so should ours be to the advantage of the world, and not degenerate into vain speculations.

[3.] This attribute is injured by swearing by creatures. To swear by the name of God in a righteous cause, † when we are lawfully called to it by a superior power, or for the necessary decision of some controversy, for the ends of charity and justice, is an act of religion and a part of worship, founded upon and directed to the honour of this attribute ; by it we acknowledge the glory of his infallible knowledge of all things. But to swear by false gods, or by any creature, is blasphemous ; it sets the creature in the place of God, and invests it in that which is the peculiar honour of the divinity ; for, when any swear truly, they intend the invocation of an infallible witness, and the bringing an undoubted testimony for what they do assert. While any therefore swear by a creature, or a false god, they profess that that creature, or that which they esteem to be a god, is an infallible witness, which to be is only the right of God ; they attribute to the creature that which is the property of God alone, to know the heart, and to be a witness whether they speak true or no, and this was accounted by all nations the true design of an oath. As to swear falsely is a plain denial of the all-knowledge of God, so to swear by any creature is to set the creature upon the throne of God, in ascribing that perfection to the creature which sovereignly belongs to the Creator, for it is not in the power of any to witness to the truth of the heart, but of him that is the searcher of hearts.

[4.] We sin against this attribute by censuring the hearts of others. An open crime indeed falls under our cognisance, and therefore under our judgment ; for whatsoever falls under the authority of man to be punished, falls under the judgment of man to be censured, as an act contrary to the law of God. Yet when a censure is built upon the evil of the act which is obvious to the view, if we take a step farther, to judge the heart and state, we leave the revealed rule of the law, and ambitiously erect a tribunal equal with God's, and usurp a judicial power, pertaining only to the supreme governor of the world ; and consequently pretend to be possessed of this perfection of omniscience, which is necessary to render him capable of the exercise of that sovereign authority. For it is in respect of his dominion that God hath the supreme right to judge ; and in respect of his knowledge that he hath an incommunicable capacity to judge.

In an action that is doubtful, the good or evil whereof depends only upon God's determination, and wherein much of the judgment depends upon the discerning the intention of the agent, we cannot judge any man without a manifest invasion of God's peculiar right. Such actions are to be tried by God's knowledge, not by our surmises. God only is the master in such cases, to whom a person ' stands or falls,' Rom. xiv. 4. Till the true principle and ends of an action be known by the confession of the party acting it, a true judgment of it is not in our power. Principles and ends lie deep and hid from us ; and it is intolerable pride to pretend to have a joint key with God, to open that cabinet which he hath reserved to himself.

Besides the violation of the rule of charity in misconstruing actions,

* Qu. ' buy '?—ED.　　　　　　　† Cajetan, Sum. p. 190.

which may be great and generous in their root and principle, we invade God's right, as if our ungrounded imaginations and conjectures were in joint commission with this sovereign perfection; and thereby we become usurping 'judges of evil thoughts,' James ii. 4. It is therefore a boldness worthy to be punished by the judge, to assume to ourselves the capacity and authority of him who is the only judge. For as the execution of the divine law for the inward violation of it belongs only to God, so is the right of judging a prerogative belonging only to his omniscience; his right is therefore invaded if we pretend to a knowledge of it. This humour of men the apostle checks, when he saith, 1 Cor. iv. 5, 'He that judgeth me is the Lord: therefore judge nothing before the time, until the Lord come, who will manifest the counsels of all hearts.' It is not the time yet for God to erect a tribunal for the trial of men's hearts, and the principles of their actions; he hath reserved the glorious discovery of this attribute for another season. We must not therefore presume to judge of the counsels of men's hearts, till God hath revealed them by opening the treasuries of his own knowledge.

Much less are we to judge any man's final condition. Manasseh may sacrifice to devils, and unconverted Paul tear the church in pieces; but God had mercy on them and called them. The action may be censured, not the state, for we know not whom God may call. In censuring men, we may doubly imitate the devil, in a false accusation of the brethren, as well as in an ambitious usurpation of the rights of God.

(2.) This perfection is injured, by presuming upon it, or making an ill use of it : as in the neglect of prayer for the supply of man's wants, because God knows them already; so that that which is an encouragement to prayer, they make the reason of restraining it before God. Prayer is not to administer knowledge to God, but to acknowledge this admirable perfection of the divine nature. If God did not know, there were indeed no use of prayer; it would be as vain a thing to send up our prayers to heaven, as to implore the senseless statue or picture of a prince for a protection. We pray because God knows, for though he know our wants with a knowledge of vision, yet he will not know them with a knowledge of supply, till he be sought unto, Mat. vi. 32, 33. All the excellencies of God are ground of adoration; and this excellency is the ground of that part of worship we call prayer, Mat. vii. 11. If God be to be worshipped, he is to be called upon : invocations of his name in our necessities is a chief act of worship, whence the temple, the place of solemn worship, was not called the house of sacrifice, but ' the house of prayer.'

Prayer was not appointed for God's information as if he were ignorant, but for the expression of our desires; not to furnish him with a knowledge of what we want, but to manifest to him by some rational sign convenient to our nature, our sense of that want, which he knows by himself. So that prayer is not designed to acquaint God with our wants, but to express the desire of a remedy of our wants. God knows our wants, but hath not made promises barely to our wants but to our asking, that his omniscience in hearing, as well as his sufficiency in supplying, may have a sensible honour in our acknowledgments and receipts. It is therefore an ill use of this excellency of God to neglect prayer to him as needless, because he knows already.

(3.) This perfection of God is wronged by a practical denial of it. It is the language of every sin, and so God takes it when he comes to reckon with men for their impieties. Upon this he charges the greatness of the iniquity of Israel, the overflowing of blood in the land, and the perverseness of the city : 'They say, The Lord hath forsaken the earth, and the Lord sees not,' Ezek. ix. 9. They deny his eyes to see, and his resolution to punish.

[1.] It will appear in forbearing sin from a sense of man's knowledge, not of God's. Open impieties are refrained [from] because of the eye of man ; but secret sins are not checked because of the eye of God. Wickedness is committed in darkness, that is restrained in light ; as if darkness were as great a clog to God's eyes as it is to ours, as though his eyes were muffled with the curtains of the night, Job xxii. 14. This it is likely was at the root of Jonah's flight ; he might have some secret thought that his master's eye could not follow him, as though the close hatches of a ship could secure him from the knowledge of God, as well as the sides of the ship could from the dashing of the waves. What lies most upon the conscience when it is graciously wounded, is least regarded, or contemned when it is basely inclined. David's heart smote him not only for his sin in the gross, but as particularly circumstantiated by the commission of it in the sight of God : Ps. li 4, 'Against thee, thee only, have I sinned, and done this evil in thy sight.' None knew the reason of Uriah's death but myself, and because others knew it not, I neglected any regard to this divine eye. When Jacob's sons used their brother Joseph so barbarously, they took care to hide it from their father, but cast away all thoughts of God, from whom it could not be concealed.

Doth not the presence of a child bridle a man from the act of a longed for sin, when the eye of God is of no force to restrain him ? As if God's knowledge were of less value than the sight of a little boy or girl, as if a child only could see, and God were blind. He that will forbear an unworthy action for fear of an informer, will not forbear it for God ; as if God's omniscience were not as full an intelligencer to him, as man can be an informer to a magistrate. As we acknowledge the power of men seeing us when we are ashamed to commit a filthy action in their view, so we discover * the power of God seeing us when we regard not what we do before the light of his eyes. Secret sins are more against God than open. Open sins are against the law, secret sins are against the law and this prime perfection of his nature. The majesty of God is not only violated, but the omniscience of God disowned, who is the only witness. We must, in all of them, either imagine him to be without eyes to behold us, or without an arm of justice to punish us. And often it is, I believe, in such cases, that if any thoughts of God's knowledge strike upon men, they quickly damp them, lest they should begin to know what they fear, and fear that they might not eat their pleasant sinful morsels.

[2.] It appears in partial confessions before God. As by a free, full, and ingenuous confession we offer a due glory to this attribute, so by a feigned and curtailed confession we deny him the honour of it ; for though by any confession we in part own him to be a sovereign and judge, yet by a half and pared acknowledgment, we own him to be no more than a human and ignorant one. Achan's full confession gave God the glory of his omniscience, manifested in the discovery of his secret crime : Joshua vii. 19, 'And Joshua said to Achan, My son, give glory to the Lord God of Israel, and make confession unto him.' And so, Ps. l. 23, 'Whoso offereth praise glorifieth me,' or confession, as the word signifieth, in which sense I would rather take it, referring to this attribute, which God seems to tax sinners with the denial of, ver. 21, telling them that he would open the records of their sins before them, and indict them particularly for every one. If there-

* Qu. 'disown'?—ED.

fore you would glorify this attribute, which shall one day break open your consciences, offer to me a sincere confession. When David speaks of the happiness of a pardoned man, Ps. xxxii. 1, 2, he adds, 'in whose spirit there is no guile,' not meaning a sincerity in general, but that ingenuity in confessing.* To excuse or extenuate sin, is to deny God the knowledge of the depths of our deceitful hearts. When we will mince it rather than aggravate it, lay it upon the inducements of others when it was the free act of our own wills, study shifts to deceive our judge, this is to 'speak lies of him,' as the expression is, Hosea vii. 13 ; as though he were a God easy to be cheated, and knew no more than we are willing to declare. What did Saul's transferring his sin from himself to the people, 1 Sam. xv. 15, but charge God with a defect in this attribute ? When man could not be like God in his knowledge, he would fancy a God like to him in his ignorance, and imagine a possibility of hiding himself from his knowledge ; and all men tread more or less in their father's steps, and are fruitful to devise distinctions to disguise errors in doctrine, and excuses to palliate errors in practice. This crime Job removes from himself, when he speaks of several acts of his sincerity : 'If I covered my transgression as Adam, by hiding my iniquity in my bosom,' Job xxxi. 33, I hid not any of my sins in my own conscience, but acknowledged God a witness of them, and gave God the glory of his knowledge by a free confession. I did not conceal it from God as Adam did, or as men ordinarily do, as if God could understand no more of their secret crimes than they will let him, and had no more sense of their faults than they would furnish him with. As the first rise of confession is the owning of this attribute (for the justice of God would not scare men, nor the holiness of God awe them without a sense of his knowledge of their iniquities), so to drop out some fragments of confession, discover some sins, and conceal others, is a plain denial of the extensiveness of the divine knowledge.

[3.] It is discovered by putting God off with an outside worship. Men are often flatterers of God, and think to bend him by formal glavering devotions, without the concurrence of their hearts, as though he could not pierce into the darkness of the mind, but did as little know us as one man knows another. There are such things as 'feigned lips,' Ps. xvii. 1 ; a contradiction between the heart and the tongue, a clamour in the voice and scoffing in the soul, a crying to God, 'Thou art my father, the guide of my youth,' and yet speaking and doing evil to the utmost of our power, Jer. iii. 4, 5 ; as if God could be imposed upon by fawning pretences, and, like old Isaac, take Jacob for Esau, and be cozened by the smell of his garments ; as if he could not discern the negro heart under an angel's garb. Thus Ephraim, the ten tribes, apostatised from the true religion, would go with their flocks and their herds to seek the Lord, Hosea v. 6 ; would sacrifice multitudes of sheep and heifers, which was the main outside of the Jewish religion ; only with their flocks and their herds, not with their hearts, with those inward qualifications of deep humiliation and repentance for sin, as though outside appearances limited God's observation, whereas God had told them before that he 'knew Ephraim, and Israel was not hid from him' ver. 3. Thus to do is to put a cheat upon God, and think to blind his all-seeing eye, and therefore it is called deceit : Ps. lxxviii. 36, 'They did flatter him with their mouths.' The word פתה signifies to deceive as well as to flatter ; not that they or any else can deceive God, but it implies an endeavour to deceive him by a few dissembling words and gestures, or an imagination that God was satisfied with bare professions, and would not

* Camero. p. 89, col. 1.

concern himself in a further inquisition. This is an unworthy conceit of God, to fancy that we can satisfy for inward sins, and avert approaching judgments by external offerings, by a loud voice, with a false heart, as if God (like children) would be pleased with the glittering of an empty shell, or the rattling of stones, the chinking of money, a mere voice, and crying without inward frames and intentions of service.

[4.] In cherishing multitudes of evil thoughts. No man but would blush for shame if the base, impure, slovenly thoughts, either in or out of duties of worship, were visible to the understanding of man. How diligent would he be to curb his luxuriant and unworthy fancies, as well as bite in his words; but when we give the reins to the motions of our hearts, and suffer them to run at random without a curb, it is an evidence we are not concerned for their falling under the notice of the eye of God, and it argues a very weak belief of this perfection, or scarce any belief at all. Who can think any man's heart possessed with a sense of this infinite excellency, that suffers his mind, in his meditation on God, to wander into every sty, and be picking up stones upon a dunghill? What doth it intimate but that those thoughts are as invisible or inaudible to God as they are to men without the garments of words?* When a man thinks of obscene things, his own natural notions, if revived, would tell him that God discerns what he thinks, that the depths of his heart are open to him; and the voice of those notions is, deface those vain imaginations out of your minds. But what is done? Men cast away rational light, muster up conceits, that God sees them not, knows them not, and so sink into the puddle of their sordid imaginations as though they remained in darkness to God.

I might further instance,

[5.] In omission of prayer, which arises sometimes from a flat atheism. Who will call upon a God that believes no such being? Or from partial atheism, either a denial of God's sufficiency to help, or of his omniscience to know, as if God were like the statue of Jupiter in Crete, framed without ears.

[6.] In the hypocritical pretences of men to exempt them from the service God calls them to; when men pretend one thing, and intend another. This lurks in the veins sometimes of the best men; sometimes it ariseth from the fear of man, when men are more afraid of the power of man than of dissembling with the Almighty. It will pretend a virtue to cover a secret wile, and 'choose the tongue of the crafty,' as the expression in Job, chap. xv. 5.

The case is plain in Moses, who, when ordered to undertake an eminent service, pretends a want of eloquence, and an ungrateful slowness of speech, Exod. iv. 10. This generous soul, that before was not afraid to discover himself in the midst of Egypt for his countrymen, answers sneakingly to God, and would veil his carnal fear with a pretence of insufficiency and humility. 'Who am I, that I should go unto Pharaoh?' Exod. iii. 11. He could not well allege an inability to go to Pharaoh, since he had had an education in the Egyptian learning, which rendered him capable to appear at court. God at last uncaseth him, and shews it all to be a dissimulation; and whatsoever was the pretence, fear lay at the bottom. He was afraid of his life upon his appearance before Pharaoh, from whose face he had fled upon the slaying the Egyptian, which God intimates to him, Exod. iv. 19, 'Go, and return unto Egypt, for all the men are dead which sought thy life.' What doth this carriage speak, but as if God's eye were not upon our inward parts; as though we could lock him out of our hearts that cannot be shut out from any creek of the hearts of men and angels.

* Drexel Nicetas, lib. ii. cap. x. p. 357.

Use 2. The second use is of comfort. It is a ground of great comfort under the present dispensation wherein we are. We have heard the doctrinal part, and God hath given us the experimental part of it in his special providence this day* upon the stage of world. And blessed be God that he hath given us a ground of comfort without going out of our ordinary course to fetch it, whereby it seems to be peculiarly of God's ordering for us.

1. It is a comfort in all the clandestine contrivances of men against the church. His eyes pierce as far as the depths of hell. Not one of his church's adversaries lies in a mist; all are as plain as the stars which he numbers. 'Mine adversaries are all before thee,' Ps. lxix. 19; more exactly known to thee than I can recount them. It is a prophecy of Christ, wherein Christ is brought in speaking to God, of his own and the church's enemies. He comforts himself with this, that God hath his eye upon every particular person among his adversaries. He knows where they repose themselves when they go out to consult, and when they come in with their resolves. He discerns all the rage that spirits their hearts, in what corner it lurks, how it acts; all the disorders, motions of it, and every object of that rage. He cannot be deceived by the closest and subtilest person. Thus God speaks concerning Sennacherib and his host against Jerusalem, Isa. xxxvii. 28, 29. After he had spoke of the forming of his church and the weakness of it, he adds, 'But I know thy abode, and thy going out and thy coming in, and thy rage against me; because thy rage against me, and thy tumult is come up into mine ears, therefore will I put my hook in thy nose, and my bridle in thy lips, and I will turn thee back,' &c. He knows all the methods of the counsels, the stages they had laid, the manner of execution of their designs, all the ways whither they turned themselves, and would use them no better than men do devouring fish and untamed beasts, with a hook in the nose and a bridle in the mouth. Those statesmen in Isa. xxix. 15, thought their contrivances too deep for God to fathom, and too close for God to frustrate: 'They seek deep to hide their counsels from the Lord; surely your turning of things upside down shall be esteemed as the potter's clay,' of no more force and understanding than a potter's vessel, which understands not its own form wrought by the artificer, nor the use it is put to by the buyer and possessor; or shall be esteemed as a potter's vessel, that can be as easily flung back into the mass from whence it was taken, as preserved in the figure it is now endued with. No secret designer is shrouded from God's sight, or can be sheltered from God's arm. He understands the venom of their hearts better than we can feel it, and discovers their inward fury more plainly than we can see the sting or teeth of a viper when they are opened for mischief; and to what purpose doth God know and see them, but in order to deliver his people from them in his own due time: 'I know their sorrow, and am come down to deliver them,' Exod. iii. 7, 8. The walls of Jerusalem are continually before him; he knows, therefore, all that would undermine and demolish them. None can hurt Zion by any ignorance or inadvertency in God.

It is observable that our Saviour, assuming to himself a different title in every epistle to the seven churches, doth particularly ascribe to himself this of knowledge and wrath in that to Thyatira, an emblem or description of the Romish state: Rev. ii. 19, 'And unto the angel of the church at Thyatira write: These things saith the Son of God, who hath his eyes like to a flame of fire, and his feet like fine brass.' His eyes, like a flame of fire, are of a piercing nature, insinuating themselves into all the pores and parts of the body they encounter with; and his feet, like

* Nov. 1678, when the popish plot was discovered.

brass, to crush them with, is explained, verse 23, ' I will kill her children with death, and all the churches shall know that I am he which searches the reins and the heart : and I will give to every one of you according to your works.' He knows every design of the Romish party, designed by that church of Thyatira.* Jezebel, there, signifies a whorish church, such a church as shall act as Jezebel, Ahab's wife, who was not only a worshipper of idols, but propagated idolatry in Israel, slew the prophets, persecuted Elijah, murdered Naboth, the name whereof signifies *prophecy*, seized upon his possession. And if it be said that, verse 19, this church was commended for her works, faith, patience, it is true Rome did at first strongly profess Christianity, and maintained the interest of it, but afterwards fell into the practice of Jezebel, and committed spiritual adultery. And is she to be owned for a wife that now plays the harlot, because she was honest and modest at her first marriage? And though she shall be destroyed, yet not speedily : † verse 22, ' I will cast her into a bed,' seems to intimate the destruction of Jezebel not to be at once and speedily, but in a lingering way, and by degrees, as sickness consumes a body.

2. This perfection of God fits him to be a special object of trust. If he were forgetful, what comfort could we have in any promise? How could we depend upon him if he were ignorant of our state? His compassions to pity us, his readiness to relieve us, his power to protect and assist us, would be insignificant, without his omniscience to inform his goodness and direct the arm of his power. This perfection is, as it were, God's office of intelligence. As you go to your memorandum-book to know what you are to do, so doth God to his omniscience. This perfection is God's eye, to acquaint him with the necessities of his church, and directs all his other attributes in their exercise for and about his people. You may depend upon his mercy that hath promised, and upon his truth to perform, upon his sufficiency to supply you and his goodness to relieve you, and his righteousness to reward you, because he hath an infinite understanding to know you and your wants, you and your services. And without this knowledge of his, no comfort could be drawn from any other perfection ; none of them could be a sure nail to hang our hopes and confidence upon. This is that the church always celebrated : Ps. cv. 8, ' He hath remembered his covenant for ever, and the word which he hath commanded to a thousand generations ; ' and verse 42, ' He remembered his holy promise ; ' and Ps. cvi. 45, ' He remembered for them his covenant.' He remembers and understands his covenant, therefore his promise to perform it, and therefore our wants to supply them.

3. And the rather, because God knows the persons of all his own. He hath in his infinite understanding the exact number of all the individual persons that belong to him : 2 Tim. ii. 19, ' The Lord knows them that are his.' He knows all things, because he hath created them ; and he knows his people, because he hath not only made them, but also chose them. He could no more choose he knew not what, than he could create he knew not what. He knows them under a double title : of creation, as creatures, in the common mass of creation ; as new creatures, by a particular act of separation. He cannot be ignorant of them in time whom he foreknew from eternity. His knowledge in time is the same he had from eternity. He foreknew them that he intended to give the grace of faith unto ; and he knows them after they believe, because he knows his own act in bestowing grace upon them, and his own mark and seal wherewith he hath stamped

---

* For the evidence of it I refer you to Dr More's Exposition of the Seven Churches, worthy every learned and understanding man's reading, and of every sober Romanist. † Coc. *in loc.*

them. No doubt but he that ' calls the stars of heaven by their names,' Ps. cxlvii. 4, knows the number of those living stars that sparkle in the firmament of his church. He cannot be ignorant of their persons, when he numbers the hairs of their heads, and hath registered their names in the book of life. As he only had an infinite mercy to make the choice, so he only hath an infinite understanding to comprehend their persons. We only know the elect of God by a moral assurance in the judgment of charity, when the conversation of men is according to the doctrine of God. We have not an infallible knowledge of them, we may be often mistaken ; Judas, a devil, may be judged by man for a saint, till he be stripped of his disguise. God only hath an infallible knowledge of them; he knows his own records, and the counterparts in the hearts of his people. None can counterfeit his seal, nor can any raze it out. When the church is either scattered like dust by persecution, or overgrown with superstition and idolatry, that there is scarce any grain of true religion appearing, as in the time of Elijah, who complained that he was left alone, as if the church had been rooted out of that corner of the world, 1 Kings xix. 14, 18, yet God knew that he had a number fed in a cave, and had reserved ' seven thousand men ' that had preserved the purity of his worship, and ' not bowed their knee to Baal.' * Christ knew his sheep as well as he is known of them, yea, better than they can know him. History acquaints us that Cyrus had so vast a memory that he knew the name of every particular soldier in his army, which consisted of divers nations. Shall it be too hard for an infinite understanding to know every one of that host that march under his banners ? May he not as well know them as know the number, qualities, influences of those stars which lie concealed from our eye, as well as those that are visible to our sense ? Yes, he knows them, as a general, to employ them, as a shepherd, to preserve them. He knows them in the world to guard them, and he knows them, when they are out of the world, to gather them, and cull out their bodies, though wrapped up in a cloud of the putrified carcasses of the wicked. As he knew them from all eternity to elect them, so he knows them in time to clothe their persons with righteousness, to protect their persons in calamity, according to his good pleasure, and at last to raise, and reward them according to his promise.

4. We may take comfort from hence, that our sincerity cannot be unknown to an infinite understanding. Not a way of the righteous is concealed from him, and therefore they shall ' stand in judgment before him.' Ps. i. 6, ' The Lord knows the way of the righteous ;' he knows them to observe them, and he knows them to reward them. How comfortable is it to appeal to this attribute of God for our integrity, with Hezekiah : 2 Kings xx. 3, ' Remember, Lord, how I have walked before thee in truth, and with a perfect heart.' Christ himself is brought in this prophetical psalm drawing out the comfort of this attribute : Ps. xl. 9, ' I have not refrained my lips, O Lord, thou knowest,' meaning his faithfulness in declaring the righteousness of God. Job follows the same steps : ' Also now, behold, my record is in heaven, and my witness is on high,' Job xvi. 19; my innocence hath the testimony of men, but my greatest support is in the records of God. *Also now*, or besides the testimony of my own heart, I have another witness in heaven that knows the heart, and can only judge of the principles of my actions, and clear me from the scorn of my friends, and the accusations of men, with a justification of my innocence. He repeats it twice, to take the greater comfort in it. God knows that we do that in the simplicity of our hearts, which may be judged by men to be done for

* Turrettine's Sermons, p. 362.

unworthy and sordid ends. He knows not only the outward action, but the inward affection, and praises that which men often dispraise; and writes down that with an *euge*, 'Well done, good and faithful servant,' which men daub with their severest censures, Rom. ii. 29. How refreshing is it to consider that God never mistakes the appearance for reality, nor is led by the judgment of man! He sits in heaven, and laughs at their follies and censures. If God had no sounder and no more piercing a judgment than man, woe be to the sincerest souls, that are often judged hypocrites by some. What a happiness is it for integrity to have a judge of infinite understanding, who will one day wipe off the dirt of worldly reproaches!

'Again, God knows the least dram of grace and righteousness in the hearts of his people, though but as a 'smoking flax,' or as the least bruise of a saving conviction, Mat. xii. 20, and knows it so as to cherish it. He knows that work he hath begun, and never hath his eye off from it to abandon it.

5. The consideration of this excellent perfection in God may comfort us in our secret prayers, sighs, and works. If God were not of infinite understanding, to pierce into the heart, what comfort hath a poor creature that hath a scantiness of expressions, but a heart in a flame? If God did not understand the heart, faith and prayer, which are internal works, would be in vain. How could he give that mercy our hearts plead for, if he were ignorant of our inward affections? Hypocrites might scale heaven by lofty expressions, and a sincere soul come short of the happiness he is prepared for, for want of flourishing gifts. Prayer is an internal work, words are but the garment of prayer; meditation is the body, and affections the soul and life, of prayer: 'Give ear to my words, O Lord; consider my meditation,' Ps. v. 1. Prayer is a rational act, an act of the mind, not the act of a parrot; prayer is an act of the heart, though the speaking prayer is the work of the tongue. Now, God gives ear to the words, but he considers the meditation, the frame of the heart. Consideration is a more exact notice than hearing, the act only of the ear. Were not God of an infinite understanding, an omniscient, he might take fine clothes, a heap of garments, for the man himself, and be put off by glittering words, without a spiritual frame. What matter of rejoicing is it, that we call not upon a deaf and ignorant idol, but on one that listens to our secret petitions to give them a despatch, that knows our desires afar off, and from the infiniteness of his mercy, joined with his omniscience, stands ready to give us a return! Hath he not a book of remembrance for them that fear him, and for their sighs and ejaculations to him as well as their discourses of him, Mal. iii. 16; and not only what prayers they utter, but what gracious and holy thoughts they have of him, 'that thought upon his name'? Though millions of supplications be put up at the same time, yet they have all a distinct file (as I may say) in an infinite understanding, which perceives and comprehends them all. As he observes millions of sins committed at the same time by a vast number of persons, to record them in order to punishment, so he distinctly discerns an infinite number of cries at the same moment to register them in order to an answer.

A sigh cannot escape an infinite understanding, though crowded among a mighty multitude of cries from others, or covered with many unwelcome distractions in ourselves, no more than a believing touch from the woman that had the bloody issue could be concealed from Christ, and be undiscerned from the press of the thronging multitudes. Our groans are as audible and intelligible to him as our words, and he knows what is the mind of his own Spirit, though expressed in no plainer language than sobs and heavings,

Rom. viii. 27. Thus David cheers up himself under the neglects of his friends: Ps. xxxviii. 9, 'Lord, my desire is before thee; and my groaning is not hid from thee.' Not a groan of a panting spirit shall be lost till God hath lost his knowledge, not a petition forgotten while God hath a record, nor a tear dried while God hath a bottle to reserve it in, Ps. lvi. 8.

Our secret works are also known and observed by him, not only our outward labour, but our inward love in it, Heb. vi. 10. If with Isaac we go privately into the field to meditate, or secretly 'cast our bread upon the waters,' he keeps his eye upon us to reward us, and returns the fruit into our own bosoms, Mat. vi. 4, 6; yea, though it be but a cup of cold water, from an inward spring of love given to a disciple. He sees your works and your labours, and faith and patience in working them, Rev. ii. 2, all the marks of your industry, and strength of your intentions, and will be as exact at last in order to a due praise, as to open sins in order to a just recompence, 1 Cor. iv. 5.

6. The consideration of this excellent attribute affords comfort in the afflictions of good men. He knows their pressures, as well as hears their cries, Exod. iii. 7. His knowledge comes not by information from us, but his compassionate listening to our cries springs from his own inspection into our sorrows; he is affected with them before we make discovery of them. He is not ignorant of the best season, when they may be usefully inflicted, and when they may be profitably removed. The tribulation and poverty of his church is not unknown to him: Rev. ii. 8, 9, 'I know thy works and tribulation,' &c. He knows their works, and what tribulation they meet with for him; he sees their extremities, when they are toiling against the wind and tide of the world, Mark vi. 48; yea, the natural exigencies of the multitude are not neglected by him, he discerns to take care of them. Our Saviour considered the three days' fasting of his followers, and miraculously provides a dish for them in the wilderness. No good man is ever out of God's mind, and therefore never out of his compassionate care; his eye pierceth into their dungeons, and pities their miseries. Joseph may forget his brethren, and the disciples not know Christ when he walks upon the midnight waves and turbulent sea,* but a lion's den cannot obscure a Daniel from his sight, nor the depths of the whale's belly bury Jonah from the divine understanding. He discerns Peter in his chains, and Stephen under the stones of martyrdom; he knows Lazarus under his tattered rags, and Abel wallowing in his blood; his eye and knowledge goes along with his people when they are transplanted into foreign countries, and sold for slaves into the islands of the Grecians; for 'he will raise them out of the place,' Joel iii. 6, 7. He would defeat the hopes of the persecutors, and applaud the patience of his people. He knows his people in the tabernacle of life, and in the 'valley of the shadow of death,' Ps. xxiii. He knows all penal evils, because he commissions and directs them. He knows the instruments, because they are his sword, Ps. xvii. 13; and he knows his gracious sufferer, because he hath his mark. He discerns Job in his anguish, and the devil in his malice. By the direction of this attribute he orders calamities, and rescues from them: 'Thou hast seen it, for thou beholdest mischief and spite,' Ps. x. 14. That is the comfort of the psalmist, and the comfort of every believer, and the ground of committing themselves to God under all the injustice of men.

7. It is a comfort in all our infirmities. As he knows our sins to charge them, so he knows the weakness of our nature to pity us. As his infinite understanding may scare us, because he knows our transgressions, so it may

* Barlow's Man's Refuge, p. 29, 30.

relieve us, because he knows our natural mutability in our first creation : ' He knows our frame, he remembers that we are dust,' Ps. ciii. 14.   It is the reason of the precedent verses, why he removes our transgression from us, why he is so backward in punishing, so patient in waiting, so forward in pitying; why ?   He doth not only remember our sins, but remember our frame or forming, what brittle, though clear glasses we are by creation, how easy to be cracked.   He remembers our impotent and weak condition by corruption ; what a sink we have of vain imaginations that remain in us after regeneration ; he doth not only consider that we were made according to his image, and therefore able to stand, but that we were made of dust and weak matter, and had a sensitive soul, like that of beasts, as well as an intellectual nature, like that of angels, and therefore liable to follow the dictates of it without exact care and watchfulness.   If he remembered only the first, there would be no issue but indignation ; but the consideration of the latter moves his compassion.   How miserable should we be for want of this perfection in the divine nature, whereby God remembers and reflects upon his past act in our first frame, and the mindfulness of our condition excites the motion of his bowels to us !   Had he lost the knowledge how he first framed us, did he not still remember the mutability of our nature as we were formed and stamped in his mint, how much more wretched would our condition be than it is !   If his remembrance of our original be one ground of his pity, the sense of his omniscience should be a ground of our comfort in the stirring of our infirmities ; he remembers we were but dust when he made us, and yet remembers we are but dust while he preserves and forbears us.

8. It is some comfort in the fears of some lurking corruption in our hearts.   We know by this whither to address ourselves for the search and discovery of it.   Perhaps some blessings we want are retarded, some calamities we understand not the particular cause of are inflicted, some petitions we have put up hang too long for an answer, and the chariot wheels of divine goodness move slow, and are long in coming.   Let us beg the aid of this attribute to open to us the *remoras*, to discover what base affection there is that retards the mercies we want, or attracts the affliction we feel, or bars the door against the return of our supplications.   What our dim sight cannot discover, the clear eye of God can make visible to us.   Job x. 2, ' Shew me wherefore thou contendest with me.'   As in want of pardon, we particularly plead his mercy, and in our desires for the performance of his promise we argue with him from his faithfulness, so in the fear of any insincerity or hidden corruption we should implore his omniscience.   For as God is a God in covenant, our God, our God in the whole of his nature, so the perfections of his nature are employed in their several stations as assistances of his creatures.   This was David's practice and comfort.   After that large meditation on the omniscience and omnipresence of God, he turns his thoughts of it into petitions for the employment of it in the concerns of his soul, and begs a mercy suitable to the glory of this perfection: Ps. cxxxix. 23, ' Search me, O God, and try my heart ; try me, and know my thoughts ;' dive to the bottom : ver. 24, ' And see if there be any wicked way in me, and lead me in the way everlasting.'   His desire is not barely that God should know him, for it would be senseless to beg of God that he should have mercy, or faithfulness, or power, or knowledge in his nature ; but he desires the exercise of this attribute in the discovery of himself to himself, in order to his sight of any wicked way, and humiliation for it, and reformation of it in order to his conduct to everlasting life.   As we may appeal to this perfection to judge us, when the sincerity of our actions is censured by

others, so we may implore it to search us when our sincerity is questioned by ourselves, that our minds may be enlightened by a beam from his knowledge, and the little thieves may be pulled out of their dens in our hearts by the hand of his power. In particular, it is our comfort that we can, and our necessity that we must, address particularly to this, when we engage solemnly in a work of self-examination ; that we may have a clearer eye to direct us than our own, that we may not mistake brass for gold, or counterfeit graces for true ; that nothing that is filthy and fit to be cast out may escape our sight, and preserve its stations. And we need not question the laying at the door of this neglect (viz., not calling in this attribute to our aid, whose proper office it is, as I may so say, to search and inquire) all the mistakes, ill success, and fruitlessness of our endeavours in self-examination, because we would engage in it in the pitiful strength of our own dimness, and not in the light of God's countenance, and the assistance of his eye, which can discern what we cannot see, and discover that to us which we cannot manifest to ourselves. It is a comfort to a learner of an art, to have a skilful eye to overlook his work, and inform him of the defects. Beg the help of the eye of God in all your searches and self-examinations.

9. The consideration of this attribute is comfortable in our assurances of, and reflections upon, the pardon of sin, or seeking of it. As God punishes men for sin according to his knowledge of them, which is greater than the knowledge their own consciences have of them, so he pardons according to his knowledge. He pardons not only according to our knowledge, but according to his own. He is greater than any man's heart, to condemn for that which a man is at present ignorant of, and greater than our hearts, to pardon that which is not at present visible to us ; he knows that which the most watchful conscience cannot take a survey of. If God had not an infinite understanding of us, how could we have a perfect and full pardon from him ? It would not stand with his honour to pardon he knew not what. He knows what crimes we have to be pardoned, when we know not all of them ourselves, that stand in need of a gracious remission ; his omniscience beholds every sin, to charge it upon our Saviour. If he knows our sins that are black, he knows every mite of Christ's righteousness, which is pure, and the utmost extent of his merits, as well as the demerit of our iniquities. As he knows the filth of our sin, he also knows the covering of our Saviour ; he knows the value of the Redeemer's sufferings, and exactly understands every plea in the intercession of our advocate. Though God knows our sins *oculo indice*, yet he doth not see them *oculo judice*, with a judicial eye. His omniscience stirs not up his justice to revenge, but his mercy to pity. His infinite understanding of what Christ hath done directs him to disarm his justice, and sound an alarm to his bowels. As he understands better than we what we have committed, so he understands better than we what our Saviour hath merited, and his eye directs his hand in the blotting out guilt, and applying the remedy.

Use 3. The third use shall be to sinners to humble them, and put them upon serious consideration. This attribute speaks terrible things to a profligate sinner. Basil thinks that the ripping open the sins of the damned to their faces by this perfection of God is more terrible than their other torments in hell. God knows the persons of wicked men, not one is exempted from his eye, he sees all the actions of men as well as he knows their persons : Job xi. 11, 'He knows vain men, he sees wickedness also.' Job xxxiv. 21, 'His eye is upon all their goings.' He hears the most private whispers, Ps. cxxxix. 4 ; the scope, manner, circumstance of speaking he knows it altogether; 'he understands all our thoughts,' the first bubblings of that bitter spring, ver. 2. The quickest glances of the fancy, the closest musings of the mind, and the abortive wouldings or wishes of the will, the language of the heart as well as the language of the tongue; not a foolish thought or an idle word, not a wanton glance or a dishonest action; not a negligent service, or a distracting fancy, but is more visible to him than the filth of a dunghill can be to any man by the help of a sunbeam. How much better would it be for desperate sinners to have their crimes known to all angels in heaven, and men upon earth, and devils in hell, than that they should be known to their sovereign, whose laws they have violated, and to their judge, whose righteousness obligeth him to revenge the injury!

1. Consider, what a poor refuge is secrecy to a sinner! Not the mists of a foggy day, not the obscurity of the darkest night, not the closest curtains, nor the deepest dungeon, can hide any sin from the eye of God. Adam is known in his thickets, and Jonah in his cabin. Achan's wedge of gold is discerned by him, though buried in the earth, and hooded with a tent. Shall Sarah be unseen by him, when she mockingly laughs behind the door? Shall Gehazi tell a lie, and comfort himself with an imagination of his master's ignorance, as long as God knows it? Whatsoever works men do, are not hid from God, whether done in the darkness or daylight, in the midnight darkness or the noonday sun. He is all eye to see, and he hath a great wrath to punish. The wheels in Ezekiel are full of eyes: a piercing eye to behold the sinner, and a swift wheel of wrath to overtake him. God is light, and of all things light is most difficultly kept out. The 'secretest sins are set in the light of his countenance,' Ps. xc. 8, as legible to him as if writ with a sunbeam; more visible to him than the greatest print to the sharpest eye. The fornications of the Samaritan woman, perhaps known only to her own conscience, were manifest to Christ, John iv. 16. There is nothing so secretly done, but there is an infallible witness to prepare a charge. Though God be invisible to us, we must not imagine we are so to him; it is a vanity therefore to think we can conceal ourselves from God, by concealing the notions of God from our sense and practice. If men be as close from the eyes of all men, as from those of the sun; yea, if they could separate themselves from their own shadow; they could not draw themselves from God's understanding. How then can darkness shelter us, or crafty artifices defend us? With what shame will sinners be filled, when God, who hath traced their steps, and writ their sins in a book, shall make a repetition of their ways, and unveil the web of their wickedness.

2. What a dreadful consideration is this to the juggling hypocrite, that masks himself with an appearance of piety! An infinite understanding judges not according to the veils and shadows, but according to truth: 'He judges not according to appearance,' 1 Sam. xvi. 7. The outward comeliness of a work imposeth not on him; his knowledge, and therefore his estimations, are quite of another nature than those of men. By this perfection God looks through the veil, and beholds the litter of abominations in the secrets of the soul, the true quality and principle of every work, and judges of them as they are, and not as they appear. Disguised pretexts cannot deceive him; the disguises are known afar off before they are weaved, he pierceth into the depths of the most abstruse wills; all secret ends are dissected before. Every action is naked in its outside, and open in its inside, all are as clear to him as if their bodies were of crystal, so that if there be any secret reserves, he will certainly reprove us, Job xiii. 10. We are often deceived, we may take wolves for sheep, and hypocrites for believers; for the eyes of men are no better than flesh, and dive no further than appear-

ance; but an infinite understanding, that fathoms the secret depths of the heart, is too knowing to let a dream pass for a truth, or mistake a shadow for a body. Though we call God Father all our days, speak the language of angels, or be endowed with the gift of miracles, he can discern whether we have his mark upon us ; he can espy the treason of Judas in a kiss ; Herod's intent of murdering under a specious pretence of worship ; a Pharisee's fraud under a broad philactery ; a ravenous wolf under the softness of a sheep's skin ; and the devil in Samuel's mantle, or when he would shroud himself among the sons of God, Job i. 6, 7. All the rooms of the heart, and every atom of dust in the least chink of it, is clear to his eye. He can strip sin from the fairest excuses, pierce into the heart with more ease than the sun can through the thinnest cloud or vapour, and look through all Ephraim's ingenious inventions to excuse his idolatry, Hosea v. 3. Hypocrisy then is a senseless thing, since it cannot escape unmasking by an infinite understanding. As all our force cannot stop his arm, when he is resolved to punish, so all our sophistry cannot blind his understanding, when he comes to judge. Woe to the hypocrite, for God sees him ; all his juggling is open and naked to infinite understanding.

3. Is it not also a senseless thing to be careless of sins committed long ago ? The old sins forgotten by men, stick fast in an infinite understanding. Time cannot raze out that which hath been known from eternity. Why should they be forgotten many years after they were acted, since they were foreknown in an eternity before they were committed, or the criminal capable to practise them ? Amalek must pay their arrears of their ancient unkindness to Israel in the time of Saul, though the generation that committed them were rotten in their graves, 1 Sam. xv. 2. Old sins are written in a book, which lies always before God ; and not only our own sins, but the sins of our fathers, to be requited upon their posterity: Isa. lxv. 6, ' Behold it is written.' What a vanity is it, then, to be regardless of the sins of an age that went before us ; because they are in some measure out of our knowledge, are they therefore blotted out of God's remembrance ? Sins are bound up with him, as men do bonds, till they resolve to sue for the debt: ' The iniquity of Ephraim is bound up,' Hosea xiii. 12. As his foreknowledge extends to all acts that shall be done, so his remembrance extends to all acts that have been done. We may as well say, God foreknows nothing that shall be done to the end of the world, as that he forgets any things that hath been done from the beginning of the world. The former ages of the world are no further distant from him than the latter. God hath a calendar (as it were) or an account-book of men's sins ever since the beginning of the world, what they did in their childhood, what in their youth, what in their manhood, and what in their old age. He hath them ' in store among his treasure,' Deut. xxxii. 34. He hath neither lost his understanding to know them, nor his resolution to revenge them. As it follows: ver. 35, ' To me vengeance belongs.' He intends to enrich his justice with a glorious manifestation, by rendering a due recompence. And it is to be observed, that God doth not only necessarily remember them, but sometimes binds himself by an oath to do it: Amos viii. 7, ' The Lord hath sworn by the excellency of Jacob, Surely I will never forget any of their works ;' or in the Hebrew, ' If I ever forget any of their works ;' that is, let me not be accounted a God for ever, if I do forget ; let me lose my Godhead, if I lose my remembrance. It is not less a misery to the wicked, than it is a comfort to the godly, that their record is in heaven.

4. Let it be observed, that this infinite understanding doth exactly know the sins of men ; he knows so as to consider. He doth not only know them,

but intently behold them : Ps. xi. 4, ' His eyelids try the children of men,'
a metaphor taken from men, that contract the eyelids when they would
wistly and accurately behold a thing ; it is not a transient and careless
look : Ps. x. 14, ' Thou hast seen it ;' thou hast intently beheld it, as the
word properly signifies.   He beholds and knows the actions of every particular man, as if there were none but he in the world ; and doth not only
know, but ponder, Prov. v. 21, and ' consider their works,' Ps. xxxiii. 15.
He is not a bare spectator, but a diligent observer : ' By him actions are
weighed,' 1 Sam. ii. 3, to see what degree of good or evil there is in
them, what there is to blemish them, what to advantage them, what the
quality and quantity of every action is.   Consideration takes in every circumstance of the considered object.   Notice is taken of the place where, the
minute when, the mercy against which it is committed ; the number of them
is exact in God's book : ' They have tempted me now these ten times,'
Num. xiv. 22, against the demonstrations of my glory in Egypt and the
wilderness. The whole guilt in every circumstance is spread before him. His
knowledge of men's sins is not confused, such an imperfection an infinite
understanding cannot be subject to ; it is exact, for ' iniquity is marked before
him,' Jer. ii. 22.

5. God knows men's miscarriage so as to judge.   This use his omniscience is put to, to maintain his sovereign authority in the exercise of his
justice.   His notice of the sins of men is in order to a just retribution: Ps.
x. 14, ' Thou hast seen mischief, to requite it with thy hand.'   The eye of
his knowledge directs the hand of his justice, and no sinful action that falls
under his cognizance but will fall under his revenge ; they can as little
escape his censure as they can his knowledge.   He is a witness in his
omniscience, that he may be a judge in his righteousness.   ' He knows the
hearts of the wicked' so as to hate their works, and testify his abhorrency
of that which is of high value with men, Luke xvi. 15.   Sin is not preserved in his understanding, or written down in his books to be moth-eaten
as an old manuscript, but to be opened one day and copied out in the consciences of men.   He writes them to publish them, and sets them in the
light of his countenance, to bring them to the light of their consciences.   What
a terrible consideration is it, to think that the sins of a day are upon record
in an infallible understanding, much more the sins of a week.   What a number, then, do the sins of a month, a year, ten or forty years arise to !   How
many actions against charity, against sincerity !   What an infinite number
is there of them, all bound up in the court-rolls of God's omniscience, in
order to a trial, to be brought out before the eyes of men !   Who can seriously consider all those bonds, reserved in the cabinet of God's knowledge,
to be sued out against the sinner in due time, without an unexpressible
horror ?

Use 4. The fourth use is of exhortation.   Let us have a sense of God's
knowledge upon our hearts.   All wickedness hath a spring from a want of
due consideration and sense of it.   David concludes it so, Ps. lxxxvi. 14 ;
the proud rose up against him, and violent men sought after his soul, because they did not set God before them.   They think God doth not know,
and therefore care not what nor how they act.   When the fear of this attribute is removed, a door is opened to all impiety.   What is there so villanous but the minds of men will attempt to act ?   What reverence of a Deity
can be left, when the sense of his infinite understanding is extinguished ?
What faith could there be in judgment, in witnesess ?   How would the
foundations of human society be overturned !   the pillars upon which commerce stands be utterly broken and dissolved !   What society can be

preserved if this be not truly believed and faithfully stuck to? But how easily would oaths be swallowed and quickly violated if the sense of this perfection were rooted out of the minds of men! What fear could they have of calling to witness a being they imagine blind and ignorant? Men secretly imagine that God knows not, or soon forgets, and then make bold to sin against him, Ezek. viii. 12. How much does it therefore concern us to cherish and keep alive the sense of this? If God 'writes us upon the palms of his hands,' as the expression is, to remember us, let us engrave him upon the tables of our hearts to remember him. It would be a good motto to write upon our minds, God knows all, he is of infinite understanding.

1. This would give check to much iniquity. Can a man's conscience easily and delightfully swallow that which he is sensible falls under the cognizance of God, when it is hateful to the eye of his holiness, and renders the actor odious to him? 'Doth he not see my ways, and count all my steps,' saith Job, chap. xxxi. 4. To what end doth he fix this consideration? To keep him from wanton glances. Temptations have no encouragement to come near him that is constantly armed with the thoughts that his sin is booked in God's omniscience. If any impudent devil hath the face to tempt us, we should not have the impudence to join issue with him under the sense of an infinite understanding. How fruitless would his wiles be against this consideration! How easily would his snares be cracked by one sensible thought of this! This doth Solomon prescribe to allay the heat of carnal imaginations, Prov. v. 20, 21. It were a useful question to ask at the appearance of every temptation, at the entrance upon every action, as the church did in temptations to idolatry, Ps. xliv. 21, 'Shall not God search this out, for he knows the secrets of the heart?' His understanding comprehends us more than our consciences can our acts, or our understanding our thoughts. Who durst speak treason against a prince if he were sure he heard him, or that it would come to his knowledge? A sense of God's knowledge of wickedness in the first motion and inward contrivance would bar the accomplishment and execution. The consideration of God's infinite understanding would cry *Stand* to the first glances of the heart to sin.

2. It would make us watchful over our hearts and thoughts. Should we harbour any unworthy thoughts in our cabinet, if our heads and hearts were possessed with this useful truth, that God knows everything which comes into our minds, we should as much blush at the rising of impure thoughts before the understanding of God as at the discovery of unworthy actions to the knowledge of men. If we lived under a sense that not a thought of all those millions which flutter about our minds can be concealed from him, how watchful and careful should we be of our hearts and thoughts!

3. It would be a good preparation to every duty. This consideration should be the preface to every service,—The divine understanding knows how I now act. This would engage us to serious intention, and quell wandering and distracting fancies. Who would come before God with a careless and ignorant soul, under a sense of his infinite understanding, and prerogative of searching the heart? 'O thou that sittest in heaven' was a consideration the psalmist had at the beginning of his prayer, Ps. cxxiii. 1, whereby he testifies not only an apprehension of the majesty and power of God, but of his omniscience, as one sitting above beholds all that is below. Would we offer to God such raw and undigested petitions; would there be so much flatness in our services; should our hearts so often give us the slip; would any hang down their heads like a bulrush by an affected or

counterfeit humility while the heart is filled with pride, if we did actuate faith in this attribute ?   No ; our prayers would be more sound, our devotions more vigorous, our hearts more close, our spirits like the chariots of Amminadab, more swift in their motions.   Everything would be done by us with all our might, which would be very feeble and faint if we conceived God to be of a finite understanding like ourselves.   Let us therefore before every duty, not draw, but open the curtains between God and our souls, and think that we are going before him that sees us, Gen. xvi. 13, before him that knows us.   And the stronger impressions of the divine knowledge are upon our minds, the better would our preparation be for, and the more active our frames in every service.   And certainly we may judge of the suitableness of our preparations by the strength of such impressions upon us.

4. This would tend to make us sincere in our whole course.   This prescription David gave to Solomon, to maintain a soundness and health of spirit in his walk before God : 1 Chron. xxviii. 9, 'And thou Solomon, my son, know the God of thy fathers, and serve him with a perfect heart; for the Lord understands all the imaginations of the thoughts.'   Josephus* gives this reason for Abel's holiness, that he believed God was ignorant of nothing.   As the doctrine of omniscience is the foundation of all religion, so the impression of it would promote the practice of all religion. When all our ways are imagined by us to be before the Lord, we shall then keep his precepts, Ps. cxix. 168.   And we can never be perfect or sincere till we walk before God, Gen. xvii. 1, as under the eye of God's knowledge.   What we speak, what we think, what we act, is in his sight. He knows every place where we are, everything that we do, as well as Christ knew Nathanael under the fig-tree.   As he is too powerful to be vanquished, so he is too understanding to be deceived.   The sense of this would make us walk with as much care as if the understanding of all men did comprehend us and our actions.

5. The consideration of this attribute would make us humble.   How dejected would a person be, if he were sure all the angels in heaven and men upon earth did perfectly know his crimes, with all their aggravations !   But what is created knowledge to an infinite and just censuring understanding ? When we consider that he knows our actions, whereof there are multitudes, and our thoughts, whereof there are millions ; that he views all the blessings bestowed upon us, all the injuries we have returned to him ; that he exactly knows his own bounty, and our ingratitude ; all the idolatry, blasphemy, and secret enmity in every man's heart against him ; all tyrannical oppressions, hidden lusts, omissions of necessary duties, violation of plain precepts, every foolish imagination, with all the circumstances of them, and that perfectly in their full anatomy, every mite of unworthiness and wickedness in every circumstance ; and add to this his knowledge, the wonders of his patience, which are miraculous upon the score of his omniscience, that he is not as quick in his revenge as he is in his understanding, but is so far from inflicting punishment that he continues his former benefits, arms not his justice against us, but solicits our repentance, and waits to be gracious with all this knowledge of our crimes : should not the consideration of this melt our hearts into humiliation before him, and make us earnest in begging pardon and forgiveness of him ?

Again, Do we not all find a worm in our best fruit, a flaw in our soundest duties ? Shall any of us vaunt, as if God beheld only the gold, and not any dross ; as if he knew one thing only, and not another.   If we knew something by ourselves to cheer us, do we not also know something, yea, many

* Antiquit., lib. i. cap. 3.

things, to condemn us, and therefore to humble us? Let the sense of God's infinite knowledge, therefore, be an incentive and argument for more humiliation in us. If we know enough to render ourselves vile in our own eyes, how much more doth God know to render us vile in his!

6. The consideration of this excellent perfection should make us to acquiesce in God, and rely upon him in every strait. In public, in private, he knows all cases, and he knows all remedies. He knows the seasons of bringing them, and he knows the seasons of removing them, for his own glory. What is contingent in respect of us, and of our foreknowledge, and in respect of second causes, it is not so in regard of God's, who hath the knowledge of the futurition of all things. He knows all causes in themselves, and therefore knows what every cause will produce, what will be the event of every counsel and of every action. How should we commit ourselves to this God of infinite understanding, who knows all things, and foreknows everything; that cannot be forced through ignorance to take new counsel, or be surprised with anything that can happen to us. This use the psalmist makes of it: Ps. x. 14, ' Thou hast seen it, the poor committeth himself unto thee.' Though ' some trust in chariots and horses,' Ps. xx. 7, some in counsels and counsellors, some in their arms and courage, and some in mere vanity and nothing, yet let us ' remember the name' and nature ' of the Lord our God,' his divine perfections, of which this of his infinite understanding and omniscience is none of the least, but so necessary, that without it he could not be God, and the whole world would be a mere chaos and confusion.

END OF VOL. I.